CRIME STATE RANKINGS
2001

Crime in the 50 United States

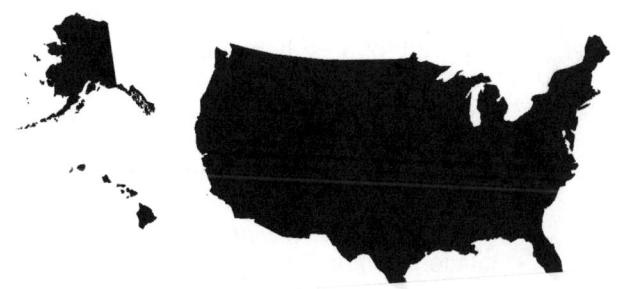

D1301278

Editors:

Kathleen O'Leary Morgan and Scott Morgan

Morgan Quitno Press
© Copyright 2001, All Rights Reserved

512 East 9th Street, P.O. Box 1656
Lawrence, KS 66044-8656
USA

800-457-0742 or 785-841-3534
www.statestats.com

Eighth Edition

ISBN:
0-7401-0031-9
ISSN:
1077-4408

Crime State Rankings 2001 sells for $52.95 ($5.00 shipping) and is only available in paper binding. For those who prefer ranking information tailored to a particular state, we also offer *Crime State Perspectives*, state-specific reports for each of the 50 states. These individual guides provide information on a state's data and rank for each of the categories featured in the national *Crime State Rankings* volume. Perspectives sell for $19.00 or $9.50 if ordered with *Crime State Rankings*. If you are interested in city and metropolitan crime data, we offer *City Crime Rankings, 7th Edition* ($39.95 paper). Those interested in health statistics should check out our annual *Health Care State Rankings* ($52.95 paper). If you are interested in a general view of the states, please ask about our annual *State Rankings* ($52.95 paper). We also offer the data in our books on diskette.   Shipping is $5.00 per order.

Eighth Edition
Printed in the United States of America
April 2001

PREFACE

This eighth edition of *Crime State Rankings* provides a huge collection of state crime statistics. Crime numbers, rates and trends; prison and other corrections data; law enforcement personnel and finance; juvenile crime and delinquency; drugs and alcohol, arrests and crime clearances are examined state-by-state in 508 easy-to-understand tables. Find out how your state compares in violent and property crime rates. What percentage of Americans is serving time? How much does your state spend for law enforcement and justice? Answers to these and hundreds of other crime-related questions are found in *Crime State Rankings 2001*.

Important Notes About *Crime State Rankings 2001*

Making complicated and often convoluted crime data easier to understand and more accessible is our primary goal in publishing *Crime State Rankings*. This newly revised and updated edition is the product of our rigorous annual review process in which each table in the previous year's book is carefully examined. Most tables are updated, others that no longer are pertinent are removed and new data of interest are added. With 508 tables of state crime comparisons, this eighth edition is a solid collection of valuable crime and law enforcement information.

While you will find a number of changes and updates, many of the organizational features that have made this book so popular with both reviewers and researchers have not changed. Data are presented in both alphabetical and rank order so that readers may quickly find information for a particular state and then just as quickly learn which states rank above and below that state. Source information and other important footnotes are clearly shown at the bottom of each page and national totals, rates and percentages are prominently displayed at the top of each table. Every other line is shaded in gray for easier reading. In addition, numerous information-finding tools are provided: a thorough table of contents, table listings at the beginning of each chapter, a detailed index and a chapter thumb index. Also included is a roster of sources showing addresses, phone numbers and websites.

As in all of our reference books, the numbers shown in *Crime State Rankings 2001* are "complete" numbers, meaning that no additional calculations are required to convert them to thousands, millions, etc. All states are ranked on a high to low basis. Any ties among states are shown alphabetically for a given ranking. Numbers reported in parentheses "( )" are negative numbers. For tables with national totals (as opposed to rates, per capita's, etc.) we include a separate column showing what percent of the national total each individual state's total represents. This column is headed by "% of USA." This percentage figure is particularly interesting when compared with a state's share of the nation's population for a particular year. The appendix contains population tables to aid in these comparisons.

For those interested in focusing on crime information for just one state, we once again are offering our *Crime State Perspective* series of publications. These 21-page, comb-bound reports feature data and ranking information for an individual state pulled from *Crime State Rankings 2001*. (For example, *New York Crime in Perspective* contains crime information about the state of New York only.) When purchased individually, *Crime State Perspectives* sell for $19. When purchased with a copy of *Crime State Rankings 2001,* these handy quick reference guides are just $9.50.

Other Books from Morgan Quitno Press

For up-to-date crime information for cities, our *City Crime Rankings* reference book compares all cities of 75,000 population or more and all metropolitan areas (some as small as 65,000 population) in 40 categories of crime. Crime numbers, rates and trends are presented for all major crime categories reported by the FBI. (7th edition, $39.95 paper; S/H $5 per order).

For general state statistics or state health care information, check out *State Rankings* and *Health Care State Rankings*. *State Rankings* is an annual book featuring statistics for a wide variety of categories including agriculture, transportation, government finance, health, population, crime, education, social welfare, energy and environment. Our annual *Health Care State Rankings* book includes data on health care facilities, providers, insurance and finance, incidence of disease, mortality, physical fitness, natality and reproductive health. *State Rankings* and *Health Care State Rankings* sell for $52.95 each (paper; S/H $5 per order). Also available are *State Perspectives* and *Health Care State Perspectives* for each of these books, selling for $19 individually or $9.50 if purchased with their corresponding national volume. The data in all of our reference books are available on CD-ROM. These electronic editions provide a searchable PDF version of each book as well as the raw data in .dbf, Excel and ASCII formats. CD-ROM and book sets are $152.95 each.

State Statistical Trends is our popular monthly journal that compares changes in life and government for the 50 United States. Each 100-page monthly issue examines a different subject and provides a collection of tables, graphics and commentary showing state multi-year trends. For further information about *Trends* or any of our other publications, please call us toll-free at 1-800-457-0742 or check out our website at www.statestats.com.

Finally, many thanks to the many hard working librarians and government workers who help us every year with information, explanations and general support. Thanks also to you, our readers. We always welcome your thoughts and suggestions, so please give us a call, send us an e-mail or drop us a note with your ideas.

- THE EDITORS

WHICH STATE IS THE MOST DANGEROUS?

 We still think New Mexico is a beautiful and an "enchanting land." However, once again it is also a land of crime when compared to its fellow states. While crime continues to drop across the country, New Mexico held tight to the #1 spot in our year 2001 Most Dangerous State review. In fact, the "top" four states were repeats, with Florida, Nevada and Louisiana finishing in second, third and fourth respectively. On the safer end of the ranking scale, North Dakota wins our Safest State Award for a record fifth year in a row.

The Methodology

The methodology to determine the Safest and Most Dangerous States involves a four-step process. First, rates for six crime categories — murder, rape, robbery, aggravated assault, burglary and motor vehicle theft — are plugged into a formula that measures how a state compares to the national average for a given crime category.

Second, the outcome of this equation is then multiplied by a weight assigned to each crime category. For this year's award, we again gave each crime category equal weight. Thus state comparisons are based purely on crime rates and how these rates stack up to the national average for a given crime category.

Third, the weighted numbers are added together to achieve state's score ("SUM.") In the fourth and final step, these composite scores are ranked from highest to lowest to determine which states are the most dangerous and safest. Thus the farther below the national average a state's crime rate is, the lower (and safer) it ranks. The farther above the national average, the higher (and more dangerous) a state ranks in the final list.

Morgan Quitno Press takes pride in presenting facts in a nonbiased, objective manner. While a central theme of our books is our clear presentation of data, with the analysis and interpretation left to our readers, we stray from this policy once a year and issue these awards. Annually since 1991 we have named the Most Livable State based on data from our *State Rankings* series. In 1993, we began the Healthiest State Award based on data from our *Health Care State Rankings* series. In 1994, we initiated the annual Safest and Most Dangerous City Award based on data from our *City Crime Rankings* book.

North Dakota continues to "own" the Safest State Award. With crime rates lower than it's average temperature (e.g. a robbery rate of 8.8 compared to the national rate of 150.2) it may be awhile before another state takes away the title.

New Mexico is not as fortunate. While the national violent crime rate is down by more than 20% in the five years from 1995 to 1999 (the most recent year for which final state crime data are available) New Mexico's rate has risen by approximately 2%. However, a one-year comparison from 1998 to 1999 offers hope. New Mexico's violent crime rate dropped more than 13%, while the national average fell 7.5%. Perhaps New Mexico can lose its "honor" with another better than average year.

— THE EDITORS

2001 MOST DANGEROUS STATE

RANK	STATE	SUM	'00	RANK	STATE	SUM	'00
1	New Mexico	48.85	1	26	Colorado	(17.38)	26
2	Florida	43.43	2	27	Oregon	(17.67)	24
3	Nevada	42.42	3	28	Ohio	(18.97)	28
4	Louisiana	36.27	4	29	Pennsylvania	(19.88)	31
5	Alaska	30.32	13	30	Massachusetts	(20.67)	29
6	Maryland	30.29	5	31	New Jersey	(21.13)	30
7	Arizona	27.08	7	32	Rhode Island	(22.42)	38
8	South Carolina	25.65	6	33	Hawaii	(25.77)	35
9	Tennessee	23.25	8	34	Nebraska	(26.12)	37
10	Delaware	21.08	11	35	Virginia	(29.75)	36
11	Illinois	20.10	9	36	Minnesota	(30.11)	33
12	Michigan	19.68	10	37	Connecticut	(30.27)	34
13	Georgia	12.22	14	38	Kentucky	(30.69)	39
14	North Carolina	11.36	15	39	Utah	(31.02)	32
15	Texas	10.56	17	40	West Virginia	(38.58)	44
16	Mississippi	7.61	16	41	Wisconsin	(42.60)	41
17	California	7.19	12	42	Idaho	(46.48)	40
18	Oklahoma	5.47	18	43	Iowa	(47.12)	42
19	Alabama	1.42	21	44	South Dakota	(48.30)	47
20	Washington	(0.97)	19	45	Montana	(49.89)	45
21	Missouri	(2.64)	20	46	Wyoming	(52.30)	43
22	New York	(8.86)	23	47	Vermont	(55.85)	46
23	Kansas	(13.73)	27	48	Maine	(59.76)	48
24	Indiana	(14.34)	25	49	New Hampshire	(65.25)	49
25	Arkansas	(16.41)	22	50	North Dakota	(66.79)	50

FACTORS CONSIDERED (all given equal weight):
(all rates per 100,000 population)

1. Murder Rate (Table 328)
2. Rape Rate (Table 347)
3. Robbery Rate (Table 353)
4. Aggravated Assault Rate (Table 368)
5. Burglary Rate (Table 388)
6. Motor Vehicle Theft Rate (Table 398)

TABLE OF CONTENTS

I. Arrests

1   Reported Arrests in 1999
2   Reported Arrest Rate in 1999
3   Reported Arrests for Crime Index Offenses in 1999
4   Reported Arrest Rate for Crime Index Offenses in 1999
5   Reported Arrests for Violent Crime in 1999
6   Reported Arrest Rate for Violent Crime in 1999
7   Reported Arrests for Murder in 1999
8   Reported Arrest Rate for Murder in 1999
9   Reported Arrests for Rape in 1999
10   Reported Arrest Rate for Rape in 1999
11   Reported Arrests for Robbery in 1999
12   Reported Arrest Rate for Robbery in 1999
13   Reported Arrests for Aggravated Assault in 1999
14   Reported Arrest Rate for Aggravated Assault in 1999
15   Reported Arrests for Property Crime in 1999
16   Reported Arrest Rate for Property Crime in 1999
17   Reported Arrests for Burglary in 1999
18   Reported Arrest Rate for Burglary in 1999
19   Reported Arrests for Larceny and Theft in 1999
20   Reported Arrest Rate for Larceny and Theft in 1999
21   Reported Arrests for Motor Vehicle Theft in 1999
22   Reported Arrest Rate for Motor Vehicle Theft in 1999
23   Reported Arrests for Arson in 1999
24   Reported Arrest Rate for Arson in 1999
25   Reported Arrests for Weapons Violations in 1999
26   Reported Arrest Rate for Weapons Violations in 1999
27   Reported Arrests for Driving Under the Influence in 1999
28   Reported Arrest Rate for Driving Under the Influence in 1999
29   Reported Arrests for Drug Abuse Violations in 1999
30   Reported Arrest Rate for Drug Abuse Violations in 1999
31   Reported Arrests for Sex Offenses in 1999
32   Reported Arrest Rate for Sex Offenses in 1999
33   Reported Arrests for Prostitution and Commercialized Vice in 1999
34   Reported Arrest Rate for Prostitution and Commercialized Vice in 1999
35   Reported Arrests for Offenses Against Families and Children in 1999
36   Reported Arrest Rate for Offenses Against Families and Children in 1999
37   Percent of Crimes Cleared in 1998
38   Percent of Violent Crimes Cleared in 1998
39   Percent of Murders Cleared in 1998
40   Percent of Rapes Cleared in 1998
41   Percent of Robberies Cleared in 1998
42   Percent of Aggravated Assaults Cleared in 1998
43   Percent of Property Crimes Cleared in 1998
44   Percent of Burglaries Cleared in 1998
45   Percent of Larcenies and Thefts Cleared in 1998
46   Percent of Motor Vehicle Thefts Cleared in 1998

II. Corrections

47   Prisoners in State Correctional Institutions: Year End 1999
48   Percent Change in Number of State Prisoners: 1998 to 1999
49   State Prisoners Sentenced to More than One Year in 1999
50   State Prisoner Incarceration Rate in 1999
51   Percent Change in State Prisoner Incarceration Rate: 1998 to 1999
52   State Prison Population as a Percent of Highest Capacity in 1999
53   Female Prisoners in State Correctional Institutions in 1999
54   Female State Prisoner Incarceration Rate in 1999
55   Female Prisoners in State Correctional Institutions as a Percent of All State Prisoners in 1999
56   Percent Change in Female State Prisoner Population: 1998 to 1999
57   White Prisoners in State Correctional Institutions in 1998
58   White State Prisoner Incarceration Rate in 1998

TABLE OF CONTENTS (continued)

59   White State Prisoners in State Correctional Institutions as a Percent of All State Prisoners in 1998
60   Black Prisoners in State Correctional Institutions in 1998
61   Black State Prisoner Incarceration Rate in 1998
62   Black State Prisoners in State Correctional Institutions as a Percent of All State Prisoners in 1998
63   Prisoners Under Sentence of Death in 1999
64   Male Prisoners Under Sentence of Death in 1999
65   Female Prisoners Under Sentence of Death in 1999
66   Percent of Prisoners Under Sentence of Death Who Are Female: 1999
67   White Prisoners Under Sentence of Death in 1999
68   Percent of Prisoners Under Sentence of Death Who Are White: 1999
69   Black Prisoners Under Sentence of Death in 1999
70   Percent of Prisoners Under Sentence of Death Who Are Black: 1999
71   Prisoners Executed in 1999
72   Prisoners Executed: 1930 to 1999
73   Prisoners Executed: 1977 to 1999
74   Prisoners Sentenced to Death: 1973 to 1999
75   Death Sentences Overturned or Commuted: 1973 to 1999
76   Percent of Death Penalty Sentences Overturned or Commuted: 1973 to 1999
77   Sentenced Prisoners Admitted to State Correctional Institutions in 1998
78   Sentenced Prisoners Admitted to State Correctional Institutions Through New Court Commitments in 1998
79   Parole Violators Returned to State Prisons in 1998
80   Escapees Returned to State Prisons in 1998
81   Prisoners Released from State Correctional Institutions in 1998
82   State Prisoners Released with Conditions in 1998
83   State Prisoners Released Conditionally as a Percent of All Releases in 1998
84   State Prisoners Released on Parole in 1998
85   State Prisoners Released on Probation in 1998
86   State Prisoners Released on Supervised Mandatory Release in 1998
87   State Prisoners Released Unconditionally in 1998
88   State Prisoners Released Unconditionally as a Percent of All Releases in 1998
89   State Prisoners Released on Appeal or Bond in 1998
90   State Prisoners Escaped in 1998
91   State Prisoner Deaths in 1998
92   Death Rate of State Prisoners in 1998
93   State Prisoner Deaths by Illness or Other Natural Causes in 1998
94   Deaths of State Prisoners by Illness or Other Natural Causes as a Percent of All State Prison Deaths in 1998
95   Deaths of State Prisoners by AIDS in 1998
96   AIDS-Related Death Rate for State Prisoners in 1998
97   Deaths of State Prisoners by AIDS as a Percent of All Prison Deaths in 1998
98   State Prisoners Known to be Positive for HIV Infection/AIDS in 1997
99   State Prisoners Known to be Positive for HIV Infection/AIDS as a Percent of Total Prison Population in 1997
100 Deaths by State Prisoners by Suicide in 1998
101 Deaths of State Prisoners by Suicide as a Percent of All Prison Deaths in 1998
102 Adults Under State Correctional Supervision in 1993
103 Percent of Population Under State Correctional Supervision in 1993
104 Adults on State Probation in 1999
105 Rate of Adults on State Probation in 1999
106 Adults on State Parole in 1999
107 Rate of Adults on State Parole in 1999
108 State and Local Government Employees in Corrections in 1999
109 State and Local Government Employees in Corrections as a Percent of All State and Local Government Employees in 1999
110 State Government Employees in Corrections in 1999
111 State Government Employees in Corrections as a Percent of All State Government Employees in 1999
112 State Correctional Officers in 1998
113 Male Correctional Officers in 1998
114 Female Correctional Officers in 1998
115 State Prisoners per Correctional Officer in 1998
116 Turnover Rate of Correctional Officers in 1998
117 Jail and Detention Centers in 1993
118 Inmates in Local Jails in 1993

TABLE OF CONTENTS (continued)

III. Drugs and Alcohol

119   Alcohol and Other Drug Treatment Units in 1997
120   Alcohol and Other Drug Treatment Admissions in 1997
121   Male Admissions to Alcohol and Other Drug Treatment Programs in 1997
122   Male Admissions to Alcohol and Drug Treatment Programs as a Percent of All Admissions in 1997
123   Female Admissions to Alcohol and Other Drug Treatment Programs in 1997
124   Female Admissions to Alcohol and Other Drug Treatment Programs as a Percent of All Admissions in 1997
125   White Admissions to Alcohol and Other Drug Treatment Programs in 1997
126   White Admissions to Alcohol and Other Drug Treatment Programs as a Percent of All Admissions in 1997
127   Black Admissions to Alcohol and Other Drug Treatment Programs in 1997
128   Black Admissions to Alcohol and Other Drug Treatment Programs as a Percent of All Admissions in 1997
129   Hispanic Admissions to Alcohol and Other Drug Treatment Programs in 1997
130   Hispanic Admissions to Alcohol and Other Drug Treatment Programs as a Percent of All Admissions in 1997
131   Expenditures for State-Supported Alcohol and Other Drug Abuse Services: 1997
132   Per Capita Expenditures for State-Supported Alcohol and Other Drug Abuse Services in 1997
133   Expenditures for State-Supported Alcohol and Other Drug Abuse Treatment Programs in 1997
134   Expenditures per Alcohol and Other Drug Treatment Admission in 1997
135   Per Capita Expenditures for State-Supported Alcohol and Other Drug Abuse Treatment Programs in 1997
136   Expenditures for State-Supported Alcohol and Other Drug Abuse Prevention Programs in 1997
137   Per Capita Expenditures for State-Supported Alcohol and Other Drug Abuse Prevention Programs in 1997

IV. Finance

138   State and Local Government Expenditures for Justice Activities in 1997
139   Per Capita State & Local Government Expenditures for Justice Activities: 1997
140   State and Local Government Expenditures for Justice Activities as a Percent of All Direct General Expenditures in 1997
141   State Government Expenditures for Justice Activities in 1997
142   Per Capita State Government Expenditures for Justice Activities in 1997
143   State Government Expenditures for Justice Activities as a Percent of All Direct General Expenditures in 1997
144   Local Government Expenditures for Justice Activities in 1997
145   Per Capita Local Government Expenditures for Justice Activities in 1997
146   Local Government Expenditures for Justice Activities as a Percent of All Direct General Expenditures in 1997
147   State and Local Government Expenditures for Police Protection in 1997
148   Per Capita State & Local Government Expenditures for Police Protection: 1997
149   State and Local Government Expenditures for Police Protection as a Percent of All Direct General Expenditures in 1997
150   State Government Expenditures for Police Protection in 1997
151   Per Capita State Government Expenditures for Police Protection in 1997
152   State Government Expenditures for Police Protection as a Percent of All Direct General Expenditures in 1997
153   Local Government Expenditures for Police Protection in 1997
154   Per Capita Local Government Expenditures for Police Protection in 1997
155   Local Government Expenditures for Police Protection as a Percent of All Direct General Expenditures in 1997
156   State and Local Government Expenditures for Corrections in 1997
157   Per Capita State and Local Government Expenditures for Corrections in 1997
158   State and Local Government Expenditures for Corrections as a Percent of All Direct General Expenditures in 1997
159   State Government Expenditures for Corrections in 1997
160   Per Capita State Government Expenditures for Corrections in 1997
161   State Government Expenditures for Corrections as a Percent of All Direct General Expenditures in 1997
162   Expenditures for State Prisons in 1996
163   Operating Expenditures for State Prisons in 1996
164   Annual Operating Expenditures per Inmate in 1996
165   Daily Operating Expenditures per Inmate in 1996
166   Local Government Expenditures for Corrections in 1997
167   Per Capita Local Government Expenditures for Corrections in 1997
168   Local Government Expenditures for Corrections as a Percent of All Direct General Expenditures in 1997
169   State and Local Government Expenditures for Judicial and Legal Services: 1997
170   Per Capita State and Local Government Expenditures for Judicial and Legal Services in 1997
171   State and Local Government Expenditures for Judicial and Legal Services as a Percent of All Direct General Expenditures in 1997
172   State Government Expenditures for Judicial and Legal Services in 1997
173   Per Capita State Government Expenditures for Judicial and Legal Services: 1997
174   State Government Expenditures for Judicial and Legal Services as a Percent of All Direct General Expenditures in 1997
175   Local Government Expenditures for Judicial and Legal Services in 1997
176   Per Capita Local Government Expenditures for Judicial & Legal Services: 1997

TABLE OF CONTENTS (continued)

177 Local Government Expenditures for Judicial and Legal Services as a Percent of All Direct General Expenditures in 1997
178 State and Local Government Judicial and Legal Payroll in 1999
179 State and Local Government Police Protection Payroll in 1999
180 State and Local Government Corrections Payroll in 1999
181 Base Salary for Justices of States' Highest Courts in 2000
182 Base Salary for Judges of Intermediate Appellate Courts in 2000
183 Base Salary for Judges of General Trial Courts in 2000

V. Juveniles

184 Reported Arrests of Juveniles in 1999
185 Reported Juvenile Arrest Rate in 1999
186 Reported Arrests of Juveniles as a Percent of All Arrests in 1999
187 Reported Arrests of Juveniles for Crime Index Offenses in 1999
188 Reported Juvenile Arrest Rate for Crime Index Offenses in 1999
189 Reported Arrests of Juveniles for Crime Index Offenses as a Percent of All Such Arrests in 1999
190 Reported Arrests of Juveniles for Violent Crime in 1999
191 Reported Juvenile Arrest Rate for Violent Crime in 1999
192 Reported Arrests of Juveniles for Violent Crime as a Percent of All Such Arrests in 1999
193 Reported Arrests of Juveniles for Murder in 1999
194 Reported Juvenile Arrest Rate for Murder in 1999
195 Reported Arrests of Juveniles for Murder as a Percent of All Such Arrests in 1999
196 Reported Arrests of Juveniles for Rape in 1999
197 Reported Juvenile Arrest Rate for Rape in 1999
198 Reported Arrests of Juveniles for Rape as a Percent of All Such Arrests in 1999
199 Reported Arrests of Juveniles for Robbery in 1999
200 Reported Juvenile Arrest Rate for Robbery in 1999
201 Reported Arrests of Juveniles for Robbery as a Percent of All Such Arrests in 1999
202 Reported Arrests of Juveniles for Aggravated Assault in 1999
203 Reported Juvenile Arrest Rate for Aggravated Assault in 1999
204 Reported Arrests of Juveniles for Aggravated Assault as a Percent of All Such Arrests in 1999
205 Reported Arrests of Juveniles for Property Crime in 1999
206 Reported Juvenile Arrest Rate for Property Crime in 1999
207 Reported Arrests of Juveniles for Property Crime as a Percent of All Such Arrests in 1999
208 Reported Arrests of Juveniles for Burglary in 1999
209 Reported Juvenile Arrest Rate for Burglary in 1999
210 Reported Arrests of Juveniles for Burglary as a Percent of All Such Arrests in 1999
211 Reported Arrests of Juveniles for Larceny and Theft in 1999
212 Reported Juvenile Arrest Rate for Larceny and Theft in 1999
213 Reported Arrests of Juveniles for Larceny and Theft as a Percent of All Such Arrests in 1999
214 Reported Arrests of Juveniles for Motor Vehicle Theft in 1999
215 Reported Juvenile Arrest Rate for Motor Vehicle Theft in 1999
216 Reported Arrests of Juveniles for Motor Vehicle Theft as a Percent of All Such Arrests in 1999
217 Reported Arrests of Juveniles for Arson in 1999
218 Reported Juvenile Arrest Rate for Arson in 1999
219 Reported Arrests of Juveniles for Arson as a Percent of All Such Arrests in 1999
220 Reported Arrests of Juveniles for Weapons Violations in 1999
221 Reported Juvenile Arrest Rate for Weapons Violations in 1999
222 Reported Arrests of Juveniles for Weapons Violations as a Percent of All Such Arrests in 1999
223 Reported Arrests of Juveniles for Driving Under the Influence in 1999
224 Reported Juvenile Arrest Rate for Driving Under the Influence in 1999
225 Reported Arrests of Juveniles for Driving Under the Influence as a Percent of All Such Arrests in 1999
226 Reported Arrests of Juveniles for Drug Abuse Violations in 1999
227 Reported Juvenile Arrest Rate for Drug Abuse Violations in 1999
228 Reported Arrests of Juveniles for Drug Abuse Violations as a Percent of All Such Arrests in 1999
229 Reported Arrests of Juveniles for Sex Offenses in 1999
230 Reported Juvenile Arrest Rate for Sex Offenses in 1999
231 Reported Arrests of Juveniles for Sex Offenses as a Percent of All Such Arrests in 1999
232 Reported Arrests of Juveniles for Prostitution and Commercialized Vice in 1999
233 Reported Juvenile Arrest Rate for Prostitution and Commercialized Vice in 1999
234 Reported Arrests of Juveniles for Prostitution and Commercialized Vice as a Percent of All Such Arrests in 1999
235 Reported Arrests of Juveniles for Offenses Against Families & Children in 1999
236 Reported Juvenile Arrest Rate for Offenses Against Families & Children in 1999
237 Reported Arrests of Juveniles for Offenses Against Families and Children as a Percent of All Such Arrests in 1999

TABLE OF CONTENTS (continued)

238 Juvenile Death Sentences: 1973 to 2000
239 Juveniles in Custody in 1997
240 Rate of Juveniles in Custody in 1997
241 White Juvenile Custody Rate in 1997
242 Black Juvenile Custody Rate in 1997
243 High School Dropout Rate in 1998
244 Percent of High School Students Who Carried a Weapon on School Property in the Previous Month: 1999
245 Percent of High School Students Threatened or Injured with a Weapon on School Property in 1999
246 Percent of Teens Who Drink Alcohol: 1999
247 Percent of Teens Who Use Marijuana: 1999
248 Admissions of Juveniles to Alcohol and Other Drug Treatment Programs in 1997
249 Admissions of Juveniles to Alcohol and Other Drug Treatment Programs as a Percent of All Admissions in 1997
250 Victims of Child Abuse and Neglect in 1998
251 Rate of Child Abuse and Neglect in 1998
252 Physically Abused Children in 1998
253 Rate of Physically Abused Children in 1998
254 Sexually Abused Children in 1998
255 Rate of Sexually Abused Children in 1998
256 Emotionally Abused Children in 1998
257 Rate of Emotionally Abused Children in 1998
258 Neglected Children in 1998
259 Rate of Neglected Children in 1998
260 Child Abuse and Neglect Fatalities in 1998
261 Rate of Child Abuse and Neglect Fatalities in 1998

VI. Law Enforcement

262 Federal Law Enforcement Officers in 1998
263 Rate of Federal Law Enforcement Officers in 1998
264 State and Local Justice System Employment in 1999
265 Rate of State and Local Justice System Employment in 1999
266 State and Local Judicial and Legal Employment in 1999
267 Rate of State and Local Judicial and Legal Employment in 1999
268 State and Local Police Officers in 1999
269 Rate of State and Local Police Officers in 1999
270 Law Enforcement Agencies in 1996
271 Population per Law Enforcement Agency in 1996
272 Law Enforcement Agencies per 1,000 Square Miles in 1996
273 Full-Time Sworn Officers in Law Enforcement Agencies in 1996
274 Percent of Full-Time Law Enforcement Agency Employees Who are Sworn Officers: 1996
275 Rate of Full-Time Sworn Officers in Law Enforcement Agencies in 1996
276 Full-Time Sworn Law Enforcement Officers per 1,000 Square Miles in 1996
277 Full-Time Employees in Law Enforcement Agencies in 1996
278 Rate of Full-Time Employees in Law Enforcement Agencies in 1996
279 Full-Time Sworn Officers in State Police Departments in 1996
280 Percent of Full-Time State Police Department Employees Who are Sworn Officers: 1996
281 Rate of Full-Time Sworn Officers in State Police Departments in 1996
282 State Government Law Enforcement Officers in 1999
283 Male State Government Law Enforcement Officers in 1999
284 Female State Government Law Enforcement Officers in 1999
285 Female State Government Law Enforcement Officers as a Percent of All Officers: 1999
286 Local Police Departments in 1996
287 Full-Time Officers in Local Police Departments in 1996
288 Percent of Full-Time Local Police Department Employees Who Are Sworn Officers: 1996
289 Rate of Full-Time Officers in Local Police Departments in 1996
290 Full-Time Employees in Local Police Departments in 1996
291 Sheriffs' Departments in 1996
292 Full-Time Officers in Sheriffs' Departments in 1996
293 Percent of Full-Time Sheriffs' Department Employees Who Are Sworn Officers: 1996
294 Rate of Full-Time Sworn Officers in Sheriffs' Departments in 1996
295 Full-Time Employees in Sheriffs' Departments in 1996
296 Special Police Agencies in 1996
297 Full-Time Sworn Officers in Special Police Departments in 1996
298 Percent of Full-Time Special Police Department Employees Who Are Sworn Officers: 1996

TABLE OF CONTENTS (continued)

299 Rate of Full-Time Sworn Officers in Special Police Departments in 1996
300 Full-Time Employees in Special Police Departments in 1996
301 Law Enforcement Officers Feloniously Killed in 1998
302 Law Enforcement Officers Feloniously Killed: 1989 to 1998
303 U.S. District Court Judges in 1999
304 Population per U.S. District Judge in 1999
305 Felony Criminal Cases Filed in U.S. District Courts in 1999
306 Felony Criminal Cases Filed per U.S. District Judge in 1999
307 Median Length of Federal Criminal Cases in 1999
308 Authorized Wiretaps in 1999

VII. Offenses

309 Crimes in 1999
310 Average Time Between Crimes in 1999
311 Crimes per Square Mile in 1999
312 Percent Change in Number of Crimes: 1998 to 1999
313 Crime Rate in 1999
314 Percent Change in Crime Rate: 1998 to 1999
315 Violent Crimes in 1999
316 Average Time Between Violent Crimes in 1999
317 Violent Crimes per Square Mile in 1999
318 Percent Change in Number of Violent Crimes: 1998 to 1999
319 Violent Crime Rate in 1999
320 Percent Change in Violent Crime Rate: 1998 to 1999
321 Violent Crimes with Firearms in 1999
322 Violent Crime Rate with Firearms in 1999
323 Percent of Violent Crimes Involving Firearms in 1999
324 Bombings in 1997
325 Murders in 1999
326 Average Time Between Murders in 1999
327 Percent Change in Number of Murders: 1998 to 1999
328 Murder Rate in 1999
329 Percent Change in Murder Rate: 1998 to 1999
330 Murders with Firearms in 1999
331 Murder Rate with Firearms in 1999
332 Percent of Murders Involving Firearms in 1999
333 Murders with Handguns in 1999
334 Murder Rate with Handguns in 1999
335 Percent of Murders Involving Handguns in 1999
336 Murders with Rifles in 1999
337 Percent of Murders Involving Rifles in 1999
338 Murders with Shotguns in 1999
339 Percent of Murders Involving Shotguns in 1999
340 Murders with Knives or Cutting Instruments in 1999
341 Percent of Murders Involving Knives or Cutting Instruments in 1999
342 Murders by Hands, Fists or Feet in 1999
343 Percent of Murders Involving Hands, Fists or Feet in 1999
344 Rapes in 1999
345 Average Time Between Rapes in 1999
346 Percent Change in Number of Rapes: 1998 to 1999
347 Rape Rate in 1999
348 Percent Change in Rape Rate: 1998 to 1999
349 Rape Rate per 100,000 Female Population in 1999
350 Robberies in 1999
351 Average Time Between Robberies in 1999
352 Percent Change in Number of Robberies: 1998 to 1999
353 Robbery Rate in 1999
354 Percent Change in Robbery Rate: 1998 to 1999
355 Robberies with Firearms in 1999
356 Robbery Rate with Firearms in 1999
357 Percent of Robberies Involving Firearms in 1999
358 Robberies with Knives or Cutting Instruments in 1999
359 Percent of Robberies Involving Knives or Cutting Instruments in 1999

TABLE OF CONTENTS (continued)

360   Robberies with Blunt Objects and Other Dangerous Weapons in 1999
361   Percent of Robberies Involving Blunt Objects and Other Dangerous Weapons in 1999
362   Robberies Committed with Hands, Fists or Feet in 1999
363   Percent of Robberies Committed with Hands, Fists or Feet in 1999
364   Bank Robberies in 1999
365   Aggravated Assaults in 1999
366   Average Time Between Aggravated Assaults in 1999
367   Percent Change in Number of Aggravated Assaults: 1998 to 1999
368   Aggravated Assault Rate in 1999
369   Percent Change in Aggravated Assault Rate: 1998 to 1999
370   Aggravated Assaults with Firearms in 1999
371   Aggravated Assault Rate with Firearms in 1999
372   Percent of Aggravated Assaults Involving Firearms in 1999
373   Aggravated Assaults with Knives or Cutting Instruments in 1999
374   Percent of Aggravated Assaults Involving Knives or Cutting Instruments in 1999
375   Aggravated Assaults with Blunt Objects and Other Dangerous Weapons in 1999
376   Percent of Aggravated Assaults Involving Blunt Objects and Other Dangerous Weapons in 1999
377   Aggravated Assaults Committed with Hands, Fists or Feet in 1999
378   Percent of Aggravated Assaults Committed with Hands, Fists or Feet in 1999
379   Property Crimes in 1999
380   Average Time Between Property Crimes in 1999
381   Property Crimes per Square Mile in 1999
382   Percent Change in Number of Property Crimes: 1998 to 1999
383   Property Crime Rate in 1999
384   Percent Change in Property Crime Rate: 1998 to 1999
385   Burglaries in 1999
386   Average Time Between Burglaries in 1999
387   Percent Change in Number of Burglaries: 1998 to 1999
388   Burglary Rate in 1999
389   Percent Change in Burglary Rate: 1998 to 1999
390   Larcenies and Thefts in 1999
391   Average Time Between Larcenies and Thefts in 1999
392   Percent Change in Number of Larcenies and Thefts: 1998 to 1999
393   Larceny and Theft Rate in 1999
394   Percent Change in Larceny and Theft Rate: 1998 to 1999
395   Motor Vehicle Thefts in 1999
396   Average Time Between Motor Vehicle Thefts in 1999
397   Percent Change in Number of Motor Vehicle Thefts: 1998 to 1999
398   Motor Vehicle Theft Rate in 1999
399   Percent Change in Motor Vehicle Theft Rate: 1998 to 1999

Urban/Rural Crime

400   Crimes in Urban Areas in 1999
401   Urban Crime Rate in 1999
402   Percent of Crimes Occurring in Urban Areas in 1999
403   Crimes in Rural Areas in 1999
404   Rural Crime Rate in 1999
405   Percent of Crimes Occurring in Rural Areas in 1999
406   Violent Crimes in Urban Areas in 1999
407   Urban Violent Crime Rate in 1999
408   Percent of Violent Crimes Occurring in Urban Areas in 1999
409   Violent Crimes in Rural Areas in 1999
410   Rural Violent Crime Rate in 1999
411   Percent of Violent Crimes Occurring in Rural Areas in 1999
412   Murders in Urban Areas in 1999
413   Urban Murder Rate in 1999
414   Percent of Murders Occurring in Urban Areas in 1999
415   Murders in Rural Areas in 1999
416   Rural Murder Rate in 1999
417   Percent of Murders Occurring in Rural Areas in 1999
418   Rapes in Urban Areas in 1999
419   Urban Rape Rate in 1999
420   Percent of Rapes Occurring in Urban Areas in 1999

TABLE OF CONTENTS (continued)

421 Rapes in Rural Areas in 1999
422 Rural Rape Rate in 1999
423 Percent of Rapes Occurring in Rural Areas in 1999
424 Robberies in Urban Areas in 1999
425 Urban Robbery Rate in 1999
426 Percent of Robberies Occurring in Urban Areas in 1999
427 Robberies in Rural Areas in 1999
428 Rural Robbery Rate in 1999
429 Percent of Robberies Occurring in Rural Areas in 1999
430 Aggravated Assaults in Urban Areas in 1999
431 Urban Aggravated Assault Rate in 1999
432 Percent of Aggravated Assaults Occurring in Urban Areas in 1999
433 Aggravated Assaults in Rural Areas in 1999
434 Rural Aggravated Assault Rate in 1999
435 Percent of Aggravated Assaults Occurring in Rural Areas in 1999
436 Property Crimes in Urban Areas in 1999
437 Urban Property Crime Rate in 1999
438 Percent of Property Crimes Occurring in Urban Areas in 1999
439 Property Crimes in Rural Areas in 1999
440 Rural Property Crime Rate in 1999
441 Percent of Property Crimes Occurring in Rural Areas in 1999
442 Burglaries in Urban Areas in 1999
443 Urban Burglary Rate in 1999
444 Percent of Burglaries Occurring in Urban Areas in 1999
445 Burglaries in Rural Areas in 1999
446 Rural Burglary Rate in 1999
447 Percent of Burglaries Occurring in Rural Areas in 1999
448 Larcenies and Thefts in Urban Areas in 1999
449 Urban Larceny and Theft Rate in 1999
450 Percent of Larcenies and Thefts Occurring in Urban Areas in 1999
451 Larcenies and Thefts in Rural Areas in 1999
452 Rural Larceny and Theft Rate in 1999
453 Percent of Larcenies and Thefts Occurring in Rural Areas in 1999
454 Motor Vehicle Thefts in Urban Areas in 1999
455 Urban Motor Vehicle Theft Rate in 1999
456 Percent of Motor Vehicle Thefts Occurring in Urban Areas in 1999
457 Motor Vehicle Thefts in Rural Areas in 1999
458 Rural Motor Vehicle Theft Rate in 1999
459 Percent of Motor Vehicle Thefts Occurring in Rural Areas in 1999
460 Crimes Reported at Universities and Colleges in 1999
461 Crimes Reported at Universities and Colleges as a Percent of All Crimes in 1999
462 Violent Crimes Reported at Universities and Colleges in 1999
463 Violent Crimes Reported at Universities and Colleges as a Percent of All Violent Crimes in 1999
464 Property Crimes Reported at Universities and Colleges in 1999
465 Property Crimes at Universities and Colleges as a Percent of All Property Crimes in 1999

1995 Crimes

466 Crimes in 1995
467 Percent Change in Number of Crimes: 1995 to 1999
468 Crime Rate in 1995
469 Percent Change in Crime Rate: 1995 to 1999
470 Violent Crimes in 1995
471 Percent Change in Number of Violent Crimes: 1995 to 1999
472 Violent Crime Rate in 1995
473 Percent Change in Violent Crime Rate: 1995 to 1999
474 Murders in 1995
475 Percent Change in Number of Murders: 1995 to 1999
476 Murder Rate in 1995
477 Percent Change in Murder Rate: 1995 to 1999
478 Rapes in 1995
479 Percent Change in Number of Rapes: 1995 to 1999
480 Rape Rate in 1995
481 Percent Change in Rape Rate: 1995 to 1999

TABLE OF CONTENTS (continued)

482 Robberies in 1995
483 Percent Change in Number of Robberies: 1995 to 1999
484 Robbery Rate in 1995
485 Percent Change in Robbery Rate: 1995 to 1999
486 Aggravated Assaults in 1995
487 Percent Change in Number of Aggravated Assaults: 1995 to 1999
488 Aggravated Assault Rate in 1995
489 Percent Change in Aggravated Assault Rate: 1995 to 1999
490 Property Crimes in 1995
491 Percent Change in Number of Property Crimes: 1995 to 1999
492 Property Crime Rate in 1995
493 Percent Change in Property Crime Rate: 1995 to 1999
494 Burglaries in 1995
495 Percent Change in Number of Burglaries: 1995 to 1999
496 Burglary Rate in 1995
497 Percent Change in Burglary Rate: 1995 to 1999
498 Larcenies and Thefts in 1995
499 Percent Change in Number of Larcenies and Thefts: 1995 to 1999
500 Larceny and Theft Rate in 1995
501 Percent Change in Larceny and Theft Rate: 1995 to 1999
502 Motor Vehicle Thefts in 1995
503 Percent Change in Number of Motor Vehicle Thefts: 1995 to 1999
504 Motor Vehicle Theft Rate in 1995
505 Percent Change in Motor Vehicle Theft Rate: 1995 to 1999
506 Hate Crimes in 1999
507 Rate of Hate Crimes in 1999
508 Criminal Victimization in 1999

VIII. Appendix

A-1 Population in 2000
A-2 Population in 1999
A-3 Population in 1995
A-4 Urban Population in 1999
A-5 Rural Population in 1999
A-6 Population 10 to 17 Years Old in 1999
A-7 Total Area of States in Square Miles in 1999

IX. Sources

X. Index

I. ARRESTS

1   Reported Arrests in 1999
2   Reported Arrest Rate in 1999
3   Reported Arrests for Crime Index Offenses in 1999
4   Reported Arrest Rate for Crime Index Offenses in 1999
5   Reported Arrests for Violent Crime in 1999
6   Reported Arrest Rate for Violent Crime in 1999
7   Reported Arrests for Murder in 1999
8   Reported Arrest Rate for Murder in 1999
9   Reported Arrests for Rape in 1999
10   Reported Arrest Rate for Rape in 1999
11   Reported Arrests for Robbery in 1999
12   Reported Arrest Rate for Robbery in 1999
13   Reported Arrests for Aggravated Assaults in 1999
14   Reported Arrest Rate for Aggravated Assault in 1999
15   Reported Arrests for Property Crime in 1999
16   Reported Arrest Rate for Property Crime in 1999
17   Reported Arrests for Burglary in 1999
18   Reported Arrest Rate for Burglary in 1999
19   Reported Arrests for Larceny and Theft in 1999
20   Reported Arrest Rate for Larceny and Theft in 1999
21   Reported Arrests for Motor Vehicle Theft in 1999
22   Reported Arrest Rate for Motor Vehicle Theft in 1999
23   Reported Arrests for Arson in 1999
24   Reported Arrest Rate for Arson in 1999
25   Reported Arrests for Weapons Violations in 1999
26   Reported Arrest Rate for Weapons Violations in 1999
27   Reported Arrests for Driving Under the Influence in 1999
28   Reported Arrest Rate for Driving Under the Influence in 1999
29   Reported Arrests for Drug Abuse Violations in 1999
30   Reported Arrest Rate for Drug Abuse Violations in 1999
31   Reported Arrests for Sex Offenses in 1999
32   Reported Arrest Rate for Sex Offenses in 1999
33   Reported Arrests for Prostitution and Commercialized Vice in 1999
34   Reported Arrest Rate for Prostitution and Commercialized Vice in 1999
35   Reported Arrests for Offenses Against Families and Children in 1999
36   Reported Arrest Rate for Offenses Against Families and Children in 1999
37   Percent of Crimes Cleared in 1998
38   Percent of Violent Crimes Cleared in 1998
39   Percent of Murders Cleared in 1998
40   Percent of Rapes Cleared in 1998
41   Percent of Robberies Cleared in 1998
42   Percent of Aggravated Assaults Cleared in 1998
43   Percent of Property Crimes Cleared in 1998
44   Percent of Burglaries Cleared in 1998
45   Percent of Larcenies and Thefts Cleared in 1998
46   Percent of Motor Vehicle Thefts Cleared in 1998

Important Note Regarding Arrest Numbers

The state arrest numbers reported by the FBI and shown in tables 1 to 36 are only from those law enforcement agencies that submitted complete arrests reports for 12 months in 1999. The arrest rates were calculated by the editors using population totals provided by the FBI for those jurisdictions reporting. Reports from law enforcement agencies in Georgia, Illinois, Kentucky, Mississippi, Montana, New Hampshire, New York and South Carolina represented less than half of their state populations. Thus rates for these states should be interpreted with caution. Reports from Ohio, Tennessee and West Virginia represented just over half of their state population. No arrest data were available for Kansas, Maine, Oklahoma, Wisconsin and the District of Columbia.

Reported Arrests in 1999

National Total = 10,038,790 Reported Arrests*

<u>ALPHA ORDER</u>

RANK	STATE	ARRESTS	% of USA
20	Alabama	176,153	1.8%
39	Alaska	36,234	0.4%
9	Arizona	272,281	2.7%
18	Arkansas	214,854	2.1%
1	California	1,494,099	14.9%
16	Colorado	220,383	2.2%
24	Connecticut	153,212	1.5%
38	Delaware	38,212	0.4%
3	Florida	897,589	8.9%
23	Georgia	157,361	1.6%
35	Hawaii	51,874	0.5%
34	Idaho	63,073	0.6%
12	Illinois	248,861	2.5%
19	Indiana	188,426	1.9%
28	Iowa	102,278	1.0%
NA	Kansas**	NA	NA
36	Kentucky	45,302	0.5%
15	Louisiana	225,942	2.3%
NA	Maine**	NA	NA
21	Maryland	173,127	1.7%
27	Massachusetts	127,383	1.3%
7	Michigan	339,994	3.4%
14	Minnesota	231,986	2.3%
29	Mississippi	98,684	1.0%
13	Missouri	247,319	2.5%
46	Montana	13,769	0.1%
30	Nebraska	95,330	0.9%
25	Nevada	138,029	1.4%
44	New Hampshire	22,389	0.2%
5	New Jersey	378,090	3.8%
33	New Mexico	67,632	0.7%
11	New York	268,170	2.7%
4	North Carolina	463,626	4.6%
43	North Dakota	24,061	0.2%
8	Ohio	289,536	2.9%
NA	Oklahoma**	NA	NA
26	Oregon	136,451	1.4%
6	Pennsylvania	375,205	3.7%
37	Rhode Island	40,149	0.4%
32	South Carolina	70,602	0.7%
41	South Dakota	32,997	0.3%
22	Tennessee	169,144	1.7%
2	Texas	984,426	9.8%
31	Utah	93,725	0.9%
45	Vermont	14,223	0.1%
10	Virginia	271,518	2.7%
17	Washington	218,541	2.2%
42	West Virginia	32,279	0.3%
NA	Wisconsin**	NA	NA
40	Wyoming	34,271	0.3%

<u>RANK ORDER</u>

RANK	STATE	ARRESTS	% of USA
1	California	1,494,099	14.9%
2	Texas	984,426	9.8%
3	Florida	897,589	8.9%
4	North Carolina	463,626	4.6%
5	New Jersey	378,090	3.8%
6	Pennsylvania	375,205	3.7%
7	Michigan	339,994	3.4%
8	Ohio	289,536	2.9%
9	Arizona	272,281	2.7%
10	Virginia	271,518	2.7%
11	New York	268,170	2.7%
12	Illinois	248,861	2.5%
13	Missouri	247,319	2.5%
14	Minnesota	231,986	2.3%
15	Louisiana	225,942	2.3%
16	Colorado	220,383	2.2%
17	Washington	218,541	2.2%
18	Arkansas	214,854	2.1%
19	Indiana	188,426	1.9%
20	Alabama	176,153	1.8%
21	Maryland	173,127	1.7%
22	Tennessee	169,144	1.7%
23	Georgia	157,361	1.6%
24	Connecticut	153,212	1.5%
25	Nevada	138,029	1.4%
26	Oregon	136,451	1.4%
27	Massachusetts	127,383	1.3%
28	Iowa	102,278	1.0%
29	Mississippi	98,684	1.0%
30	Nebraska	95,330	0.9%
31	Utah	93,725	0.9%
32	South Carolina	70,602	0.7%
33	New Mexico	67,632	0.7%
34	Idaho	63,073	0.6%
35	Hawaii	51,874	0.5%
36	Kentucky	45,302	0.5%
37	Rhode Island	40,149	0.4%
38	Delaware	38,212	0.4%
39	Alaska	36,234	0.4%
40	Wyoming	34,271	0.3%
41	South Dakota	32,997	0.3%
42	West Virginia	32,279	0.3%
43	North Dakota	24,061	0.2%
44	New Hampshire	22,389	0.2%
45	Vermont	14,223	0.1%
46	Montana	13,769	0.1%
NA	Kansas**	NA	NA
NA	Maine**	NA	NA
NA	Oklahoma**	NA	NA
NA	Wisconsin**	NA	NA
	District of Columbia**	NA	NA

Source: Federal Bureau of Investigation
   "Crime in the United States 1999" (Uniform Crime Reports, October 15, 2000)
*By law enforcement agencies submitting complete reports to the F.B.I. for 12 months in 1999. The F.B.I. estimates
14,031,070 reported and unreported arrests occurred in 1999. See important note at beginning of this chapter.
**Not available.

Reported Arrest Rate in 1999

National Rate = 5,370.0 Reported Arrests per 100,000 Population*

ALPHA ORDER

RANK	STATE	RATE
39	Alabama	4,343.0
13	Alaska	6,493.5
18	Arizona	6,175.6
3	Arkansas	8,849.0
36	California	4,522.5
5	Colorado	8,738.4
31	Connecticut	4,915.4
29	Delaware	5,067.9
20	Florida	5,940.0
15	Georgia	6,433.4
30	Hawaii	4,973.5
22	Idaho	5,850.9
4	Illinois	8,821.7
25	Indiana	5,463.2
37	Iowa	4,399.1
NA	Kansas**	NA
1	Kentucky	10,157.4
10	Louisiana	6,871.7
NA	Maine**	NA
24	Maryland	5,608.3
46	Massachusetts	2,647.7
40	Michigan	4,214.1
23	Minnesota	5,712.5
2	Mississippi	8,922.6
6	Missouri	7,861.4
44	Montana	3,179.9
17	Nebraska	6,206.4
8	Nevada	7,842.6
32	New Hampshire	4,835.6
33	New Jersey	4,825.0
12	New Mexico	6,824.6
35	New York	4,661.4
11	North Carolina	6,868.5
28	North Dakota	5,108.5
34	Ohio	4,819.2
NA	Oklahoma**	NA
38	Oregon	4,379.0
41	Pennsylvania	4,087.6
42	Rhode Island	4,051.4
7	South Carolina	7,853.4
16	South Dakota	6,333.4
19	Tennessee	6,069.0
26	Texas	5,450.9
14	Utah	6,481.7
45	Vermont	2,944.7
21	Virginia	5,851.7
27	Washington	5,164.0
43	West Virginia	3,405.0
NA	Wisconsin**	NA
9	Wyoming	7,276.2

RANK ORDER

RANK	STATE	RATE
1	Kentucky	10,157.4
2	Mississippi	8,922.6
3	Arkansas	8,849.0
4	Illinois	8,821.7
5	Colorado	8,738.4
6	Missouri	7,861.4
7	South Carolina	7,853.4
8	Nevada	7,842.6
9	Wyoming	7,276.2
10	Louisiana	6,871.7
11	North Carolina	6,868.5
12	New Mexico	6,824.6
13	Alaska	6,493.5
14	Utah	6,481.7
15	Georgia	6,433.4
16	South Dakota	6,333.4
17	Nebraska	6,206.4
18	Arizona	6,175.6
19	Tennessee	6,069.0
20	Florida	5,940.0
21	Virginia	5,851.7
22	Idaho	5,850.9
23	Minnesota	5,712.5
24	Maryland	5,608.3
25	Indiana	5,463.2
26	Texas	5,450.9
27	Washington	5,164.0
28	North Dakota	5,108.5
29	Delaware	5,067.9
30	Hawaii	4,973.5
31	Connecticut	4,915.4
32	New Hampshire	4,835.6
33	New Jersey	4,825.0
34	Ohio	4,819.2
35	New York	4,661.4
36	California	4,522.5
37	Iowa	4,399.1
38	Oregon	4,379.0
39	Alabama	4,343.0
40	Michigan	4,214.1
41	Pennsylvania	4,087.6
42	Rhode Island	4,051.4
43	West Virginia	3,405.0
44	Montana	3,179.9
45	Vermont	2,944.7
46	Massachusetts	2,647.7
NA	Kansas**	NA
NA	Maine**	NA
NA	Oklahoma**	NA
NA	Wisconsin**	NA
	District of Columbia**	NA

Source: Morgan Quitno Press using data from Federal Bureau of Investigation
"Crime in the United States 1999" (Uniform Crime Reports, October 15, 2000)
*By law enforcement agencies submitting complete reports to the F.B.I. for 12 months in 1999. These rates based on population estimates for areas under the jurisdiction of those agencies reporting. Arrest rate based on the F.B.I. estimate of total arrests is 5,145.4 reported and unreported arrests per 100,000 population. See important note at beginning of this chapter. **Not available.

Reported Arrests for Crime Index Offenses in 1999

National Total = 1,699,893 Reported Arrests*

ALPHA ORDER

RANK	STATE	ARRESTS	% of USA
24	Alabama	24,775	1.5%
39	Alaska	5,677	0.3%
8	Arizona	47,721	2.8%
25	Arkansas	23,318	1.4%
1	California	308,560	18.2%
21	Colorado	28,241	1.7%
22	Connecticut	25,278	1.5%
34	Delaware	8,629	0.5%
2	Florida	187,820	11.0%
26	Georgia	20,675	1.2%
35	Hawaii	8,058	0.5%
36	Idaho	7,932	0.5%
10	Illinois	45,881	2.7%
16	Indiana	31,359	1.8%
28	Iowa	17,064	1.0%
NA	Kansas**	NA	NA
37	Kentucky	6,712	0.4%
11	Louisiana	45,086	2.7%
NA	Maine**	NA	NA
23	Maryland	25,091	1.5%
20	Massachusetts	29,236	1.7%
7	Michigan	49,119	2.9%
17	Minnesota	31,236	1.8%
31	Mississippi	12,997	0.8%
14	Missouri	39,807	2.3%
41	Montana	4,485	0.3%
30	Nebraska	13,203	0.8%
27	Nevada	19,555	1.2%
45	New Hampshire	1,941	0.1%
6	New Jersey	56,140	3.3%
33	New Mexico	9,918	0.6%
9	New York	47,072	2.8%
4	North Carolina	78,632	4.6%
44	North Dakota	2,569	0.2%
13	Ohio	43,419	2.6%
NA	Oklahoma**	NA	NA
18	Oregon	31,023	1.8%
5	Pennsylvania	71,482	4.2%
38	Rhode Island	5,722	0.3%
32	South Carolina	10,154	0.6%
42	South Dakota	3,920	0.2%
19	Tennessee	29,827	1.8%
3	Texas	135,818	8.0%
29	Utah	15,193	0.9%
46	Vermont	1,649	0.1%
15	Virginia	34,497	2.0%
12	Washington	44,346	2.6%
40	West Virginia	5,307	0.3%
NA	Wisconsin**	NA	NA
43	Wyoming	3,749	0.2%

RANK ORDER

RANK	STATE	ARRESTS	% of USA
1	California	308,560	18.2%
2	Florida	187,820	11.0%
3	Texas	135,818	8.0%
4	North Carolina	78,632	4.6%
5	Pennsylvania	71,482	4.2%
6	New Jersey	56,140	3.3%
7	Michigan	49,119	2.9%
8	Arizona	47,721	2.8%
9	New York	47,072	2.8%
10	Illinois	45,881	2.7%
11	Louisiana	45,086	2.7%
12	Washington	44,346	2.6%
13	Ohio	43,419	2.6%
14	Missouri	39,807	2.3%
15	Virginia	34,497	2.0%
16	Indiana	31,359	1.8%
17	Minnesota	31,236	1.8%
18	Oregon	31,023	1.8%
19	Tennessee	29,827	1.8%
20	Massachusetts	29,236	1.7%
21	Colorado	28,241	1.7%
22	Connecticut	25,278	1.5%
23	Maryland	25,091	1.5%
24	Alabama	24,775	1.5%
25	Arkansas	23,318	1.4%
26	Georgia	20,675	1.2%
27	Nevada	19,555	1.2%
28	Iowa	17,064	1.0%
29	Utah	15,193	0.9%
30	Nebraska	13,203	0.8%
31	Mississippi	12,997	0.8%
32	South Carolina	10,154	0.6%
33	New Mexico	9,918	0.6%
34	Delaware	8,629	0.5%
35	Hawaii	8,058	0.5%
36	Idaho	7,932	0.5%
37	Kentucky	6,712	0.4%
38	Rhode Island	5,722	0.3%
39	Alaska	5,677	0.3%
40	West Virginia	5,307	0.3%
41	Montana	4,485	0.3%
42	South Dakota	3,920	0.2%
43	Wyoming	3,749	0.2%
44	North Dakota	2,569	0.2%
45	New Hampshire	1,941	0.1%
46	Vermont	1,649	0.1%
NA	Kansas**	NA	NA
NA	Maine**	NA	NA
NA	Oklahoma**	NA	NA
NA	Wisconsin**	NA	NA
	District of Columbia**	NA	NA

Source: Federal Bureau of Investigation
"Crime in the United States 1999" (Uniform Crime Reports, October 15, 2000)
*By law enforcement agencies submitting complete reports to the F.B.I. for 12 months in 1999. The F.B.I. estimates 2,280,500 reported and unreported arrests for crime index offenses occurred in 1999. Crime index offenses consist of murder, forcible rape, robbery, aggravated assault, burglary, larceny-theft, motor vehicle theft and arson. See important note at beginning of this chapter. **Not available.

3

Reported Arrest Rate for Crime Index Offenses in 1999

National Rate = 909.3 Reported Arrests per 100,000 Population*

ALPHA ORDER

RANK	STATE	RATE
39	Alabama	610.8
17	Alaska	1,017.4
12	Arizona	1,082.4
20	Arkansas	960.4
21	California	934.0
10	Colorado	1,119.8
27	Connecticut	811.0
8	Delaware	1,144.4
5	Florida	1,242.9
24	Georgia	845.3
30	Hawaii	772.6
35	Idaho	735.8
1	Illinois	1,626.4
22	Indiana	909.2
36	Iowa	733.9
NA	Kansas**	NA
2	Kentucky	1,504.9
3	Louisiana	1,371.2
NA	Maine**	NA
26	Maryland	812.8
41	Massachusetts	607.7
40	Michigan	608.8
31	Minnesota	769.2
6	Mississippi	1,175.1
4	Missouri	1,265.3
16	Montana	1,035.8
23	Nebraska	859.6
11	Nevada	1,111.1
45	New Hampshire	419.2
38	New Jersey	716.4
18	New Mexico	1,000.8
25	New York	818.2
7	North Carolina	1,164.9
44	North Dakota	545.4
37	Ohio	722.7
NA	Oklahoma**	NA
19	Oregon	995.6
29	Pennsylvania	778.8
42	Rhode Island	577.4
9	South Carolina	1,129.5
32	South Dakota	752.4
13	Tennessee	1,070.2
33	Texas	752.0
14	Utah	1,050.7
46	Vermont	341.4
34	Virginia	743.5
15	Washington	1,047.9
43	West Virginia	559.8
NA	Wisconsin**	NA
28	Wyoming	796.0

RANK ORDER

RANK	STATE	RATE
1	Illinois	1,626.4
2	Kentucky	1,504.9
3	Louisiana	1,371.2
4	Missouri	1,265.3
5	Florida	1,242.9
6	Mississippi	1,175.1
7	North Carolina	1,164.9
8	Delaware	1,144.4
9	South Carolina	1,129.5
10	Colorado	1,119.8
11	Nevada	1,111.1
12	Arizona	1,082.4
13	Tennessee	1,070.2
14	Utah	1,050.7
15	Washington	1,047.9
16	Montana	1,035.8
17	Alaska	1,017.4
18	New Mexico	1,000.8
19	Oregon	995.6
20	Arkansas	960.4
21	California	934.0
22	Indiana	909.2
23	Nebraska	859.6
24	Georgia	845.3
25	New York	818.2
26	Maryland	812.8
27	Connecticut	811.0
28	Wyoming	796.0
29	Pennsylvania	778.8
30	Hawaii	772.6
31	Minnesota	769.2
32	South Dakota	752.4
33	Texas	752.0
34	Virginia	743.5
35	Idaho	735.8
36	Iowa	733.9
37	Ohio	722.7
38	New Jersey	716.4
39	Alabama	610.8
40	Michigan	608.8
41	Massachusetts	607.7
42	Rhode Island	577.4
43	West Virginia	559.8
44	North Dakota	545.4
45	New Hampshire	419.2
46	Vermont	341.4
NA	Kansas**	NA
NA	Maine**	NA
NA	Oklahoma**	NA
NA	Wisconsin**	NA
	District of Columbia**	NA

Source: Morgan Quitno Press using data from Federal Bureau of Investigation
"Crime in the United States 1999" (Uniform Crime Reports, October 15, 2000)
*By law enforcement agencies submitting complete reports to the F.B.I. for 12 months in 1999. These rates based on population estimates for areas under the jurisdiction of those agencies reporting. Arrest rate based on the F.B.I. estimate of reported and unreported arrests for crime index offenses is 836.3 arrests per 100,000 population. See important note at beginning of this chapter. **Not available.

Reported Arrests for Violent Crime in 1999

National Total = 475,823 Reported Arrests*

ALPHA ORDER

ALPHA ORDER

RANK ORDER

RANK	STATE	ARRESTS	% of USA		RANK	STATE	ARRESTS	% of USA
19	Alabama	6,684	1.4%		1	California	133,086	28.0%
36	Alaska	1,447	0.3%		2	Florida	55,667	11.7%
15	Arizona	7,813	1.6%		3	Texas	29,013	6.1%
22	Arkansas	5,458	1.1%		4	North Carolina	24,074	5.1%
1	California	133,086	28.0%		5	Pennsylvania	22,365	4.7%
23	Colorado	5,166	1.1%		6	Michigan	17,180	3.6%
20	Connecticut	6,173	1.3%		7	New Jersey	15,913	3.3%
30	Delaware	2,896	0.6%		8	Massachusetts	13,659	2.9%
2	Florida	55,667	11.7%		9	Louisiana	11,607	2.4%
25	Georgia	4,241	0.9%		10	Illinois	11,345	2.4%
40	Hawaii	1,116	0.2%		11	Ohio	10,690	2.2%
39	Idaho	1,152	0.2%		12	New York	10,255	2.2%
10	Illinois	11,345	2.4%		13	Indiana	9,257	1.9%
13	Indiana	9,257	1.9%		14	Missouri	8,261	1.7%
26	Iowa	4,213	0.9%		15	Arizona	7,813	1.6%
NA	Kansas**	NA	NA		16	Virginia	7,358	1.5%
32	Kentucky	2,490	0.5%		17	Tennessee	7,186	1.5%
9	Louisiana	11,607	2.4%		18	Washington	7,144	1.5%
NA	Maine**	NA	NA		19	Alabama	6,684	1.4%
24	Maryland	4,813	1.0%		20	Connecticut	6,173	1.3%
8	Massachusetts	13,659	2.9%		21	Minnesota	5,641	1.2%
6	Michigan	17,180	3.6%		22	Arkansas	5,458	1.1%
21	Minnesota	5,641	1.2%		23	Colorado	5,166	1.1%
33	Mississippi	2,087	0.4%		24	Maryland	4,813	1.0%
14	Missouri	8,261	1.7%		25	Georgia	4,241	0.9%
41	Montana	605	0.1%		26	Iowa	4,213	0.9%
37	Nebraska	1,394	0.3%		27	Oregon	3,381	0.7%
28	Nevada	3,175	0.7%		28	Nevada	3,175	0.7%
45	New Hampshire	278	0.1%		29	South Carolina	2,999	0.6%
7	New Jersey	15,913	3.3%		30	Delaware	2,896	0.6%
31	New Mexico	2,521	0.5%		31	New Mexico	2,521	0.5%
12	New York	10,255	2.2%		32	Kentucky	2,490	0.5%
4	North Carolina	24,074	5.1%		33	Mississippi	2,087	0.4%
46	North Dakota	167	0.0%		34	Utah	1,697	0.4%
11	Ohio	10,690	2.2%		35	West Virginia	1,645	0.3%
NA	Oklahoma**	NA	NA		36	Alaska	1,447	0.3%
27	Oregon	3,381	0.7%		37	Nebraska	1,394	0.3%
5	Pennsylvania	22,365	4.7%		38	Rhode Island	1,201	0.3%
38	Rhode Island	1,201	0.3%		39	Idaho	1,152	0.2%
29	South Carolina	2,999	0.6%		40	Hawaii	1,116	0.2%
42	South Dakota	518	0.1%		41	Montana	605	0.1%
17	Tennessee	7,186	1.5%		42	South Dakota	518	0.1%
3	Texas	29,013	6.1%		43	Wyoming	504	0.1%
34	Utah	1,697	0.4%		44	Vermont	288	0.1%
44	Vermont	288	0.1%		45	New Hampshire	278	0.1%
16	Virginia	7,358	1.5%		46	North Dakota	167	0.0%
18	Washington	7,144	1.5%		NA	Kansas**	NA	NA
35	West Virginia	1,645	0.3%		NA	Maine**	NA	NA
NA	Wisconsin**	NA	NA		NA	Oklahoma**	NA	NA
43	Wyoming	504	0.1%		NA	Wisconsin**	NA	NA
						District of Columbia**	NA	NA

Source: Federal Bureau of Investigation
   "Crime in the United States 1999" (Uniform Crime Reports, October 15, 2000)
*By law enforcement agencies submitting complete reports to the F.B.I. for 12 months in 1999. The F.B.I. estimates
636,000 reported and unreported arrests for violent crimes occurred in 1999. Violent crimes are offenses of murder,
forcible rape, robbery and aggravated assault. See important note at beginning of this chapter.
**Not available.

Reported Arrest Rate for Violent Crime in 1999

National Rate = 254.5 Reported Arrests per 100,000 Population*

ALPHA ORDER

RANK	STATE	RATE
30	Alabama	164.8
12	Alaska	259.3
26	Arizona	177.2
16	Arkansas	224.8
2	California	402.8
18	Colorado	204.8
20	Connecticut	198.0
4	Delaware	384.1
5	Florida	368.4
28	Georgia	173.4
39	Hawaii	107.0
41	Idaho	106.9
3	Illinois	402.2
10	Indiana	268.4
22	Iowa	181.2
NA	Kansas**	NA
1	Kentucky	558.3
7	Louisiana	353.0
NA	Maine**	NA
33	Maryland	155.9
9	Massachusetts	283.9
17	Michigan	212.9
35	Minnesota	138.9
21	Mississippi	188.7
11	Missouri	262.6
34	Montana	139.7
43	Nebraska	90.8
23	Nevada	180.4
44	New Hampshire	60.0
19	New Jersey	203.1
14	New Mexico	254.4
24	New York	178.3
6	North Carolina	356.7
46	North Dakota	35.5
25	Ohio	177.9
NA	Oklahoma**	NA
38	Oregon	108.5
15	Pennsylvania	243.7
36	Rhode Island	121.2
8	South Carolina	333.6
42	South Dakota	99.4
13	Tennessee	257.8
31	Texas	160.6
37	Utah	117.4
45	Vermont	59.6
32	Virginia	158.6
29	Washington	168.8
27	West Virginia	173.5
NA	Wisconsin**	NA
39	Wyoming	107.0

RANK ORDER

RANK	STATE	RATE
1	Kentucky	558.3
2	California	402.8
3	Illinois	402.2
4	Delaware	384.1
5	Florida	368.4
6	North Carolina	356.7
7	Louisiana	353.0
8	South Carolina	333.6
9	Massachusetts	283.9
10	Indiana	268.4
11	Missouri	262.6
12	Alaska	259.3
13	Tennessee	257.8
14	New Mexico	254.4
15	Pennsylvania	243.7
16	Arkansas	224.8
17	Michigan	212.9
18	Colorado	204.8
19	New Jersey	203.1
20	Connecticut	198.0
21	Mississippi	188.7
22	Iowa	181.2
23	Nevada	180.4
24	New York	178.3
25	Ohio	177.9
26	Arizona	177.2
27	West Virginia	173.5
28	Georgia	173.4
29	Washington	168.8
30	Alabama	164.8
31	Texas	160.6
32	Virginia	158.6
33	Maryland	155.9
34	Montana	139.7
35	Minnesota	138.9
36	Rhode Island	121.2
37	Utah	117.4
38	Oregon	108.5
39	Hawaii	107.0
39	Wyoming	107.0
41	Idaho	106.9
42	South Dakota	99.4
43	Nebraska	90.8
44	New Hampshire	60.0
45	Vermont	59.6
46	North Dakota	35.5
NA	Kansas**	NA
NA	Maine**	NA
NA	Oklahoma**	NA
NA	Wisconsin**	NA
	District of Columbia**	NA

Source: Morgan Quitno Press using data from Federal Bureau of Investigation
"Crime in the United States 1999" (Uniform Crime Reports, October 15, 2000)
*By law enforcement agencies submitting complete reports to the F.B.I. for 12 months in 1999. These rates based on population estimates for areas under the jurisdiction of those agencies reporting. Arrest rate based on the F.B.I. estimate of reported and unreported arrests for violent crimes is 233.2 arrests per 100,000 population. See important note at beginning of this chapter. **Not available.

Reported Arrests for Murder in 1999

National Total = 10,468 Reported Arrests*

ALPHA ORDER

RANK	STATE	ARRESTS	% of USA
9	Alabama	265	2.5%
34	Alaska	36	0.3%
13	Arizona	243	2.3%
17	Arkansas	171	1.6%
1	California	1,770	16.9%
25	Colorado	99	0.9%
26	Connecticut	90	0.9%
39	Delaware	23	0.2%
4	Florida	741	7.1%
22	Georgia	122	1.2%
32	Hawaii	44	0.4%
41	Idaho	14	0.1%
6	Illinois	637	6.1%
12	Indiana	244	2.3%
38	Iowa	24	0.2%
NA	Kansas**	NA	NA
36	Kentucky	29	0.3%
11	Louisiana	248	2.4%
NA	Maine**	NA	NA
27	Maryland	73	0.7%
28	Massachusetts	69	0.7%
2	Michigan	1,275	12.2%
19	Minnesota	142	1.4%
20	Mississippi	135	1.3%
10	Missouri	251	2.4%
40	Montana	17	0.2%
31	Nebraska	46	0.4%
21	Nevada	123	1.2%
46	New Hampshire	2	0.0%
14	New Jersey	240	2.3%
29	New Mexico	68	0.6%
18	New York	165	1.6%
5	North Carolina	669	6.4%
45	North Dakota	5	0.0%
16	Ohio	185	1.8%
NA	Oklahoma**	NA	NA
24	Oregon	103	1.0%
7	Pennsylvania	477	4.6%
35	Rhode Island	30	0.3%
30	South Carolina	55	0.5%
43	South Dakota	8	0.1%
8	Tennessee	326	3.1%
3	Texas	773	7.4%
37	Utah	26	0.2%
44	Vermont	7	0.1%
15	Virginia	228	2.2%
23	Washington	120	1.1%
33	West Virginia	41	0.4%
NA	Wisconsin**	NA	NA
42	Wyoming	9	0.1%

RANK ORDER

RANK	STATE	ARRESTS	% of USA
1	California	1,770	16.9%
2	Michigan	1,275	12.2%
3	Texas	773	7.4%
4	Florida	741	7.1%
5	North Carolina	669	6.4%
6	Illinois	637	6.1%
7	Pennsylvania	477	4.6%
8	Tennessee	326	3.1%
9	Alabama	265	2.5%
10	Missouri	251	2.4%
11	Louisiana	248	2.4%
12	Indiana	244	2.3%
13	Arizona	243	2.3%
14	New Jersey	240	2.3%
15	Virginia	228	2.2%
16	Ohio	185	1.8%
17	Arkansas	171	1.6%
18	New York	165	1.6%
19	Minnesota	142	1.4%
20	Mississippi	135	1.3%
21	Nevada	123	1.2%
22	Georgia	122	1.2%
23	Washington	120	1.1%
24	Oregon	103	1.0%
25	Colorado	99	0.9%
26	Connecticut	90	0.9%
27	Maryland	73	0.7%
28	Massachusetts	69	0.7%
29	New Mexico	68	0.6%
30	South Carolina	55	0.5%
31	Nebraska	46	0.4%
32	Hawaii	44	0.4%
33	West Virginia	41	0.4%
34	Alaska	36	0.3%
35	Rhode Island	30	0.3%
36	Kentucky	29	0.3%
37	Utah	26	0.2%
38	Iowa	24	0.2%
39	Delaware	23	0.2%
40	Montana	17	0.2%
41	Idaho	14	0.1%
42	Wyoming	9	0.1%
43	South Dakota	8	0.1%
44	Vermont	7	0.1%
45	North Dakota	5	0.0%
46	New Hampshire	2	0.0%
NA	Kansas**	NA	NA
NA	Maine**	NA	NA
NA	Oklahoma**	NA	NA
NA	Wisconsin**	NA	NA
	District of Columbia**	NA	NA

Source: Federal Bureau of Investigation
   "Crime in the United States 1999" (Uniform Crime Reports, October 15, 2000)
By law enforcement agencies submitting complete reports to the F.B.I. for 12 months in 1999. The F.B.I. estimates 14,790 reported and unreported arrests for murder occurred in 1999. Murder includes nonnegligent manslaughter. See important note at beginning of this chapter.
**Not available.*

Reported Arrest Rate for Murder in 1999

National Rate = 5.6 Reported Arrests per 100,000 Population*

ALPHA ORDER

RANK	STATE	RATE
12	Alabama	6.5
12	Alaska	6.5
16	Arizona	5.5
9	Arkansas	7.0
17	California	5.4
25	Colorado	3.9
34	Connecticut	2.9
29	Delaware	3.1
20	Florida	4.9
19	Georgia	5.0
24	Hawaii	4.2
43	Idaho	1.3
1	Illinois	22.6
8	Indiana	7.1
45	Iowa	1.0
NA	Kansas**	NA
12	Kentucky	6.5
7	Louisiana	7.5
NA	Maine**	NA
37	Maryland	2.4
41	Massachusetts	1.4
2	Michigan	15.8
27	Minnesota	3.5
3	Mississippi	12.2
6	Missouri	8.0
25	Montana	3.9
32	Nebraska	3.0
9	Nevada	7.0
46	New Hampshire	0.4
29	New Jersey	3.1
11	New Mexico	6.9
34	New York	2.9
5	North Carolina	9.9
44	North Dakota	1.1
29	Ohio	3.1
NA	Oklahoma**	NA
28	Oregon	3.3
18	Pennsylvania	5.2
32	Rhode Island	3.0
15	South Carolina	6.1
40	South Dakota	1.5
4	Tennessee	11.7
22	Texas	4.3
39	Utah	1.8
41	Vermont	1.4
20	Virginia	4.9
36	Washington	2.8
22	West Virginia	4.3
NA	Wisconsin**	NA
38	Wyoming	1.9

RANK ORDER

RANK	STATE	RATE
1	Illinois	22.6
2	Michigan	15.8
3	Mississippi	12.2
4	Tennessee	11.7
5	North Carolina	9.9
6	Missouri	8.0
7	Louisiana	7.5
8	Indiana	7.1
9	Arkansas	7.0
9	Nevada	7.0
11	New Mexico	6.9
12	Alabama	6.5
12	Alaska	6.5
12	Kentucky	6.5
15	South Carolina	6.1
16	Arizona	5.5
17	California	5.4
18	Pennsylvania	5.2
19	Georgia	5.0
20	Florida	4.9
20	Virginia	4.9
22	Texas	4.3
22	West Virginia	4.3
24	Hawaii	4.2
25	Colorado	3.9
25	Montana	3.9
27	Minnesota	3.5
28	Oregon	3.3
29	Delaware	3.1
29	New Jersey	3.1
29	Ohio	3.1
32	Nebraska	3.0
32	Rhode Island	3.0
34	Connecticut	2.9
34	New York	2.9
36	Washington	2.8
37	Maryland	2.4
38	Wyoming	1.9
39	Utah	1.8
40	South Dakota	1.5
41	Massachusetts	1.4
41	Vermont	1.4
43	Idaho	1.3
44	North Dakota	1.1
45	Iowa	1.0
46	New Hampshire	0.4
NA	Kansas**	NA
NA	Maine**	NA
NA	Oklahoma**	NA
NA	Wisconsin**	NA
	District of Columbia**	NA

Source: Morgan Quitno Press using data from Federal Bureau of Investigation
   "Crime in the United States 1999" (Uniform Crime Reports, October 15, 2000)
*By law enforcement agencies submitting complete reports to the F.B.I. for 12 months in 1999. These rates based on population estimates for areas under the jurisdiction of those agencies reporting. Arrest rate based on the F.B.I. estimate of reported and unreported arrests for murder is 5.4 arrests per 100,000 population. See important note at beginning of this chapter. **Not available.

Reported Arrests for Rape in 1999

National Total = 21,033 Reported Arrests*

<u>ALPHA ORDER</u>

RANK	STATE	ARRESTS	% of USA
20	Alabama	294	1.4%
33	Alaska	134	0.6%
29	Arizona	171	0.8%
18	Arkansas	391	1.9%
1	California	2,885	13.7%
11	Colorado	511	2.4%
21	Connecticut	289	1.4%
19	Delaware	312	1.5%
2	Florida	2,274	10.8%
26	Georgia	219	1.0%
36	Hawaii	84	0.4%
38	Idaho	77	0.4%
8	Illinois	700	3.3%
25	Indiana	221	1.1%
35	Iowa	122	0.6%
NA	Kansas**	NA	NA
40	Kentucky	49	0.2%
16	Louisiana	449	2.1%
NA	Maine**	NA	NA
22	Maryland	233	1.1%
13	Massachusetts	463	2.2%
4	Michigan	1,254	6.0%
9	Minnesota	698	3.3%
28	Mississippi	191	0.9%
15	Missouri	450	2.1%
44	Montana	36	0.2%
30	Nebraska	161	0.8%
24	Nevada	228	1.1%
45	New Hampshire	21	0.1%
10	New Jersey	647	3.1%
36	New Mexico	84	0.4%
14	New York	456	2.2%
12	North Carolina	498	2.4%
46	North Dakota	20	0.1%
6	Ohio	817	3.9%
NA	Oklahoma**	NA	NA
23	Oregon	229	1.1%
5	Pennsylvania	1,186	5.6%
34	Rhode Island	131	0.6%
31	South Carolina	151	0.7%
42	South Dakota	46	0.2%
27	Tennessee	213	1.0%
3	Texas	2,185	10.4%
32	Utah	143	0.7%
39	Vermont	65	0.3%
17	Virginia	440	2.1%
7	Washington	712	3.4%
41	West Virginia	47	0.2%
NA	Wisconsin**	NA	NA
42	Wyoming	46	0.2%

<u>RANK ORDER</u>

RANK	STATE	ARRESTS	% of USA
1	California	2,885	13.7%
2	Florida	2,274	10.8%
3	Texas	2,185	10.4%
4	Michigan	1,254	6.0%
5	Pennsylvania	1,186	5.6%
6	Ohio	817	3.9%
7	Washington	712	3.4%
8	Illinois	700	3.3%
9	Minnesota	698	3.3%
10	New Jersey	647	3.1%
11	Colorado	511	2.4%
12	North Carolina	498	2.4%
13	Massachusetts	463	2.2%
14	New York	456	2.2%
15	Missouri	450	2.1%
16	Louisiana	449	2.1%
17	Virginia	440	2.1%
18	Arkansas	391	1.9%
19	Delaware	312	1.5%
20	Alabama	294	1.4%
21	Connecticut	289	1.4%
22	Maryland	233	1.1%
23	Oregon	229	1.1%
24	Nevada	228	1.1%
25	Indiana	221	1.1%
26	Georgia	219	1.0%
27	Tennessee	213	1.0%
28	Mississippi	191	0.9%
29	Arizona	171	0.8%
30	Nebraska	161	0.8%
31	South Carolina	151	0.7%
32	Utah	143	0.7%
33	Alaska	134	0.6%
34	Rhode Island	131	0.6%
35	Iowa	122	0.6%
36	Hawaii	84	0.4%
36	New Mexico	84	0.4%
38	Idaho	77	0.4%
39	Vermont	65	0.3%
40	Kentucky	49	0.2%
41	West Virginia	47	0.2%
42	South Dakota	46	0.2%
42	Wyoming	46	0.2%
44	Montana	36	0.2%
45	New Hampshire	21	0.1%
46	North Dakota	20	0.1%
NA	Kansas**	NA	NA
NA	Maine**	NA	NA
NA	Oklahoma**	NA	NA
NA	Wisconsin**	NA	NA
	District of Columbia**	NA	NA

Source: Federal Bureau of Investigation
   "Crime in the United States 1999" (Uniform Crime Reports, October 15, 2000)
*By law enforcement agencies submitting complete reports to the F.B.I. for 12 months in 1999. The F.B.I. estimates 28,830 reported and unreported arrests for rape occurred in 1999. Forcible rape is the carnal knowledge of a female forcibly and against her will. Assaults or attempts to commit rape by force or threat of force are included. See important note at beginning of this chapter. **Not available.

Reported Arrest Rate for Rape in 1999

National Rate = 11.3 Reported Arrests per 100,000 Population*

ALPHA ORDER

RANK ORDER

RANK	STATE	RATE	RANK	STATE	RATE
39	Alabama	7.2	1	Delaware	41.4
3	Alaska	24.0	2	Illinois	24.8
46	Arizona	3.9	3	Alaska	24.0
9	Arkansas	16.1	4	Colorado	20.3
29	California	8.7	5	Mississippi	17.3
4	Colorado	20.3	6	Minnesota	17.2
26	Connecticut	9.3	7	South Carolina	16.8
1	Delaware	41.4	7	Washington	16.8
11	Florida	15.0	9	Arkansas	16.1
27	Georgia	9.0	10	Michigan	15.5
33	Hawaii	8.1	11	Florida	15.0
40	Idaho	7.1	12	Missouri	14.3
2	Illinois	24.8	13	Louisiana	13.7
41	Indiana	6.4	14	Ohio	13.6
42	Iowa	5.2	15	Vermont	13.5
NA	Kansas**	NA	16	Rhode Island	13.2
20	Kentucky	11.0	17	Nevada	13.0
13	Louisiana	13.7	18	Pennsylvania	12.9
NA	Maine**	NA	19	Texas	12.1
36	Maryland	7.5	20	Kentucky	11.0
24	Massachusetts	9.6	21	Nebraska	10.5
10	Michigan	15.5	22	Utah	9.9
6	Minnesota	17.2	23	Wyoming	9.8
5	Mississippi	17.3	24	Massachusetts	9.6
12	Missouri	14.3	25	Virginia	9.5
31	Montana	8.3	26	Connecticut	9.3
21	Nebraska	10.5	27	Georgia	9.0
17	Nevada	13.0	28	South Dakota	8.8
44	New Hampshire	4.5	29	California	8.7
31	New Jersey	8.3	30	New Mexico	8.5
30	New Mexico	8.5	31	Montana	8.3
34	New York	7.9	31	New Jersey	8.3
37	North Carolina	7.4	33	Hawaii	8.1
45	North Dakota	4.2	34	New York	7.9
14	Ohio	13.6	35	Tennessee	7.6
NA	Oklahoma**	NA	36	Maryland	7.5
38	Oregon	7.3	37	North Carolina	7.4
18	Pennsylvania	12.9	38	Oregon	7.3
16	Rhode Island	13.2	39	Alabama	7.2
7	South Carolina	16.8	40	Idaho	7.1
28	South Dakota	8.8	41	Indiana	6.4
35	Tennessee	7.6	42	Iowa	5.2
19	Texas	12.1	43	West Virginia	5.0
22	Utah	9.9	44	New Hampshire	4.5
15	Vermont	13.5	45	North Dakota	4.2
25	Virginia	9.5	46	Arizona	3.9
7	Washington	16.8	NA	Kansas**	NA
43	West Virginia	5.0	NA	Maine**	NA
NA	Wisconsin**	NA	NA	Oklahoma**	NA
23	Wyoming	9.8	NA	Wisconsin**	NA
				District of Columbia**	NA

Source: Morgan Quitno Press using data from Federal Bureau of Investigation
   "Crime in the United States 1999" (Uniform Crime Reports, October 15, 2000)
*By law enforcement agencies submitting complete reports to the F.B.I. for 12 months in 1999. These rates based
on population estimates for areas under the jurisdiction of those agencies reporting. Arrest rate based on the F.B.I.
estimate of reported and unreported arrests for rape is 10.6 arrests per 100,000 population. See important note at
beginning of this chapter. **Not available.

Reported Arrests for Robbery in 1999

National Total = 83,247 Reported Arrests*

ALPHA ORDER

RANK	STATE	ARRESTS	% of USA
14	Alabama	1,413	1.7%
38	Alaska	188	0.2%
18	Arizona	1,359	1.6%
25	Arkansas	779	0.9%
1	California	18,746	22.5%
27	Colorado	634	0.8%
17	Connecticut	1,378	1.7%
28	Delaware	574	0.7%
2	Florida	9,628	11.6%
26	Georgia	755	0.9%
32	Hawaii	376	0.5%
41	Idaho	84	0.1%
7	Illinois	3,173	3.8%
13	Indiana	1,427	1.7%
33	Iowa	359	0.4%
NA	Kansas**	NA	NA
31	Kentucky	457	0.5%
15	Louisiana	1,409	1.7%
NA	Maine**	NA	NA
22	Maryland	1,039	1.2%
16	Massachusetts	1,393	1.7%
8	Michigan	2,819	3.4%
23	Minnesota	1,020	1.2%
29	Mississippi	549	0.7%
11	Missouri	1,731	2.1%
42	Montana	74	0.1%
34	Nebraska	323	0.4%
20	Nevada	1,146	1.4%
40	New Hampshire	92	0.1%
5	New Jersey	4,190	5.0%
35	New Mexico	254	0.3%
9	New York	2,283	2.7%
6	North Carolina	3,705	4.5%
45	North Dakota	20	0.0%
10	Ohio	2,027	2.4%
NA	Oklahoma**	NA	NA
24	Oregon	988	1.2%
3	Pennsylvania	6,154	7.4%
36	Rhode Island	242	0.3%
30	South Carolina	492	0.6%
43	South Dakota	46	0.1%
21	Tennessee	1,047	1.3%
4	Texas	5,714	6.9%
36	Utah	242	0.3%
46	Vermont	4	0.0%
12	Virginia	1,431	1.7%
19	Washington	1,349	1.6%
39	West Virginia	99	0.1%
NA	Wisconsin**	NA	NA
44	Wyoming	35	0.0%

RANK ORDER

RANK	STATE	ARRESTS	% of USA
1	California	18,746	22.5%
2	Florida	9,628	11.6%
3	Pennsylvania	6,154	7.4%
4	Texas	5,714	6.9%
5	New Jersey	4,190	5.0%
6	North Carolina	3,705	4.5%
7	Illinois	3,173	3.8%
8	Michigan	2,819	3.4%
9	New York	2,283	2.7%
10	Ohio	2,027	2.4%
11	Missouri	1,731	2.1%
12	Virginia	1,431	1.7%
13	Indiana	1,427	1.7%
14	Alabama	1,413	1.7%
15	Louisiana	1,409	1.7%
16	Massachusetts	1,393	1.7%
17	Connecticut	1,378	1.7%
18	Arizona	1,359	1.6%
19	Washington	1,349	1.6%
20	Nevada	1,146	1.4%
21	Tennessee	1,047	1.3%
22	Maryland	1,039	1.2%
23	Minnesota	1,020	1.2%
24	Oregon	988	1.2%
25	Arkansas	779	0.9%
26	Georgia	755	0.9%
27	Colorado	634	0.8%
28	Delaware	574	0.7%
29	Mississippi	549	0.7%
30	South Carolina	492	0.6%
31	Kentucky	457	0.5%
32	Hawaii	376	0.5%
33	Iowa	359	0.4%
34	Nebraska	323	0.4%
35	New Mexico	254	0.3%
36	Rhode Island	242	0.3%
36	Utah	242	0.3%
38	Alaska	188	0.2%
39	West Virginia	99	0.1%
40	New Hampshire	92	0.1%
41	Idaho	84	0.1%
42	Montana	74	0.1%
43	South Dakota	46	0.1%
44	Wyoming	35	0.0%
45	North Dakota	20	0.0%
46	Vermont	4	0.0%
NA	Kansas**	NA	NA
NA	Maine**	NA	NA
NA	Oklahoma**	NA	NA
NA	Wisconsin**	NA	NA
	District of Columbia**	NA	NA

Source: Federal Bureau of Investigation
"Crime in the United States 1999" (Uniform Crime Reports, October 15, 2000)
By law enforcement agencies submitting complete reports to the F.B.I. for 12 months in 1999. The F.B.I. estimates 108,850 reported and unreported arrests for robbery occurred in 1999. Robbery is the taking or attempting to take anything of value by force or threat of force. See important note at beginning of this chapter.
**Not available.*

Reported Arrest Rate for Robbery in 1999

National Rate = 44.5 Reported Arrests per 100,000 Population*

ALPHA ORDER

RANK ORDER

RANK	STATE	RATE
20	Alabama	34.8
21	Alaska	33.7
29	Arizona	30.8
24	Arkansas	32.1
7	California	56.7
33	Colorado	25.1
13	Connecticut	44.2
3	Delaware	76.1
6	Florida	63.7
28	Georgia	30.9
18	Hawaii	36.0
43	Idaho	7.8
1	Illinois	112.5
15	Indiana	41.4
40	Iowa	15.4
NA	Kansas**	NA
2	Kentucky	102.5
14	Louisiana	42.9
NA	Maine**	NA
21	Maryland	33.7
31	Massachusetts	29.0
19	Michigan	34.9
33	Minnesota	25.1
12	Mississippi	49.6
8	Missouri	55.0
38	Montana	17.1
36	Nebraska	21.0
5	Nevada	65.1
37	New Hampshire	19.9
11	New Jersey	53.5
32	New Mexico	25.6
16	New York	39.7
9	North Carolina	54.9
45	North Dakota	4.2
21	Ohio	33.7
NA	Oklahoma**	NA
26	Oregon	31.7
4	Pennsylvania	67.0
35	Rhode Island	24.4
10	South Carolina	54.7
42	South Dakota	8.8
17	Tennessee	37.6
27	Texas	31.6
39	Utah	16.7
46	Vermont	0.8
29	Virginia	30.8
25	Washington	31.9
41	West Virginia	10.4
NA	Wisconsin**	NA
44	Wyoming	7.4

RANK	STATE	RATE
1	Illinois	112.5
2	Kentucky	102.5
3	Delaware	76.1
4	Pennsylvania	67.0
5	Nevada	65.1
6	Florida	63.7
7	California	56.7
8	Missouri	55.0
9	North Carolina	54.9
10	South Carolina	54.7
11	New Jersey	53.5
12	Mississippi	49.6
13	Connecticut	44.2
14	Louisiana	42.9
15	Indiana	41.4
16	New York	39.7
17	Tennessee	37.6
18	Hawaii	36.0
19	Michigan	34.9
20	Alabama	34.8
21	Alaska	33.7
21	Maryland	33.7
21	Ohio	33.7
24	Arkansas	32.1
25	Washington	31.9
26	Oregon	31.7
27	Texas	31.6
28	Georgia	30.9
29	Arizona	30.8
29	Virginia	30.8
31	Massachusetts	29.0
32	New Mexico	25.6
33	Colorado	25.1
33	Minnesota	25.1
35	Rhode Island	24.4
36	Nebraska	21.0
37	New Hampshire	19.9
38	Montana	17.1
39	Utah	16.7
40	Iowa	15.4
41	West Virginia	10.4
42	South Dakota	8.8
43	Idaho	7.8
44	Wyoming	7.4
45	North Dakota	4.2
46	Vermont	0.8
NA	Kansas**	NA
NA	Maine**	NA
NA	Oklahoma**	NA
NA	Wisconsin**	NA
	District of Columbia**	NA

Source: Morgan Quitno Press using data from Federal Bureau of Investigation
"Crime in the United States 1999" (Uniform Crime Reports, October 15, 2000)
*By law enforcement agencies submitting complete reports to the F.B.I. for 12 months in 1999. These rates based on population estimates for areas under the jurisdiction of those agencies reporting. Arrest rate based on the F.B.I. estimate of reported and unreported arrests for robbery is 39.9 arrests per 100,000 population. See important note at beginning of this chapter. **Not available.

Reported Arrests for Aggravated Assault in 1999

National Total = 361,075 Reported Arrests*

ALPHA ORDER

RANK	STATE	ARRESTS	% of USA
19	Alabama	4,712	1.3%
36	Alaska	1,089	0.3%
14	Arizona	6,040	1.7%
21	Arkansas	4,117	1.1%
1	California	109,685	30.4%
22	Colorado	3,922	1.1%
20	Connecticut	4,416	1.2%
30	Delaware	1,987	0.6%
2	Florida	43,024	11.9%
26	Georgia	3,145	0.9%
40	Hawaii	612	0.2%
37	Idaho	977	0.3%
13	Illinois	6,835	1.9%
11	Indiana	7,365	2.0%
24	Iowa	3,708	1.0%
NA	Kansas**	NA	NA
31	Kentucky	1,955	0.5%
9	Louisiana	9,501	2.6%
NA	Maine**	NA	NA
25	Maryland	3,468	1.0%
7	Massachusetts	11,734	3.2%
6	Michigan	11,832	3.3%
23	Minnesota	3,781	1.0%
35	Mississippi	1,212	0.3%
15	Missouri	5,829	1.6%
41	Montana	478	0.1%
38	Nebraska	864	0.2%
32	Nevada	1,678	0.5%
45	New Hampshire	163	0.0%
8	New Jersey	10,836	3.0%
28	New Mexico	2,115	0.6%
12	New York	7,351	2.0%
4	North Carolina	19,202	5.3%
46	North Dakota	122	0.0%
10	Ohio	7,661	2.1%
NA	Oklahoma**	NA	NA
29	Oregon	2,061	0.6%
5	Pennsylvania	14,548	4.0%
39	Rhode Island	798	0.2%
27	South Carolina	2,301	0.6%
42	South Dakota	418	0.1%
16	Tennessee	5,600	1.6%
3	Texas	20,341	5.6%
34	Utah	1,286	0.4%
44	Vermont	212	0.1%
17	Virginia	5,259	1.5%
18	Washington	4,963	1.4%
33	West Virginia	1,458	0.4%
NA	Wisconsin**	NA	NA
43	Wyoming	414	0.1%

RANK ORDER

RANK	STATE	ARRESTS	% of USA
1	California	109,685	30.4%
2	Florida	43,024	11.9%
3	Texas	20,341	5.6%
4	North Carolina	19,202	5.3%
5	Pennsylvania	14,548	4.0%
6	Michigan	11,832	3.3%
7	Massachusetts	11,734	3.2%
8	New Jersey	10,836	3.0%
9	Louisiana	9,501	2.6%
10	Ohio	7,661	2.1%
11	Indiana	7,365	2.0%
12	New York	7,351	2.0%
13	Illinois	6,835	1.9%
14	Arizona	6,040	1.7%
15	Missouri	5,829	1.6%
16	Tennessee	5,600	1.6%
17	Virginia	5,259	1.5%
18	Washington	4,963	1.4%
19	Alabama	4,712	1.3%
20	Connecticut	4,416	1.2%
21	Arkansas	4,117	1.1%
22	Colorado	3,922	1.1%
23	Minnesota	3,781	1.0%
24	Iowa	3,708	1.0%
25	Maryland	3,468	1.0%
26	Georgia	3,145	0.9%
27	South Carolina	2,301	0.6%
28	New Mexico	2,115	0.6%
29	Oregon	2,061	0.6%
30	Delaware	1,987	0.6%
31	Kentucky	1,955	0.5%
32	Nevada	1,678	0.5%
33	West Virginia	1,458	0.4%
34	Utah	1,286	0.4%
35	Mississippi	1,212	0.3%
36	Alaska	1,089	0.3%
37	Idaho	977	0.3%
38	Nebraska	864	0.2%
39	Rhode Island	798	0.2%
40	Hawaii	612	0.2%
41	Montana	478	0.1%
42	South Dakota	418	0.1%
43	Wyoming	414	0.1%
44	Vermont	212	0.1%
45	New Hampshire	163	0.0%
46	North Dakota	122	0.0%
NA	Kansas**	NA	NA
NA	Maine**	NA	NA
NA	Oklahoma**	NA	NA
NA	Wisconsin**	NA	NA
	District of Columbia**	NA	NA

Source: Federal Bureau of Investigation
   "Crime in the United States 1999" (Uniform Crime Reports, October 15, 2000)
*By law enforcement agencies submitting complete reports to the F.B.I. for 12 months in 1999. The F.B.I. estimates
483,530 reported and unreported arrests for aggravated assault occurred in 1999. Aggravated assault is an attack
for the purpose of inflicting severe bodily injury. See important note at beginning of this chapter.
**Not available.

Reported Arrest Rate for Aggravated Assault in 1999

National Rate = 193.1 Reported Arrests per 100,000 Population*

ALPHA ORDER				RANK ORDER		
RANK	STATE	RATE		RANK	STATE	RATE
28	Alabama	116.2		1	Kentucky	438.3
13	Alaska	195.2		2	California	332.0
23	Arizona	137.0		3	Louisiana	289.0
15	Arkansas	169.6		4	Florida	284.7
2	California	332.0		5	North Carolina	284.5
18	Colorado	155.5		6	Delaware	263.5
21	Connecticut	141.7		7	South Carolina	256.0
6	Delaware	263.5		8	Massachusetts	243.9
4	Florida	284.7		9	Illinois	242.3
24	Georgia	128.6		10	Indiana	213.5
42	Hawaii	58.7		11	New Mexico	213.4
36	Idaho	90.6		12	Tennessee	200.9
9	Illinois	242.3		13	Alaska	195.2
10	Indiana	213.5		14	Missouri	185.3
16	Iowa	159.5		15	Arkansas	169.6
NA	Kansas**	NA		16	Iowa	159.5
1	Kentucky	438.3		17	Pennsylvania	158.5
3	Louisiana	289.0		18	Colorado	155.5
NA	Maine**	NA		19	West Virginia	153.8
31	Maryland	112.3		20	Michigan	146.7
8	Massachusetts	243.9		21	Connecticut	141.7
20	Michigan	146.7		22	New Jersey	138.3
35	Minnesota	93.1		23	Arizona	137.0
33	Mississippi	109.6		24	Georgia	128.6
14	Missouri	185.3		25	New York	127.8
32	Montana	110.4		26	Ohio	127.5
43	Nebraska	56.3		27	Washington	117.3
34	Nevada	95.3		28	Alabama	116.2
45	New Hampshire	35.2		29	Virginia	113.3
22	New Jersey	138.3		30	Texas	112.6
11	New Mexico	213.4		31	Maryland	112.3
25	New York	127.8		32	Montana	110.4
5	North Carolina	284.5		33	Mississippi	109.6
46	North Dakota	25.9		34	Nevada	95.3
26	Ohio	127.5		35	Minnesota	93.1
NA	Oklahoma**	NA		36	Idaho	90.6
41	Oregon	66.1		37	Utah	88.9
17	Pennsylvania	158.5		38	Wyoming	87.9
39	Rhode Island	80.5		39	Rhode Island	80.5
7	South Carolina	256.0		40	South Dakota	80.2
40	South Dakota	80.2		41	Oregon	66.1
12	Tennessee	200.9		42	Hawaii	58.7
30	Texas	112.6		43	Nebraska	56.3
37	Utah	88.9		44	Vermont	43.9
44	Vermont	43.9		45	New Hampshire	35.2
29	Virginia	113.3		46	North Dakota	25.9
27	Washington	117.3		NA	Kansas**	NA
19	West Virginia	153.8		NA	Maine**	NA
NA	Wisconsin**	NA		NA	Oklahoma**	NA
38	Wyoming	87.9		NA	Wisconsin**	NA
					District of Columbia**	NA

Source: Morgan Quitno Press using data from Federal Bureau of Investigation
  "Crime in the United States 1999" (Uniform Crime Reports, October 15, 2000)
*By law enforcement agencies submitting complete reports to the F.B.I. for 12 months in 1999. These rates based on population estimates for areas under the jurisdiction of those agencies reporting. Arrest rate based on the F.B.I. estimate of reported and unreported arrests for aggravated assault is 177.3 arrests per 100,000 population. See important note at beginning of this chapter. **Not available.

Reported Arrests for Property Crime in 1999

National Total = 1,224,070 Reported Arrests*

ALPHA ORDER

RANK	STATE	ARRESTS	% of USA
23	Alabama	18,091	1.5%
38	Alaska	4,230	0.3%
7	Arizona	39,908	3.3%
24	Arkansas	17,860	1.5%
1	California	175,474	14.3%
18	Colorado	23,075	1.9%
22	Connecticut	19,105	1.6%
36	Delaware	5,733	0.5%
2	Florida	132,153	10.8%
25	Georgia	16,434	1.3%
34	Hawaii	6,942	0.6%
35	Idaho	6,780	0.6%
10	Illinois	34,536	2.8%
20	Indiana	22,102	1.8%
29	Iowa	12,851	1.0%
NA	Kansas**	NA	NA
39	Kentucky	4,222	0.3%
11	Louisiana	33,479	2.7%
NA	Maine**	NA	NA
21	Maryland	20,278	1.7%
27	Massachusetts	15,577	1.3%
13	Michigan	31,939	2.6%
17	Minnesota	25,595	2.1%
31	Mississippi	10,910	0.9%
14	Missouri	31,546	2.6%
40	Montana	3,880	0.3%
30	Nebraska	11,809	1.0%
26	Nevada	16,380	1.3%
45	New Hampshire	1,663	0.1%
6	New Jersey	40,227	3.3%
32	New Mexico	7,397	0.6%
9	New York	36,817	3.0%
4	North Carolina	54,558	4.5%
44	North Dakota	2,402	0.2%
12	Ohio	32,729	2.7%
NA	Oklahoma**	NA	NA
15	Oregon	27,642	2.3%
5	Pennsylvania	49,117	4.0%
37	Rhode Island	4,521	0.4%
33	South Carolina	7,155	0.6%
42	South Dakota	3,402	0.3%
19	Tennessee	22,641	1.8%
3	Texas	106,805	8.7%
28	Utah	13,496	1.1%
46	Vermont	1,361	0.1%
16	Virginia	27,139	2.2%
8	Washington	37,202	3.0%
41	West Virginia	3,662	0.3%
NA	Wisconsin**	NA	NA
43	Wyoming	3,245	0.3%

RANK ORDER

RANK	STATE	ARRESTS	% of USA
1	California	175,474	14.3%
2	Florida	132,153	10.8%
3	Texas	106,805	8.7%
4	North Carolina	54,558	4.5%
5	Pennsylvania	49,117	4.0%
6	New Jersey	40,227	3.3%
7	Arizona	39,908	3.3%
8	Washington	37,202	3.0%
9	New York	36,817	3.0%
10	Illinois	34,536	2.8%
11	Louisiana	33,479	2.7%
12	Ohio	32,729	2.7%
13	Michigan	31,939	2.6%
14	Missouri	31,546	2.6%
15	Oregon	27,642	2.3%
16	Virginia	27,139	2.2%
17	Minnesota	25,595	2.1%
18	Colorado	23,075	1.9%
19	Tennessee	22,641	1.8%
20	Indiana	22,102	1.8%
21	Maryland	20,278	1.7%
22	Connecticut	19,105	1.6%
23	Alabama	18,091	1.5%
24	Arkansas	17,860	1.5%
25	Georgia	16,434	1.3%
26	Nevada	16,380	1.3%
27	Massachusetts	15,577	1.3%
28	Utah	13,496	1.1%
29	Iowa	12,851	1.0%
30	Nebraska	11,809	1.0%
31	Mississippi	10,910	0.9%
32	New Mexico	7,397	0.6%
33	South Carolina	7,155	0.6%
34	Hawaii	6,942	0.6%
35	Idaho	6,780	0.6%
36	Delaware	5,733	0.5%
37	Rhode Island	4,521	0.4%
38	Alaska	4,230	0.3%
39	Kentucky	4,222	0.3%
40	Montana	3,880	0.3%
41	West Virginia	3,662	0.3%
42	South Dakota	3,402	0.3%
43	Wyoming	3,245	0.3%
44	North Dakota	2,402	0.2%
45	New Hampshire	1,663	0.1%
46	Vermont	1,361	0.1%
NA	Kansas**	NA	NA
NA	Maine**	NA	NA
NA	Oklahoma**	NA	NA
NA	Wisconsin**	NA	NA
	District of Columbia**	NA	NA

Source: Federal Bureau of Investigation
   "Crime in the United States 1999" (Uniform Crime Reports, October 15, 2000)
*By law enforcement agencies submitting complete reports to the F.B.I. for 12 months in 1999. The F.B.I. estimates
1,645,045 reported and unreported arrests for property crime occurred in 1999. Property crimes are offenses of
burglary, larceny-theft, motor vehicle theft and arson.   See important note at beginning of this chapter.
**Not available.

Reported Arrest Rate for Property Crime in 1999

National Rate = 654.8 Reported Arrests per 100,000 Population*

ALPHA ORDER

RANK	STATE	RATE
41	Alabama	446.0
19	Alaska	758.1
9	Arizona	905.1
21	Arkansas	735.6
37	California	531.1
8	Colorado	914.9
31	Connecticut	612.9
18	Delaware	760.3
13	Florida	874.5
23	Georgia	671.9
24	Hawaii	665.6
30	Idaho	628.9
1	Illinois	1,224.2
27	Indiana	640.8
34	Iowa	552.7
NA	Kansas**	NA
5	Kentucky	946.6
2	Louisiana	1,018.2
NA	Maine**	NA
25	Maryland	656.9
45	Massachusetts	323.8
42	Michigan	395.9
29	Minnesota	630.3
4	Mississippi	986.4
3	Missouri	1,002.7
10	Montana	896.1
17	Nebraska	768.8
7	Nevada	930.7
44	New Hampshire	359.2
38	New Jersey	513.4
20	New Mexico	746.4
28	New York	640.0
15	North Carolina	808.3
39	North Dakota	510.0
35	Ohio	544.8
NA	Oklahoma**	NA
11	Oregon	887.1
36	Pennsylvania	535.1
40	Rhode Island	456.2
16	South Carolina	795.9
26	South Dakota	653.0
14	Tennessee	812.4
32	Texas	591.4
6	Utah	933.3
46	Vermont	281.8
33	Virginia	584.9
12	Washington	879.1
43	West Virginia	386.3
NA	Wisconsin**	NA
22	Wyoming	689.0

RANK ORDER

RANK	STATE	RATE
1	Illinois	1,224.2
2	Louisiana	1,018.2
3	Missouri	1,002.7
4	Mississippi	986.4
5	Kentucky	946.6
6	Utah	933.3
7	Nevada	930.7
8	Colorado	914.9
9	Arizona	905.1
10	Montana	896.1
11	Oregon	887.1
12	Washington	879.1
13	Florida	874.5
14	Tennessee	812.4
15	North Carolina	808.3
16	South Carolina	795.9
17	Nebraska	768.8
18	Delaware	760.3
19	Alaska	758.1
20	New Mexico	746.4
21	Arkansas	735.6
22	Wyoming	689.0
23	Georgia	671.9
24	Hawaii	665.6
25	Maryland	656.9
26	South Dakota	653.0
27	Indiana	640.8
28	New York	640.0
29	Minnesota	630.3
30	Idaho	628.9
31	Connecticut	612.9
32	Texas	591.4
33	Virginia	584.9
34	Iowa	552.7
35	Ohio	544.8
36	Pennsylvania	535.1
37	California	531.1
38	New Jersey	513.4
39	North Dakota	510.0
40	Rhode Island	456.2
41	Alabama	446.0
42	Michigan	395.9
43	West Virginia	386.3
44	New Hampshire	359.2
45	Massachusetts	323.8
46	Vermont	281.8
NA	Kansas**	NA
NA	Maine**	NA
NA	Oklahoma**	NA
NA	Wisconsin**	NA
	District of Columbia**	NA

Source: Morgan Quitno Press using data from Federal Bureau of Investigation
"Crime in the United States 1999" (Uniform Crime Reports, October 15, 2000)
*By law enforcement agencies submitting complete reports to the F.B.I. for 12 months in 1999. These rates based on population estimates for areas under the jurisdiction of those agencies reporting. Arrest rate based on the F.B.I. estimate of reported and unreported arrests for property crime is 603.3 arrests per 100,000 population. See important note at beginning of this chapter. **Not available.

Reported Arrests for Burglary in 1999

National Total = 220,286 Reported Arrests*

ALPHA ORDER

RANK	STATE	ARRESTS	% of USA
25	Alabama	2,617	1.2%
39	Alaska	605	0.3%
12	Arizona	4,632	2.1%
18	Arkansas	3,384	1.5%
1	California	49,307	22.4%
27	Colorado	2,212	1.0%
24	Connecticut	2,724	1.2%
32	Delaware	1,080	0.5%
2	Florida	27,716	12.6%
22	Georgia	2,902	1.3%
36	Hawaii	885	0.4%
33	Idaho	976	0.4%
14	Illinois	4,174	1.9%
23	Indiana	2,858	1.3%
29	Iowa	1,839	0.8%
NA	Kansas**	NA	NA
35	Kentucky	886	0.4%
6	Louisiana	6,545	3.0%
NA	Maine**	NA	NA
17	Maryland	3,667	1.7%
21	Massachusetts	2,943	1.3%
9	Michigan	5,796	2.6%
20	Minnesota	3,134	1.4%
28	Mississippi	2,160	1.0%
13	Missouri	4,368	2.0%
45	Montana	269	0.1%
31	Nebraska	1,139	0.5%
16	Nevada	3,719	1.7%
46	New Hampshire	195	0.1%
7	New Jersey	6,479	2.9%
37	New Mexico	830	0.4%
8	New York	6,009	2.7%
4	North Carolina	13,279	6.0%
43	North Dakota	321	0.1%
11	Ohio	5,159	2.3%
NA	Oklahoma**	NA	NA
19	Oregon	3,216	1.5%
5	Pennsylvania	8,899	4.0%
38	Rhode Island	782	0.4%
34	South Carolina	939	0.4%
40	South Dakota	560	0.3%
26	Tennessee	2,447	1.1%
3	Texas	16,619	7.5%
30	Utah	1,154	0.5%
44	Vermont	319	0.1%
15	Virginia	4,072	1.8%
10	Washington	5,548	2.5%
41	West Virginia	536	0.2%
NA	Wisconsin**	NA	NA
42	Wyoming	386	0.2%

RANK ORDER

RANK	STATE	ARRESTS	% of USA
1	California	49,307	22.4%
2	Florida	27,716	12.6%
3	Texas	16,619	7.5%
4	North Carolina	13,279	6.0%
5	Pennsylvania	8,899	4.0%
6	Louisiana	6,545	3.0%
7	New Jersey	6,479	2.9%
8	New York	6,009	2.7%
9	Michigan	5,796	2.6%
10	Washington	5,548	2.5%
11	Ohio	5,159	2.3%
12	Arizona	4,632	2.1%
13	Missouri	4,368	2.0%
14	Illinois	4,174	1.9%
15	Virginia	4,072	1.8%
16	Nevada	3,719	1.7%
17	Maryland	3,667	1.7%
18	Arkansas	3,384	1.5%
19	Oregon	3,216	1.5%
20	Minnesota	3,134	1.4%
21	Massachusetts	2,943	1.3%
22	Georgia	2,902	1.3%
23	Indiana	2,858	1.3%
24	Connecticut	2,724	1.2%
25	Alabama	2,617	1.2%
26	Tennessee	2,447	1.1%
27	Colorado	2,212	1.0%
28	Mississippi	2,160	1.0%
29	Iowa	1,839	0.8%
30	Utah	1,154	0.5%
31	Nebraska	1,139	0.5%
32	Delaware	1,080	0.5%
33	Idaho	976	0.4%
34	South Carolina	939	0.4%
35	Kentucky	886	0.4%
36	Hawaii	885	0.4%
37	New Mexico	830	0.4%
38	Rhode Island	782	0.4%
39	Alaska	605	0.3%
40	South Dakota	560	0.3%
41	West Virginia	536	0.2%
42	Wyoming	386	0.2%
43	North Dakota	321	0.1%
44	Vermont	319	0.1%
45	Montana	269	0.1%
46	New Hampshire	195	0.1%
NA	Kansas**	NA	NA
NA	Maine**	NA	NA
NA	Oklahoma**	NA	NA
NA	Wisconsin**	NA	NA
	District of Columbia**	NA	NA

Source: Federal Bureau of Investigation
     "Crime in the United States 1999" (Uniform Crime Reports, October 15, 2000)
*By law enforcement agencies submitting complete reports to the F.B.I. for 12 months in 1999. The F.B.I. estimates 296,100 reported and unreported arrests for burglary occurred in 1999. Burglary is the unlawful entry of a structure to commit a felony or theft. Attempts are included.   See important note at beginning of this chapter.
**Not available.

Reported Arrest Rate for Burglary in 1999

National Rate = 117.8 Reported Arrests per 100,000 Population*

ALPHA ORDER

RANK	STATE	RATE
42	Alabama	64.5
15	Alaska	108.4
17	Arizona	105.1
10	Arkansas	139.4
7	California	149.2
26	Colorado	87.7
27	Connecticut	87.4
9	Delaware	143.2
6	Florida	183.4
14	Georgia	118.6
29	Hawaii	84.9
23	Idaho	90.5
8	Illinois	148.0
31	Indiana	82.9
35	Iowa	79.1
NA	Kansas**	NA
3	Kentucky	198.7
2	Louisiana	199.1
NA	Maine**	NA
13	Maryland	118.8
44	Massachusetts	61.2
39	Michigan	71.8
37	Minnesota	77.2
5	Mississippi	195.3
11	Missouri	138.8
43	Montana	62.1
38	Nebraska	74.2
1	Nevada	211.3
46	New Hampshire	42.1
32	New Jersey	82.7
30	New Mexico	83.8
18	New York	104.4
4	North Carolina	196.7
40	North Dakota	68.2
28	Ohio	85.9
NA	Oklahoma**	NA
20	Oregon	103.2
21	Pennsylvania	96.9
36	Rhode Island	78.9
18	South Carolina	104.4
16	South Dakota	107.5
24	Tennessee	87.8
22	Texas	92.0
34	Utah	79.8
41	Vermont	66.0
24	Virginia	87.8
12	Washington	131.1
45	West Virginia	56.5
NA	Wisconsin**	NA
33	Wyoming	82.0

RANK ORDER

RANK	STATE	RATE
1	Nevada	211.3
2	Louisiana	199.1
3	Kentucky	198.7
4	North Carolina	196.7
5	Mississippi	195.3
6	Florida	183.4
7	California	149.2
8	Illinois	148.0
9	Delaware	143.2
10	Arkansas	139.4
11	Missouri	138.8
12	Washington	131.1
13	Maryland	118.8
14	Georgia	118.6
15	Alaska	108.4
16	South Dakota	107.5
17	Arizona	105.1
18	New York	104.4
18	South Carolina	104.4
20	Oregon	103.2
21	Pennsylvania	96.9
22	Texas	92.0
23	Idaho	90.5
24	Tennessee	87.8
24	Virginia	87.8
26	Colorado	87.7
27	Connecticut	87.4
28	Ohio	85.9
29	Hawaii	84.9
30	New Mexico	83.8
31	Indiana	82.9
32	New Jersey	82.7
33	Wyoming	82.0
34	Utah	79.8
35	Iowa	79.1
36	Rhode Island	78.9
37	Minnesota	77.2
38	Nebraska	74.2
39	Michigan	71.8
40	North Dakota	68.2
41	Vermont	66.0
42	Alabama	64.5
43	Montana	62.1
44	Massachusetts	61.2
45	West Virginia	56.5
46	New Hampshire	42.1
NA	Kansas**	NA
NA	Maine**	NA
NA	Oklahoma**	NA
NA	Wisconsin**	NA
	District of Columbia**	NA

Source: Morgan Quitno Press using data from Federal Bureau of Investigation
"Crime in the United States 1999" (Uniform Crime Reports, October 15, 2000)
*By law enforcement agencies submitting complete reports to the F.B.I. for 12 months in 1999. These rates based on population estimates for areas under the jurisdiction of those agencies reporting. Arrest rate based on the F.B.I. estimate of reported and unreported arrests for burglary is 108.6 arrests per 100,000 population. See important note at beginning of this chapter. **Not available.

Reported Arrests for Larceny and Theft in 1999

National Total = 885,006 Reported Arrests*

ALPHA ORDER

ALPHA ORDER

RANK	STATE	ARRESTS	% of USA
23	Alabama	14,252	1.6%
39	Alaska	3,166	0.4%
7	Arizona	31,589	3.6%
24	Arkansas	13,824	1.6%
1	California	104,527	11.8%
18	Colorado	18,842	2.1%
21	Connecticut	15,002	1.7%
36	Delaware	4,370	0.5%
2	Florida	90,805	10.3%
25	Georgia	12,418	1.4%
35	Hawaii	5,179	0.6%
34	Idaho	5,394	0.6%
19	Illinois	17,921	2.0%
20	Indiana	17,142	1.9%
29	Iowa	10,253	1.2%
NA	Kansas**	NA	NA
41	Kentucky	2,779	0.3%
10	Louisiana	25,273	2.9%
NA	Maine**	NA	NA
22	Maryland	14,831	1.7%
27	Massachusetts	11,313	1.3%
12	Michigan	23,425	2.6%
16	Minnesota	19,455	2.2%
31	Mississippi	7,914	0.9%
13	Missouri	23,405	2.6%
37	Montana	3,365	0.4%
30	Nebraska	10,023	1.1%
28	Nevada	10,986	1.2%
45	New Hampshire	1,356	0.2%
6	New Jersey	31,797	3.6%
32	New Mexico	6,269	0.7%
9	New York	28,481	3.2%
4	North Carolina	38,529	4.4%
44	North Dakota	1,818	0.2%
11	Ohio	25,119	2.8%
NA	Oklahoma**	NA	NA
14	Oregon	21,808	2.5%
5	Pennsylvania	33,048	3.7%
38	Rhode Island	3,195	0.4%
33	South Carolina	5,887	0.7%
43	South Dakota	2,653	0.3%
17	Tennessee	18,879	2.1%
3	Texas	80,852	9.1%
26	Utah	11,575	1.3%
46	Vermont	955	0.1%
15	Virginia	20,803	2.4%
8	Washington	28,987	3.3%
40	West Virginia	2,834	0.3%
NA	Wisconsin**	NA	NA
42	Wyoming	2,708	0.3%

RANK ORDER

RANK	STATE	ARRESTS	% of USA
1	California	104,527	11.8%
2	Florida	90,805	10.3%
3	Texas	80,852	9.1%
4	North Carolina	38,529	4.4%
5	Pennsylvania	33,048	3.7%
6	New Jersey	31,797	3.6%
7	Arizona	31,589	3.6%
8	Washington	28,987	3.3%
9	New York	28,481	3.2%
10	Louisiana	25,273	2.9%
11	Ohio	25,119	2.8%
12	Michigan	23,425	2.6%
13	Missouri	23,405	2.6%
14	Oregon	21,808	2.5%
15	Virginia	20,803	2.4%
16	Minnesota	19,455	2.2%
17	Tennessee	18,879	2.1%
18	Colorado	18,842	2.1%
19	Illinois	17,921	2.0%
20	Indiana	17,142	1.9%
21	Connecticut	15,002	1.7%
22	Maryland	14,831	1.7%
23	Alabama	14,252	1.6%
24	Arkansas	13,824	1.6%
25	Georgia	12,418	1.4%
26	Utah	11,575	1.3%
27	Massachusetts	11,313	1.3%
28	Nevada	10,986	1.2%
29	Iowa	10,253	1.2%
30	Nebraska	10,023	1.1%
31	Mississippi	7,914	0.9%
32	New Mexico	6,269	0.7%
33	South Carolina	5,887	0.7%
34	Idaho	5,394	0.6%
35	Hawaii	5,179	0.6%
36	Delaware	4,370	0.5%
37	Montana	3,365	0.4%
38	Rhode Island	3,195	0.4%
39	Alaska	3,166	0.4%
40	West Virginia	2,834	0.3%
41	Kentucky	2,779	0.3%
42	Wyoming	2,708	0.3%
43	South Dakota	2,653	0.3%
44	North Dakota	1,818	0.2%
45	New Hampshire	1,356	0.2%
46	Vermont	955	0.1%
NA	Kansas**	NA	NA
NA	Maine**	NA	NA
NA	Oklahoma**	NA	NA
NA	Wisconsin**	NA	NA
	District of Columbia**	NA	NA

Source: Federal Bureau of Investigation
"Crime in the United States 1999" (Uniform Crime Reports, October 15, 2000)
*By law enforcement agencies submitting complete reports to the F.B.I. for 12 months in 1999. The F.B.I. estimates 1,189,400 reported and unreported arrests for larceny and theft occurred in 1999. Larceny and theft is the unlawful taking of property without use of force, violence or fraud. Attempts are included. Motor vehicle thefts are excluded. See important note at beginning of this chapter. **Not available.

Reported Arrest Rate for Larceny and Theft in 1999

National Rate = 473.4 Reported Arrests per 100,000 Population*

ALPHA ORDER

RANK ORDER

RANK	STATE	RATE		RANK	STATE	RATE
39	Alabama	351.4		1	Utah	800.5
22	Alaska	567.4		2	Montana	777.1
6	Arizona	716.5		3	Louisiana	768.6
21	Arkansas	569.4		4	Colorado	747.1
41	California	316.4		5	Missouri	744.0
4	Colorado	747.1		6	Arizona	716.5
29	Connecticut	481.3		7	Mississippi	715.6
18	Delaware	579.6		8	Oregon	699.9
17	Florida	600.9		9	Washington	684.9
24	Georgia	507.7		10	Tennessee	677.4
27	Hawaii	496.5		11	South Carolina	654.8
25	Idaho	500.4		12	Nebraska	652.5
13	Illinois	635.3		13	Illinois	635.3
26	Indiana	497.0		14	New Mexico	632.6
34	Iowa	441.0		15	Nevada	624.2
NA	Kansas**	NA		16	Kentucky	623.1
16	Kentucky	623.1		17	Florida	600.9
3	Louisiana	768.6		18	Delaware	579.6
NA	Maine**	NA		19	Wyoming	574.9
30	Maryland	480.4		20	North Carolina	570.8
45	Massachusetts	235.1		21	Arkansas	569.4
44	Michigan	290.3		22	Alaska	567.4
31	Minnesota	479.1		23	South Dakota	509.2
7	Mississippi	715.6		24	Georgia	507.7
5	Missouri	744.0		25	Idaho	500.4
2	Montana	777.1		26	Indiana	497.0
12	Nebraska	652.5		27	Hawaii	496.5
15	Nevada	624.2		28	New York	495.1
43	New Hampshire	292.9		29	Connecticut	481.3
36	New Jersey	405.8		30	Maryland	480.4
14	New Mexico	632.6		31	Minnesota	479.1
28	New York	495.1		32	Virginia	448.3
20	North Carolina	570.8		33	Texas	447.7
37	North Dakota	386.0		34	Iowa	441.0
35	Ohio	418.1		35	Ohio	418.1
NA	Oklahoma**	NA		36	New Jersey	405.8
8	Oregon	699.9		37	North Dakota	386.0
38	Pennsylvania	360.0		38	Pennsylvania	360.0
40	Rhode Island	322.4		39	Alabama	351.4
11	South Carolina	654.8		40	Rhode Island	322.4
23	South Dakota	509.2		41	California	316.4
10	Tennessee	677.4		42	West Virginia	298.9
33	Texas	447.7		43	New Hampshire	292.9
1	Utah	800.5		44	Michigan	290.3
46	Vermont	197.7		45	Massachusetts	235.1
32	Virginia	448.3		46	Vermont	197.7
9	Washington	684.9		NA	Kansas**	NA
42	West Virginia	298.9		NA	Maine**	NA
NA	Wisconsin**	NA		NA	Oklahoma**	NA
19	Wyoming	574.9		NA	Wisconsin**	NA
					District of Columbia**	NA

Source: Morgan Quitno Press using data from Federal Bureau of Investigation
    "Crime in the United States 1999" (Uniform Crime Reports, October 15, 2000)
*By law enforcement agencies submitting complete reports to the F.B.I. for 12 months in 1999. These rates based
on population estimates for areas under the jurisdiction of those agencies reporting. Arrest rate based on the F.B.I.
estimate of reported and unreported arrests for larceny and theft is 436.2 arrests per 100,000 population. See
important note at beginning of this chapter. **Not available.

Reported Arrests for Motor Vehicle Theft in 1999

National Total = 107,305 Reported Arrests*

ALPHA ORDER

RANK	STATE	ARRESTS	% of USA
25	Alabama	1,150	1.1%
35	Alaska	441	0.4%
7	Arizona	3,418	3.2%
31	Arkansas	537	0.5%
1	California	19,857	18.5%
17	Colorado	1,801	1.7%
22	Connecticut	1,234	1.1%
42	Delaware	218	0.2%
2	Florida	12,970	12.1%
26	Georgia	931	0.9%
27	Hawaii	857	0.8%
36	Idaho	351	0.3%
3	Illinois	12,233	11.4%
14	Indiana	1,969	1.8%
30	Iowa	643	0.6%
NA	Kansas**	NA	NA
32	Kentucky	503	0.5%
19	Louisiana	1,434	1.3%
NA	Maine**	NA	NA
20	Maryland	1,430	1.3%
23	Massachusetts	1,188	1.1%
12	Michigan	2,189	2.0%
8	Minnesota	2,760	2.6%
28	Mississippi	762	0.7%
6	Missouri	3,462	3.2%
41	Montana	221	0.2%
33	Nebraska	484	0.5%
18	Nevada	1,580	1.5%
45	New Hampshire	83	0.1%
21	New Jersey	1,383	1.3%
37	New Mexico	276	0.3%
13	New York	2,003	1.9%
11	North Carolina	2,275	2.1%
40	North Dakota	251	0.2%
15	Ohio	1,886	1.8%
NA	Oklahoma**	NA	NA
9	Oregon	2,312	2.2%
5	Pennsylvania	6,354	5.9%
34	Rhode Island	468	0.4%
38	South Carolina	264	0.2%
44	South Dakota	141	0.1%
24	Tennessee	1,180	1.1%
4	Texas	8,535	8.0%
29	Utah	659	0.6%
46	Vermont	73	0.1%
16	Virginia	1,853	1.7%
10	Washington	2,292	2.1%
39	West Virginia	252	0.2%
NA	Wisconsin**	NA	NA
43	Wyoming	142	0.1%

RANK ORDER

RANK	STATE	ARRESTS	% of USA
1	California	19,857	18.5%
2	Florida	12,970	12.1%
3	Illinois	12,233	11.4%
4	Texas	8,535	8.0%
5	Pennsylvania	6,354	5.9%
6	Missouri	3,462	3.2%
7	Arizona	3,418	3.2%
8	Minnesota	2,760	2.6%
9	Oregon	2,312	2.2%
10	Washington	2,292	2.1%
11	North Carolina	2,275	2.1%
12	Michigan	2,189	2.0%
13	New York	2,003	1.9%
14	Indiana	1,969	1.8%
15	Ohio	1,886	1.8%
16	Virginia	1,853	1.7%
17	Colorado	1,801	1.7%
18	Nevada	1,580	1.5%
19	Louisiana	1,434	1.3%
20	Maryland	1,430	1.3%
21	New Jersey	1,383	1.3%
22	Connecticut	1,234	1.1%
23	Massachusetts	1,188	1.1%
24	Tennessee	1,180	1.1%
25	Alabama	1,150	1.1%
26	Georgia	931	0.9%
27	Hawaii	857	0.8%
28	Mississippi	762	0.7%
29	Utah	659	0.6%
30	Iowa	643	0.6%
31	Arkansas	537	0.5%
32	Kentucky	503	0.5%
33	Nebraska	484	0.5%
34	Rhode Island	468	0.4%
35	Alaska	441	0.4%
36	Idaho	351	0.3%
37	New Mexico	276	0.3%
38	South Carolina	264	0.2%
39	West Virginia	252	0.2%
40	North Dakota	251	0.2%
41	Montana	221	0.2%
42	Delaware	218	0.2%
43	Wyoming	142	0.1%
44	South Dakota	141	0.1%
45	New Hampshire	83	0.1%
46	Vermont	73	0.1%
NA	Kansas**	NA	NA
NA	Maine**	NA	NA
NA	Oklahoma**	NA	NA
NA	Wisconsin**	NA	NA
	District of Columbia**	NA	NA

Source: Federal Bureau of Investigation
    "Crime in the United States 1999" (Uniform Crime Reports, October 15, 2000)
*By law enforcement agencies submitting complete reports to the F.B.I. for 12 months in 1999. The F.B.I. estimates 142,200 reported and unreported arrests for motor vehicle theft occurred in 1999. Motor vehicle theft includes the theft or attempted theft of a self-propelled vehicle. Excludes motorboats, construction equipment, airplanes and farming equipment. See important note at beginning of this chapter. **Not available.*

Reported Arrest Rate for Motor Vehicle Theft in 1999

National Rate = 57.4 Reported Arrests per 100,000 Population*

ALPHA ORDER

RANK	STATE	RATE
36	Alabama	28.4
7	Alaska	79.0
8	Arizona	77.5
43	Arkansas	22.1
14	California	60.1
10	Colorado	71.4
26	Connecticut	39.6
35	Delaware	28.9
5	Florida	85.8
27	Georgia	38.1
6	Hawaii	82.2
30	Idaho	32.6
1	Illinois	433.6
15	Indiana	57.1
38	Iowa	27.7
NA	Kansas**	NA
2	Kentucky	112.8
23	Louisiana	43.6
NA	Maine**	NA
21	Maryland	46.3
42	Massachusetts	24.7
39	Michigan	27.1
13	Minnesota	68.0
12	Mississippi	68.9
3	Missouri	110.0
18	Montana	51.0
31	Nebraska	31.5
4	Nevada	89.8
44	New Hampshire	17.9
45	New Jersey	17.6
37	New Mexico	27.9
28	New York	34.8
29	North Carolina	33.7
17	North Dakota	53.3
32	Ohio	31.4
NA	Oklahoma**	NA
9	Oregon	74.2
11	Pennsylvania	69.2
20	Rhode Island	47.2
34	South Carolina	29.4
39	South Dakota	27.1
24	Tennessee	42.3
19	Texas	47.3
22	Utah	45.6
46	Vermont	15.1
25	Virginia	39.9
16	Washington	54.2
41	West Virginia	26.6
NA	Wisconsin**	NA
33	Wyoming	30.1

RANK ORDER

RANK	STATE	RATE
1	Illinois	433.6
2	Kentucky	112.8
3	Missouri	110.0
4	Nevada	89.8
5	Florida	85.8
6	Hawaii	82.2
7	Alaska	79.0
8	Arizona	77.5
9	Oregon	74.2
10	Colorado	71.4
11	Pennsylvania	69.2
12	Mississippi	68.9
13	Minnesota	68.0
14	California	60.1
15	Indiana	57.1
16	Washington	54.2
17	North Dakota	53.3
18	Montana	51.0
19	Texas	47.3
20	Rhode Island	47.2
21	Maryland	46.3
22	Utah	45.6
23	Louisiana	43.6
24	Tennessee	42.3
25	Virginia	39.9
26	Connecticut	39.6
27	Georgia	38.1
28	New York	34.8
29	North Carolina	33.7
30	Idaho	32.6
31	Nebraska	31.5
32	Ohio	31.4
33	Wyoming	30.1
34	South Carolina	29.4
35	Delaware	28.9
36	Alabama	28.4
37	New Mexico	27.9
38	Iowa	27.7
39	Michigan	27.1
39	South Dakota	27.1
41	West Virginia	26.6
42	Massachusetts	24.7
43	Arkansas	22.1
44	New Hampshire	17.9
45	New Jersey	17.6
46	Vermont	15.1
NA	Kansas**	NA
NA	Maine**	NA
NA	Oklahoma**	NA
NA	Wisconsin**	NA
	District of Columbia**	NA

Source: Morgan Quitno Press using data from Federal Bureau of Investigation
   "Crime in the United States 1999" (Uniform Crime Reports, October 15, 2000)
*By law enforcement agencies submitting complete reports to the F.B.I. for 12 months in 1999. These rates based on population estimates for areas under the jurisdiction of those agencies reporting. Arrest rate based on the F.B.I. estimate of reported and unreported arrests for motor vehicle theft is 52.1 arrests per 100,000 population. See important note at beginning of this chapter. **Not available.

Reported Arrests for Arson in 1999

National Total = 11,473 Reported Arrests*

ALPHA ORDER

RANK	STATE	ARRESTS	% of USA
32	Alabama	72	0.6%
43	Alaska	18	0.2%
15	Arizona	269	2.3%
27	Arkansas	115	1.0%
1	California	1,783	15.5%
18	Colorado	220	1.9%
22	Connecticut	145	1.3%
33	Delaware	65	0.6%
4	Florida	662	5.8%
20	Georgia	183	1.6%
42	Hawaii	21	0.2%
35	Idaho	59	0.5%
19	Illinois	208	1.8%
24	Indiana	133	1.2%
26	Iowa	116	1.0%
NA	Kansas**	NA	NA
36	Kentucky	54	0.5%
17	Louisiana	227	2.0%
NA	Maine**	NA	NA
11	Maryland	350	3.1%
24	Massachusetts	133	1.2%
7	Michigan	529	4.6%
16	Minnesota	246	2.1%
31	Mississippi	74	0.6%
13	Missouri	311	2.7%
40	Montana	25	0.2%
21	Nebraska	163	1.4%
29	Nevada	95	0.8%
39	New Hampshire	29	0.3%
5	New Jersey	568	5.0%
41	New Mexico	22	0.2%
12	New York	324	2.8%
8	North Carolina	475	4.1%
45	North Dakota	12	0.1%
6	Ohio	565	4.9%
NA	Oklahoma**	NA	NA
14	Oregon	306	2.7%
2	Pennsylvania	816	7.1%
30	Rhode Island	76	0.7%
33	South Carolina	65	0.6%
37	South Dakota	48	0.4%
23	Tennessee	135	1.2%
3	Texas	799	7.0%
28	Utah	108	0.9%
44	Vermont	14	0.1%
9	Virginia	411	3.6%
10	Washington	375	3.3%
38	West Virginia	40	0.3%
NA	Wisconsin**	NA	NA
46	Wyoming	9	0.1%

RANK ORDER

RANK	STATE	ARRESTS	% of USA
1	California	1,783	15.5%
2	Pennsylvania	816	7.1%
3	Texas	799	7.0%
4	Florida	662	5.8%
5	New Jersey	568	5.0%
6	Ohio	565	4.9%
7	Michigan	529	4.6%
8	North Carolina	475	4.1%
9	Virginia	411	3.6%
10	Washington	375	3.3%
11	Maryland	350	3.1%
12	New York	324	2.8%
13	Missouri	311	2.7%
14	Oregon	306	2.7%
15	Arizona	269	2.3%
16	Minnesota	246	2.1%
17	Louisiana	227	2.0%
18	Colorado	220	1.9%
19	Illinois	208	1.8%
20	Georgia	183	1.6%
21	Nebraska	163	1.4%
22	Connecticut	145	1.3%
23	Tennessee	135	1.2%
24	Indiana	133	1.2%
24	Massachusetts	133	1.2%
26	Iowa	116	1.0%
27	Arkansas	115	1.0%
28	Utah	108	0.9%
29	Nevada	95	0.8%
30	Rhode Island	76	0.7%
31	Mississippi	74	0.6%
32	Alabama	72	0.6%
33	Delaware	65	0.6%
33	South Carolina	65	0.6%
35	Idaho	59	0.5%
36	Kentucky	54	0.5%
37	South Dakota	48	0.4%
38	West Virginia	40	0.3%
39	New Hampshire	29	0.3%
40	Montana	25	0.2%
41	New Mexico	22	0.2%
42	Hawaii	21	0.2%
43	Alaska	18	0.2%
44	Vermont	14	0.1%
45	North Dakota	12	0.1%
46	Wyoming	9	0.1%
NA	Kansas**	NA	NA
NA	Maine**	NA	NA
NA	Oklahoma**	NA	NA
NA	Wisconsin**	NA	NA
	District of Columbia**	NA	NA

Source: Federal Bureau of Investigation
"Crime in the United States 1999" (Uniform Crime Reports, October 15, 2000)
By law enforcement agencies submitting complete reports to the F.B.I. for 12 months in 1999. The F.B.I. estimates 16,800 reported and unreported arrests for arson occurred in 1999. Arson is the willful burning of or attempt to burn a building, vehicle or another's personal property. See important note at beginning of this chapter.
***Not available.*

Reported Arrest Rate for Arson in 1999

National Rate = 6.1 Reported Arrests per 100,000 Population*

ALPHA ORDER				RANK ORDER		
RANK	STATE	RATE		RANK	STATE	RATE
46	Alabama	1.8		1	Kentucky	12.1
39	Alaska	3.2		2	Maryland	11.3
24	Arizona	6.1		3	Nebraska	10.6
33	Arkansas	4.7		4	Missouri	9.9
29	California	5.4		5	Oregon	9.8
11	Colorado	8.7		6	Ohio	9.4
33	Connecticut	4.7		7	South Dakota	9.2
12	Delaware	8.6		8	Pennsylvania	8.9
35	Florida	4.4		8	Virginia	8.9
14	Georgia	7.5		8	Washington	8.9
44	Hawaii	2.0		11	Colorado	8.7
28	Idaho	5.5		12	Delaware	8.6
16	Illinois	7.4		13	Rhode Island	7.7
38	Indiana	3.9		14	Georgia	7.5
31	Iowa	5.0		14	Utah	7.5
NA	Kansas**	NA		16	Illinois	7.4
1	Kentucky	12.1		17	New Jersey	7.2
20	Louisiana	6.9		17	South Carolina	7.2
NA	Maine**	NA		19	North Carolina	7.0
2	Maryland	11.3		20	Louisiana	6.9
41	Massachusetts	2.8		21	Mississippi	6.7
22	Michigan	6.6		22	Michigan	6.6
24	Minnesota	6.1		23	New Hampshire	6.3
21	Mississippi	6.7		24	Arizona	6.1
4	Missouri	9.9		24	Minnesota	6.1
26	Montana	5.8		26	Montana	5.8
3	Nebraska	10.6		27	New York	5.6
29	Nevada	5.4		28	Idaho	5.5
23	New Hampshire	6.3		29	California	5.4
17	New Jersey	7.2		29	Nevada	5.4
43	New Mexico	2.2		31	Iowa	5.0
27	New York	5.6		32	Tennessee	4.8
19	North Carolina	7.0		33	Arkansas	4.7
42	North Dakota	2.5		33	Connecticut	4.7
6	Ohio	9.4		35	Florida	4.4
NA	Oklahoma**	NA		35	Texas	4.4
5	Oregon	9.8		37	West Virginia	4.2
8	Pennsylvania	8.9		38	Indiana	3.9
13	Rhode Island	7.7		39	Alaska	3.2
17	South Carolina	7.2		40	Vermont	2.9
7	South Dakota	9.2		41	Massachusetts	2.8
32	Tennessee	4.8		42	North Dakota	2.5
35	Texas	4.4		43	New Mexico	2.2
14	Utah	7.5		44	Hawaii	2.0
40	Vermont	2.9		45	Wyoming	1.9
8	Virginia	8.9		46	Alabama	1.8
8	Washington	8.9		NA	Kansas**	NA
37	West Virginia	4.2		NA	Maine**	NA
NA	Wisconsin**	NA		NA	Oklahoma**	NA
45	Wyoming	1.9		NA	Wisconsin**	NA
					District of Columbia**	NA

Source: Morgan Quitno Press using data from Federal Bureau of Investigation
   "Crime in the United States 1999" (Uniform Crime Reports, October 15, 2000)
*By law enforcement agencies submitting complete reports to the F.B.I. for 12 months in 1999. These rates based on population estimates for areas under the jurisdiction of those agencies reporting. Arrest rate based on the F.B.I. estimate of reported and unreported arrests for arson is 6.2 arrests per 100,000 population. See important note at beginning of this chapter. **Not available.

Reported Arrests for Weapons Violations in 1999

National Total = 122,173 Reported Arrests*

ALPHA ORDER

RANK	STATE	ARRESTS	% of USA
25	Alabama	1,490	1.2%
34	Alaska	532	0.4%
12	Arizona	2,911	2.4%
16	Arkansas	2,399	2.0%
1	California	22,738	18.6%
18	Colorado	2,275	1.9%
24	Connecticut	1,657	1.4%
37	Delaware	458	0.4%
3	Florida	8,293	6.8%
21	Georgia	1,729	1.4%
40	Hawaii	241	0.2%
36	Idaho	494	0.4%
4	Illinois	7,417	6.1%
26	Indiana	1,481	1.2%
33	Iowa	598	0.5%
NA	Kansas**	NA	NA
32	Kentucky	689	0.6%
19	Louisiana	1,970	1.6%
NA	Maine**	NA	NA
22	Maryland	1,720	1.4%
29	Massachusetts	872	0.7%
6	Michigan	5,927	4.9%
17	Minnesota	2,318	1.9%
31	Mississippi	768	0.6%
9	Missouri	3,519	2.9%
45	Montana	72	0.1%
28	Nebraska	1,098	0.9%
20	Nevada	1,828	1.5%
44	New Hampshire	78	0.1%
7	New Jersey	4,959	4.1%
35	New Mexico	505	0.4%
14	New York	2,785	2.3%
5	North Carolina	6,589	5.4%
43	North Dakota	82	0.1%
11	Ohio	3,247	2.7%
NA	Oklahoma**	NA	NA
23	Oregon	1,714	1.4%
10	Pennsylvania	3,399	2.8%
38	Rhode Island	449	0.4%
27	South Carolina	1,120	0.9%
42	South Dakota	151	0.1%
13	Tennessee	2,851	2.3%
2	Texas	10,941	9.0%
30	Utah	782	0.6%
46	Vermont	9	0.0%
8	Virginia	3,941	3.2%
15	Washington	2,602	2.1%
39	West Virginia	316	0.3%
NA	Wisconsin**	NA	NA
41	Wyoming	159	0.1%

RANK ORDER

RANK	STATE	ARRESTS	% of USA
1	California	22,738	18.6%
2	Texas	10,941	9.0%
3	Florida	8,293	6.8%
4	Illinois	7,417	6.1%
5	North Carolina	6,589	5.4%
6	Michigan	5,927	4.9%
7	New Jersey	4,959	4.1%
8	Virginia	3,941	3.2%
9	Missouri	3,519	2.9%
10	Pennsylvania	3,399	2.8%
11	Ohio	3,247	2.7%
12	Arizona	2,911	2.4%
13	Tennessee	2,851	2.3%
14	New York	2,785	2.3%
15	Washington	2,602	2.1%
16	Arkansas	2,399	2.0%
17	Minnesota	2,318	1.9%
18	Colorado	2,275	1.9%
19	Louisiana	1,970	1.6%
20	Nevada	1,828	1.5%
21	Georgia	1,729	1.4%
22	Maryland	1,720	1.4%
23	Oregon	1,714	1.4%
24	Connecticut	1,657	1.4%
25	Alabama	1,490	1.2%
26	Indiana	1,481	1.2%
27	South Carolina	1,120	0.9%
28	Nebraska	1,098	0.9%
29	Massachusetts	872	0.7%
30	Utah	782	0.6%
31	Mississippi	768	0.6%
32	Kentucky	689	0.6%
33	Iowa	598	0.5%
34	Alaska	532	0.4%
35	New Mexico	505	0.4%
36	Idaho	494	0.4%
37	Delaware	458	0.4%
38	Rhode Island	449	0.4%
39	West Virginia	316	0.3%
40	Hawaii	241	0.2%
41	Wyoming	159	0.1%
42	South Dakota	151	0.1%
43	North Dakota	82	0.1%
44	New Hampshire	78	0.1%
45	Montana	72	0.1%
46	Vermont	9	0.0%
NA	Kansas**	NA	NA
NA	Maine**	NA	NA
NA	Oklahoma**	NA	NA
NA	Wisconsin**	NA	NA
	District of Columbia**	NA	NA

Source: Federal Bureau of Investigation
    "Crime in the United States 1999" (Uniform Crime Reports, October 15, 2000)
*By law enforcement agencies submitting complete reports to the F.B.I. for 12 months in 1999. The F.B.I. estimates
172,400 reported and unreported arrests for weapons violations occurred in 1999. Weapons violations include
illegal carrying and possession. See important note at beginning of this chapter.
**Not available.

Reported Arrest Rate for Weapons Violations in 1999

National Rate = 65.4 Reported Arrests per 100,000 Population*

ALPHA ORDER

RANK	STATE	RATE
36	Alabama	36.7
9	Alaska	95.3
17	Arizona	66.0
7	Arkansas	98.8
16	California	68.8
10	Colorado	90.2
29	Connecticut	53.2
20	Delaware	60.7
26	Florida	54.9
14	Georgia	70.7
41	Hawaii	23.1
32	Idaho	45.8
1	Illinois	262.9
34	Indiana	42.9
40	Iowa	25.7
NA	Kansas**	NA
2	Kentucky	154.5
22	Louisiana	59.9
NA	Maine**	NA
24	Maryland	55.7
42	Massachusetts	18.1
12	Michigan	73.5
23	Minnesota	57.1
15	Mississippi	69.4
4	Missouri	111.9
45	Montana	16.6
13	Nebraska	71.5
5	Nevada	103.9
44	New Hampshire	16.8
18	New Jersey	63.3
30	New Mexico	51.0
31	New York	48.4
8	North Carolina	97.6
43	North Dakota	17.4
28	Ohio	54.0
NA	Oklahoma**	NA
25	Oregon	55.0
35	Pennsylvania	37.0
33	Rhode Island	45.3
3	South Carolina	124.6
39	South Dakota	29.0
6	Tennessee	102.3
21	Texas	60.6
27	Utah	54.1
46	Vermont	1.9
11	Virginia	84.9
19	Washington	61.5
38	West Virginia	33.3
NA	Wisconsin**	NA
37	Wyoming	33.8

RANK ORDER

RANK	STATE	RATE
1	Illinois	262.9
2	Kentucky	154.5
3	South Carolina	124.6
4	Missouri	111.9
5	Nevada	103.9
6	Tennessee	102.3
7	Arkansas	98.8
8	North Carolina	97.6
9	Alaska	95.3
10	Colorado	90.2
11	Virginia	84.9
12	Michigan	73.5
13	Nebraska	71.5
14	Georgia	70.7
15	Mississippi	69.4
16	California	68.8
17	Arizona	66.0
18	New Jersey	63.3
19	Washington	61.5
20	Delaware	60.7
21	Texas	60.6
22	Louisiana	59.9
23	Minnesota	57.1
24	Maryland	55.7
25	Oregon	55.0
26	Florida	54.9
27	Utah	54.1
28	Ohio	54.0
29	Connecticut	53.2
30	New Mexico	51.0
31	New York	48.4
32	Idaho	45.8
33	Rhode Island	45.3
34	Indiana	42.9
35	Pennsylvania	37.0
36	Alabama	36.7
37	Wyoming	33.8
38	West Virginia	33.3
39	South Dakota	29.0
40	Iowa	25.7
41	Hawaii	23.1
42	Massachusetts	18.1
43	North Dakota	17.4
44	New Hampshire	16.8
45	Montana	16.6
46	Vermont	1.9
NA	Kansas**	NA
NA	Maine**	NA
NA	Oklahoma**	NA
NA	Wisconsin**	NA
	District of Columbia**	NA

Source: Morgan Quitno Press using data from Federal Bureau of Investigation
"Crime in the United States 1999" (Uniform Crime Reports, October 15, 2000)
*By law enforcement agencies submitting complete reports to the F.B.I. for 12 months in 1999. These rates based on population estimates for areas under the jurisdiction of those agencies reporting. Arrest rate based on the F.B.I. estimate of reported and unreported arrests for weapons violations is 63.2 arrests per 100,000 population. See important note at beginning of this chapter. **Not available.

Reported Arrests for Driving Under the Influence in 1999

National Total = 988,950 Reported Arrests*

ALPHA ORDER

RANK	STATE	ARRESTS	% of USA
20	Alabama	15,954	1.6%
35	Alaska	4,316	0.4%
8	Arizona	31,746	3.2%
17	Arkansas	18,290	1.8%
1	California	189,349	19.1%
10	Colorado	30,564	3.1%
28	Connecticut	9,691	1.0%
45	Delaware	223	0.0%
3	Florida	57,715	5.8%
16	Georgia	20,366	2.1%
38	Hawaii	3,661	0.4%
29	Idaho	9,209	0.9%
NA	Illinois**	NA	NA
19	Indiana	16,849	1.7%
25	Iowa	12,091	1.2%
NA	Kansas**	NA	NA
39	Kentucky	3,468	0.4%
23	Louisiana	14,239	1.4%
NA	Maine**	NA	NA
15	Maryland	20,727	2.1%
26	Massachusetts	11,562	1.2%
5	Michigan	47,191	4.8%
6	Minnesota	40,604	4.1%
27	Mississippi	10,087	1.0%
18	Missouri	18,259	1.8%
44	Montana	1,053	0.1%
24	Nebraska	12,755	1.3%
32	Nevada	7,771	0.8%
42	New Hampshire	2,237	0.2%
13	New Jersey	23,770	2.4%
30	New Mexico	8,966	0.9%
9	New York	30,776	3.1%
4	North Carolina	56,617	5.7%
40	North Dakota	3,456	0.3%
14	Ohio	22,245	2.2%
NA	Oklahoma**	NA	NA
21	Oregon	15,744	1.6%
7	Pennsylvania	32,757	3.3%
43	Rhode Island	1,841	0.2%
31	South Carolina	8,132	0.8%
37	South Dakota	4,214	0.4%
22	Tennessee	14,744	1.5%
2	Texas	82,809	8.4%
34	Utah	5,601	0.6%
41	Vermont	3,048	0.3%
12	Virginia	24,227	2.4%
11	Washington	29,919	3.0%
33	West Virginia	5,836	0.6%
NA	Wisconsin**	NA	NA
36	Wyoming	4,271	0.4%

RANK ORDER

RANK	STATE	ARRESTS	% of USA
1	California	189,349	19.1%
2	Texas	82,809	8.4%
3	Florida	57,715	5.8%
4	North Carolina	56,617	5.7%
5	Michigan	47,191	4.8%
6	Minnesota	40,604	4.1%
7	Pennsylvania	32,757	3.3%
8	Arizona	31,746	3.2%
9	New York	30,776	3.1%
10	Colorado	30,564	3.1%
11	Washington	29,919	3.0%
12	Virginia	24,227	2.4%
13	New Jersey	23,770	2.4%
14	Ohio	22,245	2.2%
15	Maryland	20,727	2.1%
16	Georgia	20,366	2.1%
17	Arkansas	18,290	1.8%
18	Missouri	18,259	1.8%
19	Indiana	16,849	1.7%
20	Alabama	15,954	1.6%
21	Oregon	15,744	1.6%
22	Tennessee	14,744	1.5%
23	Louisiana	14,239	1.4%
24	Nebraska	12,755	1.3%
25	Iowa	12,091	1.2%
26	Massachusetts	11,562	1.2%
27	Mississippi	10,087	1.0%
28	Connecticut	9,691	1.0%
29	Idaho	9,209	0.9%
30	New Mexico	8,966	0.9%
31	South Carolina	8,132	0.8%
32	Nevada	7,771	0.8%
33	West Virginia	5,836	0.6%
34	Utah	5,601	0.6%
35	Alaska	4,316	0.4%
36	Wyoming	4,271	0.4%
37	South Dakota	4,214	0.4%
38	Hawaii	3,661	0.4%
39	Kentucky	3,468	0.4%
40	North Dakota	3,456	0.3%
41	Vermont	3,048	0.3%
42	New Hampshire	2,237	0.2%
43	Rhode Island	1,841	0.2%
44	Montana	1,053	0.1%
45	Delaware	223	0.0%
NA	Illinois**	NA	NA
NA	Kansas**	NA	NA
NA	Maine**	NA	NA
NA	Oklahoma**	NA	NA
NA	Wisconsin**	NA	NA
	District of Columbia**	NA	NA

Source: Federal Bureau of Investigation
"Crime in the United States 1999" (Uniform Crime Reports, October 15, 2000)
*By law enforcement agencies submitting complete reports to the F.B.I. for 12 months in 1999. The F.B.I. estimates 1,511,300 reported and unreported arrests for driving under the influence occurred in 1999. Includes driving any vehicle while drunk or under the influence of liquor or narcotics. See important note at beginning of this chapter.
**Not available.

Reported Arrest Rate for Driving Under the Influence in 1999

National Rate = 529.0 Reported Arrests per 100,000 Population*

ALPHA ORDER

RANK ORDER

RANK	STATE	RATE
34	Alabama	393.3
13	Alaska	773.5
16	Arizona	720.0
14	Arkansas	753.3
23	California	573.1
1	Colorado	1,211.9
40	Connecticut	310.9
45	Delaware	29.6
36	Florida	381.9
9	Georgia	832.6
39	Hawaii	351.0
7	Idaho	854.3
NA	Illinois**	NA
29	Indiana	488.5
27	Iowa	520.0
NA	Kansas**	NA
12	Kentucky	777.6
33	Louisiana	433.1
NA	Maine**	NA
18	Maryland	671.4
43	Massachusetts	240.3
21	Michigan	584.9
2	Minnesota	999.9
3	Mississippi	912.0
22	Missouri	580.4
42	Montana	243.2
10	Nebraska	830.4
32	Nevada	441.5
30	New Hampshire	483.2
41	New Jersey	303.3
5	New Mexico	904.7
24	New York	535.0
8	North Carolina	838.8
15	North Dakota	733.8
37	Ohio	370.3
NA	Oklahoma**	NA
28	Oregon	505.3
38	Pennsylvania	356.9
44	Rhode Island	185.8
6	South Carolina	904.6
11	South Dakota	808.8
25	Tennessee	529.0
31	Texas	458.5
35	Utah	387.3
19	Vermont	631.1
26	Virginia	522.1
17	Washington	707.0
20	West Virginia	615.6
NA	Wisconsin**	NA
4	Wyoming	906.8

RANK	STATE	RATE
1	Colorado	1,211.9
2	Minnesota	999.9
3	Mississippi	912.0
4	Wyoming	906.8
5	New Mexico	904.7
6	South Carolina	904.6
7	Idaho	854.3
8	North Carolina	838.8
9	Georgia	832.6
10	Nebraska	830.4
11	South Dakota	808.8
12	Kentucky	777.6
13	Alaska	773.5
14	Arkansas	753.3
15	North Dakota	733.8
16	Arizona	720.0
17	Washington	707.0
18	Maryland	671.4
19	Vermont	631.1
20	West Virginia	615.6
21	Michigan	584.9
22	Missouri	580.4
23	California	573.1
24	New York	535.0
25	Tennessee	529.0
26	Virginia	522.1
27	Iowa	520.0
28	Oregon	505.3
29	Indiana	488.5
30	New Hampshire	483.2
31	Texas	458.5
32	Nevada	441.5
33	Louisiana	433.1
34	Alabama	393.3
35	Utah	387.3
36	Florida	381.9
37	Ohio	370.3
38	Pennsylvania	356.9
39	Hawaii	351.0
40	Connecticut	310.9
41	New Jersey	303.3
42	Montana	243.2
43	Massachusetts	240.3
44	Rhode Island	185.8
45	Delaware	29.6
NA	Illinois**	NA
NA	Kansas**	NA
NA	Maine**	NA
NA	Oklahoma**	NA
NA	Wisconsin**	NA
	District of Columbia**	NA

Source: Morgan Quitno Press using data from Federal Bureau of Investigation
"Crime in the United States 1999" (Uniform Crime Reports, October 15, 2000)
*By law enforcement agencies submitting complete reports to the F.B.I. for 12 months in 1999. These rates based on population estimates for areas under the jurisdiction of those agencies reporting. Arrest rate based on the F.B.I. estimate of reported and unreported arrests for driving under the influence is 554.2 arrests per 100,000 population. See important note at beginning of this chapter. **Not available.

Reported Arrests for Drug Abuse Violations in 1999

National Total = 1,148,721 Reported Arrests*

ALPHA ORDER

RANK	STATE	ARRESTS	% of USA
25	Alabama	13,449	1.2%
42	Alaska	1,841	0.2%
10	Arizona	28,322	2.5%
24	Arkansas	14,615	1.3%
1	California	253,820	22.1%
19	Colorado	16,765	1.5%
17	Connecticut	18,161	1.6%
37	Delaware	3,290	0.3%
2	Florida	141,719	12.3%
21	Georgia	15,753	1.4%
38	Hawaii	2,492	0.2%
34	Idaho	4,470	0.4%
4	Illinois	54,679	4.8%
20	Indiana	15,965	1.4%
30	Iowa	8,887	0.8%
NA	Kansas**	NA	NA
32	Kentucky	6,229	0.5%
12	Louisiana	22,077	1.9%
NA	Maine**	NA	NA
18	Maryland	17,142	1.5%
22	Massachusetts	15,690	1.4%
9	Michigan	30,955	2.7%
16	Minnesota	19,518	1.7%
28	Mississippi	9,816	0.9%
11	Missouri	24,042	2.1%
46	Montana	229	0.0%
29	Nebraska	8,955	0.8%
27	Nevada	10,432	0.9%
43	New Hampshire	1,726	0.2%
5	New Jersey	54,465	4.7%
36	New Mexico	4,324	0.4%
8	New York	34,606	3.0%
7	North Carolina	36,640	3.2%
44	North Dakota	1,091	0.1%
13	Ohio	21,555	1.9%
NA	Oklahoma**	NA	NA
26	Oregon	12,930	1.1%
6	Pennsylvania	41,891	3.6%
35	Rhode Island	4,383	0.4%
31	South Carolina	8,713	0.8%
39	South Dakota	2,409	0.2%
23	Tennessee	15,283	1.3%
3	Texas	96,559	8.4%
33	Utah	6,153	0.5%
45	Vermont	1,089	0.1%
14	Virginia	21,310	1.9%
15	Washington	19,692	1.7%
41	West Virginia	2,272	0.2%
NA	Wisconsin**	NA	NA
40	Wyoming	2,317	0.2%

RANK ORDER

RANK	STATE	ARRESTS	% of USA
1	California	253,820	22.1%
2	Florida	141,719	12.3%
3	Texas	96,559	8.4%
4	Illinois	54,679	4.8%
5	New Jersey	54,465	4.7%
6	Pennsylvania	41,891	3.6%
7	North Carolina	36,640	3.2%
8	New York	34,606	3.0%
9	Michigan	30,955	2.7%
10	Arizona	28,322	2.5%
11	Missouri	24,042	2.1%
12	Louisiana	22,077	1.9%
13	Ohio	21,555	1.9%
14	Virginia	21,310	1.9%
15	Washington	19,692	1.7%
16	Minnesota	19,518	1.7%
17	Connecticut	18,161	1.6%
18	Maryland	17,142	1.5%
19	Colorado	16,765	1.5%
20	Indiana	15,965	1.4%
21	Georgia	15,753	1.4%
22	Massachusetts	15,690	1.4%
23	Tennessee	15,283	1.3%
24	Arkansas	14,615	1.3%
25	Alabama	13,449	1.2%
26	Oregon	12,930	1.1%
27	Nevada	10,432	0.9%
28	Mississippi	9,816	0.9%
29	Nebraska	8,955	0.8%
30	Iowa	8,887	0.8%
31	South Carolina	8,713	0.8%
32	Kentucky	6,229	0.5%
33	Utah	6,153	0.5%
34	Idaho	4,470	0.4%
35	Rhode Island	4,383	0.4%
36	New Mexico	4,324	0.4%
37	Delaware	3,290	0.3%
38	Hawaii	2,492	0.2%
39	South Dakota	2,409	0.2%
40	Wyoming	2,317	0.2%
41	West Virginia	2,272	0.2%
42	Alaska	1,841	0.2%
43	New Hampshire	1,726	0.2%
44	North Dakota	1,091	0.1%
45	Vermont	1,089	0.1%
46	Montana	229	0.0%
NA	Kansas**	NA	NA
NA	Maine**	NA	NA
NA	Oklahoma**	NA	NA
NA	Wisconsin**	NA	NA
	District of Columbia**	NA	NA

Source: Federal Bureau of Investigation
   "Crime in the United States 1999" (Uniform Crime Reports, October 15, 2000)
*By law enforcement agencies submitting complete reports to the F.B.I. for 12 months in 1999. The F.B.I. estimates 1,532,200 reported and unreported arrests for drug abuse violations occurred in 1999. Includes offenses relating to possession, sale, use, growing and manufacturing of narcotic drugs. See important note at beginning of this chapter.
**Not available.

Reported Arrest Rate for Drug Abuse Violations in 1999

National Rate = 614.5 Reported Arrests per 100,000 Population*

ALPHA ORDER				RANK ORDER		
RANK	STATE	RATE		RANK	STATE	RATE
39	Alabama	331.6		1	Illinois	1,938.3
40	Alaska	329.9		2	Kentucky	1,396.6
12	Arizona	642.4		3	South Carolina	969.2
13	Arkansas	601.9		4	Florida	937.9
6	California	768.3		5	Mississippi	887.5
10	Colorado	664.8		6	California	768.3
17	Connecticut	582.6		7	Missouri	764.2
30	Delaware	436.3		8	New Jersey	695.1
4	Florida	937.9		9	Louisiana	671.4
11	Georgia	644.0		10	Colorado	664.8
43	Hawaii	238.9		11	Georgia	644.0
34	Idaho	414.7		12	Arizona	642.4
1	Illinois	1,938.3		13	Arkansas	601.9
25	Indiana	462.9		14	New York	601.5
36	Iowa	382.2		15	Nevada	592.7
NA	Kansas**	NA		16	Nebraska	583.0
2	Kentucky	1,396.6		17	Connecticut	582.6
9	Louisiana	671.4		18	Maryland	555.3
NA	Maine**	NA		19	Tennessee	548.4
18	Maryland	555.3		20	North Carolina	542.8
41	Massachusetts	326.1		21	Texas	534.7
35	Michigan	383.7		22	Wyoming	491.9
23	Minnesota	480.6		23	Minnesota	480.6
5	Mississippi	887.5		24	Washington	465.3
7	Missouri	764.2		25	Indiana	462.9
46	Montana	52.9		26	South Dakota	462.4
16	Nebraska	583.0		27	Virginia	459.3
15	Nevada	592.7		28	Pennsylvania	456.4
37	New Hampshire	372.8		29	Rhode Island	442.3
8	New Jersey	695.1		30	Delaware	436.3
30	New Mexico	436.3		30	New Mexico	436.3
14	New York	601.5		32	Utah	425.5
20	North Carolina	542.8		33	Oregon	415.0
44	North Dakota	231.6		34	Idaho	414.7
38	Ohio	358.8		35	Michigan	383.7
NA	Oklahoma**	NA		36	Iowa	382.2
33	Oregon	415.0		37	New Hampshire	372.8
28	Pennsylvania	456.4		38	Ohio	358.8
29	Rhode Island	442.3		39	Alabama	331.6
3	South Carolina	969.2		40	Alaska	329.9
26	South Dakota	462.4		41	Massachusetts	326.1
19	Tennessee	548.4		42	West Virginia	239.7
21	Texas	534.7		43	Hawaii	238.9
32	Utah	425.5		44	North Dakota	231.6
45	Vermont	225.5		45	Vermont	225.5
27	Virginia	459.3		46	Montana	52.9
24	Washington	465.3		NA	Kansas**	NA
42	West Virginia	239.7		NA	Maine**	NA
NA	Wisconsin**	NA		NA	Oklahoma**	NA
22	Wyoming	491.9		NA	Wisconsin**	NA
					District of Columbia**	NA

Source: Morgan Quitno Press using data from Federal Bureau of Investigation
   "Crime in the United States 1999" (Uniform Crime Reports, October 15, 2000)
*By law enforcement agencies submitting complete reports to the F.B.I. for 12 months in 1999. These rates based on population estimates for areas under the jurisdiction of those agencies reporting. Arrest rate based on the F.B.I. estimate of reported and unreported arrests for drug abuse violations is 561.9 arrests per 100,000 population. See important note at beginning of this chapter. **Not available.

Reported Arrests for Sex Offenses in 1999

National Total = 64,236 Reported Arrests*

ALPHA ORDER

RANK	STATE	ARRESTS	% of USA
31	Alabama	361	0.6%
32	Alaska	304	0.5%
6	Arizona	2,179	3.4%
25	Arkansas	705	1.1%
1	California	16,474	25.6%
18	Colorado	1,207	1.9%
28	Connecticut	615	1.0%
29	Delaware	427	0.7%
3	Florida	4,116	6.4%
19	Georgia	1,206	1.9%
30	Hawaii	397	0.6%
33	Idaho	286	0.4%
13	Illinois	1,415	2.2%
20	Indiana	1,058	1.6%
34	Iowa	235	0.4%
NA	Kansas**	NA	NA
37	Kentucky	205	0.3%
11	Louisiana	1,425	2.2%
NA	Maine**	NA	NA
22	Maryland	810	1.3%
23	Massachusetts	787	1.2%
15	Michigan	1,355	2.1%
21	Minnesota	934	1.5%
34	Mississippi	235	0.4%
8	Missouri	2,002	3.1%
42	Montana	82	0.1%
27	Nebraska	627	1.0%
12	Nevada	1,417	2.2%
43	New Hampshire	75	0.1%
9	New Jersey	1,988	3.1%
44	New Mexico	53	0.1%
4	New York	3,255	5.1%
7	North Carolina	2,111	3.3%
45	North Dakota	51	0.1%
10	Ohio	1,752	2.7%
NA	Oklahoma**	NA	NA
16	Oregon	1,325	2.1%
5	Pennsylvania	3,060	4.8%
38	Rhode Island	203	0.3%
39	South Carolina	159	0.2%
36	South Dakota	219	0.3%
24	Tennessee	721	1.1%
2	Texas	4,815	7.5%
26	Utah	703	1.1%
46	Vermont	27	0.0%
17	Virginia	1,251	1.9%
14	Washington	1,359	2.1%
40	West Virginia	127	0.2%
NA	Wisconsin**	NA	NA
41	Wyoming	118	0.2%

RANK ORDER

RANK	STATE	ARRESTS	% of USA
1	California	16,474	25.6%
2	Texas	4,815	7.5%
3	Florida	4,116	6.4%
4	New York	3,255	5.1%
5	Pennsylvania	3,060	4.8%
6	Arizona	2,179	3.4%
7	North Carolina	2,111	3.3%
8	Missouri	2,002	3.1%
9	New Jersey	1,988	3.1%
10	Ohio	1,752	2.7%
11	Louisiana	1,425	2.2%
12	Nevada	1,417	2.2%
13	Illinois	1,415	2.2%
14	Washington	1,359	2.1%
15	Michigan	1,355	2.1%
16	Oregon	1,325	2.1%
17	Virginia	1,251	1.9%
18	Colorado	1,207	1.9%
19	Georgia	1,206	1.9%
20	Indiana	1,058	1.6%
21	Minnesota	934	1.5%
22	Maryland	810	1.3%
23	Massachusetts	787	1.2%
24	Tennessee	721	1.1%
25	Arkansas	705	1.1%
26	Utah	703	1.1%
27	Nebraska	627	1.0%
28	Connecticut	615	1.0%
29	Delaware	427	0.7%
30	Hawaii	397	0.6%
31	Alabama	361	0.6%
32	Alaska	304	0.5%
33	Idaho	286	0.4%
34	Iowa	235	0.4%
34	Mississippi	235	0.4%
36	South Dakota	219	0.3%
37	Kentucky	205	0.3%
38	Rhode Island	203	0.3%
39	South Carolina	159	0.2%
40	West Virginia	127	0.2%
41	Wyoming	118	0.2%
42	Montana	82	0.1%
43	New Hampshire	75	0.1%
44	New Mexico	53	0.1%
45	North Dakota	51	0.1%
46	Vermont	27	0.0%
NA	Kansas**	NA	NA
NA	Maine**	NA	NA
NA	Oklahoma**	NA	NA
NA	Wisconsin**	NA	NA
	District of Columbia**	NA	NA

Source: Federal Bureau of Investigation
   "Crime in the United States 1999" (Uniform Crime Reports, October 15, 2000)
*By law enforcement agencies submitting complete reports to the F.B.I. for 12 months in 1999. The F.B.I. estimates
92,400 reported and unreported arrests for sex offenses occurred in 1999. Excludes forcible rape, prostitution and
commercialized vice. Includes statutory rape and offenses against chastity, common decency, morals and the like.
See important note at beginning of this chapter. **Not available.

Reported Arrest Rate for Sex Offenses in 1999

National Rate = 34.4 Reported Arrests per 100,000 Population*

ALPHA ORDER

RANK	STATE	RATE
44	Alabama	8.9
5	Alaska	54.5
8	Arizona	49.4
23	Arkansas	29.0
7	California	49.9
11	Colorado	47.9
35	Connecticut	19.7
3	Delaware	56.6
24	Florida	27.2
9	Georgia	49.3
17	Hawaii	38.1
27	Idaho	26.5
6	Illinois	50.2
21	Indiana	30.7
43	Iowa	10.1
NA	Kansas**	NA
12	Kentucky	46.0
13	Louisiana	43.3
NA	Maine**	NA
28	Maryland	26.2
39	Massachusetts	16.4
38	Michigan	16.8
32	Minnesota	23.0
33	Mississippi	21.2
2	Missouri	63.6
36	Montana	18.9
16	Nebraska	40.8
1	Nevada	80.5
40	New Hampshire	16.2
30	New Jersey	25.4
46	New Mexico	5.3
3	New York	56.6
20	North Carolina	31.3
42	North Dakota	10.8
22	Ohio	29.2
NA	Oklahoma**	NA
14	Oregon	42.5
18	Pennsylvania	33.3
34	Rhode Island	20.5
37	South Carolina	17.7
15	South Dakota	42.0
29	Tennessee	25.9
26	Texas	26.7
10	Utah	48.6
45	Vermont	5.6
25	Virginia	27.0
19	Washington	32.1
41	West Virginia	13.4
NA	Wisconsin**	NA
31	Wyoming	25.1

RANK ORDER

RANK	STATE	RATE
1	Nevada	80.5
2	Missouri	63.6
3	Delaware	56.6
3	New York	56.6
5	Alaska	54.5
6	Illinois	50.2
7	California	49.9
8	Arizona	49.4
9	Georgia	49.3
10	Utah	48.6
11	Colorado	47.9
12	Kentucky	46.0
13	Louisiana	43.3
14	Oregon	42.5
15	South Dakota	42.0
16	Nebraska	40.8
17	Hawaii	38.1
18	Pennsylvania	33.3
19	Washington	32.1
20	North Carolina	31.3
21	Indiana	30.7
22	Ohio	29.2
23	Arkansas	29.0
24	Florida	27.2
25	Virginia	27.0
26	Texas	26.7
27	Idaho	26.5
28	Maryland	26.2
29	Tennessee	25.9
30	New Jersey	25.4
31	Wyoming	25.1
32	Minnesota	23.0
33	Mississippi	21.2
34	Rhode Island	20.5
35	Connecticut	19.7
36	Montana	18.9
37	South Carolina	17.7
38	Michigan	16.8
39	Massachusetts	16.4
40	New Hampshire	16.2
41	West Virginia	13.4
42	North Dakota	10.8
43	Iowa	10.1
44	Alabama	8.9
45	Vermont	5.6
46	New Mexico	5.3
NA	Kansas**	NA
NA	Maine**	NA
NA	Oklahoma**	NA
NA	Wisconsin**	NA
	District of Columbia**	NA

Source: Morgan Quitno Press using data from Federal Bureau of Investigation
   "Crime in the United States 1999" (Uniform Crime Reports, October 15, 2000)
*By law enforcement agencies submitting complete reports to the F.B.I. for 12 months in 1999. These rates based on population estimates for areas under the jurisdiction of those agencies reporting. Arrest rate based on the F.B.I. estimate of reported and unreported arrests for sex offenses is 33.9 arrests per 100,000 population. See important note at beginning of this chapter. **Not available.*

Reported Arrests for Prostitution and Commercialized Vice in 1999

National Total = 78,475 Reported Arrests*

ALPHA ORDER

RANK	STATE	ARRESTS	% of USA
34	Alabama	182	0.2%
35	Alaska	180	0.2%
8	Arizona	2,262	2.9%
31	Arkansas	276	0.4%
1	California	14,706	18.7%
17	Colorado	1,130	1.4%
20	Connecticut	654	0.8%
37	Delaware	131	0.2%
2	Florida	14,548	18.5%
39	Georgia	64	0.1%
27	Hawaii	427	0.5%
43	Idaho	7	0.0%
4	Illinois	6,662	8.5%
16	Indiana	1,283	1.6%
32	Iowa	242	0.3%
NA	Kansas**	NA	NA
25	Kentucky	445	0.6%
21	Louisiana	550	0.7%
NA	Maine**	NA	NA
33	Maryland	220	0.3%
13	Massachusetts	1,572	2.0%
9	Michigan	2,107	2.7%
12	Minnesota	1,646	2.1%
36	Mississippi	155	0.2%
10	Missouri	2,010	2.6%
40	Montana	39	0.0%
30	Nebraska	355	0.5%
5	Nevada	4,422	5.6%
41	New Hampshire	9	0.0%
6	New Jersey	2,969	3.8%
23	New Mexico	511	0.7%
15	New York	1,326	1.7%
18	North Carolina	922	1.2%
46	North Dakota	0	0.0%
11	Ohio	1,993	2.5%
NA	Oklahoma**	NA	NA
22	Oregon	517	0.7%
7	Pennsylvania	2,928	3.7%
28	Rhode Island	404	0.5%
29	South Carolina	383	0.5%
44	South Dakota	4	0.0%
14	Tennessee	1,426	1.8%
3	Texas	7,067	9.0%
25	Utah	445	0.6%
45	Vermont	2	0.0%
24	Virginia	469	0.6%
19	Washington	703	0.9%
38	West Virginia	113	0.1%
NA	Wisconsin**	NA	NA
41	Wyoming	9	0.0%

RANK ORDER

RANK	STATE	ARRESTS	% of USA
1	California	14,706	18.7%
2	Florida	14,548	18.5%
3	Texas	7,067	9.0%
4	Illinois	6,662	8.5%
5	Nevada	4,422	5.6%
6	New Jersey	2,969	3.8%
7	Pennsylvania	2,928	3.7%
8	Arizona	2,262	2.9%
9	Michigan	2,107	2.7%
10	Missouri	2,010	2.6%
11	Ohio	1,993	2.5%
12	Minnesota	1,646	2.1%
13	Massachusetts	1,572	2.0%
14	Tennessee	1,426	1.8%
15	New York	1,326	1.7%
16	Indiana	1,283	1.6%
17	Colorado	1,130	1.4%
18	North Carolina	922	1.2%
19	Washington	703	0.9%
20	Connecticut	654	0.8%
21	Louisiana	550	0.7%
22	Oregon	517	0.7%
23	New Mexico	511	0.7%
24	Virginia	469	0.6%
25	Kentucky	445	0.6%
25	Utah	445	0.6%
27	Hawaii	427	0.5%
28	Rhode Island	404	0.5%
29	South Carolina	383	0.5%
30	Nebraska	355	0.5%
31	Arkansas	276	0.4%
32	Iowa	242	0.3%
33	Maryland	220	0.3%
34	Alabama	182	0.2%
35	Alaska	180	0.2%
36	Mississippi	155	0.2%
37	Delaware	131	0.2%
38	West Virginia	113	0.1%
39	Georgia	64	0.1%
40	Montana	39	0.0%
41	New Hampshire	9	0.0%
41	Wyoming	9	0.0%
43	Idaho	7	0.0%
44	South Dakota	4	0.0%
45	Vermont	2	0.0%
46	North Dakota	0	0.0%
NA	Kansas**	NA	NA
NA	Maine**	NA	NA
NA	Oklahoma**	NA	NA
NA	Wisconsin**	NA	NA
	District of Columbia**	NA	NA

Source: Federal Bureau of Investigation
"Crime in the United States 1999" (Uniform Crime Reports, October 15, 2000)
*By law enforcement agencies submitting complete reports to the F.B.I. for 12 months in 1999. The F.B.I. estimates 92,100 reported and unreported arrests for prostitution and commercialized vice occurred in 1999. Includes keeping a bawdy house, procuring or transporting women for immoral purposes. Attempts are included. See important note at beginning of this chapter. **Not available.*

Reported Arrest Rate for Prostitution and Commercialized Vice in 1999

National Rate = 42.0 Reported Arrests per 100,000 Population*

ALPHA ORDER

RANK ORDER

RANK	STATE	RATE		RANK	STATE	RATE
39	Alabama	4.5		1	Nevada	251.3
20	Alaska	32.3		2	Illinois	236.2
7	Arizona	51.3		3	Kentucky	99.8
34	Arkansas	11.4		4	Florida	96.3
10	California	44.5		5	Missouri	63.9
9	Colorado	44.8		6	New Mexico	51.6
26	Connecticut	21.0		7	Arizona	51.3
27	Delaware	17.4		8	Tennessee	51.2
4	Florida	96.3		9	Colorado	44.8
40	Georgia	2.6		10	California	44.5
12	Hawaii	40.9		11	South Carolina	42.6
44	Idaho	0.6		12	Hawaii	40.9
2	Illinois	236.2		13	Rhode Island	40.8
17	Indiana	37.2		14	Minnesota	40.5
35	Iowa	10.4		15	Texas	39.1
NA	Kansas**	NA		16	New Jersey	37.9
3	Kentucky	99.8		17	Indiana	37.2
28	Louisiana	16.7		18	Ohio	33.2
NA	Maine**	NA		19	Massachusetts	32.7
38	Maryland	7.1		20	Alaska	32.3
19	Massachusetts	32.7		21	Pennsylvania	31.9
23	Michigan	26.1		22	Utah	30.8
14	Minnesota	40.5		23	Michigan	26.1
31	Mississippi	14.0		24	Nebraska	23.1
5	Missouri	63.9		25	New York	23.0
37	Montana	9.0		26	Connecticut	21.0
24	Nebraska	23.1		27	Delaware	17.4
1	Nevada	251.3		28	Louisiana	16.7
41	New Hampshire	1.9		29	Oregon	16.6
16	New Jersey	37.9		29	Washington	16.6
6	New Mexico	51.6		31	Mississippi	14.0
25	New York	23.0		32	North Carolina	13.7
32	North Carolina	13.7		33	West Virginia	11.9
46	North Dakota	0.0		34	Arkansas	11.4
18	Ohio	33.2		35	Iowa	10.4
NA	Oklahoma**	NA		36	Virginia	10.1
29	Oregon	16.6		37	Montana	9.0
21	Pennsylvania	31.9		38	Maryland	7.1
13	Rhode Island	40.8		39	Alabama	4.5
11	South Carolina	42.6		40	Georgia	2.6
43	South Dakota	0.8		41	New Hampshire	1.9
8	Tennessee	51.2		41	Wyoming	1.9
15	Texas	39.1		43	South Dakota	0.8
22	Utah	30.8		44	Idaho	0.6
45	Vermont	0.4		45	Vermont	0.4
36	Virginia	10.1		46	North Dakota	0.0
29	Washington	16.6		NA	Kansas**	NA
33	West Virginia	11.9		NA	Maine**	NA
NA	Wisconsin**	NA		NA	Oklahoma**	NA
41	Wyoming	1.9		NA	Wisconsin**	NA
					District of Columbia**	NA

Source: Morgan Quitno Press using data from Federal Bureau of Investigation
"Crime in the United States 1999" (Uniform Crime Reports, October 15, 2000)
*By law enforcement agencies submitting complete reports to the F.B.I. for 12 months in 1999. These rates based on population estimates for areas under the jurisdiction of those agencies reporting. Arrest rate based on the F.B.I. estimate of reported and unreported arrests for prostitution and commercialized vice is 33.8 arrests per 100,000 population. See important note at beginning of this chapter. **Not available.

Reported Arrests for Offenses Against Families and Children in 1999

National Total = 92,849 Reported Arrests*

ALPHA ORDER

RANK	STATE	ARRESTS	% of USA
23	Alabama	947	1.0%
34	Alaska	378	0.4%
12	Arizona	2,040	2.2%
15	Arkansas	1,929	2.1%
25	California	849	0.9%
16	Colorado	1,758	1.9%
9	Connecticut	2,346	2.5%
37	Delaware	267	0.3%
NA	Florida**	NA	NA
7	Georgia	3,017	3.2%
17	Hawaii	1,657	1.8%
35	Idaho	336	0.4%
45	Illinois	34	0.0%
21	Indiana	1,093	1.2%
32	Iowa	453	0.5%
NA	Kansas**	NA	NA
26	Kentucky	830	0.9%
13	Louisiana	1,990	2.1%
NA	Maine**	NA	NA
11	Maryland	2,078	2.2%
10	Massachusetts	2,301	2.5%
4	Michigan	4,432	4.8%
28	Minnesota	701	0.8%
14	Mississippi	1,979	2.1%
8	Missouri	2,700	2.9%
41	Montana	128	0.1%
19	Nebraska	1,474	1.6%
20	Nevada	1,119	1.2%
44	New Hampshire	55	0.1%
2	New Jersey	15,656	16.9%
29	New Mexico	640	0.7%
6	New York	3,050	3.3%
3	North Carolina	5,670	6.1%
40	North Dakota	184	0.2%
1	Ohio	20,399	22.0%
NA	Oklahoma**	NA	NA
30	Oregon	494	0.5%
24	Pennsylvania	875	0.9%
31	Rhode Island	469	0.5%
42	South Carolina	77	0.1%
36	South Dakota	312	0.3%
27	Tennessee	792	0.9%
5	Texas	3,888	4.2%
22	Utah	975	1.1%
33	Vermont	415	0.4%
18	Virginia	1,533	1.7%
39	Washington	227	0.2%
43	West Virginia	73	0.1%
NA	Wisconsin**	NA	NA
38	Wyoming	229	0.2%

RANK ORDER

RANK	STATE	ARRESTS	% of USA
1	Ohio	20,399	22.0%
2	New Jersey	15,656	16.9%
3	North Carolina	5,670	6.1%
4	Michigan	4,432	4.8%
5	Texas	3,888	4.2%
6	New York	3,050	3.3%
7	Georgia	3,017	3.2%
8	Missouri	2,700	2.9%
9	Connecticut	2,346	2.5%
10	Massachusetts	2,301	2.5%
11	Maryland	2,078	2.2%
12	Arizona	2,040	2.2%
13	Louisiana	1,990	2.1%
14	Mississippi	1,979	2.1%
15	Arkansas	1,929	2.1%
16	Colorado	1,758	1.9%
17	Hawaii	1,657	1.8%
18	Virginia	1,533	1.7%
19	Nebraska	1,474	1.6%
20	Nevada	1,119	1.2%
21	Indiana	1,093	1.2%
22	Utah	975	1.1%
23	Alabama	947	1.0%
24	Pennsylvania	875	0.9%
25	California	849	0.9%
26	Kentucky	830	0.9%
27	Tennessee	792	0.9%
28	Minnesota	701	0.8%
29	New Mexico	640	0.7%
30	Oregon	494	0.5%
31	Rhode Island	469	0.5%
32	Iowa	453	0.5%
33	Vermont	415	0.4%
34	Alaska	378	0.4%
35	Idaho	336	0.4%
36	South Dakota	312	0.3%
37	Delaware	267	0.3%
38	Wyoming	229	0.2%
39	Washington	227	0.2%
40	North Dakota	184	0.2%
41	Montana	128	0.1%
42	South Carolina	77	0.1%
43	West Virginia	73	0.1%
44	New Hampshire	55	0.1%
45	Illinois	34	0.0%
NA	Florida**	NA	NA
NA	Kansas**	NA	NA
NA	Maine**	NA	NA
NA	Oklahoma**	NA	NA
NA	Wisconsin**	NA	NA
	District of Columbia**	NA	NA

Source: Federal Bureau of Investigation
   "Crime in the United States 1999" (Uniform Crime Reports, October 15, 2000)
By law enforcement agencies submitting complete reports to the F.B.I. for 12 months in 1999. The F.B.I. estimates 151,200 reported and unreported arrests for offenses against families and children occurred in 1999. Includes nonsupport, neglect, desertion or abuse of family and children. See important note at beginning of this chapter.
**Not available.*

35

Reported Arrest Rate for Offenses Against Families and Children in 1999

National Rate = 49.7 Reported Arrests per 100,000 Population*

ALPHA ORDER

RANK	STATE	RATE
34	Alabama	23.3
14	Alaska	67.7
26	Arizona	46.3
11	Arkansas	79.4
44	California	2.6
13	Colorado	69.7
12	Connecticut	75.3
28	Delaware	35.4
NA	Florida**	NA
6	Georgia	123.3
5	Hawaii	158.9
31	Idaho	31.2
45	Illinois	1.2
30	Indiana	31.7
36	Iowa	19.5
NA	Kansas**	NA
3	Kentucky	186.1
19	Louisiana	60.5
NA	Maine**	NA
16	Maryland	67.3
24	Massachusetts	47.8
21	Michigan	54.9
37	Minnesota	17.3
4	Mississippi	178.9
9	Missouri	85.8
32	Montana	29.6
7	Nebraska	96.0
18	Nevada	63.6
39	New Hampshire	11.9
2	New Jersey	199.8
17	New Mexico	64.6
22	New York	53.0
10	North Carolina	84.0
27	North Dakota	39.1
1	Ohio	339.5
NA	Oklahoma**	NA
38	Oregon	15.9
40	Pennsylvania	9.5
25	Rhode Island	47.3
41	South Carolina	8.6
20	South Dakota	59.9
33	Tennessee	28.4
35	Texas	21.5
15	Utah	67.4
8	Vermont	85.9
29	Virginia	33.0
43	Washington	5.4
42	West Virginia	7.7
NA	Wisconsin**	NA
23	Wyoming	48.6

RANK ORDER

RANK	STATE	RATE
1	Ohio	339.5
2	New Jersey	199.8
3	Kentucky	186.1
4	Mississippi	178.9
5	Hawaii	158.9
6	Georgia	123.3
7	Nebraska	96.0
8	Vermont	85.9
9	Missouri	85.8
10	North Carolina	84.0
11	Arkansas	79.4
12	Connecticut	75.3
13	Colorado	69.7
14	Alaska	67.7
15	Utah	67.4
16	Maryland	67.3
17	New Mexico	64.6
18	Nevada	63.6
19	Louisiana	60.5
20	South Dakota	59.9
21	Michigan	54.9
22	New York	53.0
23	Wyoming	48.6
24	Massachusetts	47.8
25	Rhode Island	47.3
26	Arizona	46.3
27	North Dakota	39.1
28	Delaware	35.4
29	Virginia	33.0
30	Indiana	31.7
31	Idaho	31.2
32	Montana	29.6
33	Tennessee	28.4
34	Alabama	23.3
35	Texas	21.5
36	Iowa	19.5
37	Minnesota	17.3
38	Oregon	15.9
39	New Hampshire	11.9
40	Pennsylvania	9.5
41	South Carolina	8.6
42	West Virginia	7.7
43	Washington	5.4
44	California	2.6
45	Illinois	1.2
NA	Florida**	NA
NA	Kansas**	NA
NA	Maine**	NA
NA	Oklahoma**	NA
NA	Wisconsin**	NA

District of Columbia**   NA

Source: Morgan Quitno Press using data from Federal Bureau of Investigation
"Crime in the United States 1999" (Uniform Crime Reports, October 15, 2000)
*By law enforcement agencies submitting complete reports to the F.B.I. for 12 months in 1999. These rates based on population estimates for areas under the jurisdiction of those agencies reporting. Arrest rate based on the F.B.I. estimate of reported and unreported arrests for offenses against families and children is 55.4 arrests per 100,000 population. See important note at beginning of this chapter. **Not available.

Percent of Crimes Cleared in 1998

National Percent = 21.5% Cleared*

ALPHA ORDER

RANK	STATE	PERCENT
34	Alabama	20.0
3	Alaska	28.0
44	Arizona	18.0
7	Arkansas	25.7
27	California	21.2
21	Colorado	22.3
33	Connecticut	20.1
6	Delaware	25.8
19	Florida	22.7
32	Georgia	20.4
40	Hawaii	18.9
15	Idaho	23.8
NA	Illinois**	NA
34	Indiana	20.0
39	Iowa	19.3
NA	Kansas**	NA
10	Kentucky	25.4
5	Louisiana	26.2
2	Maine	28.1
17	Maryland	22.9
24	Massachusetts	22.1
47	Michigan	13.4
12	Minnesota	25.1
37	Mississippi	19.8
25	Missouri	21.9
20	Montana	22.6
13	Nebraska	24.9
22	Nevada	22.2
4	New Hampshire	27.6
29	New Jersey	20.9
45	New Mexico	17.7
9	New York	25.6
18	North Carolina	22.8
31	North Dakota	20.5
38	Ohio	19.5
36	Oklahoma	19.9
25	Oregon	21.9
10	Pennsylvania	25.4
42	Rhode Island	18.3
28	South Carolina	21.1
7	South Dakota	25.7
16	Tennessee	23.2
29	Texas	20.9
22	Utah	22.2
48	Vermont	12.0
14	Virginia	24.3
43	Washington	18.1
41	West Virginia	18.6
46	Wisconsin	17.1
1	Wyoming	30.3

RANK ORDER

RANK	STATE	PERCENT
1	Wyoming	30.3
2	Maine	28.1
3	Alaska	28.0
4	New Hampshire	27.6
5	Louisiana	26.2
6	Delaware	25.8
7	Arkansas	25.7
7	South Dakota	25.7
9	New York	25.6
10	Kentucky	25.4
10	Pennsylvania	25.4
12	Minnesota	25.1
13	Nebraska	24.9
14	Virginia	24.3
15	Idaho	23.8
16	Tennessee	23.2
17	Maryland	22.9
18	North Carolina	22.8
19	Florida	22.7
20	Montana	22.6
21	Colorado	22.3
22	Nevada	22.2
22	Utah	22.2
24	Massachusetts	22.1
25	Missouri	21.9
25	Oregon	21.9
27	California	21.2
28	South Carolina	21.1
29	New Jersey	20.9
29	Texas	20.9
31	North Dakota	20.5
32	Georgia	20.4
33	Connecticut	20.1
34	Alabama	20.0
34	Indiana	20.0
36	Oklahoma	19.9
37	Mississippi	19.8
38	Ohio	19.5
39	Iowa	19.3
40	Hawaii	18.9
41	West Virginia	18.6
42	Rhode Island	18.3
43	Washington	18.1
44	Arizona	18.0
45	New Mexico	17.7
46	Wisconsin	17.1
47	Michigan	13.4
48	Vermont	12.0
NA	Illinois**	NA
NA	Kansas**	NA
	District of Columbia	11.2

Source: Federal Bureau of Investigation (unpublished data)
*Includes murder, rape, robbery, aggravated assault, burglary, larceny-theft and motor vehicle theft. A crime is considered cleared when at least one person is arrested, charged and turned over to the court for prosecution. Clearances recorded in 1998 may be for crimes which occurred in prior years. Several crimes may be cleared by the arrest of one person while the arrest of many persons may clear only one crime.
**Not available.

Percent of Violent Crimes Cleared in 1998

National Percent = 49.4% Cleared*

RANK	STATE	PERCENT	RANK	STATE	PERCENT
40	Alabama	43.5	1	Wyoming	73.6
4	Alaska	61.1	2	Nebraska	62.8
44	Arizona	39.5	3	Minnesota	62.6
11	Arkansas	55.0	4	Alaska	61.1
20	California	51.8	5	South Dakota	60.4
7	Colorado	59.8	6	Maine	60.1
29	Connecticut	49.5	7	Colorado	59.8
7	Delaware	59.8	7	Delaware	59.8
15	Florida	53.7	9	Virginia	58.2
41	Georgia	43.1	10	Idaho	57.3
35	Hawaii	46.6	11	Arkansas	55.0
10	Idaho	57.3	12	Iowa	54.8
NA	Illinois**	NA	13	North Carolina	54.7
31	Indiana	48.0	14	Oklahoma	53.8
12	Iowa	54.8	15	Florida	53.7
NA	Kansas**	NA	16	Louisiana	53.6
18	Kentucky	53.0	17	Montana	53.5
16	Louisiana	53.6	18	Kentucky	53.0
6	Maine	60.1	19	New York	51.9
33	Maryland	47.3	20	California	51.8
23	Massachusetts	50.4	21	South Carolina	51.5
46	Michigan	35.4	22	Tennessee	50.5
3	Minnesota	62.6	23	Massachusetts	50.4
48	Mississippi	13.2	24	West Virginia	50.3
30	Missouri	49.1	25	Utah	49.9
17	Montana	53.5	26	Pennsylvania	49.7
2	Nebraska	62.8	27	North Dakota	49.6
45	Nevada	37.6	27	Texas	49.6
34	New Hampshire	46.9	29	Connecticut	49.5
32	New Jersey	47.8	30	Missouri	49.1
42	New Mexico	43.0	31	Indiana	48.0
19	New York	51.9	32	New Jersey	47.8
13	North Carolina	54.7	33	Maryland	47.3
27	North Dakota	49.6	34	New Hampshire	46.9
39	Ohio	43.7	35	Hawaii	46.6
14	Oklahoma	53.8	36	Washington	46.5
37	Oregon	44.2	37	Oregon	44.2
26	Pennsylvania	49.7	38	Vermont	43.8
47	Rhode Island	28.1	39	Ohio	43.7
21	South Carolina	51.5	40	Alabama	43.5
5	South Dakota	60.4	41	Georgia	43.1
22	Tennessee	50.5	42	New Mexico	43.0
27	Texas	49.6	43	Wisconsin	41.4
25	Utah	49.9	44	Arizona	39.5
38	Vermont	43.8	45	Nevada	37.6
9	Virginia	58.2	46	Michigan	35.4
36	Washington	46.5	47	Rhode Island	28.1
24	West Virginia	50.3	48	Mississippi	13.2
43	Wisconsin	41.4	NA	Illinois**	NA
1	Wyoming	73.6	NA	Kansas**	NA
				District of Columbia	30.4

Source: Federal Bureau of Investigation (unpublished data)
*Includes murder, rape, robbery and aggravated assault. A crime is considered cleared when at least one person is arrested, charged and turned over to the court for prosecution. Clearances recorded in 1998 may be for crimes which occurred in prior years. Several crimes may be cleared by the arrest of one person while the arrest of many persons may clear only one crime.
**Not available.

Percent of Murders Cleared in 1998

National Percent = 68.4% Cleared*

ALPHA ORDER

RANK	STATE	PERCENT
40	Alabama	58.0
9	Alaska	83.3
41	Arizona	56.4
6	Arkansas	87.1
35	California	63.1
16	Colorado	75.6
23	Connecticut	71.1
33	Delaware	65.2
25	Florida	70.4
38	Georgia	61.0
1	Hawaii	100.0
3	Idaho	88.9
NA	Illinois**	NA
28	Indiana	69.5
21	Iowa	71.4
NA	Kansas**	NA
32	Kentucky	65.5
26	Louisiana	70.2
46	Maine	42.3
44	Maryland	48.9
37	Massachusetts	61.7
45	Michigan	48.1
16	Minnesota	75.6
19	Mississippi	74.0
24	Missouri	70.7
30	Montana	66.7
4	Nebraska	88.2
43	Nevada	53.5
NA	New Hampshire**	NA
15	New Jersey	76.3
42	New Mexico	54.2
7	New York	84.2
10	North Carolina	82.9
21	North Dakota	71.4
20	Ohio	72.0
8	Oklahoma	83.8
39	Oregon	60.0
13	Pennsylvania	79.2
18	Rhode Island	75.0
11	South Carolina	82.6
1	South Dakota	100.0
29	Tennessee	68.5
27	Texas	70.0
36	Utah	62.3
47	Vermont	37.5
12	Virginia	82.4
31	Washington	66.2
14	West Virginia	78.2
5	Wisconsin	87.4
34	Wyoming	64.3

RANK ORDER

RANK	STATE	PERCENT
1	Hawaii	100.0
1	South Dakota	100.0
3	Idaho	88.9
4	Nebraska	88.2
5	Wisconsin	87.4
6	Arkansas	87.1
7	New York	84.2
8	Oklahoma	83.8
9	Alaska	83.3
10	North Carolina	82.9
11	South Carolina	82.6
12	Virginia	82.4
13	Pennsylvania	79.2
14	West Virginia	78.2
15	New Jersey	76.3
16	Colorado	75.6
16	Minnesota	75.6
18	Rhode Island	75.0
19	Mississippi	74.0
20	Ohio	72.0
21	Iowa	71.4
21	North Dakota	71.4
23	Connecticut	71.1
24	Missouri	70.7
25	Florida	70.4
26	Louisiana	70.2
27	Texas	70.0
28	Indiana	69.5
29	Tennessee	68.5
30	Montana	66.7
31	Washington	66.2
32	Kentucky	65.5
33	Delaware	65.2
34	Wyoming	64.3
35	California	63.1
36	Utah	62.3
37	Massachusetts	61.7
38	Georgia	61.0
39	Oregon	60.0
40	Alabama	58.0
41	Arizona	56.4
42	New Mexico	54.2
43	Nevada	53.5
44	Maryland	48.9
45	Michigan	48.1
46	Maine	42.3
47	Vermont	37.5
NA	Illinois**	NA
NA	Kansas**	NA
NA	New Hampshire**	NA
	District of Columbia	40.0

Source: Federal Bureau of Investigation (unpublished data)
*Includes nonnegligent manslaughter. A crime is considered cleared when at least one person is arrested, charged and turned over to the court for prosecution. Clearances recorded in 1998 may be for crimes which occurred in prior years. Several crimes may be cleared by the arrest of one person while the arrest of many persons may clear only one crime.
**Not available.

Percent of Rapes Cleared in 1998

National Percent = 50.5% Cleared*

<table>
<tr><td colspan="3">ALPHA ORDER</td><td colspan="3">RANK ORDER</td></tr>
<tr><td>RANK</td><td>STATE</td><td>PERCENT</td><td>RANK</td><td>STATE</td><td>PERCENT</td></tr>
<tr><td>28</td><td>Alabama</td><td>45.7</td><td>1</td><td>Wisconsin</td><td>78.0</td></tr>
<tr><td>35</td><td>Alaska</td><td>39.0</td><td>2</td><td>Hawaii</td><td>72.7</td></tr>
<tr><td>46</td><td>Arizona</td><td>28.7</td><td>3</td><td>Virginia</td><td>63.2</td></tr>
<tr><td>10</td><td>Arkansas</td><td>57.0</td><td>4</td><td>Nebraska</td><td>62.3</td></tr>
<tr><td>20</td><td>California</td><td>50.6</td><td>5</td><td>North Carolina</td><td>61.9</td></tr>
<tr><td>12</td><td>Colorado</td><td>56.0</td><td>6</td><td>Oklahoma</td><td>61.3</td></tr>
<tr><td>24</td><td>Connecticut</td><td>47.8</td><td>7</td><td>Missouri</td><td>60.3</td></tr>
<tr><td>NA</td><td>Delaware**</td><td>NA</td><td>8</td><td>Maryland</td><td>59.5</td></tr>
<tr><td>14</td><td>Florida</td><td>55.8</td><td>9</td><td>New York</td><td>57.3</td></tr>
<tr><td>21</td><td>Georgia</td><td>50.2</td><td>10</td><td>Arkansas</td><td>57.0</td></tr>
<tr><td>2</td><td>Hawaii</td><td>72.7</td><td>11</td><td>Pennsylvania</td><td>56.6</td></tr>
<tr><td>34</td><td>Idaho</td><td>40.7</td><td>12</td><td>Colorado</td><td>56.0</td></tr>
<tr><td>NA</td><td>Illinois**</td><td>NA</td><td>12</td><td>New Jersey</td><td>56.0</td></tr>
<tr><td>29</td><td>Indiana</td><td>45.4</td><td>14</td><td>Florida</td><td>55.8</td></tr>
<tr><td>42</td><td>Iowa</td><td>34.7</td><td>15</td><td>Texas</td><td>54.6</td></tr>
<tr><td>NA</td><td>Kansas**</td><td>NA</td><td>16</td><td>Wyoming</td><td>54.5</td></tr>
<tr><td>22</td><td>Kentucky</td><td>49.6</td><td>17</td><td>Minnesota</td><td>54.3</td></tr>
<tr><td>24</td><td>Louisiana</td><td>47.8</td><td>18</td><td>Ohio</td><td>51.7</td></tr>
<tr><td>40</td><td>Maine</td><td>36.0</td><td>19</td><td>Tennessee</td><td>51.3</td></tr>
<tr><td>8</td><td>Maryland</td><td>59.5</td><td>20</td><td>California</td><td>50.6</td></tr>
<tr><td>23</td><td>Massachusetts</td><td>49.5</td><td>21</td><td>Georgia</td><td>50.2</td></tr>
<tr><td>43</td><td>Michigan</td><td>32.9</td><td>22</td><td>Kentucky</td><td>49.6</td></tr>
<tr><td>17</td><td>Minnesota</td><td>54.3</td><td>23</td><td>Massachusetts</td><td>49.5</td></tr>
<tr><td>32</td><td>Mississippi</td><td>42.9</td><td>24</td><td>Connecticut</td><td>47.8</td></tr>
<tr><td>7</td><td>Missouri</td><td>60.3</td><td>24</td><td>Louisiana</td><td>47.8</td></tr>
<tr><td>37</td><td>Montana</td><td>37.8</td><td>26</td><td>South Carolina</td><td>46.9</td></tr>
<tr><td>4</td><td>Nebraska</td><td>62.3</td><td>27</td><td>Rhode Island</td><td>46.2</td></tr>
<tr><td>41</td><td>Nevada</td><td>35.8</td><td>28</td><td>Alabama</td><td>45.7</td></tr>
<tr><td>45</td><td>New Hampshire</td><td>31.0</td><td>29</td><td>Indiana</td><td>45.4</td></tr>
<tr><td>12</td><td>New Jersey</td><td>56.0</td><td>30</td><td>New Mexico</td><td>44.4</td></tr>
<tr><td>30</td><td>New Mexico</td><td>44.4</td><td>31</td><td>South Dakota</td><td>44.1</td></tr>
<tr><td>9</td><td>New York</td><td>57.3</td><td>32</td><td>Mississippi</td><td>42.9</td></tr>
<tr><td>5</td><td>North Carolina</td><td>61.9</td><td>33</td><td>Washington</td><td>42.7</td></tr>
<tr><td>39</td><td>North Dakota</td><td>37.6</td><td>34</td><td>Idaho</td><td>40.7</td></tr>
<tr><td>18</td><td>Ohio</td><td>51.7</td><td>35</td><td>Alaska</td><td>39.0</td></tr>
<tr><td>6</td><td>Oklahoma</td><td>61.3</td><td>36</td><td>Utah</td><td>38.1</td></tr>
<tr><td>37</td><td>Oregon</td><td>37.8</td><td>37</td><td>Montana</td><td>37.8</td></tr>
<tr><td>11</td><td>Pennsylvania</td><td>56.6</td><td>37</td><td>Oregon</td><td>37.8</td></tr>
<tr><td>27</td><td>Rhode Island</td><td>46.2</td><td>39</td><td>North Dakota</td><td>37.6</td></tr>
<tr><td>26</td><td>South Carolina</td><td>46.9</td><td>40</td><td>Maine</td><td>36.0</td></tr>
<tr><td>31</td><td>South Dakota</td><td>44.1</td><td>41</td><td>Nevada</td><td>35.8</td></tr>
<tr><td>19</td><td>Tennessee</td><td>51.3</td><td>42</td><td>Iowa</td><td>34.7</td></tr>
<tr><td>15</td><td>Texas</td><td>54.6</td><td>43</td><td>Michigan</td><td>32.9</td></tr>
<tr><td>36</td><td>Utah</td><td>38.1</td><td>44</td><td>Vermont</td><td>31.4</td></tr>
<tr><td>44</td><td>Vermont</td><td>31.4</td><td>45</td><td>New Hampshire</td><td>31.0</td></tr>
<tr><td>3</td><td>Virginia</td><td>63.2</td><td>46</td><td>Arizona</td><td>28.7</td></tr>
<tr><td>33</td><td>Washington</td><td>42.7</td><td>47</td><td>West Virginia</td><td>28.5</td></tr>
<tr><td>47</td><td>West Virginia</td><td>28.5</td><td>NA</td><td>Delaware**</td><td>NA</td></tr>
<tr><td>1</td><td>Wisconsin</td><td>78.0</td><td>NA</td><td>Illinois**</td><td>NA</td></tr>
<tr><td>16</td><td>Wyoming</td><td>54.5</td><td>NA</td><td>Kansas**</td><td>NA</td></tr>
<tr><td></td><td></td><td></td><td></td><td>District of Columbia</td><td>42.1</td></tr>
</table>

Source: Federal Bureau of Investigation (unpublished data)

*Forcible rape including attempts. However, statutory rape without force and other sex offenses are excluded. A crime is considered cleared when at least one person is arrested, charged and turned over to the court for prosecution. Clearances recorded in 1998 may be for crimes which occurred in prior years. Several crimes may be cleared by the arrest of one person while the arrest of many persons may clear only one crime.
**Not available.

Percent of Robberies Cleared in 1998

National Percent = 28.3% Cleared*

ALPHA ORDER

RANK	STATE	PERCENT
20	Alabama	30.7
37	Alaska	26.5
47	Arizona	20.7
10	Arkansas	34.6
31	California	27.7
3	Colorado	38.0
35	Connecticut	26.6
19	Delaware	31.0
22	Florida	29.6
41	Georgia	24.3
16	Hawaii	31.4
9	Idaho	34.7
NA	Illinois**	NA
26	Indiana	28.5
37	Iowa	26.5
NA	Kansas**	NA
25	Kentucky	29.1
29	Louisiana	28.4
1	Maine	41.2
43	Maryland	24.1
26	Massachusetts	28.5
48	Michigan	12.2
6	Minnesota	36.2
45	Mississippi	22.9
35	Missouri	26.6
11	Montana	34.5
17	Nebraska	31.3
40	Nevada	24.7
4	New Hampshire	37.9
30	New Jersey	28.1
41	New Mexico	24.3
12	New York	34.1
8	North Carolina	34.9
14	North Dakota	33.3
32	Ohio	27.2
5	Oklahoma	36.5
12	Oregon	34.1
22	Pennsylvania	29.6
32	Rhode Island	27.2
21	South Carolina	30.6
26	South Dakota	28.5
17	Tennessee	31.3
24	Texas	29.3
15	Utah	31.7
44	Vermont	23.8
7	Virginia	35.4
34	Washington	26.7
39	West Virginia	24.8
46	Wisconsin	22.8
2	Wyoming	40.3

RANK ORDER

RANK	STATE	PERCENT
1	Maine	41.2
2	Wyoming	40.3
3	Colorado	38.0
4	New Hampshire	37.9
5	Oklahoma	36.5
6	Minnesota	36.2
7	Virginia	35.4
8	North Carolina	34.9
9	Idaho	34.7
10	Arkansas	34.6
11	Montana	34.5
12	New York	34.1
12	Oregon	34.1
14	North Dakota	33.3
15	Utah	31.7
16	Hawaii	31.4
17	Nebraska	31.3
17	Tennessee	31.3
19	Delaware	31.0
20	Alabama	30.7
21	South Carolina	30.6
22	Florida	29.6
22	Pennsylvania	29.6
24	Texas	29.3
25	Kentucky	29.1
26	Indiana	28.5
26	Massachusetts	28.5
26	South Dakota	28.5
29	Louisiana	28.4
30	New Jersey	28.1
31	California	27.7
32	Ohio	27.2
32	Rhode Island	27.2
34	Washington	26.7
35	Connecticut	26.6
35	Missouri	26.6
37	Alaska	26.5
37	Iowa	26.5
39	West Virginia	24.8
40	Nevada	24.7
41	Georgia	24.3
41	New Mexico	24.3
43	Maryland	24.1
44	Vermont	23.8
45	Mississippi	22.9
46	Wisconsin	22.8
47	Arizona	20.7
48	Michigan	12.2
NA	Illinois**	NA
NA	Kansas**	NA
	District of Columbia	12.0

Source: Federal Bureau of Investigation (unpublished data)
*Robbery is the taking of anything of value by force or threat of force. Attempts are included. A crime is considered cleared when at least one person is arrested, charged and turned over to the court for prosecution. Clearances recorded in 1998 may be for crimes which occurred in prior years. Several crimes may be cleared by the arrest of one person while the arrest of many persons may clear only one crime.
**Not available.

Percent of Aggravated Assaults Cleared in 1998

National Percent = 58.6% Cleared*

ALPHA ORDER				RANK ORDER		
RANK	**STATE**	**PERCENT**		**RANK**	**STATE**	**PERCENT**
45	Alabama	47.1		1	Wyoming	79.1
4	Alaska	71.5		2	Minnesota	73.9
42	Arizona	48.1		3	South Dakota	73.0
24	Arkansas	59.7		4	Alaska	71.5
16	California	62.9		5	Delaware	70.8
9	Colorado	68.3		6	Maine	70.4
12	Connecticut	64.2		7	Nebraska	69.8
5	Delaware	70.8		8	Virginia	69.7
22	Florida	61.2		9	Colorado	68.3
39	Georgia	52.2		10	New Hampshire	65.8
38	Hawaii	52.6		11	New York	65.3
20	Idaho	61.4		12	Connecticut	64.2
NA	Illinois**	NA		13	Louisiana	63.4
30	Indiana	56.8		13	Pennsylvania	63.4
17	Iowa	62.5		15	Kentucky	63.0
NA	Kansas**	NA		16	California	62.9
15	Kentucky	63.0		17	Iowa	62.5
13	Louisiana	63.4		17	New Jersey	62.5
6	Maine	70.4		19	Maryland	61.6
19	Maryland	61.6		20	Idaho	61.4
35	Massachusetts	54.8		21	North Carolina	61.3
46	Michigan	44.4		22	Florida	61.2
2	Minnesota	73.9		22	North Dakota	61.2
48	Mississippi	2.2		24	Arkansas	59.7
26	Missouri	57.9		25	Utah	58.2
28	Montana	57.8		26	Missouri	57.9
7	Nebraska	69.8		26	Tennessee	57.9
44	Nevada	47.5		28	Montana	57.8
10	New Hampshire	65.8		29	West Virginia	57.0
17	New Jersey	62.5		30	Indiana	56.8
43	New Mexico	47.6		31	Oklahoma	56.5
11	New York	65.3		31	Texas	56.5
21	North Carolina	61.3		33	South Carolina	56.2
22	North Dakota	61.2		34	Washington	55.6
37	Ohio	54.2		35	Massachusetts	54.8
31	Oklahoma	56.5		36	Wisconsin	54.4
41	Oregon	48.7		37	Ohio	54.2
13	Pennsylvania	63.4		38	Hawaii	52.6
47	Rhode Island	24.9		39	Georgia	52.2
33	South Carolina	56.2		40	Vermont	50.4
3	South Dakota	73.0		41	Oregon	48.7
26	Tennessee	57.9		42	Arizona	48.1
31	Texas	56.5		43	New Mexico	47.6
25	Utah	58.2		44	Nevada	47.5
40	Vermont	50.4		45	Alabama	47.1
8	Virginia	69.7		46	Michigan	44.4
34	Washington	55.6		47	Rhode Island	24.9
29	West Virginia	57.0		48	Mississippi	2.2
36	Wisconsin	54.4		NA	Illinois**	NA
1	Wyoming	79.1		NA	Kansas**	NA
					District of Columbia	42.9

Source: Federal Bureau of Investigation (unpublished data)
*Aggravated assault is an attack for the purpose of inflicting severe bodily injury. A crime is considered cleared when at least one person is arrested, charged and turned over to the court for prosecution. Clearances recorded in 1998 may be for crimes which occurred in prior years. Several crimes may be cleared by the arrest of one person while the arrest of many persons may clear only one crime.
**Not available.

Percent of Property Crimes Cleared in 1998

National Percent = 17.5% Cleared*

ALPHA ORDER

RANK	STATE	PERCENT
33	Alabama	17.1
6	Alaska	22.9
38	Arizona	15.9
8	Arkansas	21.9
44	California	15.2
26	Colorado	18.3
35	Connecticut	16.9
14	Delaware	20.6
27	Florida	18.1
29	Georgia	17.5
28	Hawaii	17.6
10	Idaho	21.0
NA	Illinois**	NA
36	Indiana	16.7
37	Iowa	16.0
NA	Kansas**	NA
12	Kentucky	20.8
7	Louisiana	22.3
2	Maine	26.7
23	Maryland	18.7
38	Massachusetts	15.9
48	Michigan	9.9
5	Minnesota	23.2
17	Mississippi	20.4
25	Missouri	18.4
12	Montana	20.8
14	Nebraska	20.6
18	Nevada	20.1
3	New Hampshire	26.5
32	New Jersey	17.2
45	New Mexico	13.8
20	New York	19.5
22	North Carolina	18.9
20	North Dakota	19.5
33	Ohio	17.1
40	Oklahoma	15.8
18	Oregon	20.1
9	Pennsylvania	21.7
30	Rhode Island	17.3
42	South Carolina	15.5
4	South Dakota	23.4
23	Tennessee	18.7
30	Texas	17.3
16	Utah	20.5
47	Vermont	10.8
10	Virginia	21.0
40	Washington	15.8
43	West Virginia	15.3
45	Wisconsin	13.8
1	Wyoming	27.3

RANK ORDER

RANK	STATE	PERCENT
1	Wyoming	27.3
2	Maine	26.7
3	New Hampshire	26.5
4	South Dakota	23.4
5	Minnesota	23.2
6	Alaska	22.9
7	Louisiana	22.3
8	Arkansas	21.9
9	Pennsylvania	21.7
10	Idaho	21.0
10	Virginia	21.0
12	Kentucky	20.8
12	Montana	20.8
14	Delaware	20.6
14	Nebraska	20.6
16	Utah	20.5
17	Mississippi	20.4
18	Nevada	20.1
18	Oregon	20.1
20	New York	19.5
20	North Dakota	19.5
22	North Carolina	18.9
23	Maryland	18.7
23	Tennessee	18.7
25	Missouri	18.4
26	Colorado	18.3
27	Florida	18.1
28	Hawaii	17.6
29	Georgia	17.5
30	Rhode Island	17.3
30	Texas	17.3
32	New Jersey	17.2
33	Alabama	17.1
33	Ohio	17.1
35	Connecticut	16.9
36	Indiana	16.7
37	Iowa	16.0
38	Arizona	15.9
38	Massachusetts	15.9
40	Oklahoma	15.8
40	Washington	15.8
42	South Carolina	15.5
43	West Virginia	15.3
44	California	15.2
45	New Mexico	13.8
45	Wisconsin	13.8
47	Vermont	10.8
48	Michigan	9.9
NA	Illinois**	NA
NA	Kansas**	NA
	District of Columbia	6.6

Source: Federal Bureau of Investigation (unpublished data)
*Property crimes are offenses of burglary, larceny-theft and motor vehicle theft. A crime is considered cleared when at least one person is arrested, charged and turned over to the court for prosecution. Clearances recorded in 1998 may be for crimes which occurred in prior years. Several crimes may be cleared by the arrest of one person while the arrest of many persons may clear only one crime.
**Not available.

43

Percent of Burglaries Cleared in 1998

National Percent = 13.8% Cleared*

<table>
<tr><td colspan="3">ALPHA ORDER</td><td colspan="3">RANK ORDER</td></tr>
<tr><td>RANK</td><td>STATE</td><td>PERCENT</td><td>RANK</td><td>STATE</td><td>PERCENT</td></tr>
<tr><td>36</td><td>Alabama</td><td>12.2</td><td>1</td><td>Wyoming</td><td>21.2</td></tr>
<tr><td>4</td><td>Alaska</td><td>19.5</td><td>2</td><td>Nevada</td><td>20.2</td></tr>
<tr><td>46</td><td>Arizona</td><td>8.2</td><td>3</td><td>Virginia</td><td>20.1</td></tr>
<tr><td>9</td><td>Arkansas</td><td>17.2</td><td>4</td><td>Alaska</td><td>19.5</td></tr>
<tr><td>28</td><td>California</td><td>13.5</td><td>5</td><td>Maine</td><td>19.4</td></tr>
<tr><td>19</td><td>Colorado</td><td>14.7</td><td>6</td><td>New Hampshire</td><td>19.2</td></tr>
<tr><td>38</td><td>Connecticut</td><td>12.1</td><td>7</td><td>New York</td><td>18.0</td></tr>
<tr><td>12</td><td>Delaware</td><td>16.9</td><td>8</td><td>Pennsylvania</td><td>17.4</td></tr>
<tr><td>16</td><td>Florida</td><td>15.7</td><td>9</td><td>Arkansas</td><td>17.2</td></tr>
<tr><td>30</td><td>Georgia</td><td>13.4</td><td>10</td><td>Louisiana</td><td>17.0</td></tr>
<tr><td>32</td><td>Hawaii</td><td>12.8</td><td>10</td><td>South Dakota</td><td>17.0</td></tr>
<tr><td>31</td><td>Idaho</td><td>13.3</td><td>12</td><td>Delaware</td><td>16.9</td></tr>
<tr><td>NA</td><td>Illinois**</td><td>NA</td><td>13</td><td>Maryland</td><td>16.8</td></tr>
<tr><td>41</td><td>Indiana</td><td>10.9</td><td>14</td><td>North Carolina</td><td>16.5</td></tr>
<tr><td>45</td><td>Iowa</td><td>9.3</td><td>15</td><td>Montana</td><td>16.4</td></tr>
<tr><td>NA</td><td>Kansas**</td><td>NA</td><td>16</td><td>Florida</td><td>15.7</td></tr>
<tr><td>18</td><td>Kentucky</td><td>15.1</td><td>16</td><td>Mississippi</td><td>15.7</td></tr>
<tr><td>10</td><td>Louisiana</td><td>17.0</td><td>18</td><td>Kentucky</td><td>15.1</td></tr>
<tr><td>5</td><td>Maine</td><td>19.4</td><td>19</td><td>Colorado</td><td>14.7</td></tr>
<tr><td>13</td><td>Maryland</td><td>16.8</td><td>20</td><td>Minnesota</td><td>14.2</td></tr>
<tr><td>21</td><td>Massachusetts</td><td>14.1</td><td>21</td><td>Massachusetts</td><td>14.1</td></tr>
<tr><td>47</td><td>Michigan</td><td>7.4</td><td>21</td><td>Rhode Island</td><td>14.1</td></tr>
<tr><td>20</td><td>Minnesota</td><td>14.2</td><td>21</td><td>Tennessee</td><td>14.1</td></tr>
<tr><td>16</td><td>Mississippi</td><td>15.7</td><td>24</td><td>Missouri</td><td>13.9</td></tr>
<tr><td>24</td><td>Missouri</td><td>13.9</td><td>25</td><td>Wisconsin</td><td>13.7</td></tr>
<tr><td>15</td><td>Montana</td><td>16.4</td><td>26</td><td>Nebraska</td><td>13.6</td></tr>
<tr><td>26</td><td>Nebraska</td><td>13.6</td><td>26</td><td>Ohio</td><td>13.6</td></tr>
<tr><td>2</td><td>Nevada</td><td>20.2</td><td>28</td><td>California</td><td>13.5</td></tr>
<tr><td>6</td><td>New Hampshire</td><td>19.2</td><td>28</td><td>New Jersey</td><td>13.5</td></tr>
<tr><td>28</td><td>New Jersey</td><td>13.5</td><td>30</td><td>Georgia</td><td>13.4</td></tr>
<tr><td>44</td><td>New Mexico</td><td>9.8</td><td>31</td><td>Idaho</td><td>13.3</td></tr>
<tr><td>7</td><td>New York</td><td>18.0</td><td>32</td><td>Hawaii</td><td>12.8</td></tr>
<tr><td>14</td><td>North Carolina</td><td>16.5</td><td>33</td><td>North Dakota</td><td>12.7</td></tr>
<tr><td>33</td><td>North Dakota</td><td>12.7</td><td>34</td><td>Oklahoma</td><td>12.4</td></tr>
<tr><td>26</td><td>Ohio</td><td>13.6</td><td>35</td><td>Texas</td><td>12.3</td></tr>
<tr><td>34</td><td>Oklahoma</td><td>12.4</td><td>36</td><td>Alabama</td><td>12.2</td></tr>
<tr><td>38</td><td>Oregon</td><td>12.1</td><td>36</td><td>South Carolina</td><td>12.2</td></tr>
<tr><td>8</td><td>Pennsylvania</td><td>17.4</td><td>38</td><td>Connecticut</td><td>12.1</td></tr>
<tr><td>21</td><td>Rhode Island</td><td>14.1</td><td>38</td><td>Oregon</td><td>12.1</td></tr>
<tr><td>36</td><td>South Carolina</td><td>12.2</td><td>40</td><td>Utah</td><td>12.0</td></tr>
<tr><td>10</td><td>South Dakota</td><td>17.0</td><td>41</td><td>Indiana</td><td>10.9</td></tr>
<tr><td>21</td><td>Tennessee</td><td>14.1</td><td>42</td><td>Washington</td><td>10.8</td></tr>
<tr><td>35</td><td>Texas</td><td>12.3</td><td>43</td><td>West Virginia</td><td>10.3</td></tr>
<tr><td>40</td><td>Utah</td><td>12.0</td><td>44</td><td>New Mexico</td><td>9.8</td></tr>
<tr><td>48</td><td>Vermont</td><td>5.7</td><td>45</td><td>Iowa</td><td>9.3</td></tr>
<tr><td>3</td><td>Virginia</td><td>20.1</td><td>46</td><td>Arizona</td><td>8.2</td></tr>
<tr><td>42</td><td>Washington</td><td>10.8</td><td>47</td><td>Michigan</td><td>7.4</td></tr>
<tr><td>43</td><td>West Virginia</td><td>10.3</td><td>48</td><td>Vermont</td><td>5.7</td></tr>
<tr><td>25</td><td>Wisconsin</td><td>13.7</td><td>NA</td><td>Illinois**</td><td>NA</td></tr>
<tr><td>1</td><td>Wyoming</td><td>21.2</td><td>NA</td><td>Kansas**</td><td>NA</td></tr>
<tr><td></td><td></td><td></td><td></td><td>District of Columbia</td><td>15.7</td></tr>
</table>

Source: Federal Bureau of Investigation (unpublished data)

*Burglary is the unlawful entry of a structure to commit a felony or theft. Attempts are included. A crime is considered cleared when at least one person is arrested, charged and turned over to the court for prosecution. Clearances recorded in 1998 may be for crimes which occurred in prior years. Several crimes may be cleared by the arrest of one person while the arrest of many persons may clear only one crime.

**Not available.

Percent of Larcenies and Thefts Cleared in 1998

National Percent = 19.2% Cleared*

ALPHA ORDER

RANK	STATE	PERCENT
36	Alabama	18.3
7	Alaska	23.7
30	Arizona	19.0
13	Arkansas	22.6
42	California	17.2
31	Colorado	18.9
27	Connecticut	19.1
10	Delaware	22.9
31	Florida	18.9
33	Georgia	18.6
27	Hawaii	19.1
10	Idaho	22.9
NA	Illinois**	NA
36	Indiana	18.3
39	Iowa	17.6
NA	Kansas**	NA
9	Kentucky	23.0
4	Louisiana	24.9
2	Maine	28.3
24	Maryland	20.1
39	Massachusetts	17.6
48	Michigan	11.0
6	Minnesota	24.5
12	Mississippi	22.7
25	Missouri	19.8
19	Montana	21.0
16	Nebraska	22.2
15	Nevada	22.4
1	New Hampshire	28.7
22	New Jersey	20.7
45	New Mexico	15.7
18	New York	21.6
26	North Carolina	19.2
23	North Dakota	20.4
35	Ohio	18.5
43	Oklahoma	16.9
13	Oregon	22.6
8	Pennsylvania	23.5
33	Rhode Island	18.6
43	South Carolina	16.9
5	South Dakota	24.6
20	Tennessee	20.9
27	Texas	19.1
17	Utah	22.1
47	Vermont	12.1
20	Virginia	20.9
38	Washington	18.1
41	West Virginia	17.5
46	Wisconsin	14.3
3	Wyoming	27.9

RANK ORDER

RANK	STATE	PERCENT
1	New Hampshire	28.7
2	Maine	28.3
3	Wyoming	27.9
4	Louisiana	24.9
5	South Dakota	24.6
6	Minnesota	24.5
7	Alaska	23.7
8	Pennsylvania	23.5
9	Kentucky	23.0
10	Delaware	22.9
10	Idaho	22.9
12	Mississippi	22.7
13	Arkansas	22.6
13	Oregon	22.6
15	Nevada	22.4
16	Nebraska	22.2
17	Utah	22.1
18	New York	21.6
19	Montana	21.0
20	Tennessee	20.9
20	Virginia	20.9
22	New Jersey	20.7
23	North Dakota	20.4
24	Maryland	20.1
25	Missouri	19.8
26	North Carolina	19.2
27	Connecticut	19.1
27	Hawaii	19.1
27	Texas	19.1
30	Arizona	19.0
31	Colorado	18.9
31	Florida	18.9
33	Georgia	18.6
33	Rhode Island	18.6
35	Ohio	18.5
36	Alabama	18.3
36	Indiana	18.3
38	Washington	18.1
39	Iowa	17.6
39	Massachusetts	17.6
41	West Virginia	17.5
42	California	17.2
43	Oklahoma	16.9
43	South Carolina	16.9
45	New Mexico	15.7
46	Wisconsin	14.3
47	Vermont	12.1
48	Michigan	11.0
NA	Illinois**	NA
NA	Kansas**	NA
	District of Columbia	5.0

Source: Federal Bureau of Investigation (unpublished data)
*Larceny and theft is the unlawful taking of property without use of force, violence or fraud. Attempts are included. Motor vehicle thefts are excluded. A crime is considered cleared when at least one person is arrested, charged and turned over to the court for prosecution. Clearances recorded in 1998 may be for crimes which occurred in prior years. Several crimes may be cleared by the arrest of one person while the arrest of many persons may clear only one crime. **Not available.

Percent of Motor Vehicle Thefts Cleared in 1998

National Percent = 14.4% Cleared*

ALPHA ORDER				RANK ORDER		
RANK	STATE	PERCENT		RANK	STATE	PERCENT
14	Alabama	20.7		1	Wyoming	40.4
11	Alaska	22.6		2	Maine	39.3
38	Arizona	12.2		3	Minnesota	31.1
4	Arkansas	30.8		4	Arkansas	30.8
44	California	10.3		5	Montana	29.6
13	Colorado	21.2		6	South Dakota	27.9
37	Connecticut	12.5		7	North Carolina	26.2
46	Delaware	10.1		8	Idaho	24.7
21	Florida	18.5		9	Virginia	23.8
20	Georgia	18.6		10	North Dakota	23.3
33	Hawaii	15.1		11	Alaska	22.6
8	Idaho	24.7		12	Utah	21.5
NA	Illinois**	NA		13	Colorado	21.2
24	Indiana	17.9		14	Alabama	20.7
22	Iowa	18.4		15	Kentucky	20.1
NA	Kansas**	NA		16	New Hampshire	19.9
15	Kentucky	20.1		17	Nebraska	19.4
27	Louisiana	16.3		18	Mississippi	18.9
2	Maine	39.3		19	Vermont	18.7
35	Maryland	13.5		20	Georgia	18.6
42	Massachusetts	10.7		21	Florida	18.5
47	Michigan	9.0		22	Iowa	18.4
3	Minnesota	31.1		23	Pennsylvania	18.2
18	Mississippi	18.9		24	Indiana	17.9
26	Missouri	17.3		25	Oklahoma	17.8
5	Montana	29.6		26	Missouri	17.3
17	Nebraska	19.4		27	Louisiana	16.3
40	Nevada	11.8		28	Oregon	16.2
16	New Hampshire	19.9		28	Tennessee	16.2
48	New Jersey	5.4		28	Texas	16.2
42	New Mexico	10.7		31	Ohio	15.7
41	New York	11.1		32	Rhode Island	15.3
7	North Carolina	26.2		33	Hawaii	15.1
10	North Dakota	23.3		34	West Virginia	13.6
31	Ohio	15.7		35	Maryland	13.5
25	Oklahoma	17.8		35	South Carolina	13.5
28	Oregon	16.2		37	Connecticut	12.5
23	Pennsylvania	18.2		38	Arizona	12.2
32	Rhode Island	15.3		39	Wisconsin	12.0
35	South Carolina	13.5		40	Nevada	11.8
6	South Dakota	27.9		41	New York	11.1
28	Tennessee	16.2		42	Massachusetts	10.7
28	Texas	16.2		42	New Mexico	10.7
12	Utah	21.5		44	California	10.3
19	Vermont	18.7		45	Washington	10.2
9	Virginia	23.8		46	Delaware	10.1
45	Washington	10.2		47	Michigan	9.0
34	West Virginia	13.6		48	New Jersey	5.4
39	Wisconsin	12.0		NA	Illinois**	NA
1	Wyoming	40.4		NA	Kansas**	NA
					District of Columbia	3.7

Source: Federal Bureau of Investigation (unpublished data)
*Motor vehicle theft includes the theft or attempted theft of a self-propelled vehicle. Excludes motorboats, construction equipment, airplanes and farming equipment. A crime is considered cleared when at least one person is arrested, charged and turned over to the court for prosecution. Clearances recorded in 1998 may be for crimes which occurred in prior years. Several crimes may be cleared by the arrest of one person while the arrest of many persons may clear only one crime. **Not available.*

II. CORRECTIONS

47   Prisoners in State Correctional Institutions: Year End 1999
48   Percent Change in Number of State Prisoners: 1998 to 1999
49   State Prisoners Sentenced to More than One Year in 1999
50   State Prisoner Incarceration Rate in 1999
51   Percent Change in State Prisoner Incarceration Rate: 1998 to 1999
52   State Prison Population as a Percent of Highest Capacity in 1999
53   Female Prisoners in State Correctional Institutions in 1999
54   Female State Prisoner Incarceration Rate in 1999
55   Female Prisoners in State Correctional Institutions as a Percent of All State Prisoners in 1999
56   Percent Change in Female State Prisoner Population: 1998 to 1999
57   White Prisoners in State Correctional Institutions in 1998
58   White State Prisoner Incarceration Rate in 1998
59   White State Prisoners in State Correctional Institutions as a Percent of All State Prisoners in 1998
60   Black Prisoners in State Correctional Institutions in 1998
61   Black State Prisoner Incarceration Rate in 1998
62   Black State Prisoners in State Correctional Institutions as a Percent of All State Prisoners in 1998
63   Prisoners Under Sentence of Death in 1999
64   Male Prisoners Under Sentence of Death in 1999
65   Female Prisoners Under Sentence of Death in 1999
66   Percent of Prisoners Under Sentence of Death Who Are Female: 1999
67   White Prisoners Under Sentence of Death in 1999
68   Percent of Prisoners Under Sentence of Death Who Are White: 1999
69   Black Prisoners Under Sentence of Death in 1999
70   Percent of Prisoners Under Sentence of Death Who Are Black: 1999
71   Prisoners Executed in 1999
72   Prisoners Executed: 1930 to 1999
73   Prisoners Executed: 1977 to 1999
74   Prisoners Sentenced to Death: 1973 to 1999
75   Death Sentences Overturned or Commuted: 1973 to 1999
76   Percent of Death Penalty Sentences Overturned or Commuted: 1973 to 1999
77   Sentenced Prisoners Admitted to State Correctional Institutions in 1998
78   Sentenced Prisoners Admitted to State Correctional Institutions Through New Court Commitments in 1998
79   Parole Violators Returned to State Prisons in 1998
80   Escapees Returned to State Prisons in 1998
81   Prisoners Released from State Correctional Institutions in 1998
82   State Prisoners Released with Conditions in 1998
83   State Prisoners Released Conditionally as a Percent of All Releases in 1998
84   State Prisoners Released on Parole in 1998
85   State Prisoners Released on Probation in 1998
86   State Prisoners Released on Supervised Mandatory Release in 1998
87   State Prisoners Released Unconditionally in 1998
88   State Prisoners Released Unconditionally as a Percent of All Releases in 1998
89   State Prisoners Released on Appeal or Bond in 1998
90   State Prisoners Escaped in 1998
91   State Prisoner Deaths in 1998
92   Death Rate of State Prisoners in 1998
93   State Prisoner Deaths by Illness or Other Natural Causes in 1998
94   Deaths of State Prisoners by Illness or Other Natural Causes as a Percent of All State Prison Deaths in 1998
95   Deaths of State Prisoners by AIDS in 1998
96   AIDS-Related Death Rate for State Prisoners in 1998
97   Deaths of State Prisoners by AIDS as a Percent of All Prison Deaths in 1998
98   State Prisoners Known to be Positive for HIV Infection/AIDS in 1997
99   State Prisoners Known to be Positive for HIV Infection/AIDS as a Percent of Total Prison Population in 1997
100   Deaths by State Prisoners by Suicide in 1998
101   Deaths of State Prisoners by Suicide as a Percent of All Prison Deaths in 1998
102   Adults Under State Correctional Supervision in 1993
103   Percent of Population Under State Correctional Supervision in 1993
104   Adults on State Probation in 1999
105   Rate of Adults on State Probation in 1999
106   Adults on State Parole in 1999
107   Rate of Adults on State Parole in 1999
108   State and Local Government Employees in Corrections in 1999

II. CORRECTIONS (continued)

109 State and Local Government Employees in Corrections as a Percent of All State and Local Government Employees in 1999
110 State Government Employees in Corrections in 1999
111 State Government Employees in Corrections as a Percent of All State Government Employees in 1999
112 State Correctional Officers in 1998
113 Male Correctional Officers in 1998
114 Female Correctional Officers in 1998
115 State Prisoners per Correctional Officer in 1998
116 Turnover Rate of Correctional Officers in 1998
117 Jail and Detention Centers in 1993
118 Inmates in Local Jails in 1993

Prisoners in State Correctional Institutions: Year End 1999

National Total = 1,231,475 State Prisoners*

ALPHA ORDER

RANK ORDER

RANK	STATE	PRISONERS	% of USA		RANK	STATE	PRISONERS	% of USA
16	Alabama	24,658	2.0%		1	Texas	163,190	13.3%
40	Alaska	3,949	0.3%		2	California	163,067	13.2%
15	Arizona	25,986	2.1%		3	New York	73,233	5.9%
28	Arkansas	11,415	0.9%		4	Florida	69,596	5.7%
2	California	163,067	13.2%		5	Ohio	46,842	3.8%
25	Colorado	15,670	1.3%		6	Michigan	46,617	3.8%
23	Connecticut	18,639	1.5%		7	Illinois	44,660	3.6%
34	Delaware	6,983	0.6%		8	Georgia	42,091	3.4%
4	Florida	69,596	5.7%		9	Pennsylvania	36,525	3.0%
8	Georgia	42,091	3.4%		10	Louisiana	34,066	2.8%
38	Hawaii	4,903	0.4%		11	Virginia	32,453	2.6%
39	Idaho	4,842	0.4%		12	New Jersey	31,493	2.6%
7	Illinois	44,660	3.6%		13	North Carolina	31,086	2.5%
22	Indiana	19,309	1.6%		14	Missouri	26,155	2.1%
33	Iowa	7,232	0.6%		15	Arizona	25,986	2.1%
32	Kansas	8,567	0.7%		16	Alabama	24,658	2.0%
26	Kentucky	15,317	1.2%		17	Maryland	23,095	1.9%
10	Louisiana	34,066	2.8%		18	Tennessee	22,502	1.8%
47	Maine	1,716	0.1%		19	Oklahoma	22,393	1.8%
17	Maryland	23,095	1.9%		20	South Carolina	22,008	1.8%
29	Massachusetts	11,356	0.9%		21	Wisconsin	20,417	1.7%
6	Michigan	46,617	3.8%		22	Indiana	19,309	1.6%
35	Minnesota	5,969	0.5%		23	Connecticut	18,639	1.5%
24	Mississippi	18,247	1.5%		24	Mississippi	18,247	1.5%
14	Missouri	26,155	2.1%		25	Colorado	15,670	1.3%
44	Montana	2,954	0.2%		26	Kentucky	15,317	1.2%
41	Nebraska	3,688	0.3%		27	Washington	14,590	1.2%
31	Nevada	9,494	0.8%		28	Arkansas	11,415	0.9%
46	New Hampshire	2,257	0.2%		29	Massachusetts	11,356	0.9%
12	New Jersey	31,493	2.6%		30	Oregon	9,810	0.8%
37	New Mexico	5,124	0.4%		31	Nevada	9,494	0.8%
3	New York	73,233	5.9%		32	Kansas	8,567	0.7%
13	North Carolina	31,086	2.5%		33	Iowa	7,232	0.6%
50	North Dakota	943	0.1%		34	Delaware	6,983	0.6%
5	Ohio	46,842	3.8%		35	Minnesota	5,969	0.5%
19	Oklahoma	22,393	1.8%		36	Utah	5,426	0.4%
30	Oregon	9,810	0.8%		37	New Mexico	5,124	0.4%
9	Pennsylvania	36,525	3.0%		38	Hawaii	4,903	0.4%
43	Rhode Island	3,003	0.2%		39	Idaho	4,842	0.4%
20	South Carolina	22,008	1.8%		40	Alaska	3,949	0.3%
45	South Dakota	2,506	0.2%		41	Nebraska	3,688	0.3%
18	Tennessee	22,502	1.8%		42	West Virginia	3,532	0.3%
1	Texas	163,190	13.3%		43	Rhode Island	3,003	0.2%
36	Utah	5,426	0.4%		44	Montana	2,954	0.2%
49	Vermont	1,536	0.1%		45	South Dakota	2,506	0.2%
11	Virginia	32,453	2.6%		46	New Hampshire	2,257	0.2%
27	Washington	14,590	1.2%		47	Maine	1,716	0.1%
42	West Virginia	3,532	0.3%		48	Wyoming	1,713	0.1%
21	Wisconsin	20,417	1.7%		49	Vermont	1,536	0.1%
48	Wyoming	1,713	0.1%		50	North Dakota	943	0.1%
						District of Columbia	8,652	0.7%

Source: U.S. Department of Justice, Bureau of Justice Statistics
   "Prisoners in 1999" (August 2000, NCJ-183476)
*As of December 31, 1999. Totals reflect all prisoners, including those sentenced to a year or less and those unsentenced. National total does not include 135,246 prisoners under federal jurisdiction. State and federal prisoners combined total 1,366,721.

Percent Change in Number of State Prisoners: 1998 to 1999

National Percent Change = 2.7% Increase*

ALPHA ORDER

RANK	STATE	PERCENT CHANGE
7	Alabama	8.7
47	Alaska	(3.6)
31	Arizona	1.8
9	Arkansas	7.3
38	California	0.7
3	Colorado	9.5
14	Connecticut	5.9
NA	Delaware**	NA
23	Florida	3.5
10	Georgia	7.2
42	Hawaii	(0.4)
1	Idaho	12.9
22	Illinois	3.7
39	Indiana	0.6
44	Iowa	(2.2)
17	Kansas	4.7
29	Kentucky	2.2
15	Louisiana	5.7
34	Maine	1.5
28	Maryland	2.3
48	Massachusetts	(3.8)
32	Michigan	1.6
13	Minnesota	7.1
4	Mississippi	9.4
16	Missouri	4.7
8	Montana	8.0
41	Nebraska	0.3
43	Nevada	(1.6)
21	New Hampshire	4.1
35	New Jersey	1.2
37	New Mexico	0.9
27	New York	2.6
45	North Carolina	(2.7)
25	North Dakota	3.1
46	Ohio	(3.3)
12	Oklahoma	7.2
5	Oregon	9.2
40	Pennsylvania	0.4
49	Rhode Island	(12.8)
36	South Carolina	1.1
24	South Dakota	3.5
18	Tennessee	4.5
30	Texas	1.9
20	Utah	4.2
19	Vermont	4.3
11	Virginia	7.2
26	Washington	3.0
33	West Virginia	1.6
2	Wisconsin	10.9
6	Wyoming	9.0

RANK ORDER

RANK	STATE	PERCENT CHANGE
1	Idaho	12.9
2	Wisconsin	10.9
3	Colorado	9.5
4	Mississippi	9.4
5	Oregon	9.2
6	Wyoming	9.0
7	Alabama	8.7
8	Montana	8.0
9	Arkansas	7.3
10	Georgia	7.2
11	Virginia	7.2
12	Oklahoma	7.2
13	Minnesota	7.1
14	Connecticut	5.9
15	Louisiana	5.7
16	Missouri	4.7
17	Kansas	4.7
18	Tennessee	4.5
19	Vermont	4.3
20	Utah	4.2
21	New Hampshire	4.1
22	Illinois	3.7
23	Florida	3.5
24	South Dakota	3.5
25	North Dakota	3.1
26	Washington	3.0
27	New York	2.6
28	Maryland	2.3
29	Kentucky	2.2
30	Texas	1.9
31	Arizona	1.8
32	Michigan	1.6
33	West Virginia	1.6
34	Maine	1.5
35	New Jersey	1.2
36	South Carolina	1.1
37	New Mexico	0.9
38	California	0.7
39	Indiana	0.6
40	Pennsylvania	0.4
41	Nebraska	0.3
42	Hawaii	(0.4)
43	Nevada	(1.6)
44	Iowa	(2.2)
45	North Carolina	(2.7)
46	Ohio	(3.3)
47	Alaska	(3.6)
48	Massachusetts	(3.8)
49	Rhode Island	(12.8)
NA	Delaware**	NA
	District of Columbia	(12.0)

Source: U.S. Department of Justice, Bureau of Justice Statistics
     "Prisoners in 1999" (August 2000, NCJ-183476)
From December 31, 1998 to December 31, 1999. Includes inmates sentenced to more than one year and those sentenced to a year or less or with no sentence. The percent change in number of prisoners under federal jurisdiction during the same period was a 9.9% increase. The combined state and federal increase was 3.4%.
**Not available.*

State Prisoners Sentenced to More than One Year in 1999

National Total = 1,191,118 State Prisoners*

ALPHA ORDER

RANK	STATE	PRISONERS	% of USA
15	Alabama	24,109	2.0%
44	Alaska	2,325	0.2%
16	Arizona	23,944	2.0%
28	Arkansas	11,336	1.0%
1	California	160,517	13.5%
24	Colorado	15,670	1.3%
27	Connecticut	13,032	1.1%
39	Delaware	3,730	0.3%
4	Florida	69,594	5.8%
8	Georgia	42,008	3.5%
38	Hawaii	3,817	0.3%
36	Idaho	4,842	0.4%
7	Illinois	44,660	3.7%
22	Indiana	19,260	1.6%
33	Iowa	7,232	0.6%
32	Kansas	8,567	0.7%
25	Kentucky	15,317	1.3%
10	Louisiana	34,066	2.9%
48	Maine	1,663	0.1%
19	Maryland	22,184	1.9%
29	Massachusetts	10,282	0.9%
6	Michigan	46,617	3.9%
34	Minnesota	5,955	0.5%
23	Mississippi	17,410	1.5%
14	Missouri	26,133	2.2%
42	Montana	2,954	0.2%
40	Nebraska	3,632	0.3%
31	Nevada	9,413	0.8%
45	New Hampshire	2,257	0.2%
11	New Jersey	31,493	2.6%
37	New Mexico	4,730	0.4%
3	New York	72,896	6.1%
13	North Carolina	26,635	2.2%
50	North Dakota	866	0.1%
5	Ohio	46,842	3.9%
18	Oklahoma	22,393	1.9%
30	Oregon	9,792	0.8%
9	Pennsylvania	36,525	3.1%
46	Rhode Island	1,908	0.2%
20	South Carolina	21,228	1.8%
43	South Dakota	2,498	0.2%
17	Tennessee	22,502	1.9%
2	Texas	154,865	13.0%
35	Utah	5,271	0.4%
49	Vermont	1,178	0.1%
12	Virginia	30,738	2.6%
26	Washington	14,558	1.2%
41	West Virginia	3,532	0.3%
21	Wisconsin	19,699	1.7%
47	Wyoming	1,713	0.1%

RANK ORDER

RANK	STATE	PRISONERS	% of USA
1	California	160,517	13.5%
2	Texas	154,865	13.0%
3	New York	72,896	6.1%
4	Florida	69,594	5.8%
5	Ohio	46,842	3.9%
6	Michigan	46,617	3.9%
7	Illinois	44,660	3.7%
8	Georgia	42,008	3.5%
9	Pennsylvania	36,525	3.1%
10	Louisiana	34,066	2.9%
11	New Jersey	31,493	2.6%
12	Virginia	30,738	2.6%
13	North Carolina	26,635	2.2%
14	Missouri	26,133	2.2%
15	Alabama	24,109	2.0%
16	Arizona	23,944	2.0%
17	Tennessee	22,502	1.9%
18	Oklahoma	22,393	1.9%
19	Maryland	22,184	1.9%
20	South Carolina	21,228	1.8%
21	Wisconsin	19,699	1.7%
22	Indiana	19,260	1.6%
23	Mississippi	17,410	1.5%
24	Colorado	15,670	1.3%
25	Kentucky	15,317	1.3%
26	Washington	14,558	1.2%
27	Connecticut	13,032	1.1%
28	Arkansas	11,336	1.0%
29	Massachusetts	10,282	0.9%
30	Oregon	9,792	0.8%
31	Nevada	9,413	0.8%
32	Kansas	8,567	0.7%
33	Iowa	7,232	0.6%
34	Minnesota	5,955	0.5%
35	Utah	5,271	0.4%
36	Idaho	4,842	0.4%
37	New Mexico	4,730	0.4%
38	Hawaii	3,817	0.3%
39	Delaware	3,730	0.3%
40	Nebraska	3,632	0.3%
41	West Virginia	3,532	0.3%
42	Montana	2,954	0.2%
43	South Dakota	2,498	0.2%
44	Alaska	2,325	0.2%
45	New Hampshire	2,257	0.2%
46	Rhode Island	1,908	0.2%
47	Wyoming	1,713	0.1%
48	Maine	1,663	0.1%
49	Vermont	1,178	0.1%
50	North Dakota	866	0.1%
	District of Columbia	6,730	0.6%

Source: U.S. Department of Justice, Bureau of Justice Statistics
"Prisoners in 1999" (August 2000, NCJ-183476)
*Advance figures as of December 31, 1999. Does not include 114,275 prisoners under federal jurisdiction sentenced to more than one year. State and federal prisoners sentenced to more than one year total 1,305,393.

State Prisoner Incarceration Rate in 1999

National Rate = 434.0 State Prisoners per 100,000 Population*

ALPHA ORDER

RANK	STATE	RATE
5	Alabama	548.6
27	Alaska	374.4
9	Arizona	494.8
16	Arkansas	442.6
11	California	481.1
25	Colorado	383.3
21	Connecticut	396.8
10	Delaware	493.4
14	Florida	455.7
7	Georgia	532.1
35	Hawaii	320.5
23	Idaho	384.9
28	Illinois	368.3
33	Indiana	323.7
40	Iowa	251.5
34	Kansas	320.9
22	Kentucky	385.2
1	Louisiana	776.0
49	Maine	133.3
17	Maryland	427.3
39	Massachusetts	266.1
13	Michigan	472.3
50	Minnesota	124.6
4	Mississippi	626.0
12	Missouri	476.7
32	Montana	334.5
43	Nebraska	217.5
8	Nevada	509.4
47	New Hampshire	187.3
24	New Jersey	384.2
38	New Mexico	269.7
20	New York	400.3
30	North Carolina	345.1
48	North Dakota	136.8
18	Ohio	417.0
3	Oklahoma	662.1
37	Oregon	293.3
36	Pennsylvania	304.8
46	Rhode Island	192.7
6	South Carolina	543.3
31	South Dakota	338.9
19	Tennessee	407.7
2	Texas	762.4
42	Utah	244.9
44	Vermont	198.0
15	Virginia	447.4
41	Washington	251.1
45	West Virginia	195.6
26	Wisconsin	374.9
29	Wyoming	355.4

RANK ORDER

RANK	STATE	RATE
1	Louisiana	776.0
2	Texas	762.4
3	Oklahoma	662.1
4	Mississippi	626.0
5	Alabama	548.6
6	South Carolina	543.3
7	Georgia	532.1
8	Nevada	509.4
9	Arizona	494.8
10	Delaware	493.4
11	California	481.1
12	Missouri	476.7
13	Michigan	472.3
14	Florida	455.7
15	Virginia	447.4
16	Arkansas	442.6
17	Maryland	427.3
18	Ohio	417.0
19	Tennessee	407.7
20	New York	400.3
21	Connecticut	396.8
22	Kentucky	385.2
23	Idaho	384.9
24	New Jersey	384.2
25	Colorado	383.3
26	Wisconsin	374.9
27	Alaska	374.4
28	Illinois	368.3
29	Wyoming	355.4
30	North Carolina	345.1
31	South Dakota	338.9
32	Montana	334.5
33	Indiana	323.7
34	Kansas	320.9
35	Hawaii	320.5
36	Pennsylvania	304.8
37	Oregon	293.3
38	New Mexico	269.7
39	Massachusetts	266.1
40	Iowa	251.5
41	Washington	251.1
42	Utah	244.9
43	Nebraska	217.5
44	Vermont	198.0
45	West Virginia	195.6
46	Rhode Island	192.7
47	New Hampshire	187.3
48	North Dakota	136.8
49	Maine	133.3
50	Minnesota	124.6
	District of Columbia	1,314.5

Source: U.S. Department of Justice, Bureau of Justice Statistics
"Prisoners in 1999" (August 2000, NCJ-183476)

*As of December 31, 1999. Includes only inmates sentenced to more than one year. Does not include federal incarceration rate of 42 prisoners per 100,000 population. State and federal combined incarceration rate is 476 prisoners per 100,000 population.

Percent Change in State Prisoner Incarceration Rate: 1998 to 1999

National Percent Change = 2.6% Increase*

ALPHA ORDER

RANK	STATE	PERCENT CHANGE
18	Alabama	5.7
48	Alaska	(9.3)
42	Arizona	(2.4)
12	Arkansas	6.7
39	California	(0.4)
10	Colorado	7.4
12	Connecticut	6.7
NA	Delaware**	NA
29	Florida	2.0
17	Georgia	6.0
22	Hawaii	4.4
3	Idaho	16.6
25	Illinois	3.2
35	Indiana	0.8
43	Iowa	(2.5)
24	Kansas	3.5
32	Kentucky	1.6
19	Louisiana	5.4
14	Maine	6.6
28	Maryland	2.2
44	Massachusetts	(3.3)
33	Michigan	1.4
15	Minnesota	6.5
7	Mississippi	9.1
23	Missouri	4.3
9	Montana	7.9
34	Nebraska	1.2
47	Nevada	(6.0)
27	New Hampshire	2.9
37	New Jersey	0.6
40	New Mexico	(0.5)
35	New York	0.8
46	North Carolina	(3.6)
11	North Dakota	6.9
45	Ohio	(3.5)
15	Oklahoma	6.5
4	Oregon	12.8
37	Pennsylvania	0.6
49	Rhode Island	(12.4)
41	South Carolina	(1.2)
26	South Dakota	3.0
1	Tennessee	25.5
20	Texas	5.3
2	Utah	19.5
20	Vermont	5.3
6	Virginia	12.1
31	Washington	1.7
30	West Virginia	1.9
5	Wisconsin	12.2
8	Wyoming	8.7

RANK ORDER

RANK	STATE	PERCENT CHANGE
1	Tennessee	25.5
2	Utah	19.5
3	Idaho	16.6
4	Oregon	12.8
5	Wisconsin	12.2
6	Virginia	12.1
7	Mississippi	9.1
8	Wyoming	8.7
9	Montana	7.9
10	Colorado	7.4
11	North Dakota	6.9
12	Arkansas	6.7
12	Connecticut	6.7
14	Maine	6.6
15	Minnesota	6.5
15	Oklahoma	6.5
17	Georgia	6.0
18	Alabama	5.7
19	Louisiana	5.4
20	Texas	5.3
20	Vermont	5.3
22	Hawaii	4.4
23	Missouri	4.3
24	Kansas	3.5
25	Illinois	3.2
26	South Dakota	3.0
27	New Hampshire	2.9
28	Maryland	2.2
29	Florida	2.0
30	West Virginia	1.9
31	Washington	1.7
32	Kentucky	1.6
33	Michigan	1.4
34	Nebraska	1.2
35	Indiana	0.8
35	New York	0.8
37	New Jersey	0.6
37	Pennsylvania	0.6
39	California	(0.4)
40	New Mexico	(0.5)
41	South Carolina	(1.2)
42	Arizona	(2.4)
43	Iowa	(2.5)
44	Massachusetts	(3.3)
45	Ohio	(3.5)
46	North Carolina	(3.6)
47	Nevada	(6.0)
48	Alaska	(9.3)
49	Rhode Island	(12.4)
NA	Delaware**	NA
	District of Columbia	(31.3)

Source: Morgan Quitno Press using data from U.S. Department of Justice, Bureau of Justice Statistics
    "Prisoners in 1999" (August 2000, NCJ-183476)
*From December 31, 1998 to December 31, 1999. Includes only inmates sentenced to more than one year. The percent change in rate of prisoners under federal jurisdiction during the same period was a 10.5% increase. The combined state and federal increase was 3.3%.
**Not available.

State Prison Population as a Percent of Highest Capacity in 1999

National Percent = 101% of Highest Capacity*

ALPHA ORDER   RANK ORDER

RANK	STATE	PERCENT		RANK	STATE	PERCENT
28	Alabama	97		1	New Jersey	143
38	Alaska	94		2	Wisconsin	139
17	Arizona	101		3	Illinois	138
20	Arkansas	100		4	Ohio	125
17	California	101		5	Massachusetts	122
8	Colorado	116		6	Nebraska	120
NA	Connecticut**	NA		7	Washington	119
NA	Delaware**	NA		8	Colorado	116
47	Florida	82		8	Iowa	116
44	Georgia	89		10	Utah	115
15	Hawaii	102		11	Pennsylvania	113
28	Idaho	97		12	New Hampshire	109
3	Illinois	138		12	North Carolina	109
33	Indiana	96		14	New York	108
8	Iowa	116		15	Hawaii	102
28	Kansas	97		15	Mississippi	102
40	Kentucky	93		17	Arizona	101
46	Louisiana	83		17	California	101
20	Maine	100		17	Wyoming	101
28	Maryland	97		20	Arkansas	100
5	Massachusetts	122		20	Maine	100
26	Michigan	98		20	Montana	100
26	Minnesota	98		23	Nevada	99
15	Mississippi	102		23	Oklahoma	99
36	Missouri	95		23	Oregon	99
20	Montana	100		26	Michigan	98
6	Nebraska	120		26	Minnesota	98
23	Nevada	99		28	Alabama	97
12	New Hampshire	109		28	Idaho	97
1	New Jersey	143		28	Kansas	97
41	New Mexico	92		28	Maryland	97
14	New York	108		28	Texas	97
12	North Carolina	109		33	Indiana	96
42	North Dakota	91		33	South Dakota	96
4	Ohio	125		33	Tennessee	96
23	Oklahoma	99		36	Missouri	95
23	Oregon	99		36	Vermont	95
11	Pennsylvania	113		38	Alaska	94
48	Rhode Island	76		38	West Virginia	94
44	South Carolina	89		40	Kentucky	93
33	South Dakota	96		41	New Mexico	92
33	Tennessee	96		42	North Dakota	91
28	Texas	97		42	Virginia	91
10	Utah	115		44	Georgia	89
36	Vermont	95		44	South Carolina	89
42	Virginia	91		46	Louisiana	83
7	Washington	119		47	Florida	82
38	West Virginia	94		48	Rhode Island	76
2	Wisconsin	139		NA	Connecticut**	NA
17	Wyoming	101		NA	Delaware**	NA
					District of Columbia	85

Source: U.S. Department of Justice, Bureau of Justice Statistics
   "Prisoners in 1999" (August 2000, NCJ-183476)
*As of December 31, 1999. Federal prison population is at 132% of highest rated capacity. Because of a change in calculating operational capacity the national figure is not comparable to previous years' figures. This year's comparable figure would be 109%. Figures exclude inmates sentenced to prison but held in local jails or private facilities unless these facilities are included in reported capacity. **Not available.

Female Prisoners in State Correctional Institutions in 1999

National Total = 80,755 Female State Prisoners*

ALPHA ORDER

RANK	STATE	PRISONERS	% of USA
16	Alabama	1,668	2.1%
40	Alaska	288	0.4%
15	Arizona	1,855	2.3%
28	Arkansas	788	1.0%
2	California	11,368	14.1%
24	Colorado	1,213	1.5%
18	Connecticut	1,459	1.8%
31	Delaware	612	0.8%
3	Florida	3,820	4.7%
7	Georgia	2,607	3.2%
34	Hawaii	553	0.7%
37	Idaho	399	0.5%
6	Illinois	2,802	3.5%
23	Indiana	1,222	1.5%
35	Iowa	539	0.7%
33	Kansas	570	0.7%
27	Kentucky	1,097	1.4%
9	Louisiana	2,268	2.8%
49	Maine	65	0.1%
25	Maryland	1,113	1.4%
29	Massachusetts	742	0.9%
11	Michigan	2,027	2.5%
39	Minnesota	355	0.4%
20	Mississippi	1,405	1.7%
12	Missouri	1,891	2.3%
41	Montana	262	0.3%
42	Nebraska	251	0.3%
30	Nevada	731	0.9%
47	New Hampshire	117	0.1%
14	New Jersey	1,862	2.3%
36	New Mexico	460	0.6%
4	New York	3,644	4.5%
13	North Carolina	1,880	2.3%
48	North Dakota	70	0.1%
5	Ohio	2,841	3.5%
8	Oklahoma	2,316	2.9%
32	Oregon	583	0.7%
17	Pennsylvania	1,618	2.0%
45	Rhode Island	188	0.2%
19	South Carolina	1,447	1.8%
44	South Dakota	189	0.2%
22	Tennessee	1,368	1.7%
1	Texas	12,502	15.5%
38	Utah	368	0.5%
50	Vermont	59	0.1%
10	Virginia	2,119	2.6%
26	Washington	1,111	1.4%
43	West Virginia	239	0.3%
21	Wisconsin	1,386	1.7%
46	Wyoming	142	0.2%

RANK ORDER

RANK	STATE	PRISONERS	% of USA
1	Texas	12,502	15.5%
2	California	11,368	14.1%
3	Florida	3,820	4.7%
4	New York	3,644	4.5%
5	Ohio	2,841	3.5%
6	Illinois	2,802	3.5%
7	Georgia	2,607	3.2%
8	Oklahoma	2,316	2.9%
9	Louisiana	2,268	2.8%
10	Virginia	2,119	2.6%
11	Michigan	2,027	2.5%
12	Missouri	1,891	2.3%
13	North Carolina	1,880	2.3%
14	New Jersey	1,862	2.3%
15	Arizona	1,855	2.3%
16	Alabama	1,668	2.1%
17	Pennsylvania	1,618	2.0%
18	Connecticut	1,459	1.8%
19	South Carolina	1,447	1.8%
20	Mississippi	1,405	1.7%
21	Wisconsin	1,386	1.7%
22	Tennessee	1,368	1.7%
23	Indiana	1,222	1.5%
24	Colorado	1,213	1.5%
25	Maryland	1,113	1.4%
26	Washington	1,111	1.4%
27	Kentucky	1,097	1.4%
28	Arkansas	788	1.0%
29	Massachusetts	742	0.9%
30	Nevada	731	0.9%
31	Delaware	612	0.8%
32	Oregon	583	0.7%
33	Kansas	570	0.7%
34	Hawaii	553	0.7%
35	Iowa	539	0.7%
36	New Mexico	460	0.6%
37	Idaho	399	0.5%
38	Utah	368	0.5%
39	Minnesota	355	0.4%
40	Alaska	288	0.4%
41	Montana	262	0.3%
42	Nebraska	251	0.3%
43	West Virginia	239	0.3%
44	South Dakota	189	0.2%
45	Rhode Island	188	0.2%
46	Wyoming	142	0.2%
47	New Hampshire	117	0.1%
48	North Dakota	70	0.1%
49	Maine	65	0.1%
50	Vermont	59	0.1%
	District of Columbia	276	0.3%

Source: U.S. Department of Justice, Bureau of Justice Statistics
"Prisoners in 1999" (August 2000, NCJ-183476)
*As of December 31, 1999. Does not include 9,913 female prisoners under federal jurisdiction. State and federal female prisoners total 90,668.

Female State Prisoner Incarceration Rate in 1999

National Rate = 53 State Female Prisoners per 100,000 Female Population*

ALPHA ORDER			RANK ORDER		
RANK	STATE	RATE	RANK	STATE	RATE
7	Alabama	70	1	Oklahoma	134
27	Alaska	45	2	Louisiana	100
11	Arizona	64	2	Texas	100
14	Arkansas	59	4	Mississippi	89
9	California	65	5	Nevada	81
14	Colorado	59	6	Hawaii	80
25	Connecticut	48	7	Alabama	70
19	Delaware	56	8	Missouri	67
23	Florida	49	9	California	65
11	Georgia	64	9	South Carolina	65
6	Hawaii	80	11	Arizona	64
13	Idaho	63	11	Georgia	64
27	Illinois	45	13	Idaho	63
32	Indiana	40	14	Arkansas	59
36	Iowa	37	14	Colorado	59
31	Kansas	42	14	Montana	59
20	Kentucky	54	14	Wyoming	59
2	Louisiana	100	18	Virginia	57
50	Maine	9	19	Delaware	56
36	Maryland	37	20	Kentucky	54
48	Massachusetts	13	21	South Dakota	51
32	Michigan	40	21	Wisconsin	51
46	Minnesota	15	23	Florida	49
4	Mississippi	89	23	Ohio	49
8	Missouri	67	25	Connecticut	48
14	Montana	59	25	Tennessee	48
41	Nebraska	28	27	Alaska	45
5	Nevada	81	27	Illinois	45
45	New Hampshire	19	29	New Jersey	44
29	New Jersey	44	29	New Mexico	44
29	New Mexico	44	31	Kansas	42
34	New York	38	32	Indiana	40
39	North Carolina	34	32	Michigan	40
44	North Dakota	20	34	New York	38
23	Ohio	49	34	Washington	38
1	Oklahoma	134	36	Iowa	37
38	Oregon	35	36	Maryland	37
42	Pennsylvania	26	38	Oregon	35
49	Rhode Island	11	39	North Carolina	34
9	South Carolina	65	40	Utah	33
21	South Dakota	51	41	Nebraska	28
25	Tennessee	48	42	Pennsylvania	26
2	Texas	100	42	West Virginia	26
40	Utah	33	44	North Dakota	20
47	Vermont	14	45	New Hampshire	19
18	Virginia	57	46	Minnesota	15
34	Washington	38	47	Vermont	14
42	West Virginia	26	48	Massachusetts	13
21	Wisconsin	51	49	Rhode Island	11
14	Wyoming	59	50	Maine	9
				District of Columbia	31

Source: U.S. Department of Justice, Bureau of Justice Statistics
    "Prisoners in 1999" (August 2000, NCJ-183476)
*As of December 31, 1999. Rate is for female prisoners sentenced to more than one year. National rate does not include federal female inmates. Federal female incarceration rate is six federal female prisoners per 100,000 female population. The combined federal and state female incarceration rate is 59 female prisoners per 100,000 female population.

Female Prisoners in State Correctional Institutions
As a Percent of All State Prisoners in 1999
National Percent = 6.6% of State Prisoners are Female*

ALPHA ORDER

RANK	STATE	PERCENT
23	Alabama	6.8
17	Alaska	7.3
20	Arizona	7.1
22	Arkansas	6.9
21	California	7.0
9	Colorado	7.7
8	Connecticut	7.8
5	Delaware	8.8
43	Florida	5.5
36	Georgia	6.2
1	Hawaii	11.3
7	Idaho	8.2
33	Illinois	6.3
33	Indiana	6.3
14	Iowa	7.5
28	Kansas	6.7
18	Kentucky	7.2
28	Louisiana	6.7
49	Maine	3.8
46	Maryland	4.8
31	Massachusetts	6.5
48	Michigan	4.3
40	Minnesota	5.9
9	Mississippi	7.7
18	Missouri	7.2
4	Montana	8.9
23	Nebraska	6.8
9	Nevada	7.7
44	New Hampshire	5.2
40	New Jersey	5.9
3	New Mexico	9.0
45	New York	5.0
39	North Carolina	6.0
16	North Dakota	7.4
37	Ohio	6.1
2	Oklahoma	10.3
40	Oregon	5.9
47	Pennsylvania	4.4
33	Rhode Island	6.3
30	South Carolina	6.6
14	South Dakota	7.5
37	Tennessee	6.1
9	Texas	7.7
23	Utah	6.8
49	Vermont	3.8
31	Virginia	6.5
13	Washington	7.6
23	West Virginia	6.8
23	Wisconsin	6.8
6	Wyoming	8.3

RANK ORDER

RANK	STATE	PERCENT
1	Hawaii	11.3
2	Oklahoma	10.3
3	New Mexico	9.0
4	Montana	8.9
5	Delaware	8.8
6	Wyoming	8.3
7	Idaho	8.2
8	Connecticut	7.8
9	Colorado	7.7
9	Mississippi	7.7
9	Nevada	7.7
9	Texas	7.7
13	Washington	7.6
14	Iowa	7.5
14	South Dakota	7.5
16	North Dakota	7.4
17	Alaska	7.3
18	Kentucky	7.2
18	Missouri	7.2
20	Arizona	7.1
21	California	7.0
22	Arkansas	6.9
23	Alabama	6.8
23	Nebraska	6.8
23	Utah	6.8
23	West Virginia	6.8
23	Wisconsin	6.8
28	Kansas	6.7
28	Louisiana	6.7
30	South Carolina	6.6
31	Massachusetts	6.5
31	Virginia	6.5
33	Illinois	6.3
33	Indiana	6.3
33	Rhode Island	6.3
36	Georgia	6.2
37	Ohio	6.1
37	Tennessee	6.1
39	North Carolina	6.0
40	Minnesota	5.9
40	New Jersey	5.9
40	Oregon	5.9
43	Florida	5.5
44	New Hampshire	5.2
45	New York	5.0
46	Maryland	4.8
47	Pennsylvania	4.4
48	Michigan	4.3
49	Maine	3.8
49	Vermont	3.8
	District of Columbia	3.2

Source: Morgan Quitno Press using data from U.S. Department of Justice, Bureau of Justice Statistics "Prisoners in 1999" (August 2000, NCJ-183476)

As of December 31, 1999. Rate does not include federal female inmates. Federal female inmates constitute 7.3% of federal inmates. The federal and state combined rate is 6.6%.

Percent Change in Female State Prisoner Population: 1998 to 1999

National Percent Change = 3.9% Increase*

<table>
<tr><td colspan="3">ALPHA ORDER</td><td colspan="3">RANK ORDER</td></tr>
<tr><td>RANK</td><td>STATE</td><td>PERCENT CHANGE</td><td>RANK</td><td>STATE</td><td>PERCENT CHANGE</td></tr>
<tr><td>6</td><td>Alabama</td><td>14.2</td><td>1</td><td>Hawaii</td><td>28.6</td></tr>
<tr><td>46</td><td>Alaska</td><td>(4.6)</td><td>2</td><td>Minnesota</td><td>23.3</td></tr>
<tr><td>30</td><td>Arizona</td><td>3.2</td><td>3</td><td>Wisconsin</td><td>18.7</td></tr>
<tr><td>11</td><td>Arkansas</td><td>13.2</td><td>4</td><td>Idaho</td><td>16.8</td></tr>
<tr><td>44</td><td>California</td><td>(2.8)</td><td>5</td><td>Mississippi</td><td>15.8</td></tr>
<tr><td>9</td><td>Colorado</td><td>13.4</td><td>6</td><td>Alabama</td><td>14.2</td></tr>
<tr><td>22</td><td>Connecticut</td><td>7.5</td><td>7</td><td>Virginia</td><td>14.1</td></tr>
<tr><td>NA</td><td>Delaware**</td><td>NA</td><td>8</td><td>Vermont</td><td>13.5</td></tr>
<tr><td>21</td><td>Florida</td><td>8.3</td><td>9</td><td>Colorado</td><td>13.4</td></tr>
<tr><td>26</td><td>Georgia</td><td>5.4</td><td>10</td><td>West Virginia</td><td>13.3</td></tr>
<tr><td>1</td><td>Hawaii</td><td>28.6</td><td>11</td><td>Arkansas</td><td>13.2</td></tr>
<tr><td>4</td><td>Idaho</td><td>16.8</td><td>12</td><td>New Jersey</td><td>12.6</td></tr>
<tr><td>24</td><td>Illinois</td><td>5.9</td><td>13</td><td>Tennessee</td><td>11.7</td></tr>
<tr><td>32</td><td>Indiana</td><td>2.0</td><td>14</td><td>Oregon</td><td>11.3</td></tr>
<tr><td>16</td><td>Iowa</td><td>9.8</td><td>15</td><td>Oklahoma</td><td>10.8</td></tr>
<tr><td>19</td><td>Kansas</td><td>9.0</td><td>16</td><td>Iowa</td><td>9.8</td></tr>
<tr><td>27</td><td>Kentucky</td><td>4.9</td><td>17</td><td>Utah</td><td>9.6</td></tr>
<tr><td>29</td><td>Louisiana</td><td>4.0</td><td>18</td><td>Washington</td><td>9.1</td></tr>
<tr><td>48</td><td>Maine</td><td>(7.1)</td><td>19</td><td>Kansas</td><td>9.0</td></tr>
<tr><td>42</td><td>Maryland</td><td>(2.4)</td><td>20</td><td>Wyoming</td><td>8.4</td></tr>
<tr><td>39</td><td>Massachusetts</td><td>(0.5)</td><td>21</td><td>Florida</td><td>8.3</td></tr>
<tr><td>40</td><td>Michigan</td><td>(1.2)</td><td>22</td><td>Connecticut</td><td>7.5</td></tr>
<tr><td>2</td><td>Minnesota</td><td>23.3</td><td>23</td><td>Pennsylvania</td><td>6.7</td></tr>
<tr><td>5</td><td>Mississippi</td><td>15.8</td><td>24</td><td>Illinois</td><td>5.9</td></tr>
<tr><td>38</td><td>Missouri</td><td>0.6</td><td>25</td><td>Montana</td><td>5.6</td></tr>
<tr><td>25</td><td>Montana</td><td>5.6</td><td>26</td><td>Georgia</td><td>5.4</td></tr>
<tr><td>37</td><td>Nebraska</td><td>0.8</td><td>27</td><td>Kentucky</td><td>4.9</td></tr>
<tr><td>41</td><td>Nevada</td><td>(1.6)</td><td>28</td><td>South Carolina</td><td>4.6</td></tr>
<tr><td>36</td><td>New Hampshire</td><td>0.9</td><td>29</td><td>Louisiana</td><td>4.0</td></tr>
<tr><td>12</td><td>New Jersey</td><td>12.6</td><td>30</td><td>Arizona</td><td>3.2</td></tr>
<tr><td>31</td><td>New Mexico</td><td>2.2</td><td>31</td><td>New Mexico</td><td>2.2</td></tr>
<tr><td>35</td><td>New York</td><td>0.9</td><td>32</td><td>Indiana</td><td>2.0</td></tr>
<tr><td>45</td><td>North Carolina</td><td>(3.0)</td><td>33</td><td>North Dakota</td><td>1.4</td></tr>
<tr><td>33</td><td>North Dakota</td><td>1.4</td><td>34</td><td>Texas</td><td>1.1</td></tr>
<tr><td>43</td><td>Ohio</td><td>(2.4)</td><td>35</td><td>New York</td><td>0.9</td></tr>
<tr><td>15</td><td>Oklahoma</td><td>10.8</td><td>36</td><td>New Hampshire</td><td>0.9</td></tr>
<tr><td>14</td><td>Oregon</td><td>11.3</td><td>37</td><td>Nebraska</td><td>0.8</td></tr>
<tr><td>23</td><td>Pennsylvania</td><td>6.7</td><td>38</td><td>Missouri</td><td>0.6</td></tr>
<tr><td>49</td><td>Rhode Island</td><td>(20.0)</td><td>39</td><td>Massachusetts</td><td>(0.5)</td></tr>
<tr><td>28</td><td>South Carolina</td><td>4.6</td><td>40</td><td>Michigan</td><td>(1.2)</td></tr>
<tr><td>47</td><td>South Dakota</td><td>(6.9)</td><td>41</td><td>Nevada</td><td>(1.6)</td></tr>
<tr><td>13</td><td>Tennessee</td><td>11.7</td><td>42</td><td>Maryland</td><td>(2.4)</td></tr>
<tr><td>34</td><td>Texas</td><td>1.1</td><td>43</td><td>Ohio</td><td>(2.4)</td></tr>
<tr><td>17</td><td>Utah</td><td>9.6</td><td>44</td><td>California</td><td>(2.8)</td></tr>
<tr><td>8</td><td>Vermont</td><td>13.5</td><td>45</td><td>North Carolina</td><td>(3.0)</td></tr>
<tr><td>7</td><td>Virginia</td><td>14.1</td><td>46</td><td>Alaska</td><td>(4.6)</td></tr>
<tr><td>18</td><td>Washington</td><td>9.1</td><td>47</td><td>South Dakota</td><td>(6.9)</td></tr>
<tr><td>10</td><td>West Virginia</td><td>13.3</td><td>48</td><td>Maine</td><td>(7.1)</td></tr>
<tr><td>3</td><td>Wisconsin</td><td>18.7</td><td>49</td><td>Rhode Island</td><td>(20.0)</td></tr>
<tr><td>20</td><td>Wyoming</td><td>8.4</td><td>NA</td><td>Delaware**</td><td>NA</td></tr>
<tr><td></td><td></td><td></td><td></td><td>District of Columbia</td><td>(23.1)</td></tr>
</table>

Source: U.S. Department of Justice, Bureau of Justice Statistics
   "Prisoners in 1999" (August 2000, NCJ-183476)
*As of December 31, 1999. Rate does not include federal female inmates. Federal female inmates increased by
7.9%. The combined federal and state female prison population grew by 4.4%.

White Prisoners in State Correctional Institutions in 1998

National Total = 462,119 White State Prisoners*

ALPHA ORDER

RANK	STATE	PRISONERS	% of USA
22	Alabama	7,693	1.7%
43	Alaska	1,878	0.4%
6	Arizona	20,141	4.4%
30	Arkansas	4,868	1.1%
1	California	47,595	10.3%
13	Colorado	10,492	2.3%
32	Connecticut	4,691	1.0%
42	Delaware	2,028	0.4%
4	Florida	28,632	6.2%
9	Georgia	13,055	2.8%
49	Hawaii	1,039	0.2%
36	Idaho	3,327	0.7%
15	Illinois	10,371	2.2%
12	Indiana	11,016	2.4%
28	Iowa	5,117	1.1%
31	Kansas	4,853	1.1%
18	Kentucky	9,373	2.0%
23	Louisiana	7,559	1.6%
46	Maine	1,525	0.3%
29	Maryland	5,039	1.1%
26	Massachusetts	5,325	1.2%
7	Michigan	19,067	4.1%
38	Minnesota	2,619	0.6%
33	Mississippi	4,150	0.9%
8	Missouri	13,617	2.9%
40	Montana	2,108	0.5%
39	Nebraska	2,520	0.5%
27	Nevada	5,324	1.2%
41	New Hampshire	2,031	0.4%
21	New Jersey	7,880	1.7%
34	New Mexico	4,140	0.9%
3	New York	30,806	6.7%
14	North Carolina	10,419	2.3%
50	North Dakota	703	0.2%
5	Ohio	22,434	4.9%
11	Oklahoma	11,397	2.5%
25	Oregon	6,561	1.4%
10	Pennsylvania	12,287	2.7%
44	Rhode Island	1,845	0.4%
24	South Carolina	6,651	1.4%
45	South Dakota	1,826	0.4%
20	Tennessee	8,615	1.9%
2	Texas	41,383	9.0%
35	Utah	3,825	0.8%
47	Vermont	1,216	0.3%
17	Virginia	9,958	2.2%
16	Washington	10,006	2.2%
37	West Virginia	2,923	0.6%
19	Wisconsin	8,902	1.9%
48	Wyoming	1,196	0.3%

RANK ORDER

RANK	STATE	PRISONERS	% of USA
1	California	47,595	10.3%
2	Texas	41,383	9.0%
3	New York	30,806	6.7%
4	Florida	28,632	6.2%
5	Ohio	22,434	4.9%
6	Arizona	20,141	4.4%
7	Michigan	19,067	4.1%
8	Missouri	13,617	2.9%
9	Georgia	13,055	2.8%
10	Pennsylvania	12,287	2.7%
11	Oklahoma	11,397	2.5%
12	Indiana	11,016	2.4%
13	Colorado	10,492	2.3%
14	North Carolina	10,419	2.3%
15	Illinois	10,371	2.2%
16	Washington	10,006	2.2%
17	Virginia	9,958	2.2%
18	Kentucky	9,373	2.0%
19	Wisconsin	8,902	1.9%
20	Tennessee	8,615	1.9%
21	New Jersey	7,880	1.7%
22	Alabama	7,693	1.7%
23	Louisiana	7,559	1.6%
24	South Carolina	6,651	1.4%
25	Oregon	6,561	1.4%
26	Massachusetts	5,325	1.2%
27	Nevada	5,324	1.2%
28	Iowa	5,117	1.1%
29	Maryland	5,039	1.1%
30	Arkansas	4,868	1.1%
31	Kansas	4,853	1.1%
32	Connecticut	4,691	1.0%
33	Mississippi	4,150	0.9%
34	New Mexico	4,140	0.9%
35	Utah	3,825	0.8%
36	Idaho	3,327	0.7%
37	West Virginia	2,923	0.6%
38	Minnesota	2,619	0.6%
39	Nebraska	2,520	0.5%
40	Montana	2,108	0.5%
41	New Hampshire	2,031	0.4%
42	Delaware	2,028	0.4%
43	Alaska	1,878	0.4%
44	Rhode Island	1,845	0.4%
45	South Dakota	1,826	0.4%
46	Maine	1,525	0.3%
47	Vermont	1,216	0.3%
48	Wyoming	1,196	0.3%
49	Hawaii	1,039	0.2%
50	North Dakota	703	0.2%
	District of Columbia	93	0.0%

Source: U.S. Department of Justice, Bureau of Justice Statistics
   "Correctional Populations in the United States, 1998" (forthcoming in 2001)
*Preliminary data as of December 31, 1998. National total does not include 71,119 white federal prisoners.

White State Prisoner Incarceration Rate in 1998

National Rate = 207 White State Prisoners per 100,000 White Population*

ALPHA ORDER				RANK ORDER		
RANK	STATE	RATE		RANK	STATE	RATE
19	Alabama	242		1	Arizona	486
3	Alaska	406		2	Oklahoma	410
1	Arizona	486		3	Alaska	406
22	Arkansas	232		4	Nevada	355
37	California	183		5	Delaware	349
7	Colorado	286		6	Missouri	287
41	Connecticut	163		7	Colorado	286
5	Delaware	349		8	Idaho	279
22	Florida	232		9	New Mexico	275
18	Georgia	247		10	South Dakota	273
11	Hawaii	263		11	Hawaii	263
8	Idaho	279		12	Louisiana	262
48	Illinois	106		13	Kentucky	259
28	Indiana	206		13	Wyoming	259
35	Iowa	185		15	Montana	258
30	Kansas	202		16	South Carolina	251
13	Kentucky	259		17	Texas	248
12	Louisiana	262		18	Georgia	247
44	Maine	125		19	Alabama	242
43	Maryland	145		20	Mississippi	241
49	Massachusetts	97		21	Michigan	233
21	Michigan	233		22	Arkansas	232
50	Minnesota	59		22	Florida	232
20	Mississippi	241		24	Ohio	230
6	Missouri	287		25	New York	222
15	Montana	258		26	Oregon	214
42	Nebraska	162		27	Vermont	209
4	Nevada	355		28	Indiana	206
39	New Hampshire	175		29	Rhode Island	203
45	New Jersey	122		30	Kansas	202
9	New Mexico	275		31	Washington	198
25	New York	222		32	Tennessee	193
37	North Carolina	183		32	Virginia	193
46	North Dakota	117		34	Utah	191
24	Ohio	230		35	Iowa	185
2	Oklahoma	410		35	Wisconsin	185
26	Oregon	214		37	California	183
47	Pennsylvania	116		37	North Carolina	183
29	Rhode Island	203		39	New Hampshire	175
16	South Carolina	251		40	West Virginia	168
10	South Dakota	273		41	Connecticut	163
32	Tennessee	193		42	Nebraska	162
17	Texas	248		43	Maryland	145
34	Utah	191		44	Maine	125
27	Vermont	209		45	New Jersey	122
32	Virginia	193		46	North Dakota	117
31	Washington	198		47	Pennsylvania	116
40	West Virginia	168		48	Illinois	106
35	Wisconsin	185		49	Massachusetts	97
13	Wyoming	259		50	Minnesota	59
					District of Columbia	52

Source: Morgan Quitno Press using data from U.S. Department of Justice, Bureau of Justice Statistics
"Correctional Populations in the United States, 1998" (forthcoming in 2001)
*Preliminary data as of December 31, 1998. National rate does not include 71,119 white federal prisoners.
Federal rate is 32 white prisoners per 100,000 white population. The combined federal/state rate is 239 white
prisoners per 100,000 white population.

White State Prisoners in State Correctional Institutions
As a Percent of All State Prisoners in 1998
National Percent = 39.3% White*

ALPHA ORDER

RANK	STATE	PERCENT
36	Alabama	33.9
29	Alaska	45.8
8	Arizona	79.6
29	Arkansas	45.8
42	California	29.7
14	Colorado	73.3
44	Connecticut	26.6
35	Delaware	36.5
33	Florida	42.6
38	Georgia	33.3
50	Hawaii	21.1
7	Idaho	81.5
47	Illinois	24.1
20	Indiana	57.4
16	Iowa	69.2
19	Kansas	59.3
18	Kentucky	62.5
48	Louisiana	23.5
3	Maine	85.6
49	Maryland	22.3
31	Massachusetts	45.1
34	Michigan	41.6
27	Minnesota	47.0
46	Mississippi	24.9
23	Missouri	54.5
9	Montana	77.1
17	Nebraska	68.6
21	Nevada	55.2
1	New Hampshire	93.6
45	New Jersey	25.3
5	New Mexico	83.0
32	New York	44.0
40	North Carolina	32.6
10	North Dakota	76.8
28	Ohio	46.3
22	Oklahoma	54.6
13	Oregon	73.5
37	Pennsylvania	33.8
24	Rhode Island	53.6
41	South Carolina	30.1
12	South Dakota	75.4
25	Tennessee	48.6
43	Texas	28.6
2	Utah	85.9
6	Vermont	82.6
39	Virginia	32.9
15	Washington	70.7
4	West Virginia	84.0
26	Wisconsin	47.8
11	Wyoming	76.1

RANK ORDER

RANK	STATE	PERCENT
1	New Hampshire	93.6
2	Utah	85.9
3	Maine	85.6
4	West Virginia	84.0
5	New Mexico	83.0
6	Vermont	82.6
7	Idaho	81.5
8	Arizona	79.6
9	Montana	77.1
10	North Dakota	76.8
11	Wyoming	76.1
12	South Dakota	75.4
13	Oregon	73.5
14	Colorado	73.3
15	Washington	70.7
16	Iowa	69.2
17	Nebraska	68.6
18	Kentucky	62.5
19	Kansas	59.3
20	Indiana	57.4
21	Nevada	55.2
22	Oklahoma	54.6
23	Missouri	54.5
24	Rhode Island	53.6
25	Tennessee	48.6
26	Wisconsin	47.8
27	Minnesota	47.0
28	Ohio	46.3
29	Alaska	45.8
29	Arkansas	45.8
31	Massachusetts	45.1
32	New York	44.0
33	Florida	42.6
34	Michigan	41.6
35	Delaware	36.5
36	Alabama	33.9
37	Pennsylvania	33.8
38	Georgia	33.3
39	Virginia	32.9
40	North Carolina	32.6
41	South Carolina	30.1
42	California	29.7
43	Texas	28.6
44	Connecticut	26.6
45	New Jersey	25.3
46	Mississippi	24.9
47	Illinois	24.1
48	Louisiana	23.5
49	Maryland	22.3
50	Hawaii	21.1
	District of Columbia	0.9

Source: Morgan Quitno Press using data from U.S. Department of Justice, Bureau of Justice Statistics
   "Correctional Populations in the United States, 1998" (forthcoming in 2001)
*Preliminary data as of December 31, 1998. National percent does not include white federal prisoners. Federal prison population is 57.8% white. Combined state and federal percentage is 41.0% white.

Black Prisoners in State Correctional Institutions in 1998

National Total = 568,259 Black State Prisoners*

RANK	STATE	PRISONERS	% of USA	RANK	STATE	PRISONERS	% of USA
16	Alabama	14,905	2.6%	1	Texas	65,133	11.5%
39	Alaska	556	0.1%	2	California	50,052	8.8%
26	Arizona	3,739	0.7%	3	New York	38,284	6.7%
24	Arkansas	5,699	1.0%	4	Florida	37,143	6.5%
2	California	50,052	8.8%	5	Illinois	28,220	5.0%
29	Colorado	3,376	0.6%	6	Georgia	26,022	4.6%
21	Connecticut	8,290	1.5%	7	Ohio	25,798	4.5%
27	Delaware	3,521	0.6%	8	Michigan	25,336	4.5%
4	Florida	37,143	6.5%	9	Louisiana	24,621	4.3%
6	Georgia	26,022	4.6%	10	Pennsylvania	20,413	3.6%
42	Hawaii	220	0.0%	11	North Carolina	20,355	3.6%
46	Idaho	57	0.0%	12	New Jersey	20,323	3.6%
5	Illinois	28,220	5.0%	13	Virginia	20,050	3.5%
22	Indiana	8,109	1.4%	14	Maryland	17,495	3.1%
34	Iowa	1,770	0.3%	15	South Carolina	15,339	2.7%
31	Kansas	3,050	0.5%	16	Alabama	14,905	2.6%
25	Kentucky	5,574	1.0%	17	Mississippi	12,442	2.2%
9	Louisiana	24,621	4.3%	18	Missouri	11,243	2.0%
46	Maine	57	0.0%	19	Wisconsin	9,016	1.6%
14	Maryland	17,495	3.1%	20	Tennessee	8,993	1.6%
28	Massachusetts	3,384	0.6%	21	Connecticut	8,290	1.5%
8	Michigan	25,336	4.5%	22	Indiana	8,109	1.4%
33	Minnesota	2,088	0.4%	23	Oklahoma	7,119	1.3%
17	Mississippi	12,442	2.2%	24	Arkansas	5,699	1.0%
18	Missouri	11,243	2.0%	25	Kentucky	5,574	1.0%
48	Montana	49	0.0%	26	Arizona	3,739	0.7%
37	Nebraska	979	0.2%	27	Delaware	3,521	0.6%
32	Nevada	2,657	0.5%	28	Massachusetts	3,384	0.6%
43	New Hampshire	115	0.0%	29	Colorado	3,376	0.6%
12	New Jersey	20,323	3.6%	30	Washington	3,255	0.6%
38	New Mexico	560	0.1%	31	Kansas	3,050	0.5%
3	New York	38,284	6.7%	32	Nevada	2,657	0.5%
11	North Carolina	20,355	3.6%	33	Minnesota	2,088	0.4%
50	North Dakota	31	0.0%	34	Iowa	1,770	0.3%
7	Ohio	25,798	4.5%	35	Oregon	1,136	0.2%
23	Oklahoma	7,119	1.3%	36	Rhode Island	992	0.2%
35	Oregon	1,136	0.2%	37	Nebraska	979	0.2%
10	Pennsylvania	20,413	3.6%	38	New Mexico	560	0.1%
36	Rhode Island	992	0.2%	39	Alaska	556	0.1%
15	South Carolina	15,339	2.7%	40	West Virginia	552	0.1%
44	South Dakota	97	0.0%	41	Utah	346	0.1%
20	Tennessee	8,993	1.6%	42	Hawaii	220	0.0%
1	Texas	65,133	11.5%	43	New Hampshire	115	0.0%
41	Utah	346	0.1%	44	South Dakota	97	0.0%
49	Vermont	46	0.0%	45	Wyoming	78	0.0%
13	Virginia	20,050	3.5%	46	Idaho	57	0.0%
30	Washington	3,255	0.6%	46	Maine	57	0.0%
40	West Virginia	552	0.1%	48	Montana	49	0.0%
19	Wisconsin	9,016	1.6%	49	Vermont	46	0.0%
45	Wyoming	78	0.0%	50	North Dakota	31	0.0%
					District of Columbia	9,574	1.7%

ALPHA ORDER — RANK ORDER

Source: U.S. Department of Justice, Bureau of Justice Statistics
"Correctional Populations in the United States, 1998" (forthcoming in 2001)
*Preliminary data as of December 31, 1998. National total does not include 47,847 black federal prisoners.

Black State Prisoner Incarceration Rate in 1998

National Rate = 1,650 Black State Prisoners per 100,000 Black Population*

ALPHA ORDER

RANK ORDER

RANK	STATE	RATE
37	Alabama	1,316
7	Alaska	2,339
8	Arizona	2,210
34	Arkansas	1,398
9	California	2,038
14	Colorado	1,964
3	Connecticut	2,729
6	Delaware	2,439
27	Florida	1,638
42	Georgia	1,193
50	Hawaii	629
48	Idaho	796
28	Illinois	1,534
25	Indiana	1,653
1	Iowa	3,112
13	Kansas	1,971
15	Kentucky	1,957
22	Louisiana	1,750
46	Maine	902
40	Maryland	1,225
47	Massachusetts	857
21	Michigan	1,804
30	Minnesota	1,485
39	Mississippi	1,240
20	Missouri	1,835
29	Montana	1,522
33	Nebraska	1,457
12	Nevada	1,992
35	New Hampshire	1,352
24	New Jersey	1,710
38	New Mexico	1,241
43	New York	1,189
41	North Carolina	1,222
49	North Dakota	775
11	Ohio	2,000
4	Oklahoma	2,718
18	Oregon	1,864
22	Pennsylvania	1,750
10	Rhode Island	2,005
36	South Carolina	1,337
17	South Dakota	1,895
44	Tennessee	1,000
5	Texas	2,680
19	Utah	1,853
32	Vermont	1,470
31	Virginia	1,471
26	Washington	1,641
45	West Virginia	950
2	Wisconsin	3,103
16	Wyoming	1,911

RANK	STATE	RATE
1	Iowa	3,112
2	Wisconsin	3,103
3	Connecticut	2,729
4	Oklahoma	2,718
5	Texas	2,680
6	Delaware	2,439
7	Alaska	2,339
8	Arizona	2,210
9	California	2,038
10	Rhode Island	2,005
11	Ohio	2,000
12	Nevada	1,992
13	Kansas	1,971
14	Colorado	1,964
15	Kentucky	1,957
16	Wyoming	1,911
17	South Dakota	1,895
18	Oregon	1,864
19	Utah	1,853
20	Missouri	1,835
21	Michigan	1,804
22	Louisiana	1,750
22	Pennsylvania	1,750
24	New Jersey	1,710
25	Indiana	1,653
26	Washington	1,641
27	Florida	1,638
28	Illinois	1,534
29	Montana	1,522
30	Minnesota	1,485
31	Virginia	1,471
32	Vermont	1,470
33	Nebraska	1,457
34	Arkansas	1,398
35	New Hampshire	1,352
36	South Carolina	1,337
37	Alabama	1,316
38	New Mexico	1,241
39	Mississippi	1,240
40	Maryland	1,225
41	North Carolina	1,222
42	Georgia	1,193
43	New York	1,189
44	Tennessee	1,000
45	West Virginia	950
46	Maine	902
47	Massachusetts	857
48	Idaho	796
49	North Dakota	775
50	Hawaii	629

District of Columbia   2,938

Source: Morgan Quitno Press using data from U.S. Department of Justice, Bureau of Justice Statistics
   "Correctional Populations in the United States, 1998" (forthcoming in 2001)
*Preliminary data as of December 31, 1998. National rate does not include 47,847 black federal prisoners. Federal rate is 139 black prisoners per 100,000 black population. The combined federal/state rate is 1,789 black prisoners per 100,000 black population.

Black State Prisoners in State Correctional Institutions
As a Percent of All State Prisoners in 1998
National Percent = 48.3% Black*

ALPHA ORDER

RANK	STATE	PERCENT
7	Alabama	65.7
38	Alaska	13.6
37	Arizona	14.8
16	Arkansas	53.6
28	California	31.3
34	Colorado	23.6
20	Connecticut	47.1
11	Delaware	63.4
13	Florida	55.3
5	Georgia	66.3
44	Hawaii	4.5
50	Idaho	1.4
8	Illinois	65.6
23	Indiana	42.2
33	Iowa	23.9
25	Kansas	37.3
26	Kentucky	37.2
2	Louisiana	76.4
47	Maine	3.2
1	Maryland	77.5
30	Massachusetts	28.7
14	Michigan	55.2
24	Minnesota	37.5
3	Mississippi	74.6
22	Missouri	45.0
49	Montana	1.8
32	Nebraska	26.6
31	Nevada	27.5
42	New Hampshire	5.3
9	New Jersey	65.3
40	New Mexico	11.2
15	New York	54.7
10	North Carolina	63.7
46	North Dakota	3.4
17	Ohio	53.2
27	Oklahoma	34.1
39	Oregon	12.7
12	Pennsylvania	56.1
29	Rhode Island	28.8
4	South Carolina	69.4
45	South Dakota	4.0
18	Tennessee	50.7
21	Texas	45.1
41	Utah	7.8
48	Vermont	3.1
6	Virginia	66.2
35	Washington	23.0
36	West Virginia	15.9
19	Wisconsin	48.4
43	Wyoming	5.0

RANK ORDER

RANK	STATE	PERCENT
1	Maryland	77.5
2	Louisiana	76.4
3	Mississippi	74.6
4	South Carolina	69.4
5	Georgia	66.3
6	Virginia	66.2
7	Alabama	65.7
8	Illinois	65.6
9	New Jersey	65.3
10	North Carolina	63.7
11	Delaware	63.4
12	Pennsylvania	56.1
13	Florida	55.3
14	Michigan	55.2
15	New York	54.7
16	Arkansas	53.6
17	Ohio	53.2
18	Tennessee	50.7
19	Wisconsin	48.4
20	Connecticut	47.1
21	Texas	45.1
22	Missouri	45.0
23	Indiana	42.2
24	Minnesota	37.5
25	Kansas	37.3
26	Kentucky	37.2
27	Oklahoma	34.1
28	California	31.3
29	Rhode Island	28.8
30	Massachusetts	28.7
31	Nevada	27.5
32	Nebraska	26.6
33	Iowa	23.9
34	Colorado	23.6
35	Washington	23.0
36	West Virginia	15.9
37	Arizona	14.8
38	Alaska	13.6
39	Oregon	12.7
40	New Mexico	11.2
41	Utah	7.8
42	New Hampshire	5.3
43	Wyoming	5.0
44	Hawaii	4.5
45	South Dakota	4.0
46	North Dakota	3.4
47	Maine	3.2
48	Vermont	3.1
49	Montana	1.8
50	Idaho	1.4
	District of Columbia	97.4

Source: Morgan Quitno Press using data from U.S. Department of Justice, Bureau of Justice Statistics
"Correctional Populations in the United States, 1998" (forthcoming in 2001)
*Preliminary data as of December 31, 1998. National percent does not include black federal prisoners. Federal prison population is 38.9% black. Combined state and federal percentage is 47.4% black.

Prisoners Under Sentence of Death in 1999

National Total = 3,507 State Prisoners*

ALPHA ORDER

RANK	STATE	PRISONERS	% of USA
7	Alabama	180	5.1%
NA	Alaska**	NA	NA
10	Arizona	116	3.3%
19	Arkansas	40	1.1%
1	California	553	15.8%
33	Colorado	4	0.1%
30	Connecticut	6	0.2%
24	Delaware	17	0.5%
3	Florida	365	10.4%
10	Georgia	116	3.3%
NA	Hawaii**	NA	NA
23	Idaho	21	0.6%
8	Illinois	156	4.4%
18	Indiana	43	1.2%
NA	Iowa**	NA	NA
35	Kansas	3	0.1%
20	Kentucky	39	1.1%
14	Louisiana	85	2.4%
NA	Maine**	NA	NA
24	Maryland	17	0.5%
NA	Massachusetts**	NA	NA
NA	Michigan**	NA	NA
NA	Minnesota**	NA	NA
17	Mississippi	60	1.7%
15	Missouri	83	2.4%
30	Montana	6	0.2%
29	Nebraska	9	0.3%
13	Nevada	86	2.5%
38	New Hampshire	0	0.0%
26	New Jersey	14	0.4%
33	New Mexico	4	0.1%
32	New York	5	0.1%
5	North Carolina	202	5.8%
NA	North Dakota**	NA	NA
6	Ohio	199	5.7%
9	Oklahoma	139	4.0%
22	Oregon	25	0.7%
4	Pennsylvania	230	6.6%
NA	Rhode Island**	NA	NA
16	South Carolina	65	1.9%
35	South Dakota	3	0.1%
12	Tennessee	100	2.9%
2	Texas	460	13.1%
28	Utah	10	0.3%
NA	Vermont**	NA	NA
21	Virginia	31	0.9%
27	Washington	13	0.4%
NA	West Virginia**	NA	NA
NA	Wisconsin**	NA	NA
37	Wyoming	2	0.1%

RANK ORDER

RANK	STATE	PRISONERS	% of USA
1	California	553	15.8%
2	Texas	460	13.1%
3	Florida	365	10.4%
4	Pennsylvania	230	6.6%
5	North Carolina	202	5.8%
6	Ohio	199	5.7%
7	Alabama	180	5.1%
8	Illinois	156	4.4%
9	Oklahoma	139	4.0%
10	Arizona	116	3.3%
10	Georgia	116	3.3%
12	Tennessee	100	2.9%
13	Nevada	86	2.5%
14	Louisiana	85	2.4%
15	Missouri	83	2.4%
16	South Carolina	65	1.9%
17	Mississippi	60	1.7%
18	Indiana	43	1.2%
19	Arkansas	40	1.1%
20	Kentucky	39	1.1%
21	Virginia	31	0.9%
22	Oregon	25	0.7%
23	Idaho	21	0.6%
24	Delaware	17	0.5%
24	Maryland	17	0.5%
26	New Jersey	14	0.4%
27	Washington	13	0.4%
28	Utah	10	0.3%
29	Nebraska	9	0.3%
30	Connecticut	6	0.2%
30	Montana	6	0.2%
32	New York	5	0.1%
33	Colorado	4	0.1%
33	New Mexico	4	0.1%
35	Kansas	3	0.1%
35	South Dakota	3	0.1%
37	Wyoming	2	0.1%
38	New Hampshire	0	0.0%
NA	Alaska**	NA	NA
NA	Hawaii**	NA	NA
NA	Iowa**	NA	NA
NA	Maine**	NA	NA
NA	Massachusetts**	NA	NA
NA	Michigan**	NA	NA
NA	Minnesota**	NA	NA
NA	North Dakota**	NA	NA
NA	Rhode Island**	NA	NA
NA	Vermont**	NA	NA
NA	West Virginia**	NA	NA
NA	Wisconsin**	NA	NA
	District of Columbia**	NA	NA

Source: U.S. Department of Justice, Bureau of Justice Statistics
   "Capital Punishment 1999" (Bulletin, December 2000, NCJ-184795)
As of December 31, 1999. Does not include 20 federal prisoners under sentence of death. There were 98 executions in 1999.
**No death penalty as of 12/31/99.*

Male Prisoners Under Sentence of Death in 1999

National Total = 3,457 Male State Prisoners*

ALPHA ORDER

RANK	STATE	PRISONERS	% of USA
7	Alabama	178	5.1%
NA	Alaska**	NA	NA
10	Arizona	115	3.3%
19	Arkansas	39	1.1%
1	California	542	15.7%
33	Colorado	4	0.1%
30	Connecticut	6	0.2%
24	Delaware	17	0.5%
3	Florida	361	10.4%
10	Georgia	115	3.3%
NA	Hawaii**	NA	NA
23	Idaho	20	0.6%
8	Illinois	153	4.4%
18	Indiana	42	1.2%
NA	Iowa**	NA	NA
35	Kansas	3	0.1%
19	Kentucky	39	1.1%
14	Louisiana	84	2.4%
NA	Maine**	NA	NA
24	Maryland	17	0.5%
NA	Massachusetts**	NA	NA
NA	Michigan**	NA	NA
NA	Minnesota**	NA	NA
17	Mississippi	59	1.7%
15	Missouri	82	2.4%
30	Montana	6	0.2%
29	Nebraska	9	0.3%
13	Nevada	85	2.5%
38	New Hampshire	0	0.0%
26	New Jersey	14	0.4%
33	New Mexico	4	0.1%
32	New York	5	0.1%
6	North Carolina	198	5.7%
NA	North Dakota**	NA	NA
5	Ohio	199	5.8%
9	Oklahoma	136	3.9%
22	Oregon	25	0.7%
4	Pennsylvania	227	6.6%
NA	Rhode Island**	NA	NA
16	South Carolina	65	1.9%
35	South Dakota	3	0.1%
12	Tennessee	98	2.8%
2	Texas	451	13.0%
28	Utah	10	0.3%
NA	Vermont**	NA	NA
21	Virginia	31	0.9%
27	Washington	13	0.4%
NA	West Virginia**	NA	NA
NA	Wisconsin**	NA	NA
37	Wyoming	2	0.1%

RANK ORDER

RANK	STATE	PRISONERS	% of USA
1	California	542	15.7%
2	Texas	451	13.0%
3	Florida	361	10.4%
4	Pennsylvania	227	6.6%
5	Ohio	199	5.8%
6	North Carolina	198	5.7%
7	Alabama	178	5.1%
8	Illinois	153	4.4%
9	Oklahoma	136	3.9%
10	Arizona	115	3.3%
10	Georgia	115	3.3%
12	Tennessee	98	2.8%
13	Nevada	85	2.5%
14	Louisiana	84	2.4%
15	Missouri	82	2.4%
16	South Carolina	65	1.9%
17	Mississippi	59	1.7%
18	Indiana	42	1.2%
19	Arkansas	39	1.1%
19	Kentucky	39	1.1%
21	Virginia	31	0.9%
22	Oregon	25	0.7%
23	Idaho	20	0.6%
24	Delaware	17	0.5%
24	Maryland	17	0.5%
26	New Jersey	14	0.4%
27	Washington	13	0.4%
28	Utah	10	0.3%
29	Nebraska	9	0.3%
30	Connecticut	6	0.2%
30	Montana	6	0.2%
32	New York	5	0.1%
33	Colorado	4	0.1%
33	New Mexico	4	0.1%
35	Kansas	3	0.1%
35	South Dakota	3	0.1%
37	Wyoming	2	0.1%
38	New Hampshire	0	0.0%
NA	Alaska**	NA	NA
NA	Hawaii**	NA	NA
NA	Iowa**	NA	NA
NA	Maine**	NA	NA
NA	Massachusetts**	NA	NA
NA	Michigan**	NA	NA
NA	Minnesota**	NA	NA
NA	North Dakota**	NA	NA
NA	Rhode Island**	NA	NA
NA	Vermont**	NA	NA
NA	West Virginia**	NA	NA
NA	Wisconsin**	NA	NA
	District of Columbia**	NA	NA

Source: Morgan Quitno Press using data from U.S. Department of Justice, Bureau of Justice Statistics
    "Capital Punishment 1999" (Bulletin, December 2000, NCJ-184795)
*As of December 31, 1999. Does not include 20 male federal prisoners under sentence of death. There were 98
executions in 1999. All were male.
**No death penalty as of 12/31/99.

Female Prisoners Under Sentence of Death in 1999

National Total = 50 Female State Prisoners*

ALPHA ORDER

RANK	STATE	PRISONERS	% of USA
8	Alabama	2	4.0%
NA	Alaska**	NA	NA
10	Arizona	1	2.0%
10	Arkansas	1	2.0%
1	California	11	22.0%
19	Colorado	0	0.0%
19	Connecticut	0	0.0%
19	Delaware	0	0.0%
3	Florida	4	8.0%
10	Georgia	1	2.0%
NA	Hawaii**	NA	NA
10	Idaho	1	2.0%
5	Illinois	3	6.0%
10	Indiana	1	2.0%
NA	Iowa**	NA	NA
19	Kansas	0	0.0%
19	Kentucky	0	0.0%
10	Louisiana	1	2.0%
NA	Maine**	NA	NA
19	Maryland	0	0.0%
NA	Massachusetts**	NA	NA
NA	Michigan**	NA	NA
NA	Minnesota**	NA	NA
10	Mississippi	1	2.0%
10	Missouri	1	2.0%
19	Montana	0	0.0%
19	Nebraska	0	0.0%
10	Nevada	1	2.0%
19	New Hampshire	0	0.0%
19	New Jersey	0	0.0%
19	New Mexico	0	0.0%
19	New York	0	0.0%
3	North Carolina	4	8.0%
NA	North Dakota**	NA	NA
19	Ohio	0	0.0%
5	Oklahoma	3	6.0%
19	Oregon	0	0.0%
5	Pennsylvania	3	6.0%
NA	Rhode Island**	NA	NA
19	South Carolina	0	0.0%
19	South Dakota	0	0.0%
8	Tennessee	2	4.0%
2	Texas	9	18.0%
19	Utah	0	0.0%
NA	Vermont**	NA	NA
19	Virginia	0	0.0%
19	Washington	0	0.0%
NA	West Virginia**	NA	NA
NA	Wisconsin**	NA	NA
19	Wyoming	0	0.0%

RANK ORDER

RANK	STATE	PRISONERS	% of USA
1	California	11	22.0%
2	Texas	9	18.0%
3	Florida	4	8.0%
3	North Carolina	4	8.0%
5	Illinois	3	6.0%
5	Oklahoma	3	6.0%
5	Pennsylvania	3	6.0%
8	Alabama	2	4.0%
8	Tennessee	2	4.0%
10	Arizona	1	2.0%
10	Arkansas	1	2.0%
10	Georgia	1	2.0%
10	Idaho	1	2.0%
10	Indiana	1	2.0%
10	Louisiana	1	2.0%
10	Mississippi	1	2.0%
10	Missouri	1	2.0%
10	Nevada	1	2.0%
19	Colorado	0	0.0%
19	Connecticut	0	0.0%
19	Delaware	0	0.0%
19	Kansas	0	0.0%
19	Kentucky	0	0.0%
19	Maryland	0	0.0%
19	Montana	0	0.0%
19	Nebraska	0	0.0%
19	New Hampshire	0	0.0%
19	New Jersey	0	0.0%
19	New Mexico	0	0.0%
19	New York	0	0.0%
19	Ohio	0	0.0%
19	Oregon	0	0.0%
19	South Carolina	0	0.0%
19	South Dakota	0	0.0%
19	Utah	0	0.0%
19	Virginia	0	0.0%
19	Washington	0	0.0%
19	Wyoming	0	0.0%
NA	Alaska**	NA	NA
NA	Hawaii**	NA	NA
NA	Iowa**	NA	NA
NA	Maine**	NA	NA
NA	Massachusetts**	NA	NA
NA	Michigan**	NA	NA
NA	Minnesota**	NA	NA
NA	North Dakota**	NA	NA
NA	Rhode Island**	NA	NA
NA	Vermont**	NA	NA
NA	West Virginia**	NA	NA
NA	Wisconsin**	NA	NA
	District of Columbia**	NA	NA

Source: U.S. Department of Justice, Bureau of Justice Statistics
   "Capital Punishment 1999" (Bulletin, December 2000, NCJ-184795)
*As of December 31, 1999. There were no federal female prisoners under sentence of death. There were 98 executions in 1999, none of whom was female.
**No death penalty as of 12/31/99.

Percent of Prisoners Under Sentence of Death Who Are Female: 1999

National Percent = 1.4% of State Death Sentence Prisoners*

ALPHA ORDER

RANK	STATE	PERCENT
15	Alabama	1.1
NA	Alaska**	NA
17	Arizona	0.9
2	Arkansas	2.5
5	California	2.0
19	Colorado	0.0
19	Connecticut	0.0
19	Delaware	0.0
15	Florida	1.1
17	Georgia	0.9
NA	Hawaii**	NA
1	Idaho	4.8
9	Illinois	1.9
3	Indiana	2.3
NA	Iowa**	NA
19	Kansas	0.0
19	Kentucky	0.0
12	Louisiana	1.2
NA	Maine**	NA
19	Maryland	0.0
NA	Massachusetts**	NA
NA	Michigan**	NA
NA	Minnesota**	NA
10	Mississippi	1.7
12	Missouri	1.2
19	Montana	0.0
19	Nebraska	0.0
12	Nevada	1.2
19	New Hampshire	0.0
19	New Jersey	0.0
19	New Mexico	0.0
19	New York	0.0
5	North Carolina	2.0
NA	North Dakota**	NA
19	Ohio	0.0
4	Oklahoma	2.2
19	Oregon	0.0
11	Pennsylvania	1.3
NA	Rhode Island**	NA
19	South Carolina	0.0
19	South Dakota	0.0
5	Tennessee	2.0
5	Texas	2.0
19	Utah	0.0
NA	Vermont**	NA
19	Virginia	0.0
19	Washington	0.0
NA	West Virginia**	NA
NA	Wisconsin**	NA
19	Wyoming	0.0

RANK ORDER

RANK	STATE	PERCENT
1	Idaho	4.8
2	Arkansas	2.5
3	Indiana	2.3
4	Oklahoma	2.2
5	California	2.0
5	North Carolina	2.0
5	Tennessee	2.0
5	Texas	2.0
9	Illinois	1.9
10	Mississippi	1.7
11	Pennsylvania	1.3
12	Louisiana	1.2
12	Missouri	1.2
12	Nevada	1.2
15	Alabama	1.1
15	Florida	1.1
17	Arizona	0.9
17	Georgia	0.9
19	Colorado	0.0
19	Connecticut	0.0
19	Delaware	0.0
19	Kansas	0.0
19	Kentucky	0.0
19	Maryland	0.0
19	Montana	0.0
19	Nebraska	0.0
19	New Hampshire	0.0
19	New Jersey	0.0
19	New Mexico	0.0
19	New York	0.0
19	Ohio	0.0
19	Oregon	0.0
19	South Carolina	0.0
19	South Dakota	0.0
19	Utah	0.0
19	Virginia	0.0
19	Washington	0.0
19	Wyoming	0.0
NA	Alaska**	NA
NA	Hawaii**	NA
NA	Iowa**	NA
NA	Maine**	NA
NA	Massachusetts**	NA
NA	Michigan**	NA
NA	Minnesota**	NA
NA	North Dakota**	NA
NA	Rhode Island**	NA
NA	Vermont**	NA
NA	West Virginia**	NA
NA	Wisconsin**	NA
	District of Columbia**	NA

Source: Morgan Quitno Press using data from U.S. Department of Justice, Bureau of Justice Statistics
    "Capital Punishment 1999" (Bulletin, December 2000, NCJ-184795)
*As of December 31, 1999. There were no federal female prisoners under sentence of death. There were 98 executions in 1999, none was female.
**No death penalty as of 12/31/99.

White Prisoners Under Sentence of Death in 1999

National Total = 1,943 White State Prisoners*

ALPHA ORDER

RANK	STATE	PRISONERS	% of USA
6	Alabama	94	4.8%
NA	Alaska**	NA	NA
4	Arizona	100	5.1%
23	Arkansas	16	0.8%
1	California	335	17.2%
36	Colorado	2	0.1%
33	Connecticut	3	0.2%
25	Delaware	8	0.4%
3	Florida	235	12.1%
11	Georgia	60	3.1%
NA	Hawaii**	NA	NA
21	Idaho	21	1.1%
12	Illinois	56	2.9%
17	Indiana	30	1.5%
NA	Iowa**	NA	NA
33	Kansas	3	0.2%
16	Kentucky	32	1.6%
18	Louisiana	27	1.4%
NA	Maine**	NA	NA
30	Maryland	4	0.2%
NA	Massachusetts**	NA	NA
NA	Michigan**	NA	NA
NA	Minnesota**	NA	NA
19	Mississippi	26	1.3%
14	Missouri	47	2.4%
29	Montana	5	0.3%
25	Nebraska	8	0.4%
13	Nevada	51	2.6%
38	New Hampshire	0	0.0%
25	New Jersey	8	0.4%
30	New Mexico	4	0.2%
30	New York	4	0.2%
8	North Carolina	82	4.2%
NA	North Dakota**	NA	NA
5	Ohio	99	5.1%
7	Oklahoma	85	4.4%
20	Oregon	24	1.2%
9	Pennsylvania	74	3.8%
NA	Rhode Island**	NA	NA
15	South Carolina	33	1.7%
33	South Dakota	3	0.2%
10	Tennessee	63	3.2%
2	Texas	266	13.7%
28	Utah	6	0.3%
NA	Vermont**	NA	NA
22	Virginia	18	0.9%
24	Washington	9	0.5%
NA	West Virginia**	NA	NA
NA	Wisconsin**	NA	NA
36	Wyoming	2	0.1%

RANK ORDER

RANK	STATE	PRISONERS	% of USA
1	California	335	17.2%
2	Texas	266	13.7%
3	Florida	235	12.1%
4	Arizona	100	5.1%
5	Ohio	99	5.1%
6	Alabama	94	4.8%
7	Oklahoma	85	4.4%
8	North Carolina	82	4.2%
9	Pennsylvania	74	3.8%
10	Tennessee	63	3.2%
11	Georgia	60	3.1%
12	Illinois	56	2.9%
13	Nevada	51	2.6%
14	Missouri	47	2.4%
15	South Carolina	33	1.7%
16	Kentucky	32	1.6%
17	Indiana	30	1.5%
18	Louisiana	27	1.4%
19	Mississippi	26	1.3%
20	Oregon	24	1.2%
21	Idaho	21	1.1%
22	Virginia	18	0.9%
23	Arkansas	16	0.8%
24	Washington	9	0.5%
25	Delaware	8	0.4%
25	Nebraska	8	0.4%
25	New Jersey	8	0.4%
28	Utah	6	0.3%
29	Montana	5	0.3%
30	Maryland	4	0.2%
30	New Mexico	4	0.2%
30	New York	4	0.2%
33	Connecticut	3	0.2%
33	Kansas	3	0.2%
33	South Dakota	3	0.2%
36	Colorado	2	0.1%
36	Wyoming	2	0.1%
38	New Hampshire	0	0.0%
NA	Alaska**	NA	NA
NA	Hawaii**	NA	NA
NA	Iowa**	NA	NA
NA	Maine**	NA	NA
NA	Massachusetts**	NA	NA
NA	Michigan**	NA	NA
NA	Minnesota**	NA	NA
NA	North Dakota**	NA	NA
NA	Rhode Island**	NA	NA
NA	Vermont**	NA	NA
NA	West Virginia**	NA	NA
NA	Wisconsin**	NA	NA
	District of Columbia**	NA	NA

Source: U.S. Department of Justice, Bureau of Justice Statistics
   "Capital Punishment 1999" (Bulletin, December 2000, NCJ-184795)
*As of December 31, 1999. Does not include five white federal prisoners under sentence of death. There were 98 executions in 1999, 61 of whom were white prisoners.
**No death penalty as of 12/31/99.

Percent of Prisoners Under Sentence of Death Who Are White: 1999

National Percent = 55.4% of State Death Sentence Prisoners*

ALPHA ORDER

RANK	STATE	PERCENT
24	Alabama	52.2
NA	Alaska**	NA
8	Arizona	86.2
33	Arkansas	40.0
17	California	60.6
27	Colorado	50.0
27	Connecticut	50.0
30	Delaware	47.1
14	Florida	64.4
25	Georgia	51.7
NA	Hawaii**	NA
1	Idaho	100.0
34	Illinois	35.9
12	Indiana	69.8
NA	Iowa**	NA
1	Kansas	100.0
10	Kentucky	82.1
36	Louisiana	31.8
NA	Maine**	NA
37	Maryland	23.5
NA	Massachusetts**	NA
NA	Michigan**	NA
NA	Minnesota**	NA
31	Mississippi	43.3
23	Missouri	56.6
9	Montana	83.3
7	Nebraska	88.9
19	Nevada	59.3
38	New Hampshire	0.0
22	New Jersey	57.1
1	New Mexico	100.0
11	New York	80.0
32	North Carolina	40.6
NA	North Dakota**	NA
29	Ohio	49.7
16	Oklahoma	61.2
6	Oregon	96.0
35	Pennsylvania	32.2
NA	Rhode Island**	NA
26	South Carolina	50.8
1	South Dakota	100.0
15	Tennessee	63.0
21	Texas	57.8
18	Utah	60.0
NA	Vermont**	NA
20	Virginia	58.1
13	Washington	69.2
NA	West Virginia**	NA
NA	Wisconsin**	NA
1	Wyoming	100.0

RANK ORDER

RANK	STATE	PERCENT
1	Idaho	100.0
1	Kansas	100.0
1	New Mexico	100.0
1	South Dakota	100.0
1	Wyoming	100.0
6	Oregon	96.0
7	Nebraska	88.9
8	Arizona	86.2
9	Montana	83.3
10	Kentucky	82.1
11	New York	80.0
12	Indiana	69.8
13	Washington	69.2
14	Florida	64.4
15	Tennessee	63.0
16	Oklahoma	61.2
17	California	60.6
18	Utah	60.0
19	Nevada	59.3
20	Virginia	58.1
21	Texas	57.8
22	New Jersey	57.1
23	Missouri	56.6
24	Alabama	52.2
25	Georgia	51.7
26	South Carolina	50.8
27	Colorado	50.0
27	Connecticut	50.0
29	Ohio	49.7
30	Delaware	47.1
31	Mississippi	43.3
32	North Carolina	40.6
33	Arkansas	40.0
34	Illinois	35.9
35	Pennsylvania	32.2
36	Louisiana	31.8
37	Maryland	23.5
38	New Hampshire	0.0
NA	Alaska**	NA
NA	Hawaii**	NA
NA	Iowa**	NA
NA	Maine**	NA
NA	Massachusetts**	NA
NA	Michigan**	NA
NA	Minnesota**	NA
NA	North Dakota**	NA
NA	Rhode Island**	NA
NA	Vermont**	NA
NA	West Virginia**	NA
NA	Wisconsin**	NA
	District of Columbia**	NA

Source: Morgan Quitno Press using data from U.S. Department of Justice, Bureau of Justice Statistics
    "Capital Punishment 1999" (Bulletin, December 2000, NCJ-184795)
*As of December 31, 1999. Does not federal prisoners under sentence of death, 25.0% of whom are white prisoners. Of the 98 executions in 1999, 62.2% were white prisoners.
**No death penalty as of 12/31/99.

Black Prisoners Under Sentence of Death in 1999

National Total = 1,500 Black State Prisoners*

ALPHA ORDER					RANK ORDER			
RANK	STATE	PRISONERS	% of USA		RANK	STATE	PRISONERS	% of USA
8	Alabama	85	5.7%		1	California	200	13.3%
NA	Alaska**	NA	NA		2	Texas	190	12.7%
21	Arizona	12	0.8%		3	Pennsylvania	144	9.6%
17	Arkansas	24	1.6%		4	Florida	129	8.6%
1	California	200	13.3%		5	North Carolina	113	7.5%
27	Colorado	2	0.1%		6	Illinois	100	6.7%
26	Connecticut	3	0.2%		7	Ohio	99	6.6%
22	Delaware	9	0.6%		8	Alabama	85	5.7%
4	Florida	129	8.6%		9	Louisiana	57	3.8%
10	Georgia	55	3.7%		10	Georgia	55	3.7%
NA	Hawaii**	NA	NA		11	Oklahoma	48	3.2%
30	Idaho	0	0.0%		12	Missouri	36	2.4%
6	Illinois	100	6.7%		13	Tennessee	35	2.3%
18	Indiana	13	0.9%		14	Mississippi	34	2.3%
NA	Iowa**	NA	NA		14	Nevada	34	2.3%
30	Kansas	0	0.0%		16	South Carolina	32	2.1%
23	Kentucky	7	0.5%		17	Arkansas	24	1.6%
9	Louisiana	57	3.8%		18	Indiana	13	0.9%
NA	Maine**	NA	NA		18	Maryland	13	0.9%
18	Maryland	13	0.9%		18	Virginia	13	0.9%
NA	Massachusetts**	NA	NA		21	Arizona	12	0.8%
NA	Michigan**	NA	NA		22	Delaware	9	0.6%
NA	Minnesota**	NA	NA		23	Kentucky	7	0.5%
14	Mississippi	34	2.3%		24	New Jersey	6	0.4%
12	Missouri	36	2.4%		25	Washington	4	0.3%
30	Montana	0	0.0%		26	Connecticut	3	0.2%
30	Nebraska	0	0.0%		27	Colorado	2	0.1%
14	Nevada	34	2.3%		27	Utah	2	0.1%
30	New Hampshire	0	0.0%		29	New York	1	0.1%
24	New Jersey	6	0.4%		30	Idaho	0	0.0%
30	New Mexico	0	0.0%		30	Kansas	0	0.0%
29	New York	1	0.1%		30	Montana	0	0.0%
5	North Carolina	113	7.5%		30	Nebraska	0	0.0%
NA	North Dakota**	NA	NA		30	New Hampshire	0	0.0%
7	Ohio	99	6.6%		30	New Mexico	0	0.0%
11	Oklahoma	48	3.2%		30	Oregon	0	0.0%
30	Oregon	0	0.0%		30	South Dakota	0	0.0%
3	Pennsylvania	144	9.6%		30	Wyoming	0	0.0%
NA	Rhode Island**	NA	NA		NA	Alaska**	NA	NA
16	South Carolina	32	2.1%		NA	Hawaii**	NA	NA
30	South Dakota	0	0.0%		NA	Iowa**	NA	NA
13	Tennessee	35	2.3%		NA	Maine**	NA	NA
2	Texas	190	12.7%		NA	Massachusetts**	NA	NA
27	Utah	2	0.1%		NA	Michigan**	NA	NA
NA	Vermont**	NA	NA		NA	Minnesota**	NA	NA
18	Virginia	13	0.9%		NA	North Dakota**	NA	NA
25	Washington	4	0.3%		NA	Rhode Island**	NA	NA
NA	West Virginia**	NA	NA		NA	Vermont**	NA	NA
NA	Wisconsin**	NA	NA		NA	West Virginia**	NA	NA
30	Wyoming	0	0.0%		NA	Wisconsin**	NA	NA
						District of Columbia**	NA	NA

Source: U.S. Department of Justice, Bureau of Justice Statistics
    "Capital Punishment 1999" (Bulletin, December 2000, NCJ-184795)
*As of December 31, 1999. Does not include 14 black federal prisoners under sentence of death. There were
98 executions in 1999, 33 of whom were black prisoners.
**No death penalty as of 12/31/99.

Percent of Prisoners Under Sentence of Death Who Are Black: 1999

National Percent = 42.8% of State Death Sentence Prisoners*

ALPHA ORDER				RANK ORDER		
RANK	STATE	PERCENT		RANK	STATE	PERCENT
14	Alabama	47.2		1	Maryland	76.5
NA	Alaska**	NA		2	Louisiana	67.1
29	Arizona	10.3		3	Illinois	64.1
5	Arkansas	60.0		4	Pennsylvania	62.6
20	California	36.2		5	Arkansas	60.0
9	Colorado	50.0		6	Mississippi	56.7
9	Connecticut	50.0		7	North Carolina	55.9
8	Delaware	52.9		8	Delaware	52.9
21	Florida	35.3		9	Colorado	50.0
13	Georgia	47.4		9	Connecticut	50.0
NA	Hawaii**	NA		11	Ohio	49.7
30	Idaho	0.0		12	South Carolina	49.2
3	Illinois	64.1		13	Georgia	47.4
25	Indiana	30.2		14	Alabama	47.2
NA	Iowa**	NA		15	Missouri	43.4
30	Kansas	0.0		16	New Jersey	42.9
28	Kentucky	17.9		17	Virginia	41.9
2	Louisiana	67.1		18	Texas	41.3
NA	Maine**	NA		19	Nevada	39.5
1	Maryland	76.5		20	California	36.2
NA	Massachusetts**	NA		21	Florida	35.3
NA	Michigan**	NA		22	Tennessee	35.0
NA	Minnesota**	NA		23	Oklahoma	34.5
6	Mississippi	56.7		24	Washington	30.8
15	Missouri	43.4		25	Indiana	30.2
30	Montana	0.0		26	New York	20.0
30	Nebraska	0.0		26	Utah	20.0
19	Nevada	39.5		28	Kentucky	17.9
30	New Hampshire	0.0		29	Arizona	10.3
16	New Jersey	42.9		30	Idaho	0.0
30	New Mexico	0.0		30	Kansas	0.0
26	New York	20.0		30	Montana	0.0
7	North Carolina	55.9		30	Nebraska	0.0
NA	North Dakota**	NA		30	New Hampshire	0.0
11	Ohio	49.7		30	New Mexico	0.0
23	Oklahoma	34.5		30	Oregon	0.0
30	Oregon	0.0		30	South Dakota	0.0
4	Pennsylvania	62.6		30	Wyoming	0.0
NA	Rhode Island**	NA		NA	Alaska**	NA
12	South Carolina	49.2		NA	Hawaii**	NA
30	South Dakota	0.0		NA	Iowa**	NA
22	Tennessee	35.0		NA	Maine**	NA
18	Texas	41.3		NA	Massachusetts**	NA
26	Utah	20.0		NA	Michigan**	NA
NA	Vermont**	NA		NA	Minnesota**	NA
17	Virginia	41.9		NA	North Dakota**	NA
24	Washington	30.8		NA	Rhode Island**	NA
NA	West Virginia**	NA		NA	Vermont**	NA
NA	Wisconsin**	NA		NA	West Virginia**	NA
30	Wyoming	0.0		NA	Wisconsin**	NA
					District of Columbia**	NA

Source: Morgan Quitno Press using data from U.S. Department of Justice, Bureau of Justice Statistics
    "Capital Punishment 1999" (Bulletin, December 2000, NCJ-184795)
*As of December 31, 1999. Does not federal prisoners under sentence of death, 70.0% of whom are black
prisoners. Of the 98 executions in 1999, 33.7% were black prisoners.
**No death penalty as of 12/31/99.

Prisoners Executed in 1999

National Total = 98 Executed*

ALPHA ORDER				RANK ORDER			
RANK	STATE	EXECUTED	% of USA	RANK	STATE	EXECUTED	% of USA
9	Alabama	2	2.0%	1	Texas	35	35.7%
NA	Alaska**	NA	NA	2	Virginia	14	14.3%
4	Arizona	7	7.1%	3	Missouri	9	9.2%
6	Arkansas	4	4.1%	4	Arizona	7	7.1%
9	California	2	2.0%	5	Oklahoma	6	6.1%
21	Colorado	0	0.0%	6	Arkansas	4	4.1%
21	Connecticut	0	0.0%	6	North Carolina	4	4.1%
9	Delaware	2	2.0%	6	South Carolina	4	4.1%
12	Florida	1	1.0%	9	Alabama	2	2.0%
21	Georgia	0	0.0%	9	California	2	2.0%
NA	Hawaii**	NA	NA	9	Delaware	2	2.0%
21	Idaho	0	0.0%	12	Florida	1	1.0%
12	Illinois	1	1.0%	12	Illinois	1	1.0%
12	Indiana	1	1.0%	12	Indiana	1	1.0%
NA	Iowa**	NA	NA	12	Kentucky	1	1.0%
21	Kansas	0	0.0%	12	Louisiana	1	1.0%
12	Kentucky	1	1.0%	12	Nevada	1	1.0%
12	Louisiana	1	1.0%	12	Ohio	1	1.0%
NA	Maine**	NA	NA	12	Pennsylvania	1	1.0%
21	Maryland	0	0.0%	12	Utah	1	1.0%
NA	Massachusetts**	NA	NA	21	Colorado	0	0.0%
NA	Michigan**	NA	NA	21	Connecticut	0	0.0%
NA	Minnesota**	NA	NA	21	Georgia	0	0.0%
21	Mississippi	0	0.0%	21	Idaho	0	0.0%
3	Missouri	9	9.2%	21	Kansas	0	0.0%
21	Montana	0	0.0%	21	Maryland	0	0.0%
21	Nebraska	0	0.0%	21	Mississippi	0	0.0%
12	Nevada	1	1.0%	21	Montana	0	0.0%
21	New Hampshire	0	0.0%	21	Nebraska	0	0.0%
21	New Jersey	0	0.0%	21	New Hampshire	0	0.0%
21	New Mexico	0	0.0%	21	New Jersey	0	0.0%
21	New York	0	0.0%	21	New Mexico	0	0.0%
6	North Carolina	4	4.1%	21	New York	0	0.0%
NA	North Dakota**	NA	NA	21	Oregon	0	0.0%
12	Ohio	1	1.0%	21	South Dakota	0	0.0%
5	Oklahoma	6	6.1%	21	Tennessee	0	0.0%
21	Oregon	0	0.0%	21	Washington	0	0.0%
12	Pennsylvania	1	1.0%	21	Wyoming	0	0.0%
NA	Rhode Island**	NA	NA	NA	Alaska**	NA	NA
6	South Carolina	4	4.1%	NA	Hawaii**	NA	NA
21	South Dakota	0	0.0%	NA	Iowa**	NA	NA
21	Tennessee	0	0.0%	NA	Maine**	NA	NA
1	Texas	35	35.7%	NA	Massachusetts**	NA	NA
12	Utah	1	1.0%	NA	Michigan**	NA	NA
NA	Vermont**	NA	NA	NA	Minnesota**	NA	NA
2	Virginia	14	14.3%	NA	North Dakota**	NA	NA
21	Washington	0	0.0%	NA	Rhode Island**	NA	NA
NA	West Virginia**	NA	NA	NA	Vermont**	NA	NA
NA	Wisconsin**	NA	NA	NA	West Virginia**	NA	NA
21	Wyoming	0	0.0%	NA	Wisconsin**	NA	NA
					District of Columbia**	NA	NA

Source: U.S. Department of Justice, Bureau of Justice Statistics
   "Capital Punishment 1999" (Bulletin, December 2000, NCJ-184795)
*No federal prisoners were executed in 1999
**No death penalty as of 12/31/99.

Prisoners Executed: 1930 to 1999

National Total = 4,457 Prisoners*

ALPHA ORDER

RANK	STATE	PRISONERS	% of USA
13	Alabama	154	3.5%
43	Alaska	0	0.0%
22	Arizona	57	1.3%
14	Arkansas	139	3.1%
4	California	299	6.7%
24	Colorado	48	1.1%
30	Connecticut	21	0.5%
29	Delaware	22	0.5%
6	Florida	214	4.8%
2	Georgia	389	8.7%
43	Hawaii	0	0.0%
39	Idaho	4	0.1%
17	Illinois	102	2.3%
24	Indiana	48	1.1%
33	Iowa	18	0.4%
34	Kansas	15	0.3%
15	Kentucky	105	2.4%
10	Louisiana	158	3.5%
43	Maine	0	0.0%
21	Maryland	71	1.6%
28	Massachusetts	27	0.6%
43	Michigan	0	0.0%
43	Minnesota	0	0.0%
10	Mississippi	158	3.5%
16	Missouri	103	2.3%
35	Montana	8	0.2%
38	Nebraska	7	0.2%
27	Nevada	37	0.8%
41	New Hampshire	1	0.0%
20	New Jersey	74	1.7%
35	New Mexico	8	0.2%
3	New York	329	7.4%
5	North Carolina	278	6.2%
43	North Dakota	0	0.0%
8	Ohio	173	3.9%
19	Oklahoma	79	1.8%
30	Oregon	21	0.5%
12	Pennsylvania	155	3.5%
43	Rhode Island	0	0.0%
7	South Carolina	186	4.2%
41	South Dakota	1	0.0%
18	Tennessee	93	2.1%
1	Texas	496	11.1%
32	Utah	19	0.4%
39	Vermont	4	0.1%
9	Virginia	165	3.7%
23	Washington	50	1.1%
26	West Virginia	40	0.9%
43	Wisconsin	0	0.0%
35	Wyoming	8	0.2%

RANK ORDER

RANK	STATE	PRISONERS	% of USA
1	Texas	496	11.1%
2	Georgia	389	8.7%
3	New York	329	7.4%
4	California	299	6.7%
5	North Carolina	278	6.2%
6	Florida	214	4.8%
7	South Carolina	186	4.2%
8	Ohio	173	3.9%
9	Virginia	165	3.7%
10	Louisiana	158	3.5%
10	Mississippi	158	3.5%
12	Pennsylvania	155	3.5%
13	Alabama	154	3.5%
14	Arkansas	139	3.1%
15	Kentucky	105	2.4%
16	Missouri	103	2.3%
17	Illinois	102	2.3%
18	Tennessee	93	2.1%
19	Oklahoma	79	1.8%
20	New Jersey	74	1.7%
21	Maryland	71	1.6%
22	Arizona	57	1.3%
23	Washington	50	1.1%
24	Colorado	48	1.1%
24	Indiana	48	1.1%
26	West Virginia	40	0.9%
27	Nevada	37	0.8%
28	Massachusetts	27	0.6%
29	Delaware	22	0.5%
30	Connecticut	21	0.5%
30	Oregon	21	0.5%
32	Utah	19	0.4%
33	Iowa	18	0.4%
34	Kansas	15	0.3%
35	Montana	8	0.2%
35	New Mexico	8	0.2%
35	Wyoming	8	0.2%
38	Nebraska	7	0.2%
39	Idaho	4	0.1%
39	Vermont	4	0.1%
41	New Hampshire	1	0.0%
41	South Dakota	1	0.0%
43	Alaska	0	0.0%
43	Hawaii	0	0.0%
43	Maine	0	0.0%
43	Michigan	0	0.0%
43	Minnesota	0	0.0%
43	North Dakota	0	0.0%
43	Rhode Island	0	0.0%
43	Wisconsin	0	0.0%
	District of Columbia	40	0.9%

Source: U.S. Department of Justice, Bureau of Justice Statistics
   "Capital Punishment 1999" (Bulletin, December 2000, NCJ-184795)
*Includes 33 executions by the federal government. Does not include 160 executions carried out under military
authority. There were no executions from 1968 to 1976.

Prisoners Executed: 1977 to 1999

National Total = 598 Prisoners*

RANK	STATE	PRISONERS	% of USA
9	Alabama	19	3.2%
31	Alaska	0	0.0%
9	Arizona	19	3.2%
8	Arkansas	21	3.5%
16	California	7	1.2%
27	Colorado	1	0.2%
31	Connecticut	0	0.0%
14	Delaware	10	1.7%
3	Florida	44	7.4%
7	Georgia	23	3.8%
31	Hawaii	0	0.0%
27	Idaho	1	0.2%
13	Illinois	12	2.0%
16	Indiana	7	1.2%
31	Iowa	0	0.0%
31	Kansas	0	0.0%
24	Kentucky	2	0.3%
5	Louisiana	25	4.2%
31	Maine	0	0.0%
20	Maryland	3	0.5%
31	Massachusetts	0	0.0%
31	Michigan	0	0.0%
31	Minnesota	0	0.0%
19	Mississippi	4	0.7%
4	Missouri	41	6.9%
24	Montana	2	0.3%
20	Nebraska	3	0.5%
15	Nevada	8	1.3%
31	New Hampshire	0	0.0%
31	New Jersey	0	0.0%
31	New Mexico	0	0.0%
31	New York	0	0.0%
12	North Carolina	15	2.5%
31	North Dakota	0	0.0%
27	Ohio	1	0.2%
9	Oklahoma	19	3.2%
24	Oregon	2	0.3%
20	Pennsylvania	3	0.5%
31	Rhode Island	0	0.0%
6	South Carolina	24	4.0%
31	South Dakota	0	0.0%
31	Tennessee	0	0.0%
1	Texas	199	33.3%
18	Utah	6	1.0%
31	Vermont	0	0.0%
2	Virginia	73	12.2%
20	Washington	3	0.5%
31	West Virginia	0	0.0%
31	Wisconsin	0	0.0%
27	Wyoming	1	0.2%

RANK ORDER

RANK	STATE	PRISONERS	% of USA
1	Texas	199	33.3%
2	Virginia	73	12.2%
3	Florida	44	7.4%
4	Missouri	41	6.9%
5	Louisiana	25	4.2%
6	South Carolina	24	4.0%
7	Georgia	23	3.8%
8	Arkansas	21	3.5%
9	Alabama	19	3.2%
9	Arizona	19	3.2%
9	Oklahoma	19	3.2%
12	North Carolina	15	2.5%
13	Illinois	12	2.0%
14	Delaware	10	1.7%
15	Nevada	8	1.3%
16	California	7	1.2%
16	Indiana	7	1.2%
18	Utah	6	1.0%
19	Mississippi	4	0.7%
20	Maryland	3	0.5%
20	Nebraska	3	0.5%
20	Pennsylvania	3	0.5%
20	Washington	3	0.5%
24	Kentucky	2	0.3%
24	Montana	2	0.3%
24	Oregon	2	0.3%
27	Colorado	1	0.2%
27	Idaho	1	0.2%
27	Ohio	1	0.2%
27	Wyoming	1	0.2%
31	Alaska	0	0.0%
31	Connecticut	0	0.0%
31	Hawaii	0	0.0%
31	Iowa	0	0.0%
31	Kansas	0	0.0%
31	Maine	0	0.0%
31	Massachusetts	0	0.0%
31	Michigan	0	0.0%
31	Minnesota	0	0.0%
31	New Hampshire	0	0.0%
31	New Jersey	0	0.0%
31	New Mexico	0	0.0%
31	New York	0	0.0%
31	North Dakota	0	0.0%
31	Rhode Island	0	0.0%
31	South Dakota	0	0.0%
31	Tennessee	0	0.0%
31	Vermont	0	0.0%
31	West Virginia	0	0.0%
31	Wisconsin	0	0.0%
	District of Columbia	0	0.0%

Source: U.S. Department of Justice, Bureau of Justice Statistics
   "Capital Punishment 1999" (Bulletin, December 2000, NCJ-184795)
*As of December 31, 1999. All executions since 1977 have been for murder. In this time period, there have been no executions by the federal government. The most common method of executions was lethal injection (438) followed by electrocution (144), lethal gas (11), hanging (3) and firing squad (2).

Prisoners Sentenced to Death: 1973 to 1999

National Total = 6,685 State Death Sentences*

ALPHA ORDER

RANK	STATE	SENTENCES	% of USA
7	Alabama	314	4.7%
40	Alaska	0	0.0%
11	Arizona	223	3.3%
19	Arkansas	94	1.4%
3	California	722	10.8%
31	Colorado	17	0.3%
35	Connecticut	7	0.1%
25	Delaware	40	0.6%
2	Florida	821	12.3%
9	Georgia	289	4.3%
40	Hawaii	0	0.0%
26	Idaho	37	0.6%
10	Illinois	273	4.1%
20	Indiana	92	1.4%
40	Iowa	0	0.0%
37	Kansas	3	0.0%
21	Kentucky	71	1.1%
12	Louisiana	196	2.9%
40	Maine	0	0.0%
22	Maryland	48	0.7%
36	Massachusetts	4	0.1%
40	Michigan	0	0.0%
40	Minnesota	0	0.0%
14	Mississippi	163	2.4%
16	Missouri	158	2.4%
32	Montana	15	0.2%
30	Nebraska	24	0.4%
17	Nevada	127	1.9%
40	New Hampshire	0	0.0%
22	New Jersey	48	0.7%
28	New Mexico	26	0.4%
34	New York	8	0.1%
4	North Carolina	468	7.0%
40	North Dakota	0	0.0%
5	Ohio	351	5.3%
8	Oklahoma	294	4.4%
24	Oregon	46	0.7%
6	Pennsylvania	323	4.8%
39	Rhode Island	2	0.0%
14	South Carolina	163	2.4%
37	South Dakota	3	0.0%
13	Tennessee	192	2.9%
1	Texas	829	12.4%
28	Utah	26	0.4%
40	Vermont	0	0.0%
18	Virginia	123	1.8%
27	Washington	34	0.5%
40	West Virginia	0	0.0%
40	Wisconsin	0	0.0%
33	Wyoming	11	0.2%

RANK ORDER

RANK	STATE	SENTENCES	% of USA
1	Texas	829	12.4%
2	Florida	821	12.3%
3	California	722	10.8%
4	North Carolina	468	7.0%
5	Ohio	351	5.3%
6	Pennsylvania	323	4.8%
7	Alabama	314	4.7%
8	Oklahoma	294	4.4%
9	Georgia	289	4.3%
10	Illinois	273	4.1%
11	Arizona	223	3.3%
12	Louisiana	196	2.9%
13	Tennessee	192	2.9%
14	Mississippi	163	2.4%
14	South Carolina	163	2.4%
16	Missouri	158	2.4%
17	Nevada	127	1.9%
18	Virginia	123	1.8%
19	Arkansas	94	1.4%
20	Indiana	92	1.4%
21	Kentucky	71	1.1%
22	Maryland	48	0.7%
22	New Jersey	48	0.7%
24	Oregon	46	0.7%
25	Delaware	40	0.6%
26	Idaho	37	0.6%
27	Washington	34	0.5%
28	New Mexico	26	0.4%
28	Utah	26	0.4%
30	Nebraska	24	0.4%
31	Colorado	17	0.3%
32	Montana	15	0.2%
33	Wyoming	11	0.2%
34	New York	8	0.1%
35	Connecticut	7	0.1%
36	Massachusetts	4	0.1%
37	Kansas	3	0.0%
37	South Dakota	3	0.0%
39	Rhode Island	2	0.0%
40	Alaska	0	0.0%
40	Hawaii	0	0.0%
40	Iowa	0	0.0%
40	Maine	0	0.0%
40	Michigan	0	0.0%
40	Minnesota	0	0.0%
40	New Hampshire	0	0.0%
40	North Dakota	0	0.0%
40	Vermont	0	0.0%
40	West Virginia	0	0.0%
40	Wisconsin	0	0.0%
	District of Columbia	0	0.0%

Source: U.S. Department of Justice, Bureau of Justice Statistics
  "Capital Punishment 1999" (Bulletin, December 2000, NCJ-184795)
*As of December 31, 1999. Does not include 22 federal prisoners sentenced to death. For those sentenced to death more than once, the numbers are based on the most recent death sentence.

Death Sentences Overturned or Commuted: 1973 to 1999

National Total = 2,345 Sentences*

ALPHA ORDER

RANK	STATE	SENTENCES	% of USA
8	Alabama	102	4.3%
NA	Alaska**	NA	NA
14	Arizona	78	3.3%
17	Arkansas	32	1.4%
6	California	131	5.6%
29	Colorado	11	0.5%
37	Connecticut	1	0.0%
28	Delaware	13	0.6%
1	Florida	381	16.2%
5	Georgia	140	6.0%
NA	Hawaii**	NA	NA
27	Idaho	14	0.6%
10	Illinois	88	3.8%
16	Indiana	39	1.7%
NA	Iowa**	NA	NA
38	Kansas	0	0.0%
18	Kentucky	28	1.2%
11	Louisiana	82	3.5%
NA	Maine**	NA	NA
20	Maryland	27	1.2%
34	Massachusetts	4	0.2%
NA	Michigan**	NA	NA
NA	Minnesota**	NA	NA
9	Mississippi	94	4.0%
20	Missouri	27	1.2%
32	Montana	7	0.3%
30	Nebraska	10	0.4%
18	Nevada	28	1.2%
NA	New Hampshire**	NA	NA
22	New Jersey	23	1.0%
23	New Mexico	21	0.9%
35	New York	3	0.1%
2	North Carolina	242	10.3%
NA	North Dakota**	NA	NA
4	Ohio	142	6.1%
7	Oklahoma	129	5.5%
24	Oregon	18	0.8%
13	Pennsylvania	80	3.4%
36	Rhode Island	2	0.1%
15	South Carolina	70	3.0%
38	South Dakota	0	0.0%
12	Tennessee	81	3.5%
3	Texas	148	6.3%
30	Utah	10	0.4%
NA	Vermont**	NA	NA
26	Virginia	15	0.6%
25	Washington	17	0.7%
NA	West Virginia**	NA	NA
NA	Wisconsin**	NA	NA
32	Wyoming	7	0.3%

RANK ORDER

RANK	STATE	SENTENCES	% of USA
1	Florida	381	16.2%
2	North Carolina	242	10.3%
3	Texas	148	6.3%
4	Ohio	142	6.1%
5	Georgia	140	6.0%
6	California	131	5.6%
7	Oklahoma	129	5.5%
8	Alabama	102	4.3%
9	Mississippi	94	4.0%
10	Illinois	88	3.8%
11	Louisiana	82	3.5%
12	Tennessee	81	3.5%
13	Pennsylvania	80	3.4%
14	Arizona	78	3.3%
15	South Carolina	70	3.0%
16	Indiana	39	1.7%
17	Arkansas	32	1.4%
18	Kentucky	28	1.2%
18	Nevada	28	1.2%
20	Maryland	27	1.2%
20	Missouri	27	1.2%
22	New Jersey	23	1.0%
23	New Mexico	21	0.9%
24	Oregon	18	0.8%
25	Washington	17	0.7%
26	Virginia	15	0.6%
27	Idaho	14	0.6%
28	Delaware	13	0.6%
29	Colorado	11	0.5%
30	Nebraska	10	0.4%
30	Utah	10	0.4%
32	Montana	7	0.3%
32	Wyoming	7	0.3%
34	Massachusetts	4	0.2%
35	New York	3	0.1%
36	Rhode Island	2	0.1%
37	Connecticut	1	0.0%
38	Kansas	0	0.0%
38	South Dakota	0	0.0%
NA	Alaska**	NA	NA
NA	Hawaii**	NA	NA
NA	Iowa**	NA	NA
NA	Maine**	NA	NA
NA	Michigan**	NA	NA
NA	Minnesota**	NA	NA
NA	New Hampshire**	NA	NA
NA	North Dakota**	NA	NA
NA	Vermont**	NA	NA
NA	West Virginia**	NA	NA
NA	Wisconsin**	NA	NA
	District of Columbia**	NA	NA

Source: U.S. Department of Justice, Bureau of Justice Statistics
    "Capital Punishment 1999" (Bulletin, December 2000, NCJ-184795)
*As of December 31, 1999. Does not include two federal prisoners whose sentences were overturned.
**Not applicable.

Percent of Death Penalty Sentences Overturned or Commuted: 1973 to 1999

National Percent = 35.0% of Sentences*

<table>
<tr><td colspan="3">ALPHA ORDER</td><td colspan="3">RANK ORDER</td></tr>
<tr><td>RANK</td><td>STATE</td><td>PERCENT</td><td>RANK</td><td>STATE</td><td>PERCENT</td></tr>
<tr><td>28</td><td>Alabama</td><td>32.5</td><td>1</td><td>Massachusetts</td><td>100.0</td></tr>
<tr><td>NA</td><td>Alaska**</td><td>NA</td><td>1</td><td>Rhode Island</td><td>100.0</td></tr>
<tr><td>26</td><td>Arizona</td><td>35.0</td><td>3</td><td>New Mexico</td><td>80.8</td></tr>
<tr><td>27</td><td>Arkansas</td><td>34.0</td><td>4</td><td>Colorado</td><td>64.7</td></tr>
<tr><td>33</td><td>California</td><td>18.1</td><td>5</td><td>Wyoming</td><td>63.6</td></tr>
<tr><td>4</td><td>Colorado</td><td>64.7</td><td>6</td><td>Mississippi</td><td>57.7</td></tr>
<tr><td>36</td><td>Connecticut</td><td>14.3</td><td>7</td><td>Maryland</td><td>56.3</td></tr>
<tr><td>28</td><td>Delaware</td><td>32.5</td><td>8</td><td>North Carolina</td><td>51.7</td></tr>
<tr><td>13</td><td>Florida</td><td>46.4</td><td>9</td><td>Washington</td><td>50.0</td></tr>
<tr><td>10</td><td>Georgia</td><td>48.4</td><td>10</td><td>Georgia</td><td>48.4</td></tr>
<tr><td>NA</td><td>Hawaii**</td><td>NA</td><td>11</td><td>New Jersey</td><td>47.9</td></tr>
<tr><td>24</td><td>Idaho</td><td>37.8</td><td>12</td><td>Montana</td><td>46.7</td></tr>
<tr><td>30</td><td>Illinois</td><td>32.2</td><td>13</td><td>Florida</td><td>46.4</td></tr>
<tr><td>16</td><td>Indiana</td><td>42.4</td><td>14</td><td>Oklahoma</td><td>43.9</td></tr>
<tr><td>NA</td><td>Iowa**</td><td>NA</td><td>15</td><td>South Carolina</td><td>42.9</td></tr>
<tr><td>38</td><td>Kansas</td><td>0.0</td><td>16</td><td>Indiana</td><td>42.4</td></tr>
<tr><td>21</td><td>Kentucky</td><td>39.4</td><td>17</td><td>Tennessee</td><td>42.2</td></tr>
<tr><td>18</td><td>Louisiana</td><td>41.8</td><td>18</td><td>Louisiana</td><td>41.8</td></tr>
<tr><td>NA</td><td>Maine**</td><td>NA</td><td>19</td><td>Nebraska</td><td>41.7</td></tr>
<tr><td>7</td><td>Maryland</td><td>56.3</td><td>20</td><td>Ohio</td><td>40.5</td></tr>
<tr><td>1</td><td>Massachusetts</td><td>100.0</td><td>21</td><td>Kentucky</td><td>39.4</td></tr>
<tr><td>NA</td><td>Michigan**</td><td>NA</td><td>22</td><td>Oregon</td><td>39.1</td></tr>
<tr><td>NA</td><td>Minnesota**</td><td>NA</td><td>23</td><td>Utah</td><td>38.5</td></tr>
<tr><td>6</td><td>Mississippi</td><td>57.7</td><td>24</td><td>Idaho</td><td>37.8</td></tr>
<tr><td>35</td><td>Missouri</td><td>17.1</td><td>25</td><td>New York</td><td>37.5</td></tr>
<tr><td>12</td><td>Montana</td><td>46.7</td><td>26</td><td>Arizona</td><td>35.0</td></tr>
<tr><td>19</td><td>Nebraska</td><td>41.7</td><td>27</td><td>Arkansas</td><td>34.0</td></tr>
<tr><td>32</td><td>Nevada</td><td>22.0</td><td>28</td><td>Alabama</td><td>32.5</td></tr>
<tr><td>NA</td><td>New Hampshire**</td><td>NA</td><td>28</td><td>Delaware</td><td>32.5</td></tr>
<tr><td>11</td><td>New Jersey</td><td>47.9</td><td>30</td><td>Illinois</td><td>32.2</td></tr>
<tr><td>3</td><td>New Mexico</td><td>80.8</td><td>31</td><td>Pennsylvania</td><td>24.8</td></tr>
<tr><td>25</td><td>New York</td><td>37.5</td><td>32</td><td>Nevada</td><td>22.0</td></tr>
<tr><td>8</td><td>North Carolina</td><td>51.7</td><td>33</td><td>California</td><td>18.1</td></tr>
<tr><td>NA</td><td>North Dakota**</td><td>NA</td><td>34</td><td>Texas</td><td>17.9</td></tr>
<tr><td>20</td><td>Ohio</td><td>40.5</td><td>35</td><td>Missouri</td><td>17.1</td></tr>
<tr><td>14</td><td>Oklahoma</td><td>43.9</td><td>36</td><td>Connecticut</td><td>14.3</td></tr>
<tr><td>22</td><td>Oregon</td><td>39.1</td><td>37</td><td>Virginia</td><td>12.2</td></tr>
<tr><td>31</td><td>Pennsylvania</td><td>24.8</td><td>38</td><td>Kansas</td><td>0.0</td></tr>
<tr><td>1</td><td>Rhode Island</td><td>100.0</td><td>38</td><td>South Dakota</td><td>0.0</td></tr>
<tr><td>15</td><td>South Carolina</td><td>42.9</td><td>NA</td><td>Alaska**</td><td>NA</td></tr>
<tr><td>38</td><td>South Dakota</td><td>0.0</td><td>NA</td><td>Hawaii**</td><td>NA</td></tr>
<tr><td>17</td><td>Tennessee</td><td>42.2</td><td>NA</td><td>Iowa**</td><td>NA</td></tr>
<tr><td>34</td><td>Texas</td><td>17.9</td><td>NA</td><td>Maine**</td><td>NA</td></tr>
<tr><td>23</td><td>Utah</td><td>38.5</td><td>NA</td><td>Michigan**</td><td>NA</td></tr>
<tr><td>NA</td><td>Vermont**</td><td>NA</td><td>NA</td><td>Minnesota**</td><td>NA</td></tr>
<tr><td>37</td><td>Virginia</td><td>12.2</td><td>NA</td><td>New Hampshire**</td><td>NA</td></tr>
<tr><td>9</td><td>Washington</td><td>50.0</td><td>NA</td><td>North Dakota**</td><td>NA</td></tr>
<tr><td>NA</td><td>West Virginia**</td><td>NA</td><td>NA</td><td>Vermont**</td><td>NA</td></tr>
<tr><td>NA</td><td>Wisconsin**</td><td>NA</td><td>NA</td><td>West Virginia**</td><td>NA</td></tr>
<tr><td>5</td><td>Wyoming</td><td>63.6</td><td>NA</td><td>Wisconsin**</td><td>NA</td></tr>
<tr><td></td><td></td><td></td><td></td><td>District of Columbia**</td><td>NA</td></tr>
</table>

Source: Morgan Quitno Press using data from U.S. Department of Justice, Bureau of Justice Statistics
   "Capital Punishment 1999" (Bulletin, December 2000, NCJ-184795)
*As of December 31, 1999. Does not include two federal prisoners whose sentences were overturned.
**Not applicable.

Sentenced Prisoners Admitted to State Correctional Institutions in 1998

National Total = 576,038 Prisoners Admitted*

ALPHA ORDER

RANK ORDER

RANK	STATE	ADMISSIONS	% of USA
22	Alabama	7,750	1.3%
36	Alaska	2,647	0.5%
16	Arizona	10,175	1.8%
27	Arkansas	6,204	1.1%
1	California	134,485	23.3%
25	Colorado	6,881	1.2%
39	Connecticut	1,933	0.3%
40	Delaware	1,888	0.3%
5	Florida	25,524	4.4%
9	Georgia	15,471	2.7%
33	Hawaii	3,481	0.6%
37	Idaho	2,621	0.5%
4	Illinois	27,362	4.8%
15	Indiana	10,566	1.8%
28	Iowa	4,798	0.8%
30	Kansas	4,517	0.8%
21	Kentucky	7,989	1.4%
7	Louisiana	17,079	3.0%
48	Maine	795	0.1%
13	Maryland	11,078	1.9%
34	Massachusetts	3,227	0.6%
10	Michigan	14,435	2.5%
31	Minnesota	4,307	0.7%
26	Mississippi	6,670	1.2%
11	Missouri	13,660	2.4%
44	Montana	1,289	0.2%
41	Nebraska	1,791	0.3%
29	Nevada	4,773	0.8%
45	New Hampshire	1,000	0.2%
8	New Jersey	16,801	2.9%
38	New Mexico	2,347	0.4%
3	New York	28,871	5.0%
12	North Carolina	11,403	2.0%
49	North Dakota	765	0.1%
6	Ohio	20,637	3.6%
23	Oklahoma	7,297	1.3%
32	Oregon	3,688	0.6%
14	Pennsylvania	10,679	1.9%
46	Rhode Island	991	0.2%
18	South Carolina	8,914	1.5%
43	South Dakota	1,337	0.2%
20	Tennessee	8,770	1.5%
2	Texas	59,340	10.3%
35	Utah	3,076	0.5%
47	Vermont	824	0.1%
17	Virginia	10,152	1.8%
24	Washington	7,151	1.2%
42	West Virginia	1,444	0.3%
19	Wisconsin	8,785	1.5%
50	Wyoming	757	0.1%

RANK	STATE	ADMISSIONS	% of USA
1	California	134,485	23.3%
2	Texas	59,340	10.3%
3	New York	28,871	5.0%
4	Illinois	27,362	4.8%
5	Florida	25,524	4.4%
6	Ohio	20,637	3.6%
7	Louisiana	17,079	3.0%
8	New Jersey	16,801	2.9%
9	Georgia	15,471	2.7%
10	Michigan	14,435	2.5%
11	Missouri	13,660	2.4%
12	North Carolina	11,403	2.0%
13	Maryland	11,078	1.9%
14	Pennsylvania	10,679	1.9%
15	Indiana	10,566	1.8%
16	Arizona	10,175	1.8%
17	Virginia	10,152	1.8%
18	South Carolina	8,914	1.5%
19	Wisconsin	8,785	1.5%
20	Tennessee	8,770	1.5%
21	Kentucky	7,989	1.4%
22	Alabama	7,750	1.3%
23	Oklahoma	7,297	1.3%
24	Washington	7,151	1.2%
25	Colorado	6,881	1.2%
26	Mississippi	6,670	1.2%
27	Arkansas	6,204	1.1%
28	Iowa	4,798	0.8%
29	Nevada	4,773	0.8%
30	Kansas	4,517	0.8%
31	Minnesota	4,307	0.7%
32	Oregon	3,688	0.6%
33	Hawaii	3,481	0.6%
34	Massachusetts	3,227	0.6%
35	Utah	3,076	0.5%
36	Alaska	2,647	0.5%
37	Idaho	2,621	0.5%
38	New Mexico	2,347	0.4%
39	Connecticut	1,933	0.3%
40	Delaware	1,888	0.3%
41	Nebraska	1,791	0.3%
42	West Virginia	1,444	0.3%
43	South Dakota	1,337	0.2%
44	Montana	1,289	0.2%
45	New Hampshire	1,000	0.2%
46	Rhode Island	991	0.2%
47	Vermont	824	0.1%
48	Maine	795	0.1%
49	North Dakota	765	0.1%
50	Wyoming	757	0.1%
	District of Columbia	7,613	1.3%

Source: U.S. Department of Justice, Bureau of Justice Statistics
"Correctional Populations in the United States, 1998" (forthcoming in 2001)
*Preliminary data. Includes sentenced prisoners admitted because of new court commitments, parole violators returned, escapees returned and others. Does not include 39,188 new federal admissions.

Sentenced Prisoners Admitted to State Correctional Institutions
Through New Court Commitments in 1998
National Total = 347,270 New Prisoners*

ALPHA ORDER

RANK	STATE	PRISONERS	% of USA
17	Alabama	6,664	1.9%
36	Alaska	1,612	0.5%
14	Arizona	7,709	2.2%
27	Arkansas	3,732	1.1%
1	California	46,529	13.4%
26	Colorado	4,585	1.3%
43	Connecticut	947	0.3%
41	Delaware	1,118	0.3%
3	Florida	21,937	6.3%
7	Georgia	11,329	3.3%
34	Hawaii	2,003	0.6%
39	Idaho	1,331	0.4%
4	Illinois	19,655	5.7%
10	Indiana	9,495	2.7%
29	Iowa	3,312	1.0%
31	Kansas	2,886	0.8%
22	Kentucky	6,171	1.8%
16	Louisiana	7,367	2.1%
49	Maine	449	0.1%
15	Maryland	7,552	2.2%
33	Massachusetts	2,154	0.6%
12	Michigan	8,024	2.3%
30	Minnesota	3,001	0.9%
23	Mississippi	5,301	1.5%
13	Missouri	7,822	2.3%
45	Montana	638	0.2%
37	Nebraska	1,462	0.4%
28	Nevada	3,617	1.0%
46	New Hampshire	629	0.2%
8	New Jersey	9,938	2.9%
35	New Mexico	1,631	0.5%
5	New York	19,497	5.6%
9	North Carolina	9,582	2.8%
47	North Dakota	613	0.2%
6	Ohio	17,652	5.1%
20	Oklahoma	6,302	1.8%
32	Oregon	2,267	0.7%
18	Pennsylvania	6,650	1.9%
44	Rhode Island	700	0.2%
19	South Carolina	6,521	1.9%
42	South Dakota	1,087	0.3%
24	Tennessee	4,855	1.4%
2	Texas	34,876	10.0%
38	Utah	1,378	0.4%
50	Vermont	211	0.1%
11	Virginia	8,659	2.5%
21	Washington	6,211	1.8%
40	West Virginia	1,259	0.4%
25	Wisconsin	4,790	1.4%
48	Wyoming	461	0.1%

RANK ORDER

RANK	STATE	PRISONERS	% of USA
1	California	46,529	13.4%
2	Texas	34,876	10.0%
3	Florida	21,937	6.3%
4	Illinois	19,655	5.7%
5	New York	19,497	5.6%
6	Ohio	17,652	5.1%
7	Georgia	11,329	3.3%
8	New Jersey	9,938	2.9%
9	North Carolina	9,582	2.8%
10	Indiana	9,495	2.7%
11	Virginia	8,659	2.5%
12	Michigan	8,024	2.3%
13	Missouri	7,822	2.3%
14	Arizona	7,709	2.2%
15	Maryland	7,552	2.2%
16	Louisiana	7,367	2.1%
17	Alabama	6,664	1.9%
18	Pennsylvania	6,650	1.9%
19	South Carolina	6,521	1.9%
20	Oklahoma	6,302	1.8%
21	Washington	6,211	1.8%
22	Kentucky	6,171	1.8%
23	Mississippi	5,301	1.5%
24	Tennessee	4,855	1.4%
25	Wisconsin	4,790	1.4%
26	Colorado	4,585	1.3%
27	Arkansas	3,732	1.1%
28	Nevada	3,617	1.0%
29	Iowa	3,312	1.0%
30	Minnesota	3,001	0.9%
31	Kansas	2,886	0.8%
32	Oregon	2,267	0.7%
33	Massachusetts	2,154	0.6%
34	Hawaii	2,003	0.6%
35	New Mexico	1,631	0.5%
36	Alaska	1,612	0.5%
37	Nebraska	1,462	0.4%
38	Utah	1,378	0.4%
39	Idaho	1,331	0.4%
40	West Virginia	1,259	0.4%
41	Delaware	1,118	0.3%
42	South Dakota	1,087	0.3%
43	Connecticut	947	0.3%
44	Rhode Island	700	0.2%
45	Montana	638	0.2%
46	New Hampshire	629	0.2%
47	North Dakota	613	0.2%
48	Wyoming	461	0.1%
49	Maine	449	0.1%
50	Vermont	211	0.1%
	District of Columbia	3,099	0.9%

Source: U.S. Department of Justice, Bureau of Justice Statistics
   "Correctional Populations in the United States, 1998" (forthcoming in 2001)
*Preliminary data. Does not include 34,376 new federal court commitments.

Parole Violators Returned to State Prisons in 1998

National Total = 206,152 Prisoners*

ALPHA ORDER					RANK ORDER			

RANK	STATE	PRISONERS	% of USA		RANK	STATE	PRISONERS	% of USA
34	Alabama	700	0.3%		1	California	87,539	42.5%
29	Alaska	993	0.5%		2	Texas	23,784	11.5%
14	Arizona	2,398	1.2%		3	Louisiana	8,853	4.3%
19	Arkansas	1,694	0.8%		4	New York	7,613	3.7%
1	California	87,539	42.5%		5	New Jersey	6,822	3.3%
17	Colorado	1,951	0.9%		6	Illinois	6,802	3.3%
31	Connecticut	849	0.4%		7	Michigan	4,453	2.2%
39	Delaware	513	0.2%		8	Georgia	4,078	2.0%
15	Florida	2,362	1.1%		9	Missouri	3,965	1.9%
8	Georgia	4,078	2.0%		10	Tennessee	3,836	1.9%
25	Hawaii	1,408	0.7%		11	Pennsylvania	3,665	1.8%
NA	Idaho**	NA	NA		12	Maryland	3,408	1.7%
6	Illinois	6,802	3.3%		13	Ohio	2,961	1.4%
28	Indiana	1,052	0.5%		14	Arizona	2,398	1.2%
37	Iowa	660	0.3%		15	Florida	2,362	1.1%
22	Kansas	1,595	0.8%		16	South Carolina	2,140	1.0%
18	Kentucky	1,700	0.8%		17	Colorado	1,951	0.9%
3	Louisiana	8,853	4.3%		18	Kentucky	1,700	0.8%
43	Maine	303	0.1%		19	Arkansas	1,694	0.8%
12	Maryland	3,408	1.7%		20	Utah	1,683	0.8%
35	Massachusetts	682	0.3%		21	North Carolina	1,681	0.8%
7	Michigan	4,453	2.2%		22	Kansas	1,595	0.8%
26	Minnesota	1,306	0.6%		23	Wisconsin	1,567	0.8%
40	Mississippi	454	0.2%		24	Virginia	1,493	0.7%
9	Missouri	3,965	1.9%		25	Hawaii	1,408	0.7%
38	Montana	616	0.3%		26	Minnesota	1,306	0.6%
42	Nebraska	309	0.1%		27	Oregon	1,271	0.6%
32	Nevada	794	0.4%		28	Indiana	1,052	0.5%
41	New Hampshire	358	0.2%		29	Alaska	993	0.5%
5	New Jersey	6,822	3.3%		30	Oklahoma	879	0.4%
36	New Mexico	671	0.3%		31	Connecticut	849	0.4%
4	New York	7,613	3.7%		32	Nevada	794	0.4%
21	North Carolina	1,681	0.8%		33	Washington	788	0.4%
48	North Dakota	150	0.1%		34	Alabama	700	0.3%
13	Ohio	2,961	1.4%		35	Massachusetts	682	0.3%
30	Oklahoma	879	0.4%		36	New Mexico	671	0.3%
27	Oregon	1,271	0.6%		37	Iowa	660	0.3%
11	Pennsylvania	3,665	1.8%		38	Montana	616	0.3%
45	Rhode Island	270	0.1%		39	Delaware	513	0.2%
16	South Carolina	2,140	1.0%		40	Mississippi	454	0.2%
46	South Dakota	208	0.1%		41	New Hampshire	358	0.2%
10	Tennessee	3,836	1.9%		42	Nebraska	309	0.1%
2	Texas	23,784	11.5%		43	Maine	303	0.1%
20	Utah	1,683	0.8%		44	Wyoming	287	0.1%
49	Vermont	122	0.1%		45	Rhode Island	270	0.1%
24	Virginia	1,493	0.7%		46	South Dakota	208	0.1%
33	Washington	788	0.4%		47	West Virginia	181	0.1%
47	West Virginia	181	0.1%		48	North Dakota	150	0.1%
23	Wisconsin	1,567	0.8%		49	Vermont	122	0.1%
44	Wyoming	287	0.1%		NA	Idaho**	NA	NA
						District of Columbia	2,285	1.1%

Source: U.S. Department of Justice, Bureau of Justice Statistics
   "Correctional Populations in the United States, 1998" (forthcoming in 2001)
*Preliminary data. Includes other conditional release violators. Does not include 3,630 federal parole violators
returned to prison.
**Not available.

Escapees Returned to State Prisons in 1998

National Total = 7,175 Prisoners*

ALPHA ORDER

RANK	STATE	PRISONERS	% of USA
7	Alabama	217	3.0%
24	Alaska	40	0.6%
31	Arizona	15	0.2%
32	Arkansas	14	0.2%
8	California	209	2.9%
6	Colorado	322	4.5%
11	Connecticut	131	1.8%
25	Delaware	33	0.5%
9	Florida	167	2.3%
20	Georgia	51	0.7%
27	Hawaii	26	0.4%
44	Idaho	0	0.0%
3	Illinois	892	12.4%
29	Indiana	17	0.2%
5	Iowa	618	8.6%
36	Kansas	8	0.1%
17	Kentucky	88	1.2%
15	Louisiana	97	1.4%
36	Maine	8	0.1%
14	Maryland	102	1.4%
30	Massachusetts	16	0.2%
2	Michigan	1,067	14.9%
44	Minnesota	0	0.0%
23	Mississippi	44	0.6%
4	Missouri	760	10.6%
25	Montana	33	0.5%
28	Nebraska	20	0.3%
44	Nevada	0	0.0%
33	New Hampshire	13	0.2%
44	New Jersey	0	0.0%
34	New Mexico	10	0.1%
1	New York	1,092	15.2%
13	North Carolina	111	1.5%
43	North Dakota	1	0.0%
39	Ohio	6	0.1%
12	Oklahoma	116	1.6%
20	Oregon	51	0.7%
18	Pennsylvania	72	1.0%
34	Rhode Island	10	0.1%
22	South Carolina	48	0.7%
40	South Dakota	5	0.1%
19	Tennessee	53	0.7%
44	Texas	0	0.0%
38	Utah	7	0.1%
16	Vermont	94	1.3%
44	Virginia	0	0.0%
10	Washington	139	1.9%
42	West Virginia	2	0.0%
44	Wisconsin	0	0.0%
41	Wyoming	3	0.0%

RANK ORDER

RANK	STATE	PRISONERS	% of USA
1	New York	1,092	15.2%
2	Michigan	1,067	14.9%
3	Illinois	892	12.4%
4	Missouri	760	10.6%
5	Iowa	618	8.6%
6	Colorado	322	4.5%
7	Alabama	217	3.0%
8	California	209	2.9%
9	Florida	167	2.3%
10	Washington	139	1.9%
11	Connecticut	131	1.8%
12	Oklahoma	116	1.6%
13	North Carolina	111	1.5%
14	Maryland	102	1.4%
15	Louisiana	97	1.4%
16	Vermont	94	1.3%
17	Kentucky	88	1.2%
18	Pennsylvania	72	1.0%
19	Tennessee	53	0.7%
20	Georgia	51	0.7%
20	Oregon	51	0.7%
22	South Carolina	48	0.7%
23	Mississippi	44	0.6%
24	Alaska	40	0.6%
25	Delaware	33	0.5%
25	Montana	33	0.5%
27	Hawaii	26	0.4%
28	Nebraska	20	0.3%
29	Indiana	17	0.2%
30	Massachusetts	16	0.2%
31	Arizona	15	0.2%
32	Arkansas	14	0.2%
33	New Hampshire	13	0.2%
34	New Mexico	10	0.1%
34	Rhode Island	10	0.1%
36	Kansas	8	0.1%
36	Maine	8	0.1%
38	Utah	7	0.1%
39	Ohio	6	0.1%
40	South Dakota	5	0.1%
41	Wyoming	3	0.0%
42	West Virginia	2	0.0%
43	North Dakota	1	0.0%
44	Idaho	0	0.0%
44	Minnesota	0	0.0%
44	Nevada	0	0.0%
44	New Jersey	0	0.0%
44	Texas	0	0.0%
44	Virginia	0	0.0%
44	Wisconsin	0	0.0%
	District of Columbia	347	4.8%

Source: U.S. Department of Justice, Bureau of Justice Statistics
"Correctional Populations in the United States, 1998" (forthcoming in 2001)
*Preliminary data. Includes AWOLs returned. Federal data were not reported.

Prisoners Released from State Correctional Institutions in 1998

National Total = 531,312 Prisoners*

ALPHA ORDER

RANK	STATE	PRISONERS	% of USA
21	Alabama	7,280	1.4%
35	Alaska	2,677	0.5%
17	Arizona	8,573	1.6%
26	Arkansas	5,579	1.1%
1	California	129,800	24.4%
25	Colorado	6,030	1.1%
40	Connecticut	1,660	0.3%
39	Delaware	1,941	0.4%
5	Florida	22,905	4.3%
10	Georgia	12,607	2.4%
33	Hawaii	3,259	0.6%
37	Idaho	2,486	0.5%
4	Illinois	25,099	4.7%
14	Indiana	9,280	1.7%
28	Iowa	4,342	0.8%
29	Kansas	4,245	0.8%
20	Kentucky	7,602	1.4%
7	Louisiana	14,116	2.7%
50	Maine	606	0.1%
13	Maryland	10,626	2.0%
32	Massachusetts	3,330	0.6%
9	Michigan	13,327	2.5%
31	Minnesota	4,056	0.8%
27	Mississippi	4,491	0.8%
11	Missouri	12,374	2.3%
44	Montana	1,096	0.2%
41	Nebraska	1,532	0.3%
30	Nevada	4,146	0.8%
45	New Hampshire	999	0.2%
8	New Jersey	14,041	2.6%
38	New Mexico	2,264	0.4%
3	New York	27,978	5.3%
12	North Carolina	11,726	2.2%
49	North Dakota	646	0.1%
6	Ohio	20,203	3.8%
22	Oklahoma	6,947	1.3%
35	Oregon	2,677	0.5%
15	Pennsylvania	9,270	1.7%
46	Rhode Island	916	0.2%
18	South Carolina	7,942	1.5%
42	South Dakota	1,162	0.2%
19	Tennessee	7,691	1.4%
2	Texas	55,181	10.4%
34	Utah	2,954	0.6%
48	Vermont	695	0.1%
16	Virginia	9,004	1.7%
24	Washington	6,204	1.2%
43	West Virginia	1,114	0.2%
23	Wisconsin	6,464	1.2%
47	Wyoming	735	0.1%

RANK ORDER

RANK	STATE	PRISONERS	% of USA
1	California	129,800	24.4%
2	Texas	55,181	10.4%
3	New York	27,978	5.3%
4	Illinois	25,099	4.7%
5	Florida	22,905	4.3%
6	Ohio	20,203	3.8%
7	Louisiana	14,116	2.7%
8	New Jersey	14,041	2.6%
9	Michigan	13,327	2.5%
10	Georgia	12,607	2.4%
11	Missouri	12,374	2.3%
12	North Carolina	11,726	2.2%
13	Maryland	10,626	2.0%
14	Indiana	9,280	1.7%
15	Pennsylvania	9,270	1.7%
16	Virginia	9,004	1.7%
17	Arizona	8,573	1.6%
18	South Carolina	7,942	1.5%
19	Tennessee	7,691	1.4%
20	Kentucky	7,602	1.4%
21	Alabama	7,280	1.4%
22	Oklahoma	6,947	1.3%
23	Wisconsin	6,464	1.2%
24	Washington	6,204	1.2%
25	Colorado	6,030	1.1%
26	Arkansas	5,579	1.1%
27	Mississippi	4,491	0.8%
28	Iowa	4,342	0.8%
29	Kansas	4,245	0.8%
30	Nevada	4,146	0.8%
31	Minnesota	4,056	0.8%
32	Massachusetts	3,330	0.6%
33	Hawaii	3,259	0.6%
34	Utah	2,954	0.6%
35	Alaska	2,677	0.5%
35	Oregon	2,677	0.5%
37	Idaho	2,486	0.5%
38	New Mexico	2,264	0.4%
39	Delaware	1,941	0.4%
40	Connecticut	1,660	0.3%
41	Nebraska	1,532	0.3%
42	South Dakota	1,162	0.2%
43	West Virginia	1,114	0.2%
44	Montana	1,096	0.2%
45	New Hampshire	999	0.2%
46	Rhode Island	916	0.2%
47	Wyoming	735	0.1%
48	Vermont	695	0.1%
49	North Dakota	646	0.1%
50	Maine	606	0.1%
	District of Columbia	9,434	1.8%

Source: U.S. Department of Justice, Bureau of Justice Statistics
"Correctional Populations in the United States, 1998" (forthcoming in 2001)
*Preliminary data. Includes conditional releases, unconditional releases, escapees, out on appeal, deaths and other releases. Does not include 29,708 federal prisoners released.

State Prisoners Released with Conditions in 1998

National Total = 403,902 Prisoners*

ALPHA ORDER

RANK	STATE	PRISONERS	% of USA
20	Alabama	4,420	1.1%
36	Alaska	1,862	0.5%
15	Arizona	6,917	1.7%
18	Arkansas	4,854	1.2%
1	California	122,094	30.2%
21	Colorado	4,387	1.1%
38	Connecticut	1,104	0.3%
48	Delaware	454	0.1%
11	Florida	8,674	2.1%
13	Georgia	8,602	2.1%
35	Hawaii	2,042	0.5%
34	Idaho	2,127	0.5%
4	Illinois	22,662	5.6%
12	Indiana	8,603	2.1%
28	Iowa	3,366	0.8%
25	Kansas	3,910	1.0%
26	Kentucky	3,739	0.9%
5	Louisiana	13,179	3.3%
50	Maine	352	0.1%
10	Maryland	9,205	2.3%
39	Massachusetts	953	0.2%
8	Michigan	10,500	2.6%
27	Minnesota	3,544	0.9%
33	Mississippi	2,193	0.5%
7	Missouri	10,636	2.6%
41	Montana	839	0.2%
44	Nebraska	702	0.2%
32	Nevada	2,255	0.6%
43	New Hampshire	768	0.2%
9	New Jersey	9,654	2.4%
37	New Mexico	1,421	0.4%
3	New York	24,197	6.0%
16	North Carolina	6,560	1.6%
47	North Dakota	499	0.1%
6	Ohio	11,643	2.9%
29	Oklahoma	3,104	0.8%
31	Oregon	2,584	0.6%
14	Pennsylvania	7,285	1.8%
40	Rhode Island	877	0.2%
23	South Carolina	4,134	1.0%
42	South Dakota	793	0.2%
17	Tennessee	5,288	1.3%
2	Texas	40,550	10.0%
30	Utah	2,673	0.7%
46	Vermont	608	0.2%
22	Virginia	4,193	1.0%
24	Washington	3,983	1.0%
45	West Virginia	686	0.2%
19	Wisconsin	4,523	1.1%
49	Wyoming	420	0.1%

RANK ORDER

RANK	STATE	PRISONERS	% of USA
1	California	122,094	30.2%
2	Texas	40,550	10.0%
3	New York	24,197	6.0%
4	Illinois	22,662	5.6%
5	Louisiana	13,179	3.3%
6	Ohio	11,643	2.9%
7	Missouri	10,636	2.6%
8	Michigan	10,500	2.6%
9	New Jersey	9,654	2.4%
10	Maryland	9,205	2.3%
11	Florida	8,674	2.1%
12	Indiana	8,603	2.1%
13	Georgia	8,602	2.1%
14	Pennsylvania	7,285	1.8%
15	Arizona	6,917	1.7%
16	North Carolina	6,560	1.6%
17	Tennessee	5,288	1.3%
18	Arkansas	4,854	1.2%
19	Wisconsin	4,523	1.1%
20	Alabama	4,420	1.1%
21	Colorado	4,387	1.1%
22	Virginia	4,193	1.0%
23	South Carolina	4,134	1.0%
24	Washington	3,983	1.0%
25	Kansas	3,910	1.0%
26	Kentucky	3,739	0.9%
27	Minnesota	3,544	0.9%
28	Iowa	3,366	0.8%
29	Oklahoma	3,104	0.8%
30	Utah	2,673	0.7%
31	Oregon	2,584	0.6%
32	Nevada	2,255	0.6%
33	Mississippi	2,193	0.5%
34	Idaho	2,127	0.5%
35	Hawaii	2,042	0.5%
36	Alaska	1,862	0.5%
37	New Mexico	1,421	0.4%
38	Connecticut	1,104	0.3%
39	Massachusetts	953	0.2%
40	Rhode Island	877	0.2%
41	Montana	839	0.2%
42	South Dakota	793	0.2%
43	New Hampshire	768	0.2%
44	Nebraska	702	0.2%
45	West Virginia	686	0.2%
46	Vermont	608	0.2%
47	North Dakota	499	0.1%
48	Delaware	454	0.1%
49	Wyoming	420	0.1%
50	Maine	352	0.1%
	District of Columbia	3,284	0.8%

Source: U.S. Department of Justice, Bureau of Justice Statistics
   "Correctional Populations in the United States, 1998" (forthcoming in 2001)
*Preliminary data. Released on parole, probation, supervised mandatory release or other conditions. Does not include 2,148 federal prisoners released with conditions.

State Prisoners Released Conditionally as a Percent of All Releases in 1998

National Percent = 76.0% of Prisoners Released*

ALPHA ORDER				RANK ORDER		
RANK	STATE	PERCENT		RANK	STATE	PERCENT
36	Alabama	60.7		1	Oregon	96.5
26	Alaska	69.6		2	Rhode Island	95.7
16	Arizona	80.7		3	California	94.1
11	Arkansas	87.0		4	Louisiana	93.4
3	California	94.1		5	Indiana	92.7
24	Colorado	72.8		6	Kansas	92.1
31	Connecticut	66.5		7	Utah	90.5
50	Delaware	23.4		8	Illinois	90.3
48	Florida	37.9		9	Vermont	87.5
29	Georgia	68.2		10	Minnesota	87.4
34	Hawaii	62.7		11	Arkansas	87.0
15	Idaho	85.6		12	Maryland	86.6
8	Illinois	90.3		13	New York	86.5
5	Indiana	92.7		14	Missouri	86.0
19	Iowa	77.5		15	Idaho	85.6
6	Kansas	92.1		16	Arizona	80.7
43	Kentucky	49.2		17	Michigan	78.8
4	Louisiana	93.4		18	Pennsylvania	78.6
37	Maine	58.1		19	Iowa	77.5
12	Maryland	86.6		20	North Dakota	77.2
49	Massachusetts	28.6		21	New Hampshire	76.9
17	Michigan	78.8		22	Montana	76.6
10	Minnesota	87.4		23	Texas	73.5
44	Mississippi	48.8		24	Colorado	72.8
14	Missouri	86.0		25	Wisconsin	70.0
22	Montana	76.6		26	Alaska	69.6
46	Nebraska	45.8		27	New Jersey	68.8
41	Nevada	54.4		27	Tennessee	68.8
21	New Hampshire	76.9		29	Georgia	68.2
27	New Jersey	68.8		29	South Dakota	68.2
33	New Mexico	62.8		31	Connecticut	66.5
13	New York	86.5		32	Washington	64.2
40	North Carolina	55.9		33	New Mexico	62.8
20	North Dakota	77.2		34	Hawaii	62.7
38	Ohio	57.6		35	West Virginia	61.6
47	Oklahoma	44.7		36	Alabama	60.7
1	Oregon	96.5		37	Maine	58.1
18	Pennsylvania	78.6		38	Ohio	57.6
2	Rhode Island	95.7		39	Wyoming	57.1
42	South Carolina	52.1		40	North Carolina	55.9
29	South Dakota	68.2		41	Nevada	54.4
27	Tennessee	68.8		42	South Carolina	52.1
23	Texas	73.5		43	Kentucky	49.2
7	Utah	90.5		44	Mississippi	48.8
9	Vermont	87.5		45	Virginia	46.6
45	Virginia	46.6		46	Nebraska	45.8
32	Washington	64.2		47	Oklahoma	44.7
35	West Virginia	61.6		48	Florida	37.9
25	Wisconsin	70.0		49	Massachusetts	28.6
39	Wyoming	57.1		50	Delaware	23.4
					District of Columbia	34.8

Source: Morgan Quitno Press using data from U.S. Department of Justice, Bureau of Justice Statistics
     "Correctional Populations in the United States, 1998" (forthcoming in 2001)
*Preliminary data. Released on parole, probation, supervised mandatory release or other conditions. Does not
include federal prisoners released with conditions. Federal percent is 7.2% of releases. The combined state and
federal percent is 72.4% of prisoners released are released with conditions.

State Prisoners Released on Parole in 1998

National Total = 135,138 Prisoners*

ALPHA ORDER

RANK	STATE	PRISONERS	% of USA
14	Alabama	2,688	2.0%
43	Alaska	80	0.1%
35	Arizona	600	0.4%
10	Arkansas	4,428	3.3%
49	California	0	0.0%
13	Colorado	3,011	2.2%
41	Connecticut	211	0.2%
46	Delaware	26	0.0%
42	Florida	160	0.1%
6	Georgia	7,195	5.3%
29	Hawaii	852	0.6%
26	Idaho	988	0.7%
45	Illinois	32	0.0%
49	Indiana	0	0.0%
22	Iowa	1,729	1.3%
11	Kansas	3,691	2.7%
18	Kentucky	2,611	1.9%
27	Louisiana	978	0.7%
48	Maine	3	0.0%
12	Maryland	3,352	2.5%
28	Massachusetts	953	0.7%
3	Michigan	10,500	7.8%
47	Minnesota	10	0.0%
25	Mississippi	1,084	0.8%
9	Missouri	4,828	3.6%
34	Montana	634	0.5%
30	Nebraska	702	0.5%
21	Nevada	2,255	1.7%
33	New Hampshire	636	0.5%
4	New Jersey	8,821	6.5%
23	New Mexico	1,420	1.1%
1	New York	18,367	13.6%
7	North Carolina	6,560	4.9%
39	North Dakota	285	0.2%
8	Ohio	5,656	4.2%
37	Oklahoma	317	0.2%
20	Oregon	2,386	1.8%
5	Pennsylvania	7,285	5.4%
36	Rhode Island	427	0.3%
15	South Carolina	2,687	2.0%
31	South Dakota	688	0.5%
17	Tennessee	2,626	1.9%
2	Texas	13,037	9.6%
16	Utah	2,673	2.0%
40	Vermont	231	0.2%
24	Virginia	1,356	1.0%
44	Washington	63	0.0%
32	West Virginia	664	0.5%
19	Wisconsin	2,609	1.9%
38	Wyoming	311	0.2%

RANK ORDER

RANK	STATE	PRISONERS	% of USA
1	New York	18,367	13.6%
2	Texas	13,037	9.6%
3	Michigan	10,500	7.8%
4	New Jersey	8,821	6.5%
5	Pennsylvania	7,285	5.4%
6	Georgia	7,195	5.3%
7	North Carolina	6,560	4.9%
8	Ohio	5,656	4.2%
9	Missouri	4,828	3.6%
10	Arkansas	4,428	3.3%
11	Kansas	3,691	2.7%
12	Maryland	3,352	2.5%
13	Colorado	3,011	2.2%
14	Alabama	2,688	2.0%
15	South Carolina	2,687	2.0%
16	Utah	2,673	2.0%
17	Tennessee	2,626	1.9%
18	Kentucky	2,611	1.9%
19	Wisconsin	2,609	1.9%
20	Oregon	2,386	1.8%
21	Nevada	2,255	1.7%
22	Iowa	1,729	1.3%
23	New Mexico	1,420	1.1%
24	Virginia	1,356	1.0%
25	Mississippi	1,084	0.8%
26	Idaho	988	0.7%
27	Louisiana	978	0.7%
28	Massachusetts	953	0.7%
29	Hawaii	852	0.6%
30	Nebraska	702	0.5%
31	South Dakota	688	0.5%
32	West Virginia	664	0.5%
33	New Hampshire	636	0.5%
34	Montana	634	0.5%
35	Arizona	600	0.4%
36	Rhode Island	427	0.3%
37	Oklahoma	317	0.2%
38	Wyoming	311	0.2%
39	North Dakota	285	0.2%
40	Vermont	231	0.2%
41	Connecticut	211	0.2%
42	Florida	160	0.1%
43	Alaska	80	0.1%
44	Washington	63	0.0%
45	Illinois	32	0.0%
46	Delaware	26	0.0%
47	Minnesota	10	0.0%
48	Maine	3	0.0%
49	California	0	0.0%
49	Indiana	0	0.0%
	District of Columbia	2,432	1.8%

Source: U.S. Department of Justice, Bureau of Justice Statistics
"Correctional Populations in the United States, 1998" (forthcoming in 2001)
Preliminary data. Does not include 1,328 federal prisoners released on parole.

State Prisoners Released on Probation in 1998

National Total = 37,085 Prisoners*

<table>
<tr><td colspan="4">ALPHA ORDER</td><td colspan="4">RANK ORDER</td></tr>
<tr><th>RANK</th><th>STATE</th><th>PRISONERS</th><th>% of USA</th><th>RANK</th><th>STATE</th><th>PRISONERS</th><th>% of USA</th></tr>
<tr><td>8</td><td>Alabama</td><td>1,644</td><td>4.4%</td><td>1</td><td>Texas</td><td>7,649</td><td>20.6%</td></tr>
<tr><td>11</td><td>Alaska</td><td>1,156</td><td>3.1%</td><td>2</td><td>Indiana</td><td>4,290</td><td>11.6%</td></tr>
<tr><td>27</td><td>Arizona</td><td>30</td><td>0.1%</td><td>3</td><td>Florida</td><td>3,898</td><td>10.5%</td></tr>
<tr><td>30</td><td>Arkansas</td><td>0</td><td>0.0%</td><td>4</td><td>Missouri</td><td>3,647</td><td>9.8%</td></tr>
<tr><td>30</td><td>California</td><td>0</td><td>0.0%</td><td>5</td><td>Oklahoma</td><td>2,532</td><td>6.8%</td></tr>
<tr><td>18</td><td>Colorado</td><td>215</td><td>0.6%</td><td>6</td><td>Ohio</td><td>1,990</td><td>5.4%</td></tr>
<tr><td>30</td><td>Connecticut</td><td>0</td><td>0.0%</td><td>7</td><td>Tennessee</td><td>1,791</td><td>4.8%</td></tr>
<tr><td>30</td><td>Delaware</td><td>0</td><td>0.0%</td><td>8</td><td>Alabama</td><td>1,644</td><td>4.4%</td></tr>
<tr><td>3</td><td>Florida</td><td>3,898</td><td>10.5%</td><td>9</td><td>South Carolina</td><td>1,424</td><td>3.8%</td></tr>
<tr><td>25</td><td>Georgia</td><td>42</td><td>0.1%</td><td>10</td><td>Hawaii</td><td>1,186</td><td>3.2%</td></tr>
<tr><td>10</td><td>Hawaii</td><td>1,186</td><td>3.2%</td><td>11</td><td>Alaska</td><td>1,156</td><td>3.1%</td></tr>
<tr><td>12</td><td>Idaho</td><td>1,139</td><td>3.1%</td><td>12</td><td>Idaho</td><td>1,139</td><td>3.1%</td></tr>
<tr><td>30</td><td>Illinois</td><td>0</td><td>0.0%</td><td>13</td><td>Kentucky</td><td>1,128</td><td>3.0%</td></tr>
<tr><td>2</td><td>Indiana</td><td>4,290</td><td>11.6%</td><td>14</td><td>Mississippi</td><td>1,109</td><td>3.0%</td></tr>
<tr><td>15</td><td>Iowa</td><td>694</td><td>1.9%</td><td>15</td><td>Iowa</td><td>694</td><td>1.9%</td></tr>
<tr><td>23</td><td>Kansas</td><td>59</td><td>0.2%</td><td>16</td><td>Rhode Island</td><td>444</td><td>1.2%</td></tr>
<tr><td>13</td><td>Kentucky</td><td>1,128</td><td>3.0%</td><td>17</td><td>Maine</td><td>311</td><td>0.8%</td></tr>
<tr><td>24</td><td>Louisiana</td><td>43</td><td>0.1%</td><td>18</td><td>Colorado</td><td>215</td><td>0.6%</td></tr>
<tr><td>17</td><td>Maine</td><td>311</td><td>0.8%</td><td>19</td><td>North Dakota</td><td>206</td><td>0.6%</td></tr>
<tr><td>30</td><td>Maryland</td><td>0</td><td>0.0%</td><td>20</td><td>Montana</td><td>205</td><td>0.6%</td></tr>
<tr><td>30</td><td>Massachusetts</td><td>0</td><td>0.0%</td><td>21</td><td>Wyoming</td><td>109</td><td>0.3%</td></tr>
<tr><td>30</td><td>Michigan</td><td>0</td><td>0.0%</td><td>22</td><td>New Hampshire</td><td>89</td><td>0.2%</td></tr>
<tr><td>30</td><td>Minnesota</td><td>0</td><td>0.0%</td><td>23</td><td>Kansas</td><td>59</td><td>0.2%</td></tr>
<tr><td>14</td><td>Mississippi</td><td>1,109</td><td>3.0%</td><td>24</td><td>Louisiana</td><td>43</td><td>0.1%</td></tr>
<tr><td>4</td><td>Missouri</td><td>3,647</td><td>9.8%</td><td>25</td><td>Georgia</td><td>42</td><td>0.1%</td></tr>
<tr><td>20</td><td>Montana</td><td>205</td><td>0.6%</td><td>26</td><td>Vermont</td><td>32</td><td>0.1%</td></tr>
<tr><td>30</td><td>Nebraska</td><td>0</td><td>0.0%</td><td>27</td><td>Arizona</td><td>30</td><td>0.1%</td></tr>
<tr><td>30</td><td>Nevada</td><td>0</td><td>0.0%</td><td>28</td><td>West Virginia</td><td>22</td><td>0.1%</td></tr>
<tr><td>22</td><td>New Hampshire</td><td>89</td><td>0.2%</td><td>29</td><td>New Mexico</td><td>1</td><td>0.0%</td></tr>
<tr><td>30</td><td>New Jersey</td><td>0</td><td>0.0%</td><td>30</td><td>Arkansas</td><td>0</td><td>0.0%</td></tr>
<tr><td>29</td><td>New Mexico</td><td>1</td><td>0.0%</td><td>30</td><td>California</td><td>0</td><td>0.0%</td></tr>
<tr><td>30</td><td>New York</td><td>0</td><td>0.0%</td><td>30</td><td>Connecticut</td><td>0</td><td>0.0%</td></tr>
<tr><td>30</td><td>North Carolina</td><td>0</td><td>0.0%</td><td>30</td><td>Delaware</td><td>0</td><td>0.0%</td></tr>
<tr><td>19</td><td>North Dakota</td><td>206</td><td>0.6%</td><td>30</td><td>Illinois</td><td>0</td><td>0.0%</td></tr>
<tr><td>6</td><td>Ohio</td><td>1,990</td><td>5.4%</td><td>30</td><td>Maryland</td><td>0</td><td>0.0%</td></tr>
<tr><td>5</td><td>Oklahoma</td><td>2,532</td><td>6.8%</td><td>30</td><td>Massachusetts</td><td>0</td><td>0.0%</td></tr>
<tr><td>30</td><td>Oregon</td><td>0</td><td>0.0%</td><td>30</td><td>Michigan</td><td>0</td><td>0.0%</td></tr>
<tr><td>30</td><td>Pennsylvania</td><td>0</td><td>0.0%</td><td>30</td><td>Minnesota</td><td>0</td><td>0.0%</td></tr>
<tr><td>16</td><td>Rhode Island</td><td>444</td><td>1.2%</td><td>30</td><td>Nebraska</td><td>0</td><td>0.0%</td></tr>
<tr><td>9</td><td>South Carolina</td><td>1,424</td><td>3.8%</td><td>30</td><td>Nevada</td><td>0</td><td>0.0%</td></tr>
<tr><td>30</td><td>South Dakota</td><td>0</td><td>0.0%</td><td>30</td><td>New Jersey</td><td>0</td><td>0.0%</td></tr>
<tr><td>7</td><td>Tennessee</td><td>1,791</td><td>4.8%</td><td>30</td><td>New York</td><td>0</td><td>0.0%</td></tr>
<tr><td>1</td><td>Texas</td><td>7,649</td><td>20.6%</td><td>30</td><td>North Carolina</td><td>0</td><td>0.0%</td></tr>
<tr><td>30</td><td>Utah</td><td>0</td><td>0.0%</td><td>30</td><td>Oregon</td><td>0</td><td>0.0%</td></tr>
<tr><td>26</td><td>Vermont</td><td>32</td><td>0.1%</td><td>30</td><td>Pennsylvania</td><td>0</td><td>0.0%</td></tr>
<tr><td>30</td><td>Virginia</td><td>0</td><td>0.0%</td><td>30</td><td>South Dakota</td><td>0</td><td>0.0%</td></tr>
<tr><td>30</td><td>Washington</td><td>0</td><td>0.0%</td><td>30</td><td>Utah</td><td>0</td><td>0.0%</td></tr>
<tr><td>28</td><td>West Virginia</td><td>22</td><td>0.1%</td><td>30</td><td>Virginia</td><td>0</td><td>0.0%</td></tr>
<tr><td>30</td><td>Wisconsin</td><td>0</td><td>0.0%</td><td>30</td><td>Washington</td><td>0</td><td>0.0%</td></tr>
<tr><td>21</td><td>Wyoming</td><td>109</td><td>0.3%</td><td>30</td><td>Wisconsin</td><td>0</td><td>0.0%</td></tr>
<tr><td></td><td></td><td></td><td></td><td></td><td>District of Columbia</td><td>0</td><td>0.0%</td></tr>
</table>

Source: U.S. Department of Justice, Bureau of Justice Statistics
  "Correctional Populations in the United States, 1998" (forthcoming in 2001)
*Preliminary data. Does not include 79 federal prisoners released on probation.

State Prisoners Released on Supervised Mandatory Release in 1998

National Total = 210,394 Prisoners*

ALPHA ORDER

RANK	STATE	PRISONERS	% of USA
18	Alabama	0	0.0%
15	Alaska	327	0.2%
17	Arizona	65	0.0%
18	Arkansas	0	0.0%
1	California	122,094	58.0%
13	Colorado	1,161	0.6%
18	Connecticut	0	0.0%
14	Delaware	428	0.2%
18	Florida	0	0.0%
18	Georgia	0	0.0%
18	Hawaii	0	0.0%
18	Idaho	0	0.0%
2	Illinois	22,630	10.8%
7	Indiana	4,313	2.0%
18	Iowa	0	0.0%
18	Kansas	0	0.0%
18	Kentucky	0	0.0%
4	Louisiana	12,158	5.8%
18	Maine	0	0.0%
5	Maryland	5,845	2.8%
18	Massachusetts	0	0.0%
18	Michigan	0	0.0%
11	Minnesota	2,738	1.3%
18	Mississippi	0	0.0%
18	Missouri	0	0.0%
18	Montana	0	0.0%
18	Nebraska	0	0.0%
18	Nevada	0	0.0%
18	New Hampshire	0	0.0%
18	New Jersey	0	0.0%
18	New Mexico	0	0.0%
6	New York	5,830	2.8%
18	North Carolina	0	0.0%
18	North Dakota	0	0.0%
8	Ohio	3,997	1.9%
18	Oklahoma	0	0.0%
18	Oregon	0	0.0%
18	Pennsylvania	0	0.0%
18	Rhode Island	0	0.0%
18	South Carolina	0	0.0%
16	South Dakota	105	0.0%
18	Tennessee	0	0.0%
3	Texas	19,864	9.4%
18	Utah	0	0.0%
18	Vermont	0	0.0%
10	Virginia	2,837	1.3%
9	Washington	3,920	1.9%
18	West Virginia	0	0.0%
12	Wisconsin	1,913	0.9%
18	Wyoming	0	0.0%

RANK ORDER

RANK	STATE	PRISONERS	% of USA
1	California	122,094	58.0%
2	Illinois	22,630	10.8%
3	Texas	19,864	9.4%
4	Louisiana	12,158	5.8%
5	Maryland	5,845	2.8%
6	New York	5,830	2.8%
7	Indiana	4,313	2.0%
8	Ohio	3,997	1.9%
9	Washington	3,920	1.9%
10	Virginia	2,837	1.3%
11	Minnesota	2,738	1.3%
12	Wisconsin	1,913	0.9%
13	Colorado	1,161	0.6%
14	Delaware	428	0.2%
15	Alaska	327	0.2%
16	South Dakota	105	0.0%
17	Arizona	65	0.0%
18	Alabama	0	0.0%
18	Arkansas	0	0.0%
18	Connecticut	0	0.0%
18	Florida	0	0.0%
18	Georgia	0	0.0%
18	Hawaii	0	0.0%
18	Idaho	0	0.0%
18	Iowa	0	0.0%
18	Kansas	0	0.0%
18	Kentucky	0	0.0%
18	Maine	0	0.0%
18	Massachusetts	0	0.0%
18	Michigan	0	0.0%
18	Mississippi	0	0.0%
18	Missouri	0	0.0%
18	Montana	0	0.0%
18	Nebraska	0	0.0%
18	Nevada	0	0.0%
18	New Hampshire	0	0.0%
18	New Jersey	0	0.0%
18	New Mexico	0	0.0%
18	North Carolina	0	0.0%
18	North Dakota	0	0.0%
18	Oklahoma	0	0.0%
18	Oregon	0	0.0%
18	Pennsylvania	0	0.0%
18	Rhode Island	0	0.0%
18	South Carolina	0	0.0%
18	Tennessee	0	0.0%
18	Utah	0	0.0%
18	Vermont	0	0.0%
18	West Virginia	0	0.0%
18	Wyoming	0	0.0%
	District of Columbia	169	0.1%

Source: U.S. Department of Justice, Bureau of Justice Statistics
  "Correctional Populations in the United States, 1998" (forthcoming in 2001)
  *Preliminary data. Does not include 741 federal prisoners released on supervised mandatory release.

State Prisoners Released Unconditionally in 1998

National Total = 102,147 Prisoners*

RANK	STATE	PRISONERS	% of USA
12	Alabama	2,375	2.3%
29	Alaska	746	0.7%
21	Arizona	1,268	1.2%
33	Arkansas	584	0.6%
11	California	2,603	2.5%
24	Colorado	1,103	1.1%
41	Connecticut	238	0.2%
26	Delaware	911	0.9%
1	Florida	13,504	13.2%
10	Georgia	3,431	3.4%
45	Hawaii	205	0.2%
37	Idaho	331	0.3%
20	Illinois	1,409	1.4%
32	Indiana	614	0.6%
28	Iowa	748	0.7%
38	Kansas	301	0.3%
8	Kentucky	3,629	3.6%
31	Louisiana	671	0.7%
42	Maine	229	0.2%
22	Maryland	1,225	1.2%
16	Massachusetts	1,923	1.9%
23	Michigan	1,174	1.1%
34	Minnesota	504	0.5%
13	Mississippi	2,170	2.1%
25	Missouri	1,036	1.0%
43	Montana	216	0.2%
27	Nebraska	809	0.8%
17	Nevada	1,862	1.8%
44	New Hampshire	206	0.2%
6	New Jersey	4,116	4.0%
30	New Mexico	712	0.7%
18	New York	1,648	1.6%
4	North Carolina	5,007	4.9%
47	North Dakota	140	0.1%
3	Ohio	8,372	8.2%
7	Oklahoma	3,685	3.6%
50	Oregon	4	0.0%
19	Pennsylvania	1,608	1.6%
49	Rhode Island	6	0.0%
9	South Carolina	3,488	3.4%
36	South Dakota	356	0.3%
14	Tennessee	2,168	2.1%
2	Texas	12,922	12.7%
40	Utah	253	0.2%
48	Vermont	81	0.1%
5	Virginia	4,743	4.6%
15	Washington	2,037	2.0%
35	West Virginia	410	0.4%
46	Wisconsin	195	0.2%
39	Wyoming	277	0.3%

RANK	STATE	PRISONERS	% of USA
1	Florida	13,504	13.2%
2	Texas	12,922	12.7%
3	Ohio	8,372	8.2%
4	North Carolina	5,007	4.9%
5	Virginia	4,743	4.6%
6	New Jersey	4,116	4.0%
7	Oklahoma	3,685	3.6%
8	Kentucky	3,629	3.6%
9	South Carolina	3,488	3.4%
10	Georgia	3,431	3.4%
11	California	2,603	2.5%
12	Alabama	2,375	2.3%
13	Mississippi	2,170	2.1%
14	Tennessee	2,168	2.1%
15	Washington	2,037	2.0%
16	Massachusetts	1,923	1.9%
17	Nevada	1,862	1.8%
18	New York	1,648	1.6%
19	Pennsylvania	1,608	1.6%
20	Illinois	1,409	1.4%
21	Arizona	1,268	1.2%
22	Maryland	1,225	1.2%
23	Michigan	1,174	1.1%
24	Colorado	1,103	1.1%
25	Missouri	1,036	1.0%
26	Delaware	911	0.9%
27	Nebraska	809	0.8%
28	Iowa	748	0.7%
29	Alaska	746	0.7%
30	New Mexico	712	0.7%
31	Louisiana	671	0.7%
32	Indiana	614	0.6%
33	Arkansas	584	0.6%
34	Minnesota	504	0.5%
35	West Virginia	410	0.4%
36	South Dakota	356	0.3%
37	Idaho	331	0.3%
38	Kansas	301	0.3%
39	Wyoming	277	0.3%
40	Utah	253	0.2%
41	Connecticut	238	0.2%
42	Maine	229	0.2%
43	Montana	216	0.2%
44	New Hampshire	206	0.2%
45	Hawaii	205	0.2%
46	Wisconsin	195	0.2%
47	North Dakota	140	0.1%
48	Vermont	81	0.1%
49	Rhode Island	6	0.0%
50	Oregon	4	0.0%
	District of Columbia	3,894	3.8%

Source: U.S. Department of Justice, Bureau of Justice Statistics
"Correctional Populations in the United States, 1998" (forthcoming in 2001)
*Preliminary data. Does not include 23,939 federal prisoners released without conditions.

State Prisoners Released Unconditionally as a Percent of All Releases in 1998

National Percent = 19.2% of Released Prisoners*

ALPHA ORDER

RANK	STATE	PERCENT
17	Alabama	32.6
22	Alaska	27.9
31	Arizona	14.8
37	Arkansas	10.5
48	California	2.0
28	Colorado	18.3
32	Connecticut	14.3
8	Delaware	46.9
1	Florida	59.0
23	Georgia	27.2
43	Hawaii	6.3
33	Idaho	13.3
45	Illinois	5.6
42	Indiana	6.6
30	Iowa	17.2
41	Kansas	7.1
7	Kentucky	47.7
46	Louisiana	4.8
13	Maine	37.8
36	Maryland	11.5
2	Massachusetts	57.7
38	Michigan	8.8
34	Minnesota	12.4
6	Mississippi	48.3
40	Missouri	8.4
27	Montana	19.7
4	Nebraska	52.8
9	Nevada	44.9
26	New Hampshire	20.6
20	New Jersey	29.3
18	New Mexico	31.4
44	New York	5.9
11	North Carolina	42.7
25	North Dakota	21.7
12	Ohio	41.4
3	Oklahoma	53.0
50	Oregon	0.1
29	Pennsylvania	17.3
49	Rhode Island	0.7
10	South Carolina	43.9
19	South Dakota	30.6
21	Tennessee	28.2
24	Texas	23.4
39	Utah	8.6
35	Vermont	11.7
5	Virginia	52.7
16	Washington	32.8
15	West Virginia	36.8
47	Wisconsin	3.0
14	Wyoming	37.7

RANK ORDER

RANK	STATE	PERCENT
1	Florida	59.0
2	Massachusetts	57.7
3	Oklahoma	53.0
4	Nebraska	52.8
5	Virginia	52.7
6	Mississippi	48.3
7	Kentucky	47.7
8	Delaware	46.9
9	Nevada	44.9
10	South Carolina	43.9
11	North Carolina	42.7
12	Ohio	41.4
13	Maine	37.8
14	Wyoming	37.7
15	West Virginia	36.8
16	Washington	32.8
17	Alabama	32.6
18	New Mexico	31.4
19	South Dakota	30.6
20	New Jersey	29.3
21	Tennessee	28.2
22	Alaska	27.9
23	Georgia	27.2
24	Texas	23.4
25	North Dakota	21.7
26	New Hampshire	20.6
27	Montana	19.7
28	Colorado	18.3
29	Pennsylvania	17.3
30	Iowa	17.2
31	Arizona	14.8
32	Connecticut	14.3
33	Idaho	13.3
34	Minnesota	12.4
35	Vermont	11.7
36	Maryland	11.5
37	Arkansas	10.5
38	Michigan	8.8
39	Utah	8.6
40	Missouri	8.4
41	Kansas	7.1
42	Indiana	6.6
43	Hawaii	6.3
44	New York	5.9
45	Illinois	5.6
46	Louisiana	4.8
47	Wisconsin	3.0
48	California	2.0
49	Rhode Island	0.7
50	Oregon	0.1
	District of Columbia	41.3

Source: Morgan Quitno Press using data from U.S. Department of Justice, Bureau of Justice Statistics
    "Correctional Populations in the United States, 1998" (forthcoming in 2001)
*Preliminary data. Does not include federal prisoners released without conditions. Federal percent is 80.6% of releases. The combined state and federal percent is 22.5% of prisoners released are released without conditions.

State Prisoners Released on Appeal or Bond in 1998

National Total = 797 Prisoners*

<table>
<tr><td colspan="4">ALPHA ORDER</td><td colspan="4">RANK ORDER</td></tr>
<tr><td>RANK</td><td>STATE</td><td>PRISONERS</td><td>% of USA</td><td>RANK</td><td>STATE</td><td>PRISONERS</td><td>% of USA</td></tr>
<tr><td>5</td><td>Alabama</td><td>86</td><td>10.8%</td><td>1</td><td>Hawaii</td><td>125</td><td>15.7%</td></tr>
<tr><td>21</td><td>Alaska</td><td>3</td><td>0.4%</td><td>2</td><td>Michigan</td><td>105</td><td>13.2%</td></tr>
<tr><td>30</td><td>Arizona</td><td>0</td><td>0.0%</td><td>2</td><td>New York</td><td>105</td><td>13.2%</td></tr>
<tr><td>8</td><td>Arkansas</td><td>40</td><td>5.0%</td><td>4</td><td>New Jersey</td><td>102</td><td>12.8%</td></tr>
<tr><td>30</td><td>California</td><td>0</td><td>0.0%</td><td>5</td><td>Alabama</td><td>86</td><td>10.8%</td></tr>
<tr><td>12</td><td>Colorado</td><td>14</td><td>1.8%</td><td>6</td><td>Iowa</td><td>56</td><td>7.0%</td></tr>
<tr><td>26</td><td>Connecticut</td><td>1</td><td>0.1%</td><td>7</td><td>Ohio</td><td>43</td><td>5.4%</td></tr>
<tr><td>30</td><td>Delaware</td><td>0</td><td>0.0%</td><td>8</td><td>Arkansas</td><td>40</td><td>5.0%</td></tr>
<tr><td>26</td><td>Florida</td><td>1</td><td>0.1%</td><td>9</td><td>Missouri</td><td>20</td><td>2.5%</td></tr>
<tr><td>30</td><td>Georgia</td><td>0</td><td>0.0%</td><td>10</td><td>Utah</td><td>16</td><td>2.0%</td></tr>
<tr><td>1</td><td>Hawaii</td><td>125</td><td>15.7%</td><td>11</td><td>Washington</td><td>15</td><td>1.9%</td></tr>
<tr><td>30</td><td>Idaho</td><td>0</td><td>0.0%</td><td>12</td><td>Colorado</td><td>14</td><td>1.8%</td></tr>
<tr><td>13</td><td>Illinois</td><td>11</td><td>1.4%</td><td>13</td><td>Illinois</td><td>11</td><td>1.4%</td></tr>
<tr><td>30</td><td>Indiana</td><td>0</td><td>0.0%</td><td>13</td><td>South Carolina</td><td>11</td><td>1.4%</td></tr>
<tr><td>6</td><td>Iowa</td><td>56</td><td>7.0%</td><td>15</td><td>Kansas</td><td>7</td><td>0.9%</td></tr>
<tr><td>15</td><td>Kansas</td><td>7</td><td>0.9%</td><td>15</td><td>Oregon</td><td>7</td><td>0.9%</td></tr>
<tr><td>30</td><td>Kentucky</td><td>0</td><td>0.0%</td><td>17</td><td>North Dakota</td><td>5</td><td>0.6%</td></tr>
<tr><td>30</td><td>Louisiana</td><td>0</td><td>0.0%</td><td>18</td><td>Maine</td><td>4</td><td>0.5%</td></tr>
<tr><td>18</td><td>Maine</td><td>4</td><td>0.5%</td><td>18</td><td>Montana</td><td>4</td><td>0.5%</td></tr>
<tr><td>30</td><td>Maryland</td><td>0</td><td>0.0%</td><td>18</td><td>Pennsylvania</td><td>4</td><td>0.5%</td></tr>
<tr><td>30</td><td>Massachusetts</td><td>0</td><td>0.0%</td><td>21</td><td>Alaska</td><td>3</td><td>0.4%</td></tr>
<tr><td>2</td><td>Michigan</td><td>105</td><td>13.2%</td><td>21</td><td>Rhode Island</td><td>3</td><td>0.4%</td></tr>
<tr><td>30</td><td>Minnesota</td><td>0</td><td>0.0%</td><td>21</td><td>Wyoming</td><td>3</td><td>0.4%</td></tr>
<tr><td>30</td><td>Mississippi</td><td>0</td><td>0.0%</td><td>24</td><td>Nevada</td><td>2</td><td>0.3%</td></tr>
<tr><td>9</td><td>Missouri</td><td>20</td><td>2.5%</td><td>24</td><td>West Virginia</td><td>2</td><td>0.3%</td></tr>
<tr><td>18</td><td>Montana</td><td>4</td><td>0.5%</td><td>26</td><td>Connecticut</td><td>1</td><td>0.1%</td></tr>
<tr><td>30</td><td>Nebraska</td><td>0</td><td>0.0%</td><td>26</td><td>Florida</td><td>1</td><td>0.1%</td></tr>
<tr><td>24</td><td>Nevada</td><td>2</td><td>0.3%</td><td>26</td><td>New Mexico</td><td>1</td><td>0.1%</td></tr>
<tr><td>30</td><td>New Hampshire</td><td>0</td><td>0.0%</td><td>26</td><td>South Dakota</td><td>1</td><td>0.1%</td></tr>
<tr><td>4</td><td>New Jersey</td><td>102</td><td>12.8%</td><td>30</td><td>Arizona</td><td>0</td><td>0.0%</td></tr>
<tr><td>26</td><td>New Mexico</td><td>1</td><td>0.1%</td><td>30</td><td>California</td><td>0</td><td>0.0%</td></tr>
<tr><td>2</td><td>New York</td><td>105</td><td>13.2%</td><td>30</td><td>Delaware</td><td>0</td><td>0.0%</td></tr>
<tr><td>30</td><td>North Carolina</td><td>0</td><td>0.0%</td><td>30</td><td>Georgia</td><td>0</td><td>0.0%</td></tr>
<tr><td>17</td><td>North Dakota</td><td>5</td><td>0.6%</td><td>30</td><td>Idaho</td><td>0</td><td>0.0%</td></tr>
<tr><td>7</td><td>Ohio</td><td>43</td><td>5.4%</td><td>30</td><td>Indiana</td><td>0</td><td>0.0%</td></tr>
<tr><td>30</td><td>Oklahoma</td><td>0</td><td>0.0%</td><td>30</td><td>Kentucky</td><td>0</td><td>0.0%</td></tr>
<tr><td>15</td><td>Oregon</td><td>7</td><td>0.9%</td><td>30</td><td>Louisiana</td><td>0</td><td>0.0%</td></tr>
<tr><td>18</td><td>Pennsylvania</td><td>4</td><td>0.5%</td><td>30</td><td>Maryland</td><td>0</td><td>0.0%</td></tr>
<tr><td>21</td><td>Rhode Island</td><td>3</td><td>0.4%</td><td>30</td><td>Massachusetts</td><td>0</td><td>0.0%</td></tr>
<tr><td>13</td><td>South Carolina</td><td>11</td><td>1.4%</td><td>30</td><td>Minnesota</td><td>0</td><td>0.0%</td></tr>
<tr><td>26</td><td>South Dakota</td><td>1</td><td>0.1%</td><td>30</td><td>Mississippi</td><td>0</td><td>0.0%</td></tr>
<tr><td>30</td><td>Tennessee</td><td>0</td><td>0.0%</td><td>30</td><td>Nebraska</td><td>0</td><td>0.0%</td></tr>
<tr><td>30</td><td>Texas</td><td>0</td><td>0.0%</td><td>30</td><td>New Hampshire</td><td>0</td><td>0.0%</td></tr>
<tr><td>10</td><td>Utah</td><td>16</td><td>2.0%</td><td>30</td><td>North Carolina</td><td>0</td><td>0.0%</td></tr>
<tr><td>30</td><td>Vermont</td><td>0</td><td>0.0%</td><td>30</td><td>Oklahoma</td><td>0</td><td>0.0%</td></tr>
<tr><td>30</td><td>Virginia</td><td>0</td><td>0.0%</td><td>30</td><td>Tennessee</td><td>0</td><td>0.0%</td></tr>
<tr><td>11</td><td>Washington</td><td>15</td><td>1.9%</td><td>30</td><td>Texas</td><td>0</td><td>0.0%</td></tr>
<tr><td>24</td><td>West Virginia</td><td>2</td><td>0.3%</td><td>30</td><td>Vermont</td><td>0</td><td>0.0%</td></tr>
<tr><td>30</td><td>Wisconsin</td><td>0</td><td>0.0%</td><td>30</td><td>Virginia</td><td>0</td><td>0.0%</td></tr>
<tr><td>21</td><td>Wyoming</td><td>3</td><td>0.4%</td><td>30</td><td>Wisconsin</td><td>0</td><td>0.0%</td></tr>
<tr><td></td><td></td><td></td><td></td><td></td><td>District of Columbia</td><td>0</td><td>0.0%</td></tr>
</table>

Source: U.S. Department of Justice, Bureau of Justice Statistics
"Correctional Populations in the United States, 1998" (forthcoming in 2001)
*Preliminary data. Numbers of federal prisoners released on appeal or bond were not available.

State Prisoners Escaped in 1998

National Total = 6,530 Prisoners*

ALPHA ORDER

RANK	STATE	PRISONERS	% of USA
7	Alabama	221	3.4%
21	Alaska	41	0.6%
32	Arizona	10	0.2%
29	Arkansas	13	0.2%
6	California	319	4.9%
5	Colorado	347	5.3%
14	Connecticut	94	1.4%
44	Delaware	0	0.0%
8	Florida	144	2.2%
20	Georgia	47	0.7%
23	Hawaii	27	0.4%
25	Idaho	17	0.3%
3	Illinois	894	13.7%
25	Indiana	17	0.3%
39	Iowa	3	0.0%
34	Kansas	6	0.1%
15	Kentucky	93	1.4%
12	Louisiana	103	1.6%
34	Maine	6	0.1%
10	Maryland	118	1.8%
27	Massachusetts	16	0.2%
1	Michigan	1,249	19.1%
44	Minnesota	0	0.0%
16	Mississippi	73	1.1%
4	Missouri	622	9.5%
24	Montana	20	0.3%
27	Nebraska	16	0.2%
44	Nevada	0	0.0%
29	New Hampshire	13	0.2%
44	New Jersey	0	0.0%
42	New Mexico	1	0.0%
2	New York	1,117	17.1%
11	North Carolina	111	1.7%
42	North Dakota	1	0.0%
38	Ohio	4	0.1%
13	Oklahoma	101	1.5%
18	Oregon	64	1.0%
17	Pennsylvania	72	1.1%
34	Rhode Island	6	0.1%
22	South Carolina	39	0.6%
34	South Dakota	6	0.1%
19	Tennessee	63	1.0%
44	Texas	0	0.0%
33	Utah	7	0.1%
44	Vermont	0	0.0%
39	Virginia	3	0.0%
9	Washington	123	1.9%
31	West Virginia	11	0.2%
44	Wisconsin	0	0.0%
39	Wyoming	3	0.0%

RANK ORDER

RANK	STATE	PRISONERS	% of USA
1	Michigan	1,249	19.1%
2	New York	1,117	17.1%
3	Illinois	894	13.7%
4	Missouri	622	9.5%
5	Colorado	347	5.3%
6	California	319	4.9%
7	Alabama	221	3.4%
8	Florida	144	2.2%
9	Washington	123	1.9%
10	Maryland	118	1.8%
11	North Carolina	111	1.7%
12	Louisiana	103	1.6%
13	Oklahoma	101	1.5%
14	Connecticut	94	1.4%
15	Kentucky	93	1.4%
16	Mississippi	73	1.1%
17	Pennsylvania	72	1.1%
18	Oregon	64	1.0%
19	Tennessee	63	1.0%
20	Georgia	47	0.7%
21	Alaska	41	0.6%
22	South Carolina	39	0.6%
23	Hawaii	27	0.4%
24	Montana	20	0.3%
25	Idaho	17	0.3%
25	Indiana	17	0.3%
27	Massachusetts	16	0.2%
27	Nebraska	16	0.2%
29	Arkansas	13	0.2%
29	New Hampshire	13	0.2%
31	West Virginia	11	0.2%
32	Arizona	10	0.2%
33	Utah	7	0.1%
34	Kansas	6	0.1%
34	Maine	6	0.1%
34	Rhode Island	6	0.1%
34	South Dakota	6	0.1%
38	Ohio	4	0.1%
39	Iowa	3	0.0%
39	Virginia	3	0.0%
39	Wyoming	3	0.0%
42	New Mexico	1	0.0%
42	North Dakota	1	0.0%
44	Delaware	0	0.0%
44	Minnesota	0	0.0%
44	Nevada	0	0.0%
44	New Jersey	0	0.0%
44	Texas	0	0.0%
44	Vermont	0	0.0%
44	Wisconsin	0	0.0%
	District of Columbia	269	4.1%

Source: U.S. Department of Justice, Bureau of Justice Statistics
  "Correctional Populations in the United States, 1998" (forthcoming in 2001)
*Preliminary data. Includes AWOLs. Numbers of escaped federal prisoners were not available.

State Prisoner Deaths in 1998

National Total = 2,795 Deaths*

<u>ALPHA ORDER</u>

RANK	STATE	DEATHS	% of USA
11	Alabama	76	2.7%
43	Alaska	4	0.1%
15	Arizona	62	2.2%
24	Arkansas	35	1.3%
2	California	284	10.2%
29	Colorado	26	0.9%
26	Connecticut	33	1.2%
35	Delaware	9	0.3%
4	Florida	207	7.4%
8	Georgia	98	3.5%
33	Hawaii	11	0.4%
33	Idaho	11	0.4%
7	Illinois	99	3.5%
20	Indiana	46	1.6%
38	Iowa	7	0.3%
31	Kansas	21	0.8%
27	Kentucky	30	1.1%
10	Louisiana	80	2.9%
46	Maine	2	0.1%
20	Maryland	46	1.6%
30	Massachusetts	24	0.9%
9	Michigan	96	3.4%
36	Minnesota	8	0.3%
17	Mississippi	49	1.8%
22	Missouri	42	1.5%
38	Montana	7	0.3%
41	Nebraska	5	0.2%
28	Nevada	27	1.0%
36	New Hampshire	8	0.3%
13	New Jersey	69	2.5%
46	New Mexico	2	0.1%
3	New York	213	7.6%
18	North Carolina	48	1.7%
49	North Dakota	1	0.0%
5	Ohio	140	5.0%
16	Oklahoma	57	2.0%
32	Oregon	13	0.5%
6	Pennsylvania	127	4.5%
40	Rhode Island	6	0.2%
12	South Carolina	70	2.5%
46	South Dakota	2	0.1%
18	Tennessee	48	1.7%
1	Texas	373	13.3%
45	Utah	3	0.1%
49	Vermont	1	0.0%
14	Virginia	65	2.3%
23	Washington	41	1.5%
41	West Virginia	5	0.2%
25	Wisconsin	34	1.2%
43	Wyoming	4	0.1%

<u>RANK ORDER</u>

RANK	STATE	DEATHS	% of USA
1	Texas	373	13.3%
2	California	284	10.2%
3	New York	213	7.6%
4	Florida	207	7.4%
5	Ohio	140	5.0%
6	Pennsylvania	127	4.5%
7	Illinois	99	3.5%
8	Georgia	98	3.5%
9	Michigan	96	3.4%
10	Louisiana	80	2.9%
11	Alabama	76	2.7%
12	South Carolina	70	2.5%
13	New Jersey	69	2.5%
14	Virginia	65	2.3%
15	Arizona	62	2.2%
16	Oklahoma	57	2.0%
17	Mississippi	49	1.8%
18	North Carolina	48	1.7%
18	Tennessee	48	1.7%
20	Indiana	46	1.6%
20	Maryland	46	1.6%
22	Missouri	42	1.5%
23	Washington	41	1.5%
24	Arkansas	35	1.3%
25	Wisconsin	34	1.2%
26	Connecticut	33	1.2%
27	Kentucky	30	1.1%
28	Nevada	27	1.0%
29	Colorado	26	0.9%
30	Massachusetts	24	0.9%
31	Kansas	21	0.8%
32	Oregon	13	0.5%
33	Hawaii	11	0.4%
33	Idaho	11	0.4%
35	Delaware	9	0.3%
36	Minnesota	8	0.3%
36	New Hampshire	8	0.3%
38	Iowa	7	0.3%
38	Montana	7	0.3%
40	Rhode Island	6	0.2%
41	Nebraska	5	0.2%
41	West Virginia	5	0.2%
43	Alaska	4	0.1%
43	Wyoming	4	0.1%
45	Utah	3	0.1%
46	Maine	2	0.1%
46	New Mexico	2	0.1%
46	South Dakota	2	0.1%
49	North Dakota	1	0.0%
49	Vermont	1	0.0%
	District of Columbia	20	0.7%

Source: U.S. Department of Justice, Bureau of Justice Statistics
"Correctional Populations in the United States, 1998" (forthcoming in 2001)
*Preliminary data. Does not include 223 deaths of federal prisoners.

Death Rate of State Prisoners in 1998

National Rate = 2.4 State Prisoner Deaths per 1,000 Inmates*

ALPHA ORDER

RANK	STATE	RATE
3	Alabama	3.4
45	Alaska	1.0
21	Arizona	2.4
4	Arkansas	3.3
32	California	1.8
32	Colorado	1.8
31	Connecticut	1.9
37	Delaware	1.6
6	Florida	3.1
18	Georgia	2.5
24	Hawaii	2.2
12	Idaho	2.7
23	Illinois	2.3
21	Indiana	2.4
46	Iowa	0.9
15	Kansas	2.6
28	Kentucky	2.0
18	Louisiana	2.5
43	Maine	1.2
28	Maryland	2.0
28	Massachusetts	2.0
26	Michigan	2.1
39	Minnesota	1.4
8	Mississippi	2.9
35	Missouri	1.7
15	Montana	2.6
39	Nebraska	1.4
11	Nevada	2.8
1	New Hampshire	3.7
24	New Jersey	2.2
50	New Mexico	0.4
7	New York	3.0
38	North Carolina	1.5
44	North Dakota	1.1
8	Ohio	2.9
12	Oklahoma	2.7
39	Oregon	1.4
2	Pennsylvania	3.5
35	Rhode Island	1.7
5	South Carolina	3.2
47	South Dakota	0.8
12	Tennessee	2.7
15	Texas	2.6
48	Utah	0.7
48	Vermont	0.7
26	Virginia	2.1
8	Washington	2.9
39	West Virginia	1.4
32	Wisconsin	1.8
18	Wyoming	2.5

RANK ORDER

RANK	STATE	RATE
1	New Hampshire	3.7
2	Pennsylvania	3.5
3	Alabama	3.4
4	Arkansas	3.3
5	South Carolina	3.2
6	Florida	3.1
7	New York	3.0
8	Mississippi	2.9
8	Ohio	2.9
8	Washington	2.9
11	Nevada	2.8
12	Idaho	2.7
12	Oklahoma	2.7
12	Tennessee	2.7
15	Kansas	2.6
15	Montana	2.6
15	Texas	2.6
18	Georgia	2.5
18	Louisiana	2.5
18	Wyoming	2.5
21	Arizona	2.4
21	Indiana	2.4
23	Illinois	2.3
24	Hawaii	2.2
24	New Jersey	2.2
26	Michigan	2.1
26	Virginia	2.1
28	Kentucky	2.0
28	Maryland	2.0
28	Massachusetts	2.0
31	Connecticut	1.9
32	California	1.8
32	Colorado	1.8
32	Wisconsin	1.8
35	Missouri	1.7
35	Rhode Island	1.7
37	Delaware	1.6
38	North Carolina	1.5
39	Minnesota	1.4
39	Nebraska	1.4
39	Oregon	1.4
39	West Virginia	1.4
43	Maine	1.2
44	North Dakota	1.1
45	Alaska	1.0
46	Iowa	0.9
47	South Dakota	0.8
48	Utah	0.7
48	Vermont	0.7
50	New Mexico	0.4
	District of Columbia	2.0

Source: Morgan Quitno Press using data from U.S. Department of Justice, Bureau of Justice Statistics "Correctional Populations in the United States, 1998" (forthcoming in 2001)
Preliminary data. Does not include deaths of federal prisoners. Federal death rate is 1.8 deaths per 1,000 federal inmates. The combined federal and state rate is 2.3 prisoner deaths per 1,000 inmates.

State Prisoner Deaths by Illness or Other Natural Causes in 1998

National Total = 1,831 Deaths*

ALPHA ORDER

RANK	STATE	DEATHS	% of USA
NA	Alabama**	NA	NA
40	Alaska	4	0.2%
10	Arizona	50	2.7%
21	Arkansas	30	1.6%
1	California	208	11.4%
28	Colorado	18	1.0%
29	Connecticut	16	0.9%
30	Delaware	8	0.4%
4	Florida	130	7.1%
8	Georgia	70	3.8%
30	Hawaii	8	0.4%
30	Idaho	8	0.4%
9	Illinois	63	3.4%
13	Indiana	45	2.5%
34	Iowa	6	0.3%
26	Kansas	19	1.0%
21	Kentucky	30	1.6%
NA	Louisiana**	NA	NA
44	Maine	1	0.1%
23	Maryland	25	1.4%
25	Massachusetts	20	1.1%
7	Michigan	80	4.4%
34	Minnesota	6	0.3%
14	Mississippi	44	2.4%
20	Missouri	31	1.7%
36	Montana	5	0.3%
36	Nebraska	5	0.3%
26	Nevada	19	1.0%
36	New Hampshire	5	0.3%
18	New Jersey	36	2.0%
NA	New Mexico**	NA	NA
3	New York	158	8.6%
16	North Carolina	37	2.0%
44	North Dakota	1	0.1%
5	Ohio	124	6.8%
11	Oklahoma	47	2.6%
33	Oregon	7	0.4%
6	Pennsylvania	89	4.9%
43	Rhode Island	2	0.1%
12	South Carolina	46	2.5%
47	South Dakota	0	0.0%
15	Tennessee	38	2.1%
2	Texas	170	9.3%
41	Utah	3	0.2%
44	Vermont	1	0.1%
16	Virginia	37	2.0%
19	Washington	34	1.9%
36	West Virginia	5	0.3%
24	Wisconsin	24	1.3%
41	Wyoming	3	0.2%

RANK ORDER

RANK	STATE	DEATHS	% of USA
1	California	208	11.4%
2	Texas	170	9.3%
3	New York	158	8.6%
4	Florida	130	7.1%
5	Ohio	124	6.8%
6	Pennsylvania	89	4.9%
7	Michigan	80	4.4%
8	Georgia	70	3.8%
9	Illinois	63	3.4%
10	Arizona	50	2.7%
11	Oklahoma	47	2.6%
12	South Carolina	46	2.5%
13	Indiana	45	2.5%
14	Mississippi	44	2.4%
15	Tennessee	38	2.1%
16	North Carolina	37	2.0%
16	Virginia	37	2.0%
18	New Jersey	36	2.0%
19	Washington	34	1.9%
20	Missouri	31	1.7%
21	Arkansas	30	1.6%
21	Kentucky	30	1.6%
23	Maryland	25	1.4%
24	Wisconsin	24	1.3%
25	Massachusetts	20	1.1%
26	Kansas	19	1.0%
26	Nevada	19	1.0%
28	Colorado	18	1.0%
29	Connecticut	16	0.9%
30	Delaware	8	0.4%
30	Hawaii	8	0.4%
30	Idaho	8	0.4%
33	Oregon	7	0.4%
34	Iowa	6	0.3%
34	Minnesota	6	0.3%
36	Montana	5	0.3%
36	Nebraska	5	0.3%
36	New Hampshire	5	0.3%
36	West Virginia	5	0.3%
40	Alaska	4	0.2%
41	Utah	3	0.2%
41	Wyoming	3	0.2%
43	Rhode Island	2	0.1%
44	Maine	1	0.1%
44	North Dakota	1	0.1%
44	Vermont	1	0.1%
47	South Dakota	0	0.0%
NA	Alabama**	NA	NA
NA	Louisiana**	NA	NA
NA	New Mexico**	NA	NA
	District of Columbia	15	0.8%

Source: U.S. Department of Justice, Bureau of Justice Statistics
"Correctional Populations in the United States, 1998" (forthcoming in 2001)
*Preliminary data. Excludes AIDS. Federal data were not reported.
**Not available.

Deaths of State Prisoners by Illness or Other Natural Causes
As a Percent of All State Prison Deaths in 1998
National Percent = 65.5% of Deaths*

ALPHA ORDER

RANK ORDER

RANK	STATE	PERCENT		RANK	STATE	PERCENT
NA	Alabama**	NA		1	Alaska	100.0
1	Alaska	100.0		1	Kentucky	100.0
19	Arizona	80.6		1	Nebraska	100.0
13	Arkansas	85.7		1	North Dakota	100.0
26	California	73.2		1	Utah	100.0
34	Colorado	69.2		1	Vermont	100.0
44	Connecticut	48.5		1	West Virginia	100.0
11	Delaware	88.9		8	Indiana	97.8
37	Florida	62.8		9	Kansas	90.5
29	Georgia	71.4		10	Mississippi	89.8
27	Hawaii	72.7		11	Delaware	88.9
27	Idaho	72.7		12	Ohio	88.6
36	Illinois	63.6		13	Arkansas	85.7
8	Indiana	97.8		13	Iowa	85.7
13	Iowa	85.7		15	Massachusetts	83.3
9	Kansas	90.5		15	Michigan	83.3
1	Kentucky	100.0		17	Washington	82.9
NA	Louisiana**	NA		18	Oklahoma	82.5
43	Maine	50.0		19	Arizona	80.6
40	Maryland	54.3		20	Tennessee	79.2
15	Massachusetts	83.3		21	North Carolina	77.1
15	Michigan	83.3		22	Minnesota	75.0
22	Minnesota	75.0		22	Wyoming	75.0
10	Mississippi	89.8		24	New York	74.2
25	Missouri	73.8		25	Missouri	73.8
29	Montana	71.4		26	California	73.2
1	Nebraska	100.0		27	Hawaii	72.7
32	Nevada	70.4		27	Idaho	72.7
38	New Hampshire	62.5		29	Georgia	71.4
42	New Jersey	52.2		29	Montana	71.4
NA	New Mexico**	NA		31	Wisconsin	70.6
24	New York	74.2		32	Nevada	70.4
21	North Carolina	77.1		33	Pennsylvania	70.1
1	North Dakota	100.0		34	Colorado	69.2
12	Ohio	88.6		35	South Carolina	65.7
18	Oklahoma	82.5		36	Illinois	63.6
41	Oregon	53.8		37	Florida	62.8
33	Pennsylvania	70.1		38	New Hampshire	62.5
46	Rhode Island	33.3		39	Virginia	56.9
35	South Carolina	65.7		40	Maryland	54.3
47	South Dakota	0.0		41	Oregon	53.8
20	Tennessee	79.2		42	New Jersey	52.2
45	Texas	45.6		43	Maine	50.0
1	Utah	100.0		44	Connecticut	48.5
1	Vermont	100.0		45	Texas	45.6
39	Virginia	56.9		46	Rhode Island	33.3
17	Washington	82.9		47	South Dakota	0.0
1	West Virginia	100.0		NA	Alabama**	NA
31	Wisconsin	70.6		NA	Louisiana**	NA
22	Wyoming	75.0		NA	New Mexico**	NA

District of Columbia 75.0

Source: Morgan Quitno Press using data from U.S. Department of Justice, Bureau of Justice Statistics
"Correctional Populations in the United States, 1998" (forthcoming in 2001)
*Preliminary data. Excludes AIDS. Federal data were not reported.
**Not available.

Deaths of State Prisoners by AIDS in 1998

National Total = 339 Deaths*

ALPHA ORDER				RANK ORDER			
RANK	STATE	DEATHS	% of USA	RANK	STATE	DEATHS	% of USA
NA	Alabama**	NA	NA	1	Florida	61	18.0%
28	Alaska	0	0.0%	2	Texas	58	17.1%
28	Arizona	0	0.0%	3	New York	39	11.5%
28	Arkansas	0	0.0%	4	California	29	8.6%
4	California	29	8.6%	5	Pennsylvania	20	5.9%
28	Colorado	0	0.0%	6	New Jersey	16	4.7%
8	Connecticut	14	4.1%	7	Georgia	15	4.4%
28	Delaware	0	0.0%	8	Connecticut	14	4.1%
1	Florida	61	18.0%	8	Illinois	14	4.1%
7	Georgia	15	4.4%	8	South Carolina	14	4.1%
22	Hawaii	1	0.3%	11	Virginia	12	3.5%
22	Idaho	1	0.3%	12	Maryland	11	3.2%
8	Illinois	14	4.1%	13	Ohio	7	2.1%
NA	Indiana**	NA	NA	14	North Carolina	6	1.8%
28	Iowa	0	0.0%	15	Massachusetts	3	0.9%
28	Kansas	0	0.0%	15	Michigan	3	0.9%
28	Kentucky	0	0.0%	15	Rhode Island	3	0.9%
NA	Louisiana**	NA	NA	18	Mississippi	2	0.6%
28	Maine	0	0.0%	18	Oklahoma	2	0.6%
12	Maryland	11	3.2%	18	Tennessee	2	0.6%
15	Massachusetts	3	0.9%	18	Washington	2	0.6%
15	Michigan	3	0.9%	22	Hawaii	1	0.3%
22	Minnesota	1	0.3%	22	Idaho	1	0.3%
18	Mississippi	2	0.6%	22	Minnesota	1	0.3%
28	Missouri	0	0.0%	22	Nevada	1	0.3%
28	Montana	0	0.0%	22	New Hampshire	1	0.3%
28	Nebraska	0	0.0%	22	Wisconsin	1	0.3%
22	Nevada	1	0.3%	28	Alaska	0	0.0%
22	New Hampshire	1	0.3%	28	Arizona	0	0.0%
6	New Jersey	16	4.7%	28	Arkansas	0	0.0%
NA	New Mexico**	NA	NA	28	Colorado	0	0.0%
3	New York	39	11.5%	28	Delaware	0	0.0%
14	North Carolina	6	1.8%	28	Iowa	0	0.0%
28	North Dakota	0	0.0%	28	Kansas	0	0.0%
13	Ohio	7	2.1%	28	Kentucky	0	0.0%
18	Oklahoma	2	0.6%	28	Maine	0	0.0%
28	Oregon	0	0.0%	28	Missouri	0	0.0%
5	Pennsylvania	20	5.9%	28	Montana	0	0.0%
15	Rhode Island	3	0.9%	28	Nebraska	0	0.0%
8	South Carolina	14	4.1%	28	North Dakota	0	0.0%
28	South Dakota	0	0.0%	28	Oregon	0	0.0%
18	Tennessee	2	0.6%	28	South Dakota	0	0.0%
2	Texas	58	17.1%	28	Utah	0	0.0%
28	Utah	0	0.0%	28	Vermont	0	0.0%
28	Vermont	0	0.0%	28	West Virginia	0	0.0%
11	Virginia	12	3.5%	28	Wyoming	0	0.0%
18	Washington	2	0.6%	NA	Alabama**	NA	NA
28	West Virginia	0	0.0%	NA	Indiana**	NA	NA
22	Wisconsin	1	0.3%	NA	Louisiana**	NA	NA
28	Wyoming	0	0.0%	NA	New Mexico**	NA	NA
					District of Columbia**	NA	NA

Source: U.S. Department of Justice, Bureau of Justice Statistics
  "Correctional Populations in the United States, 1998" (forthcoming in 2001)
*Preliminary data. Federal data were not reported.
**Not available.

AIDS-Related Death Rate for State Prisoners in 1998

National Rate = 29 State Prisoner Deaths per 100,000 Prison Population*

ALPHA ORDER

RANK	STATE	RATE
NA	Alabama**	NA
28	Alaska	0
28	Arizona	0
28	Arkansas	0
18	California	18
28	Colorado	0
3	Connecticut	80
28	Delaware	0
1	Florida	91
12	Georgia	38
16	Hawaii	20
15	Idaho	24
13	Illinois	33
NA	Indiana**	NA
28	Iowa	0
28	Kansas	0
28	Kentucky	0
NA	Louisiana**	NA
28	Maine	0
8	Maryland	49
14	Massachusetts	25
26	Michigan	7
18	Minnesota	18
22	Mississippi	12
28	Missouri	0
28	Montana	0
28	Nebraska	0
24	Nevada	10
9	New Hampshire	46
7	New Jersey	51
NA	New Mexico**	NA
5	New York	56
17	North Carolina	19
28	North Dakota	0
20	Ohio	14
24	Oklahoma	10
28	Oregon	0
6	Pennsylvania	55
2	Rhode Island	87
4	South Carolina	63
28	South Dakota	0
23	Tennessee	11
10	Texas	40
28	Utah	0
28	Vermont	0
10	Virginia	40
20	Washington	14
28	West Virginia	0
27	Wisconsin	5
28	Wyoming	0

RANK ORDER

RANK	STATE	RATE
1	Florida	91
2	Rhode Island	87
3	Connecticut	80
4	South Carolina	63
5	New York	56
6	Pennsylvania	55
7	New Jersey	51
8	Maryland	49
9	New Hampshire	46
10	Texas	40
10	Virginia	40
12	Georgia	38
13	Illinois	33
14	Massachusetts	25
15	Idaho	24
16	Hawaii	20
17	North Carolina	19
18	California	18
18	Minnesota	18
20	Ohio	14
20	Washington	14
22	Mississippi	12
23	Tennessee	11
24	Nevada	10
24	Oklahoma	10
26	Michigan	7
27	Wisconsin	5
28	Alaska	0
28	Arizona	0
28	Arkansas	0
28	Colorado	0
28	Delaware	0
28	Iowa	0
28	Kansas	0
28	Kentucky	0
28	Maine	0
28	Missouri	0
28	Montana	0
28	Nebraska	0
28	North Dakota	0
28	Oregon	0
28	South Dakota	0
28	Utah	0
28	Vermont	0
28	West Virginia	0
28	Wyoming	0
NA	Alabama**	NA
NA	Indiana**	NA
NA	Louisiana**	NA
NA	New Mexico**	NA
	District of Columbia**	NA

Source: Morgan Quitno Press using data from U.S. Department of Justice, Bureau of Justice Statistics
"Correctional Populations in the United States, 1998" (forthcoming in 2001)
*Preliminary data. Federal data were not reported.
**Not available.

Deaths of State Prisoners by AIDS as a Percent of All Prison Deaths in 1998

National Percent = 12.1% of Deaths*

ALPHA ORDER

RANK ORDER

RANK	STATE	PERCENT		RANK	STATE	PERCENT
NA	Alabama**	NA		1	Rhode Island	50.0
28	Alaska	0.0		2	Connecticut	42.4
28	Arizona	0.0		3	Florida	29.5
28	Arkansas	0.0		4	Maryland	23.9
17	California	10.2		5	New Jersey	23.2
28	Colorado	0.0		6	South Carolina	20.0
2	Connecticut	42.4		7	Virginia	18.5
28	Delaware	0.0		8	New York	18.3
3	Florida	29.5		9	Pennsylvania	15.7
11	Georgia	15.3		10	Texas	15.5
18	Hawaii	9.1		11	Georgia	15.3
18	Idaho	9.1		12	Illinois	14.1
12	Illinois	14.1		13	Massachusetts	12.5
NA	Indiana**	NA		13	Minnesota	12.5
28	Iowa	0.0		13	New Hampshire	12.5
28	Kansas	0.0		13	North Carolina	12.5
28	Kentucky	0.0		17	California	10.2
NA	Louisiana**	NA		18	Hawaii	9.1
28	Maine	0.0		18	Idaho	9.1
4	Maryland	23.9		20	Ohio	5.0
13	Massachusetts	12.5		21	Washington	4.9
26	Michigan	3.1		22	Tennessee	4.2
13	Minnesota	12.5		23	Mississippi	4.1
23	Mississippi	4.1		24	Nevada	3.7
28	Missouri	0.0		25	Oklahoma	3.5
28	Montana	0.0		26	Michigan	3.1
28	Nebraska	0.0		27	Wisconsin	2.9
24	Nevada	3.7		28	Alaska	0.0
13	New Hampshire	12.5		28	Arizona	0.0
5	New Jersey	23.2		28	Arkansas	0.0
NA	New Mexico**	NA		28	Colorado	0.0
8	New York	18.3		28	Delaware	0.0
13	North Carolina	12.5		28	Iowa	0.0
28	North Dakota	0.0		28	Kansas	0.0
20	Ohio	5.0		28	Kentucky	0.0
25	Oklahoma	3.5		28	Maine	0.0
28	Oregon	0.0		28	Missouri	0.0
9	Pennsylvania	15.7		28	Montana	0.0
1	Rhode Island	50.0		28	Nebraska	0.0
6	South Carolina	20.0		28	North Dakota	0.0
28	South Dakota	0.0		28	Oregon	0.0
22	Tennessee	4.2		28	South Dakota	0.0
10	Texas	15.5		28	Utah	0.0
28	Utah	0.0		28	Vermont	0.0
28	Vermont	0.0		28	West Virginia	0.0
7	Virginia	18.5		28	Wyoming	0.0
21	Washington	4.9		NA	Alabama**	NA
28	West Virginia	0.0		NA	Indiana**	NA
27	Wisconsin	2.9		NA	Louisiana**	NA
28	Wyoming	0.0		NA	New Mexico**	NA
					District of Columbia**	NA

Source: Morgan Quitno Press using data from U.S. Department of Justice, Bureau of Justice Statistics
    "Correctional Populations in the United States, 1998" (forthcoming in 2001)
*Preliminary data. Federal data were not reported.
**Not available.

State Prisoners Known to be Positive for HIV Infection/AIDS in 1997

National Total = 22,518 Inmates*

ALPHA ORDER

RANK	STATE	INMATES	% of USA
18	Alabama	212	0.9%
38	Alaska	10	0.0%
26	Arizona	105	0.5%
27	Arkansas	86	0.4%
4	California	1,328	5.9%
23	Colorado	110	0.5%
7	Connecticut	798	3.5%
NA	Delaware**	NA	NA
2	Florida	2,325	10.3%
6	Georgia	861	3.8%
37	Hawaii	16	0.1%
38	Idaho	10	0.0%
10	Illinois	655	2.9%
NA	Indiana**	NA	NA
32	Iowa	34	0.2%
44	Kansas	4	0.0%
30	Kentucky	55	0.2%
15	Louisiana	397	1.8%
NA	Maine**	NA	NA
8	Maryland	766	3.4%
14	Massachusetts	402	1.8%
13	Michigan	419	1.9%
33	Minnesota	31	0.1%
19	Mississippi	189	0.8%
17	Missouri	227	1.0%
41	Montana	8	0.0%
35	Nebraska	22	0.1%
20	Nevada	139	0.6%
36	New Hampshire	17	0.1%
5	New Jersey	867	3.9%
34	New Mexico	23	0.1%
1	New York	7,500	33.3%
11	North Carolina	519	2.3%
42	North Dakota	7	0.0%
16	Ohio	365	1.6%
24	Oklahoma	107	0.5%
31	Oregon	54	0.2%
9	Pennsylvania	697	3.1%
24	Rhode Island	107	0.5%
12	South Carolina	432	1.9%
46	South Dakota	1	0.0%
21	Tennessee	131	0.6%
3	Texas	2,126	9.4%
29	Utah	60	0.3%
43	Vermont	6	0.0%
NA	Virginia**	NA	NA
22	Washington	119	0.5%
38	West Virginia	10	0.0%
28	Wisconsin	84	0.4%
45	Wyoming	2	0.0%

RANK ORDER

RANK	STATE	INMATES	% of USA
1	New York	7,500	33.3%
2	Florida	2,325	10.3%
3	Texas	2,126	9.4%
4	California	1,328	5.9%
5	New Jersey	867	3.9%
6	Georgia	861	3.8%
7	Connecticut	798	3.5%
8	Maryland	766	3.4%
9	Pennsylvania	697	3.1%
10	Illinois	655	2.9%
11	North Carolina	519	2.3%
12	South Carolina	432	1.9%
13	Michigan	419	1.9%
14	Massachusetts	402	1.8%
15	Louisiana	397	1.8%
16	Ohio	365	1.6%
17	Missouri	227	1.0%
18	Alabama	212	0.9%
19	Mississippi	189	0.8%
20	Nevada	139	0.6%
21	Tennessee	131	0.6%
22	Washington	119	0.5%
23	Colorado	110	0.5%
24	Oklahoma	107	0.5%
24	Rhode Island	107	0.5%
26	Arizona	105	0.5%
27	Arkansas	86	0.4%
28	Wisconsin	84	0.4%
29	Utah	60	0.3%
30	Kentucky	55	0.2%
31	Oregon	54	0.2%
32	Iowa	34	0.2%
33	Minnesota	31	0.1%
34	New Mexico	23	0.1%
35	Nebraska	22	0.1%
36	New Hampshire	17	0.1%
37	Hawaii	16	0.1%
38	Alaska	10	0.0%
38	Idaho	10	0.0%
38	West Virginia	10	0.0%
41	Montana	8	0.0%
42	North Dakota	7	0.0%
43	Vermont	6	0.0%
44	Kansas	4	0.0%
45	Wyoming	2	0.0%
46	South Dakota	1	0.0%
NA	Delaware**	NA	NA
NA	Indiana**	NA	NA
NA	Maine**	NA	NA
NA	Virginia**	NA	NA
	District of Columbia	75	0.3%

Source: U.S. Department of Justice, Bureau of Justice Statistics
"HIV in Prisons 1997" (Bulletin, November 1999, NCJ-178284)
*Does not include 1,030 positive federal inmates.
**Not available.

State Prisoners Known to be Positive for HIV Infection/AIDS
As a Percent of Total Prison Population in 1997
National Percent = 2.2% of State Prisoners*

ALPHA ORDER

RANK	STATE	PERCENT
19	Alabama	1.0
42	Alaska	0.3
38	Arizona	0.4
20	Arkansas	1.0
25	California	0.9
18	Colorado	1.0
2	Connecticut	5.1
NA	Delaware**	NA
4	Florida	3.6
8	Georgia	2.4
41	Hawaii	0.4
43	Idaho	0.3
15	Illinois	1.6
NA	Indiana**	NA
36	Iowa	0.5
45	Kansas	0.1
35	Kentucky	0.5
9	Louisiana	2.1
NA	Maine**	NA
5	Maryland	3.5
3	Massachusetts	3.7
22	Michigan	0.9
34	Minnesota	0.6
12	Mississippi	1.8
21	Missouri	0.9
39	Montana	0.4
31	Nebraska	0.7
14	Nevada	1.6
27	New Hampshire	0.8
6	New Jersey	3.4
32	New Mexico	0.6
1	New York	10.8
13	North Carolina	1.7
26	North Dakota	0.9
28	Ohio	0.8
29	Oklahoma	0.7
30	Oregon	0.7
11	Pennsylvania	2.0
7	Rhode Island	3.2
10	South Carolina	2.1
46	South Dakota	0.0
24	Tennessee	0.9
16	Texas	1.5
17	Utah	1.2
37	Vermont	0.5
NA	Virginia**	NA
23	Washington	0.9
40	West Virginia	0.4
33	Wisconsin	0.6
44	Wyoming	0.1

RANK ORDER

RANK	STATE	PERCENT
1	New York	10.8
2	Connecticut	5.1
3	Massachusetts	3.7
4	Florida	3.6
5	Maryland	3.5
6	New Jersey	3.4
7	Rhode Island	3.2
8	Georgia	2.4
9	Louisiana	2.1
10	South Carolina	2.1
11	Pennsylvania	2.0
12	Mississippi	1.8
13	North Carolina	1.7
14	Nevada	1.6
15	Illinois	1.6
16	Texas	1.5
17	Utah	1.2
18	Colorado	1.0
19	Alabama	1.0
20	Arkansas	1.0
21	Missouri	0.9
22	Michigan	0.9
23	Washington	0.9
24	Tennessee	0.9
25	California	0.9
26	North Dakota	0.9
27	New Hampshire	0.8
28	Ohio	0.8
29	Oklahoma	0.7
30	Oregon	0.7
31	Nebraska	0.7
32	New Mexico	0.6
33	Wisconsin	0.6
34	Minnesota	0.6
35	Kentucky	0.5
36	Iowa	0.5
37	Vermont	0.5
38	Arizona	0.4
39	Montana	0.4
40	West Virginia	0.4
41	Hawaii	0.4
42	Alaska	0.3
43	Idaho	0.3
44	Wyoming	0.1
45	Kansas	0.1
46	South Dakota	0.0
NA	Delaware**	NA
NA	Indiana**	NA
NA	Maine**	NA
NA	Virginia**	NA
	District of Columbia	1.1

Source: U.S. Department of Justice, Bureau of Justice Statistics
   "HIV in Prisons 1997" (Bulletin, November 1999, NCJ-178284)
Federal rate is 1.0%, combined state and federal rate is 2.1%.
**Not available.*

Deaths of State Prisoners by Suicide in 1998

National Total = 176 Suicides*

RANK	STATE	SUICIDES	% of USA
NA	Alabama**	NA	NA
39	Alaska	0	0.0%
10	Arizona	5	2.8%
16	Arkansas	3	1.7%
2	California	21	11.9%
10	Colorado	5	2.8%
27	Connecticut	1	0.6%
27	Delaware	1	0.6%
9	Florida	6	3.4%
10	Georgia	5	2.8%
27	Hawaii	1	0.6%
27	Idaho	1	0.6%
4	Illinois	12	6.8%
NA	Indiana**	NA	NA
27	Iowa	1	0.6%
27	Kansas	1	0.6%
39	Kentucky	0	0.0%
NA	Louisiana**	NA	NA
27	Maine	1	0.6%
19	Maryland	2	1.1%
27	Massachusetts	1	0.6%
6	Michigan	7	4.0%
27	Minnesota	1	0.6%
19	Mississippi	2	1.1%
6	Missouri	7	4.0%
27	Montana	1	0.6%
39	Nebraska	0	0.0%
19	Nevada	2	1.1%
27	New Hampshire	1	0.6%
19	New Jersey	2	1.1%
NA	New Mexico**	NA	NA
3	New York	14	8.0%
19	North Carolina	2	1.1%
39	North Dakota	0	0.0%
6	Ohio	7	4.0%
19	Oklahoma	2	1.1%
10	Oregon	5	2.8%
5	Pennsylvania	11	6.3%
39	Rhode Island	0	0.0%
16	South Carolina	3	1.7%
19	South Dakota	2	1.1%
10	Tennessee	5	2.8%
1	Texas	22	12.5%
39	Utah	0	0.0%
39	Vermont	0	0.0%
19	Virginia	2	1.1%
16	Washington	3	1.7%
39	West Virginia	0	0.0%
10	Wisconsin	5	2.8%
27	Wyoming	1	0.6%

RANK	STATE	SUICIDES	% of USA
1	Texas	22	12.5%
2	California	21	11.9%
3	New York	14	8.0%
4	Illinois	12	6.8%
5	Pennsylvania	11	6.3%
6	Michigan	7	4.0%
6	Missouri	7	4.0%
6	Ohio	7	4.0%
9	Florida	6	3.4%
10	Arizona	5	2.8%
10	Colorado	5	2.8%
10	Georgia	5	2.8%
10	Oregon	5	2.8%
10	Tennessee	5	2.8%
10	Wisconsin	5	2.8%
16	Arkansas	3	1.7%
16	South Carolina	3	1.7%
16	Washington	3	1.7%
19	Maryland	2	1.1%
19	Mississippi	2	1.1%
19	Nevada	2	1.1%
19	New Jersey	2	1.1%
19	North Carolina	2	1.1%
19	Oklahoma	2	1.1%
19	South Dakota	2	1.1%
19	Virginia	2	1.1%
27	Connecticut	1	0.6%
27	Delaware	1	0.6%
27	Hawaii	1	0.6%
27	Idaho	1	0.6%
27	Iowa	1	0.6%
27	Kansas	1	0.6%
27	Maine	1	0.6%
27	Massachusetts	1	0.6%
27	Minnesota	1	0.6%
27	Montana	1	0.6%
27	New Hampshire	1	0.6%
27	Wyoming	1	0.6%
39	Alaska	0	0.0%
39	Kentucky	0	0.0%
39	Nebraska	0	0.0%
39	North Dakota	0	0.0%
39	Rhode Island	0	0.0%
39	Utah	0	0.0%
39	Vermont	0	0.0%
39	West Virginia	0	0.0%
NA	Alabama**	NA	NA
NA	Indiana**	NA	NA
NA	Louisiana**	NA	NA
NA	New Mexico**	NA	NA
	District of Columbia	2	1.1%

Source: U.S. Department of Justice, Bureau of Justice Statistics
   "Correctional Populations in the United States, 1998" (forthcoming in 2001)
*Preliminary data. Federal data were not reported.
**Not available.

Deaths of State Prisoners by Suicide as a Percent of All Prison Deaths in 1998

National Percent = 6.3% of Deaths*

ALPHA ORDER

RANK	STATE	PERCENT
NA	Alabama**	NA
39	Alaska	0.0
19	Arizona	8.1
18	Arkansas	8.6
20	California	7.4
5	Colorado	19.2
36	Connecticut	3.0
13	Delaware	11.1
37	Florida	2.9
26	Georgia	5.1
15	Hawaii	9.1
15	Idaho	9.1
12	Illinois	12.1
NA	Indiana**	NA
8	Iowa	14.3
28	Kansas	4.8
39	Kentucky	0.0
NA	Louisiana**	NA
2	Maine	50.0
29	Maryland	4.3
31	Massachusetts	4.2
22	Michigan	7.3
10	Minnesota	12.5
33	Mississippi	4.1
6	Missouri	16.7
8	Montana	14.3
39	Nebraska	0.0
20	Nevada	7.4
10	New Hampshire	12.5
37	New Jersey	2.9
NA	New Mexico**	NA
24	New York	6.6
31	North Carolina	4.2
39	North Dakota	0.0
27	Ohio	5.0
34	Oklahoma	3.5
3	Oregon	38.5
17	Pennsylvania	8.7
39	Rhode Island	0.0
29	South Carolina	4.3
1	South Dakota	100.0
14	Tennessee	10.4
25	Texas	5.9
39	Utah	0.0
39	Vermont	0.0
35	Virginia	3.1
22	Washington	7.3
39	West Virginia	0.0
7	Wisconsin	14.7
4	Wyoming	25.0

RANK ORDER

RANK	STATE	PERCENT
1	South Dakota	100.0
2	Maine	50.0
3	Oregon	38.5
4	Wyoming	25.0
5	Colorado	19.2
6	Missouri	16.7
7	Wisconsin	14.7
8	Iowa	14.3
8	Montana	14.3
10	Minnesota	12.5
10	New Hampshire	12.5
12	Illinois	12.1
13	Delaware	11.1
14	Tennessee	10.4
15	Hawaii	9.1
15	Idaho	9.1
17	Pennsylvania	8.7
18	Arkansas	8.6
19	Arizona	8.1
20	California	7.4
20	Nevada	7.4
22	Michigan	7.3
22	Washington	7.3
24	New York	6.6
25	Texas	5.9
26	Georgia	5.1
27	Ohio	5.0
28	Kansas	4.8
29	Maryland	4.3
29	South Carolina	4.3
31	Massachusetts	4.2
31	North Carolina	4.2
33	Mississippi	4.1
34	Oklahoma	3.5
35	Virginia	3.1
36	Connecticut	3.0
37	Florida	2.9
37	New Jersey	2.9
39	Alaska	0.0
39	Kentucky	0.0
39	Nebraska	0.0
39	North Dakota	0.0
39	Rhode Island	0.0
39	Utah	0.0
39	Vermont	0.0
39	West Virginia	0.0
NA	Alabama**	NA
NA	Indiana**	NA
NA	Louisiana**	NA
NA	New Mexico**	NA
	District of Columbia	10.0

Source: Morgan Quitno Press using data from U.S. Department of Justice, Bureau of Justice Statistics
   "Correctional Populations in the United States, 1998" (forthcoming in 2001)
*Preliminary data. Federal data were not reported.
**Not available.

Adults Under State Correctional Supervision in 1993

National Total = 4,711,500 Adults*

ALPHA ORDER

RANK	STATE	ADULTS	% of USA
22	Alabama	66,400	1.4%
47	Alaska	6,600	0.1%
24	Arizona	65,700	1.4%
30	Arkansas	31,900	0.7%
2	California	557,000	11.8%
27	Colorado	53,400	1.1%
25	Connecticut	64,900	1.4%
35	Delaware	20,600	0.4%
3	Florida	302,800	6.4%
5	Georgia	216,400	4.6%
39	Hawaii	14,500	0.3%
43	Idaho	9,600	0.2%
10	Illinois	148,700	3.2%
14	Indiana	108,400	2.3%
33	Iowa	22,800	0.5%
29	Kansas	39,700	0.8%
31	Kentucky	31,000	0.7%
16	Louisiana	78,800	1.7%
41	Maine	10,800	0.2%
13	Maryland	123,300	2.6%
18	Massachusetts	69,400	1.5%
7	Michigan	205,400	4.4%
15	Minnesota	83,900	1.8%
32	Mississippi	25,000	0.5%
20	Missouri	67,700	1.4%
46	Montana	7,000	0.2%
37	Nebraska	19,500	0.4%
34	Nevada	21,400	0.5%
45	New Hampshire	7,700	0.2%
8	New Jersey	180,600	3.8%
38	New Mexico	15,400	0.3%
4	New York	301,400	6.4%
12	North Carolina	134,400	2.9%
50	North Dakota	2,900	0.1%
9	Ohio	157,100	3.3%
28	Oklahoma	44,300	0.9%
26	Oregon	61,900	1.3%
6	Pennsylvania	205,500	4.4%
36	Rhode Island	19,700	0.4%
21	South Carolina	67,103	1.4%
47	South Dakota	6,600	0.1%
17	Tennessee	78,000	1.7%
1	Texas	620,000	13.2%
39	Utah	14,500	0.3%
44	Vermont	7,800	0.2%
19	Virginia	67,900	1.4%
11	Washington	135,600	2.9%
42	West Virginia	10,600	0.2%
23	Wisconsin	66,300	1.4%
49	Wyoming	4,900	0.1%

RANK ORDER

RANK	STATE	ADULTS	% of USA
1	Texas	620,000	13.2%
2	California	557,000	11.8%
3	Florida	302,800	6.4%
4	New York	301,400	6.4%
5	Georgia	216,400	4.6%
6	Pennsylvania	205,500	4.4%
7	Michigan	205,400	4.4%
8	New Jersey	180,600	3.8%
9	Ohio	157,100	3.3%
10	Illinois	148,700	3.2%
11	Washington	135,600	2.9%
12	North Carolina	134,400	2.9%
13	Maryland	123,300	2.6%
14	Indiana	108,400	2.3%
15	Minnesota	83,900	1.8%
16	Louisiana	78,800	1.7%
17	Tennessee	78,000	1.7%
18	Massachusetts	69,400	1.5%
19	Virginia	67,900	1.4%
20	Missouri	67,700	1.4%
21	South Carolina	67,103	1.4%
22	Alabama	66,400	1.4%
23	Wisconsin	66,300	1.4%
24	Arizona	65,700	1.4%
25	Connecticut	64,900	1.4%
26	Oregon	61,900	1.3%
27	Colorado	53,400	1.1%
28	Oklahoma	44,300	0.9%
29	Kansas	39,700	0.8%
30	Arkansas	31,900	0.7%
31	Kentucky	31,000	0.7%
32	Mississippi	25,000	0.5%
33	Iowa	22,800	0.5%
34	Nevada	21,400	0.5%
35	Delaware	20,600	0.4%
36	Rhode Island	19,700	0.4%
37	Nebraska	19,500	0.4%
38	New Mexico	15,400	0.3%
39	Hawaii	14,500	0.3%
39	Utah	14,500	0.3%
41	Maine	10,800	0.2%
42	West Virginia	10,600	0.2%
43	Idaho	9,600	0.2%
44	Vermont	7,800	0.2%
45	New Hampshire	7,700	0.2%
46	Montana	7,000	0.2%
47	Alaska	6,600	0.1%
47	South Dakota	6,600	0.1%
49	Wyoming	4,900	0.1%
50	North Dakota	2,900	0.1%
	District of Columbia	29,000	0.6%

Source: U.S. Department of Justice, Bureau of Justice Statistics
    "Correctional Populations in the United States, 1993" (October 1995, NCJ-156241)
Includes adults in prison or jail, on probation or parole. Does not include 168,000 adults under federal correctional supervision.

Percent of Population Under State Correctional Supervision in 1993

National Percent = 2.5% of Adult Population*

ALPHA ORDER				RANK ORDER		
RANK	STATE	PERCENT		RANK	STATE	PERCENT
22	Alabama	2.1		1	Texas	4.8
35	Alaska	1.6		2	Georgia	4.3
18	Arizona	2.3		3	Delaware	3.9
28	Arkansas	1.8		4	Washington	3.5
16	California	2.5		5	Maryland	3.3
24	Colorado	2.0		6	Michigan	3.0
10	Connecticut	2.6		6	New Jersey	3.0
3	Delaware	3.9		8	Florida	2.9
8	Florida	2.9		9	Oregon	2.8
2	Georgia	4.3		10	Connecticut	2.6
32	Hawaii	1.7		10	Indiana	2.6
40	Idaho	1.3		10	Louisiana	2.6
32	Illinois	1.7		10	Minnesota	2.6
10	Indiana	2.6		10	North Carolina	2.6
46	Iowa	1.1		10	Rhode Island	2.6
19	Kansas	2.2		16	California	2.5
46	Kentucky	1.1		16	South Carolina	2.5
10	Louisiana	2.6		18	Arizona	2.3
43	Maine	1.2		19	Kansas	2.2
5	Maryland	3.3		19	New York	2.2
36	Massachusetts	1.5		19	Pennsylvania	2.2
6	Michigan	3.0		22	Alabama	2.1
10	Minnesota	2.6		22	Nevada	2.1
40	Mississippi	1.3		24	Colorado	2.0
28	Missouri	1.8		24	Tennessee	2.0
43	Montana	1.2		26	Ohio	1.9
32	Nebraska	1.7		26	Oklahoma	1.9
22	Nevada	2.1		28	Arkansas	1.8
48	New Hampshire	0.9		28	Missouri	1.8
6	New Jersey	3.0		28	Vermont	1.8
38	New Mexico	1.4		28	Wisconsin	1.8
19	New York	2.2		32	Hawaii	1.7
10	North Carolina	2.6		32	Illinois	1.7
50	North Dakota	0.6		32	Nebraska	1.7
26	Ohio	1.9		35	Alaska	1.6
26	Oklahoma	1.9		36	Massachusetts	1.5
9	Oregon	2.8		36	Wyoming	1.5
19	Pennsylvania	2.2		38	New Mexico	1.4
10	Rhode Island	2.6		38	Virginia	1.4
16	South Carolina	2.5		40	Idaho	1.3
40	South Dakota	1.3		40	Mississippi	1.3
24	Tennessee	2.0		40	South Dakota	1.3
1	Texas	4.8		43	Maine	1.2
43	Utah	1.2		43	Montana	1.2
28	Vermont	1.8		43	Utah	1.2
38	Virginia	1.4		46	Iowa	1.1
4	Washington	3.5		46	Kentucky	1.1
49	West Virginia	0.8		48	New Hampshire	0.9
28	Wisconsin	1.8		49	West Virginia	0.8
36	Wyoming	1.5		50	North Dakota	0.6
					District of Columbia	6.3

Source: U.S. Department of Justice, Bureau of Justice Statistics
    "Correctional Populations in the United States, 1993" (October 1995, NCJ-156241)
*Includes adults in prison or jail, on probation or parole. Does not include adults under federal correctional supervision. Federal percent is 0.1% making a combined state and federal percent of 2.6% of adult population is under state or federal correctional supervision.

Adults on State Probation in 1999

National Total = 3,740,808 Adults*

ALPHA ORDER			
RANK	STATE	ADULTS	% of USA
24	Alabama	41,757	1.1%
46	Alaska	4,517	0.1%
16	Arizona	57,076	1.5%
29	Arkansas	30,480	0.8%
2	California	332,414	8.9%
22	Colorado	45,339	1.2%
17	Connecticut	55,070	1.5%
32	Delaware	20,976	0.6%
4	Florida	292,399	7.8%
3	Georgia	307,653	8.2%
37	Hawaii	15,707	0.4%
26	Idaho	36,705	1.0%
9	Illinois	134,270	3.6%
12	Indiana	105,871	2.8%
34	Iowa	19,675	0.5%
36	Kansas	17,767	0.5%
35	Kentucky	18,988	0.5%
27	Louisiana	35,118	0.9%
43	Maine	7,524	0.2%
15	Maryland	81,286	2.2%
20	Massachusetts	46,267	1.2%
7	Michigan	170,978	4.6%
14	Minnesota	104,615	2.8%
38	Mississippi	12,448	0.3%
19	Missouri	52,493	1.4%
45	Montana	5,906	0.2%
33	Nebraska	20,462	0.5%
39	Nevada	11,787	0.3%
49	New Hampshire	3,160	0.1%
10	New Jersey	128,634	3.4%
40	New Mexico	11,291	0.3%
6	New York	183,686	4.9%
13	North Carolina	105,095	2.8%
50	North Dakota	2,729	0.1%
5	Ohio	184,867	4.9%
30	Oklahoma	27,997	0.7%
21	Oregon	45,490	1.2%
11	Pennsylvania	118,635	3.2%
31	Rhode Island	21,753	0.6%
23	South Carolina	44,929	1.2%
48	South Dakota	3,461	0.1%
25	Tennessee	40,060	1.1%
1	Texas	447,100	12.0%
42	Utah	9,426	0.3%
41	Vermont	10,541	0.3%
28	Virginia	32,098	0.9%
8	Washington	158,213	4.2%
44	West Virginia	5,994	0.2%
18	Wisconsin	54,131	1.4%
47	Wyoming	3,841	0.1%

RANK ORDER			
RANK	STATE	ADULTS	% of USA
1	Texas	447,100	12.0%
2	California	332,414	8.9%
3	Georgia	307,653	8.2%
4	Florida	292,399	7.8%
5	Ohio	184,867	4.9%
6	New York	183,686	4.9%
7	Michigan	170,978	4.6%
8	Washington	158,213	4.2%
9	Illinois	134,270	3.6%
10	New Jersey	128,634	3.4%
11	Pennsylvania	118,635	3.2%
12	Indiana	105,871	2.8%
13	North Carolina	105,095	2.8%
14	Minnesota	104,615	2.8%
15	Maryland	81,286	2.2%
16	Arizona	57,076	1.5%
17	Connecticut	55,070	1.5%
18	Wisconsin	54,131	1.4%
19	Missouri	52,493	1.4%
20	Massachusetts	46,267	1.2%
21	Oregon	45,490	1.2%
22	Colorado	45,339	1.2%
23	South Carolina	44,929	1.2%
24	Alabama	41,757	1.1%
25	Tennessee	40,060	1.1%
26	Idaho	36,705	1.0%
27	Louisiana	35,118	0.9%
28	Virginia	32,098	0.9%
29	Arkansas	30,480	0.8%
30	Oklahoma	27,997	0.7%
31	Rhode Island	21,753	0.6%
32	Delaware	20,976	0.6%
33	Nebraska	20,462	0.5%
34	Iowa	19,675	0.5%
35	Kentucky	18,988	0.5%
36	Kansas	17,767	0.5%
37	Hawaii	15,707	0.4%
38	Mississippi	12,448	0.3%
39	Nevada	11,787	0.3%
40	New Mexico	11,291	0.3%
41	Vermont	10,541	0.3%
42	Utah	9,426	0.3%
43	Maine	7,524	0.2%
44	West Virginia	5,994	0.2%
45	Montana	5,906	0.2%
46	Alaska	4,517	0.1%
47	Wyoming	3,841	0.1%
48	South Dakota	3,461	0.1%
49	New Hampshire	3,160	0.1%
50	North Dakota	2,729	0.1%
	District of Columbia	12,129	0.3%

Source: U.S. Department of Justice, Bureau of Justice Statistics
   "Probation and Parole in the United States, 1999" (Press Release, July 2000, NCJ-183508)
*As of December 31, 1999. Does not include 32,816 adults on federal probation.

Rate of Adults on State Probation in 1999

National Rate = 1,847 Adults on State Probation per 100,000 Adult Population*

ALPHA ORDER

RANK	STATE	RATE
30	Alabama	1,264
34	Alaska	1,069
20	Arizona	1,657
21	Arkansas	1,612
26	California	1,372
23	Colorado	1,516
12	Connecticut	2,244
4	Delaware	3,673
8	Florida	2,533
1	Georgia	5,368
18	Hawaii	1,753
2	Idaho	4,073
24	Illinois	1,501
9	Indiana	2,399
37	Iowa	915
38	Kansas	909
45	Kentucky	634
32	Louisiana	1,104
42	Maine	782
14	Maryland	2,105
35	Massachusetts	983
10	Michigan	2,341
6	Minnesota	2,986
46	Mississippi	618
29	Missouri	1,290
40	Montana	896
19	Nebraska	1,674
41	Nevada	894
NA	New Hampshire**	NA
15	New Jersey	2,095
39	New Mexico	907
27	New York	1,335
16	North Carolina	1,841
48	North Dakota	576
13	Ohio	2,198
31	Oklahoma	1,131
17	Oregon	1,828
28	Pennsylvania	1,298
7	Rhode Island	2,902
22	South Carolina	1,534
44	South Dakota	647
36	Tennessee	967
5	Texas	3,121
43	Utah	663
11	Vermont	2,320
47	Virginia	616
3	Washington	3,705
49	West Virginia	427
25	Wisconsin	1,387
33	Wyoming	1,089

RANK ORDER

RANK	STATE	RATE
1	Georgia	5,368
2	Idaho	4,073
3	Washington	3,705
4	Delaware	3,673
5	Texas	3,121
6	Minnesota	2,986
7	Rhode Island	2,902
8	Florida	2,533
9	Indiana	2,399
10	Michigan	2,341
11	Vermont	2,320
12	Connecticut	2,244
13	Ohio	2,198
14	Maryland	2,105
15	New Jersey	2,095
16	North Carolina	1,841
17	Oregon	1,828
18	Hawaii	1,753
19	Nebraska	1,674
20	Arizona	1,657
21	Arkansas	1,612
22	South Carolina	1,534
23	Colorado	1,516
24	Illinois	1,501
25	Wisconsin	1,387
26	California	1,372
27	New York	1,335
28	Pennsylvania	1,298
29	Missouri	1,290
30	Alabama	1,264
31	Oklahoma	1,131
32	Louisiana	1,104
33	Wyoming	1,089
34	Alaska	1,069
35	Massachusetts	983
36	Tennessee	967
37	Iowa	915
38	Kansas	909
39	New Mexico	907
40	Montana	896
41	Nevada	894
42	Maine	782
43	Utah	663
44	South Dakota	647
45	Kentucky	634
46	Mississippi	618
47	Virginia	616
48	North Dakota	576
49	West Virginia	427
NA	New Hampshire**	NA
	District of Columbia	2,863

Source: U.S. Department of Justice, Bureau of Justice Statistics
"Probation and Parole in the United States, 1999" (Press Release, July 2000, NCJ-183508)
*As of December 31, 1999. Federal rate is 16 adults on federal probation per 100,000 adult population.

Adults on State Parole in 1999

National Total = 641,693 Adults*

ALPHA ORDER

ALPHA ORDER

RANK	STATE	ADULTS	% of USA
21	Alabama	5,005	0.8%
45	Alaska	493	0.1%
28	Arizona	3,715	0.6%
15	Arkansas	7,645	1.2%
1	California	114,046	17.8%
20	Colorado	5,263	0.8%
35	Connecticut	1,526	0.2%
42	Delaware	634	0.1%
17	Florida	6,418	1.0%
6	Georgia	22,003	3.4%
32	Hawaii	2,252	0.4%
38	Idaho	1,310	0.2%
5	Illinois	30,484	4.8%
23	Indiana	4,539	0.7%
31	Iowa	2,514	0.4%
18	Kansas	5,909	0.9%
22	Kentucky	4,868	0.8%
7	Louisiana	21,904	3.4%
50	Maine	31	0.0%
11	Maryland	15,007	2.3%
25	Massachusetts	4,304	0.7%
10	Michigan	15,541	2.4%
30	Minnesota	3,151	0.5%
37	Mississippi	1,356	0.2%
13	Missouri	11,448	1.8%
44	Montana	549	0.1%
43	Nebraska	612	0.1%
27	Nevada	3,893	0.6%
40	New Hampshire	1,146	0.2%
12	New Jersey	12,968	2.0%
33	New Mexico	1,922	0.3%
4	New York	57,956	9.0%
24	North Carolina	4,389	0.7%
49	North Dakota	157	0.0%
9	Ohio	15,776	2.5%
34	Oklahoma	1,527	0.2%
8	Oregon	17,874	2.8%
3	Pennsylvania	83,702	13.0%
47	Rhode Island	413	0.1%
26	South Carolina	3,944	0.6%
36	South Dakota	1,360	0.2%
16	Tennessee	7,338	1.1%
2	Texas	109,310	17.0%
29	Utah	3,388	0.5%
41	Vermont	794	0.1%
19	Virginia	5,860	0.9%
48	Washington	200	0.0%
39	West Virginia	1,158	0.2%
14	Wisconsin	8,530	1.3%
46	Wyoming	458	0.1%

RANK ORDER

RANK	STATE	ADULTS	% of USA
1	California	114,046	17.8%
2	Texas	109,310	17.0%
3	Pennsylvania	83,702	13.0%
4	New York	57,956	9.0%
5	Illinois	30,484	4.8%
6	Georgia	22,003	3.4%
7	Louisiana	21,904	3.4%
8	Oregon	17,874	2.8%
9	Ohio	15,776	2.5%
10	Michigan	15,541	2.4%
11	Maryland	15,007	2.3%
12	New Jersey	12,968	2.0%
13	Missouri	11,448	1.8%
14	Wisconsin	8,530	1.3%
15	Arkansas	7,645	1.2%
16	Tennessee	7,338	1.1%
17	Florida	6,418	1.0%
18	Kansas	5,909	0.9%
19	Virginia	5,860	0.9%
20	Colorado	5,263	0.8%
21	Alabama	5,005	0.8%
22	Kentucky	4,868	0.8%
23	Indiana	4,539	0.7%
24	North Carolina	4,389	0.7%
25	Massachusetts	4,304	0.7%
26	South Carolina	3,944	0.6%
27	Nevada	3,893	0.6%
28	Arizona	3,715	0.6%
29	Utah	3,388	0.5%
30	Minnesota	3,151	0.5%
31	Iowa	2,514	0.4%
32	Hawaii	2,252	0.4%
33	New Mexico	1,922	0.3%
34	Oklahoma	1,527	0.2%
35	Connecticut	1,526	0.2%
36	South Dakota	1,360	0.2%
37	Mississippi	1,356	0.2%
38	Idaho	1,310	0.2%
39	West Virginia	1,158	0.2%
40	New Hampshire	1,146	0.2%
41	Vermont	794	0.1%
42	Delaware	634	0.1%
43	Nebraska	612	0.1%
44	Montana	549	0.1%
45	Alaska	493	0.1%
46	Wyoming	458	0.1%
47	Rhode Island	413	0.1%
48	Washington	200	0.0%
49	North Dakota	157	0.0%
50	Maine	31	0.0%
	District of Columbia	5,103	0.8%

Source: U.S. Department of Justice, Bureau of Justice Statistics
    "Probation and Parole in the United States, 1999" (Press Release, July 2000, NCJ-183508)
As of December 31, 1999. Does not include 71,020 adults on federal parole.

Rate of Adults on State Parole in 1999

National Rate = 317 Adults on State Parole per 100,000 Adult Population*

ALPHA ORDER

RANK	STATE	RATE
26	Alabama	151
31	Alaska	117
35	Arizona	108
7	Arkansas	404
5	California	471
22	Colorado	176
43	Connecticut	62
34	Delaware	111
45	Florida	56
9	Georgia	384
15	Hawaii	251
27	Idaho	145
10	Illinois	341
36	Indiana	103
31	Iowa	117
11	Kansas	302
24	Kentucky	163
4	Louisiana	688
50	Maine	3
8	Maryland	389
37	Massachusetts	91
18	Michigan	213
38	Minnesota	90
42	Mississippi	67
13	Missouri	281
39	Montana	83
47	Nebraska	50
12	Nevada	295
30	New Hampshire	128
19	New Jersey	211
25	New Mexico	154
6	New York	421
41	North Carolina	77
48	North Dakota	33
20	Ohio	188
43	Oklahoma	62
3	Oregon	718
1	Pennsylvania	916
46	Rhode Island	55
28	South Carolina	135
14	South Dakota	254
21	Tennessee	177
2	Texas	763
16	Utah	238
23	Vermont	175
33	Virginia	113
49	Washington	5
39	West Virginia	83
17	Wisconsin	219
29	Wyoming	130

RANK ORDER

RANK	STATE	RATE
1	Pennsylvania	916
2	Texas	763
3	Oregon	718
4	Louisiana	688
5	California	471
6	New York	421
7	Arkansas	404
8	Maryland	389
9	Georgia	384
10	Illinois	341
11	Kansas	302
12	Nevada	295
13	Missouri	281
14	South Dakota	254
15	Hawaii	251
16	Utah	238
17	Wisconsin	219
18	Michigan	213
19	New Jersey	211
20	Ohio	188
21	Tennessee	177
22	Colorado	176
23	Vermont	175
24	Kentucky	163
25	New Mexico	154
26	Alabama	151
27	Idaho	145
28	South Carolina	135
29	Wyoming	130
30	New Hampshire	128
31	Alaska	117
31	Iowa	117
33	Virginia	113
34	Delaware	111
35	Arizona	108
36	Indiana	103
37	Massachusetts	91
38	Minnesota	90
39	Montana	83
39	West Virginia	83
41	North Carolina	77
42	Mississippi	67
43	Connecticut	62
43	Oklahoma	62
45	Florida	56
46	Rhode Island	55
47	Nebraska	50
48	North Dakota	33
49	Washington	5
50	Maine	3
	District of Columbia	1,204

Source: U.S. Department of Justice, Bureau of Justice Statistics
   "Probation and Parole in the United States, 1999" (Press Release, July 2000, NCJ-183508)
*As of December 31, 1999. Federal rate is 35 adults on federal parole per 100,000 adult population.

State and Local Government Employees in Corrections in 1999

National Total = 678,178 Employees*

ALPHA ORDER

RANK	STATE	EMPLOYEES	% of USA
28	Alabama	7,091	1.0%
46	Alaska	1,399	0.2%
15	Arizona	12,672	1.9%
33	Arkansas	5,169	0.8%
1	California	75,878	11.2%
24	Colorado	8,755	1.3%
25	Connecticut	8,750	1.3%
39	Delaware	2,334	0.3%
4	Florida	45,736	6.7%
5	Georgia	25,778	3.8%
40	Hawaii	2,289	0.3%
38	Idaho	2,584	0.4%
8	Illinois	25,000	3.7%
23	Indiana	10,577	1.6%
35	Iowa	4,117	0.6%
30	Kansas	5,769	0.9%
29	Kentucky	6,133	0.9%
18	Louisiana	12,182	1.8%
42	Maine	1,787	0.3%
13	Maryland	14,265	2.1%
17	Massachusetts	12,307	1.8%
9	Michigan	22,882	3.4%
27	Minnesota	7,660	1.1%
31	Mississippi	5,525	0.8%
14	Missouri	13,681	2.0%
45	Montana	1,519	0.2%
37	Nebraska	2,950	0.4%
34	Nevada	4,695	0.7%
43	New Hampshire	1,668	0.2%
12	New Jersey	15,839	2.3%
32	New Mexico	5,502	0.8%
3	New York	61,406	9.1%
10	North Carolina	22,880	3.4%
50	North Dakota	787	0.1%
7	Ohio	25,682	3.8%
16	Oklahoma	12,545	1.8%
26	Oregon	7,787	1.1%
6	Pennsylvania	25,724	3.8%
41	Rhode Island	1,798	0.3%
22	South Carolina	10,887	1.6%
47	South Dakota	1,320	0.2%
21	Tennessee	11,165	1.6%
2	Texas	68,308	10.1%
36	Utah	3,893	0.6%
49	Vermont	921	0.1%
11	Virginia	21,853	3.2%
19	Washington	11,809	1.7%
44	West Virginia	1,539	0.2%
20	Wisconsin	11,505	1.7%
48	Wyoming	1,001	0.1%

RANK ORDER

RANK	STATE	EMPLOYEES	% of USA
1	California	75,878	11.2%
2	Texas	68,308	10.1%
3	New York	61,406	9.1%
4	Florida	45,736	6.7%
5	Georgia	25,778	3.8%
6	Pennsylvania	25,724	3.8%
7	Ohio	25,682	3.8%
8	Illinois	25,000	3.7%
9	Michigan	22,882	3.4%
10	North Carolina	22,880	3.4%
11	Virginia	21,853	3.2%
12	New Jersey	15,839	2.3%
13	Maryland	14,265	2.1%
14	Missouri	13,681	2.0%
15	Arizona	12,672	1.9%
16	Oklahoma	12,545	1.8%
17	Massachusetts	12,307	1.8%
18	Louisiana	12,182	1.8%
19	Washington	11,809	1.7%
20	Wisconsin	11,505	1.7%
21	Tennessee	11,165	1.6%
22	South Carolina	10,887	1.6%
23	Indiana	10,577	1.6%
24	Colorado	8,755	1.3%
25	Connecticut	8,750	1.3%
26	Oregon	7,787	1.1%
27	Minnesota	7,660	1.1%
28	Alabama	7,091	1.0%
29	Kentucky	6,133	0.9%
30	Kansas	5,769	0.9%
31	Mississippi	5,525	0.8%
32	New Mexico	5,502	0.8%
33	Arkansas	5,169	0.8%
34	Nevada	4,695	0.7%
35	Iowa	4,117	0.6%
36	Utah	3,893	0.6%
37	Nebraska	2,950	0.4%
38	Idaho	2,584	0.4%
39	Delaware	2,334	0.3%
40	Hawaii	2,289	0.3%
41	Rhode Island	1,798	0.3%
42	Maine	1,787	0.3%
43	New Hampshire	1,668	0.2%
44	West Virginia	1,539	0.2%
45	Montana	1,519	0.2%
46	Alaska	1,399	0.2%
47	South Dakota	1,320	0.2%
48	Wyoming	1,001	0.1%
49	Vermont	921	0.1%
50	North Dakota	787	0.1%
	District of Columbia	2,875	0.4%

Source: U.S. Bureau of the Census, Governments Division
"State and Local Employment and Payroll - March 1999" (http://www.census.gov/govs/www/apesstl99.html)
*Full-time equivalent as of March 1999.

State and Local Government Employees in Corrections as a Percent of All State and Local Government Employees in 1999
National Percent = 4.6% of Employees*

ALPHA ORDER

RANK	STATE	PERCENT
43	Alabama	2.7
38	Alaska	2.9
7	Arizona	5.4
29	Arkansas	3.5
14	California	4.8
25	Colorado	3.9
11	Connecticut	5.2
7	Delaware	5.4
1	Florida	6.2
5	Georgia	5.7
31	Hawaii	3.4
29	Idaho	3.5
23	Illinois	4.1
31	Indiana	3.4
48	Iowa	2.4
31	Kansas	3.4
38	Kentucky	2.9
19	Louisiana	4.4
46	Maine	2.6
10	Maryland	5.3
25	Massachusetts	3.9
14	Michigan	4.8
41	Minnesota	2.8
38	Mississippi	2.9
18	Missouri	4.5
37	Montana	3.0
41	Nebraska	2.8
6	Nevada	5.5
43	New Hampshire	2.7
28	New Jersey	3.6
14	New Mexico	4.8
7	New York	5.4
11	North Carolina	5.2
49	North Dakota	2.1
19	Ohio	4.4
2	Oklahoma	6.1
19	Oregon	4.4
13	Pennsylvania	4.9
34	Rhode Island	3.3
17	South Carolina	4.7
34	South Dakota	3.3
27	Tennessee	3.7
3	Texas	6.0
36	Utah	3.2
43	Vermont	2.7
4	Virginia	5.9
24	Washington	4.0
50	West Virginia	1.6
22	Wisconsin	4.2
46	Wyoming	2.6

RANK ORDER

RANK	STATE	PERCENT
1	Florida	6.2
2	Oklahoma	6.1
3	Texas	6.0
4	Virginia	5.9
5	Georgia	5.7
6	Nevada	5.5
7	Arizona	5.4
7	Delaware	5.4
7	New York	5.4
10	Maryland	5.3
11	Connecticut	5.2
11	North Carolina	5.2
13	Pennsylvania	4.9
14	California	4.8
14	Michigan	4.8
14	New Mexico	4.8
17	South Carolina	4.7
18	Missouri	4.5
19	Louisiana	4.4
19	Ohio	4.4
19	Oregon	4.4
22	Wisconsin	4.2
23	Illinois	4.1
24	Washington	4.0
25	Colorado	3.9
25	Massachusetts	3.9
27	Tennessee	3.7
28	New Jersey	3.6
29	Arkansas	3.5
29	Idaho	3.5
31	Hawaii	3.4
31	Indiana	3.4
31	Kansas	3.4
34	Rhode Island	3.3
34	South Dakota	3.3
36	Utah	3.2
37	Montana	3.0
38	Alaska	2.9
38	Kentucky	2.9
38	Mississippi	2.9
41	Minnesota	2.8
41	Nebraska	2.8
43	Alabama	2.7
43	New Hampshire	2.7
43	Vermont	2.7
46	Maine	2.6
46	Wyoming	2.6
48	Iowa	2.4
49	North Dakota	2.1
50	West Virginia	1.6

	District of Columbia	6.7

Source: Morgan Quitno Press using data from U.S. Bureau of the Census, Governments Division
"State and Local Employment and Payroll - March 1999" (http://www.census.gov/govs/www/apesstl99.html)
*Full-time equivalent as of March 1999.

State Government Employees in Corrections in 1999

National Total = 457,185 Employees*

ALPHA ORDER

RANK	STATE	EMPLOYEES	% of USA
26	Alabama	4,443	1.0%
42	Alaska	1,280	0.3%
17	Arizona	8,855	1.9%
30	Arkansas	3,658	0.8%
1	California	47,122	10.3%
25	Colorado	5,448	1.2%
18	Connecticut	8,750	1.9%
37	Delaware	2,334	0.5%
4	Florida	31,872	7.0%
6	Georgia	18,608	4.1%
38	Hawaii	2,289	0.5%
41	Idaho	1,627	0.4%
9	Illinois	15,761	3.4%
24	Indiana	5,984	1.3%
35	Iowa	3,123	0.7%
32	Kansas	3,533	0.8%
33	Kentucky	3,519	0.8%
22	Louisiana	6,789	1.5%
43	Maine	1,199	0.3%
14	Maryland	11,442	2.5%
21	Massachusetts	6,909	1.5%
8	Michigan	17,784	3.9%
31	Minnesota	3,632	0.8%
29	Mississippi	4,068	0.9%
13	Missouri	11,461	2.5%
46	Montana	997	0.2%
39	Nebraska	1,937	0.4%
34	Nevada	3,134	0.7%
45	New Hampshire	1,175	0.3%
15	New Jersey	9,384	2.1%
28	New Mexico	4,161	0.9%
3	New York	35,315	7.7%
5	North Carolina	19,121	4.2%
50	North Dakota	545	0.1%
7	Ohio	17,894	3.9%
12	Oklahoma	11,536	2.5%
27	Oregon	4,330	0.9%
11	Pennsylvania	14,806	3.2%
40	Rhode Island	1,798	0.4%
16	South Carolina	8,944	2.0%
48	South Dakota	863	0.2%
23	Tennessee	6,328	1.4%
2	Texas	46,752	10.2%
36	Utah	2,874	0.6%
47	Vermont	921	0.2%
10	Virginia	15,577	3.4%
20	Washington	7,503	1.6%
44	West Virginia	1,186	0.3%
19	Wisconsin	7,869	1.7%
49	Wyoming	745	0.2%

RANK ORDER

RANK	STATE	EMPLOYEES	% of USA
1	California	47,122	10.3%
2	Texas	46,752	10.2%
3	New York	35,315	7.7%
4	Florida	31,872	7.0%
5	North Carolina	19,121	4.2%
6	Georgia	18,608	4.1%
7	Ohio	17,894	3.9%
8	Michigan	17,784	3.9%
9	Illinois	15,761	3.4%
10	Virginia	15,577	3.4%
11	Pennsylvania	14,806	3.2%
12	Oklahoma	11,536	2.5%
13	Missouri	11,461	2.5%
14	Maryland	11,442	2.5%
15	New Jersey	9,384	2.1%
16	South Carolina	8,944	2.0%
17	Arizona	8,855	1.9%
18	Connecticut	8,750	1.9%
19	Wisconsin	7,869	1.7%
20	Washington	7,503	1.6%
21	Massachusetts	6,909	1.5%
22	Louisiana	6,789	1.5%
23	Tennessee	6,328	1.4%
24	Indiana	5,984	1.3%
25	Colorado	5,448	1.2%
26	Alabama	4,443	1.0%
27	Oregon	4,330	0.9%
28	New Mexico	4,161	0.9%
29	Mississippi	4,068	0.9%
30	Arkansas	3,658	0.8%
31	Minnesota	3,632	0.8%
32	Kansas	3,533	0.8%
33	Kentucky	3,519	0.8%
34	Nevada	3,134	0.7%
35	Iowa	3,123	0.7%
36	Utah	2,874	0.6%
37	Delaware	2,334	0.5%
38	Hawaii	2,289	0.5%
39	Nebraska	1,937	0.4%
40	Rhode Island	1,798	0.4%
41	Idaho	1,627	0.4%
42	Alaska	1,280	0.3%
43	Maine	1,199	0.3%
44	West Virginia	1,186	0.3%
45	New Hampshire	1,175	0.3%
46	Montana	997	0.2%
47	Vermont	921	0.2%
48	South Dakota	863	0.2%
49	Wyoming	745	0.2%
50	North Dakota	545	0.1%
	District of Columbia**	NA	NA

Source: U.S. Bureau of the Census, Governments Division
  "1999 State Government Employment and Payroll" (http://www.census.gov/govs/www/apesst99.html)
Full-time equivalent as of March 1999.
***Not applicable.*

State Government Employees in Corrections
As a Percent of All State Government Employees in 1999
National Percent = 11.3% of Employees*

ALPHA ORDER

RANK	STATE	PERCENT
44	Alabama	5.5
43	Alaska	5.7
6	Arizona	14.1
32	Arkansas	7.1
10	California	13.5
23	Colorado	8.8
8	Connecticut	13.8
19	Delaware	10.4
1	Florida	17.7
3	Georgia	16.1
48	Hawaii	4.3
35	Idaho	6.8
18	Illinois	11.2
29	Indiana	7.3
41	Iowa	5.9
24	Kansas	8.2
47	Kentucky	5.0
32	Louisiana	7.1
40	Maine	6.0
14	Maryland	12.9
25	Massachusetts	7.9
13	Michigan	13.0
46	Minnesota	5.1
28	Mississippi	7.5
16	Missouri	12.4
45	Montana	5.3
38	Nebraska	6.5
11	Nevada	13.4
39	New Hampshire	6.3
30	New Jersey	7.2
21	New Mexico	9.4
6	New York	14.1
5	North Carolina	15.3
50	North Dakota	3.5
12	Ohio	13.1
4	Oklahoma	15.8
25	Oregon	7.9
20	Pennsylvania	10.1
22	Rhode Island	9.1
17	South Carolina	11.3
37	South Dakota	6.6
27	Tennessee	7.8
2	Texas	17.4
41	Utah	5.9
30	Vermont	7.2
9	Virginia	13.7
34	Washington	6.9
49	West Virginia	3.6
15	Wisconsin	12.5
36	Wyoming	6.7

RANK ORDER

RANK	STATE	PERCENT
1	Florida	17.7
2	Texas	17.4
3	Georgia	16.1
4	Oklahoma	15.8
5	North Carolina	15.3
6	Arizona	14.1
6	New York	14.1
8	Connecticut	13.8
9	Virginia	13.7
10	California	13.5
11	Nevada	13.4
12	Ohio	13.1
13	Michigan	13.0
14	Maryland	12.9
15	Wisconsin	12.5
16	Missouri	12.4
17	South Carolina	11.3
18	Illinois	11.2
19	Delaware	10.4
20	Pennsylvania	10.1
21	New Mexico	9.4
22	Rhode Island	9.1
23	Colorado	8.8
24	Kansas	8.2
25	Massachusetts	7.9
25	Oregon	7.9
27	Tennessee	7.8
28	Mississippi	7.5
29	Indiana	7.3
30	New Jersey	7.2
30	Vermont	7.2
32	Arkansas	7.1
32	Louisiana	7.1
34	Washington	6.9
35	Idaho	6.8
36	Wyoming	6.7
37	South Dakota	6.6
38	Nebraska	6.5
39	New Hampshire	6.3
40	Maine	6.0
41	Iowa	5.9
41	Utah	5.9
43	Alaska	5.7
44	Alabama	5.5
45	Montana	5.3
46	Minnesota	5.1
47	Kentucky	5.0
48	Hawaii	4.3
49	West Virginia	3.6
50	North Dakota	3.5

District of Columbia**	NA

Source: Morgan Quitno Press using data from U.S. Bureau of the Census, Governments Division
   "1999 State Government Employment and Payroll" (http://www.census.gov/govs/www/apesst99.html)
*Full-time equivalent as of March 1999.
**Not applicable.

State Correctional Officers in 1998

National Total = 222,654 Officers*

ALPHA ORDER

RANK	STATE	OFFICERS	% of USA	RANK	STATE	OFFICERS	% of USA
24	Alabama	2,268	1.0%	1	Texas	27,199	12.2%
41	Alaska	688	0.3%	2	New York	21,796	9.8%
13	Arizona	5,175	2.3%	3	California	21,096	9.5%
27	Arkansas	1,942	0.9%	4	Florida	15,134	6.8%
3	California	21,096	9.5%	5	Michigan	10,268	4.6%
25	Colorado**	2,242	1.0%	6	North Carolina	10,204	4.6%
17	Connecticut	4,393	2.0%	7	Illinois	8,969	4.0%
36	Delaware**	948	0.4%	8	Georgia	8,642	3.9%
4	Florida	15,134	6.8%	9	Ohio	8,428	3.8%
8	Georgia	8,642	3.9%	10	Pennsylvania	7,312	3.3%
34	Hawaii	1,138	0.5%	11	Virginia	7,088	3.2%
39	Idaho	706	0.3%	12	New Jersey	6,243	2.8%
7	Illinois	8,969	4.0%	13	Arizona	5,175	2.3%
NA	Indiana***	NA	NA	14	Missouri	4,936	2.2%
31	Iowa	1,604	0.7%	15	Maryland**	4,923	2.2%
29	Kansas	1,811	0.8%	16	South Carolina	4,474	2.0%
28	Kentucky	1,821	0.8%	17	Connecticut	4,393	2.0%
18	Louisiana	4,046	1.8%	18	Louisiana	4,046	1.8%
NA	Maine***	NA	NA	19	Massachusetts	3,827	1.7%
15	Maryland**	4,923	2.2%	20	Wisconsin	3,203	1.4%
19	Massachusetts	3,827	1.7%	21	Washington	2,927	1.3%
5	Michigan	10,268	4.6%	22	Tennessee	2,726	1.2%
30	Minnesota	1,624	0.7%	23	Mississippi	2,433	1.1%
23	Mississippi	2,433	1.1%	24	Alabama	2,268	1.0%
14	Missouri	4,936	2.2%	25	Colorado**	2,242	1.0%
44	Montana	386	0.2%	26	Oklahoma	2,062	0.9%
38	Nebraska	711	0.3%	27	Arkansas	1,942	0.9%
33	Nevada**	1,312	0.6%	28	Kentucky	1,821	0.8%
42	New Hampshire**	493	0.2%	29	Kansas	1,811	0.8%
12	New Jersey	6,243	2.8%	30	Minnesota	1,624	0.7%
35	New Mexico	1,047	0.5%	31	Iowa	1,604	0.7%
2	New York	21,796	9.8%	32	Oregon**	1,540	0.7%
6	North Carolina	10,204	4.6%	33	Nevada**	1,312	0.6%
47	North Dakota	194	0.1%	34	Hawaii	1,138	0.5%
9	Ohio	8,428	3.8%	35	New Mexico	1,047	0.5%
26	Oklahoma	2,062	0.9%	36	Delaware**	948	0.4%
32	Oregon**	1,540	0.7%	37	Rhode Island	922	0.4%
10	Pennsylvania	7,312	3.3%	38	Nebraska	711	0.3%
37	Rhode Island	922	0.4%	39	Idaho	706	0.3%
16	South Carolina	4,474	2.0%	40	West Virginia**	705	0.3%
45	South Dakota	369	0.2%	41	Alaska	688	0.3%
22	Tennessee	2,726	1.2%	42	New Hampshire**	493	0.2%
1	Texas	27,199	12.2%	43	Vermont**	416	0.2%
NA	Utah***	NA	NA	44	Montana	386	0.2%
43	Vermont**	416	0.2%	45	South Dakota	369	0.2%
11	Virginia	7,088	3.2%	46	Wyoming	263	0.1%
21	Washington	2,927	1.3%	47	North Dakota	194	0.1%
40	West Virginia**	705	0.3%	NA	Indiana***	NA	NA
20	Wisconsin	3,203	1.4%	NA	Maine***	NA	NA
46	Wyoming	263	0.1%	NA	Utah***	NA	NA
					District of Columbia***	NA	NA

RANK ORDER

Source: Morgan Quitno Press using data with permission from American Correctional Association (Lanham, MD)
"2000 Directory of Juvenile and Adult Directory"
As of June 30, 1998. Total does not include 12,918 federal correctional officers.
***These states' figures are as of June 30, 1997.**
****Not available.***

Male Correctional Officers in 1998

National Total = 174,484 Male Officers*

<table>
<tr><td colspan="4"><u>ALPHA ORDER</u></td><td colspan="4"><u>RANK ORDER</u></td></tr>
<tr><td>RANK</td><td>STATE</td><td>OFFICERS</td><td>% of USA</td><td>RANK</td><td>STATE</td><td>OFFICERS</td><td>% of USA</td></tr>
<tr><td>23</td><td>Alabama</td><td>1,821</td><td>1.0%</td><td>1</td><td>New York</td><td>19,990</td><td>11.5%</td></tr>
<tr><td>NA</td><td>Alaska***</td><td>NA</td><td>NA</td><td>2</td><td>Texas</td><td>18,563</td><td>10.6%</td></tr>
<tr><td>13</td><td>Arizona</td><td>4,104</td><td>2.4%</td><td>3</td><td>California</td><td>17,867</td><td>10.2%</td></tr>
<tr><td>32</td><td>Arkansas</td><td>1,210</td><td>0.7%</td><td>4</td><td>Florida</td><td>10,896</td><td>6.2%</td></tr>
<tr><td>3</td><td>California</td><td>17,867</td><td>10.2%</td><td>5</td><td>Michigan</td><td>8,105</td><td>4.6%</td></tr>
<tr><td>24</td><td>Colorado**</td><td>1,759</td><td>1.0%</td><td>6</td><td>Illinois</td><td>7,716</td><td>4.4%</td></tr>
<tr><td>16</td><td>Connecticut</td><td>3,684</td><td>2.1%</td><td>7</td><td>North Carolina</td><td>7,714</td><td>4.4%</td></tr>
<tr><td>37</td><td>Delaware**</td><td>785</td><td>0.4%</td><td>8</td><td>Pennsylvania</td><td>6,739</td><td>3.9%</td></tr>
<tr><td>4</td><td>Florida</td><td>10,896</td><td>6.2%</td><td>9</td><td>Ohio</td><td>6,551</td><td>3.8%</td></tr>
<tr><td>10</td><td>Georgia</td><td>6,141</td><td>3.5%</td><td>10</td><td>Georgia</td><td>6,141</td><td>3.5%</td></tr>
<tr><td>34</td><td>Hawaii</td><td>967</td><td>0.6%</td><td>11</td><td>New Jersey</td><td>5,377</td><td>3.1%</td></tr>
<tr><td>39</td><td>Idaho</td><td>597</td><td>0.3%</td><td>12</td><td>Virginia</td><td>4,966</td><td>2.8%</td></tr>
<tr><td>6</td><td>Illinois</td><td>7,716</td><td>4.4%</td><td>13</td><td>Arizona</td><td>4,104</td><td>2.4%</td></tr>
<tr><td>NA</td><td>Indiana***</td><td>NA</td><td>NA</td><td>14</td><td>Missouri</td><td>3,810</td><td>2.2%</td></tr>
<tr><td>28</td><td>Iowa</td><td>1,329</td><td>0.8%</td><td>15</td><td>Maryland**</td><td>3,760</td><td>2.2%</td></tr>
<tr><td>26</td><td>Kansas</td><td>1,475</td><td>0.8%</td><td>16</td><td>Connecticut</td><td>3,684</td><td>2.1%</td></tr>
<tr><td>27</td><td>Kentucky</td><td>1,465</td><td>0.8%</td><td>17</td><td>Massachusetts</td><td>3,424</td><td>2.0%</td></tr>
<tr><td>18</td><td>Louisiana</td><td>2,927</td><td>1.7%</td><td>18</td><td>Louisiana</td><td>2,927</td><td>1.7%</td></tr>
<tr><td>NA</td><td>Maine***</td><td>NA</td><td>NA</td><td>19</td><td>South Carolina</td><td>2,780</td><td>1.6%</td></tr>
<tr><td>15</td><td>Maryland**</td><td>3,760</td><td>2.2%</td><td>20</td><td>Wisconsin</td><td>2,605</td><td>1.5%</td></tr>
<tr><td>17</td><td>Massachusetts</td><td>3,424</td><td>2.0%</td><td>21</td><td>Washington</td><td>2,301</td><td>1.3%</td></tr>
<tr><td>5</td><td>Michigan</td><td>8,105</td><td>4.6%</td><td>22</td><td>Tennessee</td><td>2,142</td><td>1.2%</td></tr>
<tr><td>31</td><td>Minnesota</td><td>1,212</td><td>0.7%</td><td>23</td><td>Alabama</td><td>1,821</td><td>1.0%</td></tr>
<tr><td>30</td><td>Mississippi</td><td>1,235</td><td>0.7%</td><td>24</td><td>Colorado**</td><td>1,759</td><td>1.0%</td></tr>
<tr><td>14</td><td>Missouri</td><td>3,810</td><td>2.2%</td><td>25</td><td>Oklahoma</td><td>1,712</td><td>1.0%</td></tr>
<tr><td>46</td><td>Montana</td><td>0</td><td>0.0%</td><td>26</td><td>Kansas</td><td>1,475</td><td>0.8%</td></tr>
<tr><td>40</td><td>Nebraska</td><td>562</td><td>0.3%</td><td>27</td><td>Kentucky</td><td>1,465</td><td>0.8%</td></tr>
<tr><td>33</td><td>Nevada**</td><td>1,092</td><td>0.6%</td><td>28</td><td>Iowa</td><td>1,329</td><td>0.8%</td></tr>
<tr><td>41</td><td>New Hampshire**</td><td>443</td><td>0.3%</td><td>29</td><td>Oregon**</td><td>1,258</td><td>0.7%</td></tr>
<tr><td>11</td><td>New Jersey</td><td>5,377</td><td>3.1%</td><td>30</td><td>Mississippi</td><td>1,235</td><td>0.7%</td></tr>
<tr><td>35</td><td>New Mexico</td><td>965</td><td>0.6%</td><td>31</td><td>Minnesota</td><td>1,212</td><td>0.7%</td></tr>
<tr><td>1</td><td>New York</td><td>19,990</td><td>11.5%</td><td>32</td><td>Arkansas</td><td>1,210</td><td>0.7%</td></tr>
<tr><td>7</td><td>North Carolina</td><td>7,714</td><td>4.4%</td><td>33</td><td>Nevada**</td><td>1,092</td><td>0.6%</td></tr>
<tr><td>45</td><td>North Dakota</td><td>149</td><td>0.1%</td><td>34</td><td>Hawaii</td><td>967</td><td>0.6%</td></tr>
<tr><td>9</td><td>Ohio</td><td>6,551</td><td>3.8%</td><td>35</td><td>New Mexico</td><td>965</td><td>0.6%</td></tr>
<tr><td>25</td><td>Oklahoma</td><td>1,712</td><td>1.0%</td><td>36</td><td>Rhode Island</td><td>839</td><td>0.5%</td></tr>
<tr><td>29</td><td>Oregon**</td><td>1,258</td><td>0.7%</td><td>37</td><td>Delaware**</td><td>785</td><td>0.4%</td></tr>
<tr><td>8</td><td>Pennsylvania</td><td>6,739</td><td>3.9%</td><td>38</td><td>West Virginia**</td><td>600</td><td>0.3%</td></tr>
<tr><td>36</td><td>Rhode Island</td><td>839</td><td>0.5%</td><td>39</td><td>Idaho</td><td>597</td><td>0.3%</td></tr>
<tr><td>19</td><td>South Carolina</td><td>2,780</td><td>1.6%</td><td>40</td><td>Nebraska</td><td>562</td><td>0.3%</td></tr>
<tr><td>43</td><td>South Dakota</td><td>280</td><td>0.2%</td><td>41</td><td>New Hampshire**</td><td>443</td><td>0.3%</td></tr>
<tr><td>22</td><td>Tennessee</td><td>2,142</td><td>1.2%</td><td>42</td><td>Vermont**</td><td>371</td><td>0.2%</td></tr>
<tr><td>2</td><td>Texas</td><td>18,563</td><td>10.6%</td><td>43</td><td>South Dakota</td><td>280</td><td>0.2%</td></tr>
<tr><td>NA</td><td>Utah***</td><td>NA</td><td>NA</td><td>44</td><td>Wyoming</td><td>196</td><td>0.1%</td></tr>
<tr><td>42</td><td>Vermont**</td><td>371</td><td>0.2%</td><td>45</td><td>North Dakota</td><td>149</td><td>0.1%</td></tr>
<tr><td>12</td><td>Virginia</td><td>4,966</td><td>2.8%</td><td>46</td><td>Montana</td><td>0</td><td>0.0%</td></tr>
<tr><td>21</td><td>Washington</td><td>2,301</td><td>1.3%</td><td>NA</td><td>Alaska***</td><td>NA</td><td>NA</td></tr>
<tr><td>38</td><td>West Virginia**</td><td>600</td><td>0.3%</td><td>NA</td><td>Indiana***</td><td>NA</td><td>NA</td></tr>
<tr><td>20</td><td>Wisconsin</td><td>2,605</td><td>1.5%</td><td>NA</td><td>Maine***</td><td>NA</td><td>NA</td></tr>
<tr><td>44</td><td>Wyoming</td><td>196</td><td>0.1%</td><td>NA</td><td>Utah***</td><td>NA</td><td>NA</td></tr>
<tr><td></td><td></td><td></td><td></td><td></td><td>District of Columbia***</td><td>NA</td><td>NA</td></tr>
</table>

Source: Morgan Quitno Press using data with permission from American Correctional Association (Lanham, MD)
   "2000 Directory of Juvenile and Adult Directory"
As of June 30, 1998. Total does not include 11,332 male federal correctional officers.
**These states' figures are as of June 30, 1997.*
***Not available.*

Female Correctional Officers in 1998

National Total = 47,401 Female Officers*

RANK	STATE	OFFICERS	% of USA
25	Alabama	447	0.9%
NA	Alaska***	NA	NA
16	Arizona	1,071	2.3%
18	Arkansas	732	1.5%
3	California	3,735	7.9%
24	Colorado**	483	1.0%
19	Connecticut	709	1.5%
35	Delaware**	163	0.3%
2	Florida	4,238	8.9%
4	Georgia	2,501	5.3%
34	Hawaii	171	0.4%
37	Idaho	109	0.2%
11	Illinois	1,253	2.6%
NA	Indiana***	NA	NA
32	Iowa	275	0.6%
30	Kansas	336	0.7%
28	Kentucky	356	0.8%
15	Louisiana	1,119	2.4%
NA	Maine***	NA	NA
13	Maryland**	1,163	2.5%
27	Massachusetts	403	0.9%
6	Michigan	2,163	4.6%
26	Minnesota	412	0.9%
12	Mississippi	1,198	2.5%
14	Missouri	1,126	2.4%
46	Montana	0	0.0%
36	Nebraska	149	0.3%
33	Nevada**	220	0.5%
43	New Hampshire**	50	0.1%
17	New Jersey	866	1.8%
41	New Mexico	82	0.2%
9	New York	1,806	3.8%
5	North Carolina	2,490	5.3%
44	North Dakota	45	0.1%
8	Ohio	1,877	4.0%
29	Oklahoma	350	0.7%
31	Oregon**	282	0.6%
23	Pennsylvania	573	1.2%
40	Rhode Island	83	0.2%
10	South Carolina	1,494	3.2%
39	South Dakota	88	0.2%
22	Tennessee	584	1.2%
1	Texas	8,636	18.2%
NA	Utah***	NA	NA
44	Vermont**	45	0.1%
7	Virginia	2,122	4.5%
20	Washington	626	1.3%
38	West Virginia**	105	0.2%
21	Wisconsin	598	1.3%
42	Wyoming	67	0.1%

RANK	STATE	OFFICERS	% of USA
1	Texas	8,636	18.2%
2	Florida	4,238	8.9%
3	California	3,735	7.9%
4	Georgia	2,501	5.3%
5	North Carolina	2,490	5.3%
6	Michigan	2,163	4.6%
7	Virginia	2,122	4.5%
8	Ohio	1,877	4.0%
9	New York	1,806	3.8%
10	South Carolina	1,494	3.2%
11	Illinois	1,253	2.6%
12	Mississippi	1,198	2.5%
13	Maryland**	1,163	2.5%
14	Missouri	1,126	2.4%
15	Louisiana	1,119	2.4%
16	Arizona	1,071	2.3%
17	New Jersey	866	1.8%
18	Arkansas	732	1.5%
19	Connecticut	709	1.5%
20	Washington	626	1.3%
21	Wisconsin	598	1.3%
22	Tennessee	584	1.2%
23	Pennsylvania	573	1.2%
24	Colorado**	483	1.0%
25	Alabama	447	0.9%
26	Minnesota	412	0.9%
27	Massachusetts	403	0.9%
28	Kentucky	356	0.8%
29	Oklahoma	350	0.7%
30	Kansas	336	0.7%
31	Oregon**	282	0.6%
32	Iowa	275	0.6%
33	Nevada**	220	0.5%
34	Hawaii	171	0.4%
35	Delaware**	163	0.3%
36	Nebraska	149	0.3%
37	Idaho	109	0.2%
38	West Virginia**	105	0.2%
39	South Dakota	88	0.2%
40	Rhode Island	83	0.2%
41	New Mexico	82	0.2%
42	Wyoming	67	0.1%
43	New Hampshire**	50	0.1%
44	North Dakota	45	0.1%
44	Vermont**	45	0.1%
46	Montana	0	0.0%
NA	Alaska***	NA	NA
NA	Indiana***	NA	NA
NA	Maine***	NA	NA
NA	Utah***	NA	NA
	District of Columbia**	NA	NA

Source: Morgan Quitno Press using data with permission from American Correctional Association (Lanham, MD)
"2000 Directory of Juvenile and Adult Directory"
As of June 30, 1998. Total does not include 1,575 female federal correctional officers.
**These states' figures are as of June 30, 1997.*
***Not available.*

State Prisoners per Correctional Officer in 1998

National Average = 4.8 Prisoners per Officer*

ALPHA ORDER

RANK	STATE	RATE
2	Alabama	8.8
11	Alaska	5.1
20	Arizona	4.8
8	Arkansas	5.6
3	California	8.0
27	Colorado**	4.1
32	Connecticut	3.7
6	Delaware**	5.7
25	Florida	4.4
NA	Georgia***	NA
37	Hawaii	3.2
6	Idaho	5.7
12	Illinois	5.0
29	Indiana	4.0
21	Iowa	4.6
24	Kansas	4.5
NA	Kentucky***	NA
39	Louisiana	3.0
NA	Maine***	NA
29	Maryland**	4.0
NA	Massachusetts***	NA
26	Michigan	4.3
35	Minnesota	3.4
12	Mississippi	5.0
NA	Missouri***	NA
NA	Montana***	NA
12	Nebraska	5.0
34	Nevada**	3.6
27	New Hampshire**	4.1
31	New Jersey	3.9
39	New Mexico	3.0
36	New York	3.3
39	North Carolina	3.0
12	North Dakota	5.0
4	Ohio	6.5
1	Oklahoma	10.0
12	Oregon**	5.0
18	Pennsylvania	4.9
NA	Rhode Island***	NA
18	South Carolina	4.9
4	South Dakota	6.5
21	Tennessee	4.6
10	Texas	5.3
NA	Utah***	NA
38	Vermont**	3.1
32	Virginia	3.7
21	Washington	4.6
39	West Virginia**	3.0
12	Wisconsin	5.0
8	Wyoming	5.6

RANK ORDER

RANK	STATE	RATE
1	Oklahoma	10.0
2	Alabama	8.8
3	California	8.0
4	Ohio	6.5
4	South Dakota	6.5
6	Delaware**	5.7
6	Idaho	5.7
8	Arkansas	5.6
8	Wyoming	5.6
10	Texas	5.3
11	Alaska	5.1
12	Illinois	5.0
12	Mississippi	5.0
12	Nebraska	5.0
12	North Dakota	5.0
12	Oregon**	5.0
12	Wisconsin	5.0
18	Pennsylvania	4.9
18	South Carolina	4.9
20	Arizona	4.8
21	Iowa	4.6
21	Tennessee	4.6
21	Washington	4.6
24	Kansas	4.5
25	Florida	4.4
26	Michigan	4.3
27	Colorado**	4.1
27	New Hampshire**	4.1
29	Indiana	4.0
29	Maryland**	4.0
31	New Jersey	3.9
32	Connecticut	3.7
32	Virginia	3.7
34	Nevada**	3.6
35	Minnesota	3.4
36	New York	3.3
37	Hawaii	3.2
38	Vermont**	3.1
39	Louisiana	3.0
39	New Mexico	3.0
39	North Carolina	3.0
39	West Virginia**	3.0
NA	Georgia***	NA
NA	Kentucky***	NA
NA	Maine***	NA
NA	Massachusetts***	NA
NA	Missouri***	NA
NA	Montana***	NA
NA	Rhode Island***	NA
NA	Utah***	NA
	District of Columbia***	NA

Source: With permission from American Correctional Association (Lanham, MD)
"2000 Directory of Juvenile and Adult Directory"
As of June 30, 1998 in adult systems. National rate does not include federal correctional officers or prisoners.
***These states' figures are as of June 30, 1997.*
****Not available.*

Turnover Rate of Correctional Officers in 1998

National Average = 22.39%*

ALPHA ORDER

RANK	STATE	TURNOVER RATE
NA	Alabama***	NA
24	Alaska	12.00
7	Arizona	25.50
1	Arkansas	39.80
NA	California***	NA
25	Colorado**	10.00
34	Connecticut	5.00
30	Delaware**	6.00
3	Florida	30.30
NA	Georgia***	NA
NA	Hawaii***	NA
6	Idaho	25.80
33	Illinois	5.20
15	Indiana	18.00
27	Iowa	9.38
9	Kansas	22.47
11	Kentucky	22.00
4	Louisiana	29.00
NA	Maine***	NA
18	Maryland**	17.00
34	Massachusetts	5.00
38	Michigan	4.20
32	Minnesota	5.90
NA	Mississippi***	NA
17	Missouri	17.40
NA	Montana***	NA
10	Nebraska	22.09
28	Nevada**	8.20
22	New Hampshire**	12.90
36	New Jersey	4.40
14	New Mexico	18.90
39	New York	3.80
13	North Carolina	20.20
30	North Dakota	6.00
20	Ohio	15.00
21	Oklahoma	14.40
29	Oregon**	7.00
37	Pennsylvania	4.30
40	Rhode Island	3.30
8	South Carolina	22.50
5	South Dakota	28.00
2	Tennessee	34.00
16	Texas	17.42
NA	Utah***	NA
23	Vermont**	12.50
19	Virginia	16.53
NA	Washington***	NA
25	West Virginia**	10.00
NA	Wisconsin***	NA
12	Wyoming	21.60

RANK ORDER

RANK	STATE	TURNOVER RATE
1	Arkansas	39.80
2	Tennessee	34.00
3	Florida	30.30
4	Louisiana	29.00
5	South Dakota	28.00
6	Idaho	25.80
7	Arizona	25.50
8	South Carolina	22.50
9	Kansas	22.47
10	Nebraska	22.09
11	Kentucky	22.00
12	Wyoming	21.60
13	North Carolina	20.20
14	New Mexico	18.90
15	Indiana	18.00
16	Texas	17.42
17	Missouri	17.40
18	Maryland**	17.00
19	Virginia	16.53
20	Ohio	15.00
21	Oklahoma	14.40
22	New Hampshire**	12.90
23	Vermont**	12.50
24	Alaska	12.00
25	Colorado**	10.00
25	West Virginia**	10.00
27	Iowa	9.38
28	Nevada**	8.20
29	Oregon**	7.00
30	Delaware**	6.00
30	North Dakota	6.00
32	Minnesota	5.90
33	Illinois	5.20
34	Connecticut	5.00
34	Massachusetts	5.00
36	New Jersey	4.40
37	Pennsylvania	4.30
38	Michigan	4.20
39	New York	3.80
40	Rhode Island	3.30
NA	Alabama***	NA
NA	California***	NA
NA	Georgia***	NA
NA	Hawaii***	NA
NA	Maine***	NA
NA	Mississippi***	NA
NA	Montana***	NA
NA	Utah***	NA
NA	Washington***	NA
NA	Wisconsin***	NA
	District of Columbia***	NA

Source: With permission from American Correctional Association (Lanham, MD)
"2000 Directory of Juvenile and Adult Directory"
*As of June 30, 1998 in adult systems. National rate does not include federal correctional officers.
**These states' figures are as of June 30, 1997.
***Not available.

Jail and Detention Centers in 1993

National Total = 3,304 Jails*

ALPHA ORDER

RANK	STATE	JAILS	% of USA
4	Alabama	129	3.9%
45	Alaska	5	0.2%
34	Arizona	33	1.0%
19	Arkansas	83	2.5%
3	California	136	4.1%
26	Colorado	61	1.9%
NA	Connecticut**	NA	NA
NA	Delaware**	NA	NA
9	Florida	100	3.0%
2	Georgia	202	6.1%
NA	Hawaii**	NA	NA
32	Idaho	39	1.2%
14	Illinois	93	2.8%
18	Indiana	88	2.7%
16	Iowa	90	2.7%
11	Kansas	96	2.9%
20	Kentucky	81	2.5%
11	Louisiana	96	2.9%
43	Maine	15	0.5%
34	Maryland	33	1.0%
41	Massachusetts	20	0.6%
17	Michigan	89	2.7%
23	Minnesota	75	2.3%
13	Mississippi	95	2.9%
5	Missouri	127	3.8%
29	Montana	44	1.3%
25	Nebraska	64	1.9%
41	Nevada	20	0.6%
44	New Hampshire	11	0.3%
37	New Jersey	25	0.8%
33	New Mexico	34	1.0%
22	New York	78	2.4%
8	North Carolina	104	3.2%
37	North Dakota	25	0.8%
6	Ohio	120	3.6%
9	Oklahoma	100	3.0%
30	Oregon	43	1.3%
21	Pennsylvania	79	2.4%
NA	Rhode Island**	NA	NA
28	South Carolina	55	1.7%
36	South Dakota	28	0.9%
7	Tennessee	111	3.4%
1	Texas	267	8.1%
37	Utah	25	0.8%
NA	Vermont**	NA	NA
14	Virginia	93	2.8%
27	Washington	56	1.7%
31	West Virginia	41	1.2%
24	Wisconsin	72	2.2%
40	Wyoming	22	0.7%

RANK ORDER

RANK	STATE	JAILS	% of USA
1	Texas	267	8.1%
2	Georgia	202	6.1%
3	California	136	4.1%
4	Alabama	129	3.9%
5	Missouri	127	3.8%
6	Ohio	120	3.6%
7	Tennessee	111	3.4%
8	North Carolina	104	3.2%
9	Florida	100	3.0%
9	Oklahoma	100	3.0%
11	Kansas	96	2.9%
11	Louisiana	96	2.9%
13	Mississippi	95	2.9%
14	Illinois	93	2.8%
14	Virginia	93	2.8%
16	Iowa	90	2.7%
17	Michigan	89	2.7%
18	Indiana	88	2.7%
19	Arkansas	83	2.5%
20	Kentucky	81	2.5%
21	Pennsylvania	79	2.4%
22	New York	78	2.4%
23	Minnesota	75	2.3%
24	Wisconsin	72	2.2%
25	Nebraska	64	1.9%
26	Colorado	61	1.9%
27	Washington	56	1.7%
28	South Carolina	55	1.7%
29	Montana	44	1.3%
30	Oregon	43	1.3%
31	West Virginia	41	1.2%
32	Idaho	39	1.2%
33	New Mexico	34	1.0%
34	Arizona	33	1.0%
34	Maryland	33	1.0%
36	South Dakota	28	0.9%
37	New Jersey	25	0.8%
37	North Dakota	25	0.8%
37	Utah	25	0.8%
40	Wyoming	22	0.7%
41	Massachusetts	20	0.6%
41	Nevada	20	0.6%
43	Maine	15	0.5%
44	New Hampshire	11	0.3%
45	Alaska	5	0.2%
NA	Connecticut**	NA	NA
NA	Delaware**	NA	NA
NA	Hawaii**	NA	NA
NA	Rhode Island**	NA	NA
NA	Vermont**	NA	NA
	District of Columbia	1	0.0%

Source: U.S. Department of Justice, Bureau of Justice Statistics
    "Jail and Jail Inmates 1993-94" (Bulletin, April 1995, NCJ-151651)
*As of July 1, 1993. Jails are locally operated correctional facilities that confine persons before or after adjudication. Inmates sentenced to jail usually have a sentence of a year or less.
**These states have combined state and local jail systems and are excluded from this count.

Inmates in Local Jails in 1993

National Total = 459,804 Inmates*

ALPHA ORDER | | | | RANK ORDER

RANK	STATE	INMATES	% of USA
21	Alabama	7,072	1.5%
45	Alaska	31	0.0%
20	Arizona	7,231	1.6%
32	Arkansas	2,846	0.6%
1	California	69,298	15.1%
23	Colorado	6,316	1.4%
NA	Connecticut**	NA	NA
NA	Delaware**	NA	NA
3	Florida	34,183	7.4%
5	Georgia	22,663	4.9%
NA	Hawaii**	NA	NA
38	Idaho	1,485	0.3%
10	Illinois	14,549	3.2%
16	Indiana	8,297	1.8%
37	Iowa	1,602	0.4%
33	Kansas	2,797	0.6%
22	Kentucky	6,813	1.5%
7	Louisiana	16,208	3.5%
40	Maine	704	0.2%
14	Maryland	9,358	2.0%
18	Massachusetts	7,878	1.7%
12	Michigan	12,479	2.7%
29	Minnesota	3,654	0.8%
26	Mississippi	4,851	1.1%
25	Missouri	5,030	1.1%
41	Montana	680	0.2%
36	Nebraska	1,680	0.4%
31	Nevada	2,987	0.7%
39	New Hampshire	1,127	0.3%
8	New Jersey	15,122	3.3%
30	New Mexico	3,058	0.7%
4	New York	29,809	6.5%
15	North Carolina	8,939	1.9%
44	North Dakota	361	0.1%
13	Ohio	11,695	2.5%
27	Oklahoma	4,102	0.9%
28	Oregon	3,777	0.8%
6	Pennsylvania	19,231	4.2%
NA	Rhode Island**	NA	NA
24	South Carolina	5,713	1.2%
42	South Dakota	623	0.1%
11	Tennessee	14,375	3.1%
2	Texas	55,395	12.1%
34	Utah	1,895	0.4%
NA	Vermont**	NA	NA
9	Virginia	14,623	3.2%
19	Washington	7,435	1.6%
35	West Virginia	1,771	0.4%
17	Wisconsin	7,879	1.7%
43	Wyoming	495	0.1%

RANK	STATE	INMATES	% of USA
1	California	69,298	15.1%
2	Texas	55,395	12.1%
3	Florida	34,183	7.4%
4	New York	29,809	6.5%
5	Georgia	22,663	4.9%
6	Pennsylvania	19,231	4.2%
7	Louisiana	16,208	3.5%
8	New Jersey	15,122	3.3%
9	Virginia	14,623	3.2%
10	Illinois	14,549	3.2%
11	Tennessee	14,375	3.1%
12	Michigan	12,479	2.7%
13	Ohio	11,695	2.5%
14	Maryland	9,358	2.0%
15	North Carolina	8,939	1.9%
16	Indiana	8,297	1.8%
17	Wisconsin	7,879	1.7%
18	Massachusetts	7,878	1.7%
19	Washington	7,435	1.6%
20	Arizona	7,231	1.6%
21	Alabama	7,072	1.5%
22	Kentucky	6,813	1.5%
23	Colorado	6,316	1.4%
24	South Carolina	5,713	1.2%
25	Missouri	5,030	1.1%
26	Mississippi	4,851	1.1%
27	Oklahoma	4,102	0.9%
28	Oregon	3,777	0.8%
29	Minnesota	3,654	0.8%
30	New Mexico	3,058	0.7%
31	Nevada	2,987	0.7%
32	Arkansas	2,846	0.6%
33	Kansas	2,797	0.6%
34	Utah	1,895	0.4%
35	West Virginia	1,771	0.4%
36	Nebraska	1,680	0.4%
37	Iowa	1,602	0.4%
38	Idaho	1,485	0.3%
39	New Hampshire	1,127	0.3%
40	Maine	704	0.2%
41	Montana	680	0.2%
42	South Dakota	623	0.1%
43	Wyoming	495	0.1%
44	North Dakota	361	0.1%
45	Alaska	31	0.0%
NA	Connecticut**	NA	NA
NA	Delaware**	NA	NA
NA	Hawaii**	NA	NA
NA	Rhode Island**	NA	NA
NA	Vermont**	NA	NA
	District of Columbia	1,687	0.4%

Source: U.S. Department of Justice, Bureau of Justice Statistics
    "Jail and Jail Inmates 1993-94" (Bulletin, April 1995, NCJ-151651)
*As of July 1, 1993. Jails are locally operated correctional facilities that confine persons before or after adjudication. Inmates sentenced to jail usually have a sentence of a year or less.
**These states have combined state and local jail systems and are excluded from this count.

III. DRUGS AND ALCOHOL

119   Alcohol and Other Drug Treatment Units in 1997
120   Alcohol and Other Drug Treatment Admissions in 1997
121   Male Admissions to Alcohol and Other Drug Treatment Programs in 1997
122   Male Admissions to Alcohol and Drug Treatment Programs as a Percent of All Admissions in 1997
123   Female Admissions to Alcohol and Other Drug Treatment Programs in 1997
124   Female Admissions to Alcohol and Other Drug Treatment Programs as a Percent of All Admissions in 1997
125   White Admissions to Alcohol and Other Drug Treatment Programs in 1997
126   White Admissions to Alcohol and Other Drug Treatment Programs as a Percent of All Admissions in 1997
127   Black Admissions to Alcohol and Other Drug Treatment Programs in 1997
128   Black Admissions to Alcohol and Other Drug Treatment Programs as a Percent of All Admissions in 1997
129   Hispanic Admissions to Alcohol and Other Drug Treatment Programs in 1997
130   Hispanic Admissions to Alcohol and Other Drug Treatment Programs as a Percent of All Admissions in 1997
131   Expenditures for State-Supported Alcohol and Other Drug Abuse Services: 1997
132   Per Capita Expenditures for State-Supported Alcohol and Other Drug Abuse Services in 1997
133   Expenditures for State-Supported Alcohol and Other Drug Abuse Treatment Programs in 1997
134   Expenditures per Alcohol and Other Drug Treatment Admission in 1997
135   Per Capita Expenditures for State-Supported Alcohol and Other Drug Abuse Treatment Programs in 1997
136   Expenditures for State-Supported Alcohol and Other Drug Abuse Prevention Programs in 1997
137   Per Capita Expenditures for State-Supported Alcohol and Other Drug Abuse Prevention Programs in 1997

Alcohol and Other Drug Treatment Units in 1997

National Total = 6,837 Units*

ALPHA ORDER

RANK	STATE	UNITS	% of USA
32	Alabama	37	0.5%
31	Alaska	38	0.6%
18	Arizona	121	1.8%
39	Arkansas	31	0.5%
2	California	860	12.6%
9	Colorado	174	2.5%
10	Connecticut	162	2.4%
38	Delaware	32	0.5%
15	Florida	136	2.0%
20	Georgia	95	1.4%
44	Hawaii	20	0.3%
NA	Idaho**	NA	NA
NA	Illinois**	NA	NA
35	Indiana	35	0.5%
32	Iowa	37	0.5%
25	Kansas	54	0.8%
7	Kentucky	218	3.2%
19	Louisiana	119	1.7%
36	Maine	33	0.5%
16	Maryland	131	1.9%
5	Massachusetts	257	3.8%
6	Michigan	253	3.7%
NA	Minnesota**	NA	NA
22	Mississippi	76	1.1%
21	Missouri	88	1.3%
41	Montana	23	0.3%
17	Nebraska	125	1.8%
27	Nevada	44	0.6%
43	New Hampshire	21	0.3%
12	New Jersey	147	2.2%
28	New Mexico	43	0.6%
1	New York	1,300	19.0%
28	North Carolina	43	0.6%
45	North Dakota	8	0.1%
4	Ohio	341	5.0%
24	Oklahoma	58	0.8%
11	Oregon	150	2.2%
3	Pennsylvania	754	11.0%
34	Rhode Island	36	0.5%
NA	South Carolina**	NA	NA
26	South Dakota	47	0.7%
23	Tennessee	60	0.9%
14	Texas	140	2.0%
39	Utah	31	0.5%
42	Vermont	22	0.3%
30	Virginia	40	0.6%
8	Washington	204	3.0%
36	West Virginia	33	0.5%
13	Wisconsin	142	2.1%
NA	Wyoming**	NA	NA

RANK ORDER

RANK	STATE	UNITS	% of USA
1	New York	1,300	19.0%
2	California	860	12.6%
3	Pennsylvania	754	11.0%
4	Ohio	341	5.0%
5	Massachusetts	257	3.8%
6	Michigan	253	3.7%
7	Kentucky	218	3.2%
8	Washington	204	3.0%
9	Colorado	174	2.5%
10	Connecticut	162	2.4%
11	Oregon	150	2.2%
12	New Jersey	147	2.2%
13	Wisconsin	142	2.1%
14	Texas	140	2.0%
15	Florida	136	2.0%
16	Maryland	131	1.9%
17	Nebraska	125	1.8%
18	Arizona	121	1.8%
19	Louisiana	119	1.7%
20	Georgia	95	1.4%
21	Missouri	88	1.3%
22	Mississippi	76	1.1%
23	Tennessee	60	0.9%
24	Oklahoma	58	0.8%
25	Kansas	54	0.8%
26	South Dakota	47	0.7%
27	Nevada	44	0.6%
28	New Mexico	43	0.6%
28	North Carolina	43	0.6%
30	Virginia	40	0.6%
31	Alaska	38	0.6%
32	Alabama	37	0.5%
32	Iowa	37	0.5%
34	Rhode Island	36	0.5%
35	Indiana	35	0.5%
36	Maine	33	0.5%
36	West Virginia	33	0.5%
38	Delaware	32	0.5%
39	Arkansas	31	0.5%
39	Utah	31	0.5%
41	Montana	23	0.3%
42	Vermont	22	0.3%
43	New Hampshire	21	0.3%
44	Hawaii	20	0.3%
45	North Dakota	8	0.1%
NA	Idaho**	NA	NA
NA	Illinois**	NA	NA
NA	Minnesota**	NA	NA
NA	South Carolina**	NA	NA
NA	Wyoming**	NA	NA
	District of Columbia	18	0.3%

Source: National Association of State Alcohol and Drug Abuse Directors
   "State Resources and Services Related to Alcohol and Other Drug Problems-Fiscal Year 1997" (July 1999)
*Does not include 58 units in Puerto Rico. Data are only from treatment units that received at least some funds administered by a state's alcohol/drug agency in fiscal year 1997.
**Not available.

Alcohol and Other Drug Treatment Admissions in 1997

National Total = 1,781,857 Admissions*

ALPHA ORDER			

RANK	STATE	ADMISSIONS	% of USA
32	Alabama	14,208	0.8%
33	Alaska	12,887	0.7%
19	Arizona	29,987	1.7%
31	Arkansas	14,959	0.8%
1	California	181,091	10.2%
11	Colorado	56,028	3.1%
17	Connecticut	32,493	1.8%
45	Delaware	5,873	0.3%
3	Florida	118,885	6.7%
10	Georgia	56,776	3.2%
46	Hawaii	4,892	0.3%
NA	Idaho**	NA	NA
4	Illinois	112,777	6.3%
26	Indiana	17,721	1.0%
25	Iowa	19,368	1.1%
30	Kansas	15,116	0.8%
35	Kentucky	12,670	0.7%
20	Louisiana	27,298	1.5%
39	Maine	8,885	0.5%
18	Maryland	30,460	1.7%
5	Massachusetts	102,997	5.8%
6	Michigan	81,820	4.6%
NA	Minnesota**	NA	NA
23	Mississippi	23,244	1.3%
16	Missouri	36,538	2.1%
44	Montana	6,429	0.4%
24	Nebraska	19,951	1.1%
40	Nevada	8,867	0.5%
41	New Hampshire	7,687	0.4%
14	New Jersey	45,809	2.6%
37	New Mexico	10,949	0.6%
2	New York	165,140	9.3%
15	North Carolina	38,315	2.2%
47	North Dakota	3,461	0.2%
7	Ohio	78,323	4.4%
29	Oklahoma	15,872	0.9%
13	Oregon	46,101	2.6%
8	Pennsylvania	70,625	4.0%
36	Rhode Island	11,980	0.7%
21	South Carolina	26,521	1.5%
34	South Dakota	12,878	0.7%
42	Tennessee	7,241	0.4%
22	Texas	25,515	1.4%
27	Utah	17,071	1.0%
43	Vermont	7,000	0.4%
9	Virginia	62,435	3.5%
12	Washington	47,498	2.7%
28	West Virginia	16,106	0.9%
38	Wisconsin	9,350	0.5%
NA	Wyoming**	NA	NA

RANK ORDER			

RANK	STATE	ADMISSIONS	% of USA
1	California	181,091	10.2%
2	New York	165,140	9.3%
3	Florida	118,885	6.7%
4	Illinois	112,777	6.3%
5	Massachusetts	102,997	5.8%
6	Michigan	81,820	4.6%
7	Ohio	78,323	4.4%
8	Pennsylvania	70,625	4.0%
9	Virginia	62,435	3.5%
10	Georgia	56,776	3.2%
11	Colorado	56,028	3.1%
12	Washington	47,498	2.7%
13	Oregon	46,101	2.6%
14	New Jersey	45,809	2.6%
15	North Carolina	38,315	2.2%
16	Missouri	36,538	2.1%
17	Connecticut	32,493	1.8%
18	Maryland	30,460	1.7%
19	Arizona	29,987	1.7%
20	Louisiana	27,298	1.5%
21	South Carolina	26,521	1.5%
22	Texas	25,515	1.4%
23	Mississippi	23,244	1.3%
24	Nebraska	19,951	1.1%
25	Iowa	19,368	1.1%
26	Indiana	17,721	1.0%
27	Utah	17,071	1.0%
28	West Virginia	16,106	0.9%
29	Oklahoma	15,872	0.9%
30	Kansas	15,116	0.8%
31	Arkansas	14,959	0.8%
32	Alabama	14,208	0.8%
33	Alaska	12,887	0.7%
34	South Dakota	12,878	0.7%
35	Kentucky	12,670	0.7%
36	Rhode Island	11,980	0.7%
37	New Mexico	10,949	0.6%
38	Wisconsin	9,350	0.5%
39	Maine	8,885	0.5%
40	Nevada	8,867	0.5%
41	New Hampshire	7,687	0.4%
42	Tennessee	7,241	0.4%
43	Vermont	7,000	0.4%
44	Montana	6,429	0.4%
45	Delaware	5,873	0.3%
46	Hawaii	4,892	0.3%
47	North Dakota	3,461	0.2%
NA	Idaho**	NA	NA
NA	Minnesota**	NA	NA
NA	Wyoming**	NA	NA
	District of Columbia	3,760	0.2%

Source: National Association of State Alcohol and Drug Abuse Directors
"State Resources and Services Related to Alcohol and Other Drug Problems-Fiscal Year 1997" (July 1999)
*Does not include 25,544 admissions in Puerto Rico. Data are only from treatment units that received at least some funds administered by a state's alcohol/drug agency in fiscal year 1997. National total is only for reporting states.
**Not available.

Male Admissions to Alcohol and Other Drug Treatment Programs in 1997

National Total = 1,228,209 Male Admissions*

ALPHA ORDER

RANK	STATE	ADMISSIONS	% of USA
31	Alabama	10,477	0.9%
34	Alaska	8,690	0.7%
19	Arizona	20,392	1.7%
28	Arkansas	11,395	0.9%
2	California	114,533	9.3%
14	Colorado	30,176	2.5%
17	Connecticut	23,338	1.9%
44	Delaware	4,350	0.4%
3	Florida	85,604	7.0%
10	Georgia	39,777	3.2%
45	Hawaii	3,137	0.3%
NA	Idaho**	NA	NA
4	Illinois	75,206	6.1%
27	Indiana	12,283	1.0%
25	Iowa	13,918	1.1%
29	Kansas	11,055	0.9%
33	Kentucky	9,107	0.7%
21	Louisiana	19,838	1.6%
38	Maine	6,413	0.5%
18	Maryland	21,201	1.7%
5	Massachusetts	74,228	6.0%
6	Michigan	58,001	4.7%
NA	Minnesota**	NA	NA
23	Mississippi	15,495	1.3%
16	Missouri	26,241	2.1%
46	Montana	3,013	0.2%
24	Nebraska	15,146	1.2%
39	Nevada	5,793	0.5%
41	New Hampshire	5,605	0.5%
11	New Jersey	32,219	2.6%
36	New Mexico	8,005	0.7%
1	New York	120,437	9.8%
15	North Carolina	28,282	2.3%
47	North Dakota	2,343	0.2%
7	Ohio	53,750	4.4%
30	Oklahoma	10,802	0.9%
13	Oregon	31,804	2.6%
8	Pennsylvania	50,623	4.1%
35	Rhode Island	8,352	0.7%
20	South Carolina	20,045	1.6%
32	South Dakota	9,506	0.8%
42	Tennessee	5,252	0.4%
22	Texas	16,086	1.3%
40	Utah	5,787	0.5%
43	Vermont	4,868	0.4%
9	Virginia	41,582	3.4%
12	Washington	31,834	2.6%
26	West Virginia	12,445	1.0%
37	Wisconsin	7,072	0.6%
NA	Wyoming**	NA	NA

RANK ORDER

RANK	STATE	ADMISSIONS	% of USA
1	New York	120,437	9.8%
2	California	114,533	9.3%
3	Florida	85,604	7.0%
4	Illinois	75,206	6.1%
5	Massachusetts	74,228	6.0%
6	Michigan	58,001	4.7%
7	Ohio	53,750	4.4%
8	Pennsylvania	50,623	4.1%
9	Virginia	41,582	3.4%
10	Georgia	39,777	3.2%
11	New Jersey	32,219	2.6%
12	Washington	31,834	2.6%
13	Oregon	31,804	2.6%
14	Colorado	30,176	2.5%
15	North Carolina	28,282	2.3%
16	Missouri	26,241	2.1%
17	Connecticut	23,338	1.9%
18	Maryland	21,201	1.7%
19	Arizona	20,392	1.7%
20	South Carolina	20,045	1.6%
21	Louisiana	19,838	1.6%
22	Texas	16,086	1.3%
23	Mississippi	15,495	1.3%
24	Nebraska	15,146	1.2%
25	Iowa	13,918	1.1%
26	West Virginia	12,445	1.0%
27	Indiana	12,283	1.0%
28	Arkansas	11,395	0.9%
29	Kansas	11,055	0.9%
30	Oklahoma	10,802	0.9%
31	Alabama	10,477	0.9%
32	South Dakota	9,506	0.8%
33	Kentucky	9,107	0.7%
34	Alaska	8,690	0.7%
35	Rhode Island	8,352	0.7%
36	New Mexico	8,005	0.7%
37	Wisconsin	7,072	0.6%
38	Maine	6,413	0.5%
39	Nevada	5,793	0.5%
40	Utah	5,787	0.5%
41	New Hampshire	5,605	0.5%
42	Tennessee	5,252	0.4%
43	Vermont	4,868	0.4%
44	Delaware	4,350	0.4%
45	Hawaii	3,137	0.3%
46	Montana	3,013	0.2%
47	North Dakota	2,343	0.2%
NA	Idaho**	NA	NA
NA	Minnesota**	NA	NA
NA	Wyoming**	NA	NA
	District of Columbia	2,703	0.2%

Source: National Association of State Alcohol and Drug Abuse Directors
"State Resources and Services Related to Alcohol and Other Drug Problems-Fiscal Year 1997" (July 1999)
*Does not include 9,880 male admissions in Puerto Rico. Data are only from treatment units that received at least some funds administered by a state's alcohol/drug agency in fiscal year 1997. An additional 42,078 admissions were not reported by sex. National total is only for reporting states.
**Not available.

121

Male Admissions to Alcohol and Drug Treatment Programs
As a Percent of All Admissions in 1997
National Percent = 68.9% Males*

ALPHA ORDER

RANK	STATE	PERCENT
9	Alabama	73.7
36	Alaska	67.4
34	Arizona	68.0
2	Arkansas	76.2
43	California	63.2
NA	Colorado**	NA
21	Connecticut	71.8
6	Delaware	74.1
18	Florida	72.0
26	Georgia	70.1
42	Hawaii	64.1
NA	Idaho**	NA
38	Illinois	66.7
30	Indiana	69.3
19	Iowa	71.9
10	Kansas	73.1
19	Kentucky	71.9
14	Louisiana	72.7
16	Maine	72.2
28	Maryland	69.6
17	Massachusetts	72.1
24	Michigan	70.9
NA	Minnesota**	NA
38	Mississippi	66.7
21	Missouri	71.8
NA	Montana**	NA
3	Nebraska	75.9
41	Nevada	65.3
12	New Hampshire	72.9
25	New Jersey	70.3
10	New Mexico	73.1
12	New York	72.9
7	North Carolina	73.8
35	North Dakota	67.7
32	Ohio	68.6
33	Oklahoma	68.1
31	Oregon	69.0
23	Pennsylvania	71.7
27	Rhode Island	69.7
4	South Carolina	75.6
7	South Dakota	73.8
15	Tennessee	72.5
44	Texas	63.0
NA	Utah**	NA
29	Vermont	69.5
40	Virginia	66.6
37	Washington	67.0
1	West Virginia	77.3
4	Wisconsin	75.6
NA	Wyoming**	NA

RANK ORDER

RANK	STATE	PERCENT
1	West Virginia	77.3
2	Arkansas	76.2
3	Nebraska	75.9
4	South Carolina	75.6
4	Wisconsin	75.6
6	Delaware	74.1
7	North Carolina	73.8
7	South Dakota	73.8
9	Alabama	73.7
10	Kansas	73.1
10	New Mexico	73.1
12	New Hampshire	72.9
12	New York	72.9
14	Louisiana	72.7
15	Tennessee	72.5
16	Maine	72.2
17	Massachusetts	72.1
18	Florida	72.0
19	Iowa	71.9
19	Kentucky	71.9
21	Connecticut	71.8
21	Missouri	71.8
23	Pennsylvania	71.7
24	Michigan	70.9
25	New Jersey	70.3
26	Georgia	70.1
27	Rhode Island	69.7
28	Maryland	69.6
29	Vermont	69.5
30	Indiana	69.3
31	Oregon	69.0
32	Ohio	68.6
33	Oklahoma	68.1
34	Arizona	68.0
35	North Dakota	67.7
36	Alaska	67.4
37	Washington	67.0
38	Illinois	66.7
38	Mississippi	66.7
40	Virginia	66.6
41	Nevada	65.3
42	Hawaii	64.1
43	California	63.2
44	Texas	63.0
NA	Colorado**	NA
NA	Idaho**	NA
NA	Minnesota**	NA
NA	Montana**	NA
NA	Utah**	NA
NA	Wyoming**	NA

District of Columbia 71.9

*Source: Morgan Quitno Press using data from National Association of State Alcohol and Drug Abuse Directors
"State Resources and Services Related to Alcohol and Other Drug Problems-Fiscal Year 1997" (July 1999)
*Does not include admissions in U.S. territories. Data are only from treatment units that received at least some
funds administered by a state's alcohol/drug agency in fiscal year 1997. An additional 42,078 admissions were not
reported by sex.
**Not available.*

Female Admissions to Alcohol and Other Drug Treatment Programs in 1997

National Total = 520,955 Female Admissions*

ALPHA ORDER

RANK	STATE	ADMISSIONS	% of USA
29	Alabama	3,731	0.7%
27	Alaska	4,197	0.8%
16	Arizona	9,595	1.8%
32	Arkansas	3,564	0.7%
1	California	66,518	12.8%
NA	Colorado**	NA	NA
19	Connecticut	9,155	1.8%
43	Delaware	1,523	0.3%
4	Florida	32,743	6.3%
10	Georgia	16,999	3.3%
42	Hawaii	1,755	0.3%
NA	Idaho**	NA	NA
3	Illinois	37,571	7.2%
24	Indiana	5,438	1.0%
23	Iowa	5,450	1.0%
28	Kansas	4,061	0.8%
33	Kentucky	3,563	0.7%
21	Louisiana	7,460	1.4%
37	Maine	2,472	0.5%
18	Maryland	9,259	1.8%
5	Massachusetts	28,756	5.5%
7	Michigan	23,689	4.5%
NA	Minnesota**	NA	NA
20	Mississippi	7,749	1.5%
14	Missouri	10,297	2.0%
NA	Montana**	NA	NA
26	Nebraska	4,805	0.9%
36	Nevada	2,768	0.5%
40	New Hampshire	2,072	0.4%
13	New Jersey	13,590	2.6%
35	New Mexico	2,944	0.6%
2	New York	44,703	8.6%
15	North Carolina	9,995	1.9%
44	North Dakota	1,118	0.2%
6	Ohio	24,573	4.7%
25	Oklahoma	4,995	1.0%
12	Oregon	14,297	2.7%
8	Pennsylvania	20,002	3.8%
31	Rhode Island	3,628	0.7%
22	South Carolina	6,476	1.2%
34	South Dakota	3,372	0.6%
41	Tennessee	1,989	0.4%
17	Texas	9,429	1.8%
NA	Utah**	NA	NA
39	Vermont	2,119	0.4%
9	Virginia	19,332	3.7%
11	Washington	15,664	3.0%
30	West Virginia	3,661	0.7%
38	Wisconsin	2,278	0.4%
NA	Wyoming**	NA	NA

RANK ORDER

RANK	STATE	ADMISSIONS	% of USA
1	California	66,518	12.8%
2	New York	44,703	8.6%
3	Illinois	37,571	7.2%
4	Florida	32,743	6.3%
5	Massachusetts	28,756	5.5%
6	Ohio	24,573	4.7%
7	Michigan	23,689	4.5%
8	Pennsylvania	20,002	3.8%
9	Virginia	19,332	3.7%
10	Georgia	16,999	3.3%
11	Washington	15,664	3.0%
12	Oregon	14,297	2.7%
13	New Jersey	13,590	2.6%
14	Missouri	10,297	2.0%
15	North Carolina	9,995	1.9%
16	Arizona	9,595	1.8%
17	Texas	9,429	1.8%
18	Maryland	9,259	1.8%
19	Connecticut	9,155	1.8%
20	Mississippi	7,749	1.5%
21	Louisiana	7,460	1.4%
22	South Carolina	6,476	1.2%
23	Iowa	5,450	1.0%
24	Indiana	5,438	1.0%
25	Oklahoma	4,995	1.0%
26	Nebraska	4,805	0.9%
27	Alaska	4,197	0.8%
28	Kansas	4,061	0.8%
29	Alabama	3,731	0.7%
30	West Virginia	3,661	0.7%
31	Rhode Island	3,628	0.7%
32	Arkansas	3,564	0.7%
33	Kentucky	3,563	0.7%
34	South Dakota	3,372	0.6%
35	New Mexico	2,944	0.6%
36	Nevada	2,768	0.5%
37	Maine	2,472	0.5%
38	Wisconsin	2,278	0.4%
39	Vermont	2,119	0.4%
40	New Hampshire	2,072	0.4%
41	Tennessee	1,989	0.4%
42	Hawaii	1,755	0.3%
43	Delaware	1,523	0.3%
44	North Dakota	1,118	0.2%
NA	Colorado**	NA	NA
NA	Idaho**	NA	NA
NA	Minnesota**	NA	NA
NA	Montana**	NA	NA
NA	Utah**	NA	NA
NA	Wyoming**	NA	NA
	District of Columbia	1,057	0.2%

Source: National Association of State Alcohol and Drug Abuse Directors
"State Resources and Services Related to Alcohol and Other Drug Problems-Fiscal Year 1997" (July 1999)
*Does not include 475 female admissions in Puerto Rico. Data are only from treatment units that received at least some funds administered by a state's alcohol/drug agency in fiscal year 1997. An additional 42,078 admissions were not reported by sex. National total is only for reporting states.
**Not available.

Female Admissions to Alcohol and Other Drug Treatment Programs
As a Percent of All Admissions in 1997
National Percent = 29.2% Female*

ALPHA ORDER			RANK ORDER		
RANK	STATE	PERCENT	RANK	STATE	PERCENT
36	Alabama	26.3	1	Texas	37.0
7	Alaska	32.6	2	California	36.7
9	Arizona	32.0	3	Hawaii	35.9
43	Arkansas	23.8	4	Illinois	33.3
2	California	36.7	4	Mississippi	33.3
NA	Colorado**	NA	6	Washington	33.0
23	Connecticut	28.2	7	Alaska	32.6
39	Delaware	25.9	8	North Dakota	32.3
29	Florida	27.5	9	Arizona	32.0
19	Georgia	29.9	10	Oklahoma	31.5
3	Hawaii	35.9	11	Ohio	31.4
NA	Idaho**	NA	12	Nevada	31.2
4	Illinois	33.3	13	Oregon	31.0
15	Indiana	30.7	13	Virginia	31.0
25	Iowa	28.1	15	Indiana	30.7
34	Kansas	26.9	16	Maryland	30.4
25	Kentucky	28.1	17	Rhode Island	30.3
31	Louisiana	27.3	17	Vermont	30.3
28	Maine	27.8	19	Georgia	29.9
16	Maryland	30.4	20	New Jersey	29.7
27	Massachusetts	27.9	21	Michigan	29.0
21	Michigan	29.0	22	Pennsylvania	28.3
NA	Minnesota**	NA	23	Connecticut	28.2
4	Mississippi	33.3	23	Missouri	28.2
23	Missouri	28.2	25	Iowa	28.1
NA	Montana**	NA	25	Kentucky	28.1
42	Nebraska	24.1	27	Massachusetts	27.9
12	Nevada	31.2	28	Maine	27.8
33	New Hampshire	27.0	29	Florida	27.5
20	New Jersey	29.7	29	Tennessee	27.5
34	New Mexico	26.9	31	Louisiana	27.3
32	New York	27.1	32	New York	27.1
38	North Carolina	26.1	33	New Hampshire	27.0
8	North Dakota	32.3	34	Kansas	26.9
11	Ohio	31.4	34	New Mexico	26.9
10	Oklahoma	31.5	36	Alabama	26.3
13	Oregon	31.0	37	South Dakota	26.2
22	Pennsylvania	28.3	38	North Carolina	26.1
17	Rhode Island	30.3	39	Delaware	25.9
40	South Carolina	24.4	40	South Carolina	24.4
37	South Dakota	26.2	40	Wisconsin	24.4
29	Tennessee	27.5	42	Nebraska	24.1
1	Texas	37.0	43	Arkansas	23.8
NA	Utah**	NA	44	West Virginia	22.7
17	Vermont	30.3	NA	Colorado**	NA
13	Virginia	31.0	NA	Idaho**	NA
6	Washington	33.0	NA	Minnesota**	NA
44	West Virginia	22.7	NA	Montana**	NA
40	Wisconsin	24.4	NA	Utah**	NA
NA	Wyoming**	NA	NA	Wyoming**	NA

District of Columbia   28.1

Source: Morgan Quitno Press using data from National Association of State Alcohol and Drug Abuse Directors
"State Resources and Services Related to Alcohol and Other Drug Problems-Fiscal Year 1997" (July 1999)
*Does not include admissions in U.S. territories. Data are only from treatment units that received at least some funds administered by a state's alcohol/drug agency in fiscal year 1997. An additional 42,078 admissions were not reported by sex.
**Not available.

White Admissions to Alcohol and Other Drug Treatment Programs in 1997

National Total = 1,015,090 White Admissions*

<u>ALPHA ORDER</u>

RANK	STATE	ADMISSIONS	% of USA
34	Alabama	8,155	0.8%
38	Alaska	5,264	0.5%
16	Arizona	18,220	1.8%
29	Arkansas	10,055	1.0%
1	California	92,330	9.1%
NA	Colorado**	NA	NA
17	Connecticut	18,006	1.8%
41	Delaware	3,467	0.3%
3	Florida	66,793	6.6%
12	Georgia	32,405	3.2%
44	Hawaii	1,606	0.2%
NA	Idaho**	NA	NA
7	Illinois	46,272	4.6%
24	Indiana	13,080	1.3%
18	Iowa	16,674	1.6%
28	Kansas	10,284	1.0%
30	Kentucky	9,925	1.0%
23	Louisiana	13,130	1.3%
33	Maine	8,540	0.8%
20	Maryland	14,916	1.5%
2	Massachusetts	72,340	7.1%
5	Michigan	52,717	5.2%
NA	Minnesota**	NA	NA
27	Mississippi	11,392	1.1%
13	Missouri	24,269	2.4%
39	Montana	5,194	0.5%
22	Nebraska	14,100	1.4%
37	Nevada	6,125	0.6%
35	New Hampshire	7,309	0.7%
14	New Jersey	22,572	2.2%
42	New Mexico	3,308	0.3%
4	New York	66,425	6.5%
15	North Carolina	20,151	2.0%
43	North Dakota	2,583	0.3%
6	Ohio	49,743	4.9%
26	Oklahoma	11,544	1.1%
10	Oregon	37,206	3.7%
8	Pennsylvania	41,676	4.1%
32	Rhode Island	9,131	0.9%
19	South Carolina	15,611	1.5%
31	South Dakota	9,162	0.9%
40	Tennessee	4,643	0.5%
25	Texas	12,869	1.3%
NA	Utah**	NA	NA
36	Vermont	6,565	0.6%
9	Virginia	39,701	3.9%
11	Washington	34,384	3.4%
21	West Virginia	14,438	1.4%
NA	Wisconsin**	NA	NA
NA	Wyoming**	NA	NA

<u>RANK ORDER</u>

RANK	STATE	ADMISSIONS	% of USA
1	California	92,330	9.1%
2	Massachusetts	72,340	7.1%
3	Florida	66,793	6.6%
4	New York	66,425	6.5%
5	Michigan	52,717	5.2%
6	Ohio	49,743	4.9%
7	Illinois	46,272	4.6%
8	Pennsylvania	41,676	4.1%
9	Virginia	39,701	3.9%
10	Oregon	37,206	3.7%
11	Washington	34,384	3.4%
12	Georgia	32,405	3.2%
13	Missouri	24,269	2.4%
14	New Jersey	22,572	2.2%
15	North Carolina	20,151	2.0%
16	Arizona	18,220	1.8%
17	Connecticut	18,006	1.8%
18	Iowa	16,674	1.6%
19	South Carolina	15,611	1.5%
20	Maryland	14,916	1.5%
21	West Virginia	14,438	1.4%
22	Nebraska	14,100	1.4%
23	Louisiana	13,130	1.3%
24	Indiana	13,080	1.3%
25	Texas	12,869	1.3%
26	Oklahoma	11,544	1.1%
27	Mississippi	11,392	1.1%
28	Kansas	10,284	1.0%
29	Arkansas	10,055	1.0%
30	Kentucky	9,925	1.0%
31	South Dakota	9,162	0.9%
32	Rhode Island	9,131	0.9%
33	Maine	8,540	0.8%
34	Alabama	8,155	0.8%
35	New Hampshire	7,309	0.7%
36	Vermont	6,565	0.6%
37	Nevada	6,125	0.6%
38	Alaska	5,264	0.5%
39	Montana	5,194	0.5%
40	Tennessee	4,643	0.5%
41	Delaware	3,467	0.3%
42	New Mexico	3,308	0.3%
43	North Dakota	2,583	0.3%
44	Hawaii	1,606	0.2%
NA	Colorado**	NA	NA
NA	Idaho**	NA	NA
NA	Minnesota**	NA	NA
NA	Utah**	NA	NA
NA	Wisconsin**	NA	NA
NA	Wyoming**	NA	NA
	District of Columbia	48	0.0%

Source: National Association of State Alcohol and Drug Abuse Directors
"State Resources and Services Related to Alcohol and Other Drug Problems-Fiscal Year 1997" (July 1999)
*Data are only from treatment units that received at least some funds administered by a state's alcohol/drug agency in fiscal year 1997. An additional 35,953 admissions were not reported by race.
**Not available.

White Admissions to Alcohol and Other Drug Treatment Programs
As a Percent of All Admissions in 1997
National Percent = 57.0% of Admissions*

ALPHA ORDER

RANK	STATE	PERCENT
29	Alabama	57.4
41	Alaska	40.8
25	Arizona	60.8
19	Arkansas	67.2
34	California	51.0
NA	Colorado**	NA
32	Connecticut	55.4
26	Delaware	59.0
31	Florida	56.2
30	Georgia	57.1
43	Hawaii	32.8
NA	Idaho**	NA
40	Illinois	41.0
11	Indiana	73.8
5	Iowa	86.1
18	Kansas	68.0
8	Kentucky	78.3
39	Louisiana	48.1
1	Maine	96.1
37	Maryland	49.0
16	Massachusetts	70.2
21	Michigan	64.4
NA	Minnesota**	NA
37	Mississippi	49.0
20	Missouri	66.4
6	Montana	80.8
15	Nebraska	70.7
17	Nevada	69.1
2	New Hampshire	95.1
36	New Jersey	49.3
44	New Mexico	30.2
42	New York	40.2
33	North Carolina	52.6
10	North Dakota	74.6
24	Ohio	63.5
12	Oklahoma	72.7
7	Oregon	80.7
26	Pennsylvania	59.0
9	Rhode Island	76.2
28	South Carolina	58.9
14	South Dakota	71.1
22	Tennessee	64.1
35	Texas	50.4
NA	Utah**	NA
3	Vermont	93.8
23	Virginia	63.6
13	Washington	72.4
4	West Virginia	89.6
NA	Wisconsin**	NA
NA	Wyoming**	NA

RANK ORDER

RANK	STATE	PERCENT
1	Maine	96.1
2	New Hampshire	95.1
3	Vermont	93.8
4	West Virginia	89.6
5	Iowa	86.1
6	Montana	80.8
7	Oregon	80.7
8	Kentucky	78.3
9	Rhode Island	76.2
10	North Dakota	74.6
11	Indiana	73.8
12	Oklahoma	72.7
13	Washington	72.4
14	South Dakota	71.1
15	Nebraska	70.7
16	Massachusetts	70.2
17	Nevada	69.1
18	Kansas	68.0
19	Arkansas	67.2
20	Missouri	66.4
21	Michigan	64.4
22	Tennessee	64.1
23	Virginia	63.6
24	Ohio	63.5
25	Arizona	60.8
26	Delaware	59.0
26	Pennsylvania	59.0
28	South Carolina	58.9
29	Alabama	57.4
30	Georgia	57.1
31	Florida	56.2
32	Connecticut	55.4
33	North Carolina	52.6
34	California	51.0
35	Texas	50.4
36	New Jersey	49.3
37	Maryland	49.0
37	Mississippi	49.0
39	Louisiana	48.1
40	Illinois	41.0
41	Alaska	40.8
42	New York	40.2
43	Hawaii	32.8
44	New Mexico	30.2
NA	Colorado**	NA
NA	Idaho**	NA
NA	Minnesota**	NA
NA	Utah**	NA
NA	Wisconsin**	NA
NA	Wyoming**	NA

District of Columbia 1.3

Source: Morgan Quitno Press using data from National Association of State Alcohol and Drug Abuse Directors "State Resources and Services Related to Alcohol and Other Drug Problems-Fiscal Year 1997" (July 1999)
Data are only from treatment units that received at least some funds administered by a state's alcohol/drug agency in fiscal year 1997. An additional 35,953 admissions were not reported by race.
**Not available.*

Black Admissions to Alcohol and Other Drug Treatment Programs in 1997

National Total = 470,002 Black Admissions*

ALPHA ORDER

RANK	STATE	ADMISSIONS	% of USA
20	Alabama	5,928	1.3%
36	Alaska	582	0.1%
26	Arizona	2,399	0.5%
21	Arkansas	4,649	1.0%
3	California	34,449	7.3%
NA	Colorado**	NA	NA
18	Connecticut	8,588	1.8%
29	Delaware	2,198	0.5%
4	Florida	34,098	7.3%
7	Georgia	23,783	5.1%
39	Hawaii	167	0.0%
NA	Idaho**	NA	NA
2	Illinois	55,058	11.7%
23	Indiana	3,730	0.8%
32	Iowa	1,612	0.3%
24	Kansas	2,787	0.6%
30	Kentucky	2,173	0.5%
14	Louisiana	13,923	3.0%
41	Maine	111	0.0%
13	Maryland	14,603	3.1%
12	Massachusetts	14,952	3.2%
6	Michigan	24,617	5.2%
NA	Minnesota**	NA	NA
17	Mississippi	10,092	2.1%
15	Missouri	11,425	2.4%
43	Montana	51	0.0%
31	Nebraska	2,057	0.4%
35	Nevada	1,134	0.2%
40	New Hampshire	157	0.0%
11	New Jersey	16,000	3.4%
37	New Mexico	289	0.1%
1	New York	63,754	13.6%
9	North Carolina	16,670	3.5%
44	North Dakota	33	0.0%
5	Ohio	25,620	5.5%
28	Oklahoma	2,244	0.5%
27	Oregon	2,387	0.5%
10	Pennsylvania	16,067	3.4%
34	Rhode Island	1,181	0.3%
16	South Carolina	10,413	2.2%
38	South Dakota	233	0.0%
25	Tennessee	2,463	0.5%
19	Texas	6,184	1.3%
NA	Utah**	NA	NA
42	Vermont	90	0.0%
8	Virginia	19,065	4.1%
22	Washington	4,608	1.0%
33	West Virginia	1,337	0.3%
NA	Wisconsin**	NA	NA
NA	Wyoming**	NA	NA

RANK ORDER

RANK	STATE	ADMISSIONS	% of USA
1	New York	63,754	13.6%
2	Illinois	55,058	11.7%
3	California	34,449	7.3%
4	Florida	34,098	7.3%
5	Ohio	25,620	5.5%
6	Michigan	24,617	5.2%
7	Georgia	23,783	5.1%
8	Virginia	19,065	4.1%
9	North Carolina	16,670	3.5%
10	Pennsylvania	16,067	3.4%
11	New Jersey	16,000	3.4%
12	Massachusetts	14,952	3.2%
13	Maryland	14,603	3.1%
14	Louisiana	13,923	3.0%
15	Missouri	11,425	2.4%
16	South Carolina	10,413	2.2%
17	Mississippi	10,092	2.1%
18	Connecticut	8,588	1.8%
19	Texas	6,184	1.3%
20	Alabama	5,928	1.3%
21	Arkansas	4,649	1.0%
22	Washington	4,608	1.0%
23	Indiana	3,730	0.8%
24	Kansas	2,787	0.6%
25	Tennessee	2,463	0.5%
26	Arizona	2,399	0.5%
27	Oregon	2,387	0.5%
28	Oklahoma	2,244	0.5%
29	Delaware	2,198	0.5%
30	Kentucky	2,173	0.5%
31	Nebraska	2,057	0.4%
32	Iowa	1,612	0.3%
33	West Virginia	1,337	0.3%
34	Rhode Island	1,181	0.3%
35	Nevada	1,134	0.2%
36	Alaska	582	0.1%
37	New Mexico	289	0.1%
38	South Dakota	233	0.0%
39	Hawaii	167	0.0%
40	New Hampshire	157	0.0%
41	Maine	111	0.0%
42	Vermont	90	0.0%
43	Montana	51	0.0%
44	North Dakota	33	0.0%
NA	Colorado**	NA	NA
NA	Idaho**	NA	NA
NA	Minnesota**	NA	NA
NA	Utah**	NA	NA
NA	Wisconsin**	NA	NA
NA	Wyoming**	NA	NA
	District of Columbia	3,534	0.8%

Source: National Association of State Alcohol and Drug Abuse Directors
   "State Resources and Services Related to Alcohol and Other Drug Problems-Fiscal Year 1997" (July 1999)
*Data are only from treatment units that received at least some funds administered by a state's alcohol/drug agency in fiscal year 1997. An additional 35,953 admissions were not reported by race.
**Not available.

Black Admissions to Alcohol and Other Drug Treatment Programs
As a Percent of All Admissions in 1997
National Percent = 26.4% of Admissions*

ALPHA ORDER

RANK	STATE	PERCENT
7	Alabama	41.7
36	Alaska	4.5
34	Arizona	8.0
15	Arkansas	31.1
23	California	19.0
NA	Colorado**	NA
19	Connecticut	26.4
10	Delaware	37.4
18	Florida	28.7
6	Georgia	41.9
37	Hawaii	3.4
NA	Idaho**	NA
2	Illinois	48.8
22	Indiana	21.0
32	Iowa	8.3
24	Kansas	18.4
25	Kentucky	17.2
1	Louisiana	51.0
42	Maine	1.2
3	Maryland	47.9
26	Massachusetts	14.5
17	Michigan	30.1
NA	Minnesota**	NA
5	Mississippi	43.4
14	Missouri	31.3
44	Montana	0.8
29	Nebraska	10.3
28	Nevada	12.8
39	New Hampshire	2.0
11	New Jersey	34.9
38	New Mexico	2.6
9	New York	38.6
4	North Carolina	43.5
43	North Dakota	1.0
13	Ohio	32.7
27	Oklahoma	14.1
35	Oregon	5.2
21	Pennsylvania	22.7
30	Rhode Island	9.9
8	South Carolina	39.3
40	South Dakota	1.8
12	Tennessee	34.0
20	Texas	24.2
NA	Utah**	NA
41	Vermont	1.3
16	Virginia	30.5
31	Washington	9.7
32	West Virginia	8.3
NA	Wisconsin**	NA
NA	Wyoming**	NA

RANK ORDER

RANK	STATE	PERCENT
1	Louisiana	51.0
2	Illinois	48.8
3	Maryland	47.9
4	North Carolina	43.5
5	Mississippi	43.4
6	Georgia	41.9
7	Alabama	41.7
8	South Carolina	39.3
9	New York	38.6
10	Delaware	37.4
11	New Jersey	34.9
12	Tennessee	34.0
13	Ohio	32.7
14	Missouri	31.3
15	Arkansas	31.1
16	Virginia	30.5
17	Michigan	30.1
18	Florida	28.7
19	Connecticut	26.4
20	Texas	24.2
21	Pennsylvania	22.7
22	Indiana	21.0
23	California	19.0
24	Kansas	18.4
25	Kentucky	17.2
26	Massachusetts	14.5
27	Oklahoma	14.1
28	Nevada	12.8
29	Nebraska	10.3
30	Rhode Island	9.9
31	Washington	9.7
32	Iowa	8.3
32	West Virginia	8.3
34	Arizona	8.0
35	Oregon	5.2
36	Alaska	4.5
37	Hawaii	3.4
38	New Mexico	2.6
39	New Hampshire	2.0
40	South Dakota	1.8
41	Vermont	1.3
42	Maine	1.2
43	North Dakota	1.0
44	Montana	0.8
NA	Colorado**	NA
NA	Idaho**	NA
NA	Minnesota**	NA
NA	Utah**	NA
NA	Wisconsin**	NA
NA	Wyoming**	NA

District of Columbia   94.0

Source: Morgan Quitno Press using data from National Association of State Alcohol and Drug Abuse Directors
"State Resources and Services Related to Alcohol and Other Drug Problems-Fiscal Year 1997" (July 1999)
*Data are only from treatment units that received at least some funds administered by a state's alcohol/drug agency in fiscal year 1997. An additional 35,853 admissions were not reported by race.
**Not available.

Hispanic Admissions to Alcohol and Other Drug Treatment Programs in 1997

National Total = 167,824 Hispanic Admissions*

ALPHA ORDER				RANK ORDER			
RANK	STATE	ADMISSIONS	% of USA	RANK	STATE	ADMISSIONS	% of USA
36	Alabama	0	0.0%	1	California	44,286	26.4%
36	Alaska	0	0.0%	2	New York	31,429	18.7%
6	Arizona	6,897	4.1%	3	Florida	15,173	9.0%
32	Arkansas	109	0.1%	4	Massachusetts	12,566	7.5%
1	California	44,286	26.4%	5	Illinois	7,439	4.4%
NA	Colorado**	NA	NA	6	Arizona	6,897	4.1%
9	Connecticut	5,581	3.3%	7	New Jersey	6,510	3.9%
36	Delaware	0	0.0%	8	Texas	6,085	3.6%
3	Florida	15,173	9.0%	9	Connecticut	5,581	3.3%
29	Georgia	146	0.1%	10	New Mexico	5,544	3.3%
27	Hawaii	181	0.1%	11	Pennsylvania	4,515	2.7%
NA	Idaho**	NA	NA	12	Oregon	3,692	2.2%
5	Illinois	7,439	4.4%	13	Washington	3,633	2.2%
22	Indiana	445	0.3%	14	Michigan	2,805	1.7%
21	Iowa	609	0.4%	15	Ohio	2,013	1.2%
17	Kansas	1,469	0.9%	16	Nebraska	1,477	0.9%
23	Kentucky	413	0.2%	17	Kansas	1,469	0.9%
36	Louisiana	0	0.0%	18	Rhode Island	1,049	0.6%
NA	Maine**	NA	NA	19	Nevada	778	0.5%
20	Maryland	624	0.4%	20	Maryland	624	0.4%
4	Massachusetts	12,566	7.5%	21	Iowa	609	0.4%
14	Michigan	2,805	1.7%	22	Indiana	445	0.3%
NA	Minnesota**	NA	NA	23	Kentucky	413	0.2%
36	Mississippi	0	0.0%	24	Oklahoma	353	0.2%
26	Missouri	213	0.1%	25	South Carolina	270	0.2%
31	Montana	128	0.1%	26	Missouri	213	0.1%
16	Nebraska	1,477	0.9%	27	Hawaii	181	0.1%
19	Nevada	778	0.5%	28	West Virginia	152	0.1%
33	New Hampshire	92	0.1%	29	Georgia	146	0.1%
7	New Jersey	6,510	3.9%	30	South Dakota	145	0.1%
10	New Mexico	5,544	3.3%	31	Montana	128	0.1%
2	New York	31,429	18.7%	32	Arkansas	109	0.1%
36	North Carolina	0	0.0%	33	New Hampshire	92	0.1%
36	North Dakota	0	0.0%	34	Vermont	59	0.0%
15	Ohio	2,013	1.2%	35	Tennessee	42	0.0%
24	Oklahoma	353	0.2%	36	Alabama	0	0.0%
12	Oregon	3,692	2.2%	36	Alaska	0	0.0%
11	Pennsylvania	4,515	2.7%	36	Delaware	0	0.0%
18	Rhode Island	1,049	0.6%	36	Louisiana	0	0.0%
25	South Carolina	270	0.2%	36	Mississippi	0	0.0%
30	South Dakota	145	0.1%	36	North Carolina	0	0.0%
35	Tennessee	42	0.0%	36	North Dakota	0	0.0%
8	Texas	6,085	3.6%	36	Virginia	0	0.0%
NA	Utah**	NA	NA	NA	Colorado**	NA	NA
34	Vermont	59	0.0%	NA	Idaho**	NA	NA
36	Virginia	0	0.0%	NA	Maine**	NA	NA
13	Washington	3,633	2.2%	NA	Minnesota**	NA	NA
28	West Virginia	152	0.1%	NA	Utah**	NA	NA
NA	Wisconsin**	NA	NA	NA	Wisconsin**	NA	NA
NA	Wyoming**	NA	NA	NA	Wyoming**	NA	NA
					District of Columbia	73	0.0%

Source: National Association of State Alcohol and Drug Abuse Directors
  "State Resources and Services Related to Alcohol and Other Drug Problems-Fiscal Year 1997" (July 1999)
*Data are only from treatment units that received at least some funds administered by a state's alcohol/drug agency
in fiscal year 1997. Total does not include 25,096 admissions in Puerto Rico. An additional 35,953 admissions
were not reported by race.
**Not available.

Hispanic Admissions to Alcohol and Other Drug Treatment Programs
As a Percent of All Admissions in 1997
National Percent = 9.4% of Admissions*

ALPHA ORDER

RANK	STATE	PERCENT
36	Alabama	0.0
36	Alaska	0.0
4	Arizona	23.0
32	Arkansas	0.7
2	California	24.5
NA	Colorado**	NA
6	Connecticut	17.2
36	Delaware	0.0
8	Florida	12.8
35	Georgia	0.3
18	Hawaii	3.7
NA	Idaho**	NA
16	Illinois	6.6
23	Indiana	2.5
21	Iowa	3.1
10	Kansas	9.7
20	Kentucky	3.3
36	Louisiana	0.0
NA	Maine**	NA
25	Maryland	2.0
9	Massachusetts	12.2
19	Michigan	3.4
NA	Minnesota**	NA
36	Mississippi	0.0
33	Missouri	0.6
25	Montana	2.0
15	Nebraska	7.4
11	Nevada	8.8
27	New Hampshire	1.2
7	New Jersey	14.2
1	New Mexico	50.6
5	New York	19.0
36	North Carolina	0.0
36	North Dakota	0.0
22	Ohio	2.6
24	Oklahoma	2.2
13	Oregon	8.0
17	Pennsylvania	6.4
11	Rhode Island	8.8
29	South Carolina	1.0
28	South Dakota	1.1
33	Tennessee	0.6
3	Texas	23.8
NA	Utah**	NA
31	Vermont	0.8
36	Virginia	0.0
14	Washington	7.6
30	West Virginia	0.9
NA	Wisconsin**	NA
NA	Wyoming**	NA

RANK ORDER

RANK	STATE	PERCENT
1	New Mexico	50.6
2	California	24.5
3	Texas	23.8
4	Arizona	23.0
5	New York	19.0
6	Connecticut	17.2
7	New Jersey	14.2
8	Florida	12.8
9	Massachusetts	12.2
10	Kansas	9.7
11	Nevada	8.8
11	Rhode Island	8.8
13	Oregon	8.0
14	Washington	7.6
15	Nebraska	7.4
16	Illinois	6.6
17	Pennsylvania	6.4
18	Hawaii	3.7
19	Michigan	3.4
20	Kentucky	3.3
21	Iowa	3.1
22	Ohio	2.6
23	Indiana	2.5
24	Oklahoma	2.2
25	Maryland	2.0
25	Montana	2.0
27	New Hampshire	1.2
28	South Dakota	1.1
29	South Carolina	1.0
30	West Virginia	0.9
31	Vermont	0.8
32	Arkansas	0.7
33	Missouri	0.6
33	Tennessee	0.6
35	Georgia	0.3
36	Alabama	0.0
36	Alaska	0.0
36	Delaware	0.0
36	Louisiana	0.0
36	Mississippi	0.0
36	North Carolina	0.0
36	North Dakota	0.0
36	Virginia	0.0
NA	Colorado**	NA
NA	Idaho**	NA
NA	Maine**	NA
NA	Minnesota**	NA
NA	Utah**	NA
NA	Wisconsin**	NA
NA	Wyoming**	NA

District of Columbia   1.9

Source: Morgan Quitno Press using data from National Association of State Alcohol and Drug Abuse Directors
"State Resources and Services Related to Alcohol and Other Drug Problems-Fiscal Year 1997" (July 1999)
*Data are only from treatment units that received at least some funds administered by a state's alcohol/drug agency in fiscal year 1997. An additional 35,953 admissions were not reported by race.
**Not available.

Expenditures for State-Supported Alcohol and Other Drug Abuse Services: 1997

National Total = $3,986,640,705*

ALPHA ORDER

RANK	STATE	EXPENDITURES	% of USA
31	Alabama	$25,407,964	0.6%
28	Alaska	28,097,100	0.7%
25	Arizona	38,280,597	1.0%
36	Arkansas	18,489,899	0.5%
2	California	507,437,000	12.7%
19	Colorado	58,504,360	1.5%
8	Connecticut	125,667,292	3.2%
41	Delaware	11,633,740	0.3%
3	Florida	271,428,774	6.8%
17	Georgia	75,936,993	1.9%
34	Hawaii	20,502,912	0.5%
NA	Idaho**	NA	NA
5	Illinois	175,355,857	4.4%
21	Indiana	52,781,285	1.3%
22	Iowa	44,905,196	1.1%
35	Kansas	19,035,918	0.5%
30	Kentucky	25,915,027	0.7%
23	Louisiana	41,533,151	1.0%
39	Maine	14,291,566	0.4%
16	Maryland	76,365,798	1.9%
15	Massachusetts	77,088,000	1.9%
7	Michigan	137,694,562	3.5%
NA	Minnesota**	NA	NA
37	Mississippi	16,592,739	0.4%
20	Missouri	55,683,450	1.4%
42	Montana	11,036,347	0.3%
38	Nebraska	15,283,912	0.4%
43	Nevada	10,773,800	0.3%
44	New Hampshire	8,329,052	0.2%
11	New Jersey	95,434,406	2.4%
40	New Mexico	14,258,058	0.4%
1	New York	789,129,988	19.8%
18	North Carolina	67,852,682	1.7%
47	North Dakota	4,730,557	0.1%
4	Ohio	192,364,274	4.8%
32	Oklahoma	24,387,599	0.6%
14	Oregon	85,170,703	2.1%
6	Pennsylvania	147,412,010	3.7%
33	Rhode Island	21,637,808	0.5%
26	South Carolina	34,723,852	0.9%
45	South Dakota	7,656,092	0.2%
27	Tennessee	29,082,929	0.7%
10	Texas	112,505,607	2.8%
24	Utah	39,308,084	1.0%
46	Vermont	7,444,830	0.2%
12	Virginia	90,932,666	2.3%
13	Washington	85,679,708	2.1%
29	West Virginia	27,575,707	0.7%
9	Wisconsin	123,531,584	3.1%
NA	Wyoming**	NA	NA

RANK ORDER

RANK	STATE	EXPENDITURES	% of USA
1	New York	$789,129,988	19.8%
2	California	507,437,000	12.7%
3	Florida	271,428,774	6.8%
4	Ohio	192,364,274	4.8%
5	Illinois	175,355,857	4.4%
6	Pennsylvania	147,412,010	3.7%
7	Michigan	137,694,562	3.5%
8	Connecticut	125,667,292	3.2%
9	Wisconsin	123,531,584	3.1%
10	Texas	112,505,607	2.8%
11	New Jersey	95,434,406	2.4%
12	Virginia	90,932,666	2.3%
13	Washington	85,679,708	2.1%
14	Oregon	85,170,703	2.1%
15	Massachusetts	77,088,000	1.9%
16	Maryland	76,365,798	1.9%
17	Georgia	75,936,993	1.9%
18	North Carolina	67,852,682	1.7%
19	Colorado	58,504,360	1.5%
20	Missouri	55,683,450	1.4%
21	Indiana	52,781,285	1.3%
22	Iowa	44,905,196	1.1%
23	Louisiana	41,533,151	1.0%
24	Utah	39,308,084	1.0%
25	Arizona	38,280,597	1.0%
26	South Carolina	34,723,852	0.9%
27	Tennessee	29,082,929	0.7%
28	Alaska	28,097,100	0.7%
29	West Virginia	27,575,707	0.7%
30	Kentucky	25,915,027	0.7%
31	Alabama	25,407,964	0.6%
32	Oklahoma	24,387,599	0.6%
33	Rhode Island	21,637,808	0.5%
34	Hawaii	20,502,912	0.5%
35	Kansas	19,035,918	0.5%
36	Arkansas	18,489,899	0.5%
37	Mississippi	16,592,739	0.4%
38	Nebraska	15,283,912	0.4%
39	Maine	14,291,566	0.4%
40	New Mexico	14,258,058	0.4%
41	Delaware	11,633,740	0.3%
42	Montana	11,036,347	0.3%
43	Nevada	10,773,800	0.3%
44	New Hampshire	8,329,052	0.2%
45	South Dakota	7,656,092	0.2%
46	Vermont	7,444,830	0.2%
47	North Dakota	4,730,557	0.1%
NA	Idaho**	NA	NA
NA	Minnesota**	NA	NA
NA	Wyoming**	NA	NA
	District of Columbia	21,769,270	0.5%

Source: National Association of State Alcohol and Drug Abuse Directors
   "State Resources and Services Related to Alcohol and Other Drug Problems-Fiscal Year 1997" (July 1999)
Funds for treatment and prevention programs as well as "other" costs (e.g. administration, capital construction and research.) Total does not include expenditures in U.S. territories and is only for reporting states.
***Not available.*

Per Capita Expenditures for State-Supported Alcohol and Other Drug Abuse Services in 1997
National Per Capita = $15.25*

ALPHA ORDER

RANK	STATE	PER CAPITA
45	Alabama	$5.88
1	Alaska	46.15
35	Arizona	8.41
39	Arkansas	7.33
12	California	15.75
16	Colorado	15.03
3	Connecticut	38.45
11	Delaware	15.83
8	Florida	18.49
29	Georgia	10.14
9	Hawaii	17.24
NA	Idaho**	NA
18	Illinois	14.60
34	Indiana	8.99
13	Iowa	15.73
40	Kansas	7.28
42	Kentucky	6.63
30	Louisiana	9.54
26	Maine	11.48
17	Maryland	14.99
22	Massachusetts	12.61
19	Michigan	14.07
NA	Minnesota**	NA
44	Mississippi	6.07
28	Missouri	10.30
23	Montana	12.56
31	Nebraska	9.23
43	Nevada	6.43
41	New Hampshire	7.10
25	New Jersey	11.85
36	New Mexico	8.28
2	New York	43.49
33	North Carolina	9.13
37	North Dakota	7.38
10	Ohio	17.16
38	Oklahoma	7.36
4	Oregon	26.26
24	Pennsylvania	12.27
6	Rhode Island	21.92
32	South Carolina	9.16
27	South Dakota	10.48
47	Tennessee	5.41
46	Texas	5.81
7	Utah	19.03
21	Vermont	12.65
20	Virginia	13.51
14	Washington	15.29
15	West Virginia	15.19
5	Wisconsin	23.76
NA	Wyoming**	NA

RANK ORDER

RANK	STATE	PER CAPITA
1	Alaska	$46.15
2	New York	43.49
3	Connecticut	38.45
4	Oregon	26.26
5	Wisconsin	23.76
6	Rhode Island	21.92
7	Utah	19.03
8	Florida	18.49
9	Hawaii	17.24
10	Ohio	17.16
11	Delaware	15.83
12	California	15.75
13	Iowa	15.73
14	Washington	15.29
15	West Virginia	15.19
16	Colorado	15.03
17	Maryland	14.99
18	Illinois	14.60
19	Michigan	14.07
20	Virginia	13.51
21	Vermont	12.65
22	Massachusetts	12.61
23	Montana	12.56
24	Pennsylvania	12.27
25	New Jersey	11.85
26	Maine	11.48
27	South Dakota	10.48
28	Missouri	10.30
29	Georgia	10.14
30	Louisiana	9.54
31	Nebraska	9.23
32	South Carolina	9.16
33	North Carolina	9.13
34	Indiana	8.99
35	Arizona	8.41
36	New Mexico	8.28
37	North Dakota	7.38
38	Oklahoma	7.36
39	Arkansas	7.33
40	Kansas	7.28
41	New Hampshire	7.10
42	Kentucky	6.63
43	Nevada	6.43
44	Mississippi	6.07
45	Alabama	5.88
46	Texas	5.81
47	Tennessee	5.41
NA	Idaho**	NA
NA	Minnesota**	NA
NA	Wyoming**	NA

District of Columbia   41.17

Source: Morgan Quitno Press using data from National Association of State Alcohol and Drug Abuse Directors "State Resources and Services Related to Alcohol and Other Drug Problems-Fiscal Year 1997" (July 1999)
Funds for treatment and prevention programs as well as "other" costs (e.g. administration, capital construction and research.) National per capita does not include expenditures or population in U.S. territories and is only for reporting states.
**Not available.

Expenditures for State-Supported Alcohol and Other Drug Abuse Treatment Programs in 1997
National Total = $3,121,118,872*

ALPHA ORDER

RANK	STATE	EXPENDITURES	% of USA
29	Alabama	$20,743,243	0.7%
28	Alaska	23,263,200	0.7%
25	Arizona	28,919,296	0.9%
37	Arkansas	12,803,172	0.4%
2	California	352,384,000	11.3%
18	Colorado	49,720,721	1.6%
7	Connecticut	115,650,242	3.7%
40	Delaware	10,070,102	0.3%
3	Florida	260,162,031	8.3%
12	Georgia	69,150,525	2.2%
32	Hawaii	16,846,053	0.5%
NA	Idaho**	NA	NA
5	Illinois	133,521,813	4.3%
20	Indiana	43,103,359	1.4%
22	Iowa	37,048,489	1.2%
36	Kansas	13,353,046	0.4%
33	Kentucky	15,994,160	0.5%
23	Louisiana	35,599,664	1.1%
42	Maine	9,571,670	0.3%
14	Maryland	65,508,245	2.1%
13	Massachusetts	67,062,000	2.1%
8	Michigan	96,442,998	3.1%
NA	Minnesota**	NA	NA
35	Mississippi	13,397,503	0.4%
19	Missouri	46,663,741	1.5%
41	Montana	9,959,905	0.3%
38	Nebraska	12,007,062	0.4%
43	Nevada	6,482,315	0.2%
44	New Hampshire	6,416,708	0.2%
9	New Jersey	80,542,834	2.6%
39	New Mexico	11,455,406	0.4%
1	New York	650,593,229	20.8%
17	North Carolina	57,157,462	1.8%
47	North Dakota	4,154,943	0.1%
4	Ohio	148,347,923	4.8%
30	Oklahoma	19,752,932	0.6%
21	Oregon	39,932,889	1.3%
6	Pennsylvania	117,229,244	3.8%
34	Rhode Island	13,426,443	0.4%
26	South Carolina	28,573,171	0.9%
45	South Dakota	6,263,725	0.2%
31	Tennessee	18,561,572	0.6%
16	Texas	59,550,993	1.9%
24	Utah	31,547,819	1.0%
46	Vermont	5,708,154	0.2%
10	Virginia	75,980,289	2.4%
15	Washington	60,629,017	1.9%
27	West Virginia	25,476,718	0.8%
11	Wisconsin	75,337,398	2.4%
NA	Wyoming**	NA	NA

RANK ORDER

RANK	STATE	EXPENDITURES	% of USA
1	New York	$650,593,229	20.8%
2	California	352,384,000	11.3%
3	Florida	260,162,031	8.3%
4	Ohio	148,347,923	4.8%
5	Illinois	133,521,813	4.3%
6	Pennsylvania	117,229,244	3.8%
7	Connecticut	115,650,242	3.7%
8	Michigan	96,442,998	3.1%
9	New Jersey	80,542,834	2.6%
10	Virginia	75,980,289	2.4%
11	Wisconsin	75,337,398	2.4%
12	Georgia	69,150,525	2.2%
13	Massachusetts	67,062,000	2.1%
14	Maryland	65,508,245	2.1%
15	Washington	60,629,017	1.9%
16	Texas	59,550,993	1.9%
17	North Carolina	57,157,462	1.8%
18	Colorado	49,720,721	1.6%
19	Missouri	46,663,741	1.5%
20	Indiana	43,103,359	1.4%
21	Oregon	39,932,889	1.3%
22	Iowa	37,048,489	1.2%
23	Louisiana	35,599,664	1.1%
24	Utah	31,547,819	1.0%
25	Arizona	28,919,296	0.9%
26	South Carolina	28,573,171	0.9%
27	West Virginia	25,476,718	0.8%
28	Alaska	23,263,200	0.7%
29	Alabama	20,743,243	0.7%
30	Oklahoma	19,752,932	0.6%
31	Tennessee	18,561,572	0.6%
32	Hawaii	16,846,053	0.5%
33	Kentucky	15,994,160	0.5%
34	Rhode Island	13,426,443	0.4%
35	Mississippi	13,397,503	0.4%
36	Kansas	13,353,046	0.4%
37	Arkansas	12,803,172	0.4%
38	Nebraska	12,007,062	0.4%
39	New Mexico	11,455,406	0.4%
40	Delaware	10,070,102	0.3%
41	Montana	9,959,905	0.3%
42	Maine	9,571,670	0.3%
43	Nevada	6,482,315	0.2%
44	New Hampshire	6,416,708	0.2%
45	South Dakota	6,263,725	0.2%
46	Vermont	5,708,154	0.2%
47	North Dakota	4,154,943	0.1%
NA	Idaho**	NA	NA
NA	Minnesota**	NA	NA
NA	Wyoming**	NA	NA
	District of Columbia	19,051,448	0.6%

Source: National Association of State Alcohol and Drug Abuse Directors
    "State Resources and Services Related to Alcohol and Other Drug Problems-Fiscal Year 1997" (July 1999)
*Total does not include expenditures in U.S. territories and is only for reporting states.
**Not available.

Expenditures per Alcohol and Other Drug Treatment Admission in 1997

National Rate = $1,752 in Treatment Expenditures per Admission*

ALPHA ORDER

RANK	STATE	RATE
21	Alabama	$1,460
14	Alaska	1,805
36	Arizona	964
40	Arkansas	856
10	California	1,946
37	Colorado	887
3	Connecticut	3,559
16	Delaware	1,715
8	Florida	2,188
27	Georgia	1,218
4	Hawaii	3,444
NA	Idaho**	NA
30	Illinois	1,184
6	Indiana	2,432
11	Iowa	1,913
38	Kansas	883
25	Kentucky	1,262
22	Louisiana	1,304
33	Maine	1,077
9	Maryland	2,151
44	Massachusetts	651
31	Michigan	1,179
NA	Minnesota**	NA
46	Mississippi	576
23	Missouri	1,277
19	Montana	1,549
45	Nebraska	602
43	Nevada	731
41	New Hampshire	835
15	New Jersey	1,758
35	New Mexico	1,046
2	New York	3,940
20	North Carolina	1,492
29	North Dakota	1,201
12	Ohio	1,894
26	Oklahoma	1,245
39	Oregon	866
17	Pennsylvania	1,660
32	Rhode Island	1,121
33	South Carolina	1,077
47	South Dakota	486
5	Tennessee	2,563
7	Texas	2,334
13	Utah	1,848
42	Vermont	815
28	Virginia	1,217
24	Washington	1,276
18	West Virginia	1,582
1	Wisconsin	8,057
NA	Wyoming**	NA

RANK ORDER

RANK	STATE	RATE
1	Wisconsin	$8,057
2	New York	3,940
3	Connecticut	3,559
4	Hawaii	3,444
5	Tennessee	2,563
6	Indiana	2,432
7	Texas	2,334
8	Florida	2,188
9	Maryland	2,151
10	California	1,946
11	Iowa	1,913
12	Ohio	1,894
13	Utah	1,848
14	Alaska	1,805
15	New Jersey	1,758
16	Delaware	1,715
17	Pennsylvania	1,660
18	West Virginia	1,582
19	Montana	1,549
20	North Carolina	1,492
21	Alabama	1,460
22	Louisiana	1,304
23	Missouri	1,277
24	Washington	1,276
25	Kentucky	1,262
26	Oklahoma	1,245
27	Georgia	1,218
28	Virginia	1,217
29	North Dakota	1,201
30	Illinois	1,184
31	Michigan	1,179
32	Rhode Island	1,121
33	Maine	1,077
33	South Carolina	1,077
35	New Mexico	1,046
36	Arizona	964
37	Colorado	887
38	Kansas	883
39	Oregon	866
40	Arkansas	856
41	New Hampshire	835
42	Vermont	815
43	Nevada	731
44	Massachusetts	651
45	Nebraska	602
46	Mississippi	576
47	South Dakota	486
NA	Idaho**	NA
NA	Minnesota**	NA
NA	Wyoming**	NA
	District of Columbia	5,067

Source: Morgan Quitno Press using data from National Association of State Alcohol and Drug Abuse Directors "State Resources and Services Related to Alcohol and Other Drug Problems-Fiscal Year 1997" (July 1999)
*Does not include admissions in U.S. territories. Data are only from treatment units that received at least some funds administered by a state's alcohol/drug agency in fiscal year 1997.
**Not available.

Per Capita Expenditures for State-Supported Alcohol and Other Drug Abuse Treatment Programs in 1997
National Per Capita = $11.94*

<u>ALPHA ORDER</u>

RANK	STATE	PER CAPITA
43	Alabama	$4.80
1	Alaska	38.21
37	Arizona	6.35
41	Arkansas	5.07
20	California	10.94
14	Colorado	12.78
3	Connecticut	35.38
9	Delaware	13.70
4	Florida	17.72
26	Georgia	9.24
7	Hawaii	14.16
NA	Idaho**	NA
18	Illinois	11.12
33	Indiana	7.34
12	Iowa	12.98
40	Kansas	5.10
44	Kentucky	4.09
29	Louisiana	8.18
30	Maine	7.69
13	Maryland	12.86
19	Massachusetts	10.97
23	Michigan	9.86
NA	Minnesota**	NA
42	Mississippi	4.90
27	Missouri	8.63
16	Montana	11.33
34	Nebraska	7.25
45	Nevada	3.87
39	New Hampshire	5.47
22	New Jersey	10.00
35	New Mexico	6.65
2	New York	35.86
30	North Carolina	7.69
36	North Dakota	6.48
11	Ohio	13.23
38	Oklahoma	5.96
15	Oregon	12.31
24	Pennsylvania	9.76
10	Rhode Island	13.60
32	South Carolina	7.54
28	South Dakota	8.57
46	Tennessee	3.45
47	Texas	3.08
5	Utah	15.27
25	Vermont	9.70
17	Virginia	11.28
21	Washington	10.82
8	West Virginia	14.03
6	Wisconsin	14.49
NA	Wyoming**	NA

<u>RANK ORDER</u>

RANK	STATE	PER CAPITA
1	Alaska	$38.21
2	New York	35.86
3	Connecticut	35.38
4	Florida	17.72
5	Utah	15.27
6	Wisconsin	14.49
7	Hawaii	14.16
8	West Virginia	14.03
9	Delaware	13.70
10	Rhode Island	13.60
11	Ohio	13.23
12	Iowa	12.98
13	Maryland	12.86
14	Colorado	12.78
15	Oregon	12.31
16	Montana	11.33
17	Virginia	11.28
18	Illinois	11.12
19	Massachusetts	10.97
20	California	10.94
21	Washington	10.82
22	New Jersey	10.00
23	Michigan	9.86
24	Pennsylvania	9.76
25	Vermont	9.70
26	Georgia	9.24
27	Missouri	8.63
28	South Dakota	8.57
29	Louisiana	8.18
30	Maine	7.69
30	North Carolina	7.69
32	South Carolina	7.54
33	Indiana	7.34
34	Nebraska	7.25
35	New Mexico	6.65
36	North Dakota	6.48
37	Arizona	6.35
38	Oklahoma	5.96
39	New Hampshire	5.47
40	Kansas	5.10
41	Arkansas	5.07
42	Mississippi	4.90
43	Alabama	4.80
44	Kentucky	4.09
45	Nevada	3.87
46	Tennessee	3.45
47	Texas	3.08
NA	Idaho**	NA
NA	Minnesota**	NA
NA	Wyoming**	NA
	District of Columbia	36.03

Source: Morgan Quitno Press using data from National Association of State Alcohol and Drug Abuse Directors "State Resources and Services Related to Alcohol and Other Drug Problems-Fiscal Year 1997" (July 1999)
National per capita does not include expenditures or population in U.S. territories and is only for reporting states.
***Not available.*

Expenditures for State-Supported Alcohol and Other Drug Abuse Prevention Programs in 1997
National Total = $504,469,872*

ALPHA ORDER

RANK	STATE	EXPENDITURES	% of USA
33	Alabama	$3,751,701	0.7%
36	Alaska	2,612,200	0.5%
15	Arizona	8,931,301	1.8%
31	Arkansas	3,982,254	0.8%
2	California	63,945,000	12.7%
24	Colorado	5,371,677	1.1%
23	Connecticut	6,143,634	1.2%
44	Delaware	1,123,072	0.2%
12	Florida	10,708,419	2.1%
22	Georgia	6,786,468	1.3%
40	Hawaii	1,756,021	0.3%
NA	Idaho**	NA	NA
7	Illinois	18,402,194	3.6%
17	Indiana	8,297,219	1.6%
18	Iowa	7,856,707	1.6%
26	Kansas	4,770,909	0.9%
30	Kentucky	4,251,151	0.8%
29	Louisiana	4,307,301	0.9%
34	Maine	3,096,116	0.6%
20	Maryland	7,364,176	1.5%
16	Massachusetts	8,723,000	1.7%
3	Michigan	32,831,560	6.5%
NA	Minnesota**	NA	NA
38	Mississippi	2,250,061	0.4%
25	Missouri	4,863,994	1.0%
46	Montana	651,692	0.1%
35	Nebraska	2,688,874	0.5%
39	Nevada	2,242,146	0.4%
42	New Hampshire	1,425,169	0.3%
11	New Jersey	11,566,948	2.3%
37	New Mexico	2,451,652	0.5%
1	New York	88,681,667	17.6%
14	North Carolina	9,356,281	1.9%
47	North Dakota	575,614	0.1%
4	Ohio	29,309,047	5.8%
32	Oklahoma	3,923,714	0.8%
6	Oregon	20,070,866	4.0%
9	Pennsylvania	15,148,317	3.0%
28	Rhode Island	4,568,216	0.9%
27	South Carolina	4,623,333	0.9%
45	South Dakota	1,064,141	0.2%
21	Tennessee	6,804,237	1.3%
8	Texas	17,371,673	3.4%
19	Utah	7,760,265	1.5%
43	Vermont	1,229,586	0.2%
10	Virginia	12,765,100	2.5%
13	Washington	9,392,143	1.9%
41	West Virginia	1,511,723	0.3%
5	Wisconsin	25,554,970	5.1%
NA	Wyoming**	NA	NA

RANK ORDER

RANK	STATE	EXPENDITURES	% of USA
1	New York	$88,681,667	17.6%
2	California	63,945,000	12.7%
3	Michigan	32,831,560	6.5%
4	Ohio	29,309,047	5.8%
5	Wisconsin	25,554,970	5.1%
6	Oregon	20,070,866	4.0%
7	Illinois	18,402,194	3.6%
8	Texas	17,371,673	3.4%
9	Pennsylvania	15,148,317	3.0%
10	Virginia	12,765,100	2.5%
11	New Jersey	11,566,948	2.3%
12	Florida	10,708,419	2.1%
13	Washington	9,392,143	1.9%
14	North Carolina	9,356,281	1.9%
15	Arizona	8,931,301	1.8%
16	Massachusetts	8,723,000	1.7%
17	Indiana	8,297,219	1.6%
18	Iowa	7,856,707	1.6%
19	Utah	7,760,265	1.5%
20	Maryland	7,364,176	1.5%
21	Tennessee	6,804,237	1.3%
22	Georgia	6,786,468	1.3%
23	Connecticut	6,143,634	1.2%
24	Colorado	5,371,677	1.1%
25	Missouri	4,863,994	1.0%
26	Kansas	4,770,909	0.9%
27	South Carolina	4,623,333	0.9%
28	Rhode Island	4,568,216	0.9%
29	Louisiana	4,307,301	0.9%
30	Kentucky	4,251,151	0.8%
31	Arkansas	3,982,254	0.8%
32	Oklahoma	3,923,714	0.8%
33	Alabama	3,751,701	0.7%
34	Maine	3,096,116	0.6%
35	Nebraska	2,688,874	0.5%
36	Alaska	2,612,200	0.5%
37	New Mexico	2,451,652	0.5%
38	Mississippi	2,250,061	0.4%
39	Nevada	2,242,146	0.4%
40	Hawaii	1,756,021	0.3%
41	West Virginia	1,511,723	0.3%
42	New Hampshire	1,425,169	0.3%
43	Vermont	1,229,586	0.2%
44	Delaware	1,123,072	0.2%
45	South Dakota	1,064,141	0.2%
46	Montana	651,692	0.1%
47	North Dakota	575,614	0.1%
NA	Idaho**	NA	NA
NA	Minnesota**	NA	NA
NA	Wyoming**	NA	NA
	District of Columbia	1,606,363	0.3%

Source: National Association of State Alcohol and Drug Abuse Directors
   "State Resources and Services Related to Alcohol and Other Drug Problems-Fiscal Year 1997" (July 1999)
*Total does not include expenditures in U.S. territories and is only for reporting states.
**Not available.

Per Capita Expenditures for State-Supported Alcohol and Other Drug Abuse Prevention Programs in 1997
National Per Capita = $1.93*

ALPHA ORDER

RANK	STATE	PER CAPITA
43	Alabama	$0.87
5	Alaska	4.29
13	Arizona	1.96
19	Arkansas	1.58
12	California	1.98
29	Colorado	1.38
15	Connecticut	1.88
20	Delaware	1.53
47	Florida	0.73
39	Georgia	0.91
22	Hawaii	1.48
NA	Idaho**	NA
20	Illinois	1.53
28	Indiana	1.41
8	Iowa	2.75
16	Kansas	1.82
37	Kentucky	1.09
38	Louisiana	0.99
10	Maine	2.49
24	Maryland	1.45
26	Massachusetts	1.43
7	Michigan	3.36
NA	Minnesota**	NA
45	Mississippi	0.82
40	Missouri	0.90
46	Montana	0.74
18	Nebraska	1.62
30	Nevada	1.34
35	New Hampshire	1.21
25	New Jersey	1.44
27	New Mexico	1.42
3	New York	4.89
32	North Carolina	1.26
40	North Dakota	0.90
9	Ohio	2.61
36	Oklahoma	1.18
1	Oregon	6.19
32	Pennsylvania	1.26
4	Rhode Island	4.63
34	South Carolina	1.22
23	South Dakota	1.46
31	Tennessee	1.27
40	Texas	0.90
6	Utah	3.76
11	Vermont	2.09
14	Virginia	1.90
17	Washington	1.68
44	West Virginia	0.83
2	Wisconsin	4.91
NA	Wyoming**	NA

RANK ORDER

RANK	STATE	PER CAPITA
1	Oregon	$6.19
2	Wisconsin	4.91
3	New York	4.89
4	Rhode Island	4.63
5	Alaska	4.29
6	Utah	3.76
7	Michigan	3.36
8	Iowa	2.75
9	Ohio	2.61
10	Maine	2.49
11	Vermont	2.09
12	California	1.98
13	Arizona	1.96
14	Virginia	1.90
15	Connecticut	1.88
16	Kansas	1.82
17	Washington	1.68
18	Nebraska	1.62
19	Arkansas	1.58
20	Delaware	1.53
20	Illinois	1.53
22	Hawaii	1.48
23	South Dakota	1.46
24	Maryland	1.45
25	New Jersey	1.44
26	Massachusetts	1.43
27	New Mexico	1.42
28	Indiana	1.41
29	Colorado	1.38
30	Nevada	1.34
31	Tennessee	1.27
32	North Carolina	1.26
32	Pennsylvania	1.26
34	South Carolina	1.22
35	New Hampshire	1.21
36	Oklahoma	1.18
37	Kentucky	1.09
38	Louisiana	0.99
39	Georgia	0.91
40	Missouri	0.90
40	North Dakota	0.90
40	Texas	0.90
43	Alabama	0.87
44	West Virginia	0.83
45	Mississippi	0.82
46	Montana	0.74
47	Florida	0.73
NA	Idaho**	NA
NA	Minnesota**	NA
NA	Wyoming**	NA
	District of Columbia	3.04

Source: Morgan Quitno Press using data from National Association of State Alcohol and Drug Abuse Directors "State Resources and Services Related to Alcohol and Other Drug Problems-Fiscal Year 1997" (July 1999)
*National per capita does not include expenditures or population in U.S. territories and is only for reporting states.
**Not available.

IV. FINANCE

138   State and Local Government Expenditures for Justice Activities in 1997
139   Per Capita State & Local Government Expenditures for Justice Activities: 1997
140   State and Local Government Expenditures for Justice Activities as a Percent of All Direct General Expenditures in 1997
141   State Government Expenditures for Justice Activities in 1997
142   Per Capita State Government Expenditures for Justice Activities in 1997
143   State Government Expenditures for Justice Activities as a Percent of All Direct General Expenditures in 1997
144   Local Government Expenditures for Justice Activities in 1997
145   Per Capita Local Government Expenditures for Justice Activities in 1997
146   Local Government Expenditures for Justice Activities as a Percent of All Direct General Expenditures in 1997
147   State and Local Government Expenditures for Police Protection in 1997
148   Per Capita State & Local Government Expenditures for Police Protection: 1997
149   State and Local Government Expenditures for Police Protection as a Percent of All Direct General Expenditures in 1997
150   State Government Expenditures for Police Protection in 1997
151   Per Capita State Government Expenditures for Police Protection in 1997
152   State Government Expenditures for Police Protection as a Percent of All Direct General Expenditures in 1997
153   Local Government Expenditures for Police Protection in 1997
154   Per Capita Local Government Expenditures for Police Protection in 1997
155   Local Government Expenditures for Police Protection as a Percent of All Direct General Expenditures in 1997
156   State and Local Government Expenditures for Corrections in 1997
157   Per Capita State and Local Government Expenditures for Corrections in 1997
158   State and Local Government Expenditures for Corrections as a Percent of All Direct General Expenditures in 1997
159   State Government Expenditures for Corrections in 1997
160   Per Capita State Government Expenditures for Corrections in 1997
161   State Government Expenditures for Corrections as a Percent of All Direct General Expenditures in 1997
162   Expenditures for State Prisons in 1996
163   Operating Expenditures for State Prisons in 1996
164   Annual Operating Expenditures per Inmate in 1996
165   Daily Operating Expenditures per Inmate in 1996
166   Local Government Expenditures for Corrections in 1997
167   Per Capita Local Government Expenditures for Corrections in 1997
168   Local Government Expenditures for Corrections as a Percent of All Direct General Expenditures in 1997
169   State and Local Government Expenditures for Judicial and Legal Services: 1997
170   Per Capita State and Local Government Expenditures for Judicial and Legal Services in 1997
171   State and Local Government Expenditures for Judicial and Legal Services as a Percent of All Direct General Expenditures in 1997
172   State Government Expenditures for Judicial and Legal Services in 1997
173   Per Capita State Government Expenditures for Judicial and Legal Services: 1997
174   State Government Expenditures for Judicial and Legal Services as a Percent of All Direct General Expenditures in 1997
175   Local Government Expenditures for Judicial and Legal Services in 1997
176   Per Capita Local Government Expenditures for Judicial & Legal Services: 1997
177   Local Government Expenditures for Judicial and Legal Services as a Percent of All Direct General Expenditures in 1997
178   State and Local Government Judicial and Legal Payroll in 1999
179   State and Local Government Police Protection Payroll in 1999
180   State and Local Government Corrections Payroll in 1999
181   Base Salary for Justices of States' Highest Courts in 2000
182   Base Salary for Judges of Intermediate Appellate Courts in 2000
183   Base Salary for Judges of General Trial Courts in 2000

State and Local Government Expenditures for Justice Activities in 1997

National Total = $109,210,974,000*

ALPHA ORDER

RANK	STATE	EXPENDITURES	% of USA
27	Alabama	$1,089,836,000	1.0%
38	Alaska	447,528,000	0.4%
16	Arizona	2,023,736,000	1.9%
36	Arkansas	649,888,000	0.6%
1	California	17,872,447,000	16.4%
21	Colorado	1,535,881,000	1.4%
25	Connecticut	1,379,356,000	1.3%
43	Delaware	329,899,000	0.3%
4	Florida	6,026,666,000	5.5%
10	Georgia	2,637,532,000	2.4%
37	Hawaii	468,778,000	0.4%
40	Idaho	388,481,000	0.4%
5	Illinois	4,515,100,000	4.1%
23	Indiana	1,492,940,000	1.4%
32	Iowa	755,773,000	0.7%
31	Kansas	796,572,000	0.7%
28	Kentucky	977,872,000	0.9%
22	Louisiana	1,511,023,000	1.4%
45	Maine	282,312,000	0.3%
15	Maryland	2,138,192,000	2.0%
11	Massachusetts	2,558,618,000	2.3%
9	Michigan	3,882,480,000	3.6%
20	Minnesota	1,549,568,000	1.4%
35	Mississippi	682,916,000	0.6%
19	Missouri	1,580,606,000	1.4%
46	Montana	257,107,000	0.2%
39	Nebraska	428,806,000	0.4%
30	Nevada	882,423,000	0.8%
44	New Hampshire	316,531,000	0.3%
8	New Jersey	3,998,471,000	3.7%
34	New Mexico	692,004,000	0.6%
2	New York	11,054,672,000	10.1%
12	North Carolina	2,489,397,000	2.3%
50	North Dakota	128,026,000	0.1%
7	Ohio	4,211,775,000	3.9%
29	Oklahoma	922,333,000	0.8%
24	Oregon	1,473,423,000	1.3%
6	Pennsylvania	4,446,126,000	4.1%
41	Rhode Island	386,686,000	0.4%
26	South Carolina	1,181,479,000	1.1%
47	South Dakota	187,629,000	0.2%
18	Tennessee	1,678,949,000	1.5%
3	Texas	7,005,010,000	6.4%
33	Utah	730,773,000	0.7%
49	Vermont	141,631,000	0.1%
13	Virginia	2,310,901,000	2.1%
14	Washington	2,245,854,000	2.1%
42	West Virginia	346,367,000	0.3%
17	Wisconsin	1,985,013,000	1.8%
48	Wyoming	175,409,000	0.2%

RANK ORDER

RANK	STATE	EXPENDITURES	% of USA
1	California	$17,872,447,000	16.4%
2	New York	11,054,672,000	10.1%
3	Texas	7,005,010,000	6.4%
4	Florida	6,026,666,000	5.5%
5	Illinois	4,515,100,000	4.1%
6	Pennsylvania	4,446,126,000	4.1%
7	Ohio	4,211,775,000	3.9%
8	New Jersey	3,998,471,000	3.7%
9	Michigan	3,882,480,000	3.6%
10	Georgia	2,637,532,000	2.4%
11	Massachusetts	2,558,618,000	2.3%
12	North Carolina	2,489,397,000	2.3%
13	Virginia	2,310,901,000	2.1%
14	Washington	2,245,854,000	2.1%
15	Maryland	2,138,192,000	2.0%
16	Arizona	2,023,736,000	1.9%
17	Wisconsin	1,985,013,000	1.8%
18	Tennessee	1,678,949,000	1.5%
19	Missouri	1,580,606,000	1.4%
20	Minnesota	1,549,568,000	1.4%
21	Colorado	1,535,881,000	1.4%
22	Louisiana	1,511,023,000	1.4%
23	Indiana	1,492,940,000	1.4%
24	Oregon	1,473,423,000	1.3%
25	Connecticut	1,379,356,000	1.3%
26	South Carolina	1,181,479,000	1.1%
27	Alabama	1,089,836,000	1.0%
28	Kentucky	977,872,000	0.9%
29	Oklahoma	922,333,000	0.8%
30	Nevada	882,423,000	0.8%
31	Kansas	796,572,000	0.7%
32	Iowa	755,773,000	0.7%
33	Utah	730,773,000	0.7%
34	New Mexico	692,004,000	0.6%
35	Mississippi	682,916,000	0.6%
36	Arkansas	649,888,000	0.6%
37	Hawaii	468,778,000	0.4%
38	Alaska	447,528,000	0.4%
39	Nebraska	428,806,000	0.4%
40	Idaho	388,481,000	0.4%
41	Rhode Island	386,686,000	0.4%
42	West Virginia	346,367,000	0.3%
43	Delaware	329,899,000	0.3%
44	New Hampshire	316,531,000	0.3%
45	Maine	282,312,000	0.3%
46	Montana	257,107,000	0.2%
47	South Dakota	187,629,000	0.2%
48	Wyoming	175,409,000	0.2%
49	Vermont	141,631,000	0.1%
50	North Dakota	128,026,000	0.1%
	District of Columbia	733,950,000	0.7%

Source: Morgan Quitno Press using data from U.S. Bureau of the Census
"Compendium of Government Finances 1997" (GC97(4)-5, December 2000)
*Direct general expenditures. Includes Police Protection, Corrections and Judicial and Legal Services.

Per Capita State & Local Government Expenditures for Justice Activities: 1997

National Per Capita = $408*

ALPHA ORDER

ALPHA ORDER

RANK	STATE	PER CAPITA
44	Alabama	$252
1	Alaska	735
8	Arizona	445
41	Arkansas	257
3	California	555
16	Colorado	395
9	Connecticut	422
7	Delaware	449
12	Florida	410
26	Georgia	352
17	Hawaii	394
31	Idaho	321
20	Illinois	376
43	Indiana	254
39	Iowa	265
34	Kansas	304
45	Kentucky	250
27	Louisiana	347
48	Maine	227
10	Maryland	420
11	Massachusetts	418
15	Michigan	397
30	Minnesota	331
45	Mississippi	250
36	Missouri	292
35	Montana	293
40	Nebraska	259
4	Nevada	527
38	New Hampshire	270
5	New Jersey	496
13	New Mexico	402
2	New York	609
29	North Carolina	335
49	North Dakota	200
20	Ohio	376
37	Oklahoma	278
6	Oregon	454
22	Pennsylvania	370
18	Rhode Island	392
32	South Carolina	312
41	South Dakota	257
32	Tennessee	312
24	Texas	362
25	Utah	354
47	Vermont	241
28	Virginia	343
14	Washington	401
50	West Virginia	191
19	Wisconsin	382
23	Wyoming	365

RANK ORDER

RANK	STATE	PER CAPITA
1	Alaska	$735
2	New York	609
3	California	555
4	Nevada	527
5	New Jersey	496
6	Oregon	454
7	Delaware	449
8	Arizona	445
9	Connecticut	422
10	Maryland	420
11	Massachusetts	418
12	Florida	410
13	New Mexico	402
14	Washington	401
15	Michigan	397
16	Colorado	395
17	Hawaii	394
18	Rhode Island	392
19	Wisconsin	382
20	Illinois	376
20	Ohio	376
22	Pennsylvania	370
23	Wyoming	365
24	Texas	362
25	Utah	354
26	Georgia	352
27	Louisiana	347
28	Virginia	343
29	North Carolina	335
30	Minnesota	331
31	Idaho	321
32	South Carolina	312
32	Tennessee	312
34	Kansas	304
35	Montana	293
36	Missouri	292
37	Oklahoma	278
38	New Hampshire	270
39	Iowa	265
40	Nebraska	259
41	Arkansas	257
41	South Dakota	257
43	Indiana	254
44	Alabama	252
45	Kentucky	250
45	Mississippi	250
47	Vermont	241
48	Maine	227
49	North Dakota	200
50	West Virginia	191

District of Columbia   1,388

Source: Morgan Quitno Press using data from U.S. Bureau of the Census
"Compendium of Government Finances 1997" (GC97(4)-5, December 2000)
*Direct general expenditures. Includes Police Protection, Corrections and Judicial and Legal Services.

State and Local Government Expenditures for Justice Activities
As a Percent of All Direct General Expenditures in 1997
National Percent = 8.7% of Direct General Expenditures*

ALPHA ORDER

RANK ORDER

RANK	STATE	PERCENT
40	Alabama	6.3
35	Alaska	6.7
1	Arizona	11.4
34	Arkansas	6.9
2	California	11.1
9	Colorado	8.8
26	Connecticut	7.8
14	Delaware	8.4
5	Florida	9.5
17	Georgia	8.1
33	Hawaii	7.0
21	Idaho	8.0
12	Illinois	8.5
37	Indiana	6.4
45	Iowa	5.9
32	Kansas	7.2
40	Kentucky	6.3
21	Louisiana	8.0
48	Maine	4.9
6	Maryland	9.4
17	Massachusetts	8.1
12	Michigan	8.5
43	Minnesota	6.2
44	Mississippi	6.1
29	Missouri	7.7
36	Montana	6.6
46	Nebraska	5.8
2	Nevada	11.1
37	New Hampshire	6.4
4	New Jersey	9.8
16	New Mexico	8.3
9	New York	8.8
21	North Carolina	8.0
50	North Dakota	4.3
9	Ohio	8.8
30	Oklahoma	7.5
8	Oregon	8.9
14	Pennsylvania	8.4
24	Rhode Island	7.9
31	South Carolina	7.4
37	South Dakota	6.4
24	Tennessee	7.9
7	Texas	9.2
17	Utah	8.1
47	Vermont	5.1
17	Virginia	8.1
26	Washington	7.8
49	West Virginia	4.5
26	Wisconsin	7.8
40	Wyoming	6.3

RANK	STATE	PERCENT
1	Arizona	11.4
2	California	11.1
2	Nevada	11.1
4	New Jersey	9.8
5	Florida	9.5
6	Maryland	9.4
7	Texas	9.2
8	Oregon	8.9
9	Colorado	8.8
9	New York	8.8
9	Ohio	8.8
12	Illinois	8.5
12	Michigan	8.5
14	Delaware	8.4
14	Pennsylvania	8.4
16	New Mexico	8.3
17	Georgia	8.1
17	Massachusetts	8.1
17	Utah	8.1
17	Virginia	8.1
21	Idaho	8.0
21	Louisiana	8.0
21	North Carolina	8.0
24	Rhode Island	7.9
24	Tennessee	7.9
26	Connecticut	7.8
26	Washington	7.8
26	Wisconsin	7.8
29	Missouri	7.7
30	Oklahoma	7.5
31	South Carolina	7.4
32	Kansas	7.2
33	Hawaii	7.0
34	Arkansas	6.9
35	Alaska	6.7
36	Montana	6.6
37	Indiana	6.4
37	New Hampshire	6.4
37	South Dakota	6.4
40	Alabama	6.3
40	Kentucky	6.3
40	Wyoming	6.3
43	Minnesota	6.2
44	Mississippi	6.1
45	Iowa	5.9
46	Nebraska	5.8
47	Vermont	5.1
48	Maine	4.9
49	West Virginia	4.5
50	North Dakota	4.3

District of Columbia   16.9

Source: Morgan Quitno Press using data from U.S. Bureau of the Census
   "Compendium of Government Finances 1997" (GC97(4)-5, December 2000)
*Includes Police Protection, Corrections and Judicial and Legal Services.

State Government Expenditures for Justice Activities in 1997

National Total = $42,353,331,000*

ALPHA ORDER

RANK ORDER

RANK	STATE	EXPENDITURES	% of USA	RANK	STATE	EXPENDITURES	% of USA
29	Alabama	$454,685,000	1.1%	1	California	$5,197,179,000	12.3%
33	Alaska	335,501,000	0.8%	2	New York	3,623,637,000	8.6%
17	Arizona	731,339,000	1.7%	3	Texas	2,838,742,000	6.7%
35	Arkansas	315,171,000	0.7%	4	Pennsylvania	1,924,145,000	4.5%
1	California	5,197,179,000	12.3%	5	Michigan	1,622,805,000	3.8%
21	Colorado	628,050,000	1.5%	6	New Jersey	1,573,861,000	3.7%
15	Connecticut	868,944,000	2.1%	7	Ohio	1,510,877,000	3.6%
39	Delaware	239,973,000	0.6%	8	Florida	1,460,888,000	3.4%
8	Florida	1,460,888,000	3.4%	9	North Carolina	1,419,365,000	3.4%
13	Georgia	1,101,936,000	2.6%	10	Illinois	1,416,824,000	3.3%
37	Hawaii	248,360,000	0.6%	11	Massachusetts	1,286,435,000	3.0%
42	Idaho	177,017,000	0.4%	12	Maryland	1,146,420,000	2.7%
10	Illinois	1,416,824,000	3.3%	13	Georgia	1,101,936,000	2.6%
19	Indiana	634,481,000	1.5%	14	Virginia	962,231,000	2.3%
31	Iowa	360,360,000	0.9%	15	Connecticut	868,944,000	2.1%
34	Kansas	331,115,000	0.8%	16	Washington	757,339,000	1.8%
26	Kentucky	550,426,000	1.3%	17	Arizona	731,339,000	1.7%
25	Louisiana	606,800,000	1.4%	18	Wisconsin	705,569,000	1.7%
45	Maine	147,762,000	0.3%	19	Indiana	634,481,000	1.5%
12	Maryland	1,146,420,000	2.7%	20	South Carolina	632,965,000	1.5%
11	Massachusetts	1,286,435,000	3.0%	21	Colorado	628,050,000	1.5%
5	Michigan	1,622,805,000	3.8%	22	Oregon	625,094,000	1.5%
28	Minnesota	491,181,000	1.2%	23	Tennessee	617,154,000	1.5%
36	Mississippi	300,816,000	0.7%	24	Missouri	613,225,000	1.4%
24	Missouri	613,225,000	1.4%	25	Louisiana	606,800,000	1.4%
46	Montana	118,606,000	0.3%	26	Kentucky	550,426,000	1.3%
43	Nebraska	176,603,000	0.4%	27	Oklahoma	495,359,000	1.2%
38	Nevada	245,678,000	0.6%	28	Minnesota	491,181,000	1.2%
44	New Hampshire	154,350,000	0.4%	29	Alabama	454,685,000	1.1%
6	New Jersey	1,573,861,000	3.7%	30	Utah	362,359,000	0.9%
32	New Mexico	359,869,000	0.8%	31	Iowa	360,360,000	0.9%
2	New York	3,623,637,000	8.6%	32	New Mexico	359,869,000	0.8%
9	North Carolina	1,419,365,000	3.4%	33	Alaska	335,501,000	0.8%
50	North Dakota	58,465,000	0.1%	34	Kansas	331,115,000	0.8%
7	Ohio	1,510,877,000	3.6%	35	Arkansas	315,171,000	0.7%
27	Oklahoma	495,359,000	1.2%	36	Mississippi	300,816,000	0.7%
22	Oregon	625,094,000	1.5%	37	Hawaii	248,360,000	0.6%
4	Pennsylvania	1,924,145,000	4.5%	38	Nevada	245,678,000	0.6%
40	Rhode Island	235,761,000	0.6%	39	Delaware	239,973,000	0.6%
20	South Carolina	632,965,000	1.5%	40	Rhode Island	235,761,000	0.6%
48	South Dakota	93,475,000	0.2%	41	West Virginia	190,022,000	0.4%
23	Tennessee	617,154,000	1.5%	42	Idaho	177,017,000	0.4%
3	Texas	2,838,742,000	6.7%	43	Nebraska	176,603,000	0.4%
30	Utah	362,359,000	0.9%	44	New Hampshire	154,350,000	0.4%
47	Vermont	103,896,000	0.2%	45	Maine	147,762,000	0.3%
14	Virginia	962,231,000	2.3%	46	Montana	118,606,000	0.3%
16	Washington	757,339,000	1.8%	47	Vermont	103,896,000	0.2%
41	West Virginia	190,022,000	0.4%	48	South Dakota	93,475,000	0.2%
18	Wisconsin	705,569,000	1.7%	49	Wyoming	73,393,000	0.2%
49	Wyoming	73,393,000	0.2%	50	North Dakota	58,465,000	0.1%
					District of Columbia**	NA	NA

Source: Morgan Quitno Press using data from U.S. Bureau of the Census
"Compendium of Government Finances 1997" (GC97(4)-5, December 2000)
*Direct general expenditures. Includes Police Protection, Corrections and Judicial and Legal Services.
**Not applicable.

Per Capita State Government Expenditures for Justice Activities in 1997

National Per Capita = $158*

<table>
<tr><td colspan="3"><u>ALPHA ORDER</u></td><td colspan="3"><u>RANK ORDER</u></td></tr>
<tr><td>RANK</td><td>STATE</td><td>PER CAPITA</td><td>RANK</td><td>STATE</td><td>PER CAPITA</td></tr>
<tr><td>46</td><td>Alabama</td><td>$105</td><td>1</td><td>Alaska</td><td>$551</td></tr>
<tr><td>1</td><td>Alaska</td><td>551</td><td>2</td><td>Delaware</td><td>326</td></tr>
<tr><td>17</td><td>Arizona</td><td>161</td><td>3</td><td>Connecticut</td><td>266</td></tr>
<tr><td>38</td><td>Arkansas</td><td>125</td><td>4</td><td>Rhode Island</td><td>239</td></tr>
<tr><td>17</td><td>California</td><td>161</td><td>5</td><td>Maryland</td><td>225</td></tr>
<tr><td>17</td><td>Colorado</td><td>161</td><td>6</td><td>Massachusetts</td><td>210</td></tr>
<tr><td>3</td><td>Connecticut</td><td>266</td><td>7</td><td>Hawaii</td><td>209</td></tr>
<tr><td>2</td><td>Delaware</td><td>326</td><td>7</td><td>New Mexico</td><td>209</td></tr>
<tr><td>49</td><td>Florida</td><td>99</td><td>9</td><td>New York</td><td>200</td></tr>
<tr><td>23</td><td>Georgia</td><td>147</td><td>10</td><td>New Jersey</td><td>195</td></tr>
<tr><td>7</td><td>Hawaii</td><td>209</td><td>11</td><td>Oregon</td><td>193</td></tr>
<tr><td>26</td><td>Idaho</td><td>146</td><td>12</td><td>North Carolina</td><td>191</td></tr>
<tr><td>40</td><td>Illinois</td><td>118</td><td>13</td><td>Vermont</td><td>176</td></tr>
<tr><td>44</td><td>Indiana</td><td>108</td><td>14</td><td>Utah</td><td>175</td></tr>
<tr><td>37</td><td>Iowa</td><td>126</td><td>15</td><td>South Carolina</td><td>167</td></tr>
<tr><td>36</td><td>Kansas</td><td>127</td><td>16</td><td>Michigan</td><td>166</td></tr>
<tr><td>28</td><td>Kentucky</td><td>141</td><td>17</td><td>Arizona</td><td>161</td></tr>
<tr><td>29</td><td>Louisiana</td><td>139</td><td>17</td><td>California</td><td>161</td></tr>
<tr><td>39</td><td>Maine</td><td>119</td><td>17</td><td>Colorado</td><td>161</td></tr>
<tr><td>5</td><td>Maryland</td><td>225</td><td>20</td><td>Pennsylvania</td><td>160</td></tr>
<tr><td>6</td><td>Massachusetts</td><td>210</td><td>21</td><td>Wyoming</td><td>153</td></tr>
<tr><td>16</td><td>Michigan</td><td>166</td><td>22</td><td>Oklahoma</td><td>149</td></tr>
<tr><td>46</td><td>Minnesota</td><td>105</td><td>23</td><td>Georgia</td><td>147</td></tr>
<tr><td>43</td><td>Mississippi</td><td>110</td><td>23</td><td>Nevada</td><td>147</td></tr>
<tr><td>42</td><td>Missouri</td><td>113</td><td>23</td><td>Texas</td><td>147</td></tr>
<tr><td>31</td><td>Montana</td><td>135</td><td>26</td><td>Idaho</td><td>146</td></tr>
<tr><td>45</td><td>Nebraska</td><td>107</td><td>27</td><td>Virginia</td><td>143</td></tr>
<tr><td>23</td><td>Nevada</td><td>147</td><td>28</td><td>Kentucky</td><td>141</td></tr>
<tr><td>34</td><td>New Hampshire</td><td>132</td><td>29</td><td>Louisiana</td><td>139</td></tr>
<tr><td>10</td><td>New Jersey</td><td>195</td><td>30</td><td>Wisconsin</td><td>136</td></tr>
<tr><td>7</td><td>New Mexico</td><td>209</td><td>31</td><td>Montana</td><td>135</td></tr>
<tr><td>9</td><td>New York</td><td>200</td><td>31</td><td>Ohio</td><td>135</td></tr>
<tr><td>12</td><td>North Carolina</td><td>191</td><td>31</td><td>Washington</td><td>135</td></tr>
<tr><td>50</td><td>North Dakota</td><td>91</td><td>34</td><td>New Hampshire</td><td>132</td></tr>
<tr><td>31</td><td>Ohio</td><td>135</td><td>35</td><td>South Dakota</td><td>128</td></tr>
<tr><td>22</td><td>Oklahoma</td><td>149</td><td>36</td><td>Kansas</td><td>127</td></tr>
<tr><td>11</td><td>Oregon</td><td>193</td><td>37</td><td>Iowa</td><td>126</td></tr>
<tr><td>20</td><td>Pennsylvania</td><td>160</td><td>38</td><td>Arkansas</td><td>125</td></tr>
<tr><td>4</td><td>Rhode Island</td><td>239</td><td>39</td><td>Maine</td><td>119</td></tr>
<tr><td>15</td><td>South Carolina</td><td>167</td><td>40</td><td>Illinois</td><td>118</td></tr>
<tr><td>35</td><td>South Dakota</td><td>128</td><td>41</td><td>Tennessee</td><td>115</td></tr>
<tr><td>41</td><td>Tennessee</td><td>115</td><td>42</td><td>Missouri</td><td>113</td></tr>
<tr><td>23</td><td>Texas</td><td>147</td><td>43</td><td>Mississippi</td><td>110</td></tr>
<tr><td>14</td><td>Utah</td><td>175</td><td>44</td><td>Indiana</td><td>108</td></tr>
<tr><td>13</td><td>Vermont</td><td>176</td><td>45</td><td>Nebraska</td><td>107</td></tr>
<tr><td>27</td><td>Virginia</td><td>143</td><td>46</td><td>Alabama</td><td>105</td></tr>
<tr><td>31</td><td>Washington</td><td>135</td><td>46</td><td>Minnesota</td><td>105</td></tr>
<tr><td>46</td><td>West Virginia</td><td>105</td><td>46</td><td>West Virginia</td><td>105</td></tr>
<tr><td>30</td><td>Wisconsin</td><td>136</td><td>49</td><td>Florida</td><td>99</td></tr>
<tr><td>21</td><td>Wyoming</td><td>153</td><td>50</td><td>North Dakota</td><td>91</td></tr>
<tr><td></td><td></td><td></td><td></td><td>District of Columbia**</td><td>NA</td></tr>
</table>

Source: Morgan Quitno Press using data from U.S. Bureau of the Census
   "Compendium of Government Finances 1997" (GC97(4)-5, December 2000)
*Direct general expenditures. Includes Police Protection, Corrections and Judicial and Legal Services.
**Not applicable.

State Government Expenditures for Justice Activities
As a Percent of All Direct General Expenditures in 1997
National Percent = 8.1% of Direct General Expenditures*

ALPHA ORDER

RANK ORDER

RANK	STATE	PERCENT
44	Alabama	5.4
17	Alaska	8.1
2	Arizona	10.9
40	Arkansas	6.1
5	California	9.8
4	Colorado	9.9
9	Connecticut	9.2
7	Delaware	9.5
29	Florida	6.4
21	Georgia	7.7
47	Hawaii	4.7
17	Idaho	8.1
29	Illinois	6.4
29	Indiana	6.4
33	Iowa	6.3
26	Kansas	7.3
33	Kentucky	6.3
33	Louisiana	6.3
48	Maine	4.6
1	Maryland	11.0
27	Massachusetts	7.2
11	Michigan	8.8
46	Minnesota	5.0
42	Mississippi	5.6
28	Missouri	6.7
42	Montana	5.6
45	Nebraska	5.3
6	Nevada	9.6
37	New Hampshire	6.2
8	New Jersey	9.4
14	New Mexico	8.2
14	New York	8.2
3	North Carolina	10.4
50	North Dakota	3.5
25	Ohio	7.5
12	Oklahoma	8.7
12	Oregon	8.7
17	Pennsylvania	8.1
14	Rhode Island	8.2
21	South Carolina	7.7
37	South Dakota	6.2
29	Tennessee	6.4
10	Texas	9.1
20	Utah	7.9
33	Vermont	6.3
21	Virginia	7.7
41	Washington	5.8
49	West Virginia	4.2
24	Wisconsin	7.6
37	Wyoming	6.2

RANK	STATE	PERCENT
1	Maryland	11.0
2	Arizona	10.9
3	North Carolina	10.4
4	Colorado	9.9
5	California	9.8
6	Nevada	9.6
7	Delaware	9.5
8	New Jersey	9.4
9	Connecticut	9.2
10	Texas	9.1
11	Michigan	8.8
12	Oklahoma	8.7
12	Oregon	8.7
14	New Mexico	8.2
14	New York	8.2
14	Rhode Island	8.2
17	Alaska	8.1
17	Idaho	8.1
17	Pennsylvania	8.1
20	Utah	7.9
21	Georgia	7.7
21	South Carolina	7.7
21	Virginia	7.7
24	Wisconsin	7.6
25	Ohio	7.5
26	Kansas	7.3
27	Massachusetts	7.2
28	Missouri	6.7
29	Florida	6.4
29	Illinois	6.4
29	Indiana	6.4
29	Tennessee	6.4
33	Iowa	6.3
33	Kentucky	6.3
33	Louisiana	6.3
33	Vermont	6.3
37	New Hampshire	6.2
37	South Dakota	6.2
37	Wyoming	6.2
40	Arkansas	6.1
41	Washington	5.8
42	Mississippi	5.6
42	Montana	5.6
44	Alabama	5.4
45	Nebraska	5.3
46	Minnesota	5.0
47	Hawaii	4.7
48	Maine	4.6
49	West Virginia	4.2
50	North Dakota	3.5

District of Columbia**   NA

Source: Morgan Quitno Press using data from U.S. Bureau of the Census
    "Compendium of Government Finances 1997" (GC97(4)-5, December 2000)
*Includes Police Protection, Corrections and Judicial and Legal Services.
**Not applicable.

Local Government Expenditures for Justice Activities in 1997

National Total = $66,857,643,000*

ALPHA ORDER

RANK	STATE	EXPENDITURES	% of USA
26	Alabama	$635,151,000	1.0%
45	Alaska	112,027,000	0.2%
13	Arizona	1,292,397,000	1.9%
35	Arkansas	334,717,000	0.5%
1	California	12,675,268,000	19.0%
21	Colorado	907,831,000	1.4%
28	Connecticut	510,412,000	0.8%
48	Delaware	89,926,000	0.1%
3	Florida	4,565,778,000	6.8%
10	Georgia	1,535,596,000	2.3%
38	Hawaii	220,418,000	0.3%
39	Idaho	211,464,000	0.3%
5	Illinois	3,098,276,000	4.6%
23	Indiana	858,459,000	1.3%
32	Iowa	395,413,000	0.6%
29	Kansas	465,457,000	0.7%
30	Kentucky	427,446,000	0.6%
22	Louisiana	904,223,000	1.4%
44	Maine	134,550,000	0.2%
19	Maryland	991,772,000	1.5%
15	Massachusetts	1,272,183,000	1.9%
9	Michigan	2,259,675,000	3.4%
18	Minnesota	1,058,387,000	1.6%
33	Mississippi	382,100,000	0.6%
20	Missouri	967,381,000	1.4%
43	Montana	138,501,000	0.2%
37	Nebraska	252,203,000	0.4%
25	Nevada	636,745,000	1.0%
40	New Hampshire	162,181,000	0.2%
8	New Jersey	2,424,610,000	3.6%
36	New Mexico	332,135,000	0.5%
2	New York	7,431,035,000	11.1%
16	North Carolina	1,070,032,000	1.6%
49	North Dakota	69,561,000	0.1%
6	Ohio	2,700,898,000	4.0%
31	Oklahoma	426,974,000	0.6%
24	Oregon	848,329,000	1.3%
7	Pennsylvania	2,521,981,000	3.8%
42	Rhode Island	150,925,000	0.2%
27	South Carolina	548,514,000	0.8%
47	South Dakota	94,154,000	0.1%
17	Tennessee	1,061,795,000	1.6%
4	Texas	4,166,268,000	6.2%
34	Utah	368,414,000	0.6%
50	Vermont	37,735,000	0.1%
12	Virginia	1,348,670,000	2.0%
11	Washington	1,488,515,000	2.2%
41	West Virginia	156,345,000	0.2%
14	Wisconsin	1,279,444,000	1.9%
46	Wyoming	102,016,000	0.2%

RANK ORDER

RANK	STATE	EXPENDITURES	% of USA
1	California	$12,675,268,000	19.0%
2	New York	7,431,035,000	11.1%
3	Florida	4,565,778,000	6.8%
4	Texas	4,166,268,000	6.2%
5	Illinois	3,098,276,000	4.6%
6	Ohio	2,700,898,000	4.0%
7	Pennsylvania	2,521,981,000	3.8%
8	New Jersey	2,424,610,000	3.6%
9	Michigan	2,259,675,000	3.4%
10	Georgia	1,535,596,000	2.3%
11	Washington	1,488,515,000	2.2%
12	Virginia	1,348,670,000	2.0%
13	Arizona	1,292,397,000	1.9%
14	Wisconsin	1,279,444,000	1.9%
15	Massachusetts	1,272,183,000	1.9%
16	North Carolina	1,070,032,000	1.6%
17	Tennessee	1,061,795,000	1.6%
18	Minnesota	1,058,387,000	1.6%
19	Maryland	991,772,000	1.5%
20	Missouri	967,381,000	1.4%
21	Colorado	907,831,000	1.4%
22	Louisiana	904,223,000	1.4%
23	Indiana	858,459,000	1.3%
24	Oregon	848,329,000	1.3%
25	Nevada	636,745,000	1.0%
26	Alabama	635,151,000	1.0%
27	South Carolina	548,514,000	0.8%
28	Connecticut	510,412,000	0.8%
29	Kansas	465,457,000	0.7%
30	Kentucky	427,446,000	0.6%
31	Oklahoma	426,974,000	0.6%
32	Iowa	395,413,000	0.6%
33	Mississippi	382,100,000	0.6%
34	Utah	368,414,000	0.6%
35	Arkansas	334,717,000	0.5%
36	New Mexico	332,135,000	0.5%
37	Nebraska	252,203,000	0.4%
38	Hawaii	220,418,000	0.3%
39	Idaho	211,464,000	0.3%
40	New Hampshire	162,181,000	0.2%
41	West Virginia	156,345,000	0.2%
42	Rhode Island	150,925,000	0.2%
43	Montana	138,501,000	0.2%
44	Maine	134,550,000	0.2%
45	Alaska	112,027,000	0.2%
46	Wyoming	102,016,000	0.2%
47	South Dakota	94,154,000	0.1%
48	Delaware	89,926,000	0.1%
49	North Dakota	69,561,000	0.1%
50	Vermont	37,735,000	0.1%
	District of Columbia	733,950,000	1.1%

Source: Morgan Quitno Press using data from U.S. Bureau of the Census
   "Compendium of Government Finances 1997" (GC97(4)-5, December 2000)
*Direct general expenditures. Includes Police Protection, Corrections and Judicial and Legal Services.

Per Capita Local Government Expenditures for Justice Activities in 1997

National Per Capita = $250*

ALPHA ORDER

RANK ORDER

RANK	STATE	PER CAPITA
35	Alabama	$147
26	Alaska	184
6	Arizona	284
42	Arkansas	133
2	California	393
12	Colorado	233
32	Connecticut	156
45	Delaware	122
4	Florida	311
20	Georgia	205
25	Hawaii	185
30	Idaho	175
9	Illinois	258
36	Indiana	146
40	Iowa	139
28	Kansas	178
46	Kentucky	109
18	Louisiana	208
48	Maine	108
23	Maryland	195
18	Massachusetts	208
13	Michigan	231
14	Minnesota	226
39	Mississippi	140
27	Missouri	179
31	Montana	158
34	Nebraska	152
3	Nevada	380
41	New Hampshire	138
5	New Jersey	301
24	New Mexico	193
1	New York	410
38	North Carolina	144
46	North Dakota	109
11	Ohio	241
43	Oklahoma	129
8	Oregon	262
17	Pennsylvania	210
33	Rhode Island	153
37	South Carolina	145
43	South Dakota	129
22	Tennessee	197
15	Texas	215
28	Utah	178
50	Vermont	64
21	Virginia	200
7	Washington	266
49	West Virginia	86
10	Wisconsin	246
16	Wyoming	213

RANK	STATE	PER CAPITA
1	New York	$410
2	California	393
3	Nevada	380
4	Florida	311
5	New Jersey	301
6	Arizona	284
7	Washington	266
8	Oregon	262
9	Illinois	258
10	Wisconsin	246
11	Ohio	241
12	Colorado	233
13	Michigan	231
14	Minnesota	226
15	Texas	215
16	Wyoming	213
17	Pennsylvania	210
18	Louisiana	208
18	Massachusetts	208
20	Georgia	205
21	Virginia	200
22	Tennessee	197
23	Maryland	195
24	New Mexico	193
25	Hawaii	185
26	Alaska	184
27	Missouri	179
28	Kansas	178
28	Utah	178
30	Idaho	175
31	Montana	158
32	Connecticut	156
33	Rhode Island	153
34	Nebraska	152
35	Alabama	147
36	Indiana	146
37	South Carolina	145
38	North Carolina	144
39	Mississippi	140
40	Iowa	139
41	New Hampshire	138
42	Arkansas	133
43	Oklahoma	129
43	South Dakota	129
45	Delaware	122
46	Kentucky	109
46	North Dakota	109
48	Maine	108
49	West Virginia	86
50	Vermont	64

District of Columbia 1,388

Source: Morgan Quitno Press using data from U.S. Bureau of the Census
    "Compendium of Government Finances 1997" (GC97(4)-5, December 2000)
*Direct general expenditures. Includes Police Protection, Corrections and Judicial and Legal Services.

Local Government Expenditures for Justice Activities
As a Percent of All Direct General Expenditures in 1997
National Percent = 9.2% of Direct General Expenditures*

ALPHA ORDER

RANK	STATE	PERCENT
30	Alabama	7.2
49	Alaska	4.6
4	Arizona	11.7
27	Arkansas	7.8
2	California	12.0
22	Colorado	8.2
43	Connecticut	6.1
39	Delaware	6.3
5	Florida	11.2
18	Georgia	8.4
1	Hawaii	15.3
26	Idaho	7.9
6	Illinois	10.0
38	Indiana	6.4
45	Iowa	5.6
31	Kansas	7.1
41	Kentucky	6.2
8	Louisiana	9.8
47	Maine	5.2
24	Maryland	8.0
11	Massachusetts	9.3
22	Michigan	8.2
33	Minnesota	6.9
35	Mississippi	6.6
17	Missouri	8.5
28	Montana	7.7
41	Nebraska	6.2
3	Nevada	11.9
35	New Hampshire	6.6
6	New Jersey	10.0
18	New Mexico	8.4
12	New York	9.2
43	North Carolina	6.1
46	North Dakota	5.3
9	Ohio	9.7
35	Oklahoma	6.6
15	Oregon	9.0
16	Pennsylvania	8.7
29	Rhode Island	7.6
31	South Carolina	7.1
34	South Dakota	6.7
12	Tennessee	9.2
12	Texas	9.2
18	Utah	8.4
50	Vermont	3.4
18	Virginia	8.4
10	Washington	9.5
48	West Virginia	4.8
24	Wisconsin	8.0
39	Wyoming	6.3

RANK ORDER

RANK	STATE	PERCENT
1	Hawaii	15.3
2	California	12.0
3	Nevada	11.9
4	Arizona	11.7
5	Florida	11.2
6	Illinois	10.0
6	New Jersey	10.0
8	Louisiana	9.8
9	Ohio	9.7
10	Washington	9.5
11	Massachusetts	9.3
12	New York	9.2
12	Tennessee	9.2
12	Texas	9.2
15	Oregon	9.0
16	Pennsylvania	8.7
17	Missouri	8.5
18	Georgia	8.4
18	New Mexico	8.4
18	Utah	8.4
18	Virginia	8.4
22	Colorado	8.2
22	Michigan	8.2
24	Maryland	8.0
24	Wisconsin	8.0
26	Idaho	7.9
27	Arkansas	7.8
28	Montana	7.7
29	Rhode Island	7.6
30	Alabama	7.2
31	Kansas	7.1
31	South Carolina	7.1
33	Minnesota	6.9
34	South Dakota	6.7
35	Mississippi	6.6
35	New Hampshire	6.6
35	Oklahoma	6.6
38	Indiana	6.4
39	Delaware	6.3
39	Wyoming	6.3
41	Kentucky	6.2
41	Nebraska	6.2
43	Connecticut	6.1
43	North Carolina	6.1
45	Iowa	5.6
46	North Dakota	5.3
47	Maine	5.2
48	West Virginia	4.8
49	Alaska	4.6
50	Vermont	3.4
	District of Columbia	16.9

Source: Morgan Quitno Press using data from U.S. Bureau of the Census
"Compendium of Government Finances 1997" (GC97(4)-5, December 2000)
*Includes Police Protection, Corrections and Judicial and Legal Services.

State and Local Government Expenditures for Police Protection in 1997

National Total = $47,618,740,000*

ALPHA ORDER

RANK	STATE	EXPENDITURES	% of USA
26	Alabama	$541,374,000	1.1%
41	Alaska	151,192,000	0.3%
16	Arizona	869,854,000	1.8%
36	Arkansas	292,379,000	0.6%
1	California	7,712,594,000	16.2%
22	Colorado	649,137,000	1.4%
24	Connecticut	592,738,000	1.2%
45	Delaware	131,700,000	0.3%
3	Florida	3,230,857,000	6.8%
11	Georgia	1,050,368,000	2.2%
38	Hawaii	192,287,000	0.4%
40	Idaho	167,159,000	0.4%
5	Illinois	2,404,047,000	5.0%
23	Indiana	644,382,000	1.4%
32	Iowa	350,462,000	0.7%
30	Kansas	377,403,000	0.8%
29	Kentucky	390,992,000	0.8%
19	Louisiana	759,222,000	1.6%
44	Maine	137,768,000	0.3%
15	Maryland	885,188,000	1.9%
10	Massachusetts	1,114,761,000	2.3%
9	Michigan	1,563,311,000	3.3%
21	Minnesota	702,137,000	1.5%
33	Mississippi	320,027,000	0.7%
18	Missouri	762,310,000	1.6%
46	Montana	111,796,000	0.2%
37	Nebraska	194,494,000	0.4%
31	Nevada	372,323,000	0.8%
42	New Hampshire	151,104,000	0.3%
8	New Jersey	1,763,319,000	3.7%
35	New Mexico	297,668,000	0.6%
2	New York	5,132,773,000	10.8%
12	North Carolina	1,029,038,000	2.2%
50	North Dakota	56,525,000	0.1%
7	Ohio	1,809,547,000	3.8%
28	Oklahoma	401,634,000	0.8%
25	Oregon	582,016,000	1.2%
6	Pennsylvania	1,838,949,000	3.9%
39	Rhode Island	174,864,000	0.4%
27	South Carolina	494,197,000	1.0%
48	South Dakota	75,560,000	0.2%
20	Tennessee	745,792,000	1.6%
4	Texas	2,760,918,000	5.8%
34	Utah	305,346,000	0.6%
49	Vermont	65,119,000	0.1%
13	Virginia	981,619,000	2.1%
17	Washington	866,316,000	1.8%
43	West Virginia	139,666,000	0.3%
14	Wisconsin	915,904,000	1.9%
47	Wyoming	78,799,000	0.2%

RANK ORDER

RANK	STATE	EXPENDITURES	% of USA
1	California	$7,712,594,000	16.2%
2	New York	5,132,773,000	10.8%
3	Florida	3,230,857,000	6.8%
4	Texas	2,760,918,000	5.8%
5	Illinois	2,404,047,000	5.0%
6	Pennsylvania	1,838,949,000	3.9%
7	Ohio	1,809,547,000	3.8%
8	New Jersey	1,763,319,000	3.7%
9	Michigan	1,563,311,000	3.3%
10	Massachusetts	1,114,761,000	2.3%
11	Georgia	1,050,368,000	2.2%
12	North Carolina	1,029,038,000	2.2%
13	Virginia	981,619,000	2.1%
14	Wisconsin	915,904,000	1.9%
15	Maryland	885,188,000	1.9%
16	Arizona	869,854,000	1.8%
17	Washington	866,316,000	1.8%
18	Missouri	762,310,000	1.6%
19	Louisiana	759,222,000	1.6%
20	Tennessee	745,792,000	1.6%
21	Minnesota	702,137,000	1.5%
22	Colorado	649,137,000	1.4%
23	Indiana	644,382,000	1.4%
24	Connecticut	592,738,000	1.2%
25	Oregon	582,016,000	1.2%
26	Alabama	541,374,000	1.1%
27	South Carolina	494,197,000	1.0%
28	Oklahoma	401,634,000	0.8%
29	Kentucky	390,992,000	0.8%
30	Kansas	377,403,000	0.8%
31	Nevada	372,323,000	0.8%
32	Iowa	350,462,000	0.7%
33	Mississippi	320,027,000	0.7%
34	Utah	305,346,000	0.6%
35	New Mexico	297,668,000	0.6%
36	Arkansas	292,379,000	0.6%
37	Nebraska	194,494,000	0.4%
38	Hawaii	192,287,000	0.4%
39	Rhode Island	174,864,000	0.4%
40	Idaho	167,159,000	0.4%
41	Alaska	151,192,000	0.3%
42	New Hampshire	151,104,000	0.3%
43	West Virginia	139,666,000	0.3%
44	Maine	137,768,000	0.3%
45	Delaware	131,700,000	0.3%
46	Montana	111,796,000	0.2%
47	Wyoming	78,799,000	0.2%
48	South Dakota	75,560,000	0.2%
49	Vermont	65,119,000	0.1%
50	North Dakota	56,525,000	0.1%
	District of Columbia	279,805,000	0.6%

Source: Morgan Quitno Press using data from U.S. Bureau of the Census
  "Compendium of Government Finances 1997" (GC97(4)-5, December 2000)
*Direct general expenditures.

Per Capita State & Local Government Expenditures for Police Protection: 1997

National Per Capita = $178*

ALPHA ORDER

ALPHA ORDER

RANK	STATE	PER CAPITA
38	Alabama	$125
2	Alaska	248
8	Arizona	191
43	Arkansas	116
3	California	239
18	Colorado	167
10	Connecticut	181
11	Delaware	179
5	Florida	220
31	Georgia	140
20	Hawaii	162
34	Idaho	138
7	Illinois	200
46	Indiana	110
39	Iowa	123
28	Kansas	144
48	Kentucky	100
15	Louisiana	174
44	Maine	111
15	Maryland	174
9	Massachusetts	182
22	Michigan	160
25	Minnesota	150
41	Mississippi	117
30	Missouri	141
37	Montana	127
41	Nebraska	117
4	Nevada	222
36	New Hampshire	129
6	New Jersey	219
17	New Mexico	173
1	New York	283
32	North Carolina	139
49	North Dakota	88
21	Ohio	161
40	Oklahoma	121
11	Oregon	179
24	Pennsylvania	153
13	Rhode Island	177
35	South Carolina	130
47	South Dakota	103
32	Tennessee	139
29	Texas	143
26	Utah	148
44	Vermont	111
27	Virginia	146
23	Washington	155
50	West Virginia	77
14	Wisconsin	176
19	Wyoming	164

RANK ORDER

RANK	STATE	PER CAPITA
1	New York	$283
2	Alaska	248
3	California	239
4	Nevada	222
5	Florida	220
6	New Jersey	219
7	Illinois	200
8	Arizona	191
9	Massachusetts	182
10	Connecticut	181
11	Delaware	179
11	Oregon	179
13	Rhode Island	177
14	Wisconsin	176
15	Louisiana	174
15	Maryland	174
17	New Mexico	173
18	Colorado	167
19	Wyoming	164
20	Hawaii	162
21	Ohio	161
22	Michigan	160
23	Washington	155
24	Pennsylvania	153
25	Minnesota	150
26	Utah	148
27	Virginia	146
28	Kansas	144
29	Texas	143
30	Missouri	141
31	Georgia	140
32	North Carolina	139
32	Tennessee	139
34	Idaho	138
35	South Carolina	130
36	New Hampshire	129
37	Montana	127
38	Alabama	125
39	Iowa	123
40	Oklahoma	121
41	Mississippi	117
41	Nebraska	117
43	Arkansas	116
44	Maine	111
44	Vermont	111
46	Indiana	110
47	South Dakota	103
48	Kentucky	100
49	North Dakota	88
50	West Virginia	77
	District of Columbia	529

Source: Morgan Quitno Press using data from U.S. Bureau of the Census
"Compendium of Government Finances 1997" (GC97(4)-5, December 2000)
*Direct general expenditures.

State and Local Government Expenditures for Police Protection
As a Percent of All Direct General Expenditures in 1997
National Percent = 3.8% of Direct General Expenditures

ALPHA ORDER

RANK ORDER

RANK	STATE	PERCENT
31	Alabama	3.1
47	Alaska	2.3
2	Arizona	4.9
31	Arkansas	3.1
3	California	4.8
11	Colorado	3.7
26	Connecticut	3.3
26	Delaware	3.3
1	Florida	5.1
30	Georgia	3.2
36	Hawaii	2.9
21	Idaho	3.4
5	Illinois	4.5
39	Indiana	2.8
42	Iowa	2.7
21	Kansas	3.4
45	Kentucky	2.5
8	Louisiana	4.0
46	Maine	2.4
9	Maryland	3.9
17	Massachusetts	3.5
21	Michigan	3.4
39	Minnesota	2.8
36	Mississippi	2.9
11	Missouri	3.7
36	Montana	2.9
43	Nebraska	2.6
4	Nevada	4.7
31	New Hampshire	3.1
6	New Jersey	4.3
13	New Mexico	3.6
7	New York	4.1
26	North Carolina	3.3
49	North Dakota	1.9
10	Ohio	3.8
26	Oklahoma	3.3
17	Oregon	3.5
17	Pennsylvania	3.5
13	Rhode Island	3.6
31	South Carolina	3.1
43	South Dakota	2.6
17	Tennessee	3.5
13	Texas	3.6
21	Utah	3.4
47	Vermont	2.3
21	Virginia	3.4
35	Washington	3.0
50	West Virginia	1.8
13	Wisconsin	3.6
39	Wyoming	2.8

RANK	STATE	PERCENT
1	Florida	5.1
2	Arizona	4.9
3	California	4.8
4	Nevada	4.7
5	Illinois	4.5
6	New Jersey	4.3
7	New York	4.1
8	Louisiana	4.0
9	Maryland	3.9
10	Ohio	3.8
11	Colorado	3.7
11	Missouri	3.7
13	New Mexico	3.6
13	Rhode Island	3.6
13	Texas	3.6
13	Wisconsin	3.6
17	Massachusetts	3.5
17	Oregon	3.5
17	Pennsylvania	3.5
17	Tennessee	3.5
21	Idaho	3.4
21	Kansas	3.4
21	Michigan	3.4
21	Utah	3.4
21	Virginia	3.4
26	Connecticut	3.3
26	Delaware	3.3
26	North Carolina	3.3
26	Oklahoma	3.3
30	Georgia	3.2
31	Alabama	3.1
31	Arkansas	3.1
31	New Hampshire	3.1
31	South Carolina	3.1
35	Washington	3.0
36	Hawaii	2.9
36	Mississippi	2.9
36	Montana	2.9
39	Indiana	2.8
39	Minnesota	2.8
39	Wyoming	2.8
42	Iowa	2.7
43	Nebraska	2.6
43	South Dakota	2.6
45	Kentucky	2.5
46	Maine	2.4
47	Alaska	2.3
47	Vermont	2.3
49	North Dakota	1.9
50	West Virginia	1.8
	District of Columbia	6.5

Source: Morgan Quitno Press using data from U.S. Bureau of the Census
"Compendium of Government Finances 1997" (GC97(4)-5, December 2000)

State Government Expenditures for Police Protection in 1997

National Total = $6,669,520,000*

ALPHA ORDER					RANK ORDER			

RANK	STATE	EXPENDITURES	% of USA		RANK	STATE	EXPENDITURES	% of USA
25	Alabama	$79,940,000	1.2%		1	California	$925,709,000	13.9%
35	Alaska	49,854,000	0.7%		2	Pennsylvania	636,266,000	9.5%
19	Arizona	123,777,000	1.9%		3	New York	318,217,000	4.8%
27	Arkansas	59,135,000	0.9%		4	Florida	317,387,000	4.8%
1	California	925,709,000	13.9%		5	Texas	287,534,000	4.3%
32	Colorado	55,222,000	0.8%		6	Illinois	280,479,000	4.2%
21	Connecticut	109,523,000	1.6%		7	New Jersey	233,626,000	3.5%
36	Delaware	49,833,000	0.7%		8	Michigan	224,827,000	3.4%
4	Florida	317,387,000	4.8%		9	Massachusetts	212,812,000	3.2%
13	Georgia	169,029,000	2.5%		10	North Carolina	201,385,000	3.0%
50	Hawaii	2,632,000	0.0%		11	Ohio	189,923,000	2.8%
43	Idaho	30,724,000	0.5%		12	Maryland	177,278,000	2.7%
6	Illinois	280,479,000	4.2%		13	Georgia	169,029,000	2.5%
17	Indiana	149,918,000	2.2%		14	Virginia	161,214,000	2.4%
28	Iowa	57,881,000	0.9%		15	Louisiana	155,732,000	2.3%
37	Kansas	41,166,000	0.6%		16	South Carolina	153,363,000	2.3%
22	Kentucky	108,444,000	1.6%		17	Indiana	149,918,000	2.2%
15	Louisiana	155,732,000	2.3%		18	Washington	129,404,000	1.9%
40	Maine	38,632,000	0.6%		19	Arizona	123,777,000	1.9%
12	Maryland	177,278,000	2.7%		20	Missouri	119,084,000	1.8%
9	Massachusetts	212,812,000	3.2%		21	Connecticut	109,523,000	1.6%
8	Michigan	224,827,000	3.4%		22	Kentucky	108,444,000	1.6%
26	Minnesota	78,075,000	1.2%		23	Oregon	104,600,000	1.6%
33	Mississippi	54,999,000	0.8%		24	Tennessee	90,203,000	1.4%
20	Missouri	119,084,000	1.8%		25	Alabama	79,940,000	1.2%
46	Montana	23,360,000	0.4%		26	Minnesota	78,075,000	1.2%
41	Nebraska	36,764,000	0.6%		27	Arkansas	59,135,000	0.9%
39	Nevada	39,172,000	0.6%		28	Iowa	57,881,000	0.9%
45	New Hampshire	29,158,000	0.4%		29	New Mexico	57,658,000	0.9%
7	New Jersey	233,626,000	3.5%		30	Wisconsin	57,631,000	0.9%
29	New Mexico	57,658,000	0.9%		31	Utah	57,567,000	0.9%
3	New York	318,217,000	4.8%		32	Colorado	55,222,000	0.8%
10	North Carolina	201,385,000	3.0%		33	Mississippi	54,999,000	0.8%
49	North Dakota	8,617,000	0.1%		34	Oklahoma	52,519,000	0.8%
11	Ohio	189,923,000	2.8%		35	Alaska	49,854,000	0.7%
34	Oklahoma	52,519,000	0.8%		36	Delaware	49,833,000	0.7%
23	Oregon	104,600,000	1.6%		37	Kansas	41,166,000	0.6%
2	Pennsylvania	636,266,000	9.5%		38	West Virginia	41,030,000	0.6%
42	Rhode Island	31,945,000	0.5%		39	Nevada	39,172,000	0.6%
16	South Carolina	153,363,000	2.3%		40	Maine	38,632,000	0.6%
47	South Dakota	16,159,000	0.2%		41	Nebraska	36,764,000	0.6%
24	Tennessee	90,203,000	1.4%		42	Rhode Island	31,945,000	0.5%
5	Texas	287,534,000	4.3%		43	Idaho	30,724,000	0.5%
31	Utah	57,567,000	0.9%		44	Vermont	29,606,000	0.4%
44	Vermont	29,606,000	0.4%		45	New Hampshire	29,158,000	0.4%
14	Virginia	161,214,000	2.4%		46	Montana	23,360,000	0.4%
18	Washington	129,404,000	1.9%		47	South Dakota	16,159,000	0.2%
38	West Virginia	41,030,000	0.6%		48	Wyoming	10,507,000	0.2%
30	Wisconsin	57,631,000	0.9%		49	North Dakota	8,617,000	0.1%
48	Wyoming	10,507,000	0.2%		50	Hawaii	2,632,000	0.0%
						District of Columbia**	NA	NA

Source: Morgan Quitno Press using data from U.S. Bureau of the Census
   "Compendium of Government Finances 1997" (GC97(4)-5, December 2000)
*Direct general expenditures.
**Not applicable.

Per Capita State Government Expenditures for Police Protection in 1997

National Per Capita = $24.91*

ALPHA ORDER

ALPHA ORDER

RANK	STATE	PER CAPITA
39	Alabama	$18.50
1	Alaska	81.88
18	Arizona	27.19
25	Arkansas	23.43
15	California	28.73
47	Colorado	14.19
9	Connecticut	33.51
2	Delaware	67.80
36	Florida	21.62
31	Georgia	22.58
50	Hawaii	2.21
22	Idaho	25.38
27	Illinois	23.35
21	Indiana	25.53
37	Iowa	20.28
45	Kansas	15.73
17	Kentucky	27.75
6	Louisiana	35.79
13	Maine	31.02
7	Maryland	34.81
8	Massachusetts	34.80
29	Michigan	22.98
43	Minnesota	16.66
38	Mississippi	20.13
34	Missouri	22.02
20	Montana	26.58
32	Nebraska	22.20
26	Nevada	23.38
23	New Hampshire	24.85
14	New Jersey	29.01
10	New Mexico	33.46
40	New York	17.54
19	North Carolina	27.11
48	North Dakota	13.44
41	Ohio	16.94
44	Oklahoma	15.85
12	Oregon	32.25
3	Pennsylvania	52.95
11	Rhode Island	32.37
5	South Carolina	40.46
33	South Dakota	22.11
42	Tennessee	16.77
46	Texas	14.86
16	Utah	27.87
4	Vermont	50.29
24	Virginia	23.94
28	Washington	23.09
30	West Virginia	22.60
49	Wisconsin	11.08
35	Wyoming	21.89

RANK ORDER

RANK	STATE	PER CAPITA
1	Alaska	$81.88
2	Delaware	67.80
3	Pennsylvania	52.95
4	Vermont	50.29
5	South Carolina	40.46
6	Louisiana	35.79
7	Maryland	34.81
8	Massachusetts	34.80
9	Connecticut	33.51
10	New Mexico	33.46
11	Rhode Island	32.37
12	Oregon	32.25
13	Maine	31.02
14	New Jersey	29.01
15	California	28.73
16	Utah	27.87
17	Kentucky	27.75
18	Arizona	27.19
19	North Carolina	27.11
20	Montana	26.58
21	Indiana	25.53
22	Idaho	25.38
23	New Hampshire	24.85
24	Virginia	23.94
25	Arkansas	23.43
26	Nevada	23.38
27	Illinois	23.35
28	Washington	23.09
29	Michigan	22.98
30	West Virginia	22.60
31	Georgia	22.58
32	Nebraska	22.20
33	South Dakota	22.11
34	Missouri	22.02
35	Wyoming	21.89
36	Florida	21.62
37	Iowa	20.28
38	Mississippi	20.13
39	Alabama	18.50
40	New York	17.54
41	Ohio	16.94
42	Tennessee	16.77
43	Minnesota	16.66
44	Oklahoma	15.85
45	Kansas	15.73
46	Texas	14.86
47	Colorado	14.19
48	North Dakota	13.44
49	Wisconsin	11.08
50	Hawaii	2.21

	District of Columbia**	NA

Source: Morgan Quitno Press using data from U.S. Bureau of the Census
    "Compendium of Government Finances 1997" (GC97(4)-5, December 2000)
*Direct general expenditures.
**Not applicable.

State Government Expenditures for Police Protection
As a Percent of All Direct General Expenditures in 1997
National Percent = 1.3% of Direct General Expenditures

ALPHA ORDER

RANK	STATE	PERCENT
34	Alabama	1.0
20	Alaska	1.2
4	Arizona	1.8
20	Arkansas	1.2
6	California	1.7
38	Colorado	0.9
20	Connecticut	1.2
2	Delaware	2.0
13	Florida	1.4
20	Georgia	1.2
50	Hawaii	0.0
13	Idaho	1.4
16	Illinois	1.3
9	Indiana	1.5
34	Iowa	1.0
38	Kansas	0.9
20	Kentucky	1.2
8	Louisiana	1.6
20	Maine	1.2
6	Maryland	1.7
20	Massachusetts	1.2
20	Michigan	1.2
46	Minnesota	0.8
34	Mississippi	1.0
16	Missouri	1.3
30	Montana	1.1
30	Nebraska	1.1
9	Nevada	1.5
20	New Hampshire	1.2
13	New Jersey	1.4
16	New Mexico	1.3
47	New York	0.7
9	North Carolina	1.5
49	North Dakota	0.5
38	Ohio	0.9
38	Oklahoma	0.9
9	Oregon	1.5
1	Pennsylvania	2.7
30	Rhode Island	1.1
3	South Carolina	1.9
30	South Dakota	1.1
38	Tennessee	0.9
38	Texas	0.9
20	Utah	1.2
4	Vermont	1.8
16	Virginia	1.3
34	Washington	1.0
38	West Virginia	0.9
48	Wisconsin	0.6
38	Wyoming	0.9

RANK ORDER

RANK	STATE	PERCENT
1	Pennsylvania	2.7
2	Delaware	2.0
3	South Carolina	1.9
4	Arizona	1.8
4	Vermont	1.8
6	California	1.7
6	Maryland	1.7
8	Louisiana	1.6
9	Indiana	1.5
9	Nevada	1.5
9	North Carolina	1.5
9	Oregon	1.5
13	Florida	1.4
13	Idaho	1.4
13	New Jersey	1.4
16	Illinois	1.3
16	Missouri	1.3
16	New Mexico	1.3
16	Virginia	1.3
20	Alaska	1.2
20	Arkansas	1.2
20	Connecticut	1.2
20	Georgia	1.2
20	Kentucky	1.2
20	Maine	1.2
20	Massachusetts	1.2
20	Michigan	1.2
20	New Hampshire	1.2
20	Utah	1.2
30	Montana	1.1
30	Nebraska	1.1
30	Rhode Island	1.1
30	South Dakota	1.1
34	Alabama	1.0
34	Iowa	1.0
34	Mississippi	1.0
34	Washington	1.0
38	Colorado	0.9
38	Kansas	0.9
38	Ohio	0.9
38	Oklahoma	0.9
38	Tennessee	0.9
38	Texas	0.9
38	West Virginia	0.9
38	Wyoming	0.9
46	Minnesota	0.8
47	New York	0.7
48	Wisconsin	0.6
49	North Dakota	0.5
50	Hawaii	0.0

District of Columbia*   NA

Source: Morgan Quitno Press using data from U.S. Bureau of the Census
"Compendium of Government Finances 1997" (GC97(4)-5, December 2000)
*Not applicable.

Local Government Expenditures for Police Protection in 1997

National Total = $40,949,220,000*

ALPHA ORDER

RANK	STATE	EXPENDITURES	% of USA
26	Alabama	$461,434,000	1.1%
42	Alaska	101,338,000	0.2%
15	Arizona	746,077,000	1.8%
36	Arkansas	233,244,000	0.6%
1	California	6,786,885,000	16.6%
22	Colorado	593,915,000	1.5%
24	Connecticut	483,215,000	1.2%
46	Delaware	81,867,000	0.2%
3	Florida	2,913,470,000	7.1%
11	Georgia	881,339,000	2.2%
37	Hawaii	189,655,000	0.5%
40	Idaho	136,435,000	0.3%
5	Illinois	2,123,568,000	5.2%
23	Indiana	494,464,000	1.2%
31	Iowa	292,581,000	0.7%
29	Kansas	336,237,000	0.8%
32	Kentucky	282,548,000	0.7%
21	Louisiana	603,490,000	1.5%
43	Maine	99,136,000	0.2%
17	Maryland	707,910,000	1.7%
10	Massachusetts	901,949,000	2.2%
8	Michigan	1,338,484,000	3.3%
20	Minnesota	624,062,000	1.5%
33	Mississippi	265,028,000	0.6%
19	Missouri	643,226,000	1.6%
45	Montana	88,436,000	0.2%
38	Nebraska	157,730,000	0.4%
30	Nevada	333,151,000	0.8%
41	New Hampshire	121,946,000	0.3%
7	New Jersey	1,529,693,000	3.7%
35	New Mexico	240,010,000	0.6%
2	New York	4,814,556,000	11.8%
13	North Carolina	827,653,000	2.0%
49	North Dakota	47,908,000	0.1%
6	Ohio	1,619,624,000	4.0%
27	Oklahoma	349,115,000	0.9%
25	Oregon	477,416,000	1.2%
9	Pennsylvania	1,202,683,000	2.9%
39	Rhode Island	142,919,000	0.3%
28	South Carolina	340,834,000	0.8%
48	South Dakota	59,401,000	0.1%
18	Tennessee	655,589,000	1.6%
4	Texas	2,473,384,000	6.0%
34	Utah	247,779,000	0.6%
50	Vermont	35,513,000	0.1%
14	Virginia	820,405,000	2.0%
16	Washington	736,912,000	1.8%
44	West Virginia	98,636,000	0.2%
12	Wisconsin	858,273,000	2.1%
47	Wyoming	68,292,000	0.2%

RANK ORDER

RANK	STATE	EXPENDITURES	% of USA
1	California	$6,786,885,000	16.6%
2	New York	4,814,556,000	11.8%
3	Florida	2,913,470,000	7.1%
4	Texas	2,473,384,000	6.0%
5	Illinois	2,123,568,000	5.2%
6	Ohio	1,619,624,000	4.0%
7	New Jersey	1,529,693,000	3.7%
8	Michigan	1,338,484,000	3.3%
9	Pennsylvania	1,202,683,000	2.9%
10	Massachusetts	901,949,000	2.2%
11	Georgia	881,339,000	2.2%
12	Wisconsin	858,273,000	2.1%
13	North Carolina	827,653,000	2.0%
14	Virginia	820,405,000	2.0%
15	Arizona	746,077,000	1.8%
16	Washington	736,912,000	1.8%
17	Maryland	707,910,000	1.7%
18	Tennessee	655,589,000	1.6%
19	Missouri	643,226,000	1.6%
20	Minnesota	624,062,000	1.5%
21	Louisiana	603,490,000	1.5%
22	Colorado	593,915,000	1.5%
23	Indiana	494,464,000	1.2%
24	Connecticut	483,215,000	1.2%
25	Oregon	477,416,000	1.2%
26	Alabama	461,434,000	1.1%
27	Oklahoma	349,115,000	0.9%
28	South Carolina	340,834,000	0.8%
29	Kansas	336,237,000	0.8%
30	Nevada	333,151,000	0.8%
31	Iowa	292,581,000	0.7%
32	Kentucky	282,548,000	0.7%
33	Mississippi	265,028,000	0.6%
34	Utah	247,779,000	0.6%
35	New Mexico	240,010,000	0.6%
36	Arkansas	233,244,000	0.6%
37	Hawaii	189,655,000	0.5%
38	Nebraska	157,730,000	0.4%
39	Rhode Island	142,919,000	0.3%
40	Idaho	136,435,000	0.3%
41	New Hampshire	121,946,000	0.3%
42	Alaska	101,338,000	0.2%
43	Maine	99,136,000	0.2%
44	West Virginia	98,636,000	0.2%
45	Montana	88,436,000	0.2%
46	Delaware	81,867,000	0.2%
47	Wyoming	68,292,000	0.2%
48	South Dakota	59,401,000	0.1%
49	North Dakota	47,908,000	0.1%
50	Vermont	35,513,000	0.1%
	District of Columbia	279,805,000	0.7%

Source: Morgan Quitno Press using data from U.S. Bureau of the Census
"Compendium of Government Finances 1997" (GC97(4)-5, December 2000)
*Direct general expenditures.

Per Capita Local Government Expenditures for Police Protection in 1997

National Per Capita = $153*

ALPHA ORDER

RANK ORDER

RANK	STATE	PER CAPITA
34	Alabama	$107
7	Alaska	166
9	Arizona	164
42	Arkansas	92
2	California	211
11	Colorado	153
12	Connecticut	148
32	Delaware	111
4	Florida	198
30	Georgia	118
10	Hawaii	159
31	Idaho	113
6	Illinois	177
44	Indiana	84
37	Iowa	103
24	Kansas	129
48	Kentucky	72
18	Louisiana	139
46	Maine	80
18	Maryland	139
13	Massachusetts	147
21	Michigan	137
22	Minnesota	133
40	Mississippi	97
29	Missouri	119
38	Montana	101
41	Nebraska	95
3	Nevada	199
36	New Hampshire	104
5	New Jersey	190
18	New Mexico	139
1	New York	265
32	North Carolina	111
47	North Dakota	75
16	Ohio	144
35	Oklahoma	105
13	Oregon	147
39	Pennsylvania	100
15	Rhode Island	145
43	South Carolina	90
45	South Dakota	81
26	Tennessee	122
25	Texas	128
28	Utah	120
49	Vermont	60
26	Virginia	122
23	Washington	131
50	West Virginia	54
8	Wisconsin	165
17	Wyoming	142

RANK	STATE	PER CAPITA
1	New York	$265
2	California	211
3	Nevada	199
4	Florida	198
5	New Jersey	190
6	Illinois	177
7	Alaska	166
8	Wisconsin	165
9	Arizona	164
10	Hawaii	159
11	Colorado	153
12	Connecticut	148
13	Massachusetts	147
13	Oregon	147
15	Rhode Island	145
16	Ohio	144
17	Wyoming	142
18	Louisiana	139
18	Maryland	139
18	New Mexico	139
21	Michigan	137
22	Minnesota	133
23	Washington	131
24	Kansas	129
25	Texas	128
26	Tennessee	122
26	Virginia	122
28	Utah	120
29	Missouri	119
30	Georgia	118
31	Idaho	113
32	Delaware	111
32	North Carolina	111
34	Alabama	107
35	Oklahoma	105
36	New Hampshire	104
37	Iowa	103
38	Montana	101
39	Pennsylvania	100
40	Mississippi	97
41	Nebraska	95
42	Arkansas	92
43	South Carolina	90
44	Indiana	84
45	South Dakota	81
46	Maine	80
47	North Dakota	75
48	Kentucky	72
49	Vermont	60
50	West Virginia	54

District of Columbia   529

Source: Morgan Quitno Press using data from U.S. Bureau of the Census
    "Compendium of Government Finances 1997" (GC97(4)-5, December 2000)
*Direct general expenditures.

Local Government Expenditures for Police Protection
As a Percent of All Direct General Expenditures in 1997
National Percent = 5.7% of Direct General Expenditures

ALPHA ORDER

RANK ORDER

RANK	STATE	PERCENT
25	Alabama	5.2
40	Alaska	4.1
4	Arizona	6.8
20	Arkansas	5.5
8	California	6.4
24	Colorado	5.3
13	Connecticut	5.8
13	Delaware	5.8
2	Florida	7.2
33	Georgia	4.8
1	Hawaii	13.2
26	Idaho	5.1
4	Illinois	6.8
47	Indiana	3.7
40	Iowa	4.1
26	Kansas	5.1
40	Kentucky	4.1
6	Louisiana	6.6
46	Maine	3.8
16	Maryland	5.7
6	Massachusetts	6.6
31	Michigan	4.9
40	Minnesota	4.1
36	Mississippi	4.6
16	Missouri	5.7
31	Montana	4.9
45	Nebraska	3.9
10	Nevada	6.2
30	New Hampshire	5.0
9	New Jersey	6.3
11	New Mexico	6.1
12	New York	5.9
34	North Carolina	4.7
48	North Dakota	3.6
13	Ohio	5.8
22	Oklahoma	5.4
26	Oregon	5.1
40	Pennsylvania	4.1
2	Rhode Island	7.2
37	South Carolina	4.4
38	South Dakota	4.2
16	Tennessee	5.7
20	Texas	5.5
19	Utah	5.6
49	Vermont	3.2
26	Virginia	5.1
34	Washington	4.7
50	West Virginia	3.0
22	Wisconsin	5.4
38	Wyoming	4.2

RANK	STATE	PERCENT
1	Hawaii	13.2
2	Florida	7.2
2	Rhode Island	7.2
4	Arizona	6.8
4	Illinois	6.8
6	Louisiana	6.6
6	Massachusetts	6.6
8	California	6.4
9	New Jersey	6.3
10	Nevada	6.2
11	New Mexico	6.1
12	New York	5.9
13	Connecticut	5.8
13	Delaware	5.8
13	Ohio	5.8
16	Maryland	5.7
16	Missouri	5.7
16	Tennessee	5.7
19	Utah	5.6
20	Arkansas	5.5
20	Texas	5.5
22	Oklahoma	5.4
22	Wisconsin	5.4
24	Colorado	5.3
25	Alabama	5.2
26	Idaho	5.1
26	Kansas	5.1
26	Oregon	5.1
26	Virginia	5.1
30	New Hampshire	5.0
31	Michigan	4.9
31	Montana	4.9
33	Georgia	4.8
34	North Carolina	4.7
34	Washington	4.7
36	Mississippi	4.6
37	South Carolina	4.4
38	South Dakota	4.2
38	Wyoming	4.2
40	Alaska	4.1
40	Iowa	4.1
40	Kentucky	4.1
40	Minnesota	4.1
40	Pennsylvania	4.1
45	Nebraska	3.9
46	Maine	3.8
47	Indiana	3.7
48	North Dakota	3.6
49	Vermont	3.2
50	West Virginia	3.0
	District of Columbia	6.5

Source: Morgan Quitno Press using data from U.S. Bureau of the Census
"Compendium of Government Finances 1997" (GC97(4)-5, December 2000)

State and Local Government Expenditures for Corrections in 1997

National Total = $39,946,460,000*

ALPHA ORDER

RANK	STATE	EXPENDITURES	% of USA
30	Alabama	$323,350,000	0.8%
38	Alaska	149,823,000	0.4%
17	Arizona	701,806,000	1.8%
35	Arkansas	240,695,000	0.6%
1	California	6,209,434,000	15.5%
18	Colorado	600,124,000	1.5%
24	Connecticut	493,772,000	1.2%
41	Delaware	123,147,000	0.3%
6	Florida	1,526,928,000	3.8%
10	Georgia	1,199,638,000	3.0%
40	Hawaii	127,535,000	0.3%
39	Idaho	132,669,000	0.3%
8	Illinois	1,310,529,000	3.3%
19	Indiana	589,048,000	1.5%
36	Iowa	210,014,000	0.5%
32	Kansas	246,709,000	0.6%
28	Kentucky	353,178,000	0.9%
26	Louisiana	473,284,000	1.2%
44	Maine	93,664,000	0.2%
13	Maryland	872,988,000	2.2%
14	Massachusetts	848,654,000	2.1%
5	Michigan	1,564,842,000	3.9%
25	Minnesota	481,101,000	1.2%
33	Mississippi	245,104,000	0.6%
23	Missouri	503,566,000	1.3%
46	Montana	85,844,000	0.2%
37	Nebraska	151,592,000	0.4%
29	Nevada	337,816,000	0.8%
45	New Hampshire	86,026,000	0.2%
9	New Jersey	1,255,491,000	3.1%
31	New Mexico	257,714,000	0.6%
2	New York	3,908,022,000	9.8%
11	North Carolina	1,088,339,000	2.7%
50	North Dakota	30,251,000	0.1%
7	Ohio	1,513,243,000	3.8%
27	Oklahoma	374,792,000	0.9%
21	Oregon	579,867,000	1.5%
4	Pennsylvania	1,740,743,000	4.4%
43	Rhode Island	119,698,000	0.3%
22	South Carolina	527,347,000	1.3%
47	South Dakota	77,435,000	0.2%
20	Tennessee	587,255,000	1.5%
3	Texas	3,114,693,000	7.8%
34	Utah	243,543,000	0.6%
49	Vermont	43,827,000	0.1%
12	Virginia	947,965,000	2.4%
15	Washington	848,304,000	2.1%
42	West Virginia	121,779,000	0.3%
16	Wisconsin	702,983,000	1.8%
48	Wyoming	53,309,000	0.1%

RANK ORDER

RANK	STATE	EXPENDITURES	% of USA
1	California	$6,209,434,000	15.5%
2	New York	3,908,022,000	9.8%
3	Texas	3,114,693,000	7.8%
4	Pennsylvania	1,740,743,000	4.4%
5	Michigan	1,564,842,000	3.9%
6	Florida	1,526,928,000	3.8%
7	Ohio	1,513,243,000	3.8%
8	Illinois	1,310,529,000	3.3%
9	New Jersey	1,255,491,000	3.1%
10	Georgia	1,199,638,000	3.0%
11	North Carolina	1,088,339,000	2.7%
12	Virginia	947,965,000	2.4%
13	Maryland	872,988,000	2.2%
14	Massachusetts	848,654,000	2.1%
15	Washington	848,304,000	2.1%
16	Wisconsin	702,983,000	1.8%
17	Arizona	701,806,000	1.8%
18	Colorado	600,124,000	1.5%
19	Indiana	589,048,000	1.5%
20	Tennessee	587,255,000	1.5%
21	Oregon	579,867,000	1.5%
22	South Carolina	527,347,000	1.3%
23	Missouri	503,566,000	1.3%
24	Connecticut	493,772,000	1.2%
25	Minnesota	481,101,000	1.2%
26	Louisiana	473,284,000	1.2%
27	Oklahoma	374,792,000	0.9%
28	Kentucky	353,178,000	0.9%
29	Nevada	337,816,000	0.8%
30	Alabama	323,350,000	0.8%
31	New Mexico	257,714,000	0.6%
32	Kansas	246,709,000	0.6%
33	Mississippi	245,104,000	0.6%
34	Utah	243,543,000	0.6%
35	Arkansas	240,695,000	0.6%
36	Iowa	210,014,000	0.5%
37	Nebraska	151,592,000	0.4%
38	Alaska	149,823,000	0.4%
39	Idaho	132,669,000	0.3%
40	Hawaii	127,535,000	0.3%
41	Delaware	123,147,000	0.3%
42	West Virginia	121,779,000	0.3%
43	Rhode Island	119,698,000	0.3%
44	Maine	93,664,000	0.2%
45	New Hampshire	86,026,000	0.2%
46	Montana	85,844,000	0.2%
47	South Dakota	77,435,000	0.2%
48	Wyoming	53,309,000	0.1%
49	Vermont	43,827,000	0.1%
50	North Dakota	30,251,000	0.1%
	District of Columbia	300,157,000	0.8%

Source: Morgan Quitno Press using data from U.S. Bureau of the Census
   "Compendium of Government Finances 1997" (GC97(4)-5, December 2000)
*Direct general expenditures.

Per Capita State and Local Government Expenditures for Corrections in 1997

National Per Capita = $149*

ALPHA ORDER

RANK	STATE	PER CAPITA
44	Alabama	$75
1	Alaska	246
12	Arizona	154
38	Arkansas	95
4	California	193
12	Colorado	154
14	Connecticut	151
7	Delaware	168
34	Florida	104
9	Georgia	160
32	Hawaii	107
28	Idaho	110
29	Illinois	109
36	Indiana	100
46	Iowa	74
39	Kansas	94
42	Kentucky	90
29	Louisiana	109
44	Maine	75
6	Maryland	171
20	Massachusetts	139
9	Michigan	160
35	Minnesota	103
42	Mississippi	90
40	Missouri	93
37	Montana	98
41	Nebraska	92
3	Nevada	202
48	New Hampshire	73
11	New Jersey	156
16	New Mexico	150
2	New York	215
17	North Carolina	147
50	North Dakota	47
22	Ohio	135
26	Oklahoma	113
5	Oregon	179
18	Pennsylvania	145
24	Rhode Island	121
20	South Carolina	139
33	South Dakota	106
29	Tennessee	109
8	Texas	161
25	Utah	118
46	Vermont	74
19	Virginia	141
14	Washington	151
49	West Virginia	67
22	Wisconsin	135
27	Wyoming	111

RANK ORDER

RANK	STATE	PER CAPITA
1	Alaska	$246
2	New York	215
3	Nevada	202
4	California	193
5	Oregon	179
6	Maryland	171
7	Delaware	168
8	Texas	161
9	Georgia	160
9	Michigan	160
11	New Jersey	156
12	Arizona	154
12	Colorado	154
14	Connecticut	151
14	Washington	151
16	New Mexico	150
17	North Carolina	147
18	Pennsylvania	145
19	Virginia	141
20	Massachusetts	139
20	South Carolina	139
22	Ohio	135
22	Wisconsin	135
24	Rhode Island	121
25	Utah	118
26	Oklahoma	113
27	Wyoming	111
28	Idaho	110
29	Illinois	109
29	Louisiana	109
29	Tennessee	109
32	Hawaii	107
33	South Dakota	106
34	Florida	104
35	Minnesota	103
36	Indiana	100
37	Montana	98
38	Arkansas	95
39	Kansas	94
40	Missouri	93
41	Nebraska	92
42	Kentucky	90
42	Mississippi	90
44	Alabama	75
44	Maine	75
46	Iowa	74
46	Vermont	74
48	New Hampshire	73
49	West Virginia	67
50	North Dakota	47

| | District of Columbia | 568 |

Source: Morgan Quitno Press using data from U.S. Bureau of the Census
   "Compendium of Government Finances 1997" (GC97(4)-5, December 2000)
*Direct general expenditures.

State and Local Government Expenditures for Corrections
As a Percent of All Direct General Expenditures in 1997
National Percent = 3.2% of Direct General Expenditures

ALPHA ORDER

RANK	STATE	PERCENT
41	Alabama	1.9
36	Alaska	2.2
3	Arizona	3.9
28	Arkansas	2.6
3	California	3.9
9	Colorado	3.4
21	Connecticut	2.8
14	Delaware	3.1
34	Florida	2.4
6	Georgia	3.7
41	Hawaii	1.9
24	Idaho	2.7
29	Illinois	2.5
29	Indiana	2.5
46	Iowa	1.6
36	Kansas	2.2
35	Kentucky	2.3
29	Louisiana	2.5
46	Maine	1.6
5	Maryland	3.8
24	Massachusetts	2.7
9	Michigan	3.4
41	Minnesota	1.9
36	Mississippi	2.2
29	Missouri	2.5
36	Montana	2.2
40	Nebraska	2.0
1	Nevada	4.3
45	New Hampshire	1.7
14	New Jersey	3.1
14	New Mexico	3.1
14	New York	3.1
7	North Carolina	3.5
50	North Dakota	1.0
14	Ohio	3.1
14	Oklahoma	3.1
7	Oregon	3.5
11	Pennsylvania	3.3
29	Rhode Island	2.5
11	South Carolina	3.3
24	South Dakota	2.7
21	Tennessee	2.8
2	Texas	4.1
24	Utah	2.7
46	Vermont	1.6
11	Virginia	3.3
20	Washington	2.9
46	West Virginia	1.6
21	Wisconsin	2.8
41	Wyoming	1.9

RANK ORDER

RANK	STATE	PERCENT
1	Nevada	4.3
2	Texas	4.1
3	Arizona	3.9
3	California	3.9
5	Maryland	3.8
6	Georgia	3.7
7	North Carolina	3.5
7	Oregon	3.5
9	Colorado	3.4
9	Michigan	3.4
11	Pennsylvania	3.3
11	South Carolina	3.3
11	Virginia	3.3
14	Delaware	3.1
14	New Jersey	3.1
14	New Mexico	3.1
14	New York	3.1
14	Ohio	3.1
14	Oklahoma	3.1
20	Washington	2.9
21	Connecticut	2.8
21	Tennessee	2.8
21	Wisconsin	2.8
24	Idaho	2.7
24	Massachusetts	2.7
24	South Dakota	2.7
24	Utah	2.7
28	Arkansas	2.6
29	Illinois	2.5
29	Indiana	2.5
29	Louisiana	2.5
29	Missouri	2.5
29	Rhode Island	2.5
34	Florida	2.4
35	Kentucky	2.3
36	Alaska	2.2
36	Kansas	2.2
36	Mississippi	2.2
36	Montana	2.2
40	Nebraska	2.0
41	Alabama	1.9
41	Hawaii	1.9
41	Minnesota	1.9
41	Wyoming	1.9
45	New Hampshire	1.7
46	Iowa	1.6
46	Maine	1.6
46	Vermont	1.6
46	West Virginia	1.6
50	North Dakota	1.0

District of Columbia   6.9

Source: Morgan Quitno Press using data from U.S. Bureau of the Census
"Compendium of Government Finances 1997" (GC97(4)-5, December 2000)

State Government Expenditures for Corrections in 1997

National Total = $27,116,873,000*

ALPHA ORDER

ALPHA ORDER

RANK	STATE	EXPENDITURES	% of USA
29	Alabama	$228,662,000	0.8%
37	Alaska	149,454,000	0.6%
16	Arizona	504,701,000	1.9%
31	Arkansas	192,804,000	0.7%
1	California	3,860,134,000	14.2%
20	Colorado	426,372,000	1.6%
17	Connecticut	493,772,000	1.8%
39	Delaware	123,147,000	0.5%
12	Florida	621,514,000	2.3%
10	Georgia	857,325,000	3.2%
38	Hawaii	127,535,000	0.5%
42	Idaho	102,262,000	0.4%
7	Illinois	909,214,000	3.4%
21	Indiana	406,248,000	1.5%
36	Iowa	155,730,000	0.6%
32	Kansas	187,388,000	0.7%
28	Kentucky	244,113,000	0.9%
25	Louisiana	337,446,000	1.2%
45	Maine	66,013,000	0.2%
11	Maryland	733,190,000	2.7%
15	Massachusetts	528,875,000	2.0%
4	Michigan	1,260,171,000	4.6%
27	Minnesota	269,320,000	1.0%
30	Mississippi	197,732,000	0.7%
24	Missouri	364,571,000	1.3%
44	Montana	73,189,000	0.3%
41	Nebraska	105,630,000	0.4%
34	Nevada	179,642,000	0.7%
47	New Hampshire	59,409,000	0.2%
9	New Jersey	892,747,000	3.3%
33	New Mexico	185,300,000	0.7%
3	New York	2,032,323,000	7.5%
8	North Carolina	902,328,000	3.3%
50	North Dakota	20,692,000	0.1%
5	Ohio	1,154,282,000	4.3%
26	Oklahoma	336,073,000	1.2%
23	Oregon	378,965,000	1.4%
6	Pennsylvania	1,039,058,000	3.8%
40	Rhode Island	119,698,000	0.4%
19	South Carolina	429,244,000	1.6%
46	South Dakota	59,728,000	0.2%
22	Tennessee	390,015,000	1.4%
2	Texas	2,165,352,000	8.0%
35	Utah	175,358,000	0.6%
48	Vermont	43,703,000	0.2%
13	Virginia	618,320,000	2.3%
14	Washington	562,335,000	2.1%
43	West Virginia	94,905,000	0.3%
18	Wisconsin	487,002,000	1.8%
49	Wyoming	37,059,000	0.1%

RANK ORDER

RANK	STATE	EXPENDITURES	% of USA
1	California	$3,860,134,000	14.2%
2	Texas	2,165,352,000	8.0%
3	New York	2,032,323,000	7.5%
4	Michigan	1,260,171,000	4.6%
5	Ohio	1,154,282,000	4.3%
6	Pennsylvania	1,039,058,000	3.8%
7	Illinois	909,214,000	3.4%
8	North Carolina	902,328,000	3.3%
9	New Jersey	892,747,000	3.3%
10	Georgia	857,325,000	3.2%
11	Maryland	733,190,000	2.7%
12	Florida	621,514,000	2.3%
13	Virginia	618,320,000	2.3%
14	Washington	562,335,000	2.1%
15	Massachusetts	528,875,000	2.0%
16	Arizona	504,701,000	1.9%
17	Connecticut	493,772,000	1.8%
18	Wisconsin	487,002,000	1.8%
19	South Carolina	429,244,000	1.6%
20	Colorado	426,372,000	1.6%
21	Indiana	406,248,000	1.5%
22	Tennessee	390,015,000	1.4%
23	Oregon	378,965,000	1.4%
24	Missouri	364,571,000	1.3%
25	Louisiana	337,446,000	1.2%
26	Oklahoma	336,073,000	1.2%
27	Minnesota	269,320,000	1.0%
28	Kentucky	244,113,000	0.9%
29	Alabama	228,662,000	0.8%
30	Mississippi	197,732,000	0.7%
31	Arkansas	192,804,000	0.7%
32	Kansas	187,388,000	0.7%
33	New Mexico	185,300,000	0.7%
34	Nevada	179,642,000	0.7%
35	Utah	175,358,000	0.6%
36	Iowa	155,730,000	0.6%
37	Alaska	149,454,000	0.6%
38	Hawaii	127,535,000	0.5%
39	Delaware	123,147,000	0.5%
40	Rhode Island	119,698,000	0.4%
41	Nebraska	105,630,000	0.4%
42	Idaho	102,262,000	0.4%
43	West Virginia	94,905,000	0.3%
44	Montana	73,189,000	0.3%
45	Maine	66,013,000	0.2%
46	South Dakota	59,728,000	0.2%
47	New Hampshire	59,409,000	0.2%
48	Vermont	43,703,000	0.2%
49	Wyoming	37,059,000	0.1%
50	North Dakota	20,692,000	0.1%
	District of Columbia**	NA	NA

Source: Morgan Quitno Press using data from U.S. Bureau of the Census
   "Compendium of Government Finances 1997" (GC97(4)-5, December 2000)
*Direct general expenditures.
**Not applicable.

Per Capita State Government Expenditures for Corrections in 1997

National Per Capita = $101*

ALPHA ORDER

RANK	STATE	PER CAPITA
45	Alabama	$53
1	Alaska	245
14	Arizona	111
33	Arkansas	76
8	California	120
16	Colorado	110
3	Connecticut	151
2	Delaware	168
49	Florida	42
10	Georgia	115
18	Hawaii	107
28	Idaho	84
33	Illinois	76
39	Indiana	69
44	Iowa	55
37	Kansas	72
42	Kentucky	62
31	Louisiana	78
45	Maine	53
4	Maryland	144
25	Massachusetts	86
5	Michigan	129
43	Minnesota	57
37	Mississippi	72
40	Missouri	67
29	Montana	83
41	Nebraska	64
18	Nevada	107
48	New Hampshire	51
14	New Jersey	111
17	New Mexico	108
12	New York	112
6	North Carolina	121
50	North Dakota	32
20	Ohio	103
21	Oklahoma	101
9	Oregon	117
25	Pennsylvania	86
6	Rhode Island	121
11	South Carolina	113
30	South Dakota	82
36	Tennessee	73
12	Texas	112
27	Utah	85
35	Vermont	74
24	Virginia	92
22	Washington	100
47	West Virginia	52
23	Wisconsin	94
32	Wyoming	77

RANK ORDER

RANK	STATE	PER CAPITA
1	Alaska	$245
2	Delaware	168
3	Connecticut	151
4	Maryland	144
5	Michigan	129
6	North Carolina	121
6	Rhode Island	121
8	California	120
9	Oregon	117
10	Georgia	115
11	South Carolina	113
12	New York	112
12	Texas	112
14	Arizona	111
14	New Jersey	111
16	Colorado	110
17	New Mexico	108
18	Hawaii	107
18	Nevada	107
20	Ohio	103
21	Oklahoma	101
22	Washington	100
23	Wisconsin	94
24	Virginia	92
25	Massachusetts	86
25	Pennsylvania	86
27	Utah	85
28	Idaho	84
29	Montana	83
30	South Dakota	82
31	Louisiana	78
32	Wyoming	77
33	Arkansas	76
33	Illinois	76
35	Vermont	74
36	Tennessee	73
37	Kansas	72
37	Mississippi	72
39	Indiana	69
40	Missouri	67
41	Nebraska	64
42	Kentucky	62
43	Minnesota	57
44	Iowa	55
45	Alabama	53
45	Maine	53
47	West Virginia	52
48	New Hampshire	51
49	Florida	42
50	North Dakota	32
	District of Columbia**	NA

Source: Morgan Quitno Press using data from U.S. Bureau of the Census
    "Compendium of Government Finances 1997" (GC97(4)-5, December 2000)
*Direct general expenditures.
**Not applicable.

State Government Expenditures for Corrections
As a Percent of All Direct General Expenditures in 1997
National Percent = 5.2% of Direct General Expenditures

ALPHA ORDER

RANK	STATE	PERCENT
41	Alabama	2.7
34	Alaska	3.6
1	Arizona	7.5
31	Arkansas	3.8
2	California	7.3
7	Colorado	6.7
15	Connecticut	5.2
18	Delaware	4.9
41	Florida	2.7
9	Georgia	6.0
46	Hawaii	2.4
19	Idaho	4.7
25	Illinois	4.1
25	Indiana	4.1
41	Iowa	2.7
25	Kansas	4.1
40	Kentucky	2.8
35	Louisiana	3.5
48	Maine	2.1
3	Maryland	7.0
39	Massachusetts	2.9
6	Michigan	6.8
41	Minnesota	2.7
33	Mississippi	3.7
28	Missouri	4.0
35	Montana	3.5
37	Nebraska	3.2
3	Nevada	7.0
46	New Hampshire	2.4
12	New Jersey	5.4
23	New Mexico	4.2
20	New York	4.6
8	North Carolina	6.6
50	North Dakota	1.2
11	Ohio	5.7
10	Oklahoma	5.9
13	Oregon	5.3
21	Pennsylvania	4.4
23	Rhode Island	4.2
15	South Carolina	5.2
28	South Dakota	4.0
28	Tennessee	4.0
5	Texas	6.9
31	Utah	3.8
45	Vermont	2.6
17	Virginia	5.0
22	Washington	4.3
48	West Virginia	2.1
13	Wisconsin	5.3
37	Wyoming	3.2

RANK ORDER

RANK	STATE	PERCENT
1	Arizona	7.5
2	California	7.3
3	Maryland	7.0
3	Nevada	7.0
5	Texas	6.9
6	Michigan	6.8
7	Colorado	6.7
8	North Carolina	6.6
9	Georgia	6.0
10	Oklahoma	5.9
11	Ohio	5.7
12	New Jersey	5.4
13	Oregon	5.3
13	Wisconsin	5.3
15	Connecticut	5.2
15	South Carolina	5.2
17	Virginia	5.0
18	Delaware	4.9
19	Idaho	4.7
20	New York	4.6
21	Pennsylvania	4.4
22	Washington	4.3
23	New Mexico	4.2
23	Rhode Island	4.2
25	Illinois	4.1
25	Indiana	4.1
25	Kansas	4.1
28	Missouri	4.0
28	South Dakota	4.0
28	Tennessee	4.0
31	Arkansas	3.8
31	Utah	3.8
33	Mississippi	3.7
34	Alaska	3.6
35	Louisiana	3.5
35	Montana	3.5
37	Nebraska	3.2
37	Wyoming	3.2
39	Massachusetts	2.9
40	Kentucky	2.8
41	Alabama	2.7
41	Florida	2.7
41	Iowa	2.7
41	Minnesota	2.7
45	Vermont	2.6
46	Hawaii	2.4
46	New Hampshire	2.4
48	Maine	2.1
48	West Virginia	2.1
50	North Dakota	1.2

	District of Columbia*	NA

Source: Morgan Quitno Press using data from U.S. Bureau of the Census
    "Compendium of Government Finances 1997" (GC97(4)-5, December 2000)
*Not applicable.

Expenditures for State Prisons in 1996

National Total = $22,033,214,000*

RANK	STATE	EXPENDITURES	% of USA
30	Alabama	$168,989,000	0.8%
36	Alaska	116,664,000	0.5%
15	Arizona	418,094,000	1.9%
33	Arkansas	133,729,000	0.6%
1	California	3,031,047,000	13.8%
25	Colorado	249,833,000	1.1%
13	Connecticut	497,838,000	2.3%
39	Delaware	87,961,000	0.4%
4	Florida	1,224,933,000	5.6%
11	Georgia	560,358,000	2.5%
40	Hawaii	87,417,000	0.4%
42	Idaho	56,957,000	0.3%
10	Illinois	740,423,000	3.4%
19	Indiana	338,195,000	1.5%
32	Iowa	146,069,000	0.7%
29	Kansas	170,848,000	0.8%
26	Kentucky	208,706,000	0.9%
20	Louisiana	316,245,000	1.4%
43	Maine	51,713,000	0.2%
12	Maryland	520,263,000	2.4%
22	Massachusetts	309,674,000	1.4%
5	Michigan	1,167,610,000	5.3%
28	Minnesota	185,983,000	0.8%
31	Mississippi	148,852,000	0.7%
23	Missouri	262,787,000	1.2%
46	Montana	42,448,000	0.2%
41	Nebraska	69,867,000	0.3%
35	Nevada	121,960,000	0.6%
45	New Hampshire	42,970,000	0.2%
8	New Jersey	839,308,000	3.8%
34	New Mexico	125,602,000	0.6%
2	New York	2,220,586,000	10.1%
9	North Carolina	756,829,000	3.4%
50	North Dakota	10,749,000	0.0%
6	Ohio	1,014,917,000	4.6%
27	Oklahoma	198,290,000	0.9%
24	Oregon	254,330,000	1.2%
7	Pennsylvania	978,769,000	4.4%
38	Rhode Island	109,596,000	0.5%
21	South Carolina	315,539,000	1.4%
47	South Dakota	34,152,000	0.2%
18	Tennessee	350,575,000	1.6%
3	Texas	1,713,935,000	7.8%
37	Utah	113,394,000	0.5%
48	Vermont	33,505,000	0.2%
14	Virginia	476,715,000	2.2%
17	Washington	357,862,000	1.6%
44	West Virginia	46,949,000	0.2%
16	Wisconsin	360,439,000	1.6%
49	Wyoming	29,025,000	0.1%

RANK	STATE	EXPENDITURES	% of USA
1	California	$3,031,047,000	13.8%
2	New York	2,220,586,000	10.1%
3	Texas	1,713,935,000	7.8%
4	Florida	1,224,933,000	5.6%
5	Michigan	1,167,610,000	5.3%
6	Ohio	1,014,917,000	4.6%
7	Pennsylvania	978,769,000	4.4%
8	New Jersey	839,308,000	3.8%
9	North Carolina	756,829,000	3.4%
10	Illinois	740,423,000	3.4%
11	Georgia	560,358,000	2.5%
12	Maryland	520,263,000	2.4%
13	Connecticut	497,838,000	2.3%
14	Virginia	476,715,000	2.2%
15	Arizona	418,094,000	1.9%
16	Wisconsin	360,439,000	1.6%
17	Washington	357,862,000	1.6%
18	Tennessee	350,575,000	1.6%
19	Indiana	338,195,000	1.5%
20	Louisiana	316,245,000	1.4%
21	South Carolina	315,539,000	1.4%
22	Massachusetts	309,674,000	1.4%
23	Missouri	262,787,000	1.2%
24	Oregon	254,330,000	1.2%
25	Colorado	249,833,000	1.1%
26	Kentucky	208,706,000	0.9%
27	Oklahoma	198,290,000	0.9%
28	Minnesota	185,983,000	0.8%
29	Kansas	170,848,000	0.8%
30	Alabama	168,989,000	0.8%
31	Mississippi	148,852,000	0.7%
32	Iowa	146,069,000	0.7%
33	Arkansas	133,729,000	0.6%
34	New Mexico	125,602,000	0.6%
35	Nevada	121,960,000	0.6%
36	Alaska	116,664,000	0.5%
37	Utah	113,394,000	0.5%
38	Rhode Island	109,596,000	0.5%
39	Delaware	87,961,000	0.4%
40	Hawaii	87,417,000	0.4%
41	Nebraska	69,867,000	0.3%
42	Idaho	56,957,000	0.3%
43	Maine	51,713,000	0.2%
44	West Virginia	46,949,000	0.2%
45	New Hampshire	42,970,000	0.2%
46	Montana	42,448,000	0.2%
47	South Dakota	34,152,000	0.2%
48	Vermont	33,505,000	0.2%
49	Wyoming	29,025,000	0.1%
50	North Dakota	10,749,000	0.0%
	District of Columbia	213,716,000	1.0%

Source: U.S. Department of Justice, Bureau of Justice Statistics
"State Prison Expenditures, 1996" (August 1999, NCJ-172211)
State government expenditures, including adult prison operations and capital outlays. They do not include state juvenile justice activities, probation and parole services or nonresidential community corrections. Expenditures are net amounts after deductions for revenue from prison farms, industries and services.

Operating Expenditures for State Prisons in 1996

National Total = $20,737,888,000*

ALPHA ORDER

RANK	STATE	EXPENDITURES	% of USA
29	Alabama	$165,760,000	0.8%
36	Alaska	112,350,000	0.5%
15	Arizona	409,167,000	2.0%
33	Arkansas	124,513,000	0.6%
1	California	2,918,845,000	14.1%
25	Colorado	234,503,000	1.1%
13	Connecticut	475,367,000	2.3%
39	Delaware	87,253,000	0.4%
5	Florida	1,100,655,000	5.3%
11	Georgia	547,490,000	2.6%
40	Hawaii	83,921,000	0.4%
42	Idaho	55,017,000	0.3%
10	Illinois	732,824,000	3.5%
17	Indiana	325,700,000	1.6%
32	Iowa	143,774,000	0.7%
30	Kansas	158,454,000	0.8%
26	Kentucky	198,775,000	1.0%
18	Louisiana	313,463,000	1.5%
43	Maine	48,206,000	0.2%
12	Maryland	480,880,000	2.3%
21	Massachusetts	304,483,000	1.5%
4	Michigan	1,161,142,000	5.6%
28	Minnesota	184,359,000	0.9%
31	Mississippi	143,914,000	0.7%
24	Missouri	249,414,000	1.2%
46	Montana	41,875,000	0.2%
41	Nebraska	67,904,000	0.3%
35	Nevada	119,026,000	0.6%
45	New Hampshire	42,429,000	0.2%
8	New Jersey	827,115,000	4.0%
34	New Mexico	123,892,000	0.6%
2	New York	1,948,752,000	9.4%
9	North Carolina	733,775,000	3.5%
50	North Dakota	10,584,000	0.1%
7	Ohio	873,584,000	4.2%
27	Oklahoma	193,567,000	0.9%
23	Oregon	253,421,000	1.2%
6	Pennsylvania	902,244,000	4.4%
38	Rhode Island	108,683,000	0.5%
22	South Carolina	277,868,000	1.3%
47	South Dakota	33,582,000	0.2%
16	Tennessee	349,177,000	1.7%
3	Texas	1,565,214,000	7.5%
37	Utah	111,808,000	0.5%
48	Vermont	33,426,000	0.2%
14	Virginia	452,358,000	2.2%
20	Washington	311,122,000	1.5%
44	West Virginia	43,716,000	0.2%
19	Wisconsin	313,366,000	1.5%
49	Wyoming	27,024,000	0.1%

RANK ORDER

RANK	STATE	EXPENDITURES	% of USA
1	California	$2,918,845,000	14.1%
2	New York	1,948,752,000	9.4%
3	Texas	1,565,214,000	7.5%
4	Michigan	1,161,142,000	5.6%
5	Florida	1,100,655,000	5.3%
6	Pennsylvania	902,244,000	4.4%
7	Ohio	873,584,000	4.2%
8	New Jersey	827,115,000	4.0%
9	North Carolina	733,775,000	3.5%
10	Illinois	732,824,000	3.5%
11	Georgia	547,490,000	2.6%
12	Maryland	480,880,000	2.3%
13	Connecticut	475,367,000	2.3%
14	Virginia	452,358,000	2.2%
15	Arizona	409,167,000	2.0%
16	Tennessee	349,177,000	1.7%
17	Indiana	325,700,000	1.6%
18	Louisiana	313,463,000	1.5%
19	Wisconsin	313,366,000	1.5%
20	Washington	311,122,000	1.5%
21	Massachusetts	304,483,000	1.5%
22	South Carolina	277,868,000	1.3%
23	Oregon	253,421,000	1.2%
24	Missouri	249,414,000	1.2%
25	Colorado	234,503,000	1.1%
26	Kentucky	198,775,000	1.0%
27	Oklahoma	193,567,000	0.9%
28	Minnesota	184,359,000	0.9%
29	Alabama	165,760,000	0.8%
30	Kansas	158,454,000	0.8%
31	Mississippi	143,914,000	0.7%
32	Iowa	143,774,000	0.7%
33	Arkansas	124,513,000	0.6%
34	New Mexico	123,892,000	0.6%
35	Nevada	119,026,000	0.6%
36	Alaska	112,350,000	0.5%
37	Utah	111,808,000	0.5%
38	Rhode Island	108,683,000	0.5%
39	Delaware	87,253,000	0.4%
40	Hawaii	83,921,000	0.4%
41	Nebraska	67,904,000	0.3%
42	Idaho	55,017,000	0.3%
43	Maine	48,206,000	0.2%
44	West Virginia	43,716,000	0.2%
45	New Hampshire	42,429,000	0.2%
46	Montana	41,875,000	0.2%
47	South Dakota	33,582,000	0.2%
48	Vermont	33,426,000	0.2%
49	Wyoming	27,024,000	0.1%
50	North Dakota	10,584,000	0.1%
	District of Columbia	212,148,000	1.0%

Source: U.S. Department of Justice, Bureau of Justice Statistics
   "State Prison Expenditures, 1996" (August 1999, NCJ-172211)
*State government expenditures, including adult prison operations but not capital outlays. They do not include
state juvenile justice activities, probation and parole services or nonresidential community corrections.
Expenditures are net amounts after deductions for revenue from prison farms, industries and services.*

Annual Operating Expenditures per Inmate in 1996

National Annual Average = $20,142 per Inmate*

ALPHA ORDER

RANK	STATE	PER INMATE
50	Alabama	$7,987
4	Alaska	32,415
32	Arizona	19,091
44	Arkansas	13,341
24	California	21,385
25	Colorado	21,020
6	Connecticut	31,912
33	Delaware	17,987
35	Florida	17,327
41	Georgia	15,933
19	Hawaii	23,318
40	Idaho	16,277
31	Illinois	19,351
28	Indiana	20,188
18	Iowa	24,286
23	Kansas	22,242
38	Kentucky	16,320
46	Louisiana	12,304
3	Maine	33,711
22	Maryland	22,247
16	Massachusetts	26,002
12	Michigan	28,067
1	Minnesota	37,825
48	Mississippi	11,156
45	Missouri	12,832
27	Montana	20,782
21	Nebraska	22,271
42	Nevada	15,370
26	New Hampshire	20,839
9	New Jersey	30,773
10	New Mexico	29,491
11	New York	28,426
17	North Carolina	25,303
37	North Dakota	17,154
29	Ohio	19,613
49	Oklahoma	10,601
7	Oregon	31,837
13	Pennsylvania	28,063
2	Rhode Island	35,739
43	South Carolina	13,977
34	South Dakota	17,787
20	Tennessee	22,904
47	Texas	12,215
5	Utah	32,361
8	Vermont	31,094
39	Virginia	16,306
15	Washington	26,662
36	West Virginia	17,245
14	Wisconsin	27,771
30	Wyoming	19,456

RANK ORDER

RANK	STATE	PER INMATE
1	Minnesota	$37,825
2	Rhode Island	35,739
3	Maine	33,711
4	Alaska	32,415
5	Utah	32,361
6	Connecticut	31,912
7	Oregon	31,837
8	Vermont	31,094
9	New Jersey	30,773
10	New Mexico	29,491
11	New York	28,426
12	Michigan	28,067
13	Pennsylvania	28,063
14	Wisconsin	27,771
15	Washington	26,662
16	Massachusetts	26,002
17	North Carolina	25,303
18	Iowa	24,286
19	Hawaii	23,318
20	Tennessee	22,904
21	Nebraska	22,271
22	Maryland	22,247
23	Kansas	22,242
24	California	21,385
25	Colorado	21,020
26	New Hampshire	20,839
27	Montana	20,782
28	Indiana	20,188
29	Ohio	19,613
30	Wyoming	19,456
31	Illinois	19,351
32	Arizona	19,091
33	Delaware	17,987
34	South Dakota	17,787
35	Florida	17,327
36	West Virginia	17,245
37	North Dakota	17,154
38	Kentucky	16,320
39	Virginia	16,306
40	Idaho	16,277
41	Georgia	15,933
42	Nevada	15,370
43	South Carolina	13,977
44	Arkansas	13,341
45	Missouri	12,832
46	Louisiana	12,304
47	Texas	12,215
48	Mississippi	11,156
49	Oklahoma	10,601
50	Alabama	7,987

District of Columbia   21,296

Source: U.S. Department of Justice, Bureau of Justice Statistics
   "State Prison Expenditures, 1996" (August 1999, NCJ-172211)
*Based on estimated average daily number of inmates, June 1995 to June 1996. State government expenditures, including adult prison operations but not capital outlays. They do not include state juvenile justice activities, probation and parole services or nonresidential community corrections. Expenditures are net amounts after deductions for revenue from prison farms, industries and services.

Daily Operating Expenditures per Inmate in 1996

National Daily Average = $55.18 per Inmate*

ALPHA ORDER				RANK ORDER		
RANK	STATE	PER INMATE		RANK	STATE	PER INMATE
50	Alabama	$21.88		1	Minnesota	$103.63
4	Alaska	88.81		2	Rhode Island	97.92
32	Arizona	52.30		3	Maine	92.36
44	Arkansas	36.55		4	Alaska	88.81
24	California	58.59		5	Utah	88.66
25	Colorado	57.59		6	Connecticut	87.43
6	Connecticut	87.43		7	Oregon	87.22
33	Delaware	49.28		8	Vermont	85.19
35	Florida	47.47		9	New Jersey	84.31
41	Georgia	43.65		10	New Mexico	80.80
19	Hawaii	63.88		11	New York	77.88
40	Idaho	44.60		12	Michigan	76.89
31	Illinois	53.02		13	Pennsylvania	76.88
28	Indiana	55.31		14	Wisconsin	76.08
18	Iowa	66.54		15	Washington	73.05
23	Kansas	60.94		16	Massachusetts	71.24
38	Kentucky	44.71		17	North Carolina	69.32
46	Louisiana	33.71		18	Iowa	66.54
3	Maine	92.36		19	Hawaii	63.88
22	Maryland	60.95		20	Tennessee	62.75
16	Massachusetts	71.24		21	Nebraska	61.02
12	Michigan	76.89		22	Maryland	60.95
1	Minnesota	103.63		23	Kansas	60.94
48	Mississippi	30.56		24	California	58.59
45	Missouri	35.16		25	Colorado	57.59
27	Montana	56.94		26	New Hampshire	57.09
21	Nebraska	61.02		27	Montana	56.94
42	Nevada	42.11		28	Indiana	55.31
26	New Hampshire	57.09		29	Ohio	53.74
9	New Jersey	84.31		30	Wyoming	53.30
10	New Mexico	80.80		31	Illinois	53.02
11	New York	77.88		32	Arizona	52.30
17	North Carolina	69.32		33	Delaware	49.28
37	North Dakota	47.00		34	South Dakota	48.73
29	Ohio	53.74		35	Florida	47.47
49	Oklahoma	29.04		36	West Virginia	47.25
7	Oregon	87.22		37	North Dakota	47.00
13	Pennsylvania	76.88		38	Kentucky	44.71
2	Rhode Island	97.92		39	Virginia	44.67
43	South Carolina	38.29		40	Idaho	44.60
34	South Dakota	48.73		41	Georgia	43.65
20	Tennessee	62.75		42	Nevada	42.11
47	Texas	33.47		43	South Carolina	38.29
5	Utah	88.66		44	Arkansas	36.55
8	Vermont	85.19		45	Missouri	35.16
39	Virginia	44.67		46	Louisiana	33.71
15	Washington	73.05		47	Texas	33.47
36	West Virginia	47.25		48	Mississippi	30.56
14	Wisconsin	76.08		49	Oklahoma	29.04
30	Wyoming	53.30		50	Alabama	21.88
					District of Columbia	58.34

Source: U.S. Department of Justice, Bureau of Justice Statistics
    "State Prison Expenditures, 1996" (August 1999, NCJ-172211)
*Based on estimated average daily number of inmates, June 1995 to June 1996. State government expenditures,
including adult prison operations but not capital outlays. They do not include state juvenile justice activities,
probation and parole services or nonresidential community corrections. Expenditures are net amounts after
deductions for revenue from prison farms, industries and services.

Local Government Expenditures for Corrections in 1997

National Total = $12,829,587,000*

ALPHA ORDER

RANK	STATE	EXPENDITURES	% of USA
28	Alabama	$94,688,000	0.7%
45	Alaska	369,000	0.0%
18	Arizona	197,105,000	1.5%
33	Arkansas	47,891,000	0.4%
1	California	2,349,300,000	18.3%
21	Colorado	173,752,000	1.4%
47	Connecticut	0	0.0%
47	Delaware	0	0.0%
4	Florida	905,414,000	7.1%
9	Georgia	342,313,000	2.7%
47	Hawaii	0	0.0%
37	Idaho	30,407,000	0.2%
6	Illinois	401,315,000	3.1%
20	Indiana	182,800,000	1.4%
32	Iowa	54,284,000	0.4%
31	Kansas	59,321,000	0.5%
26	Kentucky	109,065,000	0.9%
25	Louisiana	135,838,000	1.1%
38	Maine	27,651,000	0.2%
23	Maryland	139,798,000	1.1%
11	Massachusetts	319,779,000	2.5%
12	Michigan	304,671,000	2.4%
15	Minnesota	211,781,000	1.7%
34	Mississippi	47,372,000	0.4%
24	Missouri	138,995,000	1.1%
43	Montana	12,655,000	0.1%
35	Nebraska	45,962,000	0.4%
22	Nevada	158,174,000	1.2%
40	New Hampshire	26,617,000	0.2%
7	New Jersey	362,744,000	2.8%
29	New Mexico	72,414,000	0.6%
2	New York	1,875,699,000	14.6%
19	North Carolina	186,011,000	1.4%
44	North Dakota	9,559,000	0.1%
8	Ohio	358,961,000	2.8%
36	Oklahoma	38,719,000	0.3%
16	Oregon	200,902,000	1.6%
5	Pennsylvania	701,685,000	5.5%
47	Rhode Island	0	0.0%
27	South Carolina	98,103,000	0.8%
41	South Dakota	17,707,000	0.1%
17	Tennessee	197,240,000	1.5%
3	Texas	949,341,000	7.4%
30	Utah	68,185,000	0.5%
46	Vermont	124,000	0.0%
10	Virginia	329,645,000	2.6%
13	Washington	285,969,000	2.2%
39	West Virginia	26,874,000	0.2%
14	Wisconsin	215,981,000	1.7%
42	Wyoming	16,250,000	0.1%

RANK ORDER

RANK	STATE	EXPENDITURES	% of USA
1	California	$2,349,300,000	18.3%
2	New York	1,875,699,000	14.6%
3	Texas	949,341,000	7.4%
4	Florida	905,414,000	7.1%
5	Pennsylvania	701,685,000	5.5%
6	Illinois	401,315,000	3.1%
7	New Jersey	362,744,000	2.8%
8	Ohio	358,961,000	2.8%
9	Georgia	342,313,000	2.7%
10	Virginia	329,645,000	2.6%
11	Massachusetts	319,779,000	2.5%
12	Michigan	304,671,000	2.4%
13	Washington	285,969,000	2.2%
14	Wisconsin	215,981,000	1.7%
15	Minnesota	211,781,000	1.7%
16	Oregon	200,902,000	1.6%
17	Tennessee	197,240,000	1.5%
18	Arizona	197,105,000	1.5%
19	North Carolina	186,011,000	1.4%
20	Indiana	182,800,000	1.4%
21	Colorado	173,752,000	1.4%
22	Nevada	158,174,000	1.2%
23	Maryland	139,798,000	1.1%
24	Missouri	138,995,000	1.1%
25	Louisiana	135,838,000	1.1%
26	Kentucky	109,065,000	0.9%
27	South Carolina	98,103,000	0.8%
28	Alabama	94,688,000	0.7%
29	New Mexico	72,414,000	0.6%
30	Utah	68,185,000	0.5%
31	Kansas	59,321,000	0.5%
32	Iowa	54,284,000	0.4%
33	Arkansas	47,891,000	0.4%
34	Mississippi	47,372,000	0.4%
35	Nebraska	45,962,000	0.4%
36	Oklahoma	38,719,000	0.3%
37	Idaho	30,407,000	0.2%
38	Maine	27,651,000	0.2%
39	West Virginia	26,874,000	0.2%
40	New Hampshire	26,617,000	0.2%
41	South Dakota	17,707,000	0.1%
42	Wyoming	16,250,000	0.1%
43	Montana	12,655,000	0.1%
44	North Dakota	9,559,000	0.1%
45	Alaska	369,000	0.0%
46	Vermont	124,000	0.0%
47	Connecticut	0	0.0%
47	Delaware	0	0.0%
47	Hawaii	0	0.0%
47	Rhode Island	0	0.0%
	District of Columbia	300,157,000	2.3%

Source: Morgan Quitno Press using data from U.S. Bureau of the Census
"Compendium of Government Finances 1997" (GC97(4)-5, December 2000)
Direct general expenditures.

Per Capita Local Government Expenditures for Corrections in 1997

National Per Capita = $47.91*

ALPHA ORDER

RANK	STATE	PER CAPITA
37	Alabama	$21.92
45	Alaska	0.61
15	Arizona	43.30
39	Arkansas	18.97
3	California	72.92
14	Colorado	44.65
47	Connecticut	0.00
47	Delaware	0.00
5	Florida	61.66
11	Georgia	45.73
47	Hawaii	0.00
31	Idaho	25.12
20	Illinois	33.41
25	Indiana	31.13
38	Iowa	19.02
35	Kansas	22.67
26	Kentucky	27.91
23	Louisiana	31.22
36	Maine	22.21
28	Maryland	27.45
7	Massachusetts	52.29
24	Michigan	31.14
12	Minnesota	45.18
40	Mississippi	17.34
30	Missouri	25.71
43	Montana	14.40
27	Nebraska	27.75
2	Nevada	94.40
34	New Hampshire	22.69
13	New Jersey	45.04
16	New Mexico	42.03
1	New York	103.38
32	North Carolina	25.04
41	North Dakota	14.91
22	Ohio	32.01
44	Oklahoma	11.68
4	Oregon	61.94
6	Pennsylvania	58.40
47	Rhode Island	0.00
29	South Carolina	25.88
33	South Dakota	24.23
18	Tennessee	36.67
9	Texas	49.05
21	Utah	33.01
46	Vermont	0.21
10	Virginia	48.96
8	Washington	51.03
42	West Virginia	14.80
17	Wisconsin	41.53
19	Wyoming	33.85

RANK ORDER

RANK	STATE	PER CAPITA
1	New York	$103.38
2	Nevada	94.40
3	California	72.92
4	Oregon	61.94
5	Florida	61.66
6	Pennsylvania	58.40
7	Massachusetts	52.29
8	Washington	51.03
9	Texas	49.05
10	Virginia	48.96
11	Georgia	45.73
12	Minnesota	45.18
13	New Jersey	45.04
14	Colorado	44.65
15	Arizona	43.30
16	New Mexico	42.03
17	Wisconsin	41.53
18	Tennessee	36.67
19	Wyoming	33.85
20	Illinois	33.41
21	Utah	33.01
22	Ohio	32.01
23	Louisiana	31.22
24	Michigan	31.14
25	Indiana	31.13
26	Kentucky	27.91
27	Nebraska	27.75
28	Maryland	27.45
29	South Carolina	25.88
30	Missouri	25.71
31	Idaho	25.12
32	North Carolina	25.04
33	South Dakota	24.23
34	New Hampshire	22.69
35	Kansas	22.67
36	Maine	22.21
37	Alabama	21.92
38	Iowa	19.02
39	Arkansas	18.97
40	Mississippi	17.34
41	North Dakota	14.91
42	West Virginia	14.80
43	Montana	14.40
44	Oklahoma	11.68
45	Alaska	0.61
46	Vermont	0.21
47	Connecticut	0.00
47	Delaware	0.00
47	Hawaii	0.00
47	Rhode Island	0.00
	District of Columbia	567.67

*Source: Morgan Quitno Press using data from U.S. Bureau of the Census
"Compendium of Government Finances 1997" (GC97(4)-5, December 2000)*

*Direct general expenditures.

Local Government Expenditures for Corrections
As a Percent of All Direct General Expenditures in 1997
National Percent = 1.8% of Direct General Expenditures

ALPHA ORDER

RANK ORDER

RANK	STATE	PERCENT	RANK	STATE	PERCENT
28	Alabama	1.1	1	Nevada	3.0
45	Alaska	0.0	2	Pennsylvania	2.4
11	Arizona	1.8	3	Massachusetts	2.3
28	Arkansas	1.1	3	New York	2.3
5	California	2.2	5	California	2.2
15	Colorado	1.6	5	Florida	2.2
45	Connecticut	0.0	7	Oregon	2.1
45	Delaware	0.0	7	Texas	2.1
5	Florida	2.2	7	Virginia	2.1
10	Georgia	1.9	10	Georgia	1.9
45	Hawaii	0.0	11	Arizona	1.8
28	Idaho	1.1	11	New Mexico	1.8
23	Illinois	1.3	11	Washington	1.8
20	Indiana	1.4	14	Tennessee	1.7
39	Iowa	0.8	15	Colorado	1.6
38	Kansas	0.9	15	Kentucky	1.6
15	Kentucky	1.6	15	Utah	1.6
18	Louisiana	1.5	18	Louisiana	1.5
28	Maine	1.1	18	New Jersey	1.5
28	Maryland	1.1	20	Indiana	1.4
3	Massachusetts	2.3	20	Minnesota	1.4
28	Michigan	1.1	20	Wisconsin	1.4
20	Minnesota	1.4	23	Illinois	1.3
39	Mississippi	0.8	23	Ohio	1.3
27	Missouri	1.2	23	South Carolina	1.3
42	Montana	0.7	23	South Dakota	1.3
28	Nebraska	1.1	27	Missouri	1.2
1	Nevada	3.0	28	Alabama	1.1
28	New Hampshire	1.1	28	Arkansas	1.1
18	New Jersey	1.5	28	Idaho	1.1
11	New Mexico	1.8	28	Maine	1.1
3	New York	2.3	28	Maryland	1.1
28	North Carolina	1.1	28	Michigan	1.1
42	North Dakota	0.7	28	Nebraska	1.1
23	Ohio	1.3	28	New Hampshire	1.1
44	Oklahoma	0.6	28	North Carolina	1.1
7	Oregon	2.1	37	Wyoming	1.0
2	Pennsylvania	2.4	38	Kansas	0.9
45	Rhode Island	0.0	39	Iowa	0.8
23	South Carolina	1.3	39	Mississippi	0.8
23	South Dakota	1.3	39	West Virginia	0.8
14	Tennessee	1.7	42	Montana	0.7
7	Texas	2.1	42	North Dakota	0.7
15	Utah	1.6	44	Oklahoma	0.6
45	Vermont	0.0	45	Alaska	0.0
7	Virginia	2.1	45	Connecticut	0.0
11	Washington	1.8	45	Delaware	0.0
39	West Virginia	0.8	45	Hawaii	0.0
20	Wisconsin	1.4	45	Rhode Island	0.0
37	Wyoming	1.0	45	Vermont	0.0
				District of Columbia	6.9

Source: Morgan Quitno Press using data from U.S. Bureau of the Census
"Compendium of Government Finances 1997" (GC97(4)-5, December 2000)

State and Local Government Expenditures for Judicial and Legal Services: 1997

National Total = $21,645,774,000*

RANK	STATE	EXPENDITURES	% of USA
27	Alabama	$225,112,000	1.0%
34	Alaska	146,513,000	0.7%
12	Arizona	452,076,000	2.1%
38	Arkansas	116,814,000	0.5%
1	California	3,950,419,000	18.3%
23	Colorado	286,620,000	1.3%
22	Connecticut	292,846,000	1.4%
44	Delaware	75,052,000	0.3%
3	Florida	1,268,881,000	5.9%
13	Georgia	387,526,000	1.8%
33	Hawaii	148,956,000	0.7%
40	Idaho	88,653,000	0.4%
8	Illinois	800,524,000	3.7%
25	Indiana	259,510,000	1.2%
28	Iowa	195,297,000	0.9%
30	Kansas	172,460,000	0.8%
26	Kentucky	233,702,000	1.1%
24	Louisiana	278,517,000	1.3%
46	Maine	50,880,000	0.2%
15	Maryland	380,016,000	1.8%
10	Massachusetts	595,203,000	2.7%
9	Michigan	754,327,000	3.5%
17	Minnesota	366,330,000	1.7%
37	Mississippi	117,785,000	0.5%
20	Missouri	314,730,000	1.5%
45	Montana	59,467,000	0.3%
42	Nebraska	82,720,000	0.4%
31	Nevada	172,284,000	0.8%
43	New Hampshire	79,401,000	0.4%
5	New Jersey	979,661,000	4.5%
36	New Mexico	136,622,000	0.6%
2	New York	2,013,877,000	9.3%
16	North Carolina	372,020,000	1.7%
48	North Dakota	41,250,000	0.2%
6	Ohio	888,985,000	4.1%
35	Oklahoma	145,907,000	0.7%
21	Oregon	311,540,000	1.4%
7	Pennsylvania	866,434,000	4.0%
39	Rhode Island	92,124,000	0.4%
32	South Carolina	159,935,000	0.7%
49	South Dakota	34,634,000	0.2%
19	Tennessee	345,902,000	1.6%
4	Texas	1,129,399,000	5.2%
29	Utah	181,884,000	0.8%
50	Vermont	32,685,000	0.2%
14	Virginia	381,317,000	1.8%
11	Washington	531,234,000	2.5%
41	West Virginia	84,922,000	0.4%
18	Wisconsin	366,126,000	1.7%
47	Wyoming	43,301,000	0.2%

RANK	STATE	EXPENDITURES	% of USA
1	California	$3,950,419,000	18.3%
2	New York	2,013,877,000	9.3%
3	Florida	1,268,881,000	5.9%
4	Texas	1,129,399,000	5.2%
5	New Jersey	979,661,000	4.5%
6	Ohio	888,985,000	4.1%
7	Pennsylvania	866,434,000	4.0%
8	Illinois	800,524,000	3.7%
9	Michigan	754,327,000	3.5%
10	Massachusetts	595,203,000	2.7%
11	Washington	531,234,000	2.5%
12	Arizona	452,076,000	2.1%
13	Georgia	387,526,000	1.8%
14	Virginia	381,317,000	1.8%
15	Maryland	380,016,000	1.8%
16	North Carolina	372,020,000	1.7%
17	Minnesota	366,330,000	1.7%
18	Wisconsin	366,126,000	1.7%
19	Tennessee	345,902,000	1.6%
20	Missouri	314,730,000	1.5%
21	Oregon	311,540,000	1.4%
22	Connecticut	292,846,000	1.4%
23	Colorado	286,620,000	1.3%
24	Louisiana	278,517,000	1.3%
25	Indiana	259,510,000	1.2%
26	Kentucky	233,702,000	1.1%
27	Alabama	225,112,000	1.0%
28	Iowa	195,297,000	0.9%
29	Utah	181,884,000	0.8%
30	Kansas	172,460,000	0.8%
31	Nevada	172,284,000	0.8%
32	South Carolina	159,935,000	0.7%
33	Hawaii	148,956,000	0.7%
34	Alaska	146,513,000	0.7%
35	Oklahoma	145,907,000	0.7%
36	New Mexico	136,622,000	0.6%
37	Mississippi	117,785,000	0.5%
38	Arkansas	116,814,000	0.5%
39	Rhode Island	92,124,000	0.4%
40	Idaho	88,653,000	0.4%
41	West Virginia	84,922,000	0.4%
42	Nebraska	82,720,000	0.4%
43	New Hampshire	79,401,000	0.4%
44	Delaware	75,052,000	0.3%
45	Montana	59,467,000	0.3%
46	Maine	50,880,000	0.2%
47	Wyoming	43,301,000	0.2%
48	North Dakota	41,250,000	0.2%
49	South Dakota	34,634,000	0.2%
50	Vermont	32,685,000	0.2%
	District of Columbia	153,988,000	0.7%

Source: Morgan Quitno Press using data from U.S. Bureau of the Census
"Compendium of Government Finances 1997" (GC97(4)-5, December 2000)
*Direct general expenditures. Includes Courts, Prosecution and Legal Services and Public Defense.

Per Capita State and Local Government Expenditures
For Judicial and Legal Services in 1997
National Per Capita = $80.83*

ALPHA ORDER

RANK	STATE	PER CAPITA
39	Alabama	$52.11
1	Alaska	240.64
8	Arizona	99.31
45	Arkansas	46.28
3	California	122.62
22	Colorado	73.66
14	Connecticut	89.60
7	Delaware	102.11
16	Florida	86.42
40	Georgia	51.77
2	Hawaii	125.24
23	Idaho	73.23
29	Illinois	66.65
46	Indiana	44.19
26	Iowa	68.42
30	Kansas	65.92
34	Kentucky	59.80
33	Louisiana	64.01
50	Maine	40.86
21	Maryland	74.62
9	Massachusetts	97.33
20	Michigan	77.09
19	Minnesota	78.15
48	Mississippi	43.12
36	Missouri	58.21
27	Montana	67.68
42	Nebraska	49.95
6	Nevada	102.82
27	New Hampshire	67.68
4	New Jersey	121.63
17	New Mexico	79.30
5	New York	111.00
41	North Carolina	50.08
31	North Dakota	64.36
18	Ohio	79.29
47	Oklahoma	44.02
10	Oregon	96.06
24	Pennsylvania	72.11
12	Rhode Island	93.34
49	South Carolina	42.20
43	South Dakota	47.39
32	Tennessee	64.31
35	Texas	58.35
15	Utah	88.06
38	Vermont	55.52
37	Virginia	56.64
11	Washington	94.79
44	West Virginia	46.77
25	Wisconsin	70.41
13	Wyoming	90.20

RANK ORDER

RANK	STATE	PER CAPITA
1	Alaska	$240.64
2	Hawaii	125.24
3	California	122.62
4	New Jersey	121.63
5	New York	111.00
6	Nevada	102.82
7	Delaware	102.11
8	Arizona	99.31
9	Massachusetts	97.33
10	Oregon	96.06
11	Washington	94.79
12	Rhode Island	93.34
13	Wyoming	90.20
14	Connecticut	89.60
15	Utah	88.06
16	Florida	86.42
17	New Mexico	79.30
18	Ohio	79.29
19	Minnesota	78.15
20	Michigan	77.09
21	Maryland	74.62
22	Colorado	73.66
23	Idaho	73.23
24	Pennsylvania	72.11
25	Wisconsin	70.41
26	Iowa	68.42
27	Montana	67.68
27	New Hampshire	67.68
29	Illinois	66.65
30	Kansas	65.92
31	North Dakota	64.36
32	Tennessee	64.31
33	Louisiana	64.01
34	Kentucky	59.80
35	Texas	58.35
36	Missouri	58.21
37	Virginia	56.64
38	Vermont	55.52
39	Alabama	52.11
40	Georgia	51.77
41	North Carolina	50.08
42	Nebraska	49.95
43	South Dakota	47.39
44	West Virginia	46.77
45	Arkansas	46.28
46	Indiana	44.19
47	Oklahoma	44.02
48	Mississippi	43.12
49	South Carolina	42.20
50	Maine	40.86
	District of Columbia	291.23

Source: Morgan Quitno Press using data from U.S. Bureau of the Census
"Compendium of Government Finances 1997" (GC97(4)-5, December 2000)
*Direct general expenditures. Includes Courts, Prosecution and Legal Services and Public Defense.

State and Local Government Expenditures for Judicial and Legal Services As a Percent of All Direct General Expenditures in 1997
National Percent = 1.7% of Direct General Expenditures*

ALPHA ORDER

RANK	STATE	PERCENT
37	Alabama	1.3
4	Alaska	2.2
1	Arizona	2.5
39	Arkansas	1.2
1	California	2.5
17	Colorado	1.6
17	Connecticut	1.6
9	Delaware	1.9
7	Florida	2.0
39	Georgia	1.2
4	Hawaii	2.2
13	Idaho	1.8
26	Illinois	1.5
45	Indiana	1.1
26	Iowa	1.5
17	Kansas	1.6
26	Kentucky	1.5
26	Louisiana	1.5
50	Maine	0.9
16	Maryland	1.7
9	Massachusetts	1.9
17	Michigan	1.6
26	Minnesota	1.5
45	Mississippi	1.1
26	Missouri	1.5
26	Montana	1.5
45	Nebraska	1.1
4	Nevada	2.2
17	New Hampshire	1.6
3	New Jersey	2.4
17	New Mexico	1.6
17	New York	1.6
39	North Carolina	1.2
35	North Dakota	1.4
13	Ohio	1.8
39	Oklahoma	1.2
9	Oregon	1.9
17	Pennsylvania	1.6
9	Rhode Island	1.9
49	South Carolina	1.0
39	South Dakota	1.2
17	Tennessee	1.6
26	Texas	1.5
7	Utah	2.0
39	Vermont	1.2
37	Virginia	1.3
13	Washington	1.8
45	West Virginia	1.1
35	Wisconsin	1.4
26	Wyoming	1.5

RANK ORDER

RANK	STATE	PERCENT
1	Arizona	2.5
1	California	2.5
3	New Jersey	2.4
4	Alaska	2.2
4	Hawaii	2.2
4	Nevada	2.2
7	Florida	2.0
7	Utah	2.0
9	Delaware	1.9
9	Massachusetts	1.9
9	Oregon	1.9
9	Rhode Island	1.9
13	Idaho	1.8
13	Ohio	1.8
13	Washington	1.8
16	Maryland	1.7
17	Colorado	1.6
17	Connecticut	1.6
17	Kansas	1.6
17	Michigan	1.6
17	New Hampshire	1.6
17	New Mexico	1.6
17	New York	1.6
17	Pennsylvania	1.6
17	Tennessee	1.6
26	Illinois	1.5
26	Iowa	1.5
26	Kentucky	1.5
26	Louisiana	1.5
26	Minnesota	1.5
26	Missouri	1.5
26	Montana	1.5
26	Texas	1.5
26	Wyoming	1.5
35	North Dakota	1.4
35	Wisconsin	1.4
37	Alabama	1.3
37	Virginia	1.3
39	Arkansas	1.2
39	Georgia	1.2
39	North Carolina	1.2
39	Oklahoma	1.2
39	South Dakota	1.2
39	Vermont	1.2
45	Indiana	1.1
45	Mississippi	1.1
45	Nebraska	1.1
45	West Virginia	1.1
49	South Carolina	1.0
50	Maine	0.9

District of Columbia	3.6

Source: Morgan Quitno Press using data from U.S. Bureau of the Census
"Compendium of Government Finances 1997" (GC97(4)-5, December 2000)
*Includes Courts, Prosecution and Legal Services and Public Defense.

State Government Expenditures for Judicial and Legal Services in 1997

National Total = $8,566,938,000*

ALPHA ORDER

RANK	STATE	EXPENDITURES	% of USA
18	Alabama	$146,083,000	1.7%
23	Alaska	136,193,000	1.6%
30	Arizona	102,861,000	1.2%
38	Arkansas	63,232,000	0.7%
5	California	411,336,000	4.8%
17	Colorado	146,456,000	1.7%
8	Connecticut	265,649,000	3.1%
35	Delaware	66,993,000	0.8%
3	Florida	521,987,000	6.1%
34	Georgia	75,582,000	0.9%
26	Hawaii	118,193,000	1.4%
42	Idaho	44,031,000	0.5%
11	Illinois	227,131,000	2.7%
33	Indiana	78,315,000	0.9%
16	Iowa	146,749,000	1.7%
31	Kansas	102,561,000	1.2%
12	Kentucky	197,869,000	2.3%
28	Louisiana	113,622,000	1.3%
43	Maine	43,117,000	0.5%
10	Maryland	235,952,000	2.8%
2	Massachusetts	544,748,000	6.4%
21	Michigan	137,807,000	1.6%
19	Minnesota	143,786,000	1.7%
41	Mississippi	48,085,000	0.6%
24	Missouri	129,570,000	1.5%
49	Montana	22,057,000	0.3%
44	Nebraska	34,209,000	0.4%
47	Nevada	26,864,000	0.3%
36	New Hampshire	65,783,000	0.8%
4	New Jersey	447,488,000	5.2%
27	New Mexico	116,911,000	1.4%
1	New York	1,273,097,000	14.9%
7	North Carolina	315,652,000	3.7%
46	North Dakota	29,156,000	0.3%
14	Ohio	166,672,000	1.9%
29	Oklahoma	106,767,000	1.2%
20	Oregon	141,529,000	1.7%
9	Pennsylvania	248,821,000	2.9%
32	Rhode Island	84,118,000	1.0%
40	South Carolina	50,358,000	0.6%
50	South Dakota	17,588,000	0.2%
22	Tennessee	136,936,000	1.6%
6	Texas	385,856,000	4.5%
25	Utah	129,434,000	1.5%
45	Vermont	30,587,000	0.4%
13	Virginia	182,697,000	2.1%
37	Washington	65,600,000	0.8%
39	West Virginia	54,087,000	0.6%
15	Wisconsin	160,936,000	1.9%
48	Wyoming	25,827,000	0.3%

RANK ORDER

RANK	STATE	EXPENDITURES	% of USA
1	New York	$1,273,097,000	14.9%
2	Massachusetts	544,748,000	6.4%
3	Florida	521,987,000	6.1%
4	New Jersey	447,488,000	5.2%
5	California	411,336,000	4.8%
6	Texas	385,856,000	4.5%
7	North Carolina	315,652,000	3.7%
8	Connecticut	265,649,000	3.1%
9	Pennsylvania	248,821,000	2.9%
10	Maryland	235,952,000	2.8%
11	Illinois	227,131,000	2.7%
12	Kentucky	197,869,000	2.3%
13	Virginia	182,697,000	2.1%
14	Ohio	166,672,000	1.9%
15	Wisconsin	160,936,000	1.9%
16	Iowa	146,749,000	1.7%
17	Colorado	146,456,000	1.7%
18	Alabama	146,083,000	1.7%
19	Minnesota	143,786,000	1.7%
20	Oregon	141,529,000	1.7%
21	Michigan	137,807,000	1.6%
22	Tennessee	136,936,000	1.6%
23	Alaska	136,193,000	1.6%
24	Missouri	129,570,000	1.5%
25	Utah	129,434,000	1.5%
26	Hawaii	118,193,000	1.4%
27	New Mexico	116,911,000	1.4%
28	Louisiana	113,622,000	1.3%
29	Oklahoma	106,767,000	1.2%
30	Arizona	102,861,000	1.2%
31	Kansas	102,561,000	1.2%
32	Rhode Island	84,118,000	1.0%
33	Indiana	78,315,000	0.9%
34	Georgia	75,582,000	0.9%
35	Delaware	66,993,000	0.8%
36	New Hampshire	65,783,000	0.8%
37	Washington	65,600,000	0.8%
38	Arkansas	63,232,000	0.7%
39	West Virginia	54,087,000	0.6%
40	South Carolina	50,358,000	0.6%
41	Mississippi	48,085,000	0.6%
42	Idaho	44,031,000	0.5%
43	Maine	43,117,000	0.5%
44	Nebraska	34,209,000	0.4%
45	Vermont	30,587,000	0.4%
46	North Dakota	29,156,000	0.3%
47	Nevada	26,864,000	0.3%
48	Wyoming	25,827,000	0.3%
49	Montana	22,057,000	0.3%
50	South Dakota	17,588,000	0.2%
	District of Columbia**	NA	NA

Source: Morgan Quitno Press using data from U.S. Bureau of the Census
     "Compendium of Government Finances 1997" (GC97(4)-5, December 2000)
*Direct general expenditures. Includes Courts, Prosecution and Legal Services and Public Defense.
**Not applicable.

Per Capita State Government Expenditures for Judicial and Legal Services: 1997

National Per Capita = $31.99*

ALPHA ORDER

RANK	STATE	PER CAPITA
25	Alabama	$33.81
1	Alaska	223.69
37	Arizona	22.60
34	Arkansas	25.05
48	California	12.77
21	Colorado	37.64
6	Connecticut	81.28
3	Delaware	91.14
23	Florida	35.55
50	Georgia	10.10
2	Hawaii	99.38
22	Idaho	36.37
41	Illinois	18.91
46	Indiana	13.34
14	Iowa	51.41
20	Kansas	39.20
15	Kentucky	50.63
31	Louisiana	26.11
24	Maine	34.63
16	Maryland	46.33
4	Massachusetts	89.08
45	Michigan	14.08
28	Minnesota	30.67
42	Mississippi	17.60
36	Missouri	23.96
33	Montana	25.10
39	Nebraska	20.66
43	Nevada	16.03
10	New Hampshire	56.07
11	New Jersey	55.56
8	New Mexico	67.86
7	New York	70.17
19	North Carolina	42.49
17	North Dakota	45.49
44	Ohio	14.86
26	Oklahoma	32.21
18	Oregon	43.64
38	Pennsylvania	20.71
5	Rhode Island	85.23
47	South Carolina	13.29
35	South Dakota	24.06
32	Tennessee	25.46
40	Texas	19.94
9	Utah	62.67
13	Vermont	51.96
30	Virginia	27.14
49	Washington	11.71
29	West Virginia	29.79
27	Wisconsin	30.95
12	Wyoming	53.80

RANK ORDER

RANK	STATE	PER CAPITA
1	Alaska	$223.69
2	Hawaii	99.38
3	Delaware	91.14
4	Massachusetts	89.08
5	Rhode Island	85.23
6	Connecticut	81.28
7	New York	70.17
8	New Mexico	67.86
9	Utah	62.67
10	New Hampshire	56.07
11	New Jersey	55.56
12	Wyoming	53.80
13	Vermont	51.96
14	Iowa	51.41
15	Kentucky	50.63
16	Maryland	46.33
17	North Dakota	45.49
18	Oregon	43.64
19	North Carolina	42.49
20	Kansas	39.20
21	Colorado	37.64
22	Idaho	36.37
23	Florida	35.55
24	Maine	34.63
25	Alabama	33.81
26	Oklahoma	32.21
27	Wisconsin	30.95
28	Minnesota	30.67
29	West Virginia	29.79
30	Virginia	27.14
31	Louisiana	26.11
32	Tennessee	25.46
33	Montana	25.10
34	Arkansas	25.05
35	South Dakota	24.06
36	Missouri	23.96
37	Arizona	22.60
38	Pennsylvania	20.71
39	Nebraska	20.66
40	Texas	19.94
41	Illinois	18.91
42	Mississippi	17.60
43	Nevada	16.03
44	Ohio	14.86
45	Michigan	14.08
46	Indiana	13.34
47	South Carolina	13.29
48	California	12.77
49	Washington	11.71
50	Georgia	10.10

District of Columbia**   NA

Source: Morgan Quitno Press using data from U.S. Bureau of the Census
   "Compendium of Government Finances 1997" (GC97(4)-5, December 2000)
*Direct general expenditures. Includes Courts, Prosecution and Legal Services and Public Defense.
**Not applicable.

State Government Expenditures for Judicial and Legal Services
As a Percent of All Direct General Expenditures in 1997
National Percent = 1.6% of Direct General Expenditures*

ALPHA ORDER

RANK	STATE	PERCENT
24	Alabama	1.7
1	Alaska	3.3
27	Arizona	1.5
33	Arkansas	1.2
44	California	0.8
12	Colorado	2.3
5	Connecticut	2.8
7	Delaware	2.7
12	Florida	2.3
49	Georgia	0.5
18	Hawaii	2.2
20	Idaho	2.0
39	Illinois	1.0
44	Indiana	0.8
11	Iowa	2.6
12	Kansas	2.3
12	Kentucky	2.3
33	Louisiana	1.2
30	Maine	1.4
12	Maryland	2.3
2	Massachusetts	3.0
47	Michigan	0.7
27	Minnesota	1.5
43	Mississippi	0.9
30	Missouri	1.4
39	Montana	1.0
39	Nebraska	1.0
38	Nevada	1.1
7	New Hampshire	2.7
7	New Jersey	2.7
7	New Mexico	2.7
3	New York	2.9
12	North Carolina	2.3
24	North Dakota	1.7
44	Ohio	0.8
22	Oklahoma	1.9
20	Oregon	2.0
39	Pennsylvania	1.0
3	Rhode Island	2.9
48	South Carolina	0.6
33	South Dakota	1.2
30	Tennessee	1.4
33	Texas	1.2
5	Utah	2.8
23	Vermont	1.8
27	Virginia	1.5
49	Washington	0.5
33	West Virginia	1.2
24	Wisconsin	1.7
18	Wyoming	2.2

RANK ORDER

RANK	STATE	PERCENT
1	Alaska	3.3
2	Massachusetts	3.0
3	New York	2.9
3	Rhode Island	2.9
5	Connecticut	2.8
5	Utah	2.8
7	Delaware	2.7
7	New Hampshire	2.7
7	New Jersey	2.7
7	New Mexico	2.7
11	Iowa	2.6
12	Colorado	2.3
12	Florida	2.3
12	Kansas	2.3
12	Kentucky	2.3
12	Maryland	2.3
12	North Carolina	2.3
18	Hawaii	2.2
18	Wyoming	2.2
20	Idaho	2.0
20	Oregon	2.0
22	Oklahoma	1.9
23	Vermont	1.8
24	Alabama	1.7
24	North Dakota	1.7
24	Wisconsin	1.7
27	Arizona	1.5
27	Minnesota	1.5
27	Virginia	1.5
30	Maine	1.4
30	Missouri	1.4
30	Tennessee	1.4
33	Arkansas	1.2
33	Louisiana	1.2
33	South Dakota	1.2
33	Texas	1.2
33	West Virginia	1.2
38	Nevada	1.1
39	Illinois	1.0
39	Montana	1.0
39	Nebraska	1.0
39	Pennsylvania	1.0
43	Mississippi	0.9
44	California	0.8
44	Indiana	0.8
44	Ohio	0.8
47	Michigan	0.7
48	South Carolina	0.6
49	Georgia	0.5
49	Washington	0.5
	District of Columbia**	NA

Source: Morgan Quitno Press using data from U.S. Bureau of the Census
   "Compendium of Government Finances 1997" (GC97(4)-5, December 2000)
*Includes Courts, Prosecution and Legal Services and Public Defense.
**Not applicable.

Local Government Expenditures for Judicial and Legal Services in 1997

National Total = $13,078,836,000*

ALPHA ORDER

RANK	STATE	EXPENDITURES	% of USA
25	Alabama	$79,029,000	0.6%
46	Alaska	10,320,000	0.1%
11	Arizona	349,215,000	2.7%
29	Arkansas	53,582,000	0.4%
1	California	3,539,083,000	27.1%
23	Colorado	140,164,000	1.1%
40	Connecticut	27,197,000	0.2%
47	Delaware	8,059,000	0.1%
2	Florida	746,894,000	5.7%
12	Georgia	311,944,000	2.4%
39	Hawaii	30,763,000	0.2%
34	Idaho	44,622,000	0.3%
8	Illinois	573,393,000	4.4%
18	Indiana	181,195,000	1.4%
32	Iowa	48,548,000	0.4%
26	Kansas	69,899,000	0.5%
37	Kentucky	35,833,000	0.3%
20	Louisiana	164,895,000	1.3%
49	Maine	7,763,000	0.1%
22	Maryland	144,064,000	1.1%
31	Massachusetts	50,455,000	0.4%
7	Michigan	616,520,000	4.7%
13	Minnesota	222,544,000	1.7%
27	Mississippi	69,700,000	0.5%
17	Missouri	185,160,000	1.4%
36	Montana	37,410,000	0.3%
33	Nebraska	48,511,000	0.4%
21	Nevada	145,420,000	1.1%
44	New Hampshire	13,618,000	0.1%
9	New Jersey	532,173,000	4.1%
41	New Mexico	19,711,000	0.2%
4	New York	740,780,000	5.7%
28	North Carolina	56,368,000	0.4%
45	North Dakota	12,094,000	0.1%
5	Ohio	722,313,000	5.5%
35	Oklahoma	39,140,000	0.3%
19	Oregon	170,011,000	1.3%
6	Pennsylvania	617,613,000	4.7%
48	Rhode Island	8,006,000	0.1%
24	South Carolina	109,577,000	0.8%
43	South Dakota	17,046,000	0.1%
14	Tennessee	208,966,000	1.6%
3	Texas	743,543,000	5.7%
30	Utah	52,450,000	0.4%
50	Vermont	2,098,000	0.0%
16	Virginia	198,620,000	1.5%
10	Washington	465,634,000	3.6%
38	West Virginia	30,835,000	0.2%
15	Wisconsin	205,190,000	1.6%
42	Wyoming	17,474,000	0.1%

RANK ORDER

RANK	STATE	EXPENDITURES	% of USA
1	California	$3,539,083,000	27.1%
2	Florida	746,894,000	5.7%
3	Texas	743,543,000	5.7%
4	New York	740,780,000	5.7%
5	Ohio	722,313,000	5.5%
6	Pennsylvania	617,613,000	4.7%
7	Michigan	616,520,000	4.7%
8	Illinois	573,393,000	4.4%
9	New Jersey	532,173,000	4.1%
10	Washington	465,634,000	3.6%
11	Arizona	349,215,000	2.7%
12	Georgia	311,944,000	2.4%
13	Minnesota	222,544,000	1.7%
14	Tennessee	208,966,000	1.6%
15	Wisconsin	205,190,000	1.6%
16	Virginia	198,620,000	1.5%
17	Missouri	185,160,000	1.4%
18	Indiana	181,195,000	1.4%
19	Oregon	170,011,000	1.3%
20	Louisiana	164,895,000	1.3%
21	Nevada	145,420,000	1.1%
22	Maryland	144,064,000	1.1%
23	Colorado	140,164,000	1.1%
24	South Carolina	109,577,000	0.8%
25	Alabama	79,029,000	0.6%
26	Kansas	69,899,000	0.5%
27	Mississippi	69,700,000	0.5%
28	North Carolina	56,368,000	0.4%
29	Arkansas	53,582,000	0.4%
30	Utah	52,450,000	0.4%
31	Massachusetts	50,455,000	0.4%
32	Iowa	48,548,000	0.4%
33	Nebraska	48,511,000	0.4%
34	Idaho	44,622,000	0.3%
35	Oklahoma	39,140,000	0.3%
36	Montana	37,410,000	0.3%
37	Kentucky	35,833,000	0.3%
38	West Virginia	30,835,000	0.2%
39	Hawaii	30,763,000	0.2%
40	Connecticut	27,197,000	0.2%
41	New Mexico	19,711,000	0.2%
42	Wyoming	17,474,000	0.1%
43	South Dakota	17,046,000	0.1%
44	New Hampshire	13,618,000	0.1%
45	North Dakota	12,094,000	0.1%
46	Alaska	10,320,000	0.1%
47	Delaware	8,059,000	0.1%
48	Rhode Island	8,006,000	0.1%
49	Maine	7,763,000	0.1%
50	Vermont	2,098,000	0.0%
	District of Columbia	153,988,000	1.2%

Source: Morgan Quitno Press using data from U.S. Bureau of the Census
"Compendium of Government Finances 1997" (GC97(4)-5, December 2000)
*Direct general expenditures. Includes Courts, Prosecution and Legal Services and Public Defense.

Per Capita Local Government Expenditures for Judicial & Legal Services: 1997

National Per Capita = $48.84*

ALPHA ORDER

RANK ORDER

RANK	STATE	PER CAPITA		RANK	STATE	PER CAPITA
36	Alabama	$18.29		1	California	$109.85
39	Alaska	16.95		2	Nevada	86.79
4	Arizona	76.71		3	Washington	83.09
34	Arkansas	21.23		4	Arizona	76.71
1	California	109.85		5	New Jersey	66.07
22	Colorado	36.02		6	Ohio	64.42
45	Connecticut	8.32		7	Michigan	63.00
43	Delaware	10.96		8	Oregon	52.42
10	Florida	50.87		9	Pennsylvania	51.40
14	Georgia	41.67		10	Florida	50.87
30	Hawaii	25.87		11	Illinois	47.74
20	Idaho	36.86		12	Minnesota	47.47
11	Illinois	47.74		13	Montana	42.57
24	Indiana	30.86		14	Georgia	41.67
37	Iowa	17.01		15	New York	40.83
29	Kansas	26.72		16	Wisconsin	39.46
44	Kentucky	9.17		17	Tennessee	38.85
19	Louisiana	37.89		18	Texas	38.42
49	Maine	6.23		19	Louisiana	37.89
28	Maryland	28.29		20	Idaho	36.86
46	Massachusetts	8.25		21	Wyoming	36.40
7	Michigan	63.00		22	Colorado	36.02
12	Minnesota	47.47		23	Missouri	34.24
31	Mississippi	25.51		24	Indiana	30.86
23	Missouri	34.24		25	Virginia	29.50
13	Montana	42.57		26	Nebraska	29.29
26	Nebraska	29.29		27	South Carolina	28.91
2	Nevada	86.79		28	Maryland	28.29
41	New Hampshire	11.61		29	Kansas	26.72
5	New Jersey	66.07		30	Hawaii	25.87
42	New Mexico	11.44		31	Mississippi	25.51
15	New York	40.83		32	Utah	25.39
48	North Carolina	7.59		33	South Dakota	23.32
35	North Dakota	18.87		34	Arkansas	21.23
6	Ohio	64.42		35	North Dakota	18.87
40	Oklahoma	11.81		36	Alabama	18.29
8	Oregon	52.42		37	Iowa	17.01
9	Pennsylvania	51.40		38	West Virginia	16.98
47	Rhode Island	8.11		39	Alaska	16.95
27	South Carolina	28.91		40	Oklahoma	11.81
33	South Dakota	23.32		41	New Hampshire	11.61
17	Tennessee	38.85		42	New Mexico	11.44
18	Texas	38.42		43	Delaware	10.96
32	Utah	25.39		44	Kentucky	9.17
50	Vermont	3.56		45	Connecticut	8.32
25	Virginia	29.50		46	Massachusetts	8.25
3	Washington	83.09		47	Rhode Island	8.11
38	West Virginia	16.98		48	North Carolina	7.59
16	Wisconsin	39.46		49	Maine	6.23
21	Wyoming	36.40		50	Vermont	3.56

District of Columbia   291.23

Source: Morgan Quitno Press using data from U.S. Bureau of the Census
   "Compendium of Government Finances 1997" (GC97(4)-5, December 2000)
*Direct general expenditures. Includes Courts, Prosecution and Legal Services and Public Defense.

Local Government Expenditures for Judicial and Legal Services
As a Percent of All Direct General Expenditures in 1997
National Percent = 1.8% of Direct General Expenditures*

ALPHA ORDER

RANK ORDER

RANK	STATE	PERCENT		RANK	STATE	PERCENT
34	Alabama	0.9		1	California	3.4
44	Alaska	0.4		2	Arizona	3.2
2	Arizona	3.2		3	Washington	3.0
22	Arkansas	1.3		4	Nevada	2.7
1	California	3.4		5	Ohio	2.6
22	Colorado	1.3		6	Michigan	2.2
47	Connecticut	0.3		6	New Jersey	2.2
39	Delaware	0.6		8	Hawaii	2.1
11	Florida	1.8		8	Montana	2.1
16	Georgia	1.7		8	Pennsylvania	2.1
8	Hawaii	2.1		11	Florida	1.8
16	Idaho	1.7		11	Illinois	1.8
11	Illinois	1.8		11	Louisiana	1.8
22	Indiana	1.3		11	Oregon	1.8
38	Iowa	0.7		11	Tennessee	1.8
32	Kansas	1.1		16	Georgia	1.7
42	Kentucky	0.5		16	Idaho	1.7
11	Louisiana	1.8		18	Missouri	1.6
47	Maine	0.3		18	Texas	1.6
26	Maryland	1.2		20	Minnesota	1.5
44	Massachusetts	0.4		21	South Carolina	1.4
6	Michigan	2.2		22	Arkansas	1.3
20	Minnesota	1.5		22	Colorado	1.3
26	Mississippi	1.2		22	Indiana	1.3
18	Missouri	1.6		22	Wisconsin	1.3
8	Montana	2.1		26	Maryland	1.2
26	Nebraska	1.2		26	Mississippi	1.2
4	Nevada	2.7		26	Nebraska	1.2
39	New Hampshire	0.6		26	South Dakota	1.2
6	New Jersey	2.2		26	Utah	1.2
42	New Mexico	0.5		26	Virginia	1.2
34	New York	0.9		32	Kansas	1.1
47	North Carolina	0.3		32	Wyoming	1.1
34	North Dakota	0.9		34	Alabama	0.9
5	Ohio	2.6		34	New York	0.9
39	Oklahoma	0.6		34	North Dakota	0.9
11	Oregon	1.8		34	West Virginia	0.9
8	Pennsylvania	2.1		38	Iowa	0.7
44	Rhode Island	0.4		39	Delaware	0.6
21	South Carolina	1.4		39	New Hampshire	0.6
26	South Dakota	1.2		39	Oklahoma	0.6
11	Tennessee	1.8		42	Kentucky	0.5
18	Texas	1.6		42	New Mexico	0.5
26	Utah	1.2		44	Alaska	0.4
50	Vermont	0.2		44	Massachusetts	0.4
26	Virginia	1.2		44	Rhode Island	0.4
3	Washington	3.0		47	Connecticut	0.3
34	West Virginia	0.9		47	Maine	0.3
22	Wisconsin	1.3		47	North Carolina	0.3
32	Wyoming	1.1		50	Vermont	0.2
					District of Columbia	3.6

Source: Morgan Quitno Press using data from U.S. Bureau of the Census
    "Compendium of Government Finances 1997" (GC97(4)-5, December 2000)
Includes Courts, Prosecution and Legal Services and Public Defense.

State and Local Government Judicial and Legal Payroll in 1999

National Total = $15,104,785,416*

ALPHA ORDER

RANK	STATE	PAYROLL	% of USA
27	Alabama	$169,819,608	1.1%
37	Alaska	66,094,104	0.4%
10	Arizona	341,037,180	2.3%
41	Arkansas	56,998,896	0.4%
1	California	2,590,501,020	17.2%
20	Colorado	228,810,036	1.5%
24	Connecticut	183,405,756	1.2%
40	Delaware	57,395,328	0.4%
3	Florida	996,086,460	6.6%
12	Georgia	324,901,164	2.2%
33	Hawaii	106,426,920	0.7%
43	Idaho	49,817,652	0.3%
6	Illinois	653,631,216	4.3%
23	Indiana	193,410,564	1.3%
29	Iowa	129,362,364	0.9%
30	Kansas	121,285,596	0.8%
25	Kentucky	178,230,912	1.2%
21	Louisiana	194,651,952	1.3%
46	Maine	29,910,312	0.2%
15	Maryland	265,492,848	1.8%
13	Massachusetts	276,606,108	1.8%
9	Michigan	473,779,152	3.1%
16	Minnesota	256,810,932	1.7%
36	Mississippi	85,592,436	0.6%
19	Missouri	233,290,572	1.5%
45	Montana	32,116,884	0.2%
38	Nebraska	59,071,848	0.4%
28	Nevada	155,200,080	1.0%
44	New Hampshire	42,966,756	0.3%
4	New Jersey	906,377,484	6.0%
35	New Mexico	96,127,488	0.6%
2	New York	1,524,823,224	10.1%
17	North Carolina	252,528,720	1.7%
47	North Dakota	26,595,528	0.2%
7	Ohio	643,884,504	4.3%
31	Oklahoma	116,425,308	0.8%
26	Oregon	172,986,768	1.1%
8	Pennsylvania	602,876,316	4.0%
42	Rhode Island	51,935,544	0.3%
32	South Carolina	108,448,572	0.7%
48	South Dakota	26,172,624	0.2%
22	Tennessee	193,519,776	1.3%
5	Texas	773,359,368	5.1%
34	Utah	97,404,720	0.6%
49	Vermont	23,794,368	0.2%
14	Virginia	266,189,880	1.8%
11	Washington	331,635,804	2.2%
39	West Virginia	58,459,872	0.4%
18	Wisconsin	237,283,236	1.6%
50	Wyoming	22,606,956	0.1%

RANK ORDER

RANK	STATE	PAYROLL	% of USA
1	California	$2,590,501,020	17.2%
2	New York	1,524,823,224	10.1%
3	Florida	996,086,460	6.6%
4	New Jersey	906,377,484	6.0%
5	Texas	773,359,368	5.1%
6	Illinois	653,631,216	4.3%
7	Ohio	643,884,504	4.3%
8	Pennsylvania	602,876,316	4.0%
9	Michigan	473,779,152	3.1%
10	Arizona	341,037,180	2.3%
11	Washington	331,635,804	2.2%
12	Georgia	324,901,164	2.2%
13	Massachusetts	276,606,108	1.8%
14	Virginia	266,189,880	1.8%
15	Maryland	265,492,848	1.8%
16	Minnesota	256,810,932	1.7%
17	North Carolina	252,528,720	1.7%
18	Wisconsin	237,283,236	1.6%
19	Missouri	233,290,572	1.5%
20	Colorado	228,810,036	1.5%
21	Louisiana	194,651,952	1.3%
22	Tennessee	193,519,776	1.3%
23	Indiana	193,410,564	1.3%
24	Connecticut	183,405,756	1.2%
25	Kentucky	178,230,912	1.2%
26	Oregon	172,986,768	1.1%
27	Alabama	169,819,608	1.1%
28	Nevada	155,200,080	1.0%
29	Iowa	129,362,364	0.9%
30	Kansas	121,285,596	0.8%
31	Oklahoma	116,425,308	0.8%
32	South Carolina	108,448,572	0.7%
33	Hawaii	106,426,920	0.7%
34	Utah	97,404,720	0.6%
35	New Mexico	96,127,488	0.6%
36	Mississippi	85,592,436	0.6%
37	Alaska	66,094,104	0.4%
38	Nebraska	59,071,848	0.4%
39	West Virginia	58,459,872	0.4%
40	Delaware	57,395,328	0.4%
41	Arkansas	56,998,896	0.4%
42	Rhode Island	51,935,544	0.3%
43	Idaho	49,817,652	0.3%
44	New Hampshire	42,966,756	0.3%
45	Montana	32,116,884	0.2%
46	Maine	29,910,312	0.2%
47	North Dakota	26,595,528	0.2%
48	South Dakota	26,172,624	0.2%
49	Vermont	23,794,368	0.2%
50	Wyoming	22,606,956	0.1%
	District of Columbia	18,644,700	0.1%

Source: U.S. Bureau of the Census, Governments Division
"State and Local Employment and Payroll - March 1999" (http://www.census.gov/govs/www/apesstl99.html)
*Twelve times the March 1999 full-time equivalent payroll. Includes court and court related activities (except probation and parole which are part of corrections), court activities of sheriffs' offices, prosecuting attorneys' and public defenders' offices, legal departments and attorneys providing government-wide legal service.

State and Local Government Police Protection Payroll in 1999

National Total = $36,118,988,112*

ALPHA ORDER

RANK	STATE	PAYROLL	% of USA
26	Alabama	$380,037,960	1.1%
45	Alaska	88,516,668	0.2%
14	Arizona	686,118,960	1.9%
34	Arkansas	206,934,876	0.6%
1	California	5,286,548,868	14.6%
21	Colorado	534,222,540	1.5%
22	Connecticut	517,147,824	1.4%
43	Delaware	103,151,364	0.3%
4	Florida	2,098,111,932	5.8%
13	Georgia	721,543,932	2.0%
37	Hawaii	165,620,664	0.5%
41	Idaho	112,843,992	0.3%
3	Illinois	2,315,841,852	6.4%
19	Indiana	545,525,616	1.5%
32	Iowa	245,806,608	0.7%
30	Kansas	303,803,676	0.8%
29	Kentucky	313,140,552	0.9%
24	Louisiana	438,777,660	1.2%
42	Maine	104,437,584	0.3%
11	Maryland	752,690,412	2.1%
10	Massachusetts	1,044,197,088	2.9%
9	Michigan	1,055,667,456	2.9%
23	Minnesota	478,924,512	1.3%
33	Mississippi	217,569,708	0.6%
18	Missouri	577,014,048	1.6%
46	Montana	68,507,376	0.2%
38	Nebraska	150,890,712	0.4%
31	Nevada	295,855,584	0.8%
40	New Hampshire	120,183,924	0.3%
6	New Jersey	1,762,309,656	4.9%
36	New Mexico	178,356,144	0.5%
2	New York	4,429,115,448	12.3%
12	North Carolina	735,922,968	2.0%
50	North Dakota	44,364,096	0.1%
8	Ohio	1,246,536,648	3.5%
28	Oklahoma	327,910,692	0.9%
27	Oregon	378,393,924	1.0%
7	Pennsylvania	1,312,593,300	3.6%
39	Rhode Island	140,927,388	0.4%
25	South Carolina	386,090,220	1.1%
49	South Dakota	50,075,316	0.1%
20	Tennessee	539,655,396	1.5%
5	Texas	2,075,304,792	5.7%
35	Utah	196,033,896	0.5%
47	Vermont	51,229,680	0.1%
15	Virginia	676,027,452	1.9%
16	Washington	671,027,904	1.9%
44	West Virginia	99,257,160	0.3%
17	Wisconsin	617,301,000	1.7%
48	Wyoming	50,610,828	0.1%

RANK ORDER

RANK	STATE	PAYROLL	% of USA
1	California	$5,286,548,868	14.6%
2	New York	4,429,115,448	12.3%
3	Illinois	2,315,841,852	6.4%
4	Florida	2,098,111,932	5.8%
5	Texas	2,075,304,792	5.7%
6	New Jersey	1,762,309,656	4.9%
7	Pennsylvania	1,312,593,300	3.6%
8	Ohio	1,246,536,648	3.5%
9	Michigan	1,055,667,456	2.9%
10	Massachusetts	1,044,197,088	2.9%
11	Maryland	752,690,412	2.1%
12	North Carolina	735,922,968	2.0%
13	Georgia	721,543,932	2.0%
14	Arizona	686,118,960	1.9%
15	Virginia	676,027,452	1.9%
16	Washington	671,027,904	1.9%
17	Wisconsin	617,301,000	1.7%
18	Missouri	577,014,048	1.6%
19	Indiana	545,525,616	1.5%
20	Tennessee	539,655,396	1.5%
21	Colorado	534,222,540	1.5%
22	Connecticut	517,147,824	1.4%
23	Minnesota	478,924,512	1.3%
24	Louisiana	438,777,660	1.2%
25	South Carolina	386,090,220	1.1%
26	Alabama	380,037,960	1.1%
27	Oregon	378,393,924	1.0%
28	Oklahoma	327,910,692	0.9%
29	Kentucky	313,140,552	0.9%
30	Kansas	303,803,676	0.8%
31	Nevada	295,855,584	0.8%
32	Iowa	245,806,608	0.7%
33	Mississippi	217,569,708	0.6%
34	Arkansas	206,934,876	0.6%
35	Utah	196,033,896	0.5%
36	New Mexico	178,356,144	0.5%
37	Hawaii	165,620,664	0.5%
38	Nebraska	150,890,712	0.4%
39	Rhode Island	140,927,388	0.4%
40	New Hampshire	120,183,924	0.3%
41	Idaho	112,843,992	0.3%
42	Maine	104,437,584	0.3%
43	Delaware	103,151,364	0.3%
44	West Virginia	99,257,160	0.3%
45	Alaska	88,516,668	0.2%
46	Montana	68,507,376	0.2%
47	Vermont	51,229,680	0.1%
48	Wyoming	50,610,828	0.1%
49	South Dakota	50,075,316	0.1%
50	North Dakota	44,364,096	0.1%
	District of Columbia	220,310,256	0.6%

Source: U.S. Bureau of the Census, Governments Division
"State and Local Employment and Payroll - March 1999" (http://www.census.gov/govs/www/apesstl99.html)
*Twelve times the March 1999 full-time equivalent payroll. Includes all activities concerned with the enforcement of law and order, including coroners' offices, police training academies, investigation bureaus and local jails.

State and Local Government Corrections Payroll in 1999

National Total = $23,871,383,676*

ALPHA ORDER

RANK ORDER

RANK	STATE	PAYROLL	% of USA		RANK	STATE	PAYROLL	% of USA
28	Alabama	$210,262,080	0.9%		1	California	$3,559,022,856	14.9%
42	Alaska	65,708,688	0.3%		2	New York	2,744,364,060	11.5%
17	Arizona	394,878,960	1.7%		3	Texas	1,794,477,540	7.5%
34	Arkansas	126,228,528	0.5%		4	Florida	1,736,256,480	7.3%
1	California	3,559,022,856	14.9%		5	Illinois	955,859,700	4.0%
20	Colorado	337,587,708	1.4%		6	Michigan	939,815,472	3.9%
19	Connecticut	339,714,456	1.4%		7	Pennsylvania	890,920,812	3.7%
39	Delaware	77,816,256	0.3%		8	Ohio	890,853,372	3.7%
4	Florida	1,736,256,480	7.3%		9	New Jersey	744,097,596	3.1%
10	Georgia	725,075,748	3.0%		10	Georgia	725,075,748	3.0%
41	Hawaii	66,883,896	0.3%		11	North Carolina	700,947,168	2.9%
40	Idaho	76,302,660	0.3%		12	Virginia	627,501,048	2.6%
5	Illinois	955,859,700	4.0%		13	Maryland	515,609,916	2.2%
25	Indiana	285,514,992	1.2%		14	Massachusetts	490,145,436	2.1%
33	Iowa	139,486,740	0.6%		15	Washington	462,120,948	1.9%
30	Kansas	173,123,124	0.7%		16	Wisconsin	395,803,644	1.7%
31	Kentucky	161,823,324	0.7%		17	Arizona	394,878,960	1.7%
22	Louisiana	306,687,984	1.3%		18	Missouri	340,534,908	1.4%
44	Maine	48,781,332	0.2%		19	Connecticut	339,714,456	1.4%
13	Maryland	515,609,916	2.2%		20	Colorado	337,587,708	1.4%
14	Massachusetts	490,145,436	2.1%		21	Minnesota	309,052,104	1.3%
6	Michigan	939,815,472	3.9%		22	Louisiana	306,687,984	1.3%
21	Minnesota	309,052,104	1.3%		23	Tennessee	289,096,008	1.2%
35	Mississippi	120,505,488	0.5%		24	Oregon	286,180,968	1.2%
18	Missouri	340,534,908	1.4%		25	Indiana	285,514,992	1.2%
45	Montana	40,979,340	0.2%		26	South Carolina	281,035,092	1.2%
38	Nebraska	80,755,836	0.3%		27	Oklahoma	232,703,520	1.0%
29	Nevada	196,578,108	0.8%		28	Alabama	210,262,080	0.9%
43	New Hampshire	54,327,864	0.2%		29	Nevada	196,578,108	0.8%
9	New Jersey	744,097,596	3.1%		30	Kansas	173,123,124	0.7%
32	New Mexico	156,907,908	0.7%		31	Kentucky	161,823,324	0.7%
2	New York	2,744,364,060	11.5%		32	New Mexico	156,907,908	0.7%
11	North Carolina	700,947,168	2.9%		33	Iowa	139,486,740	0.6%
50	North Dakota	20,311,500	0.1%		34	Arkansas	126,228,528	0.5%
8	Ohio	890,853,372	3.7%		35	Mississippi	120,505,488	0.5%
27	Oklahoma	232,703,520	1.0%		36	Utah	119,711,964	0.5%
24	Oregon	286,180,968	1.2%		37	Rhode Island	87,852,468	0.4%
7	Pennsylvania	890,920,812	3.7%		38	Nebraska	80,755,836	0.3%
37	Rhode Island	87,852,468	0.4%		39	Delaware	77,816,256	0.3%
26	South Carolina	281,035,092	1.2%		40	Idaho	76,302,660	0.3%
47	South Dakota	32,608,944	0.1%		41	Hawaii	66,883,896	0.3%
23	Tennessee	289,096,008	1.2%		42	Alaska	65,708,688	0.3%
3	Texas	1,794,477,540	7.5%		43	New Hampshire	54,327,864	0.2%
36	Utah	119,711,964	0.5%		44	Maine	48,781,332	0.2%
48	Vermont	31,670,628	0.1%		45	Montana	40,979,340	0.2%
12	Virginia	627,501,048	2.6%		46	West Virginia	35,047,740	0.1%
15	Washington	462,120,948	1.9%		47	South Dakota	32,608,944	0.1%
46	West Virginia	35,047,740	0.1%		48	Vermont	31,670,628	0.1%
16	Wisconsin	395,803,644	1.7%		49	Wyoming	26,168,508	0.1%
49	Wyoming	26,168,508	0.1%		50	North Dakota	20,311,500	0.1%
						District of Columbia	145,682,256	0.6%

Source: U.S. Bureau of the Census, Governments Division
"State and Local Employment and Payroll - March 1999" (http://www.census.gov/govs/www/apesstl99.html)
*Twelve times the March 1999 full-time equivalent payroll. Includes all activities pertaining to the confinement and correction of adults and minors accused or convicted of criminal offenses. Includes any pardon, probation or parole activity.

Base Salary for Justices of States' Highest Courts in 2000

National Average = $116,184

ALPHA ORDER

RANK	STATE	SALARY
7	Alabama	$140,950
30	Alaska	112,224
18	Arizona	120,500
21	Arkansas	117,296
4	California	149,686
40	Colorado	99,986
14	Connecticut	124,683
9	Delaware	132,100
3	Florida	150,000
5	Georgia	147,909
38	Hawaii	101,432
43	Idaho	97,727
1	Illinois	153,052
25	Indiana	115,000
28	Iowa	113,200
33	Kansas	109,756
27	Kentucky	114,373
36	Louisiana	103,336
39	Maine	100,169
17	Maryland	121,600
12	Massachusetts	126,943
8	Michigan	140,816
32	Minnesota	110,998
37	Mississippi	102,300
16	Missouri	123,000
50	Montana	83,550
31	Nebraska	111,003
13	Nevada	126,103
35	New Hampshire	106,518
6	New Jersey	145,881
48	New Mexico	90,407
2	New York	151,200
24	North Carolina	115,336
49	North Dakota	85,483
22	Ohio	117,250
42	Oklahoma	97,807
46	Oregon	93,600
10	Pennsylvania	131,022
19	Rhode Island	118,650
23	South Carolina	117,167
45	South Dakota	94,886
26	Tennessee	114,528
29	Texas	113,000
34	Utah	109,700
41	Vermont	99,489
11	Virginia	128,352
15	Washington	123,600
44	West Virginia	95,000
20	Wisconsin	117,998
47	Wyoming	93,000

RANK ORDER

RANK	STATE	SALARY
1	Illinois	$153,052
2	New York	151,200
3	Florida	150,000
4	California	149,686
5	Georgia	147,909
6	New Jersey	145,881
7	Alabama	140,950
8	Michigan	140,816
9	Delaware	132,100
10	Pennsylvania	131,022
11	Virginia	128,352
12	Massachusetts	126,943
13	Nevada	126,103
14	Connecticut	124,683
15	Washington	123,600
16	Missouri	123,000
17	Maryland	121,600
18	Arizona	120,500
19	Rhode Island	118,650
20	Wisconsin	117,998
21	Arkansas	117,296
22	Ohio	117,250
23	South Carolina	117,167
24	North Carolina	115,336
25	Indiana	115,000
26	Tennessee	114,528
27	Kentucky	114,373
28	Iowa	113,200
29	Texas	113,000
30	Alaska	112,224
31	Nebraska	111,003
32	Minnesota	110,998
33	Kansas	109,756
34	Utah	109,700
35	New Hampshire	106,518
36	Louisiana	103,336
37	Mississippi	102,300
38	Hawaii	101,432
39	Maine	100,169
40	Colorado	99,986
41	Vermont	99,489
42	Oklahoma	97,807
43	Idaho	97,727
44	West Virginia	95,000
45	South Dakota	94,886
46	Oregon	93,600
47	Wyoming	93,000
48	New Mexico	90,407
49	North Dakota	85,483
50	Montana	83,550
	District of Columbia	149,900

Source: National Center for State Courts
  "Survey of Judicial Salaries-Winter 2000" (Volume 26, Number 1)

Base Salary for Judges of Intermediate Appellate Courts in 2000

National Average = $114,280

ALPHA ORDER

RANK	STATE	SALARY
6	Alabama	$139,580
27	Alaska	106,020
11	Arizona	118,000
18	Arkansas	113,586
5	California	140,332
36	Colorado	95,486
14	Connecticut	116,267
NA	Delaware*	NA
7	Florida	138,500
1	Georgia	146,994
33	Hawaii	97,106
34	Idaho	96,727
2	Illinois	144,049
21	Indiana	110,000
25	Iowa	108,900
28	Kansas	105,955
22	Kentucky	109,705
32	Louisiana	97,928
NA	Maine*	NA
16	Maryland	114,400
12	Massachusetts	117,467
8	Michigan	129,551
31	Minnesota	104,589
35	Mississippi	95,500
15	Missouri	115,000
NA	Montana*	NA
29	Nebraska	105,543
NA	Nevada*	NA
NA	New Hampshire*	NA
4	New Jersey	141,176
39	New Mexico	85,887
3	New York	144,000
20	North Carolina	110,530
NA	North Dakota*	NA
23	Ohio	109,250
37	Oklahoma	93,530
38	Oregon	91,500
9	Pennsylvania	126,919
NA	Rhode Island*	NA
17	South Carolina	114,237
NA	South Dakota*	NA
24	Tennessee	109,200
26	Texas	107,350
30	Utah	104,700
NA	Vermont*	NA
10	Virginia	121,936
13	Washington	117,420
NA	West Virginia*	NA
19	Wisconsin	112,100
NA	Wyoming*	NA

RANK ORDER

RANK	STATE	SALARY
1	Georgia	$146,994
2	Illinois	144,049
3	New York	144,000
4	New Jersey	141,176
5	California	140,332
6	Alabama	139,580
7	Florida	138,500
8	Michigan	129,551
9	Pennsylvania	126,919
10	Virginia	121,936
11	Arizona	118,000
12	Massachusetts	117,467
13	Washington	117,420
14	Connecticut	116,267
15	Missouri	115,000
16	Maryland	114,400
17	South Carolina	114,237
18	Arkansas	113,586
19	Wisconsin	112,100
20	North Carolina	110,530
21	Indiana	110,000
22	Kentucky	109,705
23	Ohio	109,250
24	Tennessee	109,200
25	Iowa	108,900
26	Texas	107,350
27	Alaska	106,020
28	Kansas	105,955
29	Nebraska	105,543
30	Utah	104,700
31	Minnesota	104,589
32	Louisiana	97,928
33	Hawaii	97,106
34	Idaho	96,727
35	Mississippi	95,500
36	Colorado	95,486
37	Oklahoma	93,530
38	Oregon	91,500
39	New Mexico	85,887
NA	Delaware*	NA
NA	Maine*	NA
NA	Montana*	NA
NA	Nevada*	NA
NA	New Hampshire*	NA
NA	North Dakota*	NA
NA	Rhode Island*	NA
NA	South Dakota*	NA
NA	Vermont*	NA
NA	West Virginia*	NA
NA	Wyoming*	NA
	District of Columbia*	NA

Source: National Center for State Courts
"Survey of Judicial Salaries-Winter 2000" (Volume 26, Number 1)
*No intermediate court.

Base Salary for Judges of General Trial Courts in 2000

National Average = $104,349

ALPHA ORDER

RANK	STATE	SALARY
29	Alabama	$100,526
25	Alaska	103,776
10	Arizona	115,500
18	Arkansas	109,871
7	California	122,628
41	Colorado	90,986
15	Connecticut	111,279
6	Delaware	125,900
4	Florida	130,000
5	Georgia	127,938
38	Hawaii	93,861
40	Idaho	91,596
3	Illinois	132,182
42	Indiana	90,000
26	Iowa	103,500
34	Kansas	95,847
22	Kentucky	105,037
39	Louisiana	92,520
37	Maine	93,908
16	Maryland	110,500
12	Massachusetts	112,777
8	Michigan	119,694
33	Minnesota	98,180
35	Mississippi	94,700
19	Missouri	108,000
50	Montana	77,439
27	Nebraska	102,678
17	Nevada	110,000
31	New Hampshire	99,860
2	New Jersey	133,330
48	New Mexico	81,593
1	New York	136,700
23	North Carolina	104,523
49	North Dakota	78,887
30	Ohio	100,500
45	Oklahoma	88,511
46	Oregon	85,300
11	Pennsylvania	113,789
20	Rhode Island	106,825
14	South Carolina	111,309
44	South Dakota	88,630
24	Tennessee	104,484
28	Texas	101,700
32	Utah	99,700
36	Vermont	94,504
9	Virginia	119,154
13	Washington	111,549
42	West Virginia	90,000
21	Wisconsin	105,755
47	Wyoming	83,700

RANK ORDER

RANK	STATE	SALARY
1	New York	$136,700
2	New Jersey	133,330
3	Illinois	132,182
4	Florida	130,000
5	Georgia	127,938
6	Delaware	125,900
7	California	122,628
8	Michigan	119,694
9	Virginia	119,154
10	Arizona	115,500
11	Pennsylvania	113,789
12	Massachusetts	112,777
13	Washington	111,549
14	South Carolina	111,309
15	Connecticut	111,279
16	Maryland	110,500
17	Nevada	110,000
18	Arkansas	109,871
19	Missouri	108,000
20	Rhode Island	106,825
21	Wisconsin	105,755
22	Kentucky	105,037
23	North Carolina	104,523
24	Tennessee	104,484
25	Alaska	103,776
26	Iowa	103,500
27	Nebraska	102,678
28	Texas	101,700
29	Alabama	100,526
30	Ohio	100,500
31	New Hampshire	99,860
32	Utah	99,700
33	Minnesota	98,180
34	Kansas	95,847
35	Mississippi	94,700
36	Vermont	94,504
37	Maine	93,908
38	Hawaii	93,861
39	Louisiana	92,520
40	Idaho	91,596
41	Colorado	90,986
42	Indiana	90,000
42	West Virginia	90,000
44	South Dakota	88,630
45	Oklahoma	88,511
46	Oregon	85,300
47	Wyoming	83,700
48	New Mexico	81,593
49	North Dakota	78,887
50	Montana	77,439
	District of Columbia	141,300

Source: National Center for State Courts
"Survey of Judicial Salaries-Winter 2000" (Volume 26, Number 1)

V. JUVENILES

184   Reported Arrests of Juveniles in 1999
185   Reported Juvenile Arrest Rate in 1999
186   Reported Arrests of Juveniles as a Percent of All Arrests in 1999
187   Reported Arrests of Juveniles for Crime Index Offenses in 1999
188   Reported Juvenile Arrest Rate for Crime Index Offenses in 1999
189   Reported Arrests of Juveniles for Crime Index Offenses as a Percent of All Such Arrests in 1999
190   Reported Arrests of Juveniles for Violent Crime in 1999
191   Reported Juvenile Arrest Rate for Violent Crime in 1999
192   Reported Arrests of Juveniles for Violent Crime as a Percent of All Such Arrests in 1999
193   Reported Arrests of Juveniles for Murder in 1999
194   Reported Juvenile Arrest Rate for Murder in 1999
195   Reported Arrests of Juveniles for Murder as a Percent of All Such Arrests in 1999
196   Reported Arrests of Juveniles for Rape in 1999
197   Reported Juvenile Arrest Rate for Rape in 1999
198   Reported Arrests of Juveniles for Rape as a Percent of All Such Arrests in 1999
199   Reported Arrests of Juveniles for Robbery in 1999
200   Reported Juvenile Arrest Rate for Robbery in 1999
201   Reported Arrests of Juveniles for Robbery as a Percent of All Such Arrests in 1999
202   Reported Arrests of Juveniles for Aggravated Assault in 1999
203   Reported Juvenile Arrest Rate for Aggravated Assault in 1999
204   Reported Arrests of Juveniles for Aggravated Assault as a Percent of All Such Arrests in 1999
205   Reported Arrests of Juveniles for Property Crime in 1999
206   Reported Juvenile Arrest Rate for Property Crime in 1999
207   Reported Arrests of Juveniles for Property Crime as a Percent of All Such Arrests in 1999
208   Reported Arrests of Juveniles for Burglary in 1999
209   Reported Juvenile Arrest Rate for Burglary in 1999
210   Reported Arrests of Juveniles for Burglary as a Percent of All Such Arrests in 1999
211   Reported Arrests of Juveniles for Larceny and Theft in 1999
212   Reported Juvenile Arrest Rate for Larceny and Theft in 1999
213   Reported Arrests of Juveniles for Larceny and Theft as a Percent of All Such Arrests in 1999
214   Reported Arrests of Juveniles for Motor Vehicle Theft in 1999
215   Reported Juvenile Arrest Rate for Motor Vehicle Theft in 1999
216   Reported Arrests of Juveniles for Motor Vehicle Theft as a Percent of All Such Arrests in 1999
217   Reported Arrests of Juveniles for Arson in 1999
218   Reported Juvenile Arrest Rate for Arson in 1999
219   Reported Arrests of Juveniles for Arson as a Percent of All Such Arrests in 1999
220   Reported Arrests of Juveniles for Weapons Violations in 1999
221   Reported Juvenile Arrest Rate for Weapons Violations in 1999
222   Reported Arrests of Juveniles for Weapons Violations as a Percent of All Such Arrests in 1999
223   Reported Arrests of Juveniles for Driving Under the Influence in 1999
224   Reported Juvenile Arrest Rate for Driving Under the Influence in 1999
225   Reported Arrests of Juveniles for Driving Under the Influence as a Percent of All Such Arrests in 1999
226   Reported Arrests of Juveniles for Drug Abuse Violations in 1999
227   Reported Juvenile Arrest Rate for Drug Abuse Violations in 1999
228   Reported Arrests of Juveniles for Drug Abuse Violations as a Percent of All Such Arrests in 1999
229   Reported Arrests of Juveniles for Sex Offenses in 1999
230   Reported Juvenile Arrest Rate for Sex Offenses in 1999
231   Reported Arrests of Juveniles for Sex Offenses as a Percent of All Such Arrests in 1999
232   Reported Arrests of Juveniles for Prostitution and Commercialized Vice in 1999
233   Reported Juvenile Arrest Rate for Prostitution and Commercialized Vice in 1999
234   Reported Arrests of Juveniles for Prostitution and Commercialized Vice as a Percent of All Such Arrests in 1999
235   Reported Arrests of Juveniles for Offenses Against Families & Children in 1999
236   Reported Juvenile Arrest Rate for Offenses Against Families & Children in 1999
237   Reported Arrests of Juveniles for Offenses Against Families and Children as a Percent of All Such Arrests in 1999
238   Juvenile Death Sentences: 1973 to 2000
239   Juveniles in Custody in 1997
240   Rate of Juveniles in Custody in 1997
241   White Juvenile Custody Rate in 1997
242   Black Juvenile Custody Rate in 1997
243   High School Dropout Rate in 1998
244   Percent of High School Students Who Carried a Weapon on School Property in the Previous Month: 1999

V. JUVENILES (continued)

245 Percent of High School Students Threatened or Injured with a Weapon on School Property in 1999
246 Percent of Teens Who Drink Alcohol: 1999
247 Percent of Teens Who Use Marijuana: 1999
248 Admissions of Juveniles to Alcohol and Other Drug Treatment Programs in 1997
249 Admissions of Juveniles to Alcohol and Other Drug Treatment Programs as a Percent of All Admissions in 1997
250 Victims of Child Abuse and Neglect in 1998
251 Rate of Child Abuse and Neglect in 1998
252 Physically Abused Children in 1998
253 Rate of Physically Abused Children in 1998
254 Sexually Abused Children in 1998
255 Rate of Sexually Abused Children in 1998
256 Emotionally Abused Children in 1998
257 Rate of Emotionally Abused Children in 1998
258 Neglected Children in 1998
259 Rate of Neglected Children in 1998
260 Child Abuse and Neglect Fatalities in 1998
261 Rate of Child Abuse and Neglect Fatalities in 1998

Important Note Regarding Juvenile Arrest Rates

The juvenile arrest rates shown in tables 185 to 236 were calculated by the editors as follows:

The state arrest numbers reported by the FBI are only from those law enforcement agencies that submitted complete arrests reports for 12 months in 1999. Included in the FBI report are population totals of these reporting jurisdictions by state. Using these FBI population figures, we first determined what percentage the FBI numbers represented of each state's total resident population. Next, using 1999 US Census Bureau state estimates for 10 to 17-year-olds, we multiplied the percentages derived from the FBI population figures into the Census Bureau's total juvenile population estimates. The resulting juvenile population is the base that was used to determine juvenile arrests per 100,000 juvenile population. The national rate was calculated in the same manner.

Reports from law enforcement agencies in Georgia, Illinois, Kentucky, Mississippi, Montana, New Hampshire, New York and South Carolina represented less than half of their state populations. Thus rates for these states should be interpreted with caution. Reports from Ohio, Tennessee and West Virginia represented just over half of their state population. No arrest data were available for Kansas, Maine, Oklahoma, Wisconsin and the District of Columbia.

Reported Arrests of Juveniles in 1999

National Total = 1,720,169 Reported Arrests*

ALPHA ORDER

RANK ORDER

RANK	STATE	ARRESTS	% of USA	RANK	STATE	ARRESTS	% of USA
31	Alabama	13,577	0.8%	1	California	258,091	15.0%
41	Alaska	5,470	0.3%	2	Texas	183,097	10.6%
8	Arizona	56,492	3.3%	3	Florida	131,330	7.6%
28	Arkansas	18,386	1.1%	4	Pennsylvania	89,469	5.2%
1	California	258,091	15.0%	5	New Jersey	69,658	4.0%
15	Colorado	41,895	2.4%	6	Minnesota	61,255	3.6%
22	Connecticut	24,206	1.4%	7	Ohio	58,824	3.4%
39	Delaware	6,895	0.4%	8	Arizona	56,492	3.3%
3	Florida	131,330	7.6%	9	North Carolina	50,964	3.0%
26	Georgia	21,846	1.3%	10	Washington	46,081	2.7%
33	Hawaii	11,580	0.7%	11	Illinois	45,448	2.6%
30	Idaho	16,975	1.0%	12	New York	44,925	2.6%
11	Illinois	45,448	2.6%	13	Michigan	44,535	2.6%
18	Indiana	33,526	1.9%	14	Louisiana	42,419	2.5%
25	Iowa	22,414	1.3%	15	Colorado	41,895	2.4%
NA	Kansas**	NA	NA	16	Oregon	35,349	2.1%
44	Kentucky	4,382	0.3%	17	Virginia	34,365	2.0%
14	Louisiana	42,419	2.5%	18	Indiana	33,526	1.9%
NA	Maine**	NA	NA	19	Missouri	31,867	1.9%
20	Maryland	27,771	1.6%	20	Maryland	27,771	1.6%
29	Massachusetts	18,346	1.1%	21	Nevada	25,075	1.5%
13	Michigan	44,535	2.6%	22	Connecticut	24,206	1.4%
6	Minnesota	61,255	3.6%	23	Utah	23,287	1.4%
32	Mississippi	13,347	0.8%	24	Tennessee	22,692	1.3%
19	Missouri	31,867	1.9%	25	Iowa	22,414	1.3%
42	Montana	5,129	0.3%	26	Georgia	21,846	1.3%
27	Nebraska	19,380	1.1%	27	Nebraska	19,380	1.1%
21	Nevada	25,075	1.5%	28	Arkansas	18,386	1.1%
43	New Hampshire	4,801	0.3%	29	Massachusetts	18,346	1.1%
5	New Jersey	69,658	4.0%	30	Idaho	16,975	1.0%
34	New Mexico	10,294	0.6%	31	Alabama	13,577	0.8%
12	New York	44,925	2.6%	32	Mississippi	13,347	0.8%
9	North Carolina	50,964	3.0%	33	Hawaii	11,580	0.7%
40	North Dakota	6,535	0.4%	34	New Mexico	10,294	0.6%
7	Ohio	58,824	3.4%	35	South Carolina	8,560	0.5%
NA	Oklahoma**	NA	NA	36	Wyoming	8,535	0.5%
16	Oregon	35,349	2.1%	37	South Dakota	8,215	0.5%
4	Pennsylvania	89,469	5.2%	38	Rhode Island	7,261	0.4%
38	Rhode Island	7,261	0.4%	39	Delaware	6,895	0.4%
35	South Carolina	8,560	0.5%	40	North Dakota	6,535	0.4%
37	South Dakota	8,215	0.5%	41	Alaska	5,470	0.3%
24	Tennessee	22,692	1.3%	42	Montana	5,129	0.3%
2	Texas	183,097	10.6%	43	New Hampshire	4,801	0.3%
23	Utah	23,287	1.4%	44	Kentucky	4,382	0.3%
46	Vermont	2,398	0.1%	45	West Virginia	3,222	0.2%
17	Virginia	34,365	2.0%	46	Vermont	2,398	0.1%
10	Washington	46,081	2.7%	NA	Kansas**	NA	NA
45	West Virginia	3,222	0.2%	NA	Maine**	NA	NA
NA	Wisconsin**	NA	NA	NA	Oklahoma**	NA	NA
36	Wyoming	8,535	0.5%	NA	Wisconsin**	NA	NA
					District of Columbia**	NA	NA

Source: Federal Bureau of Investigation
    "Crime in the United States 1999" (Uniform Crime Reports, October 15, 2000)
*Arrests of youths 17 years and younger by law enforcement agencies submitting complete reports to the F.B.I. for 12 months in 1999. See important note at beginning of this chapter.
**Not available.

Reported Juvenile Arrest Rate in 1999

National Rate = 8,001.5 Reported Arrests per 100,000 Juvenile Population*

ALPHA ORDER

RANK	STATE	RATE
46	Alabama	3,071.0
39	Alaska	6,668.6
10	Arizona	10,767.1
41	Arkansas	6,417.4
35	California	6,975.2
2	Colorado	13,843.2
36	Connecticut	6,872.4
21	Delaware	8,546.3
28	Florida	8,199.1
32	Georgia	7,699.4
11	Hawaii	10,675.6
6	Idaho	12,020.4
1	Illinois	14,132.1
24	Indiana	8,379.7
29	Iowa	8,033.7
NA	Kansas**	NA
18	Kentucky	8,851.5
12	Louisiana	10,239.0
NA	Maine**	NA
31	Maryland	7,961.2
44	Massachusetts	3,597.5
42	Michigan	4,600.0
7	Minnesota	11,876.9
15	Mississippi	9,732.1
22	Missouri	8,512.1
16	Montana	9,327.0
13	Nebraska	10,013.6
4	Nevada	12,388.8
23	New Hampshire	8,499.5
26	New Jersey	8,307.9
30	New Mexico	7,990.4
34	New York	7,437.1
38	North Carolina	6,741.3
9	North Dakota	11,099.8
25	Ohio	8,368.3
NA	Oklahoma**	NA
14	Oregon	9,779.6
19	Pennsylvania	8,702.8
40	Rhode Island	6,660.9
20	South Carolina	8,578.1
5	South Dakota	12,129.0
33	Tennessee	7,469.8
27	Texas	8,242.5
8	Utah	11,106.5
43	Vermont	4,243.4
37	Virginia	6,857.6
17	Washington	9,150.2
45	West Virginia	3,206.4
NA	Wisconsin**	NA
3	Wyoming	13,624.8

RANK ORDER

RANK	STATE	RATE
1	Illinois	14,132.1
2	Colorado	13,843.2
3	Wyoming	13,624.8
4	Nevada	12,388.8
5	South Dakota	12,129.0
6	Idaho	12,020.4
7	Minnesota	11,876.9
8	Utah	11,106.5
9	North Dakota	11,099.8
10	Arizona	10,767.1
11	Hawaii	10,675.6
12	Louisiana	10,239.0
13	Nebraska	10,013.6
14	Oregon	9,779.6
15	Mississippi	9,732.1
16	Montana	9,327.0
17	Washington	9,150.2
18	Kentucky	8,851.5
19	Pennsylvania	8,702.8
20	South Carolina	8,578.1
21	Delaware	8,546.3
22	Missouri	8,512.1
23	New Hampshire	8,499.5
24	Indiana	8,379.7
25	Ohio	8,368.3
26	New Jersey	8,307.9
27	Texas	8,242.5
28	Florida	8,199.1
29	Iowa	8,033.7
30	New Mexico	7,990.4
31	Maryland	7,961.2
32	Georgia	7,699.4
33	Tennessee	7,469.8
34	New York	7,437.1
35	California	6,975.2
36	Connecticut	6,872.4
37	Virginia	6,857.6
38	North Carolina	6,741.3
39	Alaska	6,668.6
40	Rhode Island	6,660.9
41	Arkansas	6,417.4
42	Michigan	4,600.0
43	Vermont	4,243.4
44	Massachusetts	3,597.5
45	West Virginia	3,206.4
46	Alabama	3,071.0
NA	Kansas**	NA
NA	Maine**	NA
NA	Oklahoma**	NA
NA	Wisconsin**	NA
	District of Columbia**	NA

Source: Morgan Quitno Press using data from Federal Bureau of Investigation
"Crime in the United States 1999" (Uniform Crime Reports, October 15, 2000)
*By law enforcement agencies submitting complete reports to the F.B.I. for 12 months in 1999. Arrests of youths 17 years and younger divided into population of 10 to 17 year olds. See important note at beginning of this chapter.
**Not available.

Reported Arrests of Juveniles as a Percent of All Arrests in 1999

National Percent = 17.1% of Reported Arrests*

<table>
<tr><td colspan="3">ALPHA ORDER</td><td colspan="3">RANK ORDER</td></tr>
<tr><td>RANK</td><td>STATE</td><td>PERCENT</td><td>RANK</td><td>STATE</td><td>PERCENT</td></tr>
<tr><td>46</td><td>Alabama</td><td>7.7</td><td>1</td><td>Montana</td><td>37.3</td></tr>
<tr><td>32</td><td>Alaska</td><td>15.1</td><td>2</td><td>North Dakota</td><td>27.2</td></tr>
<tr><td>14</td><td>Arizona</td><td>20.7</td><td>3</td><td>Idaho</td><td>26.9</td></tr>
<tr><td>45</td><td>Arkansas</td><td>8.6</td><td>4</td><td>Minnesota</td><td>26.4</td></tr>
<tr><td>26</td><td>California</td><td>17.3</td><td>5</td><td>Oregon</td><td>25.9</td></tr>
<tr><td>17</td><td>Colorado</td><td>19.0</td><td>6</td><td>South Dakota</td><td>24.9</td></tr>
<tr><td>30</td><td>Connecticut</td><td>15.8</td><td>6</td><td>Wyoming</td><td>24.9</td></tr>
<tr><td>24</td><td>Delaware</td><td>18.0</td><td>8</td><td>Utah</td><td>24.8</td></tr>
<tr><td>33</td><td>Florida</td><td>14.6</td><td>9</td><td>Pennsylvania</td><td>23.8</td></tr>
<tr><td>35</td><td>Georgia</td><td>13.9</td><td>10</td><td>Hawaii</td><td>22.3</td></tr>
<tr><td>10</td><td>Hawaii</td><td>22.3</td><td>11</td><td>Iowa</td><td>21.9</td></tr>
<tr><td>3</td><td>Idaho</td><td>26.9</td><td>12</td><td>New Hampshire</td><td>21.4</td></tr>
<tr><td>21</td><td>Illinois</td><td>18.3</td><td>13</td><td>Washington</td><td>21.1</td></tr>
<tr><td>25</td><td>Indiana</td><td>17.8</td><td>14</td><td>Arizona</td><td>20.7</td></tr>
<tr><td>11</td><td>Iowa</td><td>21.9</td><td>15</td><td>Nebraska</td><td>20.3</td></tr>
<tr><td>NA</td><td>Kansas**</td><td>NA</td><td>15</td><td>Ohio</td><td>20.3</td></tr>
<tr><td>44</td><td>Kentucky</td><td>9.7</td><td>17</td><td>Colorado</td><td>19.0</td></tr>
<tr><td>18</td><td>Louisiana</td><td>18.8</td><td>18</td><td>Louisiana</td><td>18.8</td></tr>
<tr><td>NA</td><td>Maine**</td><td>NA</td><td>19</td><td>Texas</td><td>18.6</td></tr>
<tr><td>29</td><td>Maryland</td><td>16.0</td><td>20</td><td>New Jersey</td><td>18.4</td></tr>
<tr><td>34</td><td>Massachusetts</td><td>14.4</td><td>21</td><td>Illinois</td><td>18.3</td></tr>
<tr><td>38</td><td>Michigan</td><td>13.1</td><td>22</td><td>Nevada</td><td>18.2</td></tr>
<tr><td>4</td><td>Minnesota</td><td>26.4</td><td>23</td><td>Rhode Island</td><td>18.1</td></tr>
<tr><td>36</td><td>Mississippi</td><td>13.5</td><td>24</td><td>Delaware</td><td>18.0</td></tr>
<tr><td>39</td><td>Missouri</td><td>12.9</td><td>25</td><td>Indiana</td><td>17.8</td></tr>
<tr><td>1</td><td>Montana</td><td>37.3</td><td>26</td><td>California</td><td>17.3</td></tr>
<tr><td>15</td><td>Nebraska</td><td>20.3</td><td>27</td><td>Vermont</td><td>16.9</td></tr>
<tr><td>22</td><td>Nevada</td><td>18.2</td><td>28</td><td>New York</td><td>16.8</td></tr>
<tr><td>12</td><td>New Hampshire</td><td>21.4</td><td>29</td><td>Maryland</td><td>16.0</td></tr>
<tr><td>20</td><td>New Jersey</td><td>18.4</td><td>30</td><td>Connecticut</td><td>15.8</td></tr>
<tr><td>31</td><td>New Mexico</td><td>15.2</td><td>31</td><td>New Mexico</td><td>15.2</td></tr>
<tr><td>28</td><td>New York</td><td>16.8</td><td>32</td><td>Alaska</td><td>15.1</td></tr>
<tr><td>42</td><td>North Carolina</td><td>11.0</td><td>33</td><td>Florida</td><td>14.6</td></tr>
<tr><td>2</td><td>North Dakota</td><td>27.2</td><td>34</td><td>Massachusetts</td><td>14.4</td></tr>
<tr><td>15</td><td>Ohio</td><td>20.3</td><td>35</td><td>Georgia</td><td>13.9</td></tr>
<tr><td>NA</td><td>Oklahoma**</td><td>NA</td><td>36</td><td>Mississippi</td><td>13.5</td></tr>
<tr><td>5</td><td>Oregon</td><td>25.9</td><td>37</td><td>Tennessee</td><td>13.4</td></tr>
<tr><td>9</td><td>Pennsylvania</td><td>23.8</td><td>38</td><td>Michigan</td><td>13.1</td></tr>
<tr><td>23</td><td>Rhode Island</td><td>18.1</td><td>39</td><td>Missouri</td><td>12.9</td></tr>
<tr><td>41</td><td>South Carolina</td><td>12.1</td><td>40</td><td>Virginia</td><td>12.7</td></tr>
<tr><td>6</td><td>South Dakota</td><td>24.9</td><td>41</td><td>South Carolina</td><td>12.1</td></tr>
<tr><td>37</td><td>Tennessee</td><td>13.4</td><td>42</td><td>North Carolina</td><td>11.0</td></tr>
<tr><td>19</td><td>Texas</td><td>18.6</td><td>43</td><td>West Virginia</td><td>10.0</td></tr>
<tr><td>8</td><td>Utah</td><td>24.8</td><td>44</td><td>Kentucky</td><td>9.7</td></tr>
<tr><td>27</td><td>Vermont</td><td>16.9</td><td>45</td><td>Arkansas</td><td>8.6</td></tr>
<tr><td>40</td><td>Virginia</td><td>12.7</td><td>46</td><td>Alabama</td><td>7.7</td></tr>
<tr><td>13</td><td>Washington</td><td>21.1</td><td>NA</td><td>Kansas**</td><td>NA</td></tr>
<tr><td>43</td><td>West Virginia</td><td>10.0</td><td>NA</td><td>Maine**</td><td>NA</td></tr>
<tr><td>NA</td><td>Wisconsin**</td><td>NA</td><td>NA</td><td>Oklahoma**</td><td>NA</td></tr>
<tr><td>6</td><td>Wyoming</td><td>24.9</td><td>NA</td><td>Wisconsin**</td><td>NA</td></tr>
<tr><td></td><td></td><td></td><td colspan="2">District of Columbia**</td><td>NA</td></tr>
</table>

Source: Morgan Quitno Press using data from Federal Bureau of Investigation
    "Crime in the United States 1999" (Uniform Crime Reports, October 15, 2000)
*Arrests of youths 17 years and younger by law enforcement agencies submitting complete reports to the F.B.I. for 12 months in 1999.
**Not available.

Reported Arrests of Juveniles for Crime Index Offenses in 1999

National Total = 474,510 Reported Arrests*

<u>ALPHA ORDER</u>

RANK	STATE	ARRESTS	% of USA
30	Alabama	4,790	1.0%
37	Alaska	2,120	0.4%
8	Arizona	13,902	2.9%
28	Arkansas	5,175	1.1%
1	California	79,163	16.7%
17	Colorado	9,586	2.0%
21	Connecticut	6,306	1.3%
36	Delaware	2,230	0.5%
2	Florida	53,967	11.4%
29	Georgia	5,059	1.1%
35	Hawaii	2,479	0.5%
31	Idaho	3,864	0.8%
13	Illinois	11,907	2.5%
18	Indiana	8,409	1.8%
22	Iowa	6,298	1.3%
NA	Kansas**	NA	NA
42	Kentucky	1,393	0.3%
14	Louisiana	11,756	2.5%
NA	Maine**	NA	NA
20	Maryland	7,995	1.7%
25	Massachusetts	6,055	1.3%
10	Michigan	12,643	2.7%
9	Minnesota	13,707	2.9%
32	Mississippi	3,120	0.7%
16	Missouri	9,675	2.0%
38	Montana	2,092	0.4%
27	Nebraska	5,496	1.2%
26	Nevada	5,718	1.2%
45	New Hampshire	781	0.2%
7	New Jersey	15,372	3.2%
33	New Mexico	2,999	0.6%
11	New York	12,625	2.7%
6	North Carolina	15,453	3.3%
43	North Dakota	1,321	0.3%
12	Ohio	12,325	2.6%
NA	Oklahoma**	NA	NA
15	Oregon	9,847	2.1%
4	Pennsylvania	18,925	4.0%
39	Rhode Island	1,980	0.4%
34	South Carolina	2,514	0.5%
40	South Dakota	1,723	0.4%
23	Tennessee	6,244	1.3%
3	Texas	42,725	9.0%
24	Utah	6,124	1.3%
46	Vermont	484	0.1%
19	Virginia	8,323	1.8%
5	Washington	17,113	3.6%
44	West Virginia	1,103	0.2%
NA	Wisconsin**	NA	NA
41	Wyoming	1,624	0.3%

<u>RANK ORDER</u>

RANK	STATE	ARRESTS	% of USA
1	California	79,163	16.7%
2	Florida	53,967	11.4%
3	Texas	42,725	9.0%
4	Pennsylvania	18,925	4.0%
5	Washington	17,113	3.6%
6	North Carolina	15,453	3.3%
7	New Jersey	15,372	3.2%
8	Arizona	13,902	2.9%
9	Minnesota	13,707	2.9%
10	Michigan	12,643	2.7%
11	New York	12,625	2.7%
12	Ohio	12,325	2.6%
13	Illinois	11,907	2.5%
14	Louisiana	11,756	2.5%
15	Oregon	9,847	2.1%
16	Missouri	9,675	2.0%
17	Colorado	9,586	2.0%
18	Indiana	8,409	1.8%
19	Virginia	8,323	1.8%
20	Maryland	7,995	1.7%
21	Connecticut	6,306	1.3%
22	Iowa	6,298	1.3%
23	Tennessee	6,244	1.3%
24	Utah	6,124	1.3%
25	Massachusetts	6,055	1.3%
26	Nevada	5,718	1.2%
27	Nebraska	5,496	1.2%
28	Arkansas	5,175	1.1%
29	Georgia	5,059	1.1%
30	Alabama	4,790	1.0%
31	Idaho	3,864	0.8%
32	Mississippi	3,120	0.7%
33	New Mexico	2,999	0.6%
34	South Carolina	2,514	0.5%
35	Hawaii	2,479	0.5%
36	Delaware	2,230	0.5%
37	Alaska	2,120	0.4%
38	Montana	2,092	0.4%
39	Rhode Island	1,980	0.4%
40	South Dakota	1,723	0.4%
41	Wyoming	1,624	0.3%
42	Kentucky	1,393	0.3%
43	North Dakota	1,321	0.3%
44	West Virginia	1,103	0.2%
45	New Hampshire	781	0.2%
46	Vermont	484	0.1%
NA	Kansas**	NA	NA
NA	Maine**	NA	NA
NA	Oklahoma**	NA	NA
NA	Wisconsin**	NA	NA
	District of Columbia**	NA	NA

Source: Federal Bureau of Investigation
   "Crime in the United States 1999" (Uniform Crime Reports, October 15, 2000)
*Arrests of youths 17 years and younger by law enforcement agencies submitting complete reports to the F.B.I. for 12 months in 1999. Crime index offenses consist of murder, forcible rape, robbery, aggravated assault, burglary, larceny-theft, motor vehicle theft and arson. See important note at beginning of this chapter.
**Not available.

Reported Juvenile Arrest Rate for Crime Index Offenses in 1999

National Rate = 2,207.2 Reported Arrests per 100,000 Juvenile Population*

ALPHA ORDER

RANK	STATE	RATE
45	Alabama	1,083.5
17	Alaska	2,584.5
15	Arizona	2,649.7
36	Arkansas	1,806.3
27	California	2,139.5
5	Colorado	3,167.5
37	Connecticut	1,790.4
11	Delaware	2,764.1
4	Florida	3,369.2
38	Georgia	1,783.0
23	Hawaii	2,285.4
12	Idaho	2,736.2
2	Illinois	3,702.5
28	Indiana	2,101.8
25	Iowa	2,257.3
NA	Kansas**	NA
10	Kentucky	2,813.8
8	Louisiana	2,837.6
NA	Maine**	NA
22	Maryland	2,291.9
43	Massachusetts	1,187.3
42	Michigan	1,305.9
14	Minnesota	2,657.7
24	Mississippi	2,275.0
18	Missouri	2,584.3
1	Montana	3,804.3
7	Nebraska	2,839.8
9	Nevada	2,825.1
41	New Hampshire	1,382.6
34	New Jersey	1,833.4
21	New Mexico	2,327.9
29	New York	2,090.0
31	North Carolina	2,044.0
26	North Dakota	2,243.7
39	Ohio	1,753.4
NA	Oklahoma**	NA
13	Oregon	2,724.3
33	Pennsylvania	1,840.9
35	Rhode Island	1,816.3
20	South Carolina	2,519.3
19	South Dakota	2,543.9
30	Tennessee	2,055.4
32	Texas	1,923.4
6	Utah	2,920.8
46	Vermont	856.5
40	Virginia	1,660.9
3	Washington	3,398.1
44	West Virginia	1,097.6
NA	Wisconsin**	NA
16	Wyoming	2,592.5

RANK ORDER

RANK	STATE	RATE
1	Montana	3,804.3
2	Illinois	3,702.5
3	Washington	3,398.1
4	Florida	3,369.2
5	Colorado	3,167.5
6	Utah	2,920.8
7	Nebraska	2,839.8
8	Louisiana	2,837.6
9	Nevada	2,825.1
10	Kentucky	2,813.8
11	Delaware	2,764.1
12	Idaho	2,736.2
13	Oregon	2,724.3
14	Minnesota	2,657.7
15	Arizona	2,649.7
16	Wyoming	2,592.5
17	Alaska	2,584.5
18	Missouri	2,584.3
19	South Dakota	2,543.9
20	South Carolina	2,519.3
21	New Mexico	2,327.9
22	Maryland	2,291.9
23	Hawaii	2,285.4
24	Mississippi	2,275.0
25	Iowa	2,257.3
26	North Dakota	2,243.7
27	California	2,139.5
28	Indiana	2,101.8
29	New York	2,090.0
30	Tennessee	2,055.4
31	North Carolina	2,044.0
32	Texas	1,923.4
33	Pennsylvania	1,840.9
34	New Jersey	1,833.4
35	Rhode Island	1,816.3
36	Arkansas	1,806.3
37	Connecticut	1,790.4
38	Georgia	1,783.0
39	Ohio	1,753.4
40	Virginia	1,660.9
41	New Hampshire	1,382.6
42	Michigan	1,305.9
43	Massachusetts	1,187.3
44	West Virginia	1,097.6
45	Alabama	1,083.5
46	Vermont	856.5
NA	Kansas**	NA
NA	Maine**	NA
NA	Oklahoma**	NA
NA	Wisconsin**	NA
	District of Columbia**	NA

Source: Morgan Quitno Press using data from Federal Bureau of Investigation
    "Crime in the United States 1999" (Uniform Crime Reports, October 15, 2000)
Arrests of youths 17 years and younger by law enforcement agencies submitting complete reports to the F.B.I. for 12 months in 1999. Crime index offenses consist of murder, forcible rape, robbery, aggravated assault, burglary, larceny-theft, motor vehicle theft and arson.
**Not available.*

Reported Arrests of Juveniles for Crime Index Offenses
As a Percent of All Such Arrests in 1999
National Percent = 27.9% of Reported Crime Index Offense Arrests*

ALPHA ORDER

RANK	STATE	PERCENT
46	Alabama	19.3
11	Alaska	37.3
22	Arizona	29.1
40	Arkansas	22.2
32	California	25.7
14	Colorado	33.9
34	Connecticut	24.9
31	Delaware	25.8
23	Florida	28.7
36	Georgia	24.5
18	Hawaii	30.8
2	Idaho	48.7
30	Illinois	26.0
26	Indiana	26.8
12	Iowa	36.9
NA	Kansas**	NA
42	Kentucky	20.8
29	Louisiana	26.1
NA	Maine**	NA
15	Maryland	31.9
44	Massachusetts	20.7
32	Michigan	25.7
5	Minnesota	43.9
39	Mississippi	24.0
37	Missouri	24.3
3	Montana	46.6
7	Nebraska	41.6
21	Nevada	29.2
9	New Hampshire	40.2
25	New Jersey	27.4
19	New Mexico	30.2
26	New York	26.8
45	North Carolina	19.7
1	North Dakota	51.4
24	Ohio	28.4
NA	Oklahoma**	NA
16	Oregon	31.7
28	Pennsylvania	26.5
13	Rhode Island	34.6
35	South Carolina	24.8
4	South Dakota	44.0
41	Tennessee	20.9
17	Texas	31.5
8	Utah	40.3
20	Vermont	29.4
38	Virginia	24.1
10	Washington	38.6
42	West Virginia	20.8
NA	Wisconsin**	NA
6	Wyoming	43.3

RANK ORDER

RANK	STATE	PERCENT
1	North Dakota	51.4
2	Idaho	48.7
3	Montana	46.6
4	South Dakota	44.0
5	Minnesota	43.9
6	Wyoming	43.3
7	Nebraska	41.6
8	Utah	40.3
9	New Hampshire	40.2
10	Washington	38.6
11	Alaska	37.3
12	Iowa	36.9
13	Rhode Island	34.6
14	Colorado	33.9
15	Maryland	31.9
16	Oregon	31.7
17	Texas	31.5
18	Hawaii	30.8
19	New Mexico	30.2
20	Vermont	29.4
21	Nevada	29.2
22	Arizona	29.1
23	Florida	28.7
24	Ohio	28.4
25	New Jersey	27.4
26	Indiana	26.8
26	New York	26.8
28	Pennsylvania	26.5
29	Louisiana	26.1
30	Illinois	26.0
31	Delaware	25.8
32	California	25.7
32	Michigan	25.7
34	Connecticut	24.9
35	South Carolina	24.8
36	Georgia	24.5
37	Missouri	24.3
38	Virginia	24.1
39	Mississippi	24.0
40	Arkansas	22.2
41	Tennessee	20.9
42	Kentucky	20.8
42	West Virginia	20.8
44	Massachusetts	20.7
45	North Carolina	19.7
46	Alabama	19.3
NA	Kansas**	NA
NA	Maine**	NA
NA	Oklahoma**	NA
NA	Wisconsin**	NA
	District of Columbia**	NA

Source: Morgan Quitno Press using data from Federal Bureau of Investigation
"Crime in the United States 1999" (Uniform Crime Reports, October 15, 2000)
*Arrests of youths 17 years and younger by law enforcement agencies submitting complete reports to the F.B.I. for 12 months in 1999. Crime index offenses consist of murder, forcible rape, robbery, aggravated assault, burglary, larceny-theft, motor vehicle theft and arson.
**Not available.

Reported Arrests of Juveniles for Violent Crime in 1999

National Total = 78,624 Reported Arrests*

RANK	STATE	ARRESTS	% of USA		RANK	STATE	ARRESTS	% of USA
25	Alabama	657	0.8%		1	California	18,422	23.4%
39	Alaska	229	0.3%		2	Florida	10,708	13.6%
14	Arizona	1,659	2.1%		3	Texas	5,234	6.7%
26	Arkansas	655	0.8%		4	Pennsylvania	4,322	5.5%
1	California	18,422	23.4%		5	New Jersey	3,445	4.4%
21	Colorado	905	1.2%		6	Illinois	3,409	4.3%
17	Connecticut	1,198	1.5%		7	North Carolina	2,516	3.2%
27	Delaware	617	0.8%		8	Massachusetts	2,314	2.9%
2	Florida	10,708	13.6%		9	New York	2,038	2.6%
29	Georgia	530	0.7%		10	Louisiana	1,906	2.4%
37	Hawaii	237	0.3%		11	Michigan	1,893	2.4%
33	Idaho	276	0.4%		12	Ohio	1,737	2.2%
6	Illinois	3,409	4.3%		13	Washington	1,682	2.1%
15	Indiana	1,575	2.0%		14	Arizona	1,659	2.1%
23	Iowa	743	0.9%		15	Indiana	1,575	2.0%
NA	Kansas**	NA	NA		16	Minnesota	1,418	1.8%
36	Kentucky	256	0.3%		17	Connecticut	1,198	1.5%
10	Louisiana	1,906	2.4%		18	Missouri	1,169	1.5%
NA	Maine**	NA	NA		19	Maryland	1,064	1.4%
19	Maryland	1,064	1.4%		20	Virginia	956	1.2%
8	Massachusetts	2,314	2.9%		21	Colorado	905	1.2%
11	Michigan	1,893	2.4%		22	Tennessee	759	1.0%
16	Minnesota	1,418	1.8%		23	Iowa	743	0.9%
35	Mississippi	258	0.3%		24	Oregon	732	0.9%
18	Missouri	1,169	1.5%		25	Alabama	657	0.8%
40	Montana	173	0.2%		26	Arkansas	655	0.8%
38	Nebraska	230	0.3%		27	Delaware	617	0.8%
28	Nevada	586	0.7%		28	Nevada	586	0.7%
44	New Hampshire	70	0.1%		29	Georgia	530	0.7%
5	New Jersey	3,445	4.4%		29	Utah	530	0.7%
31	New Mexico	460	0.6%		31	New Mexico	460	0.6%
9	New York	2,038	2.6%		32	South Carolina	400	0.5%
7	North Carolina	2,516	3.2%		33	Idaho	276	0.4%
45	North Dakota	54	0.1%		34	Rhode Island	268	0.3%
12	Ohio	1,737	2.2%		35	Mississippi	258	0.3%
NA	Oklahoma**	NA	NA		36	Kentucky	256	0.3%
24	Oregon	732	0.9%		37	Hawaii	237	0.3%
4	Pennsylvania	4,322	5.5%		38	Nebraska	230	0.3%
34	Rhode Island	268	0.3%		39	Alaska	229	0.3%
32	South Carolina	400	0.5%		40	Montana	173	0.2%
41	South Dakota	113	0.1%		41	South Dakota	113	0.1%
22	Tennessee	759	1.0%		42	West Virginia	96	0.1%
3	Texas	5,234	6.7%		43	Wyoming	91	0.1%
29	Utah	530	0.7%		44	New Hampshire	70	0.1%
46	Vermont	34	0.0%		45	North Dakota	54	0.1%
20	Virginia	956	1.2%		46	Vermont	34	0.0%
13	Washington	1,682	2.1%		NA	Kansas**	NA	NA
42	West Virginia	96	0.1%		NA	Maine**	NA	NA
NA	Wisconsin**	NA	NA		NA	Oklahoma**	NA	NA
43	Wyoming	91	0.1%		NA	Wisconsin**	NA	NA
						District of Columbia**	NA	NA

Source: Federal Bureau of Investigation
"Crime in the United States 1999" (Uniform Crime Reports, October 15, 2000)
*Arrests of youths 17 years and younger by law enforcement agencies submitting complete reports to the F.B.I. for 12 months in 1999. Violent crimes are offenses of murder, forcible rape, robbery and aggravated assault. See important note at beginning of this chapter.
**Not available.

Reported Juvenile Arrest Rate for Violent Crime in 1999

National Rate = 365.7 Reported Arrests per 100,000 Juvenile Population*

ALPHA ORDER

RANK ORDER

RANK	STATE	RATE	RANK	STATE	RATE
40	Alabama	148.6	1	Illinois	1,060.0
23	Alaska	279.2	2	Delaware	764.8
17	Arizona	316.2	3	Florida	668.5
31	Arkansas	228.6	4	Kentucky	517.1
5	California	497.9	5	California	497.9
21	Colorado	299.0	6	Louisiana	460.1
13	Connecticut	340.1	7	Massachusetts	453.8
2	Delaware	764.8	8	Pennsylvania	420.4
3	Florida	668.5	9	New Jersey	410.9
38	Georgia	186.8	10	South Carolina	400.8
32	Hawaii	218.5	11	Indiana	393.7
35	Idaho	195.4	12	New Mexico	357.1
1	Illinois	1,060.0	13	Connecticut	340.1
11	Indiana	393.7	14	New York	337.4
25	Iowa	266.3	15	Washington	334.0
NA	Kansas**	NA	16	North Carolina	332.8
4	Kentucky	517.1	17	Arizona	316.2
6	Louisiana	460.1	18	Montana	314.6
NA	Maine**	NA	19	Missouri	312.3
20	Maryland	305.0	20	Maryland	305.0
7	Massachusetts	453.8	21	Colorado	299.0
34	Michigan	195.5	22	Nevada	289.5
24	Minnesota	274.9	23	Alaska	279.2
37	Mississippi	188.1	24	Minnesota	274.9
19	Missouri	312.3	25	Iowa	266.3
18	Montana	314.6	26	Utah	252.8
43	Nebraska	118.8	27	Tennessee	249.8
22	Nevada	289.5	28	Ohio	247.1
42	New Hampshire	123.9	29	Rhode Island	245.8
9	New Jersey	410.9	30	Texas	235.6
12	New Mexico	357.1	31	Arkansas	228.6
14	New York	337.4	32	Hawaii	218.5
16	North Carolina	332.8	33	Oregon	202.5
45	North Dakota	91.7	34	Michigan	195.5
28	Ohio	247.1	35	Idaho	195.4
NA	Oklahoma**	NA	36	Virginia	190.8
33	Oregon	202.5	37	Mississippi	188.1
8	Pennsylvania	420.4	38	Georgia	186.8
29	Rhode Island	245.8	39	South Dakota	166.8
10	South Carolina	400.8	40	Alabama	148.6
39	South Dakota	166.8	41	Wyoming	145.3
27	Tennessee	249.8	42	New Hampshire	123.9
30	Texas	235.6	43	Nebraska	118.8
26	Utah	252.8	44	West Virginia	95.5
46	Vermont	60.2	45	North Dakota	91.7
36	Virginia	190.8	46	Vermont	60.2
15	Washington	334.0	NA	Kansas**	NA
44	West Virginia	95.5	NA	Maine**	NA
NA	Wisconsin**	NA	NA	Oklahoma**	NA
41	Wyoming	145.3	NA	Wisconsin**	NA
				District of Columbia**	NA

Source: Morgan Quitno Press using data from Federal Bureau of Investigation
   "Crime in the United States 1999" (Uniform Crime Reports, October 15, 2000)
*By law enforcement agencies submitting complete reports to the F.B.I. for 12 months in 1999. Arrests of youths 17
years and younger divided into population of 10 to 17 year olds. See important note at beginning of this chapter.
Violent crimes are offenses of murder, forcible rape, robbery and aggravated assault.
**Not available.

Reported Arrests of Juveniles for Violent Crime
As a Percent of All Such Arrests in 1999
National Percent = 16.5% of Reported Violent Crime Arrests*

ALPHA ORDER

RANK	STATE	PERCENT
45	Alabama	9.8
32	Alaska	15.8
15	Arizona	21.2
39	Arkansas	12.0
34	California	13.8
26	Colorado	17.5
18	Connecticut	19.4
14	Delaware	21.3
20	Florida	19.2
37	Georgia	12.5
15	Hawaii	21.2
7	Idaho	24.0
3	Illinois	30.0
27	Indiana	17.0
25	Iowa	17.6
NA	Kansas**	NA
44	Kentucky	10.3
30	Louisiana	16.4
NA	Maine**	NA
10	Maryland	22.1
28	Massachusetts	16.9
41	Michigan	11.0
6	Minnesota	25.1
38	Mississippi	12.4
33	Missouri	14.2
4	Montana	28.6
29	Nebraska	16.5
21	Nevada	18.5
5	New Hampshire	25.2
13	New Jersey	21.6
22	New Mexico	18.2
17	New York	19.9
43	North Carolina	10.5
1	North Dakota	32.3
31	Ohio	16.2
NA	Oklahoma**	NA
12	Oregon	21.7
19	Pennsylvania	19.3
9	Rhode Island	22.3
35	South Carolina	13.3
11	South Dakota	21.8
42	Tennessee	10.6
24	Texas	18.0
2	Utah	31.2
40	Vermont	11.8
36	Virginia	13.0
8	Washington	23.5
46	West Virginia	5.8
NA	Wisconsin**	NA
23	Wyoming	18.1

RANK ORDER

RANK	STATE	PERCENT
1	North Dakota	32.3
2	Utah	31.2
3	Illinois	30.0
4	Montana	28.6
5	New Hampshire	25.2
6	Minnesota	25.1
7	Idaho	24.0
8	Washington	23.5
9	Rhode Island	22.3
10	Maryland	22.1
11	South Dakota	21.8
12	Oregon	21.7
13	New Jersey	21.6
14	Delaware	21.3
15	Arizona	21.2
15	Hawaii	21.2
17	New York	19.9
18	Connecticut	19.4
19	Pennsylvania	19.3
20	Florida	19.2
21	Nevada	18.5
22	New Mexico	18.2
23	Wyoming	18.1
24	Texas	18.0
25	Iowa	17.6
26	Colorado	17.5
27	Indiana	17.0
28	Massachusetts	16.9
29	Nebraska	16.5
30	Louisiana	16.4
31	Ohio	16.2
32	Alaska	15.8
33	Missouri	14.2
34	California	13.8
35	South Carolina	13.3
36	Virginia	13.0
37	Georgia	12.5
38	Mississippi	12.4
39	Arkansas	12.0
40	Vermont	11.8
41	Michigan	11.0
42	Tennessee	10.6
43	North Carolina	10.5
44	Kentucky	10.3
45	Alabama	9.8
46	West Virginia	5.8
NA	Kansas**	NA
NA	Maine**	NA
NA	Oklahoma**	NA
NA	Wisconsin**	NA
	District of Columbia**	NA

Source: Morgan Quitno Press using data from Federal Bureau of Investigation
    "Crime in the United States 1999" (Uniform Crime Reports, October 15, 2000)
*Arrests of youths 17 years and younger by law enforcement agencies submitting complete reports to the F.B.I. for 12 months in 1999. Violent crimes are offenses of murder, forcible rape, robbery and aggravated assault.
**Not available.

Reported Arrests of Juveniles for Murder in 1999

National Total = 999 Reported Arrests*

ALPHA ORDER

RANK	STATE	ARRESTS	% of USA
15	Alabama	18	1.8%
30	Alaska	5	0.5%
10	Arizona	26	2.6%
18	Arkansas	17	1.7%
1	California	183	18.3%
14	Colorado	20	2.0%
27	Connecticut	6	0.6%
41	Delaware	0	0.0%
4	Florida	80	8.0%
20	Georgia	15	1.5%
38	Hawaii	2	0.2%
41	Idaho	0	0.0%
3	Illinois	89	8.9%
8	Indiana	31	3.1%
33	Iowa	4	0.4%
NA	Kansas**	NA	NA
33	Kentucky	4	0.4%
9	Louisiana	27	2.7%
NA	Maine**	NA	NA
25	Maryland	8	0.8%
30	Massachusetts	5	0.5%
5	Michigan	58	5.8%
27	Minnesota	6	0.6%
23	Mississippi	11	1.1%
11	Missouri	25	2.5%
27	Montana	6	0.6%
36	Nebraska	3	0.3%
21	Nevada	12	1.2%
41	New Hampshire	0	0.0%
15	New Jersey	18	1.8%
25	New Mexico	8	0.8%
15	New York	18	1.8%
6	North Carolina	50	5.0%
39	North Dakota	1	0.1%
24	Ohio	9	0.9%
NA	Oklahoma**	NA	NA
21	Oregon	12	1.2%
7	Pennsylvania	42	4.2%
33	Rhode Island	4	0.4%
30	South Carolina	5	0.5%
39	South Dakota	1	0.1%
13	Tennessee	21	2.1%
2	Texas	108	10.8%
36	Utah	3	0.3%
41	Vermont	0	0.0%
12	Virginia	22	2.2%
19	Washington	16	1.6%
41	West Virginia	0	0.0%
NA	Wisconsin**	NA	NA
41	Wyoming	0	0.0%

RANK ORDER

RANK	STATE	ARRESTS	% of USA
1	California	183	18.3%
2	Texas	108	10.8%
3	Illinois	89	8.9%
4	Florida	80	8.0%
5	Michigan	58	5.8%
6	North Carolina	50	5.0%
7	Pennsylvania	42	4.2%
8	Indiana	31	3.1%
9	Louisiana	27	2.7%
10	Arizona	26	2.6%
11	Missouri	25	2.5%
12	Virginia	22	2.2%
13	Tennessee	21	2.1%
14	Colorado	20	2.0%
15	Alabama	18	1.8%
15	New Jersey	18	1.8%
15	New York	18	1.8%
18	Arkansas	17	1.7%
19	Washington	16	1.6%
20	Georgia	15	1.5%
21	Nevada	12	1.2%
21	Oregon	12	1.2%
23	Mississippi	11	1.1%
24	Ohio	9	0.9%
25	Maryland	8	0.8%
25	New Mexico	8	0.8%
27	Connecticut	6	0.6%
27	Minnesota	6	0.6%
27	Montana	6	0.6%
30	Alaska	5	0.5%
30	Massachusetts	5	0.5%
30	South Carolina	5	0.5%
33	Iowa	4	0.4%
33	Kentucky	4	0.4%
33	Rhode Island	4	0.4%
36	Nebraska	3	0.3%
36	Utah	3	0.3%
38	Hawaii	2	0.2%
39	North Dakota	1	0.1%
39	South Dakota	1	0.1%
41	Delaware	0	0.0%
41	Idaho	0	0.0%
41	New Hampshire	0	0.0%
41	Vermont	0	0.0%
41	West Virginia	0	0.0%
41	Wyoming	0	0.0%
NA	Kansas**	NA	NA
NA	Maine**	NA	NA
NA	Oklahoma**	NA	NA
NA	Wisconsin**	NA	NA
	District of Columbia**	NA	NA

Source: Federal Bureau of Investigation
"Crime in the United States 1999" (Uniform Crime Reports, October 15, 2000)
*Arrests of youths 17 years and younger by law enforcement agencies submitting complete reports to the F.B.I. for 12 months in 1999. Includes nonnegligent manslaughter. See important note at beginning of this chapter.
**Not available.

Reported Juvenile Arrest Rate for Murder in 1999

National Rate = 4.6 Reported Arrests per 100,000 Juvenile Population*

ALPHA ORDER

RANK	STATE	RATE
23	Alabama	4.1
12	Alaska	6.1
17	Arizona	5.0
14	Arkansas	5.9
20	California	4.9
8	Colorado	6.6
32	Connecticut	1.7
41	Delaware	0.0
17	Florida	5.0
16	Georgia	5.3
31	Hawaii	1.8
41	Idaho	0.0
1	Illinois	27.7
5	Indiana	7.7
36	Iowa	1.4
NA	Kansas**	NA
3	Kentucky	8.1
10	Louisiana	6.5
NA	Maine**	NA
29	Maryland	2.3
40	Massachusetts	1.0
13	Michigan	6.0
39	Minnesota	1.2
4	Mississippi	8.0
7	Missouri	6.7
2	Montana	10.9
34	Nebraska	1.6
14	Nevada	5.9
41	New Hampshire	0.0
30	New Jersey	2.1
11	New Mexico	6.2
28	New York	3.0
8	North Carolina	6.6
32	North Dakota	1.7
38	Ohio	1.3
NA	Oklahoma**	NA
26	Oregon	3.3
23	Pennsylvania	4.1
25	Rhode Island	3.7
17	South Carolina	5.0
35	South Dakota	1.5
6	Tennessee	6.9
20	Texas	4.9
36	Utah	1.4
41	Vermont	0.0
22	Virginia	4.4
27	Washington	3.2
41	West Virginia	0.0
NA	Wisconsin**	NA
41	Wyoming	0.0

RANK ORDER

RANK	STATE	RATE
1	Illinois	27.7
2	Montana	10.9
3	Kentucky	8.1
4	Mississippi	8.0
5	Indiana	7.7
6	Tennessee	6.9
7	Missouri	6.7
8	Colorado	6.6
8	North Carolina	6.6
10	Louisiana	6.5
11	New Mexico	6.2
12	Alaska	6.1
13	Michigan	6.0
14	Arkansas	5.9
14	Nevada	5.9
16	Georgia	5.3
17	Arizona	5.0
17	Florida	5.0
17	South Carolina	5.0
20	California	4.9
20	Texas	4.9
22	Virginia	4.4
23	Alabama	4.1
23	Pennsylvania	4.1
25	Rhode Island	3.7
26	Oregon	3.3
27	Washington	3.2
28	New York	3.0
29	Maryland	2.3
30	New Jersey	2.1
31	Hawaii	1.8
32	Connecticut	1.7
32	North Dakota	1.7
34	Nebraska	1.6
35	South Dakota	1.5
36	Iowa	1.4
36	Utah	1.4
38	Ohio	1.3
39	Minnesota	1.2
40	Massachusetts	1.0
41	Delaware	0.0
41	Idaho	0.0
41	New Hampshire	0.0
41	Vermont	0.0
41	West Virginia	0.0
41	Wyoming	0.0
NA	Kansas**	NA
NA	Maine**	NA
NA	Oklahoma**	NA
NA	Wisconsin**	NA
	District of Columbia**	NA

Source: Morgan Quitno Press using data from Federal Bureau of Investigation
    "Crime in the United States 1999" (Uniform Crime Reports, October 15, 2000)
*By law enforcement agencies submitting complete reports to the F.B.I. for 12 months in 1999. Includes
nonnegligent manslaughter. Arrests of youths 17 years and younger divided into population of 10 to 17 year olds.
See important note at beginning of this chapter.
**Not available.

Reported Arrests of Juveniles for Murder
As a Percent of All Such Arrests in 1999
National Percent = 9.5% of Reported Murder Arrests*

ALPHA ORDER

RANK ORDER

RANK	STATE	PERCENT
33	Alabama	6.8
7	Alaska	13.9
21	Arizona	10.7
24	Arkansas	9.9
22	California	10.3
2	Colorado	20.2
34	Connecticut	6.7
41	Delaware	0.0
20	Florida	10.8
13	Georgia	12.3
38	Hawaii	4.5
41	Idaho	0.0
5	Illinois	14.0
11	Indiana	12.7
4	Iowa	16.7
NA	Kansas**	NA
8	Kentucky	13.8
18	Louisiana	10.9
NA	Maine**	NA
17	Maryland	11.0
32	Massachusetts	7.2
38	Michigan	4.5
40	Minnesota	4.2
29	Mississippi	8.1
23	Missouri	10.0
1	Montana	35.3
35	Nebraska	6.5
25	Nevada	9.8
41	New Hampshire	0.0
30	New Jersey	7.5
14	New Mexico	11.8
18	New York	10.9
30	North Carolina	7.5
3	North Dakota	20.0
37	Ohio	4.9
NA	Oklahoma**	NA
15	Oregon	11.7
28	Pennsylvania	8.8
9	Rhode Island	13.3
27	South Carolina	9.1
12	South Dakota	12.5
36	Tennessee	6.4
5	Texas	14.0
16	Utah	11.5
41	Vermont	0.0
26	Virginia	9.6
9	Washington	13.3
41	West Virginia	0.0
NA	Wisconsin**	NA
41	Wyoming	0.0

RANK	STATE	PERCENT
1	Montana	35.3
2	Colorado	20.2
3	North Dakota	20.0
4	Iowa	16.7
5	Illinois	14.0
5	Texas	14.0
7	Alaska	13.9
8	Kentucky	13.8
9	Rhode Island	13.3
9	Washington	13.3
11	Indiana	12.7
12	South Dakota	12.5
13	Georgia	12.3
14	New Mexico	11.8
15	Oregon	11.7
16	Utah	11.5
17	Maryland	11.0
18	Louisiana	10.9
18	New York	10.9
20	Florida	10.8
21	Arizona	10.7
22	California	10.3
23	Missouri	10.0
24	Arkansas	9.9
25	Nevada	9.8
26	Virginia	9.6
27	South Carolina	9.1
28	Pennsylvania	8.8
29	Mississippi	8.1
30	New Jersey	7.5
30	North Carolina	7.5
32	Massachusetts	7.2
33	Alabama	6.8
34	Connecticut	6.7
35	Nebraska	6.5
36	Tennessee	6.4
37	Ohio	4.9
38	Hawaii	4.5
38	Michigan	4.5
40	Minnesota	4.2
41	Delaware	0.0
41	Idaho	0.0
41	New Hampshire	0.0
41	Vermont	0.0
41	West Virginia	0.0
41	Wyoming	0.0
NA	Kansas**	NA
NA	Maine**	NA
NA	Oklahoma**	NA
NA	Wisconsin**	NA

District of Columbia** NA

Source: Morgan Quitno Press using data from Federal Bureau of Investigation
  "Crime in the United States 1999" (Uniform Crime Reports, October 15, 2000)
*Arrests of youths 17 years and younger by law enforcement agencies submitting complete reports to the F.B.I. for
12 months in 1999. Includes nonnegligent manslaughter.
**Not available.

Reported Arrests of Juveniles for Rape in 1999

National Total = 3,550 Reported Arrests*

<table>
<tr><td colspan="4">ALPHA ORDER</td><td colspan="4">RANK ORDER</td></tr>
<tr><td>RANK</td><td>STATE</td><td>ARRESTS</td><td>% of USA</td><td>RANK</td><td>STATE</td><td>ARRESTS</td><td>% of USA</td></tr>
<tr><td>34</td><td>Alabama</td><td>19</td><td>0.5%</td><td>1</td><td>California</td><td>396</td><td>11.2%</td></tr>
<tr><td>31</td><td>Alaska</td><td>22</td><td>0.6%</td><td>2</td><td>Texas</td><td>393</td><td>11.1%</td></tr>
<tr><td>26</td><td>Arizona</td><td>31</td><td>0.9%</td><td>3</td><td>Florida</td><td>368</td><td>10.4%</td></tr>
<tr><td>19</td><td>Arkansas</td><td>44</td><td>1.2%</td><td>4</td><td>Ohio</td><td>214</td><td>6.0%</td></tr>
<tr><td>1</td><td>California</td><td>396</td><td>11.2%</td><td>5</td><td>Pennsylvania</td><td>206</td><td>5.8%</td></tr>
<tr><td>10</td><td>Colorado</td><td>145</td><td>4.1%</td><td>6</td><td>Illinois</td><td>182</td><td>5.1%</td></tr>
<tr><td>16</td><td>Connecticut</td><td>56</td><td>1.6%</td><td>7</td><td>Michigan</td><td>180</td><td>5.1%</td></tr>
<tr><td>13</td><td>Delaware</td><td>73</td><td>2.1%</td><td>8</td><td>Minnesota</td><td>156</td><td>4.4%</td></tr>
<tr><td>3</td><td>Florida</td><td>368</td><td>10.4%</td><td>9</td><td>Washington</td><td>152</td><td>4.3%</td></tr>
<tr><td>23</td><td>Georgia</td><td>36</td><td>1.0%</td><td>10</td><td>Colorado</td><td>145</td><td>4.1%</td></tr>
<tr><td>38</td><td>Hawaii</td><td>14</td><td>0.4%</td><td>11</td><td>New Jersey</td><td>99</td><td>2.8%</td></tr>
<tr><td>33</td><td>Idaho</td><td>20</td><td>0.6%</td><td>12</td><td>Louisiana</td><td>82</td><td>2.3%</td></tr>
<tr><td>6</td><td>Illinois</td><td>182</td><td>5.1%</td><td>13</td><td>Delaware</td><td>73</td><td>2.1%</td></tr>
<tr><td>26</td><td>Indiana</td><td>31</td><td>0.9%</td><td>14</td><td>Missouri</td><td>67</td><td>1.9%</td></tr>
<tr><td>23</td><td>Iowa</td><td>36</td><td>1.0%</td><td>15</td><td>North Carolina</td><td>62</td><td>1.7%</td></tr>
<tr><td>NA</td><td>Kansas**</td><td>NA</td><td>NA</td><td>16</td><td>Connecticut</td><td>56</td><td>1.6%</td></tr>
<tr><td>44</td><td>Kentucky</td><td>4</td><td>0.1%</td><td>17</td><td>Massachusetts</td><td>55</td><td>1.5%</td></tr>
<tr><td>12</td><td>Louisiana</td><td>82</td><td>2.3%</td><td>18</td><td>New York</td><td>48</td><td>1.4%</td></tr>
<tr><td>NA</td><td>Maine**</td><td>NA</td><td>NA</td><td>19</td><td>Arkansas</td><td>44</td><td>1.2%</td></tr>
<tr><td>21</td><td>Maryland</td><td>37</td><td>1.0%</td><td>20</td><td>Oregon</td><td>39</td><td>1.1%</td></tr>
<tr><td>17</td><td>Massachusetts</td><td>55</td><td>1.5%</td><td>21</td><td>Maryland</td><td>37</td><td>1.0%</td></tr>
<tr><td>7</td><td>Michigan</td><td>180</td><td>5.1%</td><td>21</td><td>Virginia</td><td>37</td><td>1.0%</td></tr>
<tr><td>8</td><td>Minnesota</td><td>156</td><td>4.4%</td><td>23</td><td>Georgia</td><td>36</td><td>1.0%</td></tr>
<tr><td>26</td><td>Mississippi</td><td>31</td><td>0.9%</td><td>23</td><td>Iowa</td><td>36</td><td>1.0%</td></tr>
<tr><td>14</td><td>Missouri</td><td>67</td><td>1.9%</td><td>25</td><td>Utah</td><td>32</td><td>0.9%</td></tr>
<tr><td>39</td><td>Montana</td><td>12</td><td>0.3%</td><td>26</td><td>Arizona</td><td>31</td><td>0.9%</td></tr>
<tr><td>34</td><td>Nebraska</td><td>19</td><td>0.5%</td><td>26</td><td>Indiana</td><td>31</td><td>0.9%</td></tr>
<tr><td>29</td><td>Nevada</td><td>30</td><td>0.8%</td><td>26</td><td>Mississippi</td><td>31</td><td>0.9%</td></tr>
<tr><td>45</td><td>New Hampshire</td><td>3</td><td>0.1%</td><td>29</td><td>Nevada</td><td>30</td><td>0.8%</td></tr>
<tr><td>11</td><td>New Jersey</td><td>99</td><td>2.8%</td><td>30</td><td>South Carolina</td><td>27</td><td>0.8%</td></tr>
<tr><td>34</td><td>New Mexico</td><td>19</td><td>0.5%</td><td>31</td><td>Alaska</td><td>22</td><td>0.6%</td></tr>
<tr><td>18</td><td>New York</td><td>48</td><td>1.4%</td><td>31</td><td>Tennessee</td><td>22</td><td>0.6%</td></tr>
<tr><td>15</td><td>North Carolina</td><td>62</td><td>1.7%</td><td>33</td><td>Idaho</td><td>20</td><td>0.6%</td></tr>
<tr><td>42</td><td>North Dakota</td><td>5</td><td>0.1%</td><td>34</td><td>Alabama</td><td>19</td><td>0.5%</td></tr>
<tr><td>4</td><td>Ohio</td><td>214</td><td>6.0%</td><td>34</td><td>Nebraska</td><td>19</td><td>0.5%</td></tr>
<tr><td>NA</td><td>Oklahoma**</td><td>NA</td><td>NA</td><td>34</td><td>New Mexico</td><td>19</td><td>0.5%</td></tr>
<tr><td>20</td><td>Oregon</td><td>39</td><td>1.1%</td><td>37</td><td>Rhode Island</td><td>18</td><td>0.5%</td></tr>
<tr><td>5</td><td>Pennsylvania</td><td>206</td><td>5.8%</td><td>38</td><td>Hawaii</td><td>14</td><td>0.4%</td></tr>
<tr><td>37</td><td>Rhode Island</td><td>18</td><td>0.5%</td><td>39</td><td>Montana</td><td>12</td><td>0.3%</td></tr>
<tr><td>30</td><td>South Carolina</td><td>27</td><td>0.8%</td><td>40</td><td>South Dakota</td><td>11</td><td>0.3%</td></tr>
<tr><td>40</td><td>South Dakota</td><td>11</td><td>0.3%</td><td>41</td><td>Vermont</td><td>10</td><td>0.3%</td></tr>
<tr><td>31</td><td>Tennessee</td><td>22</td><td>0.6%</td><td>42</td><td>North Dakota</td><td>5</td><td>0.1%</td></tr>
<tr><td>2</td><td>Texas</td><td>393</td><td>11.1%</td><td>42</td><td>Wyoming</td><td>5</td><td>0.1%</td></tr>
<tr><td>25</td><td>Utah</td><td>32</td><td>0.9%</td><td>44</td><td>Kentucky</td><td>4</td><td>0.1%</td></tr>
<tr><td>41</td><td>Vermont</td><td>10</td><td>0.3%</td><td>45</td><td>New Hampshire</td><td>3</td><td>0.1%</td></tr>
<tr><td>21</td><td>Virginia</td><td>37</td><td>1.0%</td><td>46</td><td>West Virginia</td><td>2</td><td>0.1%</td></tr>
<tr><td>9</td><td>Washington</td><td>152</td><td>4.3%</td><td>NA</td><td>Kansas**</td><td>NA</td><td>NA</td></tr>
<tr><td>46</td><td>West Virginia</td><td>2</td><td>0.1%</td><td>NA</td><td>Maine**</td><td>NA</td><td>NA</td></tr>
<tr><td>NA</td><td>Wisconsin**</td><td>NA</td><td>NA</td><td>NA</td><td>Oklahoma**</td><td>NA</td><td>NA</td></tr>
<tr><td>42</td><td>Wyoming</td><td>5</td><td>0.1%</td><td>NA</td><td>Wisconsin**</td><td>NA</td><td>NA</td></tr>
<tr><td></td><td></td><td></td><td></td><td></td><td>District of Columbia**</td><td>NA</td><td>NA</td></tr>
</table>

Source: Federal Bureau of Investigation
"Crime in the United States 1999" (Uniform Crime Reports, October 15, 2000)
*Arrests of youths 17 years and younger by law enforcement agencies submitting complete reports to the F.B.I. for 12 months in 1999. Forcible rape is the carnal knowledge of a female forcibly and against her will. Assaults or attempts to commit rape by force or threat of force are included. However, statutory rape without force and other sex offenses are excluded. See important note at beginning of this chapter. **Not available.

Reported Juvenile Arrest Rate for Rape in 1999

National Rate = 16.5 Reported Arrests per 100,000 Juvenile Population*

ALPHA ORDER

RANK	STATE	RATE
45	Alabama	4.3
8	Alaska	26.8
43	Arizona	5.9
21	Arkansas	15.4
32	California	10.7
3	Colorado	47.9
20	Connecticut	15.9
1	Delaware	90.5
9	Florida	23.0
28	Georgia	12.7
26	Hawaii	12.9
25	Idaho	14.2
2	Illinois	56.6
40	Indiana	7.7
26	Iowa	12.9
NA	Kansas**	NA
37	Kentucky	8.1
13	Louisiana	19.8
NA	Maine**	NA
33	Maryland	10.6
30	Massachusetts	10.8
14	Michigan	18.6
5	Minnesota	30.2
10	Mississippi	22.6
15	Missouri	17.9
11	Montana	21.8
34	Nebraska	9.8
23	Nevada	14.8
44	New Hampshire	5.3
29	New Jersey	11.8
24	New Mexico	14.7
39	New York	7.9
36	North Carolina	8.2
35	North Dakota	8.5
4	Ohio	30.4
NA	Oklahoma**	NA
30	Oregon	10.8
12	Pennsylvania	20.0
18	Rhode Island	16.5
7	South Carolina	27.1
19	South Dakota	16.2
42	Tennessee	7.2
16	Texas	17.7
22	Utah	15.3
16	Vermont	17.7
41	Virginia	7.4
5	Washington	30.2
46	West Virginia	2.0
NA	Wisconsin**	NA
38	Wyoming	8.0

RANK ORDER

RANK	STATE	RATE
1	Delaware	90.5
2	Illinois	56.6
3	Colorado	47.9
4	Ohio	30.4
5	Minnesota	30.2
5	Washington	30.2
7	South Carolina	27.1
8	Alaska	26.8
9	Florida	23.0
10	Mississippi	22.6
11	Montana	21.8
12	Pennsylvania	20.0
13	Louisiana	19.8
14	Michigan	18.6
15	Missouri	17.9
16	Texas	17.7
16	Vermont	17.7
18	Rhode Island	16.5
19	South Dakota	16.2
20	Connecticut	15.9
21	Arkansas	15.4
22	Utah	15.3
23	Nevada	14.8
24	New Mexico	14.7
25	Idaho	14.2
26	Hawaii	12.9
26	Iowa	12.9
28	Georgia	12.7
29	New Jersey	11.8
30	Massachusetts	10.8
30	Oregon	10.8
32	California	10.7
33	Maryland	10.6
34	Nebraska	9.8
35	North Dakota	8.5
36	North Carolina	8.2
37	Kentucky	8.1
38	Wyoming	8.0
39	New York	7.9
40	Indiana	7.7
41	Virginia	7.4
42	Tennessee	7.2
43	Arizona	5.9
44	New Hampshire	5.3
45	Alabama	4.3
46	West Virginia	2.0
NA	Kansas**	NA
NA	Maine**	NA
NA	Oklahoma**	NA
NA	Wisconsin**	NA
	District of Columbia**	NA

Source: Morgan Quitno Press using data from Federal Bureau of Investigation
"Crime in the United States 1999" (Uniform Crime Reports, October 15, 2000)
*By law enforcement agencies submitting complete reports to the F.B.I. for 12 months in 1999. Arrests of youths 17 years and younger divided into population of 10 to 17 year olds. See important note at beginning of this chapter. Forcible rape is the carnal knowledge of a female forcibly and against her will. Assaults or attempts to commit rape by force or threat of force are included. **Not available.

Reported Arrests of Juveniles for Rape
As a Percent of All Such Arrests in 1999
National Percent = 16.9% of Reported Rape Arrests*

ALPHA ORDER

RANK	STATE	PERCENT
45	Alabama	6.5
22	Alaska	16.4
16	Arizona	18.1
39	Arkansas	11.3
33	California	13.7
3	Colorado	28.4
14	Connecticut	19.4
9	Delaware	23.4
24	Florida	16.2
22	Georgia	16.4
21	Hawaii	16.7
5	Idaho	26.0
5	Illinois	26.0
32	Indiana	14.0
2	Iowa	29.5
NA	Kansas**	NA
44	Kentucky	8.2
15	Louisiana	18.3
NA	Maine**	NA
26	Maryland	15.9
37	Massachusetts	11.9
30	Michigan	14.4
12	Minnesota	22.3
24	Mississippi	16.2
29	Missouri	14.9
1	Montana	33.3
38	Nebraska	11.8
35	Nevada	13.2
31	New Hampshire	14.3
28	New Jersey	15.3
10	New Mexico	22.6
41	New York	10.5
36	North Carolina	12.4
7	North Dakota	25.0
4	Ohio	26.2
NA	Oklahoma**	NA
20	Oregon	17.0
19	Pennsylvania	17.4
33	Rhode Island	13.7
18	South Carolina	17.9
8	South Dakota	23.9
42	Tennessee	10.3
17	Texas	18.0
11	Utah	22.4
27	Vermont	15.4
43	Virginia	8.4
13	Washington	21.3
46	West Virginia	4.3
NA	Wisconsin**	NA
40	Wyoming	10.9

RANK ORDER

RANK	STATE	PERCENT
1	Montana	33.3
2	Iowa	29.5
3	Colorado	28.4
4	Ohio	26.2
5	Idaho	26.0
5	Illinois	26.0
7	North Dakota	25.0
8	South Dakota	23.9
9	Delaware	23.4
10	New Mexico	22.6
11	Utah	22.4
12	Minnesota	22.3
13	Washington	21.3
14	Connecticut	19.4
15	Louisiana	18.3
16	Arizona	18.1
17	Texas	18.0
18	South Carolina	17.9
19	Pennsylvania	17.4
20	Oregon	17.0
21	Hawaii	16.7
22	Alaska	16.4
22	Georgia	16.4
24	Florida	16.2
24	Mississippi	16.2
26	Maryland	15.9
27	Vermont	15.4
28	New Jersey	15.3
29	Missouri	14.9
30	Michigan	14.4
31	New Hampshire	14.3
32	Indiana	14.0
33	California	13.7
33	Rhode Island	13.7
35	Nevada	13.2
36	North Carolina	12.4
37	Massachusetts	11.9
38	Nebraska	11.8
39	Arkansas	11.3
40	Wyoming	10.9
41	New York	10.5
42	Tennessee	10.3
43	Virginia	8.4
44	Kentucky	8.2
45	Alabama	6.5
46	West Virginia	4.3
NA	Kansas**	NA
NA	Maine**	NA
NA	Oklahoma**	NA
NA	Wisconsin**	NA
	District of Columbia**	NA

Source: Morgan Quitno Press using data from Federal Bureau of Investigation
    "Crime in the United States 1999" (Uniform Crime Reports, October 15, 2000)
*Arrests of youths 17 years and younger by law enforcement agencies submitting complete reports to the F.B.I. for 12 months in 1999. Forcible rape is the carnal knowledge of a female forcibly and against her will. Assaults or attempts to commit rape by force or threat of force are included. However, statutory rape without force and other sex offenses are excluded. **Not available.

Reported Arrests of Juveniles for Robbery in 1999

National Total = 21,357 Reported Arrests*

ALPHA ORDER

RANK	STATE	ARRESTS	% of USA
22	Alabama	252	1.2%
37	Alaska	48	0.2%
18	Arizona	290	1.4%
27	Arkansas	140	0.7%
1	California	5,711	26.7%
24	Colorado	166	0.8%
17	Connecticut	291	1.4%
26	Delaware	149	0.7%
2	Florida	2,622	12.3%
28	Georgia	114	0.5%
29	Hawaii	104	0.5%
41	Idaho	18	0.1%
6	Illinois	1,204	5.6%
20	Indiana	274	1.3%
34	Iowa	87	0.4%
NA	Kansas**	NA	NA
36	Kentucky	53	0.2%
19	Louisiana	282	1.3%
NA	Maine**	NA	NA
15	Maryland	308	1.4%
12	Massachusetts	401	1.9%
10	Michigan	426	2.0%
14	Minnesota	334	1.6%
30	Mississippi	99	0.5%
13	Missouri	381	1.8%
39	Montana	32	0.1%
33	Nebraska	89	0.4%
21	Nevada	256	1.2%
39	New Hampshire	32	0.1%
5	New Jersey	1,231	5.8%
38	New Mexico	42	0.2%
7	New York	704	3.3%
8	North Carolina	639	3.0%
45	North Dakota	7	0.0%
9	Ohio	478	2.2%
NA	Oklahoma**	NA	NA
23	Oregon	209	1.0%
4	Pennsylvania	1,359	6.4%
31	Rhode Island	93	0.4%
32	South Carolina	91	0.4%
43	South Dakota	14	0.1%
25	Tennessee	158	0.7%
3	Texas	1,384	6.5%
35	Utah	57	0.3%
46	Vermont	0	0.0%
16	Virginia	296	1.4%
11	Washington	407	1.9%
42	West Virginia	17	0.1%
NA	Wisconsin**	NA	NA
44	Wyoming	8	0.0%

RANK ORDER

RANK	STATE	ARRESTS	% of USA
1	California	5,711	26.7%
2	Florida	2,622	12.3%
3	Texas	1,384	6.5%
4	Pennsylvania	1,359	6.4%
5	New Jersey	1,231	5.8%
6	Illinois	1,204	5.6%
7	New York	704	3.3%
8	North Carolina	639	3.0%
9	Ohio	478	2.2%
10	Michigan	426	2.0%
11	Washington	407	1.9%
12	Massachusetts	401	1.9%
13	Missouri	381	1.8%
14	Minnesota	334	1.6%
15	Maryland	308	1.4%
16	Virginia	296	1.4%
17	Connecticut	291	1.4%
18	Arizona	290	1.4%
19	Louisiana	282	1.3%
20	Indiana	274	1.3%
21	Nevada	256	1.2%
22	Alabama	252	1.2%
23	Oregon	209	1.0%
24	Colorado	166	0.8%
25	Tennessee	158	0.7%
26	Delaware	149	0.7%
27	Arkansas	140	0.7%
28	Georgia	114	0.5%
29	Hawaii	104	0.5%
30	Mississippi	99	0.5%
31	Rhode Island	93	0.4%
32	South Carolina	91	0.4%
33	Nebraska	89	0.4%
34	Iowa	87	0.4%
35	Utah	57	0.3%
36	Kentucky	53	0.2%
37	Alaska	48	0.2%
38	New Mexico	42	0.2%
39	Montana	32	0.1%
39	New Hampshire	32	0.1%
41	Idaho	18	0.1%
42	West Virginia	17	0.1%
43	South Dakota	14	0.1%
44	Wyoming	8	0.0%
45	North Dakota	7	0.0%
46	Vermont	0	0.0%
NA	Kansas**	NA	NA
NA	Maine**	NA	NA
NA	Oklahoma**	NA	NA
NA	Wisconsin**	NA	NA
	District of Columbia**	NA	NA

Source: Federal Bureau of Investigation
    "Crime in the United States 1999" (Uniform Crime Reports, October 15, 2000)
*Arrests of youths 17 years and younger by law enforcement agencies submitting complete reports to the F.B.I. for 12 months in 1999. Robbery is the taking or attempting to take anything of value by force or threat of force. See important note at beginning of this chapter. **Not available.

Reported Juvenile Arrest Rate for Robbery in 1999

National Rate = 99.3 Reported Arrests per 100,000 Juvenile Population*

ALPHA ORDER

RANK ORDER

RANK	STATE	RATE		RANK	STATE	RATE
29	Alabama	57.0		1	Illinois	374.4
26	Alaska	58.5		2	Delaware	184.7
31	Arizona	55.3		3	Florida	163.7
34	Arkansas	48.9		4	California	154.3
4	California	154.3		5	New Jersey	146.8
32	Colorado	54.9		6	Pennsylvania	132.2
16	Connecticut	82.6		7	Nevada	126.5
2	Delaware	184.7		8	New York	116.5
3	Florida	163.7		9	Kentucky	107.1
37	Georgia	40.2		10	Missouri	101.8
11	Hawaii	95.9		11	Hawaii	95.9
44	Idaho	12.7		12	South Carolina	91.2
1	Illinois	374.4		13	Maryland	88.3
20	Indiana	68.5		14	Rhode Island	85.3
39	Iowa	31.2		15	North Carolina	84.5
NA	Kansas**	NA		16	Connecticut	82.6
9	Kentucky	107.1		17	Washington	80.8
21	Louisiana	68.1		18	Massachusetts	78.6
NA	Maine**	NA		19	Mississippi	72.2
13	Maryland	88.3		20	Indiana	68.5
18	Massachusetts	78.6		21	Louisiana	68.1
36	Michigan	44.0		22	Ohio	68.0
23	Minnesota	64.8		23	Minnesota	64.8
19	Mississippi	72.2		24	Texas	62.3
10	Missouri	101.8		25	Virginia	59.1
27	Montana	58.2		26	Alaska	58.5
35	Nebraska	46.0		27	Montana	58.2
7	Nevada	126.5		28	Oregon	57.8
30	New Hampshire	56.7		29	Alabama	57.0
5	New Jersey	146.8		30	New Hampshire	56.7
38	New Mexico	32.6		31	Arizona	55.3
8	New York	116.5		32	Colorado	54.9
15	North Carolina	84.5		33	Tennessee	52.0
45	North Dakota	11.9		34	Arkansas	48.9
22	Ohio	68.0		35	Nebraska	46.0
NA	Oklahoma**	NA		36	Michigan	44.0
28	Oregon	57.8		37	Georgia	40.2
6	Pennsylvania	132.2		38	New Mexico	32.6
14	Rhode Island	85.3		39	Iowa	31.2
12	South Carolina	91.2		40	Utah	27.2
41	South Dakota	20.7		41	South Dakota	20.7
33	Tennessee	52.0		42	West Virginia	16.9
24	Texas	62.3		43	Wyoming	12.8
40	Utah	27.2		44	Idaho	12.7
46	Vermont	0.0		45	North Dakota	11.9
25	Virginia	59.1		46	Vermont	0.0
17	Washington	80.8		NA	Kansas**	NA
42	West Virginia	16.9		NA	Maine**	NA
NA	Wisconsin**	NA		NA	Oklahoma**	NA
43	Wyoming	12.8		NA	Wisconsin**	NA
					District of Columbia**	NA

Source: Morgan Quitno Press using data from Federal Bureau of Investigation
  "Crime in the United States 1999" (Uniform Crime Reports, October 15, 2000)
*By law enforcement agencies submitting complete reports to the F.B.I. for 12 months in 1999. Arrests of youths 17 years and younger divided into population of 10 to 17 year olds. See important note at beginning of this chapter. Robbery is the taking or attempting to take anything of value by force or threat of force.
**Not available.

Reported Arrests of Juveniles for Robbery
As a Percent of All Such Arrests in 1999
National Percent = 25.7% of Reported Robbery Arrests*

ALPHA ORDER

RANK	STATE	PERCENT
38	Alabama	17.8
19	Alaska	25.5
29	Arizona	21.3
36	Arkansas	18.0
8	California	30.5
17	Colorado	26.2
31	Connecticut	21.1
18	Delaware	26.0
16	Florida	27.2
42	Georgia	15.1
14	Hawaii	27.7
28	Idaho	21.4
3	Illinois	37.9
34	Indiana	19.2
20	Iowa	24.2
NA	Kansas**	NA
45	Kentucky	11.6
33	Louisiana	20.0
NA	Maine**	NA
11	Maryland	29.6
13	Massachusetts	28.8
42	Michigan	15.1
6	Minnesota	32.7
36	Mississippi	18.0
27	Missouri	22.0
1	Montana	43.2
15	Nebraska	27.6
25	Nevada	22.3
5	New Hampshire	34.8
12	New Jersey	29.4
41	New Mexico	16.5
7	New York	30.8
39	North Carolina	17.2
4	North Dakota	35.0
22	Ohio	23.6
NA	Oklahoma**	NA
30	Oregon	21.2
26	Pennsylvania	22.1
2	Rhode Island	38.4
35	South Carolina	18.5
9	South Dakota	30.4
42	Tennessee	15.1
20	Texas	24.2
22	Utah	23.6
46	Vermont	0.0
32	Virginia	20.7
10	Washington	30.2
39	West Virginia	17.2
NA	Wisconsin**	NA
24	Wyoming	22.9

RANK ORDER

RANK	STATE	PERCENT
1	Montana	43.2
2	Rhode Island	38.4
3	Illinois	37.9
4	North Dakota	35.0
5	New Hampshire	34.8
6	Minnesota	32.7
7	New York	30.8
8	California	30.5
9	South Dakota	30.4
10	Washington	30.2
11	Maryland	29.6
12	New Jersey	29.4
13	Massachusetts	28.8
14	Hawaii	27.7
15	Nebraska	27.6
16	Florida	27.2
17	Colorado	26.2
18	Delaware	26.0
19	Alaska	25.5
20	Iowa	24.2
20	Texas	24.2
22	Ohio	23.6
22	Utah	23.6
24	Wyoming	22.9
25	Nevada	22.3
26	Pennsylvania	22.1
27	Missouri	22.0
28	Idaho	21.4
29	Arizona	21.3
30	Oregon	21.2
31	Connecticut	21.1
32	Virginia	20.7
33	Louisiana	20.0
34	Indiana	19.2
35	South Carolina	18.5
36	Arkansas	18.0
36	Mississippi	18.0
38	Alabama	17.8
39	North Carolina	17.2
39	West Virginia	17.2
41	New Mexico	16.5
42	Georgia	15.1
42	Michigan	15.1
42	Tennessee	15.1
45	Kentucky	11.6
46	Vermont	0.0
NA	Kansas**	NA
NA	Maine**	NA
NA	Oklahoma**	NA
NA	Wisconsin**	NA
	District of Columbia**	NA

Source: Morgan Quitno Press using data from Federal Bureau of Investigation
    "Crime in the United States 1999" (Uniform Crime Reports, October 15, 2000)
*Arrests of youths 17 years and younger by law enforcement agencies submitting complete reports to the F.B.I. for 12 months in 1999. Robbery is the taking or attempting to take anything of value by force or threat of force.
**Not available.

Reported Arrests of Juveniles for Aggravated Assault in 1999

National Total = 52,718 Reported Arrests*

<table>
<tr><td colspan="4">ALPHA ORDER</td><td colspan="4">RANK ORDER</td></tr>
<tr><td>RANK</td><td>STATE</td><td>ARRESTS</td><td>% of USA</td><td>RANK</td><td>STATE</td><td>ARRESTS</td><td>% of USA</td></tr>
<tr><td>29</td><td>Alabama</td><td>368</td><td>0.7%</td><td>1</td><td>California</td><td>12,132</td><td>23.0%</td></tr>
<tr><td>35</td><td>Alaska</td><td>154</td><td>0.3%</td><td>2</td><td>Florida</td><td>7,638</td><td>14.5%</td></tr>
<tr><td>10</td><td>Arizona</td><td>1,312</td><td>2.5%</td><td>3</td><td>Texas</td><td>3,349</td><td>6.4%</td></tr>
<tr><td>25</td><td>Arkansas</td><td>454</td><td>0.9%</td><td>4</td><td>Pennsylvania</td><td>2,715</td><td>5.2%</td></tr>
<tr><td>1</td><td>California</td><td>12,132</td><td>23.0%</td><td>5</td><td>New Jersey</td><td>2,097</td><td>4.0%</td></tr>
<tr><td>22</td><td>Colorado</td><td>574</td><td>1.1%</td><td>6</td><td>Illinois</td><td>1,934</td><td>3.7%</td></tr>
<tr><td>17</td><td>Connecticut</td><td>845</td><td>1.6%</td><td>7</td><td>Massachusetts</td><td>1,853</td><td>3.5%</td></tr>
<tr><td>27</td><td>Delaware</td><td>395</td><td>0.7%</td><td>8</td><td>North Carolina</td><td>1,765</td><td>3.3%</td></tr>
<tr><td>2</td><td>Florida</td><td>7,638</td><td>14.5%</td><td>9</td><td>Louisiana</td><td>1,515</td><td>2.9%</td></tr>
<tr><td>30</td><td>Georgia</td><td>365</td><td>0.7%</td><td>10</td><td>Arizona</td><td>1,312</td><td>2.5%</td></tr>
<tr><td>39</td><td>Hawaii</td><td>117</td><td>0.2%</td><td>11</td><td>New York</td><td>1,268</td><td>2.4%</td></tr>
<tr><td>33</td><td>Idaho</td><td>238</td><td>0.5%</td><td>12</td><td>Indiana</td><td>1,239</td><td>2.4%</td></tr>
<tr><td>6</td><td>Illinois</td><td>1,934</td><td>3.7%</td><td>13</td><td>Michigan</td><td>1,229</td><td>2.3%</td></tr>
<tr><td>12</td><td>Indiana</td><td>1,239</td><td>2.4%</td><td>14</td><td>Washington</td><td>1,107</td><td>2.1%</td></tr>
<tr><td>20</td><td>Iowa</td><td>616</td><td>1.2%</td><td>15</td><td>Ohio</td><td>1,036</td><td>2.0%</td></tr>
<tr><td>NA</td><td>Kansas**</td><td>NA</td><td>NA</td><td>16</td><td>Minnesota</td><td>922</td><td>1.7%</td></tr>
<tr><td>34</td><td>Kentucky</td><td>195</td><td>0.4%</td><td>17</td><td>Connecticut</td><td>845</td><td>1.6%</td></tr>
<tr><td>9</td><td>Louisiana</td><td>1,515</td><td>2.9%</td><td>18</td><td>Maryland</td><td>711</td><td>1.3%</td></tr>
<tr><td>NA</td><td>Maine**</td><td>NA</td><td>NA</td><td>19</td><td>Missouri</td><td>696</td><td>1.3%</td></tr>
<tr><td>18</td><td>Maryland</td><td>711</td><td>1.3%</td><td>20</td><td>Iowa</td><td>616</td><td>1.2%</td></tr>
<tr><td>7</td><td>Massachusetts</td><td>1,853</td><td>3.5%</td><td>21</td><td>Virginia</td><td>601</td><td>1.1%</td></tr>
<tr><td>13</td><td>Michigan</td><td>1,229</td><td>2.3%</td><td>22</td><td>Colorado</td><td>574</td><td>1.1%</td></tr>
<tr><td>16</td><td>Minnesota</td><td>922</td><td>1.7%</td><td>23</td><td>Tennessee</td><td>558</td><td>1.1%</td></tr>
<tr><td>39</td><td>Mississippi</td><td>117</td><td>0.2%</td><td>24</td><td>Oregon</td><td>472</td><td>0.9%</td></tr>
<tr><td>19</td><td>Missouri</td><td>696</td><td>1.3%</td><td>25</td><td>Arkansas</td><td>454</td><td>0.9%</td></tr>
<tr><td>37</td><td>Montana</td><td>123</td><td>0.2%</td><td>26</td><td>Utah</td><td>438</td><td>0.8%</td></tr>
<tr><td>38</td><td>Nebraska</td><td>119</td><td>0.2%</td><td>27</td><td>Delaware</td><td>395</td><td>0.7%</td></tr>
<tr><td>31</td><td>Nevada</td><td>288</td><td>0.5%</td><td>28</td><td>New Mexico</td><td>391</td><td>0.7%</td></tr>
<tr><td>45</td><td>New Hampshire</td><td>35</td><td>0.1%</td><td>29</td><td>Alabama</td><td>368</td><td>0.7%</td></tr>
<tr><td>5</td><td>New Jersey</td><td>2,097</td><td>4.0%</td><td>30</td><td>Georgia</td><td>365</td><td>0.7%</td></tr>
<tr><td>28</td><td>New Mexico</td><td>391</td><td>0.7%</td><td>31</td><td>Nevada</td><td>288</td><td>0.5%</td></tr>
<tr><td>11</td><td>New York</td><td>1,268</td><td>2.4%</td><td>32</td><td>South Carolina</td><td>277</td><td>0.5%</td></tr>
<tr><td>8</td><td>North Carolina</td><td>1,765</td><td>3.3%</td><td>33</td><td>Idaho</td><td>238</td><td>0.5%</td></tr>
<tr><td>44</td><td>North Dakota</td><td>41</td><td>0.1%</td><td>34</td><td>Kentucky</td><td>195</td><td>0.4%</td></tr>
<tr><td>15</td><td>Ohio</td><td>1,036</td><td>2.0%</td><td>35</td><td>Alaska</td><td>154</td><td>0.3%</td></tr>
<tr><td>NA</td><td>Oklahoma**</td><td>NA</td><td>NA</td><td>36</td><td>Rhode Island</td><td>153</td><td>0.3%</td></tr>
<tr><td>24</td><td>Oregon</td><td>472</td><td>0.9%</td><td>37</td><td>Montana</td><td>123</td><td>0.2%</td></tr>
<tr><td>4</td><td>Pennsylvania</td><td>2,715</td><td>5.2%</td><td>38</td><td>Nebraska</td><td>119</td><td>0.2%</td></tr>
<tr><td>36</td><td>Rhode Island</td><td>153</td><td>0.3%</td><td>39</td><td>Hawaii</td><td>117</td><td>0.2%</td></tr>
<tr><td>32</td><td>South Carolina</td><td>277</td><td>0.5%</td><td>39</td><td>Mississippi</td><td>117</td><td>0.2%</td></tr>
<tr><td>41</td><td>South Dakota</td><td>87</td><td>0.2%</td><td>41</td><td>South Dakota</td><td>87</td><td>0.2%</td></tr>
<tr><td>23</td><td>Tennessee</td><td>558</td><td>1.1%</td><td>42</td><td>Wyoming</td><td>78</td><td>0.1%</td></tr>
<tr><td>3</td><td>Texas</td><td>3,349</td><td>6.4%</td><td>43</td><td>West Virginia</td><td>77</td><td>0.1%</td></tr>
<tr><td>26</td><td>Utah</td><td>438</td><td>0.8%</td><td>44</td><td>North Dakota</td><td>41</td><td>0.1%</td></tr>
<tr><td>46</td><td>Vermont</td><td>24</td><td>0.0%</td><td>45</td><td>New Hampshire</td><td>35</td><td>0.1%</td></tr>
<tr><td>21</td><td>Virginia</td><td>601</td><td>1.1%</td><td>46</td><td>Vermont</td><td>24</td><td>0.0%</td></tr>
<tr><td>14</td><td>Washington</td><td>1,107</td><td>2.1%</td><td>NA</td><td>Kansas**</td><td>NA</td><td>NA</td></tr>
<tr><td>43</td><td>West Virginia</td><td>77</td><td>0.1%</td><td>NA</td><td>Maine**</td><td>NA</td><td>NA</td></tr>
<tr><td>NA</td><td>Wisconsin**</td><td>NA</td><td>NA</td><td>NA</td><td>Oklahoma**</td><td>NA</td><td>NA</td></tr>
<tr><td>42</td><td>Wyoming</td><td>78</td><td>0.1%</td><td>NA</td><td>Wisconsin**</td><td>NA</td><td>NA</td></tr>
<tr><td></td><td></td><td></td><td></td><td></td><td>District of Columbia**</td><td>NA</td><td>NA</td></tr>
</table>

Source: Federal Bureau of Investigation
"Crime in the United States 1999" (Uniform Crime Reports, October 15, 2000)
*Arrests of youths 17 years and younger by law enforcement agencies submitting complete reports to the F.B.I. for 12 months in 1999. Aggravated assault is an attack for the purpose of inflicting severe bodily injury. See important note at beginning of this chapter.
**Not available.

Reported Juvenile Arrest Rate for Aggravated Assault in 1999

National Rate = 245.2 Reported Arrests per 100,000 Juvenile Population*

ALPHA ORDER

RANK ORDER

RANK	STATE	RATE
41	Alabama	83.2
23	Alaska	187.7
12	Arizona	250.1
28	Arkansas	158.5
7	California	327.9
22	Colorado	189.7
14	Connecticut	239.9
2	Delaware	489.6
3	Florida	476.8
34	Georgia	128.6
39	Hawaii	107.9
27	Idaho	168.5
1	Illinois	601.4
8	Indiana	309.7
17	Iowa	220.8
NA	Kansas**	NA
4	Kentucky	393.9
5	Louisiana	365.7
NA	Maine**	NA
21	Maryland	203.8
6	Massachusetts	363.4
36	Michigan	126.9
26	Minnesota	178.8
40	Mississippi	85.3
24	Missouri	185.9
16	Montana	223.7
45	Nebraska	61.5
31	Nevada	142.3
44	New Hampshire	62.0
12	New Jersey	250.1
9	New Mexico	303.5
19	New York	209.9
15	North Carolina	233.5
43	North Dakota	69.6
30	Ohio	147.4
NA	Oklahoma**	NA
33	Oregon	130.6
11	Pennsylvania	264.1
32	Rhode Island	140.4
10	South Carolina	277.6
35	South Dakota	128.5
25	Tennessee	183.7
29	Texas	150.8
20	Utah	208.9
46	Vermont	42.5
38	Virginia	119.9
18	Washington	219.8
42	West Virginia	76.6
NA	Wisconsin**	NA
37	Wyoming	124.5

RANK	STATE	RATE
1	Illinois	601.4
2	Delaware	489.6
3	Florida	476.8
4	Kentucky	393.9
5	Louisiana	365.7
6	Massachusetts	363.4
7	California	327.9
8	Indiana	309.7
9	New Mexico	303.5
10	South Carolina	277.6
11	Pennsylvania	264.1
12	Arizona	250.1
12	New Jersey	250.1
14	Connecticut	239.9
15	North Carolina	233.5
16	Montana	223.7
17	Iowa	220.8
18	Washington	219.8
19	New York	209.9
20	Utah	208.9
21	Maryland	203.8
22	Colorado	189.7
23	Alaska	187.7
24	Missouri	185.9
25	Tennessee	183.7
26	Minnesota	178.8
27	Idaho	168.5
28	Arkansas	158.5
29	Texas	150.8
30	Ohio	147.4
31	Nevada	142.3
32	Rhode Island	140.4
33	Oregon	130.6
34	Georgia	128.6
35	South Dakota	128.5
36	Michigan	126.9
37	Wyoming	124.5
38	Virginia	119.9
39	Hawaii	107.9
40	Mississippi	85.3
41	Alabama	83.2
42	West Virginia	76.6
43	North Dakota	69.6
44	New Hampshire	62.0
45	Nebraska	61.5
46	Vermont	42.5
NA	Kansas**	NA
NA	Maine**	NA
NA	Oklahoma**	NA
NA	Wisconsin**	NA
	District of Columbia**	NA

Source: Morgan Quitno Press using data from Federal Bureau of Investigation
   "Crime in the United States 1999" (Uniform Crime Reports, October 15, 2000)
*By law enforcement agencies submitting complete reports to the F.B.I. for 12 months in 1999. Arrests of youths 17 years and younger divided into population of 10 to 17 year olds. See important note at beginning of this chapter. Aggravated assault is an attack for the purpose of inflicting severe bodily injury.
**Not available.

Reported Arrests of Juveniles for Aggravated Assault
As a Percent of All Such Arrests in 1999
National Percent = 14.6% of Reported Aggravated Assault Arrests*

ALPHA ORDER

RANK	STATE	PERCENT
45	Alabama	7.8
30	Alaska	14.1
9	Arizona	21.7
39	Arkansas	11.0
38	California	11.1
29	Colorado	14.6
16	Connecticut	19.1
13	Delaware	19.9
21	Florida	17.8
35	Georgia	11.6
16	Hawaii	19.1
5	Idaho	24.4
3	Illinois	28.3
24	Indiana	16.8
25	Iowa	16.6
NA	Kansas**	NA
41	Kentucky	10.0
27	Louisiana	15.9
NA	Maine**	NA
12	Maryland	20.5
28	Massachusetts	15.8
40	Michigan	10.4
5	Minnesota	24.4
43	Mississippi	9.7
34	Missouri	11.9
4	Montana	25.7
31	Nebraska	13.8
22	Nevada	17.2
10	New Hampshire	21.5
14	New Jersey	19.4
20	New Mexico	18.5
22	New York	17.2
44	North Carolina	9.2
2	North Dakota	33.6
32	Ohio	13.5
NA	Oklahoma**	NA
7	Oregon	22.9
19	Pennsylvania	18.7
15	Rhode Island	19.2
33	South Carolina	12.0
11	South Dakota	20.8
41	Tennessee	10.0
26	Texas	16.5
1	Utah	34.1
37	Vermont	11.3
36	Virginia	11.4
8	Washington	22.3
46	West Virginia	5.3
NA	Wisconsin**	NA
18	Wyoming	18.8

RANK ORDER

RANK	STATE	PERCENT
1	Utah	34.1
2	North Dakota	33.6
3	Illinois	28.3
4	Montana	25.7
5	Idaho	24.4
5	Minnesota	24.4
7	Oregon	22.9
8	Washington	22.3
9	Arizona	21.7
10	New Hampshire	21.5
11	South Dakota	20.8
12	Maryland	20.5
13	Delaware	19.9
14	New Jersey	19.4
15	Rhode Island	19.2
16	Connecticut	19.1
16	Hawaii	19.1
18	Wyoming	18.8
19	Pennsylvania	18.7
20	New Mexico	18.5
21	Florida	17.8
22	Nevada	17.2
22	New York	17.2
24	Indiana	16.8
25	Iowa	16.6
26	Texas	16.5
27	Louisiana	15.9
28	Massachusetts	15.8
29	Colorado	14.6
30	Alaska	14.1
31	Nebraska	13.8
32	Ohio	13.5
33	South Carolina	12.0
34	Missouri	11.9
35	Georgia	11.6
36	Virginia	11.4
37	Vermont	11.3
38	California	11.1
39	Arkansas	11.0
40	Michigan	10.4
41	Kentucky	10.0
41	Tennessee	10.0
43	Mississippi	9.7
44	North Carolina	9.2
45	Alabama	7.8
46	West Virginia	5.3
NA	Kansas**	NA
NA	Maine**	NA
NA	Oklahoma**	NA
NA	Wisconsin**	NA
	District of Columbia**	NA

Source: Morgan Quitno Press using data from Federal Bureau of Investigation
    "Crime in the United States 1999" (Uniform Crime Reports, October 15, 2000)
*Arrests of youths 17 years and younger by law enforcement agencies submitting complete reports to the F.B.I. for 12 months in 1999. Aggravated assault is an attack for the purpose of inflicting severe bodily injury.
**Not available.

Reported Arrests of Juveniles for Property Crime in 1999

National Total = 395,886 Reported Arrests*

ALPHA ORDER

RANK	STATE	ARRESTS	% of USA
29	Alabama	4,133	1.0%
37	Alaska	1,891	0.5%
8	Arizona	12,243	3.1%
28	Arkansas	4,520	1.1%
1	California	60,741	15.3%
15	Colorado	8,681	2.2%
26	Connecticut	5,108	1.3%
39	Delaware	1,613	0.4%
2	Florida	43,259	10.9%
27	Georgia	4,529	1.1%
34	Hawaii	2,242	0.6%
31	Idaho	3,588	0.9%
17	Illinois	8,498	2.1%
20	Indiana	6,834	1.7%
22	Iowa	5,555	1.4%
NA	Kansas**	NA	NA
43	Kentucky	1,137	0.3%
13	Louisiana	9,850	2.5%
NA	Maine**	NA	NA
19	Maryland	6,931	1.8%
30	Massachusetts	3,741	0.9%
10	Michigan	10,750	2.7%
7	Minnesota	12,289	3.1%
32	Mississippi	2,862	0.7%
16	Missouri	8,506	2.1%
36	Montana	1,919	0.5%
24	Nebraska	5,266	1.3%
25	Nevada	5,132	1.3%
45	New Hampshire	711	0.2%
9	New Jersey	11,927	3.0%
33	New Mexico	2,539	0.6%
12	New York	10,587	2.7%
6	North Carolina	12,937	3.3%
42	North Dakota	1,267	0.3%
11	Ohio	10,588	2.7%
NA	Oklahoma**	NA	NA
14	Oregon	9,115	2.3%
5	Pennsylvania	14,603	3.7%
38	Rhode Island	1,712	0.4%
35	South Carolina	2,114	0.5%
40	South Dakota	1,610	0.4%
23	Tennessee	5,485	1.4%
3	Texas	37,491	9.5%
21	Utah	5,594	1.4%
46	Vermont	450	0.1%
18	Virginia	7,367	1.9%
4	Washington	15,431	3.9%
44	West Virginia	1,007	0.3%
NA	Wisconsin**	NA	NA
41	Wyoming	1,533	0.4%

RANK ORDER

RANK	STATE	ARRESTS	% of USA
1	California	60,741	15.3%
2	Florida	43,259	10.9%
3	Texas	37,491	9.5%
4	Washington	15,431	3.9%
5	Pennsylvania	14,603	3.7%
6	North Carolina	12,937	3.3%
7	Minnesota	12,289	3.1%
8	Arizona	12,243	3.1%
9	New Jersey	11,927	3.0%
10	Michigan	10,750	2.7%
11	Ohio	10,588	2.7%
12	New York	10,587	2.7%
13	Louisiana	9,850	2.5%
14	Oregon	9,115	2.3%
15	Colorado	8,681	2.2%
16	Missouri	8,506	2.1%
17	Illinois	8,498	2.1%
18	Virginia	7,367	1.9%
19	Maryland	6,931	1.8%
20	Indiana	6,834	1.7%
21	Utah	5,594	1.4%
22	Iowa	5,555	1.4%
23	Tennessee	5,485	1.4%
24	Nebraska	5,266	1.3%
25	Nevada	5,132	1.3%
26	Connecticut	5,108	1.3%
27	Georgia	4,529	1.1%
28	Arkansas	4,520	1.1%
29	Alabama	4,133	1.0%
30	Massachusetts	3,741	0.9%
31	Idaho	3,588	0.9%
32	Mississippi	2,862	0.7%
33	New Mexico	2,539	0.6%
34	Hawaii	2,242	0.6%
35	South Carolina	2,114	0.5%
36	Montana	1,919	0.5%
37	Alaska	1,891	0.5%
38	Rhode Island	1,712	0.4%
39	Delaware	1,613	0.4%
40	South Dakota	1,610	0.4%
41	Wyoming	1,533	0.4%
42	North Dakota	1,267	0.3%
43	Kentucky	1,137	0.3%
44	West Virginia	1,007	0.3%
45	New Hampshire	711	0.2%
46	Vermont	450	0.1%
NA	Kansas**	NA	NA
NA	Maine**	NA	NA
NA	Oklahoma**	NA	NA
NA	Wisconsin**	NA	NA
	District of Columbia**	NA	NA

Source: Federal Bureau of Investigation
"Crime in the United States 1999" (Uniform Crime Reports, October 15, 2000)
*Arrests of youths 17 years and younger by law enforcement agencies submitting complete reports to the F.B.I. for 12 months in 1999. Property crimes are offenses of burglary, larceny-theft, motor vehicle theft and arson. See important note at beginning of this chapter.
**Not available.

Reported Juvenile Arrest Rate for Property Crime in 1999

National Rate = 1,841.5 Reported Arrests per 100,000 Juvenile Population*

ALPHA ORDER

RANK ORDER

RANK	STATE	RATE		RANK	STATE	RATE
44	Alabama	934.8		1	Montana	3,489.7
16	Alaska	2,305.4		2	Washington	3,064.1
15	Arizona	2,333.5		3	Colorado	2,868.4
34	Arkansas	1,577.6		4	Nebraska	2,720.9
32	California	1,641.6		5	Florida	2,700.7
3	Colorado	2,868.4		6	Utah	2,668.0
38	Connecticut	1,450.2		7	Illinois	2,642.5
23	Delaware	1,999.3		8	Idaho	2,540.8
5	Florida	2,700.7		9	Nevada	2,535.6
33	Georgia	1,596.2		10	Oregon	2,521.7
22	Hawaii	2,066.9		11	Wyoming	2,447.2
8	Idaho	2,540.8		12	Minnesota	2,382.8
7	Illinois	2,642.5		13	Louisiana	2,377.6
30	Indiana	1,708.1		14	South Dakota	2,377.1
24	Iowa	1,991.0		15	Arizona	2,333.5
NA	Kansas**	NA		16	Alaska	2,305.4
17	Kentucky	2,296.7		17	Kentucky	2,296.7
13	Louisiana	2,377.6		18	Missouri	2,272.1
NA	Maine**	NA		19	North Dakota	2,152.0
25	Maryland	1,986.9		20	South Carolina	2,118.5
46	Massachusetts	733.6		21	Mississippi	2,086.9
42	Michigan	1,110.4		22	Hawaii	2,066.9
12	Minnesota	2,382.8		23	Delaware	1,999.3
21	Mississippi	2,086.9		24	Iowa	1,991.0
18	Missouri	2,272.1		25	Maryland	1,986.9
1	Montana	3,489.7		26	New Mexico	1,970.8
4	Nebraska	2,720.9		27	Tennessee	1,805.6
9	Nevada	2,535.6		28	New York	1,752.6
41	New Hampshire	1,258.7		29	North Carolina	1,711.2
39	New Jersey	1,422.5		30	Indiana	1,708.1
26	New Mexico	1,970.8		31	Texas	1,687.7
28	New York	1,752.6		32	California	1,641.6
29	North Carolina	1,711.2		33	Georgia	1,596.2
19	North Dakota	2,152.0		34	Arkansas	1,577.6
36	Ohio	1,506.3		35	Rhode Island	1,570.5
NA	Oklahoma**	NA		36	Ohio	1,506.3
10	Oregon	2,521.7		37	Virginia	1,470.1
40	Pennsylvania	1,420.5		38	Connecticut	1,450.2
35	Rhode Island	1,570.5		39	New Jersey	1,422.5
20	South Carolina	2,118.5		40	Pennsylvania	1,420.5
14	South Dakota	2,377.1		41	New Hampshire	1,258.7
27	Tennessee	1,805.6		42	Michigan	1,110.4
31	Texas	1,687.7		43	West Virginia	1,002.1
6	Utah	2,668.0		44	Alabama	934.8
45	Vermont	796.3		45	Vermont	796.3
37	Virginia	1,470.1		46	Massachusetts	733.6
2	Washington	3,064.1		NA	Kansas**	NA
43	West Virginia	1,002.1		NA	Maine**	NA
NA	Wisconsin**	NA		NA	Oklahoma**	NA
11	Wyoming	2,447.2		NA	Wisconsin**	NA
					District of Columbia**	NA

Source: Morgan Quitno Press using data from Federal Bureau of Investigation
    "Crime in the United States 1999" (Uniform Crime Reports, October 15, 2000)
*By law enforcement agencies submitting complete reports to the F.B.I. for 12 months in 1999. Arrests of youths 17 years and younger divided into population of 10 to 17 year olds. See important note at beginning of this chapter. Property crimes are offenses of burglary, larceny-theft, motor vehicle theft and arson.
**Not available.

Reported Arrests of Juveniles for Property Crime
As a Percent of All Such Arrests in 1999
National Percent = 32.3% of Reported Property Crime Arrests*

ALPHA ORDER

RANK	STATE	PERCENT
46	Alabama	22.8
7	Alaska	44.7
27	Arizona	30.7
41	Arkansas	25.3
16	California	34.6
14	Colorado	37.6
39	Connecticut	26.7
33	Delaware	28.1
22	Florida	32.7
34	Georgia	27.6
24	Hawaii	32.3
1	Idaho	52.9
42	Illinois	24.6
26	Indiana	30.9
9	Iowa	43.2
NA	Kansas**	NA
38	Kentucky	26.9
31	Louisiana	29.4
NA	Maine**	NA
18	Maryland	34.2
44	Massachusetts	24.0
19	Michigan	33.7
4	Minnesota	48.0
40	Mississippi	26.2
37	Missouri	27.0
3	Montana	49.5
8	Nebraska	44.6
25	Nevada	31.3
10	New Hampshire	42.8
29	New Jersey	29.6
17	New Mexico	34.3
32	New York	28.8
45	North Carolina	23.7
2	North Dakota	52.7
23	Ohio	32.4
NA	Oklahoma**	NA
21	Oregon	33.0
28	Pennsylvania	29.7
13	Rhode Island	37.9
30	South Carolina	29.5
5	South Dakota	47.3
43	Tennessee	24.2
15	Texas	35.1
12	Utah	41.4
20	Vermont	33.1
36	Virginia	27.1
11	Washington	41.5
35	West Virginia	27.5
NA	Wisconsin**	NA
6	Wyoming	47.2

RANK ORDER

RANK	STATE	PERCENT
1	Idaho	52.9
2	North Dakota	52.7
3	Montana	49.5
4	Minnesota	48.0
5	South Dakota	47.3
6	Wyoming	47.2
7	Alaska	44.7
8	Nebraska	44.6
9	Iowa	43.2
10	New Hampshire	42.8
11	Washington	41.5
12	Utah	41.4
13	Rhode Island	37.9
14	Colorado	37.6
15	Texas	35.1
16	California	34.6
17	New Mexico	34.3
18	Maryland	34.2
19	Michigan	33.7
20	Vermont	33.1
21	Oregon	33.0
22	Florida	32.7
23	Ohio	32.4
24	Hawaii	32.3
25	Nevada	31.3
26	Indiana	30.9
27	Arizona	30.7
28	Pennsylvania	29.7
29	New Jersey	29.6
30	South Carolina	29.5
31	Louisiana	29.4
32	New York	28.8
33	Delaware	28.1
34	Georgia	27.6
35	West Virginia	27.5
36	Virginia	27.1
37	Missouri	27.0
38	Kentucky	26.9
39	Connecticut	26.7
40	Mississippi	26.2
41	Arkansas	25.3
42	Illinois	24.6
43	Tennessee	24.2
44	Massachusetts	24.0
45	North Carolina	23.7
46	Alabama	22.8
NA	Kansas**	NA
NA	Maine**	NA
NA	Oklahoma**	NA
NA	Wisconsin**	NA
	District of Columbia**	NA

Source: Morgan Quitno Press using data from Federal Bureau of Investigation
    "Crime in the United States 1999" (Uniform Crime Reports, October 15, 2000)
*Arrests of youths 17 years and younger by law enforcement agencies submitting complete reports to the F.B.I. for
12 months in 1999. Property crimes are offenses of burglary, larceny-theft, motor vehicle theft and arson.
**Not available.

Reported Arrests of Juveniles for Burglary in 1999

National Total = 74,737 Reported Arrests*

ALPHA ORDER

RANK	STATE	ARRESTS	% of USA
27	Alabama	685	0.9%
34	Alaska	341	0.5%
10	Arizona	1,847	2.5%
21	Arkansas	910	1.2%
1	California	17,096	22.9%
20	Colorado	949	1.3%
24	Connecticut	789	1.1%
34	Delaware	341	0.5%
2	Florida	10,256	13.7%
22	Georgia	902	1.2%
33	Hawaii	365	0.5%
30	Idaho	514	0.7%
14	Illinois	1,315	1.8%
25	Indiana	783	1.0%
26	Iowa	725	1.0%
NA	Kansas**	NA	NA
40	Kentucky	204	0.3%
8	Louisiana	2,182	2.9%
NA	Maine**	NA	NA
15	Maryland	1,309	1.8%
23	Massachusetts	873	1.2%
12	Michigan	1,535	2.1%
13	Minnesota	1,375	1.8%
28	Mississippi	637	0.9%
17	Missouri	1,175	1.6%
44	Montana	136	0.2%
31	Nebraska	492	0.7%
19	Nevada	1,064	1.4%
46	New Hampshire	83	0.1%
9	New Jersey	1,940	2.6%
38	New Mexico	279	0.4%
7	New York	2,261	3.0%
4	North Carolina	3,101	4.1%
41	North Dakota	172	0.2%
11	Ohio	1,844	2.5%
NA	Oklahoma**	NA	NA
16	Oregon	1,222	1.6%
5	Pennsylvania	2,573	3.4%
36	Rhode Island	325	0.4%
37	South Carolina	294	0.4%
39	South Dakota	243	0.3%
29	Tennessee	566	0.8%
3	Texas	6,599	8.8%
32	Utah	479	0.6%
45	Vermont	119	0.2%
18	Virginia	1,147	1.5%
6	Washington	2,412	3.2%
43	West Virginia	138	0.2%
NA	Wisconsin**	NA	NA
42	Wyoming	140	0.2%

RANK ORDER

RANK	STATE	ARRESTS	% of USA
1	California	17,096	22.9%
2	Florida	10,256	13.7%
3	Texas	6,599	8.8%
4	North Carolina	3,101	4.1%
5	Pennsylvania	2,573	3.4%
6	Washington	2,412	3.2%
7	New York	2,261	3.0%
8	Louisiana	2,182	2.9%
9	New Jersey	1,940	2.6%
10	Arizona	1,847	2.5%
11	Ohio	1,844	2.5%
12	Michigan	1,535	2.1%
13	Minnesota	1,375	1.8%
14	Illinois	1,315	1.8%
15	Maryland	1,309	1.8%
16	Oregon	1,222	1.6%
17	Missouri	1,175	1.6%
18	Virginia	1,147	1.5%
19	Nevada	1,064	1.4%
20	Colorado	949	1.3%
21	Arkansas	910	1.2%
22	Georgia	902	1.2%
23	Massachusetts	873	1.2%
24	Connecticut	789	1.1%
25	Indiana	783	1.0%
26	Iowa	725	1.0%
27	Alabama	685	0.9%
28	Mississippi	637	0.9%
29	Tennessee	566	0.8%
30	Idaho	514	0.7%
31	Nebraska	492	0.7%
32	Utah	479	0.6%
33	Hawaii	365	0.5%
34	Alaska	341	0.5%
34	Delaware	341	0.5%
36	Rhode Island	325	0.4%
37	South Carolina	294	0.4%
38	New Mexico	279	0.4%
39	South Dakota	243	0.3%
40	Kentucky	204	0.3%
41	North Dakota	172	0.2%
42	Wyoming	140	0.2%
43	West Virginia	138	0.2%
44	Montana	136	0.2%
45	Vermont	119	0.2%
46	New Hampshire	83	0.1%
NA	Kansas**	NA	NA
NA	Maine**	NA	NA
NA	Oklahoma**	NA	NA
NA	Wisconsin**	NA	NA
	District of Columbia**	NA	NA

Source: Federal Bureau of Investigation
    "Crime in the United States 1999" (Uniform Crime Reports, October 15, 2000)
*Arrests of youths 17 years and younger by law enforcement agencies submitting complete reports to the F.B.I. for 12 months in 1999. Burglary is the unlawful entry of a structure to commit a felony or theft. Attempts are included. See important note at beginning of this chapter.
**Not available.

Reported Juvenile Arrest Rate for Burglary in 1999

National Rate = 347.6 Reported Arrests per 100,000 Juvenile Population*

ALPHA ORDER

RANK	STATE	RATE
44	Alabama	154.9
8	Alaska	415.7
16	Arizona	352.0
20	Arkansas	317.6
6	California	462.0
22	Colorado	313.6
36	Connecticut	224.0
7	Delaware	422.7
1	Florida	640.3
19	Georgia	317.9
18	Hawaii	336.5
14	Idaho	364.0
11	Illinois	408.9
40	Indiana	195.7
29	Iowa	259.9
NA	Kansas**	NA
9	Kentucky	412.1
2	Louisiana	526.7
NA	Maine**	NA
12	Maryland	375.3
42	Massachusetts	171.2
43	Michigan	158.5
27	Minnesota	266.6
5	Mississippi	464.5
21	Missouri	313.9
32	Montana	247.3
30	Nebraska	254.2
3	Nevada	525.7
45	New Hampshire	146.9
33	New Jersey	231.4
38	New Mexico	216.6
13	New York	374.3
10	North Carolina	410.2
26	North Dakota	292.1
28	Ohio	262.3
NA	Oklahoma**	NA
17	Oregon	338.1
31	Pennsylvania	250.3
23	Rhode Island	298.1
25	South Carolina	294.6
15	South Dakota	358.8
41	Tennessee	186.3
24	Texas	297.1
35	Utah	228.5
39	Vermont	210.6
34	Virginia	228.9
4	Washington	478.9
46	West Virginia	137.3
NA	Wisconsin**	NA
37	Wyoming	223.5

RANK ORDER

RANK	STATE	RATE
1	Florida	640.3
2	Louisiana	526.7
3	Nevada	525.7
4	Washington	478.9
5	Mississippi	464.5
6	California	462.0
7	Delaware	422.7
8	Alaska	415.7
9	Kentucky	412.1
10	North Carolina	410.2
11	Illinois	408.9
12	Maryland	375.3
13	New York	374.3
14	Idaho	364.0
15	South Dakota	358.8
16	Arizona	352.0
17	Oregon	338.1
18	Hawaii	336.5
19	Georgia	317.9
20	Arkansas	317.6
21	Missouri	313.9
22	Colorado	313.6
23	Rhode Island	298.1
24	Texas	297.1
25	South Carolina	294.6
26	North Dakota	292.1
27	Minnesota	266.6
28	Ohio	262.3
29	Iowa	259.9
30	Nebraska	254.2
31	Pennsylvania	250.3
32	Montana	247.3
33	New Jersey	231.4
34	Virginia	228.9
35	Utah	228.5
36	Connecticut	224.0
37	Wyoming	223.5
38	New Mexico	216.6
39	Vermont	210.6
40	Indiana	195.7
41	Tennessee	186.3
42	Massachusetts	171.2
43	Michigan	158.5
44	Alabama	154.9
45	New Hampshire	146.9
46	West Virginia	137.3
NA	Kansas**	NA
NA	Maine**	NA
NA	Oklahoma**	NA
NA	Wisconsin**	NA
	District of Columbia**	NA

Source: Morgan Quitno Press using data from Federal Bureau of Investigation
    "Crime in the United States 1999" (Uniform Crime Reports, October 15, 2000)
*By law enforcement agencies submitting complete reports to the F.B.I. for 12 months in 1999. Arrests of youths 17
years and younger divided into population of 10 to 17 year olds. See important note at beginning of this chapter.
Burglary is the unlawful entry of a structure to commit a felony or theft. Attempts are included.
**Not available.

Reported Arrests of Juveniles for Burglary
As a Percent of All Such Arrests in 1999
National Percent = 33.9% of Reported Burglary Arrests*

ALPHA ORDER

RANK	STATE	PERCENT
42	Alabama	26.2
1	Alaska	56.4
14	Arizona	39.9
39	Arkansas	26.9
24	California	34.7
9	Colorado	42.9
34	Connecticut	29.0
27	Delaware	31.6
20	Florida	37.0
30	Georgia	31.1
13	Hawaii	41.2
3	Idaho	52.7
28	Illinois	31.5
38	Indiana	27.4
16	Iowa	39.4
NA	Kansas**	NA
46	Kentucky	23.0
26	Louisiana	33.3
NA	Maine**	NA
22	Maryland	35.7
32	Massachusetts	29.7
41	Michigan	26.5
5	Minnesota	43.9
33	Mississippi	29.5
39	Missouri	26.9
4	Montana	50.6
8	Nebraska	43.2
36	Nevada	28.6
10	New Hampshire	42.6
31	New Jersey	29.9
25	New Mexico	33.6
18	New York	37.6
44	North Carolina	23.4
2	North Dakota	53.6
22	Ohio	35.7
NA	Oklahoma**	NA
17	Oregon	38.0
35	Pennsylvania	28.9
11	Rhode Island	41.6
29	South Carolina	31.3
7	South Dakota	43.4
45	Tennessee	23.1
15	Texas	39.7
12	Utah	41.5
19	Vermont	37.3
37	Virginia	28.2
6	Washington	43.5
43	West Virginia	25.7
NA	Wisconsin**	NA
21	Wyoming	36.3

RANK ORDER

RANK	STATE	PERCENT
1	Alaska	56.4
2	North Dakota	53.6
3	Idaho	52.7
4	Montana	50.6
5	Minnesota	43.9
6	Washington	43.5
7	South Dakota	43.4
8	Nebraska	43.2
9	Colorado	42.9
10	New Hampshire	42.6
11	Rhode Island	41.6
12	Utah	41.5
13	Hawaii	41.2
14	Arizona	39.9
15	Texas	39.7
16	Iowa	39.4
17	Oregon	38.0
18	New York	37.6
19	Vermont	37.3
20	Florida	37.0
21	Wyoming	36.3
22	Maryland	35.7
22	Ohio	35.7
24	California	34.7
25	New Mexico	33.6
26	Louisiana	33.3
27	Delaware	31.6
28	Illinois	31.5
29	South Carolina	31.3
30	Georgia	31.1
31	New Jersey	29.9
32	Massachusetts	29.7
33	Mississippi	29.5
34	Connecticut	29.0
35	Pennsylvania	28.9
36	Nevada	28.6
37	Virginia	28.2
38	Indiana	27.4
39	Arkansas	26.9
39	Missouri	26.9
41	Michigan	26.5
42	Alabama	26.2
43	West Virginia	25.7
44	North Carolina	23.4
45	Tennessee	23.1
46	Kentucky	23.0
NA	Kansas**	NA
NA	Maine**	NA
NA	Oklahoma**	NA
NA	Wisconsin**	NA
	District of Columbia**	NA

Source: Morgan Quitno Press using data from Federal Bureau of Investigation
   "Crime in the United States 1999" (Uniform Crime Reports, October 15, 2000)
*Arrests of youths 17 years and younger by law enforcement agencies submitting complete reports to the F.B.I. for 12 months in 1999. Burglary is the unlawful entry of a structure to commit a felony or theft. Attempts are included.
**Not available.

Reported Arrests of Juveniles for Larceny and Theft in 1999

National Total = 277,109 Reported Arrests*

ALPHA ORDER

RANK	STATE	ARRESTS	% of USA
28	Alabama	3,227	1.2%
37	Alaska	1,350	0.5%
7	Arizona	9,116	3.3%
26	Arkansas	3,404	1.2%
1	California	35,886	13.0%
15	Colorado	6,792	2.5%
24	Connecticut	3,780	1.4%
40	Delaware	1,142	0.4%
2	Florida	28,009	10.1%
27	Georgia	3,306	1.2%
36	Hawaii	1,634	0.6%
30	Idaho	2,818	1.0%
29	Illinois	2,847	1.0%
17	Indiana	5,327	1.9%
22	Iowa	4,456	1.6%
NA	Kansas**	NA	NA
44	Kentucky	731	0.3%
13	Louisiana	7,135	2.6%
NA	Maine**	NA	NA
19	Maryland	4,908	1.8%
31	Massachusetts	2,416	0.9%
10	Michigan	8,200	3.0%
6	Minnesota	9,420	3.4%
33	Mississippi	2,027	0.7%
16	Missouri	6,229	2.2%
35	Montana	1,654	0.6%
23	Nebraska	4,399	1.6%
25	Nevada	3,471	1.3%
45	New Hampshire	569	0.2%
8	New Jersey	9,109	3.3%
32	New Mexico	2,142	0.8%
12	New York	7,520	2.7%
9	North Carolina	8,971	3.2%
42	North Dakota	928	0.3%
11	Ohio	7,528	2.7%
NA	Oklahoma**	NA	NA
14	Oregon	7,005	2.5%
5	Pennsylvania	9,437	3.4%
41	Rhode Island	1,122	0.4%
34	South Carolina	1,694	0.6%
39	South Dakota	1,268	0.5%
21	Tennessee	4,571	1.6%
3	Texas	27,478	9.9%
20	Utah	4,690	1.7%
46	Vermont	291	0.1%
18	Virginia	5,316	1.9%
4	Washington	11,708	4.2%
43	West Virginia	762	0.3%
NA	Wisconsin**	NA	NA
38	Wyoming	1,316	0.5%

RANK ORDER

RANK	STATE	ARRESTS	% of USA
1	California	35,886	13.0%
2	Florida	28,009	10.1%
3	Texas	27,478	9.9%
4	Washington	11,708	4.2%
5	Pennsylvania	9,437	3.4%
6	Minnesota	9,420	3.4%
7	Arizona	9,116	3.3%
8	New Jersey	9,109	3.3%
9	North Carolina	8,971	3.2%
10	Michigan	8,200	3.0%
11	Ohio	7,528	2.7%
12	New York	7,520	2.7%
13	Louisiana	7,135	2.6%
14	Oregon	7,005	2.5%
15	Colorado	6,792	2.5%
16	Missouri	6,229	2.2%
17	Indiana	5,327	1.9%
18	Virginia	5,316	1.9%
19	Maryland	4,908	1.8%
20	Utah	4,690	1.7%
21	Tennessee	4,571	1.6%
22	Iowa	4,456	1.6%
23	Nebraska	4,399	1.6%
24	Connecticut	3,780	1.4%
25	Nevada	3,471	1.3%
26	Arkansas	3,404	1.2%
27	Georgia	3,306	1.2%
28	Alabama	3,227	1.2%
29	Illinois	2,847	1.0%
30	Idaho	2,818	1.0%
31	Massachusetts	2,416	0.9%
32	New Mexico	2,142	0.8%
33	Mississippi	2,027	0.7%
34	South Carolina	1,694	0.6%
35	Montana	1,654	0.6%
36	Hawaii	1,634	0.6%
37	Alaska	1,350	0.5%
38	Wyoming	1,316	0.5%
39	South Dakota	1,268	0.5%
40	Delaware	1,142	0.4%
41	Rhode Island	1,122	0.4%
42	North Dakota	928	0.3%
43	West Virginia	762	0.3%
44	Kentucky	731	0.3%
45	New Hampshire	569	0.2%
46	Vermont	291	0.1%
NA	Kansas**	NA	NA
NA	Maine**	NA	NA
NA	Oklahoma**	NA	NA
NA	Wisconsin**	NA	NA
	District of Columbia**	NA	NA

Source: Federal Bureau of Investigation
    "Crime in the United States 1999" (Uniform Crime Reports, October 15, 2000)
*Arrests of youths 17 years and younger by law enforcement agencies submitting complete reports to the F.B.I. for
12 months in 1999. Larceny and theft is the unlawful taking of property without use of force, violence or fraud.
Attempts are included. Motor vehicle thefts are excluded. See important note at beginning of this chapter.
**Not available.

Reported Juvenile Arrest Rate for Larceny and Theft in 1999

National Rate = 1,289.0 Reported Arrests per 100,000 Juvenile Population*

ALPHA ORDER

RANK	STATE	RATE
44	Alabama	729.9
18	Alaska	1,645.8
12	Arizona	1,737.5
30	Arkansas	1,188.1
39	California	969.9
4	Colorado	2,244.3
34	Connecticut	1,073.2
25	Delaware	1,415.5
11	Florida	1,748.6
32	Georgia	1,165.2
21	Hawaii	1,506.4
7	Idaho	1,995.5
41	Illinois	885.3
27	Indiana	1,331.5
19	Iowa	1,597.1
NA	Kansas**	NA
24	Kentucky	1,476.6
13	Louisiana	1,722.2
NA	Maine**	NA
26	Maryland	1,407.0
46	Massachusetts	473.8
42	Michigan	847.0
10	Minnesota	1,826.5
23	Mississippi	1,478.0
16	Missouri	1,663.8
1	Montana	3,007.8
3	Nebraska	2,273.0
14	Nevada	1,714.9
38	New Hampshire	1,007.3
33	New Jersey	1,086.4
17	New Mexico	1,662.7
28	New York	1,244.9
31	North Carolina	1,186.6
20	North Dakota	1,576.2
35	Ohio	1,070.9
NA	Oklahoma**	NA
8	Oregon	1,938.0
40	Pennsylvania	918.0
37	Rhode Island	1,029.3
15	South Carolina	1,697.6
9	South Dakota	1,872.1
22	Tennessee	1,504.7
29	Texas	1,237.0
5	Utah	2,236.8
45	Vermont	514.9
36	Virginia	1,060.8
2	Washington	2,324.8
43	West Virginia	758.3
NA	Wisconsin**	NA
6	Wyoming	2,100.8

RANK ORDER

RANK	STATE	RATE
1	Montana	3,007.8
2	Washington	2,324.8
3	Nebraska	2,273.0
4	Colorado	2,244.3
5	Utah	2,236.8
6	Wyoming	2,100.8
7	Idaho	1,995.5
8	Oregon	1,938.0
9	South Dakota	1,872.1
10	Minnesota	1,826.5
11	Florida	1,748.6
12	Arizona	1,737.5
13	Louisiana	1,722.2
14	Nevada	1,714.9
15	South Carolina	1,697.6
16	Missouri	1,663.8
17	New Mexico	1,662.7
18	Alaska	1,645.8
19	Iowa	1,597.1
20	North Dakota	1,576.2
21	Hawaii	1,506.4
22	Tennessee	1,504.7
23	Mississippi	1,478.0
24	Kentucky	1,476.6
25	Delaware	1,415.5
26	Maryland	1,407.0
27	Indiana	1,331.5
28	New York	1,244.9
29	Texas	1,237.0
30	Arkansas	1,188.1
31	North Carolina	1,186.6
32	Georgia	1,165.2
33	New Jersey	1,086.4
34	Connecticut	1,073.2
35	Ohio	1,070.9
36	Virginia	1,060.8
37	Rhode Island	1,029.3
38	New Hampshire	1,007.3
39	California	969.9
40	Pennsylvania	918.0
41	Illinois	885.3
42	Michigan	847.0
43	West Virginia	758.3
44	Alabama	729.9
45	Vermont	514.9
46	Massachusetts	473.8
NA	Kansas**	NA
NA	Maine**	NA
NA	Oklahoma**	NA
NA	Wisconsin**	NA
	District of Columbia**	NA

Source: Morgan Quitno Press using data from Federal Bureau of Investigation
   "Crime in the United States 1999" (Uniform Crime Reports, October 15, 2000)
*By law enforcement agencies submitting complete reports to the F.B.I. for 12 months in 1999. Arrests of youths 17 years and younger divided into population of 10 to 17 year olds. See important note at beginning of this chapter. Larceny and theft is the unlawful taking of property without use of force, violence or fraud. Attempts are included. Motor vehicle thefts are excluded. **Not available.

Reported Arrests of Juveniles for Larceny and Theft
As a Percent of All Such Arrests in 1999
National Percent = 31.3% of Reported Larceny and Theft Arrests*

ALPHA ORDER

RANK	STATE	PERCENT
44	Alabama	22.6
9	Alaska	42.6
27	Arizona	28.9
41	Arkansas	24.6
16	California	34.3
13	Colorado	36.0
40	Connecticut	25.2
37	Delaware	26.1
24	Florida	30.8
33	Georgia	26.6
21	Hawaii	31.6
1	Idaho	52.2
46	Illinois	15.9
23	Indiana	31.1
8	Iowa	43.5
NA	Kansas**	NA
36	Kentucky	26.3
31	Louisiana	28.2
NA	Maine**	NA
19	Maryland	33.1
45	Massachusetts	21.4
15	Michigan	35.0
5	Minnesota	48.4
38	Mississippi	25.6
33	Missouri	26.6
3	Montana	49.2
7	Nebraska	43.9
21	Nevada	31.6
10	New Hampshire	42.0
29	New Jersey	28.6
17	New Mexico	34.2
35	New York	26.4
43	North Carolina	23.3
2	North Dakota	51.0
26	Ohio	30.0
NA	Oklahoma**	NA
20	Oregon	32.1
29	Pennsylvania	28.6
14	Rhode Island	35.1
28	South Carolina	28.8
6	South Dakota	47.8
42	Tennessee	24.2
18	Texas	34.0
11	Utah	40.5
25	Vermont	30.5
38	Virginia	25.6
12	Washington	40.4
32	West Virginia	26.9
NA	Wisconsin**	NA
4	Wyoming	48.6

RANK ORDER

RANK	STATE	PERCENT
1	Idaho	52.2
2	North Dakota	51.0
3	Montana	49.2
4	Wyoming	48.6
5	Minnesota	48.4
6	South Dakota	47.8
7	Nebraska	43.9
8	Iowa	43.5
9	Alaska	42.6
10	New Hampshire	42.0
11	Utah	40.5
12	Washington	40.4
13	Colorado	36.0
14	Rhode Island	35.1
15	Michigan	35.0
16	California	34.3
17	New Mexico	34.2
18	Texas	34.0
19	Maryland	33.1
20	Oregon	32.1
21	Hawaii	31.6
21	Nevada	31.6
23	Indiana	31.1
24	Florida	30.8
25	Vermont	30.5
26	Ohio	30.0
27	Arizona	28.9
28	South Carolina	28.8
29	New Jersey	28.6
29	Pennsylvania	28.6
31	Louisiana	28.2
32	West Virginia	26.9
33	Georgia	26.6
33	Missouri	26.6
35	New York	26.4
36	Kentucky	26.3
37	Delaware	26.1
38	Mississippi	25.6
38	Virginia	25.6
40	Connecticut	25.2
41	Arkansas	24.6
42	Tennessee	24.2
43	North Carolina	23.3
44	Alabama	22.6
45	Massachusetts	21.4
46	Illinois	15.9
NA	Kansas**	NA
NA	Maine**	NA
NA	Oklahoma**	NA
NA	Wisconsin**	NA
	District of Columbia**	NA

Source: Morgan Quitno Press using data from Federal Bureau of Investigation
   "Crime in the United States 1999" (Uniform Crime Reports, October 15, 2000)
*Arrests of youths 17 years and younger by law enforcement agencies submitting complete reports to the F.B.I. for 12 months in 1999. Larceny and theft is the unlawful taking of property without use of force, violence or fraud. Attempts are included. Motor vehicle thefts are excluded.
**Not available.

Reported Arrests of Juveniles for Motor Vehicle Theft in 1999

National Total = 37,947 Reported Arrests*

ALPHA ORDER

RANK	STATE	ARRESTS	% of USA
31	Alabama	209	0.6%
33	Alaska	191	0.5%
7	Arizona	1,111	2.9%
34	Arkansas	183	0.5%
1	California	6,637	17.5%
12	Colorado	793	2.1%
21	Connecticut	479	1.3%
40	Delaware	97	0.3%
2	Florida	4,692	12.4%
27	Georgia	278	0.7%
29	Hawaii	233	0.6%
32	Idaho	203	0.5%
3	Illinois	4,238	11.2%
15	Indiana	651	1.7%
26	Iowa	289	0.8%
NA	Kansas**	NA	NA
35	Kentucky	180	0.5%
22	Louisiana	417	1.1%
NA	Maine**	NA	NA
19	Maryland	519	1.4%
23	Massachusetts	392	1.0%
11	Michigan	840	2.2%
6	Minnesota	1,318	3.5%
36	Mississippi	177	0.5%
9	Missouri	964	2.5%
38	Montana	112	0.3%
28	Nebraska	253	0.7%
18	Nevada	522	1.4%
45	New Hampshire	38	0.1%
20	New Jersey	516	1.4%
39	New Mexico	106	0.3%
17	New York	634	1.7%
16	North Carolina	649	1.7%
37	North Dakota	160	0.4%
10	Ohio	902	2.4%
NA	Oklahoma**	NA	NA
14	Oregon	668	1.8%
5	Pennsylvania	2,215	5.8%
30	Rhode Island	229	0.6%
42	South Carolina	95	0.3%
44	South Dakota	68	0.2%
25	Tennessee	291	0.8%
4	Texas	3,056	8.1%
24	Utah	343	0.9%
46	Vermont	36	0.1%
13	Virginia	711	1.9%
8	Washington	1,083	2.9%
41	West Virginia	96	0.3%
NA	Wisconsin**	NA	NA
43	Wyoming	73	0.2%

RANK ORDER

RANK	STATE	ARRESTS	% of USA
1	California	6,637	17.5%
2	Florida	4,692	12.4%
3	Illinois	4,238	11.2%
4	Texas	3,056	8.1%
5	Pennsylvania	2,215	5.8%
6	Minnesota	1,318	3.5%
7	Arizona	1,111	2.9%
8	Washington	1,083	2.9%
9	Missouri	964	2.5%
10	Ohio	902	2.4%
11	Michigan	840	2.2%
12	Colorado	793	2.1%
13	Virginia	711	1.9%
14	Oregon	668	1.8%
15	Indiana	651	1.7%
16	North Carolina	649	1.7%
17	New York	634	1.7%
18	Nevada	522	1.4%
19	Maryland	519	1.4%
20	New Jersey	516	1.4%
21	Connecticut	479	1.3%
22	Louisiana	417	1.1%
23	Massachusetts	392	1.0%
24	Utah	343	0.9%
25	Tennessee	291	0.8%
26	Iowa	289	0.8%
27	Georgia	278	0.7%
28	Nebraska	253	0.7%
29	Hawaii	233	0.6%
30	Rhode Island	229	0.6%
31	Alabama	209	0.6%
32	Idaho	203	0.5%
33	Alaska	191	0.5%
34	Arkansas	183	0.5%
35	Kentucky	180	0.5%
36	Mississippi	177	0.5%
37	North Dakota	160	0.4%
38	Montana	112	0.3%
39	New Mexico	106	0.3%
40	Delaware	97	0.3%
41	West Virginia	96	0.3%
42	South Carolina	95	0.3%
43	Wyoming	73	0.2%
44	South Dakota	68	0.2%
45	New Hampshire	38	0.1%
46	Vermont	36	0.1%
NA	Kansas**	NA	NA
NA	Maine**	NA	NA
NA	Oklahoma**	NA	NA
NA	Wisconsin**	NA	NA
	District of Columbia**	NA	NA

Source: Federal Bureau of Investigation
   "Crime in the United States 1999" (Uniform Crime Reports, October 15, 2000)
*Arrests of youths 17 years and younger by law enforcement agencies submitting complete reports to the F.B.I. for 12 months in 1999. Motor vehicle theft includes the theft or attempted theft of a self-propelled vehicle. Excludes motorboats, construction equipment, airplanes and farming equipment. See important note at beginning of this chapter. **Not available.

Reported Juvenile Arrest Rate for Motor Vehicle Theft in 1999

National Rate = 176.5 Reported Arrests per 100,000 Juvenile Population*

ALPHA ORDER

RANK	STATE	RATE
46	Alabama	47.3
9	Alaska	232.9
13	Arizona	211.8
43	Arkansas	63.9
17	California	179.4
5	Colorado	262.0
24	Connecticut	136.0
28	Delaware	120.2
3	Florida	292.9
34	Georgia	98.0
12	Hawaii	214.8
21	Idaho	143.7
1	Illinois	1,317.8
19	Indiana	162.7
31	Iowa	103.6
NA	Kansas**	NA
2	Kentucky	363.6
32	Louisiana	100.7
NA	Maine**	NA
20	Maryland	148.8
41	Massachusetts	76.9
38	Michigan	86.8
8	Minnesota	255.6
26	Mississippi	129.1
7	Missouri	257.5
15	Montana	203.7
25	Nebraska	130.7
6	Nevada	257.9
42	New Hampshire	67.3
45	New Jersey	61.5
40	New Mexico	82.3
30	New York	105.0
39	North Carolina	85.8
4	North Dakota	271.8
27	Ohio	128.3
NA	Oklahoma**	NA
16	Oregon	184.8
10	Pennsylvania	215.5
14	Rhode Island	210.1
37	South Carolina	95.2
33	South Dakota	100.4
35	Tennessee	95.8
23	Texas	137.6
18	Utah	163.6
44	Vermont	63.7
22	Virginia	141.9
11	Washington	215.0
36	West Virginia	95.5
NA	Wisconsin**	NA
29	Wyoming	116.5

RANK ORDER

RANK	STATE	RATE
1	Illinois	1,317.8
2	Kentucky	363.6
3	Florida	292.9
4	North Dakota	271.8
5	Colorado	262.0
6	Nevada	257.9
7	Missouri	257.5
8	Minnesota	255.6
9	Alaska	232.9
10	Pennsylvania	215.5
11	Washington	215.0
12	Hawaii	214.8
13	Arizona	211.8
14	Rhode Island	210.1
15	Montana	203.7
16	Oregon	184.8
17	California	179.4
18	Utah	163.6
19	Indiana	162.7
20	Maryland	148.8
21	Idaho	143.7
22	Virginia	141.9
23	Texas	137.6
24	Connecticut	136.0
25	Nebraska	130.7
26	Mississippi	129.1
27	Ohio	128.3
28	Delaware	120.2
29	Wyoming	116.5
30	New York	105.0
31	Iowa	103.6
32	Louisiana	100.7
33	South Dakota	100.4
34	Georgia	98.0
35	Tennessee	95.8
36	West Virginia	95.5
37	South Carolina	95.2
38	Michigan	86.8
39	North Carolina	85.8
40	New Mexico	82.3
41	Massachusetts	76.9
42	New Hampshire	67.3
43	Arkansas	63.9
44	Vermont	63.7
45	New Jersey	61.5
46	Alabama	47.3
NA	Kansas**	NA
NA	Maine**	NA
NA	Oklahoma**	NA
NA	Wisconsin**	NA
	District of Columbia**	NA

Source: Morgan Quitno Press using data from Federal Bureau of Investigation
"Crime in the United States 1999" (Uniform Crime Reports, October 15, 2000)
*By law enforcement agencies submitting complete reports to the F.B.I. for 12 months in 1999. Arrests of youths 17 years and younger divided into population of 10 to 17 year olds. See important note at beginning of this chapter. Motor vehicle theft includes the theft or attempted theft of a self-propelled vehicle. Excludes motorboats, construction equipment, airplanes and farming equipment. **Not available.*

Reported Arrests of Juveniles for Motor Vehicle Theft
As a Percent of All Such Arrests in 1999
National Percent = 35.4% of Reported Motor Vehicle Theft Arrests*

ALPHA ORDER

RANK	STATE	PERCENT
46	Alabama	18.2
17	Alaska	43.3
36	Arizona	32.5
31	Arkansas	34.1
32	California	33.4
16	Colorado	44.0
18	Connecticut	38.8
15	Delaware	44.5
25	Florida	36.2
38	Georgia	29.9
43	Hawaii	27.2
2	Idaho	57.8
30	Illinois	34.6
33	Indiana	33.1
14	Iowa	44.9
NA	Kansas**	NA
27	Kentucky	35.8
39	Louisiana	29.1
NA	Maine**	NA
24	Maryland	36.3
34	Massachusetts	33.0
19	Michigan	38.4
10	Minnesota	47.8
45	Mississippi	23.2
42	Missouri	27.8
6	Montana	50.7
3	Nebraska	52.3
34	Nevada	33.0
13	New Hampshire	45.8
23	New Jersey	37.3
19	New Mexico	38.4
37	New York	31.7
41	North Carolina	28.5
1	North Dakota	63.7
10	Ohio	47.8
NA	Oklahoma**	NA
40	Oregon	28.9
29	Pennsylvania	34.9
8	Rhode Island	48.9
26	South Carolina	36.0
9	South Dakota	48.2
44	Tennessee	24.7
27	Texas	35.8
4	Utah	52.0
7	Vermont	49.3
19	Virginia	38.4
12	Washington	47.3
22	West Virginia	38.1
NA	Wisconsin**	NA
5	Wyoming	51.4

RANK ORDER

RANK	STATE	PERCENT
1	North Dakota	63.7
2	Idaho	57.8
3	Nebraska	52.3
4	Utah	52.0
5	Wyoming	51.4
6	Montana	50.7
7	Vermont	49.3
8	Rhode Island	48.9
9	South Dakota	48.2
10	Minnesota	47.8
10	Ohio	47.8
12	Washington	47.3
13	New Hampshire	45.8
14	Iowa	44.9
15	Delaware	44.5
16	Colorado	44.0
17	Alaska	43.3
18	Connecticut	38.8
19	Michigan	38.4
19	New Mexico	38.4
19	Virginia	38.4
22	West Virginia	38.1
23	New Jersey	37.3
24	Maryland	36.3
25	Florida	36.2
26	South Carolina	36.0
27	Kentucky	35.8
27	Texas	35.8
29	Pennsylvania	34.9
30	Illinois	34.6
31	Arkansas	34.1
32	California	33.4
33	Indiana	33.1
34	Massachusetts	33.0
34	Nevada	33.0
36	Arizona	32.5
37	New York	31.7
38	Georgia	29.9
39	Louisiana	29.1
40	Oregon	28.9
41	North Carolina	28.5
42	Missouri	27.8
43	Hawaii	27.2
44	Tennessee	24.7
45	Mississippi	23.2
46	Alabama	18.2
NA	Kansas**	NA
NA	Maine**	NA
NA	Oklahoma**	NA
NA	Wisconsin**	NA
	District of Columbia**	NA

Source: Morgan Quitno Press using data from Federal Bureau of Investigation
   "Crime in the United States 1999" (Uniform Crime Reports, October 15, 2000)
*Arrests of youths 17 years and younger by law enforcement agencies submitting complete reports to the F.B.I. for 12 months in 1999. Motor vehicle theft includes the theft or attempted theft of a self-propelled vehicle. Excludes motorboats, construction equipment, airplanes and farming equipment.
**Not available.

Reported Arrests of Juveniles for Arson in 1999

National Total = 6,093 Reported Arrests*

ALPHA ORDER

RANK	STATE	ARRESTS	% of USA
39	Alabama	12	0.2%
43	Alaska	9	0.1%
15	Arizona	169	2.8%
34	Arkansas	23	0.4%
1	California	1,122	18.4%
16	Colorado	147	2.4%
25	Connecticut	60	1.0%
31	Delaware	33	0.5%
6	Florida	302	5.0%
29	Georgia	43	0.7%
42	Hawaii	10	0.2%
28	Idaho	53	0.9%
20	Illinois	98	1.6%
24	Indiana	73	1.2%
21	Iowa	85	1.4%
NA	Kansas**	NA	NA
35	Kentucky	22	0.4%
19	Louisiana	116	1.9%
NA	Maine**	NA	NA
10	Maryland	195	3.2%
25	Massachusetts	60	1.0%
13	Michigan	175	2.9%
12	Minnesota	176	2.9%
36	Mississippi	21	0.3%
17	Missouri	138	2.3%
38	Montana	17	0.3%
18	Nebraska	122	2.0%
23	Nevada	75	1.2%
36	New Hampshire	21	0.3%
3	New Jersey	362	5.9%
39	New Mexico	12	0.2%
14	New York	172	2.8%
9	North Carolina	216	3.5%
44	North Dakota	7	0.1%
5	Ohio	314	5.2%
NA	Oklahoma**	NA	NA
8	Oregon	220	3.6%
2	Pennsylvania	378	6.2%
30	Rhode Island	36	0.6%
32	South Carolina	31	0.5%
32	South Dakota	31	0.5%
27	Tennessee	57	0.9%
4	Texas	358	5.9%
22	Utah	82	1.3%
45	Vermont	4	0.1%
11	Virginia	193	3.2%
7	Washington	228	3.7%
41	West Virginia	11	0.2%
NA	Wisconsin**	NA	NA
45	Wyoming	4	0.1%

RANK ORDER

RANK	STATE	ARRESTS	% of USA
1	California	1,122	18.4%
2	Pennsylvania	378	6.2%
3	New Jersey	362	5.9%
4	Texas	358	5.9%
5	Ohio	314	5.2%
6	Florida	302	5.0%
7	Washington	228	3.7%
8	Oregon	220	3.6%
9	North Carolina	216	3.5%
10	Maryland	195	3.2%
11	Virginia	193	3.2%
12	Minnesota	176	2.9%
13	Michigan	175	2.9%
14	New York	172	2.8%
15	Arizona	169	2.8%
16	Colorado	147	2.4%
17	Missouri	138	2.3%
18	Nebraska	122	2.0%
19	Louisiana	116	1.9%
20	Illinois	98	1.6%
21	Iowa	85	1.4%
22	Utah	82	1.3%
23	Nevada	75	1.2%
24	Indiana	73	1.2%
25	Connecticut	60	1.0%
25	Massachusetts	60	1.0%
27	Tennessee	57	0.9%
28	Idaho	53	0.9%
29	Georgia	43	0.7%
30	Rhode Island	36	0.6%
31	Delaware	33	0.5%
32	South Carolina	31	0.5%
32	South Dakota	31	0.5%
34	Arkansas	23	0.4%
35	Kentucky	22	0.4%
36	Mississippi	21	0.3%
36	New Hampshire	21	0.3%
38	Montana	17	0.3%
39	Alabama	12	0.2%
39	New Mexico	12	0.2%
41	West Virginia	11	0.2%
42	Hawaii	10	0.2%
43	Alaska	9	0.1%
44	North Dakota	7	0.1%
45	Vermont	4	0.1%
45	Wyoming	4	0.1%
NA	Kansas**	NA	NA
NA	Maine**	NA	NA
NA	Oklahoma**	NA	NA
NA	Wisconsin**	NA	NA
	District of Columbia**	NA	NA

Source: Federal Bureau of Investigation
   "Crime in the United States 1999" (Uniform Crime Reports, October 15, 2000)
Arrests of youths 17 years and younger by law enforcement agencies submitting complete reports to the F.B.I. for 12 months in 1999. Arson is the willful burning of or attempt to burn a building, vehicle or another's personal property. See important note at beginning of this chapter.
**Not available.*

Reported Juvenile Arrest Rate for Arson in 1999

National Rate = 28.3 Reported Arrests per 100,000 Juvenile Population*

ALPHA ORDER

RANK	STATE	RATE
46	Alabama	2.7
39	Alaska	11.0
20	Arizona	32.2
43	Arkansas	8.0
25	California	30.3
4	Colorado	48.6
33	Connecticut	17.0
10	Delaware	40.9
29	Florida	18.9
36	Georgia	15.2
42	Hawaii	9.2
13	Idaho	37.5
23	Illinois	30.5
31	Indiana	18.2
23	Iowa	30.5
NA	Kansas**	NA
8	Kentucky	44.4
28	Louisiana	28.0
NA	Maine**	NA
3	Maryland	55.9
38	Massachusetts	11.8
32	Michigan	18.1
18	Minnesota	34.1
35	Mississippi	15.3
16	Missouri	36.9
22	Montana	30.9
1	Nebraska	63.0
15	Nevada	37.1
14	New Hampshire	37.2
9	New Jersey	43.2
41	New Mexico	9.3
27	New York	28.5
26	North Carolina	28.6
37	North Dakota	11.9
7	Ohio	44.7
NA	Oklahoma**	NA
2	Oregon	60.9
17	Pennsylvania	36.8
19	Rhode Island	33.0
21	South Carolina	31.1
5	South Dakota	45.8
30	Tennessee	18.8
34	Texas	16.1
11	Utah	39.1
44	Vermont	7.1
12	Virginia	38.5
6	Washington	45.3
40	West Virginia	10.9
NA	Wisconsin**	NA
45	Wyoming	6.4

RANK ORDER

RANK	STATE	RATE
1	Nebraska	63.0
2	Oregon	60.9
3	Maryland	55.9
4	Colorado	48.6
5	South Dakota	45.8
6	Washington	45.3
7	Ohio	44.7
8	Kentucky	44.4
9	New Jersey	43.2
10	Delaware	40.9
11	Utah	39.1
12	Virginia	38.5
13	Idaho	37.5
14	New Hampshire	37.2
15	Nevada	37.1
16	Missouri	36.9
17	Pennsylvania	36.8
18	Minnesota	34.1
19	Rhode Island	33.0
20	Arizona	32.2
21	South Carolina	31.1
22	Montana	30.9
23	Illinois	30.5
23	Iowa	30.5
25	California	30.3
26	North Carolina	28.6
27	New York	28.5
28	Louisiana	28.0
29	Florida	18.9
30	Tennessee	18.8
31	Indiana	18.2
32	Michigan	18.1
33	Connecticut	17.0
34	Texas	16.1
35	Mississippi	15.3
36	Georgia	15.2
37	North Dakota	11.9
38	Massachusetts	11.8
39	Alaska	11.0
40	West Virginia	10.9
41	New Mexico	9.3
42	Hawaii	9.2
43	Arkansas	8.0
44	Vermont	7.1
45	Wyoming	6.4
46	Alabama	2.7
NA	Kansas**	NA
NA	Maine**	NA
NA	Oklahoma**	NA
NA	Wisconsin**	NA
	District of Columbia**	NA

Source: Morgan Quitno Press using data from Federal Bureau of Investigation
     "Crime in the United States 1999" (Uniform Crime Reports, October 15, 2000)
*By law enforcement agencies submitting complete reports to the F.B.I. for 12 months in 1999. Arrests of youths 17 years and younger divided into population of 10 to 17 year olds. See important note at beginning of this chapter. Arson is the willful burning of or attempt to burn a building, vehicle or another's personal property.
**Not available.

Reported Arrests of Juveniles for Arson
As a Percent of All Such Arrests in 1999
National Percent = 53.1% of Reported Arson Arrests*

ALPHA ORDER

RANK	STATE	PERCENT
46	Alabama	16.7
24	Alaska	50.0
14	Arizona	62.8
45	Arkansas	20.0
13	California	62.9
10	Colorado	66.8
38	Connecticut	41.4
23	Delaware	50.8
31	Florida	45.6
44	Georgia	23.5
26	Hawaii	47.6
1	Idaho	89.8
28	Illinois	47.1
19	Indiana	54.9
5	Iowa	73.3
NA	Kansas**	NA
39	Kentucky	40.7
22	Louisiana	51.1
NA	Maine**	NA
17	Maryland	55.7
33	Massachusetts	45.1
40	Michigan	33.1
8	Minnesota	71.5
42	Mississippi	28.4
35	Missouri	44.4
9	Montana	68.0
4	Nebraska	74.8
2	Nevada	78.9
6	New Hampshire	72.4
12	New Jersey	63.7
20	New Mexico	54.5
21	New York	53.1
32	North Carolina	45.5
16	North Dakota	58.3
18	Ohio	55.6
NA	Oklahoma**	NA
7	Oregon	71.9
30	Pennsylvania	46.3
27	Rhode Island	47.4
25	South Carolina	47.7
11	South Dakota	64.6
37	Tennessee	42.2
34	Texas	44.8
3	Utah	75.9
41	Vermont	28.6
29	Virginia	47.0
15	Washington	60.8
43	West Virginia	27.5
NA	Wisconsin**	NA
35	Wyoming	44.4

RANK ORDER

RANK	STATE	PERCENT
1	Idaho	89.8
2	Nevada	78.9
3	Utah	75.9
4	Nebraska	74.8
5	Iowa	73.3
6	New Hampshire	72.4
7	Oregon	71.9
8	Minnesota	71.5
9	Montana	68.0
10	Colorado	66.8
11	South Dakota	64.6
12	New Jersey	63.7
13	California	62.9
14	Arizona	62.8
15	Washington	60.8
16	North Dakota	58.3
17	Maryland	55.7
18	Ohio	55.6
19	Indiana	54.9
20	New Mexico	54.5
21	New York	53.1
22	Louisiana	51.1
23	Delaware	50.8
24	Alaska	50.0
25	South Carolina	47.7
26	Hawaii	47.6
27	Rhode Island	47.4
28	Illinois	47.1
29	Virginia	47.0
30	Pennsylvania	46.3
31	Florida	45.6
32	North Carolina	45.5
33	Massachusetts	45.1
34	Texas	44.8
35	Missouri	44.4
35	Wyoming	44.4
37	Tennessee	42.2
38	Connecticut	41.4
39	Kentucky	40.7
40	Michigan	33.1
41	Vermont	28.6
42	Mississippi	28.4
43	West Virginia	27.5
44	Georgia	23.5
45	Arkansas	20.0
46	Alabama	16.7
NA	Kansas**	NA
NA	Maine**	NA
NA	Oklahoma**	NA
NA	Wisconsin**	NA
	District of Columbia**	NA

Source: Morgan Quitno Press using data from Federal Bureau of Investigation
    "Crime in the United States 1999" (Uniform Crime Reports, October 15, 2000)
*Arrests of youths 17 years and younger by law enforcement agencies submitting complete reports to the F.B.I. for 12 months in 1999. Arson is the willful burning of or attempt to burn a building, vehicle or another's personal property.
**Not available.

Reported Arrests of Juveniles for Weapons Violations in 1999

National Total = 29,505 Reported Arrests*

ALPHA ORDER

RANK	STATE	ARRESTS	% of USA
25	Alabama	279	0.9%
36	Alaska	123	0.4%
15	Arizona	547	1.9%
26	Arkansas	252	0.9%
1	California	7,260	24.6%
14	Colorado	575	1.9%
20	Connecticut	437	1.5%
37	Delaware	90	0.3%
3	Florida	1,909	6.5%
21	Georgia	380	1.3%
41	Hawaii	39	0.1%
33	Idaho	158	0.5%
2	Illinois	2,383	8.1%
31	Indiana	182	0.6%
29	Iowa	190	0.6%
NA	Kansas**	NA	NA
39	Kentucky	73	0.2%
18	Louisiana	475	1.6%
NA	Maine**	NA	NA
17	Maryland	528	1.8%
34	Massachusetts	156	0.5%
9	Michigan	749	2.5%
8	Minnesota	912	3.1%
30	Mississippi	183	0.6%
16	Missouri	538	1.8%
42	Montana	28	0.1%
27	Nebraska	221	0.7%
19	Nevada	456	1.5%
45	New Hampshire	17	0.1%
5	New Jersey	1,571	5.3%
28	New Mexico	196	0.7%
11	New York	688	2.3%
6	North Carolina	1,501	5.1%
44	North Dakota	21	0.1%
12	Ohio	672	2.3%
NA	Oklahoma**	NA	NA
23	Oregon	326	1.1%
7	Pennsylvania	1,052	3.6%
35	Rhode Island	146	0.5%
32	South Carolina	179	0.6%
38	South Dakota	75	0.3%
22	Tennessee	361	1.2%
4	Texas	1,864	6.3%
24	Utah	305	1.0%
46	Vermont	7	0.0%
13	Virginia	576	2.0%
10	Washington	733	2.5%
42	West Virginia	28	0.1%
NA	Wisconsin**	NA	NA
40	Wyoming	64	0.2%

RANK ORDER

RANK	STATE	ARRESTS	% of USA
1	California	7,260	24.6%
2	Illinois	2,383	8.1%
3	Florida	1,909	6.5%
4	Texas	1,864	6.3%
5	New Jersey	1,571	5.3%
6	North Carolina	1,501	5.1%
7	Pennsylvania	1,052	3.6%
8	Minnesota	912	3.1%
9	Michigan	749	2.5%
10	Washington	733	2.5%
11	New York	688	2.3%
12	Ohio	672	2.3%
13	Virginia	576	2.0%
14	Colorado	575	1.9%
15	Arizona	547	1.9%
16	Missouri	538	1.8%
17	Maryland	528	1.8%
18	Louisiana	475	1.6%
19	Nevada	456	1.5%
20	Connecticut	437	1.5%
21	Georgia	380	1.3%
22	Tennessee	361	1.2%
23	Oregon	326	1.1%
24	Utah	305	1.0%
25	Alabama	279	0.9%
26	Arkansas	252	0.9%
27	Nebraska	221	0.7%
28	New Mexico	196	0.7%
29	Iowa	190	0.6%
30	Mississippi	183	0.6%
31	Indiana	182	0.6%
32	South Carolina	179	0.6%
33	Idaho	158	0.5%
34	Massachusetts	156	0.5%
35	Rhode Island	146	0.5%
36	Alaska	123	0.4%
37	Delaware	90	0.3%
38	South Dakota	75	0.3%
39	Kentucky	73	0.2%
40	Wyoming	64	0.2%
41	Hawaii	39	0.1%
42	Montana	28	0.1%
42	West Virginia	28	0.1%
44	North Dakota	21	0.1%
45	New Hampshire	17	0.1%
46	Vermont	7	0.0%
NA	Kansas**	NA	NA
NA	Maine**	NA	NA
NA	Oklahoma**	NA	NA
NA	Wisconsin**	NA	NA
	District of Columbia**	NA	NA

Source: Federal Bureau of Investigation
   "Crime in the United States 1999" (Uniform Crime Reports, October 15, 2000)
Arrests of youths 17 years and younger by law enforcement agencies submitting complete reports to the F.B.I. for 12 months in 1999. Weapons violations include illegal carrying and possession. See important note at beginning of this chapter.
***Not available.*

Reported Juvenile Arrest Rate for Weapons Violations in 1999

National Rate = 137.2 Reported Arrests per 100,000 Juvenile Population*

ALPHA ORDER

RANK	STATE	RATE
38	Alabama	63.1
11	Alaska	150.0
29	Arizona	104.3
34	Arkansas	88.0
4	California	196.2
5	Colorado	190.0
19	Connecticut	124.1
27	Delaware	111.6
20	Florida	119.2
16	Georgia	133.9
41	Hawaii	36.0
26	Idaho	111.9
1	Illinois	741.0
40	Indiana	45.5
37	Iowa	68.1
NA	Kansas**	NA
12	Kentucky	147.5
23	Louisiana	114.7
NA	Maine**	NA
10	Maryland	151.4
43	Massachusetts	30.6
36	Michigan	77.4
8	Minnesota	176.8
18	Mississippi	133.4
15	Missouri	143.7
39	Montana	50.9
24	Nebraska	114.2
2	Nevada	225.3
44	New Hampshire	30.1
6	New Jersey	187.4
9	New Mexico	152.1
25	New York	113.9
3	North Carolina	198.5
42	North Dakota	35.7
32	Ohio	95.6
NA	Oklahoma**	NA
33	Oregon	90.2
30	Pennsylvania	102.3
16	Rhode Island	133.9
7	South Carolina	179.4
28	South Dakota	110.7
21	Tennessee	118.8
35	Texas	83.9
13	Utah	145.5
46	Vermont	12.4
22	Virginia	114.9
13	Washington	145.5
45	West Virginia	27.9
NA	Wisconsin**	NA
31	Wyoming	102.2

RANK ORDER

RANK	STATE	RATE
1	Illinois	741.0
2	Nevada	225.3
3	North Carolina	198.5
4	California	196.2
5	Colorado	190.0
6	New Jersey	187.4
7	South Carolina	179.4
8	Minnesota	176.8
9	New Mexico	152.1
10	Maryland	151.4
11	Alaska	150.0
12	Kentucky	147.5
13	Utah	145.5
13	Washington	145.5
15	Missouri	143.7
16	Georgia	133.9
16	Rhode Island	133.9
18	Mississippi	133.4
19	Connecticut	124.1
20	Florida	119.2
21	Tennessee	118.8
22	Virginia	114.9
23	Louisiana	114.7
24	Nebraska	114.2
25	New York	113.9
26	Idaho	111.9
27	Delaware	111.6
28	South Dakota	110.7
29	Arizona	104.3
30	Pennsylvania	102.3
31	Wyoming	102.2
32	Ohio	95.6
33	Oregon	90.2
34	Arkansas	88.0
35	Texas	83.9
36	Michigan	77.4
37	Iowa	68.1
38	Alabama	63.1
39	Montana	50.9
40	Indiana	45.5
41	Hawaii	36.0
42	North Dakota	35.7
43	Massachusetts	30.6
44	New Hampshire	30.1
45	West Virginia	27.9
46	Vermont	12.4
NA	Kansas**	NA
NA	Maine**	NA
NA	Oklahoma**	NA
NA	Wisconsin**	NA
	District of Columbia**	NA

Source: Morgan Quitno Press using data from Federal Bureau of Investigation
   "Crime in the United States 1999" (Uniform Crime Reports, October 15, 2000)
*By law enforcement agencies submitting complete reports to the F.B.I. for 12 months in 1999. Arrests of youths 17 years and younger divided into population of 10 to 17 year olds. See important note at beginning of this chapter. Weapons violations include illegal carrying and possession.
**Not available.

Reported Arrests of Juveniles for Weapons Violations
As a Percent of All Such Arrests in 1999
National Percent = 24.2% of Reported Weapons Violations Arrests*

ALPHA ORDER

RANK	STATE	PERCENT
34	Alabama	18.7
24	Alaska	23.1
33	Arizona	18.8
45	Arkansas	10.5
11	California	31.9
19	Colorado	25.3
17	Connecticut	26.4
31	Delaware	19.7
25	Florida	23.0
27	Georgia	22.0
37	Hawaii	16.2
10	Idaho	32.0
9	Illinois	32.1
43	Indiana	12.3
12	Iowa	31.8
NA	Kansas**	NA
44	Kentucky	10.6
22	Louisiana	24.1
NA	Maine**	NA
15	Maryland	30.7
35	Massachusetts	17.9
42	Michigan	12.6
4	Minnesota	39.3
23	Mississippi	23.8
39	Missouri	15.3
6	Montana	38.9
30	Nebraska	20.1
20	Nevada	24.9
28	New Hampshire	21.8
13	New Jersey	31.7
7	New Mexico	38.8
21	New York	24.7
26	North Carolina	22.8
18	North Dakota	25.6
29	Ohio	20.7
NA	Oklahoma**	NA
32	Oregon	19.0
14	Pennsylvania	31.0
8	Rhode Island	32.5
38	South Carolina	16.0
2	South Dakota	49.7
41	Tennessee	12.7
36	Texas	17.0
5	Utah	39.0
1	Vermont	77.8
40	Virginia	14.6
16	Washington	28.2
46	West Virginia	8.9
NA	Wisconsin**	NA
3	Wyoming	40.3

RANK ORDER

RANK	STATE	PERCENT
1	Vermont	77.8
2	South Dakota	49.7
3	Wyoming	40.3
4	Minnesota	39.3
5	Utah	39.0
6	Montana	38.9
7	New Mexico	38.8
8	Rhode Island	32.5
9	Illinois	32.1
10	Idaho	32.0
11	California	31.9
12	Iowa	31.8
13	New Jersey	31.7
14	Pennsylvania	31.0
15	Maryland	30.7
16	Washington	28.2
17	Connecticut	26.4
18	North Dakota	25.6
19	Colorado	25.3
20	Nevada	24.9
21	New York	24.7
22	Louisiana	24.1
23	Mississippi	23.8
24	Alaska	23.1
25	Florida	23.0
26	North Carolina	22.8
27	Georgia	22.0
28	New Hampshire	21.8
29	Ohio	20.7
30	Nebraska	20.1
31	Delaware	19.7
32	Oregon	19.0
33	Arizona	18.8
34	Alabama	18.7
35	Massachusetts	17.9
36	Texas	17.0
37	Hawaii	16.2
38	South Carolina	16.0
39	Missouri	15.3
40	Virginia	14.6
41	Tennessee	12.7
42	Michigan	12.6
43	Indiana	12.3
44	Kentucky	10.6
45	Arkansas	10.5
46	West Virginia	8.9
NA	Kansas**	NA
NA	Maine**	NA
NA	Oklahoma**	NA
NA	Wisconsin**	NA
	District of Columbia**	NA

Source: Morgan Quitno Press using data from Federal Bureau of Investigation
   "Crime in the United States 1999" (Uniform Crime Reports, October 15, 2000)
*Arrests of youths 17 years and younger by law enforcement agencies submitting complete reports to the F.B.I. for
12 months in 1999. Weapons violations include illegal carrying and possession.
**Not available.

Reported Arrests of Juveniles for Driving Under the Influence in 1999

National Total = 14,284 Reported Arrests*

ALPHA ORDER

RANK	STATE	ARRESTS	% of USA
31	Alabama	138	1.0%
41	Alaska	62	0.4%
8	Arizona	492	3.4%
22	Arkansas	252	1.8%
1	California	1,761	12.3%
5	Colorado	754	5.3%
33	Connecticut	105	0.7%
45	Delaware	0	0.0%
9	Florida	481	3.4%
12	Georgia	360	2.5%
39	Hawaii	84	0.6%
20	Idaho	269	1.9%
NA	Illinois**	NA	NA
26	Indiana	160	1.1%
19	Iowa	287	2.0%
NA	Kansas**	NA	NA
42	Kentucky	43	0.3%
24	Louisiana	192	1.3%
NA	Maine**	NA	NA
17	Maryland	308	2.2%
29	Massachusetts	145	1.0%
11	Michigan	475	3.3%
3	Minnesota	876	6.1%
25	Mississippi	188	1.3%
13	Missouri	338	2.4%
32	Montana	106	0.7%
10	Nebraska	480	3.4%
28	Nevada	150	1.1%
37	New Hampshire	94	0.7%
18	New Jersey	297	2.1%
23	New Mexico	234	1.6%
16	New York	310	2.2%
4	North Carolina	839	5.9%
34	North Dakota	101	0.7%
15	Ohio	320	2.2%
NA	Oklahoma**	NA	NA
21	Oregon	257	1.8%
6	Pennsylvania	526	3.7%
44	Rhode Island	26	0.2%
37	South Carolina	94	0.7%
40	South Dakota	75	0.5%
30	Tennessee	144	1.0%
2	Texas	1,223	8.6%
27	Utah	159	1.1%
43	Vermont	34	0.2%
14	Virginia	332	2.3%
7	Washington	515	3.6%
35	West Virginia	99	0.7%
NA	Wisconsin**	NA	NA
35	Wyoming	99	0.7%

RANK ORDER

RANK	STATE	ARRESTS	% of USA
1	California	1,761	12.3%
2	Texas	1,223	8.6%
3	Minnesota	876	6.1%
4	North Carolina	839	5.9%
5	Colorado	754	5.3%
6	Pennsylvania	526	3.7%
7	Washington	515	3.6%
8	Arizona	492	3.4%
9	Florida	481	3.4%
10	Nebraska	480	3.4%
11	Michigan	475	3.3%
12	Georgia	360	2.5%
13	Missouri	338	2.4%
14	Virginia	332	2.3%
15	Ohio	320	2.2%
16	New York	310	2.2%
17	Maryland	308	2.2%
18	New Jersey	297	2.1%
19	Iowa	287	2.0%
20	Idaho	269	1.9%
21	Oregon	257	1.8%
22	Arkansas	252	1.8%
23	New Mexico	234	1.6%
24	Louisiana	192	1.3%
25	Mississippi	188	1.3%
26	Indiana	160	1.1%
27	Utah	159	1.1%
28	Nevada	150	1.1%
29	Massachusetts	145	1.0%
30	Tennessee	144	1.0%
31	Alabama	138	1.0%
32	Montana	106	0.7%
33	Connecticut	105	0.7%
34	North Dakota	101	0.7%
35	West Virginia	99	0.7%
35	Wyoming	99	0.7%
37	New Hampshire	94	0.7%
37	South Carolina	94	0.7%
39	Hawaii	84	0.6%
40	South Dakota	75	0.5%
41	Alaska	62	0.4%
42	Kentucky	43	0.3%
43	Vermont	34	0.2%
44	Rhode Island	26	0.2%
45	Delaware	0	0.0%
NA	Illinois**	NA	NA
NA	Kansas**	NA	NA
NA	Maine**	NA	NA
NA	Oklahoma**	NA	NA
NA	Wisconsin**	NA	NA
	District of Columbia**	NA	NA

Source: Federal Bureau of Investigation
   "Crime in the United States 1999" (Uniform Crime Reports, October 15, 2000)
*Arrests of youths 17 years and younger by law enforcement agencies submitting complete reports to the F.B.I. for 12 months in 1999. Includes driving any vehicle while drunk or under the influence of liquor or narcotics. See important note at beginning of this chapter.
**Not available.

Reported Juvenile Arrest Rate for Driving Under the Influence in 1999

National Rate = 66.4 Reported Arrests per 100,000 Juvenile Population*

ALPHA ORDER

RANK ORDER

RANK	STATE	RATE		RANK	STATE	RATE
40	Alabama	31.2		1	Colorado	249.1
25	Alaska	75.6		2	Nebraska	248.0
18	Arizona	93.8		3	Montana	192.8
21	Arkansas	88.0		4	Idaho	190.5
34	California	47.6		5	New Mexico	181.6
1	Colorado	249.1		6	North Dakota	171.5
42	Connecticut	29.8		7	Minnesota	169.9
45	Delaware	0.0		8	New Hampshire	166.4
41	Florida	30.0		9	Wyoming	158.0
11	Georgia	126.9		10	Mississippi	137.1
23	Hawaii	77.4		11	Georgia	126.9
4	Idaho	190.5		12	North Carolina	111.0
NA	Illinois**	NA		13	South Dakota	110.7
38	Indiana	40.0		14	Iowa	102.9
14	Iowa	102.9		15	Washington	102.3
NA	Kansas**	NA		16	West Virginia	98.5
22	Kentucky	86.9		17	South Carolina	94.2
36	Louisiana	46.3		18	Arizona	93.8
NA	Maine**	NA		19	Missouri	90.3
20	Maryland	88.3		20	Maryland	88.3
43	Massachusetts	28.4		21	Arkansas	88.0
33	Michigan	49.1		22	Kentucky	86.9
7	Minnesota	169.9		23	Hawaii	77.4
10	Mississippi	137.1		24	Utah	75.8
19	Missouri	90.3		25	Alaska	75.6
3	Montana	192.8		26	Nevada	74.1
2	Nebraska	248.0		27	Oregon	71.1
26	Nevada	74.1		28	Virginia	66.3
8	New Hampshire	166.4		29	Vermont	60.2
39	New Jersey	35.4		30	Texas	55.1
5	New Mexico	181.6		31	New York	51.3
31	New York	51.3		32	Pennsylvania	51.2
12	North Carolina	111.0		33	Michigan	49.1
6	North Dakota	171.5		34	California	47.6
37	Ohio	45.5		35	Tennessee	47.4
NA	Oklahoma**	NA		36	Louisiana	46.3
27	Oregon	71.1		37	Ohio	45.5
32	Pennsylvania	51.2		38	Indiana	40.0
44	Rhode Island	23.9		39	New Jersey	35.4
17	South Carolina	94.2		40	Alabama	31.2
13	South Dakota	110.7		41	Florida	30.0
35	Tennessee	47.4		42	Connecticut	29.8
30	Texas	55.1		43	Massachusetts	28.4
24	Utah	75.8		44	Rhode Island	23.9
29	Vermont	60.2		45	Delaware	0.0
28	Virginia	66.3		NA	Illinois**	NA
15	Washington	102.3		NA	Kansas**	NA
16	West Virginia	98.5		NA	Maine**	NA
NA	Wisconsin**	NA		NA	Oklahoma**	NA
9	Wyoming	158.0		NA	Wisconsin**	NA
					District of Columbia**	NA

Source: Morgan Quitno Press using data from Federal Bureau of Investigation
    "Crime in the United States 1999" (Uniform Crime Reports, October 15, 2000)
By law enforcement agencies submitting complete reports to the F.B.I. for 12 months in 1999. Arrests of youths 17 years and younger divided into population of 10 to 17 year olds. See important note at beginning of this chapter. Includes driving any vehicle while drunk or under the influence of liquor or narcotics.
**Not available.*

Reported Arrests of Juveniles for Driving Under the Influence
As a Percent of All Such Arrests in 1999
National Percent = 1.4% of Reported Driving Under the Influence Arrests*

ALPHA ORDER

RANK ORDER

RANK	STATE	PERCENT		RANK	STATE	PERCENT
41	Alabama	0.9		1	Montana	10.1
26	Alaska	1.4		2	New Hampshire	4.2
22	Arizona	1.5		3	Nebraska	3.8
26	Arkansas	1.4		4	Idaho	2.9
41	California	0.9		4	North Dakota	2.9
8	Colorado	2.5		6	Utah	2.8
36	Connecticut	1.1		7	New Mexico	2.6
45	Delaware	0.0		8	Colorado	2.5
44	Florida	0.8		9	Iowa	2.4
16	Georgia	1.8		10	Hawaii	2.3
10	Hawaii	2.3		10	Wyoming	2.3
4	Idaho	2.9		12	Minnesota	2.2
NA	Illinois**	NA		13	Mississippi	1.9
41	Indiana	0.9		13	Missouri	1.9
9	Iowa	2.4		13	Nevada	1.9
NA	Kansas**	NA		16	Georgia	1.8
33	Kentucky	1.2		16	South Dakota	1.8
31	Louisiana	1.3		18	Washington	1.7
NA	Maine**	NA		18	West Virginia	1.7
22	Maryland	1.5		20	Oregon	1.6
31	Massachusetts	1.3		20	Pennsylvania	1.6
38	Michigan	1.0		22	Arizona	1.5
12	Minnesota	2.2		22	Maryland	1.5
13	Mississippi	1.9		22	North Carolina	1.5
13	Missouri	1.9		22	Texas	1.5
1	Montana	10.1		26	Alaska	1.4
3	Nebraska	3.8		26	Arkansas	1.4
13	Nevada	1.9		26	Ohio	1.4
2	New Hampshire	4.2		26	Rhode Island	1.4
33	New Jersey	1.2		26	Virginia	1.4
7	New Mexico	2.6		31	Louisiana	1.3
38	New York	1.0		31	Massachusetts	1.3
22	North Carolina	1.5		33	Kentucky	1.2
4	North Dakota	2.9		33	New Jersey	1.2
26	Ohio	1.4		33	South Carolina	1.2
NA	Oklahoma**	NA		36	Connecticut	1.1
20	Oregon	1.6		36	Vermont	1.1
20	Pennsylvania	1.6		38	Michigan	1.0
26	Rhode Island	1.4		38	New York	1.0
33	South Carolina	1.2		38	Tennessee	1.0
16	South Dakota	1.8		41	Alabama	0.9
38	Tennessee	1.0		41	California	0.9
22	Texas	1.5		41	Indiana	0.9
6	Utah	2.8		44	Florida	0.8
36	Vermont	1.1		45	Delaware	0.0
26	Virginia	1.4		NA	Illinois**	NA
18	Washington	1.7		NA	Kansas**	NA
18	West Virginia	1.7		NA	Maine**	NA
NA	Wisconsin**	NA		NA	Oklahoma**	NA
10	Wyoming	2.3		NA	Wisconsin**	NA
					District of Columbia**	NA

Source: Morgan Quitno Press using data from Federal Bureau of Investigation
  "Crime in the United States 1999" (Uniform Crime Reports, October 15, 2000)
*Arrests of youths 17 years and younger by law enforcement agencies submitting complete reports to the F.B.I. for
12 months in 1999. Includes driving any vehicle while drunk or under the influence of liquor or narcotics.
**Not available.

Reported Arrests of Juveniles for Drug Abuse Violations in 1999

National Total = 143,375 Reported Arrests*

ALPHA ORDER

RANK	STATE	ARRESTS	% of USA
29	Alabama	1,195	0.8%
41	Alaska	405	0.3%
7	Arizona	4,945	3.4%
30	Arkansas	1,148	0.8%
1	California	23,406	16.3%
18	Colorado	2,535	1.8%
17	Connecticut	2,607	1.8%
39	Delaware	527	0.4%
2	Florida	15,089	10.5%
25	Georgia	1,453	1.0%
37	Hawaii	554	0.4%
34	Idaho	727	0.5%
4	Illinois	9,154	6.4%
21	Indiana	2,059	1.4%
27	Iowa	1,252	0.9%
NA	Kansas**	NA	NA
36	Kentucky	621	0.4%
13	Louisiana	2,936	2.0%
NA	Maine**	NA	NA
11	Maryland	3,314	2.3%
20	Massachusetts	2,209	1.5%
12	Michigan	3,158	2.2%
10	Minnesota	3,940	2.7%
32	Mississippi	1,052	0.7%
16	Missouri	2,632	1.8%
46	Montana	69	0.0%
26	Nebraska	1,334	0.9%
24	Nevada	1,704	1.2%
42	New Hampshire	374	0.3%
5	New Jersey	7,930	5.5%
33	New Mexico	1,045	0.7%
8	New York	4,361	3.0%
9	North Carolina	4,024	2.8%
44	North Dakota	196	0.1%
14	Ohio	2,907	2.0%
NA	Oklahoma**	NA	NA
23	Oregon	1,764	1.2%
6	Pennsylvania	5,456	3.8%
34	Rhode Island	727	0.5%
31	South Carolina	1,061	0.7%
40	South Dakota	523	0.4%
22	Tennessee	1,796	1.3%
3	Texas	14,006	9.8%
28	Utah	1,211	0.8%
45	Vermont	195	0.1%
19	Virginia	2,271	1.6%
15	Washington	2,732	1.9%
43	West Virginia	222	0.2%
NA	Wisconsin**	NA	NA
38	Wyoming	549	0.4%

RANK ORDER

RANK	STATE	ARRESTS	% of USA
1	California	23,406	16.3%
2	Florida	15,089	10.5%
3	Texas	14,006	9.8%
4	Illinois	9,154	6.4%
5	New Jersey	7,930	5.5%
6	Pennsylvania	5,456	3.8%
7	Arizona	4,945	3.4%
8	New York	4,361	3.0%
9	North Carolina	4,024	2.8%
10	Minnesota	3,940	2.7%
11	Maryland	3,314	2.3%
12	Michigan	3,158	2.2%
13	Louisiana	2,936	2.0%
14	Ohio	2,907	2.0%
15	Washington	2,732	1.9%
16	Missouri	2,632	1.8%
17	Connecticut	2,607	1.8%
18	Colorado	2,535	1.8%
19	Virginia	2,271	1.6%
20	Massachusetts	2,209	1.5%
21	Indiana	2,059	1.4%
22	Tennessee	1,796	1.3%
23	Oregon	1,764	1.2%
24	Nevada	1,704	1.2%
25	Georgia	1,453	1.0%
26	Nebraska	1,334	0.9%
27	Iowa	1,252	0.9%
28	Utah	1,211	0.8%
29	Alabama	1,195	0.8%
30	Arkansas	1,148	0.8%
31	South Carolina	1,061	0.7%
32	Mississippi	1,052	0.7%
33	New Mexico	1,045	0.7%
34	Idaho	727	0.5%
34	Rhode Island	727	0.5%
36	Kentucky	621	0.4%
37	Hawaii	554	0.4%
38	Wyoming	549	0.4%
39	Delaware	527	0.4%
40	South Dakota	523	0.4%
41	Alaska	405	0.3%
42	New Hampshire	374	0.3%
43	West Virginia	222	0.2%
44	North Dakota	196	0.1%
45	Vermont	195	0.1%
46	Montana	69	0.0%
NA	Kansas**	NA	NA
NA	Maine**	NA	NA
NA	Oklahoma**	NA	NA
NA	Wisconsin**	NA	NA
	District of Columbia**	NA	NA

Source: Federal Bureau of Investigation
    "Crime in the United States 1999" (Uniform Crime Reports, October 15, 2000)
*Arrests of youths 17 years and younger by law enforcement agencies submitting complete reports to the F.B.I. for 12 months in 1999. Includes offenses relating to possession, sale, use, growing and manufacturing of narcotic drugs. See important note at beginning of this chapter.
**Not available.

Reported Juvenile Arrest Rate for Drug Abuse Violations in 1999

National Rate = 666.9 Reported Arrests per 100,000 Juvenile Population*

ALPHA ORDER   RANK ORDER

RANK	STATE	RATE		RANK	STATE	RATE
44	Alabama	270.3		1	Illinois	2,846.4
34	Alaska	493.7		2	Kentucky	1,254.4
6	Arizona	942.5		3	South Carolina	1,063.2
40	Arkansas	400.7		4	Maryland	950.0
23	California	632.6		5	New Jersey	945.8
10	Colorado	837.6		6	Arizona	942.5
15	Connecticut	740.2		7	Florida	942.0
22	Delaware	653.2		8	Wyoming	876.4
7	Florida	942.0		9	Nevada	841.9
32	Georgia	512.1		10	Colorado	837.6
33	Hawaii	510.7		11	New Mexico	811.1
30	Idaho	514.8		12	South Dakota	772.2
1	Illinois	2,846.4		13	Mississippi	767.1
31	Indiana	514.6		14	Minnesota	763.9
37	Iowa	448.7		15	Connecticut	740.2
NA	Kansas**	NA		16	New York	721.9
2	Kentucky	1,254.4		17	Louisiana	708.7
17	Louisiana	708.7		18	Missouri	703.0
NA	Maine**	NA		19	Nebraska	689.3
4	Maryland	950.0		20	Rhode Island	666.9
38	Massachusetts	433.2		21	New Hampshire	662.1
43	Michigan	326.2		22	Delaware	653.2
14	Minnesota	763.9		23	California	632.6
13	Mississippi	767.1		24	Texas	630.5
18	Missouri	703.0		25	Tennessee	591.2
46	Montana	125.5		26	Utah	577.6
19	Nebraska	689.3		27	Washington	542.5
9	Nevada	841.9		28	North Carolina	532.3
21	New Hampshire	662.1		29	Pennsylvania	530.7
5	New Jersey	945.8		30	Idaho	514.8
11	New Mexico	811.1		31	Indiana	514.6
16	New York	721.9		32	Georgia	512.1
28	North Carolina	532.3		33	Hawaii	510.7
42	North Dakota	332.9		34	Alaska	493.7
39	Ohio	413.6		35	Oregon	488.0
NA	Oklahoma**	NA		36	Virginia	453.2
35	Oregon	488.0		37	Iowa	448.7
29	Pennsylvania	530.7		38	Massachusetts	433.2
20	Rhode Island	666.9		39	Ohio	413.6
3	South Carolina	1,063.2		40	Arkansas	400.7
12	South Dakota	772.2		41	Vermont	345.1
25	Tennessee	591.2		42	North Dakota	332.9
24	Texas	630.5		43	Michigan	326.2
26	Utah	577.6		44	Alabama	270.3
41	Vermont	345.1		45	West Virginia	220.9
36	Virginia	453.2		46	Montana	125.5
27	Washington	542.5		NA	Kansas**	NA
45	West Virginia	220.9		NA	Maine**	NA
NA	Wisconsin**	NA		NA	Oklahoma**	NA
8	Wyoming	876.4		NA	Wisconsin**	NA
					District of Columbia**	NA

Source: Morgan Quitno Press using data from Federal Bureau of Investigation
  "Crime in the United States 1999" (Uniform Crime Reports, October 15, 2000)
*By law enforcement agencies submitting complete reports to the F.B.I. for 12 months in 1999. Arrests of youths 17 years and younger divided into population of 10 to 17 year olds. See important note at beginning of this chapter. Includes offenses relating to possession, sale, use, growing and manufacturing of narcotic drugs.
**Not available.

Reported Arrests of Juveniles for Drug Abuse Violations
As a Percent of All Such Arrests in 1999
National Percent = 12.5% of Reported Drug Abuse Violation Arrests*

ALPHA ORDER

RANK ORDER

RANK	STATE	PERCENT		RANK	STATE	PERCENT
45	Alabama	8.9		1	Montana	30.1
5	Alaska	22.0		2	New Mexico	24.2
13	Arizona	17.5		3	Wyoming	23.7
46	Arkansas	7.9		4	Hawaii	22.2
43	California	9.2		5	Alaska	22.0
19	Colorado	15.1		6	New Hampshire	21.7
23	Connecticut	14.4		6	South Dakota	21.7
18	Delaware	16.0		8	Minnesota	20.2
39	Florida	10.6		9	Utah	19.7
43	Georgia	9.2		10	Maryland	19.3
4	Hawaii	22.2		11	North Dakota	18.0
16	Idaho	16.3		12	Vermont	17.9
14	Illinois	16.7		13	Arizona	17.5
31	Indiana	12.9		14	Illinois	16.7
24	Iowa	14.1		15	Rhode Island	16.6
NA	Kansas**	NA		16	Idaho	16.3
41	Kentucky	10.0		16	Nevada	16.3
29	Louisiana	13.3		18	Delaware	16.0
NA	Maine**	NA		19	Colorado	15.1
10	Maryland	19.3		20	Nebraska	14.9
24	Massachusetts	14.1		21	New Jersey	14.6
40	Michigan	10.2		22	Texas	14.5
8	Minnesota	20.2		23	Connecticut	14.4
37	Mississippi	10.7		24	Iowa	14.1
36	Missouri	10.9		24	Massachusetts	14.1
1	Montana	30.1		26	Washington	13.9
20	Nebraska	14.9		27	Oregon	13.6
16	Nevada	16.3		28	Ohio	13.5
6	New Hampshire	21.7		29	Louisiana	13.3
21	New Jersey	14.6		30	Pennsylvania	13.0
2	New Mexico	24.2		31	Indiana	12.9
32	New York	12.6		32	New York	12.6
35	North Carolina	11.0		33	South Carolina	12.2
11	North Dakota	18.0		34	Tennessee	11.8
28	Ohio	13.5		35	North Carolina	11.0
NA	Oklahoma**	NA		36	Missouri	10.9
27	Oregon	13.6		37	Mississippi	10.7
30	Pennsylvania	13.0		37	Virginia	10.7
15	Rhode Island	16.6		39	Florida	10.6
33	South Carolina	12.2		40	Michigan	10.2
6	South Dakota	21.7		41	Kentucky	10.0
34	Tennessee	11.8		42	West Virginia	9.8
22	Texas	14.5		43	California	9.2
9	Utah	19.7		43	Georgia	9.2
12	Vermont	17.9		45	Alabama	8.9
37	Virginia	10.7		46	Arkansas	7.9
26	Washington	13.9		NA	Kansas**	NA
42	West Virginia	9.8		NA	Maine**	NA
NA	Wisconsin**	NA		NA	Oklahoma**	NA
3	Wyoming	23.7		NA	Wisconsin**	NA
					District of Columbia**	NA

Source: Morgan Quitno Press using data from Federal Bureau of Investigation
   "Crime in the United States 1999" (Uniform Crime Reports, October 15, 2000)
*Arrests of youths 17 years and younger by law enforcement agencies submitting complete reports to the F.B.I. for 12 months in 1999. Includes offenses relating to possession, sale, use, growing and manufacturing of narcotic drugs.
**Not available.

Reported Arrests of Juveniles for Sex Offenses in 1999

National Total = 10,977 Reported Arrests*

ALPHA ORDER

RANK	STATE	ARRESTS	% of USA
36	Alabama	33	0.3%
33	Alaska	48	0.4%
11	Arizona	302	2.8%
27	Arkansas	94	0.9%
1	California	2,467	22.5%
20	Colorado	230	2.1%
22	Connecticut	140	1.3%
29	Delaware	85	0.8%
6	Florida	336	3.1%
8	Georgia	327	3.0%
30	Hawaii	78	0.7%
26	Idaho	96	0.9%
16	Illinois	264	2.4%
23	Indiana	120	1.1%
31	Iowa	66	0.6%
NA	Kansas**	NA	NA
40	Kentucky	25	0.2%
14	Louisiana	271	2.5%
NA	Maine**	NA	NA
21	Maryland	216	2.0%
28	Massachusetts	88	0.8%
9	Michigan	325	3.0%
19	Minnesota	232	2.1%
39	Mississippi	28	0.3%
15	Missouri	268	2.4%
37	Montana	30	0.3%
24	Nebraska	113	1.0%
25	Nevada	103	0.9%
42	New Hampshire	14	0.1%
5	New Jersey	484	4.4%
45	New Mexico	11	0.1%
3	New York	674	6.1%
7	North Carolina	332	3.0%
44	North Dakota	12	0.1%
13	Ohio	280	2.6%
NA	Oklahoma**	NA	NA
16	Oregon	264	2.4%
4	Pennsylvania	612	5.6%
37	Rhode Island	30	0.3%
35	South Carolina	34	0.3%
34	South Dakota	46	0.4%
32	Tennessee	58	0.5%
2	Texas	843	7.7%
10	Utah	315	2.9%
46	Vermont	5	0.0%
18	Virginia	259	2.4%
12	Washington	286	2.6%
43	West Virginia	13	0.1%
NA	Wisconsin**	NA	NA
41	Wyoming	20	0.2%

RANK ORDER

RANK	STATE	ARRESTS	% of USA
1	California	2,467	22.5%
2	Texas	843	7.7%
3	New York	674	6.1%
4	Pennsylvania	612	5.6%
5	New Jersey	484	4.4%
6	Florida	336	3.1%
7	North Carolina	332	3.0%
8	Georgia	327	3.0%
9	Michigan	325	3.0%
10	Utah	315	2.9%
11	Arizona	302	2.8%
12	Washington	286	2.6%
13	Ohio	280	2.6%
14	Louisiana	271	2.5%
15	Missouri	268	2.4%
16	Illinois	264	2.4%
16	Oregon	264	2.4%
18	Virginia	259	2.4%
19	Minnesota	232	2.1%
20	Colorado	230	2.1%
21	Maryland	216	2.0%
22	Connecticut	140	1.3%
23	Indiana	120	1.1%
24	Nebraska	113	1.0%
25	Nevada	103	0.9%
26	Idaho	96	0.9%
27	Arkansas	94	0.9%
28	Massachusetts	88	0.8%
29	Delaware	85	0.8%
30	Hawaii	78	0.7%
31	Iowa	66	0.6%
32	Tennessee	58	0.5%
33	Alaska	48	0.4%
34	South Dakota	46	0.4%
35	South Carolina	34	0.3%
36	Alabama	33	0.3%
37	Montana	30	0.3%
37	Rhode Island	30	0.3%
39	Mississippi	28	0.3%
40	Kentucky	25	0.2%
41	Wyoming	20	0.2%
42	New Hampshire	14	0.1%
43	West Virginia	13	0.1%
44	North Dakota	12	0.1%
45	New Mexico	11	0.1%
46	Vermont	5	0.0%
NA	Kansas**	NA	NA
NA	Maine**	NA	NA
NA	Oklahoma**	NA	NA
NA	Wisconsin**	NA	NA
	District of Columbia**	NA	NA

Source: Federal Bureau of Investigation
   "Crime in the United States 1999" (Uniform Crime Reports, October 15, 2000)
*Arrests of youths 17 years and younger by law enforcement agencies submitting complete reports to the F.B.I. for 12 months in 1999. Excludes forcible rape, prostitution and commercialized vice. Includes statutory rape and offenses against chastity, common decency, morals and the like. See important note at beginning of this chapter.
**Not available.

Reported Juvenile Arrest Rate for Sex Offenses in 1999

National Rate = 51.1 Reported Arrests per 100,000 Juvenile Population*

ALPHA ORDER

RANK	STATE	RATE
46	Alabama	7.5
16	Alaska	58.5
19	Arizona	57.6
32	Arkansas	32.8
12	California	66.7
6	Colorado	76.0
28	Connecticut	39.7
4	Delaware	105.4
38	Florida	21.0
2	Georgia	115.2
8	Hawaii	71.9
10	Idaho	68.0
5	Illinois	82.1
34	Indiana	30.0
37	Iowa	23.7
NA	Kansas**	NA
24	Kentucky	50.5
13	Louisiana	65.4
NA	Maine**	NA
14	Maryland	61.9
42	Massachusetts	17.3
31	Michigan	33.6
25	Minnesota	45.0
39	Mississippi	20.4
9	Missouri	71.6
21	Montana	54.6
17	Nebraska	58.4
23	Nevada	50.9
36	New Hampshire	24.8
18	New Jersey	57.7
45	New Mexico	8.5
3	New York	111.6
26	North Carolina	43.9
39	North Dakota	20.4
27	Ohio	39.8
NA	Oklahoma**	NA
7	Oregon	73.0
15	Pennsylvania	59.5
35	Rhode Island	27.5
30	South Carolina	34.1
11	South Dakota	67.9
41	Tennessee	19.1
29	Texas	37.9
1	Utah	150.2
44	Vermont	8.8
22	Virginia	51.7
20	Washington	56.8
43	West Virginia	12.9
NA	Wisconsin**	NA
33	Wyoming	31.9

RANK ORDER

RANK	STATE	RATE
1	Utah	150.2
2	Georgia	115.2
3	New York	111.6
4	Delaware	105.4
5	Illinois	82.1
6	Colorado	76.0
7	Oregon	73.0
8	Hawaii	71.9
9	Missouri	71.6
10	Idaho	68.0
11	South Dakota	67.9
12	California	66.7
13	Louisiana	65.4
14	Maryland	61.9
15	Pennsylvania	59.5
16	Alaska	58.5
17	Nebraska	58.4
18	New Jersey	57.7
19	Arizona	57.6
20	Washington	56.8
21	Montana	54.6
22	Virginia	51.7
23	Nevada	50.9
24	Kentucky	50.5
25	Minnesota	45.0
26	North Carolina	43.9
27	Ohio	39.8
28	Connecticut	39.7
29	Texas	37.9
30	South Carolina	34.1
31	Michigan	33.6
32	Arkansas	32.8
33	Wyoming	31.9
34	Indiana	30.0
35	Rhode Island	27.5
36	New Hampshire	24.8
37	Iowa	23.7
38	Florida	21.0
39	Mississippi	20.4
39	North Dakota	20.4
41	Tennessee	19.1
42	Massachusetts	17.3
43	West Virginia	12.9
44	Vermont	8.8
45	New Mexico	8.5
46	Alabama	7.5
NA	Kansas**	NA
NA	Maine**	NA
NA	Oklahoma**	NA
NA	Wisconsin**	NA
	District of Columbia**	NA

Source: Morgan Quitno Press using data from Federal Bureau of Investigation
"Crime in the United States 1999" (Uniform Crime Reports, October 15, 2000)
*By law enforcement agencies submitting complete reports to the F.B.I. for 12 months in 1999. Arrests of youths 17 years and younger divided into population of 10 to 17 year olds. See important note at beginning of this chapter. Excludes forcible rape, prostitution and commercialized vice. Includes statutory rape and offenses against chastity, common decency, morals and the like. **Not available.

Reported Arrests of Juveniles for Sex Offenses
As a Percent of All Such Arrests in 1999
National Percent = 17.1% of Reported Sex Offenses Arrests*

ALPHA ORDER

RANK	STATE	PERCENT
43	Alabama	9.1
31	Alaska	15.8
35	Arizona	13.9
37	Arkansas	13.3
33	California	15.0
22	Colorado	19.1
11	Connecticut	22.8
19	Delaware	19.9
44	Florida	8.2
5	Georgia	27.1
21	Hawaii	19.6
3	Idaho	33.6
24	Illinois	18.7
40	Indiana	11.3
4	Iowa	28.1
NA	Kansas**	NA
38	Kentucky	12.2
23	Louisiana	19.0
NA	Maine**	NA
6	Maryland	26.7
41	Massachusetts	11.2
9	Michigan	24.0
7	Minnesota	24.8
39	Mississippi	11.9
36	Missouri	13.4
2	Montana	36.6
27	Nebraska	18.0
46	Nevada	7.3
24	New Hampshire	18.7
8	New Jersey	24.3
15	New Mexico	20.8
16	New York	20.7
32	North Carolina	15.7
10	North Dakota	23.5
30	Ohio	16.0
NA	Oklahoma**	NA
19	Oregon	19.9
18	Pennsylvania	20.0
34	Rhode Island	14.8
12	South Carolina	21.4
13	South Dakota	21.0
45	Tennessee	8.0
28	Texas	17.5
1	Utah	44.8
26	Vermont	18.5
16	Virginia	20.7
13	Washington	21.0
42	West Virginia	10.2
NA	Wisconsin**	NA
29	Wyoming	16.9

RANK ORDER

RANK	STATE	PERCENT
1	Utah	44.8
2	Montana	36.6
3	Idaho	33.6
4	Iowa	28.1
5	Georgia	27.1
6	Maryland	26.7
7	Minnesota	24.8
8	New Jersey	24.3
9	Michigan	24.0
10	North Dakota	23.5
11	Connecticut	22.8
12	South Carolina	21.4
13	South Dakota	21.0
13	Washington	21.0
15	New Mexico	20.8
16	New York	20.7
16	Virginia	20.7
18	Pennsylvania	20.0
19	Delaware	19.9
19	Oregon	19.9
21	Hawaii	19.6
22	Colorado	19.1
23	Louisiana	19.0
24	Illinois	18.7
24	New Hampshire	18.7
26	Vermont	18.5
27	Nebraska	18.0
28	Texas	17.5
29	Wyoming	16.9
30	Ohio	16.0
31	Alaska	15.8
32	North Carolina	15.7
33	California	15.0
34	Rhode Island	14.8
35	Arizona	13.9
36	Missouri	13.4
37	Arkansas	13.3
38	Kentucky	12.2
39	Mississippi	11.9
40	Indiana	11.3
41	Massachusetts	11.2
42	West Virginia	10.2
43	Alabama	9.1
44	Florida	8.2
45	Tennessee	8.0
46	Nevada	7.3
NA	Kansas**	NA
NA	Maine**	NA
NA	Oklahoma**	NA
NA	Wisconsin**	NA
	District of Columbia**	NA

Source: Morgan Quitno Press using data from Federal Bureau of Investigation
    "Crime in the United States 1999" (Uniform Crime Reports, October 15, 2000)
*Arrests of youths 17 years and younger by law enforcement agencies submitting complete reports to the F.B.I. for 12 months in 1999. Excludes forcible rape, prostitution and commercialized vice. Includes statutory rape and offenses against chastity, common decency, morals and the like.
**Not available.

Reported Arrests of Juveniles for Prostitution and Commercialized Vice in 1999

National Total = 1,173 Reported Arrests*

ALPHA ORDER

RANK	STATE	ARRESTS	% of USA
39	Alabama	0	0.0%
28	Alaska	5	0.4%
9	Arizona	27	2.3%
23	Arkansas	7	0.6%
2	California	276	23.5%
31	Colorado	4	0.3%
34	Connecticut	2	0.2%
39	Delaware	0	0.0%
1	Florida	296	25.2%
31	Georgia	4	0.3%
17	Hawaii	15	1.3%
34	Idaho	2	0.2%
4	Illinois	50	4.3%
20	Indiana	11	0.9%
39	Iowa	0	0.0%
NA	Kansas**	NA	NA
28	Kentucky	5	0.4%
20	Louisiana	11	0.9%
NA	Maine**	NA	NA
18	Maryland	13	1.1%
6	Massachusetts	31	2.6%
7	Michigan	30	2.6%
5	Minnesota	47	4.0%
34	Mississippi	2	0.2%
19	Missouri	12	1.0%
34	Montana	2	0.2%
28	Nebraska	5	0.4%
10	Nevada	24	2.0%
26	New Hampshire	6	0.5%
11	New Jersey	22	1.9%
31	New Mexico	4	0.3%
14	New York	18	1.5%
14	North Carolina	18	1.5%
39	North Dakota	0	0.0%
8	Ohio	28	2.4%
NA	Oklahoma**	NA	NA
22	Oregon	8	0.7%
13	Pennsylvania	19	1.6%
23	Rhode Island	7	0.6%
26	South Carolina	6	0.5%
39	South Dakota	0	0.0%
16	Tennessee	16	1.4%
3	Texas	111	9.5%
39	Utah	0	0.0%
39	Vermont	0	0.0%
23	Virginia	7	0.6%
12	Washington	21	1.8%
39	West Virginia	0	0.0%
NA	Wisconsin**	NA	NA
38	Wyoming	1	0.1%

RANK ORDER

RANK	STATE	ARRESTS	% of USA
1	Florida	296	25.2%
2	California	276	23.5%
3	Texas	111	9.5%
4	Illinois	50	4.3%
5	Minnesota	47	4.0%
6	Massachusetts	31	2.6%
7	Michigan	30	2.6%
8	Ohio	28	2.4%
9	Arizona	27	2.3%
10	Nevada	24	2.0%
11	New Jersey	22	1.9%
12	Washington	21	1.8%
13	Pennsylvania	19	1.6%
14	New York	18	1.5%
14	North Carolina	18	1.5%
16	Tennessee	16	1.4%
17	Hawaii	15	1.3%
18	Maryland	13	1.1%
19	Missouri	12	1.0%
20	Indiana	11	0.9%
20	Louisiana	11	0.9%
22	Oregon	8	0.7%
23	Arkansas	7	0.6%
23	Rhode Island	7	0.6%
23	Virginia	7	0.6%
26	New Hampshire	6	0.5%
26	South Carolina	6	0.5%
28	Alaska	5	0.4%
28	Kentucky	5	0.4%
28	Nebraska	5	0.4%
31	Colorado	4	0.3%
31	Georgia	4	0.3%
31	New Mexico	4	0.3%
34	Connecticut	2	0.2%
34	Idaho	2	0.2%
34	Mississippi	2	0.2%
34	Montana	2	0.2%
38	Wyoming	1	0.1%
39	Alabama	0	0.0%
39	Delaware	0	0.0%
39	Iowa	0	0.0%
39	North Dakota	0	0.0%
39	South Dakota	0	0.0%
39	Utah	0	0.0%
39	Vermont	0	0.0%
39	West Virginia	0	0.0%
NA	Kansas**	NA	NA
NA	Maine**	NA	NA
NA	Oklahoma**	NA	NA
NA	Wisconsin**	NA	NA
	District of Columbia**	NA	NA

Source: Federal Bureau of Investigation
   "Crime in the United States 1999" (Uniform Crime Reports, October 15, 2000)
Arrests of youths 17 years and younger by law enforcement agencies submitting complete reports to the F.B.I. for 12 months in 1999. Includes keeping a bawdy house, procuring or transporting women for immoral purposes. Attempts are included. See important note at beginning of this chapter.
**Not available.*

Reported Juvenile Arrest Rate for Prostitution and Commercialized Vice in 1999

National Rate = 5.5 Reported Arrests per 100,000 Juvenile Population*

ALPHA ORDER

RANK ORDER

RANK	STATE	RATE
39	Alabama	0.0
10	Alaska	6.1
14	Arizona	5.1
28	Arkansas	2.4
8	California	7.5
37	Colorado	1.3
38	Connecticut	0.6
39	Delaware	0.0
1	Florida	18.5
34	Georgia	1.4
3	Hawaii	13.8
34	Idaho	1.4
2	Illinois	15.5
24	Indiana	2.7
39	Iowa	0.0
NA	Kansas**	NA
6	Kentucky	10.1
24	Louisiana	2.7
NA	Maine**	NA
18	Maryland	3.7
10	Massachusetts	6.1
21	Michigan	3.1
7	Minnesota	9.1
33	Mississippi	1.5
20	Missouri	3.2
19	Montana	3.6
26	Nebraska	2.6
4	Nevada	11.9
5	New Hampshire	10.6
26	New Jersey	2.6
21	New Mexico	3.1
23	New York	3.0
28	North Carolina	2.4
39	North Dakota	0.0
17	Ohio	4.0
NA	Oklahoma**	NA
30	Oregon	2.2
31	Pennsylvania	1.8
9	Rhode Island	6.4
12	South Carolina	6.0
39	South Dakota	0.0
13	Tennessee	5.3
15	Texas	5.0
39	Utah	0.0
39	Vermont	0.0
34	Virginia	1.4
16	Washington	4.2
39	West Virginia	0.0
NA	Wisconsin**	NA
32	Wyoming	1.6

RANK	STATE	RATE
1	Florida	18.5
2	Illinois	15.5
3	Hawaii	13.8
4	Nevada	11.9
5	New Hampshire	10.6
6	Kentucky	10.1
7	Minnesota	9.1
8	California	7.5
9	Rhode Island	6.4
10	Alaska	6.1
10	Massachusetts	6.1
12	South Carolina	6.0
13	Tennessee	5.3
14	Arizona	5.1
15	Texas	5.0
16	Washington	4.2
17	Ohio	4.0
18	Maryland	3.7
19	Montana	3.6
20	Missouri	3.2
21	Michigan	3.1
21	New Mexico	3.1
23	New York	3.0
24	Indiana	2.7
24	Louisiana	2.7
26	Nebraska	2.6
26	New Jersey	2.6
28	Arkansas	2.4
28	North Carolina	2.4
30	Oregon	2.2
31	Pennsylvania	1.8
32	Wyoming	1.6
33	Mississippi	1.5
34	Georgia	1.4
34	Idaho	1.4
34	Virginia	1.4
37	Colorado	1.3
38	Connecticut	0.6
39	Alabama	0.0
39	Delaware	0.0
39	Iowa	0.0
39	North Dakota	0.0
39	South Dakota	0.0
39	Utah	0.0
39	Vermont	0.0
39	West Virginia	0.0
NA	Kansas**	NA
NA	Maine**	NA
NA	Oklahoma**	NA
NA	Wisconsin**	NA
	District of Columbia**	NA

Source: Morgan Quitno Press using data from Federal Bureau of Investigation
  "Crime in the United States 1999" (Uniform Crime Reports, October 15, 2000)
*By law enforcement agencies submitting complete reports to the F.B.I. for 12 months in 1999. Arrests of youths 17
years and younger divided into population of 10 to 17 year olds. See important note at beginning of this chapter.
Includes keeping a bawdy house, procuring or transporting women for immoral purposes. Attempts are included.
**Not available.*

233

Reported Arrests of Juveniles for Prostitution and Commercialized Vice As a Percent of All Such Arrests in 1999

National Percent = 1.5% of Reported Prostitution/Commercialized Vice Arrests*

ALPHA ORDER

RANK	STATE	PERCENT
39	Alabama	0.0
10	Alaska	2.8
27	Arizona	1.2
11	Arkansas	2.5
16	California	1.9
37	Colorado	0.4
38	Connecticut	0.3
39	Delaware	0.0
12	Florida	2.0
4	Georgia	6.3
7	Hawaii	3.5
2	Idaho	28.6
31	Illinois	0.8
30	Indiana	0.9
39	Iowa	0.0
NA	Kansas**	NA
28	Kentucky	1.1
12	Louisiana	2.0
NA	Maine**	NA
5	Maryland	5.9
12	Massachusetts	2.0
22	Michigan	1.4
9	Minnesota	2.9
26	Mississippi	1.3
34	Missouri	0.6
6	Montana	5.1
22	Nebraska	1.4
36	Nevada	0.5
1	New Hampshire	66.7
33	New Jersey	0.7
31	New Mexico	0.8
22	New York	1.4
12	North Carolina	2.0
39	North Dakota	0.0
22	Ohio	1.4
NA	Oklahoma**	NA
20	Oregon	1.5
34	Pennsylvania	0.6
17	Rhode Island	1.7
18	South Carolina	1.6
39	South Dakota	0.0
28	Tennessee	1.1
18	Texas	1.6
39	Utah	0.0
39	Vermont	0.0
20	Virginia	1.5
8	Washington	3.0
39	West Virginia	0.0
NA	Wisconsin**	NA
3	Wyoming	11.1

RANK ORDER

RANK	STATE	PERCENT
1	New Hampshire	66.7
2	Idaho	28.6
3	Wyoming	11.1
4	Georgia	6.3
5	Maryland	5.9
6	Montana	5.1
7	Hawaii	3.5
8	Washington	3.0
9	Minnesota	2.9
10	Alaska	2.8
11	Arkansas	2.5
12	Florida	2.0
12	Louisiana	2.0
12	Massachusetts	2.0
12	North Carolina	2.0
16	California	1.9
17	Rhode Island	1.7
18	South Carolina	1.6
18	Texas	1.6
20	Oregon	1.5
20	Virginia	1.5
22	Michigan	1.4
22	Nebraska	1.4
22	New York	1.4
22	Ohio	1.4
26	Mississippi	1.3
27	Arizona	1.2
28	Kentucky	1.1
28	Tennessee	1.1
30	Indiana	0.9
31	Illinois	0.8
31	New Mexico	0.8
33	New Jersey	0.7
34	Missouri	0.6
34	Pennsylvania	0.6
36	Nevada	0.5
37	Colorado	0.4
38	Connecticut	0.3
39	Alabama	0.0
39	Delaware	0.0
39	Iowa	0.0
39	North Dakota	0.0
39	South Dakota	0.0
39	Utah	0.0
39	Vermont	0.0
39	West Virginia	0.0
NA	Kansas**	NA
NA	Maine**	NA
NA	Oklahoma**	NA
NA	Wisconsin**	NA
	District of Columbia**	NA

Source: Morgan Quitno Press using data from Federal Bureau of Investigation
    "Crime in the United States 1999" (Uniform Crime Reports, October 15, 2000)
*Arrests of youths 17 years and younger by law enforcement agencies submitting complete reports to the F.B.I. for 12 months in 1999. Includes keeping a bawdy house, procuring or transporting women for immoral purposes. Attempts are included.
**Not available.

Reported Arrests of Juveniles for Offenses Against Families & Children in 1999

National Total = 6,093 Reported Arrests*

ALPHA ORDER

RANK	STATE	ARRESTS	% of USA
30	Alabama	18	0.3%
25	Alaska	27	0.4%
4	Arizona	236	3.9%
20	Arkansas	66	1.1%
33	California	14	0.2%
21	Colorado	61	1.0%
9	Connecticut	151	2.5%
40	Delaware	4	0.1%
NA	Florida**	NA	NA
5	Georgia	215	3.5%
10	Hawaii	150	2.5%
28	Idaho	23	0.4%
39	Illinois	6	0.1%
6	Indiana	192	3.2%
35	Iowa	9	0.1%
NA	Kansas**	NA	NA
35	Kentucky	9	0.1%
2	Louisiana	617	10.1%
NA	Maine**	NA	NA
17	Maryland	86	1.4%
12	Massachusetts	115	1.9%
34	Michigan	11	0.2%
24	Minnesota	36	0.6%
13	Mississippi	110	1.8%
11	Missouri	139	2.3%
45	Montana	1	0.0%
27	Nebraska	26	0.4%
30	Nevada	18	0.3%
35	New Hampshire	9	0.1%
23	New Jersey	52	0.9%
29	New Mexico	22	0.4%
3	New York	399	6.5%
14	North Carolina	108	1.8%
15	North Dakota	94	1.5%
1	Ohio	2,379	39.0%
NA	Oklahoma**	NA	NA
32	Oregon	15	0.2%
19	Pennsylvania	72	1.2%
7	Rhode Island	172	2.8%
43	South Carolina	3	0.0%
18	South Dakota	83	1.4%
22	Tennessee	55	0.9%
8	Texas	155	2.5%
25	Utah	27	0.4%
40	Vermont	4	0.1%
16	Virginia	89	1.5%
40	Washington	4	0.1%
35	West Virginia	9	0.1%
NA	Wisconsin**	NA	NA
44	Wyoming	2	0.0%

RANK ORDER

RANK	STATE	ARRESTS	% of USA
1	Ohio	2,379	39.0%
2	Louisiana	617	10.1%
3	New York	399	6.5%
4	Arizona	236	3.9%
5	Georgia	215	3.5%
6	Indiana	192	3.2%
7	Rhode Island	172	2.8%
8	Texas	155	2.5%
9	Connecticut	151	2.5%
10	Hawaii	150	2.5%
11	Missouri	139	2.3%
12	Massachusetts	115	1.9%
13	Mississippi	110	1.8%
14	North Carolina	108	1.8%
15	North Dakota	94	1.5%
16	Virginia	89	1.5%
17	Maryland	86	1.4%
18	South Dakota	83	1.4%
19	Pennsylvania	72	1.2%
20	Arkansas	66	1.1%
21	Colorado	61	1.0%
22	Tennessee	55	0.9%
23	New Jersey	52	0.9%
24	Minnesota	36	0.6%
25	Alaska	27	0.4%
25	Utah	27	0.4%
27	Nebraska	26	0.4%
28	Idaho	23	0.4%
29	New Mexico	22	0.4%
30	Alabama	18	0.3%
30	Nevada	18	0.3%
32	Oregon	15	0.2%
33	California	14	0.2%
34	Michigan	11	0.2%
35	Iowa	9	0.1%
35	Kentucky	9	0.1%
35	New Hampshire	9	0.1%
35	West Virginia	9	0.1%
39	Illinois	6	0.1%
40	Delaware	4	0.1%
40	Vermont	4	0.1%
40	Washington	4	0.1%
43	South Carolina	3	0.0%
44	Wyoming	2	0.0%
45	Montana	1	0.0%
NA	Florida**	NA	NA
NA	Kansas**	NA	NA
NA	Maine**	NA	NA
NA	Oklahoma**	NA	NA
NA	Wisconsin**	NA	NA
	District of Columbia**	NA	NA

Source: Federal Bureau of Investigation
"Crime in the United States 1999" (Uniform Crime Reports, October 15, 2000)
*Arrests of youths 17 years and younger by law enforcement agencies submitting complete reports to the F.B.I. for 12 months in 1999. Includes nonsupport, neglect, desertion or abuse of family and children. See important note at beginning of this chapter.
**Not available.

Reported Juvenile Arrest Rate for Offenses Against Families & Children in 1999

National Rate = 28.3 Reported Arrests per 100,000 Juvenile Population*

ALPHA ORDER

RANK	STATE	RATE
36	Alabama	4.1
14	Alaska	32.9
11	Arizona	45.0
16	Arkansas	23.0
45	California	0.4
18	Colorado	20.2
12	Connecticut	42.9
35	Delaware	5.0
NA	Florida**	NA
8	Georgia	75.8
5	Hawaii	138.3
23	Idaho	16.3
41	Illinois	1.9
10	Indiana	48.0
38	Iowa	3.2
NA	Kansas**	NA
19	Kentucky	18.2
4	Louisiana	148.9
NA	Maine**	NA
15	Maryland	24.7
17	Massachusetts	22.6
43	Michigan	1.1
31	Minnesota	7.0
7	Mississippi	80.2
13	Missouri	37.1
42	Montana	1.8
26	Nebraska	13.4
29	Nevada	8.9
24	New Hampshire	15.9
34	New Jersey	6.2
22	New Mexico	17.1
9	New York	66.1
25	North Carolina	14.3
2	North Dakota	159.7
1	Ohio	338.4
NA	Oklahoma**	NA
36	Oregon	4.1
31	Pennsylvania	7.0
3	Rhode Island	157.8
40	South Carolina	3.0
6	South Dakota	122.5
20	Tennessee	18.1
31	Texas	7.0
27	Utah	12.9
30	Vermont	7.1
21	Virginia	17.8
44	Washington	0.8
28	West Virginia	9.0
NA	Wisconsin**	NA
38	Wyoming	3.2

RANK ORDER

RANK	STATE	RATE
1	Ohio	338.4
2	North Dakota	159.7
3	Rhode Island	157.8
4	Louisiana	148.9
5	Hawaii	138.3
6	South Dakota	122.5
7	Mississippi	80.2
8	Georgia	75.8
9	New York	66.1
10	Indiana	48.0
11	Arizona	45.0
12	Connecticut	42.9
13	Missouri	37.1
14	Alaska	32.9
15	Maryland	24.7
16	Arkansas	23.0
17	Massachusetts	22.6
18	Colorado	20.2
19	Kentucky	18.2
20	Tennessee	18.1
21	Virginia	17.8
22	New Mexico	17.1
23	Idaho	16.3
24	New Hampshire	15.9
25	North Carolina	14.3
26	Nebraska	13.4
27	Utah	12.9
28	West Virginia	9.0
29	Nevada	8.9
30	Vermont	7.1
31	Minnesota	7.0
31	Pennsylvania	7.0
31	Texas	7.0
34	New Jersey	6.2
35	Delaware	5.0
36	Alabama	4.1
36	Oregon	4.1
38	Iowa	3.2
38	Wyoming	3.2
40	South Carolina	3.0
41	Illinois	1.9
42	Montana	1.8
43	Michigan	1.1
44	Washington	0.8
45	California	0.4
NA	Florida**	NA
NA	Kansas**	NA
NA	Maine**	NA
NA	Oklahoma**	NA
NA	Wisconsin**	NA
	District of Columbia**	NA

Source: Morgan Quitno Press using data from Federal Bureau of Investigation
"Crime in the United States 1999" (Uniform Crime Reports, October 15, 2000)
By law enforcement agencies submitting complete reports to the F.B.I. for 12 months in 1999. Arrests of youths 17 years and younger divided into population of 10 to 17 year olds. See important note at beginning of this chapter. Includes nonsupport, neglect, desertion or abuse of family and children.
**Not available.*

Reported Arrests of Juveniles for Offenses Against Families and Children
As a Percent of All Such Arrests in 1999
National Percent = 6.6% of Offenses Against Families and Children Arrests*

ALPHA ORDER

RANK	STATE	PERCENT
33	Alabama	1.9
14	Alaska	7.1
11	Arizona	11.6
28	Arkansas	3.4
37	California	1.6
27	Colorado	3.5
18	Connecticut	6.4
39	Delaware	1.5
NA	Florida**	NA
14	Georgia	7.1
12	Hawaii	9.1
17	Idaho	6.8
5	Illinois	17.6
5	Indiana	17.6
32	Iowa	2.0
NA	Kansas**	NA
40	Kentucky	1.1
3	Louisiana	31.0
NA	Maine**	NA
24	Maryland	4.1
23	Massachusetts	5.0
45	Michigan	0.2
21	Minnesota	5.1
20	Mississippi	5.6
21	Missouri	5.1
43	Montana	0.8
35	Nebraska	1.8
37	Nevada	1.6
7	New Hampshire	16.4
44	New Jersey	0.3
28	New Mexico	3.4
8	New York	13.1
33	North Carolina	1.9
1	North Dakota	51.1
10	Ohio	11.7
NA	Oklahoma**	NA
30	Oregon	3.0
13	Pennsylvania	8.2
2	Rhode Island	36.7
26	South Carolina	3.9
4	South Dakota	26.6
16	Tennessee	6.9
25	Texas	4.0
31	Utah	2.8
41	Vermont	1.0
19	Virginia	5.8
35	Washington	1.8
9	West Virginia	12.3
NA	Wisconsin**	NA
42	Wyoming	0.9

RANK ORDER

RANK	STATE	PERCENT
1	North Dakota	51.1
2	Rhode Island	36.7
3	Louisiana	31.0
4	South Dakota	26.6
5	Illinois	17.6
5	Indiana	17.6
7	New Hampshire	16.4
8	New York	13.1
9	West Virginia	12.3
10	Ohio	11.7
11	Arizona	11.6
12	Hawaii	9.1
13	Pennsylvania	8.2
14	Alaska	7.1
14	Georgia	7.1
16	Tennessee	6.9
17	Idaho	6.8
18	Connecticut	6.4
19	Virginia	5.8
20	Mississippi	5.6
21	Minnesota	5.1
21	Missouri	5.1
23	Massachusetts	5.0
24	Maryland	4.1
25	Texas	4.0
26	South Carolina	3.9
27	Colorado	3.5
28	Arkansas	3.4
28	New Mexico	3.4
30	Oregon	3.0
31	Utah	2.8
32	Iowa	2.0
33	Alabama	1.9
33	North Carolina	1.9
35	Nebraska	1.8
35	Washington	1.8
37	California	1.6
37	Nevada	1.6
39	Delaware	1.5
40	Kentucky	1.1
41	Vermont	1.0
42	Wyoming	0.9
43	Montana	0.8
44	New Jersey	0.3
45	Michigan	0.2
NA	Florida**	NA
NA	Kansas**	NA
NA	Maine**	NA
NA	Oklahoma**	NA
NA	Wisconsin**	NA
	District of Columbia**	NA

Source: Morgan Quitno Press using data from Federal Bureau of Investigation
    "Crime in the United States 1999" (Uniform Crime Reports, October 15, 2000)
*Arrests of youths 17 years and younger by law enforcement agencies submitting complete reports to the F.B.I. for
12 months in 1999. Includes nonsupport, neglect, desertion or abuse of family and children.
**Not available.

Juvenile Death Sentences: 1973 to 2000

National Total = 182 Juveniles Sentenced to Death*

ALPHA ORDER

RANK	STATE	JUVENILES	% of USA
3	Alabama	20	11.0%
NA	Alaska***	NA	NA
12	Arizona	5	2.7%
17	Arkansas	2	1.1%
23	California	0	0.0%
23	Colorado	0	0.0%
23	Connecticut	0	0.0%
23	Delaware	0	0.0%
2	Florida	25	13.7%
6	Georgia	7	3.8%
NA	Hawaii***	NA	NA
23	Idaho	0	0.0%
23	Illinois	0	0.0%
15	Indiana	3	1.6%
NA	Iowa***	NA	NA
23	Kansas	0	0.0%
15	Kentucky	3	1.6%
4	Louisiana	11	6.0%
NA	Maine***	NA	NA
17	Maryland**	2	1.1%
NA	Massachusetts***	NA	NA
NA	Michigan***	NA	NA
NA	Minnesota***	NA	NA
4	Mississippi	11	6.0%
14	Missouri	4	2.2%
23	Montana	0	0.0%
20	Nebraska**	1	0.5%
17	Nevada	2	1.1%
23	New Hampshire	0	0.0%
20	New Jersey**	1	0.5%
23	New Mexico	0	0.0%
23	New York	0	0.0%
8	North Carolina	6	3.3%
NA	North Dakota***	NA	NA
8	Ohio**	6	3.3%
8	Oklahoma	6	3.3%
23	Oregon	0	0.0%
8	Pennsylvania	6	3.3%
NA	Rhode Island***	NA	NA
6	South Carolina	7	3.8%
23	South Dakota	0	0.0%
23	Tennessee	0	0.0%
1	Texas	48	26.4%
23	Utah	0	0.0%
NA	Vermont***	NA	NA
12	Virginia	5	2.7%
20	Washington**	1	0.5%
NA	West Virginia***	NA	NA
NA	Wisconsin***	NA	NA
23	Wyoming	0	0.0%

RANK ORDER

RANK	STATE	JUVENILES	% of USA
1	Texas	48	26.4%
2	Florida	25	13.7%
3	Alabama	20	11.0%
4	Louisiana	11	6.0%
4	Mississippi	11	6.0%
6	Georgia	7	3.8%
6	South Carolina	7	3.8%
8	North Carolina	6	3.3%
8	Ohio**	6	3.3%
8	Oklahoma	6	3.3%
8	Pennsylvania	6	3.3%
12	Arizona	5	2.7%
12	Virginia	5	2.7%
14	Missouri	4	2.2%
15	Indiana	3	1.6%
15	Kentucky	3	1.6%
17	Arkansas	2	1.1%
17	Maryland**	2	1.1%
17	Nevada	2	1.1%
20	Nebraska**	1	0.5%
20	New Jersey**	1	0.5%
20	Washington**	1	0.5%
23	California	0	0.0%
23	Colorado	0	0.0%
23	Connecticut	0	0.0%
23	Delaware	0	0.0%
23	Idaho	0	0.0%
23	Illinois	0	0.0%
23	Kansas	0	0.0%
23	Montana	0	0.0%
23	New Hampshire	0	0.0%
23	New Mexico	0	0.0%
23	New York	0	0.0%
23	Oregon	0	0.0%
23	South Dakota	0	0.0%
23	Tennessee	0	0.0%
23	Utah	0	0.0%
23	Wyoming	0	0.0%
NA	Alaska***	NA	NA
NA	Hawaii***	NA	NA
NA	Iowa***	NA	NA
NA	Maine***	NA	NA
NA	Massachusetts***	NA	NA
NA	Michigan***	NA	NA
NA	Minnesota***	NA	NA
NA	North Dakota***	NA	NA
NA	Rhode Island***	NA	NA
NA	Vermont***	NA	NA
NA	West Virginia***	NA	NA
NA	Wisconsin***	NA	NA
	District of Columbia***	NA	NA

Source: U.S. Department of Justice, Office of Juvenile Justice and Delinquency Prevention
   "Juveniles and the Death Penalty" (November 2000)
*These are juveniles 15 to 17 at the time of their crime. There were 196 sentences for these 182 juveniles.
**These states no longer allow the death penalty for offenders who commit crimes before age 18.
***No death penalty.

Juveniles in Custody in 1997

National Total = 105,790 Juveniles*

ALPHA ORDER

ALPHA ORDER

RANK ORDER

RANK	STATE	JUVENILES	% of USA
19	Alabama	1,685	1.6%
41	Alaska	352	0.3%
17	Arizona	1,868	1.8%
37	Arkansas	603	0.6%
1	California	19,899	18.8%
18	Colorado	1,748	1.7%
25	Connecticut	1,326	1.3%
44	Delaware	311	0.3%
3	Florida	5,975	5.6%
8	Georgia	3,622	3.4%
49	Hawaii	134	0.1%
47	Idaho	242	0.2%
9	Illinois	3,425	3.2%
12	Indiana	2,485	2.3%
30	Iowa	1,064	1.0%
26	Kansas	1,242	1.2%
28	Kentucky	1,079	1.0%
11	Louisiana	2,776	2.6%
43	Maine	318	0.3%
22	Maryland	1,498	1.4%
29	Massachusetts	1,065	1.0%
7	Michigan	3,710	3.5%
21	Minnesota	1,522	1.4%
35	Mississippi	756	0.7%
24	Missouri	1,401	1.3%
45	Montana	302	0.3%
36	Nebraska	741	0.7%
31	Nevada	857	0.8%
48	New Hampshire	186	0.2%
13	New Jersey	2,251	2.1%
33	New Mexico	778	0.7%
4	New York	4,661	4.4%
27	North Carolina	1,204	1.1%
46	North Dakota	272	0.3%
5	Ohio	4,318	4.1%
32	Oklahoma	808	0.8%
23	Oregon	1,462	1.4%
6	Pennsylvania	3,962	3.7%
39	Rhode Island	426	0.4%
20	South Carolina	1,583	1.5%
38	South Dakota	528	0.5%
15	Tennessee	2,118	2.0%
2	Texas	6,898	6.5%
34	Utah	768	0.7%
50	Vermont	49	0.0%
10	Virginia	2,879	2.7%
14	Washington	2,216	2.1%
40	West Virginia	398	0.4%
16	Wisconsin	2,013	1.9%
42	Wyoming	340	0.3%

RANK	STATE	JUVENILES	% of USA
1	California	19,899	18.8%
2	Texas	6,898	6.5%
3	Florida	5,975	5.6%
4	New York	4,661	4.4%
5	Ohio	4,318	4.1%
6	Pennsylvania	3,962	3.7%
7	Michigan	3,710	3.5%
8	Georgia	3,622	3.4%
9	Illinois	3,425	3.2%
10	Virginia	2,879	2.7%
11	Louisiana	2,776	2.6%
12	Indiana	2,485	2.3%
13	New Jersey	2,251	2.1%
14	Washington	2,216	2.1%
15	Tennessee	2,118	2.0%
16	Wisconsin	2,013	1.9%
17	Arizona	1,868	1.8%
18	Colorado	1,748	1.7%
19	Alabama	1,685	1.6%
20	South Carolina	1,583	1.5%
21	Minnesota	1,522	1.4%
22	Maryland	1,498	1.4%
23	Oregon	1,462	1.4%
24	Missouri	1,401	1.3%
25	Connecticut	1,326	1.3%
26	Kansas	1,242	1.2%
27	North Carolina	1,204	1.1%
28	Kentucky	1,079	1.0%
29	Massachusetts	1,065	1.0%
30	Iowa	1,064	1.0%
31	Nevada	857	0.8%
32	Oklahoma	808	0.8%
33	New Mexico	778	0.7%
34	Utah	768	0.7%
35	Mississippi	756	0.7%
36	Nebraska	741	0.7%
37	Arkansas	603	0.6%
38	South Dakota	528	0.5%
39	Rhode Island	426	0.4%
40	West Virginia	398	0.4%
41	Alaska	352	0.3%
42	Wyoming	340	0.3%
43	Maine	318	0.3%
44	Delaware	311	0.3%
45	Montana	302	0.3%
46	North Dakota	272	0.3%
47	Idaho	242	0.2%
48	New Hampshire	186	0.2%
49	Hawaii	134	0.1%
50	Vermont	49	0.0%
	District of Columbia	265	0.3%

Source: U.S. Department of Justice, Office of Juvenile Justice and Delinquency Prevention
"Juvenile Offenders and Victims: 1999 National Report" (NCJ 178257)
National total includes 3,401 juveniles in private facilities for whom state was not reported. All states are for ages through 17 except Georgia, Illinois, Louisiana, Massachusetts, Michigan, Missouri, New Hampshire, South Carolina, Texas and Wisconsin which are through age 16 and Connecticut, New York and North Carolina which are through age 15.

Rate of Juveniles in Custody in 1997

National Rate = 368 per 100,000 Juvenile Population*

ALPHA ORDER

RANK ORDER

RANK	STATE	RATE
22	Alabama	348
9	Alaska	418
23	Arizona	344
43	Arkansas	198
3	California	549
16	Colorado	379
5	Connecticut	508
11	Delaware	402
13	Florida	394
6	Georgia	480
49	Hawaii	106
48	Idaho	145
32	Illinois	286
18	Indiana	366
30	Iowa	307
15	Kansas	386
39	Kentucky	243
1	Louisiana	582
40	Maine	220
33	Maryland	273
46	Massachusetts	194
17	Michigan	375
36	Minnesota	258
41	Mississippi	218
37	Missouri	248
34	Montana	266
21	Nebraska	353
7	Nevada	460
47	New Hampshire	154
34	New Jersey	266
24	New Mexico	342
29	New York	323
44	North Carolina	196
25	North Dakota	336
27	Ohio	332
44	Oklahoma	196
14	Oregon	389
31	Pennsylvania	302
10	Rhode Island	412
8	South Carolina	427
2	South Dakota	556
20	Tennessee	358
28	Texas	327
38	Utah	247
50	Vermont	70
12	Virginia	399
26	Washington	335
42	West Virginia	200
19	Wisconsin	359
4	Wyoming	511

RANK	STATE	RATE
1	Louisiana	582
2	South Dakota	556
3	California	549
4	Wyoming	511
5	Connecticut	508
6	Georgia	480
7	Nevada	460
8	South Carolina	427
9	Alaska	418
10	Rhode Island	412
11	Delaware	402
12	Virginia	399
13	Florida	394
14	Oregon	389
15	Kansas	386
16	Colorado	379
17	Michigan	375
18	Indiana	366
19	Wisconsin	359
20	Tennessee	358
21	Nebraska	353
22	Alabama	348
23	Arizona	344
24	New Mexico	342
25	North Dakota	336
26	Washington	335
27	Ohio	332
28	Texas	327
29	New York	323
30	Iowa	307
31	Pennsylvania	302
32	Illinois	286
33	Maryland	273
34	Montana	266
34	New Jersey	266
36	Minnesota	258
37	Missouri	248
38	Utah	247
39	Kentucky	243
40	Maine	220
41	Mississippi	218
42	West Virginia	200
43	Arkansas	198
44	North Carolina	196
44	Oklahoma	196
46	Massachusetts	194
47	New Hampshire	154
48	Idaho	145
49	Hawaii	106
50	Vermont	70

District of Columbia 662

Source: U.S. Department of Justice, Office of Juvenile Justice and Delinquency Prevention
    "Juvenile Offenders and Victims: 1999 National Report" (NCJ 178257)
*Includes committed and detained. Based on population age 10 through upper age of juvenile as defined by each state. All states are for ages through 17 except Georgia, Illinois, Louisiana, Massachusetts, Michigan, Missouri, New Hampshire, South Carolina, Texas and Wisconsin which are through age 16 and Connecticut, New York and North Carolina which are through age 15.

White Juvenile Custody Rate in 1997

National Rate = 204 White Juveniles in Custody per 100,000 White Juveniles*

ALPHA ORDER

RANK	STATE	RATE
27	Alabama	202
6	Alaska	289
11	Arizona	244
46	Arkansas	106
5	California	299
15	Colorado	238
32	Connecticut	160
40	Delaware	132
12	Florida	243
13	Georgia	240
50	Hawaii	65
38	Idaho	139
42	Illinois	127
7	Indiana	268
14	Iowa	239
9	Kansas	249
29	Kentucky	174
18	Louisiana	231
22	Maine	210
43	Maryland	123
47	Massachusetts	96
24	Michigan	205
34	Minnesota	155
41	Mississippi	129
31	Missouri	168
20	Montana	221
17	Nebraska	234
2	Nevada	382
37	New Hampshire	143
48	New Jersey	71
30	New Mexico	169
36	New York	152
45	North Carolina	108
8	North Dakota	261
24	Ohio	205
43	Oklahoma	123
4	Oregon	326
39	Pennsylvania	137
21	Rhode Island	220
15	South Carolina	238
3	South Dakota	356
19	Tennessee	226
34	Texas	155
28	Utah	188
49	Vermont	66
26	Virginia	204
10	Washington	246
33	West Virginia	156
23	Wisconsin	206
1	Wyoming	454

RANK ORDER

RANK	STATE	RATE
1	Wyoming	454
2	Nevada	382
3	South Dakota	356
4	Oregon	326
5	California	299
6	Alaska	289
7	Indiana	268
8	North Dakota	261
9	Kansas	249
10	Washington	246
11	Arizona	244
12	Florida	243
13	Georgia	240
14	Iowa	239
15	Colorado	238
15	South Carolina	238
17	Nebraska	234
18	Louisiana	231
19	Tennessee	226
20	Montana	221
21	Rhode Island	220
22	Maine	210
23	Wisconsin	206
24	Michigan	205
24	Ohio	205
26	Virginia	204
27	Alabama	202
28	Utah	188
29	Kentucky	174
30	New Mexico	169
31	Missouri	168
32	Connecticut	160
33	West Virginia	156
34	Minnesota	155
34	Texas	155
36	New York	152
37	New Hampshire	143
38	Idaho	139
39	Pennsylvania	137
40	Delaware	132
41	Mississippi	129
42	Illinois	127
43	Maryland	123
43	Oklahoma	123
45	North Carolina	108
46	Arkansas	106
47	Massachusetts	96
48	New Jersey	71
49	Vermont	66
50	Hawaii	65
	District of Columbia	0

Source: U.S. Department of Justice, Office of Juvenile Justice and Delinquency Prevention
   "Juvenile Offenders and Victims: 1999 National Report" (NCJ 178257)
Juveniles in residential placement. National rate includes juveniles in private facilities for whom state of offense was not reported. Does not include Hispanic juveniles. Based on population age 10 through upper age of juvenile as defined by each state. All states are for ages through 17 except Georgia, Illinois, Louisiana, Massachusetts, Michigan, Missouri, New Hampshire, South Carolina, Texas and Wisconsin which are through age 16 and Connecticut, New York and North Carolina which are through age 15.

Black Juvenile Custody Rate in 1997

National Rate = 1,018 Black Juveniles in Custody per 100,000 Black Juveniles*

ALPHA ORDER				RANK ORDER		
RANK	STATE	RATE		RANK	STATE	RATE
37	Alabama	650		1	Iowa	2,250
20	Alaska	1,055		2	Connecticut	2,225
24	Arizona	975		3	California	1,819
39	Arkansas	533		4	Rhode Island	1,799
3	California	1,819		5	Kansas	1,767
12	Colorado	1,397		6	Wisconsin	1,756
2	Connecticut	2,225		7	Nebraska	1,754
15	Delaware	1,195		8	Minnesota	1,676
23	Florida	980		9	Washington	1,592
26	Georgia	952		10	Oregon	1,505
42	Hawaii	212		11	Utah	1,400
NA	Idaho**	NA		12	Colorado	1,397
27	Illinois	943		13	Pennsylvania	1,348
17	Indiana	1,168		14	West Virginia	1,230
1	Iowa	2,250		15	Delaware	1,195
5	Kansas	1,767		16	Michigan	1,171
25	Kentucky	967		17	Indiana	1,168
18	Louisiana	1,140		18	Louisiana	1,140
NA	Maine**	NA		19	Ohio	1,105
38	Maryland	592		20	Alaska	1,055
33	Massachusetts	804		21	New Jersey	1,007
16	Michigan	1,171		22	Virginia	997
8	Minnesota	1,676		23	Florida	980
41	Mississippi	319		24	Arizona	975
35	Missouri	741		25	Kentucky	967
NA	Montana**	NA		26	Georgia	952
7	Nebraska	1,754		27	Illinois	943
28	Nevada	942		28	Nevada	942
NA	New Hampshire**	NA		29	New Mexico	905
21	New Jersey	1,007		30	New York	886
29	New Mexico	905		31	Texas	853
30	New York	886		32	Tennessee	843
40	North Carolina	435		33	Massachusetts	804
NA	North Dakota**	NA		34	South Carolina	753
19	Ohio	1,105		35	Missouri	741
36	Oklahoma	688		36	Oklahoma	688
10	Oregon	1,505		37	Alabama	650
13	Pennsylvania	1,348		38	Maryland	592
4	Rhode Island	1,799		39	Arkansas	533
34	South Carolina	753		40	North Carolina	435
NA	South Dakota**	NA		41	Mississippi	319
32	Tennessee	843		42	Hawaii	212
31	Texas	853		NA	Idaho**	NA
11	Utah	1,400		NA	Maine**	NA
NA	Vermont**	NA		NA	Montana**	NA
22	Virginia	997		NA	New Hampshire**	NA
9	Washington	1,592		NA	North Dakota**	NA
14	West Virginia	1,230		NA	South Dakota**	NA
6	Wisconsin	1,756		NA	Vermont**	NA
NA	Wyoming**	NA		NA	Wyoming**	NA
					District of Columbia	855

Source: U.S. Department of Justice, Office of Juvenile Justice and Delinquency Prevention
   "Juvenile Offenders and Victims: 1999 National Report" (NCJ 178257)
*Juveniles in residential placement. National rate includes juveniles in private facilities for whom state of offense was not reported. Does not include Hispanic juveniles. Based on population age 10 through upper age of juvenile as defined by each state. See note on preceding table for individual state upper ages.
**Too few black juveniles to calculate a reliable rate.

High School Dropout Rate in 1998

National Rate = 4.8%*

ALPHA ORDER

RANK	STATE	RATE
20	Alabama	4.8
23	Alaska	4.6
3	Arizona	9.4
11	Arkansas	5.4
NA	California**	NA
9	Colorado	5.8
30	Connecticut	3.5
22	Delaware	4.7
NA	Florida**	NA
4	Georgia	7.3
NA	Hawaii**	NA
7	Idaho	6.7
6	Illinois	6.9
NA	Indiana**	NA
35	Iowa	2.9
27	Kansas	4.2
12	Kentucky	5.2
1	Louisiana	11.4
32	Maine	3.2
26	Maryland	4.3
32	Massachusetts	3.2
NA	Michigan**	NA
18	Minnesota	4.9
9	Mississippi	5.8
12	Missouri	5.2
24	Montana	4.4
24	Nebraska	4.4
2	Nevada	10.1
NA	New Hampshire**	NA
30	New Jersey	3.5
5	New Mexico	7.1
NA	New York**	NA
NA	North Carolina**	NA
36	North Dakota	2.8
16	Ohio	5.1
NA	Oklahoma**	NA
NA	Oregon**	NA
29	Pennsylvania	3.9
18	Rhode Island	4.9
NA	South Carolina**	NA
34	South Dakota	3.1
17	Tennessee	5.0
NA	Texas**	NA
12	Utah	5.2
12	Vermont	5.2
20	Virginia	4.8
NA	Washington**	NA
28	West Virginia	4.1
36	Wisconsin	2.8
8	Wyoming	6.4

RANK ORDER

RANK	STATE	RATE
1	Louisiana	11.4
2	Nevada	10.1
3	Arizona	9.4
4	Georgia	7.3
5	New Mexico	7.1
6	Illinois	6.9
7	Idaho	6.7
8	Wyoming	6.4
9	Colorado	5.8
9	Mississippi	5.8
11	Arkansas	5.4
12	Kentucky	5.2
12	Missouri	5.2
12	Utah	5.2
12	Vermont	5.2
16	Ohio	5.1
17	Tennessee	5.0
18	Minnesota	4.9
18	Rhode Island	4.9
20	Alabama	4.8
20	Virginia	4.8
22	Delaware	4.7
23	Alaska	4.6
24	Montana	4.4
24	Nebraska	4.4
26	Maryland	4.3
27	Kansas	4.2
28	West Virginia	4.1
29	Pennsylvania	3.9
30	Connecticut	3.5
30	New Jersey	3.5
32	Maine	3.2
32	Massachusetts	3.2
34	South Dakota	3.1
35	Iowa	2.9
36	North Dakota	2.8
36	Wisconsin	2.8
NA	California**	NA
NA	Florida**	NA
NA	Hawaii**	NA
NA	Indiana**	NA
NA	Michigan**	NA
NA	New Hampshire**	NA
NA	New York**	NA
NA	North Carolina**	NA
NA	Oklahoma**	NA
NA	Oregon**	NA
NA	South Carolina**	NA
NA	Texas**	NA
NA	Washington**	NA

District of Columbia   12.8

Source: U.S. Department of Education, National Center for Educational Statistics
     "Dropout Rates in the United States: 1999" (NCES 2001-022, November 2000)
*"Event" dropout rates showing the proportion of youth, ages 15-24 who dropped out of grades 10-12 in the 12 months preceding October 1998.
**Not available.

Percent of High School Students Who Carried a Weapon On School Property in the Previous Month: 1999
National Percent = 6.9% of High School Students*

ALPHA ORDER

RANK	STATE	PERCENT
7	Alabama	9.6
3	Alaska	11.4
NA	Arizona**	NA
5	Arkansas	10.4
NA	California**	NA
NA	Colorado**	NA
18	Connecticut	7.2
26	Delaware	6.2
20	Florida	7.1
NA	Georgia**	NA
27	Hawaii	6.0
NA	Idaho**	NA
24	Illinois	6.5
NA	Indiana**	NA
28	Iowa	5.7
NA	Kansas**	NA
7	Kentucky	9.6
33	Louisiana	4.3
22	Maine	6.9
NA	Maryland**	NA
17	Massachusetts	7.3
14	Michigan	7.5
NA	Minnesota**	NA
21	Mississippi	7.0
10	Missouri	8.5
9	Montana	9.2
31	Nebraska	5.1
12	Nevada	8.1
14	New Hampshire	7.5
32	New Jersey	4.5
4	New Mexico	11.0
11	New York	8.2
NA	North Carolina**	NA
14	North Dakota	7.5
29	Ohio	5.6
NA	Oklahoma**	NA
NA	Oregon**	NA
NA	Pennsylvania**	NA
NA	Rhode Island**	NA
18	South Carolina	7.2
24	South Dakota	6.5
12	Tennessee	8.1
NA	Texas**	NA
23	Utah	6.7
1	Vermont	11.9
NA	Virginia**	NA
NA	Washington**	NA
6	West Virginia	9.8
30	Wisconsin	5.5
2	Wyoming	11.8

RANK ORDER

RANK	STATE	PERCENT
1	Vermont	11.9
2	Wyoming	11.8
3	Alaska	11.4
4	New Mexico	11.0
5	Arkansas	10.4
6	West Virginia	9.8
7	Alabama	9.6
7	Kentucky	9.6
9	Montana	9.2
10	Missouri	8.5
11	New York	8.2
12	Nevada	8.1
12	Tennessee	8.1
14	Michigan	7.5
14	New Hampshire	7.5
14	North Dakota	7.5
17	Massachusetts	7.3
18	Connecticut	7.2
18	South Carolina	7.2
20	Florida	7.1
21	Mississippi	7.0
22	Maine	6.9
23	Utah	6.7
24	Illinois	6.5
24	South Dakota	6.5
26	Delaware	6.2
27	Hawaii	6.0
28	Iowa	5.7
29	Ohio	5.6
30	Wisconsin	5.5
31	Nebraska	5.1
32	New Jersey	4.5
33	Louisiana	4.3
NA	Arizona**	NA
NA	California**	NA
NA	Colorado**	NA
NA	Georgia**	NA
NA	Idaho**	NA
NA	Indiana**	NA
NA	Kansas**	NA
NA	Maryland**	NA
NA	Minnesota**	NA
NA	North Carolina**	NA
NA	Oklahoma**	NA
NA	Oregon**	NA
NA	Pennsylvania**	NA
NA	Rhode Island**	NA
NA	Texas**	NA
NA	Virginia**	NA
NA	Washington**	NA
	District of Columbia**	NA

Source: U.S. Department of Health and Human Services, Centers for Disease Control and Prevention
"Youth Risk Behavior Surveillance, United States 1999" (June 9, 2000)
(http://www.cdc.gov/mmwr/preview/mmwrhtml/ss4905a1.htm)
*Grades 9 through 12.
**Not available.

Percent of High School Students Threatened or Injured
With a Weapon on School Property in 1999
National Percent = 7.7% of High School Students*

RANK	STATE	PERCENT
26	Alabama	7.5
10	Alaska	9.2
NA	Arizona**	NA
4	Arkansas	9.8
NA	California**	NA
NA	Colorado**	NA
12	Connecticut	9.1
18	Delaware	8.2
1	Florida	10.9
NA	Georgia**	NA
31	Hawaii	6.7
NA	Idaho**	NA
27	Illinois	7.4
NA	Indiana**	NA
14	Iowa	8.8
NA	Kansas**	NA
7	Kentucky	9.5
2	Louisiana	10.0
3	Maine	9.9
NA	Maryland**	NA
15	Massachusetts	8.6
10	Michigan	9.2
NA	Minnesota**	NA
19	Mississippi	8.1
13	Missouri	8.9
32	Montana	6.5
33	Nebraska	5.5
8	Nevada	9.4
24	New Hampshire	7.6
6	New Jersey	9.6
5	New Mexico	9.7
9	New York	9.3
NA	North Carolina**	NA
22	North Dakota	8.0
19	Ohio	8.1
NA	Oklahoma**	NA
NA	Oregon**	NA
NA	Pennsylvania**	NA
NA	Rhode Island**	NA
15	South Carolina	8.6
30	South Dakota	6.8
15	Tennessee	8.6
NA	Texas**	NA
28	Utah	7.2
29	Vermont	7.0
NA	Virginia**	NA
NA	Washington**	NA
23	West Virginia	7.7
24	Wisconsin	7.6
19	Wyoming	8.1

RANK	STATE	PERCENT
1	Florida	10.9
2	Louisiana	10.0
3	Maine	9.9
4	Arkansas	9.8
5	New Mexico	9.7
6	New Jersey	9.6
7	Kentucky	9.5
8	Nevada	9.4
9	New York	9.3
10	Alaska	9.2
10	Michigan	9.2
12	Connecticut	9.1
13	Missouri	8.9
14	Iowa	8.8
15	Massachusetts	8.6
15	South Carolina	8.6
15	Tennessee	8.6
18	Delaware	8.2
19	Mississippi	8.1
19	Ohio	8.1
19	Wyoming	8.1
22	North Dakota	8.0
23	West Virginia	7.7
24	New Hampshire	7.6
24	Wisconsin	7.6
26	Alabama	7.5
27	Illinois	7.4
28	Utah	7.2
29	Vermont	7.0
30	South Dakota	6.8
31	Hawaii	6.7
32	Montana	6.5
33	Nebraska	5.5
NA	Arizona**	NA
NA	California**	NA
NA	Colorado**	NA
NA	Georgia**	NA
NA	Idaho**	NA
NA	Indiana**	NA
NA	Kansas**	NA
NA	Maryland**	NA
NA	Minnesota**	NA
NA	North Carolina**	NA
NA	Oklahoma**	NA
NA	Oregon**	NA
NA	Pennsylvania**	NA
NA	Rhode Island**	NA
NA	Texas**	NA
NA	Virginia**	NA
NA	Washington**	NA
	District of Columbia**	NA

Source: U.S. Department of Health and Human Services, Centers for Disease Control and Prevention
   "Youth Risk Behavior Surveillance, United States 1999" (June 9, 2000)
      (http://www.cdc.gov/mmwr/preview/mmwrhtml/ss4905a1.htm)
*Grades 9 through 12.
**Not available.

Percent of Teens Who Drink Alcohol: 1999

National Percent = 50.0% of Teenagers*

ALPHA ORDER

RANK	STATE	PERCENT
28	Alabama	45.4
26	Alaska	46.9
NA	Arizona**	NA
24	Arkansas	48.3
NA	California**	NA
NA	Colorado**	NA
19	Connecticut	49.6
26	Delaware	46.9
25	Florida	48.1
NA	Georgia**	NA
31	Hawaii	44.6
NA	Idaho**	NA
18	Illinois	49.7
NA	Indiana**	NA
6	Iowa	55.0
NA	Kansas**	NA
17	Kentucky	49.8
8	Louisiana	53.7
11	Maine	52.5
NA	Maryland**	NA
13	Massachusetts	51.8
23	Michigan	48.5
NA	Minnesota**	NA
32	Mississippi	42.5
16	Missouri	49.9
3	Montana	57.6
4	Nebraska	55.8
9	Nevada	53.0
11	New Hampshire	52.5
15	New Jersey	50.0
9	New Mexico	53.0
19	New York	49.6
NA	North Carolina**	NA
1	North Dakota	60.5
5	Ohio	55.5
NA	Oklahoma**	NA
NA	Oregon**	NA
NA	Pennsylvania**	NA
NA	Rhode Island**	NA
28	South Carolina	45.4
2	South Dakota	59.2
30	Tennessee	45.2
NA	Texas**	NA
33	Utah	22.7
21	Vermont	49.5
NA	Virginia**	NA
NA	Washington**	NA
22	West Virginia	48.6
13	Wisconsin	51.8
7	Wyoming	54.8

RANK ORDER

RANK	STATE	PERCENT
1	North Dakota	60.5
2	South Dakota	59.2
3	Montana	57.6
4	Nebraska	55.8
5	Ohio	55.5
6	Iowa	55.0
7	Wyoming	54.8
8	Louisiana	53.7
9	Nevada	53.0
9	New Mexico	53.0
11	Maine	52.5
11	New Hampshire	52.5
13	Massachusetts	51.8
13	Wisconsin	51.8
15	New Jersey	50.0
16	Missouri	49.9
17	Kentucky	49.8
18	Illinois	49.7
19	Connecticut	49.6
19	New York	49.6
21	Vermont	49.5
22	West Virginia	48.6
23	Michigan	48.5
24	Arkansas	48.3
25	Florida	48.1
26	Alaska	46.9
26	Delaware	46.9
28	Alabama	45.4
28	South Carolina	45.4
30	Tennessee	45.2
31	Hawaii	44.6
32	Mississippi	42.5
33	Utah	22.7
NA	Arizona**	NA
NA	California**	NA
NA	Colorado**	NA
NA	Georgia**	NA
NA	Idaho**	NA
NA	Indiana**	NA
NA	Kansas**	NA
NA	Maryland**	NA
NA	Minnesota**	NA
NA	North Carolina**	NA
NA	Oklahoma**	NA
NA	Oregon**	NA
NA	Pennsylvania**	NA
NA	Rhode Island**	NA
NA	Texas**	NA
NA	Virginia**	NA
NA	Washington**	NA
	District of Columbia**	NA

Source: U.S. Department of Health and Human Services, Centers for Disease Control and Prevention
"Youth Risk Behavior Surveillance, United States 1999" (June 9, 2000)
*Percentage of students (grades 9-12) who had at least one drink of alcohol on one or more of the past 30 days.
**Not available.

246

Percent of Teens Who Use Marijuana: 1999

National Percent = 26.7% of Teenagers*

ALPHA ORDER

RANK ORDER

RANK	STATE	PERCENT
23	Alabama	22.2
4	Alaska	30.7
NA	Arizona**	NA
18	Arkansas	24.4
NA	California**	NA
NA	Colorado**	NA
9	Connecticut	27.8
8	Delaware	29.0
21	Florida	23.1
NA	Georgia**	NA
16	Hawaii	24.7
NA	Idaho**	NA
24	Illinois	21.5
NA	Indiana**	NA
31	Iowa	18.5
NA	Kansas**	NA
19	Kentucky	23.6
28	Louisiana	20.2
3	Maine	30.9
NA	Maryland**	NA
5	Massachusetts	30.6
12	Michigan	25.9
NA	Minnesota**	NA
29	Mississippi	18.9
14	Missouri	25.6
15	Montana	25.5
32	Nebraska	15.6
12	Nevada	25.9
6	New Hampshire	30.3
22	New Jersey	22.7
2	New Mexico	31.2
20	New York	23.4
NA	North Carolina**	NA
30	North Dakota	18.8
11	Ohio	26.1
NA	Oklahoma**	NA
NA	Oregon**	NA
NA	Pennsylvania**	NA
NA	Rhode Island**	NA
17	South Carolina	24.5
27	South Dakota	20.7
10	Tennessee	26.6
NA	Texas**	NA
33	Utah	10.6
1	Vermont	33.7
NA	Virginia**	NA
NA	Washington**	NA
7	West Virginia	29.3
24	Wisconsin	21.5
26	Wyoming	21.4

RANK	STATE	PERCENT
1	Vermont	33.7
2	New Mexico	31.2
3	Maine	30.9
4	Alaska	30.7
5	Massachusetts	30.6
6	New Hampshire	30.3
7	West Virginia	29.3
8	Delaware	29.0
9	Connecticut	27.8
10	Tennessee	26.6
11	Ohio	26.1
12	Michigan	25.9
12	Nevada	25.9
14	Missouri	25.6
15	Montana	25.5
16	Hawaii	24.7
17	South Carolina	24.5
18	Arkansas	24.4
19	Kentucky	23.6
20	New York	23.4
21	Florida	23.1
22	New Jersey	22.7
23	Alabama	22.2
24	Illinois	21.5
24	Wisconsin	21.5
26	Wyoming	21.4
27	South Dakota	20.7
28	Louisiana	20.2
29	Mississippi	18.9
30	North Dakota	18.8
31	Iowa	18.5
32	Nebraska	15.6
33	Utah	10.6
NA	Arizona**	NA
NA	California**	NA
NA	Colorado**	NA
NA	Georgia**	NA
NA	Idaho**	NA
NA	Indiana**	NA
NA	Kansas**	NA
NA	Maryland**	NA
NA	Minnesota**	NA
NA	North Carolina**	NA
NA	Oklahoma**	NA
NA	Oregon**	NA
NA	Pennsylvania**	NA
NA	Rhode Island**	NA
NA	Texas**	NA
NA	Virginia**	NA
NA	Washington**	NA
	District of Columbia**	NA

Source: U.S. Department of Health and Human Services, Centers for Disease Control and Prevention
   "Youth Risk Behavior Surveillance, United States 1999" (June 9, 2000)
Percentage of students (grades 9-12) who used marijuana at least one or more times during the past 30 days.
**Not available.*

Admissions of Juveniles to Alcohol and Other Drug Treatment Programs in 1997

National Total = 133,251 Juvenile Admissions*

ALPHA ORDER

RANK	STATE	ADMISSIONS	% of USA
27	Alabama	1,208	0.9%
28	Alaska	925	0.7%
NA	Arizona**	NA	NA
29	Arkansas	751	0.6%
2	California	10,310	7.7%
NA	Colorado**	NA	NA
41	Connecticut	269	0.2%
42	Delaware	2	0.0%
1	Florida	29,989	22.5%
20	Georgia	1,816	1.4%
23	Hawaii	1,436	1.1%
NA	Idaho**	NA	NA
4	Illinois	8,387	6.3%
37	Indiana	510	0.4%
24	Iowa	1,428	1.1%
25	Kansas	1,341	1.0%
26	Kentucky	1,217	0.9%
22	Louisiana	1,776	1.3%
34	Maine	622	0.5%
10	Maryland	3,960	3.0%
11	Massachusetts	3,186	2.4%
8	Michigan	4,729	3.5%
NA	Minnesota**	NA	NA
18	Mississippi	1,837	1.4%
21	Missouri	1,792	1.3%
NA	Montana**	NA	NA
16	Nebraska	2,089	1.6%
32	Nevada	640	0.5%
30	New Hampshire	677	0.5%
12	New Jersey	3,030	2.3%
38	New Mexico	439	0.3%
7	New York	5,535	4.2%
15	North Carolina	2,659	2.0%
40	North Dakota	295	0.2%
3	Ohio	9,395	7.1%
35	Oklahoma	588	0.4%
9	Oregon	4,278	3.2%
6	Pennsylvania	5,831	4.4%
31	Rhode Island	655	0.5%
17	South Carolina	1,903	1.4%
14	South Dakota	2,740	2.1%
36	Tennessee	533	0.4%
13	Texas	2,790	2.1%
NA	Utah**	NA	NA
39	Vermont	437	0.3%
NA	Virginia**	NA	NA
5	Washington	6,265	4.7%
19	West Virginia	1,828	1.4%
33	Wisconsin	623	0.5%
NA	Wyoming**	NA	NA

RANK ORDER

RANK	STATE	ADMISSIONS	% of USA
1	Florida	29,989	22.5%
2	California	10,310	7.7%
3	Ohio	9,395	7.1%
4	Illinois	8,387	6.3%
5	Washington	6,265	4.7%
6	Pennsylvania	5,831	4.4%
7	New York	5,535	4.2%
8	Michigan	4,729	3.5%
9	Oregon	4,278	3.2%
10	Maryland	3,960	3.0%
11	Massachusetts	3,186	2.4%
12	New Jersey	3,030	2.3%
13	Texas	2,790	2.1%
14	South Dakota	2,740	2.1%
15	North Carolina	2,659	2.0%
16	Nebraska	2,089	1.6%
17	South Carolina	1,903	1.4%
18	Mississippi	1,837	1.4%
19	West Virginia	1,828	1.4%
20	Georgia	1,816	1.4%
21	Missouri	1,792	1.3%
22	Louisiana	1,776	1.3%
23	Hawaii	1,436	1.1%
24	Iowa	1,428	1.1%
25	Kansas	1,341	1.0%
26	Kentucky	1,217	0.9%
27	Alabama	1,208	0.9%
28	Alaska	925	0.7%
29	Arkansas	751	0.6%
30	New Hampshire	677	0.5%
31	Rhode Island	655	0.5%
32	Nevada	640	0.5%
33	Wisconsin	623	0.5%
34	Maine	622	0.5%
35	Oklahoma	588	0.4%
36	Tennessee	533	0.4%
37	Indiana	510	0.4%
38	New Mexico	439	0.3%
39	Vermont	437	0.3%
40	North Dakota	295	0.2%
41	Connecticut	269	0.2%
42	Delaware	2	0.0%
NA	Arizona**	NA	NA
NA	Colorado**	NA	NA
NA	Idaho**	NA	NA
NA	Minnesota**	NA	NA
NA	Montana**	NA	NA
NA	Utah**	NA	NA
NA	Virginia**	NA	NA
NA	Wyoming**	NA	NA
	District of Columbia	101	0.1%

Source: National Association of State Alcohol and Drug Abuse Directors
"State Resources and Services Related to Alcohol and Other Drug Problems-Fiscal Year 1997" (July 1999)
*Youths 17 years and younger. Data are only from treatment units that received at least some funds administered by a state's alcohol/drug agency in fiscal year 1997. An additional 126,199 admissions were not reported by age.
**Not available.

Admissions of Juveniles to Alcohol and Other Drug Treatment Programs
As a Percent of All Admissions in 1997
National Percent = 8.3% of Admissions*

ALPHA ORDER

RANK	STATE	PERCENT
14	Alabama	8.5
21	Alaska	7.2
NA	Arizona**	NA
33	Arkansas	5.0
31	California	5.7
NA	Colorado**	NA
41	Connecticut	0.8
42	Delaware	0.0
2	Florida	25.2
38	Georgia	3.2
1	Hawaii	29.4
NA	Idaho**	NA
18	Illinois	7.4
40	Indiana	2.9
18	Iowa	7.4
12	Kansas	8.9
10	Kentucky	9.6
28	Louisiana	6.5
24	Maine	7.0
5	Maryland	13.0
39	Massachusetts	3.1
30	Michigan	5.8
NA	Minnesota**	NA
17	Mississippi	7.9
34	Missouri	4.9
NA	Montana**	NA
9	Nebraska	10.5
21	Nevada	7.2
13	New Hampshire	8.8
27	New Jersey	6.6
35	New Mexico	4.0
37	New York	3.4
25	North Carolina	6.9
14	North Dakota	8.5
6	Ohio	12.0
36	Oklahoma	3.7
11	Oregon	9.3
16	Pennsylvania	8.3
32	Rhode Island	5.5
21	South Carolina	7.2
3	South Dakota	21.3
18	Tennessee	7.4
8	Texas	10.9
NA	Utah**	NA
29	Vermont	6.2
NA	Virginia**	NA
4	Washington	13.2
7	West Virginia	11.3
26	Wisconsin	6.7
NA	Wyoming**	NA

RANK ORDER

RANK	STATE	PERCENT
1	Hawaii	29.4
2	Florida	25.2
3	South Dakota	21.3
4	Washington	13.2
5	Maryland	13.0
6	Ohio	12.0
7	West Virginia	11.3
8	Texas	10.9
9	Nebraska	10.5
10	Kentucky	9.6
11	Oregon	9.3
12	Kansas	8.9
13	New Hampshire	8.8
14	Alabama	8.5
14	North Dakota	8.5
16	Pennsylvania	8.3
17	Mississippi	7.9
18	Illinois	7.4
18	Iowa	7.4
18	Tennessee	7.4
21	Alaska	7.2
21	Nevada	7.2
21	South Carolina	7.2
24	Maine	7.0
25	North Carolina	6.9
26	Wisconsin	6.7
27	New Jersey	6.6
28	Louisiana	6.5
29	Vermont	6.2
30	Michigan	5.8
31	California	5.7
32	Rhode Island	5.5
33	Arkansas	5.0
34	Missouri	4.9
35	New Mexico	4.0
36	Oklahoma	3.7
37	New York	3.4
38	Georgia	3.2
39	Massachusetts	3.1
40	Indiana	2.9
41	Connecticut	0.8
42	Delaware	0.0
NA	Arizona**	NA
NA	Colorado**	NA
NA	Idaho**	NA
NA	Minnesota**	NA
NA	Montana**	NA
NA	Utah**	NA
NA	Virginia**	NA
NA	Wyoming**	NA

District of Columbia 2.7

Source: Morgan Quitno Press using data from National Association of State Alcohol and Drug Abuse Directors
"State Resources and Services Related to Alcohol and Other Drug Problems-Fiscal Year 1997" (July 1999)
*Youths 17 years and younger. Data are only from treatment units that received at least some funds administered by a state's alcohol/drug agency in fiscal year 1997. National figure based only on states breaking admissions down by age.
**Not available.

Victims of Child Abuse and Neglect in 1998

National Total = 903,395 Children*

ALPHA ORDER

RANK ORDER

RANK	STATE	CHILDREN	% of USA		RANK	STATE	CHILDREN	% of USA
14	Alabama	16,668	1.8%		1	California	157,683	17.5%
34	Alaska	7,138	0.8%		2	New York	83,537	9.2%
25	Arizona	8,983	1.0%		3	Florida	82,119	9.1%
26	Arkansas	8,578	0.9%		4	Ohio	58,070	6.4%
1	California	157,683	17.5%		5	Texas	39,925	4.4%
35	Colorado	7,010	0.8%		6	North Carolina	37,357	4.1%
13	Connecticut	16,923	1.9%		7	Illinois	35,657	3.9%
44	Delaware	2,894	0.3%		8	Massachusetts	27,559	3.1%
3	Florida	82,119	9.1%		9	Georgia	24,567	2.7%
9	Georgia	24,567	2.7%		10	Kentucky	22,875	2.5%
46	Hawaii	2,185	0.2%		11	Michigan	22,744	2.5%
31	Idaho	7,936	0.9%		12	Indiana	18,962	2.1%
7	Illinois	35,657	3.9%		13	Connecticut	16,923	1.9%
12	Indiana	18,962	2.1%		14	Alabama	16,668	1.8%
33	Iowa	7,311	0.8%		15	Oklahoma	16,584	1.8%
38	Kansas	5,312	0.6%		16	Maryland	14,234	1.6%
10	Kentucky	22,875	2.5%		17	Louisiana	13,773	1.5%
17	Louisiana	13,773	1.5%		18	Washington	12,926	1.4%
41	Maine	3,579	0.4%		19	Missouri	12,556	1.4%
16	Maryland	14,234	1.6%		20	Minnesota	10,572	1.2%
8	Massachusetts	27,559	3.1%		21	Oregon	10,147	1.1%
11	Michigan	22,744	2.5%		22	Tennessee	9,930	1.1%
20	Minnesota	10,572	1.2%		23	New Jersey	9,851	1.1%
36	Mississippi	6,079	0.7%		24	Virginia	9,766	1.1%
19	Missouri	12,556	1.4%		25	Arizona	8,983	1.0%
43	Montana	3,292	0.4%		26	Arkansas	8,578	0.9%
40	Nebraska	4,219	0.5%		27	South Carolina	8,432	0.9%
29	Nevada	8,014	0.9%		28	Wisconsin	8,168	0.9%
47	New Hampshire	1,159	0.1%		29	Nevada	8,014	0.9%
23	New Jersey	9,851	1.1%		30	Utah	7,990	0.9%
39	New Mexico	4,241	0.5%		31	Idaho	7,936	0.9%
2	New York	83,537	9.2%		32	West Virginia	7,793	0.9%
6	North Carolina	37,357	4.1%		33	Iowa	7,311	0.8%
NA	North Dakota**	NA	NA		34	Alaska	7,138	0.8%
4	Ohio	58,070	6.4%		35	Colorado	7,010	0.8%
15	Oklahoma	16,584	1.8%		36	Mississippi	6,079	0.7%
21	Oregon	10,147	1.1%		37	Pennsylvania	5,392	0.6%
37	Pennsylvania	5,392	0.6%		38	Kansas	5,312	0.6%
42	Rhode Island	3,448	0.4%		39	New Mexico	4,241	0.5%
27	South Carolina	8,432	0.9%		40	Nebraska	4,219	0.5%
45	South Dakota	2,647	0.3%		41	Maine	3,579	0.4%
22	Tennessee	9,930	1.1%		42	Rhode Island	3,448	0.4%
5	Texas	39,925	4.4%		43	Montana	3,292	0.4%
30	Utah	7,990	0.9%		44	Delaware	2,894	0.3%
48	Vermont	887	0.1%		45	South Dakota	2,647	0.3%
24	Virginia	9,766	1.1%		46	Hawaii	2,185	0.2%
18	Washington	12,926	1.4%		47	New Hampshire	1,159	0.1%
32	West Virginia	7,793	0.9%		48	Vermont	887	0.1%
28	Wisconsin	8,168	0.9%		49	Wyoming	807	0.1%
49	Wyoming	807	0.1%		NA	North Dakota**	NA	NA
						District of Columbia	4,916	0.5%

Source: U.S. Department of Health and Human Services, Children's Bureau
   "Child Maltreatment 1998: Reports from the States" (April 2000)
*State-substantiated or indicated incidents. Some children may be counted twice if they were victims of multiple types of abuse. Fifty-four percent of maltreated children suffered neglect, 23% physical abuse, 12% sexual abuse, and the remainder suffered emotional maltreatment, medical neglect or other forms of maltreatment.
**Not available.

Rate of Child Abuse and Neglect in 1998

National Rate = 12.9 Abused Children per 1,000 Population Under 18*

ALPHA ORDER

RANK	STATE	RATE
15	Alabama	15.4
1	Alaska	37.1
40	Arizona	7.1
19	Arkansas	13.1
12	California	17.7
42	Colorado	6.7
5	Connecticut	21.4
14	Delaware	16.2
2	Florida	23.2
23	Georgia	12.1
39	Hawaii	7.3
4	Idaho	22.6
26	Illinois	11.2
20	Indiana	12.5
28	Iowa	10.1
37	Kansas	7.6
3	Kentucky	23.1
24	Louisiana	11.6
21	Maine	12.3
27	Maryland	11.1
9	Massachusetts	18.9
30	Michigan	8.9
34	Minnesota	8.4
36	Mississippi	8.0
30	Missouri	8.9
16	Montana	14.7
29	Nebraska	9.5
13	Nevada	17.2
48	New Hampshire	3.9
47	New Jersey	4.9
34	New Mexico	8.4
11	New York	18.6
7	North Carolina	19.5
NA	North Dakota**	NA
6	Ohio	20.4
9	Oklahoma	18.9
21	Oregon	12.3
49	Pennsylvania	1.9
17	Rhode Island	14.5
32	South Carolina	8.8
18	South Dakota	13.2
38	Tennessee	7.5
40	Texas	7.1
25	Utah	11.4
43	Vermont	6.3
46	Virginia	5.9
32	Washington	8.8
8	West Virginia	19.3
45	Wisconsin	6.0
44	Wyoming	6.2

RANK ORDER

RANK	STATE	RATE
1	Alaska	37.1
2	Florida	23.2
3	Kentucky	23.1
4	Idaho	22.6
5	Connecticut	21.4
6	Ohio	20.4
7	North Carolina	19.5
8	West Virginia	19.3
9	Massachusetts	18.9
9	Oklahoma	18.9
11	New York	18.6
12	California	17.7
13	Nevada	17.2
14	Delaware	16.2
15	Alabama	15.4
16	Montana	14.7
17	Rhode Island	14.5
18	South Dakota	13.2
19	Arkansas	13.1
20	Indiana	12.5
21	Maine	12.3
21	Oregon	12.3
23	Georgia	12.1
24	Louisiana	11.6
25	Utah	11.4
26	Illinois	11.2
27	Maryland	11.1
28	Iowa	10.1
29	Nebraska	9.5
30	Michigan	8.9
30	Missouri	8.9
32	South Carolina	8.8
32	Washington	8.8
34	Minnesota	8.4
34	New Mexico	8.4
36	Mississippi	8.0
37	Kansas	7.6
38	Tennessee	7.5
39	Hawaii	7.3
40	Arizona	7.1
40	Texas	7.1
42	Colorado	6.7
43	Vermont	6.3
44	Wyoming	6.2
45	Wisconsin	6.0
46	Virginia	5.9
47	New Jersey	4.9
48	New Hampshire	3.9
49	Pennsylvania	1.9
NA	North Dakota**	NA
	District of Columbia	47.7

Source: Morgan Quitno Press using data from U.S. Department of Health and Human Services, Children's Bureau
     "Child Maltreatment 1998: Reports from the States" (April 2000)
State-substantiated or indicated incidents.
**Not available.*

Physically Abused Children in 1998

National Reporting States' Total = 195,891 Children*

ALPHA ORDER

RANK	STATE	CHILDREN	% of USA
6	Alabama	6,610	3.4%
28	Alaska	1,820	0.9%
23	Arizona	2,147	1.1%
20	Arkansas	2,358	1.2%
1	California	41,351	21.1%
24	Colorado	2,051	1.0%
14	Connecticut	2,787	1.4%
41	Delaware	734	0.4%
4	Florida	15,452	7.9%
13	Georgia	3,515	1.8%
46	Hawaii	228	0.1%
19	Idaho	2,472	1.3%
11	Illinois	4,053	2.1%
8	Indiana	6,068	3.1%
29	Iowa	1,612	0.8%
30	Kansas	1,524	0.8%
7	Kentucky	6,128	3.1%
18	Louisiana	2,685	1.4%
34	Maine	1,424	0.7%
NA	Maryland**	NA	NA
NA	Massachusetts**	NA	NA
9	Michigan	4,537	2.3%
15	Minnesota	2,763	1.4%
38	Mississippi	1,196	0.6%
17	Missouri	2,728	1.4%
43	Montana	427	0.2%
37	Nebraska	1,231	0.6%
35	Nevada	1,396	0.7%
44	New Hampshire	318	0.2%
22	New Jersey	2,214	1.1%
39	New Mexico	1,054	0.5%
2	New York	18,329	9.4%
32	North Carolina	1,471	0.8%
NA	North Dakota**	NA	NA
3	Ohio	15,926	8.1%
10	Oklahoma	4,127	2.1%
33	Oregon	1,444	0.7%
21	Pennsylvania	2,217	1.1%
40	Rhode Island	998	0.5%
36	South Carolina	1,241	0.6%
42	South Dakota	618	0.3%
26	Tennessee	1,949	1.0%
5	Texas	11,919	6.1%
31	Utah	1,501	0.8%
45	Vermont	235	0.1%
16	Virginia	2,749	1.4%
12	Washington	3,862	2.0%
25	West Virginia	1,975	1.0%
27	Wisconsin	1,829	0.9%
47	Wyoming	209	0.1%

RANK ORDER

RANK	STATE	CHILDREN	% of USA
1	California	41,351	21.1%
2	New York	18,329	9.4%
3	Ohio	15,926	8.1%
4	Florida	15,452	7.9%
5	Texas	11,919	6.1%
6	Alabama	6,610	3.4%
7	Kentucky	6,128	3.1%
8	Indiana	6,068	3.1%
9	Michigan	4,537	2.3%
10	Oklahoma	4,127	2.1%
11	Illinois	4,053	2.1%
12	Washington	3,862	2.0%
13	Georgia	3,515	1.8%
14	Connecticut	2,787	1.4%
15	Minnesota	2,763	1.4%
16	Virginia	2,749	1.4%
17	Missouri	2,728	1.4%
18	Louisiana	2,685	1.4%
19	Idaho	2,472	1.3%
20	Arkansas	2,358	1.2%
21	Pennsylvania	2,217	1.1%
22	New Jersey	2,214	1.1%
23	Arizona	2,147	1.1%
24	Colorado	2,051	1.0%
25	West Virginia	1,975	1.0%
26	Tennessee	1,949	1.0%
27	Wisconsin	1,829	0.9%
28	Alaska	1,820	0.9%
29	Iowa	1,612	0.8%
30	Kansas	1,524	0.8%
31	Utah	1,501	0.8%
32	North Carolina	1,471	0.8%
33	Oregon	1,444	0.7%
34	Maine	1,424	0.7%
35	Nevada	1,396	0.7%
36	South Carolina	1,241	0.6%
37	Nebraska	1,231	0.6%
38	Mississippi	1,196	0.6%
39	New Mexico	1,054	0.5%
40	Rhode Island	998	0.5%
41	Delaware	734	0.4%
42	South Dakota	618	0.3%
43	Montana	427	0.2%
44	New Hampshire	318	0.2%
45	Vermont	235	0.1%
46	Hawaii	228	0.1%
47	Wyoming	209	0.1%
NA	Maryland**	NA	NA
NA	Massachusetts**	NA	NA
NA	North Dakota**	NA	NA
	District of Columbia	409	0.2%

Source: U.S. Department of Health and Human Services, Children's Bureau
"Child Maltreatment 1998: Reports from the States" (April 2000)
State-substantiated or indicated incidents. Some children may be counted twice if they were victims of multiple types of abuse. Fifty-four percent of maltreated children suffered neglect, 23% physical abuse, 12% sexual abuse, and the remainder suffered emotional maltreatment, medical neglect or other forms of maltreatment.
**Not available.*

Rate of Physically Abused Children in 1998

National Rate = 2.9 Physically Abused Children per 1,000 Population Under 18*

ALPHA ORDER

RANK	STATE	RATE
4	Alabama	6.1
1	Alaska	9.5
32	Arizona	1.7
15	Arkansas	3.6
9	California	4.6
28	Colorado	2.0
16	Connecticut	3.5
12	Delaware	4.1
10	Florida	4.4
32	Georgia	1.7
45	Hawaii	0.8
2	Idaho	7.0
41	Illinois	1.3
14	Indiana	4.0
22	Iowa	2.2
22	Kansas	2.2
3	Kentucky	6.2
21	Louisiana	2.3
6	Maine	4.9
NA	Maryland**	NA
NA	Massachusetts**	NA
31	Michigan	1.8
22	Minnesota	2.2
37	Mississippi	1.6
29	Missouri	1.9
29	Montana	1.9
19	Nebraska	2.8
18	Nevada	3.0
43	New Hampshire	1.1
43	New Jersey	1.1
25	New Mexico	2.1
12	New York	4.1
45	North Carolina	0.8
NA	North Dakota**	NA
5	Ohio	5.6
8	Oklahoma	4.7
32	Oregon	1.7
45	Pennsylvania	0.8
11	Rhode Island	4.2
41	South Carolina	1.3
17	South Dakota	3.1
39	Tennessee	1.5
25	Texas	2.1
25	Utah	2.1
32	Vermont	1.7
32	Virginia	1.7
20	Washington	2.6
6	West Virginia	4.9
40	Wisconsin	1.4
37	Wyoming	1.6

RANK ORDER

RANK	STATE	RATE
1	Alaska	9.5
2	Idaho	7.0
3	Kentucky	6.2
4	Alabama	6.1
5	Ohio	5.6
6	Maine	4.9
6	West Virginia	4.9
8	Oklahoma	4.7
9	California	4.6
10	Florida	4.4
11	Rhode Island	4.2
12	Delaware	4.1
12	New York	4.1
14	Indiana	4.0
15	Arkansas	3.6
16	Connecticut	3.5
17	South Dakota	3.1
18	Nevada	3.0
19	Nebraska	2.8
20	Washington	2.6
21	Louisiana	2.3
22	Iowa	2.2
22	Kansas	2.2
22	Minnesota	2.2
25	New Mexico	2.1
25	Texas	2.1
25	Utah	2.1
28	Colorado	2.0
29	Missouri	1.9
29	Montana	1.9
31	Michigan	1.8
32	Arizona	1.7
32	Georgia	1.7
32	Oregon	1.7
32	Vermont	1.7
32	Virginia	1.7
37	Mississippi	1.6
37	Wyoming	1.6
39	Tennessee	1.5
40	Wisconsin	1.4
41	Illinois	1.3
41	South Carolina	1.3
43	New Hampshire	1.1
43	New Jersey	1.1
45	Hawaii	0.8
45	North Carolina	0.8
45	Pennsylvania	0.8
NA	Maryland**	NA
NA	Massachusetts**	NA
NA	North Dakota**	NA

District of Columbia   4.0

Source: Morgan Quitno Press using data from U.S. Department of Health and Human Services, Children's Bureau "Child Maltreatment 1998: Reports from the States" (April 2000)

*State-substantiated or indicated incidents. National rate is for reporting states only. Fifty-four percent of maltreated children suffered neglect, 23% physical abuse, 12% sexual abuse, maltreated children suffered neglect, 24% physical abuse, 12% sexual abuse, 6% emotional maltreatment, 2% and the remainder suffered emotional maltreatment, medical neglect or other forms of maltreatment. **Not available.*

253

Sexually Abused Children in 1998

National Reporting States' Total = 99,278 Children*

ALPHA ORDER

RANK	STATE	CHILDREN	% of USA
8	Alabama	3,561	3.6%
32	Alaska	773	0.8%
37	Arizona	393	0.4%
10	Arkansas	2,334	2.4%
1	California	21,089	21.2%
24	Colorado	1,032	1.0%
34	Connecticut	717	0.7%
44	Delaware	248	0.2%
4	Florida	6,011	6.1%
14	Georgia	2,050	2.1%
46	Hawaii	145	0.1%
23	Idaho	1,290	1.3%
7	Illinois	3,604	3.6%
5	Indiana	4,950	5.0%
26	Iowa	964	1.0%
25	Kansas	1,023	1.0%
16	Kentucky	1,762	1.8%
27	Louisiana	904	0.9%
29	Maine	830	0.8%
NA	Maryland**	NA	NA
NA	Massachusetts**	NA	NA
18	Michigan	1,541	1.6%
28	Minnesota	861	0.9%
30	Mississippi	814	0.8%
11	Missouri	2,293	2.3%
40	Montana	320	0.3%
36	Nebraska	481	0.5%
42	Nevada	269	0.3%
39	New Hampshire	322	0.3%
31	New Jersey	788	0.8%
43	New Mexico	267	0.3%
6	New York	4,449	4.5%
19	North Carolina	1,525	1.5%
NA	North Dakota**	NA	NA
2	Ohio	8,185	8.2%
22	Oklahoma	1,406	1.4%
21	Oregon	1,434	1.4%
9	Pennsylvania	2,501	2.5%
41	Rhode Island	306	0.3%
35	South Carolina	707	0.7%
45	South Dakota	221	0.2%
13	Tennessee	2,221	2.2%
3	Texas	6,279	6.3%
15	Utah	1,852	1.9%
38	Vermont	371	0.4%
17	Virginia	1,586	1.6%
20	Washington	1,443	1.5%
33	West Virginia	744	0.7%
12	Wisconsin	2,230	2.2%
47	Wyoming	90	0.1%

RANK ORDER

RANK	STATE	CHILDREN	% of USA
1	California	21,089	21.2%
2	Ohio	8,185	8.2%
3	Texas	6,279	6.3%
4	Florida	6,011	6.1%
5	Indiana	4,950	5.0%
6	New York	4,449	4.5%
7	Illinois	3,604	3.6%
8	Alabama	3,561	3.6%
9	Pennsylvania	2,501	2.5%
10	Arkansas	2,334	2.4%
11	Missouri	2,293	2.3%
12	Wisconsin	2,230	2.2%
13	Tennessee	2,221	2.2%
14	Georgia	2,050	2.1%
15	Utah	1,852	1.9%
16	Kentucky	1,762	1.8%
17	Virginia	1,586	1.6%
18	Michigan	1,541	1.6%
19	North Carolina	1,525	1.5%
20	Washington	1,443	1.5%
21	Oregon	1,434	1.4%
22	Oklahoma	1,406	1.4%
23	Idaho	1,290	1.3%
24	Colorado	1,032	1.0%
25	Kansas	1,023	1.0%
26	Iowa	964	1.0%
27	Louisiana	904	0.9%
28	Minnesota	861	0.9%
29	Maine	830	0.8%
30	Mississippi	814	0.8%
31	New Jersey	788	0.8%
32	Alaska	773	0.8%
33	West Virginia	744	0.7%
34	Connecticut	717	0.7%
35	South Carolina	707	0.7%
36	Nebraska	481	0.5%
37	Arizona	393	0.4%
38	Vermont	371	0.4%
39	New Hampshire	322	0.3%
40	Montana	320	0.3%
41	Rhode Island	306	0.3%
42	Nevada	269	0.3%
43	New Mexico	267	0.3%
44	Delaware	248	0.2%
45	South Dakota	221	0.2%
46	Hawaii	145	0.1%
47	Wyoming	90	0.1%
NA	Maryland**	NA	NA
NA	Massachusetts**	NA	NA
NA	North Dakota**	NA	NA
	District of Columbia	92	0.1%

Source: U.S. Department of Health and Human Services, Children's Bureau
"Child Maltreatment 1998: Reports from the States" (April 2000)

*State-substantiated or indicated incidents. Some children may be counted twice if they were victims of multiple types of abuse. Fifty-four percent of maltreated children suffered neglect, 23% physical abuse, 12% sexual abuse, and the remainder suffered emotional maltreatment, medical neglect or other forms of maltreatment.
**Not available.*

Rate of Sexually Abused Children in 1998

National Rate = 1.6 Sexually Abused Children per 1,000 Population Under 18*

<table>
<tr><td colspan="3">ALPHA ORDER</td><td colspan="3">RANK ORDER</td></tr>
<tr><td>RANK</td><td>STATE</td><td>RATE</td><td>RANK</td><td>STATE</td><td>RATE</td></tr>
<tr><td>4</td><td>Alabama</td><td>3.3</td><td>1</td><td>Alaska</td><td>4.0</td></tr>
<tr><td>1</td><td>Alaska</td><td>4.0</td><td>2</td><td>Idaho</td><td>3.7</td></tr>
<tr><td>47</td><td>Arizona</td><td>0.3</td><td>3</td><td>Arkansas</td><td>3.6</td></tr>
<tr><td>3</td><td>Arkansas</td><td>3.6</td><td>4</td><td>Alabama</td><td>3.3</td></tr>
<tr><td>10</td><td>California</td><td>2.4</td><td>4</td><td>Indiana</td><td>3.3</td></tr>
<tr><td>30</td><td>Colorado</td><td>1.0</td><td>6</td><td>Ohio</td><td>2.9</td></tr>
<tr><td>35</td><td>Connecticut</td><td>0.9</td><td>7</td><td>Maine</td><td>2.8</td></tr>
<tr><td>20</td><td>Delaware</td><td>1.4</td><td>8</td><td>Utah</td><td>2.6</td></tr>
<tr><td>13</td><td>Florida</td><td>1.7</td><td>8</td><td>Vermont</td><td>2.6</td></tr>
<tr><td>30</td><td>Georgia</td><td>1.0</td><td>10</td><td>California</td><td>2.4</td></tr>
<tr><td>44</td><td>Hawaii</td><td>0.5</td><td>11</td><td>Kentucky</td><td>1.8</td></tr>
<tr><td>2</td><td>Idaho</td><td>3.7</td><td>11</td><td>West Virginia</td><td>1.8</td></tr>
<tr><td>24</td><td>Illinois</td><td>1.1</td><td>13</td><td>Florida</td><td>1.7</td></tr>
<tr><td>4</td><td>Indiana</td><td>3.3</td><td>13</td><td>Oregon</td><td>1.7</td></tr>
<tr><td>22</td><td>Iowa</td><td>1.3</td><td>13</td><td>Tennessee</td><td>1.7</td></tr>
<tr><td>19</td><td>Kansas</td><td>1.5</td><td>13</td><td>Wisconsin</td><td>1.7</td></tr>
<tr><td>11</td><td>Kentucky</td><td>1.8</td><td>17</td><td>Missouri</td><td>1.6</td></tr>
<tr><td>37</td><td>Louisiana</td><td>0.8</td><td>17</td><td>Oklahoma</td><td>1.6</td></tr>
<tr><td>7</td><td>Maine</td><td>2.8</td><td>19</td><td>Kansas</td><td>1.5</td></tr>
<tr><td>NA</td><td>Maryland**</td><td>NA</td><td>20</td><td>Delaware</td><td>1.4</td></tr>
<tr><td>NA</td><td>Massachusetts**</td><td>NA</td><td>20</td><td>Montana</td><td>1.4</td></tr>
<tr><td>42</td><td>Michigan</td><td>0.6</td><td>22</td><td>Iowa</td><td>1.3</td></tr>
<tr><td>39</td><td>Minnesota</td><td>0.7</td><td>22</td><td>Rhode Island</td><td>1.3</td></tr>
<tr><td>24</td><td>Mississippi</td><td>1.1</td><td>24</td><td>Illinois</td><td>1.1</td></tr>
<tr><td>17</td><td>Missouri</td><td>1.6</td><td>24</td><td>Mississippi</td><td>1.1</td></tr>
<tr><td>20</td><td>Montana</td><td>1.4</td><td>24</td><td>Nebraska</td><td>1.1</td></tr>
<tr><td>24</td><td>Nebraska</td><td>1.1</td><td>24</td><td>New Hampshire</td><td>1.1</td></tr>
<tr><td>42</td><td>Nevada</td><td>0.6</td><td>24</td><td>South Dakota</td><td>1.1</td></tr>
<tr><td>24</td><td>New Hampshire</td><td>1.1</td><td>24</td><td>Texas</td><td>1.1</td></tr>
<tr><td>46</td><td>New Jersey</td><td>0.4</td><td>30</td><td>Colorado</td><td>1.0</td></tr>
<tr><td>44</td><td>New Mexico</td><td>0.5</td><td>30</td><td>Georgia</td><td>1.0</td></tr>
<tr><td>30</td><td>New York</td><td>1.0</td><td>30</td><td>New York</td><td>1.0</td></tr>
<tr><td>37</td><td>North Carolina</td><td>0.8</td><td>30</td><td>Virginia</td><td>1.0</td></tr>
<tr><td>NA</td><td>North Dakota**</td><td>NA</td><td>30</td><td>Washington</td><td>1.0</td></tr>
<tr><td>6</td><td>Ohio</td><td>2.9</td><td>35</td><td>Connecticut</td><td>0.9</td></tr>
<tr><td>17</td><td>Oklahoma</td><td>1.6</td><td>35</td><td>Pennsylvania</td><td>0.9</td></tr>
<tr><td>13</td><td>Oregon</td><td>1.7</td><td>37</td><td>Louisiana</td><td>0.8</td></tr>
<tr><td>35</td><td>Pennsylvania</td><td>0.9</td><td>37</td><td>North Carolina</td><td>0.8</td></tr>
<tr><td>22</td><td>Rhode Island</td><td>1.3</td><td>39</td><td>Minnesota</td><td>0.7</td></tr>
<tr><td>39</td><td>South Carolina</td><td>0.7</td><td>39</td><td>South Carolina</td><td>0.7</td></tr>
<tr><td>24</td><td>South Dakota</td><td>1.1</td><td>39</td><td>Wyoming</td><td>0.7</td></tr>
<tr><td>13</td><td>Tennessee</td><td>1.7</td><td>42</td><td>Michigan</td><td>0.6</td></tr>
<tr><td>24</td><td>Texas</td><td>1.1</td><td>42</td><td>Nevada</td><td>0.6</td></tr>
<tr><td>8</td><td>Utah</td><td>2.6</td><td>44</td><td>Hawaii</td><td>0.5</td></tr>
<tr><td>8</td><td>Vermont</td><td>2.6</td><td>44</td><td>New Mexico</td><td>0.5</td></tr>
<tr><td>30</td><td>Virginia</td><td>1.0</td><td>46</td><td>New Jersey</td><td>0.4</td></tr>
<tr><td>30</td><td>Washington</td><td>1.0</td><td>47</td><td>Arizona</td><td>0.3</td></tr>
<tr><td>11</td><td>West Virginia</td><td>1.8</td><td>NA</td><td>Maryland**</td><td>NA</td></tr>
<tr><td>13</td><td>Wisconsin</td><td>1.7</td><td>NA</td><td>Massachusetts**</td><td>NA</td></tr>
<tr><td>39</td><td>Wyoming</td><td>0.7</td><td>NA</td><td>North Dakota**</td><td>NA</td></tr>
<tr><td></td><td></td><td></td><td></td><td>District of Columbia</td><td>0.9</td></tr>
</table>

Source: Morgan Quitno Press using data from U.S. Department of Health and Human Services, Children's Bureau
    "Child Maltreatment 1998: Reports from the States" (April 2000)
*State-substantiated or indicated incidents. National rate is for reporting states only. Fifty-four percent of maltreated children suffered neglect, 23% physical abuse, 12% sexual abuse, maltreated children suffered neglect, 24% physical abuse, 12% sexual abuse, 6% emotional maltreatment, 2% and the remainder suffered emotional maltreatment, medical neglect or other forms of maltreatment. **Not available.

Emotionally Abused Children in 1998

National Reporting States' Total = 51,618 Children*

ALPHA ORDER

RANK	STATE	CHILDREN	% of USA
13	Alabama	1,075	2.1%
29	Alaska	189	0.4%
31	Arizona	162	0.3%
36	Arkansas	87	0.2%
1	California	12,779	24.8%
15	Colorado	819	1.6%
2	Connecticut	8,937	17.3%
22	Delaware	470	0.9%
4	Florida	2,488	4.8%
14	Georgia	996	1.9%
40	Hawaii	43	0.1%
NA	Idaho**	NA	NA
23	Illinois	461	0.9%
NA	Indiana**	NA	NA
NA	Iowa**	NA	NA
17	Kansas	591	1.1%
5	Kentucky	2,472	4.8%
20	Louisiana	550	1.1%
6	Maine	2,297	4.4%
NA	Maryland**	NA	NA
NA	Massachusetts**	NA	NA
10	Michigan	1,361	2.6%
35	Minnesota	91	0.2%
32	Mississippi	152	0.3%
28	Missouri	254	0.5%
21	Montana	522	1.0%
NA	Nebraska**	NA	NA
25	Nevada	312	0.6%
39	New Hampshire	45	0.1%
26	New Jersey	284	0.6%
19	New Mexico	582	1.1%
11	New York	1,274	2.5%
33	North Carolina	138	0.3%
NA	North Dakota**	NA	NA
8	Ohio	1,801	3.5%
7	Oklahoma	1,815	3.5%
16	Oregon	758	1.5%
34	Pennsylvania	105	0.2%
41	Rhode Island	24	0.0%
38	South Carolina	72	0.1%
27	South Dakota	281	0.5%
30	Tennessee	183	0.4%
9	Texas	1,576	3.1%
3	Utah	3,219	6.2%
43	Vermont	10	0.0%
24	Virginia	403	0.8%
12	Washington	1,266	2.5%
18	West Virginia	586	1.1%
37	Wisconsin	76	0.1%
42	Wyoming	12	0.0%

RANK ORDER

RANK	STATE	CHILDREN	% of USA
1	California	12,779	24.8%
2	Connecticut	8,937	17.3%
3	Utah	3,219	6.2%
4	Florida	2,488	4.8%
5	Kentucky	2,472	4.8%
6	Maine	2,297	4.4%
7	Oklahoma	1,815	3.5%
8	Ohio	1,801	3.5%
9	Texas	1,576	3.1%
10	Michigan	1,361	2.6%
11	New York	1,274	2.5%
12	Washington	1,266	2.5%
13	Alabama	1,075	2.1%
14	Georgia	996	1.9%
15	Colorado	819	1.6%
16	Oregon	758	1.5%
17	Kansas	591	1.1%
18	West Virginia	586	1.1%
19	New Mexico	582	1.1%
20	Louisiana	550	1.1%
21	Montana	522	1.0%
22	Delaware	470	0.9%
23	Illinois	461	0.9%
24	Virginia	403	0.8%
25	Nevada	312	0.6%
26	New Jersey	284	0.6%
27	South Dakota	281	0.5%
28	Missouri	254	0.5%
29	Alaska	189	0.4%
30	Tennessee	183	0.4%
31	Arizona	162	0.3%
32	Mississippi	152	0.3%
33	North Carolina	138	0.3%
34	Pennsylvania	105	0.2%
35	Minnesota	91	0.2%
36	Arkansas	87	0.2%
37	Wisconsin	76	0.1%
38	South Carolina	72	0.1%
39	New Hampshire	45	0.1%
40	Hawaii	43	0.1%
41	Rhode Island	24	0.0%
42	Wyoming	12	0.0%
43	Vermont	10	0.0%
NA	Idaho**	NA	NA
NA	Indiana**	NA	NA
NA	Iowa**	NA	NA
NA	Maryland**	NA	NA
NA	Massachusetts**	NA	NA
NA	Nebraska**	NA	NA
NA	North Dakota**	NA	NA
	District of Columbia**	NA	NA

Source: U.S. Department of Health and Human Services, Children's Bureau
"Child Maltreatment 1998: Reports from the States" (April 2000)
*State-substantiated or indicated incidents. Some children may be counted twice if they were victims of multiple types of abuse. Fifty-four percent of maltreated children suffered neglect, 23% physical abuse, 12% sexual abuse, and the remainder suffered emotional maltreatment, medical neglect or other forms of maltreatment.
**Not available.

Rate of Emotionally Abused Children in 1998

National Rate = 0.6 Emotionally Abused Children per 1,000 Population Under 18*

ALPHA ORDER

RANK	STATE	RATE
12	Alabama	1.0
12	Alaska	1.0
30	Arizona	0.1
30	Arkansas	0.1
8	California	1.4
16	Colorado	0.8
1	Connecticut	11.3
4	Delaware	2.6
18	Florida	0.7
21	Georgia	0.5
30	Hawaii	0.1
NA	Idaho**	NA
30	Illinois	0.1
NA	Indiana**	NA
NA	Iowa**	NA
16	Kansas	0.8
5	Kentucky	2.5
21	Louisiana	0.5
2	Maine	7.9
NA	Maryland**	NA
NA	Massachusetts**	NA
21	Michigan	0.5
30	Minnesota	0.1
26	Mississippi	0.2
26	Missouri	0.2
6	Montana	2.3
NA	Nebraska**	NA
18	Nevada	0.7
26	New Hampshire	0.2
30	New Jersey	0.1
11	New Mexico	1.2
24	New York	0.3
30	North Carolina	0.1
NA	North Dakota**	NA
20	Ohio	0.6
7	Oklahoma	2.1
14	Oregon	0.9
43	Pennsylvania	0.0
30	Rhode Island	0.1
30	South Carolina	0.1
8	South Dakota	1.4
30	Tennessee	0.1
24	Texas	0.3
3	Utah	4.6
30	Vermont	0.1
26	Virginia	0.2
14	Washington	0.9
8	West Virginia	1.4
30	Wisconsin	0.1
30	Wyoming	0.1

RANK ORDER

RANK	STATE	RATE
1	Connecticut	11.3
2	Maine	7.9
3	Utah	4.6
4	Delaware	2.6
5	Kentucky	2.5
6	Montana	2.3
7	Oklahoma	2.1
8	California	1.4
8	South Dakota	1.4
8	West Virginia	1.4
11	New Mexico	1.2
12	Alabama	1.0
12	Alaska	1.0
14	Oregon	0.9
14	Washington	0.9
16	Colorado	0.8
16	Kansas	0.8
18	Florida	0.7
18	Nevada	0.7
20	Ohio	0.6
21	Georgia	0.5
21	Louisiana	0.5
21	Michigan	0.5
24	New York	0.3
24	Texas	0.3
26	Mississippi	0.2
26	Missouri	0.2
26	New Hampshire	0.2
26	Virginia	0.2
30	Arizona	0.1
30	Arkansas	0.1
30	Hawaii	0.1
30	Illinois	0.1
30	Minnesota	0.1
30	New Jersey	0.1
30	North Carolina	0.1
30	Rhode Island	0.1
30	South Carolina	0.1
30	Tennessee	0.1
30	Vermont	0.1
30	Wisconsin	0.1
30	Wyoming	0.1
43	Pennsylvania	0.0
NA	Idaho**	NA
NA	Indiana**	NA
NA	Iowa**	NA
NA	Maryland**	NA
NA	Massachusetts**	NA
NA	Nebraska**	NA
NA	North Dakota**	NA

District of Columbia**	NA

Source: Morgan Quitno Press using data from U.S. Department of Health and Human Services, Children's Bureau "Child Maltreatment 1998: Reports from the States" (April 2000)
*State-substantiated or indicated incidents. National rate is for reporting states only. Fifty-four percent of maltreated children suffered neglect, 23% physical abuse, 12% sexual abuse, maltreated children suffered neglect, 24% physical abuse, 12% sexual abuse, 6% emotional maltreatment, 2% and the remainder suffered emotional maltreatment, medical neglect or other forms of maltreatment. **Not available.*

Neglected Children in 1998

National Reporting States' Total = 461,274 Children*

ALPHA ORDER

RANK	STATE	CHILDREN	% of USA
16	Alabama	7,716	1.7%
26	Alaska	4,345	0.9%
22	Arizona	5,464	1.2%
21	Arkansas	5,763	1.2%
1	California	81,828	17.7%
24	Colorado	4,746	1.0%
11	Connecticut	14,593	3.2%
42	Delaware	1,139	0.2%
2	Florida	34,041	7.4%
10	Georgia	15,295	3.3%
47	Hawaii	182	0.0%
29	Idaho	3,773	0.8%
7	Illinois	15,961	3.5%
5	Indiana	23,564	5.1%
23	Iowa	4,762	1.0%
36	Kansas	2,416	0.5%
12	Kentucky	14,056	3.0%
14	Louisiana	9,579	2.1%
37	Maine	2,357	0.5%
NA	Maryland**	NA	NA
NA	Massachusetts**	NA	NA
13	Michigan	10,538	2.3%
17	Minnesota	7,340	1.6%
30	Mississippi	3,772	0.8%
18	Missouri	6,857	1.5%
41	Montana	1,788	0.4%
34	Nebraska	2,800	0.6%
25	Nevada	4,694	1.0%
43	New Hampshire	768	0.2%
20	New Jersey	6,230	1.4%
39	New Mexico	2,219	0.5%
8	New York	15,896	3.4%
3	North Carolina	32,591	7.1%
NA	North Dakota**	NA	NA
4	Ohio	32,047	6.9%
9	Oklahoma	15,535	3.4%
38	Oregon	2,271	0.5%
46	Pennsylvania	204	0.0%
33	Rhode Island	2,920	0.6%
28	South Carolina	3,920	0.8%
40	South Dakota	1,931	0.4%
27	Tennessee	4,266	0.9%
6	Texas	22,883	5.0%
35	Utah	2,640	0.6%
45	Vermont	326	0.1%
19	Virginia	6,385	1.4%
15	Washington	8,453	1.8%
31	West Virginia	3,082	0.7%
32	Wisconsin	3,068	0.7%
44	Wyoming	537	0.1%

RANK ORDER

RANK	STATE	CHILDREN	% of USA
1	California	81,828	17.7%
2	Florida	34,041	7.4%
3	North Carolina	32,591	7.1%
4	Ohio	32,047	6.9%
5	Indiana	23,564	5.1%
6	Texas	22,883	5.0%
7	Illinois	15,961	3.5%
8	New York	15,896	3.4%
9	Oklahoma	15,535	3.4%
10	Georgia	15,295	3.3%
11	Connecticut	14,593	3.2%
12	Kentucky	14,056	3.0%
13	Michigan	10,538	2.3%
14	Louisiana	9,579	2.1%
15	Washington	8,453	1.8%
16	Alabama	7,716	1.7%
17	Minnesota	7,340	1.6%
18	Missouri	6,857	1.5%
19	Virginia	6,385	1.4%
20	New Jersey	6,230	1.4%
21	Arkansas	5,763	1.2%
22	Arizona	5,464	1.2%
23	Iowa	4,762	1.0%
24	Colorado	4,746	1.0%
25	Nevada	4,694	1.0%
26	Alaska	4,345	0.9%
27	Tennessee	4,266	0.9%
28	South Carolina	3,920	0.8%
29	Idaho	3,773	0.8%
30	Mississippi	3,772	0.8%
31	West Virginia	3,082	0.7%
32	Wisconsin	3,068	0.7%
33	Rhode Island	2,920	0.6%
34	Nebraska	2,800	0.6%
35	Utah	2,640	0.6%
36	Kansas	2,416	0.5%
37	Maine	2,357	0.5%
38	Oregon	2,271	0.5%
39	New Mexico	2,219	0.5%
40	South Dakota	1,931	0.4%
41	Montana	1,788	0.4%
42	Delaware	1,139	0.2%
43	New Hampshire	768	0.2%
44	Wyoming	537	0.1%
45	Vermont	326	0.1%
46	Pennsylvania	204	0.0%
47	Hawaii	182	0.0%
NA	Maryland**	NA	NA
NA	Massachusetts**	NA	NA
NA	North Dakota**	NA	NA
	District of Columbia	3,733	0.8%

Source: U.S. Department of Health and Human Services, Children's Bureau
    "Child Maltreatment 1998: Reports from the States" (April 2000)
*State-substantiated or indicated incidents. Some children may be counted twice if they were victims of multiple types of abuse. Fifty-four percent of maltreated children suffered neglect, 23% physical abuse, 12% sexual abuse, and the remainder suffered emotional maltreatment, medical neglect or other forms of maltreatment.
**Not available.

Rate of Neglected Children in 1998

National Rate = 7.2 Neglected Children per 1,000 Population Under 18*

ALPHA ORDER

RANK ORDER

RANK	STATE	RATE		RANK	STATE	RATE
20	Alabama	7.1		1	Alaska	22.6
1	Alaska	22.6		2	Connecticut	18.5
31	Arizona	4.3		3	Oklahoma	17.7
14	Arkansas	8.8		4	North Carolina	17.0
13	California	9.2		5	Indiana	15.5
29	Colorado	4.6		6	Kentucky	14.2
2	Connecticut	18.5		7	Rhode Island	12.3
22	Delaware	6.4		8	Ohio	11.3
11	Florida	9.6		9	Idaho	10.7
18	Georgia	7.6		10	Nevada	10.0
46	Hawaii	0.6		11	Florida	9.6
9	Idaho	10.7		11	South Dakota	9.6
26	Illinois	5.0		13	California	9.2
5	Indiana	15.5		14	Arkansas	8.8
21	Iowa	6.6		15	Maine	8.1
38	Kansas	3.5		16	Louisiana	8.0
6	Kentucky	14.2		16	Montana	8.0
16	Louisiana	8.0		18	Georgia	7.6
15	Maine	8.1		18	West Virginia	7.6
NA	Maryland**	NA		20	Alabama	7.1
NA	Massachusetts**	NA		21	Iowa	6.6
32	Michigan	4.1		22	Delaware	6.4
24	Minnesota	5.8		23	Nebraska	6.3
26	Mississippi	5.0		24	Minnesota	5.8
28	Missouri	4.9		25	Washington	5.7
16	Montana	8.0		26	Illinois	5.0
23	Nebraska	6.3		26	Mississippi	5.0
10	Nevada	10.0		28	Missouri	4.9
43	New Hampshire	2.6		29	Colorado	4.6
41	New Jersey	3.1		30	New Mexico	4.4
30	New Mexico	4.4		31	Arizona	4.3
38	New York	3.5		32	Michigan	4.1
4	North Carolina	17.0		32	South Carolina	4.1
NA	North Dakota**	NA		32	Texas	4.1
8	Ohio	11.3		32	Wyoming	4.1
3	Oklahoma	17.7		36	Virginia	3.9
42	Oregon	2.8		37	Utah	3.8
47	Pennsylvania	0.1		38	Kansas	3.5
7	Rhode Island	12.3		38	New York	3.5
32	South Carolina	4.1		40	Tennessee	3.2
11	South Dakota	9.6		41	New Jersey	3.1
40	Tennessee	3.2		42	Oregon	2.8
32	Texas	4.1		43	New Hampshire	2.6
37	Utah	3.8		44	Vermont	2.3
44	Vermont	2.3		44	Wisconsin	2.3
36	Virginia	3.9		46	Hawaii	0.6
25	Washington	5.7		47	Pennsylvania	0.1
18	West Virginia	7.6		NA	Maryland**	NA
44	Wisconsin	2.3		NA	Massachusetts**	NA
32	Wyoming	4.1		NA	North Dakota**	NA

District of Columbia   36.3

*Source: Morgan Quitno Press using data from U.S. Department of Health and Human Services, Children's Bureau
    "Child Maltreatment 1998: Reports from the States" (April 2000)*

*State-substantiated or indicated incidents. National rate is for reporting states only. Fifty-four percent of
maltreated children suffered neglect, 23% physical abuse, 12% sexual abuse, maltreated children suffered neglect,
24% physical abuse, 12% sexual abuse, 6% emotional maltreatment, 2% and the remainder suffered emotional
maltreatment, medical neglect or other forms of maltreatment. **Not available.*

Child Abuse and Neglect Fatalities in 1998

National Total = 1,118 Fatalities*

ALPHA ORDER

RANK	STATE	FATALITIES	% of USA
17	Alabama	25	2.2%
NA	Alaska**	NA	NA
29	Arizona	10	0.9%
33	Arkansas	5	0.4%
16	California	26	2.3%
13	Colorado	28	2.5%
32	Connecticut	6	0.5%
38	Delaware	3	0.3%
5	Florida	54	4.8%
10	Georgia	37	3.3%
38	Hawaii	3	0.3%
33	Idaho	5	0.4%
4	Illinois	58	5.2%
2	Indiana	65	5.8%
29	Iowa	10	0.9%
23	Kansas	13	1.2%
20	Kentucky	18	1.6%
15	Louisiana	27	2.4%
37	Maine	4	0.4%
18	Maryland	24	2.1%
27	Massachusetts	11	1.0%
9	Michigan	40	3.6%
38	Minnesota	3	0.3%
33	Mississippi	5	0.4%
13	Missouri	28	2.5%
38	Montana	3	0.3%
NA	Nebraska**	NA	NA
23	Nevada	13	1.2%
45	New Hampshire	1	0.1%
11	New Jersey	29	2.6%
33	New Mexico	5	0.4%
3	New York	61	5.5%
19	North Carolina	23	2.1%
47	North Dakota	0	0.0%
5	Ohio	54	4.8%
8	Oklahoma	45	4.0%
21	Oregon	17	1.5%
7	Pennsylvania	52	4.7%
44	Rhode Island	2	0.2%
22	South Carolina	16	1.4%
38	South Dakota	3	0.3%
25	Tennessee	12	1.1%
1	Texas	176	15.7%
25	Utah	12	1.1%
47	Vermont	0	0.0%
11	Virginia	29	2.6%
31	Washington	8	0.7%
45	West Virginia	1	0.1%
27	Wisconsin	11	1.0%
38	Wyoming	3	0.3%

RANK ORDER

RANK	STATE	FATALITIES	% of USA
1	Texas	176	15.7%
2	Indiana	65	5.8%
3	New York	61	5.5%
4	Illinois	58	5.2%
5	Florida	54	4.8%
5	Ohio	54	4.8%
7	Pennsylvania	52	4.7%
8	Oklahoma	45	4.0%
9	Michigan	40	3.6%
10	Georgia	37	3.3%
11	New Jersey	29	2.6%
11	Virginia	29	2.6%
13	Colorado	28	2.5%
13	Missouri	28	2.5%
15	Louisiana	27	2.4%
16	California	26	2.3%
17	Alabama	25	2.2%
18	Maryland	24	2.1%
19	North Carolina	23	2.1%
20	Kentucky	18	1.6%
21	Oregon	17	1.5%
22	South Carolina	16	1.4%
23	Kansas	13	1.2%
23	Nevada	13	1.2%
25	Tennessee	12	1.1%
25	Utah	12	1.1%
27	Massachusetts	11	1.0%
27	Wisconsin	11	1.0%
29	Arizona	10	0.9%
29	Iowa	10	0.9%
31	Washington	8	0.7%
32	Connecticut	6	0.5%
33	Arkansas	5	0.4%
33	Idaho	5	0.4%
33	Mississippi	5	0.4%
33	New Mexico	5	0.4%
37	Maine	4	0.4%
38	Delaware	3	0.3%
38	Hawaii	3	0.3%
38	Minnesota	3	0.3%
38	Montana	3	0.3%
38	South Dakota	3	0.3%
38	Wyoming	3	0.3%
44	Rhode Island	2	0.2%
45	New Hampshire	1	0.1%
45	West Virginia	1	0.1%
47	North Dakota	0	0.0%
47	Vermont	0	0.0%
NA	Alaska**	NA	NA
NA	Nebraska**	NA	NA
	District of Columbia	2	0.2%

Source: U.S. Department of Health and Human Services, Children's Bureau
"Child Maltreatment 1998: Reports from the States" (April 2000)
*State-substantiated or indicated incidents. National total is an estimate of all states including states not reporting. Fifty-four percent of maltreated children suffered neglect, 23% physical abuse, 12% sexual abuse, maltreated children suffered neglect, 24% physical abuse, 12% sexual abuse, 6% emotional maltreatment, 2% and the remainder suffered emotional maltreatment, medical neglect or other forms of maltreatment. **Not available.*

Rate of Child Abuse and Neglect Fatalities in 1998

National Rate = 1.6 Fatalities per 100,000 Population Under 18*

ALPHA ORDER

RANK ORDER

RANK	STATE	RATE
6	Alabama	2.3
NA	Alaska**	NA
35	Arizona	0.8
35	Arkansas	0.8
43	California	0.3
5	Colorado	2.7
35	Connecticut	0.8
19	Delaware	1.7
23	Florida	1.5
14	Georgia	1.8
32	Hawaii	1.0
26	Idaho	1.4
14	Illinois	1.8
2	Indiana	4.3
26	Iowa	1.4
11	Kansas	1.9
14	Kentucky	1.8
6	Louisiana	2.3
26	Maine	1.4
11	Maryland	1.9
35	Massachusetts	0.8
22	Michigan	1.6
45	Minnesota	0.2
41	Mississippi	0.7
10	Missouri	2.0
30	Montana	1.3
NA	Nebraska**	NA
4	Nevada	2.8
43	New Hampshire	0.3
23	New Jersey	1.5
32	New Mexico	1.0
26	New York	1.4
31	North Carolina	1.2
47	North Dakota	0.0
11	Ohio	1.9
1	Oklahoma	5.1
9	Oregon	2.1
14	Pennsylvania	1.8
35	Rhode Island	0.8
19	South Carolina	1.7
23	South Dakota	1.5
34	Tennessee	0.9
3	Texas	3.1
19	Utah	1.7
47	Vermont	0.0
14	Virginia	1.8
42	Washington	0.5
45	West Virginia	0.2
35	Wisconsin	0.8
6	Wyoming	2.3

RANK	STATE	RATE
1	Oklahoma	5.1
2	Indiana	4.3
3	Texas	3.1
4	Nevada	2.8
5	Colorado	2.7
6	Alabama	2.3
6	Louisiana	2.3
6	Wyoming	2.3
9	Oregon	2.1
10	Missouri	2.0
11	Kansas	1.9
11	Maryland	1.9
11	Ohio	1.9
14	Georgia	1.8
14	Illinois	1.8
14	Kentucky	1.8
14	Pennsylvania	1.8
14	Virginia	1.8
19	Delaware	1.7
19	South Carolina	1.7
19	Utah	1.7
22	Michigan	1.6
23	Florida	1.5
23	New Jersey	1.5
23	South Dakota	1.5
26	Idaho	1.4
26	Iowa	1.4
26	Maine	1.4
26	New York	1.4
30	Montana	1.3
31	North Carolina	1.2
32	Hawaii	1.0
32	New Mexico	1.0
34	Tennessee	0.9
35	Arizona	0.8
35	Arkansas	0.8
35	Connecticut	0.8
35	Massachusetts	0.8
35	Rhode Island	0.8
35	Wisconsin	0.8
41	Mississippi	0.7
42	Washington	0.5
43	California	0.3
43	New Hampshire	0.3
45	Minnesota	0.2
45	West Virginia	0.2
47	North Dakota	0.0
47	Vermont	0.0
NA	Alaska**	NA
NA	Nebraska**	NA

District of Columbia   1.9

Source: Morgan Quitno Press using data from U.S. Department of Health and Human Services, Children's Bureau
"Child Maltreatment 1998: Reports from the States" (April 2000)
*State-substantiated or indicated incidents. National rate is an estimate of all states including states not reporting.
Fifty-four percent of maltreated children suffered neglect, 23% physical abuse, 12% sexual abuse, maltreated
children suffered neglect, 24% physical abuse, 12% sexual abuse, 6% emotional maltreatment, 2% and the
remainder suffered emotional maltreatment, medical neglect or other forms of maltreatment. **Not available.

VI. LAW ENFORCEMENT

262 Federal Law Enforcement Officers in 1998
263 Rate of Federal Law Enforcement Officers in 1998
264 State and Local Justice System Employment in 1999
265 Rate of State and Local Justice System Employment in 1999
266 State and Local Judicial and Legal Employment in 1999
267 Rate of State and Local Judicial and Legal Employment in 1999
268 State and Local Police Officers in 1999
269 Rate of State and Local Police Officers in 1999
270 Law Enforcement Agencies in 1996
271 Population per Law Enforcement Agency in 1996
272 Law Enforcement Agencies per 1,000 Square Miles in 1996
273 Full-Time Sworn Officers in Law Enforcement Agencies in 1996
274 Percent of Full-Time Law Enforcement Agency Employees Who are Sworn Officers: 1996
275 Rate of Full-Time Sworn Officers in Law Enforcement Agencies in 1996
276 Full-Time Sworn Law Enforcement Officers per 1,000 Square Miles in 1996
277 Full-Time Employees in Law Enforcement Agencies in 1996
278 Rate of Full-Time Employees in Law Enforcement Agencies in 1996
279 Full-Time Sworn Officers in State Police Departments in 1996
280 Percent of Full-Time State Police Department Employees Who are Sworn Officers: 1996
281 Rate of Full-Time Sworn Officers in State Police Departments in 1996
282 State Government Law Enforcement Officers in 1999
283 Male State Government Law Enforcement Officers in 1999
284 Female State Government Law Enforcement Officers in 1999
285 Female State Government Law Enforcement Officers as a Percent of All Officers: 1999
286 Local Police Departments in 1996
287 Full-Time Officers in Local Police Departments in 1996
288 Percent of Full-Time Local Police Department Employees Who Are Sworn Officers: 1996
289 Rate of Full-Time Officers in Local Police Departments in 1996
290 Full-Time Employees in Local Police Departments in 1996
291 Sheriffs' Departments in 1996
292 Full-Time Officers in Sheriffs' Departments in 1996
293 Percent of Full-Time Sheriffs' Department Employees Who Are Sworn Officers: 1996
294 Rate of Full-Time Sworn Officers in Sheriffs' Departments in 1996
295 Full-Time Employees in Sheriffs' Departments in 1996
296 Special Police Agencies in 1996
297 Full-Time Sworn Officers in Special Police Departments in 1996
298 Percent of Full-Time Special Police Department Employees Who Are Sworn Officers: 1996
299 Rate of Full-Time Sworn Officers in Special Police Departments in 1996
300 Full-Time Employees in Special Police Departments in 1996
301 Law Enforcement Officers Feloniously Killed in 1998
302 Law Enforcement Officers Feloniously Killed: 1989 to 1998
303 U.S. District Court Judges in 1999
304 Population per U.S. District Judge in 1999
305 Felony Criminal Cases Filed in U.S. District Courts in 1999
306 Felony Criminal Cases Filed per U.S. District Judge in 1999
307 Median Length of Federal Criminal Cases in 1999
308 Authorized Wiretaps in 1999

Federal Law Enforcement Officers in 1998

National Total = 83,143 Officers*

ALPHA ORDER

RANK	STATE	OFFICERS	% of USA
27	Alabama	681	0.8%
38	Alaska	317	0.4%
5	Arizona	3,174	3.8%
24	Arkansas	837	1.0%
1	California	11,868	14.3%
11	Colorado	1,512	1.8%
36	Connecticut	431	0.5%
49	Delaware	93	0.1%
4	Florida	5,343	6.4%
9	Georgia	2,116	2.5%
31	Hawaii	526	0.6%
44	Idaho	196	0.2%
7	Illinois	2,782	3.3%
30	Indiana	633	0.8%
47	Iowa	121	0.1%
35	Kansas	434	0.5%
22	Kentucky	898	1.1%
21	Louisiana	956	1.1%
40	Maine	293	0.4%
13	Maryland	1,271	1.5%
16	Massachusetts	1,126	1.4%
14	Michigan	1,249	1.5%
23	Minnesota	895	1.1%
34	Mississippi	467	0.6%
15	Missouri	1,197	1.4%
39	Montana	300	0.4%
43	Nebraska	214	0.3%
33	Nevada	479	0.6%
50	New Hampshire	67	0.1%
10	New Jersey	2,109	2.5%
18	New Mexico	982	1.2%
3	New York	6,988	8.4%
19	North Carolina	967	1.2%
42	North Dakota	227	0.3%
17	Ohio	1,026	1.2%
25	Oklahoma	743	0.9%
29	Oregon	637	0.8%
6	Pennsylvania	3,052	3.7%
48	Rhode Island	101	0.1%
28	South Carolina	667	0.8%
45	South Dakota	165	0.2%
20	Tennessee	957	1.2%
2	Texas	11,059	13.3%
37	Utah	407	0.5%
41	Vermont	269	0.3%
8	Virginia	2,278	2.7%
12	Washington	1,380	1.7%
32	West Virginia	510	0.6%
26	Wisconsin	739	0.9%
46	Wyoming	162	0.2%

RANK ORDER

RANK	STATE	OFFICERS	% of USA
1	California	11,868	14.3%
2	Texas	11,059	13.3%
3	New York	6,988	8.4%
4	Florida	5,343	6.4%
5	Arizona	3,174	3.8%
6	Pennsylvania	3,052	3.7%
7	Illinois	2,782	3.3%
8	Virginia	2,278	2.7%
9	Georgia	2,116	2.5%
10	New Jersey	2,109	2.5%
11	Colorado	1,512	1.8%
12	Washington	1,380	1.7%
13	Maryland	1,271	1.5%
14	Michigan	1,249	1.5%
15	Missouri	1,197	1.4%
16	Massachusetts	1,126	1.4%
17	Ohio	1,026	1.2%
18	New Mexico	982	1.2%
19	North Carolina	967	1.2%
20	Tennessee	957	1.2%
21	Louisiana	956	1.1%
22	Kentucky	898	1.1%
23	Minnesota	895	1.1%
24	Arkansas	837	1.0%
25	Oklahoma	743	0.9%
26	Wisconsin	739	0.9%
27	Alabama	681	0.8%
28	South Carolina	667	0.8%
29	Oregon	637	0.8%
30	Indiana	633	0.8%
31	Hawaii	526	0.6%
32	West Virginia	510	0.6%
33	Nevada	479	0.6%
34	Mississippi	467	0.6%
35	Kansas	434	0.5%
36	Connecticut	431	0.5%
37	Utah	407	0.5%
38	Alaska	317	0.4%
39	Montana	300	0.4%
40	Maine	293	0.4%
41	Vermont	269	0.3%
42	North Dakota	227	0.3%
43	Nebraska	214	0.3%
44	Idaho	196	0.2%
45	South Dakota	165	0.2%
46	Wyoming	162	0.2%
47	Iowa	121	0.1%
48	Rhode Island	101	0.1%
49	Delaware	93	0.1%
50	New Hampshire	67	0.1%
	District of Columbia	7,241	8.7%

Source: U.S. Department of Justice, Bureau of Justice Statistics
"Federal Law Enforcement Officers, 1998" (NCJ-177607, March 2000)
*Full-time officers authorized to carry firearms and make arrests. Includes F.B.I., Customs Service, Immigration and Naturalization Service, I.R.S., Postal Inspection, Drug Enforcement Administration, Secret Service, National Park Service, Bureau of Alcohol, Tobacco and Firearms, Capitol Police, U.S. Courts, Federal Bureau of Prisons, Tennessee Valley Authority, and U.S. Forest Service.

Rate of Federal Law Enforcement Officers in 1998

National Rate = 31 Officers per 100,000 Population*

ALPHA ORDER

RANK	STATE	RATE
38	Alabama	16
4	Alaska	52
1	Arizona	68
15	Arkansas	33
9	California	36
7	Colorado	38
41	Connecticut	13
41	Delaware	13
9	Florida	36
16	Georgia	28
6	Hawaii	44
38	Idaho	16
24	Illinois	23
46	Indiana	11
50	Iowa	4
35	Kansas	17
24	Kentucky	23
26	Louisiana	22
22	Maine	24
20	Maryland	25
33	Massachusetts	18
41	Michigan	13
30	Minnesota	19
35	Mississippi	17
26	Missouri	22
12	Montana	34
41	Nebraska	13
18	Nevada	27
49	New Hampshire	6
19	New Jersey	26
2	New Mexico	57
7	New York	38
41	North Carolina	13
9	North Dakota	36
48	Ohio	9
26	Oklahoma	22
30	Oregon	19
20	Pennsylvania	25
47	Rhode Island	10
35	South Carolina	17
26	South Dakota	22
33	Tennessee	18
3	Texas	56
30	Utah	19
5	Vermont	46
12	Virginia	34
22	Washington	24
16	West Virginia	28
40	Wisconsin	14
12	Wyoming	34

RANK ORDER

RANK	STATE	RATE
1	Arizona	68
2	New Mexico	57
3	Texas	56
4	Alaska	52
5	Vermont	46
6	Hawaii	44
7	Colorado	38
7	New York	38
9	California	36
9	Florida	36
9	North Dakota	36
12	Montana	34
12	Virginia	34
12	Wyoming	34
15	Arkansas	33
16	Georgia	28
16	West Virginia	28
18	Nevada	27
19	New Jersey	26
20	Maryland	25
20	Pennsylvania	25
22	Maine	24
22	Washington	24
24	Illinois	23
24	Kentucky	23
26	Louisiana	22
26	Missouri	22
26	Oklahoma	22
26	South Dakota	22
30	Minnesota	19
30	Oregon	19
30	Utah	19
33	Massachusetts	18
33	Tennessee	18
35	Kansas	17
35	Mississippi	17
35	South Carolina	17
38	Alabama	16
38	Idaho	16
40	Wisconsin	14
41	Connecticut	13
41	Delaware	13
41	Michigan	13
41	Nebraska	13
41	North Carolina	13
46	Indiana	11
47	Rhode Island	10
48	Ohio	9
49	New Hampshire	6
50	Iowa	4
	District of Columbia	1,384

Source: U.S. Department of Justice, Bureau of Justice Statistics
   "Federal Law Enforcement Officers, 1998" (NCJ-177607, March 2000)
*Full-time officers authorized to carry firearms and make arrests. Includes F.B.I., Customs Service, Immigration and Naturalization Service, I.R.S., Postal Inspection, Drug Enforcement Administration, Secret Service, National Park Service, Bureau of Alcohol, Tobacco and Firearms, Capitol Police, U.S. Courts, Federal Bureau of Prisons, Tennessee Valley Authority, and U.S. Forest Service.

State and Local Justice System Employment in 1999

National Total = 1,901,150 Employees*

ALPHA ORDER

RANK	STATE	EMPLOYEES	% of USA
25	Alabama	24,534	1.3%
46	Alaska	4,264	0.2%
16	Arizona	37,964	2.0%
32	Arkansas	14,730	0.8%
1	California	220,607	11.6%
24	Colorado	26,339	1.4%
27	Connecticut	23,057	1.2%
41	Delaware	6,258	0.3%
4	Florida	126,681	6.7%
10	Georgia	57,836	3.0%
38	Hawaii	8,556	0.5%
40	Idaho	7,229	0.4%
5	Illinois	86,611	4.6%
20	Indiana	32,584	1.7%
33	Iowa	14,233	0.7%
30	Kansas	18,224	1.0%
28	Kentucky	21,607	1.1%
17	Louisiana	34,256	1.8%
44	Maine	5,890	0.3%
14	Maryland	38,846	2.0%
13	Massachusetts	41,950	2.2%
9	Michigan	59,017	3.1%
26	Minnesota	23,880	1.3%
31	Mississippi	16,971	0.9%
15	Missouri	38,062	2.0%
45	Montana	4,693	0.2%
37	Nebraska	9,165	0.5%
34	Nevada	14,061	0.7%
43	New Hampshire	6,075	0.3%
8	New Jersey	69,403	3.7%
35	New Mexico	13,724	0.7%
2	New York	175,741	9.2%
11	North Carolina	52,240	2.7%
49	North Dakota	2,964	0.2%
6	Ohio	77,481	4.1%
23	Oklahoma	27,118	1.4%
29	Oregon	20,849	1.1%
7	Pennsylvania	73,946	3.9%
42	Rhode Island	6,089	0.3%
22	South Carolina	27,466	1.4%
47	South Dakota	3,733	0.2%
18	Tennessee	33,717	1.8%
3	Texas	148,226	7.8%
36	Utah	12,027	0.6%
50	Vermont	2,878	0.2%
12	Virginia	46,365	2.4%
19	Washington	32,899	1.7%
39	West Virginia	7,235	0.4%
21	Wisconsin	32,275	1.7%
48	Wyoming	3,209	0.2%

RANK ORDER

RANK	STATE	EMPLOYEES	% of USA
1	California	220,607	11.6%
2	New York	175,741	9.2%
3	Texas	148,226	7.8%
4	Florida	126,681	6.7%
5	Illinois	86,611	4.6%
6	Ohio	77,481	4.1%
7	Pennsylvania	73,946	3.9%
8	New Jersey	69,403	3.7%
9	Michigan	59,017	3.1%
10	Georgia	57,836	3.0%
11	North Carolina	52,240	2.7%
12	Virginia	46,365	2.4%
13	Massachusetts	41,950	2.2%
14	Maryland	38,846	2.0%
15	Missouri	38,062	2.0%
16	Arizona	37,964	2.0%
17	Louisiana	34,256	1.8%
18	Tennessee	33,717	1.8%
19	Washington	32,899	1.7%
20	Indiana	32,584	1.7%
21	Wisconsin	32,275	1.7%
22	South Carolina	27,466	1.4%
23	Oklahoma	27,118	1.4%
24	Colorado	26,339	1.4%
25	Alabama	24,534	1.3%
26	Minnesota	23,880	1.3%
27	Connecticut	23,057	1.2%
28	Kentucky	21,607	1.1%
29	Oregon	20,849	1.1%
30	Kansas	18,224	1.0%
31	Mississippi	16,971	0.9%
32	Arkansas	14,730	0.8%
33	Iowa	14,233	0.7%
34	Nevada	14,061	0.7%
35	New Mexico	13,724	0.7%
36	Utah	12,027	0.6%
37	Nebraska	9,165	0.5%
38	Hawaii	8,556	0.5%
39	West Virginia	7,235	0.4%
40	Idaho	7,229	0.4%
41	Delaware	6,258	0.3%
42	Rhode Island	6,089	0.3%
43	New Hampshire	6,075	0.3%
44	Maine	5,890	0.3%
45	Montana	4,693	0.2%
46	Alaska	4,264	0.2%
47	South Dakota	3,733	0.2%
48	Wyoming	3,209	0.2%
49	North Dakota	2,964	0.2%
50	Vermont	2,878	0.2%
	District of Columbia	7,385	0.4%

Source: U.S. Bureau of the Census, Governments Division
"State and Local Employment and Payroll - March 1999" (http://www.census.gov/govs/www/apesstl99.html)
*Full-time equivalent as of March 1999. Includes police, courts, prosecution, public defense and corrections.

Rate of State and Local Justice System Employment in 1999

National Rate = 69.7 Employees per 10,000 Population*

ALPHA ORDER

RANK	STATE	RATE
38	Alabama	56.1
18	Alaska	68.8
6	Arizona	79.5
35	Arkansas	57.7
25	California	66.6
26	Colorado	64.9
16	Connecticut	70.3
4	Delaware	83.0
3	Florida	83.8
11	Georgia	74.3
13	Hawaii	72.2
34	Idaho	57.8
14	Illinois	71.4
40	Indiana	54.8
46	Iowa	49.6
20	Kansas	68.7
41	Kentucky	54.6
8	Louisiana	78.4
48	Maine	47.0
10	Maryland	75.1
22	Massachusetts	67.9
33	Michigan	59.8
45	Minnesota	50.0
32	Mississippi	61.3
17	Missouri	69.6
42	Montana	53.2
39	Nebraska	55.0
9	Nevada	77.7
44	New Hampshire	50.6
2	New Jersey	85.2
7	New Mexico	78.9
1	New York	96.6
21	North Carolina	68.3
49	North Dakota	46.8
18	Ohio	68.8
5	Oklahoma	80.8
27	Oregon	62.9
28	Pennsylvania	61.7
29	Rhode Island	61.5
15	South Carolina	70.7
43	South Dakota	50.9
29	Tennessee	61.5
12	Texas	73.9
37	Utah	56.5
47	Vermont	48.5
23	Virginia	67.5
36	Washington	57.2
50	West Virginia	40.0
29	Wisconsin	61.5
24	Wyoming	66.9

RANK ORDER

RANK	STATE	RATE
1	New York	96.6
2	New Jersey	85.2
3	Florida	83.8
4	Delaware	83.0
5	Oklahoma	80.8
6	Arizona	79.5
7	New Mexico	78.9
8	Louisiana	78.4
9	Nevada	77.7
10	Maryland	75.1
11	Georgia	74.3
12	Texas	73.9
13	Hawaii	72.2
14	Illinois	71.4
15	South Carolina	70.7
16	Connecticut	70.3
17	Missouri	69.6
18	Alaska	68.8
18	Ohio	68.8
20	Kansas	68.7
21	North Carolina	68.3
22	Massachusetts	67.9
23	Virginia	67.5
24	Wyoming	66.9
25	California	66.6
26	Colorado	64.9
27	Oregon	62.9
28	Pennsylvania	61.7
29	Rhode Island	61.5
29	Tennessee	61.5
29	Wisconsin	61.5
32	Mississippi	61.3
33	Michigan	59.8
34	Idaho	57.8
35	Arkansas	57.7
36	Washington	57.2
37	Utah	56.5
38	Alabama	56.1
39	Nebraska	55.0
40	Indiana	54.8
41	Kentucky	54.6
42	Montana	53.2
43	South Dakota	50.9
44	New Hampshire	50.6
45	Minnesota	50.0
46	Iowa	49.6
47	Vermont	48.5
48	Maine	47.0
49	North Dakota	46.8
50	West Virginia	40.0

District of Columbia	142.3

Source: Morgan Quitno Press using data from U.S. Bureau of the Census, Governments Division
   "State and Local Employment and Payroll - March 1999" (http://www.census.gov/govs/www/apesstl99.html)
*Full-time equivalent as of March 1999. Includes police, courts, prosecution, public defense and corrections.

State and Local Judicial and Legal Employment in 1999

National Total = 373,909 Employees*

ALPHA ORDER

RANK	STATE	EMPLOYEES	% of USA
25	Alabama	4,935	1.3%
42	Alaska	1,311	0.4%
10	Arizona	9,096	2.4%
38	Arkansas	1,820	0.5%
1	California	49,958	13.4%
24	Colorado	5,364	1.4%
27	Connecticut	4,102	1.1%
40	Delaware	1,579	0.4%
3	Florida	27,558	7.4%
11	Georgia	8,937	2.4%
35	Hawaii	2,766	0.7%
41	Idaho	1,383	0.4%
8	Illinois	16,435	4.4%
19	Indiana	5,788	1.5%
32	Iowa	3,196	0.9%
29	Kansas	3,595	1.0%
20	Kentucky	5,742	1.5%
17	Louisiana	6,728	1.8%
46	Maine	840	0.2%
15	Maryland	6,912	1.8%
14	Massachusetts	6,960	1.9%
9	Michigan	11,426	3.1%
21	Minnesota	5,666	1.5%
33	Mississippi	2,910	0.8%
13	Missouri	7,132	1.9%
45	Montana	994	0.3%
39	Nebraska	1,785	0.5%
31	Nevada	3,230	0.9%
44	New Hampshire	1,144	0.3%
5	New Jersey	20,518	5.5%
34	New Mexico	2,887	0.8%
2	New York	29,585	7.9%
18	North Carolina	6,609	1.8%
47	North Dakota	745	0.2%
6	Ohio	19,984	5.3%
28	Oklahoma	3,681	1.0%
26	Oregon	4,642	1.2%
7	Pennsylvania	17,463	4.7%
43	Rhode Island	1,232	0.3%
30	South Carolina	3,456	0.9%
48	South Dakota	741	0.2%
23	Tennessee	5,372	1.4%
4	Texas	21,846	5.8%
36	Utah	2,635	0.7%
50	Vermont	629	0.2%
16	Virginia	6,763	1.8%
12	Washington	7,356	2.0%
37	West Virginia	2,044	0.5%
22	Wisconsin	5,450	1.5%
49	Wyoming	635	0.2%

RANK ORDER

RANK	STATE	EMPLOYEES	% of USA
1	California	49,958	13.4%
2	New York	29,585	7.9%
3	Florida	27,558	7.4%
4	Texas	21,846	5.8%
5	New Jersey	20,518	5.5%
6	Ohio	19,984	5.3%
7	Pennsylvania	17,463	4.7%
8	Illinois	16,435	4.4%
9	Michigan	11,426	3.1%
10	Arizona	9,096	2.4%
11	Georgia	8,937	2.4%
12	Washington	7,356	2.0%
13	Missouri	7,132	1.9%
14	Massachusetts	6,960	1.9%
15	Maryland	6,912	1.8%
16	Virginia	6,763	1.8%
17	Louisiana	6,728	1.8%
18	North Carolina	6,609	1.8%
19	Indiana	5,788	1.5%
20	Kentucky	5,742	1.5%
21	Minnesota	5,666	1.5%
22	Wisconsin	5,450	1.5%
23	Tennessee	5,372	1.4%
24	Colorado	5,364	1.4%
25	Alabama	4,935	1.3%
26	Oregon	4,642	1.2%
27	Connecticut	4,102	1.1%
28	Oklahoma	3,681	1.0%
29	Kansas	3,595	1.0%
30	South Carolina	3,456	0.9%
31	Nevada	3,230	0.9%
32	Iowa	3,196	0.9%
33	Mississippi	2,910	0.8%
34	New Mexico	2,887	0.8%
35	Hawaii	2,766	0.7%
36	Utah	2,635	0.7%
37	West Virginia	2,044	0.5%
38	Arkansas	1,820	0.5%
39	Nebraska	1,785	0.5%
40	Delaware	1,579	0.4%
41	Idaho	1,383	0.4%
42	Alaska	1,311	0.4%
43	Rhode Island	1,232	0.3%
44	New Hampshire	1,144	0.3%
45	Montana	994	0.3%
46	Maine	840	0.2%
47	North Dakota	745	0.2%
48	South Dakota	741	0.2%
49	Wyoming	635	0.2%
50	Vermont	629	0.2%
	District of Columbia	344	0.1%

Source: U.S. Bureau of the Census, Governments Division
   "State and Local Employment and Payroll - March 1999" (http://www.census.gov/govs/www/apesstl99.html)
*Full-time equivalent as of March 1999. Includes courts, prosecution and public defense.

Rate of State and Local Judicial and Legal Employment in 1999

National Rate = 13.7 Employees per 10,000 Population*

ALPHA ORDER

RANK	STATE	RATE
30	Alabama	11.3
3	Alaska	21.2
5	Arizona	19.0
49	Arkansas	7.1
12	California	15.1
19	Colorado	13.2
23	Connecticut	12.5
4	Delaware	21.0
6	Florida	18.2
29	Georgia	11.5
2	Hawaii	23.3
35	Idaho	11.0
16	Illinois	13.6
45	Indiana	9.7
34	Iowa	11.1
17	Kansas	13.5
14	Kentucky	14.5
11	Louisiana	15.4
50	Maine	6.7
18	Maryland	13.4
30	Massachusetts	11.3
28	Michigan	11.6
26	Minnesota	11.9
40	Mississippi	10.5
21	Missouri	13.0
30	Montana	11.3
38	Nebraska	10.7
7	Nevada	17.9
46	New Hampshire	9.5
1	New Jersey	25.2
9	New Mexico	16.6
10	New York	16.3
48	North Carolina	8.6
27	North Dakota	11.8
8	Ohio	17.8
35	Oklahoma	11.0
15	Oregon	14.0
13	Pennsylvania	14.6
24	Rhode Island	12.4
47	South Carolina	8.9
42	South Dakota	10.1
43	Tennessee	9.8
37	Texas	10.9
24	Utah	12.4
39	Vermont	10.6
43	Virginia	9.8
22	Washington	12.8
30	West Virginia	11.3
41	Wisconsin	10.4
19	Wyoming	13.2

RANK ORDER

RANK	STATE	RATE
1	New Jersey	25.2
2	Hawaii	23.3
3	Alaska	21.2
4	Delaware	21.0
5	Arizona	19.0
6	Florida	18.2
7	Nevada	17.9
8	Ohio	17.8
9	New Mexico	16.6
10	New York	16.3
11	Louisiana	15.4
12	California	15.1
13	Pennsylvania	14.6
14	Kentucky	14.5
15	Oregon	14.0
16	Illinois	13.6
17	Kansas	13.5
18	Maryland	13.4
19	Colorado	13.2
19	Wyoming	13.2
21	Missouri	13.0
22	Washington	12.8
23	Connecticut	12.5
24	Rhode Island	12.4
24	Utah	12.4
26	Minnesota	11.9
27	North Dakota	11.8
28	Michigan	11.6
29	Georgia	11.5
30	Alabama	11.3
30	Massachusetts	11.3
30	Montana	11.3
30	West Virginia	11.3
34	Iowa	11.1
35	Idaho	11.0
35	Oklahoma	11.0
37	Texas	10.9
38	Nebraska	10.7
39	Vermont	10.6
40	Mississippi	10.5
41	Wisconsin	10.4
42	South Dakota	10.1
43	Tennessee	9.8
43	Virginia	9.8
45	Indiana	9.7
46	New Hampshire	9.5
47	South Carolina	8.9
48	North Carolina	8.6
49	Arkansas	7.1
50	Maine	6.7

District of Columbia — 6.6

Source: Morgan Quitno Press using data from U.S. Bureau of the Census, Governments Division
"State and Local Employment and Payroll - March 1999" (http://www.census.gov/govs/www/apesstl99.html)
*Full-time equivalent as of March 1999. Includes courts, prosecution and public defense.

State and Local Police Officers in 1999

National Total = 638,305 Officers*

ALPHA ORDER

RANK	STATE	OFFICERS	% of USA
21	Alabama	9,728	1.5%
49	Alaska	976	0.2%
16	Arizona	12,717	2.0%
32	Arkansas	5,827	0.9%
2	California	63,648	10.0%
24	Colorado	8,875	1.4%
25	Connecticut	8,054	1.3%
44	Delaware	1,645	0.3%
4	Florida	36,001	5.6%
11	Georgia	18,592	2.9%
39	Hawaii	2,688	0.4%
42	Idaho	2,304	0.4%
5	Illinois	33,958	5.3%
20	Indiana	11,496	1.8%
33	Iowa	5,108	0.8%
29	Kansas	6,627	1.0%
28	Kentucky	7,098	1.1%
19	Louisiana	11,627	1.8%
43	Maine	2,272	0.4%
13	Maryland	13,496	2.1%
10	Massachusetts	18,715	2.9%
9	Michigan	19,335	3.0%
26	Minnesota	7,949	1.2%
30	Mississippi	6,051	0.9%
17	Missouri	12,090	1.9%
45	Montana	1,460	0.2%
37	Nebraska	3,278	0.5%
34	Nevada	3,909	0.6%
40	New Hampshire	2,463	0.4%
8	New Jersey	24,039	3.8%
35	New Mexico	3,874	0.6%
1	New York	73,349	11.5%
12	North Carolina	18,079	2.8%
47	North Dakota	1,127	0.2%
7	Ohio	24,239	3.8%
27	Oklahoma	7,882	1.2%
31	Oregon	5,912	0.9%
6	Pennsylvania	24,431	3.8%
41	Rhode Island	2,380	0.4%
23	South Carolina	9,602	1.5%
46	South Dakota	1,250	0.2%
15	Tennessee	13,169	2.1%
3	Texas	44,134	6.9%
36	Utah	3,824	0.6%
50	Vermont	944	0.1%
14	Virginia	13,356	2.1%
22	Washington	9,700	1.5%
38	West Virginia	2,850	0.4%
18	Wisconsin	11,668	1.8%
48	Wyoming	1,037	0.2%

RANK ORDER

RANK	STATE	OFFICERS	% of USA
1	New York	73,349	11.5%
2	California	63,648	10.0%
3	Texas	44,134	6.9%
4	Florida	36,001	5.6%
5	Illinois	33,958	5.3%
6	Pennsylvania	24,431	3.8%
7	Ohio	24,239	3.8%
8	New Jersey	24,039	3.8%
9	Michigan	19,335	3.0%
10	Massachusetts	18,715	2.9%
11	Georgia	18,592	2.9%
12	North Carolina	18,079	2.8%
13	Maryland	13,496	2.1%
14	Virginia	13,356	2.1%
15	Tennessee	13,169	2.1%
16	Arizona	12,717	2.0%
17	Missouri	12,090	1.9%
18	Wisconsin	11,668	1.8%
19	Louisiana	11,627	1.8%
20	Indiana	11,496	1.8%
21	Alabama	9,728	1.5%
22	Washington	9,700	1.5%
23	South Carolina	9,602	1.5%
24	Colorado	8,875	1.4%
25	Connecticut	8,054	1.3%
26	Minnesota	7,949	1.2%
27	Oklahoma	7,882	1.2%
28	Kentucky	7,098	1.1%
29	Kansas	6,627	1.0%
30	Mississippi	6,051	0.9%
31	Oregon	5,912	0.9%
32	Arkansas	5,827	0.9%
33	Iowa	5,108	0.8%
34	Nevada	3,909	0.6%
35	New Mexico	3,874	0.6%
36	Utah	3,824	0.6%
37	Nebraska	3,278	0.5%
38	West Virginia	2,850	0.4%
39	Hawaii	2,688	0.4%
40	New Hampshire	2,463	0.4%
41	Rhode Island	2,380	0.4%
42	Idaho	2,304	0.4%
43	Maine	2,272	0.4%
44	Delaware	1,645	0.3%
45	Montana	1,460	0.2%
46	South Dakota	1,250	0.2%
47	North Dakota	1,127	0.2%
48	Wyoming	1,037	0.2%
49	Alaska	976	0.2%
50	Vermont	944	0.1%
	District of Columbia	3,472	0.5%

Source: U.S. Bureau of the Census, Governments Division
"State and Local Employment and Payroll - March 1999" (http://www.census.gov/govs/www/apesstl99.html)
*Full-time equivalent as of March 1999. Does not include employees of police departments who are not officers.

Rate of State and Local Police Officers in 1999

National Rate = 23.4 Officers per 10,000 Population*

ALPHA ORDER

RANK	STATE	RATE
19	Alabama	22.3
49	Alaska	15.8
5	Arizona	26.6
17	Arkansas	22.8
36	California	19.2
24	Colorado	21.9
10	Connecticut	24.5
26	Delaware	21.8
14	Florida	23.8
13	Georgia	23.9
18	Hawaii	22.7
37	Idaho	18.4
4	Illinois	28.0
35	Indiana	19.3
41	Iowa	17.8
8	Kansas	25.0
40	Kentucky	17.9
5	Louisiana	26.6
38	Maine	18.1
7	Maryland	26.1
2	Massachusetts	30.3
33	Michigan	19.6
46	Minnesota	16.6
24	Mississippi	21.9
22	Missouri	22.1
47	Montana	16.5
32	Nebraska	19.7
27	Nevada	21.6
30	New Hampshire	20.5
3	New Jersey	29.5
19	New Mexico	22.3
1	New York	40.3
15	North Carolina	23.6
41	North Dakota	17.8
29	Ohio	21.5
16	Oklahoma	23.5
41	Oregon	17.8
31	Pennsylvania	20.4
11	Rhode Island	24.0
9	South Carolina	24.7
44	South Dakota	17.1
11	Tennessee	24.0
23	Texas	22.0
39	Utah	18.0
48	Vermont	15.9
34	Virginia	19.4
45	Washington	16.9
49	West Virginia	15.8
21	Wisconsin	22.2
27	Wyoming	21.6

RANK ORDER

RANK	STATE	RATE
1	New York	40.3
2	Massachusetts	30.3
3	New Jersey	29.5
4	Illinois	28.0
5	Arizona	26.6
5	Louisiana	26.6
7	Maryland	26.1
8	Kansas	25.0
9	South Carolina	24.7
10	Connecticut	24.5
11	Rhode Island	24.0
11	Tennessee	24.0
13	Georgia	23.9
14	Florida	23.8
15	North Carolina	23.6
16	Oklahoma	23.5
17	Arkansas	22.8
18	Hawaii	22.7
19	Alabama	22.3
19	New Mexico	22.3
21	Wisconsin	22.2
22	Missouri	22.1
23	Texas	22.0
24	Colorado	21.9
24	Mississippi	21.9
26	Delaware	21.8
27	Nevada	21.6
27	Wyoming	21.6
29	Ohio	21.5
30	New Hampshire	20.5
31	Pennsylvania	20.4
32	Nebraska	19.7
33	Michigan	19.6
34	Virginia	19.4
35	Indiana	19.3
36	California	19.2
37	Idaho	18.4
38	Maine	18.1
39	Utah	18.0
40	Kentucky	17.9
41	Iowa	17.8
41	North Dakota	17.8
41	Oregon	17.8
44	South Dakota	17.1
45	Washington	16.9
46	Minnesota	16.6
47	Montana	16.5
48	Vermont	15.9
49	Alaska	15.8
49	West Virginia	15.8
	District of Columbia	66.9

Source: Morgan Quitno Press using data from U.S. Bureau of the Census, Governments Division
"State and Local Employment and Payroll - March 1999" (http://www.census.gov/govs/www/apesstl99.html)
*Full-time equivalent as of March 1999. Does not include employees of police departments who are not officers.

Law Enforcement Agencies in 1996

National Total = 18,769 Agencies*

ALPHA ORDER

RANK	STATE	AGENCIES	% of USA
16	Alabama	432	2.3%
45	Alaska	69	0.4%
40	Arizona	130	0.7%
24	Arkansas	360	1.9%
12	California	524	2.8%
31	Colorado	247	1.3%
41	Connecticut	129	0.7%
49	Delaware	45	0.2%
20	Florida	385	2.1%
8	Georgia	581	3.1%
50	Hawaii	7	0.0%
43	Idaho	124	0.7%
3	Illinois	963	5.1%
11	Indiana	547	2.9%
17	Iowa	426	2.3%
22	Kansas	369	2.0%
18	Kentucky	391	2.1%
23	Louisiana	365	1.9%
37	Maine	141	0.8%
35	Maryland	147	0.8%
19	Massachusetts	390	2.1%
7	Michigan	588	3.1%
14	Minnesota	486	2.6%
26	Mississippi	317	1.7%
5	Missouri	647	3.4%
41	Montana	129	0.7%
28	Nebraska	266	1.4%
47	Nevada	58	0.3%
32	New Hampshire	233	1.2%
10	New Jersey	554	3.0%
38	New Mexico	140	0.7%
6	New York	598	3.2%
13	North Carolina	503	2.7%
36	North Dakota	142	0.8%
4	Ohio	938	5.0%
15	Oklahoma	459	2.4%
34	Oregon	184	1.0%
2	Pennsylvania	1,298	6.9%
48	Rhode Island	51	0.3%
29	South Carolina	264	1.4%
33	South Dakota	191	1.0%
21	Tennessee	374	2.0%
1	Texas	1,861	9.9%
39	Utah	138	0.7%
45	Vermont	69	0.4%
25	Virginia	330	1.8%
27	Washington	277	1.5%
30	West Virginia	250	1.3%
9	Wisconsin	567	3.0%
44	Wyoming	82	0.4%

RANK ORDER

RANK	STATE	AGENCIES	% of USA
1	Texas	1,861	9.9%
2	Pennsylvania	1,298	6.9%
3	Illinois	963	5.1%
4	Ohio	938	5.0%
5	Missouri	647	3.4%
6	New York	598	3.2%
7	Michigan	588	3.1%
8	Georgia	581	3.1%
9	Wisconsin	567	3.0%
10	New Jersey	554	3.0%
11	Indiana	547	2.9%
12	California	524	2.8%
13	North Carolina	503	2.7%
14	Minnesota	486	2.6%
15	Oklahoma	459	2.4%
16	Alabama	432	2.3%
17	Iowa	426	2.3%
18	Kentucky	391	2.1%
19	Massachusetts	390	2.1%
20	Florida	385	2.1%
21	Tennessee	374	2.0%
22	Kansas	369	2.0%
23	Louisiana	365	1.9%
24	Arkansas	360	1.9%
25	Virginia	330	1.8%
26	Mississippi	317	1.7%
27	Washington	277	1.5%
28	Nebraska	266	1.4%
29	South Carolina	264	1.4%
30	West Virginia	250	1.3%
31	Colorado	247	1.3%
32	New Hampshire	233	1.2%
33	South Dakota	191	1.0%
34	Oregon	184	1.0%
35	Maryland	147	0.8%
36	North Dakota	142	0.8%
37	Maine	141	0.8%
38	New Mexico	140	0.7%
39	Utah	138	0.7%
40	Arizona	130	0.7%
41	Connecticut	129	0.7%
41	Montana	129	0.7%
43	Idaho	124	0.7%
44	Wyoming	82	0.4%
45	Alaska	69	0.4%
45	Vermont	69	0.4%
47	Nevada	58	0.3%
48	Rhode Island	51	0.3%
49	Delaware	45	0.2%
50	Hawaii	7	0.0%
	District of Columbia	3	0.0%

Source: U.S. Department of Justice, Bureau of Justice Statistics
"Census of State and Local Law Enforcement Agencies, 1996" (Bulletin, June 1998, NCJ-164618)
*Includes state and local police, sheriffs' departments and special police agencies.

Population per Law Enforcement Agency in 1996

National Rate = 14,134 Population per Agency*

ALPHA ORDER

RANK	STATE	RATE
30	Alabama	9,891
36	Alaska	8,797
5	Arizona	34,062
42	Arkansas	6,972
2	California	60,836
16	Colorado	15,476
8	Connecticut	25,382
14	Delaware	16,108
3	Florida	37,403
22	Georgia	12,656
1	Hawaii	169,103
31	Idaho	9,591
23	Illinois	12,302
27	Indiana	10,677
45	Iowa	6,694
43	Kansas	6,971
29	Kentucky	9,933
25	Louisiana	11,919
35	Maine	8,818
4	Maryland	34,501
15	Massachusetts	15,621
13	Michigan	16,317
32	Minnesota	9,584
37	Mississippi	8,568
39	Missouri	8,282
44	Montana	6,817
46	Nebraska	6,211
7	Nevada	27,641
48	New Hampshire	4,989
19	New Jersey	14,419
24	New Mexico	12,239
6	New York	30,409
17	North Carolina	14,558
49	North Dakota	4,532
26	Ohio	11,911
41	Oklahoma	7,192
12	Oregon	17,412
33	Pennsylvania	9,288
11	Rhode Island	19,416
21	South Carolina	14,010
50	South Dakota	3,835
20	Tennessee	14,224
28	Texas	10,278
18	Utah	14,496
38	Vermont	8,531
9	Virginia	20,229
10	Washington	19,975
40	West Virginia	7,303
34	Wisconsin	9,100
47	Wyoming	5,871

RANK ORDER

RANK	STATE	RATE
1	Hawaii	169,103
2	California	60,836
3	Florida	37,403
4	Maryland	34,501
5	Arizona	34,062
6	New York	30,409
7	Nevada	27,641
8	Connecticut	25,382
9	Virginia	20,229
10	Washington	19,975
11	Rhode Island	19,416
12	Oregon	17,412
13	Michigan	16,317
14	Delaware	16,108
15	Massachusetts	15,621
16	Colorado	15,476
17	North Carolina	14,558
18	Utah	14,496
19	New Jersey	14,419
20	Tennessee	14,224
21	South Carolina	14,010
22	Georgia	12,656
23	Illinois	12,302
24	New Mexico	12,239
25	Louisiana	11,919
26	Ohio	11,911
27	Indiana	10,677
28	Texas	10,278
29	Kentucky	9,933
30	Alabama	9,891
31	Idaho	9,591
32	Minnesota	9,584
33	Pennsylvania	9,288
34	Wisconsin	9,100
35	Maine	8,818
36	Alaska	8,797
37	Mississippi	8,568
38	Vermont	8,531
39	Missouri	8,282
40	West Virginia	7,303
41	Oklahoma	7,192
42	Arkansas	6,972
43	Kansas	6,971
44	Montana	6,817
45	Iowa	6,694
46	Nebraska	6,211
47	Wyoming	5,871
48	New Hampshire	4,989
49	North Dakota	4,532
50	South Dakota	3,835

District of Columbia   181,071

*Source: Morgan Quitno Press using data from U.S. Department of Justice, Bureau of Justice Statistics
"Census of State and Local Law Enforcement Agencies, 1996" (Bulletin, June 1998, NCJ-164618)*
Includes state and local police, sheriffs' departments and special police agencies.

Law Enforcement Agencies per 1,000 Square Miles in 1996

National Rate = 5.0 Agencies per 1,000 Square Miles*

ALPHA ORDER

RANK ORDER

RANK	STATE	RATE		RANK	STATE	RATE
21	Alabama	8.3		1	New Jersey	67.4
50	Alaska	0.1		2	Massachusetts	42.2
45	Arizona	1.1		3	Rhode Island	41.4
27	Arkansas	6.8		4	Pennsylvania	28.2
37	California	3.3		5	New Hampshire	25.1
39	Colorado	2.4		6	Connecticut	23.3
6	Connecticut	23.3		7	Ohio	20.9
8	Delaware	18.8		8	Delaware	18.8
30	Florida	6.4		9	Illinois	16.6
14	Georgia	9.9		10	Indiana	15.0
45	Hawaii	1.1		11	Maryland	12.0
43	Idaho	1.5		12	New York	11.1
9	Illinois	16.6		13	West Virginia	10.3
10	Indiana	15.0		14	Georgia	9.9
23	Iowa	7.6		15	Kentucky	9.7
33	Kansas	4.5		16	North Carolina	9.5
15	Kentucky	9.7		17	Missouri	9.3
24	Louisiana	7.4		18	Tennessee	8.9
34	Maine	4.2		19	Wisconsin	8.7
11	Maryland	12.0		20	South Carolina	8.5
2	Massachusetts	42.2		21	Alabama	8.3
31	Michigan	6.1		22	Virginia	7.8
32	Minnesota	5.6		23	Iowa	7.6
28	Mississippi	6.6		24	Louisiana	7.4
17	Missouri	9.3		25	Vermont	7.2
47	Montana	0.9		26	Texas	7.0
36	Nebraska	3.4		27	Arkansas	6.8
49	Nevada	0.5		28	Mississippi	6.6
5	New Hampshire	25.1		28	Oklahoma	6.6
1	New Jersey	67.4		30	Florida	6.4
44	New Mexico	1.2		31	Michigan	6.1
12	New York	11.1		32	Minnesota	5.6
16	North Carolina	9.5		33	Kansas	4.5
40	North Dakota	2.0		34	Maine	4.2
7	Ohio	20.9		35	Washington	3.9
28	Oklahoma	6.6		36	Nebraska	3.4
41	Oregon	1.9		37	California	3.3
4	Pennsylvania	28.2		38	South Dakota	2.5
3	Rhode Island	41.4		39	Colorado	2.4
20	South Carolina	8.5		40	North Dakota	2.0
38	South Dakota	2.5		41	Oregon	1.9
18	Tennessee	8.9		42	Utah	1.6
26	Texas	7.0		43	Idaho	1.5
42	Utah	1.6		44	New Mexico	1.2
25	Vermont	7.2		45	Arizona	1.1
22	Virginia	7.8		45	Hawaii	1.1
35	Washington	3.9		47	Montana	0.9
13	West Virginia	10.3		48	Wyoming	0.8
19	Wisconsin	8.7		49	Nevada	0.5
48	Wyoming	0.8		50	Alaska	0.1
					District of Columbia**	NA

Source: Morgan Quitno Press using data from U.S. Department of Justice, Bureau of Justice Statistics
    "Census of State and Local Law Enforcement Agencies, 1996" (Bulletin, June 1998, NCJ-164618)
*Includes state and local police, sheriffs' departments and special police agencies.
**The District of Columbia has three agencies for its 68 square miles.

Full-Time Sworn Officers in Law Enforcement Agencies in 1996

National Total = 663,535 Officers*

ALPHA ORDER

RANK	STATE	OFFICERS	% of USA
22	Alabama	9,767	1.5%
48	Alaska	1,254	0.2%
20	Arizona	10,088	1.5%
31	Arkansas	5,819	0.9%
2	California	69,134	10.4%
21	Colorado	9,896	1.5%
25	Connecticut	8,525	1.3%
45	Delaware	1,660	0.3%
5	Florida	37,395	5.6%
10	Georgia	19,115	2.9%
38	Hawaii	2,989	0.5%
40	Idaho	2,524	0.4%
4	Illinois	38,192	5.8%
19	Indiana	10,931	1.6%
33	Iowa	5,043	0.8%
29	Kansas	6,183	0.9%
28	Kentucky	6,466	1.0%
14	Louisiana	16,125	2.4%
42	Maine	2,318	0.3%
15	Maryland	13,828	2.1%
12	Massachusetts	17,935	2.7%
9	Michigan	20,568	3.1%
26	Minnesota	7,994	1.2%
32	Mississippi	5,813	0.9%
16	Missouri	12,998	2.0%
44	Montana	1,682	0.3%
37	Nebraska	3,297	0.5%
34	Nevada	4,363	0.7%
43	New Hampshire	2,305	0.3%
6	New Jersey	28,058	4.2%
35	New Mexico	4,134	0.6%
1	New York	71,221	10.7%
13	North Carolina	16,953	2.6%
49	North Dakota	1,141	0.2%
8	Ohio	23,811	3.6%
27	Oklahoma	7,232	1.1%
30	Oregon	6,064	0.9%
7	Pennsylvania	24,873	3.7%
41	Rhode Island	2,422	0.4%
24	South Carolina	8,675	1.3%
46	South Dakota	1,464	0.2%
18	Tennessee	12,152	1.8%
3	Texas	47,767	7.2%
36	Utah	3,699	0.6%
50	Vermont	981	0.1%
11	Virginia	18,448	2.8%
23	Washington	9,292	1.4%
39	West Virginia	2,977	0.4%
17	Wisconsin	12,678	1.9%
47	Wyoming	1,377	0.2%

RANK ORDER

RANK	STATE	OFFICERS	% of USA
1	New York	71,221	10.7%
2	California	69,134	10.4%
3	Texas	47,767	7.2%
4	Illinois	38,192	5.8%
5	Florida	37,395	5.6%
6	New Jersey	28,058	4.2%
7	Pennsylvania	24,873	3.7%
8	Ohio	23,811	3.6%
9	Michigan	20,568	3.1%
10	Georgia	19,115	2.9%
11	Virginia	18,448	2.8%
12	Massachusetts	17,935	2.7%
13	North Carolina	16,953	2.6%
14	Louisiana	16,125	2.4%
15	Maryland	13,828	2.1%
16	Missouri	12,998	2.0%
17	Wisconsin	12,678	1.9%
18	Tennessee	12,152	1.8%
19	Indiana	10,931	1.6%
20	Arizona	10,088	1.5%
21	Colorado	9,896	1.5%
22	Alabama	9,767	1.5%
23	Washington	9,292	1.4%
24	South Carolina	8,675	1.3%
25	Connecticut	8,525	1.3%
26	Minnesota	7,994	1.2%
27	Oklahoma	7,232	1.1%
28	Kentucky	6,466	1.0%
29	Kansas	6,183	0.9%
30	Oregon	6,064	0.9%
31	Arkansas	5,819	0.9%
32	Mississippi	5,813	0.9%
33	Iowa	5,043	0.8%
34	Nevada	4,363	0.7%
35	New Mexico	4,134	0.6%
36	Utah	3,699	0.6%
37	Nebraska	3,297	0.5%
38	Hawaii	2,989	0.5%
39	West Virginia	2,977	0.4%
40	Idaho	2,524	0.4%
41	Rhode Island	2,422	0.4%
42	Maine	2,318	0.3%
43	New Hampshire	2,305	0.3%
44	Montana	1,682	0.3%
45	Delaware	1,660	0.3%
46	South Dakota	1,464	0.2%
47	Wyoming	1,377	0.2%
48	Alaska	1,254	0.2%
49	North Dakota	1,141	0.2%
50	Vermont	981	0.1%
	District of Columbia	3,909	0.6%

Source: U.S. Department of Justice, Bureau of Justice Statistics
"Census of State and Local Law Enforcement Agencies, 1996" (Bulletin, June 1998, NCJ-164618)
*Includes state and local police, sheriffs' departments and special police agencies.

Percent of Full-Time Law Enforcement Agency Employees
Who are Sworn Officers: 1996
National Percent = 72.0% of Employees are Sworn Officers*

ALPHA ORDER

RANK	STATE	PERCENT
34	Alabama	67.9
40	Alaska	66.6
50	Arizona	59.9
22	Arkansas	73.1
41	California	66.5
29	Colorado	70.7
2	Connecticut	82.6
10	Delaware	77.8
49	Florida	61.5
36	Georgia	67.8
6	Hawaii	79.8
33	Idaho	68.7
12	Illinois	76.0
39	Indiana	66.7
17	Iowa	74.2
28	Kansas	70.8
13	Kentucky	75.7
3	Louisiana	81.4
44	Maine	65.6
15	Maryland	75.2
19	Massachusetts	73.4
16	Michigan	74.8
30	Minnesota	70.6
37	Mississippi	67.7
27	Missouri	72.7
42	Montana	66.2
25	Nebraska	72.8
31	Nevada	70.0
9	New Hampshire	78.0
5	New Jersey	80.3
38	New Mexico	66.9
4	New York	80.6
24	North Carolina	72.9
17	North Dakota	74.2
25	Ohio	72.8
32	Oklahoma	68.9
34	Oregon	67.9
1	Pennsylvania	84.3
8	Rhode Island	78.2
14	South Carolina	75.5
48	South Dakota	62.0
46	Tennessee	64.8
45	Texas	65.3
21	Utah	73.2
19	Vermont	73.4
6	Virginia	79.8
43	Washington	66.1
22	West Virginia	73.1
11	Wisconsin	76.9
47	Wyoming	64.1

RANK ORDER

RANK	STATE	PERCENT
1	Pennsylvania	84.3
2	Connecticut	82.6
3	Louisiana	81.4
4	New York	80.6
5	New Jersey	80.3
6	Hawaii	79.8
6	Virginia	79.8
8	Rhode Island	78.2
9	New Hampshire	78.0
10	Delaware	77.8
11	Wisconsin	76.9
12	Illinois	76.0
13	Kentucky	75.7
14	South Carolina	75.5
15	Maryland	75.2
16	Michigan	74.8
17	Iowa	74.2
17	North Dakota	74.2
19	Massachusetts	73.4
19	Vermont	73.4
21	Utah	73.2
22	Arkansas	73.1
22	West Virginia	73.1
24	North Carolina	72.9
25	Nebraska	72.8
25	Ohio	72.8
27	Missouri	72.7
28	Kansas	70.8
29	Colorado	70.7
30	Minnesota	70.6
31	Nevada	70.0
32	Oklahoma	68.9
33	Idaho	68.7
34	Alabama	67.9
34	Oregon	67.9
36	Georgia	67.8
37	Mississippi	67.7
38	New Mexico	66.9
39	Indiana	66.7
40	Alaska	66.6
41	California	66.5
42	Montana	66.2
43	Washington	66.1
44	Maine	65.6
45	Texas	65.3
46	Tennessee	64.8
47	Wyoming	64.1
48	South Dakota	62.0
49	Florida	61.5
50	Arizona	59.9

| | District of Columbia | 84.0 |

Source: Morgan Quitno Press using data from U.S. Department of Justice, Bureau of Justice Statistics
"Census of State and Local Law Enforcement Agencies, 1996" (Bulletin, June 1998, NCJ-164618)
*Includes state and local police, sheriffs' departments and special police agencies.

Rate of Full-Time Sworn Officers in Law Enforcement Agencies in 1996

National Rate = 25 Officers per 10,000 Population*

ALPHA ORDER

RANK ORDER

RANK	STATE	RATE
21	Alabama	23
30	Alaska	21
21	Arizona	23
21	Arkansas	23
28	California	22
10	Colorado	26
10	Connecticut	26
21	Delaware	23
10	Florida	26
10	Georgia	26
14	Hawaii	25
30	Idaho	21
4	Illinois	32
39	Indiana	19
43	Iowa	18
17	Kansas	24
46	Kentucky	17
2	Louisiana	37
39	Maine	19
8	Maryland	27
5	Massachusetts	29
30	Michigan	21
46	Minnesota	17
30	Mississippi	21
17	Missouri	24
39	Montana	19
36	Nebraska	20
8	Nevada	27
36	New Hampshire	20
3	New Jersey	35
17	New Mexico	24
1	New York	39
21	North Carolina	23
43	North Dakota	18
30	Ohio	21
28	Oklahoma	22
39	Oregon	19
30	Pennsylvania	21
17	Rhode Island	24
21	South Carolina	23
36	South Dakota	20
21	Tennessee	23
14	Texas	25
43	Utah	18
46	Vermont	17
7	Virginia	28
46	Washington	17
50	West Virginia	16
14	Wisconsin	25
5	Wyoming	29

RANK	STATE	RATE
1	New York	39
2	Louisiana	37
3	New Jersey	35
4	Illinois	32
5	Massachusetts	29
5	Wyoming	29
7	Virginia	28
8	Maryland	27
8	Nevada	27
10	Colorado	26
10	Connecticut	26
10	Florida	26
10	Georgia	26
14	Hawaii	25
14	Texas	25
14	Wisconsin	25
17	Kansas	24
17	Missouri	24
17	New Mexico	24
17	Rhode Island	24
21	Alabama	23
21	Arizona	23
21	Arkansas	23
21	Delaware	23
21	North Carolina	23
21	South Carolina	23
21	Tennessee	23
28	California	22
28	Oklahoma	22
30	Alaska	21
30	Idaho	21
30	Michigan	21
30	Mississippi	21
30	Ohio	21
30	Pennsylvania	21
36	Nebraska	20
36	New Hampshire	20
36	South Dakota	20
39	Indiana	19
39	Maine	19
39	Montana	19
39	Oregon	19
43	Iowa	18
43	North Dakota	18
43	Utah	18
46	Kentucky	17
46	Minnesota	17
46	Vermont	17
46	Washington	17
50	West Virginia	16

District of Columbia   72

Source: Morgan Quitno Press using data from U.S. Department of Justice, Bureau of Justice Statistics
"Census of State and Local Law Enforcement Agencies, 1996" (Bulletin, June 1998, NCJ-164618)
*Includes state and local police, sheriffs' departments and special police agencies.

Full-Time Sworn Law Enforcement Officers per 1,000 Square Miles in 1996

National Rate = 178 Officers per 1,000 Square Miles*

<u>ALPHA ORDER</u>

RANK	STATE	RATE
24	Alabama	187
50	Alaska	2
37	Arizona	88
31	Arkansas	109
14	California	435
34	Colorado	95
4	Connecticut	1,538
7	Delaware	693
9	Florida	624
16	Georgia	324
12	Hawaii	463
45	Idaho	30
8	Illinois	659
18	Indiana	300
36	Iowa	90
38	Kansas	75
27	Kentucky	160
15	Louisiana	325
39	Maine	69
6	Maryland	1,125
3	Massachusetts	1,941
22	Michigan	213
35	Minnesota	92
30	Mississippi	120
25	Missouri	186
49	Montana	11
42	Nebraska	43
43	Nevada	39
21	New Hampshire	248
1	New Jersey	3,415
44	New Mexico	34
5	New York	1,319
17	North Carolina	322
47	North Dakota	16
11	Ohio	531
32	Oklahoma	103
40	Oregon	62
10	Pennsylvania	540
2	Rhode Island	1,968
20	South Carolina	278
46	South Dakota	19
19	Tennessee	288
26	Texas	179
41	Utah	44
33	Vermont	102
13	Virginia	436
28	Washington	132
29	West Virginia	123
23	Wisconsin	194
48	Wyoming	14

<u>RANK ORDER</u>

RANK	STATE	RATE
1	New Jersey	3,415
2	Rhode Island	1,968
3	Massachusetts	1,941
4	Connecticut	1,538
5	New York	1,319
6	Maryland	1,125
7	Delaware	693
8	Illinois	659
9	Florida	624
10	Pennsylvania	540
11	Ohio	531
12	Hawaii	463
13	Virginia	436
14	California	435
15	Louisiana	325
16	Georgia	324
17	North Carolina	322
18	Indiana	300
19	Tennessee	288
20	South Carolina	278
21	New Hampshire	248
22	Michigan	213
23	Wisconsin	194
24	Alabama	187
25	Missouri	186
26	Texas	179
27	Kentucky	160
28	Washington	132
29	West Virginia	123
30	Mississippi	120
31	Arkansas	109
32	Oklahoma	103
33	Vermont	102
34	Colorado	95
35	Minnesota	92
36	Iowa	90
37	Arizona	88
38	Kansas	75
39	Maine	69
40	Oregon	62
41	Utah	44
42	Nebraska	43
43	Nevada	39
44	New Mexico	34
45	Idaho	30
46	South Dakota	19
47	North Dakota	16
48	Wyoming	14
49	Montana	11
50	Alaska	2
	District of Columbia**	NA

Source: Morgan Quitno Press using data from U.S. Department of Justice, Bureau of Justice Statistics
"Census of State and Local Law Enforcement Agencies, 1996" (Bulletin, June 1998, NCJ-164618)
*Includes state and local police, sheriffs' departments and special police agencies.
**The District of Columbia has 3,909 sworn officers for its 68 square miles.

Full-Time Employees in Law Enforcement Agencies in 1996

National Total = 921,978 Employees*

ALPHA ORDER

RANK	STATE	EMPLOYEES	% of USA
21	Alabama	14,389	1.6%
48	Alaska	1,884	0.2%
18	Arizona	16,828	1.8%
32	Arkansas	7,958	0.9%
1	California	103,967	11.3%
23	Colorado	14,002	1.5%
27	Connecticut	10,319	1.1%
47	Delaware	2,134	0.2%
4	Florida	60,808	6.6%
9	Georgia	28,204	3.1%
39	Hawaii	3,745	0.4%
40	Idaho	3,674	0.4%
5	Illinois	50,255	5.5%
20	Indiana	16,378	1.8%
33	Iowa	6,799	0.7%
29	Kansas	8,736	0.9%
31	Kentucky	8,544	0.9%
14	Louisiana	19,817	2.1%
41	Maine	3,534	0.4%
16	Maryland	18,382	2.0%
11	Massachusetts	24,434	2.7%
10	Michigan	27,490	3.0%
25	Minnesota	11,317	1.2%
30	Mississippi	8,583	0.9%
17	Missouri	17,889	1.9%
44	Montana	2,541	0.3%
37	Nebraska	4,529	0.5%
34	Nevada	6,231	0.7%
43	New Hampshire	2,957	0.3%
6	New Jersey	34,940	3.8%
35	New Mexico	6,182	0.7%
2	New York	88,348	9.6%
12	North Carolina	23,263	2.5%
49	North Dakota	1,537	0.2%
7	Ohio	32,719	3.5%
26	Oklahoma	10,491	1.1%
28	Oregon	8,933	1.0%
8	Pennsylvania	29,506	3.2%
42	Rhode Island	3,098	0.3%
24	South Carolina	11,494	1.2%
45	South Dakota	2,360	0.3%
15	Tennessee	18,746	2.0%
3	Texas	73,112	7.9%
36	Utah	5,052	0.5%
50	Vermont	1,336	0.1%
13	Virginia	23,108	2.5%
22	Washington	14,061	1.5%
38	West Virginia	4,074	0.4%
19	Wisconsin	16,490	1.8%
46	Wyoming	2,149	0.2%

RANK ORDER

RANK	STATE	EMPLOYEES	% of USA
1	California	103,967	11.3%
2	New York	88,348	9.6%
3	Texas	73,112	7.9%
4	Florida	60,808	6.6%
5	Illinois	50,255	5.5%
6	New Jersey	34,940	3.8%
7	Ohio	32,719	3.5%
8	Pennsylvania	29,506	3.2%
9	Georgia	28,204	3.1%
10	Michigan	27,490	3.0%
11	Massachusetts	24,434	2.7%
12	North Carolina	23,263	2.5%
13	Virginia	23,108	2.5%
14	Louisiana	19,817	2.1%
15	Tennessee	18,746	2.0%
16	Maryland	18,382	2.0%
17	Missouri	17,889	1.9%
18	Arizona	16,828	1.8%
19	Wisconsin	16,490	1.8%
20	Indiana	16,378	1.8%
21	Alabama	14,389	1.6%
22	Washington	14,061	1.5%
23	Colorado	14,002	1.5%
24	South Carolina	11,494	1.2%
25	Minnesota	11,317	1.2%
26	Oklahoma	10,491	1.1%
27	Connecticut	10,319	1.1%
28	Oregon	8,933	1.0%
29	Kansas	8,736	0.9%
30	Mississippi	8,583	0.9%
31	Kentucky	8,544	0.9%
32	Arkansas	7,958	0.9%
33	Iowa	6,799	0.7%
34	Nevada	6,231	0.7%
35	New Mexico	6,182	0.7%
36	Utah	5,052	0.5%
37	Nebraska	4,529	0.5%
38	West Virginia	4,074	0.4%
39	Hawaii	3,745	0.4%
40	Idaho	3,674	0.4%
41	Maine	3,534	0.4%
42	Rhode Island	3,098	0.3%
43	New Hampshire	2,957	0.3%
44	Montana	2,541	0.3%
45	South Dakota	2,360	0.3%
46	Wyoming	2,149	0.2%
47	Delaware	2,134	0.2%
48	Alaska	1,884	0.2%
49	North Dakota	1,537	0.2%
50	Vermont	1,336	0.1%
	District of Columbia	4,651	0.5%

Source: U.S. Department of Justice, Bureau of Justice Statistics
"Census of State and Local Law Enforcement Agencies, 1996" (Bulletin, June 1998, NCJ-164618)
*Includes state and local police, sheriffs' departments and special police agencies.

Rate of Full-Time Employees in Law Enforcement Agencies in 1996

National Rate = 35 Employees per 10,000 Population*

ALPHA ORDER

RANK	STATE	RATE
17	Alabama	34
29	Alaska	31
9	Arizona	38
21	Arkansas	32
19	California	33
12	Colorado	37
21	Connecticut	32
33	Delaware	29
5	Florida	42
9	Georgia	38
21	Hawaii	32
29	Idaho	31
5	Illinois	42
37	Indiana	28
44	Iowa	24
17	Kansas	34
49	Kentucky	22
2	Louisiana	46
37	Maine	28
13	Maryland	36
7	Massachusetts	40
33	Michigan	29
44	Minnesota	24
21	Mississippi	32
19	Missouri	33
33	Montana	29
40	Nebraska	27
8	Nevada	39
41	New Hampshire	25
4	New Jersey	44
13	New Mexico	36
1	New York	49
21	North Carolina	32
44	North Dakota	24
33	Ohio	29
21	Oklahoma	32
37	Oregon	28
44	Pennsylvania	24
29	Rhode Island	31
29	South Carolina	31
21	South Dakota	32
15	Tennessee	35
9	Texas	38
41	Utah	25
48	Vermont	23
15	Virginia	35
41	Washington	25
49	West Virginia	22
21	Wisconsin	32
3	Wyoming	45

RANK ORDER

RANK	STATE	RATE
1	New York	49
2	Louisiana	46
3	Wyoming	45
4	New Jersey	44
5	Florida	42
5	Illinois	42
7	Massachusetts	40
8	Nevada	39
9	Arizona	38
9	Georgia	38
9	Texas	38
12	Colorado	37
13	Maryland	36
13	New Mexico	36
15	Tennessee	35
15	Virginia	35
17	Alabama	34
17	Kansas	34
19	California	33
19	Missouri	33
21	Arkansas	32
21	Connecticut	32
21	Hawaii	32
21	Mississippi	32
21	North Carolina	32
21	Oklahoma	32
21	South Dakota	32
21	Wisconsin	32
29	Alaska	31
29	Idaho	31
29	Rhode Island	31
29	South Carolina	31
33	Delaware	29
33	Michigan	29
33	Montana	29
33	Ohio	29
37	Indiana	28
37	Maine	28
37	Oregon	28
40	Nebraska	27
41	New Hampshire	25
41	Utah	25
41	Washington	25
44	Iowa	24
44	Minnesota	24
44	North Dakota	24
44	Pennsylvania	24
48	Vermont	23
49	Kentucky	22
49	West Virginia	22

	District of Columbia	86

Source: U.S. Department of Justice, Bureau of Justice Statistics
"Census of State and Local Law Enforcement Agencies, 1996" (Bulletin, June 1998, NCJ-164618)
Includes state and local police, sheriffs' departments and special police agencies.

Full-Time Sworn Officers in State Police Departments in 1996

National Total = 54,587 Officers*

ALPHA ORDER

RANK	STATE	OFFICERS	% of USA
27	Alabama	581	1.1%
41	Alaska	290	0.5%
18	Arizona	952	1.7%
32	Arkansas	522	1.0%
1	California	6,219	11.4%
27	Colorado	581	1.1%
15	Connecticut	1,022	1.9%
30	Delaware	540	1.0%
9	Florida	1,740	3.2%
21	Georgia	878	1.6%
50	Hawaii	0	0.0%
46	Idaho	192	0.4%
8	Illinois	1,988	3.6%
14	Indiana	1,207	2.2%
37	Iowa	433	0.8%
29	Kansas	552	1.0%
17	Kentucky	984	1.8%
22	Louisiana	873	1.6%
40	Maine	337	0.6%
11	Maryland	1,625	3.0%
6	Massachusetts	2,565	4.7%
7	Michigan	2,164	4.0%
34	Minnesota	484	0.9%
31	Mississippi	535	1.0%
16	Missouri	996	1.8%
44	Montana	212	0.4%
35	Nebraska	464	0.9%
38	Nevada	375	0.7%
43	New Hampshire	245	0.4%
5	New Jersey	2,702	4.9%
36	New Mexico	435	0.8%
3	New York	3,972	7.3%
13	North Carolina	1,380	2.5%
49	North Dakota	120	0.2%
12	Ohio	1,391	2.5%
25	Oklahoma	756	1.4%
23	Oregon	824	1.5%
2	Pennsylvania	4,114	7.5%
45	Rhode Island	193	0.4%
20	South Carolina	892	1.6%
47	South Dakota	155	0.3%
24	Tennessee	768	1.4%
4	Texas	2,873	5.3%
39	Utah	355	0.7%
41	Vermont	290	0.5%
10	Virginia	1,662	3.0%
19	Washington	906	1.7%
26	West Virginia	595	1.1%
33	Wisconsin	497	0.9%
48	Wyoming	151	0.3%

RANK ORDER

RANK	STATE	OFFICERS	% of USA
1	California	6,219	11.4%
2	Pennsylvania	4,114	7.5%
3	New York	3,972	7.3%
4	Texas	2,873	5.3%
5	New Jersey	2,702	4.9%
6	Massachusetts	2,565	4.7%
7	Michigan	2,164	4.0%
8	Illinois	1,988	3.6%
9	Florida	1,740	3.2%
10	Virginia	1,662	3.0%
11	Maryland	1,625	3.0%
12	Ohio	1,391	2.5%
13	North Carolina	1,380	2.5%
14	Indiana	1,207	2.2%
15	Connecticut	1,022	1.9%
16	Missouri	996	1.8%
17	Kentucky	984	1.8%
18	Arizona	952	1.7%
19	Washington	906	1.7%
20	South Carolina	892	1.6%
21	Georgia	878	1.6%
22	Louisiana	873	1.6%
23	Oregon	824	1.5%
24	Tennessee	768	1.4%
25	Oklahoma	756	1.4%
26	West Virginia	595	1.1%
27	Alabama	581	1.1%
27	Colorado	581	1.1%
29	Kansas	552	1.0%
30	Delaware	540	1.0%
31	Mississippi	535	1.0%
32	Arkansas	522	1.0%
33	Wisconsin	497	0.9%
34	Minnesota	484	0.9%
35	Nebraska	464	0.9%
36	New Mexico	435	0.8%
37	Iowa	433	0.8%
38	Nevada	375	0.7%
39	Utah	355	0.7%
40	Maine	337	0.6%
41	Alaska	290	0.5%
41	Vermont	290	0.5%
43	New Hampshire	245	0.4%
44	Montana	212	0.4%
45	Rhode Island	193	0.4%
46	Idaho	192	0.4%
47	South Dakota	155	0.3%
48	Wyoming	151	0.3%
49	North Dakota	120	0.2%
50	Hawaii	0	0.0%
	District of Columbia	0	0.0%

Source: U.S. Department of Justice, Bureau of Justice Statistics
"Census of State and Local Law Enforcement Agencies, 1996" (Bulletin, June 1998, NCJ-164618)
*All states except Hawaii and the District of Columbia have a state police department.

Percent of Full-Time State Police Department Employees
Who are Sworn Officers: 1996
National Percent = 65.2% of Employees*

ALPHA ORDER

RANK	STATE	PERCENT
45	Alabama	48.9
34	Alaska	64.7
39	Arizona	56.8
14	Arkansas	73.3
27	California	68.1
19	Colorado	71.9
31	Connecticut	66.1
22	Delaware	71.1
7	Florida	78.8
49	Georgia	30.5
NA	Hawaii**	NA
17	Idaho	73.0
41	Illinois	55.5
36	Indiana	64.0
1	Iowa	92.5
15	Kansas	73.2
37	Kentucky	58.4
21	Louisiana	71.2
22	Maine	71.1
29	Maryland	67.0
2	Massachusetts	88.9
24	Michigan	69.0
25	Minnesota	68.8
26	Mississippi	68.4
46	Missouri	47.8
10	Montana	76.5
18	Nebraska	72.7
20	Nevada	71.4
13	New Hampshire	73.6
11	New Jersey	74.1
42	New Mexico	52.6
4	New York	85.2
8	North Carolina	78.7
35	North Dakota	64.5
38	Ohio	58.2
40	Oklahoma	56.6
30	Oregon	66.2
9	Pennsylvania	77.6
5	Rhode Island	81.8
6	South Carolina	80.9
28	South Dakota	67.7
44	Tennessee	49.3
48	Texas	42.6
3	Utah	88.3
33	Vermont	65.2
12	Virginia	73.9
47	Washington	43.9
32	West Virginia	65.4
16	Wisconsin	73.1
43	Wyoming	50.2

RANK ORDER

RANK	STATE	PERCENT
1	Iowa	92.5
2	Massachusetts	88.9
3	Utah	88.3
4	New York	85.2
5	Rhode Island	81.8
6	South Carolina	80.9
7	Florida	78.8
8	North Carolina	78.7
9	Pennsylvania	77.6
10	Montana	76.5
11	New Jersey	74.1
12	Virginia	73.9
13	New Hampshire	73.6
14	Arkansas	73.3
15	Kansas	73.2
16	Wisconsin	73.1
17	Idaho	73.0
18	Nebraska	72.7
19	Colorado	71.9
20	Nevada	71.4
21	Louisiana	71.2
22	Delaware	71.1
22	Maine	71.1
24	Michigan	69.0
25	Minnesota	68.8
26	Mississippi	68.4
27	California	68.1
28	South Dakota	67.7
29	Maryland	67.0
30	Oregon	66.2
31	Connecticut	66.1
32	West Virginia	65.4
33	Vermont	65.2
34	Alaska	64.7
35	North Dakota	64.5
36	Indiana	64.0
37	Kentucky	58.4
38	Ohio	58.2
39	Arizona	56.8
40	Oklahoma	56.6
41	Illinois	55.5
42	New Mexico	52.6
43	Wyoming	50.2
44	Tennessee	49.3
45	Alabama	48.9
46	Missouri	47.8
47	Washington	43.9
48	Texas	42.6
49	Georgia	30.5
NA	Hawaii**	NA
	District of Columbia**	NA

Source: Morgan Quitno Press using data from U.S. Department of Justice, Bureau of Justice Statistics
    "Census of State and Local Law Enforcement Agencies, 1996" (Bulletin, June 1998, NCJ-164618)
*All states except Hawaii and the District of Columbia have a state police department.
**Not applicable.

Rate of Full-Time Sworn Officers in State Police Departments in 1996

National Rate = 2.1 Officers per 10,000 Population*

ALPHA ORDER

RANK ORDER

RANK	STATE	RATE		RANK	STATE	RATE
43	Alabama	1.4		1	Delaware	7.4
3	Alaska	4.8		2	Vermont	4.9
23	Arizona	2.1		3	Alaska	4.8
23	Arkansas	2.1		4	Massachusetts	4.2
29	California	2.0		5	New Jersey	3.4
40	Colorado	1.5		5	Pennsylvania	3.4
9	Connecticut	3.1		7	West Virginia	3.3
1	Delaware	7.4		8	Maryland	3.2
45	Florida	1.2		9	Connecticut	3.1
45	Georgia	1.2		9	Wyoming	3.1
50	Hawaii*	0.0		11	Nebraska	2.8
38	Idaho	1.6		12	Maine	2.7
37	Illinois	1.7		13	Oregon	2.6
23	Indiana	2.1		14	Kentucky	2.5
40	Iowa	1.5		14	New Mexico	2.5
23	Kansas	2.1		14	Virginia	2.5
14	Kentucky	2.5		17	Montana	2.4
29	Louisiana	2.0		17	South Carolina	2.4
12	Maine	2.7		19	Michigan	2.3
8	Maryland	3.2		19	Nevada	2.3
4	Massachusetts	4.2		19	Oklahoma	2.3
19	Michigan	2.3		22	New York	2.2
48	Minnesota	1.0		23	Arizona	2.1
29	Mississippi	2.0		23	Arkansas	2.1
32	Missouri	1.9		23	Indiana	2.1
17	Montana	2.4		23	Kansas	2.1
11	Nebraska	2.8		23	New Hampshire	2.1
19	Nevada	2.3		23	South Dakota	2.1
23	New Hampshire	2.1		29	California	2.0
5	New Jersey	3.4		29	Louisiana	2.0
14	New Mexico	2.5		29	Mississippi	2.0
22	New York	2.2		32	Missouri	1.9
32	North Carolina	1.9		32	North Carolina	1.9
32	North Dakota	1.9		32	North Dakota	1.9
45	Ohio	1.2		32	Rhode Island	1.9
19	Oklahoma	2.3		36	Utah	1.8
13	Oregon	2.6		37	Illinois	1.7
5	Pennsylvania	3.4		38	Idaho	1.6
32	Rhode Island	1.9		38	Washington	1.6
17	South Carolina	2.4		40	Colorado	1.5
23	South Dakota	2.1		40	Iowa	1.5
43	Tennessee	1.4		40	Texas	1.5
40	Texas	1.5		43	Alabama	1.4
36	Utah	1.8		43	Tennessee	1.4
2	Vermont	4.9		45	Florida	1.2
14	Virginia	2.5		45	Georgia	1.2
38	Washington	1.6		45	Ohio	1.2
7	West Virginia	3.3		48	Minnesota	1.0
48	Wisconsin	1.0		48	Wisconsin	1.0
9	Wyoming	3.1		50	Hawaii*	0.0
					District of Columbia*	0.0

Source: Morgan Quitno Press using data from U.S. Department of Justice, Bureau of Justice Statistics
"Census of State and Local Law Enforcement Agencies, 1996" (Bulletin, June 1998, NCJ-164618)
*All states except Hawaii and the District of Columbia have a state police department.

State Government Law Enforcement Officers in 1999

National Total = 66,694 Officers*

ALPHA ORDER

RANK	STATE	OFFICERS	% of USA
25	Alabama	860	1.3%
41	Alaska	293	0.4%
21	Arizona	1,101	1.7%
NA	Arkansas**	NA	NA
1	California	7,424	11.1%
32	Colorado	678	1.0%
22	Connecticut	1,066	1.6%
24	Delaware	911	1.4%
15	Florida	1,686	2.5%
11	Georgia	2,065	3.1%
49	Hawaii	0	0.0%
43	Idaho	238	0.4%
7	Illinois	2,578	3.9%
18	Indiana	1,249	1.9%
31	Iowa	698	1.0%
30	Kansas	733	1.1%
13	Kentucky	1,720	2.6%
19	Louisiana	1,122	1.7%
39	Maine	364	0.5%
6	Maryland	2,722	4.1%
8	Massachusetts	2,494	3.7%
10	Michigan	2,176	3.3%
35	Minnesota	536	0.8%
34	Mississippi	595	0.9%
20	Missouri	1,104	1.7%
45	Montana	211	0.3%
37	Nebraska	457	0.7%
38	Nevada	388	0.6%
40	New Hampshire	319	0.5%
4	New Jersey	3,275	4.9%
33	New Mexico	597	0.9%
2	New York	5,136	7.7%
14	North Carolina	1,693	2.5%
48	North Dakota	127	0.2%
17	Ohio	1,390	2.1%
27	Oklahoma	779	1.2%
26	Oregon	794	1.2%
3	Pennsylvania	4,560	6.8%
44	Rhode Island	234	0.4%
12	South Carolina	1,933	2.9%
46	South Dakota	160	0.2%
16	Tennessee	1,392	2.1%
5	Texas	3,056	4.6%
36	Utah	507	0.8%
42	Vermont	292	0.4%
9	Virginia	2,321	3.5%
23	Washington	972	1.5%
27	West Virginia	779	1.2%
29	Wisconsin	764	1.1%
47	Wyoming	145	0.2%

RANK ORDER

RANK	STATE	OFFICERS	% of USA
1	California	7,424	11.1%
2	New York	5,136	7.7%
3	Pennsylvania	4,560	6.8%
4	New Jersey	3,275	4.9%
5	Texas	3,056	4.6%
6	Maryland	2,722	4.1%
7	Illinois	2,578	3.9%
8	Massachusetts	2,494	3.7%
9	Virginia	2,321	3.5%
10	Michigan	2,176	3.3%
11	Georgia	2,065	3.1%
12	South Carolina	1,933	2.9%
13	Kentucky	1,720	2.6%
14	North Carolina	1,693	2.5%
15	Florida	1,686	2.5%
16	Tennessee	1,392	2.1%
17	Ohio	1,390	2.1%
18	Indiana	1,249	1.9%
19	Louisiana	1,122	1.7%
20	Missouri	1,104	1.7%
21	Arizona	1,101	1.7%
22	Connecticut	1,066	1.6%
23	Washington	972	1.5%
24	Delaware	911	1.4%
25	Alabama	860	1.3%
26	Oregon	794	1.2%
27	Oklahoma	779	1.2%
27	West Virginia	779	1.2%
29	Wisconsin	764	1.1%
30	Kansas	733	1.1%
31	Iowa	698	1.0%
32	Colorado	678	1.0%
33	New Mexico	597	0.9%
34	Mississippi	595	0.9%
35	Minnesota	536	0.8%
36	Utah	507	0.8%
37	Nebraska	457	0.7%
38	Nevada	388	0.6%
39	Maine	364	0.5%
40	New Hampshire	319	0.5%
41	Alaska	293	0.4%
42	Vermont	292	0.4%
43	Idaho	238	0.4%
44	Rhode Island	234	0.4%
45	Montana	211	0.3%
46	South Dakota	160	0.2%
47	Wyoming	145	0.2%
48	North Dakota	127	0.2%
49	Hawaii	0	0.0%
NA	Arkansas**	NA	NA
	District of Columbia	0	0.0%

Source: Morgan Quitno Press using data from Federal Bureau of Investigation
"Crime in the United States 1999" (Uniform Crime Reports, October 15, 2000)
Includes state police agencies and other agencies with law enforcement powers. Hawaii and the District of Columbia do not have a state police agency.
**Not available.*

Male State Government Law Enforcement Officers in 1999

National Total = 61,960 Male Officers*

ALPHA ORDER

RANK ORDER

RANK	STATE	OFFICERS	% of USA		RANK	STATE	OFFICERS	% of USA
24	Alabama	837	1.4%		1	California	6,692	10.8%
41	Alaska	276	0.4%		2	New York	4,754	7.7%
21	Arizona	1,017	1.6%		3	Pennsylvania	4,383	7.1%
NA	Arkansas**	NA	NA		4	New Jersey	3,152	5.1%
1	California	6,692	10.8%		5	Texas	2,903	4.7%
32	Colorado	649	1.0%		6	Maryland	2,386	3.9%
22	Connecticut	997	1.6%		7	Illinois	2,345	3.8%
25	Delaware	774	1.2%		8	Massachusetts	2,249	3.6%
15	Florida	1,502	2.4%		9	Virginia	2,212	3.6%
11	Georgia	1,900	3.1%		10	Michigan	1,914	3.1%
49	Hawaii	0	0.0%		11	Georgia	1,900	3.1%
43	Idaho	224	0.4%		12	South Carolina	1,786	2.9%
7	Illinois	2,345	3.8%		13	North Carolina	1,629	2.6%
18	Indiana	1,183	1.9%		14	Kentucky	1,624	2.6%
31	Iowa	654	1.1%		15	Florida	1,502	2.4%
29	Kansas	707	1.1%		16	Tennessee	1,287	2.1%
14	Kentucky	1,624	2.6%		17	Ohio	1,259	2.0%
19	Louisiana	1,086	1.8%		18	Indiana	1,183	1.9%
39	Maine	339	0.5%		19	Louisiana	1,086	1.8%
6	Maryland	2,386	3.9%		20	Missouri	1,063	1.7%
8	Massachusetts	2,249	3.6%		21	Arizona	1,017	1.6%
10	Michigan	1,914	3.1%		22	Connecticut	997	1.6%
35	Minnesota	492	0.8%		23	Washington	913	1.5%
33	Mississippi	582	0.9%		24	Alabama	837	1.4%
20	Missouri	1,063	1.7%		25	Delaware	774	1.2%
45	Montana	197	0.3%		26	Oklahoma	764	1.2%
37	Nebraska	437	0.7%		27	West Virginia	763	1.2%
38	Nevada	363	0.6%		28	Oregon	731	1.2%
40	New Hampshire	291	0.5%		29	Kansas	707	1.1%
4	New Jersey	3,152	5.1%		30	Wisconsin	673	1.1%
34	New Mexico	574	0.9%		31	Iowa	654	1.1%
2	New York	4,754	7.7%		32	Colorado	649	1.0%
13	North Carolina	1,629	2.6%		33	Mississippi	582	0.9%
48	North Dakota	122	0.2%		34	New Mexico	574	0.9%
17	Ohio	1,259	2.0%		35	Minnesota	492	0.8%
26	Oklahoma	764	1.2%		36	Utah	489	0.8%
28	Oregon	731	1.2%		37	Nebraska	437	0.7%
3	Pennsylvania	4,383	7.1%		38	Nevada	363	0.6%
44	Rhode Island	214	0.3%		39	Maine	339	0.5%
12	South Carolina	1,786	2.9%		40	New Hampshire	291	0.5%
46	South Dakota	157	0.3%		41	Alaska	276	0.4%
16	Tennessee	1,287	2.1%		42	Vermont	272	0.4%
5	Texas	2,903	4.7%		43	Idaho	224	0.4%
36	Utah	489	0.8%		44	Rhode Island	214	0.3%
42	Vermont	272	0.4%		45	Montana	197	0.3%
9	Virginia	2,212	3.6%		46	South Dakota	157	0.3%
23	Washington	913	1.5%		47	Wyoming	143	0.2%
27	West Virginia	763	1.2%		48	North Dakota	122	0.2%
30	Wisconsin	673	1.1%		49	Hawaii	0	0.0%
47	Wyoming	143	0.2%		NA	Arkansas**	NA	NA
						District of Columbia	0	0.0%

Source: Morgan Quitno Press using data from Federal Bureau of Investigation
  "Crime in the United States 1999" (Uniform Crime Reports, October 15, 2000)
*Includes state police agencies and other agencies with law enforcement powers. Hawaii and the District of
Columbia do not have a state police agency.
**Not available.

Female State Government Law Enforcement Officers in 1999

National Total = 4,734 Female Officers*

RANK	STATE	OFFICERS	% of USA
34	Alabama	23	0.5%
40	Alaska	17	0.4%
19	Arizona	84	1.8%
NA	Arkansas**	NA	NA
1	California	732	15.5%
29	Colorado	29	0.6%
20	Connecticut	69	1.5%
12	Delaware	137	2.9%
7	Florida	184	3.9%
9	Georgia	165	3.5%
49	Hawaii	0	0.0%
43	Idaho	14	0.3%
6	Illinois	233	4.9%
21	Indiana	66	1.4%
25	Iowa	44	0.9%
31	Kansas	26	0.5%
17	Kentucky	96	2.0%
28	Louisiana	36	0.8%
32	Maine	25	0.5%
3	Maryland	336	7.1%
5	Massachusetts	245	5.2%
4	Michigan	262	5.5%
25	Minnesota	44	0.9%
45	Mississippi	13	0.3%
27	Missouri	41	0.9%
43	Montana	14	0.3%
36	Nebraska	20	0.4%
32	Nevada	25	0.5%
30	New Hampshire	28	0.6%
14	New Jersey	123	2.6%
34	New Mexico	23	0.5%
2	New York	382	8.1%
22	North Carolina	64	1.4%
46	North Dakota	5	0.1%
13	Ohio	131	2.8%
42	Oklahoma	15	0.3%
23	Oregon	63	1.3%
8	Pennsylvania	177	3.7%
36	Rhode Island	20	0.4%
11	South Carolina	147	3.1%
47	South Dakota	3	0.1%
16	Tennessee	105	2.2%
10	Texas	153	3.2%
39	Utah	18	0.4%
36	Vermont	20	0.4%
15	Virginia	109	2.3%
24	Washington	59	1.2%
41	West Virginia	16	0.3%
18	Wisconsin	91	1.9%
48	Wyoming	2	0.0%

RANK	STATE	OFFICERS	% of USA
1	California	732	15.5%
2	New York	382	8.1%
3	Maryland	336	7.1%
4	Michigan	262	5.5%
5	Massachusetts	245	5.2%
6	Illinois	233	4.9%
7	Florida	184	3.9%
8	Pennsylvania	177	3.7%
9	Georgia	165	3.5%
10	Texas	153	3.2%
11	South Carolina	147	3.1%
12	Delaware	137	2.9%
13	Ohio	131	2.8%
14	New Jersey	123	2.6%
15	Virginia	109	2.3%
16	Tennessee	105	2.2%
17	Kentucky	96	2.0%
18	Wisconsin	91	1.9%
19	Arizona	84	1.8%
20	Connecticut	69	1.5%
21	Indiana	66	1.4%
22	North Carolina	64	1.4%
23	Oregon	63	1.3%
24	Washington	59	1.2%
25	Iowa	44	0.9%
25	Minnesota	44	0.9%
27	Missouri	41	0.9%
28	Louisiana	36	0.8%
29	Colorado	29	0.6%
30	New Hampshire	28	0.6%
31	Kansas	26	0.5%
32	Maine	25	0.5%
32	Nevada	25	0.5%
34	Alabama	23	0.5%
34	New Mexico	23	0.5%
36	Nebraska	20	0.4%
36	Rhode Island	20	0.4%
36	Vermont	20	0.4%
39	Utah	18	0.4%
40	Alaska	17	0.4%
41	West Virginia	16	0.3%
42	Oklahoma	15	0.3%
43	Idaho	14	0.3%
43	Montana	14	0.3%
45	Mississippi	13	0.3%
46	North Dakota	5	0.1%
47	South Dakota	3	0.1%
48	Wyoming	2	0.0%
49	Hawaii	0	0.0%
NA	Arkansas**	NA	NA
	District of Columbia	0	0.0%

Source: Morgan Quitno Press using data from Federal Bureau of Investigation
"Crime in the United States 1999" (Uniform Crime Reports, October 15, 2000)
*Includes state police agencies and other agencies with law enforcement powers. Hawaii and the District of Columbia do not have a state police agency.
**Not available.

Female State Government Law Enforcement Officers
As a Percent of All Officers: 1999
National Percent = 7.1% of Officers*

ALPHA ORDER

RANK	STATE	PERCENT
43	Alabama	2.7
27	Alaska	5.8
15	Arizona	7.6
NA	Arkansas**	NA
6	California	9.9
33	Colorado	4.3
22	Connecticut	6.5
1	Delaware	15.0
5	Florida	10.9
13	Georgia	8.0
NA	Hawaii**	NA
26	Idaho	5.9
9	Illinois	9.0
29	Indiana	5.3
24	Iowa	6.3
41	Kansas	3.5
28	Kentucky	5.6
42	Louisiana	3.2
19	Maine	6.9
2	Maryland	12.3
7	Massachusetts	9.8
3	Michigan	12.0
12	Minnesota	8.2
44	Mississippi	2.2
39	Missouri	3.7
21	Montana	6.6
32	Nebraska	4.4
23	Nevada	6.4
10	New Hampshire	8.8
37	New Jersey	3.8
34	New Mexico	3.9
18	New York	7.4
37	North Carolina	3.8
34	North Dakota	3.9
8	Ohio	9.4
46	Oklahoma	1.9
14	Oregon	7.9
34	Pennsylvania	3.9
11	Rhode Island	8.5
15	South Carolina	7.6
46	South Dakota	1.9
17	Tennessee	7.5
30	Texas	5.0
40	Utah	3.6
20	Vermont	6.8
31	Virginia	4.7
25	Washington	6.1
45	West Virginia	2.1
4	Wisconsin	11.9
48	Wyoming	1.4

RANK ORDER

RANK	STATE	PERCENT
1	Delaware	15.0
2	Maryland	12.3
3	Michigan	12.0
4	Wisconsin	11.9
5	Florida	10.9
6	California	9.9
7	Massachusetts	9.8
8	Ohio	9.4
9	Illinois	9.0
10	New Hampshire	8.8
11	Rhode Island	8.5
12	Minnesota	8.2
13	Georgia	8.0
14	Oregon	7.9
15	Arizona	7.6
15	South Carolina	7.6
17	Tennessee	7.5
18	New York	7.4
19	Maine	6.9
20	Vermont	6.8
21	Montana	6.6
22	Connecticut	6.5
23	Nevada	6.4
24	Iowa	6.3
25	Washington	6.1
26	Idaho	5.9
27	Alaska	5.8
28	Kentucky	5.6
29	Indiana	5.3
30	Texas	5.0
31	Virginia	4.7
32	Nebraska	4.4
33	Colorado	4.3
34	New Mexico	3.9
34	North Dakota	3.9
34	Pennsylvania	3.9
37	New Jersey	3.8
37	North Carolina	3.8
39	Missouri	3.7
40	Utah	3.6
41	Kansas	3.5
42	Louisiana	3.2
43	Alabama	2.7
44	Mississippi	2.2
45	West Virginia	2.1
46	Oklahoma	1.9
46	South Dakota	1.9
48	Wyoming	1.4
NA	Arkansas**	NA
NA	Hawaii**	NA
	District of Columbia**	NA

Source: Morgan Quitno Press using data from Federal Bureau of Investigation
   "Crime in the United States 1999" (Uniform Crime Reports, October 15, 2000)
*Includes state police agencies and other agencies with law enforcement powers.
**Hawaii and the District of Columbia do not have a state police agency. Arkansas' information is not available.

Local Police Departments in 1996

National Total = 13,578 Departments*

ALPHA ORDER

RANK	STATE	DEPARTMENTS	% of USA
17	Alabama	331	2.4%
44	Alaska	61	0.4%
39	Arizona	88	0.6%
21	Arkansas	261	1.9%
15	California	344	2.5%
32	Colorado	163	1.2%
36	Connecticut	107	0.8%
48	Delaware	35	0.3%
19	Florida	289	2.1%
12	Georgia	377	2.8%
50	Hawaii	4	0.0%
42	Idaho	76	0.6%
2	Illinois	809	6.0%
10	Indiana	432	3.2%
18	Iowa	318	2.3%
24	Kansas	245	1.8%
23	Kentucky	254	1.9%
20	Louisiana	271	2.0%
35	Maine	115	0.8%
41	Maryland	78	0.6%
16	Massachusetts	341	2.5%
8	Michigan	475	3.5%
11	Minnesota	384	2.8%
27	Mississippi	205	1.5%
5	Missouri	509	3.7%
43	Montana	65	0.5%
31	Nebraska	168	1.2%
49	Nevada	26	0.2%
26	New Hampshire	219	1.6%
6	New Jersey	487	3.6%
38	New Mexico	91	0.7%
7	New York	476	3.5%
13	North Carolina	370	2.7%
40	North Dakota	81	0.6%
3	Ohio	808	6.0%
14	Oklahoma	347	2.6%
33	Oregon	142	1.0%
1	Pennsylvania	1,141	8.4%
47	Rhode Island	40	0.3%
28	South Carolina	192	1.4%
34	South Dakota	119	0.9%
22	Tennessee	255	1.9%
4	Texas	735	5.4%
37	Utah	95	0.7%
46	Vermont	52	0.4%
30	Virginia	170	1.3%
25	Washington	223	1.6%
29	West Virginia	179	1.3%
9	Wisconsin	471	3.5%
45	Wyoming	53	0.4%

RANK ORDER

RANK	STATE	DEPARTMENTS	% of USA
1	Pennsylvania	1,141	8.4%
2	Illinois	809	6.0%
3	Ohio	808	6.0%
4	Texas	735	5.4%
5	Missouri	509	3.7%
6	New Jersey	487	3.6%
7	New York	476	3.5%
8	Michigan	475	3.5%
9	Wisconsin	471	3.5%
10	Indiana	432	3.2%
11	Minnesota	384	2.8%
12	Georgia	377	2.8%
13	North Carolina	370	2.7%
14	Oklahoma	347	2.6%
15	California	344	2.5%
16	Massachusetts	341	2.5%
17	Alabama	331	2.4%
18	Iowa	318	2.3%
19	Florida	289	2.1%
20	Louisiana	271	2.0%
21	Arkansas	261	1.9%
22	Tennessee	255	1.9%
23	Kentucky	254	1.9%
24	Kansas	245	1.8%
25	Washington	223	1.6%
26	New Hampshire	219	1.6%
27	Mississippi	205	1.5%
28	South Carolina	192	1.4%
29	West Virginia	179	1.3%
30	Virginia	170	1.3%
31	Nebraska	168	1.2%
32	Colorado	163	1.2%
33	Oregon	142	1.0%
34	South Dakota	119	0.9%
35	Maine	115	0.8%
36	Connecticut	107	0.8%
37	Utah	95	0.7%
38	New Mexico	91	0.7%
39	Arizona	88	0.6%
40	North Dakota	81	0.6%
41	Maryland	78	0.6%
42	Idaho	76	0.6%
43	Montana	65	0.5%
44	Alaska	61	0.4%
45	Wyoming	53	0.4%
46	Vermont	52	0.4%
47	Rhode Island	40	0.3%
48	Delaware	35	0.3%
49	Nevada	26	0.2%
50	Hawaii	4	0.0%
	District of Columbia	1	0.0%

Source: U.S. Department of Justice, Bureau of Justice Statistics
"Census of State and Local Law Enforcement Agencies, 1996" (Bulletin, June 1998, NCJ-164618)
*Includes consolidated police-sheriffs' departments.

Full-Time Officers in Local Police Departments in 1996

National Total = 410,956 Officers*

ALPHA ORDER

RANK	STATE	OFFICERS	% of USA
19	Alabama	6,484	1.6%
46	Alaska	740	0.2%
18	Arizona	6,967	1.7%
32	Arkansas	3,244	0.8%
2	California	35,939	8.7%
23	Colorado	5,451	1.3%
21	Connecticut	6,411	1.6%
44	Delaware	923	0.2%
6	Florida	19,652	4.8%
11	Georgia	10,241	2.5%
34	Hawaii	2,746	0.7%
43	Idaho	1,142	0.3%
4	Illinois	26,151	6.4%
20	Indiana	6,426	1.6%
33	Iowa	3,037	0.7%
29	Kansas	3,616	0.9%
27	Kentucky	4,089	1.0%
22	Louisiana	5,733	1.4%
41	Maine	1,426	0.3%
13	Maryland	8,923	2.2%
10	Massachusetts	13,068	3.2%
9	Michigan	13,288	3.2%
25	Minnesota	5,006	1.2%
30	Mississippi	3,326	0.8%
15	Missouri	8,836	2.2%
47	Montana	690	0.2%
38	Nebraska	1,929	0.5%
35	Nevada	2,565	0.6%
40	New Hampshire	1,862	0.5%
5	New Jersey	19,891	4.8%
36	New Mexico	2,462	0.6%
1	New York	54,657	13.3%
12	North Carolina	9,505	2.3%
49	North Dakota	561	0.1%
8	Ohio	15,932	3.9%
26	Oklahoma	4,951	1.2%
31	Oregon	3,245	0.8%
7	Pennsylvania	17,655	4.3%
37	Rhode Island	1,958	0.5%
28	South Carolina	4,004	1.0%
45	South Dakota	847	0.2%
17	Tennessee	7,076	1.7%
3	Texas	28,269	6.9%
39	Utah	1,882	0.5%
50	Vermont	548	0.1%
14	Virginia	8,911	2.2%
24	Washington	5,430	1.3%
42	West Virginia	1,416	0.3%
16	Wisconsin	7,640	1.9%
48	Wyoming	618	0.2%

RANK ORDER

RANK	STATE	OFFICERS	% of USA
1	New York	54,657	13.3%
2	California	35,939	8.7%
3	Texas	28,269	6.9%
4	Illinois	26,151	6.4%
5	New Jersey	19,891	4.8%
6	Florida	19,652	4.8%
7	Pennsylvania	17,655	4.3%
8	Ohio	15,932	3.9%
9	Michigan	13,288	3.2%
10	Massachusetts	13,068	3.2%
11	Georgia	10,241	2.5%
12	North Carolina	9,505	2.3%
13	Maryland	8,923	2.2%
14	Virginia	8,911	2.2%
15	Missouri	8,836	2.2%
16	Wisconsin	7,640	1.9%
17	Tennessee	7,076	1.7%
18	Arizona	6,967	1.7%
19	Alabama	6,484	1.6%
20	Indiana	6,426	1.6%
21	Connecticut	6,411	1.6%
22	Louisiana	5,733	1.4%
23	Colorado	5,451	1.3%
24	Washington	5,430	1.3%
25	Minnesota	5,006	1.2%
26	Oklahoma	4,951	1.2%
27	Kentucky	4,089	1.0%
28	South Carolina	4,004	1.0%
29	Kansas	3,616	0.9%
30	Mississippi	3,326	0.8%
31	Oregon	3,245	0.8%
32	Arkansas	3,244	0.8%
33	Iowa	3,037	0.7%
34	Hawaii	2,746	0.7%
35	Nevada	2,565	0.6%
36	New Mexico	2,462	0.6%
37	Rhode Island	1,958	0.5%
38	Nebraska	1,929	0.5%
39	Utah	1,882	0.5%
40	New Hampshire	1,862	0.5%
41	Maine	1,426	0.3%
42	West Virginia	1,416	0.3%
43	Idaho	1,142	0.3%
44	Delaware	923	0.2%
45	South Dakota	847	0.2%
46	Alaska	740	0.2%
47	Montana	690	0.2%
48	Wyoming	618	0.2%
49	North Dakota	561	0.1%
50	Vermont	548	0.1%
	District of Columbia	3,587	0.9%

Source: U.S. Department of Justice, Bureau of Justice Statistics
   "Census of State and Local Law Enforcement Agencies, 1996" (Bulletin, June 1998, NCJ-164618)
*Includes consolidated police-sheriffs' departments.

Percent of Full-Time Local Police Department Employees
Who Are Sworn Officers: 1996
National Percent = 78.7% of Employees*

ALPHA ORDER

RANK ORDER

RANK	STATE	PERCENT		RANK	STATE	PERCENT
35	Alabama	76.7		1	Pennsylvania	86.4
50	Alaska	63.9		2	Delaware	86.1
45	Arizona	71.9		3	West Virginia	85.7
27	Arkansas	78.7		4	Michigan	84.4
46	California	71.2		5	Massachusetts	84.3
42	Colorado	74.8		6	Connecticut	84.1
6	Connecticut	84.1		7	New Jersey	83.5
2	Delaware	86.1		8	New York	83.0
47	Florida	70.0		9	Iowa	82.9
25	Georgia	79.1		10	Minnesota	82.7
25	Hawaii	79.1		11	North Carolina	82.3
21	Idaho	80.0		12	Wisconsin	82.2
19	Illinois	80.4		13	South Carolina	82.0
17	Indiana	80.7		14	Louisiana	81.9
9	Iowa	82.9		15	North Dakota	81.8
36	Kansas	76.4		16	Maryland	81.0
23	Kentucky	79.3		17	Indiana	80.7
14	Louisiana	81.9		18	Ohio	80.5
29	Maine	78.1		19	Illinois	80.4
16	Maryland	81.0		20	Nebraska	80.1
5	Massachusetts	84.3		21	Idaho	80.0
4	Michigan	84.4		22	Utah	79.6
10	Minnesota	82.7		23	Kentucky	79.3
44	Mississippi	73.7		24	New Hampshire	79.2
37	Missouri	76.2		25	Georgia	79.1
31	Montana	77.9		25	Hawaii	79.1
20	Nebraska	80.1		27	Arkansas	78.7
49	Nevada	67.3		28	Vermont	78.3
24	New Hampshire	79.2		29	Maine	78.1
7	New Jersey	83.5		30	Oklahoma	78.0
48	New Mexico	68.5		31	Montana	77.9
8	New York	83.0		32	Rhode Island	77.5
11	North Carolina	82.3		32	Virginia	77.5
15	North Dakota	81.8		34	Tennessee	76.9
18	Ohio	80.5		35	Alabama	76.7
30	Oklahoma	78.0		36	Kansas	76.4
38	Oregon	75.4		37	Missouri	76.2
1	Pennsylvania	86.4		38	Oregon	75.4
32	Rhode Island	77.5		38	Texas	75.4
13	South Carolina	82.0		40	Wyoming	75.2
43	South Dakota	74.0		41	Washington	74.9
34	Tennessee	76.9		42	Colorado	74.8
38	Texas	75.4		43	South Dakota	74.0
22	Utah	79.6		44	Mississippi	73.7
28	Vermont	78.3		45	Arizona	71.9
32	Virginia	77.5		46	California	71.2
41	Washington	74.9		47	Florida	70.0
3	West Virginia	85.7		48	New Mexico	68.5
12	Wisconsin	82.2		49	Nevada	67.3
40	Wyoming	75.2		50	Alaska	63.9

District of Columbia   84.9

Source: Morgan Quitno Press using data from U.S. Department of Justice, Bureau of Justice Statistics
"Census of State and Local Law Enforcement Agencies, 1996" (Bulletin, June 1998, NCJ-164618)
*Includes consolidated police-sheriffs' departments.

Rate of Full-Time Officers in Local Police Departments in 1996

National Rate = 15 Officers per 10,000 Population*

ALPHA ORDER

RANK	STATE	RATE
13	Alabama	15
32	Alaska	12
9	Arizona	16
25	Arkansas	13
36	California	11
18	Colorado	14
6	Connecticut	20
25	Delaware	13
18	Florida	14
18	Georgia	14
3	Hawaii	23
43	Idaho	10
4	Illinois	22
36	Indiana	11
36	Iowa	11
18	Kansas	14
36	Kentucky	11
25	Louisiana	13
36	Maine	11
8	Maryland	18
5	Massachusetts	21
18	Michigan	14
36	Minnesota	11
32	Mississippi	12
9	Missouri	16
49	Montana	8
32	Nebraska	12
9	Nevada	16
9	New Hampshire	16
2	New Jersey	25
18	New Mexico	14
1	New York	30
25	North Carolina	13
46	North Dakota	9
18	Ohio	14
13	Oklahoma	15
43	Oregon	10
13	Pennsylvania	15
6	Rhode Island	20
36	South Carolina	11
32	South Dakota	12
25	Tennessee	13
13	Texas	15
46	Utah	9
46	Vermont	9
25	Virginia	13
43	Washington	10
49	West Virginia	8
13	Wisconsin	15
25	Wyoming	13

RANK ORDER

RANK	STATE	RATE
1	New York	30
2	New Jersey	25
3	Hawaii	23
4	Illinois	22
5	Massachusetts	21
6	Connecticut	20
6	Rhode Island	20
8	Maryland	18
9	Arizona	16
9	Missouri	16
9	Nevada	16
9	New Hampshire	16
13	Alabama	15
13	Oklahoma	15
13	Pennsylvania	15
13	Texas	15
13	Wisconsin	15
18	Colorado	14
18	Florida	14
18	Georgia	14
18	Kansas	14
18	Michigan	14
18	New Mexico	14
18	Ohio	14
25	Arkansas	13
25	Delaware	13
25	Louisiana	13
25	North Carolina	13
25	Tennessee	13
25	Virginia	13
25	Wyoming	13
32	Alaska	12
32	Mississippi	12
32	Nebraska	12
32	South Dakota	12
36	California	11
36	Indiana	11
36	Iowa	11
36	Kentucky	11
36	Maine	11
36	Minnesota	11
36	South Carolina	11
43	Idaho	10
43	Oregon	10
43	Washington	10
46	North Dakota	9
46	Utah	9
46	Vermont	9
49	Montana	8
49	West Virginia	8

District of Columbia 66

Source: U.S. Department of Justice, Bureau of Justice Statistics
"Census of State and Local Law Enforcement Agencies, 1996" (Bulletin, June 1998, NCJ-164618)
*Includes consolidated police-sheriffs' departments.

Full-Time Employees in Local Police Departments in 1996

National Total = 521,985 Employees*

ALPHA ORDER

RANK	STATE	EMPLOYEES	% of USA
19	Alabama	8,454	1.6%
44	Alaska	1,158	0.2%
16	Arizona	9,686	1.9%
32	Arkansas	4,124	0.8%
2	California	50,491	9.7%
22	Colorado	7,283	1.4%
21	Connecticut	7,625	1.5%
46	Delaware	1,072	0.2%
5	Florida	28,075	5.4%
11	Georgia	12,954	2.5%
36	Hawaii	3,471	0.7%
43	Idaho	1,428	0.3%
4	Illinois	32,522	6.2%
20	Indiana	7,965	1.5%
34	Iowa	3,664	0.7%
29	Kansas	4,732	0.9%
27	Kentucky	5,157	1.0%
24	Louisiana	7,001	1.3%
41	Maine	1,826	0.3%
15	Maryland	11,015	2.1%
10	Massachusetts	15,506	3.0%
9	Michigan	15,735	3.0%
26	Minnesota	6,053	1.2%
30	Mississippi	4,511	0.9%
12	Missouri	11,594	2.2%
47	Montana	886	0.2%
38	Nebraska	2,409	0.5%
33	Nevada	3,809	0.7%
40	New Hampshire	2,351	0.5%
6	New Jersey	23,829	4.6%
35	New Mexico	3,593	0.7%
1	New York	65,854	12.6%
13	North Carolina	11,546	2.2%
50	North Dakota	686	0.1%
8	Ohio	19,799	3.8%
25	Oklahoma	6,348	1.2%
31	Oregon	4,305	0.8%
7	Pennsylvania	20,427	3.9%
37	Rhode Island	2,527	0.5%
28	South Carolina	4,884	0.9%
45	South Dakota	1,144	0.2%
18	Tennessee	9,206	1.8%
3	Texas	37,472	7.2%
39	Utah	2,363	0.5%
49	Vermont	700	0.1%
14	Virginia	11,502	2.2%
23	Washington	7,246	1.4%
42	West Virginia	1,652	0.3%
17	Wisconsin	9,298	1.8%
48	Wyoming	822	0.2%

RANK ORDER

RANK	STATE	EMPLOYEES	% of USA
1	New York	65,854	12.6%
2	California	50,491	9.7%
3	Texas	37,472	7.2%
4	Illinois	32,522	6.2%
5	Florida	28,075	5.4%
6	New Jersey	23,829	4.6%
7	Pennsylvania	20,427	3.9%
8	Ohio	19,799	3.8%
9	Michigan	15,735	3.0%
10	Massachusetts	15,506	3.0%
11	Georgia	12,954	2.5%
12	Missouri	11,594	2.2%
13	North Carolina	11,546	2.2%
14	Virginia	11,502	2.2%
15	Maryland	11,015	2.1%
16	Arizona	9,686	1.9%
17	Wisconsin	9,298	1.8%
18	Tennessee	9,206	1.8%
19	Alabama	8,454	1.6%
20	Indiana	7,965	1.5%
21	Connecticut	7,625	1.5%
22	Colorado	7,283	1.4%
23	Washington	7,246	1.4%
24	Louisiana	7,001	1.3%
25	Oklahoma	6,348	1.2%
26	Minnesota	6,053	1.2%
27	Kentucky	5,157	1.0%
28	South Carolina	4,884	0.9%
29	Kansas	4,732	0.9%
30	Mississippi	4,511	0.9%
31	Oregon	4,305	0.8%
32	Arkansas	4,124	0.8%
33	Nevada	3,809	0.7%
34	Iowa	3,664	0.7%
35	New Mexico	3,593	0.7%
36	Hawaii	3,471	0.7%
37	Rhode Island	2,527	0.5%
38	Nebraska	2,409	0.5%
39	Utah	2,363	0.5%
40	New Hampshire	2,351	0.5%
41	Maine	1,826	0.3%
42	West Virginia	1,652	0.3%
43	Idaho	1,428	0.3%
44	Alaska	1,158	0.2%
45	South Dakota	1,144	0.2%
46	Delaware	1,072	0.2%
47	Montana	886	0.2%
48	Wyoming	822	0.2%
49	Vermont	700	0.1%
50	North Dakota	686	0.1%
	District of Columbia	4,225	0.8%

Source: U.S. Department of Justice, Bureau of Justice Statistics
  "Census of State and Local Law Enforcement Agencies, 1996" (Bulletin, June 1998, NCJ-164618)
Includes consolidated police-sheriffs' departments.

Sheriffs' Departments in 1996

National Total = 3,088 Departments*

ALPHA ORDER

RANK	STATE	DEPARTMENTS	% of USA
20	Alabama	67	2.2%
49	Alaska	0	0.0%
42	Arizona	15	0.5%
18	Arkansas	75	2.4%
26	California	58	1.9%
25	Colorado	63	2.0%
46	Connecticut	8	0.3%
48	Delaware	3	0.1%
23	Florida	65	2.1%
2	Georgia	159	5.1%
49	Hawaii	0	0.0%
32	Idaho	44	1.4%
7	Illinois	102	3.3%
12	Indiana	92	3.0%
9	Iowa	99	3.2%
6	Kansas	104	3.4%
4	Kentucky	120	3.9%
24	Louisiana	64	2.1%
40	Maine	16	0.5%
37	Maryland	24	0.8%
43	Massachusetts	14	0.5%
15	Michigan	83	2.7%
14	Minnesota	87	2.8%
16	Mississippi	82	2.7%
5	Missouri	115	3.7%
28	Montana	55	1.8%
11	Nebraska	93	3.0%
40	Nevada	16	0.5%
45	New Hampshire	10	0.3%
39	New Jersey	21	0.7%
35	New Mexico	33	1.1%
27	New York	57	1.8%
8	North Carolina	100	3.2%
30	North Dakota	53	1.7%
13	Ohio	88	2.8%
17	Oklahoma	77	2.5%
34	Oregon	36	1.2%
20	Pennsylvania	67	2.2%
47	Rhode Island	5	0.2%
31	South Carolina	46	1.5%
22	South Dakota	66	2.1%
10	Tennessee	95	3.1%
1	Texas	254	8.2%
36	Utah	29	0.9%
43	Vermont	14	0.5%
3	Virginia	125	4.0%
33	Washington	39	1.3%
28	West Virginia	55	1.8%
19	Wisconsin	72	2.3%
38	Wyoming	23	0.7%

RANK ORDER

RANK	STATE	DEPARTMENTS	% of USA
1	Texas	254	8.2%
2	Georgia	159	5.1%
3	Virginia	125	4.0%
4	Kentucky	120	3.9%
5	Missouri	115	3.7%
6	Kansas	104	3.4%
7	Illinois	102	3.3%
8	North Carolina	100	3.2%
9	Iowa	99	3.2%
10	Tennessee	95	3.1%
11	Nebraska	93	3.0%
12	Indiana	92	3.0%
13	Ohio	88	2.8%
14	Minnesota	87	2.8%
15	Michigan	83	2.7%
16	Mississippi	82	2.7%
17	Oklahoma	77	2.5%
18	Arkansas	75	2.4%
19	Wisconsin	72	2.3%
20	Alabama	67	2.2%
20	Pennsylvania	67	2.2%
22	South Dakota	66	2.1%
23	Florida	65	2.1%
24	Louisiana	64	2.1%
25	Colorado	63	2.0%
26	California	58	1.9%
27	New York	57	1.8%
28	Montana	55	1.8%
28	West Virginia	55	1.8%
30	North Dakota	53	1.7%
31	South Carolina	46	1.5%
32	Idaho	44	1.4%
33	Washington	39	1.3%
34	Oregon	36	1.2%
35	New Mexico	33	1.1%
36	Utah	29	0.9%
37	Maryland	24	0.8%
38	Wyoming	23	0.7%
39	New Jersey	21	0.7%
40	Maine	16	0.5%
40	Nevada	16	0.5%
42	Arizona	15	0.5%
43	Massachusetts	14	0.5%
43	Vermont	14	0.5%
45	New Hampshire	10	0.3%
46	Connecticut	8	0.3%
47	Rhode Island	5	0.2%
48	Delaware	3	0.1%
49	Alaska	0	0.0%
49	Hawaii	0	0.0%
	District of Columbia	0	0.0%

Source: U.S. Department of Justice, Bureau of Justice Statistics
    "Census of State and Local Law Enforcement Agencies, 1996" (Bulletin, June 1998, NCJ-164618)
*Sheriffs' departments generally operate at the county level.

Full-Time Officers in Sheriffs' Departments in 1996

National Total = 152,922 Officers*

ALPHA ORDER

RANK	STATE	OFFICERS	% of USA
21	Alabama	1,963	1.3%
49	Alaska	0	0.0%
24	Arizona	1,563	1.0%
28	Arkansas	1,410	0.9%
1	California	22,869	15.0%
14	Colorado	3,324	2.2%
37	Connecticut	886	0.6%
48	Delaware	24	0.0%
2	Florida	14,124	9.2%
6	Georgia	6,752	4.4%
49	Hawaii	0	0.0%
33	Idaho	1,053	0.7%
5	Illinois	8,426	5.5%
17	Indiana	2,618	1.7%
29	Iowa	1,343	0.9%
23	Kansas	1,683	1.1%
32	Kentucky	1,113	0.7%
4	Louisiana	8,720	5.7%
44	Maine	321	0.2%
27	Maryland	1,438	0.9%
25	Massachusetts	1,540	1.0%
11	Michigan	4,435	2.9%
20	Minnesota	2,139	1.4%
26	Mississippi	1,474	1.0%
19	Missouri	2,421	1.6%
40	Montana	616	0.4%
38	Nebraska	794	0.5%
35	Nevada	935	0.6%
46	New Hampshire	129	0.1%
15	New Jersey	3,145	2.1%
36	New Mexico	889	0.6%
8	New York	5,852	3.8%
9	North Carolina	5,264	3.4%
42	North Dakota	364	0.2%
10	Ohio	5,179	3.4%
34	Oklahoma	1,014	0.7%
22	Oregon	1,921	1.3%
30	Pennsylvania	1,239	0.8%
45	Rhode Island	153	0.1%
16	South Carolina	3,037	2.0%
43	South Dakota	344	0.2%
13	Tennessee	3,520	2.3%
3	Texas	11,326	7.4%
31	Utah	1,198	0.8%
47	Vermont	87	0.1%
7	Virginia	6,605	4.3%
18	Washington	2,553	1.7%
39	West Virginia	726	0.5%
12	Wisconsin	3,886	2.5%
41	Wyoming	507	0.3%

RANK ORDER

RANK	STATE	OFFICERS	% of USA
1	California	22,869	15.0%
2	Florida	14,124	9.2%
3	Texas	11,326	7.4%
4	Louisiana	8,720	5.7%
5	Illinois	8,426	5.5%
6	Georgia	6,752	4.4%
7	Virginia	6,605	4.3%
8	New York	5,852	3.8%
9	North Carolina	5,264	3.4%
10	Ohio	5,179	3.4%
11	Michigan	4,435	2.9%
12	Wisconsin	3,886	2.5%
13	Tennessee	3,520	2.3%
14	Colorado	3,324	2.2%
15	New Jersey	3,145	2.1%
16	South Carolina	3,037	2.0%
17	Indiana	2,618	1.7%
18	Washington	2,553	1.7%
19	Missouri	2,421	1.6%
20	Minnesota	2,139	1.4%
21	Alabama	1,963	1.3%
22	Oregon	1,921	1.3%
23	Kansas	1,683	1.1%
24	Arizona	1,563	1.0%
25	Massachusetts	1,540	1.0%
26	Mississippi	1,474	1.0%
27	Maryland	1,438	0.9%
28	Arkansas	1,410	0.9%
29	Iowa	1,343	0.9%
30	Pennsylvania	1,239	0.8%
31	Utah	1,198	0.8%
32	Kentucky	1,113	0.7%
33	Idaho	1,053	0.7%
34	Oklahoma	1,014	0.7%
35	Nevada	935	0.6%
36	New Mexico	889	0.6%
37	Connecticut	886	0.6%
38	Nebraska	794	0.5%
39	West Virginia	726	0.5%
40	Montana	616	0.4%
41	Wyoming	507	0.3%
42	North Dakota	364	0.2%
43	South Dakota	344	0.2%
44	Maine	321	0.2%
45	Rhode Island	153	0.1%
46	New Hampshire	129	0.1%
47	Vermont	87	0.1%
48	Delaware	24	0.0%
49	Alaska	0	0.0%
49	Hawaii	0	0.0%
	District of Columbia	0	0.0%

Source: U.S. Department of Justice, Bureau of Justice Statistics
   "Census of State and Local Law Enforcement Agencies, 1996" (Bulletin, June 1998, NCJ-164618)
*Sheriffs' departments generally operate at the county level.

Percent of Full-Time Sheriffs' Department Employees
Who Are Sworn Officers: 1996
National Percent = 59.3% of Employees*

ALPHA ORDER

RANK	STATE	PERCENT
39	Alabama	51.7
NA	Alaska**	NA
47	Arizona	33.9
22	Arkansas	59.5
23	California	59.2
17	Colorado	64.3
1	Connecticut	99.7
43	Delaware	46.2
40	Florida	50.6
18	Georgia	64.1
NA	Hawaii**	NA
31	Idaho	57.9
13	Illinois	69.0
44	Indiana	45.8
33	Iowa	56.8
21	Kansas	59.7
3	Kentucky	87.6
5	Louisiana	81.9
46	Maine	34.2
25	Maryland	58.8
48	Massachusetts	30.5
24	Michigan	59.1
38	Minnesota	52.0
34	Mississippi	55.5
7	Missouri	74.5
36	Montana	54.0
25	Nebraska	58.8
8	Nevada	74.1
11	New Hampshire	70.5
10	New Jersey	70.7
16	New Mexico	66.2
32	New York	57.7
25	North Carolina	58.8
15	North Dakota	67.7
28	Ohio	58.5
42	Oklahoma	47.4
28	Oregon	58.5
6	Pennsylvania	77.6
2	Rhode Island	99.4
9	South Carolina	72.9
45	South Dakota	40.4
41	Tennessee	50.4
37	Texas	52.6
19	Utah	61.0
12	Vermont	69.6
4	Virginia	84.5
20	Washington	60.5
28	West Virginia	58.5
14	Wisconsin	67.9
34	Wyoming	55.5

RANK ORDER

RANK	STATE	PERCENT
1	Connecticut	99.7
2	Rhode Island	99.4
3	Kentucky	87.6
4	Virginia	84.5
5	Louisiana	81.9
6	Pennsylvania	77.6
7	Missouri	74.5
8	Nevada	74.1
9	South Carolina	72.9
10	New Jersey	70.7
11	New Hampshire	70.5
12	Vermont	69.6
13	Illinois	69.0
14	Wisconsin	67.9
15	North Dakota	67.7
16	New Mexico	66.2
17	Colorado	64.3
18	Georgia	64.1
19	Utah	61.0
20	Washington	60.5
21	Kansas	59.7
22	Arkansas	59.5
23	California	59.2
24	Michigan	59.1
25	Maryland	58.8
25	Nebraska	58.8
25	North Carolina	58.8
28	Ohio	58.5
28	Oregon	58.5
28	West Virginia	58.5
31	Idaho	57.9
32	New York	57.7
33	Iowa	56.8
34	Mississippi	55.5
34	Wyoming	55.5
36	Montana	54.0
37	Texas	52.6
38	Minnesota	52.0
39	Alabama	51.7
40	Florida	50.6
41	Tennessee	50.4
42	Oklahoma	47.4
43	Delaware	46.2
44	Indiana	45.8
45	South Dakota	40.4
46	Maine	34.2
47	Arizona	33.9
48	Massachusetts	30.5
NA	Alaska**	NA
NA	Hawaii**	NA

District of Columbia**   NA

Source: Morgan Quitno Press using data from U.S. Department of Justice, Bureau of Justice Statistics
"Census of State and Local Law Enforcement Agencies, 1996" (Bulletin, June 1998, NCJ-164618)
*Sheriffs' departments generally operate at the county level.
**Not applicable.

Rate of Full-Time Sworn Officers in Sheriffs' Departments in 1996

National Rate = 5.8 Officers per 10,000 Population*

ALPHA ORDER

RANK	STATE	RATE
27	Alabama	4.6
49	Alaska	0.0
36	Arizona	3.5
21	Arkansas	5.6
10	California	7.2
7	Colorado	8.7
41	Connecticut	2.7
48	Delaware	0.3
4	Florida	9.8
5	Georgia	9.2
49	Hawaii	0.0
6	Idaho	8.9
12	Illinois	7.1
32	Indiana	4.5
25	Iowa	4.7
15	Kansas	6.5
39	Kentucky	2.9
1	Louisiana	20.0
42	Maine	2.6
40	Maryland	2.8
43	Massachusetts	2.5
27	Michigan	4.6
27	Minnesota	4.6
22	Mississippi	5.4
32	Missouri	4.5
13	Montana	7.0
24	Nebraska	4.8
19	Nevada	5.8
46	New Hampshire	1.1
35	New Jersey	3.9
23	New Mexico	5.2
37	New York	3.2
10	North Carolina	7.2
20	North Dakota	5.7
27	Ohio	4.6
38	Oklahoma	3.1
16	Oregon	6.0
47	Pennsylvania	1.0
44	Rhode Island	1.5
8	South Carolina	8.2
25	South Dakota	4.7
14	Tennessee	6.6
18	Texas	5.9
16	Utah	6.0
44	Vermont	1.5
3	Virginia	9.9
27	Washington	4.6
34	West Virginia	4.0
9	Wisconsin	7.5
2	Wyoming	10.5

RANK ORDER

RANK	STATE	RATE
1	Louisiana	20.0
2	Wyoming	10.5
3	Virginia	9.9
4	Florida	9.8
5	Georgia	9.2
6	Idaho	8.9
7	Colorado	8.7
8	South Carolina	8.2
9	Wisconsin	7.5
10	California	7.2
10	North Carolina	7.2
12	Illinois	7.1
13	Montana	7.0
14	Tennessee	6.6
15	Kansas	6.5
16	Oregon	6.0
16	Utah	6.0
18	Texas	5.9
19	Nevada	5.8
20	North Dakota	5.7
21	Arkansas	5.6
22	Mississippi	5.4
23	New Mexico	5.2
24	Nebraska	4.8
25	Iowa	4.7
25	South Dakota	4.7
27	Alabama	4.6
27	Michigan	4.6
27	Minnesota	4.6
27	Ohio	4.6
27	Washington	4.6
32	Indiana	4.5
32	Missouri	4.5
34	West Virginia	4.0
35	New Jersey	3.9
36	Arizona	3.5
37	New York	3.2
38	Oklahoma	3.1
39	Kentucky	2.9
40	Maryland	2.8
41	Connecticut	2.7
42	Maine	2.6
43	Massachusetts	2.5
44	Rhode Island	1.5
44	Vermont	1.5
46	New Hampshire	1.1
47	Pennsylvania	1.0
48	Delaware	0.3
49	Alaska	0.0
49	Hawaii	0.0
	District of Columbia	0.0

Source: U.S. Department of Justice, Bureau of Justice Statistics
"Census of State and Local Law Enforcement Agencies, 1996" (Bulletin, June 1998, NCJ-164618)
*Sheriffs' departments generally operate at the county level.

Full-Time Employees in Sheriffs' Departments in 1996

National Total = 257,712 Employees*

ALPHA ORDER

RANK	STATE	EMPLOYEES	% of USA	RANK	STATE	EMPLOYEES	% of USA
22	Alabama	3,796	1.5%	1	California	38,603	15.0%
49	Alaska	0	0.0%	2	Florida	27,928	10.8%
17	Arizona	4,604	1.8%	3	Texas	21,548	8.4%
28	Arkansas	2,370	0.9%	4	Illinois	12,212	4.7%
1	California	38,603	15.0%	5	Louisiana	10,652	4.1%
15	Colorado	5,168	2.0%	6	Georgia	10,537	4.1%
42	Connecticut	889	0.3%	7	New York	10,150	3.9%
48	Delaware	52	0.0%	8	North Carolina	8,948	3.5%
2	Florida	27,928	10.8%	9	Ohio	8,855	3.4%
6	Georgia	10,537	4.1%	10	Virginia	7,816	3.0%
49	Hawaii	0	0.0%	11	Michigan	7,508	2.9%
32	Idaho	1,820	0.7%	12	Tennessee	6,981	2.7%
4	Illinois	12,212	4.7%	13	Wisconsin	5,723	2.2%
14	Indiana	5,721	2.2%	14	Indiana	5,721	2.2%
29	Iowa	2,364	0.9%	15	Colorado	5,168	2.0%
25	Kansas	2,817	1.1%	16	Massachusetts	5,047	2.0%
36	Kentucky	1,270	0.5%	17	Arizona	4,604	1.8%
5	Louisiana	10,652	4.1%	18	New Jersey	4,451	1.7%
40	Maine	939	0.4%	19	Washington	4,223	1.6%
27	Maryland	2,445	0.9%	20	South Carolina	4,167	1.6%
16	Massachusetts	5,047	2.0%	21	Minnesota	4,115	1.6%
11	Michigan	7,508	2.9%	22	Alabama	3,796	1.5%
21	Minnesota	4,115	1.6%	23	Oregon	3,285	1.3%
26	Mississippi	2,657	1.0%	24	Missouri	3,250	1.3%
24	Missouri	3,250	1.3%	25	Kansas	2,817	1.1%
39	Montana	1,141	0.4%	26	Mississippi	2,657	1.0%
34	Nebraska	1,351	0.5%	27	Maryland	2,445	0.9%
37	Nevada	1,261	0.5%	28	Arkansas	2,370	0.9%
45	New Hampshire	183	0.1%	29	Iowa	2,364	0.9%
18	New Jersey	4,451	1.7%	30	Oklahoma	2,138	0.8%
35	New Mexico	1,343	0.5%	31	Utah	1,965	0.8%
7	New York	10,150	3.9%	32	Idaho	1,820	0.7%
8	North Carolina	8,948	3.5%	33	Pennsylvania	1,596	0.6%
44	North Dakota	538	0.2%	34	Nebraska	1,351	0.5%
9	Ohio	8,855	3.4%	35	New Mexico	1,343	0.5%
30	Oklahoma	2,138	0.8%	36	Kentucky	1,270	0.5%
23	Oregon	3,285	1.3%	37	Nevada	1,261	0.5%
33	Pennsylvania	1,596	0.6%	38	West Virginia	1,242	0.5%
46	Rhode Island	154	0.1%	39	Montana	1,141	0.4%
20	South Carolina	4,167	1.6%	40	Maine	939	0.4%
43	South Dakota	851	0.3%	41	Wyoming	913	0.4%
12	Tennessee	6,981	2.7%	42	Connecticut	889	0.3%
3	Texas	21,548	8.4%	43	South Dakota	851	0.3%
31	Utah	1,965	0.8%	44	North Dakota	538	0.2%
47	Vermont	125	0.0%	45	New Hampshire	183	0.1%
10	Virginia	7,816	3.0%	46	Rhode Island	154	0.1%
19	Washington	4,223	1.6%	47	Vermont	125	0.0%
38	West Virginia	1,242	0.5%	48	Delaware	52	0.0%
13	Wisconsin	5,723	2.2%	49	Alaska	0	0.0%
41	Wyoming	913	0.4%	49	Hawaii	0	0.0%
					District of Columbia	0	0.0%

Source: U.S. Department of Justice, Bureau of Justice Statistics
   "Census of State and Local Law Enforcement Agencies, 1996" (Bulletin, June 1998, NCJ-164618)
*Sheriffs' departments generally operate at the county level.

Special Police Agencies in 1996

National Total = 1,316 Agencies*

ALPHA ORDER

RANK	STATE	AGENCIES	% of USA
13	Alabama	33	2.5%
39	Alaska	7	0.5%
19	Arizona	26	2.0%
21	Arkansas	23	1.7%
2	California	121	9.2%
26	Colorado	20	1.5%
34	Connecticut	13	1.0%
41	Delaware	6	0.5%
15	Florida	30	2.3%
7	Georgia	44	3.3%
47	Hawaii	3	0.2%
47	Idaho	3	0.2%
5	Illinois	51	3.9%
24	Indiana	22	1.7%
37	Iowa	8	0.6%
27	Kansas	19	1.4%
28	Kentucky	16	1.2%
16	Louisiana	29	2.2%
36	Maine	9	0.7%
7	Maryland	44	3.3%
10	Massachusetts	34	2.6%
16	Michigan	29	2.2%
32	Minnesota	14	1.1%
16	Mississippi	29	2.2%
24	Missouri	22	1.7%
37	Montana	8	0.6%
46	Nebraska	4	0.3%
29	Nevada	15	1.1%
47	New Hampshire	3	0.2%
6	New Jersey	45	3.4%
29	New Mexico	15	1.1%
4	New York	64	4.9%
14	North Carolina	32	2.4%
39	North Dakota	7	0.5%
9	Ohio	41	3.1%
10	Oklahoma	34	2.6%
42	Oregon	5	0.4%
3	Pennsylvania	89	6.8%
42	Rhode Island	5	0.4%
20	South Carolina	25	1.9%
42	South Dakota	5	0.4%
21	Tennessee	23	1.7%
1	Texas	133	10.1%
34	Utah	13	1.0%
50	Vermont	2	0.2%
10	Virginia	34	2.6%
32	Washington	14	1.1%
29	West Virginia	15	1.1%
21	Wisconsin	23	1.7%
42	Wyoming	5	0.4%

RANK ORDER

RANK	STATE	AGENCIES	% of USA
1	Texas	133	10.1%
2	California	121	9.2%
3	Pennsylvania	89	6.8%
4	New York	64	4.9%
5	Illinois	51	3.9%
6	New Jersey	45	3.4%
7	Georgia	44	3.3%
7	Maryland	44	3.3%
9	Ohio	41	3.1%
10	Massachusetts	34	2.6%
10	Oklahoma	34	2.6%
10	Virginia	34	2.6%
13	Alabama	33	2.5%
14	North Carolina	32	2.4%
15	Florida	30	2.3%
16	Louisiana	29	2.2%
16	Michigan	29	2.2%
16	Mississippi	29	2.2%
19	Arizona	26	2.0%
20	South Carolina	25	1.9%
21	Arkansas	23	1.7%
21	Tennessee	23	1.7%
21	Wisconsin	23	1.7%
24	Indiana	22	1.7%
24	Missouri	22	1.7%
26	Colorado	20	1.5%
27	Kansas	19	1.4%
28	Kentucky	16	1.2%
29	Nevada	15	1.1%
29	New Mexico	15	1.1%
29	West Virginia	15	1.1%
32	Minnesota	14	1.1%
32	Washington	14	1.1%
34	Connecticut	13	1.0%
34	Utah	13	1.0%
36	Maine	9	0.7%
37	Iowa	8	0.6%
37	Montana	8	0.6%
39	Alaska	7	0.5%
39	North Dakota	7	0.5%
41	Delaware	6	0.5%
42	Oregon	5	0.4%
42	Rhode Island	5	0.4%
42	South Dakota	5	0.4%
42	Wyoming	5	0.4%
46	Nebraska	4	0.3%
47	Hawaii	3	0.2%
47	Idaho	3	0.2%
47	New Hampshire	3	0.2%
50	Vermont	2	0.2%
	District of Columbia	2	0.2%

Source: U.S. Department of Justice, Bureau of Justice Statistics
"Census of State and Local Law Enforcement Agencies, 1996" (Bulletin, June 1998, NCJ-164618)
*Agencies with special jurisdictions or special enforcement responsibilities.

Full-Time Sworn Officers in Special Police Departments in 1996

National Total = 43,082 Officers*

ALPHA ORDER

RANK	STATE	OFFICERS	% of USA
18	Alabama	739	1.7%
38	Alaska	224	0.5%
23	Arizona	606	1.4%
22	Arkansas	643	1.5%
2	California	4,107	9.5%
24	Colorado	540	1.3%
39	Connecticut	206	0.5%
40	Delaware	173	0.4%
5	Florida	1,879	4.4%
11	Georgia	1,244	2.9%
34	Hawaii	243	0.6%
42	Idaho	137	0.3%
8	Illinois	1,627	3.8%
20	Indiana	680	1.6%
37	Iowa	230	0.5%
31	Kansas	332	0.8%
32	Kentucky	280	0.6%
13	Louisiana	799	1.9%
36	Maine	234	0.5%
7	Maryland	1,842	4.3%
15	Massachusetts	762	1.8%
19	Michigan	681	1.6%
29	Minnesota	365	0.8%
27	Mississippi	478	1.1%
16	Missouri	745	1.7%
41	Montana	164	0.4%
45	Nebraska	110	0.3%
26	Nevada	488	1.1%
49	New Hampshire	69	0.2%
4	New Jersey	2,320	5.4%
30	New Mexico	348	0.8%
1	New York	6,740	15.6%
12	North Carolina	804	1.9%
47	North Dakota	96	0.2%
9	Ohio	1,309	3.0%
25	Oklahoma	511	1.2%
48	Oregon	74	0.2%
6	Pennsylvania	1,865	4.3%
43	Rhode Island	118	0.3%
17	South Carolina	742	1.7%
43	South Dakota	118	0.3%
14	Tennessee	788	1.8%
3	Texas	3,311	7.7%
33	Utah	264	0.6%
50	Vermont	56	0.1%
10	Virginia	1,270	2.9%
28	Washington	403	0.9%
35	West Virginia	240	0.6%
21	Wisconsin	655	1.5%
46	Wyoming	101	0.2%

RANK ORDER

RANK	STATE	OFFICERS	% of USA
1	New York	6,740	15.6%
2	California	4,107	9.5%
3	Texas	3,311	7.7%
4	New Jersey	2,320	5.4%
5	Florida	1,879	4.4%
6	Pennsylvania	1,865	4.3%
7	Maryland	1,842	4.3%
8	Illinois	1,627	3.8%
9	Ohio	1,309	3.0%
10	Virginia	1,270	2.9%
11	Georgia	1,244	2.9%
12	North Carolina	804	1.9%
13	Louisiana	799	1.9%
14	Tennessee	788	1.8%
15	Massachusetts	762	1.8%
16	Missouri	745	1.7%
17	South Carolina	742	1.7%
18	Alabama	739	1.7%
19	Michigan	681	1.6%
20	Indiana	680	1.6%
21	Wisconsin	655	1.5%
22	Arkansas	643	1.5%
23	Arizona	606	1.4%
24	Colorado	540	1.3%
25	Oklahoma	511	1.2%
26	Nevada	488	1.1%
27	Mississippi	478	1.1%
28	Washington	403	0.9%
29	Minnesota	365	0.8%
30	New Mexico	348	0.8%
31	Kansas	332	0.8%
32	Kentucky	280	0.6%
33	Utah	264	0.6%
34	Hawaii	243	0.6%
35	West Virginia	240	0.6%
36	Maine	234	0.5%
37	Iowa	230	0.5%
38	Alaska	224	0.5%
39	Connecticut	206	0.5%
40	Delaware	173	0.4%
41	Montana	164	0.4%
42	Idaho	137	0.3%
43	Rhode Island	118	0.3%
43	South Dakota	118	0.3%
45	Nebraska	110	0.3%
46	Wyoming	101	0.2%
47	North Dakota	96	0.2%
48	Oregon	74	0.2%
49	New Hampshire	69	0.2%
50	Vermont	56	0.1%
	District of Columbia	322	0.7%

Source: U.S. Department of Justice, Bureau of Justice Statistics
"Census of State and Local Law Enforcement Agencies, 1996" (Bulletin, June 1998, NCJ-164618)
Agencies with special jurisdictions or special enforcement responsibilities.

Percent of Full-Time Special Police Department Employees
Who Are Sworn Officers: 1996
National Percent = 76.6% of Employees*

ALPHA ORDER

RANK	STATE	PERCENT
25	Alabama	77.7
19	Alaska	80.6
42	Arizona	70.2
6	Arkansas	85.5
41	California	71.5
39	Colorado	72.7
20	Connecticut	79.8
43	Delaware	69.2
40	Florida	72.3
45	Georgia	67.8
3	Hawaii	88.7
11	Idaho	84.0
13	Illinois	83.8
10	Indiana	84.4
34	Iowa	75.9
28	Kansas	76.7
48	Kentucky	64.8
8	Louisiana	85.2
21	Maine	79.3
38	Maryland	73.7
31	Massachusetts	76.6
49	Michigan	61.2
18	Minnesota	81.8
36	Mississippi	75.5
26	Missouri	77.4
43	Montana	69.2
11	Nebraska	84.0
28	Nevada	76.7
28	New Hampshire	76.7
27	New Jersey	76.9
14	New Mexico	83.1
4	New York	87.7
22	North Carolina	79.1
35	North Dakota	75.6
24	Ohio	78.1
33	Oklahoma	76.4
37	Oregon	74.7
6	Pennsylvania	85.5
47	Rhode Island	65.2
50	South Carolina	55.4
5	South Dakota	86.8
23	Tennessee	78.7
46	Texas	65.7
17	Utah	82.0
9	Vermont	84.8
16	Virginia	82.4
32	Washington	76.5
2	West Virginia	88.9
15	Wisconsin	83.0
1	Wyoming	89.4

RANK ORDER

RANK	STATE	PERCENT
1	Wyoming	89.4
2	West Virginia	88.9
3	Hawaii	88.7
4	New York	87.7
5	South Dakota	86.8
6	Arkansas	85.5
6	Pennsylvania	85.5
8	Louisiana	85.2
9	Vermont	84.8
10	Indiana	84.4
11	Idaho	84.0
11	Nebraska	84.0
13	Illinois	83.8
14	New Mexico	83.1
15	Wisconsin	83.0
16	Virginia	82.4
17	Utah	82.0
18	Minnesota	81.8
19	Alaska	80.6
20	Connecticut	79.8
21	Maine	79.3
22	North Carolina	79.1
23	Tennessee	78.7
24	Ohio	78.1
25	Alabama	77.7
26	Missouri	77.4
27	New Jersey	76.9
28	Kansas	76.7
28	Nevada	76.7
28	New Hampshire	76.7
31	Massachusetts	76.6
32	Washington	76.5
33	Oklahoma	76.4
34	Iowa	75.9
35	North Dakota	75.6
36	Mississippi	75.5
37	Oregon	74.7
38	Maryland	73.7
39	Colorado	72.7
40	Florida	72.3
41	California	71.5
42	Arizona	70.2
43	Delaware	69.2
43	Montana	69.2
45	Georgia	67.8
46	Texas	65.7
47	Rhode Island	65.2
48	Kentucky	64.8
49	Michigan	61.2
50	South Carolina	55.4

	District of Columbia	75.6

Source: Morgan Quitno Press using data from U.S. Department of Justice, Bureau of Justice Statistics
"Census of State and Local Law Enforcement Agencies, 1996" (Bulletin, June 1998, NCJ-164618)
*Agencies with special jurisdictions or special enforcement responsibilities.

Rate of Full-Time Sworn Officers in Special Police Departments in 1996

National Rate = 1.6 Officers per 10,000 Population*

ALPHA ORDER

RANK	STATE	RATE
17	Alabama	1.7
1	Alaska	3.7
25	Arizona	1.4
6	Arkansas	2.6
29	California	1.3
25	Colorado	1.4
48	Connecticut	0.6
7	Delaware	2.4
29	Florida	1.3
17	Georgia	1.7
8	Hawaii	2.1
36	Idaho	1.2
25	Illinois	1.4
36	Indiana	1.2
42	Iowa	0.8
29	Kansas	1.3
44	Kentucky	0.7
15	Louisiana	1.8
12	Maine	1.9
3	Maryland	3.6
29	Massachusetts	1.3
44	Michigan	0.7
42	Minnesota	0.8
15	Mississippi	1.8
25	Missouri	1.4
12	Montana	1.9
44	Nebraska	0.7
4	Nevada	3.0
48	New Hampshire	0.6
5	New Jersey	2.9
10	New Mexico	2.0
1	New York	3.7
40	North Carolina	1.1
21	North Dakota	1.5
36	Ohio	1.2
21	Oklahoma	1.5
50	Oregon	0.2
21	Pennsylvania	1.5
36	Rhode Island	1.2
10	South Carolina	2.0
20	South Dakota	1.6
21	Tennessee	1.5
17	Texas	1.7
29	Utah	1.3
41	Vermont	1.0
12	Virginia	1.9
44	Washington	0.7
29	West Virginia	1.3
29	Wisconsin	1.3
8	Wyoming	2.1

RANK ORDER

RANK	STATE	RATE
1	Alaska	3.7
1	New York	3.7
3	Maryland	3.6
4	Nevada	3.0
5	New Jersey	2.9
6	Arkansas	2.6
7	Delaware	2.4
8	Hawaii	2.1
8	Wyoming	2.1
10	New Mexico	2.0
10	South Carolina	2.0
12	Maine	1.9
12	Montana	1.9
12	Virginia	1.9
15	Louisiana	1.8
15	Mississippi	1.8
17	Alabama	1.7
17	Georgia	1.7
17	Texas	1.7
20	South Dakota	1.6
21	North Dakota	1.5
21	Oklahoma	1.5
21	Pennsylvania	1.5
21	Tennessee	1.5
25	Arizona	1.4
25	Colorado	1.4
25	Illinois	1.4
25	Missouri	1.4
29	California	1.3
29	Florida	1.3
29	Kansas	1.3
29	Massachusetts	1.3
29	Utah	1.3
29	West Virginia	1.3
29	Wisconsin	1.3
36	Idaho	1.2
36	Indiana	1.2
36	Ohio	1.2
36	Rhode Island	1.2
40	North Carolina	1.1
41	Vermont	1.0
42	Iowa	0.8
42	Minnesota	0.8
44	Kentucky	0.7
44	Michigan	0.7
44	Nebraska	0.7
44	Washington	0.7
48	Connecticut	0.6
48	New Hampshire	0.6
50	Oregon	0.2
	District of Columbia	5.9

Source: U.S. Department of Justice, Bureau of Justice Statistics
   "Census of State and Local Law Enforcement Agencies, 1996" (Bulletin, June 1998, NCJ-164618)
*Agencies with special jurisdictions or special enforcement responsibilities.

Full-Time Employees in Special Police Departments in 1996

National Total = 56,229 Employees*

ALPHA ORDER

RANK	STATE	EMPLOYEES	% of USA
18	Alabama	951	1.7%
36	Alaska	278	0.5%
20	Arizona	863	1.5%
23	Arkansas	752	1.3%
2	California	5,741	10.2%
24	Colorado	743	1.3%
39	Connecticut	258	0.5%
40	Delaware	250	0.4%
5	Florida	2,598	4.6%
9	Georgia	1,835	3.3%
37	Hawaii	274	0.5%
43	Idaho	163	0.3%
8	Illinois	1,942	3.5%
21	Indiana	806	1.4%
34	Iowa	303	0.5%
30	Kansas	433	0.8%
31	Kentucky	432	0.8%
19	Louisiana	938	1.7%
35	Maine	295	0.5%
6	Maryland	2,498	4.4%
16	Massachusetts	995	1.8%
13	Michigan	1,113	2.0%
29	Minnesota	446	0.8%
27	Mississippi	633	1.1%
17	Missouri	962	1.7%
41	Montana	237	0.4%
45	Nebraska	131	0.2%
26	Nevada	636	1.1%
49	New Hampshire	90	0.2%
4	New Jersey	3,016	5.4%
32	New Mexico	419	0.7%
1	New York	7,681	13.7%
14	North Carolina	1,016	1.8%
46	North Dakota	127	0.2%
10	Ohio	1,675	3.0%
25	Oklahoma	669	1.2%
48	Oregon	99	0.2%
7	Pennsylvania	2,182	3.9%
42	Rhode Island	181	0.3%
12	South Carolina	1,340	2.4%
44	South Dakota	136	0.2%
15	Tennessee	1,001	1.8%
3	Texas	5,037	9.0%
33	Utah	322	0.6%
50	Vermont	66	0.1%
11	Virginia	1,541	2.7%
28	Washington	527	0.9%
38	West Virginia	270	0.5%
22	Wisconsin	789	1.4%
47	Wyoming	113	0.2%

RANK ORDER

RANK	STATE	EMPLOYEES	% of USA
1	New York	7,681	13.7%
2	California	5,741	10.2%
3	Texas	5,037	9.0%
4	New Jersey	3,016	5.4%
5	Florida	2,598	4.6%
6	Maryland	2,498	4.4%
7	Pennsylvania	2,182	3.9%
8	Illinois	1,942	3.5%
9	Georgia	1,835	3.3%
10	Ohio	1,675	3.0%
11	Virginia	1,541	2.7%
12	South Carolina	1,340	2.4%
13	Michigan	1,113	2.0%
14	North Carolina	1,016	1.8%
15	Tennessee	1,001	1.8%
16	Massachusetts	995	1.8%
17	Missouri	962	1.7%
18	Alabama	951	1.7%
19	Louisiana	938	1.7%
20	Arizona	863	1.5%
21	Indiana	806	1.4%
22	Wisconsin	789	1.4%
23	Arkansas	752	1.3%
24	Colorado	743	1.3%
25	Oklahoma	669	1.2%
26	Nevada	636	1.1%
27	Mississippi	633	1.1%
28	Washington	527	0.9%
29	Minnesota	446	0.8%
30	Kansas	433	0.8%
31	Kentucky	432	0.8%
32	New Mexico	419	0.7%
33	Utah	322	0.6%
34	Iowa	303	0.5%
35	Maine	295	0.5%
36	Alaska	278	0.5%
37	Hawaii	274	0.5%
38	West Virginia	270	0.5%
39	Connecticut	258	0.5%
40	Delaware	250	0.4%
41	Montana	237	0.4%
42	Rhode Island	181	0.3%
43	Idaho	163	0.3%
44	South Dakota	136	0.2%
45	Nebraska	131	0.2%
46	North Dakota	127	0.2%
47	Wyoming	113	0.2%
48	Oregon	99	0.2%
49	New Hampshire	90	0.2%
50	Vermont	66	0.1%
	District of Columbia	426	0.8%

Source: U.S. Department of Justice, Bureau of Justice Statistics
"Census of State and Local Law Enforcement Agencies, 1996" (Bulletin, June 1998, NCJ-164618)
*Agencies with special jurisdictions or special enforcement responsibilities.

Law Enforcement Officers Feloniously Killed in 1998

National Total = 56 Officers*

ALPHA ORDER

RANK	STATE	OFFICERS	% of USA
7	Alabama	2	3.6%
14	Alaska	1	1.8%
14	Arizona	1	1.8%
14	Arkansas	1	1.8%
1	California	7	12.5%
14	Colorado	1	1.8%
28	Connecticut	0	0.0%
28	Delaware	0	0.0%
2	Florida	5	8.9%
7	Georgia	2	3.6%
28	Hawaii	0	0.0%
14	Idaho	1	1.8%
14	Illinois	1	1.8%
7	Indiana	2	3.6%
28	Iowa	0	0.0%
14	Kansas	1	1.8%
7	Kentucky	2	3.6%
28	Louisiana	0	0.0%
28	Maine	0	0.0%
28	Maryland	0	0.0%
28	Massachusetts	0	0.0%
7	Michigan	2	3.6%
28	Minnesota	0	0.0%
4	Mississippi	3	5.4%
14	Missouri	1	1.8%
28	Montana	0	0.0%
28	Nebraska	0	0.0%
14	Nevada	1	1.8%
28	New Hampshire	0	0.0%
28	New Jersey	0	0.0%
28	New Mexico	0	0.0%
4	New York	3	5.4%
7	North Carolina	2	3.6%
28	North Dakota	0	0.0%
14	Ohio	1	1.8%
28	Oklahoma	0	0.0%
14	Oregon	1	1.8%
28	Pennsylvania	0	0.0%
28	Rhode Island	0	0.0%
14	South Carolina	1	1.8%
28	South Dakota	0	0.0%
28	Tennessee	0	0.0%
2	Texas	5	8.9%
28	Utah	0	0.0%
28	Vermont	0	0.0%
4	Virginia	3	5.4%
14	Washington	1	1.8%
14	West Virginia	1	1.8%
7	Wisconsin	2	3.6%
28	Wyoming	0	0.0%

RANK ORDER

RANK	STATE	OFFICERS	% of USA
1	California	7	12.5%
2	Florida	5	8.9%
2	Texas	5	8.9%
4	Mississippi	3	5.4%
4	New York	3	5.4%
4	Virginia	3	5.4%
7	Alabama	2	3.6%
7	Georgia	2	3.6%
7	Indiana	2	3.6%
7	Kentucky	2	3.6%
7	Michigan	2	3.6%
7	North Carolina	2	3.6%
7	Wisconsin	2	3.6%
14	Alaska	1	1.8%
14	Arizona	1	1.8%
14	Arkansas	1	1.8%
14	Colorado	1	1.8%
14	Idaho	1	1.8%
14	Illinois	1	1.8%
14	Kansas	1	1.8%
14	Missouri	1	1.8%
14	Nevada	1	1.8%
14	Ohio	1	1.8%
14	Oregon	1	1.8%
14	South Carolina	1	1.8%
14	Washington	1	1.8%
14	West Virginia	1	1.8%
28	Connecticut	0	0.0%
28	Delaware	0	0.0%
28	Hawaii	0	0.0%
28	Iowa	0	0.0%
28	Louisiana	0	0.0%
28	Maine	0	0.0%
28	Maryland	0	0.0%
28	Massachusetts	0	0.0%
28	Minnesota	0	0.0%
28	Montana	0	0.0%
28	Nebraska	0	0.0%
28	New Hampshire	0	0.0%
28	New Jersey	0	0.0%
28	New Mexico	0	0.0%
28	North Dakota	0	0.0%
28	Oklahoma	0	0.0%
28	Pennsylvania	0	0.0%
28	Rhode Island	0	0.0%
28	South Dakota	0	0.0%
28	Tennessee	0	0.0%
28	Utah	0	0.0%
28	Vermont	0	0.0%
28	Wyoming	0	0.0%
	District of Columbia	2	3.6%

Source: Federal Bureau of Investigation
"Law Enforcement Officers Killed and Assaulted 1998" (http://www.fbi.gov/ucr/killed/98killed.pdf)
*Total does not include five officers killed in Puerto Rico.

Law Enforcement Officers Feloniously Killed: 1989 to 1998

National Total = 618 Officers*

ALPHA ORDER

RANK	STATE	OFFICERS	% of USA
19	Alabama	12	1.9%
31	Alaska	5	0.8%
16	Arizona	14	2.3%
22	Arkansas	11	1.8%
1	California	64	10.4%
25	Colorado	9	1.5%
40	Connecticut	2	0.3%
47	Delaware	0	0.0%
4	Florida	30	4.9%
5	Georgia	25	4.0%
43	Hawaii	1	0.2%
31	Idaho	5	0.8%
9	Illinois	20	3.2%
19	Indiana	12	1.9%
47	Iowa	0	0.0%
29	Kansas	7	1.1%
19	Kentucky	12	1.9%
10	Louisiana	19	3.1%
43	Maine	1	0.2%
25	Maryland	9	1.5%
27	Massachusetts	8	1.3%
11	Michigan	18	2.9%
22	Minnesota	11	1.8%
7	Mississippi	24	3.9%
14	Missouri	16	2.6%
35	Montana	4	0.6%
39	Nebraska	3	0.5%
30	Nevada	6	1.0%
35	New Hampshire	4	0.6%
27	New Jersey	8	1.3%
31	New Mexico	5	0.8%
3	New York	35	5.7%
5	North Carolina	25	4.0%
40	North Dakota	2	0.3%
11	Ohio	18	2.9%
22	Oklahoma	11	1.8%
35	Oregon	4	0.6%
8	Pennsylvania	21	3.4%
43	Rhode Island	1	0.2%
13	South Carolina	17	2.8%
47	South Dakota	0	0.0%
14	Tennessee	16	2.6%
2	Texas	52	8.4%
40	Utah	2	0.3%
47	Vermont	0	0.0%
18	Virginia	13	2.1%
31	Washington	5	0.8%
35	West Virginia	4	0.6%
16	Wisconsin	14	2.3%
43	Wyoming	1	0.2%

RANK ORDER

RANK	STATE	OFFICERS	% of USA
1	California	64	10.4%
2	Texas	52	8.4%
3	New York	35	5.7%
4	Florida	30	4.9%
5	Georgia	25	4.0%
5	North Carolina	25	4.0%
7	Mississippi	24	3.9%
8	Pennsylvania	21	3.4%
9	Illinois	20	3.2%
10	Louisiana	19	3.1%
11	Michigan	18	2.9%
11	Ohio	18	2.9%
13	South Carolina	17	2.8%
14	Missouri	16	2.6%
14	Tennessee	16	2.6%
16	Arizona	14	2.3%
16	Wisconsin	14	2.3%
18	Virginia	13	2.1%
19	Alabama	12	1.9%
19	Indiana	12	1.9%
19	Kentucky	12	1.9%
22	Arkansas	11	1.8%
22	Minnesota	11	1.8%
22	Oklahoma	11	1.8%
25	Colorado	9	1.5%
25	Maryland	9	1.5%
27	Massachusetts	8	1.3%
27	New Jersey	8	1.3%
29	Kansas	7	1.1%
30	Nevada	6	1.0%
31	Alaska	5	0.8%
31	Idaho	5	0.8%
31	New Mexico	5	0.8%
31	Washington	5	0.8%
35	Montana	4	0.6%
35	New Hampshire	4	0.6%
35	Oregon	4	0.6%
35	West Virginia	4	0.6%
39	Nebraska	3	0.5%
40	Connecticut	2	0.3%
40	North Dakota	2	0.3%
40	Utah	2	0.3%
43	Hawaii	1	0.2%
43	Maine	1	0.2%
43	Rhode Island	1	0.2%
43	Wyoming	1	0.2%
47	Delaware	0	0.0%
47	Iowa	0	0.0%
47	South Dakota	0	0.0%
47	Vermont	0	0.0%
	District of Columbia	12	1.9%

Source: Federal Bureau of Investigation
"Law Enforcement Officers Killed and Assaulted 1998" (http://www.fbi.gov/ucr/killed/98killed.pdf)
*Total does not include 64 officers killed in U.S. territories (62 officers killed in Puerto Rico, one in the U.S. Virgin Islands and one in the Mariana Islands).

U.S. District Court Judges in 1999

National Total = 646 Judges*

ALPHA ORDER

RANK	STATE	JUDGES	% of USA
15	Alabama	13	2.0%
41	Alaska	3	0.5%
25	Arizona	8	1.2%
25	Arkansas	8	1.2%
1	California	56	8.7%
29	Colorado	7	1.1%
25	Connecticut	8	1.2%
37	Delaware	4	0.6%
5	Florida	31	4.8%
10	Georgia	18	2.8%
37	Hawaii	4	0.6%
48	Idaho	2	0.3%
6	Illinois	30	4.6%
20	Indiana	10	1.5%
34	Iowa	5	0.8%
31	Kansas	6	0.9%
22	Kentucky	9	1.4%
7	Louisiana	22	3.4%
41	Maine	3	0.5%
20	Maryland	10	1.5%
15	Massachusetts	13	2.0%
9	Michigan	19	2.9%
29	Minnesota	7	1.1%
22	Mississippi	9	1.4%
12	Missouri	14	2.2%
41	Montana	3	0.5%
37	Nebraska	4	0.6%
37	Nevada	4	0.6%
41	New Hampshire	3	0.5%
11	New Jersey	17	2.6%
34	New Mexico	5	0.8%
2	New York	52	8.0%
17	North Carolina	11	1.7%
48	North Dakota	2	0.3%
8	Ohio	20	3.1%
17	Oklahoma	11	1.7%
31	Oregon	6	0.9%
4	Pennsylvania	38	5.9%
41	Rhode Island	3	0.5%
22	South Carolina	9	1.4%
41	South Dakota	3	0.5%
12	Tennessee	14	2.2%
3	Texas	47	7.3%
34	Utah	5	0.8%
48	Vermont	2	0.3%
12	Virginia	14	2.2%
17	Washington	11	1.7%
25	West Virginia	8	1.2%
31	Wisconsin	6	0.9%
41	Wyoming	3	0.5%

RANK ORDER

RANK	STATE	JUDGES	% of USA
1	California	56	8.7%
2	New York	52	8.0%
3	Texas	47	7.3%
4	Pennsylvania	38	5.9%
5	Florida	31	4.8%
6	Illinois	30	4.6%
7	Louisiana	22	3.4%
8	Ohio	20	3.1%
9	Michigan	19	2.9%
10	Georgia	18	2.8%
11	New Jersey	17	2.6%
12	Missouri	14	2.2%
12	Tennessee	14	2.2%
12	Virginia	14	2.2%
15	Alabama	13	2.0%
15	Massachusetts	13	2.0%
17	North Carolina	11	1.7%
17	Oklahoma	11	1.7%
17	Washington	11	1.7%
20	Indiana	10	1.5%
20	Maryland	10	1.5%
22	Kentucky	9	1.4%
22	Mississippi	9	1.4%
22	South Carolina	9	1.4%
25	Arizona	8	1.2%
25	Arkansas	8	1.2%
25	Connecticut	8	1.2%
25	West Virginia	8	1.2%
29	Colorado	7	1.1%
29	Minnesota	7	1.1%
31	Kansas	6	0.9%
31	Oregon	6	0.9%
31	Wisconsin	6	0.9%
34	Iowa	5	0.8%
34	New Mexico	5	0.8%
34	Utah	5	0.8%
37	Delaware	4	0.6%
37	Hawaii	4	0.6%
37	Nebraska	4	0.6%
37	Nevada	4	0.6%
41	Alaska	3	0.5%
41	Maine	3	0.5%
41	Montana	3	0.5%
41	New Hampshire	3	0.5%
41	Rhode Island	3	0.5%
41	South Dakota	3	0.5%
41	Wyoming	3	0.5%
48	Idaho	2	0.3%
48	North Dakota	2	0.3%
48	Vermont	2	0.3%
	District of Columbia	15	2.3%

Source: Administrative Office of the United States Courts
    "1999 Federal Court Management Statistics" (March 2000)
*Total includes 11 judgeships in U.S. territories.

Population per U.S. District Judge in 1999

National Average = 429,434 People per U.S. District Judge*

ALPHA ORDER

RANK	STATE	RATE
35	Alabama	336,143
47	Alaska	206,500
5	Arizona	597,292
37	Arkansas	318,922
7	California	591,877
8	Colorado	579,448
28	Connecticut	410,254
49	Delaware	188,385
16	Florida	487,459
22	Georgia	432,680
43	Hawaii	296,374
4	Idaho	625,850
29	Illinois	404,279
6	Indiana	594,290
9	Iowa	573,883
20	Kansas	442,342
21	Kentucky	440,092
48	Louisiana	198,729
26	Maine	417,680
14	Maryland	517,163
18	Massachusetts	475,013
13	Michigan	519,146
3	Minnesota	682,215
40	Mississippi	307,624
32	Missouri	390,596
44	Montana	294,260
27	Nebraska	416,507
19	Nevada	452,313
30	New Hampshire	400,378
17	New Jersey	479,024
34	New Mexico	347,969
33	New York	349,935
2	North Carolina	695,526
38	North Dakota	316,833
10	Ohio	562,833
41	Oklahoma	305,277
11	Oregon	552,692
39	Pennsylvania	315,632
36	Rhode Island	330,273
23	South Carolina	431,748
45	South Dakota	244,378
31	Tennessee	391,681
24	Texas	426,471
25	Utah	425,967
42	Vermont	296,870
15	Virginia	490,922
12	Washington	523,306
46	West Virginia	225,866
1	Wisconsin	875,074
50	Wyoming	159,867

RANK ORDER

RANK	STATE	RATE
1	Wisconsin	875,074
2	North Carolina	695,526
3	Minnesota	682,215
4	Idaho	625,850
5	Arizona	597,292
6	Indiana	594,290
7	California	591,877
8	Colorado	579,448
9	Iowa	573,883
10	Ohio	562,833
11	Oregon	552,692
12	Washington	523,306
13	Michigan	519,146
14	Maryland	517,163
15	Virginia	490,922
16	Florida	487,459
17	New Jersey	479,024
18	Massachusetts	475,013
19	Nevada	452,313
20	Kansas	442,342
21	Kentucky	440,092
22	Georgia	432,680
23	South Carolina	431,748
24	Texas	426,471
25	Utah	425,967
26	Maine	417,680
27	Nebraska	416,507
28	Connecticut	410,254
29	Illinois	404,279
30	New Hampshire	400,378
31	Tennessee	391,681
32	Missouri	390,596
33	New York	349,935
34	New Mexico	347,969
35	Alabama	336,143
36	Rhode Island	330,273
37	Arkansas	318,922
38	North Dakota	316,833
39	Pennsylvania	315,632
40	Mississippi	307,624
41	Oklahoma	305,277
42	Vermont	296,870
43	Hawaii	296,374
44	Montana	294,260
45	South Dakota	244,378
46	West Virginia	225,866
47	Alaska	206,500
48	Louisiana	198,729
49	Delaware	188,385
50	Wyoming	159,867
	District of Columbia	34,600

Source: Morgan Quitno Press using data from Administrative Office of the United States Courts
   "1999 Federal Court Management Statistics" (March 2000)
*National rate does not include judgeships or population in U.S. territories.

Felony Criminal Cases Filed in U.S. District Courts in 1999

National Total = 47,112 Felony Criminal Cases*

ALPHA ORDER

RANK	STATE	CASES	% of USA
22	Alabama	565	1.2%
44	Alaska	155	0.3%
5	Arizona	2,746	5.8%
36	Arkansas	317	0.7%
2	California	6,225	13.2%
30	Colorado	391	0.8%
41	Connecticut	228	0.5%
50	Delaware	72	0.2%
4	Florida	2,855	6.1%
11	Georgia	890	1.9%
39	Hawaii	253	0.5%
48	Idaho	97	0.2%
9	Illinois	1,101	2.3%
27	Indiana	451	1.0%
26	Iowa	453	1.0%
35	Kansas	349	0.7%
20	Kentucky	621	1.3%
21	Louisiana	616	1.3%
43	Maine	158	0.3%
27	Maryland	451	1.0%
29	Massachusetts	407	0.9%
15	Michigan	810	1.7%
37	Minnesota	288	0.6%
34	Mississippi	353	0.7%
13	Missouri	849	1.8%
40	Montana	248	0.5%
33	Nebraska	361	0.8%
24	Nevada	521	1.1%
45	New Hampshire	150	0.3%
19	New Jersey	633	1.3%
8	New Mexico	1,215	2.6%
3	New York	2,887	6.1%
10	North Carolina	968	2.1%
42	North Dakota	174	0.4%
14	Ohio	814	1.7%
25	Oklahoma	471	1.0%
17	Oregon	726	1.5%
7	Pennsylvania	1,230	2.6%
46	Rhode Island	122	0.3%
18	South Carolina	659	1.4%
31	South Dakota	390	0.8%
12	Tennessee	865	1.8%
1	Texas	8,310	17.6%
23	Utah	552	1.2%
47	Vermont	113	0.2%
6	Virginia	1,342	2.8%
16	Washington	808	1.7%
32	West Virginia	364	0.8%
37	Wisconsin	288	0.6%
49	Wyoming	96	0.2%

RANK ORDER

RANK	STATE	CASES	% of USA
1	Texas	8,310	17.6%
2	California	6,225	13.2%
3	New York	2,887	6.1%
4	Florida	2,855	6.1%
5	Arizona	2,746	5.8%
6	Virginia	1,342	2.8%
7	Pennsylvania	1,230	2.6%
8	New Mexico	1,215	2.6%
9	Illinois	1,101	2.3%
10	North Carolina	968	2.1%
11	Georgia	890	1.9%
12	Tennessee	865	1.8%
13	Missouri	849	1.8%
14	Ohio	814	1.7%
15	Michigan	810	1.7%
16	Washington	808	1.7%
17	Oregon	726	1.5%
18	South Carolina	659	1.4%
19	New Jersey	633	1.3%
20	Kentucky	621	1.3%
21	Louisiana	616	1.3%
22	Alabama	565	1.2%
23	Utah	552	1.2%
24	Nevada	521	1.1%
25	Oklahoma	471	1.0%
26	Iowa	453	1.0%
27	Indiana	451	1.0%
27	Maryland	451	1.0%
29	Massachusetts	407	0.9%
30	Colorado	391	0.8%
31	South Dakota	390	0.8%
32	West Virginia	364	0.8%
33	Nebraska	361	0.8%
34	Mississippi	353	0.7%
35	Kansas	349	0.7%
36	Arkansas	317	0.7%
37	Minnesota	288	0.6%
37	Wisconsin	288	0.6%
39	Hawaii	253	0.5%
40	Montana	248	0.5%
41	Connecticut	228	0.5%
42	North Dakota	174	0.4%
43	Maine	158	0.3%
44	Alaska	155	0.3%
45	New Hampshire	150	0.3%
46	Rhode Island	122	0.3%
47	Vermont	113	0.2%
48	Idaho	97	0.2%
49	Wyoming	96	0.2%
50	Delaware	72	0.2%
	District of Columbia	406	0.9%

Source: Administrative Office of the United States Courts
     "1999 Federal Court Management Statistics" (March 2000)
*National total includes 698 cases in U.S. territories. Does not include transfers from one district to another.

Felony Criminal Cases Filed per U.S. District Judge in 1999

National Rate = 74 Felony Cases per U.S. District Judge*

ALPHA ORDER

RANK	STATE	RATE
38	Alabama	43
28	Alaska	52
1	Arizona	346
41	Arkansas	41
4	California	166
25	Colorado	56
49	Connecticut	29
50	Delaware	18
13	Florida	89
32	Georgia	48
19	Hawaii	64
31	Idaho	49
26	Illinois	55
34	Indiana	46
9	Iowa	92
23	Kansas	59
18	Kentucky	70
45	Louisiana	36
27	Maine	53
34	Maryland	46
47	Massachusetts	32
29	Michigan	50
39	Minnesota	42
43	Mississippi	39
22	Missouri	61
15	Montana	83
11	Nebraska	91
5	Nevada	132
29	New Hampshire	50
43	New Jersey	39
2	New Mexico	245
20	New York	62
11	North Carolina	91
14	North Dakota	88
39	Ohio	42
34	Oklahoma	46
7	Oregon	123
45	Pennsylvania	36
41	Rhode Island	41
17	South Carolina	74
6	South Dakota	130
20	Tennessee	62
3	Texas	175
8	Utah	112
24	Vermont	57
9	Virginia	92
16	Washington	77
34	West Virginia	46
32	Wisconsin	48
47	Wyoming	32

RANK ORDER

RANK	STATE	RATE
1	Arizona	346
2	New Mexico	245
3	Texas	175
4	California	166
5	Nevada	132
6	South Dakota	130
7	Oregon	123
8	Utah	112
9	Iowa	92
9	Virginia	92
11	Nebraska	91
11	North Carolina	91
13	Florida	89
14	North Dakota	88
15	Montana	83
16	Washington	77
17	South Carolina	74
18	Kentucky	70
19	Hawaii	64
20	New York	62
20	Tennessee	62
22	Missouri	61
23	Kansas	59
24	Vermont	57
25	Colorado	56
26	Illinois	55
27	Maine	53
28	Alaska	52
29	Michigan	50
29	New Hampshire	50
31	Idaho	49
32	Georgia	48
32	Wisconsin	48
34	Indiana	46
34	Maryland	46
34	Oklahoma	46
34	West Virginia	46
38	Alabama	43
39	Minnesota	42
39	Ohio	42
41	Arkansas	41
41	Rhode Island	41
43	Mississippi	39
43	New Jersey	39
45	Louisiana	36
45	Pennsylvania	36
47	Massachusetts	32
47	Wyoming	32
49	Connecticut	29
50	Delaware	18
	District of Columbia	28

Source: Morgan Quitno Press using data from Administrative Office of the United States Courts
"1999 Federal Court Management Statistics" (March 2000)
*National rate includes cases and judges in U.S. territories. Does not include transfers from one district to another.

Median Length of Federal Criminal Cases in 1999

National Median = 6.5 Months*

ALPHA ORDER				RANK ORDER		
RANK	STATE	MONTHS		RANK	STATE	MONTHS
35	Alabama	6.4		1	Vermont	13.1
45	Alaska	5.6		2	Massachusetts	12.4
50	Arizona	4.1		3	New York	11.1
20	Arkansas	7.6		4	Nebraska	11.0
23	California	7.2		5	Connecticut	10.3
29	Colorado	6.8		6	Michigan	9.8
5	Connecticut	10.3		7	New Hampshire	9.1
40	Delaware	6.0		8	New Jersey	8.9
34	Florida	6.5		8	North Carolina	8.9
17	Georgia	7.8		10	Iowa	8.6
11	Hawaii	8.4		11	Hawaii	8.4
18	Idaho	7.7		12	Illinois	8.3
12	Illinois	8.3		12	Tennessee	8.3
29	Indiana	6.8		14	Maryland	8.2
10	Iowa	8.6		14	Nevada	8.2
22	Kansas	7.4		16	Minnesota	8.0
29	Kentucky	6.8		17	Georgia	7.8
23	Louisiana	7.2		18	Idaho	7.7
43	Maine	5.7		18	Pennsylvania	7.7
14	Maryland	8.2		20	Arkansas	7.6
2	Massachusetts	12.4		20	Montana	7.6
6	Michigan	9.8		22	Kansas	7.4
16	Minnesota	8.0		23	California	7.2
32	Mississippi	6.7		23	Louisiana	7.2
25	Missouri	7.1		25	Missouri	7.1
20	Montana	7.6		25	Virginia	7.1
4	Nebraska	11.0		27	Ohio	7.0
14	Nevada	8.2		27	South Carolina	7.0
7	New Hampshire	9.1		29	Colorado	6.8
8	New Jersey	8.9		29	Indiana	6.8
49	New Mexico	4.3		29	Kentucky	6.8
3	New York	11.1		32	Mississippi	6.7
8	North Carolina	8.9		32	Rhode Island	6.7
48	North Dakota	4.8		34	Florida	6.5
27	Ohio	7.0		35	Alabama	6.4
40	Oklahoma	6.0		35	Utah	6.4
37	Oregon	6.3		37	Oregon	6.3
18	Pennsylvania	7.7		38	Wisconsin	6.1
32	Rhode Island	6.7		38	Wyoming	6.1
27	South Carolina	7.0		40	Delaware	6.0
46	South Dakota	5.5		40	Oklahoma	6.0
12	Tennessee	8.3		42	West Virginia	6.0
46	Texas	5.5		43	Maine	5.7
35	Utah	6.4		43	Washington	5.7
1	Vermont	13.1		45	Alaska	5.6
25	Virginia	7.1		46	South Dakota	5.5
43	Washington	5.7		46	Texas	5.5
42	West Virginia	6.0		48	North Dakota	4.8
38	Wisconsin	6.1		49	New Mexico	4.3
38	Wyoming	6.1		50	Arizona	4.1
					District of Columbia	7.3

Source: Morgan Quitno Press using data from Administrative Office of the United States Courts
   "1999 Federal Court Management Statistics" (March 2000)
*Felony criminal cases. National rate includes cases U.S. territories. Does not include transfers from one district to another.

Authorized Wiretaps in 1999

National Total = 749 State Authorized Wiretaps*

ALPHA ORDER

RANK	STATE	WIRETAPS	% of USA
NA	Alabama**	NA	NA
28	Alaska	0	0.0%
12	Arizona	8	1.1%
NA	Arkansas**	NA	NA
2	California	76	10.1%
22	Colorado	2	0.3%
7	Connecticut	15	2.0%
24	Delaware	1	0.1%
6	Florida	23	3.1%
9	Georgia	11	1.5%
28	Hawaii	0	0.0%
24	Idaho	1	0.1%
5	Illinois	50	6.7%
28	Indiana	0	0.0%
28	Iowa	0	0.0%
17	Kansas	4	0.5%
NA	Kentucky**	NA	NA
28	Louisiana	0	0.0%
NA	Maine**	NA	NA
13	Maryland	6	0.8%
7	Massachusetts	15	2.0%
NA	Michigan**	NA	NA
13	Minnesota	6	0.8%
20	Mississippi	3	0.4%
28	Missouri	0	0.0%
NA	Montana**	NA	NA
17	Nebraska	4	0.5%
10	Nevada	9	1.2%
10	New Hampshire	9	1.2%
3	New Jersey	71	9.5%
28	New Mexico	0	0.0%
1	New York	343	45.8%
28	North Carolina	0	0.0%
28	North Dakota	0	0.0%
20	Ohio	3	0.4%
13	Oklahoma	6	0.8%
24	Oregon	1	0.1%
4	Pennsylvania	69	9.2%
28	Rhode Island	0	0.0%
NA	South Carolina**	NA	NA
28	South Dakota	0	0.0%
24	Tennessee	1	0.1%
17	Texas	4	0.5%
22	Utah	2	0.3%
NA	Vermont**	NA	NA
13	Virginia	6	0.8%
28	Washington	0	0.0%
28	West Virginia	0	0.0%
28	Wisconsin	0	0.0%
28	Wyoming	0	0.0%

RANK ORDER

RANK	STATE	WIRETAPS	% of USA
1	New York	343	45.8%
2	California	76	10.1%
3	New Jersey	71	9.5%
4	Pennsylvania	69	9.2%
5	Illinois	50	6.7%
6	Florida	23	3.1%
7	Connecticut	15	2.0%
7	Massachusetts	15	2.0%
9	Georgia	11	1.5%
10	Nevada	9	1.2%
10	New Hampshire	9	1.2%
12	Arizona	8	1.1%
13	Maryland	6	0.8%
13	Minnesota	6	0.8%
13	Oklahoma	6	0.8%
13	Virginia	6	0.8%
17	Kansas	4	0.5%
17	Nebraska	4	0.5%
17	Texas	4	0.5%
20	Mississippi	3	0.4%
20	Ohio	3	0.4%
22	Colorado	2	0.3%
22	Utah	2	0.3%
24	Delaware	1	0.1%
24	Idaho	1	0.1%
24	Oregon	1	0.1%
24	Tennessee	1	0.1%
28	Alaska	0	0.0%
28	Hawaii	0	0.0%
28	Indiana	0	0.0%
28	Iowa	0	0.0%
28	Louisiana	0	0.0%
28	Missouri	0	0.0%
28	New Mexico	0	0.0%
28	North Carolina	0	0.0%
28	North Dakota	0	0.0%
28	Rhode Island	0	0.0%
28	South Dakota	0	0.0%
28	Washington	0	0.0%
28	West Virginia	0	0.0%
28	Wisconsin	0	0.0%
28	Wyoming	0	0.0%
NA	Alabama**	NA	NA
NA	Arkansas**	NA	NA
NA	Kentucky**	NA	NA
NA	Maine**	NA	NA
NA	Michigan**	NA	NA
NA	Montana**	NA	NA
NA	South Carolina**	NA	NA
NA	Vermont**	NA	NA
	District of Columbia	0	0.0%

Source: Administrative Office of the United States Courts
    "1999 Wiretap Report" (2000)
Total does not include 601 wiretaps authorized under federal statute.
**No state statute authorizing wiretaps.*

VII. OFFENSES

309 Crimes in 1999
310 Average Time Between Crimes in 1999
311 Crimes per Square Mile in 1999
312 Percent Change in Number of Crimes: 1998 to 1999
313 Crime Rate in 1999
314 Percent Change in Crime Rate: 1998 to 1999
315 Violent Crimes in 1999
316 Average Time Between Violent Crimes in 1999
317 Violent Crimes per Square Mile in 1999
318 Percent Change in Number of Violent Crimes: 1998 to 1999
319 Violent Crime Rate in 1999
320 Percent Change in Violent Crime Rate: 1998 to 1999
321 Violent Crimes with Firearms in 1999
322 Violent Crime Rate with Firearms in 1999
323 Percent of Violent Crimes Involving Firearms in 1999
324 Bombings in 1997
325 Murders in 1999
326 Average Time Between Murders in 1999
327 Percent Change in Number of Murders: 1998 to 1999
328 Murder Rate in 1999
329 Percent Change in Murder Rate: 1998 to 1999
330 Murders with Firearms in 1999
331 Murder Rate with Firearms in 1999
332 Percent of Murders Involving Firearms in 1999
333 Murders with Handguns in 1999
334 Murder Rate with Handguns in 1999
335 Percent of Murders Involving Handguns in 1999
336 Murders with Rifles in 1999
337 Percent of Murders Involving Rifles in 1999
338 Murders with Shotguns in 1999
339 Percent of Murders Involving Shotguns in 1999
340 Murders with Knives or Cutting Instruments in 1999
341 Percent of Murders Involving Knives or Cutting Instruments in 1999
342 Murders by Hands, Fists or Feet in 1999
343 Percent of Murders Involving Hands, Fists or Feet in 1999
344 Rapes in 1999
345 Average Time Between Rapes in 1999
346 Percent Change in Number of Rapes: 1998 to 1999
347 Rape Rate in 1999
348 Percent Change in Rape Rate: 1998 to 1999
349 Rape Rate per 100,000 Female Population in 1999
350 Robberies in 1999
351 Average Time Between Robberies in 1999
352 Percent Change in Number of Robberies: 1998 to 1999
353 Robbery Rate in 1999
354 Percent Change in Robbery Rate: 1998 to 1999
355 Robberies with Firearms in 1999
356 Robbery Rate with Firearms in 1999
357 Percent of Robberies Involving Firearms in 1999
358 Robberies with Knives or Cutting Instruments in 1999
359 Percent of Robberies Involving Knives or Cutting Instruments in 1999
360 Robberies with Blunt Objects and Other Dangerous Weapons in 1999
361 Percent of Robberies Involving Blunt Objects and Other Dangerous Weapons in 1999
362 Robberies Committed with Hands, Fists or Feet in 1999
363 Percent of Robberies Committed with Hands, Fists or Feet in 1999
364 Bank Robberies in 1999
365 Aggravated Assaults in 1999
366 Average Time Between Aggravated Assaults in 1999
367 Percent Change in Number of Aggravated Assaults: 1998 to 1999
368 Aggravated Assault Rate in 1999
369 Percent Change in Aggravated Assault Rate: 1998 to 1999
370 Aggravated Assaults with Firearms in 1999

VII. OFFENSES (continued)

371 Aggravated Assault Rate with Firearms in 1999
372 Percent of Aggravated Assaults Involving Firearms in 1999
373 Aggravated Assaults with Knives or Cutting Instruments in 1999
374 Percent of Aggravated Assaults Involving Knives or Cutting Instruments in 1999
375 Aggravated Assaults with Blunt Objects and Other Dangerous Weapons in 1999
376 Percent of Aggravated Assaults Involving Blunt Objects and Other Dangerous Weapons in 1999
377 Aggravated Assaults Committed with Hands, Fists or Feet in 1999
378 Percent of Aggravated Assaults Committed with Hands, Fists or Feet in 1999
379 Property Crimes in 1999
380 Average Time Between Property Crimes in 1999
381 Property Crimes per Square Mile in 1999
382 Percent Change in Number of Property Crimes: 1998 to 1999
383 Property Crime Rate in 1999
384 Percent Change in Property Crime Rate: 1998 to 1999
385 Burglaries in 1999
386 Average Time Between Burglaries in 1999
387 Percent Change in Number of Burglaries: 1998 to 1999
388 Burglary Rate in 1999
389 Percent Change in Burglary Rate: 1998 to 1999
390 Larcenies and Thefts in 1999
391 Average Time Between Larcenies and Thefts in 1999
392 Percent Change in Number of Larcenies and Thefts: 1998 to 1999
393 Larceny and Theft Rate in 1999
394 Percent Change in Larceny and Theft Rate: 1998 to 1999
395 Motor Vehicle Thefts in 1999
396 Average Time Between Motor Vehicle Thefts in 1999
397 Percent Change in Number of Motor Vehicle Thefts: 1998 to 1999
398 Motor Vehicle Theft Rate in 1999
399 Percent Change in Motor Vehicle Theft Rate: 1998 to 1999

Urban/Rural Crime

400 Crimes in Urban Areas in 1999
401 Urban Crime Rate in 1999
402 Percent of Crimes Occurring in Urban Areas in 1999
403 Crimes in Rural Areas in 1999
404 Rural Crime Rate in 1999
405 Percent of Crimes Occurring in Rural Areas in 1999
406 Violent Crimes in Urban Areas in 1999
407 Urban Violent Crime Rate in 1999
408 Percent of Violent Crimes Occurring in Urban Areas in 1999
409 Violent Crimes in Rural Areas in 1999
410 Rural Violent Crime Rate in 1999
411 Percent of Violent Crimes Occurring in Rural Areas in 1999
412 Murders in Urban Areas in 1999
413 Urban Murder Rate in 1999
414 Percent of Murders Occurring in Urban Areas in 1999
415 Murders in Rural Areas in 1999
416 Rural Murder Rate in 1999
417 Percent of Murders Occurring in Rural Areas in 1999
418 Rapes in Urban Areas in 1999
419 Urban Rape Rate in 1999
420 Percent of Rapes Occurring in Urban Areas in 1999
421 Rapes in Rural Areas in 1999
422 Rural Rape Rate in 1999
423 Percent of Rapes Occurring in Rural Areas in 1999
424 Robberies in Urban Areas in 1999
425 Urban Robbery Rate in 1999
426 Percent of Robberies Occurring in Urban Areas in 1999
427 Robberies in Rural Areas in 1999
428 Rural Robbery Rate in 1999
429 Percent of Robberies Occurring in Rural Areas in 1999

VII. OFFENSES (continued)

430 Aggravated Assaults in Urban Areas in 1999
431 Urban Aggravated Assault Rate in 1999
432 Percent of Aggravated Assaults Occurring in Urban Areas in 1999
433 Aggravated Assaults in Rural Areas in 1999
434 Rural Aggravated Assault Rate in 1999
435 Percent of Aggravated Assaults Occurring in Rural Areas in 1999
436 Property Crimes in Urban Areas in 1999
437 Urban Property Crime Rate in 1999
438 Percent of Property Crimes Occurring in Urban Areas in 1999
439 Property Crimes in Rural Areas in 1999
440 Rural Property Crime Rate in 1999
441 Percent of Property Crimes Occurring in Rural Areas in 1999
442 Burglaries in Urban Areas in 1999
443 Urban Burglary Rate in 1999
444 Percent of Burglaries Occurring in Urban Areas in 1999
445 Burglaries in Rural Areas in 1999
446 Rural Burglary Rate in 1999
447 Percent of Burglaries Occurring in Rural Areas in 1999
448 Larcenies and Thefts in Urban Areas in 1999
449 Urban Larceny and Theft Rate in 1999
450 Percent of Larcenies and Thefts Occurring in Urban Areas in 1999
451 Larcenies and Thefts in Rural Areas in 1999
452 Rural Larceny and Theft Rate in 1999
453 Percent of Larcenies and Thefts Occurring in Rural Areas in 1999
454 Motor Vehicle Thefts in Urban Areas in 1999
455 Urban Motor Vehicle Theft Rate in 1999
456 Percent of Motor Vehicle Thefts Occurring in Urban Areas in 1999
457 Motor Vehicle Thefts in Rural Areas in 1999
458 Rural Motor Vehicle Theft Rate in 1999
459 Percent of Motor Vehicle Thefts Occurring in Rural Areas in 1999
460 Crimes Reported at Universities and Colleges in 1999
461 Crimes Reported at Universities and Colleges as a Percent of All Crimes in 1999
462 Violent Crimes Reported at Universities and Colleges in 1999
463 Violent Crimes Reported at Universities and Colleges as a Percent of All Violent Crimes in 1999
464 Property Crimes Reported at Universities and Colleges in 1999
465 Property Crimes at Universities and Colleges as a Percent of All Property Crimes in 1999

1995 Crimes

466 Crimes in 1995
467 Percent Change in Number of Crimes: 1995 to 1999
468 Crime Rate in 1995
469 Percent Change in Crime Rate: 1995 to 1999
470 Violent Crimes in 1995
471 Percent Change in Number of Violent Crimes: 1995 to 1999
472 Violent Crime Rate in 1995
473 Percent Change in Violent Crime Rate: 1995 to 1999
474 Murders in 1995
475 Percent Change in Number of Murders: 1995 to 1999
476 Murder Rate in 1995
477 Percent Change in Murder Rate: 1995 to 1999
478 Rapes in 1995
479 Percent Change in Number of Rapes: 1995 to 1999
480 Rape Rate in 1995
481 Percent Change in Rape Rate: 1995 to 1999
482 Robberies in 1995
483 Percent Change in Number of Robberies: 1995 to 1999
484 Robbery Rate in 1995
485 Percent Change in Robbery Rate: 1995 to 1999
486 Aggravated Assaults in 1995
487 Percent Change in Number of Aggravated Assaults: 1995 to 1999
488 Aggravated Assault Rate in 1995

VII. OFFENSES (continued)

489   Percent Change in Aggravated Assault Rate: 1995 to 1999
490   Property Crimes in 1995
491   Percent Change in Number of Property Crimes: 1995 to 1999
492   Property Crime Rate in 1995
493   Percent Change in Property Crime Rate: 1995 to 1999
494   Burglaries in 1995
495   Percent Change in Number of Burglaries: 1995 to 1999
496   Burglary Rate in 1995
497   Percent Change in Burglary Rate: 1995 to 1999
498   Larcenies and Thefts in 1995
499   Percent Change in Number of Larcenies and Thefts: 1995 to 1999
500   Larceny and Theft Rate in 1995
501   Percent Change in Larceny and Theft Rate: 1995 to 1999
502   Motor Vehicle Thefts in 1995
503   Percent Change in Number of Motor Vehicle Thefts: 1995 to 1999
504   Motor Vehicle Theft Rate in 1995
505   Percent Change in Motor Vehicle Theft Rate: 1995 to 1999
506   Hate Crimes in 1999
507   Rate of Hate Crimes in 1999
508   Criminal Victimization in 1999

Crimes in 1999

National Total = 11,635,149 Crimes*

ALPHA ORDER

RANK	STATE	CRIMES	% of USA
22	Alabama	192,819	1.7%
46	Alaska	27,008	0.2%
12	Arizona	281,735	2.4%
34	Arkansas	103,131	0.9%
1	California	1,261,164	10.8%
26	Colorado	164,813	1.4%
31	Connecticut	111,236	1.0%
41	Delaware	36,456	0.3%
3	Florida	937,718	8.1%
8	Georgia	400,968	3.4%
38	Hawaii	57,324	0.5%
40	Idaho	39,429	0.3%
5	Illinois	546,561	4.7%
19	Indiana	223,808	1.9%
35	Iowa	92,497	0.8%
29	Kansas	117,803	1.0%
30	Kentucky	114,003	1.0%
16	Louisiana	251,252	2.2%
42	Maine	36,024	0.3%
15	Maryland	254,420	2.2%
21	Massachusetts	201,460	1.7%
7	Michigan	426,596	3.7%
24	Minnesota	171,802	1.5%
28	Mississippi	118,231	1.0%
17	Missouri	250,363	2.2%
43	Montana	35,937	0.3%
37	Nebraska	68,444	0.6%
36	Nevada	84,185	0.7%
45	New Hampshire	27,406	0.2%
13	New Jersey	276,873	2.4%
33	New Mexico	103,740	0.9%
4	New York	596,743	5.1%
9	North Carolina	395,971	3.4%
50	North Dakota	15,172	0.1%
6	Ohio	449,880	3.9%
27	Oklahoma	157,286	1.4%
25	Oregon	165,866	1.4%
10	Pennsylvania	373,452	3.2%
44	Rhode Island	35,497	0.3%
20	South Carolina	206,907	1.8%
47	South Dakota	19,386	0.2%
14	Tennessee	257,413	2.2%
2	Texas	1,008,567	8.7%
32	Utah	105,999	0.9%
48	Vermont	16,735	0.1%
18	Virginia	231,886	2.0%
11	Washington	302,509	2.6%
39	West Virginia	49,161	0.4%
23	Wisconsin	173,062	1.5%
49	Wyoming	16,583	0.1%

RANK ORDER

RANK	STATE	CRIMES	% of USA
1	California	1,261,164	10.8%
2	Texas	1,008,567	8.7%
3	Florida	937,718	8.1%
4	New York	596,743	5.1%
5	Illinois	546,561	4.7%
6	Ohio	449,880	3.9%
7	Michigan	426,596	3.7%
8	Georgia	400,968	3.4%
9	North Carolina	395,971	3.4%
10	Pennsylvania	373,452	3.2%
11	Washington	302,509	2.6%
12	Arizona	281,735	2.4%
13	New Jersey	276,873	2.4%
14	Tennessee	257,413	2.2%
15	Maryland	254,420	2.2%
16	Louisiana	251,252	2.2%
17	Missouri	250,363	2.2%
18	Virginia	231,886	2.0%
19	Indiana	223,808	1.9%
20	South Carolina	206,907	1.8%
21	Massachusetts	201,460	1.7%
22	Alabama	192,819	1.7%
23	Wisconsin	173,062	1.5%
24	Minnesota	171,802	1.5%
25	Oregon	165,866	1.4%
26	Colorado	164,813	1.4%
27	Oklahoma	157,286	1.4%
28	Mississippi	118,231	1.0%
29	Kansas	117,803	1.0%
30	Kentucky	114,003	1.0%
31	Connecticut	111,236	1.0%
32	Utah	105,999	0.9%
33	New Mexico	103,740	0.9%
34	Arkansas	103,131	0.9%
35	Iowa	92,497	0.8%
36	Nevada	84,185	0.7%
37	Nebraska	68,444	0.6%
38	Hawaii	57,324	0.5%
39	West Virginia	49,161	0.4%
40	Idaho	39,429	0.3%
41	Delaware	36,456	0.3%
42	Maine	36,024	0.3%
43	Montana	35,937	0.3%
44	Rhode Island	35,497	0.3%
45	New Hampshire	27,406	0.2%
46	Alaska	27,008	0.2%
47	South Dakota	19,386	0.2%
48	Vermont	16,735	0.1%
49	Wyoming	16,583	0.1%
50	North Dakota	15,172	0.1%
	District of Columbia	41,868	0.4%

Source: Federal Bureau of Investigation
"Crime in the United States 1999" (Uniform Crime Reports, October 15, 2000)
*Includes murder, rape, robbery, aggravated assault, burglary, larceny-theft and motor vehicle theft.

Average Time Between Crimes in 1999

National Rate = A Crime Occurs Every 3 Seconds*

ALPHA ORDER

RANK	STATE	MINUTES.SECONDS
29	Alabama	2.44
5	Alaska	19.28
39	Arizona	1.52
17	Arkansas	5.06
50	California	0.25
25	Colorado	3.11
20	Connecticut	4.44
10	Delaware	14.25
48	Florida	0.34
43	Georgia	1.19
13	Hawaii	9.10
11	Idaho	13.20
46	Illinois	0.58
32	Indiana	2.21
16	Iowa	5.41
22	Kansas	4.28
21	Kentucky	4.37
35	Louisiana	2.05
9	Maine	14.35
36	Maryland	2.04
30	Massachusetts	2.37
44	Michigan	1.14
27	Minnesota	3.04
23	Mississippi	4.27
34	Missouri	2.06
8	Montana	14.38
14	Nebraska	7.41
15	Nevada	6.14
6	New Hampshire	19.11
38	New Jersey	1.54
18	New Mexico	5.04
47	New York	0.53
42	North Carolina	1.20
1	North Dakota	34.38
45	Ohio	1.10
24	Oklahoma	3.20
26	Oregon	3.10
41	Pennsylvania	1.25
7	Rhode Island	14.49
31	South Carolina	2.32
4	South Dakota	27.07
37	Tennessee	2.02
49	Texas	0.31
19	Utah	4.58
3	Vermont	31.25
33	Virginia	2.16
40	Washington	1.44
12	West Virginia	10.41
28	Wisconsin	3.02
2	Wyoming	31.42

RANK ORDER

RANK	STATE	MINUTES.SECONDS
1	North Dakota	34.38
2	Wyoming	31.42
3	Vermont	31.25
4	South Dakota	27.07
5	Alaska	19.28
6	New Hampshire	19.11
7	Rhode Island	14.49
8	Montana	14.38
9	Maine	14.35
10	Delaware	14.25
11	Idaho	13.20
12	West Virginia	10.41
13	Hawaii	9.10
14	Nebraska	7.41
15	Nevada	6.14
16	Iowa	5.41
17	Arkansas	5.06
18	New Mexico	5.04
19	Utah	4.58
20	Connecticut	4.44
21	Kentucky	4.37
22	Kansas	4.28
23	Mississippi	4.27
24	Oklahoma	3.20
25	Colorado	3.11
26	Oregon	3.10
27	Minnesota	3.04
28	Wisconsin	3.02
29	Alabama	2.44
30	Massachusetts	2.37
31	South Carolina	2.32
32	Indiana	2.21
33	Virginia	2.16
34	Missouri	2.06
35	Louisiana	2.05
36	Maryland	2.04
37	Tennessee	2.02
38	New Jersey	1.54
39	Arizona	1.52
40	Washington	1.44
41	Pennsylvania	1.25
42	North Carolina	1.20
43	Georgia	1.19
44	Michigan	1.14
45	Ohio	1.10
46	Illinois	0.58
47	New York	0.53
48	Florida	0.34
49	Texas	0.31
50	California	0.25
	District of Columbia	12.33

Source: Morgan Quitno Press using data from Federal Bureau of Investigation
   "Crime in the United States 1999" (Uniform Crime Reports, October 15, 2000)
*Includes murder, rape, robbery, aggravated assault, burglary, larceny-theft and motor vehicle theft.

Crimes per Square Mile in 1999

National Rate = 3.1 Crimes per Square Mile*

ALPHA ORDER				RANK ORDER		
RANK	STATE	RATE		RANK	STATE	RATE
24	Alabama	3.7		1	New Jersey	33.7
50	Alaska	0.0		2	Rhode Island	28.8
29	Arizona	2.5		3	Massachusetts	21.8
34	Arkansas	1.9		4	Maryland	20.7
13	California	7.9		5	Connecticut	20.1
37	Colorado	1.6		6	Florida	15.6
5	Connecticut	20.1		7	Delaware	15.2
7	Delaware	15.2		8	New York	11.1
6	Florida	15.6		9	Ohio	10.0
15	Georgia	6.8		10	Illinois	9.4
11	Hawaii	8.9		11	Hawaii	8.9
45	Idaho	0.5		12	Pennsylvania	8.1
10	Illinois	9.4		13	California	7.9
17	Indiana	6.1		14	North Carolina	7.5
37	Iowa	1.6		15	Georgia	6.8
39	Kansas	1.4		16	South Carolina	6.6
27	Kentucky	2.8		17	Indiana	6.1
20	Louisiana	5.1		17	Tennessee	6.1
41	Maine	1.1		19	Virginia	5.5
4	Maryland	20.7		20	Louisiana	5.1
3	Massachusetts	21.8		21	Michigan	4.4
21	Michigan	4.4		22	Washington	4.3
32	Minnesota	2.0		23	Texas	3.8
30	Mississippi	2.4		24	Alabama	3.7
25	Missouri	3.6		25	Missouri	3.6
47	Montana	0.2		26	New Hampshire	3.0
42	Nebraska	0.9		27	Kentucky	2.8
44	Nevada	0.8		28	Wisconsin	2.6
26	New Hampshire	3.0		29	Arizona	2.5
1	New Jersey	33.7		30	Mississippi	2.4
42	New Mexico	0.9		31	Oklahoma	2.3
8	New York	11.1		32	Minnesota	2.0
14	North Carolina	7.5		32	West Virginia	2.0
47	North Dakota	0.2		34	Arkansas	1.9
9	Ohio	10.0		35	Oregon	1.7
31	Oklahoma	2.3		35	Vermont	1.7
35	Oregon	1.7		37	Colorado	1.6
12	Pennsylvania	8.1		37	Iowa	1.6
2	Rhode Island	28.8		39	Kansas	1.4
16	South Carolina	6.6		40	Utah	1.2
46	South Dakota	0.3		41	Maine	1.1
17	Tennessee	6.1		42	Nebraska	0.9
23	Texas	3.8		42	New Mexico	0.9
40	Utah	1.2		44	Nevada	0.8
35	Vermont	1.7		45	Idaho	0.5
19	Virginia	5.5		46	South Dakota	0.3
22	Washington	4.3		47	Montana	0.2
32	West Virginia	2.0		47	North Dakota	0.2
28	Wisconsin	2.6		47	Wyoming	0.2
47	Wyoming	0.2		50	Alaska	0.0
				District of Columbia		615.7

Source: Morgan Quitno Press using data from Federal Bureau of Investigation
"Crime in the United States 1999" (Uniform Crime Reports, October 15, 2000)
*Includes murder, rape, robbery, aggravated assault, burglary, larceny-theft and motor vehicle theft.

Percent Change in Number of Crimes: 1998 to 1999

National Percent Change = 6.8% Decrease*

ALPHA ORDER

RANK	STATE	PERCENT CHANGE
6	Alabama	(3.6)
30	Alaska	(7.9)
32	Arizona	(8.2)
13	Arkansas	(5.1)
46	California	(11.1)
27	Colorado	(7.5)
44	Connecticut	(10.3)
35	Delaware	(8.6)
36	Florida	(8.7)
7	Georgia	(4.0)
42	Hawaii	(9.9)
49	Idaho	(13.6)
19	Illinois	(6.6)
38	Indiana	(9.0)
28	Iowa	(7.7)
31	Kansas	(8.0)
24	Kentucky	(7.0)
14	Louisiana	(5.7)
11	Maine	(4.8)
28	Maryland	(7.7)
9	Massachusetts	(4.6)
25	Michigan	(7.2)
43	Minnesota	(10.1)
5	Mississippi	(2.0)
9	Missouri	(4.6)
17	Montana	(6.3)
19	Nebraska	(6.6)
36	Nevada	(8.7)
8	New Hampshire	(4.4)
19	New Jersey	(6.6)
46	New Mexico	(11.1)
34	New York	(8.5)
4	North Carolina	(1.4)
48	North Dakota	(11.3)
26	Ohio	(7.3)
16	Oklahoma	(6.1)
45	Oregon	(10.5)
12	Pennsylvania	(4.9)
1	Rhode Island	2.1
19	South Carolina	(6.6)
2	South Dakota	0.1
15	Tennessee	(5.9)
3	Texas	(0.1)
33	Utah	(8.3)
41	Vermont	(9.8)
23	Virginia	(6.7)
39	Washington	(9.4)
NA	West Virginia**	NA
18	Wisconsin	(6.5)
40	Wyoming	(9.5)

RANK ORDER

RANK	STATE	PERCENT CHANGE
1	Rhode Island	2.1
2	South Dakota	0.1
3	Texas	(0.1)
4	North Carolina	(1.4)
5	Mississippi	(2.0)
6	Alabama	(3.6)
7	Georgia	(4.0)
8	New Hampshire	(4.4)
9	Massachusetts	(4.6)
9	Missouri	(4.6)
11	Maine	(4.8)
12	Pennsylvania	(4.9)
13	Arkansas	(5.1)
14	Louisiana	(5.7)
15	Tennessee	(5.9)
16	Oklahoma	(6.1)
17	Montana	(6.3)
18	Wisconsin	(6.5)
19	Illinois	(6.6)
19	Nebraska	(6.6)
19	New Jersey	(6.6)
19	South Carolina	(6.6)
23	Virginia	(6.7)
24	Kentucky	(7.0)
25	Michigan	(7.2)
26	Ohio	(7.3)
27	Colorado	(7.5)
28	Iowa	(7.7)
28	Maryland	(7.7)
30	Alaska	(7.9)
31	Kansas	(8.0)
32	Arizona	(8.2)
33	Utah	(8.3)
34	New York	(8.5)
35	Delaware	(8.6)
36	Florida	(8.7)
36	Nevada	(8.7)
38	Indiana	(9.0)
39	Washington	(9.4)
40	Wyoming	(9.5)
41	Vermont	(9.8)
42	Hawaii	(9.9)
43	Minnesota	(10.1)
44	Connecticut	(10.3)
45	Oregon	(10.5)
46	California	(11.1)
46	New Mexico	(11.1)
48	North Dakota	(11.3)
49	Idaho	(13.6)
NA	West Virginia**	NA
	District of Columbia	(9.4)

Source: Federal Bureau of Investigation
   "Crime in the United States 1999" (Uniform Crime Reports, October 15, 2000)
*Includes murder, rape, robbery, aggravated assault, burglary, larceny-theft and motor vehicle theft.
**Not available.

Crime Rate in 1999

National Rate = 4,266.8 Crimes per 100,000 Population*

ALPHA ORDER

RANK	STATE	RATE
21	Alabama	4,412.3
22	Alaska	4,363.2
3	Arizona	5,896.5
28	Arkansas	4,042.8
30	California	3,805.0
27	Colorado	4,063.4
36	Connecticut	3,389.3
14	Delaware	4,835.0
1	Florida	6,205.5
8	Georgia	5,148.5
13	Hawaii	4,837.5
42	Idaho	3,149.3
19	Illinois	4,506.6
31	Indiana	3,765.9
41	Iowa	3,224.0
20	Kansas	4,438.7
44	Kentucky	2,878.1
4	Louisiana	5,746.8
45	Maine	2,875.0
12	Maryland	4,919.2
40	Massachusetts	3,262.5
23	Michigan	4,324.8
32	Minnesota	3,597.2
24	Mississippi	4,269.8
18	Missouri	4,578.7
26	Montana	4,069.9
25	Nebraska	4,108.3
17	Nevada	4,653.7
50	New Hampshire	2,281.9
35	New Jersey	3,400.1
2	New Mexico	5,962.1
39	New York	3,279.3
7	North Carolina	5,175.4
49	North Dakota	2,393.1
29	Ohio	3,996.4
16	Oklahoma	4,683.9
10	Oregon	5,002.0
43	Pennsylvania	3,113.7
33	Rhode Island	3,581.9
5	South Carolina	5,324.4
48	South Dakota	2,644.7
15	Tennessee	4,693.9
9	Texas	5,031.8
11	Utah	4,976.5
46	Vermont	2,817.3
37	Virginia	3,373.9
6	Washington	5,255.5
47	West Virginia	2,720.6
38	Wisconsin	3,296.4
34	Wyoming	3,454.8

RANK ORDER

RANK	STATE	RATE
1	Florida	6,205.5
2	New Mexico	5,962.1
3	Arizona	5,896.5
4	Louisiana	5,746.8
5	South Carolina	5,324.4
6	Washington	5,255.5
7	North Carolina	5,175.4
8	Georgia	5,148.5
9	Texas	5,031.8
10	Oregon	5,002.0
11	Utah	4,976.5
12	Maryland	4,919.2
13	Hawaii	4,837.5
14	Delaware	4,835.0
15	Tennessee	4,693.9
16	Oklahoma	4,683.9
17	Nevada	4,653.7
18	Missouri	4,578.7
19	Illinois	4,506.6
20	Kansas	4,438.7
21	Alabama	4,412.3
22	Alaska	4,363.2
23	Michigan	4,324.8
24	Mississippi	4,269.8
25	Nebraska	4,108.3
26	Montana	4,069.9
27	Colorado	4,063.4
28	Arkansas	4,042.8
29	Ohio	3,996.4
30	California	3,805.0
31	Indiana	3,765.9
32	Minnesota	3,597.2
33	Rhode Island	3,581.9
34	Wyoming	3,454.8
35	New Jersey	3,400.1
36	Connecticut	3,389.3
37	Virginia	3,373.9
38	Wisconsin	3,296.4
39	New York	3,279.3
40	Massachusetts	3,262.5
41	Iowa	3,224.0
42	Idaho	3,149.3
43	Pennsylvania	3,113.7
44	Kentucky	2,878.1
45	Maine	2,875.0
46	Vermont	2,817.3
47	West Virginia	2,720.6
48	South Dakota	2,644.7
49	North Dakota	2,393.1
50	New Hampshire	2,281.9
	District of Columbia	8,067.1

Source: Federal Bureau of Investigation
    "Crime in the United States 1999" (Uniform Crime Reports, October 15, 2000)
*Includes murder, rape, robbery, aggravated assault, burglary, larceny-theft and motor vehicle theft.

Percent Change in Crime Rate: 1998 to 1999

National Percent Change = 7.6% Decrease*

ALPHA ORDER

RANK	STATE	PERCENT CHANGE
6	Alabama	(4.0)
30	Alaska	(8.7)
40	Arizona	(10.3)
11	Arkansas	(5.6)
48	California	(12.4)
34	Colorado	(9.4)
42	Connecticut	(10.5)
37	Delaware	(9.8)
38	Florida	(9.9)
13	Georgia	(5.8)
32	Hawaii	(9.3)
49	Idaho	(15.2)
21	Illinois	(7.2)
36	Indiana	(9.7)
27	Iowa	(7.9)
31	Kansas	(8.9)
22	Kentucky	(7.6)
13	Louisiana	(5.8)
10	Maine	(5.5)
28	Maryland	(8.3)
8	Massachusetts	(5.0)
22	Michigan	(7.6)
44	Minnesota	(11.1)
4	Mississippi	(2.6)
9	Missouri	(5.1)
16	Montana	(6.6)
17	Nebraska	(6.7)
47	Nevada	(11.9)
12	New Hampshire	(5.7)
19	New Jersey	(7.0)
45	New Mexico	(11.3)
29	New York	(8.6)
5	North Carolina	(2.8)
43	North Dakota	(10.7)
22	Ohio	(7.6)
15	Oklahoma	(6.4)
46	Oregon	(11.4)
7	Pennsylvania	(4.9)
1	Rhode Island	1.8
25	South Carolina	(7.8)
2	South Dakota	0.8
18	Tennessee	(6.8)
3	Texas	(1.6)
35	Utah	(9.6)
39	Vermont	(10.2)
25	Virginia	(7.8)
41	Washington	(10.4)
NA	West Virginia**	NA
19	Wisconsin	(7.0)
32	Wyoming	(9.3)

RANK ORDER

RANK	STATE	PERCENT CHANGE
1	Rhode Island	1.8
2	South Dakota	0.8
3	Texas	(1.6)
4	Mississippi	(2.6)
5	North Carolina	(2.8)
6	Alabama	(4.0)
7	Pennsylvania	(4.9)
8	Massachusetts	(5.0)
9	Missouri	(5.1)
10	Maine	(5.5)
11	Arkansas	(5.6)
12	New Hampshire	(5.7)
13	Georgia	(5.8)
13	Louisiana	(5.8)
15	Oklahoma	(6.4)
16	Montana	(6.6)
17	Nebraska	(6.7)
18	Tennessee	(6.8)
19	New Jersey	(7.0)
19	Wisconsin	(7.0)
21	Illinois	(7.2)
22	Kentucky	(7.6)
22	Michigan	(7.6)
22	Ohio	(7.6)
25	South Carolina	(7.8)
25	Virginia	(7.8)
27	Iowa	(7.9)
28	Maryland	(8.3)
29	New York	(8.6)
30	Alaska	(8.7)
31	Kansas	(8.9)
32	Hawaii	(9.3)
32	Wyoming	(9.3)
34	Colorado	(9.4)
35	Utah	(9.6)
36	Indiana	(9.7)
37	Delaware	(9.8)
38	Florida	(9.9)
39	Vermont	(10.2)
40	Arizona	(10.3)
41	Washington	(10.4)
42	Connecticut	(10.5)
43	North Dakota	(10.7)
44	Minnesota	(11.1)
45	New Mexico	(11.3)
46	Oregon	(11.4)
47	Nevada	(11.9)
48	California	(12.4)
49	Idaho	(15.2)
NA	West Virginia**	NA
	District of Columbia	(8.7)

Source: Federal Bureau of Investigation
  "Crime in the United States 1999" (Uniform Crime Reports, October 15, 2000)
*Includes murder, rape, robbery, aggravated assault, burglary, larceny-theft and motor vehicle theft.
**Not available.

Violent Crimes in 1999

National Total = 1,430,693 Violent Crimes*

<u>ALPHA ORDER</u>

RANK	STATE	CRIMES	% of USA
22	Alabama	21,421	1.5%
40	Alaska	3,909	0.3%
18	Arizona	26,334	1.8%
31	Arkansas	10,848	0.8%
1	California	207,879	14.5%
25	Colorado	13,811	1.0%
30	Connecticut	11,342	0.8%
39	Delaware	5,534	0.4%
2	Florida	129,044	9.0%
8	Georgia	41,585	2.9%
43	Hawaii	2,785	0.2%
41	Idaho	3,066	0.2%
5	Illinois	88,838	6.2%
19	Indiana	22,261	1.6%
35	Iowa	8,034	0.6%
33	Kansas	10,159	0.7%
29	Kentucky	11,908	0.8%
16	Louisiana	32,033	2.2%
45	Maine	1,406	0.1%
10	Maryland	38,447	2.7%
13	Massachusetts	34,023	2.4%
6	Michigan	56,709	4.0%
26	Minnesota	13,085	0.9%
34	Mississippi	9,671	0.7%
17	Missouri	27,353	1.9%
44	Montana	1,823	0.1%
36	Nebraska	7,167	0.5%
32	Nevada	10,311	0.7%
47	New Hampshire	1,159	0.1%
14	New Jersey	33,540	2.3%
24	New Mexico	14,520	1.0%
4	New York	107,147	7.5%
9	North Carolina	41,474	2.9%
50	North Dakota	424	0.0%
12	Ohio	35,616	2.5%
23	Oklahoma	17,066	1.2%
28	Oregon	12,432	0.9%
7	Pennsylvania	50,431	3.5%
42	Rhode Island	2,840	0.2%
15	South Carolina	32,920	2.3%
46	South Dakota	1,227	0.1%
11	Tennessee	38,111	2.7%
3	Texas	112,306	7.8%
38	Utah	5,869	0.4%
49	Vermont	676	0.0%
21	Virginia	21,626	1.5%
20	Washington	21,716	1.5%
37	West Virginia	6,336	0.4%
27	Wisconsin	12,908	0.9%
48	Wyoming	1,115	0.1%

<u>RANK ORDER</u>

RANK	STATE	CRIMES	% of USA
1	California	207,879	14.5%
2	Florida	129,044	9.0%
3	Texas	112,306	7.8%
4	New York	107,147	7.5%
5	Illinois	88,838	6.2%
6	Michigan	56,709	4.0%
7	Pennsylvania	50,431	3.5%
8	Georgia	41,585	2.9%
9	North Carolina	41,474	2.9%
10	Maryland	38,447	2.7%
11	Tennessee	38,111	2.7%
12	Ohio	35,616	2.5%
13	Massachusetts	34,023	2.4%
14	New Jersey	33,540	2.3%
15	South Carolina	32,920	2.3%
16	Louisiana	32,033	2.2%
17	Missouri	27,353	1.9%
18	Arizona	26,334	1.8%
19	Indiana	22,261	1.6%
20	Washington	21,716	1.5%
21	Virginia	21,626	1.5%
22	Alabama	21,421	1.5%
23	Oklahoma	17,066	1.2%
24	New Mexico	14,520	1.0%
25	Colorado	13,811	1.0%
26	Minnesota	13,085	0.9%
27	Wisconsin	12,908	0.9%
28	Oregon	12,432	0.9%
29	Kentucky	11,908	0.8%
30	Connecticut	11,342	0.8%
31	Arkansas	10,848	0.8%
32	Nevada	10,311	0.7%
33	Kansas	10,159	0.7%
34	Mississippi	9,671	0.7%
35	Iowa	8,034	0.6%
36	Nebraska	7,167	0.5%
37	West Virginia	6,336	0.4%
38	Utah	5,869	0.4%
39	Delaware	5,534	0.4%
40	Alaska	3,909	0.3%
41	Idaho	3,066	0.2%
42	Rhode Island	2,840	0.2%
43	Hawaii	2,785	0.2%
44	Montana	1,823	0.1%
45	Maine	1,406	0.1%
46	South Dakota	1,227	0.1%
47	New Hampshire	1,159	0.1%
48	Wyoming	1,115	0.1%
49	Vermont	676	0.0%
50	North Dakota	424	0.0%
	District of Columbia	8,448	0.6%

Source: Federal Bureau of Investigation
"Crime in the United States 1999" (Uniform Crime Reports, October 15, 2000)
*Violent crimes are offenses of murder, forcible rape, robbery and aggravated assault.

Average Time Between Violent Crimes in 1999

National Rate = A Violent Crime Occurs Every 22 Seconds*

ALPHA ORDER

RANK	STATE	MINUTES.SECONDS
29	Alabama	24.32
11	Alaska	134.28
33	Arizona	19.58
20	Arkansas	48.27
50	California	2.32
26	Colorado	38.04
21	Connecticut	46.20
12	Delaware	94.59
49	Florida	4.04
43	Georgia	12.38
8	Hawaii	188.44
10	Idaho	171.26
46	Illinois	5.55
32	Indiana	23.37
16	Iowa	65.25
18	Kansas	51.44
22	Kentucky	44.08
35	Louisiana	16.25
6	Maine	373.50
41	Maryland	13.40
38	Massachusetts	15.27
45	Michigan	9.16
25	Minnesota	40.10
17	Mississippi	54.21
34	Missouri	19.13
7	Montana	288.19
15	Nebraska	73.20
19	Nevada	50.58
4	New Hampshire	453.29
37	New Jersey	15.40
27	New Mexico	36.12
47	New York	4.55
42	North Carolina	12.40
1	North Dakota	1,239.37
39	Ohio	14.46
28	Oklahoma	30.48
23	Oregon	42.17
44	Pennsylvania	10.25
9	Rhode Island	185.04
36	South Carolina	15.58
5	South Dakota	428.22
40	Tennessee	13.47
48	Texas	4.41
13	Utah	89.34
2	Vermont	777.31
30	Virginia	24.18
31	Washington	24.12
14	West Virginia	82.57
24	Wisconsin	40.43
3	Wyoming	471.23

RANK ORDER

RANK	STATE	MINUTES.SECONDS
1	North Dakota	1,239.37
2	Vermont	777.31
3	Wyoming	471.23
4	New Hampshire	453.29
5	South Dakota	428.22
6	Maine	373.50
7	Montana	288.19
8	Hawaii	188.44
9	Rhode Island	185.04
10	Idaho	171.26
11	Alaska	134.28
12	Delaware	94.59
13	Utah	89.34
14	West Virginia	82.57
15	Nebraska	73.20
16	Iowa	65.25
17	Mississippi	54.21
18	Kansas	51.44
19	Nevada	50.58
20	Arkansas	48.27
21	Connecticut	46.20
22	Kentucky	44.08
23	Oregon	42.17
24	Wisconsin	40.43
25	Minnesota	40.10
26	Colorado	38.04
27	New Mexico	36.12
28	Oklahoma	30.48
29	Alabama	24.32
30	Virginia	24.18
31	Washington	24.12
32	Indiana	23.37
33	Arizona	19.58
34	Missouri	19.13
35	Louisiana	16.25
36	South Carolina	15.58
37	New Jersey	15.40
38	Massachusetts	15.27
39	Ohio	14.46
40	Tennessee	13.47
41	Maryland	13.40
42	North Carolina	12.40
43	Georgia	12.38
44	Pennsylvania	10.25
45	Michigan	9.16
46	Illinois	5.55
47	New York	4.55
48	Texas	4.41
49	Florida	4.04
50	California	2.32
	District of Columbia	62.13

Source: Morgan Quitno Press using data from Federal Bureau of Investigation
    "Crime in the United States 1999" (Uniform Crime Reports, October 15, 2000)
*Violent crimes are offenses of murder, forcible rape, robbery and aggravated assault.

Violent Crimes per Square Mile in 1999

National Rate = 0.38 Violent Crimes per Square Mile*

ALPHA ORDER

RANK ORDER

RANK	STATE	RATE		RANK	STATE	RATE
23	Alabama	0.41		1	New Jersey	4.08
47	Alaska	0.01		2	Massachusetts	3.68
29	Arizona	0.23		3	Maryland	3.13
30	Arkansas	0.20		4	Delaware	2.31
10	California	1.31		4	Rhode Island	2.31
35	Colorado	0.13		6	Florida	2.15
7	Connecticut	2.05		7	Connecticut	2.05
4	Delaware	2.31		8	New York	1.98
6	Florida	2.15		9	Illinois	1.53
16	Georgia	0.71		10	California	1.31
21	Hawaii	0.43		11	Pennsylvania	1.09
44	Idaho	0.04		12	South Carolina	1.06
9	Illinois	1.53		13	Tennessee	0.90
18	Indiana	0.61		14	North Carolina	0.79
34	Iowa	0.14		14	Ohio	0.79
37	Kansas	0.12		16	Georgia	0.71
26	Kentucky	0.29		17	Louisiana	0.65
17	Louisiana	0.65		18	Indiana	0.61
44	Maine	0.04		19	Michigan	0.59
3	Maryland	3.13		20	Virginia	0.51
2	Massachusetts	3.68		21	Hawaii	0.43
19	Michigan	0.59		22	Texas	0.42
33	Minnesota	0.15		23	Alabama	0.41
30	Mississippi	0.20		24	Missouri	0.39
24	Missouri	0.39		25	Washington	0.31
47	Montana	0.01		26	Kentucky	0.29
40	Nebraska	0.09		27	West Virginia	0.26
40	Nevada	0.09		28	Oklahoma	0.24
37	New Hampshire	0.12		29	Arizona	0.23
1	New Jersey	4.08		30	Arkansas	0.20
37	New Mexico	0.12		30	Mississippi	0.20
8	New York	1.98		30	Wisconsin	0.20
14	North Carolina	0.79		33	Minnesota	0.15
47	North Dakota	0.01		34	Iowa	0.14
14	Ohio	0.79		35	Colorado	0.13
28	Oklahoma	0.24		35	Oregon	0.13
35	Oregon	0.13		37	Kansas	0.12
11	Pennsylvania	1.09		37	New Hampshire	0.12
4	Rhode Island	2.31		37	New Mexico	0.12
12	South Carolina	1.06		40	Nebraska	0.09
46	South Dakota	0.02		40	Nevada	0.09
13	Tennessee	0.90		42	Utah	0.07
22	Texas	0.42		42	Vermont	0.07
42	Utah	0.07		44	Idaho	0.04
42	Vermont	0.07		44	Maine	0.04
20	Virginia	0.51		46	South Dakota	0.02
25	Washington	0.31		47	Alaska	0.01
27	West Virginia	0.26		47	Montana	0.01
30	Wisconsin	0.20		47	North Dakota	0.01
47	Wyoming	0.01		47	Wyoming	0.01

District of Columbia   124.24

Source: Morgan Quitno Press using data from Federal Bureau of Investigation
"Crime in the United States 1999" (Uniform Crime Reports, October 15, 2000)
*Violent crimes are offenses of murder, forcible rape, robbery and aggravated assault.

Percent Change in Number of Violent Crimes: 1998 to 1999

National Percent Change = 6.7% Decrease*

ALPHA ORDER

RANK	STATE	PERCENT CHANGE
12	Alabama	(3.9)
11	Alaska	(2.6)
9	Arizona	(2.4)
46	Arkansas	(12.8)
35	California	(9.6)
30	Colorado	(8.0)
17	Connecticut	(5.4)
9	Delaware	(2.4)
27	Florida	(7.8)
14	Georgia	(5.0)
18	Hawaii	(5.5)
43	Idaho	(11.6)
32	Illinois	(8.7)
45	Indiana	(12.4)
37	Iowa	(9.9)
25	Kansas	(7.4)
27	Kentucky	(7.8)
20	Louisiana	(5.9)
38	Maine	(10.2)
21	Maryland	(6.0)
40	Massachusetts	(10.9)
24	Michigan	(7.0)
39	Minnesota	(10.7)
48	Mississippi	(14.4)
34	Missouri	(9.5)
3	Montana	1.4
13	Nebraska	(4.5)
31	Nevada	(8.3)
32	New Hampshire	(8.7)
22	New Jersey	(6.1)
47	New Mexico	(13.1)
26	New York	(7.6)
16	North Carolina	(5.1)
49	North Dakota	(25.6)
44	Ohio	(12.3)
18	Oklahoma	(5.5)
36	Oregon	(9.8)
5	Pennsylvania	(0.1)
29	Rhode Island	(7.9)
14	South Carolina	(5.0)
1	South Dakota	7.7
7	Tennessee	(1.9)
4	Texas	0.7
42	Utah	(11.1)
2	Vermont	7.6
8	Virginia	(2.2)
40	Washington	(10.9)
NA	West Virginia**	NA
6	Wisconsin	(0.8)
23	Wyoming	(6.4)

RANK ORDER

RANK	STATE	PERCENT CHANGE
1	South Dakota	7.7
2	Vermont	7.6
3	Montana	1.4
4	Texas	0.7
5	Pennsylvania	(0.1)
6	Wisconsin	(0.8)
7	Tennessee	(1.9)
8	Virginia	(2.2)
9	Arizona	(2.4)
9	Delaware	(2.4)
11	Alaska	(2.6)
12	Alabama	(3.9)
13	Nebraska	(4.5)
14	Georgia	(5.0)
14	South Carolina	(5.0)
16	North Carolina	(5.1)
17	Connecticut	(5.4)
18	Hawaii	(5.5)
18	Oklahoma	(5.5)
20	Louisiana	(5.9)
21	Maryland	(6.0)
22	New Jersey	(6.1)
23	Wyoming	(6.4)
24	Michigan	(7.0)
25	Kansas	(7.4)
26	New York	(7.6)
27	Florida	(7.8)
27	Kentucky	(7.8)
29	Rhode Island	(7.9)
30	Colorado	(8.0)
31	Nevada	(8.3)
32	Illinois	(8.7)
32	New Hampshire	(8.7)
34	Missouri	(9.5)
35	California	(9.6)
36	Oregon	(9.8)
37	Iowa	(9.9)
38	Maine	(10.2)
39	Minnesota	(10.7)
40	Massachusetts	(10.9)
40	Washington	(10.9)
42	Utah	(11.1)
43	Idaho	(11.6)
44	Ohio	(12.3)
45	Indiana	(12.4)
46	Arkansas	(12.8)
47	New Mexico	(13.1)
48	Mississippi	(14.4)
49	North Dakota	(25.6)
NA	West Virginia**	NA
	District of Columbia	(6.0)

Source: Federal Bureau of Investigation
   "Crime in the United States 1999" (Uniform Crime Reports, October 15, 2000)
*Violent crimes are offenses of murder, forcible rape, robbery and aggravated assault.
**Not available.

Violent Crime Rate in 1999

National Rate = 524.7 Violent Crimes per 100,000 Population*

ALPHA ORDER

RANK ORDER

RANK	STATE	RATE	RANK	STATE	RATE
21	Alabama	490.2	1	Florida	854.0
9	Alaska	631.5	2	South Carolina	847.1
15	Arizona	551.2	3	New Mexico	834.5
23	Arkansas	425.2	4	Maryland	743.4
10	California	627.2	5	Delaware	734.0
33	Colorado	340.5	6	Louisiana	732.7
32	Connecticut	345.6	7	Illinois	732.5
5	Delaware	734.0	8	Tennessee	694.9
1	Florida	854.0	9	Alaska	631.5
18	Georgia	534.0	10	California	627.2
43	Hawaii	235.0	11	New York	588.8
42	Idaho	244.9	12	Michigan	574.9
7	Illinois	732.5	13	Nevada	570.0
29	Indiana	374.6	14	Texas	560.3
38	Iowa	280.0	15	Arizona	551.2
26	Kansas	382.8	16	Massachusetts	551.0
36	Kentucky	300.6	17	North Carolina	542.1
6	Louisiana	732.7	18	Georgia	534.0
48	Maine	112.2	19	Oklahoma	508.2
4	Maryland	743.4	20	Missouri	500.2
16	Massachusetts	551.0	21	Alabama	490.2
12	Michigan	574.9	22	Nebraska	430.2
40	Minnesota	274.0	23	Arkansas	425.2
31	Mississippi	349.3	24	Pennsylvania	420.5
20	Missouri	500.2	25	New Jersey	411.9
45	Montana	206.5	26	Kansas	382.8
22	Nebraska	430.2	27	Washington	377.3
13	Nevada	570.0	28	Oregon	374.9
49	New Hampshire	96.5	29	Indiana	374.6
25	New Jersey	411.9	30	West Virginia	350.6
3	New Mexico	834.5	31	Mississippi	349.3
11	New York	588.8	32	Connecticut	345.6
17	North Carolina	542.1	33	Colorado	340.5
50	North Dakota	66.9	34	Ohio	316.4
34	Ohio	316.4	35	Virginia	314.7
19	Oklahoma	508.2	36	Kentucky	300.6
28	Oregon	374.9	37	Rhode Island	286.6
24	Pennsylvania	420.5	38	Iowa	280.0
37	Rhode Island	286.6	39	Utah	275.5
2	South Carolina	847.1	40	Minnesota	274.0
46	South Dakota	167.4	41	Wisconsin	245.9
8	Tennessee	694.9	42	Idaho	244.9
14	Texas	560.3	43	Hawaii	235.0
39	Utah	275.5	44	Wyoming	232.3
47	Vermont	113.8	45	Montana	206.5
35	Virginia	314.7	46	South Dakota	167.4
27	Washington	377.3	47	Vermont	113.8
30	West Virginia	350.6	48	Maine	112.2
41	Wisconsin	245.9	49	New Hampshire	96.5
44	Wyoming	232.3	50	North Dakota	66.9
				District of Columbia	1,627.7

Source: Federal Bureau of Investigation
    "Crime in the United States 1999" (Uniform Crime Reports, October 15, 2000)
*Violent crimes are offenses of murder, forcible rape, robbery and aggravated assault.
**Not available.

Percent Change in Violent Crime Rate: 1998 to 1999

National Percent Change = 7.5% Decrease*

ALPHA ORDER

RANK	STATE	PERCENT CHANGE
11	Alabama	(4.3)
8	Alaska	(3.4)
12	Arizona	(4.6)
47	Arkansas	(13.3)
36	California	(10.9)
31	Colorado	(9.9)
15	Connecticut	(5.7)
10	Delaware	(3.7)
29	Florida	(9.0)
23	Georgia	(6.8)
14	Hawaii	(4.8)
45	Idaho	(13.2)
30	Illinois	(9.3)
44	Indiana	(13.1)
34	Iowa	(10.1)
27	Kansas	(8.3)
27	Kentucky	(8.3)
17	Louisiana	(6.0)
36	Maine	(10.9)
22	Maryland	(6.7)
38	Massachusetts	(11.3)
24	Michigan	(7.4)
40	Minnesota	(11.7)
48	Mississippi	(15.0)
32	Missouri	(10.0)
3	Montana	1.1
13	Nebraska	(4.7)
39	Nevada	(11.4)
32	New Hampshire	(10.0)
20	New Jersey	(6.4)
45	New Mexico	(13.2)
25	New York	(7.7)
20	North Carolina	(6.4)
49	North Dakota	(25.1)
43	Ohio	(12.7)
16	Oklahoma	(5.8)
35	Oregon	(10.7)
4	Pennsylvania	0.0
26	Rhode Island	(8.2)
18	South Carolina	(6.2)
1	South Dakota	8.5
7	Tennessee	(2.8)
5	Texas	(0.8)
42	Utah	(12.3)
2	Vermont	7.1
8	Virginia	(3.4)
41	Washington	(12.0)
NA	West Virginia**	NA
6	Wisconsin	(1.3)
18	Wyoming	(6.2)

RANK ORDER

RANK	STATE	PERCENT CHANGE
1	South Dakota	8.5
2	Vermont	7.1
3	Montana	1.1
4	Pennsylvania	0.0
5	Texas	(0.8)
6	Wisconsin	(1.3)
7	Tennessee	(2.8)
8	Alaska	(3.4)
8	Virginia	(3.4)
10	Delaware	(3.7)
11	Alabama	(4.3)
12	Arizona	(4.6)
13	Nebraska	(4.7)
14	Hawaii	(4.8)
15	Connecticut	(5.7)
16	Oklahoma	(5.8)
17	Louisiana	(6.0)
18	South Carolina	(6.2)
18	Wyoming	(6.2)
20	New Jersey	(6.4)
20	North Carolina	(6.4)
22	Maryland	(6.7)
23	Georgia	(6.8)
24	Michigan	(7.4)
25	New York	(7.7)
26	Rhode Island	(8.2)
27	Kansas	(8.3)
27	Kentucky	(8.3)
29	Florida	(9.0)
30	Illinois	(9.3)
31	Colorado	(9.9)
32	Missouri	(10.0)
32	New Hampshire	(10.0)
34	Iowa	(10.1)
35	Oregon	(10.7)
36	California	(10.9)
36	Maine	(10.9)
38	Massachusetts	(11.3)
39	Nevada	(11.4)
40	Minnesota	(11.7)
41	Washington	(12.0)
42	Utah	(12.3)
43	Ohio	(12.7)
44	Indiana	(13.1)
45	Idaho	(13.2)
45	New Mexico	(13.2)
47	Arkansas	(13.3)
48	Mississippi	(15.0)
49	North Dakota	(25.1)
NA	West Virginia**	NA
	District of Columbia	(5.3)

Source: Federal Bureau of Investigation
     "Crime in the United States 1999" (Uniform Crime Reports, October 15, 2000)
*Violent crimes are offenses of murder, forcible rape, robbery and aggravated assault.
**Not available.

Violent Crimes with Firearms in 1999

National Total = 255,867 Violent Crimes*

ALPHA ORDER

RANK	STATE	CRIMES	% of USA
NA	Alabama**	NA	NA
34	Alaska	779	0.3%
9	Arizona	7,765	3.0%
21	Arkansas	2,916	1.1%
1	California	40,297	15.7%
22	Colorado	2,840	1.1%
27	Connecticut	2,069	0.8%
31	Delaware	1,201	0.5%
NA	Florida**	NA	NA
8	Georgia	8,499	3.3%
39	Hawaii	270	0.1%
37	Idaho	589	0.2%
NA	Illinois**	NA	NA
13	Indiana	4,729	1.8%
35	Iowa	776	0.3%
NA	Kansas**	NA	NA
29	Kentucky	1,744	0.7%
7	Louisiana	9,169	3.6%
NA	Maine**	NA	NA
23	Maryland	2,671	1.0%
24	Massachusetts	2,590	1.0%
3	Michigan	14,666	5.7%
33	Minnesota	888	0.3%
26	Mississippi	2,237	0.9%
10	Missouri	7,345	2.9%
40	Montana	140	0.1%
30	Nebraska	1,425	0.6%
25	Nevada	2,490	1.0%
43	New Hampshire	64	0.0%
12	New Jersey	7,088	2.8%
20	New Mexico	2,948	1.2%
19	New York	3,038	1.2%
4	North Carolina	12,262	4.8%
45	North Dakota	24	0.0%
11	Ohio	7,157	2.8%
18	Oklahoma	3,197	1.2%
28	Oregon	1,860	0.7%
5	Pennsylvania	11,591	4.5%
38	Rhode Island	472	0.2%
14	South Carolina	4,141	1.6%
41	South Dakota	117	0.0%
6	Tennessee	11,573	4.5%
2	Texas	28,351	11.1%
36	Utah	771	0.3%
44	Vermont	59	0.0%
16	Virginia	3,528	1.4%
17	Washington	3,462	1.4%
32	West Virginia	981	0.4%
15	Wisconsin	3,569	1.4%
42	Wyoming	104	0.0%

RANK ORDER

RANK	STATE	CRIMES	% of USA
1	California	40,297	15.7%
2	Texas	28,351	11.1%
3	Michigan	14,666	5.7%
4	North Carolina	12,262	4.8%
5	Pennsylvania	11,591	4.5%
6	Tennessee	11,573	4.5%
7	Louisiana	9,169	3.6%
8	Georgia	8,499	3.3%
9	Arizona	7,765	3.0%
10	Missouri	7,345	2.9%
11	Ohio	7,157	2.8%
12	New Jersey	7,088	2.8%
13	Indiana	4,729	1.8%
14	South Carolina	4,141	1.6%
15	Wisconsin	3,569	1.4%
16	Virginia	3,528	1.4%
17	Washington	3,462	1.4%
18	Oklahoma	3,197	1.2%
19	New York	3,038	1.2%
20	New Mexico	2,948	1.2%
21	Arkansas	2,916	1.1%
22	Colorado	2,840	1.1%
23	Maryland	2,671	1.0%
24	Massachusetts	2,590	1.0%
25	Nevada	2,490	1.0%
26	Mississippi	2,237	0.9%
27	Connecticut	2,069	0.8%
28	Oregon	1,860	0.7%
29	Kentucky	1,744	0.7%
30	Nebraska	1,425	0.6%
31	Delaware	1,201	0.5%
32	West Virginia	981	0.4%
33	Minnesota	888	0.3%
34	Alaska	779	0.3%
35	Iowa	776	0.3%
36	Utah	771	0.3%
37	Idaho	589	0.2%
38	Rhode Island	472	0.2%
39	Hawaii	270	0.1%
40	Montana	140	0.1%
41	South Dakota	117	0.0%
42	Wyoming	104	0.0%
43	New Hampshire	64	0.0%
44	Vermont	59	0.0%
45	North Dakota	24	0.0%
NA	Alabama**	NA	NA
NA	Florida**	NA	NA
NA	Illinois**	NA	NA
NA	Kansas**	NA	NA
NA	Maine**	NA	NA
	District of Columbia**	NA	NA

Source: Morgan Quitno Press using data from Federal Bureau of Investigation
  "Crime in the United States 1999" (Uniform Crime Reports, October 15, 2000)
*Includes murder, robbery and aggravated assault. Does not include rape. National total reflects only those violent crimes for which the type of weapon was known and reported. There were an additional 322,597 violent crimes (excluding rape) for which the type of weapon was not reported to the F.B.I.
**Not available.

Violent Crime Rate with Firearms in 1999

National Rate = 124.3 Violent Crimes per 100,000 Population*

ALPHA ORDER

RANK	STATE	RATE
NA	Alabama**	NA
14	Alaska	138.5
9	Arizona	169.4
17	Arkansas	122.7
18	California	121.6
26	Colorado	74.9
30	Connecticut	65.5
11	Delaware	159.3
NA	Florida**	NA
5	Georgia	179.5
40	Hawaii	22.8
36	Idaho	48.1
NA	Illinois**	NA
19	Indiana	117.8
39	Iowa	31.7
NA	Kansas**	NA
12	Kentucky	151.4
4	Louisiana	235.8
NA	Maine**	NA
25	Maryland	85.3
34	Massachusetts	49.7
8	Michigan	170.0
32	Minnesota	52.5
10	Mississippi	168.0
7	Missouri	173.0
38	Montana	32.4
23	Nebraska	92.8
15	Nevada	137.7
43	New Hampshire	13.8
24	New Jersey	87.4
2	New Mexico	246.2
35	New York	49.2
6	North Carolina	178.6
45	North Dakota	4.5
22	Ohio	94.7
21	Oklahoma	95.6
31	Oregon	59.7
16	Pennsylvania	128.4
33	Rhode Island	51.1
3	South Carolina	242.2
42	South Dakota	22.5
1	Tennessee	252.3
13	Texas	145.3
37	Utah	44.2
44	Vermont	12.5
29	Virginia	68.2
28	Washington	68.4
20	West Virginia	99.0
27	Wisconsin	73.3
40	Wyoming	22.8

RANK ORDER

RANK	STATE	RATE
1	Tennessee	252.3
2	New Mexico	246.2
3	South Carolina	242.2
4	Louisiana	235.8
5	Georgia	179.5
6	North Carolina	178.6
7	Missouri	173.0
8	Michigan	170.0
9	Arizona	169.4
10	Mississippi	168.0
11	Delaware	159.3
12	Kentucky	151.4
13	Texas	145.3
14	Alaska	138.5
15	Nevada	137.7
16	Pennsylvania	128.4
17	Arkansas	122.7
18	California	121.6
19	Indiana	117.8
20	West Virginia	99.0
21	Oklahoma	95.6
22	Ohio	94.7
23	Nebraska	92.8
24	New Jersey	87.4
25	Maryland	85.3
26	Colorado	74.9
27	Wisconsin	73.3
28	Washington	68.4
29	Virginia	68.2
30	Connecticut	65.5
31	Oregon	59.7
32	Minnesota	52.5
33	Rhode Island	51.1
34	Massachusetts	49.7
35	New York	49.2
36	Idaho	48.1
37	Utah	44.2
38	Montana	32.4
39	Iowa	31.7
40	Hawaii	22.8
40	Wyoming	22.8
42	South Dakota	22.5
43	New Hampshire	13.8
44	Vermont	12.5
45	North Dakota	4.5
NA	Alabama**	NA
NA	Florida**	NA
NA	Illinois**	NA
NA	Kansas**	NA
NA	Maine**	NA
	District of Columbia**	NA

Source: Morgan Quitno Press using data from Federal Bureau of Investigation
"Crime in the United States 1999" (Uniform Crime Reports, October 15, 2000)
*Based only on population of reporting jurisdictions. Includes murder, robbery and aggravated assault. Does not include rape. National rate reflects only those violent crimes for which the type of weapon was known and reported.
**Not available.

Percent of Violent Crimes Involving Firearms in 1999

National Percent = 25.1% of Violent Crimes*

ALPHA ORDER			RANK ORDER		
RANK	STATE	PERCENT	RANK	STATE	PERCENT
NA	Alabama**	NA	1	Mississippi	42.1
18	Alaska	26.1	2	Tennessee	35.6
6	Arizona	32.4	3	North Carolina	34.1
10	Arkansas	30.2	4	Louisiana	33.2
32	California	20.3	5	Georgia	33.1
20	Colorado	25.3	6	Arizona	32.4
33	Connecticut	19.9	6	Missouri	32.4
22	Delaware	24.0	8	Wisconsin	31.5
NA	Florida**	NA	9	Michigan	31.1
5	Georgia	33.1	10	Arkansas	30.2
43	Hawaii	11.1	11	Indiana	29.1
26	Idaho	22.5	12	Pennsylvania	28.9
NA	Illinois**	NA	13	New Mexico	28.3
11	Indiana	29.1	14	Texas	27.6
41	Iowa	11.6	15	Ohio	27.2
NA	Kansas**	NA	16	Nevada	26.6
25	Kentucky	22.8	16	South Carolina	26.6
4	Louisiana	33.2	18	Alaska	26.1
NA	Maine**	NA	19	Virginia	25.9
24	Maryland	23.8	20	Colorado	25.3
44	Massachusetts	9.3	20	West Virginia	25.3
9	Michigan	31.1	22	Delaware	24.0
22	Minnesota	24.0	22	Minnesota	24.0
1	Mississippi	42.1	24	Maryland	23.8
6	Missouri	32.4	25	Kentucky	22.8
35	Montana	17.9	26	Idaho	22.5
28	Nebraska	22.0	27	New Jersey	22.2
16	Nevada	26.6	28	Nebraska	22.0
40	New Hampshire	12.7	29	Rhode Island	21.4
27	New Jersey	22.2	30	Washington	20.9
13	New Mexico	28.3	31	Oklahoma	20.6
37	New York	17.0	32	California	20.3
3	North Carolina	34.1	33	Connecticut	19.9
45	North Dakota	9.0	34	Utah	18.8
15	Ohio	27.2	35	Montana	17.9
31	Oklahoma	20.6	36	Oregon	17.4
36	Oregon	17.4	37	New York	17.0
12	Pennsylvania	28.9	38	South Dakota	15.3
29	Rhode Island	21.4	39	Vermont	14.4
16	South Carolina	26.6	40	New Hampshire	12.7
38	South Dakota	15.3	41	Iowa	11.6
2	Tennessee	35.6	42	Wyoming	11.2
14	Texas	27.6	43	Hawaii	11.1
34	Utah	18.8	44	Massachusetts	9.3
39	Vermont	14.4	45	North Dakota	9.0
19	Virginia	25.9	NA	Alabama**	NA
30	Washington	20.9	NA	Florida**	NA
20	West Virginia	25.3	NA	Illinois**	NA
8	Wisconsin	31.5	NA	Kansas**	NA
42	Wyoming	11.2	NA	Maine**	NA
				District of Columbia**	NA

Source: Morgan Quitno Press using data from Federal Bureau of Investigation
   "Crime in the United States 1999" (Uniform Crime Reports, October 15, 2000)
*Includes murder, robbery and aggravated assault. Does not include rape. National percent reflects only those violent crimes for which the type of weapon was known and reported. There were an additional 322,597 violent crimes (excluding rape) for which the type of weapon was not reported to the F.B.I.
**Not available.

Bombings in 1997

National Total = 1,639 Bombings*

ALPHA ORDER

RANK	STATE	BOMBINGS	% of USA
28	Alabama	13	0.8%
47	Alaska	1	0.1%
5	Arizona	70	4.3%
38	Arkansas	4	0.2%
1	California	349	21.3%
23	Colorado	17	1.0%
35	Connecticut	6	0.4%
38	Delaware	4	0.2%
2	Florida	171	10.4%
21	Georgia	18	1.1%
50	Hawaii	0	0.0%
38	Idaho	4	0.2%
3	Illinois	121	7.4%
17	Indiana	29	1.8%
16	Iowa	30	1.8%
15	Kansas	32	2.0%
23	Kentucky	17	1.0%
32	Louisiana	10	0.6%
43	Maine	3	0.2%
13	Maryland	34	2.1%
20	Massachusetts	20	1.2%
11	Michigan	42	2.6%
14	Minnesota	33	2.0%
36	Mississippi	5	0.3%
19	Missouri	24	1.5%
38	Montana	4	0.2%
29	Nebraska	12	0.7%
33	Nevada	9	0.5%
46	New Hampshire	2	0.1%
23	New Jersey	17	1.0%
38	New Mexico	4	0.2%
8	New York	58	3.5%
26	North Carolina	15	0.9%
43	North Dakota	3	0.2%
9	Ohio	43	2.6%
29	Oklahoma	12	0.7%
7	Oregon	60	3.7%
11	Pennsylvania	42	2.6%
36	Rhode Island	5	0.3%
31	South Carolina	11	0.7%
47	South Dakota	1	0.1%
9	Tennessee	43	2.6%
5	Texas	70	4.3%
18	Utah	26	1.6%
47	Vermont	1	0.1%
21	Virginia	18	1.1%
4	Washington	94	5.7%
33	West Virginia	9	0.5%
27	Wisconsin	14	0.9%
43	Wyoming	3	0.2%

RANK ORDER

RANK	STATE	BOMBINGS	% of USA
1	California	349	21.3%
2	Florida	171	10.4%
3	Illinois	121	7.4%
4	Washington	94	5.7%
5	Arizona	70	4.3%
5	Texas	70	4.3%
7	Oregon	60	3.7%
8	New York	58	3.5%
9	Ohio	43	2.6%
9	Tennessee	43	2.6%
11	Michigan	42	2.6%
11	Pennsylvania	42	2.6%
13	Maryland	34	2.1%
14	Minnesota	33	2.0%
15	Kansas	32	2.0%
16	Iowa	30	1.8%
17	Indiana	29	1.8%
18	Utah	26	1.6%
19	Missouri	24	1.5%
20	Massachusetts	20	1.2%
21	Georgia	18	1.1%
21	Virginia	18	1.1%
23	Colorado	17	1.0%
23	Kentucky	17	1.0%
23	New Jersey	17	1.0%
26	North Carolina	15	0.9%
27	Wisconsin	14	0.9%
28	Alabama	13	0.8%
29	Nebraska	12	0.7%
29	Oklahoma	12	0.7%
31	South Carolina	11	0.7%
32	Louisiana	10	0.6%
33	Nevada	9	0.5%
33	West Virginia	9	0.5%
35	Connecticut	6	0.4%
36	Mississippi	5	0.3%
36	Rhode Island	5	0.3%
38	Arkansas	4	0.2%
38	Delaware	4	0.2%
38	Idaho	4	0.2%
38	Montana	4	0.2%
38	New Mexico	4	0.2%
43	Maine	3	0.2%
43	North Dakota	3	0.2%
43	Wyoming	3	0.2%
46	New Hampshire	2	0.1%
47	Alaska	1	0.1%
47	South Dakota	1	0.1%
47	Vermont	1	0.1%
50	Hawaii	0	0.0%
	District of Columbia	6	0.4%

Source: Morgan Quitno Press using data from Federal Bureau of Investigation, Bomb Data Center "1997 Bombing Incidents"

*Includes explosive and incendiary bombings and excludes bombing attempts. Total does not include 17 bombings in Puerto Rico or one in the Virgin Islands. There were 18 deaths and 204 injuries from bombings in 1997.

Murders in 1999

National Total = 15,533 Murders*

ALPHA ORDER

RANK	STATE	MURDERS	% of USA
18	Alabama	345	2.2%
37	Alaska	53	0.3%
16	Arizona	384	2.5%
30	Arkansas	143	0.9%
1	California	2,005	12.9%
24	Colorado	185	1.2%
33	Connecticut	107	0.7%
44	Delaware	24	0.2%
5	Florida	859	5.5%
8	Georgia	583	3.8%
38	Hawaii	44	0.3%
43	Idaho	25	0.2%
3	Illinois	937	6.0%
14	Indiana	391	2.5%
40	Iowa	43	0.3%
29	Kansas	160	1.0%
23	Kentucky	212	1.4%
10	Louisiana	468	3.0%
42	Maine	27	0.2%
11	Maryland	465	3.0%
32	Massachusetts	122	0.8%
6	Michigan	695	4.5%
31	Minnesota	134	0.9%
22	Mississippi	213	1.4%
17	Missouri	359	2.3%
45	Montana	23	0.1%
36	Nebraska	60	0.4%
28	Nevada	165	1.1%
46	New Hampshire	18	0.1%
19	New Jersey	287	1.8%
27	New Mexico	170	1.1%
4	New York	903	5.8%
9	North Carolina	552	3.6%
50	North Dakota	10	0.1%
12	Ohio	397	2.6%
21	Oklahoma	231	1.5%
34	Oregon	88	0.6%
7	Pennsylvania	592	3.8%
41	Rhode Island	36	0.2%
20	South Carolina	258	1.7%
46	South Dakota	18	0.1%
14	Tennessee	391	2.5%
2	Texas	1,217	7.8%
38	Utah	44	0.3%
48	Vermont	17	0.1%
13	Virginia	392	2.5%
26	Washington	171	1.1%
35	West Virginia	79	0.5%
25	Wisconsin	179	1.2%
49	Wyoming	11	0.1%

RANK ORDER

RANK	STATE	MURDERS	% of USA
1	California	2,005	12.9%
2	Texas	1,217	7.8%
3	Illinois	937	6.0%
4	New York	903	5.8%
5	Florida	859	5.5%
6	Michigan	695	4.5%
7	Pennsylvania	592	3.8%
8	Georgia	583	3.8%
9	North Carolina	552	3.6%
10	Louisiana	468	3.0%
11	Maryland	465	3.0%
12	Ohio	397	2.6%
13	Virginia	392	2.5%
14	Indiana	391	2.5%
14	Tennessee	391	2.5%
16	Arizona	384	2.5%
17	Missouri	359	2.3%
18	Alabama	345	2.2%
19	New Jersey	287	1.8%
20	South Carolina	258	1.7%
21	Oklahoma	231	1.5%
22	Mississippi	213	1.4%
23	Kentucky	212	1.4%
24	Colorado	185	1.2%
25	Wisconsin	179	1.2%
26	Washington	171	1.1%
27	New Mexico	170	1.1%
28	Nevada	165	1.1%
29	Kansas	160	1.0%
30	Arkansas	143	0.9%
31	Minnesota	134	0.9%
32	Massachusetts	122	0.8%
33	Connecticut	107	0.7%
34	Oregon	88	0.6%
35	West Virginia	79	0.5%
36	Nebraska	60	0.4%
37	Alaska	53	0.3%
38	Hawaii	44	0.3%
38	Utah	44	0.3%
40	Iowa	43	0.3%
41	Rhode Island	36	0.2%
42	Maine	27	0.2%
43	Idaho	25	0.2%
44	Delaware	24	0.2%
45	Montana	23	0.1%
46	New Hampshire	18	0.1%
46	South Dakota	18	0.1%
48	Vermont	17	0.1%
49	Wyoming	11	0.1%
50	North Dakota	10	0.1%
	District of Columbia	241	1.6%

Source: Federal Bureau of Investigation
"Crime in the United States 1999" (Uniform Crime Reports, October 15, 2000)
Includes nonnegligent manslaughter.

Average Time Between Murders in 1999

National Rate = A Murder Occurs Every 34 Minutes*

ALPHA ORDER

RANK	STATE	HOURS.MINUTES
33	Alabama	25.23
14	Alaska	165.17
35	Arizona	22.49
21	Arkansas	61.16
50	California	4.22
27	Colorado	47.21
18	Connecticut	81.52
7	Delaware	365.00
46	Florida	10.12
43	Georgia	15.02
12	Hawaii	199.05
8	Idaho	350.24
48	Illinois	9.21
36	Indiana	22.24
11	Iowa	203.43
22	Kansas	54.45
28	Kentucky	41.19
41	Louisiana	18.43
9	Maine	324.26
40	Maryland	18.50
19	Massachusetts	71.48
45	Michigan	12.36
20	Minnesota	65.22
29	Mississippi	41.08
34	Missouri	24.24
6	Montana	380.52
15	Nebraska	146.00
23	Nevada	53.05
4	New Hampshire	486.40
32	New Jersey	30.31
24	New Mexico	51.32
47	New York	9.42
42	North Carolina	15.52
1	North Dakota	876.00
39	Ohio	22.04
30	Oklahoma	37.55
17	Oregon	99.33
44	Pennsylvania	14.48
10	Rhode Island	243.20
31	South Carolina	33.57
4	South Dakota	486.40
36	Tennessee	22.24
49	Texas	7.12
12	Utah	199.05
3	Vermont	515.17
38	Virginia	22.21
25	Washington	51.14
16	West Virginia	110.53
26	Wisconsin	48.56
2	Wyoming	796.22

RANK ORDER

RANK	STATE	HOURS.MINUTES
1	North Dakota	876.00
2	Wyoming	796.22
3	Vermont	515.17
4	New Hampshire	486.40
4	South Dakota	486.40
6	Montana	380.52
7	Delaware	365.00
8	Idaho	350.24
9	Maine	324.26
10	Rhode Island	243.20
11	Iowa	203.43
12	Hawaii	199.05
12	Utah	199.05
14	Alaska	165.17
15	Nebraska	146.00
16	West Virginia	110.53
17	Oregon	99.33
18	Connecticut	81.52
19	Massachusetts	71.48
20	Minnesota	65.22
21	Arkansas	61.16
22	Kansas	54.45
23	Nevada	53.05
24	New Mexico	51.32
25	Washington	51.14
26	Wisconsin	48.56
27	Colorado	47.21
28	Kentucky	41.19
29	Mississippi	41.08
30	Oklahoma	37.55
31	South Carolina	33.57
32	New Jersey	30.31
33	Alabama	25.23
34	Missouri	24.24
35	Arizona	22.49
36	Indiana	22.24
36	Tennessee	22.24
38	Virginia	22.21
39	Ohio	22.04
40	Maryland	18.50
41	Louisiana	18.43
42	North Carolina	15.52
43	Georgia	15.02
44	Pennsylvania	14.48
45	Michigan	12.36
46	Florida	10.12
47	New York	9.42
48	Illinois	9.21
49	Texas	7.12
50	California	4.22

| | District of Columbia | 36.21 |

Source: Morgan Quitno Press using data from Federal Bureau of Investigation
    "Crime in the United States 1999" (Uniform Crime Reports, October 15, 2000)
*Includes nonnegligent manslaughter.

Percent Change in Number of Murders: 1998 to 1999

National Percent Change = 8.5% Decrease*

ALPHA ORDER			RANK ORDER		
RANK	STATE	PERCENT CHANGE	RANK	STATE	PERCENT CHANGE
18	Alabama	(2.5)	1	Hawaii	83.3
6	Alaska	29.3	2	South Dakota	80.0
13	Arizona	2.1	3	Rhode Island	50.0
44	Arkansas	(28.9)	4	North Dakota	42.9
27	California	(7.6)	5	Vermont	30.8
14	Colorado	1.1	6	Alaska	29.3
42	Connecticut	(20.7)	7	Montana	27.8
9	Delaware	14.3	8	Nebraska	17.6
35	Florida	(11.2)	9	Delaware	14.3
21	Georgia	(5.7)	10	Oklahoma	13.2
1	Hawaii	83.3	11	Minnesota	10.7
46	Idaho	(30.6)	12	Maine	3.8
24	Illinois	(7.0)	13	Arizona	2.1
37	Indiana	(13.9)	14	Colorado	1.1
41	Iowa	(20.4)	15	New Hampshire	0.0
26	Kansas	(7.5)	16	Massachusetts	(1.6)
33	Kentucky	(10.5)	17	New York	(2.3)
40	Louisiana	(16.4)	18	Alabama	(2.5)
12	Maine	3.8	19	Nevada	(2.9)
28	Maryland	(9.4)	20	Michigan	(3.6)
16	Massachusetts	(1.6)	21	Georgia	(5.7)
20	Michigan	(3.6)	22	Wisconsin	(5.8)
11	Minnesota	10.7	23	Pennsylvania	(6.5)
48	Mississippi	(32.4)	24	Illinois	(7.0)
31	Missouri	(10.0)	25	Virginia	(7.1)
7	Montana	27.8	26	Kansas	(7.5)
8	Nebraska	17.6	27	California	(7.6)
19	Nevada	(2.9)	28	Maryland	(9.4)
15	New Hampshire	0.0	29	Texas	(9.6)
36	New Jersey	(11.7)	30	North Carolina	(9.8)
33	New Mexico	(10.5)	31	Missouri	(10.0)
17	New York	(2.3)	32	Ohio	(10.4)
30	North Carolina	(9.8)	33	Kentucky	(10.5)
4	North Dakota	42.9	33	New Mexico	(10.5)
32	Ohio	(10.4)	35	Florida	(11.2)
10	Oklahoma	13.2	36	New Jersey	(11.7)
45	Oregon	(30.2)	37	Indiana	(13.9)
23	Pennsylvania	(6.5)	38	Tennessee	(15.0)
3	Rhode Island	50.0	39	South Carolina	(15.7)
39	South Carolina	(15.7)	40	Louisiana	(16.4)
2	South Dakota	80.0	41	Iowa	(20.4)
38	Tennessee	(15.0)	42	Connecticut	(20.7)
29	Texas	(9.6)	43	Washington	(23.7)
47	Utah	(32.3)	44	Arkansas	(28.9)
5	Vermont	30.8	45	Oregon	(30.2)
25	Virginia	(7.1)	46	Idaho	(30.6)
43	Washington	(23.7)	47	Utah	(32.3)
NA	West Virginia**	NA	48	Mississippi	(32.4)
22	Wisconsin	(5.8)	49	Wyoming	(52.2)
49	Wyoming	(52.2)	NA	West Virginia**	NA
				District of Columbia	(7.3)

Source: Federal Bureau of Investigation
   "Crime in the United States 1999" (Uniform Crime Reports, October 15, 2000)
*Includes nonnegligent manslaughter.
**Not available.

Murder Rate in 1999

National Rate = 5.7 Murders per 100,000 Population*

ALPHA ORDER

RANK	STATE	RATE
7	Alabama	7.9
5	Alaska	8.6
6	Arizona	8.0
23	Arkansas	5.6
19	California	6.0
27	Colorado	4.6
35	Connecticut	3.3
36	Delaware	3.2
21	Florida	5.7
10	Georgia	7.5
29	Hawaii	3.7
46	Idaho	2.0
8	Illinois	7.7
15	Indiana	6.6
49	Iowa	1.5
19	Kansas	6.0
24	Kentucky	5.4
1	Louisiana	10.7
44	Maine	2.2
4	Maryland	9.0
46	Massachusetts	2.0
13	Michigan	7.0
39	Minnesota	2.8
8	Mississippi	7.7
15	Missouri	6.6
41	Montana	2.6
30	Nebraska	3.6
3	Nevada	9.1
49	New Hampshire	1.5
32	New Jersey	3.5
2	New Mexico	9.8
25	New York	5.0
11	North Carolina	7.2
48	North Dakota	1.6
32	Ohio	3.5
14	Oklahoma	6.9
40	Oregon	2.7
26	Pennsylvania	4.9
30	Rhode Island	3.6
15	South Carolina	6.6
42	South Dakota	2.5
12	Tennessee	7.1
18	Texas	6.1
45	Utah	2.1
38	Vermont	2.9
21	Virginia	5.7
37	Washington	3.0
28	West Virginia	4.4
34	Wisconsin	3.4
43	Wyoming	2.3

RANK ORDER

RANK	STATE	RATE
1	Louisiana	10.7
2	New Mexico	9.8
3	Nevada	9.1
4	Maryland	9.0
5	Alaska	8.6
6	Arizona	8.0
7	Alabama	7.9
8	Illinois	7.7
8	Mississippi	7.7
10	Georgia	7.5
11	North Carolina	7.2
12	Tennessee	7.1
13	Michigan	7.0
14	Oklahoma	6.9
15	Indiana	6.6
15	Missouri	6.6
15	South Carolina	6.6
18	Texas	6.1
19	California	6.0
19	Kansas	6.0
21	Florida	5.7
21	Virginia	5.7
23	Arkansas	5.6
24	Kentucky	5.4
25	New York	5.0
26	Pennsylvania	4.9
27	Colorado	4.6
28	West Virginia	4.4
29	Hawaii	3.7
30	Nebraska	3.6
30	Rhode Island	3.6
32	New Jersey	3.5
32	Ohio	3.5
34	Wisconsin	3.4
35	Connecticut	3.3
36	Delaware	3.2
37	Washington	3.0
38	Vermont	2.9
39	Minnesota	2.8
40	Oregon	2.7
41	Montana	2.6
42	South Dakota	2.5
43	Wyoming	2.3
44	Maine	2.2
45	Utah	2.1
46	Idaho	2.0
46	Massachusetts	2.0
48	North Dakota	1.6
49	Iowa	1.5
49	New Hampshire	1.5
	District of Columbia	46.4

Source: Federal Bureau of Investigation
   "Crime in the United States 1999" (Uniform Crime Reports, October 15, 2000)
*Includes nonnegligent manslaughter.

Percent Change in Murder Rate: 1998 to 1999

National Percent Change = 9.3% Decrease*

ALPHA ORDER

RANK	STATE	PERCENT CHANGE
18	Alabama	(2.9)
6	Alaska	28.2
13	Arizona	(0.2)
44	Arkansas	(29.2)
27	California	(9.0)
14	Colorado	(1.0)
42	Connecticut	(20.9)
10	Delaware	12.8
36	Florida	(12.3)
23	Georgia	(7.4)
1	Hawaii	84.6
46	Idaho	(31.8)
24	Illinois	(7.7)
37	Indiana	(14.5)
41	Iowa	(20.6)
26	Kansas	(8.4)
34	Kentucky	(11.1)
39	Louisiana	(16.5)
12	Maine	3.1
28	Maryland	(10.0)
16	Massachusetts	(2.1)
19	Michigan	(4.1)
11	Minnesota	9.6
47	Mississippi	(32.8)
29	Missouri	(10.5)
7	Montana	27.3
8	Nebraska	17.4
20	Nevada	(6.3)
15	New Hampshire	(1.3)
35	New Jersey	(12.0)
30	New Mexico	(10.7)
17	New York	(2.4)
33	North Carolina	(11.0)
4	North Dakota	43.8
31	Ohio	(10.8)
9	Oklahoma	12.9
45	Oregon	(30.9)
22	Pennsylvania	(6.4)
3	Rhode Island	49.5
40	South Carolina	(16.8)
2	South Dakota	81.2
38	Tennessee	(15.8)
32	Texas	(10.9)
48	Utah	(33.3)
5	Vermont	30.1
25	Virginia	(8.2)
43	Washington	(24.5)
NA	West Virginia**	NA
20	Wisconsin	(6.3)
49	Wyoming	(52.1)

RANK ORDER

RANK	STATE	PERCENT CHANGE
1	Hawaii	84.6
2	South Dakota	81.2
3	Rhode Island	49.5
4	North Dakota	43.8
5	Vermont	30.1
6	Alaska	28.2
7	Montana	27.3
8	Nebraska	17.4
9	Oklahoma	12.9
10	Delaware	12.8
11	Minnesota	9.6
12	Maine	3.1
13	Arizona	(0.2)
14	Colorado	(1.0)
15	New Hampshire	(1.3)
16	Massachusetts	(2.1)
17	New York	(2.4)
18	Alabama	(2.9)
19	Michigan	(4.1)
20	Nevada	(6.3)
20	Wisconsin	(6.3)
22	Pennsylvania	(6.4)
23	Georgia	(7.4)
24	Illinois	(7.7)
25	Virginia	(8.2)
26	Kansas	(8.4)
27	California	(9.0)
28	Maryland	(10.0)
29	Missouri	(10.5)
30	New Mexico	(10.7)
31	Ohio	(10.8)
32	Texas	(10.9)
33	North Carolina	(11.0)
34	Kentucky	(11.1)
35	New Jersey	(12.0)
36	Florida	(12.3)
37	Indiana	(14.5)
38	Tennessee	(15.8)
39	Louisiana	(16.5)
40	South Carolina	(16.8)
41	Iowa	(20.6)
42	Connecticut	(20.9)
43	Washington	(24.5)
44	Arkansas	(29.2)
45	Oregon	(30.9)
46	Idaho	(31.8)
47	Mississippi	(32.8)
48	Utah	(33.3)
49	Wyoming	(52.1)
NA	West Virginia**	NA
	District of Columbia	(6.6)

Source: Federal Bureau of Investigation
   "Crime in the United States 1999" (Uniform Crime Reports, October 15, 2000)
*Includes nonnegligent manslaughter.
**Not available.

Murders with Firearms in 1999

National Total = 8,256 Murders*

ALPHA ORDER

RANK	STATE	MURDERS	% of USA
NA	Alabama**	NA	NA
33	Alaska	23	0.3%
11	Arizona	272	3.3%
23	Arkansas	97	1.2%
1	California	1,338	16.2%
21	Colorado	107	1.3%
26	Connecticut	74	0.9%
38	Delaware	17	0.2%
NA	Florida**	NA	NA
8	Georgia	360	4.4%
34	Hawaii	22	0.3%
40	Idaho	15	0.2%
5	Illinois*	458	5.5%
13	Indiana	238	2.9%
36	Iowa	21	0.3%
NA	Kansas**	NA	NA
29	Kentucky	52	0.6%
9	Louisiana	315	3.8%
38	Maine	17	0.2%
10	Maryland	293	3.5%
27	Massachusetts	66	0.8%
4	Michigan	485	5.9%
30	Minnesota	50	0.6%
20	Mississippi	112	1.4%
15	Missouri	213	2.6%
43	Montana	6	0.1%
41	Nebraska	7	0.1%
22	Nevada	103	1.2%
45	New Hampshire	4	0.0%
17	New Jersey	151	1.8%
25	New Mexico	77	0.9%
3	New York	487	5.9%
7	North Carolina	362	4.4%
45	North Dakota	4	0.0%
16	Ohio	199	2.4%
28	Oklahoma	56	0.7%
31	Oregon	46	0.6%
6	Pennsylvania	407	4.9%
37	Rhode Island	20	0.2%
18	South Carolina	146	1.8%
44	South Dakota	5	0.1%
14	Tennessee	237	2.9%
2	Texas	746	9.0%
34	Utah	22	0.3%
41	Vermont	7	0.1%
12	Virginia	243	2.9%
24	Washington	90	1.1%
32	West Virginia	44	0.5%
19	Wisconsin	126	1.5%
47	Wyoming	3	0.0%

RANK ORDER

RANK	STATE	MURDERS	% of USA
1	California	1,338	16.2%
2	Texas	746	9.0%
3	New York	487	5.9%
4	Michigan	485	5.9%
5	Illinois*	458	5.5%
6	Pennsylvania	407	4.9%
7	North Carolina	362	4.4%
8	Georgia	360	4.4%
9	Louisiana	315	3.8%
10	Maryland	293	3.5%
11	Arizona	272	3.3%
12	Virginia	243	2.9%
13	Indiana	238	2.9%
14	Tennessee	237	2.9%
15	Missouri	213	2.6%
16	Ohio	199	2.4%
17	New Jersey	151	1.8%
18	South Carolina	146	1.8%
19	Wisconsin	126	1.5%
20	Mississippi	112	1.4%
21	Colorado	107	1.3%
22	Nevada	103	1.2%
23	Arkansas	97	1.2%
24	Washington	90	1.1%
25	New Mexico	77	0.9%
26	Connecticut	74	0.9%
27	Massachusetts	66	0.8%
28	Oklahoma	56	0.7%
29	Kentucky	52	0.6%
30	Minnesota	50	0.6%
31	Oregon	46	0.6%
32	West Virginia	44	0.5%
33	Alaska	23	0.3%
34	Hawaii	22	0.3%
34	Utah	22	0.3%
36	Iowa	21	0.3%
37	Rhode Island	20	0.2%
38	Delaware	17	0.2%
38	Maine	17	0.2%
40	Idaho	15	0.2%
41	Nebraska	7	0.1%
41	Vermont	7	0.1%
43	Montana	6	0.1%
44	South Dakota	5	0.1%
45	New Hampshire	4	0.0%
45	North Dakota	4	0.0%
47	Wyoming	3	0.0%
NA	Alabama**	NA	NA
NA	Florida**	NA	NA
NA	Kansas**	NA	NA
	District of Columbia**	NA	NA

Source: Federal Bureau of Investigation
   "Crime in the United States 1999" (Uniform Crime Reports, October 15, 2000)
*Of the 12,658 murders in 1999 for which supplemental data were received by the F.B.I. There were an additional 2,875 murders for which the type of murder weapon was not reported to the F.B.I. Includes nonnegligent manslaughter. Numbers are for reporting jurisdictions only. Illinois' figure is for Chicago only.
**Not available.

Murder Rate with Firearms in 1999

National Rate = 4.3 Murders per 100,000 Population*

<u>ALPHA ORDER</u>

<u>RANK ORDER</u>

RANK	STATE	RATE		RANK	STATE	RATE
NA	Alabama**	NA		1	Illinois*	16.2
20	Alaska	4.1		2	Maryland	9.4
9	Arizona	5.9		3	South Carolina	8.5
20	Arkansas	4.1		4	Mississippi	8.4
22	California	4.0		5	Louisiana	8.1
25	Colorado	2.8		6	New York	7.9
28	Connecticut	2.3		7	Georgia	7.6
28	Delaware	2.3		8	New Mexico	6.4
NA	Florida**	NA		9	Arizona	5.9
7	Georgia	7.6		9	Indiana	5.9
31	Hawaii	1.9		11	Nevada	5.7
41	Idaho	1.2		12	Michigan	5.6
1	Illinois*	16.2		13	North Carolina	5.3
9	Indiana	5.9		14	Tennessee	5.2
43	Iowa	0.9		15	Missouri	5.0
NA	Kansas**	NA		16	Virginia	4.7
17	Kentucky	4.5		17	Kentucky	4.5
5	Louisiana	8.1		17	Pennsylvania	4.5
37	Maine	1.4		19	West Virginia	4.4
2	Maryland	9.4		20	Alaska	4.1
39	Massachusetts	1.3		20	Arkansas	4.1
12	Michigan	5.6		22	California	4.0
24	Minnesota	3.0		23	Texas	3.8
4	Mississippi	8.4		24	Minnesota	3.0
15	Missouri	5.0		25	Colorado	2.8
37	Montana	1.4		26	Ohio	2.6
47	Nebraska	0.5		26	Wisconsin	2.6
11	Nevada	5.7		28	Connecticut	2.3
43	New Hampshire	0.9		28	Delaware	2.3
31	New Jersey	1.9		30	Rhode Island	2.2
8	New Mexico	6.4		31	Hawaii	1.9
6	New York	7.9		31	New Jersey	1.9
13	North Carolina	5.3		33	Oklahoma	1.7
45	North Dakota	0.8		33	Washington	1.7
26	Ohio	2.6		35	Oregon	1.5
33	Oklahoma	1.7		35	Vermont	1.5
35	Oregon	1.5		37	Maine	1.4
17	Pennsylvania	4.5		37	Montana	1.4
30	Rhode Island	2.2		39	Massachusetts	1.3
3	South Carolina	8.5		39	Utah	1.3
42	South Dakota	1.0		41	Idaho	1.2
14	Tennessee	5.2		42	South Dakota	1.0
23	Texas	3.8		43	Iowa	0.9
39	Utah	1.3		43	New Hampshire	0.9
35	Vermont	1.5		45	North Dakota	0.8
16	Virginia	4.7		46	Wyoming	0.7
33	Washington	1.7		47	Nebraska	0.5
19	West Virginia	4.4		NA	Alabama**	NA
26	Wisconsin	2.6		NA	Florida**	NA
46	Wyoming	0.7		NA	Kansas**	NA
					District of Columbia**	NA

Source: Morgan Quitno Press using data from Federal Bureau of Investigation
"Crime in the United States 1999" (Uniform Crime Reports, October 15, 2000)
*Of the 12,658 murders in 1999 for which supplemental data were received by the F.B.I. There were an additional 2,875 murders for which the type of murder weapon was not reported to the F.B.I. Includes nonnegligent manslaughter. National and state rates based on population for reporting jurisdictions only. Illinois' rate is for Chicago only. **Not available.

Percent of Murders Involving Firearms in 1999

National Percent = 65.2% of Murders*

ALPHA ORDER				RANK ORDER		
RANK	STATE	PERCENT		RANK	STATE	PERCENT
NA	Alabama**	NA		1	Mississippi	78.3
40	Alaska	50.0		2	Maryland	74.4
6	Arizona	71.2		3	Indiana	73.5
16	Arkansas	67.8		4	Pennsylvania	72.7
18	California	66.7		5	Illinois*	71.6
27	Colorado	61.8		6	Arizona	71.2
13	Connecticut	69.2		7	West Virginia	71.0
8	Delaware	70.8		8	Delaware	70.8
NA	Florida**	NA		8	Wisconsin	70.8
11	Georgia	69.8		10	South Carolina	69.9
38	Hawaii	51.2		11	Georgia	69.8
25	Idaho	62.5		12	Louisiana	69.5
5	Illinois*	71.6		13	Connecticut	69.2
3	Indiana	73.5		14	Virginia	68.6
38	Iowa	51.2		15	Michigan	67.9
NA	Kansas**	NA		16	Arkansas	67.8
23	Kentucky	64.2		17	North Carolina	67.2
12	Louisiana	69.5		18	California	66.7
24	Maine	63.0		18	Montana	66.7
2	Maryland	74.4		18	Oklahoma	66.7
30	Massachusetts	56.4		21	Tennessee	66.2
15	Michigan	67.9		22	Missouri	65.1
43	Minnesota	38.8		23	Kentucky	64.2
1	Mississippi	78.3		24	Maine	63.0
22	Missouri	65.1		25	Idaho	62.5
18	Montana	66.7		26	Nevada	62.4
46	Nebraska	26.9		27	Colorado	61.8
26	Nevada	62.4		28	Texas	61.7
47	New Hampshire	22.2		29	Ohio	57.3
36	New Jersey	52.6		30	Massachusetts	56.4
34	New Mexico	54.6		30	New York	56.4
30	New York	56.4		32	Rhode Island	55.6
17	North Carolina	67.2		33	Utah	55.0
40	North Dakota	50.0		34	New Mexico	54.6
29	Ohio	57.3		35	Washington	54.2
18	Oklahoma	66.7		36	New Jersey	52.6
37	Oregon	52.3		37	Oregon	52.3
4	Pennsylvania	72.7		38	Hawaii	51.2
32	Rhode Island	55.6		38	Iowa	51.2
10	South Carolina	69.9		40	Alaska	50.0
44	South Dakota	38.5		40	North Dakota	50.0
21	Tennessee	66.2		42	Vermont	41.2
28	Texas	61.7		43	Minnesota	38.8
33	Utah	55.0		44	South Dakota	38.5
42	Vermont	41.2		45	Wyoming	27.3
14	Virginia	68.6		46	Nebraska	26.9
35	Washington	54.2		47	New Hampshire	22.2
7	West Virginia	71.0		NA	Alabama**	NA
8	Wisconsin	70.8		NA	Florida**	NA
45	Wyoming	27.3		NA	Kansas**	NA
					District of Columbia**	NA

Source: Morgan Quitno Press using data from Federal Bureau of Investigation
     "Crime in the United States 1999" (Uniform Crime Reports, October 15, 2000)
*Of the 12,658 murders in 1999 for which supplemental data were received by the F.B.I. There were an additional 2,875 murders for which the type of murder weapon was not reported to the F.B.I. Murder includes nonnegligent manslaughter. Illinois' percentage is for Chicago only.
**Not available.

Murders with Handguns in 1999

National Total = 6,495 Murders*

ALPHA ORDER

RANK	STATE	MURDERS	% of USA
NA	Alabama**	NA	NA
40	Alaska	6	0.1%
10	Arizona	232	3.6%
25	Arkansas	64	1.0%
1	California	1,150	17.7%
22	Colorado	78	1.2%
24	Connecticut	66	1.0%
34	Delaware	16	0.2%
NA	Florida**	NA	NA
6	Georgia	318	4.9%
33	Hawaii	20	0.3%
39	Idaho	9	0.1%
4	Illinois*	373	5.7%
11	Indiana	210	3.2%
35	Iowa	15	0.2%
NA	Kansas**	NA	NA
30	Kentucky	35	0.5%
8	Louisiana	263	4.0%
38	Maine	10	0.2%
7	Maryland	276	4.2%
27	Massachusetts	48	0.7%
12	Michigan	198	3.0%
29	Minnesota	42	0.6%
20	Mississippi	95	1.5%
13	Missouri	186	2.9%
43	Montana	2	0.0%
41	Nebraska	5	0.1%
21	Nevada	87	1.3%
42	New Hampshire	3	0.0%
17	New Jersey	139	2.1%
26	New Mexico	56	0.9%
3	New York	449	6.9%
9	North Carolina	236	3.6%
46	North Dakota	1	0.0%
14	Ohio	162	2.5%
28	Oklahoma	45	0.7%
32	Oregon	27	0.4%
5	Pennsylvania	369	5.7%
37	Rhode Island	13	0.2%
19	South Carolina	110	1.7%
43	South Dakota	2	0.0%
15	Tennessee	148	2.3%
2	Texas	527	8.1%
35	Utah	15	0.2%
46	Vermont	1	0.0%
15	Virginia	148	2.3%
23	Washington	77	1.2%
31	West Virginia	33	0.5%
18	Wisconsin	117	1.8%
43	Wyoming	2	0.0%

RANK ORDER

RANK	STATE	MURDERS	% of USA
1	California	1,150	17.7%
2	Texas	527	8.1%
3	New York	449	6.9%
4	Illinois*	373	5.7%
5	Pennsylvania	369	5.7%
6	Georgia	318	4.9%
7	Maryland	276	4.2%
8	Louisiana	263	4.0%
9	North Carolina	236	3.6%
10	Arizona	232	3.6%
11	Indiana	210	3.2%
12	Michigan	198	3.0%
13	Missouri	186	2.9%
14	Ohio	162	2.5%
15	Tennessee	148	2.3%
15	Virginia	148	2.3%
17	New Jersey	139	2.1%
18	Wisconsin	117	1.8%
19	South Carolina	110	1.7%
20	Mississippi	95	1.5%
21	Nevada	87	1.3%
22	Colorado	78	1.2%
23	Washington	77	1.2%
24	Connecticut	66	1.0%
25	Arkansas	64	1.0%
26	New Mexico	56	0.9%
27	Massachusetts	48	0.7%
28	Oklahoma	45	0.7%
29	Minnesota	42	0.6%
30	Kentucky	35	0.5%
31	West Virginia	33	0.5%
32	Oregon	27	0.4%
33	Hawaii	20	0.3%
34	Delaware	16	0.2%
35	Iowa	15	0.2%
35	Utah	15	0.2%
37	Rhode Island	13	0.2%
38	Maine	10	0.2%
39	Idaho	9	0.1%
40	Alaska	6	0.1%
41	Nebraska	5	0.1%
42	New Hampshire	3	0.0%
43	Montana	2	0.0%
43	South Dakota	2	0.0%
43	Wyoming	2	0.0%
46	North Dakota	1	0.0%
46	Vermont	1	0.0%
NA	Alabama**	NA	NA
NA	Florida**	NA	NA
NA	Kansas**	NA	NA
	District of Columbia**	NA	NA

Source: Federal Bureau of Investigation
"Crime in the United States 1999" (Uniform Crime Reports, October 15, 2000)
*Of the 12,658 murders in 1999 for which supplemental data were received by the F.B.I. There were an additional 2,875 murders for which the type of murder weapon was not reported to the F.B.I. There were also 873 murders that were reported as murders by "firearms, type unknown." Murder includes nonnegligent manslaughter. Numbers are for reporting jurisdictions only. Illinois' figure is for Chicago only. **Not available.*

Murder Rate with Handguns in 1999

National Rate = 3.4 Murders per 100,000 Population*

ALPHA ORDER

RANK	STATE	RATE
NA	Alabama**	NA
34	Alaska	1.1
9	Arizona	5.1
20	Arkansas	2.7
14	California	3.5
25	Colorado	2.1
25	Connecticut	2.1
25	Delaware	2.1
NA	Florida**	NA
6	Georgia	6.7
29	Hawaii	1.7
39	Idaho	0.7
1	Illinois*	13.2
8	Indiana	5.2
40	Iowa	0.6
NA	Kansas**	NA
18	Kentucky	3.0
5	Louisiana	6.8
38	Maine	0.8
2	Maryland	8.8
35	Massachusetts	0.9
24	Michigan	2.3
22	Minnesota	2.5
4	Mississippi	7.1
12	Missouri	4.4
42	Montana	0.5
45	Nebraska	0.3
10	Nevada	4.8
40	New Hampshire	0.6
29	New Jersey	1.7
11	New Mexico	4.7
3	New York	7.3
15	North Carolina	3.4
46	North Dakota	0.2
25	Ohio	2.1
33	Oklahoma	1.3
35	Oregon	0.9
13	Pennsylvania	4.1
32	Rhode Island	1.4
7	South Carolina	6.4
43	South Dakota	0.4
17	Tennessee	3.2
20	Texas	2.7
35	Utah	0.9
46	Vermont	0.2
19	Virginia	2.9
31	Washington	1.5
16	West Virginia	3.3
23	Wisconsin	2.4
43	Wyoming	0.4

RANK ORDER

RANK	STATE	RATE
1	Illinois*	13.2
2	Maryland	8.8
3	New York	7.3
4	Mississippi	7.1
5	Louisiana	6.8
6	Georgia	6.7
7	South Carolina	6.4
8	Indiana	5.2
9	Arizona	5.1
10	Nevada	4.8
11	New Mexico	4.7
12	Missouri	4.4
13	Pennsylvania	4.1
14	California	3.5
15	North Carolina	3.4
16	West Virginia	3.3
17	Tennessee	3.2
18	Kentucky	3.0
19	Virginia	2.9
20	Arkansas	2.7
20	Texas	2.7
22	Minnesota	2.5
23	Wisconsin	2.4
24	Michigan	2.3
25	Colorado	2.1
25	Connecticut	2.1
25	Delaware	2.1
25	Ohio	2.1
29	Hawaii	1.7
29	New Jersey	1.7
31	Washington	1.5
32	Rhode Island	1.4
33	Oklahoma	1.3
34	Alaska	1.1
35	Massachusetts	0.9
35	Oregon	0.9
35	Utah	0.9
38	Maine	0.8
39	Idaho	0.7
40	Iowa	0.6
40	New Hampshire	0.6
42	Montana	0.5
43	South Dakota	0.4
43	Wyoming	0.4
45	Nebraska	0.3
46	North Dakota	0.2
46	Vermont	0.2
NA	Alabama**	NA
NA	Florida**	NA
NA	Kansas**	NA
	District of Columbia**	NA

Source: Morgan Quitno Press using data from Federal Bureau of Investigation
    "Crime in the United States 1999" (Uniform Crime Reports, October 15, 2000)
*Of the 12,685 murders in 1999 for which supplemental data were received by the F.B.I. There were an additional 2,875 murders for which the type of murder weapon was not reported to the F.B.I. There were also 873 murders that were reported as murders by "firearms, type unknown." Murder includes nonnegligent manslaughter. Numbers are for reporting jurisdictions only. Illinois' figure is for Chicago only. **Not available.

Percent of Murders Involving Handguns in 1999

National Percent = 51.3% of Murders*

ALPHA ORDER

RANK	STATE	PERCENT
NA	Alabama**	NA
45	Alaska	13.0
9	Arizona	60.7
24	Arkansas	44.8
12	California	57.4
23	Colorado	45.1
7	Connecticut	61.7
2	Delaware	66.7
NA	Florida**	NA
8	Georgia	61.6
21	Hawaii	46.5
32	Idaho	37.5
10	Illinois*	58.3
6	Indiana	64.8
35	Iowa	36.6
NA	Kansas**	NA
27	Kentucky	43.2
11	Louisiana	58.1
34	Maine	37.0
1	Maryland	70.1
30	Massachusetts	41.0
39	Michigan	27.7
37	Minnesota	32.6
3	Mississippi	66.4
13	Missouri	56.9
40	Montana	22.2
41	Nebraska	19.2
16	Nevada	52.7
43	New Hampshire	16.7
19	New Jersey	48.4
31	New Mexico	39.7
18	New York	52.0
25	North Carolina	43.8
46	North Dakota	12.5
20	Ohio	46.7
14	Oklahoma	53.6
38	Oregon	30.7
4	Pennsylvania	65.9
36	Rhode Island	36.1
17	South Carolina	52.6
44	South Dakota	15.4
29	Tennessee	41.3
26	Texas	43.6
32	Utah	37.5
47	Vermont	5.9
28	Virginia	41.8
22	Washington	46.4
15	West Virginia	53.2
5	Wisconsin	65.7
42	Wyoming	18.2

RANK ORDER

RANK	STATE	PERCENT
1	Maryland	70.1
2	Delaware	66.7
3	Mississippi	66.4
4	Pennsylvania	65.9
5	Wisconsin	65.7
6	Indiana	64.8
7	Connecticut	61.7
8	Georgia	61.6
9	Arizona	60.7
10	Illinois*	58.3
11	Louisiana	58.1
12	California	57.4
13	Missouri	56.9
14	Oklahoma	53.6
15	West Virginia	53.2
16	Nevada	52.7
17	South Carolina	52.6
18	New York	52.0
19	New Jersey	48.4
20	Ohio	46.7
21	Hawaii	46.5
22	Washington	46.4
23	Colorado	45.1
24	Arkansas	44.8
25	North Carolina	43.8
26	Texas	43.6
27	Kentucky	43.2
28	Virginia	41.8
29	Tennessee	41.3
30	Massachusetts	41.0
31	New Mexico	39.7
32	Idaho	37.5
32	Utah	37.5
34	Maine	37.0
35	Iowa	36.6
36	Rhode Island	36.1
37	Minnesota	32.6
38	Oregon	30.7
39	Michigan	27.7
40	Montana	22.2
41	Nebraska	19.2
42	Wyoming	18.2
43	New Hampshire	16.7
44	South Dakota	15.4
45	Alaska	13.0
46	North Dakota	12.5
47	Vermont	5.9
NA	Alabama**	NA
NA	Florida**	NA
NA	Kansas**	NA
	District of Columbia**	NA

Source: Morgan Quitno Press using data from Federal Bureau of Investigation
   "Crime in the United States 1999" (Uniform Crime Reports, October 15, 2000)
*Of the 12,685 murders in 1999 for which supplemental data were received by the F.B.I. There were an additional 2,875 murders for which the type of murder weapon was not reported to the F.B.I. There were also 873 murders that were reported as murders by "firearms, type unknown." Murder includes nonnegligent manslaughter. Numbers are for reporting jurisdictions only. Illinois' figure is for Chicago only. **Not available.

Murders with Rifles in 1999

National Total = 385 Murders*

ALPHA ORDER

RANK	STATE	MURDERS	% of USA
NA	Alabama**	NA	NA
15	Alaska	7	1.8%
8	Arizona	14	3.6%
13	Arkansas	8	2.1%
1	California	62	16.1%
18	Colorado	5	1.3%
29	Connecticut	2	0.5%
40	Delaware	0	0.0%
NA	Florida**	NA	NA
10	Georgia	12	3.1%
40	Hawaii	0	0.0%
22	Idaho	4	1.0%
22	Illinois*	4	1.0%
13	Indiana	8	2.1%
40	Iowa	0	0.0%
NA	Kansas**	NA	NA
26	Kentucky	3	0.8%
5	Louisiana	19	4.9%
29	Maine	2	0.5%
22	Maryland	4	1.0%
29	Massachusetts	2	0.5%
4	Michigan	23	6.0%
29	Minnesota	2	0.5%
29	Mississippi	2	0.5%
15	Missouri	7	1.8%
29	Montana	2	0.5%
38	Nebraska	1	0.3%
26	Nevada	3	0.8%
40	New Hampshire	0	0.0%
40	New Jersey	0	0.0%
15	New Mexico	7	1.8%
11	New York	10	2.6%
3	North Carolina	27	7.0%
40	North Dakota	0	0.0%
29	Ohio	2	0.5%
18	Oklahoma	5	1.3%
38	Oregon	1	0.3%
11	Pennsylvania	10	2.6%
40	Rhode Island	0	0.0%
9	South Carolina	13	3.4%
29	South Dakota	2	0.5%
6	Tennessee	17	4.4%
2	Texas	60	15.6%
26	Utah	3	0.8%
29	Vermont	2	0.5%
7	Virginia	16	4.2%
22	Washington	4	1.0%
18	West Virginia	5	1.3%
18	Wisconsin	5	1.3%
40	Wyoming	0	0.0%

RANK ORDER

RANK	STATE	MURDERS	% of USA
1	California	62	16.1%
2	Texas	60	15.6%
3	North Carolina	27	7.0%
4	Michigan	23	6.0%
5	Louisiana	19	4.9%
6	Tennessee	17	4.4%
7	Virginia	16	4.2%
8	Arizona	14	3.6%
9	South Carolina	13	3.4%
10	Georgia	12	3.1%
11	New York	10	2.6%
11	Pennsylvania	10	2.6%
13	Arkansas	8	2.1%
13	Indiana	8	2.1%
15	Alaska	7	1.8%
15	Missouri	7	1.8%
15	New Mexico	7	1.8%
18	Colorado	5	1.3%
18	Oklahoma	5	1.3%
18	West Virginia	5	1.3%
18	Wisconsin	5	1.3%
22	Idaho	4	1.0%
22	Illinois*	4	1.0%
22	Maryland	4	1.0%
22	Washington	4	1.0%
26	Kentucky	3	0.8%
26	Nevada	3	0.8%
26	Utah	3	0.8%
29	Connecticut	2	0.5%
29	Maine	2	0.5%
29	Massachusetts	2	0.5%
29	Minnesota	2	0.5%
29	Mississippi	2	0.5%
29	Montana	2	0.5%
29	Ohio	2	0.5%
29	South Dakota	2	0.5%
29	Vermont	2	0.5%
38	Nebraska	1	0.3%
38	Oregon	1	0.3%
40	Delaware	0	0.0%
40	Hawaii	0	0.0%
40	Iowa	0	0.0%
40	New Hampshire	0	0.0%
40	New Jersey	0	0.0%
40	North Dakota	0	0.0%
40	Rhode Island	0	0.0%
40	Wyoming	0	0.0%
NA	Alabama**	NA	NA
NA	Florida**	NA	NA
NA	Kansas**	NA	NA
	District of Columbia**	NA	NA

Source: Federal Bureau of Investigation
"Crime in the United States 1999" (Uniform Crime Reports, October 15, 2000)
*Of the 12,685 murders in 1999 for which supplemental data were received by the F.B.I. There were an additional 2,875 murders for which the type of murder weapon was not reported to the F.B.I. There were also 873 murders that were reported as murders by "firearms, type unknown." Murder includes nonnegligent manslaughter. Numbers are for reporting jurisdictions only. Illinois' figure is for Chicago only. **Not available.*

Percent of Murders Involving Rifles in 1999

National Percent = 3.0% of Murders*

ALPHA ORDER				RANK ORDER		
RANK	STATE	PERCENT		RANK	STATE	PERCENT
NA	Alabama**	NA		1	Montana	22.2
4	Alaska	15.2		2	Idaho	16.7
19	Arizona	3.7		3	South Dakota	15.4
11	Arkansas	5.6		4	Alaska	15.2
22	California	3.1		5	Vermont	11.8
23	Colorado	2.9		6	West Virginia	8.1
29	Connecticut	1.9		7	Utah	7.5
40	Delaware	0.0		8	Maine	7.4
NA	Florida**	NA		9	South Carolina	6.2
27	Georgia	2.3		10	Oklahoma	6.0
40	Hawaii	0.0		11	Arkansas	5.6
2	Idaho	16.7		12	New Mexico	5.0
38	Illinois*	0.6		12	North Carolina	5.0
25	Indiana	2.5		12	Texas	5.0
40	Iowa	0.0		15	Tennessee	4.7
NA	Kansas**	NA		16	Virginia	4.5
19	Kentucky	3.7		17	Louisiana	4.2
17	Louisiana	4.2		18	Nebraska	3.8
8	Maine	7.4		19	Arizona	3.7
37	Maryland	1.0		19	Kentucky	3.7
32	Massachusetts	1.7		21	Michigan	3.2
21	Michigan	3.2		22	California	3.1
33	Minnesota	1.6		23	Colorado	2.9
34	Mississippi	1.4		24	Wisconsin	2.8
28	Missouri	2.1		25	Indiana	2.5
1	Montana	22.2		26	Washington	2.4
18	Nebraska	3.8		27	Georgia	2.3
30	Nevada	1.8		28	Missouri	2.1
40	New Hampshire	0.0		29	Connecticut	1.9
40	New Jersey	0.0		30	Nevada	1.8
12	New Mexico	5.0		30	Pennsylvania	1.8
35	New York	1.2		32	Massachusetts	1.7
12	North Carolina	5.0		33	Minnesota	1.6
40	North Dakota	0.0		34	Mississippi	1.4
38	Ohio	0.6		35	New York	1.2
10	Oklahoma	6.0		36	Oregon	1.1
36	Oregon	1.1		37	Maryland	1.0
30	Pennsylvania	1.8		38	Illinois*	0.6
40	Rhode Island	0.0		38	Ohio	0.6
9	South Carolina	6.2		40	Delaware	0.0
3	South Dakota	15.4		40	Hawaii	0.0
15	Tennessee	4.7		40	Iowa	0.0
12	Texas	5.0		40	New Hampshire	0.0
7	Utah	7.5		40	New Jersey	0.0
5	Vermont	11.8		40	North Dakota	0.0
16	Virginia	4.5		40	Rhode Island	0.0
26	Washington	2.4		40	Wyoming	0.0
6	West Virginia	8.1		NA	Alabama**	NA
24	Wisconsin	2.8		NA	Florida**	NA
40	Wyoming	0.0		NA	Kansas**	NA
					District of Columbia**	NA

Source: Morgan Quitno Press using data from Federal Bureau of Investigation
"Crime in the United States 1999" (Uniform Crime Reports, October 15, 2000)
*Of the 12,685 murders in 1999 for which supplemental data were received by the F.B.I. There were an additional 2,875 murders for which the type of murder weapon was not reported to the F.B.I. There were also 873 murders that were reported as murders by "firearms, type unknown." Murder includes nonnegligent manslaughter. Numbers are for reporting jurisdictions only. Illinois' figure is for Chicago only. **Not available.

Murders with Shotguns in 1999

National Total = 503 Murders*

ALPHA ORDER

RANK	STATE	MURDERS	% of USA
NA	Alabama**	NA	NA
25	Alaska	4	0.8%
11	Arizona	15	3.0%
13	Arkansas	11	2.2%
2	California	64	12.7%
29	Colorado	3	0.6%
25	Connecticut	4	0.8%
44	Delaware	0	0.0%
NA	Florida**	NA	NA
7	Georgia	22	4.4%
39	Hawaii	1	0.2%
44	Idaho	0	0.0%
29	Illinois*	3	0.6%
18	Indiana	7	1.4%
34	Iowa	2	0.4%
NA	Kansas**	NA	NA
25	Kentucky	4	0.8%
6	Louisiana	25	5.0%
29	Maine	3	0.6%
15	Maryland	10	2.0%
34	Massachusetts	2	0.4%
4	Michigan	28	5.6%
19	Minnesota	6	1.2%
15	Mississippi	10	2.0%
13	Missouri	11	2.2%
34	Montana	2	0.4%
39	Nebraska	1	0.2%
17	Nevada	8	1.6%
39	New Hampshire	1	0.2%
19	New Jersey	6	1.2%
19	New Mexico	6	1.2%
5	New York	26	5.2%
3	North Carolina	39	7.8%
29	North Dakota	3	0.6%
23	Ohio	5	1.0%
19	Oklahoma	6	1.2%
23	Oregon	5	1.0%
7	Pennsylvania	22	4.4%
44	Rhode Island	0	0.0%
11	South Carolina	15	3.0%
39	South Dakota	1	0.2%
10	Tennessee	18	3.6%
1	Texas	71	14.1%
44	Utah	0	0.0%
34	Vermont	2	0.4%
9	Virginia	20	4.0%
25	Washington	4	0.8%
29	West Virginia	3	0.6%
34	Wisconsin	2	0.4%
39	Wyoming	1	0.2%

RANK ORDER

RANK	STATE	MURDERS	% of USA
1	Texas	71	14.1%
2	California	64	12.7%
3	North Carolina	39	7.8%
4	Michigan	28	5.6%
5	New York	26	5.2%
6	Louisiana	25	5.0%
7	Georgia	22	4.4%
7	Pennsylvania	22	4.4%
9	Virginia	20	4.0%
10	Tennessee	18	3.6%
11	Arizona	15	3.0%
11	South Carolina	15	3.0%
13	Arkansas	11	2.2%
13	Missouri	11	2.2%
15	Maryland	10	2.0%
15	Mississippi	10	2.0%
17	Nevada	8	1.6%
18	Indiana	7	1.4%
19	Minnesota	6	1.2%
19	New Jersey	6	1.2%
19	New Mexico	6	1.2%
19	Oklahoma	6	1.2%
23	Ohio	5	1.0%
23	Oregon	5	1.0%
25	Alaska	4	0.8%
25	Connecticut	4	0.8%
25	Kentucky	4	0.8%
25	Washington	4	0.8%
29	Colorado	3	0.6%
29	Illinois*	3	0.6%
29	Maine	3	0.6%
29	North Dakota	3	0.6%
29	West Virginia	3	0.6%
34	Iowa	2	0.4%
34	Massachusetts	2	0.4%
34	Montana	2	0.4%
34	Vermont	2	0.4%
34	Wisconsin	2	0.4%
39	Hawaii	1	0.2%
39	Nebraska	1	0.2%
39	New Hampshire	1	0.2%
39	South Dakota	1	0.2%
39	Wyoming	1	0.2%
44	Delaware	0	0.0%
44	Idaho	0	0.0%
44	Rhode Island	0	0.0%
44	Utah	0	0.0%
NA	Alabama**	NA	NA
NA	Florida**	NA	NA
NA	Kansas**	NA	NA
	District of Columbia**	NA	NA

Source: Federal Bureau of Investigation
"Crime in the United States 1999" (Uniform Crime Reports, October 15, 2000)
*Of the 12,685 murders in 1999 for which supplemental data were received by the F.B.I. There were an additional 2,875 murders for which the type of murder weapon was not reported to the F.B.I. There were also 873 murders that were reported as murders by "firearms, type unknown." Murder includes nonnegligent manslaughter. Numbers are for reporting jurisdictions only. Illinois' figure is for Chicago only. **Not available.

Percent of Murders Involving Shotguns in 1999

National Percent = 4.0% of Murders*

<table>
<tr><td colspan="3">ALPHA ORDER</td><td colspan="3">RANK ORDER</td></tr>
<tr><th>RANK</th><th>STATE</th><th>PERCENT</th><th>RANK</th><th>STATE</th><th>PERCENT</th></tr>
<tr><td>NA</td><td>Alabama**</td><td>NA</td><td>1</td><td>North Dakota</td><td>37.5</td></tr>
<tr><td>6</td><td>Alaska</td><td>8.7</td><td>2</td><td>Montana</td><td>22.2</td></tr>
<tr><td>26</td><td>Arizona</td><td>3.9</td><td>3</td><td>Vermont</td><td>11.8</td></tr>
<tr><td>7</td><td>Arkansas</td><td>7.7</td><td>4</td><td>Maine</td><td>11.1</td></tr>
<tr><td>32</td><td>California</td><td>3.2</td><td>5</td><td>Wyoming</td><td>9.1</td></tr>
<tr><td>39</td><td>Colorado</td><td>1.7</td><td>6</td><td>Alaska</td><td>8.7</td></tr>
<tr><td>30</td><td>Connecticut</td><td>3.7</td><td>7</td><td>Arkansas</td><td>7.7</td></tr>
<tr><td>44</td><td>Delaware</td><td>0.0</td><td>7</td><td>South Dakota</td><td>7.7</td></tr>
<tr><td>NA</td><td>Florida**</td><td>NA</td><td>9</td><td>North Carolina</td><td>7.2</td></tr>
<tr><td>24</td><td>Georgia</td><td>4.3</td><td>9</td><td>South Carolina</td><td>7.2</td></tr>
<tr><td>36</td><td>Hawaii</td><td>2.3</td><td>11</td><td>Oklahoma</td><td>7.1</td></tr>
<tr><td>44</td><td>Idaho</td><td>0.0</td><td>12</td><td>Mississippi</td><td>7.0</td></tr>
<tr><td>43</td><td>Illinois*</td><td>0.5</td><td>13</td><td>Texas</td><td>5.9</td></tr>
<tr><td>37</td><td>Indiana</td><td>2.2</td><td>14</td><td>Oregon</td><td>5.7</td></tr>
<tr><td>19</td><td>Iowa</td><td>4.9</td><td>15</td><td>New Hampshire</td><td>5.6</td></tr>
<tr><td>NA</td><td>Kansas**</td><td>NA</td><td>15</td><td>Virginia</td><td>5.6</td></tr>
<tr><td>19</td><td>Kentucky</td><td>4.9</td><td>17</td><td>Louisiana</td><td>5.5</td></tr>
<tr><td>17</td><td>Louisiana</td><td>5.5</td><td>18</td><td>Tennessee</td><td>5.0</td></tr>
<tr><td>4</td><td>Maine</td><td>11.1</td><td>19</td><td>Iowa</td><td>4.9</td></tr>
<tr><td>34</td><td>Maryland</td><td>2.5</td><td>19</td><td>Kentucky</td><td>4.9</td></tr>
<tr><td>39</td><td>Massachusetts</td><td>1.7</td><td>21</td><td>Nevada</td><td>4.8</td></tr>
<tr><td>26</td><td>Michigan</td><td>3.9</td><td>21</td><td>West Virginia</td><td>4.8</td></tr>
<tr><td>23</td><td>Minnesota</td><td>4.7</td><td>23</td><td>Minnesota</td><td>4.7</td></tr>
<tr><td>12</td><td>Mississippi</td><td>7.0</td><td>24</td><td>Georgia</td><td>4.3</td></tr>
<tr><td>31</td><td>Missouri</td><td>3.4</td><td>24</td><td>New Mexico</td><td>4.3</td></tr>
<tr><td>2</td><td>Montana</td><td>22.2</td><td>26</td><td>Arizona</td><td>3.9</td></tr>
<tr><td>29</td><td>Nebraska</td><td>3.8</td><td>26</td><td>Michigan</td><td>3.9</td></tr>
<tr><td>21</td><td>Nevada</td><td>4.8</td><td>26</td><td>Pennsylvania</td><td>3.9</td></tr>
<tr><td>15</td><td>New Hampshire</td><td>5.6</td><td>29</td><td>Nebraska</td><td>3.8</td></tr>
<tr><td>38</td><td>New Jersey</td><td>2.1</td><td>30</td><td>Connecticut</td><td>3.7</td></tr>
<tr><td>24</td><td>New Mexico</td><td>4.3</td><td>31</td><td>Missouri</td><td>3.4</td></tr>
<tr><td>33</td><td>New York</td><td>3.0</td><td>32</td><td>California</td><td>3.2</td></tr>
<tr><td>9</td><td>North Carolina</td><td>7.2</td><td>33</td><td>New York</td><td>3.0</td></tr>
<tr><td>1</td><td>North Dakota</td><td>37.5</td><td>34</td><td>Maryland</td><td>2.5</td></tr>
<tr><td>41</td><td>Ohio</td><td>1.4</td><td>35</td><td>Washington</td><td>2.4</td></tr>
<tr><td>11</td><td>Oklahoma</td><td>7.1</td><td>36</td><td>Hawaii</td><td>2.3</td></tr>
<tr><td>14</td><td>Oregon</td><td>5.7</td><td>37</td><td>Indiana</td><td>2.2</td></tr>
<tr><td>26</td><td>Pennsylvania</td><td>3.9</td><td>38</td><td>New Jersey</td><td>2.1</td></tr>
<tr><td>44</td><td>Rhode Island</td><td>0.0</td><td>39</td><td>Colorado</td><td>1.7</td></tr>
<tr><td>9</td><td>South Carolina</td><td>7.2</td><td>39</td><td>Massachusetts</td><td>1.7</td></tr>
<tr><td>7</td><td>South Dakota</td><td>7.7</td><td>41</td><td>Ohio</td><td>1.4</td></tr>
<tr><td>18</td><td>Tennessee</td><td>5.0</td><td>42</td><td>Wisconsin</td><td>1.1</td></tr>
<tr><td>13</td><td>Texas</td><td>5.9</td><td>43</td><td>Illinois*</td><td>0.5</td></tr>
<tr><td>44</td><td>Utah</td><td>0.0</td><td>44</td><td>Delaware</td><td>0.0</td></tr>
<tr><td>3</td><td>Vermont</td><td>11.8</td><td>44</td><td>Idaho</td><td>0.0</td></tr>
<tr><td>15</td><td>Virginia</td><td>5.6</td><td>44</td><td>Rhode Island</td><td>0.0</td></tr>
<tr><td>35</td><td>Washington</td><td>2.4</td><td>44</td><td>Utah</td><td>0.0</td></tr>
<tr><td>21</td><td>West Virginia</td><td>4.8</td><td>NA</td><td>Alabama**</td><td>NA</td></tr>
<tr><td>42</td><td>Wisconsin</td><td>1.1</td><td>NA</td><td>Florida**</td><td>NA</td></tr>
<tr><td>5</td><td>Wyoming</td><td>9.1</td><td>NA</td><td>Kansas**</td><td>NA</td></tr>
<tr><td></td><td></td><td></td><td></td><td>District of Columbia**</td><td>NA</td></tr>
</table>

Source: Morgan Quitno Press using data from Federal Bureau of Investigation
"Crime in the United States 1999" (Uniform Crime Reports, October 15, 2000)
*Of the 12,685 murders in 1999 for which supplemental data were received by the F.B.I. There were an additional 2,875 murders for which the type of murder weapon was not reported to the F.B.I. There were also 873 murders that were reported as murders by "firearms, type unknown." Murder includes nonnegligent manslaughter. Numbers are for reporting jurisdictions only. Illinois' figure is for Chicago only. **Not available.

Murders with Knives or Cutting Instruments in 1999

National Total = 1,667 Murders*

ALPHA ORDER

RANK	STATE	MURDERS	% of USA
NA	Alabama**	NA	NA
31	Alaska	9	0.5%
12	Arizona	52	3.1%
26	Arkansas	20	1.2%
1	California	252	15.1%
18	Colorado	30	1.8%
28	Connecticut	16	1.0%
39	Delaware	4	0.2%
NA	Florida**	NA	NA
5	Georgia	64	3.8%
35	Hawaii	6	0.4%
41	Idaho	3	0.2%
6	Illinois*	63	3.8%
22	Indiana	24	1.4%
31	Iowa	9	0.5%
NA	Kansas**	NA	NA
33	Kentucky	8	0.5%
8	Louisiana	58	3.5%
39	Maine	4	0.2%
15	Maryland	34	2.0%
19	Massachusetts	28	1.7%
7	Michigan	61	3.7%
23	Minnesota	23	1.4%
29	Mississippi	15	0.9%
15	Missouri	34	2.0%
46	Montana	1	0.1%
37	Nebraska	5	0.3%
24	Nevada	22	1.3%
33	New Hampshire	8	0.5%
9	New Jersey	54	3.2%
19	New Mexico	28	1.7%
3	New York	166	10.0%
4	North Carolina	71	4.3%
43	North Dakota	2	0.1%
14	Ohio	40	2.4%
27	Oklahoma	18	1.1%
29	Oregon	15	0.9%
10	Pennsylvania	53	3.2%
41	Rhode Island	3	0.2%
17	South Carolina	33	2.0%
46	South Dakota	1	0.1%
13	Tennessee	42	2.5%
2	Texas	170	10.2%
37	Utah	5	0.3%
43	Vermont	2	0.1%
10	Virginia	53	3.2%
19	Washington	28	1.7%
35	West Virginia	6	0.4%
25	Wisconsin	21	1.3%
43	Wyoming	2	0.1%

RANK ORDER

RANK	STATE	MURDERS	% of USA
1	California	252	15.1%
2	Texas	170	10.2%
3	New York	166	10.0%
4	North Carolina	71	4.3%
5	Georgia	64	3.8%
6	Illinois*	63	3.8%
7	Michigan	61	3.7%
8	Louisiana	58	3.5%
9	New Jersey	54	3.2%
10	Pennsylvania	53	3.2%
10	Virginia	53	3.2%
12	Arizona	52	3.1%
13	Tennessee	42	2.5%
14	Ohio	40	2.4%
15	Maryland	34	2.0%
15	Missouri	34	2.0%
17	South Carolina	33	2.0%
18	Colorado	30	1.8%
19	Massachusetts	28	1.7%
19	New Mexico	28	1.7%
19	Washington	28	1.7%
22	Indiana	24	1.4%
23	Minnesota	23	1.4%
24	Nevada	22	1.3%
25	Wisconsin	21	1.3%
26	Arkansas	20	1.2%
27	Oklahoma	18	1.1%
28	Connecticut	16	1.0%
29	Mississippi	15	0.9%
29	Oregon	15	0.9%
31	Alaska	9	0.5%
31	Iowa	9	0.5%
33	Kentucky	8	0.5%
33	New Hampshire	8	0.5%
35	Hawaii	6	0.4%
35	West Virginia	6	0.4%
37	Nebraska	5	0.3%
37	Utah	5	0.3%
39	Delaware	4	0.2%
39	Maine	4	0.2%
41	Idaho	3	0.2%
41	Rhode Island	3	0.2%
43	North Dakota	2	0.1%
43	Vermont	2	0.1%
43	Wyoming	2	0.1%
46	Montana	1	0.1%
46	South Dakota	1	0.1%
NA	Alabama**	NA	NA
NA	Florida**	NA	NA
NA	Kansas**	NA	NA
	District of Columbia**	NA	NA

Source: Federal Bureau of Investigation
   "Crime in the United States 1999" (Uniform Crime Reports, October 15, 2000)
*Of the 12,658 murders in 1999 for which supplemental data were received by the F.B.I. There were an additional 2,875 murders for which the type of murder weapon was not reported to the F.B.I. Includes nonnegligent manslaughter. Numbers are for reporting jurisdictions only. Illinois' rate is for Chicago only.
**Not available.

Percent of Murders Involving Knives or Cutting Instruments in 1999

National Percent = 13.2% of Murders*

ALPHA ORDER

RANK ORDER

RANK	STATE	PERCENT		RANK	STATE	PERCENT
NA	Alabama**	NA		1	New Hampshire	44.4
7	Alaska	19.6		2	North Dakota	25.0
24	Arizona	13.6		3	Massachusetts	23.9
21	Arkansas	14.0		4	Iowa	22.0
28	California	12.6		5	Oklahoma	21.4
13	Colorado	17.3		6	New Mexico	19.9
18	Connecticut	15.0		7	Alaska	19.6
16	Delaware	16.7		8	Nebraska	19.2
NA	Florida**	NA		8	New York	19.2
31	Georgia	12.4		10	New Jersey	18.8
21	Hawaii	14.0		11	Wyoming	18.2
29	Idaho	12.5		12	Minnesota	17.8
40	Illinois*	9.8		13	Colorado	17.3
47	Indiana	7.4		14	Oregon	17.0
4	Iowa	22.0		15	Washington	16.9
NA	Kansas**	NA		16	Delaware	16.7
39	Kentucky	9.9		17	South Carolina	15.8
27	Louisiana	12.8		18	Connecticut	15.0
20	Maine	14.8		18	Virginia	15.0
43	Maryland	8.6		20	Maine	14.8
3	Massachusetts	23.9		21	Arkansas	14.0
44	Michigan	8.5		21	Hawaii	14.0
12	Minnesota	17.8		21	Texas	14.0
37	Mississippi	10.5		24	Arizona	13.6
38	Missouri	10.4		25	Nevada	13.3
36	Montana	11.1		26	North Carolina	13.2
8	Nebraska	19.2		27	Louisiana	12.8
25	Nevada	13.3		28	California	12.6
1	New Hampshire	44.4		29	Idaho	12.5
10	New Jersey	18.8		29	Utah	12.5
6	New Mexico	19.9		31	Georgia	12.4
8	New York	19.2		32	Vermont	11.8
26	North Carolina	13.2		32	Wisconsin	11.8
2	North Dakota	25.0		34	Tennessee	11.7
35	Ohio	11.5		35	Ohio	11.5
5	Oklahoma	21.4		36	Montana	11.1
14	Oregon	17.0		37	Mississippi	10.5
42	Pennsylvania	9.5		38	Missouri	10.4
45	Rhode Island	8.3		39	Kentucky	9.9
17	South Carolina	15.8		40	Illinois*	9.8
46	South Dakota	7.7		41	West Virginia	9.7
34	Tennessee	11.7		42	Pennsylvania	9.5
21	Texas	14.0		43	Maryland	8.6
29	Utah	12.5		44	Michigan	8.5
32	Vermont	11.8		45	Rhode Island	8.3
18	Virginia	15.0		46	South Dakota	7.7
15	Washington	16.9		47	Indiana	7.4
41	West Virginia	9.7		NA	Alabama**	NA
32	Wisconsin	11.8		NA	Florida**	NA
11	Wyoming	18.2		NA	Kansas**	NA
					District of Columbia**	NA

Source: Morgan Quitno Press using data from Federal Bureau of Investigation
   "Crime in the United States 1999" (Uniform Crime Reports, October 15, 2000)
*Of the 12,658 murders in 1999 for which supplemental data were received by the F.B.I. There were an additional 2,875 murders for which the type of murder weapon was not reported to the F.B.I. Includes nonnegligent manslaughter. Numbers are for reporting jurisdictions only. Illinois' rate is for Chicago only.
**Not available.

Murders by Hands, Fists or Feet in 1999

National Total = 850 Murders*

ALPHA ORDER

RANK	STATE	MURDERS	% of USA
NA	Alabama**	NA	NA
29	Alaska	6	0.7%
13	Arizona	19	2.2%
23	Arkansas	11	1.3%
1	California	104	12.2%
14	Colorado	18	2.1%
31	Connecticut	5	0.6%
41	Delaware	2	0.2%
NA	Florida**	NA	NA
11	Georgia	26	3.1%
26	Hawaii	8	0.9%
41	Idaho	2	0.2%
4	Illinois*	55	6.5%
19	Indiana	14	1.6%
44	Iowa	1	0.1%
NA	Kansas**	NA	NA
31	Kentucky	5	0.6%
11	Louisiana	26	3.1%
34	Maine	3	0.4%
17	Maryland	15	1.8%
44	Massachusetts	1	0.1%
6	Michigan	39	4.6%
16	Minnesota	17	2.0%
26	Mississippi	8	0.9%
9	Missouri	29	3.4%
41	Montana	2	0.2%
29	Nebraska	6	0.7%
23	Nevada	11	1.3%
34	New Hampshire	3	0.4%
7	New Jersey	32	3.8%
22	New Mexico	12	1.4%
2	New York	86	10.1%
10	North Carolina	28	3.3%
47	North Dakota	0	0.0%
7	Ohio	32	3.8%
34	Oklahoma	3	0.4%
33	Oregon	4	0.5%
5	Pennsylvania	45	5.3%
34	Rhode Island	3	0.4%
23	South Carolina	11	1.3%
34	South Dakota	3	0.4%
17	Tennessee	15	1.8%
3	Texas	80	9.4%
26	Utah	8	0.9%
44	Vermont	1	0.1%
14	Virginia	18	2.1%
19	Washington	14	1.6%
34	West Virginia	3	0.4%
21	Wisconsin	13	1.5%
34	Wyoming	3	0.4%

RANK ORDER

RANK	STATE	MURDERS	% of USA
1	California	104	12.2%
2	New York	86	10.1%
3	Texas	80	9.4%
4	Illinois*	55	6.5%
5	Pennsylvania	45	5.3%
6	Michigan	39	4.6%
7	New Jersey	32	3.8%
7	Ohio	32	3.8%
9	Missouri	29	3.4%
10	North Carolina	28	3.3%
11	Georgia	26	3.1%
11	Louisiana	26	3.1%
13	Arizona	19	2.2%
14	Colorado	18	2.1%
14	Virginia	18	2.1%
16	Minnesota	17	2.0%
17	Maryland	15	1.8%
17	Tennessee	15	1.8%
19	Indiana	14	1.6%
19	Washington	14	1.6%
21	Wisconsin	13	1.5%
22	New Mexico	12	1.4%
23	Arkansas	11	1.3%
23	Nevada	11	1.3%
23	South Carolina	11	1.3%
26	Hawaii	8	0.9%
26	Mississippi	8	0.9%
26	Utah	8	0.9%
29	Alaska	6	0.7%
29	Nebraska	6	0.7%
31	Connecticut	5	0.6%
31	Kentucky	5	0.6%
33	Oregon	4	0.5%
34	Maine	3	0.4%
34	New Hampshire	3	0.4%
34	Oklahoma	3	0.4%
34	Rhode Island	3	0.4%
34	South Dakota	3	0.4%
34	West Virginia	3	0.4%
34	Wyoming	3	0.4%
41	Delaware	2	0.2%
41	Idaho	2	0.2%
41	Montana	2	0.2%
44	Iowa	1	0.1%
44	Massachusetts	1	0.1%
44	Vermont	1	0.1%
47	North Dakota	0	0.0%
NA	Alabama**	NA	NA
NA	Florida**	NA	NA
NA	Kansas**	NA	NA
	District of Columbia**	NA	NA

Source: Federal Bureau of Investigation
    "Crime in the United States 1999" (Uniform Crime Reports, October 15, 2000)
*Of the 12,658 murders in 1999 for which supplemental data were received by the F.B.I. There were an additional
2,875 murders for which the type of murder weapon was not reported to the F.B.I. Includes nonnegligent
manslaughter. Numbers are for reporting jurisdictions only. Illinois' rate is for Chicago only.
**Not available.

Percent of Murders Involving Hands, Fists or Feet in 1999

National Percent = 6.7% of Murders*

ALPHA ORDER

RANK	STATE	PERCENT
NA	Alabama**	NA
9	Alaska	13.0
36	Arizona	5.0
23	Arkansas	7.7
33	California	5.2
12	Colorado	10.4
39	Connecticut	4.7
19	Delaware	8.3
NA	Florida**	NA
36	Georgia	5.0
6	Hawaii	18.6
19	Idaho	8.3
16	Illinois*	8.6
41	Indiana	4.3
45	Iowa	2.4
NA	Kansas**	NA
27	Kentucky	6.2
29	Louisiana	5.7
10	Maine	11.1
43	Maryland	3.8
46	Massachusetts	0.9
31	Michigan	5.5
8	Minnesota	13.2
30	Mississippi	5.6
15	Missouri	8.9
4	Montana	22.2
2	Nebraska	23.1
25	Nevada	6.7
7	New Hampshire	16.7
10	New Jersey	11.1
17	New Mexico	8.5
13	New York	10.0
33	North Carolina	5.2
47	North Dakota	0.0
14	Ohio	9.2
44	Oklahoma	3.6
40	Oregon	4.5
22	Pennsylvania	8.0
19	Rhode Island	8.3
32	South Carolina	5.3
2	South Dakota	23.1
42	Tennessee	4.2
26	Texas	6.6
5	Utah	20.0
28	Vermont	5.9
35	Virginia	5.1
18	Washington	8.4
38	West Virginia	4.8
24	Wisconsin	7.3
1	Wyoming	27.3

RANK ORDER

RANK	STATE	PERCENT
1	Wyoming	27.3
2	Nebraska	23.1
2	South Dakota	23.1
4	Montana	22.2
5	Utah	20.0
6	Hawaii	18.6
7	New Hampshire	16.7
8	Minnesota	13.2
9	Alaska	13.0
10	Maine	11.1
10	New Jersey	11.1
12	Colorado	10.4
13	New York	10.0
14	Ohio	9.2
15	Missouri	8.9
16	Illinois*	8.6
17	New Mexico	8.5
18	Washington	8.4
19	Delaware	8.3
19	Idaho	8.3
19	Rhode Island	8.3
22	Pennsylvania	8.0
23	Arkansas	7.7
24	Wisconsin	7.3
25	Nevada	6.7
26	Texas	6.6
27	Kentucky	6.2
28	Vermont	5.9
29	Louisiana	5.7
30	Mississippi	5.6
31	Michigan	5.5
32	South Carolina	5.3
33	California	5.2
33	North Carolina	5.2
35	Virginia	5.1
36	Arizona	5.0
36	Georgia	5.0
38	West Virginia	4.8
39	Connecticut	4.7
40	Oregon	4.5
41	Indiana	4.3
42	Tennessee	4.2
43	Maryland	3.8
44	Oklahoma	3.6
45	Iowa	2.4
46	Massachusetts	0.9
47	North Dakota	0.0
NA	Alabama**	NA
NA	Florida**	NA
NA	Kansas**	NA
	District of Columbia**	NA

Source: Morgan Quitno Press using data from Federal Bureau of Investigation
"Crime in the United States 1999" (Uniform Crime Reports, October 15, 2000)
*Of the 12,658 murders in 1999 for which supplemental data were received by the F.B.I. There were an additional 2,875 murders for which the type of murder weapon was not reported to the F.B.I. Includes nonnegligent manslaughter. Numbers are for reporting jurisdictions only. Illinois' rate is for Chicago only.
**Not available.

Rapes in 1999

National Total = 89,107 Rapes*

ALPHA ORDER

RANK	STATE	RAPES	% of USA
20	Alabama	1,513	1.7%
38	Alaska	517	0.6%
24	Arizona	1,383	1.6%
35	Arkansas	710	0.8%
1	California	9,363	10.5%
15	Colorado	1,679	1.9%
36	Connecticut	654	0.7%
37	Delaware	529	0.6%
3	Florida	6,990	7.8%
11	Georgia	2,319	2.6%
42	Hawaii	354	0.4%
39	Idaho	417	0.5%
5	Illinois	4,144	4.7%
17	Indiana	1,607	1.8%
34	Iowa	780	0.9%
28	Kansas	1,065	1.2%
30	Kentucky	1,040	1.2%
21	Louisiana	1,448	1.6%
47	Maine	239	0.3%
19	Maryland	1,551	1.7%
16	Massachusetts	1,663	1.9%
4	Michigan	4,849	5.4%
13	Minnesota	2,038	2.3%
27	Mississippi	1,156	1.3%
22	Missouri	1,439	1.6%
46	Montana	250	0.3%
40	Nebraska	414	0.5%
32	Nevada	943	1.1%
43	New Hampshire	345	0.4%
23	New Jersey	1,409	1.6%
31	New Mexico	944	1.1%
7	New York	3,563	4.0%
12	North Carolina	2,155	2.4%
48	North Dakota	142	0.2%
6	Ohio	4,129	4.6%
25	Oklahoma	1,375	1.5%
26	Oregon	1,219	1.4%
8	Pennsylvania	3,279	3.7%
41	Rhode Island	391	0.4%
18	South Carolina	1,587	1.8%
45	South Dakota	336	0.4%
10	Tennessee	2,415	2.7%
2	Texas	7,614	8.5%
33	Utah	806	0.9%
50	Vermont	136	0.2%
14	Virginia	1,720	1.9%
9	Washington	2,711	3.0%
44	West Virginia	337	0.4%
29	Wisconsin	1,055	1.2%
49	Wyoming	137	0.2%

RANK ORDER

RANK	STATE	RAPES	% of USA
1	California	9,363	10.5%
2	Texas	7,614	8.5%
3	Florida	6,990	7.8%
4	Michigan	4,849	5.4%
5	Illinois	4,144	4.7%
6	Ohio	4,129	4.6%
7	New York	3,563	4.0%
8	Pennsylvania	3,279	3.7%
9	Washington	2,711	3.0%
10	Tennessee	2,415	2.7%
11	Georgia	2,319	2.6%
12	North Carolina	2,155	2.4%
13	Minnesota	2,038	2.3%
14	Virginia	1,720	1.9%
15	Colorado	1,679	1.9%
16	Massachusetts	1,663	1.9%
17	Indiana	1,607	1.8%
18	South Carolina	1,587	1.8%
19	Maryland	1,551	1.7%
20	Alabama	1,513	1.7%
21	Louisiana	1,448	1.6%
22	Missouri	1,439	1.6%
23	New Jersey	1,409	1.6%
24	Arizona	1,383	1.6%
25	Oklahoma	1,375	1.5%
26	Oregon	1,219	1.4%
27	Mississippi	1,156	1.3%
28	Kansas	1,065	1.2%
29	Wisconsin	1,055	1.2%
30	Kentucky	1,040	1.2%
31	New Mexico	944	1.1%
32	Nevada	943	1.1%
33	Utah	806	0.9%
34	Iowa	780	0.9%
35	Arkansas	710	0.8%
36	Connecticut	654	0.7%
37	Delaware	529	0.6%
38	Alaska	517	0.6%
39	Idaho	417	0.5%
40	Nebraska	414	0.5%
41	Rhode Island	391	0.4%
42	Hawaii	354	0.4%
43	New Hampshire	345	0.4%
44	West Virginia	337	0.4%
45	South Dakota	336	0.4%
46	Montana	250	0.3%
47	Maine	239	0.3%
48	North Dakota	142	0.2%
49	Wyoming	137	0.2%
50	Vermont	136	0.2%
	District of Columbia	248	0.3%

Source: Federal Bureau of Investigation
      "Crime in the United States 1999" (Uniform Crime Reports, October 15, 2000)
*Forcible rape is the carnal knowledge of a female forcibly and against her will. Assaults or attempts to commit rape by force or threat of force are included. However, statutory rape without force and other sex offenses are excluded.

Average Time Between Rapes in 1999

National Rate = A Rape Occurs Every 6 Minutes*

ALPHA ORDER

RANK	STATE	HOURS.MINUTES
31	Alabama	5.47
13	Alaska	16.56
27	Arizona	6.20
16	Arkansas	12.20
50	California	0.56
36	Colorado	5.13
15	Connecticut	13.23
14	Delaware	16.34
48	Florida	1.15
40	Georgia	3.47
9	Hawaii	24.45
12	Idaho	21.01
45	Illinois	2.07
34	Indiana	5.27
17	Iowa	11.14
23	Kansas	8.14
21	Kentucky	8.25
30	Louisiana	6.03
4	Maine	36.39
32	Maryland	5.39
35	Massachusetts	5.16
47	Michigan	1.49
38	Minnesota	4.18
24	Mississippi	7.35
29	Missouri	6.05
5	Montana	35.02
11	Nebraska	21.10
19	Nevada	9.17
8	New Hampshire	25.23
28	New Jersey	6.13
19	New Mexico	9.17
44	New York	2.28
39	North Carolina	4.04
3	North Dakota	61.41
45	Ohio	2.07
26	Oklahoma	6.22
25	Oregon	7.11
43	Pennsylvania	2.40
10	Rhode Island	22.24
33	South Carolina	5.31
6	South Dakota	26.04
41	Tennessee	3.38
49	Texas	1.09
18	Utah	10.52
1	Vermont	64.25
37	Virginia	5.05
42	Washington	3.14
7	West Virginia	25.59
22	Wisconsin	8.18
2	Wyoming	63.56

RANK ORDER

RANK	STATE	HOURS.MINUTES
1	Vermont	64.25
2	Wyoming	63.56
3	North Dakota	61.41
4	Maine	36.39
5	Montana	35.02
6	South Dakota	26.04
7	West Virginia	25.59
8	New Hampshire	25.23
9	Hawaii	24.45
10	Rhode Island	22.24
11	Nebraska	21.10
12	Idaho	21.01
13	Alaska	16.56
14	Delaware	16.34
15	Connecticut	13.23
16	Arkansas	12.20
17	Iowa	11.14
18	Utah	10.52
19	Nevada	9.17
19	New Mexico	9.17
21	Kentucky	8.25
22	Wisconsin	8.18
23	Kansas	8.14
24	Mississippi	7.35
25	Oregon	7.11
26	Oklahoma	6.22
27	Arizona	6.20
28	New Jersey	6.13
29	Missouri	6.05
30	Louisiana	6.03
31	Alabama	5.47
32	Maryland	5.39
33	South Carolina	5.31
34	Indiana	5.27
35	Massachusetts	5.16
36	Colorado	5.13
37	Virginia	5.05
38	Minnesota	4.18
39	North Carolina	4.04
40	Georgia	3.47
41	Tennessee	3.38
42	Washington	3.14
43	Pennsylvania	2.40
44	New York	2.28
45	Illinois	2.07
45	Ohio	2.07
47	Michigan	1.49
48	Florida	1.15
49	Texas	1.09
50	California	0.56
	District of Columbia	35.19

Source: Morgan Quitno Press using data from Federal Bureau of Investigation
"Crime in the United States 1999" (Uniform Crime Reports, October 15, 2000)
*Forcible rape is the carnal knowledge of a female forcibly and against her will. Assaults or attempts to commit rape by force or threat of force are included. However, statutory rape without force and other sex offenses are excluded.

Percent Change in Number of Rapes: 1998 to 1999

National Percent Change = 4.3% Decrease*

ALPHA ORDER			RANK ORDER		
RANK	STATE	PERCENT CHANGE	RANK	STATE	PERCENT CHANGE
10	Alabama	4.9	1	South Dakota	30.2
2	Alaska	22.8	2	Alaska	22.8
27	Arizona	(4.7)	3	Mississippi	12.7
48	Arkansas	(20.5)	4	Rhode Island	11.4
26	California	(4.3)	5	Idaho	8.0
42	Colorado	(10.8)	6	Iowa	7.1
41	Connecticut	(10.2)	7	Montana	6.4
9	Delaware	6.0	8	Maine	6.2
29	Florida	(5.6)	9	Delaware	6.0
17	Georgia	(0.1)	10	Alabama	4.9
16	Hawaii	0.6	11	Nevada	3.5
5	Idaho	8.0	12	Wyoming	3.0
15	Illinois	1.2	13	Pennsylvania	1.7
47	Indiana	(17.7)	13	Wisconsin	1.7
6	Iowa	7.1	15	Illinois	1.2
29	Kansas	(5.6)	16	Hawaii	0.6
31	Kentucky	(6.1)	17	Georgia	(0.1)
40	Louisiana	(10.0)	18	Nebraska	(0.7)
8	Maine	6.2	19	Washington	(1.1)
38	Maryland	(9.5)	20	Massachusetts	(1.4)
20	Massachusetts	(1.4)	20	New Mexico	(1.4)
23	Michigan	(2.0)	22	Missouri	(1.6)
44	Minnesota	(13.6)	23	Michigan	(2.0)
3	Mississippi	12.7	24	Tennessee	(2.8)
22	Missouri	(1.6)	25	Texas	(3.8)
7	Montana	6.4	26	California	(4.3)
18	Nebraska	(0.7)	27	Arizona	(4.7)
11	Nevada	3.5	28	Virginia	(5.0)
45	New Hampshire	(13.8)	29	Florida	(5.6)
43	New Jersey	(13.2)	29	Kansas	(5.6)
20	New Mexico	(1.4)	31	Kentucky	(6.1)
34	New York	(7.3)	32	Oregon	(6.7)
33	North Carolina	(6.8)	33	North Carolina	(6.8)
49	North Dakota	(33.0)	34	New York	(7.3)
36	Ohio	(9.1)	35	Utah	(7.9)
36	Oklahoma	(9.1)	36	Ohio	(9.1)
32	Oregon	(6.7)	36	Oklahoma	(9.1)
13	Pennsylvania	1.7	38	Maryland	(9.5)
4	Rhode Island	11.4	38	South Carolina	(9.5)
38	South Carolina	(9.5)	40	Louisiana	(10.0)
1	South Dakota	30.2	41	Connecticut	(10.2)
24	Tennessee	(2.8)	42	Colorado	(10.8)
25	Texas	(3.8)	43	New Jersey	(13.2)
35	Utah	(7.9)	44	Minnesota	(13.6)
46	Vermont	(16.6)	45	New Hampshire	(13.8)
28	Virginia	(5.0)	46	Vermont	(16.6)
19	Washington	(1.1)	47	Indiana	(17.7)
NA	West Virginia**	NA	48	Arkansas	(20.5)
13	Wisconsin	1.7	49	North Dakota	(33.0)
12	Wyoming	3.0	NA	West Virginia**	NA
				District of Columbia	30.5

Source: Federal Bureau of Investigation
    "Crime in the United States 1999" (Uniform Crime Reports, October 15, 2000)
Forcible rape is the carnal knowledge of a female forcibly and against her will. Assaults or attempts to commit rape by force or threat of force are included. However, statutory rape without force and other sex offenses are excluded.
**Not available.*

Rape Rate in 1999

National Rate = 32.7 Rapes per 100,000 Population*

<table>
<tr><td colspan="3">ALPHA ORDER</td><td colspan="3">RANK ORDER</td></tr>
<tr><td>RANK</td><td>STATE</td><td>RATE</td><td>RANK</td><td>STATE</td><td>RATE</td></tr>
<tr><td>21</td><td>Alabama</td><td>34.6</td><td>1</td><td>Alaska</td><td>83.5</td></tr>
<tr><td>1</td><td>Alaska</td><td>83.5</td><td>2</td><td>Delaware</td><td>70.2</td></tr>
<tr><td>28</td><td>Arizona</td><td>28.9</td><td>3</td><td>New Mexico</td><td>54.3</td></tr>
<tr><td>34</td><td>Arkansas</td><td>27.8</td><td>4</td><td>Nevada</td><td>52.1</td></tr>
<tr><td>32</td><td>California</td><td>28.2</td><td>5</td><td>Michigan</td><td>49.2</td></tr>
<tr><td>12</td><td>Colorado</td><td>41.4</td><td>6</td><td>Washington</td><td>47.1</td></tr>
<tr><td>46</td><td>Connecticut</td><td>19.9</td><td>7</td><td>Florida</td><td>46.3</td></tr>
<tr><td>2</td><td>Delaware</td><td>70.2</td><td>8</td><td>South Dakota</td><td>45.8</td></tr>
<tr><td>7</td><td>Florida</td><td>46.3</td><td>9</td><td>Tennessee</td><td>44.0</td></tr>
<tr><td>27</td><td>Georgia</td><td>29.8</td><td>10</td><td>Minnesota</td><td>42.7</td></tr>
<tr><td>26</td><td>Hawaii</td><td>29.9</td><td>11</td><td>Mississippi</td><td>41.7</td></tr>
<tr><td>23</td><td>Idaho</td><td>33.3</td><td>12</td><td>Colorado</td><td>41.4</td></tr>
<tr><td>22</td><td>Illinois</td><td>34.2</td><td>13</td><td>Oklahoma</td><td>40.9</td></tr>
<tr><td>37</td><td>Indiana</td><td>27.0</td><td>14</td><td>South Carolina</td><td>40.8</td></tr>
<tr><td>36</td><td>Iowa</td><td>27.2</td><td>15</td><td>Kansas</td><td>40.1</td></tr>
<tr><td>15</td><td>Kansas</td><td>40.1</td><td>16</td><td>Rhode Island</td><td>39.5</td></tr>
<tr><td>39</td><td>Kentucky</td><td>26.3</td><td>17</td><td>Texas</td><td>38.0</td></tr>
<tr><td>24</td><td>Louisiana</td><td>33.1</td><td>18</td><td>Utah</td><td>37.8</td></tr>
<tr><td>48</td><td>Maine</td><td>19.1</td><td>19</td><td>Oregon</td><td>36.8</td></tr>
<tr><td>25</td><td>Maryland</td><td>30.0</td><td>20</td><td>Ohio</td><td>36.7</td></tr>
<tr><td>38</td><td>Massachusetts</td><td>26.9</td><td>21</td><td>Alabama</td><td>34.6</td></tr>
<tr><td>5</td><td>Michigan</td><td>49.2</td><td>22</td><td>Illinois</td><td>34.2</td></tr>
<tr><td>10</td><td>Minnesota</td><td>42.7</td><td>23</td><td>Idaho</td><td>33.3</td></tr>
<tr><td>11</td><td>Mississippi</td><td>41.7</td><td>24</td><td>Louisiana</td><td>33.1</td></tr>
<tr><td>39</td><td>Missouri</td><td>26.3</td><td>25</td><td>Maryland</td><td>30.0</td></tr>
<tr><td>31</td><td>Montana</td><td>28.3</td><td>26</td><td>Hawaii</td><td>29.9</td></tr>
<tr><td>42</td><td>Nebraska</td><td>24.8</td><td>27</td><td>Georgia</td><td>29.8</td></tr>
<tr><td>4</td><td>Nevada</td><td>52.1</td><td>28</td><td>Arizona</td><td>28.9</td></tr>
<tr><td>29</td><td>New Hampshire</td><td>28.7</td><td>29</td><td>New Hampshire</td><td>28.7</td></tr>
<tr><td>50</td><td>New Jersey</td><td>17.3</td><td>30</td><td>Wyoming</td><td>28.5</td></tr>
<tr><td>3</td><td>New Mexico</td><td>54.3</td><td>31</td><td>Montana</td><td>28.3</td></tr>
<tr><td>47</td><td>New York</td><td>19.6</td><td>32</td><td>California</td><td>28.2</td></tr>
<tr><td>32</td><td>North Carolina</td><td>28.2</td><td>32</td><td>North Carolina</td><td>28.2</td></tr>
<tr><td>44</td><td>North Dakota</td><td>22.4</td><td>34</td><td>Arkansas</td><td>27.8</td></tr>
<tr><td>20</td><td>Ohio</td><td>36.7</td><td>35</td><td>Pennsylvania</td><td>27.3</td></tr>
<tr><td>13</td><td>Oklahoma</td><td>40.9</td><td>36</td><td>Iowa</td><td>27.2</td></tr>
<tr><td>19</td><td>Oregon</td><td>36.8</td><td>37</td><td>Indiana</td><td>27.0</td></tr>
<tr><td>35</td><td>Pennsylvania</td><td>27.3</td><td>38</td><td>Massachusetts</td><td>26.9</td></tr>
<tr><td>16</td><td>Rhode Island</td><td>39.5</td><td>39</td><td>Kentucky</td><td>26.3</td></tr>
<tr><td>14</td><td>South Carolina</td><td>40.8</td><td>39</td><td>Missouri</td><td>26.3</td></tr>
<tr><td>8</td><td>South Dakota</td><td>45.8</td><td>41</td><td>Virginia</td><td>25.0</td></tr>
<tr><td>9</td><td>Tennessee</td><td>44.0</td><td>42</td><td>Nebraska</td><td>24.8</td></tr>
<tr><td>17</td><td>Texas</td><td>38.0</td><td>43</td><td>Vermont</td><td>22.9</td></tr>
<tr><td>18</td><td>Utah</td><td>37.8</td><td>44</td><td>North Dakota</td><td>22.4</td></tr>
<tr><td>43</td><td>Vermont</td><td>22.9</td><td>45</td><td>Wisconsin</td><td>20.1</td></tr>
<tr><td>41</td><td>Virginia</td><td>25.0</td><td>46</td><td>Connecticut</td><td>19.9</td></tr>
<tr><td>6</td><td>Washington</td><td>47.1</td><td>47</td><td>New York</td><td>19.6</td></tr>
<tr><td>49</td><td>West Virginia</td><td>18.6</td><td>48</td><td>Maine</td><td>19.1</td></tr>
<tr><td>45</td><td>Wisconsin</td><td>20.1</td><td>49</td><td>West Virginia</td><td>18.6</td></tr>
<tr><td>30</td><td>Wyoming</td><td>28.5</td><td>50</td><td>New Jersey</td><td>17.3</td></tr>
<tr><td></td><td></td><td></td><td></td><td>District of Columbia</td><td>47.8</td></tr>
</table>

Source: Federal Bureau of Investigation
   "Crime in the United States 1999" (Uniform Crime Reports, October 15, 2000)
*Forcible rape is the carnal knowledge of a female forcibly and against her will. Assaults or attempts to commit rape by force or threat of force are included. However, statutory rape without force and other sex offenses are excluded.

Percent Change in Rape Rate: 1998 to 1999

National Percent Change = 5.2% Decrease*

ALPHA ORDER

RANK	STATE	PERCENT CHANGE
10	Alabama	4.4
2	Alaska	21.8
31	Arizona	(6.9)
48	Arkansas	(20.9)
26	California	(5.7)
42	Colorado	(12.7)
40	Connecticut	(10.4)
9	Delaware	4.6
30	Florida	(6.8)
20	Georgia	(2.0)
13	Hawaii	1.2
6	Idaho	6.0
15	Illinois	0.5
47	Indiana	(18.3)
5	Iowa	6.9
28	Kansas	(6.5)
29	Kentucky	(6.6)
38	Louisiana	(10.1)
8	Maine	5.5
39	Maryland	(10.2)
19	Massachusetts	(1.9)
23	Michigan	(2.4)
44	Minnesota	(14.5)
3	Mississippi	12.0
21	Missouri	(2.2)
6	Montana	6.0
17	Nebraska	(0.9)
16	Nevada	0.0
45	New Hampshire	(14.9)
43	New Jersey	(13.5)
18	New Mexico	(1.5)
32	New York	(7.4)
34	North Carolina	(8.0)
49	North Dakota	(32.6)
37	Ohio	(9.5)
36	Oklahoma	(9.4)
33	Oregon	(7.7)
12	Pennsylvania	1.8
4	Rhode Island	11.1
41	South Carolina	(10.6)
1	South Dakota	31.1
24	Tennessee	(3.8)
25	Texas	(5.1)
35	Utah	(9.2)
46	Vermont	(17.0)
27	Virginia	(6.1)
21	Washington	(2.2)
NA	West Virginia**	NA
13	Wisconsin	1.2
11	Wyoming	3.2

RANK ORDER

RANK	STATE	PERCENT CHANGE
1	South Dakota	31.1
2	Alaska	21.8
3	Mississippi	12.0
4	Rhode Island	11.1
5	Iowa	6.9
6	Idaho	6.0
6	Montana	6.0
8	Maine	5.5
9	Delaware	4.6
10	Alabama	4.4
11	Wyoming	3.2
12	Pennsylvania	1.8
13	Hawaii	1.2
13	Wisconsin	1.2
15	Illinois	0.5
16	Nevada	0.0
17	Nebraska	(0.9)
18	New Mexico	(1.5)
19	Massachusetts	(1.9)
20	Georgia	(2.0)
21	Missouri	(2.2)
21	Washington	(2.2)
23	Michigan	(2.4)
24	Tennessee	(3.8)
25	Texas	(5.1)
26	California	(5.7)
27	Virginia	(6.1)
28	Kansas	(6.5)
29	Kentucky	(6.6)
30	Florida	(6.8)
31	Arizona	(6.9)
32	New York	(7.4)
33	Oregon	(7.7)
34	North Carolina	(8.0)
35	Utah	(9.2)
36	Oklahoma	(9.4)
37	Ohio	(9.5)
38	Louisiana	(10.1)
39	Maryland	(10.2)
40	Connecticut	(10.4)
41	South Carolina	(10.6)
42	Colorado	(12.7)
43	New Jersey	(13.5)
44	Minnesota	(14.5)
45	New Hampshire	(14.9)
46	Vermont	(17.0)
47	Indiana	(18.3)
48	Arkansas	(20.9)
49	North Dakota	(32.6)
NA	West Virginia**	NA

District of Columbia   31.5

Source: Federal Bureau of Investigation
"Crime in the United States 1999" (Uniform Crime Reports, October 15, 2000)
*Forcible rape is the carnal knowledge of a female forcibly and against her will. Assaults or attempts to commit rape by force or threat of force are included. However, statutory rape without force and other sex offenses are excluded.
**Not available.

Rape Rate per 100,000 Female Population in 1999

National Rate = 63.9 Rapes per 100,000 Female Population*

ALPHA ORDER				RANK ORDER		
RANK	STATE	RATE		RANK	STATE	RATE
22	Alabama	66.6		1	Alaska	175.6
1	Alaska	175.6		2	Delaware	136.6
29	Arizona	57.3		3	New Mexico	106.8
34	Arkansas	53.9		4	Nevada	106.2
30	California	56.5		5	Michigan	95.8
11	Colorado	82.1		6	Washington	93.7
46	Connecticut	38.7		7	South Dakota	90.2
2	Delaware	136.6		8	Florida	89.8
8	Florida	89.8		9	Tennessee	85.1
27	Georgia	58.0		10	Minnesota	84.1
25	Hawaii	59.7		11	Colorado	82.1
23	Idaho	66.5		12	Mississippi	80.2
21	Illinois	66.7		13	Oklahoma	80.0
36	Indiana	52.7		14	Kansas	79.0
35	Iowa	53.0		15	South Carolina	78.9
14	Kansas	79.0		16	Rhode Island	76.0
39	Kentucky	51.0		17	Utah	75.2
24	Louisiana	63.8		18	Texas	75.0
48	Maine	37.3		19	Oregon	72.6
26	Maryland	58.3		20	Ohio	71.0
38	Massachusetts	52.0		21	Illinois	66.7
5	Michigan	95.8		22	Alabama	66.6
10	Minnesota	84.1		23	Idaho	66.5
12	Mississippi	80.2		24	Louisiana	63.8
39	Missouri	51.0		25	Hawaii	59.7
32	Montana	56.3		26	Maryland	58.3
42	Nebraska	48.6		27	Georgia	58.0
4	Nevada	106.2		28	Wyoming	57.4
30	New Hampshire	56.5		29	Arizona	57.3
50	New Jersey	33.6		30	California	56.5
3	New Mexico	106.8		30	New Hampshire	56.5
47	New York	37.8		32	Montana	56.3
33	North Carolina	54.7		33	North Carolina	54.7
44	North Dakota	44.6		34	Arkansas	53.9
20	Ohio	71.0		35	Iowa	53.0
13	Oklahoma	80.0		36	Indiana	52.7
19	Oregon	72.6		37	Pennsylvania	52.6
37	Pennsylvania	52.6		38	Massachusetts	52.0
16	Rhode Island	76.0		39	Kentucky	51.0
15	South Carolina	78.9		39	Missouri	51.0
7	South Dakota	90.2		41	Virginia	48.9
9	Tennessee	85.1		42	Nebraska	48.6
18	Texas	75.0		43	Vermont	45.1
17	Utah	75.2		44	North Dakota	44.6
43	Vermont	45.1		45	Wisconsin	39.5
41	Virginia	48.9		46	Connecticut	38.7
6	Washington	93.7		47	New York	37.8
49	West Virginia	36.0		48	Maine	37.3
45	Wisconsin	39.5		49	West Virginia	36.0
28	Wyoming	57.4		50	New Jersey	33.6
					District of Columbia	89.9

Source: Morgan Quitno Press using data from Federal Bureau of Investigation
    "Crime in the United States 1999" (Uniform Crime Reports, October 15, 2000)
*Forcible rape is the carnal knowledge of a female forcibly and against her will. Assaults or attempts to commit rape by force or threat of force are included. However, statutory rape without force and other sex offenses are excluded.

Robberies in 1999

National Total = 409,670 Robberies*

ALPHA ORDER

RANK	STATE	ROBBERIES	% of USA
22	Alabama	5,297	1.3%
42	Alaska	566	0.1%
15	Arizona	7,288	1.8%
34	Arkansas	2,024	0.5%
1	California	60,039	14.7%
29	Colorado	3,056	0.7%
25	Connecticut	4,054	1.0%
35	Delaware	1,492	0.4%
3	Florida	31,969	7.8%
11	Georgia	12,962	3.2%
39	Hawaii	1,044	0.3%
46	Idaho	223	0.1%
5	Illinois	26,611	6.5%
18	Indiana	6,496	1.6%
38	Iowa	1,051	0.3%
33	Kansas	2,047	0.5%
27	Kentucky	3,168	0.8%
14	Louisiana	7,591	1.9%
44	Maine	243	0.1%
10	Maryland	13,636	3.3%
19	Massachusetts	5,931	1.4%
9	Michigan	14,103	3.4%
26	Minnesota	3,917	1.0%
28	Mississippi	3,091	0.8%
16	Missouri	7,149	1.7%
45	Montana	228	0.1%
36	Nebraska	1,264	0.3%
24	Nevada	4,209	1.0%
43	New Hampshire	257	0.1%
8	New Jersey	14,243	3.5%
32	New Mexico	2,579	0.6%
2	New York	43,821	10.7%
12	North Carolina	12,087	3.0%
50	North Dakota	56	0.0%
7	Ohio	14,405	3.5%
31	Oklahoma	2,785	0.7%
30	Oregon	2,858	0.7%
6	Pennsylvania	18,670	4.6%
40	Rhode Island	788	0.2%
21	South Carolina	5,760	1.4%
47	South Dakota	103	0.0%
13	Tennessee	8,598	2.1%
4	Texas	29,405	7.2%
37	Utah	1,158	0.3%
49	Vermont	65	0.0%
17	Virginia	6,947	1.7%
20	Washington	5,808	1.4%
41	West Virginia	661	0.2%
23	Wisconsin	4,449	1.1%
48	Wyoming	74	0.0%

RANK ORDER

RANK	STATE	ROBBERIES	% of USA
1	California	60,039	14.7%
2	New York	43,821	10.7%
3	Florida	31,969	7.8%
4	Texas	29,405	7.2%
5	Illinois	26,611	6.5%
6	Pennsylvania	18,670	4.6%
7	Ohio	14,405	3.5%
8	New Jersey	14,243	3.5%
9	Michigan	14,103	3.4%
10	Maryland	13,636	3.3%
11	Georgia	12,962	3.2%
12	North Carolina	12,087	3.0%
13	Tennessee	8,598	2.1%
14	Louisiana	7,591	1.9%
15	Arizona	7,288	1.8%
16	Missouri	7,149	1.7%
17	Virginia	6,947	1.7%
18	Indiana	6,496	1.6%
19	Massachusetts	5,931	1.4%
20	Washington	5,808	1.4%
21	South Carolina	5,760	1.4%
22	Alabama	5,297	1.3%
23	Wisconsin	4,449	1.1%
24	Nevada	4,209	1.0%
25	Connecticut	4,054	1.0%
26	Minnesota	3,917	1.0%
27	Kentucky	3,168	0.8%
28	Mississippi	3,091	0.8%
29	Colorado	3,056	0.7%
30	Oregon	2,858	0.7%
31	Oklahoma	2,785	0.7%
32	New Mexico	2,579	0.6%
33	Kansas	2,047	0.5%
34	Arkansas	2,024	0.5%
35	Delaware	1,492	0.4%
36	Nebraska	1,264	0.3%
37	Utah	1,158	0.3%
38	Iowa	1,051	0.3%
39	Hawaii	1,044	0.3%
40	Rhode Island	788	0.2%
41	West Virginia	661	0.2%
42	Alaska	566	0.1%
43	New Hampshire	257	0.1%
44	Maine	243	0.1%
45	Montana	228	0.1%
46	Idaho	223	0.1%
47	South Dakota	103	0.0%
48	Wyoming	74	0.0%
49	Vermont	65	0.0%
50	North Dakota	56	0.0%
	District of Columbia	3,344	0.8%

Source: Federal Bureau of Investigation
   "Crime in the United States 1999" (Uniform Crime Reports, October 15, 2000)
*Robbery is the taking or attempting to take anything of value by force or threat of force.

Average Time Between Robberies in 1999

National Rate = A Robbery Occurs Every 1 Minute*

ALPHA ORDER

RANK	STATE	HOURS.MINUTES
29	Alabama	1.39
9	Alaska	15.29
36	Arizona	1.12
17	Arkansas	4.20
50	California	0.09
22	Colorado	2.52
26	Connecticut	2.10
16	Delaware	5.52
48	Florida	0.16
40	Georgia	0.41
12	Hawaii	8.23
5	Idaho	39.17
46	Illinois	0.20
33	Indiana	1.21
13	Iowa	8.20
18	Kansas	4.17
24	Kentucky	2.46
37	Louisiana	1.09
7	Maine	36.03
41	Maryland	0.38
32	Massachusetts	1.29
42	Michigan	0.37
25	Minnesota	2.14
23	Mississippi	2.50
35	Missouri	1.14
6	Montana	38.25
15	Nebraska	6.56
27	Nevada	2.05
8	New Hampshire	34.05
42	New Jersey	0.37
19	New Mexico	3.24
49	New York	0.12
39	North Carolina	0.43
1	North Dakota	156.26
42	Ohio	0.37
20	Oklahoma	3.09
21	Oregon	3.04
45	Pennsylvania	0.28
11	Rhode Island	11.07
30	South Carolina	1.31
4	South Dakota	85.03
38	Tennessee	1.01
47	Texas	0.18
14	Utah	7.34
2	Vermont	134.46
34	Virginia	1.16
30	Washington	1.31
10	West Virginia	13.15
28	Wisconsin	1.58
3	Wyoming	118.23

RANK ORDER

RANK	STATE	HOURS.MINUTES
1	North Dakota	156.26
2	Vermont	134.46
3	Wyoming	118.23
4	South Dakota	85.03
5	Idaho	39.17
6	Montana	38.25
7	Maine	36.03
8	New Hampshire	34.05
9	Alaska	15.29
10	West Virginia	13.15
11	Rhode Island	11.07
12	Hawaii	8.23
13	Iowa	8.20
14	Utah	7.34
15	Nebraska	6.56
16	Delaware	5.52
17	Arkansas	4.20
18	Kansas	4.17
19	New Mexico	3.24
20	Oklahoma	3.09
21	Oregon	3.04
22	Colorado	2.52
23	Mississippi	2.50
24	Kentucky	2.46
25	Minnesota	2.14
26	Connecticut	2.10
27	Nevada	2.05
28	Wisconsin	1.58
29	Alabama	1.39
30	South Carolina	1.31
30	Washington	1.31
32	Massachusetts	1.29
33	Indiana	1.21
34	Virginia	1.16
35	Missouri	1.14
36	Arizona	1.12
37	Louisiana	1.09
38	Tennessee	1.01
39	North Carolina	0.43
40	Georgia	0.41
41	Maryland	0.38
42	Michigan	0.37
42	New Jersey	0.37
42	Ohio	0.37
45	Pennsylvania	0.28
46	Illinois	0.20
47	Texas	0.18
48	Florida	0.16
49	New York	0.12
50	California	0.09
	District of Columbia	2.37

Source: Morgan Quitno Press using data from Federal Bureau of Investigation
    "Crime in the United States 1999" (Uniform Crime Reports, October 15, 2000)
*Robbery is the taking or attempting to take anything of value by force or threat of force.

Percent Change in Number of Robberies: 1998 to 1999

National Percent Change = 8.4% Decrease*

ALPHA ORDER

RANK	STATE	PERCENT CHANGE
22	Alabama	(7.0)
3	Alaska	6.4
17	Arizona	(5.5)
46	Arkansas	(17.1)
41	California	(12.7)
19	Colorado	(5.6)
23	Connecticut	(7.4)
4	Delaware	3.3
37	Florida	(11.7)
29	Georgia	(9.4)
43	Hawaii	(14.8)
44	Idaho	(15.5)
34	Illinois	(11.1)
10	Indiana	(1.0)
48	Iowa	(27.8)
32	Kansas	(10.5)
26	Kentucky	(8.7)
40	Louisiana	(12.3)
24	Maine	(7.6)
34	Maryland	(11.1)
7	Massachusetts	(0.1)
25	Michigan	(7.8)
31	Minnesota	(10.4)
27	Mississippi	(8.9)
39	Missouri	(11.9)
11	Montana	(1.7)
12	Nebraska	(2.0)
17	Nevada	(5.5)
6	New Hampshire	0.8
21	New Jersey	(5.7)
28	New Mexico	(9.2)
33	New York	(10.8)
8	North Carolina	(0.4)
42	North Dakota	(13.8)
15	Ohio	(3.7)
30	Oklahoma	(9.5)
47	Oregon	(17.2)
19	Pennsylvania	(5.6)
1	Rhode Island	19.6
13	South Carolina	(3.1)
49	South Dakota	(30.9)
34	Tennessee	(11.1)
5	Texas	2.5
45	Utah	(16.4)
2	Vermont	16.1
13	Virginia	(3.1)
37	Washington	(11.7)
NA	West Virginia**	NA
9	Wisconsin	(0.6)
16	Wyoming	(5.1)

RANK ORDER

RANK	STATE	PERCENT CHANGE
1	Rhode Island	19.6
2	Vermont	16.1
3	Alaska	6.4
4	Delaware	3.3
5	Texas	2.5
6	New Hampshire	0.8
7	Massachusetts	(0.1)
8	North Carolina	(0.4)
9	Wisconsin	(0.6)
10	Indiana	(1.0)
11	Montana	(1.7)
12	Nebraska	(2.0)
13	South Carolina	(3.1)
13	Virginia	(3.1)
15	Ohio	(3.7)
16	Wyoming	(5.1)
17	Arizona	(5.5)
17	Nevada	(5.5)
19	Colorado	(5.6)
19	Pennsylvania	(5.6)
21	New Jersey	(5.7)
22	Alabama	(7.0)
23	Connecticut	(7.4)
24	Maine	(7.6)
25	Michigan	(7.8)
26	Kentucky	(8.7)
27	Mississippi	(8.9)
28	New Mexico	(9.2)
29	Georgia	(9.4)
30	Oklahoma	(9.5)
31	Minnesota	(10.4)
32	Kansas	(10.5)
33	New York	(10.8)
34	Illinois	(11.1)
34	Maryland	(11.1)
34	Tennessee	(11.1)
37	Florida	(11.7)
37	Washington	(11.7)
39	Missouri	(11.9)
40	Louisiana	(12.3)
41	California	(12.7)
42	North Dakota	(13.8)
43	Hawaii	(14.8)
44	Idaho	(15.5)
45	Utah	(16.4)
46	Arkansas	(17.1)
47	Oregon	(17.2)
48	Iowa	(27.8)
49	South Dakota	(30.9)
NA	West Virginia**	NA
	District of Columbia	(7.3)

Source: Federal Bureau of Investigation
   "Crime in the United States 1999" (Uniform Crime Reports, October 15, 2000)
*Robbery is the taking or attempting to take anything of value by force or threat of force.
**Not available.

Robbery Rate in 1999

National Rate = 150.2 Robberies per 100,000 Population*

ALPHA ORDER			RANK ORDER		
RANK	STATE	RATE	RANK	STATE	RATE
22	Alabama	121.2	1	Maryland	263.7
28	Alaska	91.4	2	New York	240.8
14	Arizona	152.5	3	Nevada	232.7
36	Arkansas	79.3	4	Illinois	219.4
7	California	181.1	5	Florida	211.6
39	Colorado	75.3	6	Delaware	197.9
21	Connecticut	123.5	7	California	181.1
6	Delaware	197.9	8	New Jersey	174.9
5	Florida	211.6	9	Louisiana	173.6
10	Georgia	166.4	10	Georgia	166.4
29	Hawaii	88.1	11	North Carolina	158.0
46	Idaho	17.8	12	Tennessee	156.8
4	Illinois	219.4	13	Pennsylvania	155.7
24	Indiana	109.3	14	Arizona	152.5
41	Iowa	36.6	15	New Mexico	148.2
37	Kansas	77.1	15	South Carolina	148.2
34	Kentucky	80.0	17	Texas	146.7
9	Louisiana	173.6	18	Michigan	143.0
45	Maine	19.4	19	Missouri	130.7
1	Maryland	263.7	20	Ohio	128.0
27	Massachusetts	96.0	21	Connecticut	123.5
18	Michigan	143.0	22	Alabama	121.2
33	Minnesota	82.0	23	Mississippi	111.6
23	Mississippi	111.6	24	Indiana	109.3
19	Missouri	130.7	25	Virginia	101.1
43	Montana	25.8	26	Washington	100.9
38	Nebraska	75.9	27	Massachusetts	96.0
3	Nevada	232.7	28	Alaska	91.4
44	New Hampshire	21.4	29	Hawaii	88.1
8	New Jersey	174.9	30	Oregon	86.2
15	New Mexico	148.2	31	Wisconsin	84.7
2	New York	240.8	32	Oklahoma	82.9
11	North Carolina	158.0	33	Minnesota	82.0
50	North Dakota	8.8	34	Kentucky	80.0
20	Ohio	128.0	35	Rhode Island	79.5
32	Oklahoma	82.9	36	Arkansas	79.3
30	Oregon	86.2	37	Kansas	77.1
13	Pennsylvania	155.7	38	Nebraska	75.9
35	Rhode Island	79.5	39	Colorado	75.3
15	South Carolina	148.2	40	Utah	54.4
48	South Dakota	14.1	41	Iowa	36.6
12	Tennessee	156.8	41	West Virginia	36.6
17	Texas	146.7	43	Montana	25.8
40	Utah	54.4	44	New Hampshire	21.4
49	Vermont	10.9	45	Maine	19.4
25	Virginia	101.1	46	Idaho	17.8
26	Washington	100.9	47	Wyoming	15.4
41	West Virginia	36.6	48	South Dakota	14.1
31	Wisconsin	84.7	49	Vermont	10.9
47	Wyoming	15.4	50	North Dakota	8.8
				District of Columbia	644.3

Source: Federal Bureau of Investigation
   "Crime in the United States 1999" (Uniform Crime Reports, October 15, 2000)
*Robbery is the taking or attempting to take anything of value by force or threat of force.

Percent Change in Robbery Rate: 1998 to 1999

National Percent Change = 9.2% Decrease*

ALPHA ORDER

RANK	STATE	PERCENT CHANGE
19	Alabama	(7.4)
3	Alaska	5.5
22	Arizona	(7.7)
45	Arkansas	(17.5)
42	California	(14.0)
20	Colorado	(7.6)
20	Connecticut	(7.6)
4	Delaware	1.9
40	Florida	(12.8)
31	Georgia	(11.1)
43	Hawaii	(14.2)
44	Idaho	(17.1)
34	Illinois	(11.7)
9	Indiana	(1.7)
48	Iowa	(28.0)
32	Kansas	(11.3)
26	Kentucky	(9.2)
37	Louisiana	(12.3)
24	Maine	(8.3)
34	Maryland	(11.7)
6	Massachusetts	(0.6)
23	Michigan	(8.2)
32	Minnesota	(11.3)
28	Mississippi	(9.5)
38	Missouri	(12.4)
11	Montana	(2.1)
12	Nebraska	(2.2)
25	Nevada	(8.7)
6	New Hampshire	(0.6)
18	New Jersey	(6.1)
27	New Mexico	(9.3)
30	New York	(10.9)
9	North Carolina	(1.7)
41	North Dakota	(13.3)
13	Ohio	(4.1)
29	Oklahoma	(9.8)
47	Oregon	(18.1)
17	Pennsylvania	(5.6)
1	Rhode Island	19.2
14	South Carolina	(4.3)
49	South Dakota	(30.4)
36	Tennessee	(11.9)
5	Texas	1.1
46	Utah	(17.6)
2	Vermont	15.5
14	Virginia	(4.3)
39	Washington	(12.7)
NA	West Virginia**	NA
8	Wisconsin	(1.1)
16	Wyoming	(4.9)

RANK ORDER

RANK	STATE	PERCENT CHANGE
1	Rhode Island	19.2
2	Vermont	15.5
3	Alaska	5.5
4	Delaware	1.9
5	Texas	1.1
6	Massachusetts	(0.6)
6	New Hampshire	(0.6)
8	Wisconsin	(1.1)
9	Indiana	(1.7)
9	North Carolina	(1.7)
11	Montana	(2.1)
12	Nebraska	(2.2)
13	Ohio	(4.1)
14	South Carolina	(4.3)
14	Virginia	(4.3)
16	Wyoming	(4.9)
17	Pennsylvania	(5.6)
18	New Jersey	(6.1)
19	Alabama	(7.4)
20	Colorado	(7.6)
20	Connecticut	(7.6)
22	Arizona	(7.7)
23	Michigan	(8.2)
24	Maine	(8.3)
25	Nevada	(8.7)
26	Kentucky	(9.2)
27	New Mexico	(9.3)
28	Mississippi	(9.5)
29	Oklahoma	(9.8)
30	New York	(10.9)
31	Georgia	(11.1)
32	Kansas	(11.3)
32	Minnesota	(11.3)
34	Illinois	(11.7)
34	Maryland	(11.7)
36	Tennessee	(11.9)
37	Louisiana	(12.3)
38	Missouri	(12.4)
39	Washington	(12.7)
40	Florida	(12.8)
41	North Dakota	(13.3)
42	California	(14.0)
43	Hawaii	(14.2)
44	Idaho	(17.1)
45	Arkansas	(17.5)
46	Utah	(17.6)
47	Oregon	(18.1)
48	Iowa	(28.0)
49	South Dakota	(30.4)
NA	West Virginia**	NA
	District of Columbia	(6.6)

Source: Federal Bureau of Investigation
    "Crime in the United States 1999" (Uniform Crime Reports, October 15, 2000)
*Robbery is the taking or attempting to take anything of value by force or threat of force.
**Not available.

Robberies with Firearms in 1999

National Total = 121,132 Robberies*

ALPHA ORDER

RANK	STATE	ROBBERIES	% of USA
29	Alabama	946	0.8%
38	Alaska	221	0.2%
12	Arizona	3,144	2.6%
28	Arkansas	1,058	0.9%
1	California	19,908	16.4%
26	Colorado	1,084	0.9%
20	Connecticut	1,461	1.2%
33	Delaware	561	0.5%
3	Florida	12,095	10.0%
10	Georgia	4,474	3.7%
41	Hawaii	114	0.1%
42	Idaho	64	0.1%
NA	Illinois**	NA	NA
14	Indiana	2,669	2.2%
37	Iowa	251	0.2%
35	Kansas	319	0.3%
30	Kentucky	874	0.7%
11	Louisiana	4,175	3.4%
NA	Maine**	NA	NA
23	Maryland	1,171	1.0%
22	Massachusetts	1,236	1.0%
5	Michigan	6,243	5.2%
34	Minnesota	381	0.3%
24	Mississippi	1,162	1.0%
13	Missouri	2,789	2.3%
43	Montana	41	0.0%
32	Nebraska	596	0.5%
17	Nevada	1,631	1.3%
44	New Hampshire	40	0.0%
7	New Jersey	4,680	3.9%
27	New Mexico	1,068	0.9%
18	New York	1,577	1.3%
6	North Carolina	5,560	4.6%
47	North Dakota	14	0.0%
8	Ohio	4,631	3.8%
25	Oklahoma	1,128	0.9%
31	Oregon	748	0.6%
4	Pennsylvania	6,479	5.3%
39	Rhode Island	208	0.2%
21	South Carolina	1,428	1.2%
45	South Dakota	18	0.0%
9	Tennessee	4,555	3.8%
2	Texas	12,785	10.6%
36	Utah	304	0.3%
46	Vermont	16	0.0%
16	Virginia	2,014	1.7%
19	Washington	1,537	1.3%
40	West Virginia	123	0.1%
15	Wisconsin	2,307	1.9%
48	Wyoming	13	0.0%

RANK ORDER

RANK	STATE	ROBBERIES	% of USA
1	California	19,908	16.4%
2	Texas	12,785	10.6%
3	Florida	12,095	10.0%
4	Pennsylvania	6,479	5.3%
5	Michigan	6,243	5.2%
6	North Carolina	5,560	4.6%
7	New Jersey	4,680	3.9%
8	Ohio	4,631	3.8%
9	Tennessee	4,555	3.8%
10	Georgia	4,474	3.7%
11	Louisiana	4,175	3.4%
12	Arizona	3,144	2.6%
13	Missouri	2,789	2.3%
14	Indiana	2,669	2.2%
15	Wisconsin	2,307	1.9%
16	Virginia	2,014	1.7%
17	Nevada	1,631	1.3%
18	New York	1,577	1.3%
19	Washington	1,537	1.3%
20	Connecticut	1,461	1.2%
21	South Carolina	1,428	1.2%
22	Massachusetts	1,236	1.0%
23	Maryland	1,171	1.0%
24	Mississippi	1,162	1.0%
25	Oklahoma	1,128	0.9%
26	Colorado	1,084	0.9%
27	New Mexico	1,068	0.9%
28	Arkansas	1,058	0.9%
29	Alabama	946	0.8%
30	Kentucky	874	0.7%
31	Oregon	748	0.6%
32	Nebraska	596	0.5%
33	Delaware	561	0.5%
34	Minnesota	381	0.3%
35	Kansas	319	0.3%
36	Utah	304	0.3%
37	Iowa	251	0.2%
38	Alaska	221	0.2%
39	Rhode Island	208	0.2%
40	West Virginia	123	0.1%
41	Hawaii	114	0.1%
42	Idaho	64	0.1%
43	Montana	41	0.0%
44	New Hampshire	40	0.0%
45	South Dakota	18	0.0%
46	Vermont	16	0.0%
47	North Dakota	14	0.0%
48	Wyoming	13	0.0%
NA	Illinois**	NA	NA
NA	Maine**	NA	NA
	District of Columbia	1,231	1.0%

Source: Federal Bureau of Investigation
    "Crime in the United States 1999" (Uniform Crime Reports, October 15, 2000)
*Of the 303,940 robberies in 1999 for which supplemental data were received by the F.B.I. There were an additional 105,730 robberies for which the type of weapon was not reported to the F.B.I. Robbery is the taking or attempting to take anything of value by force or threat of force.
**Not available.

Robbery Rate with Firearms in 1999

National Rate = 58.7 Robberies per 100,000 Population*

ALPHA ORDER

RANK	STATE	RATE
30	Alabama	30.8
25	Alaska	39.3
15	Arizona	68.6
24	Arkansas	44.5
20	California	60.1
32	Colorado	28.6
23	Connecticut	46.3
12	Delaware	74.4
10	Florida	80.5
4	Georgia	94.5
41	Hawaii	9.6
44	Idaho	5.2
NA	Illinois**	NA
16	Indiana	66.5
40	Iowa	10.2
3	Kansas	96.0
11	Kentucky	75.9
1	Louisiana	107.4
NA	Maine**	NA
28	Maryland	37.4
35	Massachusetts	23.7
13	Michigan	72.4
36	Minnesota	22.5
7	Mississippi	87.3
17	Missouri	65.7
42	Montana	9.5
27	Nebraska	38.8
5	Nevada	90.2
43	New Hampshire	8.6
21	New Jersey	57.7
6	New Mexico	89.2
33	New York	25.5
9	North Carolina	81.0
48	North Dakota	2.6
19	Ohio	61.3
29	Oklahoma	33.7
34	Oregon	24.0
14	Pennsylvania	71.8
36	Rhode Island	22.5
8	South Carolina	83.5
45	South Dakota	3.5
2	Tennessee	99.3
18	Texas	65.5
38	Utah	17.4
46	Vermont	3.4
26	Virginia	38.9
31	Washington	29.8
39	West Virginia	12.4
22	Wisconsin	47.4
47	Wyoming	2.8

RANK ORDER

RANK	STATE	RATE
1	Louisiana	107.4
2	Tennessee	99.3
3	Kansas	96.0
4	Georgia	94.5
5	Nevada	90.2
6	New Mexico	89.2
7	Mississippi	87.3
8	South Carolina	83.5
9	North Carolina	81.0
10	Florida	80.5
11	Kentucky	75.9
12	Delaware	74.4
13	Michigan	72.4
14	Pennsylvania	71.8
15	Arizona	68.6
16	Indiana	66.5
17	Missouri	65.7
18	Texas	65.5
19	Ohio	61.3
20	California	60.1
21	New Jersey	57.7
22	Wisconsin	47.4
23	Connecticut	46.3
24	Arkansas	44.5
25	Alaska	39.3
26	Virginia	38.9
27	Nebraska	38.8
28	Maryland	37.4
29	Oklahoma	33.7
30	Alabama	30.8
31	Washington	29.8
32	Colorado	28.6
33	New York	25.5
34	Oregon	24.0
35	Massachusetts	23.7
36	Minnesota	22.5
36	Rhode Island	22.5
38	Utah	17.4
39	West Virginia	12.4
40	Iowa	10.2
41	Hawaii	9.6
42	Montana	9.5
43	New Hampshire	8.6
44	Idaho	5.2
45	South Dakota	3.5
46	Vermont	3.4
47	Wyoming	2.8
48	North Dakota	2.6
NA	Illinois**	NA
NA	Maine**	NA

	District of Columbia	237.2

Source: Morgan Quitno Press using data from Federal Bureau of Investigation
     "Crime in the United States 1999" (Uniform Crime Reports, October 15, 2000)
Based only on population of reporting jurisdictions. Robbery is the taking or attempting to take anything of value by force or threat of force. National rate reflects only those robberies for which the type of weapon was known and reported.
***Not available.*

Percent of Robberies Involving Firearms in 1999

National Percent = 39.9% of Robberies*

ALPHA ORDER

RANK ORDER

RANK	STATE	PERCENT		RANK	STATE	PERCENT
7	Alabama	49.6		1	Louisiana	58.4
18	Alaska	42.2		2	Tennessee	55.7
17	Arizona	43.5		3	Arkansas	53.4
3	Arkansas	53.4		4	Wisconsin	52.3
31	California	33.2		5	Mississippi	51.6
26	Colorado	37.7		6	Georgia	50.1
28	Connecticut	37.3		7	Alabama	49.6
27	Delaware	37.6		8	North Carolina	49.4
25	Florida	38.0		9	Virginia	49.2
6	Georgia	50.1		10	Indiana	48.3
48	Hawaii	10.9		11	Michigan	47.8
36	Idaho	28.8		12	Nebraska	47.5
NA	Illinois**	NA		12	New Mexico	47.5
10	Indiana	48.3		14	Kansas	45.6
43	Iowa	25.0		15	Texas	44.0
14	Kansas	45.6		16	South Carolina	43.8
22	Kentucky	39.6		17	Arizona	43.5
1	Louisiana	58.4		18	Alaska	42.2
NA	Maine**	NA		19	Maryland	41.2
19	Maryland	41.2		20	Missouri	40.6
44	Massachusetts	24.2		20	Oklahoma	40.6
11	Michigan	47.8		22	Kentucky	39.6
30	Minnesota	33.8		23	Pennsylvania	38.9
5	Mississippi	51.6		24	Nevada	38.8
20	Missouri	40.6		25	Florida	38.0
38	Montana	28.3		26	Colorado	37.7
12	Nebraska	47.5		27	Delaware	37.6
24	Nevada	38.8		28	Connecticut	37.3
45	New Hampshire	20.9		29	Ohio	36.4
32	New Jersey	33.0		30	Minnesota	33.8
12	New Mexico	47.5		31	California	33.2
37	New York	28.6		32	New Jersey	33.0
8	North Carolina	49.4		33	Utah	32.4
42	North Dakota	25.5		34	Rhode Island	29.8
29	Ohio	36.4		35	West Virginia	29.6
20	Oklahoma	40.6		36	Idaho	28.8
40	Oregon	27.3		37	New York	28.6
23	Pennsylvania	38.9		38	Montana	28.3
34	Rhode Island	29.8		39	Washington	27.8
16	South Carolina	43.8		40	Oregon	27.3
46	South Dakota	18.9		41	Vermont	27.1
2	Tennessee	55.7		42	North Dakota	25.5
15	Texas	44.0		43	Iowa	25.0
33	Utah	32.4		44	Massachusetts	24.2
41	Vermont	27.1		45	New Hampshire	20.9
9	Virginia	49.2		46	South Dakota	18.9
39	Washington	27.8		47	Wyoming	17.8
35	West Virginia	29.6		48	Hawaii	10.9
4	Wisconsin	52.3		NA	Illinois**	NA
47	Wyoming	17.8		NA	Maine**	NA
					District of Columbia	36.8

Source: Morgan Quitno Press using data from Federal Bureau of Investigation
    "Crime in the United States 1999" (Uniform Crime Reports, October 15, 2000)
*Of the 303,940 robberies in 1999 for which supplemental data were received by the F.B.I. There were an additional 105,730 robberies for which the type of weapon was not reported to the F.B.I. Robbery is the taking or attempting to take anything of value by force or threat of force. Numbers are for reporting jurisdictions only.
**Not available.

Robberies with Knives or Cutting Instruments in 1999

National Total = 25,637 Robberies*

ALPHA ORDER

RANK ORDER

RANK	STATE	ROBBERIES	% of USA
28	Alabama	158	0.6%
40	Alaska	46	0.2%
9	Arizona	757	3.0%
30	Arkansas	131	0.5%
1	California	6,091	23.8%
25	Colorado	255	1.0%
17	Connecticut	382	1.5%
31	Delaware	118	0.5%
3	Florida	2,199	8.6%
15	Georgia	472	1.8%
37	Hawaii	81	0.3%
42	Idaho	25	0.1%
NA	Illinois**	NA	NA
19	Indiana	351	1.4%
34	Iowa	112	0.4%
39	Kansas	55	0.2%
29	Kentucky	157	0.6%
16	Louisiana	393	1.5%
NA	Maine**	NA	NA
22	Maryland	303	1.2%
6	Massachusetts	1,043	4.1%
7	Michigan	802	3.1%
36	Minnesota	85	0.3%
32	Mississippi	117	0.5%
14	Missouri	479	1.9%
46	Montana	11	0.0%
33	Nebraska	116	0.5%
18	Nevada	370	1.4%
45	New Hampshire	13	0.1%
4	New Jersey	1,263	4.9%
20	New Mexico	346	1.3%
11	New York	627	2.4%
7	North Carolina	802	3.1%
48	North Dakota	3	0.0%
10	Ohio	672	2.6%
27	Oklahoma	224	0.9%
26	Oregon	254	1.0%
5	Pennsylvania	1,138	4.4%
38	Rhode Island	65	0.3%
24	South Carolina	264	1.0%
43	South Dakota	18	0.1%
12	Tennessee	621	2.4%
2	Texas	2,680	10.5%
35	Utah	101	0.4%
44	Vermont	14	0.1%
21	Virginia	319	1.2%
13	Washington	507	2.0%
41	West Virginia	42	0.2%
23	Wisconsin	301	1.2%
46	Wyoming	11	0.0%

RANK	STATE	ROBBERIES	% of USA
1	California	6,091	23.8%
2	Texas	2,680	10.5%
3	Florida	2,199	8.6%
4	New Jersey	1,263	4.9%
5	Pennsylvania	1,138	4.4%
6	Massachusetts	1,043	4.1%
7	Michigan	802	3.1%
7	North Carolina	802	3.1%
9	Arizona	757	3.0%
10	Ohio	672	2.6%
11	New York	627	2.4%
12	Tennessee	621	2.4%
13	Washington	507	2.0%
14	Missouri	479	1.9%
15	Georgia	472	1.8%
16	Louisiana	393	1.5%
17	Connecticut	382	1.5%
18	Nevada	370	1.4%
19	Indiana	351	1.4%
20	New Mexico	346	1.3%
21	Virginia	319	1.2%
22	Maryland	303	1.2%
23	Wisconsin	301	1.2%
24	South Carolina	264	1.0%
25	Colorado	255	1.0%
26	Oregon	254	1.0%
27	Oklahoma	224	0.9%
28	Alabama	158	0.6%
29	Kentucky	157	0.6%
30	Arkansas	131	0.5%
31	Delaware	118	0.5%
32	Mississippi	117	0.5%
33	Nebraska	116	0.5%
34	Iowa	112	0.4%
35	Utah	101	0.4%
36	Minnesota	85	0.3%
37	Hawaii	81	0.3%
38	Rhode Island	65	0.3%
39	Kansas	55	0.2%
40	Alaska	46	0.2%
41	West Virginia	42	0.2%
42	Idaho	25	0.1%
43	South Dakota	18	0.1%
44	Vermont	14	0.1%
45	New Hampshire	13	0.1%
46	Montana	11	0.0%
46	Wyoming	11	0.0%
48	North Dakota	3	0.0%
NA	Illinois**	NA	NA
NA	Maine**	NA	NA
	District of Columbia	243	0.9%

Source: Federal Bureau of Investigation
  "Crime in the United States 1999" (Uniform Crime Reports, October 15, 2000)
*Of the 303,940 robberies in 1999 for which supplemental data were received by the F.B.I. There were an additional 105,730 robberies for which the type of weapon was not reported to the F.B.I. Robbery is the taking or attempting to take anything of value by force or threat of force. Numbers are for reporting jurisdictions only.
**Not available.

Percent of Robberies Involving Knives or Cutting Instruments in 1999

National Percent = 8.4% of Robberies*

<table>
<tr><td colspan="3">ALPHA ORDER</td><td colspan="3">RANK ORDER</td></tr>
<tr><td>RANK</td><td>STATE</td><td>PERCENT</td><td>RANK</td><td>STATE</td><td>PERCENT</td></tr>
<tr><td>24</td><td>Alabama</td><td>8.3</td><td>1</td><td>Vermont</td><td>23.7</td></tr>
<tr><td>22</td><td>Alaska</td><td>8.8</td><td>2</td><td>Massachusetts</td><td>20.4</td></tr>
<tr><td>11</td><td>Arizona</td><td>10.5</td><td>3</td><td>South Dakota</td><td>18.9</td></tr>
<tr><td>41</td><td>Arkansas</td><td>6.6</td><td>4</td><td>New Mexico</td><td>15.4</td></tr>
<tr><td>12</td><td>California</td><td>10.1</td><td>5</td><td>Wyoming</td><td>15.1</td></tr>
<tr><td>20</td><td>Colorado</td><td>8.9</td><td>6</td><td>New York</td><td>11.4</td></tr>
<tr><td>14</td><td>Connecticut</td><td>9.7</td><td>7</td><td>Idaho</td><td>11.3</td></tr>
<tr><td>27</td><td>Delaware</td><td>7.9</td><td>8</td><td>Iowa</td><td>11.2</td></tr>
<tr><td>37</td><td>Florida</td><td>6.9</td><td>9</td><td>Utah</td><td>10.8</td></tr>
<tr><td>46</td><td>Georgia</td><td>5.3</td><td>10</td><td>Maryland</td><td>10.7</td></tr>
<tr><td>29</td><td>Hawaii</td><td>7.8</td><td>11</td><td>Arizona</td><td>10.5</td></tr>
<tr><td>7</td><td>Idaho</td><td>11.3</td><td>12</td><td>California</td><td>10.1</td></tr>
<tr><td>NA</td><td>Illinois**</td><td>NA</td><td>12</td><td>West Virginia</td><td>10.1</td></tr>
<tr><td>42</td><td>Indiana</td><td>6.3</td><td>14</td><td>Connecticut</td><td>9.7</td></tr>
<tr><td>8</td><td>Iowa</td><td>11.2</td><td>15</td><td>Nebraska</td><td>9.3</td></tr>
<tr><td>27</td><td>Kansas</td><td>7.9</td><td>15</td><td>Oregon</td><td>9.3</td></tr>
<tr><td>34</td><td>Kentucky</td><td>7.1</td><td>15</td><td>Rhode Island</td><td>9.3</td></tr>
<tr><td>44</td><td>Louisiana</td><td>5.5</td><td>18</td><td>Texas</td><td>9.2</td></tr>
<tr><td>NA</td><td>Maine**</td><td>NA</td><td>18</td><td>Washington</td><td>9.2</td></tr>
<tr><td>10</td><td>Maryland</td><td>10.7</td><td>20</td><td>Colorado</td><td>8.9</td></tr>
<tr><td>2</td><td>Massachusetts</td><td>20.4</td><td>20</td><td>New Jersey</td><td>8.9</td></tr>
<tr><td>43</td><td>Michigan</td><td>6.1</td><td>22</td><td>Alaska</td><td>8.8</td></tr>
<tr><td>33</td><td>Minnesota</td><td>7.5</td><td>22</td><td>Nevada</td><td>8.8</td></tr>
<tr><td>48</td><td>Mississippi</td><td>5.2</td><td>24</td><td>Alabama</td><td>8.3</td></tr>
<tr><td>36</td><td>Missouri</td><td>7.0</td><td>25</td><td>Oklahoma</td><td>8.1</td></tr>
<tr><td>31</td><td>Montana</td><td>7.6</td><td>25</td><td>South Carolina</td><td>8.1</td></tr>
<tr><td>15</td><td>Nebraska</td><td>9.3</td><td>27</td><td>Delaware</td><td>7.9</td></tr>
<tr><td>22</td><td>Nevada</td><td>8.8</td><td>27</td><td>Kansas</td><td>7.9</td></tr>
<tr><td>38</td><td>New Hampshire</td><td>6.8</td><td>29</td><td>Hawaii</td><td>7.8</td></tr>
<tr><td>20</td><td>New Jersey</td><td>8.9</td><td>29</td><td>Virginia</td><td>7.8</td></tr>
<tr><td>4</td><td>New Mexico</td><td>15.4</td><td>31</td><td>Montana</td><td>7.6</td></tr>
<tr><td>6</td><td>New York</td><td>11.4</td><td>31</td><td>Tennessee</td><td>7.6</td></tr>
<tr><td>34</td><td>North Carolina</td><td>7.1</td><td>33</td><td>Minnesota</td><td>7.5</td></tr>
<tr><td>44</td><td>North Dakota</td><td>5.5</td><td>34</td><td>Kentucky</td><td>7.1</td></tr>
<tr><td>46</td><td>Ohio</td><td>5.3</td><td>34</td><td>North Carolina</td><td>7.1</td></tr>
<tr><td>25</td><td>Oklahoma</td><td>8.1</td><td>36</td><td>Missouri</td><td>7.0</td></tr>
<tr><td>15</td><td>Oregon</td><td>9.3</td><td>37</td><td>Florida</td><td>6.9</td></tr>
<tr><td>38</td><td>Pennsylvania</td><td>6.8</td><td>38</td><td>New Hampshire</td><td>6.8</td></tr>
<tr><td>15</td><td>Rhode Island</td><td>9.3</td><td>38</td><td>Pennsylvania</td><td>6.8</td></tr>
<tr><td>25</td><td>South Carolina</td><td>8.1</td><td>38</td><td>Wisconsin</td><td>6.8</td></tr>
<tr><td>3</td><td>South Dakota</td><td>18.9</td><td>41</td><td>Arkansas</td><td>6.6</td></tr>
<tr><td>31</td><td>Tennessee</td><td>7.6</td><td>42</td><td>Indiana</td><td>6.3</td></tr>
<tr><td>18</td><td>Texas</td><td>9.2</td><td>43</td><td>Michigan</td><td>6.1</td></tr>
<tr><td>9</td><td>Utah</td><td>10.8</td><td>44</td><td>Louisiana</td><td>5.5</td></tr>
<tr><td>1</td><td>Vermont</td><td>23.7</td><td>44</td><td>North Dakota</td><td>5.5</td></tr>
<tr><td>29</td><td>Virginia</td><td>7.8</td><td>46</td><td>Georgia</td><td>5.3</td></tr>
<tr><td>18</td><td>Washington</td><td>9.2</td><td>46</td><td>Ohio</td><td>5.3</td></tr>
<tr><td>12</td><td>West Virginia</td><td>10.1</td><td>48</td><td>Mississippi</td><td>5.2</td></tr>
<tr><td>38</td><td>Wisconsin</td><td>6.8</td><td>NA</td><td>Illinois**</td><td>NA</td></tr>
<tr><td>5</td><td>Wyoming</td><td>15.1</td><td>NA</td><td>Maine**</td><td>NA</td></tr>
<tr><td></td><td></td><td></td><td></td><td>District of Columbia</td><td>7.3</td></tr>
</table>

Source: Morgan Quitno Press using data from Federal Bureau of Investigation
"Crime in the United States 1999" (Uniform Crime Reports, October 15, 2000)
*Of the 303,940 robberies in 1999 for which supplemental data were received by the F.B.I. There were an
additional 105,730 robberies for which the type of weapon was not reported to the F.B.I. Robbery is the taking or
attempting to take anything of value by force or threat of force. Numbers are for reporting jurisdictions only.
**Not available.

Robberies with Blunt Objects and Other Dangerous Weapons in 1999

National Total = 30,169 Robberies*

RANK	STATE	ROBBERIES	% of USA
32	Alabama	128	0.4%
40	Alaska	37	0.1%
12	Arizona	711	2.4%
31	Arkansas	163	0.5%
1	California	5,861	19.4%
21	Colorado	359	1.2%
20	Connecticut	367	1.2%
34	Delaware	107	0.4%
2	Florida	3,480	11.5%
8	Georgia	1,082	3.6%
42	Hawaii	29	0.1%
43	Idaho	24	0.1%
NA	Illinois**	NA	NA
17	Indiana	419	1.4%
27	Iowa	171	0.6%
37	Kansas	69	0.2%
33	Kentucky	126	0.4%
19	Louisiana	368	1.2%
NA	Maine**	NA	NA
29	Maryland	168	0.6%
13	Massachusetts	626	2.1%
4	Michigan	1,824	6.0%
30	Minnesota	167	0.6%
25	Mississippi	222	0.7%
14	Missouri	569	1.9%
41	Montana	30	0.1%
35	Nebraska	78	0.3%
22	Nevada	331	1.1%
45	New Hampshire	20	0.1%
7	New Jersey	1,145	3.8%
26	New Mexico	179	0.6%
15	New York	495	1.6%
6	North Carolina	1,444	4.8%
44	North Dakota	22	0.1%
5	Ohio	1,578	5.2%
27	Oklahoma	171	0.6%
24	Oregon	228	0.8%
10	Pennsylvania	961	3.2%
38	Rhode Island	54	0.2%
18	South Carolina	372	1.2%
46	South Dakota	17	0.1%
11	Tennessee	857	2.8%
3	Texas	2,973	9.9%
36	Utah	77	0.3%
48	Vermont	6	0.0%
16	Virginia	470	1.6%
9	Washington	973	3.2%
39	West Virginia	46	0.2%
23	Wisconsin	318	1.1%
47	Wyoming	7	0.0%

RANK	STATE	ROBBERIES	% of USA
1	California	5,861	19.4%
2	Florida	3,480	11.5%
3	Texas	2,973	9.9%
4	Michigan	1,824	6.0%
5	Ohio	1,578	5.2%
6	North Carolina	1,444	4.8%
7	New Jersey	1,145	3.8%
8	Georgia	1,082	3.6%
9	Washington	973	3.2%
10	Pennsylvania	961	3.2%
11	Tennessee	857	2.8%
12	Arizona	711	2.4%
13	Massachusetts	626	2.1%
14	Missouri	569	1.9%
15	New York	495	1.6%
16	Virginia	470	1.6%
17	Indiana	419	1.4%
18	South Carolina	372	1.2%
19	Louisiana	368	1.2%
20	Connecticut	367	1.2%
21	Colorado	359	1.2%
22	Nevada	331	1.1%
23	Wisconsin	318	1.1%
24	Oregon	228	0.8%
25	Mississippi	222	0.7%
26	New Mexico	179	0.6%
27	Iowa	171	0.6%
27	Oklahoma	171	0.6%
29	Maryland	168	0.6%
30	Minnesota	167	0.6%
31	Arkansas	163	0.5%
32	Alabama	128	0.4%
33	Kentucky	126	0.4%
34	Delaware	107	0.4%
35	Nebraska	78	0.3%
36	Utah	77	0.3%
37	Kansas	69	0.2%
38	Rhode Island	54	0.2%
39	West Virginia	46	0.2%
40	Alaska	37	0.1%
41	Montana	30	0.1%
42	Hawaii	29	0.1%
43	Idaho	24	0.1%
44	North Dakota	22	0.1%
45	New Hampshire	20	0.1%
46	South Dakota	17	0.1%
47	Wyoming	7	0.0%
48	Vermont	6	0.0%
NA	Illinois**	NA	NA
NA	Maine**	NA	NA
	District of Columbia	240	0.8%

Source: Federal Bureau of Investigation
   "Crime in the United States 1999" (Uniform Crime Reports, October 15, 2000)
*Of the 303,940 robberies in 1999 for which supplemental data were received by the F.B.I. There were an additional 105,730 robberies for which the type of weapon was not reported to the F.B.I. Robbery is the taking or attempting to take anything of value by force or threat of force. Numbers are for reporting jurisdictions only.
**Not available.

Percent of Robberies Involving Blunt Objects
And Other Dangerous Weapons in 1999
National Percent = 9.9% of Robberies*

ALPHA ORDER

RANK	STATE	PERCENT
41	Alabama	6.7
40	Alaska	7.1
24	Arizona	9.8
31	Arkansas	8.2
24	California	9.8
9	Colorado	12.5
27	Connecticut	9.4
38	Delaware	7.2
16	Florida	10.9
12	Georgia	12.1
48	Hawaii	2.8
17	Idaho	10.8
NA	Illinois**	NA
37	Indiana	7.6
5	Iowa	17.1
22	Kansas	9.9
46	Kentucky	5.7
47	Louisiana	5.2
NA	Maine**	NA
44	Maryland	5.9
11	Massachusetts	12.3
7	Michigan	14.0
6	Minnesota	14.8
22	Mississippi	9.9
29	Missouri	8.3
2	Montana	20.7
42	Nebraska	6.2
35	Nevada	7.9
18	New Hampshire	10.5
33	New Jersey	8.1
34	New Mexico	8.0
28	New York	9.0
8	North Carolina	12.8
1	North Dakota	40.0
10	Ohio	12.4
42	Oklahoma	6.2
29	Oregon	8.3
45	Pennsylvania	5.8
36	Rhode Island	7.7
14	South Carolina	11.4
3	South Dakota	17.9
18	Tennessee	10.5
20	Texas	10.2
31	Utah	8.2
20	Vermont	10.2
13	Virginia	11.5
4	Washington	17.6
15	West Virginia	11.1
38	Wisconsin	7.2
26	Wyoming	9.6

RANK ORDER

RANK	STATE	PERCENT
1	North Dakota	40.0
2	Montana	20.7
3	South Dakota	17.9
4	Washington	17.6
5	Iowa	17.1
6	Minnesota	14.8
7	Michigan	14.0
8	North Carolina	12.8
9	Colorado	12.5
10	Ohio	12.4
11	Massachusetts	12.3
12	Georgia	12.1
13	Virginia	11.5
14	South Carolina	11.4
15	West Virginia	11.1
16	Florida	10.9
17	Idaho	10.8
18	New Hampshire	10.5
18	Tennessee	10.5
20	Texas	10.2
20	Vermont	10.2
22	Kansas	9.9
22	Mississippi	9.9
24	Arizona	9.8
24	California	9.8
26	Wyoming	9.6
27	Connecticut	9.4
28	New York	9.0
29	Missouri	8.3
29	Oregon	8.3
31	Arkansas	8.2
31	Utah	8.2
33	New Jersey	8.1
34	New Mexico	8.0
35	Nevada	7.9
36	Rhode Island	7.7
37	Indiana	7.6
38	Delaware	7.2
38	Wisconsin	7.2
40	Alaska	7.1
41	Alabama	6.7
42	Nebraska	6.2
42	Oklahoma	6.2
44	Maryland	5.9
45	Pennsylvania	5.8
46	Kentucky	5.7
47	Louisiana	5.2
48	Hawaii	2.8
NA	Illinois**	NA
NA	Maine**	NA
	District of Columbia	7.2

Source: Morgan Quitno Press using data from Federal Bureau of Investigation
   "Crime in the United States 1999" (Uniform Crime Reports, October 15, 2000)
Of the 303,940 robberies in 1999 for which supplemental data were received by the F.B.I. There were an
additional 105,730 robberies for which the type of weapon was not reported to the F.B.I. Robbery is the taking or
attempting to take anything of value by force or threat of force. Numbers are for reporting jurisdictions only.
***Not available.*

Robberies Committed with Hands, Fists or Feet in 1999

National Total = 127,002 Robberies*

ALPHA ORDER

ALPHA ORDER

RANK ORDER

RANK	STATE	ROBBERIES	% of USA		RANK	STATE	ROBBERIES	% of USA
31	Alabama	674	0.5%		1	California	28,159	22.2%
40	Alaska	220	0.2%		2	Florida	14,040	11.1%
12	Arizona	2,609	2.1%		3	Texas	10,644	8.4%
33	Arkansas	630	0.5%		4	Pennsylvania	8,071	6.4%
1	California	28,159	22.2%		5	New Jersey	7,107	5.6%
26	Colorado	1,178	0.9%		6	Ohio	5,854	4.6%
19	Connecticut	1,708	1.3%		7	Michigan	4,204	3.3%
30	Delaware	706	0.6%		8	North Carolina	3,460	2.7%
2	Florida	14,040	11.1%		9	Missouri	3,025	2.4%
10	Georgia	2,911	2.3%		10	Georgia	2,911	2.3%
28	Hawaii	820	0.6%		11	New York	2,818	2.2%
43	Idaho	109	0.1%		12	Arizona	2,609	2.1%
NA	Illinois**	NA	NA		13	Washington	2,508	2.0%
17	Indiana	2,091	1.6%		14	Louisiana	2,209	1.7%
35	Iowa	468	0.4%		15	Massachusetts	2,198	1.7%
39	Kansas	257	0.2%		16	Tennessee	2,143	1.7%
27	Kentucky	1,048	0.8%		17	Indiana	2,091	1.6%
14	Louisiana	2,209	1.7%		18	Nevada	1,877	1.5%
NA	Maine**	NA	NA		19	Connecticut	1,708	1.3%
24	Maryland	1,197	0.9%		20	Oregon	1,506	1.2%
15	Massachusetts	2,198	1.7%		21	Wisconsin	1,486	1.2%
7	Michigan	4,204	3.3%		22	Virginia	1,290	1.0%
34	Minnesota	494	0.4%		23	Oklahoma	1,254	1.0%
29	Mississippi	750	0.6%		24	Maryland	1,197	0.9%
9	Missouri	3,025	2.4%		25	South Carolina	1,195	0.9%
44	Montana	63	0.0%		26	Colorado	1,178	0.9%
36	Nebraska	464	0.4%		27	Kentucky	1,048	0.8%
18	Nevada	1,877	1.5%		28	Hawaii	820	0.6%
42	New Hampshire	118	0.1%		29	Mississippi	750	0.6%
5	New Jersey	7,107	5.6%		30	Delaware	706	0.6%
32	New Mexico	654	0.5%		31	Alabama	674	0.5%
11	New York	2,818	2.2%		32	New Mexico	654	0.5%
8	North Carolina	3,460	2.7%		33	Arkansas	630	0.5%
48	North Dakota	16	0.0%		34	Minnesota	494	0.4%
6	Ohio	5,854	4.6%		35	Iowa	468	0.4%
23	Oklahoma	1,254	1.0%		36	Nebraska	464	0.4%
20	Oregon	1,506	1.2%		37	Utah	456	0.4%
4	Pennsylvania	8,071	6.4%		38	Rhode Island	372	0.3%
38	Rhode Island	372	0.3%		39	Kansas	257	0.2%
25	South Carolina	1,195	0.9%		40	Alaska	220	0.2%
45	South Dakota	42	0.0%		41	West Virginia	204	0.2%
16	Tennessee	2,143	1.7%		42	New Hampshire	118	0.1%
3	Texas	10,644	8.4%		43	Idaho	109	0.1%
37	Utah	456	0.4%		44	Montana	63	0.0%
47	Vermont	23	0.0%		45	South Dakota	42	0.0%
22	Virginia	1,290	1.0%		45	Wyoming	42	0.0%
13	Washington	2,508	2.0%		47	Vermont	23	0.0%
41	West Virginia	204	0.2%		48	North Dakota	16	0.0%
21	Wisconsin	1,486	1.2%		NA	Illinois**	NA	NA
45	Wyoming	42	0.0%		NA	Maine**	NA	NA
						District of Columbia	1,630	1.3%

Source: Federal Bureau of Investigation
    "Crime in the United States 1999" (Uniform Crime Reports, October 15, 2000)
*Also called strong-armed robberies. Of the 303,940 robberies in 1999 for which supplemental data were received by the F.B.I. There were an additional 105,730 robberies for which the type of weapon was not reported to the F.B.I. Robbery is the taking or attempting to take anything of value by force or threat of force. Numbers are for reporting jurisdictions only. **Not available.

Percent of Robberies Committed with Hands, Fists or Feet in 1999

National Percent = 41.8% of Robberies*

<table>
<tr><td colspan="3">ALPHA ORDER</td><td colspan="3">RANK ORDER</td></tr>
<tr><td>RANK</td><td>STATE</td><td>PERCENT</td><td>RANK</td><td>STATE</td><td>PERCENT</td></tr>
<tr><td>37</td><td>Alabama</td><td>35.4</td><td>1</td><td>Hawaii</td><td>78.5</td></tr>
<tr><td>28</td><td>Alaska</td><td>42.0</td><td>2</td><td>New Hampshire</td><td>61.8</td></tr>
<tr><td>36</td><td>Arizona</td><td>36.1</td><td>3</td><td>Wyoming</td><td>57.5</td></tr>
<tr><td>42</td><td>Arkansas</td><td>31.8</td><td>4</td><td>Oregon</td><td>55.0</td></tr>
<tr><td>14</td><td>California</td><td>46.9</td><td>5</td><td>Rhode Island</td><td>53.2</td></tr>
<tr><td>29</td><td>Colorado</td><td>41.0</td><td>6</td><td>New York</td><td>51.1</td></tr>
<tr><td>24</td><td>Connecticut</td><td>43.6</td><td>7</td><td>New Jersey</td><td>50.1</td></tr>
<tr><td>13</td><td>Delaware</td><td>47.3</td><td>8</td><td>West Virginia</td><td>49.2</td></tr>
<tr><td>21</td><td>Florida</td><td>44.1</td><td>9</td><td>Idaho</td><td>49.1</td></tr>
<tr><td>40</td><td>Georgia</td><td>32.6</td><td>10</td><td>Utah</td><td>48.6</td></tr>
<tr><td>1</td><td>Hawaii</td><td>78.5</td><td>11</td><td>Pennsylvania</td><td>48.5</td></tr>
<tr><td>9</td><td>Idaho</td><td>49.1</td><td>12</td><td>Kentucky</td><td>47.5</td></tr>
<tr><td>NA</td><td>Illinois**</td><td>NA</td><td>13</td><td>Delaware</td><td>47.3</td></tr>
<tr><td>31</td><td>Indiana</td><td>37.8</td><td>14</td><td>California</td><td>46.9</td></tr>
<tr><td>15</td><td>Iowa</td><td>46.7</td><td>15</td><td>Iowa</td><td>46.7</td></tr>
<tr><td>33</td><td>Kansas</td><td>36.7</td><td>16</td><td>Ohio</td><td>46.0</td></tr>
<tr><td>12</td><td>Kentucky</td><td>47.5</td><td>17</td><td>Washington</td><td>45.4</td></tr>
<tr><td>44</td><td>Louisiana</td><td>30.9</td><td>18</td><td>Oklahoma</td><td>45.2</td></tr>
<tr><td>NA</td><td>Maine**</td><td>NA</td><td>19</td><td>Nevada</td><td>44.6</td></tr>
<tr><td>27</td><td>Maryland</td><td>42.2</td><td>20</td><td>South Dakota</td><td>44.2</td></tr>
<tr><td>26</td><td>Massachusetts</td><td>43.1</td><td>21</td><td>Florida</td><td>44.1</td></tr>
<tr><td>41</td><td>Michigan</td><td>32.2</td><td>21</td><td>Missouri</td><td>44.1</td></tr>
<tr><td>23</td><td>Minnesota</td><td>43.8</td><td>23</td><td>Minnesota</td><td>43.8</td></tr>
<tr><td>39</td><td>Mississippi</td><td>33.3</td><td>24</td><td>Connecticut</td><td>43.6</td></tr>
<tr><td>21</td><td>Missouri</td><td>44.1</td><td>25</td><td>Montana</td><td>43.4</td></tr>
<tr><td>25</td><td>Montana</td><td>43.4</td><td>26</td><td>Massachusetts</td><td>43.1</td></tr>
<tr><td>32</td><td>Nebraska</td><td>37.0</td><td>27</td><td>Maryland</td><td>42.2</td></tr>
<tr><td>19</td><td>Nevada</td><td>44.6</td><td>28</td><td>Alaska</td><td>42.0</td></tr>
<tr><td>2</td><td>New Hampshire</td><td>61.8</td><td>29</td><td>Colorado</td><td>41.0</td></tr>
<tr><td>7</td><td>New Jersey</td><td>50.1</td><td>30</td><td>Vermont</td><td>39.0</td></tr>
<tr><td>46</td><td>New Mexico</td><td>29.1</td><td>31</td><td>Indiana</td><td>37.8</td></tr>
<tr><td>6</td><td>New York</td><td>51.1</td><td>32</td><td>Nebraska</td><td>37.0</td></tr>
<tr><td>45</td><td>North Carolina</td><td>30.7</td><td>33</td><td>Kansas</td><td>36.7</td></tr>
<tr><td>46</td><td>North Dakota</td><td>29.1</td><td>33</td><td>South Carolina</td><td>36.7</td></tr>
<tr><td>16</td><td>Ohio</td><td>46.0</td><td>35</td><td>Texas</td><td>36.6</td></tr>
<tr><td>18</td><td>Oklahoma</td><td>45.2</td><td>36</td><td>Arizona</td><td>36.1</td></tr>
<tr><td>4</td><td>Oregon</td><td>55.0</td><td>37</td><td>Alabama</td><td>35.4</td></tr>
<tr><td>11</td><td>Pennsylvania</td><td>48.5</td><td>38</td><td>Wisconsin</td><td>33.7</td></tr>
<tr><td>5</td><td>Rhode Island</td><td>53.2</td><td>39</td><td>Mississippi</td><td>33.3</td></tr>
<tr><td>33</td><td>South Carolina</td><td>36.7</td><td>40</td><td>Georgia</td><td>32.6</td></tr>
<tr><td>20</td><td>South Dakota</td><td>44.2</td><td>41</td><td>Michigan</td><td>32.2</td></tr>
<tr><td>48</td><td>Tennessee</td><td>26.2</td><td>42</td><td>Arkansas</td><td>31.8</td></tr>
<tr><td>35</td><td>Texas</td><td>36.6</td><td>43</td><td>Virginia</td><td>31.5</td></tr>
<tr><td>10</td><td>Utah</td><td>48.6</td><td>44</td><td>Louisiana</td><td>30.9</td></tr>
<tr><td>30</td><td>Vermont</td><td>39.0</td><td>45</td><td>North Carolina</td><td>30.7</td></tr>
<tr><td>43</td><td>Virginia</td><td>31.5</td><td>46</td><td>New Mexico</td><td>29.1</td></tr>
<tr><td>17</td><td>Washington</td><td>45.4</td><td>46</td><td>North Dakota</td><td>29.1</td></tr>
<tr><td>8</td><td>West Virginia</td><td>49.2</td><td>48</td><td>Tennessee</td><td>26.2</td></tr>
<tr><td>38</td><td>Wisconsin</td><td>33.7</td><td>NA</td><td>Illinois**</td><td>NA</td></tr>
<tr><td>3</td><td>Wyoming</td><td>57.5</td><td>NA</td><td>Maine**</td><td>NA</td></tr>
<tr><td></td><td></td><td></td><td></td><td>District of Columbia</td><td>48.7</td></tr>
</table>

Source: Morgan Quitno Press using data from Federal Bureau of Investigation
    "Crime in the United States 1999" (Uniform Crime Reports, October 15, 2000)
*Also called strong-armed robberies. Of the 303,940 robberies in 1999 for which supplemental data were received
by the F.B.I. There were an additional 105,730 robberies for which the type of weapon was not reported to the
F.B.I. Robbery is the taking or attempting to take anything of value by force or threat of force.- Numbers are for
reporting jurisdictions only. **Not available.

Bank Robberies in 1999

National Total = 6,590 Robberies*

ALPHA ORDER

RANK	STATE	ROBBERIES	% of USA
24	Alabama	69	1.0%
38	Alaska	23	0.3%
8	Arizona	246	3.7%
41	Arkansas	18	0.3%
1	California	1,249	19.0%
22	Colorado	85	1.3%
36	Connecticut	26	0.4%
36	Delaware	26	0.4%
2	Florida	467	7.1%
16	Georgia	145	2.2%
31	Hawaii	50	0.8%
43	Idaho	14	0.2%
14	Illinois	153	2.3%
20	Indiana	94	1.4%
33	Iowa	46	0.7%
29	Kansas	56	0.8%
26	Kentucky	63	1.0%
28	Louisiana	60	0.9%
46	Maine	4	0.1%
12	Maryland	196	3.0%
15	Massachusetts	150	2.3%
6	Michigan	292	4.4%
25	Minnesota	65	1.0%
32	Mississippi	47	0.7%
23	Missouri	82	1.2%
44	Montana	7	0.1%
34	Nebraska	37	0.6%
17	Nevada	130	2.0%
39	New Hampshire	21	0.3%
19	New Jersey	95	1.4%
30	New Mexico	51	0.8%
4	New York	321	4.9%
10	North Carolina	221	3.4%
49	North Dakota	0	0.0%
3	Ohio	395	6.0%
40	Oklahoma	20	0.3%
11	Oregon	204	3.1%
7	Pennsylvania	288	4.4%
42	Rhode Island	15	0.2%
21	South Carolina	93	1.4%
47	South Dakota	2	0.0%
18	Tennessee	118	1.8%
9	Texas	223	3.4%
35	Utah	31	0.5%
47	Vermont	2	0.0%
13	Virginia	182	2.8%
5	Washington	320	4.9%
45	West Virginia	6	0.1%
27	Wisconsin	61	0.9%
49	Wyoming	0	0.0%

RANK ORDER

RANK	STATE	ROBBERIES	% of USA
1	California	1,249	19.0%
2	Florida	467	7.1%
3	Ohio	395	6.0%
4	New York	321	4.9%
5	Washington	320	4.9%
6	Michigan	292	4.4%
7	Pennsylvania	288	4.4%
8	Arizona	246	3.7%
9	Texas	223	3.4%
10	North Carolina	221	3.4%
11	Oregon	204	3.1%
12	Maryland	196	3.0%
13	Virginia	182	2.8%
14	Illinois	153	2.3%
15	Massachusetts	150	2.3%
16	Georgia	145	2.2%
17	Nevada	130	2.0%
18	Tennessee	118	1.8%
19	New Jersey	95	1.4%
20	Indiana	94	1.4%
21	South Carolina	93	1.4%
22	Colorado	85	1.3%
23	Missouri	82	1.2%
24	Alabama	69	1.0%
25	Minnesota	65	1.0%
26	Kentucky	63	1.0%
27	Wisconsin	61	0.9%
28	Louisiana	60	0.9%
29	Kansas	56	0.8%
30	New Mexico	51	0.8%
31	Hawaii	50	0.8%
32	Mississippi	47	0.7%
33	Iowa	46	0.7%
34	Nebraska	37	0.6%
35	Utah	31	0.5%
36	Connecticut	26	0.4%
36	Delaware	26	0.4%
38	Alaska	23	0.3%
39	New Hampshire	21	0.3%
40	Oklahoma	20	0.3%
41	Arkansas	18	0.3%
42	Rhode Island	15	0.2%
43	Idaho	14	0.2%
44	Montana	7	0.1%
45	West Virginia	6	0.1%
46	Maine	4	0.1%
47	South Dakota	2	0.0%
47	Vermont	2	0.0%
49	North Dakota	0	0.0%
49	Wyoming	0	0.0%
	District of Columbia	21	0.3%

Source: Federal Bureau of Investigation
"Bank Crime Statistics, Federally Insured Financial Institutions, January 1, 1999 - December 31, 1999"
Does not include 9 robberies in Puerto Rico. In addition, there were 315 bank burglaries and 74 bank larcenies. Of these 6,998 bank crimes, loot valued at $73,921,652 was taken in 6,340 cases. Of this, $11,981,524 was recovered.

Aggravated Assaults in 1999

National Total = 916,383 Aggravated Assaults*

ALPHA ORDER

ALPHA ORDER | | | | RANK ORDER | | |

RANK	STATE	ASSAULTS	% of USA	RANK	STATE	ASSAULTS	% of USA
19	Alabama	14,266	1.6%	1	California	136,472	14.9%
40	Alaska	2,773	0.3%	2	Florida	89,226	9.7%
17	Arizona	17,279	1.9%	3	Texas	74,070	8.1%
27	Arkansas	7,971	0.9%	4	New York	58,860	6.4%
1	California	136,472	14.9%	5	Illinois	57,146	6.2%
25	Colorado	8,891	1.0%	6	Michigan	37,062	4.0%
32	Connecticut	6,527	0.7%	7	Pennsylvania	27,890	3.0%
39	Delaware	3,489	0.4%	8	Tennessee	26,707	2.9%
2	Florida	89,226	9.7%	9	North Carolina	26,680	2.9%
11	Georgia	25,721	2.8%	10	Massachusetts	26,307	2.9%
43	Hawaii	1,343	0.1%	11	Georgia	25,721	2.8%
41	Idaho	2,401	0.3%	12	South Carolina	25,315	2.8%
5	Illinois	57,146	6.2%	13	Maryland	22,795	2.5%
20	Indiana	13,767	1.5%	14	Louisiana	22,526	2.5%
33	Iowa	6,160	0.7%	15	Missouri	18,406	2.0%
31	Kansas	6,887	0.8%	16	New Jersey	17,601	1.9%
28	Kentucky	7,488	0.8%	17	Arizona	17,279	1.9%
14	Louisiana	22,526	2.5%	18	Ohio	16,685	1.8%
45	Maine	897	0.1%	19	Alabama	14,266	1.6%
13	Maryland	22,795	2.5%	20	Indiana	13,767	1.5%
10	Massachusetts	26,307	2.9%	21	Washington	13,026	1.4%
6	Michigan	37,062	4.0%	22	Oklahoma	12,675	1.4%
30	Minnesota	6,996	0.8%	23	Virginia	12,567	1.4%
36	Mississippi	5,211	0.6%	24	New Mexico	10,827	1.2%
15	Missouri	18,406	2.0%	25	Colorado	8,891	1.0%
44	Montana	1,322	0.1%	26	Oregon	8,267	0.9%
34	Nebraska	5,429	0.6%	27	Arkansas	7,971	0.9%
37	Nevada	4,994	0.5%	28	Kentucky	7,488	0.8%
48	New Hampshire	539	0.1%	29	Wisconsin	7,225	0.8%
16	New Jersey	17,601	1.9%	30	Minnesota	6,996	0.8%
24	New Mexico	10,827	1.2%	31	Kansas	6,887	0.8%
4	New York	58,860	6.4%	32	Connecticut	6,527	0.7%
9	North Carolina	26,680	2.9%	33	Iowa	6,160	0.7%
50	North Dakota	216	0.0%	34	Nebraska	5,429	0.6%
18	Ohio	16,685	1.8%	35	West Virginia	5,259	0.6%
22	Oklahoma	12,675	1.4%	36	Mississippi	5,211	0.6%
26	Oregon	8,267	0.9%	37	Nevada	4,994	0.5%
7	Pennsylvania	27,890	3.0%	38	Utah	3,861	0.4%
42	Rhode Island	1,625	0.2%	39	Delaware	3,489	0.4%
12	South Carolina	25,315	2.8%	40	Alaska	2,773	0.3%
47	South Dakota	770	0.1%	41	Idaho	2,401	0.3%
8	Tennessee	26,707	2.9%	42	Rhode Island	1,625	0.2%
3	Texas	74,070	8.1%	43	Hawaii	1,343	0.1%
38	Utah	3,861	0.4%	44	Montana	1,322	0.1%
49	Vermont	458	0.0%	45	Maine	897	0.1%
23	Virginia	12,567	1.4%	46	Wyoming	893	0.1%
21	Washington	13,026	1.4%	47	South Dakota	770	0.1%
35	West Virginia	5,259	0.6%	48	New Hampshire	539	0.1%
29	Wisconsin	7,225	0.8%	49	Vermont	458	0.0%
46	Wyoming	893	0.1%	50	North Dakota	216	0.0%
					District of Columbia	4,615	0.5%

Source: Federal Bureau of Investigation
"Crime in the United States 1999" (Uniform Crime Reports, October 15, 2000)
Aggravated assault is an attack for the purpose of inflicting severe bodily injury.

Average Time Between Aggravated Assaults in 1999

National Rate = An Aggravated Assault Occurs Every 34 Seconds*

ALPHA ORDER

RANK	STATE	MINUTES.SECONDS
32	Alabama	36.50
11	Alaska	189.32
34	Arizona	30.25
24	Arkansas	65.56
50	California	3.51
26	Colorado	59.07
19	Connecticut	80.32
12	Delaware	150.38
49	Florida	5.53
40	Georgia	20.26
8	Hawaii	391.22
10	Idaho	218.55
46	Illinois	9.12
31	Indiana	38.11
18	Iowa	85.19
20	Kansas	76.19
23	Kentucky	70.11
37	Louisiana	23.20
6	Maine	585.57
38	Maryland	23.04
41	Massachusetts	19.59
45	Michigan	14.11
21	Minnesota	75.08
15	Mississippi	100.52
36	Missouri	28.34
7	Montana	397.35
17	Nebraska	96.49
14	Nevada	105.15
3	New Hampshire	975.08
35	New Jersey	29.52
27	New Mexico	48.33
47	New York	8.56
42	North Carolina	19.42
1	North Dakota	2,433.20
33	Ohio	31.30
29	Oklahoma	41.28
25	Oregon	63.35
44	Pennsylvania	18.51
9	Rhode Island	323.27
39	South Carolina	20.46
4	South Dakota	682.36
43	Tennessee	19.41
48	Texas	7.06
13	Utah	136.08
2	Vermont	1,147.36
28	Virginia	41.49
30	Washington	40.21
16	West Virginia	99.56
22	Wisconsin	72.45
5	Wyoming	588.35

RANK ORDER

RANK	STATE	MINUTES.SECONDS
1	North Dakota	2,433.20
2	Vermont	1,147.36
3	New Hampshire	975.08
4	South Dakota	682.36
5	Wyoming	588.35
6	Maine	585.57
7	Montana	397.35
8	Hawaii	391.22
9	Rhode Island	323.27
10	Idaho	218.55
11	Alaska	189.32
12	Delaware	150.38
13	Utah	136.08
14	Nevada	105.15
15	Mississippi	100.52
16	West Virginia	99.56
17	Nebraska	96.49
18	Iowa	85.19
19	Connecticut	80.32
20	Kansas	76.19
21	Minnesota	75.08
22	Wisconsin	72.45
23	Kentucky	70.11
24	Arkansas	65.56
25	Oregon	63.35
26	Colorado	59.07
27	New Mexico	48.33
28	Virginia	41.49
29	Oklahoma	41.28
30	Washington	40.21
31	Indiana	38.11
32	Alabama	36.50
33	Ohio	31.30
34	Arizona	30.25
35	New Jersey	29.52
36	Missouri	28.34
37	Louisiana	23.20
38	Maryland	23.04
39	South Carolina	20.46
40	Georgia	20.26
41	Massachusetts	19.59
42	North Carolina	19.42
43	Tennessee	19.41
44	Pennsylvania	18.51
45	Michigan	14.11
46	Illinois	9.12
47	New York	8.56
48	Texas	7.06
49	Florida	5.53
50	California	3.51
	District of Columbia	113.53

Source: Morgan Quitno Press using data from Federal Bureau of Investigation
"Crime in the United States 1999" (Uniform Crime Reports, October 15, 2000)
*Aggravated assault is an attack for the purpose of inflicting severe bodily injury.

Percent Change in Number of Aggravated Assaults: 1998 to 1999

National Percent Change = 6.2% Decrease*

ALPHA ORDER

RANK ORDER

RANK	STATE	PERCENT CHANGE
15	Alabama	(3.5)
30	Alaska	(8.2)
8	Arizona	(0.9)
38	Arkansas	(10.5)
33	California	(8.5)
32	Colorado	(8.4)
14	Connecticut	(3.3)
21	Delaware	(5.9)
22	Florida	(6.5)
12	Georgia	(3.0)
7	Hawaii	(0.1)
42	Idaho	(13.7)
30	Illinois	(8.2)
45	Indiana	(16.3)
29	Iowa	(7.8)
23	Kansas	(6.7)
28	Kentucky	(7.5)
13	Louisiana	(3.1)
43	Maine	(14.7)
11	Maryland	(2.3)
41	Massachusetts	(13.6)
27	Michigan	(7.3)
37	Minnesota	(10.4)
47	Mississippi	(20.6)
34	Missouri	(9.1)
5	Montana	0.8
19	Nebraska	(5.6)
40	Nevada	(12.5)
35	New Hampshire	(9.7)
20	New Jersey	(5.7)
44	New Mexico	(14.8)
18	New York	(5.1)
25	North Carolina	(6.9)
49	North Dakota	(24.5)
46	Ohio	(19.3)
16	Oklahoma	(4.4)
26	Oregon	(7.0)
3	Pennsylvania	4.0
48	Rhode Island	(20.7)
17	South Carolina	(5.0)
2	South Dakota	6.6
4	Tennessee	1.9
6	Texas	0.6
35	Utah	(9.7)
1	Vermont	15.7
9	Virginia	(1.1)
39	Washington	(12.2)
NA	West Virginia**	NA
9	Wisconsin	(1.1)
23	Wyoming	(6.7)

RANK	STATE	PERCENT CHANGE
1	Vermont	15.7
2	South Dakota	6.6
3	Pennsylvania	4.0
4	Tennessee	1.9
5	Montana	0.8
6	Texas	0.6
7	Hawaii	(0.1)
8	Arizona	(0.9)
9	Virginia	(1.1)
9	Wisconsin	(1.1)
11	Maryland	(2.3)
12	Georgia	(3.0)
13	Louisiana	(3.1)
14	Connecticut	(3.3)
15	Alabama	(3.5)
16	Oklahoma	(4.4)
17	South Carolina	(5.0)
18	New York	(5.1)
19	Nebraska	(5.6)
20	New Jersey	(5.7)
21	Delaware	(5.9)
22	Florida	(6.5)
23	Kansas	(6.7)
23	Wyoming	(6.7)
25	North Carolina	(6.9)
26	Oregon	(7.0)
27	Michigan	(7.3)
28	Kentucky	(7.5)
29	Iowa	(7.8)
30	Alaska	(8.2)
30	Illinois	(8.2)
32	Colorado	(8.4)
33	California	(8.5)
34	Missouri	(9.1)
35	New Hampshire	(9.7)
35	Utah	(9.7)
37	Minnesota	(10.4)
38	Arkansas	(10.5)
39	Washington	(12.2)
40	Nevada	(12.5)
41	Massachusetts	(13.6)
42	Idaho	(13.7)
43	Maine	(14.7)
44	New Mexico	(14.8)
45	Indiana	(16.3)
46	Ohio	(19.3)
47	Mississippi	(20.6)
48	Rhode Island	(20.7)
49	North Dakota	(24.5)
NA	West Virginia**	NA
	District of Columbia	(6.4)

Source: Federal Bureau of Investigation
"Crime in the United States 1999" (Uniform Crime Reports, October 15, 2000)
*Aggravated assault is an attack for the purpose of inflicting severe bodily injury.
**Not available.

Aggravated Assault Rate in 1999

National Rate = 336.1 Aggravated Assaults per 100,000 Population*

ALPHA ORDER

RANK	STATE	RATE
19	Alabama	326.5
8	Alaska	448.0
15	Arizona	361.6
22	Arkansas	312.5
11	California	411.7
30	Colorado	219.2
33	Connecticut	198.9
7	Delaware	462.7
3	Florida	590.5
18	Georgia	330.3
45	Hawaii	113.3
34	Idaho	191.8
6	Illinois	471.2
28	Indiana	231.7
32	Iowa	214.7
25	Kansas	259.5
35	Kentucky	189.0
4	Louisiana	515.2
48	Maine	71.6
9	Maryland	440.7
10	Massachusetts	426.0
13	Michigan	375.7
43	Minnesota	146.5
36	Mississippi	188.2
17	Missouri	336.6
41	Montana	149.7
20	Nebraska	325.9
24	Nevada	276.1
49	New Hampshire	44.9
31	New Jersey	216.1
2	New Mexico	622.2
21	New York	323.5
16	North Carolina	348.7
50	North Dakota	34.1
42	Ohio	148.2
12	Oklahoma	377.5
26	Oregon	249.3
27	Pennsylvania	232.5
40	Rhode Island	164.0
1	South Carolina	651.4
46	South Dakota	105.0
5	Tennessee	487.0
14	Texas	369.5
39	Utah	181.3
47	Vermont	77.1
38	Virginia	182.8
29	Washington	226.3
23	West Virginia	291.0
44	Wisconsin	137.6
37	Wyoming	186.0

RANK ORDER

RANK	STATE	RATE
1	South Carolina	651.4
2	New Mexico	622.2
3	Florida	590.5
4	Louisiana	515.2
5	Tennessee	487.0
6	Illinois	471.2
7	Delaware	462.7
8	Alaska	448.0
9	Maryland	440.7
10	Massachusetts	426.0
11	California	411.7
12	Oklahoma	377.5
13	Michigan	375.7
14	Texas	369.5
15	Arizona	361.6
16	North Carolina	348.7
17	Missouri	336.6
18	Georgia	330.3
19	Alabama	326.5
20	Nebraska	325.9
21	New York	323.5
22	Arkansas	312.5
23	West Virginia	291.0
24	Nevada	276.1
25	Kansas	259.5
26	Oregon	249.3
27	Pennsylvania	232.5
28	Indiana	231.7
29	Washington	226.3
30	Colorado	219.2
31	New Jersey	216.1
32	Iowa	214.7
33	Connecticut	198.9
34	Idaho	191.8
35	Kentucky	189.0
36	Mississippi	188.2
37	Wyoming	186.0
38	Virginia	182.8
39	Utah	181.3
40	Rhode Island	164.0
41	Montana	149.7
42	Ohio	148.2
43	Minnesota	146.5
44	Wisconsin	137.6
45	Hawaii	113.3
46	South Dakota	105.0
47	Vermont	77.1
48	Maine	71.6
49	New Hampshire	44.9
50	North Dakota	34.1
	District of Columbia	889.2

Source: Federal Bureau of Investigation
"Crime in the United States 1999" (Uniform Crime Reports, October 15, 2000)
Aggravated assault is an attack for the purpose of inflicting severe bodily injury.

Percent Change in Aggravated Assault Rate: 1998 to 1999

National Percent Change = 7.0% Decrease*

ALPHA ORDER

RANK	STATE	PERCENT CHANGE
14	Alabama	(3.9)
31	Alaska	(9.0)
12	Arizona	(3.2)
37	Arkansas	(11.0)
33	California	(9.8)
34	Colorado	(10.3)
13	Connecticut	(3.6)
22	Delaware	(7.1)
24	Florida	(7.7)
16	Georgia	(4.8)
5	Hawaii	0.5
42	Idaho	(15.3)
30	Illinois	(8.8)
45	Indiana	(17.0)
26	Iowa	(8.0)
23	Kansas	(7.6)
28	Kentucky	(8.1)
11	Louisiana	(3.1)
42	Maine	(15.3)
10	Maryland	(3.0)
40	Massachusetts	(14.0)
25	Michigan	(7.8)
38	Minnesota	(11.3)
48	Mississippi	(21.1)
32	Missouri	(9.6)
6	Montana	0.4
18	Nebraska	(5.7)
44	Nevada	(15.5)
35	New Hampshire	(10.9)
19	New Jersey	(6.0)
41	New Mexico	(15.0)
17	New York	(5.2)
29	North Carolina	(8.2)
49	North Dakota	(24.0)
46	Ohio	(19.7)
15	Oklahoma	(4.7)
26	Oregon	(8.0)
3	Pennsylvania	4.0
47	Rhode Island	(21.0)
20	South Carolina	(6.2)
2	South Dakota	7.4
4	Tennessee	0.9
7	Texas	(0.8)
35	Utah	(10.9)
1	Vermont	15.1
9	Virginia	(2.3)
39	Washington	(13.2)
NA	West Virginia**	NA
8	Wisconsin	(1.6)
21	Wyoming	(6.5)

RANK ORDER

RANK	STATE	PERCENT CHANGE
1	Vermont	15.1
2	South Dakota	7.4
3	Pennsylvania	4.0
4	Tennessee	0.9
5	Hawaii	0.5
6	Montana	0.4
7	Texas	(0.8)
8	Wisconsin	(1.6)
9	Virginia	(2.3)
10	Maryland	(3.0)
11	Louisiana	(3.1)
12	Arizona	(3.2)
13	Connecticut	(3.6)
14	Alabama	(3.9)
15	Oklahoma	(4.7)
16	Georgia	(4.8)
17	New York	(5.2)
18	Nebraska	(5.7)
19	New Jersey	(6.0)
20	South Carolina	(6.2)
21	Wyoming	(6.5)
22	Delaware	(7.1)
23	Kansas	(7.6)
24	Florida	(7.7)
25	Michigan	(7.8)
26	Iowa	(8.0)
26	Oregon	(8.0)
28	Kentucky	(8.1)
29	North Carolina	(8.2)
30	Illinois	(8.8)
31	Alaska	(9.0)
32	Missouri	(9.6)
33	California	(9.8)
34	Colorado	(10.3)
35	New Hampshire	(10.9)
35	Utah	(10.9)
37	Arkansas	(11.0)
38	Minnesota	(11.3)
39	Washington	(13.2)
40	Massachusetts	(14.0)
41	New Mexico	(15.0)
42	Idaho	(15.3)
42	Maine	(15.3)
44	Nevada	(15.5)
45	Indiana	(17.0)
46	Ohio	(19.7)
47	Rhode Island	(21.0)
48	Mississippi	(21.1)
49	North Dakota	(24.0)
NA	West Virginia**	NA

District of Columbia   (5.7)

Source: Federal Bureau of Investigation
    "Crime in the United States 1999" (Uniform Crime Reports, October 15, 2000)
*Aggravated assault is an attack for the purpose of inflicting severe bodily injury.
**Not available.

Aggravated Assaults with Firearms in 1999

National Total = 126,479 Aggravated Assaults*

ALPHA ORDER

RANK	STATE	ASSAULTS	% of USA
21	Alabama	1,645	1.3%
34	Alaska	535	0.4%
9	Arizona	4,349	3.4%
19	Arkansas	1,761	1.4%
1	California	19,051	15.1%
20	Colorado	1,649	1.3%
35	Connecticut	534	0.4%
33	Delaware	623	0.5%
3	Florida	13,607	10.8%
11	Georgia	3,665	2.9%
42	Hawaii	134	0.1%
36	Idaho	510	0.4%
NA	Illinois**	NA	NA
17	Indiana	1,822	1.4%
37	Iowa	504	0.4%
41	Kansas	242	0.2%
30	Kentucky	818	0.6%
8	Louisiana	4,679	3.7%
NA	Maine**	NA	NA
24	Maryland	1,207	1.0%
22	Massachusetts	1,288	1.0%
4	Michigan	7,938	6.3%
38	Minnesota	457	0.4%
28	Mississippi	963	0.8%
10	Missouri	4,343	3.4%
44	Montana	93	0.1%
29	Nebraska	822	0.6%
32	Nevada	756	0.6%
47	New Hampshire	20	0.0%
14	New Jersey	2,257	1.8%
18	New Mexico	1,803	1.4%
27	New York	974	0.8%
6	North Carolina	6,340	5.0%
48	North Dakota	6	0.0%
13	Ohio	2,327	1.8%
15	Oklahoma	2,013	1.6%
26	Oregon	1,066	0.8%
7	Pennsylvania	4,705	3.7%
40	Rhode Island	244	0.2%
12	South Carolina	2,567	2.0%
43	South Dakota	94	0.1%
5	Tennessee	6,781	5.4%
2	Texas	14,820	11.7%
39	Utah	445	0.4%
46	Vermont	36	0.0%
23	Virginia	1,271	1.0%
16	Washington	1,835	1.5%
31	West Virginia	814	0.6%
25	Wisconsin	1,136	0.9%
45	Wyoming	88	0.1%

RANK ORDER

RANK	STATE	ASSAULTS	% of USA
1	California	19,051	15.1%
2	Texas	14,820	11.7%
3	Florida	13,607	10.8%
4	Michigan	7,938	6.3%
5	Tennessee	6,781	5.4%
6	North Carolina	6,340	5.0%
7	Pennsylvania	4,705	3.7%
8	Louisiana	4,679	3.7%
9	Arizona	4,349	3.4%
10	Missouri	4,343	3.4%
11	Georgia	3,665	2.9%
12	South Carolina	2,567	2.0%
13	Ohio	2,327	1.8%
14	New Jersey	2,257	1.8%
15	Oklahoma	2,013	1.6%
16	Washington	1,835	1.5%
17	Indiana	1,822	1.4%
18	New Mexico	1,803	1.4%
19	Arkansas	1,761	1.4%
20	Colorado	1,649	1.3%
21	Alabama	1,645	1.3%
22	Massachusetts	1,288	1.0%
23	Virginia	1,271	1.0%
24	Maryland	1,207	1.0%
25	Wisconsin	1,136	0.9%
26	Oregon	1,066	0.8%
27	New York	974	0.8%
28	Mississippi	963	0.8%
29	Nebraska	822	0.6%
30	Kentucky	818	0.6%
31	West Virginia	814	0.6%
32	Nevada	756	0.6%
33	Delaware	623	0.5%
34	Alaska	535	0.4%
35	Connecticut	534	0.4%
36	Idaho	510	0.4%
37	Iowa	504	0.4%
38	Minnesota	457	0.4%
39	Utah	445	0.4%
40	Rhode Island	244	0.2%
41	Kansas	242	0.2%
42	Hawaii	134	0.1%
43	South Dakota	94	0.1%
44	Montana	93	0.1%
45	Wyoming	88	0.1%
46	Vermont	36	0.0%
47	New Hampshire	20	0.0%
48	North Dakota	6	0.0%
NA	Illinois**	NA	NA
NA	Maine**	NA	NA
	District of Columbia	842	0.7%

Source: Federal Bureau of Investigation
   "Crime in the United States 1999" (Uniform Crime Reports, October 15, 2000)
*Of the 702,391 aggravated assaults in 1999 for which supplemental data were received by the F.B.I. There were
an additional 213,992 aggravated assaults for which the type of weapon was not reported to the F.B.I. Aggravated
assault is an attack for the purpose of inflicting severe bodily injury. Numbers are for reporting jurisdictions only.*
**Not available.*

Aggravated Assault Rate with Firearms in 1999

National Rate = 61.3 Aggravated Assaults per 100,000 Population*

ALPHA ORDER

RANK	STATE	RATE
21	Alabama	53.5
6	Alaska	95.1
7	Arizona	94.9
15	Arkansas	74.1
20	California	57.5
25	Colorado	43.5
43	Connecticut	16.9
11	Delaware	82.6
10	Florida	90.6
13	Georgia	77.4
45	Hawaii	11.3
27	Idaho	41.7
NA	Illinois**	NA
24	Indiana	45.4
40	Iowa	20.6
16	Kansas	72.8
18	Kentucky	71.0
4	Louisiana	120.3
NA	Maine**	NA
28	Maryland	38.5
36	Massachusetts	24.7
9	Michigan	92.0
33	Minnesota	27.0
17	Mississippi	72.3
5	Missouri	102.3
39	Montana	21.5
21	Nebraska	53.5
26	Nevada	41.8
47	New Hampshire	4.3
32	New Jersey	27.8
1	New Mexico	150.6
44	New York	15.8
8	North Carolina	92.3
48	North Dakota	1.1
31	Ohio	30.8
19	Oklahoma	60.2
30	Oregon	34.2
23	Pennsylvania	52.1
34	Rhode Island	26.4
2	South Carolina	150.2
42	South Dakota	18.0
3	Tennessee	147.8
14	Texas	76.0
35	Utah	25.5
46	Vermont	7.6
37	Virginia	24.6
29	Washington	36.9
12	West Virginia	82.2
38	Wisconsin	23.3
41	Wyoming	19.3

RANK ORDER

RANK	STATE	RATE
1	New Mexico	150.6
2	South Carolina	150.2
3	Tennessee	147.8
4	Louisiana	120.3
5	Missouri	102.3
6	Alaska	95.1
7	Arizona	94.9
8	North Carolina	92.3
9	Michigan	92.0
10	Florida	90.6
11	Delaware	82.6
12	West Virginia	82.2
13	Georgia	77.4
14	Texas	76.0
15	Arkansas	74.1
16	Kansas	72.8
17	Mississippi	72.3
18	Kentucky	71.0
19	Oklahoma	60.2
20	California	57.5
21	Alabama	53.5
21	Nebraska	53.5
23	Pennsylvania	52.1
24	Indiana	45.4
25	Colorado	43.5
26	Nevada	41.8
27	Idaho	41.7
28	Maryland	38.5
29	Washington	36.9
30	Oregon	34.2
31	Ohio	30.8
32	New Jersey	27.8
33	Minnesota	27.0
34	Rhode Island	26.4
35	Utah	25.5
36	Massachusetts	24.7
37	Virginia	24.6
38	Wisconsin	23.3
39	Montana	21.5
40	Iowa	20.6
41	Wyoming	19.3
42	South Dakota	18.0
43	Connecticut	16.9
44	New York	15.8
45	Hawaii	11.3
46	Vermont	7.6
47	New Hampshire	4.3
48	North Dakota	1.1
NA	Illinois**	NA
NA	Maine**	NA

District of Columbia   162.2

Source: Morgan Quitno Press using data from Federal Bureau of Investigation
      "Crime in the United States 1999" (Uniform Crime Reports, October 15, 2000)
*Based only on population of reporting jurisdictions. Aggravated assault is an attack for the purpose of inflicting severe bodily injury. National rate reflects only those robberies for which the type of weapon was known and reported.
**Not available.

371

Percent of Aggravated Assaults Involving Firearms in 1999

National Percent = 18.0% of Aggravated Assaults*

ALPHA ORDER

RANK	STATE	PERCENT
6	Alabama	24.3
14	Alaska	22.1
4	Arizona	26.6
10	Arkansas	23.4
36	California	14.0
19	Colorado	20.2
45	Connecticut	8.4
21	Delaware	17.9
29	Florida	15.3
12	Georgia	22.5
42	Hawaii	10.0
15	Idaho	21.5
NA	Illinois**	NA
23	Indiana	17.5
43	Iowa	8.9
9	Kansas	23.5
29	Kentucky	15.3
10	Louisiana	23.4
NA	Maine**	NA
31	Maryland	15.1
47	Massachusetts	5.7
8	Michigan	23.8
20	Minnesota	18.7
1	Mississippi	33.0
3	Missouri	28.0
33	Montana	14.8
28	Nebraska	15.8
31	Nevada	15.1
46	New Hampshire	6.8
39	New Jersey	12.9
12	New Mexico	22.5
44	New York	8.5
5	North Carolina	26.3
48	North Dakota	2.9
22	Ohio	17.6
27	Oklahoma	15.9
38	Oregon	13.5
17	Pennsylvania	20.6
26	Rhode Island	16.6
16	South Carolina	21.2
34	South Dakota	14.3
2	Tennessee	28.3
18	Texas	20.4
35	Utah	14.2
40	Vermont	10.8
37	Virginia	13.9
24	Washington	16.8
7	West Virginia	24.0
24	Wisconsin	16.8
41	Wyoming	10.4

RANK ORDER

RANK	STATE	PERCENT
1	Mississippi	33.0
2	Tennessee	28.3
3	Missouri	28.0
4	Arizona	26.6
5	North Carolina	26.3
6	Alabama	24.3
7	West Virginia	24.0
8	Michigan	23.8
9	Kansas	23.5
10	Arkansas	23.4
10	Louisiana	23.4
12	Georgia	22.5
12	New Mexico	22.5
14	Alaska	22.1
15	Idaho	21.5
16	South Carolina	21.2
17	Pennsylvania	20.6
18	Texas	20.4
19	Colorado	20.2
20	Minnesota	18.7
21	Delaware	17.9
22	Ohio	17.6
23	Indiana	17.5
24	Washington	16.8
24	Wisconsin	16.8
26	Rhode Island	16.6
27	Oklahoma	15.9
28	Nebraska	15.8
29	Florida	15.3
29	Kentucky	15.3
31	Maryland	15.1
31	Nevada	15.1
33	Montana	14.8
34	South Dakota	14.3
35	Utah	14.2
36	California	14.0
37	Virginia	13.9
38	Oregon	13.5
39	New Jersey	12.9
40	Vermont	10.8
41	Wyoming	10.4
42	Hawaii	10.0
43	Iowa	8.9
44	New York	8.5
45	Connecticut	8.4
46	New Hampshire	6.8
47	Massachusetts	5.7
48	North Dakota	2.9
NA	Illinois**	NA
NA	Maine**	NA
	District of Columbia	18.2

Source: Morgan Quitno Press using data from Federal Bureau of Investigation
    "Crime in the United States 1999" (Uniform Crime Reports, October 15, 2000)
*Of the 702,391 aggravated assaults in 1999 for which supplemental data were received by the F.B.I. There were an additional 213,992 aggravated assaults for which the type of weapon was not reported to the F.B.I. Aggravated assault is an attack for the purpose of inflicting severe bodily injury. Numbers are for reporting jurisdictions only.
**Not available.

Aggravated Assaults with Knives or Cutting Instruments in 1999

National Total = 125,040 Aggravated Assaults*

ALPHA ORDER

RANK	STATE	ASSAULTS	% of USA
26	Alabama	1,223	1.0%
37	Alaska	549	0.4%
14	Arizona	2,502	2.0%
23	Arkansas	1,328	1.1%
1	California	17,629	14.1%
19	Colorado	1,814	1.5%
29	Connecticut	918	0.7%
31	Delaware	816	0.7%
2	Florida	16,394	13.1%
11	Georgia	3,221	2.6%
43	Hawaii	144	0.1%
38	Idaho	542	0.4%
NA	Illinois**	NA	NA
24	Indiana	1,300	1.0%
30	Iowa	908	0.7%
41	Kansas	223	0.2%
35	Kentucky	618	0.5%
7	Louisiana	4,126	3.3%
NA	Maine**	NA	NA
20	Maryland	1,736	1.4%
10	Massachusetts	3,324	2.7%
4	Michigan	6,971	5.6%
33	Minnesota	650	0.5%
34	Mississippi	626	0.5%
12	Missouri	2,694	2.2%
45	Montana	86	0.1%
36	Nebraska	608	0.5%
28	Nevada	1,029	0.8%
47	New Hampshire	61	0.0%
8	New Jersey	3,924	3.1%
22	New Mexico	1,346	1.1%
18	New York	1,905	1.5%
6	North Carolina	4,857	3.9%
48	North Dakota	38	0.0%
15	Ohio	2,346	1.9%
17	Oklahoma	1,911	1.5%
25	Oregon	1,264	1.0%
9	Pennsylvania	3,530	2.8%
40	Rhode Island	320	0.3%
13	South Carolina	2,649	2.1%
42	South Dakota	212	0.2%
5	Tennessee	4,946	4.0%
3	Texas	16,365	13.1%
32	Utah	680	0.5%
46	Vermont	76	0.1%
21	Virginia	1,690	1.4%
16	Washington	2,124	1.7%
39	West Virginia	441	0.4%
27	Wisconsin	1,089	0.9%
44	Wyoming	133	0.1%

RANK ORDER

RANK	STATE	ASSAULTS	% of USA
1	California	17,629	14.1%
2	Florida	16,394	13.1%
3	Texas	16,365	13.1%
4	Michigan	6,971	5.6%
5	Tennessee	4,946	4.0%
6	North Carolina	4,857	3.9%
7	Louisiana	4,126	3.3%
8	New Jersey	3,924	3.1%
9	Pennsylvania	3,530	2.8%
10	Massachusetts	3,324	2.7%
11	Georgia	3,221	2.6%
12	Missouri	2,694	2.2%
13	South Carolina	2,649	2.1%
14	Arizona	2,502	2.0%
15	Ohio	2,346	1.9%
16	Washington	2,124	1.7%
17	Oklahoma	1,911	1.5%
18	New York	1,905	1.5%
19	Colorado	1,814	1.5%
20	Maryland	1,736	1.4%
21	Virginia	1,690	1.4%
22	New Mexico	1,346	1.1%
23	Arkansas	1,328	1.1%
24	Indiana	1,300	1.0%
25	Oregon	1,264	1.0%
26	Alabama	1,223	1.0%
27	Wisconsin	1,089	0.9%
28	Nevada	1,029	0.8%
29	Connecticut	918	0.7%
30	Iowa	908	0.7%
31	Delaware	816	0.7%
32	Utah	680	0.5%
33	Minnesota	650	0.5%
34	Mississippi	626	0.5%
35	Kentucky	618	0.5%
36	Nebraska	608	0.5%
37	Alaska	549	0.4%
38	Idaho	542	0.4%
39	West Virginia	441	0.4%
40	Rhode Island	320	0.3%
41	Kansas	223	0.2%
42	South Dakota	212	0.2%
43	Hawaii	144	0.1%
44	Wyoming	133	0.1%
45	Montana	86	0.1%
46	Vermont	76	0.1%
47	New Hampshire	61	0.0%
48	North Dakota	38	0.0%
NA	Illinois**	NA	NA
NA	Maine**	NA	NA
	District of Columbia	1,154	0.9%

Source: Federal Bureau of Investigation
"Crime in the United States 1999" (Uniform Crime Reports, October 15, 2000)
Of the 702,391 aggravated assaults in 1999 for which supplemental data were received by the F.B.I. There were an additional 213,992 aggravated assaults for which the type of weapon was not reported to the F.B.I. Aggravated assault is an attack for the purpose of inflicting severe bodily injury. Numbers are for reporting jurisdictions only.
***Not available.**

Percent of Aggravated Assaults Involving Knives or Cutting Instruments in 1999

National Percent = 17.8% of Aggravated Assaults*

ALPHA ORDER

RANK	STATE	PERCENT
27	Alabama	18.1
6	Alaska	22.7
38	Arizona	15.3
29	Arkansas	17.6
44	California	12.9
9	Colorado	22.2
41	Connecticut	14.4
3	Delaware	23.4
25	Florida	18.5
22	Georgia	19.8
48	Hawaii	10.7
4	Idaho	22.9
NA	Illinois**	NA
45	Indiana	12.5
34	Iowa	16.1
14	Kansas	21.6
47	Kentucky	11.6
18	Louisiana	20.6
NA	Maine**	NA
11	Maryland	21.8
40	Massachusetts	14.8
16	Michigan	20.9
2	Minnesota	26.6
15	Mississippi	21.4
30	Missouri	17.4
42	Montana	13.7
46	Nebraska	11.7
18	Nevada	20.6
17	New Hampshire	20.8
8	New Jersey	22.4
31	New Mexico	16.8
32	New York	16.6
21	North Carolina	20.1
24	North Dakota	18.6
28	Ohio	17.7
39	Oklahoma	15.1
34	Oregon	16.1
37	Pennsylvania	15.4
13	Rhode Island	21.7
10	South Carolina	21.9
1	South Dakota	32.2
18	Tennessee	20.6
7	Texas	22.6
11	Utah	21.8
5	Vermont	22.8
26	Virginia	18.4
23	Washington	19.5
43	West Virginia	13.0
33	Wisconsin	16.2
36	Wyoming	15.7

RANK ORDER

RANK	STATE	PERCENT
1	South Dakota	32.2
2	Minnesota	26.6
3	Delaware	23.4
4	Idaho	22.9
5	Vermont	22.8
6	Alaska	22.7
7	Texas	22.6
8	New Jersey	22.4
9	Colorado	22.2
10	South Carolina	21.9
11	Maryland	21.8
11	Utah	21.8
13	Rhode Island	21.7
14	Kansas	21.6
15	Mississippi	21.4
16	Michigan	20.9
17	New Hampshire	20.8
18	Louisiana	20.6
18	Nevada	20.6
18	Tennessee	20.6
21	North Carolina	20.1
22	Georgia	19.8
23	Washington	19.5
24	North Dakota	18.6
25	Florida	18.5
26	Virginia	18.4
27	Alabama	18.1
28	Ohio	17.7
29	Arkansas	17.6
30	Missouri	17.4
31	New Mexico	16.8
32	New York	16.6
33	Wisconsin	16.2
34	Iowa	16.1
34	Oregon	16.1
36	Wyoming	15.7
37	Pennsylvania	15.4
38	Arizona	15.3
39	Oklahoma	15.1
40	Massachusetts	14.8
41	Connecticut	14.4
42	Montana	13.7
43	West Virginia	13.0
44	California	12.9
45	Indiana	12.5
46	Nebraska	11.7
47	Kentucky	11.6
48	Hawaii	10.7
NA	Illinois**	NA
NA	Maine**	NA

District of Columbia 25.0

Source: Morgan Quitno Press using data from Federal Bureau of Investigation
  "Crime in the United States 1999" (Uniform Crime Reports, October 15, 2000)
*Of the 702,391 aggravated assaults in 1999 for which supplemental data were received by the F.B.I. There were an additional 213,992 aggravated assaults for which the type of weapon was not reported to the F.B.I. Aggravated assault is an attack for the purpose of inflicting severe bodily injury. Numbers are for reporting jurisdictions only.
**Not available.

Aggravated Assaults with Blunt Objects and Other Dangerous Weapons in 1999

National Total = 247,878 Aggravated Assaults*

ALPHA ORDER

RANK	STATE	ASSAULTS	% of USA
26	Alabama	1,774	0.7%
40	Alaska	618	0.2%
13	Arizona	4,832	1.9%
28	Arkansas	1,635	0.7%
1	California	42,909	17.3%
23	Colorado	2,510	1.0%
25	Connecticut	2,369	1.0%
27	Delaware	1,659	0.7%
2	Florida	42,515	17.2%
12	Georgia	5,519	2.2%
43	Hawaii	326	0.1%
36	Idaho	848	0.3%
NA	Illinois**	NA	NA
20	Indiana	3,172	1.3%
31	Iowa	1,594	0.6%
41	Kansas	497	0.2%
33	Kentucky	1,359	0.5%
8	Louisiana	6,164	2.5%
NA	Maine**	NA	NA
18	Maryland	3,409	1.4%
5	Massachusetts	9,305	3.8%
4	Michigan	13,702	5.5%
35	Minnesota	894	0.4%
37	Mississippi	697	0.3%
11	Missouri	5,679	2.3%
42	Montana	330	0.1%
30	Nebraska	1,599	0.6%
29	Nevada	1,619	0.7%
47	New Hampshire	84	0.0%
10	New Jersey	5,812	2.3%
24	New Mexico	2,398	1.0%
19	New York	3,334	1.3%
7	North Carolina	8,095	3.3%
48	North Dakota	62	0.0%
16	Ohio	3,887	1.6%
14	Oklahoma	4,584	1.8%
22	Oregon	2,841	1.1%
9	Pennsylvania	6,073	2.4%
38	Rhode Island	658	0.3%
15	South Carolina	3,936	1.6%
45	South Dakota	200	0.1%
6	Tennessee	9,122	3.7%
3	Texas	26,719	10.8%
34	Utah	1,048	0.4%
46	Vermont	107	0.0%
21	Virginia	2,919	1.2%
17	Washington	3,850	1.6%
39	West Virginia	624	0.3%
32	Wisconsin	1,473	0.6%
44	Wyoming	293	0.1%

RANK ORDER

RANK	STATE	ASSAULTS	% of USA
1	California	42,909	17.3%
2	Florida	42,515	17.2%
3	Texas	26,719	10.8%
4	Michigan	13,702	5.5%
5	Massachusetts	9,305	3.8%
6	Tennessee	9,122	3.7%
7	North Carolina	8,095	3.3%
8	Louisiana	6,164	2.5%
9	Pennsylvania	6,073	2.4%
10	New Jersey	5,812	2.3%
11	Missouri	5,679	2.3%
12	Georgia	5,519	2.2%
13	Arizona	4,832	1.9%
14	Oklahoma	4,584	1.8%
15	South Carolina	3,936	1.6%
16	Ohio	3,887	1.6%
17	Washington	3,850	1.6%
18	Maryland	3,409	1.4%
19	New York	3,334	1.3%
20	Indiana	3,172	1.3%
21	Virginia	2,919	1.2%
22	Oregon	2,841	1.1%
23	Colorado	2,510	1.0%
24	New Mexico	2,398	1.0%
25	Connecticut	2,369	1.0%
26	Alabama	1,774	0.7%
27	Delaware	1,659	0.7%
28	Arkansas	1,635	0.7%
29	Nevada	1,619	0.7%
30	Nebraska	1,599	0.6%
31	Iowa	1,594	0.6%
32	Wisconsin	1,473	0.6%
33	Kentucky	1,359	0.5%
34	Utah	1,048	0.4%
35	Minnesota	894	0.4%
36	Idaho	848	0.3%
37	Mississippi	697	0.3%
38	Rhode Island	658	0.3%
39	West Virginia	624	0.3%
40	Alaska	618	0.2%
41	Kansas	497	0.2%
42	Montana	330	0.1%
43	Hawaii	326	0.1%
44	Wyoming	293	0.1%
45	South Dakota	200	0.1%
46	Vermont	107	0.0%
47	New Hampshire	84	0.0%
48	North Dakota	62	0.0%
NA	Illinois**	NA	NA
NA	Maine**	NA	NA
	District of Columbia	2,225	0.9%

Source: Federal Bureau of Investigation
    "Crime in the United States 1999" (Uniform Crime Reports, October 15, 2000)
*Of the 702,391 aggravated assaults in 1999 for which supplemental data were received by the F.B.I. There were
an additional 213,992 aggravated assaults for which the type of weapon was not reported to the F.B.I. Aggravated
assault is an attack for the purpose of inflicting severe bodily injury. Numbers are for reporting jurisdictions only.
**Not available.

Percent of Aggravated Assaults Involving Blunt Objects
And Other Dangerous Weapons in 1999
National Percent = 35.3% of Aggravated Assaults*

ALPHA ORDER

RANK ORDER

RANK	STATE	PERCENT
41	Alabama	26.2
42	Alaska	25.6
35	Arizona	29.6
47	Arkansas	21.7
27	California	31.5
29	Colorado	30.7
10	Connecticut	37.2
4	Delaware	47.5
3	Florida	47.9
19	Georgia	33.9
44	Hawaii	24.3
16	Idaho	35.8
NA	Illinois**	NA
31	Indiana	30.4
39	Iowa	28.2
2	Kansas	48.2
43	Kentucky	25.4
28	Louisiana	30.8
NA	Maine**	NA
6	Maryland	42.7
7	Massachusetts	41.4
8	Michigan	41.0
13	Minnesota	36.6
45	Mississippi	23.9
12	Missouri	36.7
1	Montana	52.5
29	Nebraska	30.7
24	Nevada	32.4
38	New Hampshire	28.7
22	New Jersey	33.2
34	New Mexico	29.9
37	New York	29.0
20	North Carolina	33.5
31	North Dakota	30.4
36	Ohio	29.4
14	Oklahoma	36.3
15	Oregon	36.1
40	Pennsylvania	26.5
5	Rhode Island	44.7
23	South Carolina	32.5
33	South Dakota	30.3
9	Tennessee	38.0
11	Texas	36.8
20	Utah	33.5
25	Vermont	32.0
26	Virginia	31.8
17	Washington	35.4
48	West Virginia	18.4
46	Wisconsin	21.8
18	Wyoming	34.7

RANK	STATE	PERCENT
1	Montana	52.5
2	Kansas	48.2
3	Florida	47.9
4	Delaware	47.5
5	Rhode Island	44.7
6	Maryland	42.7
7	Massachusetts	41.4
8	Michigan	41.0
9	Tennessee	38.0
10	Connecticut	37.2
11	Texas	36.8
12	Missouri	36.7
13	Minnesota	36.6
14	Oklahoma	36.3
15	Oregon	36.1
16	Idaho	35.8
17	Washington	35.4
18	Wyoming	34.7
19	Georgia	33.9
20	North Carolina	33.5
20	Utah	33.5
22	New Jersey	33.2
23	South Carolina	32.5
24	Nevada	32.4
25	Vermont	32.0
26	Virginia	31.8
27	California	31.5
28	Louisiana	30.8
29	Colorado	30.7
29	Nebraska	30.7
31	Indiana	30.4
31	North Dakota	30.4
33	South Dakota	30.3
34	New Mexico	29.9
35	Arizona	29.6
36	Ohio	29.4
37	New York	29.0
38	New Hampshire	28.7
39	Iowa	28.2
40	Pennsylvania	26.5
41	Alabama	26.2
42	Alaska	25.6
43	Kentucky	25.4
44	Hawaii	24.3
45	Mississippi	23.9
46	Wisconsin	21.8
47	Arkansas	21.7
48	West Virginia	18.4
NA	Illinois**	NA
NA	Maine**	NA

District of Columbia   48.2

Source: Morgan Quitno Press using data from Federal Bureau of Investigation
"Crime in the United States 1999" (Uniform Crime Reports, October 15, 2000)
*Of the 702,391 aggravated assaults in 1999 for which supplemental data were received by the F.B.I. There were an additional 213,992 aggravated assaults for which the type of weapon was not reported to the F.B.I. Aggravated assault is an attack for the purpose of inflicting severe bodily injury. Numbers are for reporting jurisdictions only.
**Not available.

Aggravated Assaults Committed with Hands, Fists or Feet in 1999

National Total = 202,994 Aggravated Assaults*

RANK	STATE	ASSAULTS	% of USA
30	Alabama	2,129	1.0%
36	Alaska	716	0.4%
12	Arizona	4,658	2.3%
21	Arkansas	2,802	1.4%
1	California	56,833	28.0%
28	Colorado	2,202	1.1%
26	Connecticut	2,552	1.3%
40	Delaware	391	0.2%
2	Florida	16,193	8.0%
15	Georgia	3,853	1.9%
35	Hawaii	739	0.4%
38	Idaho	471	0.2%
NA	Illinois**	NA	NA
13	Indiana	4,125	2.0%
24	Iowa	2,650	1.3%
48	Kansas	69	0.0%
25	Kentucky	2,554	1.3%
8	Louisiana	5,069	2.5%
NA	Maine**	NA	NA
31	Maryland	1,624	0.8%
4	Massachusetts	8,580	4.2%
10	Michigan	4,773	2.4%
39	Minnesota	440	0.2%
37	Mississippi	634	0.3%
22	Missouri	2,768	1.4%
45	Montana	119	0.1%
29	Nebraska	2,176	1.1%
32	Nevada	1,590	0.8%
44	New Hampshire	128	0.1%
6	New Jersey	5,522	2.7%
27	New Mexico	2,469	1.2%
7	New York	5,285	2.6%
9	North Carolina	4,859	2.4%
47	North Dakota	98	0.0%
11	Ohio	4,664	2.3%
14	Oklahoma	4,116	2.0%
23	Oregon	2,699	1.3%
5	Pennsylvania	8,577	4.2%
42	Rhode Island	251	0.1%
20	South Carolina	2,955	1.5%
43	South Dakota	153	0.1%
17	Tennessee	3,125	1.5%
3	Texas	14,663	7.2%
34	Utah	951	0.5%
46	Vermont	115	0.1%
16	Virginia	3,289	1.6%
18	Washington	3,082	1.5%
33	West Virginia	1,514	0.7%
19	Wisconsin	3,044	1.5%
41	Wyoming	331	0.2%

RANK	STATE	ASSAULTS	% of USA
1	California	56,833	28.0%
2	Florida	16,193	8.0%
3	Texas	14,663	7.2%
4	Massachusetts	8,580	4.2%
5	Pennsylvania	8,577	4.2%
6	New Jersey	5,522	2.7%
7	New York	5,285	2.6%
8	Louisiana	5,069	2.5%
9	North Carolina	4,859	2.4%
10	Michigan	4,773	2.4%
11	Ohio	4,664	2.3%
12	Arizona	4,658	2.3%
13	Indiana	4,125	2.0%
14	Oklahoma	4,116	2.0%
15	Georgia	3,853	1.9%
16	Virginia	3,289	1.6%
17	Tennessee	3,125	1.5%
18	Washington	3,082	1.5%
19	Wisconsin	3,044	1.5%
20	South Carolina	2,955	1.5%
21	Arkansas	2,802	1.4%
22	Missouri	2,768	1.4%
23	Oregon	2,699	1.3%
24	Iowa	2,650	1.3%
25	Kentucky	2,554	1.3%
26	Connecticut	2,552	1.3%
27	New Mexico	2,469	1.2%
28	Colorado	2,202	1.1%
29	Nebraska	2,176	1.1%
30	Alabama	2,129	1.0%
31	Maryland	1,624	0.8%
32	Nevada	1,590	0.8%
33	West Virginia	1,514	0.7%
34	Utah	951	0.5%
35	Hawaii	739	0.4%
36	Alaska	716	0.4%
37	Mississippi	634	0.3%
38	Idaho	471	0.2%
39	Minnesota	440	0.2%
40	Delaware	391	0.2%
41	Wyoming	331	0.2%
42	Rhode Island	251	0.1%
43	South Dakota	153	0.1%
44	New Hampshire	128	0.1%
45	Montana	119	0.1%
46	Vermont	115	0.1%
47	North Dakota	98	0.0%
48	Kansas	69	0.0%
NA	Illinois**	NA	NA
NA	Maine**	NA	NA
	District of Columbia	394	0.2%

Source: Federal Bureau of Investigation
  "Crime in the United States 1999" (Uniform Crime Reports, October 15, 2000)
*Of the 702,391 aggravated assaults in 1999 for which supplemental data were received by the F.B.I. There were
an additional 213,992 aggravated assaults for which the type of weapon was not reported to the F.B.I. Aggravated
assault is an attack for the purpose of inflicting severe bodily injury. Numbers are for reporting jurisdictions only.
**Not available.

Percent of Aggravated Assaults Committed with Hands, Fists or Feet in 1999

National Percent = 28.9% of Aggravated Assaults*

ALPHA ORDER

RANK	STATE	PERCENT
24	Alabama	31.4
27	Alaska	29.6
28	Arizona	28.5
16	Arkansas	37.2
10	California	41.7
30	Colorado	26.9
11	Connecticut	40.0
47	Delaware	11.2
41	Florida	18.3
33	Georgia	23.7
1	Hawaii	55.0
39	Idaho	19.9
NA	Illinois**	NA
12	Indiana	39.6
4	Iowa	46.9
48	Kansas	6.7
3	Kentucky	47.7
31	Louisiana	25.3
NA	Maine**	NA
36	Maryland	20.4
14	Massachusetts	38.1
45	Michigan	14.3
42	Minnesota	18.0
35	Mississippi	21.7
43	Missouri	17.9
40	Montana	18.9
9	Nebraska	41.8
22	Nevada	31.8
8	New Hampshire	43.7
23	New Jersey	31.5
25	New Mexico	30.8
5	New York	46.0
38	North Carolina	20.1
2	North Dakota	48.0
18	Ohio	35.3
21	Oklahoma	32.6
20	Oregon	34.3
15	Pennsylvania	37.5
44	Rhode Island	17.0
32	South Carolina	24.4
34	South Dakota	23.2
46	Tennessee	13.0
37	Texas	20.2
26	Utah	30.4
19	Vermont	34.4
17	Virginia	35.9
29	Washington	28.3
7	West Virginia	44.6
6	Wisconsin	45.1
13	Wyoming	39.2

RANK ORDER

RANK	STATE	PERCENT
1	Hawaii	55.0
2	North Dakota	48.0
3	Kentucky	47.7
4	Iowa	46.9
5	New York	46.0
6	Wisconsin	45.1
7	West Virginia	44.6
8	New Hampshire	43.7
9	Nebraska	41.8
10	California	41.7
11	Connecticut	40.0
12	Indiana	39.6
13	Wyoming	39.2
14	Massachusetts	38.1
15	Pennsylvania	37.5
16	Arkansas	37.2
17	Virginia	35.9
18	Ohio	35.3
19	Vermont	34.4
20	Oregon	34.3
21	Oklahoma	32.6
22	Nevada	31.8
23	New Jersey	31.5
24	Alabama	31.4
25	New Mexico	30.8
26	Utah	30.4
27	Alaska	29.6
28	Arizona	28.5
29	Washington	28.3
30	Colorado	26.9
31	Louisiana	25.3
32	South Carolina	24.4
33	Georgia	23.7
34	South Dakota	23.2
35	Mississippi	21.7
36	Maryland	20.4
37	Texas	20.2
38	North Carolina	20.1
39	Idaho	19.9
40	Montana	18.9
41	Florida	18.3
42	Minnesota	18.0
43	Missouri	17.9
44	Rhode Island	17.0
45	Michigan	14.3
46	Tennessee	13.0
47	Delaware	11.2
48	Kansas	6.7
NA	Illinois**	NA
NA	Maine**	NA
	District of Columbia	8.5

Source: Morgan Quitno Press using data from Federal Bureau of Investigation
"Crime in the United States 1999" (Uniform Crime Reports, October 15, 2000)
*Of the 702,391 aggravated assaults in 1999 for which supplemental data were received by the F.B.I. There were an additional 213,992 aggravated assaults for which the type of weapon was not reported to the F.B.I. Aggravated assault is an attack for the purpose of inflicting severe bodily injury. Numbers are for reporting jurisdictions only.
**Not available.

Property Crimes in 1999

National Total = 10,204,456 Property Crimes*

ALPHA ORDER

RANK	STATE	CRIMES	% of USA
21	Alabama	171,398	1.7%
46	Alaska	23,099	0.2%
12	Arizona	255,401	2.5%
33	Arkansas	92,283	0.9%
1	California	1,053,285	10.3%
26	Colorado	151,002	1.5%
32	Connecticut	99,894	1.0%
44	Delaware	30,922	0.3%
3	Florida	808,674	7.9%
8	Georgia	359,383	3.5%
38	Hawaii	54,539	0.5%
40	Idaho	36,363	0.4%
5	Illinois	457,723	4.5%
19	Indiana	201,547	2.0%
35	Iowa	84,463	0.8%
29	Kansas	107,644	1.1%
30	Kentucky	102,095	1.0%
16	Louisiana	219,219	2.1%
41	Maine	34,618	0.3%
17	Maryland	215,973	2.1%
22	Massachusetts	167,437	1.6%
7	Michigan	369,887	3.6%
24	Minnesota	158,717	1.6%
28	Mississippi	108,560	1.1%
14	Missouri	223,010	2.2%
42	Montana	34,114	0.3%
37	Nebraska	61,277	0.6%
36	Nevada	73,874	0.7%
45	New Hampshire	26,247	0.3%
13	New Jersey	243,333	2.4%
34	New Mexico	89,220	0.9%
4	New York	489,596	4.8%
9	North Carolina	354,497	3.5%
50	North Dakota	14,748	0.1%
6	Ohio	414,264	4.1%
27	Oklahoma	140,220	1.4%
25	Oregon	153,434	1.5%
10	Pennsylvania	323,021	3.2%
43	Rhode Island	32,657	0.3%
20	South Carolina	173,987	1.7%
47	South Dakota	18,159	0.2%
15	Tennessee	219,302	2.1%
2	Texas	896,261	8.8%
31	Utah	100,130	1.0%
48	Vermont	16,059	0.2%
18	Virginia	210,260	2.1%
11	Washington	280,793	2.8%
39	West Virginia	42,825	0.4%
23	Wisconsin	160,154	1.6%
49	Wyoming	15,468	0.2%

RANK ORDER

RANK	STATE	CRIMES	% of USA
1	California	1,053,285	10.3%
2	Texas	896,261	8.8%
3	Florida	808,674	7.9%
4	New York	489,596	4.8%
5	Illinois	457,723	4.5%
6	Ohio	414,264	4.1%
7	Michigan	369,887	3.6%
8	Georgia	359,383	3.5%
9	North Carolina	354,497	3.5%
10	Pennsylvania	323,021	3.2%
11	Washington	280,793	2.8%
12	Arizona	255,401	2.5%
13	New Jersey	243,333	2.4%
14	Missouri	223,010	2.2%
15	Tennessee	219,302	2.1%
16	Louisiana	219,219	2.1%
17	Maryland	215,973	2.1%
18	Virginia	210,260	2.1%
19	Indiana	201,547	2.0%
20	South Carolina	173,987	1.7%
21	Alabama	171,398	1.7%
22	Massachusetts	167,437	1.6%
23	Wisconsin	160,154	1.6%
24	Minnesota	158,717	1.6%
25	Oregon	153,434	1.5%
26	Colorado	151,002	1.5%
27	Oklahoma	140,220	1.4%
28	Mississippi	108,560	1.1%
29	Kansas	107,644	1.1%
30	Kentucky	102,095	1.0%
31	Utah	100,130	1.0%
32	Connecticut	99,894	1.0%
33	Arkansas	92,283	0.9%
34	New Mexico	89,220	0.9%
35	Iowa	84,463	0.8%
36	Nevada	73,874	0.7%
37	Nebraska	61,277	0.6%
38	Hawaii	54,539	0.5%
39	West Virginia	42,825	0.4%
40	Idaho	36,363	0.4%
41	Maine	34,618	0.3%
42	Montana	34,114	0.3%
43	Rhode Island	32,657	0.3%
44	Delaware	30,922	0.3%
45	New Hampshire	26,247	0.3%
46	Alaska	23,099	0.2%
47	South Dakota	18,159	0.2%
48	Vermont	16,059	0.2%
49	Wyoming	15,468	0.2%
50	North Dakota	14,748	0.1%
	District of Columbia	33,420	0.3%

Source: Federal Bureau of Investigation
"Crime in the United States 1999" (Uniform Crime Reports, October 15, 2000)
*Property crimes are offenses of burglary, larceny-theft and motor vehicle theft.

Average Time Between Property Crimes in 1999

National Rate = A Property Crime Occurs Every 3 Seconds*

ALPHA ORDER

RANK ORDER

RANK	STATE	MINUTES.SECONDS
30	Alabama	3.04
5	Alaska	22.45
39	Arizona	2.04
18	Arkansas	5.42
50	California	0.30
25	Colorado	3.29
19	Connecticut	5.16
7	Delaware	17.00
48	Florida	0.39
43	Georgia	1.28
13	Hawaii	9.38
11	Idaho	14.27
46	Illinois	1.09
32	Indiana	2.37
16	Iowa	6.13
22	Kansas	4.53
21	Kentucky	5.09
35	Louisiana	2.24
10	Maine	15.11
34	Maryland	2.26
29	Massachusetts	3.08
44	Michigan	1.25
27	Minnesota	3.19
23	Mississippi	4.50
37	Missouri	2.22
9	Montana	15.25
14	Nebraska	8.35
15	Nevada	7.07
6	New Hampshire	20.02
38	New Jersey	2.10
17	New Mexico	5.53
47	New York	1.04
42	North Carolina	1.29
1	North Dakota	35.38
45	Ohio	1.16
24	Oklahoma	3.45
26	Oregon	3.26
41	Pennsylvania	1.38
8	Rhode Island	16.05
31	South Carolina	3.01
4	South Dakota	28.56
35	Tennessee	2.24
49	Texas	0.35
20	Utah	5.15
3	Vermont	32.44
33	Virginia	2.30
40	Washington	1.52
12	West Virginia	12.16
28	Wisconsin	3.17
2	Wyoming	33.59

RANK	STATE	MINUTES.SECONDS
1	North Dakota	35.38
2	Wyoming	33.59
3	Vermont	32.44
4	South Dakota	28.56
5	Alaska	22.45
6	New Hampshire	20.02
7	Delaware	17.00
8	Rhode Island	16.05
9	Montana	15.25
10	Maine	15.11
11	Idaho	14.27
12	West Virginia	12.16
13	Hawaii	9.38
14	Nebraska	8.35
15	Nevada	7.07
16	Iowa	6.13
17	New Mexico	5.53
18	Arkansas	5.42
19	Connecticut	5.16
20	Utah	5.15
21	Kentucky	5.09
22	Kansas	4.53
23	Mississippi	4.50
24	Oklahoma	3.45
25	Colorado	3.29
26	Oregon	3.26
27	Minnesota	3.19
28	Wisconsin	3.17
29	Massachusetts	3.08
30	Alabama	3.04
31	South Carolina	3.01
32	Indiana	2.37
33	Virginia	2.30
34	Maryland	2.26
35	Louisiana	2.24
35	Tennessee	2.24
37	Missouri	2.22
38	New Jersey	2.10
39	Arizona	2.04
40	Washington	1.52
41	Pennsylvania	1.38
42	North Carolina	1.29
43	Georgia	1.28
44	Michigan	1.25
45	Ohio	1.16
46	Illinois	1.09
47	New York	1.04
48	Florida	0.39
49	Texas	0.35
50	California	0.30

District of Columbia   15.44

Source: Morgan Quitno Press using data from Federal Bureau of Investigation
"Crime in the United States 1999" (Uniform Crime Reports, October 15, 2000)
*Property crimes are offenses of burglary, larceny-theft and motor vehicle theft.

Property Crimes per Square Mile in 1999

National Rate = 2.7 Property Crimes per Square Mile*

ALPHA ORDER				RANK ORDER		
RANK	STATE	RATE		RANK	STATE	RATE
24	Alabama	3.3		1	New Jersey	29.6
50	Alaska	0.0		2	Rhode Island	26.5
29	Arizona	2.2		3	Massachusetts	18.1
34	Arkansas	1.7		4	Connecticut	18.0
14	California	6.6		5	Maryland	17.6
37	Colorado	1.5		6	Florida	13.5
4	Connecticut	18.0		7	Delaware	12.9
7	Delaware	12.9		8	Ohio	9.2
6	Florida	13.5		9	New York	9.1
15	Georgia	6.1		10	Hawaii	8.4
10	Hawaii	8.4		11	Illinois	7.9
45	Idaho	0.4		12	Pennsylvania	7.0
11	Illinois	7.9		13	North Carolina	6.7
17	Indiana	5.5		14	California	6.6
37	Iowa	1.5		15	Georgia	6.1
39	Kansas	1.3		16	South Carolina	5.6
27	Kentucky	2.5		17	Indiana	5.5
20	Louisiana	4.4		18	Tennessee	5.2
41	Maine	1.0		19	Virginia	5.0
5	Maryland	17.6		20	Louisiana	4.4
3	Massachusetts	18.1		21	Washington	4.0
22	Michigan	3.8		22	Michigan	3.8
32	Minnesota	1.8		23	Texas	3.4
29	Mississippi	2.2		24	Alabama	3.3
25	Missouri	3.2		25	Missouri	3.2
46	Montana	0.2		26	New Hampshire	2.8
42	Nebraska	0.8		27	Kentucky	2.5
43	Nevada	0.7		28	Wisconsin	2.4
26	New Hampshire	2.8		29	Arizona	2.2
1	New Jersey	29.6		29	Mississippi	2.2
43	New Mexico	0.7		31	Oklahoma	2.0
9	New York	9.1		32	Minnesota	1.8
13	North Carolina	6.7		32	West Virginia	1.8
46	North Dakota	0.2		34	Arkansas	1.7
8	Ohio	9.2		34	Vermont	1.7
31	Oklahoma	2.0		36	Oregon	1.6
36	Oregon	1.6		37	Colorado	1.5
12	Pennsylvania	7.0		37	Iowa	1.5
2	Rhode Island	26.5		39	Kansas	1.3
16	South Carolina	5.6		40	Utah	1.2
46	South Dakota	0.2		41	Maine	1.0
18	Tennessee	5.2		42	Nebraska	0.8
23	Texas	3.4		43	Nevada	0.7
40	Utah	1.2		43	New Mexico	0.7
34	Vermont	1.7		45	Idaho	0.4
19	Virginia	5.0		46	Montana	0.2
21	Washington	4.0		46	North Dakota	0.2
32	West Virginia	1.8		46	South Dakota	0.2
28	Wisconsin	2.4		46	Wyoming	0.2
46	Wyoming	0.2		50	Alaska	0.0

District of Columbia   491.5

Source: Morgan Quitno Press using data from Federal Bureau of Investigation
"Crime in the United States 1999" (Uniform Crime Reports, October 15, 2000)
*Property crimes are offenses of burglary, larceny-theft and motor vehicle theft.

Percent Change in Number of Property Crimes: 1998 to 1999

National Percent Change = 6.8% Decrease*

ALPHA ORDER

RANK	STATE	PERCENT CHANGE
7	Alabama	(3.6)
34	Alaska	(8.8)
34	Arizona	(8.8)
10	Arkansas	(4.1)
48	California	(11.4)
27	Colorado	(7.5)
45	Connecticut	(10.8)
39	Delaware	(9.7)
34	Florida	(8.8)
8	Georgia	(3.8)
41	Hawaii	(10.1)
49	Idaho	(13.8)
15	Illinois	(6.2)
32	Indiana	(8.6)
27	Iowa	(7.5)
30	Kansas	(8.1)
24	Kentucky	(7.0)
14	Louisiana	(5.7)
12	Maine	(4.5)
29	Maryland	(7.9)
6	Massachusetts	(3.2)
25	Michigan	(7.2)
41	Minnesota	(10.1)
4	Mississippi	(0.7)
9	Missouri	(4.0)
18	Montana	(6.7)
20	Nebraska	(6.8)
34	Nevada	(8.8)
11	New Hampshire	(4.2)
18	New Jersey	(6.7)
45	New Mexico	(10.8)
33	New York	(8.7)
5	North Carolina	(0.9)
45	North Dakota	(10.8)
20	Ohio	(6.8)
15	Oklahoma	(6.2)
44	Oregon	(10.6)
13	Pennsylvania	(5.6)
1	Rhode Island	3.1
22	South Carolina	(6.9)
3	South Dakota	(0.4)
17	Tennessee	(6.5)
2	Texas	(0.2)
31	Utah	(8.2)
43	Vermont	(10.4)
25	Virginia	(7.2)
38	Washington	(9.3)
NA	West Virginia**	NA
22	Wisconsin	(6.9)
39	Wyoming	(9.7)

RANK ORDER

RANK	STATE	PERCENT CHANGE
1	Rhode Island	3.1
2	Texas	(0.2)
3	South Dakota	(0.4)
4	Mississippi	(0.7)
5	North Carolina	(0.9)
6	Massachusetts	(3.2)
7	Alabama	(3.6)
8	Georgia	(3.8)
9	Missouri	(4.0)
10	Arkansas	(4.1)
11	New Hampshire	(4.2)
12	Maine	(4.5)
13	Pennsylvania	(5.6)
14	Louisiana	(5.7)
15	Illinois	(6.2)
15	Oklahoma	(6.2)
17	Tennessee	(6.5)
18	Montana	(6.7)
18	New Jersey	(6.7)
20	Nebraska	(6.8)
20	Ohio	(6.8)
22	South Carolina	(6.9)
22	Wisconsin	(6.9)
24	Kentucky	(7.0)
25	Michigan	(7.2)
25	Virginia	(7.2)
27	Colorado	(7.5)
27	Iowa	(7.5)
29	Maryland	(7.9)
30	Kansas	(8.1)
31	Utah	(8.2)
32	Indiana	(8.6)
33	New York	(8.7)
34	Alaska	(8.8)
34	Arizona	(8.8)
34	Florida	(8.8)
34	Nevada	(8.8)
38	Washington	(9.3)
39	Delaware	(9.7)
39	Wyoming	(9.7)
41	Hawaii	(10.1)
41	Minnesota	(10.1)
43	Vermont	(10.4)
44	Oregon	(10.6)
45	Connecticut	(10.8)
45	New Mexico	(10.8)
45	North Dakota	(10.8)
48	California	(11.4)
49	Idaho	(13.8)
NA	West Virginia**	NA

	District of Columbia	(10.2)

Source: Federal Bureau of Investigation
"Crime in the United States 1999" (Uniform Crime Reports, October 15, 2000)
*Property crimes are offenses of burglary, larceny-theft and motor vehicle theft.
**Not available.

Property Crime Rate in 1999

National Rate = 3,742.1 Property Crimes per 100,000 Population*

ALPHA ORDER

RANK	STATE	RATE
20	Alabama	3,922.2
25	Alaska	3,731.7
2	Arizona	5,345.4
29	Arkansas	3,617.5
34	California	3,177.8
26	Colorado	3,722.9
37	Connecticut	3,043.7
15	Delaware	4,101.1
1	Florida	5,351.6
9	Georgia	4,614.6
10	Hawaii	4,602.4
40	Idaho	2,904.4
23	Illinois	3,774.1
30	Indiana	3,391.3
39	Iowa	2,944.0
18	Kansas	4,055.9
46	Kentucky	2,577.5
4	Louisiana	5,014.2
41	Maine	2,762.8
13	Maryland	4,175.8
42	Massachusetts	2,711.5
24	Michigan	3,749.9
31	Minnesota	3,323.2
21	Mississippi	3,920.5
17	Missouri	4,078.5
22	Montana	3,863.4
28	Nebraska	3,678.1
16	Nevada	4,083.7
50	New Hampshire	2,185.4
38	New Jersey	2,988.2
3	New Mexico	5,127.6
45	New York	2,690.5
7	North Carolina	4,633.3
49	North Dakota	2,326.2
27	Ohio	3,680.1
14	Oklahoma	4,175.7
8	Oregon	4,627.1
44	Pennsylvania	2,693.2
32	Rhode Island	3,295.4
11	South Carolina	4,477.3
47	South Dakota	2,477.4
19	Tennessee	3,998.9
12	Texas	4,471.5
6	Utah	4,700.9
43	Vermont	2,703.5
35	Virginia	3,059.2
5	Washington	4,878.3
48	West Virginia	2,370.0
36	Wisconsin	3,050.6
33	Wyoming	3,222.5

RANK ORDER

RANK	STATE	RATE
1	Florida	5,351.6
2	Arizona	5,345.4
3	New Mexico	5,127.6
4	Louisiana	5,014.2
5	Washington	4,878.3
6	Utah	4,700.9
7	North Carolina	4,633.3
8	Oregon	4,627.1
9	Georgia	4,614.6
10	Hawaii	4,602.4
11	South Carolina	4,477.3
12	Texas	4,471.5
13	Maryland	4,175.8
14	Oklahoma	4,175.7
15	Delaware	4,101.1
16	Nevada	4,083.7
17	Missouri	4,078.5
18	Kansas	4,055.9
19	Tennessee	3,998.9
20	Alabama	3,922.2
21	Mississippi	3,920.5
22	Montana	3,863.4
23	Illinois	3,774.1
24	Michigan	3,749.9
25	Alaska	3,731.7
26	Colorado	3,722.9
27	Ohio	3,680.1
28	Nebraska	3,678.1
29	Arkansas	3,617.5
30	Indiana	3,391.3
31	Minnesota	3,323.2
32	Rhode Island	3,295.4
33	Wyoming	3,222.5
34	California	3,177.8
35	Virginia	3,059.2
36	Wisconsin	3,050.6
37	Connecticut	3,043.7
38	New Jersey	2,988.2
39	Iowa	2,944.0
40	Idaho	2,904.4
41	Maine	2,762.8
42	Massachusetts	2,711.5
43	Vermont	2,703.5
44	Pennsylvania	2,693.2
45	New York	2,690.5
46	Kentucky	2,577.5
47	South Dakota	2,477.4
48	West Virginia	2,370.0
49	North Dakota	2,326.2
50	New Hampshire	2,185.4
	District of Columbia	6,439.3

Source: Federal Bureau of Investigation
   "Crime in the United States 1999" (Uniform Crime Reports, October 15, 2000)
*Property crimes are offenses of burglary, larceny-theft and motor vehicle theft.

Percent Change in Property Crime Rate: 1998 to 1999

National Percent Change = 7.6% Decrease*

ALPHA ORDER

RANK	STATE	PERCENT CHANGE
7	Alabama	(4.0)
33	Alaska	(9.5)
40	Arizona	(10.9)
9	Arkansas	(4.6)
48	California	(12.7)
32	Colorado	(9.4)
44	Connecticut	(11.0)
40	Delaware	(10.9)
37	Florida	(10.0)
12	Georgia	(5.6)
33	Hawaii	(9.5)
49	Idaho	(15.4)
16	Illinois	(6.8)
31	Indiana	(9.3)
24	Iowa	(7.7)
30	Kansas	(9.0)
23	Kentucky	(7.5)
14	Louisiana	(5.7)
10	Maine	(5.2)
28	Maryland	(8.6)
6	Massachusetts	(3.7)
24	Michigan	(7.7)
45	Minnesota	(11.1)
3	Mississippi	(1.3)
8	Missouri	(4.5)
17	Montana	(7.0)
17	Nebraska	(7.0)
47	Nevada	(11.9)
11	New Hampshire	(5.5)
17	New Jersey	(7.0)
40	New Mexico	(10.9)
29	New York	(8.8)
5	North Carolina	(2.3)
38	North Dakota	(10.2)
20	Ohio	(7.2)
15	Oklahoma	(6.5)
46	Oregon	(11.5)
12	Pennsylvania	(5.6)
1	Rhode Island	2.8
26	South Carolina	(8.1)
2	South Dakota	0.3
21	Tennessee	(7.4)
4	Texas	(1.7)
33	Utah	(9.5)
40	Vermont	(10.9)
27	Virginia	(8.3)
39	Washington	(10.3)
NA	West Virginia**	NA
21	Wisconsin	(7.4)
33	Wyoming	(9.5)

RANK ORDER

RANK	STATE	PERCENT CHANGE
1	Rhode Island	2.8
2	South Dakota	0.3
3	Mississippi	(1.3)
4	Texas	(1.7)
5	North Carolina	(2.3)
6	Massachusetts	(3.7)
7	Alabama	(4.0)
8	Missouri	(4.5)
9	Arkansas	(4.6)
10	Maine	(5.2)
11	New Hampshire	(5.5)
12	Georgia	(5.6)
12	Pennsylvania	(5.6)
14	Louisiana	(5.7)
15	Oklahoma	(6.5)
16	Illinois	(6.8)
17	Montana	(7.0)
17	Nebraska	(7.0)
17	New Jersey	(7.0)
20	Ohio	(7.2)
21	Tennessee	(7.4)
21	Wisconsin	(7.4)
23	Kentucky	(7.5)
24	Iowa	(7.7)
24	Michigan	(7.7)
26	South Carolina	(8.1)
27	Virginia	(8.3)
28	Maryland	(8.6)
29	New York	(8.8)
30	Kansas	(9.0)
31	Indiana	(9.3)
32	Colorado	(9.4)
33	Alaska	(9.5)
33	Hawaii	(9.5)
33	Utah	(9.5)
33	Wyoming	(9.5)
37	Florida	(10.0)
38	North Dakota	(10.2)
39	Washington	(10.3)
40	Arizona	(10.9)
40	Delaware	(10.9)
40	New Mexico	(10.9)
40	Vermont	(10.9)
44	Connecticut	(11.0)
45	Minnesota	(11.1)
46	Oregon	(11.5)
47	Nevada	(11.9)
48	California	(12.7)
49	Idaho	(15.4)
NA	West Virginia**	NA
	District of Columbia	(9.5)

Source: Federal Bureau of Investigation
   "Crime in the United States 1999" (Uniform Crime Reports, October 15, 2000)
*Property crimes are offenses of burglary, larceny-theft and motor vehicle theft.
**Not available.

Burglaries in 1999

National Total = 2,099,739 Burglaries*

ALPHA ORDER

RANK	STATE	BURGLARIES	% of USA
20	Alabama	38,648	1.8%
44	Alaska	3,787	0.2%
13	Arizona	49,423	2.4%
31	Arkansas	21,692	1.0%
1	California	223,814	10.7%
26	Colorado	26,979	1.3%
33	Connecticut	19,298	0.9%
43	Delaware	5,245	0.2%
3	Florida	181,378	8.6%
9	Georgia	71,429	3.4%
39	Hawaii	9,421	0.4%
40	Idaho	7,641	0.4%
7	Illinois	86,390	4.1%
18	Indiana	42,463	2.0%
35	Iowa	17,012	0.8%
30	Kansas	21,874	1.0%
29	Kentucky	24,199	1.2%
14	Louisiana	47,775	2.3%
41	Maine	7,532	0.4%
16	Maryland	43,230	2.1%
22	Massachusetts	32,964	1.6%
8	Michigan	76,736	3.7%
25	Minnesota	27,706	1.3%
24	Mississippi	29,109	1.4%
17	Missouri	42,476	2.0%
45	Montana	3,784	0.2%
38	Nebraska	10,158	0.5%
34	Nevada	17,613	0.8%
46	New Hampshire	3,698	0.2%
15	New Jersey	46,998	2.2%
32	New Mexico	21,481	1.0%
5	New York	93,217	4.4%
4	North Carolina	98,457	4.7%
50	North Dakota	2,337	0.1%
6	Ohio	87,023	4.1%
21	Oklahoma	34,472	1.6%
27	Oregon	26,749	1.3%
10	Pennsylvania	56,037	2.7%
42	Rhode Island	6,341	0.3%
19	South Carolina	39,630	1.9%
48	South Dakota	3,255	0.2%
12	Tennessee	51,362	2.4%
2	Texas	190,362	9.1%
36	Utah	14,592	0.7%
47	Vermont	3,537	0.2%
23	Virginia	32,411	1.5%
11	Washington	54,652	2.6%
37	West Virginia	10,303	0.5%
28	Wisconsin	25,633	1.2%
49	Wyoming	2,349	0.1%

RANK ORDER

RANK	STATE	BURGLARIES	% of USA
1	California	223,814	10.7%
2	Texas	190,362	9.1%
3	Florida	181,378	8.6%
4	North Carolina	98,457	4.7%
5	New York	93,217	4.4%
6	Ohio	87,023	4.1%
7	Illinois	86,390	4.1%
8	Michigan	76,736	3.7%
9	Georgia	71,429	3.4%
10	Pennsylvania	56,037	2.7%
11	Washington	54,652	2.6%
12	Tennessee	51,362	2.4%
13	Arizona	49,423	2.4%
14	Louisiana	47,775	2.3%
15	New Jersey	46,998	2.2%
16	Maryland	43,230	2.1%
17	Missouri	42,476	2.0%
18	Indiana	42,463	2.0%
19	South Carolina	39,630	1.9%
20	Alabama	38,648	1.8%
21	Oklahoma	34,472	1.6%
22	Massachusetts	32,964	1.6%
23	Virginia	32,411	1.5%
24	Mississippi	29,109	1.4%
25	Minnesota	27,706	1.3%
26	Colorado	26,979	1.3%
27	Oregon	26,749	1.3%
28	Wisconsin	25,633	1.2%
29	Kentucky	24,199	1.2%
30	Kansas	21,874	1.0%
31	Arkansas	21,692	1.0%
32	New Mexico	21,481	1.0%
33	Connecticut	19,298	0.9%
34	Nevada	17,613	0.8%
35	Iowa	17,012	0.8%
36	Utah	14,592	0.7%
37	West Virginia	10,303	0.5%
38	Nebraska	10,158	0.5%
39	Hawaii	9,421	0.4%
40	Idaho	7,641	0.4%
41	Maine	7,532	0.4%
42	Rhode Island	6,341	0.3%
43	Delaware	5,245	0.2%
44	Alaska	3,787	0.2%
45	Montana	3,784	0.2%
46	New Hampshire	3,698	0.2%
47	Vermont	3,537	0.2%
48	South Dakota	3,255	0.2%
49	Wyoming	2,349	0.1%
50	North Dakota	2,337	0.1%
	District of Columbia	5,067	0.2%

Source: Federal Bureau of Investigation
"Crime in the United States 1999" (Uniform Crime Reports, October 15, 2000)
*Burglary is the unlawful entry of a structure to commit a felony or theft. Attempts are included.

Average Time Between Burglaries in 1999

National Rate = A Burglary Occurs Every 15 Seconds*

ALPHA ORDER

RANK ORDER

RANK	STATE	MINUTES.SECONDS
31	Alabama	13.36
7	Alaska	138.47
38	Arizona	10.38
20	Arkansas	24.14
50	California	2.21
25	Colorado	19.29
18	Connecticut	27.14
8	Delaware	100.13
48	Florida	2.54
42	Georgia	7.22
12	Hawaii	55.47
11	Idaho	68.47
44	Illinois	6.05
33	Indiana	12.23
16	Iowa	30.54
21	Kansas	24.02
22	Kentucky	21.43
37	Louisiana	11.00
10	Maine	69.47
35	Maryland	12.10
29	Massachusetts	15.56
43	Michigan	6.51
26	Minnesota	18.58
27	Mississippi	18.04
34	Missouri	12.22
6	Montana	138.54
13	Nebraska	51.44
17	Nevada	29.50
5	New Hampshire	142.08
36	New Jersey	11.11
19	New Mexico	24.28
46	New York	5.38
47	North Carolina	5.20
1	North Dakota	224.54
45	Ohio	6.02
30	Oklahoma	15.15
24	Oregon	19.39
41	Pennsylvania	9.23
9	Rhode Island	82.53
32	South Carolina	13.16
3	South Dakota	161.28
39	Tennessee	10.14
49	Texas	2.46
15	Utah	36.01
4	Vermont	148.36
28	Virginia	16.13
40	Washington	9.37
14	West Virginia	51.01
23	Wisconsin	20.30
2	Wyoming	223.45

RANK	STATE	MINUTES.SECONDS
1	North Dakota	224.54
2	Wyoming	223.45
3	South Dakota	161.28
4	Vermont	148.36
5	New Hampshire	142.08
6	Montana	138.54
7	Alaska	138.47
8	Delaware	100.13
9	Rhode Island	82.53
10	Maine	69.47
11	Idaho	68.47
12	Hawaii	55.47
13	Nebraska	51.44
14	West Virginia	51.01
15	Utah	36.01
16	Iowa	30.54
17	Nevada	29.50
18	Connecticut	27.14
19	New Mexico	24.28
20	Arkansas	24.14
21	Kansas	24.02
22	Kentucky	21.43
23	Wisconsin	20.30
24	Oregon	19.39
25	Colorado	19.29
26	Minnesota	18.58
27	Mississippi	18.04
28	Virginia	16.13
29	Massachusetts	15.56
30	Oklahoma	15.15
31	Alabama	13.36
32	South Carolina	13.16
33	Indiana	12.23
34	Missouri	12.22
35	Maryland	12.10
36	New Jersey	11.11
37	Louisiana	11.00
38	Arizona	10.38
39	Tennessee	10.14
40	Washington	9.37
41	Pennsylvania	9.23
42	Georgia	7.22
43	Michigan	6.51
44	Illinois	6.05
45	Ohio	6.02
46	New York	5.38
47	North Carolina	5.20
48	Florida	2.54
49	Texas	2.46
50	California	2.21
	District of Columbia	103.44

Source: Morgan Quitno Press using data from Federal Bureau of Investigation
"Crime in the United States 1999" (Uniform Crime Reports, October 15, 2000)
*Burglary is the unlawful entry of a structure to commit a felony or theft. Attempts are included.

Percent Change in Number of Burglaries: 1998 to 1999

National Percent Change = 10.0% Decrease*

RANK	STATE	PERCENT CHANGE
14	Alabama	(7.9)
12	Alaska	(7.6)
37	Arizona	(12.5)
14	Arkansas	(7.9)
47	California	(16.8)
39	Colorado	(13.6)
29	Connecticut	(11.5)
49	Delaware	(18.0)
23	Florida	(10.7)
8	Georgia	(5.7)
46	Hawaii	(15.7)
21	Idaho	(10.3)
30	Illinois	(11.7)
16	Indiana	(8.8)
32	Iowa	(11.8)
36	Kansas	(12.4)
39	Kentucky	(13.6)
10	Louisiana	(6.7)
18	Maine	(9.2)
16	Maryland	(8.8)
30	Massachusetts	(11.7)
10	Michigan	(6.7)
44	Minnesota	(14.7)
12	Mississippi	(7.6)
22	Missouri	(10.5)
48	Montana	(17.3)
5	Nebraska	(3.7)
28	Nevada	(11.4)
6	New Hampshire	(4.0)
41	New Jersey	(13.7)
27	New Mexico	(11.3)
25	New York	(11.1)
2	North Carolina	(1.5)
1	North Dakota	2.8
7	Ohio	(4.2)
20	Oklahoma	(9.9)
33	Oregon	(12.1)
33	Pennsylvania	(12.1)
3	Rhode Island	(1.7)
25	South Carolina	(11.1)
9	South Dakota	(5.9)
33	Tennessee	(12.1)
4	Texas	(2.3)
43	Utah	(14.5)
24	Vermont	(10.8)
45	Virginia	(14.9)
19	Washington	(9.6)
NA	West Virginia**	NA
42	Wisconsin	(13.8)
38	Wyoming	(12.9)

RANK	STATE	PERCENT CHANGE
1	North Dakota	2.8
2	North Carolina	(1.5)
3	Rhode Island	(1.7)
4	Texas	(2.3)
5	Nebraska	(3.7)
6	New Hampshire	(4.0)
7	Ohio	(4.2)
8	Georgia	(5.7)
9	South Dakota	(5.9)
10	Louisiana	(6.7)
10	Michigan	(6.7)
12	Alaska	(7.6)
12	Mississippi	(7.6)
14	Alabama	(7.9)
14	Arkansas	(7.9)
16	Indiana	(8.8)
16	Maryland	(8.8)
18	Maine	(9.2)
19	Washington	(9.6)
20	Oklahoma	(9.9)
21	Idaho	(10.3)
22	Missouri	(10.5)
23	Florida	(10.7)
24	Vermont	(10.8)
25	New York	(11.1)
25	South Carolina	(11.1)
27	New Mexico	(11.3)
28	Nevada	(11.4)
29	Connecticut	(11.5)
30	Illinois	(11.7)
30	Massachusetts	(11.7)
32	Iowa	(11.8)
33	Oregon	(12.1)
33	Pennsylvania	(12.1)
33	Tennessee	(12.1)
36	Kansas	(12.4)
37	Arizona	(12.5)
38	Wyoming	(12.9)
39	Colorado	(13.6)
39	Kentucky	(13.6)
41	New Jersey	(13.7)
42	Wisconsin	(13.8)
43	Utah	(14.5)
44	Minnesota	(14.7)
45	Virginia	(14.9)
46	Hawaii	(15.7)
47	California	(16.8)
48	Montana	(17.3)
49	Delaware	(18.0)
NA	West Virginia**	NA

District of Columbia   (20.3)

Source: Federal Bureau of Investigation
   "Crime in the United States 1999" (Uniform Crime Reports, October 15, 2000)
Burglary is the unlawful entry of a structure to commit a felony or theft. Attempts are included.
***Not available.*

Burglary Rate in 1999

National Rate = 770.0 Burglaries per 100,000 Population*

ALPHA ORDER

RANK	STATE	RATE
14	Alabama	884.4
30	Alaska	611.8
6	Arizona	1,034.4
15	Arkansas	850.3
27	California	675.3
28	Colorado	665.2
37	Connecticut	588.0
25	Delaware	695.6
3	Florida	1,200.3
13	Georgia	917.2
19	Hawaii	795.0
32	Idaho	610.3
24	Illinois	712.3
23	Indiana	714.5
36	Iowa	593.0
17	Kansas	824.2
31	Kentucky	610.9
4	Louisiana	1,092.7
34	Maine	601.1
16	Maryland	835.8
41	Massachusetts	533.8
20	Michigan	777.9
38	Minnesota	580.1
5	Mississippi	1,051.2
21	Missouri	776.8
48	Montana	428.5
33	Nebraska	609.7
9	Nevada	973.6
50	New Hampshire	307.9
39	New Jersey	577.2
2	New Mexico	1,234.5
42	New York	512.3
1	North Carolina	1,286.9
49	North Dakota	368.6
22	Ohio	773.1
7	Oklahoma	1,026.6
18	Oregon	806.7
46	Pennsylvania	467.2
29	Rhode Island	639.9
8	South Carolina	1,019.8
47	South Dakota	444.1
12	Tennessee	936.6
10	Texas	949.7
26	Utah	685.1
35	Vermont	595.5
45	Virginia	471.6
11	Washington	949.5
40	West Virginia	570.2
44	Wisconsin	488.2
43	Wyoming	489.4

RANK ORDER

RANK	STATE	RATE
1	North Carolina	1,286.9
2	New Mexico	1,234.5
3	Florida	1,200.3
4	Louisiana	1,092.7
5	Mississippi	1,051.2
6	Arizona	1,034.4
7	Oklahoma	1,026.6
8	South Carolina	1,019.8
9	Nevada	973.6
10	Texas	949.7
11	Washington	949.5
12	Tennessee	936.6
13	Georgia	917.2
14	Alabama	884.4
15	Arkansas	850.3
16	Maryland	835.8
17	Kansas	824.2
18	Oregon	806.7
19	Hawaii	795.0
20	Michigan	777.9
21	Missouri	776.8
22	Ohio	773.1
23	Indiana	714.5
24	Illinois	712.3
25	Delaware	695.6
26	Utah	685.1
27	California	675.3
28	Colorado	665.2
29	Rhode Island	639.9
30	Alaska	611.8
31	Kentucky	610.9
32	Idaho	610.3
33	Nebraska	609.7
34	Maine	601.1
35	Vermont	595.5
36	Iowa	593.0
37	Connecticut	588.0
38	Minnesota	580.1
39	New Jersey	577.2
40	West Virginia	570.2
41	Massachusetts	533.8
42	New York	512.3
43	Wyoming	489.4
44	Wisconsin	488.2
45	Virginia	471.6
46	Pennsylvania	467.2
47	South Dakota	444.1
48	Montana	428.5
49	North Dakota	368.6
50	New Hampshire	307.9
	District of Columbia	976.3

Source: Federal Bureau of Investigation
"Crime in the United States 1999" (Uniform Crime Reports, October 15, 2000)
*Burglary is the unlawful entry of a structure to commit a felony or theft. Attempts are included.

Percent Change in Burglary Rate: 1998 to 1999

National Percent Change = 10.8% Decrease*

ALPHA ORDER				RANK ORDER		
RANK	STATE	PERCENT CHANGE		RANK	STATE	PERCENT CHANGE
13	Alabama	(8.3)		1	North Dakota	3.4
13	Alaska	(8.3)		2	Rhode Island	(2.0)
41	Arizona	(14.5)		3	North Carolina	(2.8)
15	Arkansas	(8.4)		4	Texas	(3.7)
48	California	(18.0)		5	Nebraska	(3.8)
43	Colorado	(15.4)		6	Ohio	(4.6)
25	Connecticut	(11.7)		7	South Dakota	(5.2)
49	Delaware	(19.1)		8	New Hampshire	(5.3)
26	Florida	(11.8)		9	Louisiana	(6.8)
11	Georgia	(7.4)		10	Michigan	(7.1)
42	Hawaii	(15.1)		11	Georgia	(7.4)
27	Idaho	(11.9)		12	Mississippi	(8.2)
31	Illinois	(12.3)		13	Alabama	(8.3)
17	Indiana	(9.5)		13	Alaska	(8.3)
28	Iowa	(12.0)		15	Arkansas	(8.4)
36	Kansas	(13.3)		16	Maryland	(9.4)
38	Kentucky	(14.1)		17	Indiana	(9.5)
9	Louisiana	(6.8)		18	Maine	(9.9)
18	Maine	(9.9)		19	Oklahoma	(10.2)
16	Maryland	(9.4)		20	Washington	(10.6)
29	Massachusetts	(12.1)		21	Missouri	(11.0)
10	Michigan	(7.1)		22	New York	(11.2)
44	Minnesota	(15.6)		23	Vermont	(11.3)
12	Mississippi	(8.2)		24	New Mexico	(11.4)
21	Missouri	(11.0)		25	Connecticut	(11.7)
47	Montana	(17.6)		26	Florida	(11.8)
5	Nebraska	(3.8)		27	Idaho	(11.9)
40	Nevada	(14.4)		28	Iowa	(12.0)
8	New Hampshire	(5.3)		29	Massachusetts	(12.1)
37	New Jersey	(14.0)		29	Pennsylvania	(12.1)
24	New Mexico	(11.4)		31	Illinois	(12.3)
22	New York	(11.2)		31	South Carolina	(12.3)
3	North Carolina	(2.8)		33	Wyoming	(12.7)
1	North Dakota	3.4		34	Tennessee	(12.9)
6	Ohio	(4.6)		35	Oregon	(13.0)
19	Oklahoma	(10.2)		36	Kansas	(13.3)
35	Oregon	(13.0)		37	New Jersey	(14.0)
29	Pennsylvania	(12.1)		38	Kentucky	(14.1)
2	Rhode Island	(2.0)		39	Wisconsin	(14.2)
31	South Carolina	(12.3)		40	Nevada	(14.4)
7	South Dakota	(5.2)		41	Arizona	(14.5)
34	Tennessee	(12.9)		42	Hawaii	(15.1)
4	Texas	(3.7)		43	Colorado	(15.4)
45	Utah	(15.7)		44	Minnesota	(15.6)
23	Vermont	(11.3)		45	Utah	(15.7)
46	Virginia	(15.9)		46	Virginia	(15.9)
20	Washington	(10.6)		47	Montana	(17.6)
NA	West Virginia**	NA		48	California	(18.0)
39	Wisconsin	(14.2)		49	Delaware	(19.1)
33	Wyoming	(12.7)		NA	West Virginia**	NA
					District of Columbia	(19.7)

Source: Federal Bureau of Investigation
   "Crime in the United States 1999" (Uniform Crime Reports, October 15, 2000)
*Burglary is the unlawful entry of a structure to commit a felony or theft. Attempts are included.
**Not available.

Larcenies and Thefts in 1999

National Total = 6,957,412 Larcenies and Thefts*

ALPHA ORDER

RANK	STATE	THEFTS	% of USA
22	Alabama	119,616	1.7%
46	Alaska	16,654	0.2%
12	Arizona	167,731	2.4%
33	Arkansas	63,927	0.9%
1	California	660,991	9.5%
25	Colorado	109,228	1.6%
30	Connecticut	69,299	1.0%
43	Delaware	22,634	0.3%
3	Florida	534,105	7.7%
7	Georgia	247,834	3.6%
38	Hawaii	40,458	0.6%
41	Idaho	26,824	0.4%
5	Illinois	319,219	4.6%
19	Indiana	138,794	2.0%
34	Iowa	62,316	0.9%
28	Kansas	79,722	1.1%
31	Kentucky	69,265	1.0%
16	Louisiana	149,749	2.2%
42	Maine	25,392	0.4%
17	Maryland	147,296	2.1%
26	Massachusetts	108,845	1.6%
8	Michigan	236,351	3.4%
23	Minnesota	117,736	1.7%
32	Mississippi	65,919	0.9%
15	Missouri	157,550	2.3%
40	Montana	28,434	0.4%
36	Nebraska	45,679	0.7%
37	Nevada	43,167	0.6%
45	New Hampshire	21,195	0.3%
13	New Jersey	160,978	2.3%
35	New Mexico	59,613	0.9%
4	New York	338,118	4.9%
9	North Carolina	230,463	3.3%
50	North Dakota	11,375	0.2%
6	Ohio	288,049	4.1%
27	Oklahoma	93,616	1.3%
24	Oregon	113,052	1.6%
10	Pennsylvania	227,750	3.3%
44	Rhode Island	22,284	0.3%
21	South Carolina	119,912	1.7%
47	South Dakota	14,043	0.2%
18	Tennessee	142,685	2.1%
2	Texas	613,862	8.8%
29	Utah	78,156	1.1%
49	Vermont	11,610	0.2%
14	Virginia	159,896	2.3%
11	Washington	192,334	2.8%
39	West Virginia	28,760	0.4%
20	Wisconsin	120,702	1.7%
48	Wyoming	12,523	0.2%

RANK ORDER

RANK	STATE	THEFTS	% of USA
1	California	660,991	9.5%
2	Texas	613,862	8.8%
3	Florida	534,105	7.7%
4	New York	338,118	4.9%
5	Illinois	319,219	4.6%
6	Ohio	288,049	4.1%
7	Georgia	247,834	3.6%
8	Michigan	236,351	3.4%
9	North Carolina	230,463	3.3%
10	Pennsylvania	227,750	3.3%
11	Washington	192,334	2.8%
12	Arizona	167,731	2.4%
13	New Jersey	160,978	2.3%
14	Virginia	159,896	2.3%
15	Missouri	157,550	2.3%
16	Louisiana	149,749	2.2%
17	Maryland	147,296	2.1%
18	Tennessee	142,685	2.1%
19	Indiana	138,794	2.0%
20	Wisconsin	120,702	1.7%
21	South Carolina	119,912	1.7%
22	Alabama	119,616	1.7%
23	Minnesota	117,736	1.7%
24	Oregon	113,052	1.6%
25	Colorado	109,228	1.6%
26	Massachusetts	108,845	1.6%
27	Oklahoma	93,616	1.3%
28	Kansas	79,722	1.1%
29	Utah	78,156	1.1%
30	Connecticut	69,299	1.0%
31	Kentucky	69,265	1.0%
32	Mississippi	65,919	0.9%
33	Arkansas	63,927	0.9%
34	Iowa	62,316	0.9%
35	New Mexico	59,613	0.9%
36	Nebraska	45,679	0.7%
37	Nevada	43,167	0.6%
38	Hawaii	40,458	0.6%
39	West Virginia	28,760	0.4%
40	Montana	28,434	0.4%
41	Idaho	26,824	0.4%
42	Maine	25,392	0.4%
43	Delaware	22,634	0.3%
44	Rhode Island	22,284	0.3%
45	New Hampshire	21,195	0.3%
46	Alaska	16,654	0.2%
47	South Dakota	14,043	0.2%
48	Wyoming	12,523	0.2%
49	Vermont	11,610	0.2%
50	North Dakota	11,375	0.2%
	District of Columbia	21,701	0.3%

Source: Federal Bureau of Investigation
"Crime in the United States 1999" (Uniform Crime Reports, October 15, 2000)
*Larceny and theft is the unlawful taking of property without use of force, violence or fraud. Attempts are included. Motor vehicle thefts are excluded.

Average Time Between Larcenies and Thefts in 1999

National Rate = A Larceny Occurs Every 5 Seconds*

ALPHA ORDER

RANK	STATE	MINUTES.SECONDS
29	Alabama	4.23
5	Alaska	31.34
39	Arizona	3.08
18	Arkansas	8.13
50	California	0.48
26	Colorado	4.49
20	Connecticut	7.35
8	Delaware	23.13
48	Florida	0.59
44	Georgia	2.07
13	Hawaii	12.59
10	Idaho	19.35
46	Illinois	1.39
32	Indiana	3.47
17	Iowa	8.26
23	Kansas	6.35
20	Kentucky	7.35
35	Louisiana	3.31
9	Maine	20.42
34	Maryland	3.34
25	Massachusetts	4.50
43	Michigan	2.13
28	Minnesota	4.28
19	Mississippi	7.58
36	Missouri	3.20
11	Montana	18.29
15	Nebraska	11.31
14	Nevada	12.11
6	New Hampshire	24.48
38	New Jersey	3.16
16	New Mexico	8.49
47	New York	1.33
42	North Carolina	2.17
1	North Dakota	46.13
45	Ohio	1.49
24	Oklahoma	5.37
27	Oregon	4.39
41	Pennsylvania	2.19
7	Rhode Island	23.35
29	South Carolina	4.23
4	South Dakota	37.26
33	Tennessee	3.41
49	Texas	0.52
22	Utah	6.44
2	Vermont	45.16
37	Virginia	3.17
40	Washington	2.44
12	West Virginia	18.17
31	Wisconsin	4.21
3	Wyoming	41.58

RANK ORDER

RANK	STATE	MINUTES.SECONDS
1	North Dakota	46.13
2	Vermont	45.16
3	Wyoming	41.58
4	South Dakota	37.26
5	Alaska	31.34
6	New Hampshire	24.48
7	Rhode Island	23.35
8	Delaware	23.13
9	Maine	20.42
10	Idaho	19.35
11	Montana	18.29
12	West Virginia	18.17
13	Hawaii	12.59
14	Nevada	12.11
15	Nebraska	11.31
16	New Mexico	8.49
17	Iowa	8.26
18	Arkansas	8.13
19	Mississippi	7.58
20	Connecticut	7.35
20	Kentucky	7.35
22	Utah	6.44
23	Kansas	6.35
24	Oklahoma	5.37
25	Massachusetts	4.50
26	Colorado	4.49
27	Oregon	4.39
28	Minnesota	4.28
29	Alabama	4.23
29	South Carolina	4.23
31	Wisconsin	4.21
32	Indiana	3.47
33	Tennessee	3.41
34	Maryland	3.34
35	Louisiana	3.31
36	Missouri	3.20
37	Virginia	3.17
38	New Jersey	3.16
39	Arizona	3.08
40	Washington	2.44
41	Pennsylvania	2.19
42	North Carolina	2.17
43	Michigan	2.13
44	Georgia	2.07
45	Ohio	1.49
46	Illinois	1.39
47	New York	1.33
48	Florida	0.59
49	Texas	0.52
50	California	0.48

District of Columbia 24.13

Source: Morgan Quitno Press using data from Federal Bureau of Investigation
"Crime in the United States 1999" (Uniform Crime Reports, October 15, 2000)
*Larceny and theft is the unlawful taking of property without use of force, violence or fraud. Attempts are included. Motor vehicle thefts are excluded.

Percent Change in Number of Larcenies and Thefts: 1998 to 1999

National Percent Change = 5.7% Decrease*

ALPHA ORDER

RANK	STATE	PERCENT CHANGE
5	Alabama	(1.1)
45	Alaska	(10.5)
36	Arizona	(8.4)
8	Arkansas	(2.4)
39	California	(8.7)
22	Colorado	(5.7)
45	Connecticut	(10.5)
34	Delaware	(8.2)
32	Florida	(7.9)
9	Georgia	(3.0)
32	Hawaii	(7.9)
49	Idaho	(14.5)
20	Illinois	(5.3)
43	Indiana	(9.2)
21	Iowa	(5.6)
26	Kansas	(6.6)
12	Kentucky	(3.8)
17	Louisiana	(4.9)
14	Maine	(4.0)
30	Maryland	(7.4)
4	Massachusetts	(0.4)
37	Michigan	(8.5)
37	Minnesota	(8.5)
12	Mississippi	(3.8)
7	Missouri	(1.8)
18	Montana	(5.0)
31	Nebraska	(7.6)
41	Nevada	(8.9)
14	New Hampshire	(4.0)
24	New Jersey	(6.0)
35	New Mexico	(8.3)
27	New York	(6.9)
6	North Carolina	(1.2)
48	North Dakota	(13.4)
29	Ohio	(7.3)
16	Oklahoma	(4.1)
39	Oregon	(8.7)
10	Pennsylvania	(3.4)
1	Rhode Island	4.2
19	South Carolina	(5.1)
3	South Dakota	0.3
11	Tennessee	(3.6)
2	Texas	1.1
28	Utah	(7.2)
47	Vermont	(11.3)
24	Virginia	(6.0)
44	Washington	(10.0)
NA	West Virginia**	NA
23	Wisconsin	(5.8)
42	Wyoming	(9.0)

RANK ORDER

RANK	STATE	PERCENT CHANGE
1	Rhode Island	4.2
2	Texas	1.1
3	South Dakota	0.3
4	Massachusetts	(0.4)
5	Alabama	(1.1)
6	North Carolina	(1.2)
7	Missouri	(1.8)
8	Arkansas	(2.4)
9	Georgia	(3.0)
10	Pennsylvania	(3.4)
11	Tennessee	(3.6)
12	Kentucky	(3.8)
12	Mississippi	(3.8)
14	Maine	(4.0)
14	New Hampshire	(4.0)
16	Oklahoma	(4.1)
17	Louisiana	(4.9)
18	Montana	(5.0)
19	South Carolina	(5.1)
20	Illinois	(5.3)
21	Iowa	(5.6)
22	Colorado	(5.7)
23	Wisconsin	(5.8)
24	New Jersey	(6.0)
24	Virginia	(6.0)
26	Kansas	(6.6)
27	New York	(6.9)
28	Utah	(7.2)
29	Ohio	(7.3)
30	Maryland	(7.4)
31	Nebraska	(7.6)
32	Florida	(7.9)
32	Hawaii	(7.9)
34	Delaware	(8.2)
35	New Mexico	(8.3)
36	Arizona	(8.4)
37	Michigan	(8.5)
37	Minnesota	(8.5)
39	California	(8.7)
39	Oregon	(8.7)
41	Nevada	(8.9)
42	Wyoming	(9.0)
43	Indiana	(9.2)
44	Washington	(10.0)
45	Alaska	(10.5)
45	Connecticut	(10.5)
47	Vermont	(11.3)
48	North Dakota	(13.4)
49	Idaho	(14.5)
NA	West Virginia**	NA
	District of Columbia	(10.9)

Source: Federal Bureau of Investigation
   "Crime in the United States 1999" (Uniform Crime Reports, October 15, 2000)
*Larceny and theft is the unlawful taking of property without use of force, violence or fraud. Attempts are included.
Motor vehicle thefts are excluded.
**Not available.

Larceny and Theft Rate in 1999

National Rate = 2,551.4 Larcenies and Thefts per 100,000 Population*

ALPHA ORDER				RANK ORDER		
RANK	STATE	RATE		RANK	STATE	RATE
20	Alabama	2,737.2		1	Utah	3,669.3
22	Alaska	2,690.5		2	Florida	3,534.5
3	Arizona	3,510.5		3	Arizona	3,510.5
27	Arkansas	2,506.0		4	New Mexico	3,426.0
40	California	1,994.2		5	Louisiana	3,425.2
21	Colorado	2,693.0		6	Hawaii	3,414.2
38	Connecticut	2,111.5		7	Oregon	3,409.3
15	Delaware	3,001.9		8	Washington	3,341.5
2	Florida	3,534.5		9	Montana	3,220.2
10	Georgia	3,182.3		10	Georgia	3,182.3
6	Hawaii	3,414.2		11	South Carolina	3,085.7
37	Idaho	2,142.5		12	Texas	3,062.6
23	Illinois	2,632.1		13	North Carolina	3,012.2
32	Indiana	2,335.4		14	Kansas	3,003.8
36	Iowa	2,172.0		15	Delaware	3,001.9
14	Kansas	3,003.8		16	Missouri	2,881.3
49	Kentucky	1,748.7		17	Maryland	2,848.0
5	Louisiana	3,425.2		18	Oklahoma	2,787.8
39	Maine	2,026.5		19	Nebraska	2,741.8
17	Maryland	2,848.0		20	Alabama	2,737.2
48	Massachusetts	1,762.7		21	Colorado	2,693.0
29	Michigan	2,396.1		22	Alaska	2,690.5
28	Minnesota	2,465.2		23	Illinois	2,632.1
31	Mississippi	2,380.6		24	Wyoming	2,609.0
16	Missouri	2,881.3		25	Tennessee	2,601.8
9	Montana	3,220.2		26	Ohio	2,558.8
19	Nebraska	2,741.8		27	Arkansas	2,506.0
30	Nevada	2,386.2		28	Minnesota	2,465.2
47	New Hampshire	1,764.8		29	Michigan	2,396.1
41	New Jersey	1,976.9		30	Nevada	2,386.2
4	New Mexico	3,426.0		31	Mississippi	2,380.6
45	New York	1,858.1		32	Indiana	2,335.4
13	North Carolina	3,012.2		33	Virginia	2,326.4
46	North Dakota	1,794.2		34	Wisconsin	2,299.1
26	Ohio	2,558.8		35	Rhode Island	2,248.6
18	Oklahoma	2,787.8		36	Iowa	2,172.0
7	Oregon	3,409.3		37	Idaho	2,142.5
44	Pennsylvania	1,898.9		38	Connecticut	2,111.5
35	Rhode Island	2,248.6		39	Maine	2,026.5
11	South Carolina	3,085.7		40	California	1,994.2
43	South Dakota	1,915.8		41	New Jersey	1,976.9
25	Tennessee	2,601.8		42	Vermont	1,954.5
12	Texas	3,062.6		43	South Dakota	1,915.8
1	Utah	3,669.3		44	Pennsylvania	1,898.9
42	Vermont	1,954.5		45	New York	1,858.1
33	Virginia	2,326.4		46	North Dakota	1,794.2
8	Washington	3,341.5		47	New Hampshire	1,764.8
50	West Virginia	1,591.6		48	Massachusetts	1,762.7
34	Wisconsin	2,299.1		49	Kentucky	1,748.7
24	Wyoming	2,609.0		50	West Virginia	1,591.6
					District of Columbia	4,181.3

Source: Federal Bureau of Investigation
"Crime in the United States 1999" (Uniform Crime Reports, October 15, 2000)
*Larceny and theft is the unlawful taking of property without use of force, violence or fraud. Attempts are included. Motor vehicle thefts are excluded.

Percent Change in Larceny and Theft Rate: 1998 to 1999

National Percent Change = 6.5% Decrease*

ALPHA ORDER

RANK	STATE	PERCENT CHANGE
5	Alabama	(1.5)
45	Alaska	(11.2)
42	Arizona	(10.5)
8	Arkansas	(2.9)
41	California	(10.1)
28	Colorado	(7.7)
43	Connecticut	(10.8)
37	Delaware	(9.4)
36	Florida	(9.1)
15	Georgia	(4.8)
26	Hawaii	(7.2)
49	Idaho	(16.1)
20	Illinois	(6.0)
40	Indiana	(9.8)
19	Iowa	(5.8)
27	Kansas	(7.5)
10	Kentucky	(4.4)
16	Louisiana	(5.0)
14	Maine	(4.7)
31	Maryland	(8.0)
4	Massachusetts	(0.8)
35	Michigan	(8.9)
38	Minnesota	(9.5)
10	Mississippi	(4.4)
6	Missouri	(2.3)
18	Montana	(5.4)
28	Nebraska	(7.7)
47	Nevada	(12.0)
17	New Hampshire	(5.3)
21	New Jersey	(6.3)
32	New Mexico	(8.5)
24	New York	(7.0)
7	North Carolina	(2.6)
48	North Dakota	(12.8)
28	Ohio	(7.7)
10	Oklahoma	(4.4)
39	Oregon	(9.6)
9	Pennsylvania	(3.4)
1	Rhode Island	3.9
23	South Carolina	(6.4)
2	South Dakota	0.9
13	Tennessee	(4.6)
3	Texas	(0.3)
32	Utah	(8.5)
46	Vermont	(11.7)
25	Virginia	(7.1)
44	Washington	(11.1)
NA	West Virginia**	NA
21	Wisconsin	(6.3)
34	Wyoming	(8.8)

RANK ORDER

RANK	STATE	PERCENT CHANGE
1	Rhode Island	3.9
2	South Dakota	0.9
3	Texas	(0.3)
4	Massachusetts	(0.8)
5	Alabama	(1.5)
6	Missouri	(2.3)
7	North Carolina	(2.6)
8	Arkansas	(2.9)
9	Pennsylvania	(3.4)
10	Kentucky	(4.4)
10	Mississippi	(4.4)
10	Oklahoma	(4.4)
13	Tennessee	(4.6)
14	Maine	(4.7)
15	Georgia	(4.8)
16	Louisiana	(5.0)
17	New Hampshire	(5.3)
18	Montana	(5.4)
19	Iowa	(5.8)
20	Illinois	(6.0)
21	New Jersey	(6.3)
21	Wisconsin	(6.3)
23	South Carolina	(6.4)
24	New York	(7.0)
25	Virginia	(7.1)
26	Hawaii	(7.2)
27	Kansas	(7.5)
28	Colorado	(7.7)
28	Nebraska	(7.7)
28	Ohio	(7.7)
31	Maryland	(8.0)
32	New Mexico	(8.5)
32	Utah	(8.5)
34	Wyoming	(8.8)
35	Michigan	(8.9)
36	Florida	(9.1)
37	Delaware	(9.4)
38	Minnesota	(9.5)
39	Oregon	(9.6)
40	Indiana	(9.8)
41	California	(10.1)
42	Arizona	(10.5)
43	Connecticut	(10.8)
44	Washington	(11.1)
45	Alaska	(11.2)
46	Vermont	(11.7)
47	Nevada	(12.0)
48	North Dakota	(12.8)
49	Idaho	(16.1)
NA	West Virginia**	NA
	District of Columbia	(10.2)

Source: Federal Bureau of Investigation
   "Crime in the United States 1999" (Uniform Crime Reports, October 15, 2000)
*Larceny and theft is the unlawful taking of property without use of force, violence or fraud. Attempts are included.
Motor vehicle thefts are excluded.
**Not available.

Motor Vehicle Thefts in 1999

National Total = 1,147,305 Motor Vehicle Thefts*

<table>
<tr><td colspan="4">ALPHA ORDER</td><td colspan="4">RANK ORDER</td></tr>
<tr><td>RANK</td><td>STATE</td><td>THEFTS</td><td>% of USA</td><td>RANK</td><td>STATE</td><td>THEFTS</td><td>% of USA</td></tr>
<tr><td>27</td><td>Alabama</td><td>13,134</td><td>1.1%</td><td>1</td><td>California</td><td>168,480</td><td>14.7%</td></tr>
<tr><td>42</td><td>Alaska</td><td>2,658</td><td>0.2%</td><td>2</td><td>Florida</td><td>93,191</td><td>8.1%</td></tr>
<tr><td>10</td><td>Arizona</td><td>38,247</td><td>3.3%</td><td>3</td><td>Texas</td><td>92,037</td><td>8.0%</td></tr>
<tr><td>34</td><td>Arkansas</td><td>6,664</td><td>0.6%</td><td>4</td><td>New York</td><td>58,261</td><td>5.1%</td></tr>
<tr><td>1</td><td>California</td><td>168,480</td><td>14.7%</td><td>5</td><td>Michigan</td><td>56,800</td><td>5.0%</td></tr>
<tr><td>21</td><td>Colorado</td><td>14,795</td><td>1.3%</td><td>6</td><td>Illinois</td><td>52,114</td><td>4.5%</td></tr>
<tr><td>30</td><td>Connecticut</td><td>11,297</td><td>1.0%</td><td>7</td><td>Georgia</td><td>40,120</td><td>3.5%</td></tr>
<tr><td>41</td><td>Delaware</td><td>3,043</td><td>0.3%</td><td>8</td><td>Pennsylvania</td><td>39,234</td><td>3.4%</td></tr>
<tr><td>2</td><td>Florida</td><td>93,191</td><td>8.1%</td><td>9</td><td>Ohio</td><td>39,192</td><td>3.4%</td></tr>
<tr><td>7</td><td>Georgia</td><td>40,120</td><td>3.5%</td><td>10</td><td>Arizona</td><td>38,247</td><td>3.3%</td></tr>
<tr><td>38</td><td>Hawaii</td><td>4,660</td><td>0.4%</td><td>11</td><td>New Jersey</td><td>35,357</td><td>3.1%</td></tr>
<tr><td>43</td><td>Idaho</td><td>1,898</td><td>0.2%</td><td>12</td><td>Washington</td><td>33,807</td><td>2.9%</td></tr>
<tr><td>6</td><td>Illinois</td><td>52,114</td><td>4.5%</td><td>13</td><td>Massachusetts</td><td>25,628</td><td>2.2%</td></tr>
<tr><td>19</td><td>Indiana</td><td>20,290</td><td>1.8%</td><td>14</td><td>North Carolina</td><td>25,577</td><td>2.2%</td></tr>
<tr><td>37</td><td>Iowa</td><td>5,135</td><td>0.4%</td><td>15</td><td>Maryland</td><td>25,447</td><td>2.2%</td></tr>
<tr><td>35</td><td>Kansas</td><td>6,048</td><td>0.5%</td><td>16</td><td>Tennessee</td><td>25,255</td><td>2.2%</td></tr>
<tr><td>31</td><td>Kentucky</td><td>8,631</td><td>0.8%</td><td>17</td><td>Missouri</td><td>22,984</td><td>2.0%</td></tr>
<tr><td>18</td><td>Louisiana</td><td>21,695</td><td>1.9%</td><td>18</td><td>Louisiana</td><td>21,695</td><td>1.9%</td></tr>
<tr><td>45</td><td>Maine</td><td>1,694</td><td>0.1%</td><td>19</td><td>Indiana</td><td>20,290</td><td>1.8%</td></tr>
<tr><td>15</td><td>Maryland</td><td>25,447</td><td>2.2%</td><td>20</td><td>Virginia</td><td>17,953</td><td>1.6%</td></tr>
<tr><td>13</td><td>Massachusetts</td><td>25,628</td><td>2.2%</td><td>21</td><td>Colorado</td><td>14,795</td><td>1.3%</td></tr>
<tr><td>5</td><td>Michigan</td><td>56,800</td><td>5.0%</td><td>22</td><td>South Carolina</td><td>14,445</td><td>1.3%</td></tr>
<tr><td>26</td><td>Minnesota</td><td>13,275</td><td>1.2%</td><td>23</td><td>Wisconsin</td><td>13,819</td><td>1.2%</td></tr>
<tr><td>25</td><td>Mississippi</td><td>13,532</td><td>1.2%</td><td>24</td><td>Oregon</td><td>13,633</td><td>1.2%</td></tr>
<tr><td>17</td><td>Missouri</td><td>22,984</td><td>2.0%</td><td>25</td><td>Mississippi</td><td>13,532</td><td>1.2%</td></tr>
<tr><td>44</td><td>Montana</td><td>1,896</td><td>0.2%</td><td>26</td><td>Minnesota</td><td>13,275</td><td>1.2%</td></tr>
<tr><td>36</td><td>Nebraska</td><td>5,440</td><td>0.5%</td><td>27</td><td>Alabama</td><td>13,134</td><td>1.1%</td></tr>
<tr><td>28</td><td>Nevada</td><td>13,094</td><td>1.1%</td><td>28</td><td>Nevada</td><td>13,094</td><td>1.1%</td></tr>
<tr><td>46</td><td>New Hampshire</td><td>1,354</td><td>0.1%</td><td>29</td><td>Oklahoma</td><td>12,132</td><td>1.1%</td></tr>
<tr><td>11</td><td>New Jersey</td><td>35,357</td><td>3.1%</td><td>30</td><td>Connecticut</td><td>11,297</td><td>1.0%</td></tr>
<tr><td>32</td><td>New Mexico</td><td>8,126</td><td>0.7%</td><td>31</td><td>Kentucky</td><td>8,631</td><td>0.8%</td></tr>
<tr><td>4</td><td>New York</td><td>58,261</td><td>5.1%</td><td>32</td><td>New Mexico</td><td>8,126</td><td>0.7%</td></tr>
<tr><td>14</td><td>North Carolina</td><td>25,577</td><td>2.2%</td><td>33</td><td>Utah</td><td>7,382</td><td>0.6%</td></tr>
<tr><td>47</td><td>North Dakota</td><td>1,036</td><td>0.1%</td><td>34</td><td>Arkansas</td><td>6,664</td><td>0.6%</td></tr>
<tr><td>9</td><td>Ohio</td><td>39,192</td><td>3.4%</td><td>35</td><td>Kansas</td><td>6,048</td><td>0.5%</td></tr>
<tr><td>29</td><td>Oklahoma</td><td>12,132</td><td>1.1%</td><td>36</td><td>Nebraska</td><td>5,440</td><td>0.5%</td></tr>
<tr><td>24</td><td>Oregon</td><td>13,633</td><td>1.2%</td><td>37</td><td>Iowa</td><td>5,135</td><td>0.4%</td></tr>
<tr><td>8</td><td>Pennsylvania</td><td>39,234</td><td>3.4%</td><td>38</td><td>Hawaii</td><td>4,660</td><td>0.4%</td></tr>
<tr><td>39</td><td>Rhode Island</td><td>4,032</td><td>0.4%</td><td>39</td><td>Rhode Island</td><td>4,032</td><td>0.4%</td></tr>
<tr><td>22</td><td>South Carolina</td><td>14,445</td><td>1.3%</td><td>40</td><td>West Virginia</td><td>3,762</td><td>0.3%</td></tr>
<tr><td>49</td><td>South Dakota</td><td>861</td><td>0.1%</td><td>41</td><td>Delaware</td><td>3,043</td><td>0.3%</td></tr>
<tr><td>16</td><td>Tennessee</td><td>25,255</td><td>2.2%</td><td>42</td><td>Alaska</td><td>2,658</td><td>0.2%</td></tr>
<tr><td>3</td><td>Texas</td><td>92,037</td><td>8.0%</td><td>43</td><td>Idaho</td><td>1,898</td><td>0.2%</td></tr>
<tr><td>33</td><td>Utah</td><td>7,382</td><td>0.6%</td><td>44</td><td>Montana</td><td>1,896</td><td>0.2%</td></tr>
<tr><td>48</td><td>Vermont</td><td>912</td><td>0.1%</td><td>45</td><td>Maine</td><td>1,694</td><td>0.1%</td></tr>
<tr><td>20</td><td>Virginia</td><td>17,953</td><td>1.6%</td><td>46</td><td>New Hampshire</td><td>1,354</td><td>0.1%</td></tr>
<tr><td>12</td><td>Washington</td><td>33,807</td><td>2.9%</td><td>47</td><td>North Dakota</td><td>1,036</td><td>0.1%</td></tr>
<tr><td>40</td><td>West Virginia</td><td>3,762</td><td>0.3%</td><td>48</td><td>Vermont</td><td>912</td><td>0.1%</td></tr>
<tr><td>23</td><td>Wisconsin</td><td>13,819</td><td>1.2%</td><td>49</td><td>South Dakota</td><td>861</td><td>0.1%</td></tr>
<tr><td>50</td><td>Wyoming</td><td>596</td><td>0.1%</td><td>50</td><td>Wyoming</td><td>596</td><td>0.1%</td></tr>
<tr><td></td><td></td><td></td><td></td><td></td><td>District of Columbia</td><td>6,652</td><td>0.6%</td></tr>
</table>

Source: Federal Bureau of Investigation
   "Crime in the United States 1999" (Uniform Crime Reports, October 15, 2000)
*Includes the theft or attempted theft of a self-propelled vehicle. Excludes motorboats, construction equipment, airplanes and farming equipment.

Average Time Between Motor Vehicle Thefts in 1999

National Rate = A Motor Vehicle Theft Occurs Every 27 Seconds*

ALPHA ORDER

RANK	STATE	MINUTES.SECONDS
24	Alabama	40.01
9	Alaska	197.44
41	Arizona	13.44
17	Arkansas	78.52
50	California	3.07
30	Colorado	35.32
21	Connecticut	46.32
10	Delaware	172.43
49	Florida	5.38
44	Georgia	13.06
13	Hawaii	112.47
8	Idaho	276.55
45	Illinois	10.05
32	Indiana	25.54
14	Iowa	102.22
16	Kansas	86.54
20	Kentucky	60.54
33	Louisiana	24.14
6	Maine	310.16
36	Maryland	20.39
38	Massachusetts	20.31
46	Michigan	9.15
25	Minnesota	39.35
26	Mississippi	38.50
34	Missouri	22.52
7	Montana	277.13
15	Nebraska	96.37
23	Nevada	40.08
5	New Hampshire	388.11
40	New Jersey	14.52
19	New Mexico	64.41
47	New York	9.01
37	North Carolina	20.33
4	North Dakota	507.20
42	Ohio	13.25
22	Oklahoma	43.19
27	Oregon	38.33
43	Pennsylvania	13.24
12	Rhode Island	130.22
29	South Carolina	36.23
2	South Dakota	610.27
35	Tennessee	20.49
48	Texas	5.43
18	Utah	71.12
3	Vermont	576.19
31	Virginia	29.17
39	Washington	15.33
11	West Virginia	139.43
28	Wisconsin	38.02
1	Wyoming	881.53

RANK ORDER

RANK	STATE	MINUTES.SECONDS
1	Wyoming	881.53
2	South Dakota	610.27
3	Vermont	576.19
4	North Dakota	507.20
5	New Hampshire	388.11
6	Maine	310.16
7	Montana	277.13
8	Idaho	276.55
9	Alaska	197.44
10	Delaware	172.43
11	West Virginia	139.43
12	Rhode Island	130.22
13	Hawaii	112.47
14	Iowa	102.22
15	Nebraska	96.37
16	Kansas	86.54
17	Arkansas	78.52
18	Utah	71.12
19	New Mexico	64.41
20	Kentucky	60.54
21	Connecticut	46.32
22	Oklahoma	43.19
23	Nevada	40.08
24	Alabama	40.01
25	Minnesota	39.35
26	Mississippi	38.50
27	Oregon	38.33
28	Wisconsin	38.02
29	South Carolina	36.23
30	Colorado	35.32
31	Virginia	29.17
32	Indiana	25.54
33	Louisiana	24.14
34	Missouri	22.52
35	Tennessee	20.49
36	Maryland	20.39
37	North Carolina	20.33
38	Massachusetts	20.31
39	Washington	15.33
40	New Jersey	14.52
41	Arizona	13.44
42	Ohio	13.25
43	Pennsylvania	13.24
44	Georgia	13.06
45	Illinois	10.05
46	Michigan	9.15
47	New York	9.01
48	Texas	5.43
49	Florida	5.38
50	California	3.07
	District of Columbia	79.01

Source: Morgan Quitno Press using data from Federal Bureau of Investigation
    "Crime in the United States 1999" (Uniform Crime Reports, October 15, 2000)
*Includes the theft or attempted theft of a self-propelled vehicle. Excludes motorboats, construction equipment, airplanes and farming equipment.

Percent Change in Number of Motor Vehicle Thefts: 1998 to 1999

National Percent Change = 7.7% Decrease*

ALPHA ORDER			RANK ORDER		
RANK	STATE	PERCENT CHANGE	RANK	STATE	PERCENT CHANGE
41	Alabama	(11.7)	1	Mississippi	45.2
7	Alaska	2.0	2	South Dakota	12.8
20	Arizona	(5.3)	3	Maine	12.3
24	Arkansas	(7.3)	4	Rhode Island	5.3
43	California	(13.8)	5	Vermont	4.3
26	Colorado	(8.0)	6	North Carolina	3.9
38	Connecticut	(11.1)	7	Alaska	2.0
17	Delaware	(4.5)	8	New Jersey	0.5
35	Florida	(10.6)	9	Illinois	(1.5)
21	Georgia	(5.7)	10	Virginia	(2.2)
46	Hawaii	(16.7)	11	Michigan	(2.6)
47	Idaho	(16.8)	12	Wisconsin	(2.8)
9	Illinois	(1.5)	13	Massachusetts	(2.9)
16	Indiana	(4.2)	14	Washington	(4.0)
44	Iowa	(14.0)	15	Utah	(4.1)
38	Kansas	(11.1)	16	Indiana	(4.2)
40	Kentucky	(11.5)	17	Delaware	(4.5)
30	Louisiana	(8.3)	18	Texas	(4.8)
3	Maine	12.3	19	Nevada	(4.9)
33	Maryland	(9.8)	20	Arizona	(5.3)
13	Massachusetts	(2.9)	21	Georgia	(5.7)
11	Michigan	(2.6)	22	Nebraska	(6.0)
42	Minnesota	(13.6)	23	Missouri	(6.1)
1	Mississippi	45.2	24	Arkansas	(7.3)
23	Missouri	(6.1)	25	Montana	(7.5)
25	Montana	(7.5)	26	Colorado	(8.0)
22	Nebraska	(6.0)	26	Pennsylvania	(8.0)
19	Nevada	(4.9)	28	New Hampshire	(8.1)
28	New Hampshire	(8.1)	28	North Dakota	(8.1)
8	New Jersey	0.5	30	Louisiana	(8.3)
49	New Mexico	(24.5)	31	Ohio	(8.9)
45	New York	(14.5)	32	South Carolina	(9.4)
6	North Carolina	3.9	33	Maryland	(9.8)
28	North Dakota	(8.1)	34	Tennessee	(10.1)
31	Ohio	(8.9)	35	Florida	(10.6)
35	Oklahoma	(10.6)	35	Oklahoma	(10.6)
48	Oregon	(21.0)	37	Wyoming	(10.9)
26	Pennsylvania	(8.0)	38	Connecticut	(11.1)
4	Rhode Island	5.3	38	Kansas	(11.1)
32	South Carolina	(9.4)	40	Kentucky	(11.5)
2	South Dakota	12.8	41	Alabama	(11.7)
34	Tennessee	(10.1)	42	Minnesota	(13.6)
18	Texas	(4.8)	43	California	(13.8)
15	Utah	(4.1)	44	Iowa	(14.0)
5	Vermont	4.3	45	New York	(14.5)
10	Virginia	(2.2)	46	Hawaii	(16.7)
14	Washington	(4.0)	47	Idaho	(16.8)
NA	West Virginia**	NA	48	Oregon	(21.0)
12	Wisconsin	(2.8)	49	New Mexico	(24.5)
37	Wyoming	(10.9)	NA	West Virginia**	NA
				District of Columbia	2.3

Source: Federal Bureau of Investigation
    "Crime in the United States 1999" (Uniform Crime Reports, October 15, 2000)
*Includes the theft or attempted theft of a self-propelled vehicle. Excludes motorboats, construction equipment, airplanes and farming equipment.
**Not available.

Motor Vehicle Theft Rate in 1999

National Rate = 420.7 Motor Vehicle Thefts per 100,000 Population*

ALPHA ORDER

RANK	STATE	RATE
34	Alabama	300.5
16	Alaska	429.4
1	Arizona	800.5
37	Arkansas	261.2
7	California	508.3
24	Colorado	364.8
28	Connecticut	344.2
21	Delaware	403.6
3	Florida	616.7
6	Georgia	515.2
22	Hawaii	393.2
46	Idaho	151.6
15	Illinois	429.7
29	Indiana	341.4
43	Iowa	179.0
39	Kansas	227.9
40	Kentucky	217.9
8	Louisiana	496.2
47	Maine	135.2
9	Maryland	492.0
18	Massachusetts	415.0
5	Michigan	575.8
35	Minnesota	278.0
10	Mississippi	488.7
17	Missouri	420.3
41	Montana	214.7
32	Nebraska	326.5
2	Nevada	723.8
50	New Hampshire	112.7
14	New Jersey	434.2
11	New Mexico	467.0
33	New York	320.2
30	North Carolina	334.3
44	North Dakota	163.4
26	Ohio	348.2
25	Oklahoma	361.3
19	Oregon	411.1
31	Pennsylvania	327.1
20	Rhode Island	406.9
23	South Carolina	371.7
49	South Dakota	117.5
12	Tennessee	460.5
13	Texas	459.2
27	Utah	346.6
45	Vermont	153.5
37	Virginia	261.2
4	Washington	587.3
42	West Virginia	208.2
36	Wisconsin	263.2
48	Wyoming	124.2

RANK ORDER

RANK	STATE	RATE
1	Arizona	800.5
2	Nevada	723.8
3	Florida	616.7
4	Washington	587.3
5	Michigan	575.8
6	Georgia	515.2
7	California	508.3
8	Louisiana	496.2
9	Maryland	492.0
10	Mississippi	488.7
11	New Mexico	467.0
12	Tennessee	460.5
13	Texas	459.2
14	New Jersey	434.2
15	Illinois	429.7
16	Alaska	429.4
17	Missouri	420.3
18	Massachusetts	415.0
19	Oregon	411.1
20	Rhode Island	406.9
21	Delaware	403.6
22	Hawaii	393.2
23	South Carolina	371.7
24	Colorado	364.8
25	Oklahoma	361.3
26	Ohio	348.2
27	Utah	346.6
28	Connecticut	344.2
29	Indiana	341.4
30	North Carolina	334.3
31	Pennsylvania	327.1
32	Nebraska	326.5
33	New York	320.2
34	Alabama	300.5
35	Minnesota	278.0
36	Wisconsin	263.2
37	Arkansas	261.2
37	Virginia	261.2
39	Kansas	227.9
40	Kentucky	217.9
41	Montana	214.7
42	West Virginia	208.2
43	Iowa	179.0
44	North Dakota	163.4
45	Vermont	153.5
46	Idaho	151.6
47	Maine	135.2
48	Wyoming	124.2
49	South Dakota	117.5
50	New Hampshire	112.7
	District of Columbia	1,281.7

Source: Federal Bureau of Investigation
"Crime in the United States 1999" (Uniform Crime Reports, October 15, 2000)
Includes the theft or attempted theft of a self-propelled vehicle. Excludes motorboats, construction equipment, airplanes and farming equipment.

Percent Change in Motor Vehicle Theft Rate: 1998 to 1999

National Percent Change = 8.5% Decrease*

ALPHA ORDER				RANK ORDER		
RANK	STATE	PERCENT CHANGE		RANK	STATE	PERCENT CHANGE
40	Alabama	(12.0)		1	Mississippi	44.3
7	Alaska	1.1		2	South Dakota	13.6
21	Arizona	(7.5)		3	Maine	11.5
24	Arkansas	(7.7)		4	Rhode Island	5.0
45	California	(15.1)		5	Vermont	3.8
31	Colorado	(10.0)		6	North Carolina	2.5
37	Connecticut	(11.3)		7	Alaska	1.1
17	Delaware	(5.8)		8	New Jersey	0.1
38	Florida	(11.8)		9	Illinois	(2.2)
21	Georgia	(7.5)		10	Michigan	(3.1)
46	Hawaii	(16.1)		11	Wisconsin	(3.2)
47	Idaho	(18.4)		12	Massachusetts	(3.4)
9	Illinois	(2.2)		12	Virginia	(3.4)
14	Indiana	(4.9)		14	Indiana	(4.9)
42	Iowa	(14.3)		15	Washington	(5.1)
39	Kansas	(11.9)		16	Utah	(5.5)
41	Kentucky	(12.1)		17	Delaware	(5.8)
28	Louisiana	(8.4)		18	Texas	(6.1)
3	Maine	11.5		19	Nebraska	(6.2)
32	Maryland	(10.4)		20	Missouri	(6.6)
12	Massachusetts	(3.4)		21	Arizona	(7.5)
10	Michigan	(3.1)		21	Georgia	(7.5)
43	Minnesota	(14.5)		21	North Dakota	(7.5)
1	Mississippi	44.3		24	Arkansas	(7.7)
20	Missouri	(6.6)		25	Montana	(7.8)
25	Montana	(7.8)		26	Pennsylvania	(8.0)
19	Nebraska	(6.2)		27	Nevada	(8.1)
27	Nevada	(8.1)		28	Louisiana	(8.4)
30	New Hampshire	(9.4)		29	Ohio	(9.3)
8	New Jersey	0.1		30	New Hampshire	(9.4)
49	New Mexico	(24.7)		31	Colorado	(10.0)
44	New York	(14.6)		32	Maryland	(10.4)
6	North Carolina	2.5		33	South Carolina	(10.6)
21	North Dakota	(7.5)		34	Wyoming	(10.7)
29	Ohio	(9.3)		35	Oklahoma	(10.9)
35	Oklahoma	(10.9)		36	Tennessee	(11.0)
48	Oregon	(21.8)		37	Connecticut	(11.3)
26	Pennsylvania	(8.0)		38	Florida	(11.8)
4	Rhode Island	5.0		39	Kansas	(11.9)
33	South Carolina	(10.6)		40	Alabama	(12.0)
2	South Dakota	13.6		41	Kentucky	(12.1)
36	Tennessee	(11.0)		42	Iowa	(14.3)
18	Texas	(6.1)		43	Minnesota	(14.5)
16	Utah	(5.5)		44	New York	(14.6)
5	Vermont	3.8		45	California	(15.1)
12	Virginia	(3.4)		46	Hawaii	(16.1)
15	Washington	(5.1)		47	Idaho	(18.4)
NA	West Virginia**	NA		48	Oregon	(21.8)
11	Wisconsin	(3.2)		49	New Mexico	(24.7)
34	Wyoming	(10.7)		NA	West Virginia**	NA
					District of Columbia	3.1

Source: Federal Bureau of Investigation
   "Crime in the United States 1999" (Uniform Crime Reports, October 15, 2000)
*Includes the theft or attempted theft of a self-propelled vehicle. Excludes motorboats, construction equipment, airplanes and farming equipment.
**Not available.

Crimes in Urban Areas in 1999

National Urban Total = 11,001,777 Crimes*

ALPHA ORDER

RANK	STATE	CRIMES	% of USA
20	Alabama	181,517	1.6%
40	Alaska	22,373	0.2%
12	Arizona	275,825	2.5%
31	Arkansas	91,039	0.8%
1	California	1,245,447	11.3%
22	Colorado	159,683	1.5%
27	Connecticut	103,400	0.9%
NA	Delaware**	NA	NA
3	Florida	908,105	8.3%
7	Georgia	361,781	3.3%
35	Hawaii	42,678	0.4%
38	Idaho	33,143	0.3%
NA	Illinois**	NA	NA
18	Indiana	203,233	1.8%
32	Iowa	83,769	0.8%
NA	Kansas**	NA	NA
NA	Kentucky**	NA	NA
16	Louisiana	232,760	2.1%
39	Maine	30,014	0.3%
13	Maryland	248,170	2.3%
19	Massachusetts	201,426	1.8%
6	Michigan	401,857	3.7%
24	Minnesota	156,114	1.4%
28	Mississippi	100,908	0.9%
15	Missouri	235,217	2.1%
NA	Montana**	NA	NA
34	Nebraska	62,698	0.6%
33	Nevada	79,676	0.7%
NA	New Hampshire**	NA	NA
11	New Jersey	276,873	2.5%
30	New Mexico	95,367	0.9%
4	New York	581,324	5.3%
9	North Carolina	349,873	3.2%
43	North Dakota	13,029	0.1%
5	Ohio	427,769	3.9%
26	Oklahoma	147,042	1.3%
25	Oregon	154,634	1.4%
8	Pennsylvania	357,491	3.2%
37	Rhode Island	35,440	0.3%
21	South Carolina	172,979	1.6%
41	South Dakota	17,004	0.2%
14	Tennessee	235,722	2.1%
2	Texas	979,230	8.9%
29	Utah	100,881	0.9%
44	Vermont	12,464	0.1%
17	Virginia	214,096	1.9%
10	Washington	287,142	2.6%
36	West Virginia	36,943	0.3%
23	Wisconsin	158,119	1.4%
42	Wyoming	14,350	0.1%

RANK ORDER

RANK	STATE	CRIMES	% of USA
1	California	1,245,447	11.3%
2	Texas	979,230	8.9%
3	Florida	908,105	8.3%
4	New York	581,324	5.3%
5	Ohio	427,769	3.9%
6	Michigan	401,857	3.7%
7	Georgia	361,781	3.3%
8	Pennsylvania	357,491	3.2%
9	North Carolina	349,873	3.2%
10	Washington	287,142	2.6%
11	New Jersey	276,873	2.5%
12	Arizona	275,825	2.5%
13	Maryland	248,170	2.3%
14	Tennessee	235,722	2.1%
15	Missouri	235,217	2.1%
16	Louisiana	232,760	2.1%
17	Virginia	214,096	1.9%
18	Indiana	203,233	1.8%
19	Massachusetts	201,426	1.8%
20	Alabama	181,517	1.6%
21	South Carolina	172,979	1.6%
22	Colorado	159,683	1.5%
23	Wisconsin	158,119	1.4%
24	Minnesota	156,114	1.4%
25	Oregon	154,634	1.4%
26	Oklahoma	147,042	1.3%
27	Connecticut	103,400	0.9%
28	Mississippi	100,908	0.9%
29	Utah	100,881	0.9%
30	New Mexico	95,367	0.9%
31	Arkansas	91,039	0.8%
32	Iowa	83,769	0.8%
33	Nevada	79,676	0.7%
34	Nebraska	62,698	0.6%
35	Hawaii	42,678	0.4%
36	West Virginia	36,943	0.3%
37	Rhode Island	35,440	0.3%
38	Idaho	33,143	0.3%
39	Maine	30,014	0.3%
40	Alaska	22,373	0.2%
41	South Dakota	17,004	0.2%
42	Wyoming	14,350	0.1%
43	North Dakota	13,029	0.1%
44	Vermont	12,464	0.1%
NA	Delaware**	NA	NA
NA	Illinois**	NA	NA
NA	Kansas**	NA	NA
NA	Kentucky**	NA	NA
NA	Montana**	NA	NA
NA	New Hampshire**	NA	NA
	District of Columbia	41,868	0.4%

Source: Morgan Quitno Press using data from Federal Bureau of Investigation
    "Crime in the United States 1999" (Uniform Crime Reports, October 15, 2000)
*Estimated totals for urban areas, defined by the F.B.I. as Metropolitan Statistical Areas and other cities outside such areas. National total includes those states listed as not available. Includes murder, rape, robbery, aggravated assault, burglary, larceny-theft and motor vehicle theft.
**Not available.

Urban Crime Rate in 1999

National Urban Rate = 4,596.2 Crimes per 100,000 Population*

ALPHA ORDER

RANK ORDER

RANK	STATE	RATE		RANK	STATE	RATE
18	Alabama	5,101.6		1	New Mexico	6,681.7
16	Alaska	5,258.0		2	Louisiana	6,363.3
5	Arizona	6,156.3		3	Florida	6,361.4
17	Arkansas	5,256.3		4	Mississippi	6,187.8
31	California	3,831.5		5	Arizona	6,156.3
24	Colorado	4,331.5		6	North Carolina	5,957.8
35	Connecticut	3,688.9		7	Georgia	5,812.0
NA	Delaware**	NA		8	South Carolina	5,716.0
3	Florida	6,361.4		9	Missouri	5,565.1
7	Georgia	5,812.0		10	Oregon	5,542.8
22	Hawaii	4,925.0		11	Washington	5,510.8
30	Idaho	3,976.5		12	Oklahoma	5,429.6
NA	Illinois**	NA		13	Tennessee	5,412.4
27	Indiana	4,213.9		14	Utah	5,338.4
26	Iowa	4,242.8		15	Texas	5,334.7
NA	Kansas**	NA		16	Alaska	5,258.0
NA	Kentucky**	NA		17	Arkansas	5,256.3
2	Louisiana	6,363.3		18	Alabama	5,101.6
40	Maine	3,358.3		19	Maryland	5,081.0
19	Maryland	5,081.0		20	Nebraska	4,990.7
42	Massachusetts	3,267.4		21	Nevada	4,951.2
23	Michigan	4,590.6		22	Hawaii	4,925.0
29	Minnesota	4,020.3		23	Michigan	4,590.6
4	Mississippi	6,187.8		24	Colorado	4,331.5
9	Missouri	5,565.1		25	Ohio	4,328.9
NA	Montana**	NA		26	Iowa	4,242.8
20	Nebraska	4,990.7		27	Indiana	4,213.9
21	Nevada	4,951.2		28	Wyoming	4,109.5
NA	New Hampshire**	NA		29	Minnesota	4,020.3
39	New Jersey	3,400.1		30	Idaho	3,976.5
1	New Mexico	6,681.7		31	California	3,831.5
41	New York	3,356.4		32	South Dakota	3,761.4
6	North Carolina	5,957.8		33	Wisconsin	3,723.1
44	North Dakota	3,112.3		34	Virginia	3,698.1
25	Ohio	4,328.9		35	Connecticut	3,688.9
12	Oklahoma	5,429.6		36	Rhode Island	3,576.2
10	Oregon	5,542.8		37	West Virginia	3,543.6
43	Pennsylvania	3,263.3		38	Vermont	3,530.4
36	Rhode Island	3,576.2		39	New Jersey	3,400.1
8	South Carolina	5,716.0		40	Maine	3,358.3
32	South Dakota	3,761.4		41	New York	3,356.4
13	Tennessee	5,412.4		42	Massachusetts	3,267.4
15	Texas	5,334.7		43	Pennsylvania	3,263.3
14	Utah	5,338.4		44	North Dakota	3,112.3
38	Vermont	3,530.4		NA	Delaware**	NA
34	Virginia	3,698.1		NA	Illinois**	NA
11	Washington	5,510.8		NA	Kansas**	NA
37	West Virginia	3,543.6		NA	Kentucky**	NA
33	Wisconsin	3,723.1		NA	Montana**	NA
28	Wyoming	4,109.5		NA	New Hampshire**	NA

District of Columbia   8,067.1

Source: Morgan Quitno Press using data from Federal Bureau of Investigation
    "Crime in the United States 1999" (Uniform Crime Reports, October 15, 2000)
*Estimated rates for urban areas, defined by the F.B.I. as Metropolitan Statistical Areas and other cities outside such areas. National rate includes those states listed as not available. Includes murder, rape, robbery, aggravated assault, burglary, larceny-theft and motor vehicle theft.
**Not available.

Percent of Crimes Occurring in Urban Areas in 1999

National Percent = 94.6% of Crimes*

ALPHA ORDER

RANK	STATE	PERCENT
17	Alabama	94.1
41	Alaska	82.8
5	Arizona	97.9
33	Arkansas	88.3
4	California	98.8
9	Colorado	96.9
21	Connecticut	93.0
NA	Delaware**	NA
10	Florida	96.8
31	Georgia	90.2
43	Hawaii	74.5
38	Idaho	84.1
NA	Illinois**	NA
29	Indiana	90.8
30	Iowa	90.6
NA	Kansas**	NA
NA	Kentucky**	NA
22	Louisiana	92.6
40	Maine	83.3
6	Maryland	97.5
1	Massachusetts	100.0
16	Michigan	94.2
28	Minnesota	90.9
37	Mississippi	85.3
18	Missouri	94.0
NA	Montana**	NA
25	Nebraska	91.6
15	Nevada	94.6
NA	New Hampshire**	NA
1	New Jersey	100.0
24	New Mexico	91.9
7	New York	97.4
32	North Carolina	88.4
36	North Dakota	85.9
13	Ohio	95.1
19	Oklahoma	93.5
20	Oregon	93.2
11	Pennsylvania	95.7
3	Rhode Island	99.8
39	South Carolina	83.6
34	South Dakota	87.7
25	Tennessee	91.6
8	Texas	97.1
12	Utah	95.2
43	Vermont	74.5
23	Virginia	92.3
14	Washington	94.9
42	West Virginia	75.1
27	Wisconsin	91.4
35	Wyoming	86.5

RANK ORDER

RANK	STATE	PERCENT
1	Massachusetts	100.0
1	New Jersey	100.0
3	Rhode Island	99.8
4	California	98.8
5	Arizona	97.9
6	Maryland	97.5
7	New York	97.4
8	Texas	97.1
9	Colorado	96.9
10	Florida	96.8
11	Pennsylvania	95.7
12	Utah	95.2
13	Ohio	95.1
14	Washington	94.9
15	Nevada	94.6
16	Michigan	94.2
17	Alabama	94.1
18	Missouri	94.0
19	Oklahoma	93.5
20	Oregon	93.2
21	Connecticut	93.0
22	Louisiana	92.6
23	Virginia	92.3
24	New Mexico	91.9
25	Nebraska	91.6
25	Tennessee	91.6
27	Wisconsin	91.4
28	Minnesota	90.9
29	Indiana	90.8
30	Iowa	90.6
31	Georgia	90.2
32	North Carolina	88.4
33	Arkansas	88.3
34	South Dakota	87.7
35	Wyoming	86.5
36	North Dakota	85.9
37	Mississippi	85.3
38	Idaho	84.1
39	South Carolina	83.6
40	Maine	83.3
41	Alaska	82.8
42	West Virginia	75.1
43	Hawaii	74.5
43	Vermont	74.5
NA	Delaware**	NA
NA	Illinois**	NA
NA	Kansas**	NA
NA	Kentucky**	NA
NA	Montana**	NA
NA	New Hampshire**	NA

District of Columbia 100.0

Source: Morgan Quitno Press using data from Federal Bureau of Investigation
    "Crime in the United States 1999" (Uniform Crime Reports, October 15, 2000)
*Estimated percentages for urban areas, defined by the F.B.I. as Metropolitan Statistical Areas and other cities
outside such areas. National percent includes those states listed as not available. Includes murder, rape, robbery,
aggravated assault, burglary, larceny-theft and motor vehicle theft.
**Not available.

Crimes in Rural Areas in 1999

National Rural Total = 633,372 Crimes*

ALPHA ORDER

RANK	STATE	CRIMES	% of USA
23	Alabama	11,302	1.8%
36	Alaska	4,635	0.7%
32	Arizona	5,910	0.9%
22	Arkansas	12,092	1.9%
14	California	15,717	2.5%
34	Colorado	5,130	0.8%
28	Connecticut	7,836	1.2%
NA	Delaware**	NA	NA
4	Florida	29,613	4.7%
2	Georgia	39,187	6.2%
20	Hawaii	14,646	2.3%
29	Idaho	6,286	1.0%
NA	Illinois**	NA	NA
9	Indiana	20,575	3.2%
26	Iowa	8,728	1.4%
NA	Kansas**	NA	NA
NA	Kentucky**	NA	NA
10	Louisiana	18,492	2.9%
31	Maine	6,010	0.9%
30	Maryland	6,250	1.0%
43	Massachusetts	34	0.0%
6	Michigan	24,739	3.9%
15	Minnesota	15,688	2.5%
12	Mississippi	17,323	2.7%
18	Missouri	15,146	2.4%
NA	Montana**	NA	NA
33	Nebraska	5,746	0.9%
37	Nevada	4,509	0.7%
NA	New Hampshire**	NA	NA
44	New Jersey	0	0.0%
27	New Mexico	8,373	1.3%
16	New York	15,419	2.4%
1	North Carolina	46,098	7.3%
41	North Dakota	2,143	0.3%
7	Ohio	22,111	3.5%
25	Oklahoma	10,244	1.6%
24	Oregon	11,232	1.8%
13	Pennsylvania	15,961	2.5%
42	Rhode Island	57	0.0%
3	South Carolina	33,928	5.4%
39	South Dakota	2,382	0.4%
8	Tennessee	21,691	3.4%
5	Texas	29,337	4.6%
35	Utah	5,118	0.8%
38	Vermont	4,271	0.7%
11	Virginia	17,790	2.8%
17	Washington	15,367	2.4%
21	West Virginia	12,218	1.9%
19	Wisconsin	14,943	2.4%
40	Wyoming	2,233	0.4%

RANK ORDER

RANK	STATE	CRIMES	% of USA
1	North Carolina	46,098	7.3%
2	Georgia	39,187	6.2%
3	South Carolina	33,928	5.4%
4	Florida	29,613	4.7%
5	Texas	29,337	4.6%
6	Michigan	24,739	3.9%
7	Ohio	22,111	3.5%
8	Tennessee	21,691	3.4%
9	Indiana	20,575	3.2%
10	Louisiana	18,492	2.9%
11	Virginia	17,790	2.8%
12	Mississippi	17,323	2.7%
13	Pennsylvania	15,961	2.5%
14	California	15,717	2.5%
15	Minnesota	15,688	2.5%
16	New York	15,419	2.4%
17	Washington	15,367	2.4%
18	Missouri	15,146	2.4%
19	Wisconsin	14,943	2.4%
20	Hawaii	14,646	2.3%
21	West Virginia	12,218	1.9%
22	Arkansas	12,092	1.9%
23	Alabama	11,302	1.8%
24	Oregon	11,232	1.8%
25	Oklahoma	10,244	1.6%
26	Iowa	8,728	1.4%
27	New Mexico	8,373	1.3%
28	Connecticut	7,836	1.2%
29	Idaho	6,286	1.0%
30	Maryland	6,250	1.0%
31	Maine	6,010	0.9%
32	Arizona	5,910	0.9%
33	Nebraska	5,746	0.9%
34	Colorado	5,130	0.8%
35	Utah	5,118	0.8%
36	Alaska	4,635	0.7%
37	Nevada	4,509	0.7%
38	Vermont	4,271	0.7%
39	South Dakota	2,382	0.4%
40	Wyoming	2,233	0.4%
41	North Dakota	2,143	0.3%
42	Rhode Island	57	0.0%
43	Massachusetts	34	0.0%
44	New Jersey	0	0.0%
NA	Delaware**	NA	NA
NA	Illinois**	NA	NA
NA	Kansas**	NA	NA
NA	Kentucky**	NA	NA
NA	Montana**	NA	NA
NA	New Hampshire**	NA	NA
	District of Columbia	0	0.0%

Source: Federal Bureau of Investigation
"Crime in the United States 1999" (Uniform Crime Reports, October 15, 2000)
*Estimated totals for rural areas, defined by the F.B.I. as other than Metropolitan Statistical Areas and other cities outside such areas. National total includes those states listed as not available. Includes murder, rape, robbery, aggravated assault, burglary, larceny-theft and motor vehicle theft.
**Not available.

Rural Crime Rate in 1999

National Rural Rate = 1,900.6 Crimes per 100,000 Population*

ALPHA ORDER

RANK ORDER

RANK	STATE	RATE
36	Alabama	1,391.9
10	Alaska	2,395.4
16	Arizona	1,985.8
34	Arkansas	1,476.5
9	California	2,456.0
37	Colorado	1,388.6
26	Connecticut	1,635.9
NA	Delaware**	NA
3	Florida	3,543.5
8	Georgia	2,506.7
1	Hawaii	4,599.4
32	Idaho	1,501.9
NA	Illinois**	NA
18	Indiana	1,836.8
40	Iowa	975.6
NA	Kansas**	NA
NA	Kentucky**	NA
7	Louisiana	2,589.3
24	Maine	1,672.8
13	Maryland	2,172.3
42	Massachusetts	332.7
12	Michigan	2,228.5
21	Minnesota	1,757.1
31	Mississippi	1,521.9
38	Missouri	1,220.1
NA	Montana**	NA
35	Nebraska	1,402.5
11	Nevada	2,256.9
NA	New Hampshire**	NA
43	New Jersey	0.0
5	New Mexico	2,677.5
20	New York	1,757.8
6	North Carolina	2,591.9
39	North Dakota	995.0
27	Ohio	1,607.6
29	Oklahoma	1,576.3
14	Oregon	2,134.6
30	Pennsylvania	1,536.3
43	Rhode Island	0.0
2	South Carolina	3,946.2
41	South Dakota	847.9
17	Tennessee	1,921.6
22	Texas	1,737.8
15	Utah	2,130.0
19	Vermont	1,772.5
25	Virginia	1,641.7
4	Washington	2,817.4
28	West Virginia	1,598.2
33	Wisconsin	1,489.8
23	Wyoming	1,707.1

RANK	STATE	RATE
1	Hawaii	4,599.4
2	South Carolina	3,946.2
3	Florida	3,543.5
4	Washington	2,817.4
5	New Mexico	2,677.5
6	North Carolina	2,591.9
7	Louisiana	2,589.3
8	Georgia	2,506.7
9	California	2,456.0
10	Alaska	2,395.4
11	Nevada	2,256.9
12	Michigan	2,228.5
13	Maryland	2,172.3
14	Oregon	2,134.6
15	Utah	2,130.0
16	Arizona	1,985.8
17	Tennessee	1,921.6
18	Indiana	1,836.8
19	Vermont	1,772.5
20	New York	1,757.8
21	Minnesota	1,757.1
22	Texas	1,737.8
23	Wyoming	1,707.1
24	Maine	1,672.8
25	Virginia	1,641.7
26	Connecticut	1,635.9
27	Ohio	1,607.6
28	West Virginia	1,598.2
29	Oklahoma	1,576.3
30	Pennsylvania	1,536.3
31	Mississippi	1,521.9
32	Idaho	1,501.9
33	Wisconsin	1,489.8
34	Arkansas	1,476.5
35	Nebraska	1,402.5
36	Alabama	1,391.9
37	Colorado	1,388.6
38	Missouri	1,220.1
39	North Dakota	995.0
40	Iowa	975.6
41	South Dakota	847.9
42	Massachusetts	332.7
43	New Jersey	0.0
43	Rhode Island	0.0
NA	Delaware**	NA
NA	Illinois**	NA
NA	Kansas**	NA
NA	Kentucky**	NA
NA	Montana**	NA
NA	New Hampshire**	NA
	District of Columbia	0.0

Source: Morgan Quitno Press using data from Federal Bureau of Investigation
    "Crime in the United States 1999" (Uniform Crime Reports, October 15, 2000)
*Estimated rates for rural areas, defined by the F.B.I. as other than Metropolitan Statistical Areas and other cities outside such areas. National rate includes those states listed as not available. Includes murder, rape, robbery, aggravated assault, burglary, larceny-theft and motor vehicle theft.
**Not available.

Percent of Crimes Occurring in Rural Areas in 1999

National Percent = 5.4% of Crimes*

ALPHA ORDER

RANK	STATE	PERCENT
28	Alabama	5.9
4	Alaska	17.2
40	Arizona	2.1
12	Arkansas	11.7
41	California	1.2
36	Colorado	3.1
24	Connecticut	7.0
NA	Delaware**	NA
35	Florida	3.2
14	Georgia	9.8
1	Hawaii	25.5
7	Idaho	15.9
NA	Illinois**	NA
16	Indiana	9.2
15	Iowa	9.4
NA	Kansas**	NA
NA	Kentucky**	NA
23	Louisiana	7.4
5	Maine	16.7
39	Maryland	2.5
43	Massachusetts	0.0
29	Michigan	5.8
17	Minnesota	9.1
8	Mississippi	14.7
27	Missouri	6.0
NA	Montana**	NA
19	Nebraska	8.4
30	Nevada	5.4
NA	New Hampshire**	NA
43	New Jersey	0.0
21	New Mexico	8.1
38	New York	2.6
13	North Carolina	11.6
9	North Dakota	14.1
32	Ohio	4.9
26	Oklahoma	6.5
25	Oregon	6.8
34	Pennsylvania	4.3
42	Rhode Island	0.2
6	South Carolina	16.4
11	South Dakota	12.3
19	Tennessee	8.4
37	Texas	2.9
33	Utah	4.8
1	Vermont	25.5
22	Virginia	7.7
31	Washington	5.1
3	West Virginia	24.9
18	Wisconsin	8.6
10	Wyoming	13.5

RANK ORDER

RANK	STATE	PERCENT
1	Hawaii	25.5
1	Vermont	25.5
3	West Virginia	24.9
4	Alaska	17.2
5	Maine	16.7
6	South Carolina	16.4
7	Idaho	15.9
8	Mississippi	14.7
9	North Dakota	14.1
10	Wyoming	13.5
11	South Dakota	12.3
12	Arkansas	11.7
13	North Carolina	11.6
14	Georgia	9.8
15	Iowa	9.4
16	Indiana	9.2
17	Minnesota	9.1
18	Wisconsin	8.6
19	Nebraska	8.4
19	Tennessee	8.4
21	New Mexico	8.1
22	Virginia	7.7
23	Louisiana	7.4
24	Connecticut	7.0
25	Oregon	6.8
26	Oklahoma	6.5
27	Missouri	6.0
28	Alabama	5.9
29	Michigan	5.8
30	Nevada	5.4
31	Washington	5.1
32	Ohio	4.9
33	Utah	4.8
34	Pennsylvania	4.3
35	Florida	3.2
36	Colorado	3.1
37	Texas	2.9
38	New York	2.6
39	Maryland	2.5
40	Arizona	2.1
41	California	1.2
42	Rhode Island	0.2
43	Massachusetts	0.0
43	New Jersey	0.0
NA	Delaware**	NA
NA	Illinois**	NA
NA	Kansas**	NA
NA	Kentucky**	NA
NA	Montana**	NA
NA	New Hampshire**	NA

District of Columbia   0.0

Source: Morgan Quitno Press using data from Federal Bureau of Investigation
   "Crime in the United States 1999" (Uniform Crime Reports, October 15, 2000)
*Estimated percentages for rural areas, defined by the F.B.I. as other than Metropolitan Statistical Areas and other cities outside such areas. National percent includes those states listed as not available. Includes murder, rape, robbery, aggravated assault, burglary, larceny-theft and motor vehicle theft.
**Not available.

Violent Crimes in Urban Areas in 1999

National Urban Total = 1,357,227 Violent Crimes*

ALPHA ORDER

RANK	STATE	CRIMES	% of USA
19	Alabama	19,852	1.5%
36	Alaska	3,145	0.2%
17	Arizona	25,443	1.9%
30	Arkansas	9,641	0.7%
1	California	205,804	15.2%
23	Colorado	13,343	1.0%
28	Connecticut	10,255	0.8%
NA	Delaware**	NA	NA
2	Florida	124,219	9.2%
9	Georgia	36,624	2.7%
39	Hawaii	2,198	0.2%
38	Idaho	2,385	0.2%
NA	Illinois**	NA	NA
20	Indiana	19,382	1.4%
32	Iowa	7,456	0.5%
NA	Kansas**	NA	NA
NA	Kentucky**	NA	NA
14	Louisiana	28,265	2.1%
40	Maine	1,241	0.1%
7	Maryland	37,570	2.8%
12	Massachusetts	34,011	2.5%
5	Michigan	54,354	4.0%
25	Minnesota	12,178	0.9%
31	Mississippi	7,600	0.6%
16	Missouri	25,494	1.9%
NA	Montana**	NA	NA
33	Nebraska	6,893	0.5%
29	Nevada	9,694	0.7%
NA	New Hampshire**	NA	NA
13	New Jersey	33,540	2.5%
24	New Mexico	12,739	0.9%
4	New York	105,289	7.8%
8	North Carolina	36,807	2.7%
44	North Dakota	371	0.0%
11	Ohio	34,386	2.5%
22	Oklahoma	15,438	1.1%
27	Oregon	11,627	0.9%
6	Pennsylvania	49,002	3.6%
37	Rhode Island	2,799	0.2%
15	South Carolina	26,670	2.0%
41	South Dakota	1,035	0.1%
10	Tennessee	35,051	2.6%
3	Texas	108,464	8.0%
34	Utah	5,573	0.4%
43	Vermont	539	0.0%
21	Virginia	19,317	1.4%
18	Washington	20,794	1.5%
35	West Virginia	4,319	0.3%
26	Wisconsin	11,977	0.9%
42	Wyoming	891	0.1%

RANK ORDER

RANK	STATE	CRIMES	% of USA
1	California	205,804	15.2%
2	Florida	124,219	9.2%
3	Texas	108,464	8.0%
4	New York	105,289	7.8%
5	Michigan	54,354	4.0%
6	Pennsylvania	49,002	3.6%
7	Maryland	37,570	2.8%
8	North Carolina	36,807	2.7%
9	Georgia	36,624	2.7%
10	Tennessee	35,051	2.6%
11	Ohio	34,386	2.5%
12	Massachusetts	34,011	2.5%
13	New Jersey	33,540	2.5%
14	Louisiana	28,265	2.1%
15	South Carolina	26,670	2.0%
16	Missouri	25,494	1.9%
17	Arizona	25,443	1.9%
18	Washington	20,794	1.5%
19	Alabama	19,852	1.5%
20	Indiana	19,382	1.4%
21	Virginia	19,317	1.4%
22	Oklahoma	15,438	1.1%
23	Colorado	13,343	1.0%
24	New Mexico	12,739	0.9%
25	Minnesota	12,178	0.9%
26	Wisconsin	11,977	0.9%
27	Oregon	11,627	0.9%
28	Connecticut	10,255	0.8%
29	Nevada	9,694	0.7%
30	Arkansas	9,641	0.7%
31	Mississippi	7,600	0.6%
32	Iowa	7,456	0.5%
33	Nebraska	6,893	0.5%
34	Utah	5,573	0.4%
35	West Virginia	4,319	0.3%
36	Alaska	3,145	0.2%
37	Rhode Island	2,799	0.2%
38	Idaho	2,385	0.2%
39	Hawaii	2,198	0.2%
40	Maine	1,241	0.1%
41	South Dakota	1,035	0.1%
42	Wyoming	891	0.1%
43	Vermont	539	0.0%
44	North Dakota	371	0.0%
NA	Delaware**	NA	NA
NA	Illinois**	NA	NA
NA	Kansas**	NA	NA
NA	Kentucky**	NA	NA
NA	Montana**	NA	NA
NA	New Hampshire**	NA	NA

District of Columbia   8,448   0.6%

Source: Morgan Quitno Press using data from Federal Bureau of Investigation
   "Crime in the United States 1999" (Uniform Crime Reports, October 15, 2000)
*Estimated totals for urban areas, defined by the F.B.I. as Metropolitan Statistical Areas and other cities outside such areas. National total includes those states listed as not available. Violent crimes are offenses of murder, forcible rape, robbery and aggravated assault.
**Not available.

Urban Violent Crime Rate in 1999

National Urban Rate = 567.0 Violent Crimes per 100,000 Population*

ALPHA ORDER

RANK	STATE	RATE
18	Alabama	558.0
7	Alaska	739.1
17	Arizona	567.9
19	Arkansas	556.6
8	California	633.1
31	Colorado	361.9
30	Connecticut	365.9
NA	Delaware**	NA
3	Florida	870.2
15	Georgia	588.4
40	Hawaii	253.6
36	Idaho	286.2
NA	Illinois**	NA
27	Indiana	401.9
29	Iowa	377.6
NA	Kansas**	NA
NA	Kentucky**	NA
5	Louisiana	772.7
43	Maine	138.9
6	Maryland	769.2
20	Massachusetts	551.7
10	Michigan	620.9
34	Minnesota	313.6
22	Mississippi	466.0
12	Missouri	603.2
NA	Montana**	NA
21	Nebraska	548.7
13	Nevada	602.4
NA	New Hampshire**	NA
26	New Jersey	411.9
1	New Mexico	892.5
11	New York	607.9
9	North Carolina	626.8
44	North Dakota	88.6
32	Ohio	348.0
16	Oklahoma	570.1
24	Oregon	416.8
23	Pennsylvania	447.3
37	Rhode Island	282.4
2	South Carolina	881.3
41	South Dakota	229.0
4	Tennessee	804.8
14	Texas	590.9
35	Utah	294.9
42	Vermont	152.7
33	Virginia	333.7
28	Washington	399.1
25	West Virginia	414.3
38	Wisconsin	282.0
39	Wyoming	255.2

RANK ORDER

RANK	STATE	RATE
1	New Mexico	892.5
2	South Carolina	881.3
3	Florida	870.2
4	Tennessee	804.8
5	Louisiana	772.7
6	Maryland	769.2
7	Alaska	739.1
8	California	633.1
9	North Carolina	626.8
10	Michigan	620.9
11	New York	607.9
12	Missouri	603.2
13	Nevada	602.4
14	Texas	590.9
15	Georgia	588.4
16	Oklahoma	570.1
17	Arizona	567.9
18	Alabama	558.0
19	Arkansas	556.6
20	Massachusetts	551.7
21	Nebraska	548.7
22	Mississippi	466.0
23	Pennsylvania	447.3
24	Oregon	416.8
25	West Virginia	414.3
26	New Jersey	411.9
27	Indiana	401.9
28	Washington	399.1
29	Iowa	377.6
30	Connecticut	365.9
31	Colorado	361.9
32	Ohio	348.0
33	Virginia	333.7
34	Minnesota	313.6
35	Utah	294.9
36	Idaho	286.2
37	Rhode Island	282.4
38	Wisconsin	282.0
39	Wyoming	255.2
40	Hawaii	253.6
41	South Dakota	229.0
42	Vermont	152.7
43	Maine	138.9
44	North Dakota	88.6
NA	Delaware**	NA
NA	Illinois**	NA
NA	Kansas**	NA
NA	Kentucky**	NA
NA	Montana**	NA
NA	New Hampshire**	NA

District of Columbia 1,627.7

Source: Morgan Quitno Press using data from Federal Bureau of Investigation
"Crime in the United States 1999" (Uniform Crime Reports, October 15, 2000)
*Estimated rates for urban areas, defined by the F.B.I. as Metropolitan Statistical Areas and other cities outside such areas. National rate includes those states listed as not available. Violent crimes are offenses of murder, forcible rape, robbery and aggravated assault.
**Not available.

Percent of Violent Crimes Occurring in Urban Areas in 1999

National Percent = 94.9% of Violent Crimes*

ALPHA ORDER

RANK	STATE	PERCENT
23	Alabama	92.7
38	Alaska	80.5
8	Arizona	96.6
28	Arkansas	88.9
3	California	99.0
8	Colorado	96.6
26	Connecticut	90.4
NA	Delaware**	NA
12	Florida	96.3
32	Georgia	88.1
41	Hawaii	78.9
43	Idaho	77.8
NA	Illinois**	NA
35	Indiana	87.1
21	Iowa	92.8
NA	Kansas**	NA
NA	Kentucky**	NA
31	Louisiana	88.2
30	Maine	88.3
6	Maryland	97.7
1	Massachusetts	100.0
14	Michigan	95.8
20	Minnesota	93.1
42	Mississippi	78.6
19	Missouri	93.2
NA	Montana**	NA
13	Nebraska	96.2
17	Nevada	94.0
NA	New Hampshire**	NA
1	New Jersey	100.0
33	New Mexico	87.7
5	New York	98.3
29	North Carolina	88.7
34	North Dakota	87.5
11	Ohio	96.5
25	Oklahoma	90.5
18	Oregon	93.5
7	Pennsylvania	97.2
4	Rhode Island	98.6
37	South Carolina	81.0
36	South Dakota	84.4
24	Tennessee	92.0
8	Texas	96.6
16	Utah	95.0
40	Vermont	79.7
27	Virginia	89.3
14	Washington	95.8
44	West Virginia	68.2
21	Wisconsin	92.8
39	Wyoming	79.9

RANK ORDER

RANK	STATE	PERCENT
1	Massachusetts	100.0
1	New Jersey	100.0
3	California	99.0
4	Rhode Island	98.6
5	New York	98.3
6	Maryland	97.7
7	Pennsylvania	97.2
8	Arizona	96.6
8	Colorado	96.6
8	Texas	96.6
11	Ohio	96.5
12	Florida	96.3
13	Nebraska	96.2
14	Michigan	95.8
14	Washington	95.8
16	Utah	95.0
17	Nevada	94.0
18	Oregon	93.5
19	Missouri	93.2
20	Minnesota	93.1
21	Iowa	92.8
21	Wisconsin	92.8
23	Alabama	92.7
24	Tennessee	92.0
25	Oklahoma	90.5
26	Connecticut	90.4
27	Virginia	89.3
28	Arkansas	88.9
29	North Carolina	88.7
30	Maine	88.3
31	Louisiana	88.2
32	Georgia	88.1
33	New Mexico	87.7
34	North Dakota	87.5
35	Indiana	87.1
36	South Dakota	84.4
37	South Carolina	81.0
38	Alaska	80.5
39	Wyoming	79.9
40	Vermont	79.7
41	Hawaii	78.9
42	Mississippi	78.6
43	Idaho	77.8
44	West Virginia	68.2
NA	Delaware**	NA
NA	Illinois**	NA
NA	Kansas**	NA
NA	Kentucky**	NA
NA	Montana**	NA
NA	New Hampshire**	NA
	District of Columbia	100.0

Source: Morgan Quitno Press using data from Federal Bureau of Investigation
    "Crime in the United States 1999" (Uniform Crime Reports, October 15, 2000)
*Estimated percentages for urban areas, defined by the F.B.I. as Metropolitan Statistical Areas and other cities outside such areas. National percent includes those states listed as not available. Violent crimes are offenses of murder, forcible rape, robbery and aggravated assault.
**Not available.

Violent Crimes in Rural Areas in 1999

National Rural Total = 73,466 Violent Crimes*

ALPHA ORDER

RANK	STATE	CRIMES	% of USA
18	Alabama	1,569	2.1%
29	Alaska	764	1.0%
26	Arizona	891	1.2%
21	Arkansas	1,207	1.6%
11	California	2,075	2.8%
34	Colorado	468	0.6%
22	Connecticut	1,087	1.5%
NA	Delaware**	NA	NA
3	Florida	4,825	6.6%
2	Georgia	4,961	6.8%
32	Hawaii	587	0.8%
30	Idaho	681	0.9%
NA	Illinois**	NA	NA
8	Indiana	2,879	3.9%
33	Iowa	578	0.8%
NA	Kansas**	NA	NA
NA	Kentucky**	NA	NA
6	Louisiana	3,768	5.1%
39	Maine	165	0.2%
27	Maryland	877	1.2%
43	Massachusetts	12	0.0%
9	Michigan	2,355	3.2%
25	Minnesota	907	1.2%
12	Mississippi	2,071	2.8%
14	Missouri	1,859	2.5%
NA	Montana**	NA	NA
36	Nebraska	274	0.4%
31	Nevada	617	0.8%
NA	New Hampshire**	NA	NA
44	New Jersey	0	0.0%
16	New Mexico	1,781	2.4%
15	New York	1,858	2.5%
4	North Carolina	4,667	6.4%
41	North Dakota	53	0.1%
20	Ohio	1,230	1.7%
17	Oklahoma	1,628	2.2%
28	Oregon	805	1.1%
19	Pennsylvania	1,429	1.9%
42	Rhode Island	41	0.1%
1	South Carolina	6,250	8.5%
38	South Dakota	192	0.3%
7	Tennessee	3,060	4.2%
5	Texas	3,842	5.2%
35	Utah	296	0.4%
40	Vermont	137	0.2%
10	Virginia	2,309	3.1%
24	Washington	922	1.3%
13	West Virginia	2,017	2.7%
23	Wisconsin	931	1.3%
37	Wyoming	224	0.3%

RANK ORDER

RANK	STATE	CRIMES	% of USA
1	South Carolina	6,250	8.5%
2	Georgia	4,961	6.8%
3	Florida	4,825	6.6%
4	North Carolina	4,667	6.4%
5	Texas	3,842	5.2%
6	Louisiana	3,768	5.1%
7	Tennessee	3,060	4.2%
8	Indiana	2,879	3.9%
9	Michigan	2,355	3.2%
10	Virginia	2,309	3.1%
11	California	2,075	2.8%
12	Mississippi	2,071	2.8%
13	West Virginia	2,017	2.7%
14	Missouri	1,859	2.5%
15	New York	1,858	2.5%
16	New Mexico	1,781	2.4%
17	Oklahoma	1,628	2.2%
18	Alabama	1,569	2.1%
19	Pennsylvania	1,429	1.9%
20	Ohio	1,230	1.7%
21	Arkansas	1,207	1.6%
22	Connecticut	1,087	1.5%
23	Wisconsin	931	1.3%
24	Washington	922	1.3%
25	Minnesota	907	1.2%
26	Arizona	891	1.2%
27	Maryland	877	1.2%
28	Oregon	805	1.1%
29	Alaska	764	1.0%
30	Idaho	681	0.9%
31	Nevada	617	0.8%
32	Hawaii	587	0.8%
33	Iowa	578	0.8%
34	Colorado	468	0.6%
35	Utah	296	0.4%
36	Nebraska	274	0.4%
37	Wyoming	224	0.3%
38	South Dakota	192	0.3%
39	Maine	165	0.2%
40	Vermont	137	0.2%
41	North Dakota	53	0.1%
42	Rhode Island	41	0.1%
43	Massachusetts	12	0.0%
44	New Jersey	0	0.0%
NA	Delaware**	NA	NA
NA	Illinois**	NA	NA
NA	Kansas**	NA	NA
NA	Kentucky**	NA	NA
NA	Montana**	NA	NA
NA	New Hampshire**	NA	NA
	District of Columbia	0	0.0%

Source: Federal Bureau of Investigation
     "Crime in the United States 1999" (Uniform Crime Reports, October 15, 2000)
*Estimated totals for rural areas, defined by the F.B.I. as other than Metropolitan Statistical Areas and other cities outside such areas. National total includes those states listed as not available. Violent crimes are offenses of murder, forcible rape, robbery and aggravated assault.
**Not available.

Rural Violent Crime Rate in 1999

National Rural Rate = 220.5 Violent Crimes per 100,000 Population*

ALPHA ORDER

RANK	STATE	RATE
21	Alabama	193.2
5	Alaska	394.8
10	Arizona	299.4
29	Arkansas	147.4
6	California	324.2
31	Colorado	126.7
17	Connecticut	226.9
NA	Delaware**	NA
2	Florida	577.4
7	Georgia	317.3
22	Hawaii	184.3
26	Idaho	162.7
NA	Illinois**	NA
14	Indiana	257.0
39	Iowa	64.6
NA	Kansas**	NA
NA	Kentucky**	NA
4	Louisiana	527.6
41	Maine	45.9
9	Maryland	304.8
33	Massachusetts	117.4
19	Michigan	212.1
34	Minnesota	101.6
23	Mississippi	181.9
28	Missouri	149.8
NA	Montana**	NA
38	Nebraska	66.9
8	Nevada	308.8
NA	New Hampshire**	NA
43	New Jersey	0.0
3	New Mexico	569.5
20	New York	211.8
13	North Carolina	262.4
42	North Dakota	24.6
36	Ohio	89.4
15	Oklahoma	250.5
27	Oregon	153.0
30	Pennsylvania	137.5
43	Rhode Island	0.0
1	South Carolina	727.0
37	South Dakota	68.3
11	Tennessee	271.1
16	Texas	227.6
32	Utah	123.2
40	Vermont	56.9
18	Virginia	213.1
25	Washington	169.0
12	West Virginia	263.8
35	Wisconsin	92.8
24	Wyoming	171.2

RANK ORDER

RANK	STATE	RATE
1	South Carolina	727.0
2	Florida	577.4
3	New Mexico	569.5
4	Louisiana	527.6
5	Alaska	394.8
6	California	324.2
7	Georgia	317.3
8	Nevada	308.8
9	Maryland	304.8
10	Arizona	299.4
11	Tennessee	271.1
12	West Virginia	263.8
13	North Carolina	262.4
14	Indiana	257.0
15	Oklahoma	250.5
16	Texas	227.6
17	Connecticut	226.9
18	Virginia	213.1
19	Michigan	212.1
20	New York	211.8
21	Alabama	193.2
22	Hawaii	184.3
23	Mississippi	181.9
24	Wyoming	171.2
25	Washington	169.0
26	Idaho	162.7
27	Oregon	153.0
28	Missouri	149.8
29	Arkansas	147.4
30	Pennsylvania	137.5
31	Colorado	126.7
32	Utah	123.2
33	Massachusetts	117.4
34	Minnesota	101.6
35	Wisconsin	92.8
36	Ohio	89.4
37	South Dakota	68.3
38	Nebraska	66.9
39	Iowa	64.6
40	Vermont	56.9
41	Maine	45.9
42	North Dakota	24.6
43	New Jersey	0.0
43	Rhode Island	0.0
NA	Delaware**	NA
NA	Illinois**	NA
NA	Kansas**	NA
NA	Kentucky**	NA
NA	Montana**	NA
NA	New Hampshire**	NA

District of Columbia   0.0

Source: Morgan Quitno Press using data from Federal Bureau of Investigation
    "Crime in the United States 1999" (Uniform Crime Reports, October 15, 2000)
*Estimated rates for rural areas, defined by the F.B.I. as other than Metropolitan Statistical Areas and other cities outside such areas. National rate includes those states listed as not available. Violent crimes are offenses of murder, forcible rape, robbery and aggravated assault.
**Not available.

Percent of Violent Crimes Occurring in Rural Areas in 1999

National Percent = 5.1% of Violent Crimes*

ALPHA ORDER

RANK	STATE	PERCENT
22	Alabama	7.3
7	Alaska	19.5
35	Arizona	3.4
17	Arkansas	11.1
42	California	1.0
35	Colorado	3.4
19	Connecticut	9.6
NA	Delaware**	NA
33	Florida	3.7
13	Georgia	11.9
4	Hawaii	21.1
2	Idaho	22.2
NA	Illinois**	NA
10	Indiana	12.9
23	Iowa	7.2
NA	Kansas**	NA
NA	Kentucky**	NA
14	Louisiana	11.8
15	Maine	11.7
39	Maryland	2.3
43	Massachusetts	0.0
30	Michigan	4.2
25	Minnesota	6.9
3	Mississippi	21.4
26	Missouri	6.8
NA	Montana**	NA
32	Nebraska	3.8
28	Nevada	6.0
NA	New Hampshire**	NA
43	New Jersey	0.0
12	New Mexico	12.3
40	New York	1.7
16	North Carolina	11.3
11	North Dakota	12.5
34	Ohio	3.5
20	Oklahoma	9.5
27	Oregon	6.5
38	Pennsylvania	2.8
41	Rhode Island	1.4
8	South Carolina	19.0
9	South Dakota	15.6
21	Tennessee	8.0
35	Texas	3.4
29	Utah	5.0
5	Vermont	20.3
18	Virginia	10.7
30	Washington	4.2
1	West Virginia	31.8
23	Wisconsin	7.2
6	Wyoming	20.1

RANK ORDER

RANK	STATE	PERCENT
1	West Virginia	31.8
2	Idaho	22.2
3	Mississippi	21.4
4	Hawaii	21.1
5	Vermont	20.3
6	Wyoming	20.1
7	Alaska	19.5
8	South Carolina	19.0
9	South Dakota	15.6
10	Indiana	12.9
11	North Dakota	12.5
12	New Mexico	12.3
13	Georgia	11.9
14	Louisiana	11.8
15	Maine	11.7
16	North Carolina	11.3
17	Arkansas	11.1
18	Virginia	10.7
19	Connecticut	9.6
20	Oklahoma	9.5
21	Tennessee	8.0
22	Alabama	7.3
23	Iowa	7.2
23	Wisconsin	7.2
25	Minnesota	6.9
26	Missouri	6.8
27	Oregon	6.5
28	Nevada	6.0
29	Utah	5.0
30	Michigan	4.2
30	Washington	4.2
32	Nebraska	3.8
33	Florida	3.7
34	Ohio	3.5
35	Arizona	3.4
35	Colorado	3.4
35	Texas	3.4
38	Pennsylvania	2.8
39	Maryland	2.3
40	New York	1.7
41	Rhode Island	1.4
42	California	1.0
43	Massachusetts	0.0
43	New Jersey	0.0
NA	Delaware**	NA
NA	Illinois**	NA
NA	Kansas**	NA
NA	Kentucky**	NA
NA	Montana**	NA
NA	New Hampshire**	NA
	District of Columbia	0.0

Source: Morgan Quitno Press using data from Federal Bureau of Investigation
"Crime in the United States 1999" (Uniform Crime Reports, October 15, 2000)
*Estimated percentages for rural areas, defined by the F.B.I. as other than Metropolitan Statistical Areas and other cities outside such areas. National percent includes those states listed as not available. Violent crimes are offenses of murder, forcible rape, robbery and aggravated assault.
**Not available.

Murders in Urban Areas in 1999

National Urban Total = 14,239 Murders*

ALPHA ORDER

RANK	STATE	MURDERS	% of USA
16	Alabama	314	2.2%
38	Alaska	32	0.2%
12	Arizona	373	2.6%
29	Arkansas	114	0.8%
1	California	1,966	13.8%
20	Colorado	180	1.3%
30	Connecticut	101	0.7%
40	Delaware	23	0.2%
4	Florida	820	5.8%
7	Georgia	511	3.6%
36	Hawaii	37	0.3%
41	Idaho	15	0.1%
NA	Illinois**	NA	NA
15	Indiana	338	2.4%
34	Iowa	43	0.3%
NA	Kansas**	NA	NA
NA	Kentucky**	NA	NA
10	Louisiana	427	3.0%
39	Maine	24	0.2%
8	Maryland	454	3.2%
27	Massachusetts	122	0.9%
5	Michigan	673	4.7%
28	Minnesota	116	0.8%
25	Mississippi	149	1.0%
17	Missouri	310	2.2%
NA	Montana**	NA	NA
32	Nebraska	51	0.4%
24	Nevada	154	1.1%
NA	New Hampshire**	NA	NA
18	New Jersey	287	2.0%
26	New Mexico	136	1.0%
3	New York	883	6.2%
9	North Carolina	431	3.0%
44	North Dakota	8	0.1%
11	Ohio	385	2.7%
21	Oklahoma	175	1.2%
31	Oregon	68	0.5%
6	Pennsylvania	573	4.0%
37	Rhode Island	34	0.2%
19	South Carolina	192	1.3%
43	South Dakota	9	0.1%
13	Tennessee	350	2.5%
2	Texas	1,132	7.9%
34	Utah	43	0.3%
42	Vermont	12	0.1%
14	Virginia	344	2.4%
23	Washington	158	1.1%
33	West Virginia	45	0.3%
22	Wisconsin	165	1.2%
45	Wyoming	7	0.0%

RANK ORDER

RANK	STATE	MURDERS	% of USA
1	California	1,966	13.8%
2	Texas	1,132	7.9%
3	New York	883	6.2%
4	Florida	820	5.8%
5	Michigan	673	4.7%
6	Pennsylvania	573	4.0%
7	Georgia	511	3.6%
8	Maryland	454	3.2%
9	North Carolina	431	3.0%
10	Louisiana	427	3.0%
11	Ohio	385	2.7%
12	Arizona	373	2.6%
13	Tennessee	350	2.5%
14	Virginia	344	2.4%
15	Indiana	338	2.4%
16	Alabama	314	2.2%
17	Missouri	310	2.2%
18	New Jersey	287	2.0%
19	South Carolina	192	1.3%
20	Colorado	180	1.3%
21	Oklahoma	175	1.2%
22	Wisconsin	165	1.2%
23	Washington	158	1.1%
24	Nevada	154	1.1%
25	Mississippi	149	1.0%
26	New Mexico	136	1.0%
27	Massachusetts	122	0.9%
28	Minnesota	116	0.8%
29	Arkansas	114	0.8%
30	Connecticut	101	0.7%
31	Oregon	68	0.5%
32	Nebraska	51	0.4%
33	West Virginia	45	0.3%
34	Iowa	43	0.3%
34	Utah	43	0.3%
36	Hawaii	37	0.3%
37	Rhode Island	34	0.2%
38	Alaska	32	0.2%
39	Maine	24	0.2%
40	Delaware	23	0.2%
41	Idaho	15	0.1%
42	Vermont	12	0.1%
43	South Dakota	9	0.1%
44	North Dakota	8	0.1%
45	Wyoming	7	0.0%
NA	Illinois**	NA	NA
NA	Kansas**	NA	NA
NA	Kentucky**	NA	NA
NA	Montana**	NA	NA
NA	New Hampshire**	NA	NA
	District of Columbia	241	1.7%

Source: Morgan Quitno Press using data from Federal Bureau of Investigation
"Crime in the United States 1999" (Uniform Crime Reports, October 15, 2000)
Estimated totals for urban areas, defined by the F.B.I. as Metropolitan Statistical Areas and other cities outside such areas. National total includes those states listed as not available. Includes nonnegligent manslaughter.
**Not available.*

Urban Murder Rate in 1999

National Urban Rate = 5.9 Murders per 100,000 Population*

ALPHA ORDER

RANK	STATE	RATE
6	Alabama	8.8
11	Alaska	7.5
7	Arizona	8.3
15	Arkansas	6.6
19	California	6.0
24	Colorado	4.9
30	Connecticut	3.6
31	Delaware	3.5
21	Florida	5.7
8	Georgia	8.2
25	Hawaii	4.3
45	Idaho	1.8
NA	Illinois**	NA
14	Indiana	7.0
40	Iowa	2.2
NA	Kansas**	NA
NA	Kentucky**	NA
1	Louisiana	11.7
37	Maine	2.7
4	Maryland	9.3
41	Massachusetts	2.0
10	Michigan	7.7
35	Minnesota	3.0
5	Mississippi	9.1
12	Missouri	7.3
NA	Montana**	NA
27	Nebraska	4.1
2	Nevada	9.6
NA	New Hampshire**	NA
31	New Jersey	3.5
3	New Mexico	9.5
23	New York	5.1
12	North Carolina	7.3
44	North Dakota	1.9
28	Ohio	3.9
16	Oklahoma	6.5
38	Oregon	2.4
22	Pennsylvania	5.2
33	Rhode Island	3.4
17	South Carolina	6.3
41	South Dakota	2.0
9	Tennessee	8.0
18	Texas	6.2
39	Utah	2.3
33	Vermont	3.4
20	Virginia	5.9
35	Washington	3.0
25	West Virginia	4.3
28	Wisconsin	3.9
41	Wyoming	2.0

RANK ORDER

RANK	STATE	RATE
1	Louisiana	11.7
2	Nevada	9.6
3	New Mexico	9.5
4	Maryland	9.3
5	Mississippi	9.1
6	Alabama	8.8
7	Arizona	8.3
8	Georgia	8.2
9	Tennessee	8.0
10	Michigan	7.7
11	Alaska	7.5
12	Missouri	7.3
12	North Carolina	7.3
14	Indiana	7.0
15	Arkansas	6.6
16	Oklahoma	6.5
17	South Carolina	6.3
18	Texas	6.2
19	California	6.0
20	Virginia	5.9
21	Florida	5.7
22	Pennsylvania	5.2
23	New York	5.1
24	Colorado	4.9
25	Hawaii	4.3
25	West Virginia	4.3
27	Nebraska	4.1
28	Ohio	3.9
28	Wisconsin	3.9
30	Connecticut	3.6
31	Delaware	3.5
31	New Jersey	3.5
33	Rhode Island	3.4
33	Vermont	3.4
35	Minnesota	3.0
35	Washington	3.0
37	Maine	2.7
38	Oregon	2.4
39	Utah	2.3
40	Iowa	2.2
41	Massachusetts	2.0
41	South Dakota	2.0
41	Wyoming	2.0
44	North Dakota	1.9
45	Idaho	1.8
NA	Illinois**	NA
NA	Kansas**	NA
NA	Kentucky**	NA
NA	Montana**	NA
NA	New Hampshire**	NA

District of Columbia 46.4

Source: Morgan Quitno Press using data from Federal Bureau of Investigation
   "Crime in the United States 1999" (Uniform Crime Reports, October 15, 2000)
*Estimated rates for urban areas, defined by the F.B.I. as Metropolitan Statistical Areas and other cities outside
such areas. National rate includes those states listed as not available. Includes nonnegligent manslaughter.
**Not available.

Percent of Murders Occurring in Urban Areas in 1999

National Percent = 91.7% of Murders*

ALPHA ORDER

RANK	STATE	PERCENT
22	Alabama	91.0
42	Alaska	60.4
9	Arizona	97.1
34	Arkansas	79.7
4	California	98.1
8	Colorado	97.3
15	Connecticut	94.4
13	Delaware	95.8
14	Florida	95.5
26	Georgia	87.7
31	Hawaii	84.1
43	Idaho	60.0
NA	Illinois**	NA
28	Indiana	86.4
1	Iowa	100.0
NA	Kansas**	NA
NA	Kentucky**	NA
21	Louisiana	91.2
24	Maine	88.9
7	Maryland	97.6
1	Massachusetts	100.0
11	Michigan	96.8
27	Minnesota	86.6
40	Mississippi	70.0
28	Missouri	86.4
NA	Montana**	NA
30	Nebraska	85.0
17	Nevada	93.3
NA	New Hampshire**	NA
1	New Jersey	100.0
32	New Mexico	80.0
5	New York	97.8
35	North Carolina	78.1
32	North Dakota	80.0
10	Ohio	97.0
37	Oklahoma	75.8
36	Oregon	77.3
11	Pennsylvania	96.8
15	Rhode Island	94.4
38	South Carolina	74.4
45	South Dakota	50.0
23	Tennessee	89.5
18	Texas	93.0
6	Utah	97.7
39	Vermont	70.6
25	Virginia	87.8
19	Washington	92.4
44	West Virginia	57.0
20	Wisconsin	92.2
41	Wyoming	63.6

RANK ORDER

RANK	STATE	PERCENT
1	Iowa	100.0
1	Massachusetts	100.0
1	New Jersey	100.0
4	California	98.1
5	New York	97.8
6	Utah	97.7
7	Maryland	97.6
8	Colorado	97.3
9	Arizona	97.1
10	Ohio	97.0
11	Michigan	96.8
11	Pennsylvania	96.8
13	Delaware	95.8
14	Florida	95.5
15	Connecticut	94.4
15	Rhode Island	94.4
17	Nevada	93.3
18	Texas	93.0
19	Washington	92.4
20	Wisconsin	92.2
21	Louisiana	91.2
22	Alabama	91.0
23	Tennessee	89.5
24	Maine	88.9
25	Virginia	87.8
26	Georgia	87.7
27	Minnesota	86.6
28	Indiana	86.4
28	Missouri	86.4
30	Nebraska	85.0
31	Hawaii	84.1
32	New Mexico	80.0
32	North Dakota	80.0
34	Arkansas	79.7
35	North Carolina	78.1
36	Oregon	77.3
37	Oklahoma	75.8
38	South Carolina	74.4
39	Vermont	70.6
40	Mississippi	70.0
41	Wyoming	63.6
42	Alaska	60.4
43	Idaho	60.0
44	West Virginia	57.0
45	South Dakota	50.0
NA	Illinois**	NA
NA	Kansas**	NA
NA	Kentucky**	NA
NA	Montana**	NA
NA	New Hampshire**	NA

District of Columbia   100.0

Source: Morgan Quitno Press using data from Federal Bureau of Investigation
"Crime in the United States 1999" (Uniform Crime Reports, October 15, 2000)
Estimated percentages for urban areas, defined by the F.B.I. as Metropolitan Statistical Areas and other cities outside such areas. National percent includes those states listed as not available. Includes nonnegligent manslaughter.
**Not available.*

Murders in Rural Areas in 1999

National Rural Total = 1,294 Murders*

ALPHA ORDER

RANK	STATE	MURDERS	% of USA
16	Alabama	31	2.4%
19	Alaska	21	1.6%
27	Arizona	11	0.9%
17	Arkansas	29	2.2%
12	California	39	3.0%
35	Colorado	5	0.4%
34	Connecticut	6	0.5%
41	Delaware	1	0.1%
12	Florida	39	3.0%
3	Georgia	72	5.6%
33	Hawaii	7	0.5%
30	Idaho	10	0.8%
NA	Illinois**	NA	NA
7	Indiana	53	4.1%
43	Iowa	0	0.0%
NA	Kansas**	NA	NA
NA	Kentucky**	NA	NA
10	Louisiana	41	3.2%
38	Maine	3	0.2%
27	Maryland	11	0.9%
43	Massachusetts	0	0.0%
18	Michigan	22	1.7%
23	Minnesota	18	1.4%
5	Mississippi	64	4.9%
8	Missouri	49	3.8%
NA	Montana**	NA	NA
31	Nebraska	9	0.7%
27	Nevada	11	0.9%
NA	New Hampshire**	NA	NA
43	New Jersey	0	0.0%
14	New Mexico	34	2.6%
20	New York	20	1.5%
1	North Carolina	121	9.4%
39	North Dakota	2	0.2%
26	Ohio	12	0.9%
6	Oklahoma	56	4.3%
20	Oregon	20	1.5%
22	Pennsylvania	19	1.5%
39	Rhode Island	2	0.2%
4	South Carolina	66	5.1%
31	South Dakota	9	0.7%
10	Tennessee	41	3.2%
2	Texas	85	6.6%
41	Utah	1	0.1%
35	Vermont	5	0.4%
9	Virginia	48	3.7%
25	Washington	13	1.0%
14	West Virginia	34	2.6%
24	Wisconsin	14	1.1%
37	Wyoming	4	0.3%

RANK ORDER

RANK	STATE	MURDERS	% of USA
1	North Carolina	121	9.4%
2	Texas	85	6.6%
3	Georgia	72	5.6%
4	South Carolina	66	5.1%
5	Mississippi	64	4.9%
6	Oklahoma	56	4.3%
7	Indiana	53	4.1%
8	Missouri	49	3.8%
9	Virginia	48	3.7%
10	Louisiana	41	3.2%
10	Tennessee	41	3.2%
12	California	39	3.0%
12	Florida	39	3.0%
14	New Mexico	34	2.6%
14	West Virginia	34	2.6%
16	Alabama	31	2.4%
17	Arkansas	29	2.2%
18	Michigan	22	1.7%
19	Alaska	21	1.6%
20	New York	20	1.5%
20	Oregon	20	1.5%
22	Pennsylvania	19	1.5%
23	Minnesota	18	1.4%
24	Wisconsin	14	1.1%
25	Washington	13	1.0%
26	Ohio	12	0.9%
27	Arizona	11	0.9%
27	Maryland	11	0.9%
27	Nevada	11	0.9%
30	Idaho	10	0.8%
31	Nebraska	9	0.7%
31	South Dakota	9	0.7%
33	Hawaii	7	0.5%
34	Connecticut	6	0.5%
35	Colorado	5	0.4%
35	Vermont	5	0.4%
37	Wyoming	4	0.3%
38	Maine	3	0.2%
39	North Dakota	2	0.2%
39	Rhode Island	2	0.2%
41	Delaware	1	0.1%
41	Utah	1	0.1%
43	Iowa	0	0.0%
43	Massachusetts	0	0.0%
43	New Jersey	0	0.0%
NA	Illinois**	NA	NA
NA	Kansas**	NA	NA
NA	Kentucky**	NA	NA
NA	Montana**	NA	NA
NA	New Hampshire**	NA	NA
	District of Columbia	0	0.0%

Source: Federal Bureau of Investigation
   "Crime in the United States 1999" (Uniform Crime Reports, October 15, 2000)
*Estimated totals for rural areas, defined by the F.B.I. as other than Metropolitan Statistical Areas and other cities outside such areas. National total includes those states listed as not available. Includes nonnegligent manslaughter.
**Not available.

Rural Murder Rate in 1999

National Rural Rate = 3.9 Murders per 100,000 Population*

ALPHA ORDER			RANK ORDER		
RANK	STATE	RATE	RANK	STATE	RATE
17	Alabama	3.8	1	Alaska	10.9
1	Alaska	10.9	1	New Mexico	10.9
20	Arizona	3.7	3	Oklahoma	8.6
22	Arkansas	3.5	4	South Carolina	7.7
6	California	6.1	5	North Carolina	6.8
34	Colorado	1.4	6	California	6.1
36	Connecticut	1.3	7	Louisiana	5.7
37	Delaware	1.0	8	Mississippi	5.6
11	Florida	4.7	9	Nevada	5.5
13	Georgia	4.6	10	Texas	5.0
28	Hawaii	2.2	11	Florida	4.7
25	Idaho	2.4	11	Indiana	4.7
NA	Illinois**	NA	13	Georgia	4.6
11	Indiana	4.7	14	Virginia	4.4
42	Iowa	0.0	14	West Virginia	4.4
NA	Kansas**	NA	16	Missouri	3.9
NA	Kentucky**	NA	17	Alabama	3.8
7	Louisiana	5.7	17	Maryland	3.8
40	Maine	0.8	17	Oregon	3.8
17	Maryland	3.8	20	Arizona	3.7
42	Massachusetts	0.0	21	Tennessee	3.6
31	Michigan	2.0	22	Arkansas	3.5
31	Minnesota	2.0	23	South Dakota	3.2
8	Mississippi	5.6	24	Wyoming	3.1
16	Missouri	3.9	25	Idaho	2.4
NA	Montana**	NA	25	Washington	2.4
28	Nebraska	2.2	27	New York	2.3
9	Nevada	5.5	28	Hawaii	2.2
NA	New Hampshire**	NA	28	Nebraska	2.2
42	New Jersey	0.0	30	Vermont	2.1
1	New Mexico	10.9	31	Michigan	2.0
27	New York	2.3	31	Minnesota	2.0
5	North Carolina	6.8	33	Pennsylvania	1.8
38	North Dakota	0.9	34	Colorado	1.4
38	Ohio	0.9	34	Wisconsin	1.4
3	Oklahoma	8.6	36	Connecticut	1.3
17	Oregon	3.8	37	Delaware	1.0
33	Pennsylvania	1.8	38	North Dakota	0.9
42	Rhode Island	0.0	38	Ohio	0.9
4	South Carolina	7.7	40	Maine	0.8
23	South Dakota	3.2	41	Utah	0.4
21	Tennessee	3.6	42	Iowa	0.0
10	Texas	5.0	42	Massachusetts	0.0
41	Utah	0.4	42	New Jersey	0.0
30	Vermont	2.1	42	Rhode Island	0.0
14	Virginia	4.4	NA	Illinois**	NA
25	Washington	2.4	NA	Kansas**	NA
14	West Virginia	4.4	NA	Kentucky**	NA
34	Wisconsin	1.4	NA	Montana**	NA
24	Wyoming	3.1	NA	New Hampshire**	NA
				District of Columbia	0.0

Source: Morgan Quitno Press using data from Federal Bureau of Investigation
  "Crime in the United States 1999" (Uniform Crime Reports, October 15, 2000)
*Estimated rates for rural areas, defined by the F.B.I. as other than Metropolitan Statistical Areas and other cities outside such areas. National rate includes those states listed as not available. Includes nonnegligent manslaughter.
**Not available.

Percent of Murders Occurring in Rural Areas in 1999

National Percent = 8.3% of Murders*

ALPHA ORDER				RANK ORDER		
RANK	STATE	PERCENT		RANK	STATE	PERCENT
24	Alabama	9.0		1	South Dakota	50.0
4	Alaska	39.6		2	West Virginia	43.0
37	Arizona	2.9		3	Idaho	40.0
12	Arkansas	20.3		4	Alaska	39.6
42	California	1.9		5	Wyoming	36.4
38	Colorado	2.7		6	Mississippi	30.0
30	Connecticut	5.6		7	Vermont	29.4
33	Delaware	4.2		8	South Carolina	25.6
32	Florida	4.5		9	Oklahoma	24.2
20	Georgia	12.3		10	Oregon	22.7
15	Hawaii	15.9		11	North Carolina	21.9
3	Idaho	40.0		12	Arkansas	20.3
NA	Illinois**	NA		13	New Mexico	20.0
17	Indiana	13.6		13	North Dakota	20.0
43	Iowa	0.0		15	Hawaii	15.9
NA	Kansas**	NA		16	Nebraska	15.0
NA	Kentucky**	NA		17	Indiana	13.6
25	Louisiana	8.8		17	Missouri	13.6
22	Maine	11.1		19	Minnesota	13.4
39	Maryland	2.4		20	Georgia	12.3
43	Massachusetts	0.0		21	Virginia	12.2
34	Michigan	3.2		22	Maine	11.1
19	Minnesota	13.4		23	Tennessee	10.5
6	Mississippi	30.0		24	Alabama	9.0
17	Missouri	13.6		25	Louisiana	8.8
NA	Montana**	NA		26	Wisconsin	7.8
16	Nebraska	15.0		27	Washington	7.6
29	Nevada	6.7		28	Texas	7.0
NA	New Hampshire**	NA		29	Nevada	6.7
43	New Jersey	0.0		30	Connecticut	5.6
13	New Mexico	20.0		30	Rhode Island	5.6
41	New York	2.2		32	Florida	4.5
11	North Carolina	21.9		33	Delaware	4.2
13	North Dakota	20.0		34	Michigan	3.2
36	Ohio	3.0		34	Pennsylvania	3.2
9	Oklahoma	24.2		36	Ohio	3.0
10	Oregon	22.7		37	Arizona	2.9
34	Pennsylvania	3.2		38	Colorado	2.7
30	Rhode Island	5.6		39	Maryland	2.4
8	South Carolina	25.6		40	Utah	2.3
1	South Dakota	50.0		41	New York	2.2
23	Tennessee	10.5		42	California	1.9
28	Texas	7.0		43	Iowa	0.0
40	Utah	2.3		43	Massachusetts	0.0
7	Vermont	29.4		43	New Jersey	0.0
21	Virginia	12.2		NA	Illinois**	NA
27	Washington	7.6		NA	Kansas**	NA
2	West Virginia	43.0		NA	Kentucky**	NA
26	Wisconsin	7.8		NA	Montana**	NA
5	Wyoming	36.4		NA	New Hampshire**	NA
					District of Columbia	0.0

Source: Morgan Quitno Press using data from Federal Bureau of Investigation
    "Crime in the United States 1999" (Uniform Crime Reports, October 15, 2000)
*Estimated percentages for rural areas, defined by the F.B.I. as other than Metropolitan Statistical Areas and other cities outside such areas. National percent includes those states listed as not available. Includes nonnegligent manslaughter.
**Not available.

Rapes in Urban Areas in 1999

National Urban Total = 81,487 Rapes*

RANK	STATE	RAPES	% of USA
19	Alabama	1,358	1.7%
36	Alaska	370	0.5%
20	Arizona	1,349	1.7%
32	Arkansas	637	0.8%
1	California	9,198	11.3%
14	Colorado	1,597	2.0%
33	Connecticut	599	0.7%
NA	Delaware**	NA	NA
3	Florida	6,634	8.1%
10	Georgia	2,037	2.5%
40	Hawaii	235	0.3%
37	Idaho	302	0.4%
NA	Illinois**	NA	NA
18	Indiana	1,381	1.7%
31	Iowa	733	0.9%
NA	Kansas**	NA	NA
NA	Kentucky**	NA	NA
21	Louisiana	1,326	1.6%
41	Maine	209	0.3%
16	Maryland	1,460	1.8%
13	Massachusetts	1,663	2.0%
4	Michigan	4,136	5.1%
12	Minnesota	1,753	2.2%
26	Mississippi	931	1.1%
23	Missouri	1,257	1.5%
NA	Montana**	NA	NA
34	Nebraska	385	0.5%
28	Nevada	880	1.1%
NA	New Hampshire**	NA	NA
17	New Jersey	1,409	1.7%
29	New Mexico	788	1.0%
6	New York	3,425	4.2%
11	North Carolina	1,803	2.2%
42	North Dakota	120	0.1%
5	Ohio	3,915	4.8%
24	Oklahoma	1,249	1.5%
25	Oregon	1,109	1.4%
7	Pennsylvania	2,996	3.7%
35	Rhode Island	376	0.5%
22	South Carolina	1,303	1.6%
38	South Dakota	274	0.3%
9	Tennessee	2,217	2.7%
2	Texas	7,264	8.9%
30	Utah	764	0.9%
44	Vermont	100	0.1%
15	Virginia	1,497	1.8%
8	Washington	2,540	3.1%
39	West Virginia	238	0.3%
27	Wisconsin	927	1.1%
43	Wyoming	114	0.1%

RANK	STATE	RAPES	% of USA
1	California	9,198	11.3%
2	Texas	7,264	8.9%
3	Florida	6,634	8.1%
4	Michigan	4,136	5.1%
5	Ohio	3,915	4.8%
6	New York	3,425	4.2%
7	Pennsylvania	2,996	3.7%
8	Washington	2,540	3.1%
9	Tennessee	2,217	2.7%
10	Georgia	2,037	2.5%
11	North Carolina	1,803	2.2%
12	Minnesota	1,753	2.2%
13	Massachusetts	1,663	2.0%
14	Colorado	1,597	2.0%
15	Virginia	1,497	1.8%
16	Maryland	1,460	1.8%
17	New Jersey	1,409	1.7%
18	Indiana	1,381	1.7%
19	Alabama	1,358	1.7%
20	Arizona	1,349	1.7%
21	Louisiana	1,326	1.6%
22	South Carolina	1,303	1.6%
23	Missouri	1,257	1.5%
24	Oklahoma	1,249	1.5%
25	Oregon	1,109	1.4%
26	Mississippi	931	1.1%
27	Wisconsin	927	1.1%
28	Nevada	880	1.1%
29	New Mexico	788	1.0%
30	Utah	764	0.9%
31	Iowa	733	0.9%
32	Arkansas	637	0.8%
33	Connecticut	599	0.7%
34	Nebraska	385	0.5%
35	Rhode Island	376	0.5%
36	Alaska	370	0.5%
37	Idaho	302	0.4%
38	South Dakota	274	0.3%
39	West Virginia	238	0.3%
40	Hawaii	235	0.3%
41	Maine	209	0.3%
42	North Dakota	120	0.1%
43	Wyoming	114	0.1%
44	Vermont	100	0.1%
NA	Delaware**	NA	NA
NA	Illinois**	NA	NA
NA	Kansas**	NA	NA
NA	Kentucky**	NA	NA
NA	Montana**	NA	NA
NA	New Hampshire**	NA	NA
	District of Columbia	248	0.3%

*Source: Morgan Quitno Press using data from Federal Bureau of Investigation
"Crime in the United States 1999" (Uniform Crime Reports, October 15, 2000)*
*Estimated totals for urban areas, defined by the F.B.I. as Metropolitan Statistical Areas and other cities outside such areas. National total includes those states listed as not available. Forcible rape is the carnal knowledge of a female forcibly and against her will. Attempts are included. However, statutory rape without force and other sex offenses are excluded. **Not available.*

Urban Rape Rate in 1999

National Urban Rate = 34.0 Rapes per 100,000 Population*

ALPHA ORDER

RANK	STATE	RATE
18	Alabama	38.2
1	Alaska	87.0
28	Arizona	30.1
21	Arkansas	36.8
33	California	28.3
12	Colorado	43.3
42	Connecticut	21.4
NA	Delaware**	NA
9	Florida	46.5
24	Georgia	32.7
36	Hawaii	27.1
23	Idaho	36.2
NA	Illinois**	NA
32	Indiana	28.6
20	Iowa	37.1
NA	Kansas**	NA
NA	Kentucky**	NA
22	Louisiana	36.3
39	Maine	23.4
29	Maryland	29.9
37	Massachusetts	27.0
8	Michigan	47.2
11	Minnesota	45.1
3	Mississippi	57.1
30	Missouri	29.7
NA	Montana**	NA
27	Nebraska	30.6
5	Nevada	54.7
NA	New Hampshire**	NA
44	New Jersey	17.3
4	New Mexico	55.2
43	New York	19.8
26	North Carolina	30.7
31	North Dakota	28.7
16	Ohio	39.6
10	Oklahoma	46.1
15	Oregon	39.8
35	Pennsylvania	27.3
19	Rhode Island	37.9
13	South Carolina	43.1
2	South Dakota	60.6
6	Tennessee	50.9
16	Texas	39.6
14	Utah	40.4
33	Vermont	28.3
38	Virginia	25.9
7	Washington	48.7
40	West Virginia	22.8
41	Wisconsin	21.8
25	Wyoming	32.6

RANK ORDER

RANK	STATE	RATE
1	Alaska	87.0
2	South Dakota	60.6
3	Mississippi	57.1
4	New Mexico	55.2
5	Nevada	54.7
6	Tennessee	50.9
7	Washington	48.7
8	Michigan	47.2
9	Florida	46.5
10	Oklahoma	46.1
11	Minnesota	45.1
12	Colorado	43.3
13	South Carolina	43.1
14	Utah	40.4
15	Oregon	39.8
16	Ohio	39.6
16	Texas	39.6
18	Alabama	38.2
19	Rhode Island	37.9
20	Iowa	37.1
21	Arkansas	36.8
22	Louisiana	36.3
23	Idaho	36.2
24	Georgia	32.7
25	Wyoming	32.6
26	North Carolina	30.7
27	Nebraska	30.6
28	Arizona	30.1
29	Maryland	29.9
30	Missouri	29.7
31	North Dakota	28.7
32	Indiana	28.6
33	California	28.3
33	Vermont	28.3
35	Pennsylvania	27.3
36	Hawaii	27.1
37	Massachusetts	27.0
38	Virginia	25.9
39	Maine	23.4
40	West Virginia	22.8
41	Wisconsin	21.8
42	Connecticut	21.4
43	New York	19.8
44	New Jersey	17.3
NA	Delaware**	NA
NA	Illinois**	NA
NA	Kansas**	NA
NA	Kentucky**	NA
NA	Montana**	NA
NA	New Hampshire**	NA

District of Columbia 47.8

Source: Morgan Quitno Press using data from Federal Bureau of Investigation
   "Crime in the United States 1999" (Uniform Crime Reports, October 15, 2000)
*Estimated rates for urban areas, defined by the F.B.I. as Metropolitan Statistical Areas and other cities outside such areas. National rate includes those states listed as not available. Forcible rape is the carnal knowledge of a female forcibly and against her will. Attempts are included. However, statutory rape without force and other sex offenses are excluded. **Not available.

Percent of Rapes Occurring in Urban Areas in 1999

National Percent = 91.4% of Rapes*

ALPHA ORDER

RANK	STATE	PERCENT
23	Alabama	89.8
42	Alaska	71.6
4	Arizona	97.5
24	Arkansas	89.7
3	California	98.2
8	Colorado	95.1
18	Connecticut	91.6
NA	Delaware**	NA
9	Florida	94.9
26	Georgia	87.8
44	Hawaii	66.4
41	Idaho	72.4
NA	Illinois**	NA
31	Indiana	85.9
13	Iowa	94.0
NA	Kansas**	NA
NA	Kentucky**	NA
18	Louisiana	91.6
27	Maine	87.4
12	Maryland	94.1
1	Massachusetts	100.0
32	Michigan	85.3
30	Minnesota	86.0
39	Mississippi	80.5
27	Missouri	87.4
NA	Montana**	NA
16	Nebraska	93.0
15	Nevada	93.3
NA	New Hampshire**	NA
1	New Jersey	100.0
35	New Mexico	83.5
6	New York	96.1
34	North Carolina	83.7
33	North Dakota	84.5
10	Ohio	94.8
22	Oklahoma	90.8
21	Oregon	91.0
20	Pennsylvania	91.4
5	Rhode Island	96.2
37	South Carolina	82.1
38	South Dakota	81.5
17	Tennessee	91.8
7	Texas	95.4
10	Utah	94.8
40	Vermont	73.5
29	Virginia	87.0
14	Washington	93.7
43	West Virginia	70.6
25	Wisconsin	87.9
36	Wyoming	83.2

RANK ORDER

RANK	STATE	PERCENT
1	Massachusetts	100.0
1	New Jersey	100.0
3	California	98.2
4	Arizona	97.5
5	Rhode Island	96.2
6	New York	96.1
7	Texas	95.4
8	Colorado	95.1
9	Florida	94.9
10	Ohio	94.8
10	Utah	94.8
12	Maryland	94.1
13	Iowa	94.0
14	Washington	93.7
15	Nevada	93.3
16	Nebraska	93.0
17	Tennessee	91.8
18	Connecticut	91.6
18	Louisiana	91.6
20	Pennsylvania	91.4
21	Oregon	91.0
22	Oklahoma	90.8
23	Alabama	89.8
24	Arkansas	89.7
25	Wisconsin	87.9
26	Georgia	87.8
27	Maine	87.4
27	Missouri	87.4
29	Virginia	87.0
30	Minnesota	86.0
31	Indiana	85.9
32	Michigan	85.3
33	North Dakota	84.5
34	North Carolina	83.7
35	New Mexico	83.5
36	Wyoming	83.2
37	South Carolina	82.1
38	South Dakota	81.5
39	Mississippi	80.5
40	Vermont	73.5
41	Idaho	72.4
42	Alaska	71.6
43	West Virginia	70.6
44	Hawaii	66.4
NA	Delaware**	NA
NA	Illinois**	NA
NA	Kansas**	NA
NA	Kentucky**	NA
NA	Montana**	NA
NA	New Hampshire**	NA
	District of Columbia	100.0

Source: Morgan Quitno Press using data from Federal Bureau of Investigation
 "Crime in the United States 1999" (Uniform Crime Reports, October 15, 2000)
*Estimated percentages for urban areas, defined by the F.B.I. as Metropolitan Statistical Areas and other cities outside such areas. National percent includes those states listed as not available. Forcible rape is the carnal knowledge of a female forcibly and against her will. Attempts are included. However, statutory rape without force and other sex offenses are excluded. **Not available.*

Rapes in Rural Areas in 1999

National Rural Total = 7,620 Rapes*

RANK	STATE	RAPES	% of USA
18	Alabama	155	2.0%
19	Alaska	147	1.9%
37	Arizona	34	0.4%
30	Arkansas	73	1.0%
16	California	165	2.2%
29	Colorado	82	1.1%
33	Connecticut	55	0.7%
NA	Delaware**	NA	NA
2	Florida	356	4.7%
8	Georgia	282	3.7%
24	Hawaii	119	1.6%
25	Idaho	115	1.5%
NA	Illinois**	NA	NA
9	Indiana	226	3.0%
34	Iowa	47	0.6%
NA	Kansas**	NA	NA
NA	Kentucky**	NA	NA
23	Louisiana	122	1.6%
38	Maine	30	0.4%
28	Maryland	91	1.2%
43	Massachusetts	0	0.0%
1	Michigan	713	9.4%
5	Minnesota	285	3.7%
10	Mississippi	225	3.0%
14	Missouri	182	2.4%
NA	Montana**	NA	NA
39	Nebraska	29	0.4%
31	Nevada	63	0.8%
NA	New Hampshire**	NA	NA
43	New Jersey	0	0.0%
17	New Mexico	156	2.0%
20	New York	138	1.8%
3	North Carolina	352	4.6%
41	North Dakota	22	0.3%
12	Ohio	214	2.8%
22	Oklahoma	126	1.7%
26	Oregon	110	1.4%
7	Pennsylvania	283	3.7%
42	Rhode Island	15	0.2%
6	South Carolina	284	3.7%
32	South Dakota	62	0.8%
13	Tennessee	198	2.6%
4	Texas	350	4.6%
35	Utah	42	0.6%
36	Vermont	36	0.5%
11	Virginia	223	2.9%
15	Washington	171	2.2%
27	West Virginia	99	1.3%
21	Wisconsin	128	1.7%
40	Wyoming	23	0.3%

RANK	STATE	RAPES	% of USA
1	Michigan	713	9.4%
2	Florida	356	4.7%
3	North Carolina	352	4.6%
4	Texas	350	4.6%
5	Minnesota	285	3.7%
6	South Carolina	284	3.7%
7	Pennsylvania	283	3.7%
8	Georgia	282	3.7%
9	Indiana	226	3.0%
10	Mississippi	225	3.0%
11	Virginia	223	2.9%
12	Ohio	214	2.8%
13	Tennessee	198	2.6%
14	Missouri	182	2.4%
15	Washington	171	2.2%
16	California	165	2.2%
17	New Mexico	156	2.0%
18	Alabama	155	2.0%
19	Alaska	147	1.9%
20	New York	138	1.8%
21	Wisconsin	128	1.7%
22	Oklahoma	126	1.7%
23	Louisiana	122	1.6%
24	Hawaii	119	1.6%
25	Idaho	115	1.5%
26	Oregon	110	1.4%
27	West Virginia	99	1.3%
28	Maryland	91	1.2%
29	Colorado	82	1.1%
30	Arkansas	73	1.0%
31	Nevada	63	0.8%
32	South Dakota	62	0.8%
33	Connecticut	55	0.7%
34	Iowa	47	0.6%
35	Utah	42	0.6%
36	Vermont	36	0.5%
37	Arizona	34	0.4%
38	Maine	30	0.4%
39	Nebraska	29	0.4%
40	Wyoming	23	0.3%
41	North Dakota	22	0.3%
42	Rhode Island	15	0.2%
43	Massachusetts	0	0.0%
43	New Jersey	0	0.0%
NA	Delaware**	NA	NA
NA	Illinois**	NA	NA
NA	Kansas**	NA	NA
NA	Kentucky**	NA	NA
NA	Montana**	NA	NA
NA	New Hampshire**	NA	NA
	District of Columbia	0	0.0%

Source: Federal Bureau of Investigation
   "Crime in the United States 1999" (Uniform Crime Reports, October 15, 2000)
*Estimated totals for rural areas, defined by the F.B.I. as other than Metropolitan Statistical Areas and other cities outside such areas. National total includes those states listed as not available. Forcible rape is the carnal knowledge of a female forcibly and against her will. Attempts are included. However, statutory rape without force and other sex offenses are excluded. **Not available.

Rural Rape Rate in 1999

National Rural Rate = 22.9 Rapes per 100,000 Population*

ALPHA ORDER

RANK	STATE	RATE
23	Alabama	19.1
1	Alaska	76.0
36	Arizona	11.4
38	Arkansas	8.9
13	California	25.8
14	Colorado	22.2
35	Connecticut	11.5
NA	Delaware**	NA
4	Florida	42.6
24	Georgia	18.0
5	Hawaii	37.4
11	Idaho	27.5
NA	Illinois**	NA
19	Indiana	20.2
41	Iowa	5.3
NA	Kansas**	NA
NA	Kentucky**	NA
28	Louisiana	17.1
39	Maine	8.4
8	Maryland	31.6
42	Massachusetts	0.0
2	Michigan	64.2
7	Minnesota	31.9
20	Mississippi	19.8
32	Missouri	14.7
NA	Montana**	NA
40	Nebraska	7.1
9	Nevada	31.5
NA	New Hampshire**	NA
42	New Jersey	0.0
3	New Mexico	49.9
29	New York	15.7
20	North Carolina	19.8
37	North Dakota	10.2
30	Ohio	15.6
22	Oklahoma	19.4
16	Oregon	20.9
12	Pennsylvania	27.2
42	Rhode Island	0.0
6	South Carolina	33.0
15	South Dakota	22.1
26	Tennessee	17.5
17	Texas	20.7
26	Utah	17.5
31	Vermont	14.9
18	Virginia	20.6
10	Washington	31.4
33	West Virginia	13.0
34	Wisconsin	12.8
25	Wyoming	17.6

RANK ORDER

RANK	STATE	RATE
1	Alaska	76.0
2	Michigan	64.2
3	New Mexico	49.9
4	Florida	42.6
5	Hawaii	37.4
6	South Carolina	33.0
7	Minnesota	31.9
8	Maryland	31.6
9	Nevada	31.5
10	Washington	31.4
11	Idaho	27.5
12	Pennsylvania	27.2
13	California	25.8
14	Colorado	22.2
15	South Dakota	22.1
16	Oregon	20.9
17	Texas	20.7
18	Virginia	20.6
19	Indiana	20.2
20	Mississippi	19.8
20	North Carolina	19.8
22	Oklahoma	19.4
23	Alabama	19.1
24	Georgia	18.0
25	Wyoming	17.6
26	Tennessee	17.5
26	Utah	17.5
28	Louisiana	17.1
29	New York	15.7
30	Ohio	15.6
31	Vermont	14.9
32	Missouri	14.7
33	West Virginia	13.0
34	Wisconsin	12.8
35	Connecticut	11.5
36	Arizona	11.4
37	North Dakota	10.2
38	Arkansas	8.9
39	Maine	8.4
40	Nebraska	7.1
41	Iowa	5.3
42	Massachusetts	0.0
42	New Jersey	0.0
42	Rhode Island	0.0
NA	Delaware**	NA
NA	Illinois**	NA
NA	Kansas**	NA
NA	Kentucky**	NA
NA	Montana**	NA
NA	New Hampshire**	NA
	District of Columbia	0.0

Source: Morgan Quitno Press using data from Federal Bureau of Investigation
"Crime in the United States 1999" (Uniform Crime Reports, October 15, 2000)
*Estimated rates for rural areas, defined by the F.B.I. as other than Metropolitan Statistical Areas and other cities outside such areas. National rate includes those states listed as not available. Forcible rape is the carnal knowledge of a female forcibly and against her will. Attempts are included. However, statutory rape without force and other sex offenses are excluded. **Not available.

Percent of Rapes Occurring in Rural Areas in 1999

National Percent = 8.6% of Rapes*

<table>
<tr><td colspan="3">ALPHA ORDER</td><td colspan="3">RANK ORDER</td></tr>
<tr><th>RANK</th><th>STATE</th><th>PERCENT</th><th>RANK</th><th>STATE</th><th>PERCENT</th></tr>
<tr><td>22</td><td>Alabama</td><td>10.2</td><td>1</td><td>Hawaii</td><td>33.6</td></tr>
<tr><td>3</td><td>Alaska</td><td>28.4</td><td>2</td><td>West Virginia</td><td>29.4</td></tr>
<tr><td>41</td><td>Arizona</td><td>2.5</td><td>3</td><td>Alaska</td><td>28.4</td></tr>
<tr><td>21</td><td>Arkansas</td><td>10.3</td><td>4</td><td>Idaho</td><td>27.6</td></tr>
<tr><td>42</td><td>California</td><td>1.8</td><td>5</td><td>Vermont</td><td>26.5</td></tr>
<tr><td>37</td><td>Colorado</td><td>4.9</td><td>6</td><td>Mississippi</td><td>19.5</td></tr>
<tr><td>26</td><td>Connecticut</td><td>8.4</td><td>7</td><td>South Dakota</td><td>18.5</td></tr>
<tr><td>NA</td><td>Delaware**</td><td>NA</td><td>8</td><td>South Carolina</td><td>17.9</td></tr>
<tr><td>36</td><td>Florida</td><td>5.1</td><td>9</td><td>Wyoming</td><td>16.8</td></tr>
<tr><td>19</td><td>Georgia</td><td>12.2</td><td>10</td><td>New Mexico</td><td>16.5</td></tr>
<tr><td>1</td><td>Hawaii</td><td>33.6</td><td>11</td><td>North Carolina</td><td>16.3</td></tr>
<tr><td>4</td><td>Idaho</td><td>27.6</td><td>12</td><td>North Dakota</td><td>15.5</td></tr>
<tr><td>NA</td><td>Illinois**</td><td>NA</td><td>13</td><td>Michigan</td><td>14.7</td></tr>
<tr><td>14</td><td>Indiana</td><td>14.1</td><td>14</td><td>Indiana</td><td>14.1</td></tr>
<tr><td>32</td><td>Iowa</td><td>6.0</td><td>15</td><td>Minnesota</td><td>14.0</td></tr>
<tr><td>NA</td><td>Kansas**</td><td>NA</td><td>16</td><td>Virginia</td><td>13.0</td></tr>
<tr><td>NA</td><td>Kentucky**</td><td>NA</td><td>17</td><td>Maine</td><td>12.6</td></tr>
<tr><td>26</td><td>Louisiana</td><td>8.4</td><td>17</td><td>Missouri</td><td>12.6</td></tr>
<tr><td>17</td><td>Maine</td><td>12.6</td><td>19</td><td>Georgia</td><td>12.2</td></tr>
<tr><td>33</td><td>Maryland</td><td>5.9</td><td>20</td><td>Wisconsin</td><td>12.1</td></tr>
<tr><td>43</td><td>Massachusetts</td><td>0.0</td><td>21</td><td>Arkansas</td><td>10.3</td></tr>
<tr><td>13</td><td>Michigan</td><td>14.7</td><td>22</td><td>Alabama</td><td>10.2</td></tr>
<tr><td>15</td><td>Minnesota</td><td>14.0</td><td>23</td><td>Oklahoma</td><td>9.2</td></tr>
<tr><td>6</td><td>Mississippi</td><td>19.5</td><td>24</td><td>Oregon</td><td>9.0</td></tr>
<tr><td>17</td><td>Missouri</td><td>12.6</td><td>25</td><td>Pennsylvania</td><td>8.6</td></tr>
<tr><td>NA</td><td>Montana**</td><td>NA</td><td>26</td><td>Connecticut</td><td>8.4</td></tr>
<tr><td>29</td><td>Nebraska</td><td>7.0</td><td>26</td><td>Louisiana</td><td>8.4</td></tr>
<tr><td>30</td><td>Nevada</td><td>6.7</td><td>28</td><td>Tennessee</td><td>8.2</td></tr>
<tr><td>NA</td><td>New Hampshire**</td><td>NA</td><td>29</td><td>Nebraska</td><td>7.0</td></tr>
<tr><td>43</td><td>New Jersey</td><td>0.0</td><td>30</td><td>Nevada</td><td>6.7</td></tr>
<tr><td>10</td><td>New Mexico</td><td>16.5</td><td>31</td><td>Washington</td><td>6.3</td></tr>
<tr><td>39</td><td>New York</td><td>3.9</td><td>32</td><td>Iowa</td><td>6.0</td></tr>
<tr><td>11</td><td>North Carolina</td><td>16.3</td><td>33</td><td>Maryland</td><td>5.9</td></tr>
<tr><td>12</td><td>North Dakota</td><td>15.5</td><td>34</td><td>Ohio</td><td>5.2</td></tr>
<tr><td>34</td><td>Ohio</td><td>5.2</td><td>34</td><td>Utah</td><td>5.2</td></tr>
<tr><td>23</td><td>Oklahoma</td><td>9.2</td><td>36</td><td>Florida</td><td>5.1</td></tr>
<tr><td>24</td><td>Oregon</td><td>9.0</td><td>37</td><td>Colorado</td><td>4.9</td></tr>
<tr><td>25</td><td>Pennsylvania</td><td>8.6</td><td>38</td><td>Texas</td><td>4.6</td></tr>
<tr><td>40</td><td>Rhode Island</td><td>3.8</td><td>39</td><td>New York</td><td>3.9</td></tr>
<tr><td>8</td><td>South Carolina</td><td>17.9</td><td>40</td><td>Rhode Island</td><td>3.8</td></tr>
<tr><td>7</td><td>South Dakota</td><td>18.5</td><td>41</td><td>Arizona</td><td>2.5</td></tr>
<tr><td>28</td><td>Tennessee</td><td>8.2</td><td>42</td><td>California</td><td>1.8</td></tr>
<tr><td>38</td><td>Texas</td><td>4.6</td><td>43</td><td>Massachusetts</td><td>0.0</td></tr>
<tr><td>34</td><td>Utah</td><td>5.2</td><td>43</td><td>New Jersey</td><td>0.0</td></tr>
<tr><td>5</td><td>Vermont</td><td>26.5</td><td>NA</td><td>Delaware**</td><td>NA</td></tr>
<tr><td>16</td><td>Virginia</td><td>13.0</td><td>NA</td><td>Illinois**</td><td>NA</td></tr>
<tr><td>31</td><td>Washington</td><td>6.3</td><td>NA</td><td>Kansas**</td><td>NA</td></tr>
<tr><td>2</td><td>West Virginia</td><td>29.4</td><td>NA</td><td>Kentucky**</td><td>NA</td></tr>
<tr><td>20</td><td>Wisconsin</td><td>12.1</td><td>NA</td><td>Montana**</td><td>NA</td></tr>
<tr><td>9</td><td>Wyoming</td><td>16.8</td><td>NA</td><td>New Hampshire**</td><td>NA</td></tr>
<tr><td></td><td></td><td></td><td></td><td>District of Columbia</td><td>0.0</td></tr>
</table>

Source: Morgan Quitno Press using data from Federal Bureau of Investigation
    "Crime in the United States 1999" (Uniform Crime Reports, October 15, 2000)
*Estimated percentages for rural areas, defined by the F.B.I. as other than Metropolitan Statistical Areas and other cities outside such areas. National percent includes those states listed as not available. Forcible rape is the carnal knowledge of a female forcibly and against her will. Attempts are included. However, statutory rape without force and other sex offenses are excluded. **Not available.

Robberies in Urban Areas in 1999

National Urban Total = 404,160 Robberies*

ALPHA ORDER

RANK ORDER

RANK	STATE	ROBBERIES	% of USA	RANK	STATE	ROBBERIES	% of USA
20	Alabama	5,178	1.3%	1	California	59,899	14.8%
39	Alaska	535	0.1%	2	New York	43,759	10.8%
14	Arizona	7,246	1.8%	3	Florida	31,589	7.8%
31	Arkansas	1,956	0.5%	4	Texas	29,232	7.2%
1	California	59,899	14.8%	5	Pennsylvania	18,577	4.6%
26	Colorado	3,042	0.8%	6	Ohio	14,290	3.5%
24	Connecticut	3,972	1.0%	7	New Jersey	14,243	3.5%
32	Delaware	1,427	0.4%	8	Michigan	14,037	3.5%
3	Florida	31,589	7.8%	9	Maryland	13,548	3.4%
10	Georgia	12,583	3.1%	10	Georgia	12,583	3.1%
36	Hawaii	907	0.2%	11	North Carolina	11,417	2.8%
41	Idaho	203	0.1%	12	Tennessee	8,459	2.1%
NA	Illinois**	NA	NA	13	Louisiana	7,383	1.8%
17	Indiana	5,987	1.5%	14	Arizona	7,246	1.8%
35	Iowa	1,032	0.3%	15	Missouri	7,087	1.8%
NA	Kansas**	NA	NA	16	Virginia	6,742	1.7%
NA	Kentucky**	NA	NA	17	Indiana	5,987	1.5%
13	Louisiana	7,383	1.8%	18	Massachusetts	5,931	1.5%
40	Maine	239	0.1%	19	Washington	5,754	1.4%
9	Maryland	13,548	3.4%	20	Alabama	5,178	1.3%
18	Massachusetts	5,931	1.5%	21	South Carolina	5,039	1.2%
8	Michigan	14,037	3.5%	22	Wisconsin	4,417	1.1%
25	Minnesota	3,883	1.0%	23	Nevada	4,172	1.0%
27	Mississippi	2,874	0.7%	24	Connecticut	3,972	1.0%
15	Missouri	7,087	1.8%	25	Minnesota	3,883	1.0%
NA	Montana**	NA	NA	26	Colorado	3,042	0.8%
33	Nebraska	1,251	0.3%	27	Mississippi	2,874	0.7%
23	Nevada	4,172	1.0%	28	Oregon	2,785	0.7%
NA	New Hampshire**	NA	NA	29	Oklahoma	2,747	0.7%
7	New Jersey	14,243	3.5%	30	New Mexico	2,498	0.6%
30	New Mexico	2,498	0.6%	31	Arkansas	1,956	0.5%
2	New York	43,759	10.8%	32	Delaware	1,427	0.4%
11	North Carolina	11,417	2.8%	33	Nebraska	1,251	0.3%
45	North Dakota	55	0.0%	34	Utah	1,141	0.3%
6	Ohio	14,290	3.5%	35	Iowa	1,032	0.3%
29	Oklahoma	2,747	0.7%	36	Hawaii	907	0.2%
28	Oregon	2,785	0.7%	37	Rhode Island	779	0.2%
5	Pennsylvania	18,577	4.6%	38	West Virginia	590	0.1%
37	Rhode Island	779	0.2%	39	Alaska	535	0.1%
21	South Carolina	5,039	1.2%	40	Maine	239	0.1%
42	South Dakota	96	0.0%	41	Idaho	203	0.1%
12	Tennessee	8,459	2.1%	42	South Dakota	96	0.0%
4	Texas	29,232	7.2%	43	Wyoming	69	0.0%
34	Utah	1,141	0.3%	44	Vermont	56	0.0%
44	Vermont	56	0.0%	45	North Dakota	55	0.0%
16	Virginia	6,742	1.7%	NA	Illinois**	NA	NA
19	Washington	5,754	1.4%	NA	Kansas**	NA	NA
38	West Virginia	590	0.1%	NA	Kentucky**	NA	NA
22	Wisconsin	4,417	1.1%	NA	Montana**	NA	NA
43	Wyoming	69	0.0%	NA	New Hampshire**	NA	NA
					District of Columbia	3,344	0.8%

Source: Morgan Quitno Press using data from Federal Bureau of Investigation
    "Crime in the United States 1999" (Uniform Crime Reports, October 15, 2000)
*Estimated totals for urban areas, defined by the F.B.I. as Metropolitan Statistical Areas and other cities outside such areas. National total includes those states listed as not available. Robbery is the taking or attempting to take anything of value by force or threat of force.
**Not available.

Urban Robbery Rate in 1999

National Urban Rate = 168.8 Robberies per 100,000 Population*

RANK	STATE	RATE	RANK	STATE	RATE
	ALPHA ORDER			RANK ORDER	
20	Alabama	145.5	1	Maryland	277.4
23	Alaska	125.7	2	Nevada	259.3
17	Arizona	161.7	3	New York	252.7
26	Arkansas	112.9	4	Florida	221.3
10	California	184.3	5	Delaware	219.3
35	Colorado	82.5	6	Georgia	202.1
22	Connecticut	141.7	7	Louisiana	201.8
5	Delaware	219.3	8	North Carolina	194.4
4	Florida	221.3	9	Tennessee	194.2
6	Georgia	202.1	10	California	184.3
28	Hawaii	104.7	11	Mississippi	176.2
41	Idaho	24.4	12	New Mexico	175.0
NA	Illinois**	NA	13	New Jersey	174.9
24	Indiana	124.1	14	Pennsylvania	169.6
39	Iowa	52.3	15	Missouri	167.7
NA	Kansas**	NA	16	South Carolina	166.5
NA	Kentucky**	NA	17	Arizona	161.7
7	Louisiana	201.8	18	Michigan	160.4
40	Maine	26.7	19	Texas	159.3
1	Maryland	277.4	20	Alabama	145.5
34	Massachusetts	96.2	21	Ohio	144.6
18	Michigan	160.4	22	Connecticut	141.7
31	Minnesota	100.0	23	Alaska	125.7
11	Mississippi	176.2	24	Indiana	124.1
15	Missouri	167.7	25	Virginia	116.5
NA	Montana**	NA	26	Arkansas	112.9
33	Nebraska	99.6	27	Washington	110.4
2	Nevada	259.3	28	Hawaii	104.7
NA	New Hampshire**	NA	29	Wisconsin	104.0
13	New Jersey	174.9	30	Oklahoma	101.4
12	New Mexico	175.0	31	Minnesota	100.0
3	New York	252.7	32	Oregon	99.8
8	North Carolina	194.4	33	Nebraska	99.6
45	North Dakota	13.1	34	Massachusetts	96.2
21	Ohio	144.6	35	Colorado	82.5
30	Oklahoma	101.4	36	Rhode Island	78.6
32	Oregon	99.8	37	Utah	60.4
14	Pennsylvania	169.6	38	West Virginia	56.6
36	Rhode Island	78.6	39	Iowa	52.3
16	South Carolina	166.5	40	Maine	26.7
42	South Dakota	21.2	41	Idaho	24.4
9	Tennessee	194.2	42	South Dakota	21.2
19	Texas	159.3	43	Wyoming	19.8
37	Utah	60.4	44	Vermont	15.9
44	Vermont	15.9	45	North Dakota	13.1
25	Virginia	116.5	NA	Illinois**	NA
27	Washington	110.4	NA	Kansas**	NA
38	West Virginia	56.6	NA	Kentucky**	NA
29	Wisconsin	104.0	NA	Montana**	NA
43	Wyoming	19.8	NA	New Hampshire**	NA
				District of Columbia	644.3

Source: Morgan Quitno Press using data from Federal Bureau of Investigation
   "Crime in the United States 1999" (Uniform Crime Reports, October 15, 2000)
*Estimated rates for urban areas, defined by the F.B.I. as Metropolitan Statistical Areas and other cities outside
such areas. National rate includes those states listed as not available. Robbery is the taking or attempting to take
anything of value by force or threat of force.
**Not available.

Percent of Robberies Occurring in Urban Areas in 1999

National Percent = 98.7% of Robberies*

ALPHA ORDER

RANK ORDER

RANK	STATE	PERCENT	RANK	STATE	PERCENT
27	Alabama	97.8	1	Massachusetts	100.0
35	Alaska	94.5	1	New Jersey	100.0
8	Arizona	99.4	3	New York	99.9
33	Arkansas	96.6	4	California	99.8
4	California	99.8	5	Colorado	99.5
5	Colorado	99.5	5	Michigan	99.5
26	Connecticut	98.0	5	Pennsylvania	99.5
34	Delaware	95.6	8	Arizona	99.4
19	Florida	98.8	8	Maryland	99.4
30	Georgia	97.1	8	Texas	99.4
44	Hawaii	86.9	11	Wisconsin	99.3
41	Idaho	91.0	12	Ohio	99.2
NA	Illinois**	NA	13	Minnesota	99.1
40	Indiana	92.2	13	Missouri	99.1
24	Iowa	98.2	13	Nevada	99.1
NA	Kansas**	NA	13	Washington	99.1
NA	Kentucky**	NA	17	Nebraska	99.0
29	Louisiana	97.3	18	Rhode Island	98.9
22	Maine	98.4	19	Florida	98.8
8	Maryland	99.4	20	Oklahoma	98.6
1	Massachusetts	100.0	21	Utah	98.5
5	Michigan	99.5	22	Maine	98.4
13	Minnesota	99.1	22	Tennessee	98.4
39	Mississippi	93.0	24	Iowa	98.2
13	Missouri	99.1	24	North Dakota	98.2
NA	Montana**	NA	26	Connecticut	98.0
17	Nebraska	99.0	27	Alabama	97.8
13	Nevada	99.1	28	Oregon	97.4
NA	New Hampshire**	NA	29	Louisiana	97.3
1	New Jersey	100.0	30	Georgia	97.1
32	New Mexico	96.9	31	Virginia	97.0
3	New York	99.9	32	New Mexico	96.9
35	North Carolina	94.5	33	Arkansas	96.6
24	North Dakota	98.2	34	Delaware	95.6
12	Ohio	99.2	35	Alaska	94.5
20	Oklahoma	98.6	35	North Carolina	94.5
28	Oregon	97.4	37	South Dakota	93.2
5	Pennsylvania	99.5	37	Wyoming	93.2
18	Rhode Island	98.9	39	Mississippi	93.0
43	South Carolina	87.5	40	Indiana	92.2
37	South Dakota	93.2	41	Idaho	91.0
22	Tennessee	98.4	42	West Virginia	89.3
8	Texas	99.4	43	South Carolina	87.5
21	Utah	98.5	44	Hawaii	86.9
45	Vermont	86.2	45	Vermont	86.2
31	Virginia	97.0	NA	Illinois**	NA
13	Washington	99.1	NA	Kansas**	NA
42	West Virginia	89.3	NA	Kentucky**	NA
11	Wisconsin	99.3	NA	Montana**	NA
37	Wyoming	93.2	NA	New Hampshire**	NA

District of Columbia 100.0

Source: Morgan Quitno Press using data from Federal Bureau of Investigation
    "Crime in the United States 1999" (Uniform Crime Reports, October 15, 2000)
*Estimated percentages for urban areas, defined by the F.B.I. as Metropolitan Statistical Areas and other cities outside such areas. National percent includes those states listed as not available. Robbery is the taking or attempting to take anything of value by force or threat of force.
**Not available.

Robberies in Rural Areas in 1999

National Rural Total = 5,510 Robberies*

ALPHA ORDER

RANK ORDER

RANK	STATE	ROBBERIES	% of USA		RANK	STATE	ROBBERIES	% of USA
13	Alabama	119	2.2%		1	South Carolina	721	13.1%
32	Alaska	31	0.6%		2	North Carolina	670	12.2%
27	Arizona	42	0.8%		3	Indiana	509	9.2%
21	Arkansas	68	1.2%		4	Florida	380	6.9%
10	California	140	2.5%		5	Georgia	379	6.9%
36	Colorado	14	0.3%		6	Mississippi	217	3.9%
17	Connecticut	82	1.5%		7	Louisiana	208	3.8%
23	Delaware	65	1.2%		8	Virginia	205	3.7%
4	Florida	380	6.9%		9	Texas	173	3.1%
5	Georgia	379	6.9%		10	California	140	2.5%
12	Hawaii	137	2.5%		11	Tennessee	139	2.5%
33	Idaho	20	0.4%		12	Hawaii	137	2.5%
NA	Illinois**	NA	NA		13	Alabama	119	2.2%
3	Indiana	509	9.2%		14	Ohio	115	2.1%
34	Iowa	19	0.3%		15	Pennsylvania	93	1.7%
NA	Kansas**	NA	NA		16	Maryland	88	1.6%
NA	Kentucky**	NA	NA		17	Connecticut	82	1.5%
7	Louisiana	208	3.8%		18	New Mexico	81	1.5%
42	Maine	4	0.1%		19	Oregon	73	1.3%
16	Maryland	88	1.6%		20	West Virginia	71	1.3%
44	Massachusetts	0	0.0%		21	Arkansas	68	1.2%
22	Michigan	66	1.2%		22	Michigan	66	1.2%
30	Minnesota	34	0.6%		23	Delaware	65	1.2%
6	Mississippi	217	3.9%		24	Missouri	62	1.1%
24	Missouri	62	1.1%		24	New York	62	1.1%
NA	Montana**	NA	NA		26	Washington	54	1.0%
37	Nebraska	13	0.2%		27	Arizona	42	0.8%
29	Nevada	37	0.7%		28	Oklahoma	38	0.7%
NA	New Hampshire**	NA	NA		29	Nevada	37	0.7%
44	New Jersey	0	0.0%		30	Minnesota	34	0.6%
18	New Mexico	81	1.5%		31	Wisconsin	32	0.6%
24	New York	62	1.1%		32	Alaska	31	0.6%
2	North Carolina	670	12.2%		33	Idaho	20	0.4%
43	North Dakota	1	0.0%		34	Iowa	19	0.3%
14	Ohio	115	2.1%		35	Utah	17	0.3%
28	Oklahoma	38	0.7%		36	Colorado	14	0.3%
19	Oregon	73	1.3%		37	Nebraska	13	0.2%
15	Pennsylvania	93	1.7%		38	Rhode Island	9	0.2%
38	Rhode Island	9	0.2%		38	Vermont	9	0.2%
1	South Carolina	721	13.1%		40	South Dakota	7	0.1%
40	South Dakota	7	0.1%		41	Wyoming	5	0.1%
11	Tennessee	139	2.5%		42	Maine	4	0.1%
9	Texas	173	3.1%		43	North Dakota	1	0.0%
35	Utah	17	0.3%		44	Massachusetts	0	0.0%
38	Vermont	9	0.2%		44	New Jersey	0	0.0%
8	Virginia	205	3.7%		NA	Illinois**	NA	NA
26	Washington	54	1.0%		NA	Kansas**	NA	NA
20	West Virginia	71	1.3%		NA	Kentucky**	NA	NA
31	Wisconsin	32	0.6%		NA	Montana**	NA	NA
41	Wyoming	5	0.1%		NA	New Hampshire**	NA	NA
						District of Columbia	0	0.0%

Source: Federal Bureau of Investigation
 "Crime in the United States 1999" (Uniform Crime Reports, October 15, 2000)
*Estimated totals for rural areas, defined by the F.B.I. as other than Metropolitan Statistical Areas and other cities outside such areas. National total includes those states listed as not available. Robbery is the taking or attempting to take anything of value by force or threat of force.
**Not available.

Rural Robbery Rate in 1999

National Rural Rate = 16.5 Robberies per 100,000 Population*

ALPHA ORDER

RANK	STATE	RATE
17	Alabama	14.7
16	Alaska	16.0
18	Arizona	14.1
26	Arkansas	8.3
11	California	21.9
33	Colorado	3.8
15	Connecticut	17.1
2	Delaware	62.9
3	Florida	45.5
10	Georgia	24.2
5	Hawaii	43.0
32	Idaho	4.8
NA	Illinois**	NA
4	Indiana	45.4
40	Iowa	2.1
NA	Kansas**	NA
NA	Kentucky**	NA
8	Louisiana	29.1
41	Maine	1.1
7	Maryland	30.6
43	Massachusetts	0.0
29	Michigan	5.9
33	Minnesota	3.8
12	Mississippi	19.1
31	Missouri	5.0
NA	Montana**	NA
37	Nebraska	3.2
14	Nevada	18.5
NA	New Hampshire**	NA
43	New Jersey	0.0
9	New Mexico	25.9
27	New York	7.1
6	North Carolina	37.7
42	North Dakota	0.5
25	Ohio	8.4
30	Oklahoma	5.8
19	Oregon	13.9
24	Pennsylvania	9.0
43	Rhode Island	0.0
1	South Carolina	83.9
39	South Dakota	2.5
20	Tennessee	12.3
21	Texas	10.2
27	Utah	7.1
36	Vermont	3.7
13	Virginia	18.9
22	Washington	9.9
23	West Virginia	9.3
37	Wisconsin	3.2
33	Wyoming	3.8

RANK ORDER

RANK	STATE	RATE
1	South Carolina	83.9
2	Delaware	62.9
3	Florida	45.5
4	Indiana	45.4
5	Hawaii	43.0
6	North Carolina	37.7
7	Maryland	30.6
8	Louisiana	29.1
9	New Mexico	25.9
10	Georgia	24.2
11	California	21.9
12	Mississippi	19.1
13	Virginia	18.9
14	Nevada	18.5
15	Connecticut	17.1
16	Alaska	16.0
17	Alabama	14.7
18	Arizona	14.1
19	Oregon	13.9
20	Tennessee	12.3
21	Texas	10.2
22	Washington	9.9
23	West Virginia	9.3
24	Pennsylvania	9.0
25	Ohio	8.4
26	Arkansas	8.3
27	New York	7.1
27	Utah	7.1
29	Michigan	5.9
30	Oklahoma	5.8
31	Missouri	5.0
32	Idaho	4.8
33	Colorado	3.8
33	Minnesota	3.8
33	Wyoming	3.8
36	Vermont	3.7
37	Nebraska	3.2
37	Wisconsin	3.2
39	South Dakota	2.5
40	Iowa	2.1
41	Maine	1.1
42	North Dakota	0.5
43	Massachusetts	0.0
43	New Jersey	0.0
43	Rhode Island	0.0
NA	Illinois**	NA
NA	Kansas**	NA
NA	Kentucky**	NA
NA	Montana**	NA
NA	New Hampshire**	NA
	District of Columbia	0.0

Source: Morgan Quitno Press using data from Federal Bureau of Investigation
   "Crime in the United States 1999" (Uniform Crime Reports, October 15, 2000)
*Estimated rates for rural areas, defined by the F.B.I. as other than Metropolitan Statistical Areas and other cities outside such areas. National rate includes those states listed as not available. Robbery is the taking or attempting to take anything of value by force or threat of force.
**Not available.

Percent of Robberies Occurring in Rural Areas in 1999

National Percent = 1.3% of Robberies*

ALPHA ORDER

RANK	STATE	PERCENT
19	Alabama	2.2
10	Alaska	5.5
36	Arizona	0.6
13	Arkansas	3.4
42	California	0.2
39	Colorado	0.5
20	Connecticut	2.0
12	Delaware	4.4
27	Florida	1.2
16	Georgia	2.9
2	Hawaii	13.1
5	Idaho	9.0
NA	Illinois**	NA
6	Indiana	7.8
21	Iowa	1.8
NA	Kansas**	NA
NA	Kentucky**	NA
17	Louisiana	2.7
23	Maine	1.6
36	Maryland	0.6
44	Massachusetts	0.0
39	Michigan	0.5
30	Minnesota	0.9
7	Mississippi	7.0
30	Missouri	0.9
NA	Montana**	NA
29	Nebraska	1.0
30	Nevada	0.9
NA	New Hampshire**	NA
44	New Jersey	0.0
14	New Mexico	3.1
43	New York	0.1
10	North Carolina	5.5
21	North Dakota	1.8
34	Ohio	0.8
26	Oklahoma	1.4
18	Oregon	2.6
39	Pennsylvania	0.5
28	Rhode Island	1.1
3	South Carolina	12.5
8	South Dakota	6.8
23	Tennessee	1.6
36	Texas	0.6
25	Utah	1.5
1	Vermont	13.8
15	Virginia	3.0
30	Washington	0.9
4	West Virginia	10.7
35	Wisconsin	0.7
8	Wyoming	6.8

RANK ORDER

RANK	STATE	PERCENT
1	Vermont	13.8
2	Hawaii	13.1
3	South Carolina	12.5
4	West Virginia	10.7
5	Idaho	9.0
6	Indiana	7.8
7	Mississippi	7.0
8	South Dakota	6.8
8	Wyoming	6.8
10	Alaska	5.5
10	North Carolina	5.5
12	Delaware	4.4
13	Arkansas	3.4
14	New Mexico	3.1
15	Virginia	3.0
16	Georgia	2.9
17	Louisiana	2.7
18	Oregon	2.6
19	Alabama	2.2
20	Connecticut	2.0
21	Iowa	1.8
21	North Dakota	1.8
23	Maine	1.6
23	Tennessee	1.6
25	Utah	1.5
26	Oklahoma	1.4
27	Florida	1.2
28	Rhode Island	1.1
29	Nebraska	1.0
30	Minnesota	0.9
30	Missouri	0.9
30	Nevada	0.9
30	Washington	0.9
34	Ohio	0.8
35	Wisconsin	0.7
36	Arizona	0.6
36	Maryland	0.6
36	Texas	0.6
39	Colorado	0.5
39	Michigan	0.5
39	Pennsylvania	0.5
42	California	0.2
43	New York	0.1
44	Massachusetts	0.0
44	New Jersey	0.0
NA	Illinois**	NA
NA	Kansas**	NA
NA	Kentucky**	NA
NA	Montana**	NA
NA	New Hampshire**	NA
	District of Columbia	0.0

Source: Morgan Quitno Press using data from Federal Bureau of Investigation
    "Crime in the United States 1999" (Uniform Crime Reports, October 15, 2000)
*Estimated percentages for rural areas, defined by the F.B.I. as other than Metropolitan Statistical Areas and other cities outside such areas. National percent includes those states listed as not available. Robbery is the taking or attempting to take anything of value by force or threat of force.
**Not available.

Aggravated Assaults in Urban Areas in 1999

National Urban Total = 857,341 Aggravated Assaults*

ALPHA ORDER					RANK ORDER			
RANK	STATE		ASSAULTS	% of USA	RANK	STATE	ASSAULTS	% of USA
18	Alabama		13,002	1.5%	1	California	134,741	15.7%
37	Alaska		2,208	0.3%	2	Florida	85,176	9.9%
16	Arizona		16,475	1.9%	3	Texas	70,836	8.3%
26	Arkansas		6,934	0.8%	4	New York	57,222	6.7%
1	California		134,741	15.7%	5	Michigan	35,508	4.1%
24	Colorado		8,524	1.0%	6	Pennsylvania	26,856	3.1%
30	Connecticut		5,583	0.7%	7	Massachusetts	26,295	3.1%
36	Delaware		2,971	0.3%	8	Tennessee	24,025	2.8%
2	Florida		85,176	9.9%	9	North Carolina	23,156	2.7%
11	Georgia		21,493	2.5%	10	Maryland	22,108	2.6%
40	Hawaii		1,019	0.1%	11	Georgia	21,493	2.5%
38	Idaho		1,865	0.2%	12	South Carolina	20,136	2.3%
NA	Illinois**		NA	NA	13	Louisiana	19,129	2.2%
20	Indiana		11,676	1.4%	14	New Jersey	17,601	2.1%
29	Iowa		5,648	0.7%	15	Missouri	16,840	2.0%
NA	Kansas**		NA	NA	16	Arizona	16,475	1.9%
NA	Kentucky**		NA	NA	17	Ohio	15,796	1.8%
13	Louisiana		19,129	2.2%	18	Alabama	13,002	1.5%
41	Maine		769	0.1%	19	Washington	12,342	1.4%
10	Maryland		22,108	2.6%	20	Indiana	11,676	1.4%
7	Massachusetts		26,295	3.1%	21	Oklahoma	11,267	1.3%
5	Michigan		35,508	4.1%	22	Virginia	10,734	1.3%
28	Minnesota		6,426	0.7%	23	New Mexico	9,317	1.1%
33	Mississippi		3,646	0.4%	24	Colorado	8,524	1.0%
15	Missouri		16,840	2.0%	25	Oregon	7,665	0.9%
NA	Montana**		NA	NA	26	Arkansas	6,934	0.8%
31	Nebraska		5,206	0.6%	27	Wisconsin	6,468	0.8%
32	Nevada		4,488	0.5%	28	Minnesota	6,426	0.7%
NA	New Hampshire**		NA	NA	29	Iowa	5,648	0.7%
14	New Jersey		17,601	2.1%	30	Connecticut	5,583	0.7%
23	New Mexico		9,317	1.1%	31	Nebraska	5,206	0.6%
4	New York		57,222	6.7%	32	Nevada	4,488	0.5%
9	North Carolina		23,156	2.7%	33	Mississippi	3,646	0.4%
45	North Dakota		188	0.0%	34	Utah	3,625	0.4%
17	Ohio		15,796	1.8%	35	West Virginia	3,446	0.4%
21	Oklahoma		11,267	1.3%	36	Delaware	2,971	0.3%
25	Oregon		7,665	0.9%	37	Alaska	2,208	0.3%
6	Pennsylvania		26,856	3.1%	38	Idaho	1,865	0.2%
39	Rhode Island		1,610	0.2%	39	Rhode Island	1,610	0.2%
12	South Carolina		20,136	2.3%	40	Hawaii	1,019	0.1%
43	South Dakota		656	0.1%	41	Maine	769	0.1%
8	Tennessee		24,025	2.8%	42	Wyoming	701	0.1%
3	Texas		70,836	8.3%	43	South Dakota	656	0.1%
34	Utah		3,625	0.4%	44	Vermont	371	0.0%
44	Vermont		371	0.0%	45	North Dakota	188	0.0%
22	Virginia		10,734	1.3%	NA	Illinois**	NA	NA
19	Washington		12,342	1.4%	NA	Kansas**	NA	NA
35	West Virginia		3,446	0.4%	NA	Kentucky**	NA	NA
27	Wisconsin		6,468	0.8%	NA	Montana**	NA	NA
42	Wyoming		701	0.1%	NA	New Hampshire**	NA	NA
						District of Columbia	4,615	0.5%

Source: Morgan Quitno Press using data from Federal Bureau of Investigation
"Crime in the United States 1999" (Uniform Crime Reports, October 15, 2000)
*Estimated totals for urban areas, defined by the F.B.I. as Metropolitan Statistical Areas and other cities outside such areas. National total includes those states listed as not available. Aggravated assault is an attack for the purpose of inflicting severe bodily injury.
**Not available.

Urban Aggravated Assault Rate in 1999

National Urban Rate = 358.2 Aggravated Assaults per 100,000 Population*

ALPHA ORDER

RANK ORDER

RANK	STATE	RATE
19	Alabama	365.4
6	Alaska	518.9
18	Arizona	367.7
14	Arkansas	400.3
11	California	414.5
29	Colorado	231.2
34	Connecticut	199.2
7	Delaware	456.6
3	Florida	596.7
20	Georgia	345.3
42	Hawaii	117.6
30	Idaho	223.8
NA	Illinois**	NA
27	Indiana	242.1
23	Iowa	286.1
NA	Kansas**	NA
NA	Kentucky**	NA
5	Louisiana	523.0
44	Maine	86.0
8	Maryland	452.6
9	Massachusetts	426.5
13	Michigan	405.6
37	Minnesota	165.5
31	Mississippi	223.6
15	Missouri	398.4
NA	Montana**	NA
12	Nebraska	414.4
24	Nevada	278.9
NA	New Hampshire**	NA
32	New Jersey	216.1
2	New Mexico	652.8
22	New York	330.4
16	North Carolina	394.3
45	North Dakota	44.9
39	Ohio	159.9
10	Oklahoma	416.0
25	Oregon	274.7
26	Pennsylvania	245.1
38	Rhode Island	162.5
1	South Carolina	665.4
41	South Dakota	145.1
4	Tennessee	551.6
17	Texas	385.9
35	Utah	191.8
43	Vermont	105.1
36	Virginia	185.4
28	Washington	236.9
21	West Virginia	330.5
40	Wisconsin	152.3
33	Wyoming	200.7

RANK	STATE	RATE
1	South Carolina	665.4
2	New Mexico	652.8
3	Florida	596.7
4	Tennessee	551.6
5	Louisiana	523.0
6	Alaska	518.9
7	Delaware	456.6
8	Maryland	452.6
9	Massachusetts	426.5
10	Oklahoma	416.0
11	California	414.5
12	Nebraska	414.4
13	Michigan	405.6
14	Arkansas	400.3
15	Missouri	398.4
16	North Carolina	394.3
17	Texas	385.9
18	Arizona	367.7
19	Alabama	365.4
20	Georgia	345.3
21	West Virginia	330.5
22	New York	330.4
23	Iowa	286.1
24	Nevada	278.9
25	Oregon	274.7
26	Pennsylvania	245.1
27	Indiana	242.1
28	Washington	236.9
29	Colorado	231.2
30	Idaho	223.8
31	Mississippi	223.6
32	New Jersey	216.1
33	Wyoming	200.7
34	Connecticut	199.2
35	Utah	191.8
36	Virginia	185.4
37	Minnesota	165.5
38	Rhode Island	162.5
39	Ohio	159.9
40	Wisconsin	152.3
41	South Dakota	145.1
42	Hawaii	117.6
43	Vermont	105.1
44	Maine	86.0
45	North Dakota	44.9
NA	Illinois**	NA
NA	Kansas**	NA
NA	Kentucky**	NA
NA	Montana**	NA
NA	New Hampshire**	NA

District of Columbia 889.2

Source: Morgan Quitno Press using data from Federal Bureau of Investigation
    "Crime in the United States 1999" (Uniform Crime Reports, October 15, 2000)
*Estimated rates for urban areas, defined by the F.B.I. as Metropolitan Statistical Areas and other cities outside
such areas. National rate includes those states listed as not available. Aggravated assault is an attack for the
purpose of inflicting severe bodily injury.
**Not available.

Percent of Aggravated Assaults Occurring in Urban Areas in 1999

National Percent = 93.6% of Aggravated Assaults*

ALPHA ORDER

RANK	STATE	PERCENT
21	Alabama	91.1
39	Alaska	79.6
13	Arizona	95.3
26	Arkansas	87.0
4	California	98.7
8	Colorado	95.9
31	Connecticut	85.5
33	Delaware	85.2
12	Florida	95.5
37	Georgia	83.6
43	Hawaii	75.9
42	Idaho	77.7
NA	Illinois**	NA
36	Indiana	84.8
19	Iowa	91.7
NA	Kansas**	NA
NA	Kentucky**	NA
35	Louisiana	84.9
30	Maine	85.7
6	Maryland	97.0
1	Massachusetts	100.0
10	Michigan	95.8
18	Minnesota	91.9
44	Mississippi	70.0
20	Missouri	91.5
NA	Montana**	NA
8	Nebraska	95.9
23	Nevada	89.9
NA	New Hampshire**	NA
1	New Jersey	100.0
29	New Mexico	86.1
5	New York	97.2
28	North Carolina	86.8
26	North Dakota	87.0
14	Ohio	94.7
25	Oklahoma	88.9
17	Oregon	92.7
7	Pennsylvania	96.3
3	Rhode Island	99.1
40	South Carolina	79.5
33	South Dakota	85.2
22	Tennessee	90.0
11	Texas	95.6
16	Utah	93.9
38	Vermont	81.0
32	Virginia	85.4
14	Washington	94.7
45	West Virginia	65.5
24	Wisconsin	89.5
41	Wyoming	78.5

RANK ORDER

RANK	STATE	PERCENT
1	Massachusetts	100.0
1	New Jersey	100.0
3	Rhode Island	99.1
4	California	98.7
5	New York	97.2
6	Maryland	97.0
7	Pennsylvania	96.3
8	Colorado	95.9
8	Nebraska	95.9
10	Michigan	95.8
11	Texas	95.6
12	Florida	95.5
13	Arizona	95.3
14	Ohio	94.7
14	Washington	94.7
16	Utah	93.9
17	Oregon	92.7
18	Minnesota	91.9
19	Iowa	91.7
20	Missouri	91.5
21	Alabama	91.1
22	Tennessee	90.0
23	Nevada	89.9
24	Wisconsin	89.5
25	Oklahoma	88.9
26	Arkansas	87.0
26	North Dakota	87.0
28	North Carolina	86.8
29	New Mexico	86.1
30	Maine	85.7
31	Connecticut	85.5
32	Virginia	85.4
33	Delaware	85.2
33	South Dakota	85.2
35	Louisiana	84.9
36	Indiana	84.8
37	Georgia	83.6
38	Vermont	81.0
39	Alaska	79.6
40	South Carolina	79.5
41	Wyoming	78.5
42	Idaho	77.7
43	Hawaii	75.9
44	Mississippi	70.0
45	West Virginia	65.5
NA	Illinois**	NA
NA	Kansas**	NA
NA	Kentucky**	NA
NA	Montana**	NA
NA	New Hampshire**	NA

District of Columbia   100.0

Source: Morgan Quitno Press using data from Federal Bureau of Investigation
   "Crime in the United States 1999" (Uniform Crime Reports, October 15, 2000)
Estimated percentages for urban areas, defined by the F.B.I. as Metropolitan Statistical Areas and other cities outside such areas. National percent includes those states listed as not available. Aggravated assault is an attack for the purpose of inflicting severe bodily injury.
**Not available.*

Aggravated Assaults in Rural Areas in 1999

National Rural Total = 59,042 Aggravated Assaults*

ALPHA ORDER

RANK	STATE	ASSAULTS	% of USA
18	Alabama	1,264	2.1%
29	Alaska	565	1.0%
23	Arizona	804	1.4%
19	Arkansas	1,037	1.8%
11	California	1,731	2.9%
34	Colorado	367	0.6%
21	Connecticut	944	1.6%
31	Delaware	518	0.9%
3	Florida	4,050	6.9%
2	Georgia	4,228	7.2%
35	Hawaii	324	0.5%
30	Idaho	536	0.9%
NA	Illinois**	NA	NA
8	Indiana	2,091	3.5%
32	Iowa	512	0.9%
NA	Kansas**	NA	NA
NA	Kentucky**	NA	NA
5	Louisiana	3,397	5.8%
39	Maine	128	0.2%
25	Maryland	687	1.2%
44	Massachusetts	12	0.0%
15	Michigan	1,554	2.6%
28	Minnesota	570	1.0%
14	Mississippi	1,565	2.7%
13	Missouri	1,566	2.7%
NA	Montana**	NA	NA
37	Nebraska	223	0.4%
33	Nevada	506	0.9%
NA	New Hampshire**	NA	NA
45	New Jersey	0	0.0%
16	New Mexico	1,510	2.6%
12	New York	1,638	2.8%
4	North Carolina	3,524	6.0%
42	North Dakota	28	0.0%
22	Ohio	889	1.5%
17	Oklahoma	1,408	2.4%
27	Oregon	602	1.0%
20	Pennsylvania	1,034	1.8%
43	Rhode Island	15	0.0%
1	South Carolina	5,179	8.8%
40	South Dakota	114	0.2%
7	Tennessee	2,682	4.5%
6	Texas	3,234	5.5%
36	Utah	236	0.4%
41	Vermont	87	0.1%
9	Virginia	1,833	3.1%
26	Washington	684	1.2%
10	West Virginia	1,813	3.1%
24	Wisconsin	757	1.3%
38	Wyoming	192	0.3%

RANK ORDER

RANK	STATE	ASSAULTS	% of USA
1	South Carolina	5,179	8.8%
2	Georgia	4,228	7.2%
3	Florida	4,050	6.9%
4	North Carolina	3,524	6.0%
5	Louisiana	3,397	5.8%
6	Texas	3,234	5.5%
7	Tennessee	2,682	4.5%
8	Indiana	2,091	3.5%
9	Virginia	1,833	3.1%
10	West Virginia	1,813	3.1%
11	California	1,731	2.9%
12	New York	1,638	2.8%
13	Missouri	1,566	2.7%
14	Mississippi	1,565	2.7%
15	Michigan	1,554	2.6%
16	New Mexico	1,510	2.6%
17	Oklahoma	1,408	2.4%
18	Alabama	1,264	2.1%
19	Arkansas	1,037	1.8%
20	Pennsylvania	1,034	1.8%
21	Connecticut	944	1.6%
22	Ohio	889	1.5%
23	Arizona	804	1.4%
24	Wisconsin	757	1.3%
25	Maryland	687	1.2%
26	Washington	684	1.2%
27	Oregon	602	1.0%
28	Minnesota	570	1.0%
29	Alaska	565	1.0%
30	Idaho	536	0.9%
31	Delaware	518	0.9%
32	Iowa	512	0.9%
33	Nevada	506	0.9%
34	Colorado	367	0.6%
35	Hawaii	324	0.5%
36	Utah	236	0.4%
37	Nebraska	223	0.4%
38	Wyoming	192	0.3%
39	Maine	128	0.2%
40	South Dakota	114	0.2%
41	Vermont	87	0.1%
42	North Dakota	28	0.0%
43	Rhode Island	15	0.0%
44	Massachusetts	12	0.0%
45	New Jersey	0	0.0%
NA	Illinois**	NA	NA
NA	Kansas**	NA	NA
NA	Kentucky**	NA	NA
NA	Montana**	NA	NA
NA	New Hampshire**	NA	NA
	District of Columbia	0	0.0%

Source: Federal Bureau of Investigation
   "Crime in the United States 1999" (Uniform Crime Reports, October 15, 2000)
*Estimated totals for rural areas, defined by the F.B.I. as other than Metropolitan Statistical Areas and other cities outside such areas. National total includes those states listed as not available. Aggravated assault is an attack for the purpose of inflicting severe bodily injury.
**Not available.

Rural Aggravated Assault Rate in 1999

National Rural Rate = 177.2 Aggravated Assaults per 100,000 Population*

ALPHA ORDER

RANK	STATE	RATE
21	Alabama	155.7
6	Alaska	292.0
9	Arizona	270.1
26	Arkansas	126.6
7	California	270.5
33	Colorado	99.3
16	Connecticut	197.1
2	Delaware	501.5
3	Florida	484.6
7	Georgia	270.5
31	Hawaii	101.7
25	Idaho	128.1
NA	Illinois**	NA
18	Indiana	186.7
38	Iowa	57.2
NA	Kansas**	NA
NA	Kentucky**	NA
5	Louisiana	475.7
42	Maine	35.6
11	Maryland	238.8
29	Massachusetts	117.4
23	Michigan	140.0
37	Minnesota	63.8
24	Mississippi	137.5
27	Missouri	126.2
NA	Montana**	NA
39	Nebraska	54.4
10	Nevada	253.3
NA	New Hampshire**	NA
44	New Jersey	0.0
4	New Mexico	482.9
18	New York	186.7
15	North Carolina	198.1
43	North Dakota	13.0
36	Ohio	64.6
14	Oklahoma	216.7
30	Oregon	114.4
32	Pennsylvania	99.5
44	Rhode Island	0.0
1	South Carolina	602.4
40	South Dakota	40.6
12	Tennessee	237.6
17	Texas	191.6
34	Utah	98.2
41	Vermont	36.1
20	Virginia	169.2
28	Washington	125.4
13	West Virginia	237.2
35	Wisconsin	75.5
22	Wyoming	146.8

RANK ORDER

RANK	STATE	RATE
1	South Carolina	602.4
2	Delaware	501.5
3	Florida	484.6
4	New Mexico	482.9
5	Louisiana	475.7
6	Alaska	292.0
7	California	270.5
7	Georgia	270.5
9	Arizona	270.1
10	Nevada	253.3
11	Maryland	238.8
12	Tennessee	237.6
13	West Virginia	237.2
14	Oklahoma	216.7
15	North Carolina	198.1
16	Connecticut	197.1
17	Texas	191.6
18	Indiana	186.7
18	New York	186.7
20	Virginia	169.2
21	Alabama	155.7
22	Wyoming	146.8
23	Michigan	140.0
24	Mississippi	137.5
25	Idaho	128.1
26	Arkansas	126.6
27	Missouri	126.2
28	Washington	125.4
29	Massachusetts	117.4
30	Oregon	114.4
31	Hawaii	101.7
32	Pennsylvania	99.5
33	Colorado	99.3
34	Utah	98.2
35	Wisconsin	75.5
36	Ohio	64.6
37	Minnesota	63.8
38	Iowa	57.2
39	Nebraska	54.4
40	South Dakota	40.6
41	Vermont	36.1
42	Maine	35.6
43	North Dakota	13.0
44	New Jersey	0.0
44	Rhode Island	0.0
NA	Illinois**	NA
NA	Kansas**	NA
NA	Kentucky**	NA
NA	Montana**	NA
NA	New Hampshire**	NA

District of Columbia	0.0

Source: Morgan Quitno Press using data from Federal Bureau of Investigation
   "Crime in the United States 1999" (Uniform Crime Reports, October 15, 2000)
*Estimated rates for rural areas, defined by the F.B.I. as other than Metropolitan Statistical Areas and other cities outside such areas. National rate includes those states listed as not available. Aggravated assault is an attack for the purpose of inflicting severe bodily injury.
**Not available.

Percent of Aggravated Assaults Occurring in Rural Areas in 1999

National Percent = 6.4% of Aggravated Assaults*

ALPHA ORDER

RANK ORDER

RANK	STATE	PERCENT		RANK	STATE	PERCENT
25	Alabama	8.9		1	West Virginia	34.5
7	Alaska	20.4		2	Mississippi	30.0
33	Arizona	4.7		3	Hawaii	24.1
19	Arkansas	13.0		4	Idaho	22.3
42	California	1.3		5	Wyoming	21.5
37	Colorado	4.1		6	South Carolina	20.5
15	Connecticut	14.5		7	Alaska	20.4
12	Delaware	14.8		8	Vermont	19.0
34	Florida	4.5		9	Georgia	16.4
9	Georgia	16.4		10	Indiana	15.2
3	Hawaii	24.1		11	Louisiana	15.1
4	Idaho	22.3		12	Delaware	14.8
NA	Illinois**	NA		12	South Dakota	14.8
10	Indiana	15.2		14	Virginia	14.6
27	Iowa	8.3		15	Connecticut	14.5
NA	Kansas**	NA		16	Maine	14.3
NA	Kentucky**	NA		17	New Mexico	13.9
11	Louisiana	15.1		18	North Carolina	13.2
16	Maine	14.3		19	Arkansas	13.0
40	Maryland	3.0		19	North Dakota	13.0
44	Massachusetts	0.0		21	Oklahoma	11.1
36	Michigan	4.2		22	Wisconsin	10.5
28	Minnesota	8.1		23	Nevada	10.1
2	Mississippi	30.0		24	Tennessee	10.0
26	Missouri	8.5		25	Alabama	8.9
NA	Montana**	NA		26	Missouri	8.5
37	Nebraska	4.1		27	Iowa	8.3
23	Nevada	10.1		28	Minnesota	8.1
NA	New Hampshire**	NA		29	Oregon	7.3
44	New Jersey	0.0		30	Utah	6.1
17	New Mexico	13.9		31	Ohio	5.3
41	New York	2.8		31	Washington	5.3
18	North Carolina	13.2		33	Arizona	4.7
19	North Dakota	13.0		34	Florida	4.5
31	Ohio	5.3		35	Texas	4.4
21	Oklahoma	11.1		36	Michigan	4.2
29	Oregon	7.3		37	Colorado	4.1
39	Pennsylvania	3.7		37	Nebraska	4.1
43	Rhode Island	0.9		39	Pennsylvania	3.7
6	South Carolina	20.5		40	Maryland	3.0
12	South Dakota	14.8		41	New York	2.8
24	Tennessee	10.0		42	California	1.3
35	Texas	4.4		43	Rhode Island	0.9
30	Utah	6.1		44	Massachusetts	0.0
8	Vermont	19.0		44	New Jersey	0.0
14	Virginia	14.6		NA	Illinois**	NA
31	Washington	5.3		NA	Kansas**	NA
1	West Virginia	34.5		NA	Kentucky**	NA
22	Wisconsin	10.5		NA	Montana**	NA
5	Wyoming	21.5		NA	New Hampshire**	NA

District of Columbia   0.0

Source: Morgan Quitno Press using data from Federal Bureau of Investigation
  "Crime in the United States 1999" (Uniform Crime Reports, October 15, 2000)
*Estimated percentages for rural areas, defined by the F.B.I. as other than Metropolitan Statistical Areas and other cities outside such areas. National percent includes those states listed as not available. Aggravated assault is an attack for the purpose of inflicting severe bodily injury.
**Not available.

Property Crimes in Urban Areas in 1999

National Urban Total = 9,644,550 Property Crimes*

ALPHA ORDER					RANK ORDER			

RANK	STATE	CRIMES	% of USA		RANK	STATE	CRIMES	% of USA
20	Alabama	161,665	1.7%		1	California	1,039,643	10.8%
41	Alaska	19,228	0.2%		2	Texas	870,766	9.0%
11	Arizona	250,382	2.6%		3	Florida	783,886	8.1%
31	Arkansas	81,398	0.8%		4	New York	476,035	4.9%
1	California	1,039,643	10.8%		5	Ohio	393,383	4.1%
21	Colorado	146,340	1.5%		6	Michigan	347,503	3.6%
29	Connecticut	93,145	1.0%		7	Georgia	325,157	3.4%
40	Delaware	28,375	0.3%		8	North Carolina	313,066	3.2%
3	Florida	783,886	8.1%		9	Pennsylvania	308,489	3.2%
7	Georgia	325,157	3.4%		10	Washington	266,348	2.8%
35	Hawaii	40,480	0.4%		11	Arizona	250,382	2.6%
38	Idaho	30,758	0.3%		12	New Jersey	243,333	2.5%
NA	Illinois**	NA	NA		13	Maryland	210,600	2.2%
18	Indiana	183,851	1.9%		14	Missouri	209,723	2.2%
32	Iowa	76,313	0.8%		15	Louisiana	204,495	2.1%
NA	Kansas**	NA	NA		16	Tennessee	200,671	2.1%
NA	Kentucky**	NA	NA		17	Virginia	194,779	2.0%
15	Louisiana	204,495	2.1%		18	Indiana	183,851	1.9%
39	Maine	28,773	0.3%		19	Massachusetts	167,415	1.7%
13	Maryland	210,600	2.2%		20	Alabama	161,665	1.7%
19	Massachusetts	167,415	1.7%		21	Colorado	146,340	1.5%
6	Michigan	347,503	3.6%		22	South Carolina	146,309	1.5%
24	Minnesota	143,936	1.5%		23	Wisconsin	146,142	1.5%
28	Mississippi	93,308	1.0%		24	Minnesota	143,936	1.5%
14	Missouri	209,723	2.2%		25	Oregon	143,007	1.5%
NA	Montana**	NA	NA		26	Oklahoma	131,604	1.4%
34	Nebraska	55,805	0.6%		27	Utah	95,308	1.0%
33	Nevada	69,982	0.7%		28	Mississippi	93,308	1.0%
NA	New Hampshire**	NA	NA		29	Connecticut	93,145	1.0%
12	New Jersey	243,333	2.5%		30	New Mexico	82,628	0.9%
30	New Mexico	82,628	0.9%		31	Arkansas	81,398	0.8%
4	New York	476,035	4.9%		32	Iowa	76,313	0.8%
8	North Carolina	313,066	3.2%		33	Nevada	69,982	0.7%
44	North Dakota	12,658	0.1%		34	Nebraska	55,805	0.6%
5	Ohio	393,383	4.1%		35	Hawaii	40,480	0.4%
26	Oklahoma	131,604	1.4%		36	Rhode Island	32,641	0.3%
25	Oregon	143,007	1.5%		37	West Virginia	32,624	0.3%
9	Pennsylvania	308,489	3.2%		38	Idaho	30,758	0.3%
36	Rhode Island	32,641	0.3%		39	Maine	28,773	0.3%
22	South Carolina	146,309	1.5%		40	Delaware	28,375	0.3%
42	South Dakota	15,969	0.2%		41	Alaska	19,228	0.2%
16	Tennessee	200,671	2.1%		42	South Dakota	15,969	0.2%
2	Texas	870,766	9.0%		43	Wyoming	13,459	0.1%
27	Utah	95,308	1.0%		44	North Dakota	12,658	0.1%
45	Vermont	11,925	0.1%		45	Vermont	11,925	0.1%
17	Virginia	194,779	2.0%		NA	Illinois**	NA	NA
10	Washington	266,348	2.8%		NA	Kansas**	NA	NA
37	West Virginia	32,624	0.3%		NA	Kentucky**	NA	NA
23	Wisconsin	146,142	1.5%		NA	Montana**	NA	NA
43	Wyoming	13,459	0.1%		NA	New Hampshire**	NA	NA
						District of Columbia	33,420	0.3%

Source: Morgan Quitno Press using data from Federal Bureau of Investigation
    "Crime in the United States 1999" (Uniform Crime Reports, October 15, 2000)
*Estimated totals for urban areas, defined by the F.B.I. as Metropolitan Statistical Areas and other cities outside such areas. National total includes those states listed as not available. Property crimes are offenses of burglary, larceny-theft and motor vehicle theft.
**Not available.

Urban Property Crime Rate in 1999

National Urban Rate = 4,029.2 Property Crimes per 100,000 Population*

ALPHA ORDER				RANK ORDER		
RANK	STATE	RATE		RANK	STATE	RATE
18	Alabama	4,543.7		1	New Mexico	5,789.2
19	Alaska	4,518.9		2	Mississippi	5,721.7
4	Arizona	5,588.4		3	Louisiana	5,590.6
15	Arkansas	4,699.6		4	Arizona	5,588.4
39	California	3,198.4		5	Florida	5,491.2
26	Colorado	3,969.6		6	North Carolina	5,331.1
36	Connecticut	3,323.0		7	Georgia	5,223.7
21	Delaware	4,360.6		8	Oregon	5,126.0
5	Florida	5,491.2		9	Washington	5,111.7
7	Georgia	5,223.7		10	Utah	5,043.5
16	Hawaii	4,671.3		11	Missouri	4,961.9
31	Idaho	3,690.4		12	Oklahoma	4,859.6
NA	Illinois**	NA		13	South Carolina	4,834.7
29	Indiana	3,812.1		14	Texas	4,743.8
27	Iowa	3,865.1		15	Arkansas	4,699.6
NA	Kansas**	NA		16	Hawaii	4,671.3
NA	Kentucky**	NA		17	Tennessee	4,607.6
3	Louisiana	5,590.6		18	Alabama	4,543.7
38	Maine	3,219.4		19	Alaska	4,518.9
23	Maryland	4,311.8		20	Nebraska	4,442.0
45	Massachusetts	2,715.7		21	Delaware	4,360.6
25	Michigan	3,969.7		22	Nevada	4,348.8
30	Minnesota	3,706.7		23	Maryland	4,311.8
2	Mississippi	5,721.7		24	Ohio	3,981.0
11	Missouri	4,961.9		25	Michigan	3,969.7
NA	Montana**	NA		26	Colorado	3,969.6
20	Nebraska	4,442.0		27	Iowa	3,865.1
22	Nevada	4,348.8		28	Wyoming	3,854.3
NA	New Hampshire**	NA		29	Indiana	3,812.1
42	New Jersey	2,988.2		30	Minnesota	3,706.7
1	New Mexico	5,789.2		31	Idaho	3,690.4
44	New York	2,748.5		32	South Dakota	3,532.5
6	North Carolina	5,331.1		33	Wisconsin	3,441.1
41	North Dakota	3,023.7		34	Vermont	3,377.7
24	Ohio	3,981.0		35	Virginia	3,364.4
12	Oklahoma	4,859.6		36	Connecticut	3,323.0
8	Oregon	5,126.0		37	Rhode Island	3,293.7
43	Pennsylvania	2,816.0		38	Maine	3,219.4
37	Rhode Island	3,293.7		39	California	3,198.4
13	South Carolina	4,834.7		40	West Virginia	3,129.3
32	South Dakota	3,532.5		41	North Dakota	3,023.7
17	Tennessee	4,607.6		42	New Jersey	2,988.2
14	Texas	4,743.8		43	Pennsylvania	2,816.0
10	Utah	5,043.5		44	New York	2,748.5
34	Vermont	3,377.7		45	Massachusetts	2,715.7
35	Virginia	3,364.4		NA	Illinois**	NA
9	Washington	5,111.7		NA	Kansas**	NA
40	West Virginia	3,129.3		NA	Kentucky**	NA
33	Wisconsin	3,441.1		NA	Montana**	NA
28	Wyoming	3,854.3		NA	New Hampshire**	NA

District of Columbia   6,439.3

Source: Morgan Quitno Press using data from Federal Bureau of Investigation
    "Crime in the United States 1999" (Uniform Crime Reports, October 15, 2000)
*Estimated rates for urban areas, defined by the F.B.I. as Metropolitan Statistical Areas and other cities outside such areas. National rate includes those states listed as not available. Property crimes are offenses of burglary, larceny-theft and motor vehicle theft.
**Not available.

Percent of Property Crimes Occurring in Urban Areas in 1999

National Percent = 94.5% of Property Crimes*

ALPHA ORDER

RANK	STATE	PERCENT
16	Alabama	94.3
41	Alaska	83.2
5	Arizona	98.0
34	Arkansas	88.2
4	California	98.7
9	Colorado	96.9
21	Connecticut	93.2
25	Delaware	91.8
9	Florida	96.9
31	Georgia	90.5
45	Hawaii	74.2
39	Idaho	84.6
NA	Illinois**	NA
28	Indiana	91.2
32	Iowa	90.4
NA	Kansas**	NA
NA	Kentucky**	NA
20	Louisiana	93.3
42	Maine	83.1
6	Maryland	97.5
1	Massachusetts	100.0
18	Michigan	93.9
30	Minnesota	90.7
37	Mississippi	86.0
17	Missouri	94.0
NA	Montana**	NA
29	Nebraska	91.1
15	Nevada	94.7
NA	New Hampshire**	NA
1	New Jersey	100.0
23	New Mexico	92.6
7	New York	97.2
33	North Carolina	88.3
38	North Dakota	85.8
13	Ohio	95.0
18	Oklahoma	93.9
21	Oregon	93.2
11	Pennsylvania	95.5
1	Rhode Island	100.0
40	South Carolina	84.1
35	South Dakota	87.9
26	Tennessee	91.5
7	Texas	97.2
12	Utah	95.2
44	Vermont	74.3
23	Virginia	92.6
14	Washington	94.9
43	West Virginia	76.2
27	Wisconsin	91.3
36	Wyoming	87.0

RANK ORDER

RANK	STATE	PERCENT
1	Massachusetts	100.0
1	New Jersey	100.0
1	Rhode Island	100.0
4	California	98.7
5	Arizona	98.0
6	Maryland	97.5
7	New York	97.2
7	Texas	97.2
9	Colorado	96.9
9	Florida	96.9
11	Pennsylvania	95.5
12	Utah	95.2
13	Ohio	95.0
14	Washington	94.9
15	Nevada	94.7
16	Alabama	94.3
17	Missouri	94.0
18	Michigan	93.9
18	Oklahoma	93.9
20	Louisiana	93.3
21	Connecticut	93.2
21	Oregon	93.2
23	New Mexico	92.6
23	Virginia	92.6
25	Delaware	91.8
26	Tennessee	91.5
27	Wisconsin	91.3
28	Indiana	91.2
29	Nebraska	91.1
30	Minnesota	90.7
31	Georgia	90.5
32	Iowa	90.4
33	North Carolina	88.3
34	Arkansas	88.2
35	South Dakota	87.9
36	Wyoming	87.0
37	Mississippi	86.0
38	North Dakota	85.8
39	Idaho	84.6
40	South Carolina	84.1
41	Alaska	83.2
42	Maine	83.1
43	West Virginia	76.2
44	Vermont	74.3
45	Hawaii	74.2
NA	Illinois**	NA
NA	Kansas**	NA
NA	Kentucky**	NA
NA	Montana**	NA
NA	New Hampshire**	NA

District of Columbia 100.0

Source: Morgan Quitno Press using data from Federal Bureau of Investigation
   "Crime in the United States 1999" (Uniform Crime Reports, October 15, 2000)
*Estimated percentages for urban areas, defined by the F.B.I. as Metropolitan Statistical Areas and other cities outside such areas. National percent includes those states listed as not available. Property crimes are offenses of burglary, larceny-theft and motor vehicle theft.
**Not available.

Property Crimes in Rural Areas in 1999

National Rural Total = 559,906 Property Crimes*

ALPHA ORDER

RANK	STATE	CRIMES	% of USA
24	Alabama	9,733	1.7%
38	Alaska	3,871	0.7%
33	Arizona	5,019	0.9%
21	Arkansas	10,885	1.9%
18	California	13,642	2.4%
35	Colorado	4,662	0.8%
27	Connecticut	6,749	1.2%
39	Delaware	2,547	0.5%
5	Florida	24,788	4.4%
2	Georgia	34,226	6.1%
16	Hawaii	14,059	2.5%
30	Idaho	5,605	1.0%
NA	Illinois**	NA	NA
9	Indiana	17,696	3.2%
26	Iowa	8,150	1.5%
NA	Kansas**	NA	NA
NA	Kentucky**	NA	NA
13	Louisiana	14,724	2.6%
29	Maine	5,845	1.0%
32	Maryland	5,373	1.0%
43	Massachusetts	22	0.0%
6	Michigan	22,384	4.0%
12	Minnesota	14,781	2.6%
11	Mississippi	15,252	2.7%
20	Missouri	13,287	2.4%
NA	Montana**	NA	NA
31	Nebraska	5,472	1.0%
37	Nevada	3,892	0.7%
NA	New Hampshire**	NA	NA
45	New Jersey	0	0.0%
28	New Mexico	6,592	1.2%
19	New York	13,561	2.4%
1	North Carolina	41,431	7.4%
41	North Dakota	2,090	0.4%
7	Ohio	20,881	3.7%
25	Oklahoma	8,616	1.5%
22	Oregon	10,427	1.9%
14	Pennsylvania	14,532	2.6%
44	Rhode Island	16	0.0%
3	South Carolina	27,678	4.9%
40	South Dakota	2,190	0.4%
8	Tennessee	18,631	3.3%
4	Texas	25,495	4.6%
34	Utah	4,822	0.9%
36	Vermont	4,134	0.7%
10	Virginia	15,481	2.8%
15	Washington	14,445	2.6%
23	West Virginia	10,201	1.8%
17	Wisconsin	14,012	2.5%
42	Wyoming	2,009	0.4%

RANK ORDER

RANK	STATE	CRIMES	% of USA
1	North Carolina	41,431	7.4%
2	Georgia	34,226	6.1%
3	South Carolina	27,678	4.9%
4	Texas	25,495	4.6%
5	Florida	24,788	4.4%
6	Michigan	22,384	4.0%
7	Ohio	20,881	3.7%
8	Tennessee	18,631	3.3%
9	Indiana	17,696	3.2%
10	Virginia	15,481	2.8%
11	Mississippi	15,252	2.7%
12	Minnesota	14,781	2.6%
13	Louisiana	14,724	2.6%
14	Pennsylvania	14,532	2.6%
15	Washington	14,445	2.6%
16	Hawaii	14,059	2.5%
17	Wisconsin	14,012	2.5%
18	California	13,642	2.4%
19	New York	13,561	2.4%
20	Missouri	13,287	2.4%
21	Arkansas	10,885	1.9%
22	Oregon	10,427	1.9%
23	West Virginia	10,201	1.8%
24	Alabama	9,733	1.7%
25	Oklahoma	8,616	1.5%
26	Iowa	8,150	1.5%
27	Connecticut	6,749	1.2%
28	New Mexico	6,592	1.2%
29	Maine	5,845	1.0%
30	Idaho	5,605	1.0%
31	Nebraska	5,472	1.0%
32	Maryland	5,373	1.0%
33	Arizona	5,019	0.9%
34	Utah	4,822	0.9%
35	Colorado	4,662	0.8%
36	Vermont	4,134	0.7%
37	Nevada	3,892	0.7%
38	Alaska	3,871	0.7%
39	Delaware	2,547	0.5%
40	South Dakota	2,190	0.4%
41	North Dakota	2,090	0.4%
42	Wyoming	2,009	0.4%
43	Massachusetts	22	0.0%
44	Rhode Island	16	0.0%
45	New Jersey	0	0.0%
NA	Illinois**	NA	NA
NA	Kansas**	NA	NA
NA	Kentucky**	NA	NA
NA	Montana**	NA	NA
NA	New Hampshire**	NA	NA
	District of Columbia	0	0.0%

Source: Federal Bureau of Investigation
"Crime in the United States 1999" (Uniform Crime Reports, October 15, 2000)
*Estimated totals for rural areas, defined by the F.B.I. as other than Metropolitan Statistical Areas and other cities outside such areas. National total includes those states listed as not available. Property crimes are offenses of burglary, larceny-theft and motor vehicle theft.
**Not available.

Rural Property Crime Rate in 1999

National Rural Rate = 1,680.2 Property Crimes per 100,000 Population*

ALPHA ORDER

RANK	STATE	RATE
38	Alabama	1,198.7
13	Alaska	2,000.5
18	Arizona	1,686.4
35	Arkansas	1,329.1
8	California	2,131.7
37	Colorado	1,261.9
28	Connecticut	1,409.0
5	Delaware	2,466.1
3	Florida	2,966.2
7	Georgia	2,189.3
1	Hawaii	4,415.0
32	Idaho	1,339.2
NA	Illinois**	NA
22	Indiana	1,579.8
41	Iowa	911.0
NA	Kansas**	NA
NA	Kentucky**	NA
10	Louisiana	2,061.7
21	Maine	1,626.9
16	Maryland	1,867.5
43	Massachusetts	215.3
11	Michigan	2,016.4
19	Minnesota	1,655.5
31	Mississippi	1,340.0
39	Missouri	1,070.4
NA	Montana**	NA
33	Nebraska	1,335.6
15	Nevada	1,948.1
NA	New Hampshire**	NA
44	New Jersey	0.0
9	New Mexico	2,108.0
23	New York	1,546.0
6	North Carolina	2,329.5
40	North Dakota	970.4
25	Ohio	1,518.2
36	Oklahoma	1,325.8
14	Oregon	1,981.6
29	Pennsylvania	1,398.7
44	Rhode Island	0.0
2	South Carolina	3,219.3
42	South Dakota	779.5
20	Tennessee	1,650.5
26	Texas	1,510.2
12	Utah	2,006.8
17	Vermont	1,715.7
27	Virginia	1,428.6
4	Washington	2,648.4
34	West Virginia	1,334.4
30	Wisconsin	1,397.0
24	Wyoming	1,535.8

RANK ORDER

RANK	STATE	RATE
1	Hawaii	4,415.0
2	South Carolina	3,219.3
3	Florida	2,966.2
4	Washington	2,648.4
5	Delaware	2,466.1
6	North Carolina	2,329.5
7	Georgia	2,189.3
8	California	2,131.7
9	New Mexico	2,108.0
10	Louisiana	2,061.7
11	Michigan	2,016.4
12	Utah	2,006.8
13	Alaska	2,000.5
14	Oregon	1,981.6
15	Nevada	1,948.1
16	Maryland	1,867.5
17	Vermont	1,715.7
18	Arizona	1,686.4
19	Minnesota	1,655.5
20	Tennessee	1,650.5
21	Maine	1,626.9
22	Indiana	1,579.8
23	New York	1,546.0
24	Wyoming	1,535.8
25	Ohio	1,518.2
26	Texas	1,510.2
27	Virginia	1,428.6
28	Connecticut	1,409.0
29	Pennsylvania	1,398.7
30	Wisconsin	1,397.0
31	Mississippi	1,340.0
32	Idaho	1,339.2
33	Nebraska	1,335.6
34	West Virginia	1,334.4
35	Arkansas	1,329.1
36	Oklahoma	1,325.8
37	Colorado	1,261.9
38	Alabama	1,198.7
39	Missouri	1,070.4
40	North Dakota	970.4
41	Iowa	911.0
42	South Dakota	779.5
43	Massachusetts	215.3
44	New Jersey	0.0
44	Rhode Island	0.0
NA	Illinois**	NA
NA	Kansas**	NA
NA	Kentucky**	NA
NA	Montana**	NA
NA	New Hampshire**	NA

District of Columbia   0.0

Source: Morgan Quitno Press using data from Federal Bureau of Investigation
    "Crime in the United States 1999" (Uniform Crime Reports, October 15, 2000)
*Estimated rates for rural areas, defined by the F.B.I. as other than Metropolitan Statistical Areas and other cities outside such areas. National rate includes those states listed as not available. Property crimes are offenses of burglary, larceny-theft and motor vehicle theft.
**Not available.

Percent of Property Crimes Occurring in Rural Areas in 1999

National Percent = 5.5% of Property Crimes*

ALPHA ORDER

RANK ORDER

RANK	STATE	PERCENT		RANK	STATE	PERCENT
30	Alabama	5.7		1	Hawaii	25.8
5	Alaska	16.8		2	Vermont	25.7
41	Arizona	2.0		3	West Virginia	23.8
12	Arkansas	11.8		4	Maine	16.9
42	California	1.3		5	Alaska	16.8
36	Colorado	3.1		6	South Carolina	15.9
24	Connecticut	6.8		7	Idaho	15.4
21	Delaware	8.2		8	North Dakota	14.2
36	Florida	3.1		9	Mississippi	14.0
15	Georgia	9.5		10	Wyoming	13.0
1	Hawaii	25.8		11	South Dakota	12.1
7	Idaho	15.4		12	Arkansas	11.8
NA	Illinois**	NA		13	North Carolina	11.7
18	Indiana	8.8		14	Iowa	9.6
14	Iowa	9.6		15	Georgia	9.5
NA	Kansas**	NA		16	Minnesota	9.3
NA	Kentucky**	NA		17	Nebraska	8.9
26	Louisiana	6.7		18	Indiana	8.8
4	Maine	16.9		19	Wisconsin	8.7
40	Maryland	2.5		20	Tennessee	8.5
43	Massachusetts	0.0		21	Delaware	8.2
27	Michigan	6.1		22	New Mexico	7.4
16	Minnesota	9.3		22	Virginia	7.4
9	Mississippi	14.0		24	Connecticut	6.8
29	Missouri	6.0		24	Oregon	6.8
NA	Montana**	NA		26	Louisiana	6.7
17	Nebraska	8.9		27	Michigan	6.1
31	Nevada	5.3		27	Oklahoma	6.1
NA	New Hampshire**	NA		29	Missouri	6.0
43	New Jersey	0.0		30	Alabama	5.7
22	New Mexico	7.4		31	Nevada	5.3
38	New York	2.8		32	Washington	5.1
13	North Carolina	11.7		33	Ohio	5.0
8	North Dakota	14.2		34	Utah	4.8
33	Ohio	5.0		35	Pennsylvania	4.5
27	Oklahoma	6.1		36	Colorado	3.1
24	Oregon	6.8		36	Florida	3.1
35	Pennsylvania	4.5		38	New York	2.8
43	Rhode Island	0.0		38	Texas	2.8
6	South Carolina	15.9		40	Maryland	2.5
11	South Dakota	12.1		41	Arizona	2.0
20	Tennessee	8.5		42	California	1.3
38	Texas	2.8		43	Massachusetts	0.0
34	Utah	4.8		43	New Jersey	0.0
2	Vermont	25.7		43	Rhode Island	0.0
22	Virginia	7.4		NA	Illinois**	NA
32	Washington	5.1		NA	Kansas**	NA
3	West Virginia	23.8		NA	Kentucky**	NA
19	Wisconsin	8.7		NA	Montana**	NA
10	Wyoming	13.0		NA	New Hampshire**	NA
					District of Columbia	0.0

Source: Morgan Quitno Press using data from Federal Bureau of Investigation
    "Crime in the United States 1999" (Uniform Crime Reports, October 15, 2000)
*Estimated percentages for rural areas, defined by the F.B.I. as other than Metropolitan Statistical Areas and other cities outside such areas. National percent includes those states listed as not available. Property crimes are offenses of burglary, larceny-theft and motor vehicle theft.
**Not available.

Burglaries in Urban Areas in 1999

National Urban Total = 1,915,971 Burglaries*

ALPHA ORDER

RANK	STATE	BURGLARIES	% of USA
18	Alabama	35,027	1.8%
41	Alaska	2,635	0.1%
11	Arizona	47,915	2.5%
29	Arkansas	17,628	0.9%
1	California	218,534	11.4%
23	Colorado	25,966	1.4%
30	Connecticut	17,301	0.9%
40	Delaware	4,466	0.2%
3	Florida	173,339	9.0%
8	Georgia	62,075	3.2%
37	Hawaii	6,087	0.3%
38	Idaho	5,932	0.3%
NA	Illinois**	NA	NA
16	Indiana	37,213	1.9%
32	Iowa	14,236	0.7%
NA	Kansas**	NA	NA
NA	Kentucky**	NA	NA
14	Louisiana	43,280	2.3%
39	Maine	5,327	0.3%
15	Maryland	41,633	2.2%
19	Massachusetts	32,956	1.7%
7	Michigan	68,862	3.6%
25	Minnesota	23,113	1.2%
26	Mississippi	22,476	1.2%
17	Missouri	37,102	1.9%
NA	Montana**	NA	NA
34	Nebraska	8,636	0.5%
31	Nevada	16,602	0.9%
NA	New Hampshire**	NA	NA
12	New Jersey	46,998	2.5%
28	New Mexico	19,281	1.0%
4	New York	88,876	4.6%
6	North Carolina	80,536	4.2%
45	North Dakota	1,744	0.1%
5	Ohio	80,849	4.2%
21	Oklahoma	30,925	1.6%
24	Oregon	23,824	1.2%
9	Pennsylvania	51,251	2.7%
36	Rhode Island	6,339	0.3%
20	South Carolina	31,367	1.6%
42	South Dakota	2,572	0.1%
13	Tennessee	45,051	2.4%
2	Texas	180,291	9.4%
33	Utah	13,520	0.7%
43	Vermont	2,013	0.1%
22	Virginia	28,339	1.5%
10	Washington	49,904	2.6%
35	West Virginia	7,218	0.4%
27	Wisconsin	21,296	1.1%
44	Wyoming	1,886	0.1%

RANK ORDER

RANK	STATE	BURGLARIES	% of USA
1	California	218,534	11.4%
2	Texas	180,291	9.4%
3	Florida	173,339	9.0%
4	New York	88,876	4.6%
5	Ohio	80,849	4.2%
6	North Carolina	80,536	4.2%
7	Michigan	68,862	3.6%
8	Georgia	62,075	3.2%
9	Pennsylvania	51,251	2.7%
10	Washington	49,904	2.6%
11	Arizona	47,915	2.5%
12	New Jersey	46,998	2.5%
13	Tennessee	45,051	2.4%
14	Louisiana	43,280	2.3%
15	Maryland	41,633	2.2%
16	Indiana	37,213	1.9%
17	Missouri	37,102	1.9%
18	Alabama	35,027	1.8%
19	Massachusetts	32,956	1.7%
20	South Carolina	31,367	1.6%
21	Oklahoma	30,925	1.6%
22	Virginia	28,339	1.5%
23	Colorado	25,966	1.4%
24	Oregon	23,824	1.2%
25	Minnesota	23,113	1.2%
26	Mississippi	22,476	1.2%
27	Wisconsin	21,296	1.1%
28	New Mexico	19,281	1.0%
29	Arkansas	17,628	0.9%
30	Connecticut	17,301	0.9%
31	Nevada	16,602	0.9%
32	Iowa	14,236	0.7%
33	Utah	13,520	0.7%
34	Nebraska	8,636	0.5%
35	West Virginia	7,218	0.4%
36	Rhode Island	6,339	0.3%
37	Hawaii	6,087	0.3%
38	Idaho	5,932	0.3%
39	Maine	5,327	0.3%
40	Delaware	4,466	0.2%
41	Alaska	2,635	0.1%
42	South Dakota	2,572	0.1%
43	Vermont	2,013	0.1%
44	Wyoming	1,886	0.1%
45	North Dakota	1,744	0.1%
NA	Illinois**	NA	NA
NA	Kansas**	NA	NA
NA	Kentucky**	NA	NA
NA	Montana**	NA	NA
NA	New Hampshire**	NA	NA
	District of Columbia	5,067	0.3%

Source: Morgan Quitno Press using data from Federal Bureau of Investigation
  "Crime in the United States 1999" (Uniform Crime Reports, October 15, 2000)
*Estimated totals for urban areas, defined by the F.B.I. as Metropolitan Statistical Areas and other cities outside such areas. National total includes those states listed as not available. Burglary is the unlawful entry of a structure to commit a felony or theft. Attempts are included.
**Not available.

Urban Burglary Rate in 1999

National Urban Rate = 800.4 Burglaries per 100,000 Population*

ALPHA ORDER

RANK	STATE	RATE
13	Alabama	984.5
32	Alaska	619.3
7	Arizona	1,069.4
11	Arkansas	1,017.8
30	California	672.3
25	Colorado	704.3
33	Connecticut	617.2
29	Delaware	686.3
4	Florida	1,214.3
12	Georgia	997.2
26	Hawaii	702.4
24	Idaho	711.7
NA	Illinois**	NA
21	Indiana	771.6
22	Iowa	721.0
NA	Kansas**	NA
NA	Kentucky**	NA
5	Louisiana	1,183.2
34	Maine	596.0
18	Maryland	852.4
40	Massachusetts	534.6
20	Michigan	786.6
35	Minnesota	595.2
1	Mississippi	1,378.3
16	Missouri	877.8
NA	Montana**	NA
28	Nebraska	687.4
10	Nevada	1,031.7
NA	New Hampshire**	NA
36	New Jersey	577.2
3	New Mexico	1,350.9
41	New York	513.1
2	North Carolina	1,371.4
45	North Dakota	416.6
19	Ohio	818.2
6	Oklahoma	1,141.9
17	Oregon	854.0
44	Pennsylvania	467.8
31	Rhode Island	639.7
8	South Carolina	1,036.5
38	South Dakota	568.9
9	Tennessee	1,034.4
14	Texas	982.2
23	Utah	715.5
37	Vermont	570.2
43	Virginia	489.5
15	Washington	957.7
27	West Virginia	692.4
42	Wisconsin	501.4
39	Wyoming	540.1

RANK ORDER

RANK	STATE	RATE
1	Mississippi	1,378.3
2	North Carolina	1,371.4
3	New Mexico	1,350.9
4	Florida	1,214.3
5	Louisiana	1,183.2
6	Oklahoma	1,141.9
7	Arizona	1,069.4
8	South Carolina	1,036.5
9	Tennessee	1,034.4
10	Nevada	1,031.7
11	Arkansas	1,017.8
12	Georgia	997.2
13	Alabama	984.5
14	Texas	982.2
15	Washington	957.7
16	Missouri	877.8
17	Oregon	854.0
18	Maryland	852.4
19	Ohio	818.2
20	Michigan	786.6
21	Indiana	771.6
22	Iowa	721.0
23	Utah	715.5
24	Idaho	711.7
25	Colorado	704.3
26	Hawaii	702.4
27	West Virginia	692.4
28	Nebraska	687.4
29	Delaware	686.3
30	California	672.3
31	Rhode Island	639.7
32	Alaska	619.3
33	Connecticut	617.2
34	Maine	596.0
35	Minnesota	595.2
36	New Jersey	577.2
37	Vermont	570.2
38	South Dakota	568.9
39	Wyoming	540.1
40	Massachusetts	534.6
41	New York	513.1
42	Wisconsin	501.4
43	Virginia	489.5
44	Pennsylvania	467.8
45	North Dakota	416.6
NA	Illinois**	NA
NA	Kansas**	NA
NA	Kentucky**	NA
NA	Montana**	NA
NA	New Hampshire**	NA

District of Columbia   976.3

Source: Morgan Quitno Press using data from Federal Bureau of Investigation
   "Crime in the United States 1999" (Uniform Crime Reports, October 15, 2000)
*Estimated rates for urban areas, defined by the F.B.I. as Metropolitan Statistical Areas and other cities outside such areas. National rate includes those states listed as not available. Burglary is the unlawful entry of a structure to commit a felony or theft. Attempts are included.
**Not available.

Percent of Burglaries Occurring in Urban Areas in 1999

National Percent = 91.2% of Burglaries*

ALPHA ORDER

RANK ORDER

RANK	STATE	PERCENT	RANK	STATE	PERCENT
16	Alabama	90.6	1	Massachusetts	100.0
43	Alaska	69.6	1	New Jersey	100.0
5	Arizona	96.9	1	Rhode Island	100.0
34	Arkansas	81.3	4	California	97.6
4	California	97.6	5	Arizona	96.9
7	Colorado	96.2	6	Maryland	96.3
19	Connecticut	89.7	7	Colorado	96.2
28	Delaware	85.1	8	Florida	95.6
8	Florida	95.6	9	New York	95.3
27	Georgia	86.9	10	Texas	94.7
44	Hawaii	64.6	11	Nevada	94.3
38	Idaho	77.6	12	Ohio	92.9
NA	Illinois**	NA	13	Utah	92.7
24	Indiana	87.6	14	Pennsylvania	91.5
30	Iowa	83.7	15	Washington	91.3
NA	Kansas**	NA	16	Alabama	90.6
NA	Kentucky**	NA	16	Louisiana	90.6
16	Louisiana	90.6	18	New Mexico	89.8
41	Maine	70.7	19	Connecticut	89.7
6	Maryland	96.3	19	Michigan	89.7
1	Massachusetts	100.0	19	Oklahoma	89.7
19	Michigan	89.7	22	Oregon	89.1
31	Minnesota	83.4	23	Tennessee	87.7
39	Mississippi	77.2	24	Indiana	87.6
26	Missouri	87.3	25	Virginia	87.4
NA	Montana**	NA	26	Missouri	87.3
29	Nebraska	85.0	27	Georgia	86.9
11	Nevada	94.3	28	Delaware	85.1
NA	New Hampshire**	NA	29	Nebraska	85.0
1	New Jersey	100.0	30	Iowa	83.7
18	New Mexico	89.8	31	Minnesota	83.4
9	New York	95.3	32	Wisconsin	83.1
33	North Carolina	81.8	33	North Carolina	81.8
40	North Dakota	74.6	34	Arkansas	81.3
12	Ohio	92.9	35	Wyoming	80.3
19	Oklahoma	89.7	36	South Carolina	79.1
22	Oregon	89.1	37	South Dakota	79.0
14	Pennsylvania	91.5	38	Idaho	77.6
1	Rhode Island	100.0	39	Mississippi	77.2
36	South Carolina	79.1	40	North Dakota	74.6
37	South Dakota	79.0	41	Maine	70.7
23	Tennessee	87.7	42	West Virginia	70.1
10	Texas	94.7	43	Alaska	69.6
13	Utah	92.7	44	Hawaii	64.6
45	Vermont	56.9	45	Vermont	56.9
25	Virginia	87.4	NA	Illinois**	NA
15	Washington	91.3	NA	Kansas**	NA
42	West Virginia	70.1	NA	Kentucky**	NA
32	Wisconsin	83.1	NA	Montana**	NA
35	Wyoming	80.3	NA	New Hampshire**	NA

District of Columbia   100.0

Source: Morgan Quitno Press using data from Federal Bureau of Investigation
     "Crime in the United States 1999" (Uniform Crime Reports, October 15, 2000)
*Estimated percentages for urban areas, defined by the F.B.I. as Metropolitan Statistical Areas and other cities
outside such areas. National percent includes those states listed as not available. Burglary is the unlawful entry
of a structure to commit a felony or theft. Attempts are included.
**Not available.

Burglaries in Rural Areas in 1999

National Rural Total = 183,768 Burglaries*

ALPHA ORDER

RANK	STATE	BURGLARIES	% of USA
21	Alabama	3,621	2.0%
35	Alaska	1,152	0.6%
34	Arizona	1,508	0.8%
20	Arkansas	4,064	2.2%
11	California	5,280	2.9%
37	Colorado	1,013	0.6%
29	Connecticut	1,997	1.1%
39	Delaware	779	0.4%
5	Florida	8,039	4.4%
3	Georgia	9,354	5.1%
23	Hawaii	3,334	1.8%
30	Idaho	1,709	0.9%
NA	Illinois**	NA	NA
12	Indiana	5,250	2.9%
26	Iowa	2,776	1.5%
NA	Kansas**	NA	NA
NA	Kentucky**	NA	NA
16	Louisiana	4,495	2.4%
27	Maine	2,205	1.2%
31	Maryland	1,597	0.9%
43	Massachusetts	8	0.0%
6	Michigan	7,874	4.3%
15	Minnesota	4,593	2.5%
7	Mississippi	6,633	3.6%
10	Missouri	5,374	2.9%
NA	Montana**	NA	NA
33	Nebraska	1,522	0.8%
38	Nevada	1,011	0.6%
NA	New Hampshire**	NA	NA
45	New Jersey	0	0.0%
28	New Mexico	2,200	1.2%
17	New York	4,341	2.4%
1	North Carolina	17,921	9.8%
41	North Dakota	593	0.3%
9	Ohio	6,174	3.4%
22	Oklahoma	3,547	1.9%
25	Oregon	2,925	1.6%
13	Pennsylvania	4,786	2.6%
44	Rhode Island	2	0.0%
4	South Carolina	8,263	4.5%
40	South Dakota	683	0.4%
8	Tennessee	6,311	3.4%
2	Texas	10,071	5.5%
36	Utah	1,072	0.6%
32	Vermont	1,524	0.8%
19	Virginia	4,072	2.2%
14	Washington	4,748	2.6%
24	West Virginia	3,085	1.7%
18	Wisconsin	4,337	2.4%
42	Wyoming	463	0.3%

RANK ORDER

RANK	STATE	BURGLARIES	% of USA
1	North Carolina	17,921	9.8%
2	Texas	10,071	5.5%
3	Georgia	9,354	5.1%
4	South Carolina	8,263	4.5%
5	Florida	8,039	4.4%
6	Michigan	7,874	4.3%
7	Mississippi	6,633	3.6%
8	Tennessee	6,311	3.4%
9	Ohio	6,174	3.4%
10	Missouri	5,374	2.9%
11	California	5,280	2.9%
12	Indiana	5,250	2.9%
13	Pennsylvania	4,786	2.6%
14	Washington	4,748	2.6%
15	Minnesota	4,593	2.5%
16	Louisiana	4,495	2.4%
17	New York	4,341	2.4%
18	Wisconsin	4,337	2.4%
19	Virginia	4,072	2.2%
20	Arkansas	4,064	2.2%
21	Alabama	3,621	2.0%
22	Oklahoma	3,547	1.9%
23	Hawaii	3,334	1.8%
24	West Virginia	3,085	1.7%
25	Oregon	2,925	1.6%
26	Iowa	2,776	1.5%
27	Maine	2,205	1.2%
28	New Mexico	2,200	1.2%
29	Connecticut	1,997	1.1%
30	Idaho	1,709	0.9%
31	Maryland	1,597	0.9%
32	Vermont	1,524	0.8%
33	Nebraska	1,522	0.8%
34	Arizona	1,508	0.8%
35	Alaska	1,152	0.6%
36	Utah	1,072	0.6%
37	Colorado	1,013	0.6%
38	Nevada	1,011	0.6%
39	Delaware	779	0.4%
40	South Dakota	683	0.4%
41	North Dakota	593	0.3%
42	Wyoming	463	0.3%
43	Massachusetts	8	0.0%
44	Rhode Island	2	0.0%
45	New Jersey	0	0.0%
NA	Illinois**	NA	NA
NA	Kansas**	NA	NA
NA	Kentucky**	NA	NA
NA	Montana**	NA	NA
NA	New Hampshire**	NA	NA
	District of Columbia	0	0.0%

Source: Federal Bureau of Investigation
   "Crime in the United States 1999" (Uniform Crime Reports, October 15, 2000)
*Estimated totals for rural areas, defined by the F.B.I. as other than Metropolitan Statistical Areas and other cities outside such areas. National total includes those states listed as not available. Burglary is the unlawful entry of a structure to commit a felony or theft. Attempts are included.
**Not available.

Rural Burglary Rate in 1999

National Rural Rate = 551.5 Burglaries per 100,000 Population*

ALPHA ORDER

RANK	STATE	RATE
30	Alabama	445.9
15	Alaska	595.4
22	Arizona	506.7
24	Arkansas	496.2
6	California	825.1
41	Colorado	274.2
33	Connecticut	416.9
7	Delaware	754.3
3	Florida	962.0
13	Georgia	598.3
1	Hawaii	1,047.0
34	Idaho	408.3
NA	Illinois**	NA
26	Indiana	468.7
39	Iowa	310.3
NA	Kansas**	NA
NA	Kentucky**	NA
11	Louisiana	629.4
12	Maine	613.7
19	Maryland	555.1
43	Massachusetts	78.3
8	Michigan	709.3
21	Minnesota	514.4
16	Mississippi	582.7
31	Missouri	432.9
NA	Montana**	NA
37	Nebraska	371.5
23	Nevada	506.0
NA	New Hampshire**	NA
44	New Jersey	0.0
9	New Mexico	703.5
25	New York	494.9
2	North Carolina	1,007.6
40	North Dakota	275.3
28	Ohio	448.9
20	Oklahoma	545.8
18	Oregon	555.9
27	Pennsylvania	460.7
44	Rhode Island	0.0
4	South Carolina	961.1
42	South Dakota	243.1
17	Tennessee	559.1
14	Texas	596.6
29	Utah	446.1
10	Vermont	632.5
36	Virginia	375.8
5	Washington	870.5
35	West Virginia	403.5
32	Wisconsin	432.4
38	Wyoming	354.0

RANK ORDER

RANK	STATE	RATE
1	Hawaii	1,047.0
2	North Carolina	1,007.6
3	Florida	962.0
4	South Carolina	961.1
5	Washington	870.5
6	California	825.1
7	Delaware	754.3
8	Michigan	709.3
9	New Mexico	703.5
10	Vermont	632.5
11	Louisiana	629.4
12	Maine	613.7
13	Georgia	598.3
14	Texas	596.6
15	Alaska	595.4
16	Mississippi	582.7
17	Tennessee	559.1
18	Oregon	555.9
19	Maryland	555.1
20	Oklahoma	545.8
21	Minnesota	514.4
22	Arizona	506.7
23	Nevada	506.0
24	Arkansas	496.2
25	New York	494.9
26	Indiana	468.7
27	Pennsylvania	460.7
28	Ohio	448.9
29	Utah	446.1
30	Alabama	445.9
31	Missouri	432.9
32	Wisconsin	432.4
33	Connecticut	416.9
34	Idaho	408.3
35	West Virginia	403.5
36	Virginia	375.8
37	Nebraska	371.5
38	Wyoming	354.0
39	Iowa	310.3
40	North Dakota	275.3
41	Colorado	274.2
42	South Dakota	243.1
43	Massachusetts	78.3
44	New Jersey	0.0
44	Rhode Island	0.0
NA	Illinois**	NA
NA	Kansas**	NA
NA	Kentucky**	NA
NA	Montana**	NA
NA	New Hampshire**	NA
	District of Columbia	0.0

Source: Morgan Quitno Press using data from Federal Bureau of Investigation
     "Crime in the United States 1999" (Uniform Crime Reports, October 15, 2000)
*Estimated rates for rural areas, defined by the F.B.I. as other than Metropolitan Statistical Areas and other cities outside such areas. National rate includes those states listed as not available. Burglary is the unlawful entry of a structure to commit a felony or theft. Attempts are included.
**Not available.

Percent of Burglaries Occurring in Rural Areas in 1999

National Percent = 8.8% of Burglaries*

ALPHA ORDER

RANK ORDER

RANK	STATE	PERCENT		RANK	STATE	PERCENT
29	Alabama	9.4		1	Vermont	43.1
3	Alaska	30.4		2	Hawaii	35.4
41	Arizona	3.1		3	Alaska	30.4
12	Arkansas	18.7		4	West Virginia	29.9
42	California	2.4		5	Maine	29.3
39	Colorado	3.8		6	North Dakota	25.4
25	Connecticut	10.3		7	Mississippi	22.8
18	Delaware	14.9		8	Idaho	22.4
38	Florida	4.4		9	South Dakota	21.0
19	Georgia	13.1		10	South Carolina	20.9
2	Hawaii	35.4		11	Wyoming	19.7
8	Idaho	22.4		12	Arkansas	18.7
NA	Illinois**	NA		13	North Carolina	18.2
22	Indiana	12.4		14	Wisconsin	16.9
16	Iowa	16.3		15	Minnesota	16.6
NA	Kansas**	NA		16	Iowa	16.3
NA	Kentucky**	NA		17	Nebraska	15.0
29	Louisiana	9.4		18	Delaware	14.9
5	Maine	29.3		19	Georgia	13.1
40	Maryland	3.7		20	Missouri	12.7
43	Massachusetts	0.0		21	Virginia	12.6
25	Michigan	10.3		22	Indiana	12.4
15	Minnesota	16.6		23	Tennessee	12.3
7	Mississippi	22.8		24	Oregon	10.9
20	Missouri	12.7		25	Connecticut	10.3
NA	Montana**	NA		25	Michigan	10.3
17	Nebraska	15.0		25	Oklahoma	10.3
35	Nevada	5.7		28	New Mexico	10.2
NA	New Hampshire**	NA		29	Alabama	9.4
43	New Jersey	0.0		29	Louisiana	9.4
28	New Mexico	10.2		31	Washington	8.7
37	New York	4.7		32	Pennsylvania	8.5
13	North Carolina	18.2		33	Utah	7.3
6	North Dakota	25.4		34	Ohio	7.1
34	Ohio	7.1		35	Nevada	5.7
25	Oklahoma	10.3		36	Texas	5.3
24	Oregon	10.9		37	New York	4.7
32	Pennsylvania	8.5		38	Florida	4.4
43	Rhode Island	0.0		39	Colorado	3.8
10	South Carolina	20.9		40	Maryland	3.7
9	South Dakota	21.0		41	Arizona	3.1
23	Tennessee	12.3		42	California	2.4
36	Texas	5.3		43	Massachusetts	0.0
33	Utah	7.3		43	New Jersey	0.0
1	Vermont	43.1		43	Rhode Island	0.0
21	Virginia	12.6		NA	Illinois**	NA
31	Washington	8.7		NA	Kansas**	NA
4	West Virginia	29.9		NA	Kentucky**	NA
14	Wisconsin	16.9		NA	Montana**	NA
11	Wyoming	19.7		NA	New Hampshire**	NA
					District of Columbia	0.0

Source: Morgan Quitno Press using data from Federal Bureau of Investigation
    "Crime in the United States 1999" (Uniform Crime Reports, October 15, 2000)
*Estimated percentages for rural areas, defined by the F.B.I. as other than Metropolitan Statistical Areas and other
cities outside such areas. National percent includes those states listed as not available. Burglary is the unlawful
entry of a structure to commit a felony or theft. Attempts are included.
**Not available.

Larcenies and Thefts in Urban Areas in 1999

National Urban Total = 6,622,422 Larcenies and Thefts*

ALPHA ORDER

ALPHA ORDER

RANK	STATE	THEFTS	% of USA
19	Alabama	114,245	1.7%
41	Alaska	14,381	0.2%
11	Arizona	164,641	2.5%
30	Arkansas	58,078	0.9%
1	California	654,020	9.9%
24	Colorado	105,913	1.6%
28	Connecticut	65,221	1.0%
40	Delaware	20,981	0.3%
3	Florida	519,025	7.8%
6	Georgia	225,869	3.4%
35	Hawaii	30,396	0.5%
36	Idaho	23,319	0.4%
NA	Illinois**	NA	NA
18	Indiana	128,013	1.9%
31	Iowa	57,540	0.9%
NA	Kansas**	NA	NA
NA	Kentucky**	NA	NA
16	Louisiana	140,318	2.1%
39	Maine	22,153	0.3%
15	Maryland	143,818	2.2%
21	Massachusetts	108,835	1.6%
7	Michigan	223,201	3.4%
22	Minnesota	108,641	1.6%
29	Mississippi	58,411	0.9%
13	Missouri	150,403	2.3%
NA	Montana**	NA	NA
33	Nebraska	42,022	0.6%
34	Nevada	40,523	0.6%
NA	New Hampshire**	NA	NA
12	New Jersey	160,978	2.4%
32	New Mexico	55,909	0.8%
4	New York	329,335	5.0%
9	North Carolina	209,937	3.2%
44	North Dakota	10,019	0.2%
5	Ohio	274,656	4.1%
26	Oklahoma	89,386	1.3%
23	Oregon	106,344	1.6%
8	Pennsylvania	219,072	3.3%
38	Rhode Island	22,272	0.3%
25	South Carolina	102,707	1.6%
42	South Dakota	12,683	0.2%
17	Tennessee	132,304	2.0%
2	Texas	600,232	9.1%
27	Utah	74,712	1.1%
45	Vermont	9,351	0.1%
14	Virginia	149,724	2.3%
10	Washington	183,601	2.8%
37	West Virginia	22,575	0.3%
20	Wisconsin	111,967	1.7%
43	Wyoming	11,093	0.2%

RANK ORDER

RANK	STATE	THEFTS	% of USA
1	California	654,020	9.9%
2	Texas	600,232	9.1%
3	Florida	519,025	7.8%
4	New York	329,335	5.0%
5	Ohio	274,656	4.1%
6	Georgia	225,869	3.4%
7	Michigan	223,201	3.4%
8	Pennsylvania	219,072	3.3%
9	North Carolina	209,937	3.2%
10	Washington	183,601	2.8%
11	Arizona	164,641	2.5%
12	New Jersey	160,978	2.4%
13	Missouri	150,403	2.3%
14	Virginia	149,724	2.3%
15	Maryland	143,818	2.2%
16	Louisiana	140,318	2.1%
17	Tennessee	132,304	2.0%
18	Indiana	128,013	1.9%
19	Alabama	114,245	1.7%
20	Wisconsin	111,967	1.7%
21	Massachusetts	108,835	1.6%
22	Minnesota	108,641	1.6%
23	Oregon	106,344	1.6%
24	Colorado	105,913	1.6%
25	South Carolina	102,707	1.6%
26	Oklahoma	89,386	1.3%
27	Utah	74,712	1.1%
28	Connecticut	65,221	1.0%
29	Mississippi	58,411	0.9%
30	Arkansas	58,078	0.9%
31	Iowa	57,540	0.9%
32	New Mexico	55,909	0.8%
33	Nebraska	42,022	0.6%
34	Nevada	40,523	0.6%
35	Hawaii	30,396	0.5%
36	Idaho	23,319	0.4%
37	West Virginia	22,575	0.3%
38	Rhode Island	22,272	0.3%
39	Maine	22,153	0.3%
40	Delaware	20,981	0.3%
41	Alaska	14,381	0.2%
42	South Dakota	12,683	0.2%
43	Wyoming	11,093	0.2%
44	North Dakota	10,019	0.2%
45	Vermont	9,351	0.1%
NA	Illinois**	NA	NA
NA	Kansas**	NA	NA
NA	Kentucky**	NA	NA
NA	Montana**	NA	NA
NA	New Hampshire**	NA	NA
	District of Columbia	21,701	0.3%

Source: Morgan Quitno Press using data from Federal Bureau of Investigation
    "Crime in the United States 1999" (Uniform Crime Reports, October 15, 2000)
*Estimated totals for urban areas, defined by the F.B.I. as Metropolitan Statistical Areas and other cities outside such areas. National total includes those states listed as not available. Larceny and theft is the unlawful taking of property without use of force, violence or fraud. Attempts are included. Motor vehicle thefts are excluded.
**Not available.

Urban Larceny and Theft Rate in 1999

National Urban Rate = 2,766.6 Larcenies and Thefts per 100,000 Population*

ALPHA ORDER

RANK ORDER

RANK	STATE	RATE		RANK	STATE	RATE
20	Alabama	3,210.9		1	Utah	3,953.6
14	Alaska	3,379.8		2	New Mexico	3,917.2
5	Arizona	3,674.7		3	Louisiana	3,836.1
15	Arkansas	3,353.2		4	Oregon	3,811.9
41	California	2,012.1		5	Arizona	3,674.7
25	Colorado	2,873.0		6	Florida	3,635.8
38	Connecticut	2,326.8		7	Georgia	3,628.6
19	Delaware	3,224.3		8	Mississippi	3,581.8
6	Florida	3,635.8		9	North Carolina	3,574.9
7	Georgia	3,628.6		10	Missouri	3,558.4
12	Hawaii	3,507.6		11	Washington	3,523.6
27	Idaho	2,797.8		12	Hawaii	3,507.6
NA	Illinois**	NA		13	South Carolina	3,393.9
30	Indiana	2,654.3		14	Alaska	3,379.8
24	Iowa	2,914.3		15	Arkansas	3,353.2
NA	Kansas**	NA		16	Nebraska	3,344.9
NA	Kentucky**	NA		17	Oklahoma	3,300.6
3	Louisiana	3,836.1		18	Texas	3,270.0
36	Maine	2,478.7		19	Delaware	3,224.3
23	Maryland	2,944.5		20	Alabama	3,210.9
45	Massachusetts	1,765.4		21	Wyoming	3,176.8
34	Michigan	2,549.7		22	Tennessee	3,037.8
28	Minnesota	2,797.7		23	Maryland	2,944.5
8	Mississippi	3,581.8		24	Iowa	2,914.3
10	Missouri	3,558.4		25	Colorado	2,873.0
NA	Montana**	NA		26	South Dakota	2,805.6
16	Nebraska	3,344.9		27	Idaho	2,797.8
35	Nevada	2,518.2		28	Minnesota	2,797.7
NA	New Hampshire**	NA		29	Ohio	2,779.5
43	New Jersey	1,976.9		30	Indiana	2,654.3
2	New Mexico	3,917.2		31	Vermont	2,648.7
44	New York	1,901.5		32	Wisconsin	2,636.4
9	North Carolina	3,574.9		33	Virginia	2,586.2
37	North Dakota	2,393.3		34	Michigan	2,549.7
29	Ohio	2,779.5		35	Nevada	2,518.2
17	Oklahoma	3,300.6		36	Maine	2,478.7
4	Oregon	3,811.9		37	North Dakota	2,393.3
42	Pennsylvania	1,999.7		38	Connecticut	2,326.8
39	Rhode Island	2,247.4		39	Rhode Island	2,247.4
13	South Carolina	3,393.9		40	West Virginia	2,165.4
26	South Dakota	2,805.6		41	California	2,012.1
22	Tennessee	3,037.8		42	Pennsylvania	1,999.7
18	Texas	3,270.0		43	New Jersey	1,976.9
1	Utah	3,953.6		44	New York	1,901.5
31	Vermont	2,648.7		45	Massachusetts	1,765.4
33	Virginia	2,586.2		NA	Illinois**	NA
11	Washington	3,523.6		NA	Kansas**	NA
40	West Virginia	2,165.4		NA	Kentucky**	NA
32	Wisconsin	2,636.4		NA	Montana**	NA
21	Wyoming	3,176.8		NA	New Hampshire**	NA

District of Columbia 4,181.3

Source: Morgan Quitno Press using data from Federal Bureau of Investigation
   "Crime in the United States 1999" (Uniform Crime Reports, October 15, 2000)
*Estimated rates for urban areas, defined by the F.B.I. as Metropolitan Statistical Areas and other cities outside
such areas. National rate includes those states listed as not available. Larceny and theft is the unlawful taking of
property without use of force, violence or fraud. Attempts are included. Motor vehicle thefts are excluded.
**Not available.

449

Percent of Larcenies and Thefts Occurring in Urban Areas in 1999

National Percent = 95.2% of Larcenies and Thefts*

ALPHA ORDER

RANK ORDER

RANK	STATE	PERCENT		RANK	STATE	PERCENT
13	Alabama	95.5		1	Massachusetts	100.0
41	Alaska	86.4		1	New Jersey	100.0
5	Arizona	98.2		3	Rhode Island	99.9
34	Arkansas	90.9		4	California	98.9
4	California	98.9		5	Arizona	98.2
10	Colorado	97.0		6	Texas	97.8
19	Connecticut	94.1		7	Maryland	97.6
26	Delaware	92.7		8	New York	97.4
9	Florida	97.2		9	Florida	97.2
32	Georgia	91.1		10	Colorado	97.0
45	Hawaii	75.1		11	Pennsylvania	96.2
40	Idaho	86.9		12	Utah	95.6
NA	Illinois**	NA		13	Alabama	95.5
30	Indiana	92.2		13	Missouri	95.5
28	Iowa	92.3		13	Oklahoma	95.5
NA	Kansas**	NA		13	Washington	95.5
NA	Kentucky**	NA		17	Ohio	95.4
23	Louisiana	93.7		18	Michigan	94.4
39	Maine	87.2		19	Connecticut	94.1
7	Maryland	97.6		19	Oregon	94.1
1	Massachusetts	100.0		21	Nevada	93.9
18	Michigan	94.4		22	New Mexico	93.8
28	Minnesota	92.3		23	Louisiana	93.7
36	Mississippi	88.6		24	Virginia	93.6
13	Missouri	95.5		25	Wisconsin	92.8
NA	Montana**	NA		26	Delaware	92.7
31	Nebraska	92.0		26	Tennessee	92.7
21	Nevada	93.9		28	Iowa	92.3
NA	New Hampshire**	NA		28	Minnesota	92.3
1	New Jersey	100.0		30	Indiana	92.2
22	New Mexico	93.8		31	Nebraska	92.0
8	New York	97.4		32	Georgia	91.1
32	North Carolina	91.1		32	North Carolina	91.1
38	North Dakota	88.1		34	Arkansas	90.9
17	Ohio	95.4		35	South Dakota	90.3
13	Oklahoma	95.5		36	Mississippi	88.6
19	Oregon	94.1		36	Wyoming	88.6
11	Pennsylvania	96.2		38	North Dakota	88.1
3	Rhode Island	99.9		39	Maine	87.2
42	South Carolina	85.7		40	Idaho	86.9
35	South Dakota	90.3		41	Alaska	86.4
26	Tennessee	92.7		42	South Carolina	85.7
6	Texas	97.8		43	Vermont	80.5
12	Utah	95.6		44	West Virginia	78.5
43	Vermont	80.5		45	Hawaii	75.1
24	Virginia	93.6		NA	Illinois**	NA
13	Washington	95.5		NA	Kansas**	NA
44	West Virginia	78.5		NA	Kentucky**	NA
25	Wisconsin	92.8		NA	Montana**	NA
36	Wyoming	88.6		NA	New Hampshire**	NA

District of Columbia   100.0

Source: Morgan Quitno Press using data from Federal Bureau of Investigation
"Crime in the United States 1999" (Uniform Crime Reports, October 15, 2000)
*Estimated percentages for urban areas, defined by the F.B.I. as Metropolitan Statistical Areas and other cities outside such areas. National percent includes those states listed as not available. Larceny and theft is the unlawful taking of property without use of force, violence or fraud. Attempts are included. Motor vehicle thefts are excluded.
**Not available.

Larcenies and Thefts in Rural Areas in 1999

National Rural Total = 334,990 Larcenies and Thefts*

ALPHA ORDER

RANK	STATE	THEFTS	% of USA
24	Alabama	5,371	1.6%
37	Alaska	2,273	0.7%
35	Arizona	3,090	0.9%
23	Arkansas	5,849	1.7%
20	California	6,971	2.1%
33	Colorado	3,315	1.0%
27	Connecticut	4,078	1.2%
39	Delaware	1,653	0.5%
4	Florida	15,080	4.5%
1	Georgia	21,965	6.6%
11	Hawaii	10,062	3.0%
30	Idaho	3,505	1.0%
NA	Illinois**	NA	NA
8	Indiana	10,781	3.2%
25	Iowa	4,776	1.4%
NA	Kansas**	NA	NA
NA	Kentucky**	NA	NA
12	Louisiana	9,431	2.8%
34	Maine	3,239	1.0%
31	Maryland	3,478	1.0%
44	Massachusetts	10	0.0%
7	Michigan	13,150	3.9%
13	Minnesota	9,095	2.7%
18	Mississippi	7,508	2.2%
19	Missouri	7,147	2.1%
NA	Montana**	NA	NA
29	Nebraska	3,657	1.1%
36	Nevada	2,644	0.8%
NA	New Hampshire**	NA	NA
45	New Jersey	0	0.0%
28	New Mexico	3,704	1.1%
14	New York	8,783	2.6%
2	North Carolina	20,526	6.1%
42	North Dakota	1,356	0.4%
6	Ohio	13,393	4.0%
26	Oklahoma	4,230	1.3%
21	Oregon	6,708	2.0%
17	Pennsylvania	8,678	2.6%
43	Rhode Island	12	0.0%
3	South Carolina	17,205	5.1%
41	South Dakota	1,360	0.4%
9	Tennessee	10,381	3.1%
5	Texas	13,630	4.1%
32	Utah	3,444	1.0%
38	Vermont	2,259	0.7%
10	Virginia	10,172	3.0%
16	Washington	8,733	2.6%
22	West Virginia	6,185	1.8%
15	Wisconsin	8,735	2.6%
40	Wyoming	1,430	0.4%

RANK ORDER

RANK	STATE	THEFTS	% of USA
1	Georgia	21,965	6.6%
2	North Carolina	20,526	6.1%
3	South Carolina	17,205	5.1%
4	Florida	15,080	4.5%
5	Texas	13,630	4.1%
6	Ohio	13,393	4.0%
7	Michigan	13,150	3.9%
8	Indiana	10,781	3.2%
9	Tennessee	10,381	3.1%
10	Virginia	10,172	3.0%
11	Hawaii	10,062	3.0%
12	Louisiana	9,431	2.8%
13	Minnesota	9,095	2.7%
14	New York	8,783	2.6%
15	Wisconsin	8,735	2.6%
16	Washington	8,733	2.6%
17	Pennsylvania	8,678	2.6%
18	Mississippi	7,508	2.2%
19	Missouri	7,147	2.1%
20	California	6,971	2.1%
21	Oregon	6,708	2.0%
22	West Virginia	6,185	1.8%
23	Arkansas	5,849	1.7%
24	Alabama	5,371	1.6%
25	Iowa	4,776	1.4%
26	Oklahoma	4,230	1.3%
27	Connecticut	4,078	1.2%
28	New Mexico	3,704	1.1%
29	Nebraska	3,657	1.1%
30	Idaho	3,505	1.0%
31	Maryland	3,478	1.0%
32	Utah	3,444	1.0%
33	Colorado	3,315	1.0%
34	Maine	3,239	1.0%
35	Arizona	3,090	0.9%
36	Nevada	2,644	0.8%
37	Alaska	2,273	0.7%
38	Vermont	2,259	0.7%
39	Delaware	1,653	0.5%
40	Wyoming	1,430	0.4%
41	South Dakota	1,360	0.4%
42	North Dakota	1,356	0.4%
43	Rhode Island	12	0.0%
44	Massachusetts	10	0.0%
45	New Jersey	0	0.0%
NA	Illinois**	NA	NA
NA	Kansas**	NA	NA
NA	Kentucky**	NA	NA
NA	Montana**	NA	NA
NA	New Hampshire**	NA	NA
	District of Columbia	0	0.0%

Source: Federal Bureau of Investigation
   "Crime in the United States 1999" (Uniform Crime Reports, October 15, 2000)
Estimated totals for rural areas, defined by the F.B.I. as other than Metropolitan Statistical Areas and other cities outside such areas. National total includes those states listed as not available. Larceny and theft is the unlawful taking of property without use of force, violence or fraud. Attempts are included. Motor vehicle thefts are excluded.
***Not available.*

Rural Larceny and Theft Rate in 1999

National Rural Rate = 1,005.3 Larcenies and Thefts per 100,000 Population*

ALPHA ORDER

RANK	STATE	RATE
36	Alabama	661.5
14	Alaska	1,174.7
18	Arizona	1,038.3
35	Arkansas	714.2
17	California	1,089.3
27	Colorado	897.3
30	Connecticut	851.4
5	Delaware	1,600.5
3	Florida	1,804.5
7	Georgia	1,405.0
1	Hawaii	3,159.8
31	Idaho	837.5
NA	Illinois**	NA
22	Indiana	962.5
41	Iowa	533.9
NA	Kansas**	NA
NA	Kentucky**	NA
9	Louisiana	1,320.6
26	Maine	901.6
11	Maryland	1,208.8
43	Massachusetts	97.9
12	Michigan	1,184.6
19	Minnesota	1,018.7
37	Mississippi	659.6
40	Missouri	575.8
NA	Montana**	NA
28	Nebraska	892.6
8	Nevada	1,323.4
NA	New Hampshire**	NA
44	New Jersey	0.0
13	New Mexico	1,184.5
20	New York	1,001.3
15	North Carolina	1,154.1
39	North Dakota	629.6
21	Ohio	973.8
38	Oklahoma	650.9
10	Oregon	1,274.8
32	Pennsylvania	835.3
44	Rhode Island	0.0
2	South Carolina	2,001.1
42	South Dakota	484.1
25	Tennessee	919.7
34	Texas	807.4
6	Utah	1,433.3
24	Vermont	937.5
23	Virginia	938.7
4	Washington	1,601.1
33	West Virginia	809.1
29	Wisconsin	870.9
16	Wyoming	1,093.2

RANK ORDER

RANK	STATE	RATE
1	Hawaii	3,159.8
2	South Carolina	2,001.1
3	Florida	1,804.5
4	Washington	1,601.1
5	Delaware	1,600.5
6	Utah	1,433.3
7	Georgia	1,405.0
8	Nevada	1,323.4
9	Louisiana	1,320.6
10	Oregon	1,274.8
11	Maryland	1,208.8
12	Michigan	1,184.6
13	New Mexico	1,184.5
14	Alaska	1,174.7
15	North Carolina	1,154.1
16	Wyoming	1,093.2
17	California	1,089.3
18	Arizona	1,038.3
19	Minnesota	1,018.7
20	New York	1,001.3
21	Ohio	973.8
22	Indiana	962.5
23	Virginia	938.7
24	Vermont	937.5
25	Tennessee	919.7
26	Maine	901.6
27	Colorado	897.3
28	Nebraska	892.6
29	Wisconsin	870.9
30	Connecticut	851.4
31	Idaho	837.5
32	Pennsylvania	835.3
33	West Virginia	809.1
34	Texas	807.4
35	Arkansas	714.2
36	Alabama	661.5
37	Mississippi	659.6
38	Oklahoma	650.9
39	North Dakota	629.6
40	Missouri	575.8
41	Iowa	533.9
42	South Dakota	484.1
43	Massachusetts	97.9
44	New Jersey	0.0
44	Rhode Island	0.0
NA	Illinois**	NA
NA	Kansas**	NA
NA	Kentucky**	NA
NA	Montana**	NA
NA	New Hampshire**	NA
	District of Columbia	0.0

Source: Morgan Quitno Press using data from Federal Bureau of Investigation
"Crime in the United States 1999" (Uniform Crime Reports, October 15, 2000)
*Estimated rates for rural areas, defined by the F.B.I. as other than Metropolitan Statistical Areas and other cities outside such areas. National rate includes those states listed as not available. Larceny and theft is the unlawful taking of property without use of force, violence or fraud. Attempts are included. Motor vehicle thefts are excluded.
**Not available.

Percent of Larcenies and Thefts Occurring in Rural Areas in 1999

National Percent = 4.8% of Larcenies and Thefts*

ALPHA ORDER

RANK	STATE	PERCENT
30	Alabama	4.5
5	Alaska	13.6
41	Arizona	1.8
12	Arkansas	9.1
42	California	1.1
36	Colorado	3.0
26	Connecticut	5.9
19	Delaware	7.3
37	Florida	2.8
13	Georgia	8.9
1	Hawaii	24.9
6	Idaho	13.1
NA	Illinois**	NA
16	Indiana	7.8
17	Iowa	7.7
NA	Kansas**	NA
NA	Kentucky**	NA
23	Louisiana	6.3
7	Maine	12.8
39	Maryland	2.4
44	Massachusetts	0.0
28	Michigan	5.6
17	Minnesota	7.7
9	Mississippi	11.4
30	Missouri	4.5
NA	Montana**	NA
15	Nebraska	8.0
25	Nevada	6.1
NA	New Hampshire**	NA
44	New Jersey	0.0
24	New Mexico	6.2
38	New York	2.6
13	North Carolina	8.9
8	North Dakota	11.9
29	Ohio	4.6
30	Oklahoma	4.5
26	Oregon	5.9
35	Pennsylvania	3.8
43	Rhode Island	0.1
4	South Carolina	14.3
11	South Dakota	9.7
19	Tennessee	7.3
40	Texas	2.2
34	Utah	4.4
3	Vermont	19.5
22	Virginia	6.4
30	Washington	4.5
2	West Virginia	21.5
21	Wisconsin	7.2
9	Wyoming	11.4

RANK ORDER

RANK	STATE	PERCENT
1	Hawaii	24.9
2	West Virginia	21.5
3	Vermont	19.5
4	South Carolina	14.3
5	Alaska	13.6
6	Idaho	13.1
7	Maine	12.8
8	North Dakota	11.9
9	Mississippi	11.4
9	Wyoming	11.4
11	South Dakota	9.7
12	Arkansas	9.1
13	Georgia	8.9
13	North Carolina	8.9
15	Nebraska	8.0
16	Indiana	7.8
17	Iowa	7.7
17	Minnesota	7.7
19	Delaware	7.3
19	Tennessee	7.3
21	Wisconsin	7.2
22	Virginia	6.4
23	Louisiana	6.3
24	New Mexico	6.2
25	Nevada	6.1
26	Connecticut	5.9
26	Oregon	5.9
28	Michigan	5.6
29	Ohio	4.6
30	Alabama	4.5
30	Missouri	4.5
30	Oklahoma	4.5
30	Washington	4.5
34	Utah	4.4
35	Pennsylvania	3.8
36	Colorado	3.0
37	Florida	2.8
38	New York	2.6
39	Maryland	2.4
40	Texas	2.2
41	Arizona	1.8
42	California	1.1
43	Rhode Island	0.1
44	Massachusetts	0.0
44	New Jersey	0.0
NA	Illinois**	NA
NA	Kansas**	NA
NA	Kentucky**	NA
NA	Montana**	NA
NA	New Hampshire**	NA

District of Columbia   0.0

Source: Morgan Quitno Press using data from Federal Bureau of Investigation
   "Crime in the United States 1999" (Uniform Crime Reports, October 15, 2000)
*Estimated percentages for rural areas, defined by the F.B.I. as other than Metropolitan Statistical Areas and other
cities outside such areas. National percent includes those states listed as not available. Larceny and theft is the
unlawful taking of property without use of force, violence or fraud. Attempts are included. Motor vehicle thefts are
excluded. **Not available.*

Motor Vehicle Thefts in Urban Areas in 1999

National Urban Total = 1,106,157 Motor Vehicle Thefts*

ALPHA ORDER

RANK	STATE	THEFTS	% of USA
25	Alabama	12,393	1.2%
39	Alaska	2,212	0.2%
8	Arizona	37,826	3.6%
32	Arkansas	5,692	0.5%
1	California	167,089	15.8%
20	Colorado	14,461	1.4%
29	Connecticut	10,623	1.0%
37	Delaware	2,928	0.3%
2	Florida	91,522	8.7%
9	Georgia	37,213	3.5%
36	Hawaii	3,997	0.4%
40	Idaho	1,507	0.1%
NA	Illinois**	NA	NA
18	Indiana	18,625	1.8%
34	Iowa	4,537	0.4%
NA	Kansas**	NA	NA
NA	Kentucky**	NA	NA
17	Louisiana	20,897	2.0%
41	Maine	1,293	0.1%
13	Maryland	25,149	2.4%
12	Massachusetts	25,624	2.4%
5	Michigan	55,440	5.2%
27	Minnesota	12,182	1.2%
24	Mississippi	12,421	1.2%
16	Missouri	22,218	2.1%
NA	Montana**	NA	NA
33	Nebraska	5,147	0.5%
22	Nevada	12,857	1.2%
NA	New Hampshire**	NA	NA
10	New Jersey	35,357	3.3%
30	New Mexico	7,438	0.7%
4	New York	57,824	5.5%
15	North Carolina	22,593	2.1%
42	North Dakota	895	0.1%
7	Ohio	37,878	3.6%
28	Oklahoma	11,293	1.1%
23	Oregon	12,839	1.2%
6	Pennsylvania	38,166	3.6%
35	Rhode Island	4,030	0.4%
26	South Carolina	12,235	1.2%
43	South Dakota	714	0.1%
14	Tennessee	23,316	2.2%
3	Texas	90,243	8.5%
31	Utah	7,076	0.7%
44	Vermont	561	0.1%
19	Virginia	16,716	1.6%
11	Washington	32,843	3.1%
38	West Virginia	2,831	0.3%
21	Wisconsin	12,879	1.2%
45	Wyoming	480	0.0%

RANK ORDER

RANK	STATE	THEFTS	% of USA
1	California	167,089	15.8%
2	Florida	91,522	8.7%
3	Texas	90,243	8.5%
4	New York	57,824	5.5%
5	Michigan	55,440	5.2%
6	Pennsylvania	38,166	3.6%
7	Ohio	37,878	3.6%
8	Arizona	37,826	3.6%
9	Georgia	37,213	3.5%
10	New Jersey	35,357	3.3%
11	Washington	32,843	3.1%
12	Massachusetts	25,624	2.4%
13	Maryland	25,149	2.4%
14	Tennessee	23,316	2.2%
15	North Carolina	22,593	2.1%
16	Missouri	22,218	2.1%
17	Louisiana	20,897	2.0%
18	Indiana	18,625	1.8%
19	Virginia	16,716	1.6%
20	Colorado	14,461	1.4%
21	Wisconsin	12,879	1.2%
22	Nevada	12,857	1.2%
23	Oregon	12,839	1.2%
24	Mississippi	12,421	1.2%
25	Alabama	12,393	1.2%
26	South Carolina	12,235	1.2%
27	Minnesota	12,182	1.2%
28	Oklahoma	11,293	1.1%
29	Connecticut	10,623	1.0%
30	New Mexico	7,438	0.7%
31	Utah	7,076	0.7%
32	Arkansas	5,692	0.5%
33	Nebraska	5,147	0.5%
34	Iowa	4,537	0.4%
35	Rhode Island	4,030	0.4%
36	Hawaii	3,997	0.4%
37	Delaware	2,928	0.3%
38	West Virginia	2,831	0.3%
39	Alaska	2,212	0.2%
40	Idaho	1,507	0.1%
41	Maine	1,293	0.1%
42	North Dakota	895	0.1%
43	South Dakota	714	0.1%
44	Vermont	561	0.1%
45	Wyoming	480	0.0%
NA	Illinois**	NA	NA
NA	Kansas**	NA	NA
NA	Kentucky**	NA	NA
NA	Montana**	NA	NA
NA	New Hampshire**	NA	NA
	District of Columbia	6,652	0.6%

Source: Morgan Quitno Press using data from Federal Bureau of Investigation
"Crime in the United States 1999" (Uniform Crime Reports, October 15, 2000)
*Estimated totals for urban areas, defined by the F.B.I. as Metropolitan Statistical Areas and other cities outside such areas. National total includes those states listed as not available. Motor vehicle theft includes the theft or attempted theft of a self-propelled vehicle. Excludes motorboats, construction equipment, airplanes and farming equipment. **Not available.

Urban Motor Vehicle Theft Rate in 1999

National Urban Rate = 462.1 Motor Vehicle Thefts per 100,000 Population*

ALPHA ORDER

RANK	STATE	RATE
32	Alabama	348.3
12	Alaska	519.9
1	Arizona	844.3
34	Arkansas	328.6
14	California	514.0
25	Colorado	392.3
29	Connecticut	379.0
18	Delaware	450.0
4	Florida	641.1
7	Georgia	597.8
16	Hawaii	461.2
41	Idaho	180.8
NA	Illinois**	NA
26	Indiana	386.2
39	Iowa	229.8
NA	Kansas**	NA
NA	Kentucky**	NA
8	Louisiana	571.3
44	Maine	144.7
13	Maryland	514.9
21	Massachusetts	415.7
5	Michigan	633.3
35	Minnesota	313.7
3	Mississippi	761.7
10	Missouri	525.7
NA	Montana**	NA
22	Nebraska	409.7
2	Nevada	799.0
NA	New Hampshire**	NA
19	New Jersey	434.2
11	New Mexico	521.1
33	New York	333.9
27	North Carolina	384.7
40	North Dakota	213.8
28	Ohio	383.3
20	Oklahoma	417.0
17	Oregon	460.2
31	Pennsylvania	348.4
23	Rhode Island	406.7
24	South Carolina	404.3
43	South Dakota	157.9
9	Tennessee	535.4
15	Texas	491.6
30	Utah	374.4
42	Vermont	158.9
37	Virginia	288.7
6	Washington	630.3
38	West Virginia	271.6
36	Wisconsin	303.3
45	Wyoming	137.5

RANK ORDER

RANK	STATE	RATE
1	Arizona	844.3
2	Nevada	799.0
3	Mississippi	761.7
4	Florida	641.1
5	Michigan	633.3
6	Washington	630.3
7	Georgia	597.8
8	Louisiana	571.3
9	Tennessee	535.4
10	Missouri	525.7
11	New Mexico	521.1
12	Alaska	519.9
13	Maryland	514.9
14	California	514.0
15	Texas	491.6
16	Hawaii	461.2
17	Oregon	460.2
18	Delaware	450.0
19	New Jersey	434.2
20	Oklahoma	417.0
21	Massachusetts	415.7
22	Nebraska	409.7
23	Rhode Island	406.7
24	South Carolina	404.3
25	Colorado	392.3
26	Indiana	386.2
27	North Carolina	384.7
28	Ohio	383.3
29	Connecticut	379.0
30	Utah	374.4
31	Pennsylvania	348.4
32	Alabama	348.3
33	New York	333.9
34	Arkansas	328.6
35	Minnesota	313.7
36	Wisconsin	303.3
37	Virginia	288.7
38	West Virginia	271.6
39	Iowa	229.8
40	North Dakota	213.8
41	Idaho	180.8
42	Vermont	158.9
43	South Dakota	157.9
44	Maine	144.7
45	Wyoming	137.5
NA	Illinois**	NA
NA	Kansas**	NA
NA	Kentucky**	NA
NA	Montana**	NA
NA	New Hampshire**	NA

District of Columbia — 1,281.7

Source: Morgan Quitno Press using data from Federal Bureau of Investigation
    "Crime in the United States 1999" (Uniform Crime Reports, October 15, 2000)
*Estimated rates for urban areas, defined by the F.B.I. as Metropolitan Statistical Areas and other cities outside such areas. National rate includes those states listed as not available. Motor vehicle theft includes the theft or attempted theft of a self-propelled vehicle. Excludes motorboats, construction equipment, airplanes and farming equipment. **Not available.

455

Percent of Motor Vehicle Thefts Occurring in Urban Areas in 1999

National Percent = 96.4% of Motor Vehicle Thefts*

ALPHA ORDER

RANK	STATE	PERCENT
21	Alabama	94.4
39	Alaska	83.2
6	Arizona	98.9
37	Arkansas	85.4
4	California	99.2
11	Colorado	97.7
23	Connecticut	94.0
18	Delaware	96.2
8	Florida	98.2
27	Georgia	92.8
36	Hawaii	85.8
42	Idaho	79.4
NA	Illinois**	NA
29	Indiana	91.8
33	Iowa	88.4
NA	Kansas**	NA
NA	Kentucky**	NA
17	Louisiana	96.3
43	Maine	76.3
7	Maryland	98.8
1	Massachusetts	100.0
12	Michigan	97.6
29	Minnesota	91.8
29	Mississippi	91.8
15	Missouri	96.7
NA	Montana**	NA
20	Nebraska	94.6
8	Nevada	98.2
NA	New Hampshire**	NA
1	New Jersey	100.0
32	New Mexico	91.5
4	New York	99.2
34	North Carolina	88.3
35	North Dakota	86.4
16	Ohio	96.6
25	Oklahoma	93.1
22	Oregon	94.2
13	Pennsylvania	97.3
1	Rhode Island	100.0
38	South Carolina	84.7
40	South Dakota	82.9
28	Tennessee	92.3
10	Texas	98.1
19	Utah	95.9
45	Vermont	61.5
25	Virginia	93.1
14	Washington	97.1
44	West Virginia	75.3
24	Wisconsin	93.2
41	Wyoming	80.5

RANK ORDER

RANK	STATE	PERCENT
1	Massachusetts	100.0
1	New Jersey	100.0
1	Rhode Island	100.0
4	California	99.2
4	New York	99.2
6	Arizona	98.9
7	Maryland	98.8
8	Florida	98.2
8	Nevada	98.2
10	Texas	98.1
11	Colorado	97.7
12	Michigan	97.6
13	Pennsylvania	97.3
14	Washington	97.1
15	Missouri	96.7
16	Ohio	96.6
17	Louisiana	96.3
18	Delaware	96.2
19	Utah	95.9
20	Nebraska	94.6
21	Alabama	94.4
22	Oregon	94.2
23	Connecticut	94.0
24	Wisconsin	93.2
25	Oklahoma	93.1
25	Virginia	93.1
27	Georgia	92.8
28	Tennessee	92.3
29	Indiana	91.8
29	Minnesota	91.8
29	Mississippi	91.8
32	New Mexico	91.5
33	Iowa	88.4
34	North Carolina	88.3
35	North Dakota	86.4
36	Hawaii	85.8
37	Arkansas	85.4
38	South Carolina	84.7
39	Alaska	83.2
40	South Dakota	82.9
41	Wyoming	80.5
42	Idaho	79.4
43	Maine	76.3
44	West Virginia	75.3
45	Vermont	61.5
NA	Illinois**	NA
NA	Kansas**	NA
NA	Kentucky**	NA
NA	Montana**	NA
NA	New Hampshire**	NA
	District of Columbia	100.0

Source: Morgan Quitno Press using data from Federal Bureau of Investigation
"Crime in the United States 1999" (Uniform Crime Reports, October 15, 2000)
*Estimated percentages for urban areas, defined by the F.B.I. as Metropolitan Statistical Areas and other cities outside such areas. National percent includes those states listed as not available. Motor vehicle theft includes the theft or attempted theft of a self-propelled vehicle. Excludes motorboats, construction equipment, airplanes and farming equipment. **Not available.

Motor Vehicle Thefts in Rural Areas in 1999

National Rural Total = 41,148 Motor Vehicle Thefts*

ALPHA ORDER

RANK	STATE	THEFTS	% of USA
23	Alabama	741	1.8%
28	Alaska	446	1.1%
30	Arizona	421	1.0%
15	Arkansas	972	2.4%
8	California	1,391	3.4%
34	Colorado	334	0.8%
25	Connecticut	674	1.6%
42	Delaware	115	0.3%
6	Florida	1,669	4.1%
2	Georgia	2,907	7.1%
26	Hawaii	663	1.6%
32	Idaho	391	1.0%
NA	Illinois**	NA	NA
7	Indiana	1,665	4.0%
27	Iowa	598	1.5%
NA	Kansas**	NA	NA
NA	Kentucky**	NA	NA
20	Louisiana	798	1.9%
31	Maine	401	1.0%
36	Maryland	298	0.7%
43	Massachusetts	4	0.0%
9	Michigan	1,360	3.3%
13	Minnesota	1,093	2.7%
12	Mississippi	1,111	2.7%
22	Missouri	766	1.9%
NA	Montana**	NA	NA
37	Nebraska	293	0.7%
38	Nevada	237	0.6%
NA	New Hampshire**	NA	NA
45	New Jersey	0	0.0%
24	New Mexico	688	1.7%
29	New York	437	1.1%
1	North Carolina	2,984	7.3%
40	North Dakota	141	0.3%
10	Ohio	1,314	3.2%
19	Oklahoma	839	2.0%
21	Oregon	794	1.9%
14	Pennsylvania	1,068	2.6%
44	Rhode Island	2	0.0%
3	South Carolina	2,210	5.4%
39	South Dakota	147	0.4%
4	Tennessee	1,939	4.7%
5	Texas	1,794	4.4%
35	Utah	306	0.7%
33	Vermont	351	0.9%
11	Virginia	1,237	3.0%
16	Washington	964	2.3%
18	West Virginia	931	2.3%
17	Wisconsin	940	2.3%
41	Wyoming	116	0.3%

RANK ORDER

RANK	STATE	THEFTS	% of USA
1	North Carolina	2,984	7.3%
2	Georgia	2,907	7.1%
3	South Carolina	2,210	5.4%
4	Tennessee	1,939	4.7%
5	Texas	1,794	4.4%
6	Florida	1,669	4.1%
7	Indiana	1,665	4.0%
8	California	1,391	3.4%
9	Michigan	1,360	3.3%
10	Ohio	1,314	3.2%
11	Virginia	1,237	3.0%
12	Mississippi	1,111	2.7%
13	Minnesota	1,093	2.7%
14	Pennsylvania	1,068	2.6%
15	Arkansas	972	2.4%
16	Washington	964	2.3%
17	Wisconsin	940	2.3%
18	West Virginia	931	2.3%
19	Oklahoma	839	2.0%
20	Louisiana	798	1.9%
21	Oregon	794	1.9%
22	Missouri	766	1.9%
23	Alabama	741	1.8%
24	New Mexico	688	1.7%
25	Connecticut	674	1.6%
26	Hawaii	663	1.6%
27	Iowa	598	1.5%
28	Alaska	446	1.1%
29	New York	437	1.1%
30	Arizona	421	1.0%
31	Maine	401	1.0%
32	Idaho	391	1.0%
33	Vermont	351	0.9%
34	Colorado	334	0.8%
35	Utah	306	0.7%
36	Maryland	298	0.7%
37	Nebraska	293	0.7%
38	Nevada	237	0.6%
39	South Dakota	147	0.4%
40	North Dakota	141	0.3%
41	Wyoming	116	0.3%
42	Delaware	115	0.3%
43	Massachusetts	4	0.0%
44	Rhode Island	2	0.0%
45	New Jersey	0	0.0%
NA	Illinois**	NA	NA
NA	Kansas**	NA	NA
NA	Kentucky**	NA	NA
NA	Montana**	NA	NA
NA	New Hampshire**	NA	NA
	District of Columbia	0	0.0%

Source: Federal Bureau of Investigation
    "Crime in the United States 1999" (Uniform Crime Reports, October 15, 2000)
*Estimated totals for rural areas, defined by the F.B.I. as other than Metropolitan Statistical Areas and other cities outside such areas. National total includes those states listed as not available. Motor vehicle theft includes the theft or attempted theft of a self-propelled vehicle. Excludes motorboats, construction equipment, airplanes and farming equipment. **Not available.

Rural Motor Vehicle Theft Rate in 1999

National Rural Rate = 123.5 Motor Vehicle Thefts per 100,000 Population*

ALPHA ORDER

RANK	STATE	RATE
34	Alabama	91.3
2	Alaska	230.5
14	Arizona	141.5
21	Arkansas	118.7
4	California	217.4
35	Colorado	90.4
15	Connecticut	140.7
26	Delaware	111.3
6	Florida	199.7
7	Georgia	186.0
5	Hawaii	208.2
33	Idaho	93.4
NA	Illinois**	NA
12	Indiana	148.6
38	Iowa	66.8
NA	Kansas**	NA
NA	Kentucky**	NA
24	Louisiana	111.7
25	Maine	111.6
28	Maryland	103.6
43	Massachusetts	39.1
18	Michigan	122.5
19	Minnesota	122.4
30	Mississippi	97.6
40	Missouri	61.7
NA	Montana**	NA
37	Nebraska	71.5
22	Nevada	118.6
NA	New Hampshire**	NA
44	New Jersey	0.0
3	New Mexico	220.0
42	New York	49.8
10	North Carolina	167.8
39	North Dakota	65.5
31	Ohio	95.5
16	Oklahoma	129.1
11	Oregon	150.9
29	Pennsylvania	102.8
44	Rhode Island	0.0
1	South Carolina	257.0
41	South Dakota	52.3
9	Tennessee	171.8
27	Texas	106.3
17	Utah	127.3
13	Vermont	145.7
23	Virginia	114.2
8	Washington	176.7
20	West Virginia	121.8
32	Wisconsin	93.7
36	Wyoming	88.7

RANK ORDER

RANK	STATE	RATE
1	South Carolina	257.0
2	Alaska	230.5
3	New Mexico	220.0
4	California	217.4
5	Hawaii	208.2
6	Florida	199.7
7	Georgia	186.0
8	Washington	176.7
9	Tennessee	171.8
10	North Carolina	167.8
11	Oregon	150.9
12	Indiana	148.6
13	Vermont	145.7
14	Arizona	141.5
15	Connecticut	140.7
16	Oklahoma	129.1
17	Utah	127.3
18	Michigan	122.5
19	Minnesota	122.4
20	West Virginia	121.8
21	Arkansas	118.7
22	Nevada	118.6
23	Virginia	114.2
24	Louisiana	111.7
25	Maine	111.6
26	Delaware	111.3
27	Texas	106.3
28	Maryland	103.6
29	Pennsylvania	102.8
30	Mississippi	97.6
31	Ohio	95.5
32	Wisconsin	93.7
33	Idaho	93.4
34	Alabama	91.3
35	Colorado	90.4
36	Wyoming	88.7
37	Nebraska	71.5
38	Iowa	66.8
39	North Dakota	65.5
40	Missouri	61.7
41	South Dakota	52.3
42	New York	49.8
43	Massachusetts	39.1
44	New Jersey	0.0
44	Rhode Island	0.0
NA	Illinois**	NA
NA	Kansas**	NA
NA	Kentucky**	NA
NA	Montana**	NA
NA	New Hampshire**	NA
	District of Columbia	0.0

Source: Morgan Quitno Press using data from Federal Bureau of Investigation
"Crime in the United States 1999" (Uniform Crime Reports, October 15, 2000)
*Estimated rates for rural areas, defined by the F.B.I. as other than Metropolitan Statistical Areas and other cities outside such areas. National rate includes those states listed as not available. Motor vehicle theft includes the theft or attempted theft of a self-propelled vehicle. Excludes motorboats, construction equipment, airplanes and farming equipment. **Not available.

Percent of Motor Vehicle Thefts Occurring in Rural Areas in 1999

National Percent = 3.6% of Motor Vehicle Thefts*

ALPHA ORDER

RANK ORDER

RANK	STATE	PERCENT		RANK	STATE	PERCENT
25	Alabama	5.6		1	Vermont	38.5
7	Alaska	16.8		2	West Virginia	24.7
40	Arizona	1.1		3	Maine	23.7
9	Arkansas	14.6		4	Idaho	20.6
41	California	0.8		5	Wyoming	19.5
35	Colorado	2.3		6	South Dakota	17.1
23	Connecticut	6.0		7	Alaska	16.8
28	Delaware	3.8		8	South Carolina	15.3
37	Florida	1.8		9	Arkansas	14.6
19	Georgia	7.2		10	Hawaii	14.2
10	Hawaii	14.2		11	North Dakota	13.6
4	Idaho	20.6		12	North Carolina	11.7
NA	Illinois**	NA		13	Iowa	11.6
15	Indiana	8.2		14	New Mexico	8.5
13	Iowa	11.6		15	Indiana	8.2
NA	Kansas**	NA		15	Minnesota	8.2
NA	Kentucky**	NA		15	Mississippi	8.2
29	Louisiana	3.7		18	Tennessee	7.7
3	Maine	23.7		19	Georgia	7.2
39	Maryland	1.2		20	Oklahoma	6.9
43	Massachusetts	0.0		20	Virginia	6.9
34	Michigan	2.4		22	Wisconsin	6.8
15	Minnesota	8.2		23	Connecticut	6.0
15	Mississippi	8.2		24	Oregon	5.8
31	Missouri	3.3		25	Alabama	5.6
NA	Montana**	NA		26	Nebraska	5.4
26	Nebraska	5.4		27	Utah	4.1
37	Nevada	1.8		28	Delaware	3.8
NA	New Hampshire**	NA		29	Louisiana	3.7
43	New Jersey	0.0		30	Ohio	3.4
14	New Mexico	8.5		31	Missouri	3.3
41	New York	0.8		32	Washington	2.9
12	North Carolina	11.7		33	Pennsylvania	2.7
11	North Dakota	13.6		34	Michigan	2.4
30	Ohio	3.4		35	Colorado	2.3
20	Oklahoma	6.9		36	Texas	1.9
24	Oregon	5.8		37	Florida	1.8
33	Pennsylvania	2.7		37	Nevada	1.8
43	Rhode Island	0.0		39	Maryland	1.2
8	South Carolina	15.3		40	Arizona	1.1
6	South Dakota	17.1		41	California	0.8
18	Tennessee	7.7		41	New York	0.8
36	Texas	1.9		43	Massachusetts	0.0
27	Utah	4.1		43	New Jersey	0.0
1	Vermont	38.5		43	Rhode Island	0.0
20	Virginia	6.9		NA	Illinois**	NA
32	Washington	2.9		NA	Kansas**	NA
2	West Virginia	24.7		NA	Kentucky**	NA
22	Wisconsin	6.8		NA	Montana**	NA
5	Wyoming	19.5		NA	New Hampshire**	NA
					District of Columbia	0.0

Source: Morgan Quitno Press using data from Federal Bureau of Investigation
   "Crime in the United States 1999" (Uniform Crime Reports, October 15, 2000)
*Estimated percentages for rural areas, defined by the F.B.I. as other than Metropolitan Statistical Areas and other
cities outside such areas. National percent includes those states listed as not available. Motor vehicle theft
includes the theft or attempted theft of a self-propelled vehicle. Excludes motorboats, construction equipment,
airplanes and farming equipment. **Not available.

Crimes Reported at Universities and Colleges in 1999

National Total = 94,514 Reported Crimes*

ALPHA ORDER

RANK	STATE	CRIMES	% of USA
32	Alabama	595	0.6%
39	Alaska	124	0.1%
10	Arizona	3,205	3.4%
23	Arkansas	1,251	1.3%
1	California	12,932	13.7%
18	Colorado	1,905	2.0%
22	Connecticut	1,405	1.5%
35	Delaware	550	0.6%
6	Florida	4,225	4.5%
4	Georgia	4,798	5.1%
NA	Hawaii**	NA	NA
NA	Idaho**	NA	NA
NA	Illinois**	NA	NA
16	Indiana	2,626	2.8%
28	Iowa	911	1.0%
NA	Kansas**	NA	NA
NA	Kentucky**	NA	NA
12	Louisiana	2,900	3.1%
NA	Maine**	NA	NA
14	Maryland	2,713	2.9%
8	Massachusetts	3,606	3.8%
3	Michigan	4,888	5.2%
29	Minnesota	910	1.0%
27	Mississippi	1,128	1.2%
30	Missouri	828	0.9%
NA	Montana**	NA	NA
34	Nebraska	559	0.6%
33	Nevada	570	0.6%
NA	New Hampshire**	NA	NA
15	New Jersey	2,691	2.8%
24	New Mexico	1,247	1.3%
11	New York	3,162	3.3%
7	North Carolina	4,075	4.3%
36	North Dakota	341	0.4%
5	Ohio	4,692	5.0%
25	Oklahoma	1,235	1.3%
NA	Oregon**	NA	NA
17	Pennsylvania	2,441	2.6%
31	Rhode Island	601	0.6%
26	South Carolina	1,199	1.3%
NA	South Dakota**	NA	NA
13	Tennessee	2,880	3.0%
2	Texas	8,591	9.1%
21	Utah	1,530	1.6%
NA	Vermont**	NA	NA
9	Virginia	3,437	3.6%
19	Washington	1,735	1.8%
38	West Virginia	178	0.2%
20	Wisconsin	1,668	1.8%
37	Wyoming	182	0.2%

RANK ORDER

RANK	STATE	CRIMES	% of USA
1	California	12,932	13.7%
2	Texas	8,591	9.1%
3	Michigan	4,888	5.2%
4	Georgia	4,798	5.1%
5	Ohio	4,692	5.0%
6	Florida	4,225	4.5%
7	North Carolina	4,075	4.3%
8	Massachusetts	3,606	3.8%
9	Virginia	3,437	3.6%
10	Arizona	3,205	3.4%
11	New York	3,162	3.3%
12	Louisiana	2,900	3.1%
13	Tennessee	2,880	3.0%
14	Maryland	2,713	2.9%
15	New Jersey	2,691	2.8%
16	Indiana	2,626	2.8%
17	Pennsylvania	2,441	2.6%
18	Colorado	1,905	2.0%
19	Washington	1,735	1.8%
20	Wisconsin	1,668	1.8%
21	Utah	1,530	1.6%
22	Connecticut	1,405	1.5%
23	Arkansas	1,251	1.3%
24	New Mexico	1,247	1.3%
25	Oklahoma	1,235	1.3%
26	South Carolina	1,199	1.3%
27	Mississippi	1,128	1.2%
28	Iowa	911	1.0%
29	Minnesota	910	1.0%
30	Missouri	828	0.9%
31	Rhode Island	601	0.6%
32	Alabama	595	0.6%
33	Nevada	570	0.6%
34	Nebraska	559	0.6%
35	Delaware	550	0.6%
36	North Dakota	341	0.4%
37	Wyoming	182	0.2%
38	West Virginia	178	0.2%
39	Alaska	124	0.1%
NA	Hawaii**	NA	NA
NA	Idaho**	NA	NA
NA	Illinois**	NA	NA
NA	Kansas**	NA	NA
NA	Kentucky**	NA	NA
NA	Maine**	NA	NA
NA	Montana**	NA	NA
NA	New Hampshire**	NA	NA
NA	Oregon**	NA	NA
NA	South Dakota**	NA	NA
NA	Vermont**	NA	NA
	District of Columbia**	NA	NA

Source: Morgan Quitno Press using data from Federal Bureau of Investigation
"Crime in the United States 1999" (Uniform Crime Reports, October 15, 2000)
*Includes murder, rape, robbery, aggravated assault, burglary, larceny-theft and motor vehicle theft. Total is only for states shown separately. Many states had incomplete reports.
**Not available.

Crimes Reported at Universities and Colleges as a Percent of All Crimes in 1999

National Percent = 0.91% of Crimes*

ALPHA ORDER				RANK ORDER		
RANK	STATE	PERCENT		RANK	STATE	PERCENT
39	Alabama	0.31		1	North Dakota	2.25
35	Alaska	0.46		2	Massachusetts	1.79
15	Arizona	1.14		3	Rhode Island	1.69
8	Arkansas	1.21		4	Delaware	1.51
20	California	1.03		5	Virginia	1.48
12	Colorado	1.16		6	Utah	1.44
7	Connecticut	1.26		7	Connecticut	1.26
4	Delaware	1.51		8	Arkansas	1.21
36	Florida	0.45		9	Georgia	1.20
9	Georgia	1.20		9	New Mexico	1.20
NA	Hawaii**	NA		11	Indiana	1.17
NA	Idaho**	NA		12	Colorado	1.16
NA	Illinois**	NA		13	Louisiana	1.15
11	Indiana	1.17		13	Michigan	1.15
22	Iowa	0.98		15	Arizona	1.14
NA	Kansas**	NA		16	Tennessee	1.12
NA	Kentucky**	NA		17	Wyoming	1.10
13	Louisiana	1.15		18	Maryland	1.07
NA	Maine**	NA		19	Ohio	1.04
18	Maryland	1.07		20	California	1.03
2	Massachusetts	1.79		20	North Carolina	1.03
13	Michigan	1.15		22	Iowa	0.98
33	Minnesota	0.53		23	New Jersey	0.97
25	Mississippi	0.95		24	Wisconsin	0.96
38	Missouri	0.33		25	Mississippi	0.95
NA	Montana**	NA		26	Texas	0.85
27	Nebraska	0.82		27	Nebraska	0.82
29	Nevada	0.68		28	Oklahoma	0.79
NA	New Hampshire**	NA		29	Nevada	0.68
23	New Jersey	0.97		30	Pennsylvania	0.65
9	New Mexico	1.20		31	South Carolina	0.58
33	New York	0.53		32	Washington	0.57
20	North Carolina	1.03		33	Minnesota	0.53
1	North Dakota	2.25		33	New York	0.53
19	Ohio	1.04		35	Alaska	0.46
28	Oklahoma	0.79		36	Florida	0.45
NA	Oregon**	NA		37	West Virginia	0.36
30	Pennsylvania	0.65		38	Missouri	0.33
3	Rhode Island	1.69		39	Alabama	0.31
31	South Carolina	0.58		NA	Hawaii**	NA
NA	South Dakota**	NA		NA	Idaho**	NA
16	Tennessee	1.12		NA	Illinois**	NA
26	Texas	0.85		NA	Kansas**	NA
6	Utah	1.44		NA	Kentucky**	NA
NA	Vermont**	NA		NA	Maine**	NA
5	Virginia	1.48		NA	Montana**	NA
32	Washington	0.57		NA	New Hampshire**	NA
37	West Virginia	0.36		NA	Oregon**	NA
24	Wisconsin	0.96		NA	South Dakota**	NA
17	Wyoming	1.10		NA	Vermont**	NA
					District of Columbia**	NA

Source: Morgan Quitno Press using data from Federal Bureau of Investigation
   "Crime in the United States 1999" (Uniform Crime Reports, October 15, 2000)
*Includes murder, rape, robbery, aggravated assault, burglary, larceny-theft and motor vehicle theft. National
percent is only for states shown separately. Many states had incomplete reports.
**Not available.

Violent Crimes Reported at Universities and Colleges in 1999

National Total = 2,221 Reported Violent Crimes*

ALPHA ORDER

RANK	STATE	CRIMES	% of USA
29	Alabama	19	0.9%
33	Alaska	14	0.6%
13	Arizona	74	3.3%
25	Arkansas	25	1.1%
1	California	277	12.5%
19	Colorado	37	1.7%
22	Connecticut	28	1.3%
39	Delaware	0	0.0%
4	Florida	128	5.8%
9	Georgia	91	4.1%
NA	Hawaii**	NA	NA
NA	Idaho**	NA	NA
NA	Illinois**	NA	NA
19	Indiana	37	1.7%
17	Iowa	45	2.0%
NA	Kansas**	NA	NA
NA	Kentucky**	NA	NA
5	Louisiana	111	5.0%
NA	Maine**	NA	NA
11	Maryland	86	3.9%
3	Massachusetts	146	6.6%
8	Michigan	93	4.2%
32	Minnesota	15	0.7%
31	Mississippi	16	0.7%
28	Missouri	21	0.9%
NA	Montana**	NA	NA
35	Nebraska	7	0.3%
26	Nevada	22	1.0%
NA	New Hampshire**	NA	NA
16	New Jersey	51	2.3%
24	New Mexico	27	1.2%
15	New York	57	2.6%
7	North Carolina	101	4.5%
38	North Dakota	2	0.1%
6	Ohio	110	5.0%
18	Oklahoma	42	1.9%
NA	Oregon**	NA	NA
14	Pennsylvania	63	2.8%
34	Rhode Island	8	0.4%
22	South Carolina	28	1.3%
NA	South Dakota**	NA	NA
12	Tennessee	82	3.7%
2	Texas	187	8.4%
26	Utah	22	1.0%
NA	Vermont**	NA	NA
10	Virginia	89	4.0%
29	Washington	19	0.9%
36	West Virginia	5	0.2%
21	Wisconsin	32	1.4%
37	Wyoming	4	0.2%

RANK ORDER

RANK	STATE	CRIMES	% of USA
1	California	277	12.5%
2	Texas	187	8.4%
3	Massachusetts	146	6.6%
4	Florida	128	5.8%
5	Louisiana	111	5.0%
6	Ohio	110	5.0%
7	North Carolina	101	4.5%
8	Michigan	93	4.2%
9	Georgia	91	4.1%
10	Virginia	89	4.0%
11	Maryland	86	3.9%
12	Tennessee	82	3.7%
13	Arizona	74	3.3%
14	Pennsylvania	63	2.8%
15	New York	57	2.6%
16	New Jersey	51	2.3%
17	Iowa	45	2.0%
18	Oklahoma	42	1.9%
19	Colorado	37	1.7%
19	Indiana	37	1.7%
21	Wisconsin	32	1.4%
22	Connecticut	28	1.3%
22	South Carolina	28	1.3%
24	New Mexico	27	1.2%
25	Arkansas	25	1.1%
26	Nevada	22	1.0%
26	Utah	22	1.0%
28	Missouri	21	0.9%
29	Alabama	19	0.9%
29	Washington	19	0.9%
31	Mississippi	16	0.7%
32	Minnesota	15	0.7%
33	Alaska	14	0.6%
34	Rhode Island	8	0.4%
35	Nebraska	7	0.3%
36	West Virginia	5	0.2%
37	Wyoming	4	0.2%
38	North Dakota	2	0.1%
39	Delaware	0	0.0%
NA	Hawaii**	NA	NA
NA	Idaho**	NA	NA
NA	Illinois**	NA	NA
NA	Kansas**	NA	NA
NA	Kentucky**	NA	NA
NA	Maine**	NA	NA
NA	Montana**	NA	NA
NA	New Hampshire**	NA	NA
NA	Oregon**	NA	NA
NA	South Dakota**	NA	NA
NA	Vermont**	NA	NA
	District of Columbia**	NA	NA

Source: Morgan Quitno Press using data from Federal Bureau of Investigation
"Crime in the United States 1999" (Uniform Crime Reports, October 15, 2000)
*Includes murder, rape, robbery and aggravated assault. Total is only for states shown separately. Many states had incomplete reports.
**Not available.

Violent Crimes Reported at Universities and Colleges
As a Percent of All Violent Crimes in 1999
National Percent = 0.17% of Violent Crimes*

ALPHA ORDER

RANK	STATE	PERCENT
33	Alabama	0.09
6	Alaska	0.36
10	Arizona	0.28
17	Arkansas	0.23
28	California	0.13
12	Colorado	0.27
13	Connecticut	0.25
39	Delaware	0.00
31	Florida	0.10
18	Georgia	0.22
NA	Hawaii**	NA
NA	Idaho**	NA
NA	Illinois**	NA
23	Indiana	0.17
1	Iowa	0.56
NA	Kansas**	NA
NA	Kentucky**	NA
8	Louisiana	0.35
NA	Maine**	NA
18	Maryland	0.22
3	Massachusetts	0.43
26	Michigan	0.16
30	Minnesota	0.11
23	Mississippi	0.17
36	Missouri	0.08
NA	Montana**	NA
31	Nebraska	0.10
21	Nevada	0.21
NA	New Hampshire**	NA
27	New Jersey	0.15
22	New Mexico	0.19
38	New York	0.05
16	North Carolina	0.24
2	North Dakota	0.47
9	Ohio	0.31
13	Oklahoma	0.25
NA	Oregon**	NA
29	Pennsylvania	0.12
10	Rhode Island	0.28
33	South Carolina	0.09
NA	South Dakota**	NA
18	Tennessee	0.22
23	Texas	0.17
5	Utah	0.37
NA	Vermont**	NA
4	Virginia	0.41
33	Washington	0.09
36	West Virginia	0.08
13	Wisconsin	0.25
6	Wyoming	0.36

RANK ORDER

RANK	STATE	PERCENT
1	Iowa	0.56
2	North Dakota	0.47
3	Massachusetts	0.43
4	Virginia	0.41
5	Utah	0.37
6	Alaska	0.36
6	Wyoming	0.36
8	Louisiana	0.35
9	Ohio	0.31
10	Arizona	0.28
10	Rhode Island	0.28
12	Colorado	0.27
13	Connecticut	0.25
13	Oklahoma	0.25
13	Wisconsin	0.25
16	North Carolina	0.24
17	Arkansas	0.23
18	Georgia	0.22
18	Maryland	0.22
18	Tennessee	0.22
21	Nevada	0.21
22	New Mexico	0.19
23	Indiana	0.17
23	Mississippi	0.17
23	Texas	0.17
26	Michigan	0.16
27	New Jersey	0.15
28	California	0.13
29	Pennsylvania	0.12
30	Minnesota	0.11
31	Florida	0.10
31	Nebraska	0.10
33	Alabama	0.09
33	South Carolina	0.09
33	Washington	0.09
36	Missouri	0.08
36	West Virginia	0.08
38	New York	0.05
39	Delaware	0.00
NA	Hawaii**	NA
NA	Idaho**	NA
NA	Illinois**	NA
NA	Kansas**	NA
NA	Kentucky**	NA
NA	Maine**	NA
NA	Montana**	NA
NA	New Hampshire**	NA
NA	Oregon**	NA
NA	South Dakota**	NA
NA	Vermont**	NA
	District of Columbia**	NA

Source: Morgan Quitno Press using data from Federal Bureau of Investigation
"Crime in the United States 1999" (Uniform Crime Reports, October 15, 2000)
*Includes murder, rape, robbery and aggravated assault. Total is only for states shown separately. Many states had incomplete reports.
**Not available.

Property Crimes Reported at Universities and Colleges in 1999

National Total = 92,303 Reported Property Crimes*

ALPHA ORDER

RANK	STATE	CRIMES	% of USA
32	Alabama	576	0.6%
39	Alaska	110	0.1%
10	Arizona	3,131	3.4%
23	Arkansas	1,226	1.3%
1	California	12,655	13.7%
18	Colorado	1,868	2.0%
22	Connecticut	1,377	1.5%
34	Delaware	550	0.6%
6	Florida	4,097	4.4%
4	Georgia	4,707	5.1%
NA	Hawaii**	NA	NA
NA	Idaho**	NA	NA
NA	Illinois**	NA	NA
16	Indiana	2,589	2.8%
29	Iowa	866	0.9%
NA	Kansas**	NA	NA
NA	Kentucky**	NA	NA
13	Louisiana	2,789	3.0%
NA	Maine**	NA	NA
15	Maryland	2,627	2.8%
8	Massachusetts	3,460	3.7%
3	Michigan	4,795	5.2%
28	Minnesota	895	1.0%
27	Mississippi	1,112	1.2%
30	Missouri	807	0.9%
NA	Montana**	NA	NA
33	Nebraska	552	0.6%
35	Nevada	548	0.6%
NA	New Hampshire**	NA	NA
14	New Jersey	2,640	2.9%
24	New Mexico	1,220	1.3%
11	New York	3,105	3.4%
7	North Carolina	3,974	4.3%
36	North Dakota	339	0.4%
5	Ohio	4,582	5.0%
25	Oklahoma	1,193	1.3%
NA	Oregon**	NA	NA
17	Pennsylvania	2,378	2.6%
31	Rhode Island	593	0.6%
26	South Carolina	1,171	1.3%
NA	South Dakota**	NA	NA
12	Tennessee	2,798	3.0%
2	Texas	8,404	9.1%
21	Utah	1,518	1.6%
NA	Vermont**	NA	NA
9	Virginia	3,348	3.6%
19	Washington	1,716	1.9%
38	West Virginia	173	0.2%
20	Wisconsin	1,636	1.8%
37	Wyoming	178	0.2%

RANK ORDER

RANK	STATE	CRIMES	% of USA
1	California	12,655	13.7%
2	Texas	8,404	9.1%
3	Michigan	4,795	5.2%
4	Georgia	4,707	5.1%
5	Ohio	4,582	5.0%
6	Florida	4,097	4.4%
7	North Carolina	3,974	4.3%
8	Massachusetts	3,460	3.7%
9	Virginia	3,348	3.6%
10	Arizona	3,131	3.4%
11	New York	3,105	3.4%
12	Tennessee	2,798	3.0%
13	Louisiana	2,789	3.0%
14	New Jersey	2,640	2.9%
15	Maryland	2,627	2.8%
16	Indiana	2,589	2.8%
17	Pennsylvania	2,378	2.6%
18	Colorado	1,868	2.0%
19	Washington	1,716	1.9%
20	Wisconsin	1,636	1.8%
21	Utah	1,518	1.6%
22	Connecticut	1,377	1.5%
23	Arkansas	1,226	1.3%
24	New Mexico	1,220	1.3%
25	Oklahoma	1,193	1.3%
26	South Carolina	1,171	1.3%
27	Mississippi	1,112	1.2%
28	Minnesota	895	1.0%
29	Iowa	866	0.9%
30	Missouri	807	0.9%
31	Rhode Island	593	0.6%
32	Alabama	576	0.6%
33	Nebraska	552	0.6%
34	Delaware	550	0.6%
35	Nevada	548	0.6%
36	North Dakota	339	0.4%
37	Wyoming	178	0.2%
38	West Virginia	173	0.2%
39	Alaska	110	0.1%
NA	Hawaii**	NA	NA
NA	Idaho**	NA	NA
NA	Illinois**	NA	NA
NA	Kansas**	NA	NA
NA	Kentucky**	NA	NA
NA	Maine**	NA	NA
NA	Montana**	NA	NA
NA	New Hampshire**	NA	NA
NA	Oregon**	NA	NA
NA	South Dakota**	NA	NA
NA	Vermont**	NA	NA
	District of Columbia**	NA	NA

Source: Morgan Quitno Press using data from Federal Bureau of Investigation
"Crime in the United States 1999" (Uniform Crime Reports, October 15, 2000)
*Includes burglary, larceny-theft and motor vehicle theft. Total is only for states shown separately. Many states had incomplete reports.
**Not available.

Property Crimes at Universities and Colleges
As a Percent of All Property Crimes in 1999
National Percent = 1.01% of Property Crimes*

ALPHA ORDER

RANK	STATE	PERCENT
39	Alabama	0.34
36	Alaska	0.48
16	Arizona	1.23
9	Arkansas	1.33
18	California	1.20
15	Colorado	1.24
7	Connecticut	1.38
4	Delaware	1.78
35	Florida	0.51
10	Georgia	1.31
NA	Hawaii**	NA
NA	Idaho**	NA
NA	Illinois**	NA
12	Indiana	1.28
23	Iowa	1.03
NA	Kansas**	NA
NA	Kentucky**	NA
14	Louisiana	1.27
NA	Maine**	NA
17	Maryland	1.22
2	Massachusetts	2.07
11	Michigan	1.30
34	Minnesota	0.56
24	Mississippi	1.02
38	Missouri	0.36
NA	Montana**	NA
27	Nebraska	0.90
29	Nevada	0.74
NA	New Hampshire**	NA
22	New Jersey	1.08
8	New Mexico	1.37
32	New York	0.63
20	North Carolina	1.12
1	North Dakota	2.30
21	Ohio	1.11
28	Oklahoma	0.85
NA	Oregon**	NA
29	Pennsylvania	0.74
3	Rhode Island	1.82
31	South Carolina	0.67
NA	South Dakota**	NA
12	Tennessee	1.28
26	Texas	0.94
6	Utah	1.52
NA	Vermont**	NA
5	Virginia	1.59
33	Washington	0.61
37	West Virginia	0.40
24	Wisconsin	1.02
19	Wyoming	1.15

RANK ORDER

RANK	STATE	PERCENT
1	North Dakota	2.30
2	Massachusetts	2.07
3	Rhode Island	1.82
4	Delaware	1.78
5	Virginia	1.59
6	Utah	1.52
7	Connecticut	1.38
8	New Mexico	1.37
9	Arkansas	1.33
10	Georgia	1.31
11	Michigan	1.30
12	Indiana	1.28
12	Tennessee	1.28
14	Louisiana	1.27
15	Colorado	1.24
16	Arizona	1.23
17	Maryland	1.22
18	California	1.20
19	Wyoming	1.15
20	North Carolina	1.12
21	Ohio	1.11
22	New Jersey	1.08
23	Iowa	1.03
24	Mississippi	1.02
24	Wisconsin	1.02
26	Texas	0.94
27	Nebraska	0.90
28	Oklahoma	0.85
29	Nevada	0.74
29	Pennsylvania	0.74
31	South Carolina	0.67
32	New York	0.63
33	Washington	0.61
34	Minnesota	0.56
35	Florida	0.51
36	Alaska	0.48
37	West Virginia	0.40
38	Missouri	0.36
39	Alabama	0.34
NA	Hawaii**	NA
NA	Idaho**	NA
NA	Illinois**	NA
NA	Kansas**	NA
NA	Kentucky**	NA
NA	Maine**	NA
NA	Montana**	NA
NA	New Hampshire**	NA
NA	Oregon**	NA
NA	South Dakota**	NA
NA	Vermont**	NA
	District of Columbia**	NA

Source: Morgan Quitno Press using data from Federal Bureau of Investigation
    "Crime in the United States 1999" (Uniform Crime Reports, October 15, 2000)
*Includes burglary, larceny-theft and motor vehicle theft. Total is only for states shown separately. Many states had incomplete reports.
**Not available.

Crimes in 1995

National Total = 13,862,727 Crimes*

<u>ALPHA ORDER</u>

RANK	STATE	CRIMES	% of USA
23	Alabama	206,188	1.5%
45	Alaska	34,753	0.3%
12	Arizona	346,450	2.5%
34	Arkansas	116,521	0.8%
1	California	1,841,984	13.3%
25	Colorado	202,199	1.5%
28	Connecticut	147,481	1.1%
44	Delaware	36,988	0.3%
2	Florida	1,090,999	7.9%
8	Georgia	432,322	3.1%
37	Hawaii	85,447	0.6%
39	Idaho	51,189	0.4%
5	Illinois	645,408	4.7%
18	Indiana	268,768	1.9%
33	Iowa	116,575	0.8%
30	Kansas	125,350	0.9%
29	Kentucky	129,377	0.9%
15	Louisiana	289,873	2.1%
43	Maine	40,763	0.3%
14	Maryland	317,382	2.3%
20	Massachusetts	263,710	1.9%
6	Michigan	494,903	3.6%
22	Minnesota	207,327	1.5%
31	Mississippi	121,755	0.9%
17	Missouri	272,617	2.0%
42	Montana	41,737	0.3%
38	Nebraska	74,393	0.5%
36	Nevada	100,664	0.7%
46	New Hampshire	30,484	0.2%
11	New Jersey	373,708	2.7%
35	New Mexico	108,312	0.8%
4	New York	827,025	6.0%
10	North Carolina	405,764	2.9%
50	North Dakota	18,373	0.1%
7	Ohio	491,223	3.5%
27	Oklahoma	183,463	1.3%
24	Oregon	206,173	1.5%
9	Pennsylvania	406,209	2.9%
41	Rhode Island	42,021	0.3%
21	South Carolina	222,723	1.6%
47	South Dakota	22,312	0.2%
16	Tennessee	281,864	2.0%
3	Texas	1,064,336	7.7%
32	Utah	118,832	0.9%
49	Vermont	20,087	0.1%
19	Virginia	264,005	1.9%
13	Washington	340,513	2.5%
40	West Virginia	44,935	0.3%
26	Wisconsin	199,064	1.4%
48	Wyoming	20,737	0.1%

<u>RANK ORDER</u>

RANK	STATE	CRIMES	% of USA
1	California	1,841,984	13.3%
2	Florida	1,090,999	7.9%
3	Texas	1,064,336	7.7%
4	New York	827,025	6.0%
5	Illinois	645,408	4.7%
6	Michigan	494,903	3.6%
7	Ohio	491,223	3.5%
8	Georgia	432,322	3.1%
9	Pennsylvania	406,209	2.9%
10	North Carolina	405,764	2.9%
11	New Jersey	373,708	2.7%
12	Arizona	346,450	2.5%
13	Washington	340,513	2.5%
14	Maryland	317,382	2.3%
15	Louisiana	289,873	2.1%
16	Tennessee	281,864	2.0%
17	Missouri	272,617	2.0%
18	Indiana	268,768	1.9%
19	Virginia	264,005	1.9%
20	Massachusetts	263,710	1.9%
21	South Carolina	222,723	1.6%
22	Minnesota	207,327	1.5%
23	Alabama	206,188	1.5%
24	Oregon	206,173	1.5%
25	Colorado	202,199	1.5%
26	Wisconsin	199,064	1.4%
27	Oklahoma	183,463	1.3%
28	Connecticut	147,481	1.1%
29	Kentucky	129,377	0.9%
30	Kansas	125,350	0.9%
31	Mississippi	121,755	0.9%
32	Utah	118,832	0.9%
33	Iowa	116,575	0.8%
34	Arkansas	116,521	0.8%
35	New Mexico	108,312	0.8%
36	Nevada	100,664	0.7%
37	Hawaii	85,447	0.6%
38	Nebraska	74,393	0.5%
39	Idaho	51,189	0.4%
40	West Virginia	44,935	0.3%
41	Rhode Island	42,021	0.3%
42	Montana	41,737	0.3%
43	Maine	40,763	0.3%
44	Delaware	36,988	0.3%
45	Alaska	34,753	0.3%
46	New Hampshire	30,484	0.2%
47	South Dakota	22,312	0.2%
48	Wyoming	20,737	0.1%
49	Vermont	20,087	0.1%
50	North Dakota	18,373	0.1%
	District of Columbia	67,441	0.5%

Source: Federal Bureau of Investigation
"Crime in the United States 1996" (Uniform Crime Reports, October 4, 1997)
*Revised figures. Includes murder, rape, robbery, aggravated assault, burglary, larceny-theft and motor vehicle theft.

Percent Change in Number of Crimes: 1995 to 1999

National Percent Change = 16.1% Decrease*

ALPHA ORDER			RANK ORDER		
RANK	STATE	PERCENT CHANGE	RANK	STATE	PERCENT CHANGE
7	Alabama	(6.5)	1	Delaware	(1.4)
42	Alaska	(22.3)	2	North Carolina	(2.4)
37	Arizona	(18.7)	3	Mississippi	(2.9)
18	Arkansas	(11.5)	4	New Mexico	(4.2)
48	California	(31.5)	5	Texas	(5.2)
36	Colorado	(18.5)	6	Kansas	(6.0)
45	Connecticut	(24.6)	7	Alabama	(6.5)
1	Delaware	(1.4)	8	South Carolina	(7.1)
27	Florida	(14.0)	9	Georgia	(7.3)
9	Georgia	(7.3)	10	Nebraska	(8.0)
49	Hawaii	(32.9)	11	Pennsylvania	(8.1)
43	Idaho	(23.0)	12	Missouri	(8.2)
29	Illinois	(15.3)	13	Ohio	(8.4)
32	Indiana	(16.7)	14	Tennessee	(8.7)
41	Iowa	(20.7)	15	New Hampshire	(10.1)
6	Kansas	(6.0)	16	Utah	(10.8)
20	Kentucky	(11.9)	17	Washington	(11.2)
24	Louisiana	(13.3)	18	Arkansas	(11.5)
19	Maine	(11.6)	19	Maine	(11.6)
39	Maryland	(19.8)	20	Kentucky	(11.9)
44	Massachusetts	(23.6)	21	Virginia	(12.2)
25	Michigan	(13.8)	22	South Dakota	(13.1)
34	Minnesota	(17.1)	22	Wisconsin	(13.1)
3	Mississippi	(2.9)	24	Louisiana	(13.3)
12	Missouri	(8.2)	25	Michigan	(13.8)
26	Montana	(13.9)	26	Montana	(13.9)
10	Nebraska	(8.0)	27	Florida	(14.0)
31	Nevada	(16.4)	28	Oklahoma	(14.3)
15	New Hampshire	(10.1)	29	Illinois	(15.3)
46	New Jersey	(25.9)	30	Rhode Island	(15.5)
4	New Mexico	(4.2)	31	Nevada	(16.4)
47	New York	(27.8)	32	Indiana	(16.7)
2	North Carolina	(2.4)	32	Vermont	(16.7)
35	North Dakota	(17.4)	34	Minnesota	(17.1)
13	Ohio	(8.4)	35	North Dakota	(17.4)
28	Oklahoma	(14.3)	36	Colorado	(18.5)
38	Oregon	(19.6)	37	Arizona	(18.7)
11	Pennsylvania	(8.1)	38	Oregon	(19.6)
30	Rhode Island	(15.5)	39	Maryland	(19.8)
8	South Carolina	(7.1)	40	Wyoming	(20.0)
22	South Dakota	(13.1)	41	Iowa	(20.7)
14	Tennessee	(8.7)	42	Alaska	(22.3)
5	Texas	(5.2)	43	Idaho	(23.0)
16	Utah	(10.8)	44	Massachusetts	(23.6)
32	Vermont	(16.7)	45	Connecticut	(24.6)
21	Virginia	(12.2)	46	New Jersey	(25.9)
17	Washington	(11.2)	47	New York	(27.8)
NA	West Virginia**	NA	48	California	(31.5)
22	Wisconsin	(13.1)	49	Hawaii	(32.9)
40	Wyoming	(20.0)	NA	West Virginia**	NA
				District of Columbia	(37.9)

Source: Morgan Quitno Press using data from Federal Bureau of Investigation
   "Crime in the United States" (Uniform Crime Reports, 1996 and 1999 editions)
*Includes murder, rape, robbery, aggravated assault, burglary, larceny-theft and motor vehicle theft.
**Not comparable.

Crime Rate in 1995

National Rate = 5,275.9 Crimes per 100,000 Population*

ALPHA ORDER

RANK	STATE	RATE
25	Alabama	4,848.1
14	Alaska	5,753.8
1	Arizona	8,213.6
28	Arkansas	4,690.9
13	California	5,831.1
19	Colorado	5,396.3
33	Connecticut	4,503.2
22	Delaware	5,158.7
2	Florida	7,701.5
12	Georgia	6,003.6
3	Hawaii	7,198.6
36	Idaho	4,401.5
18	Illinois	5,455.7
29	Indiana	4,631.5
40	Iowa	4,101.9
24	Kansas	4,886.9
45	Kentucky	3,351.7
4	Louisiana	6,676.0
46	Maine	3,284.7
8	Maryland	6,294.8
37	Massachusetts	4,341.6
21	Michigan	5,182.8
34	Minnesota	4,497.3
32	Mississippi	4,514.5
23	Missouri	5,120.5
26	Montana	4,797.4
31	Nebraska	4,544.5
5	Nevada	6,579.3
49	New Hampshire	2,655.4
27	New Jersey	4,703.7
7	New Mexico	6,428.0
30	New York	4,560.1
16	North Carolina	5,639.5
48	North Dakota	2,866.3
35	Ohio	4,405.2
17	Oklahoma	5,596.8
6	Oregon	6,563.9
44	Pennsylvania	3,364.9
39	Rhode Island	4,244.5
11	South Carolina	6,063.8
47	South Dakota	3,060.6
20	Tennessee	5,362.7
15	Texas	5,684.3
10	Utah	6,090.8
43	Vermont	3,433.7
41	Virginia	3,989.2
9	Washington	6,269.8
50	West Virginia	2,458.2
42	Wisconsin	3,885.7
38	Wyoming	4,320.2

RANK ORDER

RANK	STATE	RATE
1	Arizona	8,213.6
2	Florida	7,701.5
3	Hawaii	7,198.6
4	Louisiana	6,676.0
5	Nevada	6,579.3
6	Oregon	6,563.9
7	New Mexico	6,428.0
8	Maryland	6,294.8
9	Washington	6,269.8
10	Utah	6,090.8
11	South Carolina	6,063.8
12	Georgia	6,003.6
13	California	5,831.1
14	Alaska	5,753.8
15	Texas	5,684.3
16	North Carolina	5,639.5
17	Oklahoma	5,596.8
18	Illinois	5,455.7
19	Colorado	5,396.3
20	Tennessee	5,362.7
21	Michigan	5,182.8
22	Delaware	5,158.7
23	Missouri	5,120.5
24	Kansas	4,886.9
25	Alabama	4,848.1
26	Montana	4,797.4
27	New Jersey	4,703.7
28	Arkansas	4,690.9
29	Indiana	4,631.5
30	New York	4,560.1
31	Nebraska	4,544.5
32	Mississippi	4,514.5
33	Connecticut	4,503.2
34	Minnesota	4,497.3
35	Ohio	4,405.2
36	Idaho	4,401.5
37	Massachusetts	4,341.6
38	Wyoming	4,320.2
39	Rhode Island	4,244.5
40	Iowa	4,101.9
41	Virginia	3,989.2
42	Wisconsin	3,885.7
43	Vermont	3,433.7
44	Pennsylvania	3,364.9
45	Kentucky	3,351.7
46	Maine	3,284.7
47	South Dakota	3,060.6
48	North Dakota	2,866.3
49	New Hampshire	2,655.4
50	West Virginia	2,458.2
	District of Columbia	12,173.5

Source: Federal Bureau of Investigation
    "Crime in the United States 1996" (Uniform Crime Reports, October 4, 1997)
*Revised figures. Includes murder, rape, robbery, aggravated assault, burglary, larceny-theft and motor vehicle theft.

Percent Change in Crime Rate: 1995 to 1999

National Percent Change = 19.1% Decrease*

ALPHA ORDER			RANK ORDER		
RANK	STATE	PERCENT CHANGE	RANK	STATE	PERCENT CHANGE
6	Alabama	(9.0)	1	Mississippi	(5.4)
39	Alaska	(24.2)	2	Delaware	(6.3)
45	Arizona	(28.2)	3	New Mexico	(7.2)
16	Arkansas	(13.8)	4	Pennsylvania	(7.5)
49	California	(34.7)	5	North Carolina	(8.2)
40	Colorado	(24.7)	6	Alabama	(9.0)
40	Connecticut	(24.7)	7	Kansas	(9.2)
2	Delaware	(6.3)	8	Ohio	(9.3)
33	Florida	(19.4)	9	Nebraska	(9.6)
20	Georgia	(14.2)	10	Missouri	(10.6)
48	Hawaii	(32.8)	11	Texas	(11.5)
46	Idaho	(28.4)	12	South Carolina	(12.2)
29	Illinois	(17.4)	13	Maine	(12.5)
32	Indiana	(18.7)	13	Tennessee	(12.5)
36	Iowa	(21.4)	15	South Dakota	(13.6)
7	Kansas	(9.2)	16	Arkansas	(13.8)
18	Kentucky	(14.1)	17	Louisiana	(13.9)
17	Louisiana	(13.9)	18	Kentucky	(14.1)
13	Maine	(12.5)	18	New Hampshire	(14.1)
37	Maryland	(21.9)	20	Georgia	(14.2)
42	Massachusetts	(24.9)	21	Montana	(15.2)
28	Michigan	(16.6)	21	Wisconsin	(15.2)
34	Minnesota	(20.0)	23	Virginia	(15.4)
1	Mississippi	(5.4)	24	Rhode Island	(15.6)
10	Missouri	(10.6)	25	Washington	(16.2)
21	Montana	(15.2)	26	Oklahoma	(16.3)
9	Nebraska	(9.6)	27	North Dakota	(16.5)
47	Nevada	(29.3)	28	Michigan	(16.6)
18	New Hampshire	(14.1)	29	Illinois	(17.4)
43	New Jersey	(27.7)	30	Vermont	(18.0)
3	New Mexico	(7.2)	31	Utah	(18.3)
44	New York	(28.1)	32	Indiana	(18.7)
5	North Carolina	(8.2)	33	Florida	(19.4)
27	North Dakota	(16.5)	34	Minnesota	(20.0)
8	Ohio	(9.3)	34	Wyoming	(20.0)
26	Oklahoma	(16.3)	36	Iowa	(21.4)
38	Oregon	(23.8)	37	Maryland	(21.9)
4	Pennsylvania	(7.5)	38	Oregon	(23.8)
24	Rhode Island	(15.6)	39	Alaska	(24.2)
12	South Carolina	(12.2)	40	Colorado	(24.7)
15	South Dakota	(13.6)	40	Connecticut	(24.7)
13	Tennessee	(12.5)	42	Massachusetts	(24.9)
11	Texas	(11.5)	43	New Jersey	(27.7)
31	Utah	(18.3)	44	New York	(28.1)
30	Vermont	(18.0)	45	Arizona	(28.2)
23	Virginia	(15.4)	46	Idaho	(28.4)
25	Washington	(16.2)	47	Nevada	(29.3)
NA	West Virginia**	NA	48	Hawaii	(32.8)
21	Wisconsin	(15.2)	49	California	(34.7)
34	Wyoming	(20.0)	NA	West Virginia**	NA
				District of Columbia	(33.7)

Source: Morgan Quitno Press using data from Federal Bureau of Investigation
   "Crime in the United States" (Uniform Crime Reports, 1996 and 1999 editions)
*Includes murder, rape, robbery, aggravated assault, burglary, larceny-theft and motor vehicle theft.
**Not comparable.

Violent Crimes in 1995

National Total = 1,798,792 Violent Crimes*

ALPHA ORDER

RANK	STATE	CRIMES	% of USA
20	Alabama	26,894	1.5%
39	Alaska	4,656	0.3%
19	Arizona	30,095	1.7%
31	Arkansas	13,741	0.8%
1	California	305,154	17.0%
24	Colorado	16,494	0.9%
33	Connecticut	13,293	0.7%
38	Delaware	5,198	0.3%
3	Florida	151,711	8.4%
11	Georgia	47,317	2.6%
43	Hawaii	3,509	0.2%
41	Idaho	3,745	0.2%
5	Illinois	117,836	6.6%
18	Indiana	30,451	1.7%
35	Iowa	10,071	0.6%
34	Kansas	10,792	0.6%
29	Kentucky	14,079	0.8%
13	Louisiana	43,741	2.4%
44	Maine	1,631	0.1%
9	Maryland	49,757	2.8%
14	Massachusetts	41,739	2.3%
6	Michigan	65,680	3.7%
25	Minnesota	16,416	0.9%
32	Mississippi	13,560	0.8%
17	Missouri	35,339	2.0%
46	Montana	1,491	0.1%
37	Nebraska	6,253	0.3%
27	Nevada	14,461	0.8%
47	New Hampshire	1,314	0.1%
10	New Jersey	47,652	2.6%
30	New Mexico	13,804	0.8%
2	New York	152,683	8.5%
12	North Carolina	46,508	2.6%
50	North Dakota	556	0.0%
7	Ohio	53,799	3.0%
23	Oklahoma	21,770	1.2%
26	Oregon	16,408	0.9%
8	Pennsylvania	51,586	2.9%
42	Rhode Island	3,643	0.2%
16	South Carolina	36,067	2.0%
45	South Dakota	1,513	0.1%
15	Tennessee	40,549	2.3%
4	Texas	124,303	6.9%
36	Utah	6,415	0.4%
49	Vermont	692	0.0%
22	Virginia	23,921	1.3%
21	Washington	26,300	1.5%
40	West Virginia	3,842	0.2%
28	Wisconsin	14,399	0.8%
48	Wyoming	1,220	0.1%

RANK ORDER

RANK	STATE	CRIMES	% of USA
1	California	305,154	17.0%
2	New York	152,683	8.5%
3	Florida	151,711	8.4%
4	Texas	124,303	6.9%
5	Illinois	117,836	6.6%
6	Michigan	65,680	3.7%
7	Ohio	53,799	3.0%
8	Pennsylvania	51,586	2.9%
9	Maryland	49,757	2.8%
10	New Jersey	47,652	2.6%
11	Georgia	47,317	2.6%
12	North Carolina	46,508	2.6%
13	Louisiana	43,741	2.4%
14	Massachusetts	41,739	2.3%
15	Tennessee	40,549	2.3%
16	South Carolina	36,067	2.0%
17	Missouri	35,339	2.0%
18	Indiana	30,451	1.7%
19	Arizona	30,095	1.7%
20	Alabama	26,894	1.5%
21	Washington	26,300	1.5%
22	Virginia	23,921	1.3%
23	Oklahoma	21,770	1.2%
24	Colorado	16,494	0.9%
25	Minnesota	16,416	0.9%
26	Oregon	16,408	0.9%
27	Nevada	14,461	0.8%
28	Wisconsin	14,399	0.8%
29	Kentucky	14,079	0.8%
30	New Mexico	13,804	0.8%
31	Arkansas	13,741	0.8%
32	Mississippi	13,560	0.8%
33	Connecticut	13,293	0.7%
34	Kansas	10,792	0.6%
35	Iowa	10,071	0.6%
36	Utah	6,415	0.4%
37	Nebraska	6,253	0.3%
38	Delaware	5,198	0.3%
39	Alaska	4,656	0.3%
40	West Virginia	3,842	0.2%
41	Idaho	3,745	0.2%
42	Rhode Island	3,643	0.2%
43	Hawaii	3,509	0.2%
44	Maine	1,631	0.1%
45	South Dakota	1,513	0.1%
46	Montana	1,491	0.1%
47	New Hampshire	1,314	0.1%
48	Wyoming	1,220	0.1%
49	Vermont	692	0.0%
50	North Dakota	556	0.0%
	District of Columbia	14,744	0.8%

Source: Federal Bureau of Investigation
"Crime in the United States 1996" (Uniform Crime Reports, October 4, 1997)
*Revised figures. Violent crimes are offenses of murder, forcible rape, robbery and aggravated assault.

Percent Change in Number of Violent Crimes: 1995 to 1999

National Percent Change = 20.5% Decrease*

ALPHA ORDER

ALPHA ORDER

RANK ORDER

RANK	STATE	PERCENT CHANGE	RANK	STATE	PERCENT CHANGE
32	Alabama	(20.4)	1	Montana	22.3
24	Alaska	(16.0)	2	Nebraska	14.6
18	Arizona	(12.5)	3	Delaware	6.5
34	Arkansas	(21.1)	4	New Mexico	5.2
48	California	(31.9)	5	Pennsylvania	(2.2)
25	Colorado	(16.3)	6	Vermont	(2.3)
21	Connecticut	(14.7)	7	Kansas	(5.9)
3	Delaware	6.5	8	Tennessee	(6.0)
22	Florida	(14.9)	9	Utah	(8.5)
17	Georgia	(12.1)	10	Wyoming	(8.6)
33	Hawaii	(20.6)	11	South Carolina	(8.7)
27	Idaho	(18.1)	12	Virginia	(9.6)
41	Illinois	(24.6)	13	Texas	(9.7)
43	Indiana	(26.9)	14	Wisconsin	(10.4)
30	Iowa	(20.2)	15	North Carolina	(10.8)
7	Kansas	(5.9)	16	New Hampshire	(11.8)
23	Kentucky	(15.4)	17	Georgia	(12.1)
42	Louisiana	(26.8)	18	Arizona	(12.5)
20	Maine	(13.8)	19	Michigan	(13.7)
38	Maryland	(22.7)	20	Maine	(13.8)
28	Massachusetts	(18.5)	21	Connecticut	(14.7)
19	Michigan	(13.7)	22	Florida	(14.9)
31	Minnesota	(20.3)	23	Kentucky	(15.4)
44	Mississippi	(28.7)	24	Alaska	(16.0)
37	Missouri	(22.6)	25	Colorado	(16.3)
1	Montana	22.3	26	Washington	(17.4)
2	Nebraska	14.6	27	Idaho	(18.1)
44	Nevada	(28.7)	28	Massachusetts	(18.5)
16	New Hampshire	(11.8)	29	South Dakota	(18.9)
46	New Jersey	(29.6)	30	Iowa	(20.2)
4	New Mexico	5.2	31	Minnesota	(20.3)
47	New York	(29.8)	32	Alabama	(20.4)
15	North Carolina	(10.8)	33	Hawaii	(20.6)
39	North Dakota	(23.7)	34	Arkansas	(21.1)
49	Ohio	(33.8)	35	Oklahoma	(21.6)
35	Oklahoma	(21.6)	36	Rhode Island	(22.0)
40	Oregon	(24.2)	37	Missouri	(22.6)
5	Pennsylvania	(2.2)	38	Maryland	(22.7)
36	Rhode Island	(22.0)	39	North Dakota	(23.7)
11	South Carolina	(8.7)	40	Oregon	(24.2)
29	South Dakota	(18.9)	41	Illinois	(24.6)
8	Tennessee	(6.0)	42	Louisiana	(26.8)
13	Texas	(9.7)	43	Indiana	(26.9)
9	Utah	(8.5)	44	Mississippi	(28.7)
6	Vermont	(2.3)	44	Nevada	(28.7)
12	Virginia	(9.6)	46	New Jersey	(29.6)
26	Washington	(17.4)	47	New York	(29.8)
NA	West Virginia**	NA	48	California	(31.9)
14	Wisconsin	(10.4)	49	Ohio	(33.8)
10	Wyoming	(8.6)	NA	West Virginia**	NA
				District of Columbia	(42.7)

Source: Morgan Quitno Press using data from Federal Bureau of Investigation
"Crime in the United States" (Uniform Crime Reports, 1996 and 1999 editions)
*Violent crimes are offenses of murder, forcible rape, robbery and aggravated assault.
**Not comparable.

Violent Crime Rate in 1995

National Rate = 684.6 Violent Crimes per 100,000 Population*

ALPHA ORDER

RANK	STATE	RATE
21	Alabama	632.4
11	Alaska	770.9
13	Arizona	713.5
23	Arkansas	553.2
6	California	966.0
29	Colorado	440.2
32	Connecticut	405.9
12	Delaware	725.0
1	Florida	1,071.0
19	Georgia	657.1
41	Hawaii	295.6
40	Idaho	322.0
3	Illinois	996.1
24	Indiana	524.7
38	Iowa	354.4
31	Kansas	420.7
35	Kentucky	364.7
2	Louisiana	1,007.4
47	Maine	131.4
4	Maryland	986.9
15	Massachusetts	687.2
14	Michigan	687.8
37	Minnesota	356.1
26	Mississippi	502.8
18	Missouri	663.8
46	Montana	171.4
33	Nebraska	382.0
7	Nevada	945.2
49	New Hampshire	114.5
22	New Jersey	599.8
9	New Mexico	819.2
8	New York	841.9
20	North Carolina	646.4
50	North Dakota	86.7
28	Ohio	482.5
16	Oklahoma	664.1
25	Oregon	522.4
30	Pennsylvania	427.3
34	Rhode Island	368.0
5	South Carolina	981.9
45	South Dakota	207.5
10	Tennessee	771.5
17	Texas	663.9
39	Utah	328.8
48	Vermont	118.3
36	Virginia	361.5
27	Washington	484.3
44	West Virginia	210.2
42	Wisconsin	281.1
43	Wyoming	254.2

RANK ORDER

RANK	STATE	RATE
1	Florida	1,071.0
2	Louisiana	1,007.4
3	Illinois	996.1
4	Maryland	986.9
5	South Carolina	981.9
6	California	966.0
7	Nevada	945.2
8	New York	841.9
9	New Mexico	819.2
10	Tennessee	771.5
11	Alaska	770.9
12	Delaware	725.0
13	Arizona	713.5
14	Michigan	687.8
15	Massachusetts	687.2
16	Oklahoma	664.1
17	Texas	663.9
18	Missouri	663.8
19	Georgia	657.1
20	North Carolina	646.4
21	Alabama	632.4
22	New Jersey	599.8
23	Arkansas	553.2
24	Indiana	524.7
25	Oregon	522.4
26	Mississippi	502.8
27	Washington	484.3
28	Ohio	482.5
29	Colorado	440.2
30	Pennsylvania	427.3
31	Kansas	420.7
32	Connecticut	405.9
33	Nebraska	382.0
34	Rhode Island	368.0
35	Kentucky	364.7
36	Virginia	361.5
37	Minnesota	356.1
38	Iowa	354.4
39	Utah	328.8
40	Idaho	322.0
41	Hawaii	295.6
42	Wisconsin	281.1
43	Wyoming	254.2
44	West Virginia	210.2
45	South Dakota	207.5
46	Montana	171.4
47	Maine	131.4
48	Vermont	118.3
49	New Hampshire	114.5
50	North Dakota	86.7
	District of Columbia	2,661.4

Source: Federal Bureau of Investigation
  "Crime in the United States 1996" (Uniform Crime Reports, October 4, 1997)
*Revised figures. Violent crimes are offenses of murder, forcible rape, robbery and aggravated assault.

Percent Change in Violent Crime Rate: 1995 to 1999

National Percent Change = 23.4% Decrease*

RANK	STATE	PERCENT CHANGE	RANK	STATE	PERCENT CHANGE
30	Alabama	(22.5)	1	Montana	20.5
21	Alaska	(18.1)	2	Nebraska	12.6
32	Arizona	(22.7)	3	New Mexico	1.9
34	Arkansas	(23.1)	4	Delaware	1.2
48	California	(35.1)	5	Pennsylvania	(1.6)
31	Colorado	(22.6)	6	Vermont	(3.8)
14	Connecticut	(14.9)	7	Wyoming	(8.6)
4	Delaware	1.2	8	Kansas	(9.0)
25	Florida	(20.3)	9	Tennessee	(9.9)
22	Georgia	(18.7)	10	Wisconsin	(12.5)
26	Hawaii	(20.5)	11	Virginia	(12.9)
37	Idaho	(23.9)	12	South Carolina	(13.7)
40	Illinois	(26.5)	13	Maine	(14.6)
43	Indiana	(28.6)	14	Connecticut	(14.9)
27	Iowa	(21.0)	15	Texas	(15.6)
8	Kansas	(9.0)	16	New Hampshire	(15.7)
20	Kentucky	(17.6)	17	North Carolina	(16.1)
41	Louisiana	(27.3)	18	Utah	(16.2)
13	Maine	(14.6)	19	Michigan	(16.4)
39	Maryland	(24.7)	20	Kentucky	(17.6)
24	Massachusetts	(19.8)	21	Alaska	(18.1)
19	Michigan	(16.4)	22	Georgia	(18.7)
34	Minnesota	(23.1)	23	South Dakota	(19.3)
45	Mississippi	(30.5)	24	Massachusetts	(19.8)
38	Missouri	(24.6)	25	Florida	(20.3)
1	Montana	20.5	26	Hawaii	(20.5)
2	Nebraska	12.6	27	Iowa	(21.0)
49	Nevada	(39.7)	28	Rhode Island	(22.1)
16	New Hampshire	(15.7)	28	Washington	(22.1)
46	New Jersey	(31.3)	30	Alabama	(22.5)
3	New Mexico	1.9	31	Colorado	(22.6)
44	New York	(30.1)	32	Arizona	(22.7)
17	North Carolina	(16.1)	33	North Dakota	(22.8)
33	North Dakota	(22.8)	34	Arkansas	(23.1)
47	Ohio	(34.4)	34	Minnesota	(23.1)
36	Oklahoma	(23.5)	36	Oklahoma	(23.5)
42	Oregon	(28.2)	37	Idaho	(23.9)
5	Pennsylvania	(1.6)	38	Missouri	(24.6)
28	Rhode Island	(22.1)	39	Maryland	(24.7)
12	South Carolina	(13.7)	40	Illinois	(26.5)
23	South Dakota	(19.3)	41	Louisiana	(27.3)
9	Tennessee	(9.9)	42	Oregon	(28.2)
15	Texas	(15.6)	43	Indiana	(28.6)
18	Utah	(16.2)	44	New York	(30.1)
6	Vermont	(3.8)	45	Mississippi	(30.5)
11	Virginia	(12.9)	46	New Jersey	(31.3)
28	Washington	(22.1)	47	Ohio	(34.4)
NA	West Virginia**	NA	48	California	(35.1)
10	Wisconsin	(12.5)	49	Nevada	(39.7)
7	Wyoming	(8.6)	NA	West Virginia**	NA
				District of Columbia	(38.8)

Source: Morgan Quitno Press using data from Federal Bureau of Investigation
   "Crime in the United States" (Uniform Crime Reports, 1996 and 1999 editions)
*Violent crimes are offenses of murder, forcible rape, robbery and aggravated assault.
**Not comparable.

Murders in 1995

National Total = 21,606 Murders*

ALPHA ORDER

RANK	STATE	MURDERS	% of USA
15	Alabama	475	2.2%
38	Alaska	55	0.3%
18	Arizona	439	2.0%
25	Arkansas	259	1.2%
1	California	3,531	16.3%
28	Colorado	216	1.0%
32	Connecticut	150	0.7%
44	Delaware	25	0.1%
5	Florida	1,037	4.8%
9	Georgia	683	3.2%
37	Hawaii	56	0.3%
40	Idaho	48	0.2%
4	Illinois	1,221	5.7%
17	Indiana	466	2.2%
39	Iowa	51	0.2%
31	Kansas	159	0.7%
23	Kentucky	276	1.3%
8	Louisiana	740	3.4%
44	Maine	25	0.1%
12	Maryland	596	2.8%
27	Massachusetts	217	1.0%
6	Michigan	808	3.7%
29	Minnesota	182	0.8%
21	Mississippi	348	1.6%
16	Missouri	469	2.2%
42	Montana	35	0.2%
40	Nebraska	48	0.2%
30	Nevada	163	0.8%
46	New Hampshire	21	0.1%
19	New Jersey	409	1.9%
33	New Mexico	148	0.7%
3	New York	1,550	7.2%
10	North Carolina	677	3.1%
50	North Dakota	6	0.0%
11	Ohio	600	2.8%
20	Oklahoma	400	1.9%
34	Oregon	129	0.6%
7	Pennsylvania	755	3.5%
43	Rhode Island	33	0.2%
22	South Carolina	292	1.4%
47	South Dakota	13	0.1%
13	Tennessee	557	2.6%
2	Texas	1,693	7.8%
36	Utah	76	0.4%
47	Vermont	13	0.1%
14	Virginia	503	2.3%
24	Washington	275	1.3%
35	West Virginia	89	0.4%
26	Wisconsin	219	1.0%
49	Wyoming	10	0.0%

RANK ORDER

RANK	STATE	MURDERS	% of USA
1	California	3,531	16.3%
2	Texas	1,693	7.8%
3	New York	1,550	7.2%
4	Illinois	1,221	5.7%
5	Florida	1,037	4.8%
6	Michigan	808	3.7%
7	Pennsylvania	755	3.5%
8	Louisiana	740	3.4%
9	Georgia	683	3.2%
10	North Carolina	677	3.1%
11	Ohio	600	2.8%
12	Maryland	596	2.8%
13	Tennessee	557	2.6%
14	Virginia	503	2.3%
15	Alabama	475	2.2%
16	Missouri	469	2.2%
17	Indiana	466	2.2%
18	Arizona	439	2.0%
19	New Jersey	409	1.9%
20	Oklahoma	400	1.9%
21	Mississippi	348	1.6%
22	South Carolina	292	1.4%
23	Kentucky	276	1.3%
24	Washington	275	1.3%
25	Arkansas	259	1.2%
26	Wisconsin	219	1.0%
27	Massachusetts	217	1.0%
28	Colorado	216	1.0%
29	Minnesota	182	0.8%
30	Nevada	163	0.8%
31	Kansas	159	0.7%
32	Connecticut	150	0.7%
33	New Mexico	148	0.7%
34	Oregon	129	0.6%
35	West Virginia	89	0.4%
36	Utah	76	0.4%
37	Hawaii	56	0.3%
38	Alaska	55	0.3%
39	Iowa	51	0.2%
40	Idaho	48	0.2%
40	Nebraska	48	0.2%
42	Montana	35	0.2%
43	Rhode Island	33	0.2%
44	Delaware	25	0.1%
44	Maine	25	0.1%
46	New Hampshire	21	0.1%
47	South Dakota	13	0.1%
47	Vermont	13	0.1%
49	Wyoming	10	0.0%
50	North Dakota	6	0.0%
	District of Columbia	360	1.7%

Source: Federal Bureau of Investigation
   "Crime in the United States 1996" (Uniform Crime Reports, October 4, 1997)
*Revised figures. Includes nonnegligent manslaughter.

Percent Change in Number of Murders: 1995 to 1999

National Percent Change = 28.1% Decrease*

ALPHA ORDER

RANK	STATE	PERCENT CHANGE
33	Alabama	(27.4)
11	Alaska	(3.6)
15	Arizona	(12.5)
49	Arkansas	(44.8)
47	California	(43.2)
18	Colorado	(14.4)
35	Connecticut	(28.7)
12	Delaware	(4.0)
22	Florida	(17.2)
19	Georgia	(14.6)
25	Hawaii	(21.4)
50	Idaho	(47.9)
30	Illinois	(23.3)
21	Indiana	(16.1)
20	Iowa	(15.7)
10	Kansas	0.6
29	Kentucky	(23.2)
41	Louisiana	(36.8)
8	Maine	8.0
27	Maryland	(22.0)
48	Massachusetts	(43.8)
16	Michigan	(14.0)
32	Minnesota	(26.4)
43	Mississippi	(38.8)
31	Missouri	(23.5)
40	Montana	(34.3)
4	Nebraska	25.0
9	Nevada	1.2
17	New Hampshire	(14.3)
36	New Jersey	(29.8)
5	New Mexico	14.9
44	New York	(41.7)
24	North Carolina	(18.5)
1	North Dakota	66.7
39	Ohio	(33.8)
46	Oklahoma	(42.3)
38	Oregon	(31.8)
26	Pennsylvania	(21.6)
7	Rhode Island	9.1
14	South Carolina	(11.6)
2	South Dakota	38.5
36	Tennessee	(29.8)
34	Texas	(28.1)
45	Utah	(42.1)
3	Vermont	30.8
28	Virginia	(22.1)
42	Washington	(37.8)
13	West Virginia	(11.2)
23	Wisconsin	(18.3)
6	Wyoming	10.0

RANK ORDER

RANK	STATE	PERCENT CHANGE
1	North Dakota	66.7
2	South Dakota	38.5
3	Vermont	30.8
4	Nebraska	25.0
5	New Mexico	14.9
6	Wyoming	10.0
7	Rhode Island	9.1
8	Maine	8.0
9	Nevada	1.2
10	Kansas	0.6
11	Alaska	(3.6)
12	Delaware	(4.0)
13	West Virginia	(11.2)
14	South Carolina	(11.6)
15	Arizona	(12.5)
16	Michigan	(14.0)
17	New Hampshire	(14.3)
18	Colorado	(14.4)
19	Georgia	(14.6)
20	Iowa	(15.7)
21	Indiana	(16.1)
22	Florida	(17.2)
23	Wisconsin	(18.3)
24	North Carolina	(18.5)
25	Hawaii	(21.4)
26	Pennsylvania	(21.6)
27	Maryland	(22.0)
28	Virginia	(22.1)
29	Kentucky	(23.2)
30	Illinois	(23.3)
31	Missouri	(23.5)
32	Minnesota	(26.4)
33	Alabama	(27.4)
34	Texas	(28.1)
35	Connecticut	(28.7)
36	New Jersey	(29.8)
36	Tennessee	(29.8)
38	Oregon	(31.8)
39	Ohio	(33.8)
40	Montana	(34.3)
41	Louisiana	(36.8)
42	Washington	(37.8)
43	Mississippi	(38.8)
44	New York	(41.7)
45	Utah	(42.1)
46	Oklahoma	(42.3)
47	California	(43.2)
48	Massachusetts	(43.8)
49	Arkansas	(44.8)
50	Idaho	(47.9)
	District of Columbia	(33.1)

Source: Morgan Quitno Press using data from Federal Bureau of Investigation
"Crime in the United States" (Uniform Crime Reports, 1996 and 1999 editions)
*Includes nonnegligent manslaughter.

Murder Rate in 1995

National Rate = 8.2 Murders per 100,000 Population*

ALPHA ORDER

RANK	STATE	RATE
5	Alabama	11.2
14	Alaska	9.1
9	Arizona	10.4
9	Arkansas	10.4
5	California	11.2
27	Colorado	5.8
33	Connecticut	4.6
41	Delaware	3.5
23	Florida	7.3
12	Georgia	9.5
32	Hawaii	4.7
35	Idaho	4.1
11	Illinois	10.3
20	Indiana	8.0
47	Iowa	1.8
26	Kansas	6.2
24	Kentucky	7.2
1	Louisiana	17.0
46	Maine	2.0
4	Maryland	11.8
40	Massachusetts	3.6
18	Michigan	8.5
38	Minnesota	3.9
2	Mississippi	12.9
16	Missouri	8.8
37	Montana	4.0
43	Nebraska	2.9
7	Nevada	10.7
47	New Hampshire	1.8
29	New Jersey	5.1
16	New Mexico	8.8
18	New York	8.5
13	North Carolina	9.4
50	North Dakota	0.9
28	Ohio	5.4
3	Oklahoma	12.2
35	Oregon	4.1
25	Pennsylvania	6.3
42	Rhode Island	3.3
21	South Carolina	7.9
47	South Dakota	1.8
8	Tennessee	10.6
15	Texas	9.0
38	Utah	3.9
44	Vermont	2.2
22	Virginia	7.6
29	Washington	5.1
31	West Virginia	4.9
34	Wisconsin	4.3
45	Wyoming	2.1

RANK ORDER

RANK	STATE	RATE
1	Louisiana	17.0
2	Mississippi	12.9
3	Oklahoma	12.2
4	Maryland	11.8
5	Alabama	11.2
5	California	11.2
7	Nevada	10.7
8	Tennessee	10.6
9	Arizona	10.4
9	Arkansas	10.4
11	Illinois	10.3
12	Georgia	9.5
13	North Carolina	9.4
14	Alaska	9.1
15	Texas	9.0
16	Missouri	8.8
16	New Mexico	8.8
18	Michigan	8.5
18	New York	8.5
20	Indiana	8.0
21	South Carolina	7.9
22	Virginia	7.6
23	Florida	7.3
24	Kentucky	7.2
25	Pennsylvania	6.3
26	Kansas	6.2
27	Colorado	5.8
28	Ohio	5.4
29	New Jersey	5.1
29	Washington	5.1
31	West Virginia	4.9
32	Hawaii	4.7
33	Connecticut	4.6
34	Wisconsin	4.3
35	Idaho	4.1
35	Oregon	4.1
37	Montana	4.0
38	Minnesota	3.9
38	Utah	3.9
40	Massachusetts	3.6
41	Delaware	3.5
42	Rhode Island	3.3
43	Nebraska	2.9
44	Vermont	2.2
45	Wyoming	2.1
46	Maine	2.0
47	Iowa	1.8
47	New Hampshire	1.8
47	South Dakota	1.8
50	North Dakota	0.9
	District of Columbia	65.0

Source: Federal Bureau of Investigation
"Crime in the United States 1996" (Uniform Crime Reports, October 4, 1997)
*Revised figures. Includes nonnegligent manslaughter.

Percent Change in Murder Rate: 1995 to 1999

National Percent Change = 30.5% Decrease*

ALPHA ORDER

RANK ORDER

RANK	STATE	PERCENT CHANGE
34	Alabama	(29.5)
10	Alaska	(5.5)
25	Arizona	(23.1)
47	Arkansas	(46.2)
49	California	(46.4)
19	Colorado	(20.7)
33	Connecticut	(28.3)
11	Delaware	(8.6)
23	Florida	(21.9)
21	Georgia	(21.1)
22	Hawaii	(21.3)
50	Idaho	(51.2)
31	Illinois	(25.2)
17	Indiana	(17.5)
15	Iowa	(16.7)
9	Kansas	(3.2)
28	Kentucky	(25.0)
41	Louisiana	(37.1)
6	Maine	10.0
27	Maryland	(23.7)
46	Massachusetts	(44.4)
18	Michigan	(17.6)
32	Minnesota	(28.2)
42	Mississippi	(40.3)
28	Missouri	(25.0)
39	Montana	(35.0)
4	Nebraska	24.1
13	Nevada	(15.0)
15	New Hampshire	(16.7)
35	New Jersey	(31.4)
5	New Mexico	11.4
43	New York	(41.2)
26	North Carolina	(23.4)
1	North Dakota	77.8
40	Ohio	(35.2)
45	Oklahoma	(43.4)
38	Oregon	(34.1)
24	Pennsylvania	(22.2)
8	Rhode Island	9.1
14	South Carolina	(16.5)
2	South Dakota	38.9
37	Tennessee	(33.0)
36	Texas	(32.2)
47	Utah	(46.2)
3	Vermont	31.8
28	Virginia	(25.0)
43	Washington	(41.2)
12	West Virginia	(10.2)
20	Wisconsin	(20.9)
7	Wyoming	9.5

RANK	STATE	PERCENT CHANGE
1	North Dakota	77.8
2	South Dakota	38.9
3	Vermont	31.8
4	Nebraska	24.1
5	New Mexico	11.4
6	Maine	10.0
7	Wyoming	9.5
8	Rhode Island	9.1
9	Kansas	(3.2)
10	Alaska	(5.5)
11	Delaware	(8.6)
12	West Virginia	(10.2)
13	Nevada	(15.0)
14	South Carolina	(16.5)
15	Iowa	(16.7)
15	New Hampshire	(16.7)
17	Indiana	(17.5)
18	Michigan	(17.6)
19	Colorado	(20.7)
20	Wisconsin	(20.9)
21	Georgia	(21.1)
22	Hawaii	(21.3)
23	Florida	(21.9)
24	Pennsylvania	(22.2)
25	Arizona	(23.1)
26	North Carolina	(23.4)
27	Maryland	(23.7)
28	Kentucky	(25.0)
28	Missouri	(25.0)
28	Virginia	(25.0)
31	Illinois	(25.2)
32	Minnesota	(28.2)
33	Connecticut	(28.3)
34	Alabama	(29.5)
35	New Jersey	(31.4)
36	Texas	(32.2)
37	Tennessee	(33.0)
38	Oregon	(34.1)
39	Montana	(35.0)
40	Ohio	(35.2)
41	Louisiana	(37.1)
42	Mississippi	(40.3)
43	New York	(41.2)
43	Washington	(41.2)
45	Oklahoma	(43.4)
46	Massachusetts	(44.4)
47	Arkansas	(46.2)
47	Utah	(46.2)
49	California	(46.4)
50	Idaho	(51.2)

| | District of Columbia | (28.6) |

Source: Morgan Quitno Press using data from Federal Bureau of Investigation
"Crime in the United States" (Uniform Crime Reports, 1996 and 1999 editions)
*Includes nonnegligent manslaughter.

Rapes in 1995

National Total = 97,470 Rapes*

ALPHA ORDER

RANK ORDER

RANK	STATE	RAPES	% of USA
25	Alabama	1,350	1.4%
38	Alaska	485	0.5%
24	Arizona	1,418	1.5%
33	Arkansas	925	0.9%
1	California	10,554	10.8%
22	Colorado	1,480	1.5%
35	Connecticut	776	0.8%
37	Delaware	575	0.6%
3	Florida	6,887	7.1%
11	Georgia	2,539	2.6%
40	Hawaii	336	0.3%
42	Idaho	330	0.3%
6	Illinois	4,313	4.4%
15	Indiana	1,930	2.0%
36	Iowa	619	0.6%
31	Kansas	938	1.0%
27	Kentucky	1,231	1.3%
17	Louisiana	1,855	1.9%
46	Maine	265	0.3%
14	Maryland	2,130	2.2%
19	Massachusetts	1,759	1.8%
4	Michigan	5,917	6.1%
10	Minnesota	2,593	2.7%
29	Mississippi	1,054	1.1%
21	Missouri	1,711	1.8%
47	Montana	231	0.2%
43	Nebraska	317	0.3%
32	Nevada	937	1.0%
41	New Hampshire	333	0.3%
16	New Jersey	1,927	2.0%
30	New Mexico	954	1.0%
7	New York	4,290	4.4%
13	North Carolina	2,320	2.4%
50	North Dakota	146	0.1%
5	Ohio	4,835	5.0%
23	Oklahoma	1,461	1.5%
26	Oregon	1,309	1.3%
9	Pennsylvania	3,046	3.1%
45	Rhode Island	267	0.3%
20	South Carolina	1,737	1.8%
44	South Dakota	299	0.3%
12	Tennessee	2,477	2.5%
2	Texas	8,563	8.8%
34	Utah	834	0.9%
48	Vermont	165	0.2%
18	Virginia	1,799	1.8%
8	Washington	3,214	3.3%
39	West Virginia	388	0.4%
28	Wisconsin	1,194	1.2%
48	Wyoming	165	0.2%

RANK	STATE	RAPES	% of USA
1	California	10,554	10.8%
2	Texas	8,563	8.8%
3	Florida	6,887	7.1%
4	Michigan	5,917	6.1%
5	Ohio	4,835	5.0%
6	Illinois	4,313	4.4%
7	New York	4,290	4.4%
8	Washington	3,214	3.3%
9	Pennsylvania	3,046	3.1%
10	Minnesota	2,593	2.7%
11	Georgia	2,539	2.6%
12	Tennessee	2,477	2.5%
13	North Carolina	2,320	2.4%
14	Maryland	2,130	2.2%
15	Indiana	1,930	2.0%
16	New Jersey	1,927	2.0%
17	Louisiana	1,855	1.9%
18	Virginia	1,799	1.8%
19	Massachusetts	1,759	1.8%
20	South Carolina	1,737	1.8%
21	Missouri	1,711	1.8%
22	Colorado	1,480	1.5%
23	Oklahoma	1,461	1.5%
24	Arizona	1,418	1.5%
25	Alabama	1,350	1.4%
26	Oregon	1,309	1.3%
27	Kentucky	1,231	1.3%
28	Wisconsin	1,194	1.2%
29	Mississippi	1,054	1.1%
30	New Mexico	954	1.0%
31	Kansas	938	1.0%
32	Nevada	937	1.0%
33	Arkansas	925	0.9%
34	Utah	834	0.9%
35	Connecticut	776	0.8%
36	Iowa	619	0.6%
37	Delaware	575	0.6%
38	Alaska	485	0.5%
39	West Virginia	388	0.4%
40	Hawaii	336	0.3%
41	New Hampshire	333	0.3%
42	Idaho	330	0.3%
43	Nebraska	317	0.3%
44	South Dakota	299	0.3%
45	Rhode Island	267	0.3%
46	Maine	265	0.3%
47	Montana	231	0.2%
48	Vermont	165	0.2%
48	Wyoming	165	0.2%
50	North Dakota	146	0.1%
	District of Columbia	292	0.3%

Source: Federal Bureau of Investigation
   "Crime in the United States 1996" (Uniform Crime Reports, October 4, 1997)
*Revised figures. Forcible rape is the carnal knowledge of a female forcibly and against her will. Assaults or attempts to commit rape by force or threat of force are included. However, statutory rape without force and other sex offenses are excluded.

Percent Change in Number of Rapes: 1995 to 1999

National Percent Change = 8.6% Decrease*

ALPHA ORDER

RANK	STATE	PERCENT CHANGE
8	Alabama	12.1
12	Alaska	6.6
18	Arizona	(2.5)
48	Arkansas	(23.2)
33	California	(11.3)
6	Colorado	13.4
38	Connecticut	(15.7)
28	Delaware	(8.0)
15	Florida	1.5
30	Georgia	(8.7)
13	Hawaii	5.4
3	Idaho	26.4
22	Illinois	(3.9)
41	Indiana	(16.7)
4	Iowa	26.0
5	Kansas	13.5
37	Kentucky	(15.5)
47	Louisiana	(21.9)
31	Maine	(9.8)
50	Maryland	(27.2)
24	Massachusetts	(5.5)
45	Michigan	(18.0)
46	Minnesota	(21.4)
9	Mississippi	9.7
40	Missouri	(15.9)
10	Montana	8.2
2	Nebraska	30.6
16	Nevada	0.6
14	New Hampshire	3.6
49	New Jersey	(26.9)
17	New Mexico	(1.0)
42	New York	(16.9)
27	North Carolina	(7.1)
20	North Dakota	(2.7)
36	Ohio	(14.6)
25	Oklahoma	(5.9)
26	Oregon	(6.9)
11	Pennsylvania	7.6
1	Rhode Island	46.4
29	South Carolina	(8.6)
7	South Dakota	12.4
18	Tennessee	(2.5)
32	Texas	(11.1)
21	Utah	(3.4)
44	Vermont	(17.6)
23	Virginia	(4.4)
38	Washington	(15.7)
35	West Virginia	(13.1)
34	Wisconsin	(11.6)
43	Wyoming	(17.0)

RANK ORDER

RANK	STATE	PERCENT CHANGE
1	Rhode Island	46.4
2	Nebraska	30.6
3	Idaho	26.4
4	Iowa	26.0
5	Kansas	13.5
6	Colorado	13.4
7	South Dakota	12.4
8	Alabama	12.1
9	Mississippi	9.7
10	Montana	8.2
11	Pennsylvania	7.6
12	Alaska	6.6
13	Hawaii	5.4
14	New Hampshire	3.6
15	Florida	1.5
16	Nevada	0.6
17	New Mexico	(1.0)
18	Arizona	(2.5)
18	Tennessee	(2.5)
20	North Dakota	(2.7)
21	Utah	(3.4)
22	Illinois	(3.9)
23	Virginia	(4.4)
24	Massachusetts	(5.5)
25	Oklahoma	(5.9)
26	Oregon	(6.9)
27	North Carolina	(7.1)
28	Delaware	(8.0)
29	South Carolina	(8.6)
30	Georgia	(8.7)
31	Maine	(9.8)
32	Texas	(11.1)
33	California	(11.3)
34	Wisconsin	(11.6)
35	West Virginia	(13.1)
36	Ohio	(14.6)
37	Kentucky	(15.5)
38	Connecticut	(15.7)
38	Washington	(15.7)
40	Missouri	(15.9)
41	Indiana	(16.7)
42	New York	(16.9)
43	Wyoming	(17.0)
44	Vermont	(17.6)
45	Michigan	(18.0)
46	Minnesota	(21.4)
47	Louisiana	(21.9)
48	Arkansas	(23.2)
49	New Jersey	(26.9)
50	Maryland	(27.2)
	District of Columbia	(15.1)

Source: Morgan Quitno Press using data from Federal Bureau of Investigation
   "Crime in the United States" (Uniform Crime Reports, 1996 and 1999 editions)
*Forcible rape is the carnal knowledge of a female forcibly and against her will. Assaults or attempts to commit rape by force or threat of force are included. However, statutory rape without force and other sex offenses are excluded.

Rape Rate in 1995

National Rate = 37.1 Rapes per 100,000 Population*

ALPHA ORDER

RANK	STATE	RATE
32	Alabama	31.7
1	Alaska	80.3
26	Arizona	33.6
21	Arkansas	37.2
27	California	33.4
19	Colorado	39.5
43	Connecticut	23.7
2	Delaware	80.2
8	Florida	48.6
24	Georgia	35.3
36	Hawaii	28.3
35	Idaho	28.4
23	Illinois	36.5
28	Indiana	33.3
47	Iowa	21.8
22	Kansas	36.6
31	Kentucky	31.9
14	Louisiana	42.7
48	Maine	21.4
16	Maryland	42.2
33	Massachusetts	29.0
3	Michigan	62.0
7	Minnesota	56.2
20	Mississippi	39.1
30	Missouri	32.1
40	Montana	26.6
50	Nebraska	19.4
4	Nevada	61.2
33	New Hampshire	29.0
42	New Jersey	24.3
6	New Mexico	56.6
43	New York	23.7
29	North Carolina	32.2
46	North Dakota	22.8
13	Ohio	43.4
12	Oklahoma	44.6
17	Oregon	41.7
41	Pennsylvania	25.2
39	Rhode Island	27.0
9	South Carolina	47.3
18	South Dakota	41.0
10	Tennessee	47.1
11	Texas	45.7
14	Utah	42.7
37	Vermont	28.2
38	Virginia	27.2
5	Washington	59.2
49	West Virginia	21.2
45	Wisconsin	23.3
25	Wyoming	34.4

RANK ORDER

RANK	STATE	RATE
1	Alaska	80.3
2	Delaware	80.2
3	Michigan	62.0
4	Nevada	61.2
5	Washington	59.2
6	New Mexico	56.6
7	Minnesota	56.2
8	Florida	48.6
9	South Carolina	47.3
10	Tennessee	47.1
11	Texas	45.7
12	Oklahoma	44.6
13	Ohio	43.4
14	Louisiana	42.7
14	Utah	42.7
16	Maryland	42.2
17	Oregon	41.7
18	South Dakota	41.0
19	Colorado	39.5
20	Mississippi	39.1
21	Arkansas	37.2
22	Kansas	36.6
23	Illinois	36.5
24	Georgia	35.3
25	Wyoming	34.4
26	Arizona	33.6
27	California	33.4
28	Indiana	33.3
29	North Carolina	32.2
30	Missouri	32.1
31	Kentucky	31.9
32	Alabama	31.7
33	Massachusetts	29.0
33	New Hampshire	29.0
35	Idaho	28.4
36	Hawaii	28.3
37	Vermont	28.2
38	Virginia	27.2
39	Rhode Island	27.0
40	Montana	26.6
41	Pennsylvania	25.2
42	New Jersey	24.3
43	Connecticut	23.7
43	New York	23.7
45	Wisconsin	23.3
46	North Dakota	22.8
47	Iowa	21.8
48	Maine	21.4
49	West Virginia	21.2
50	Nebraska	19.4
	District of Columbia	52.7

Source: Federal Bureau of Investigation
"Crime in the United States 1996" (Uniform Crime Reports, October 4, 1997)
*Revised figures. Forcible rape is the carnal knowledge of a female forcibly and against her will. Assaults or attempts to commit rape by force or threat of force are included. However, statutory rape without force and other sex offenses are excluded.

Percent Change in Rape Rate: 1995 to 1999

National Percent Change = 11.9% Decrease*

ALPHA ORDER

RANK	STATE	PERCENT CHANGE
7	Alabama	9.1
13	Alaska	4.0
31	Arizona	(14.0)
48	Arkansas	(25.3)
34	California	(15.6)
12	Colorado	4.8
36	Connecticut	(16.0)
28	Delaware	(12.5)
17	Florida	(4.7)
34	Georgia	(15.6)
11	Hawaii	5.7
4	Idaho	17.3
18	Illinois	(6.3)
43	Indiana	(18.9)
3	Iowa	24.8
6	Kansas	9.6
40	Kentucky	(17.6)
46	Louisiana	(22.5)
23	Maine	(10.7)
50	Maryland	(28.9)
20	Massachusetts	(7.2)
45	Michigan	(20.6)
47	Minnesota	(24.0)
9	Mississippi	6.6
41	Missouri	(18.1)
10	Montana	6.4
2	Nebraska	27.8
32	Nevada	(14.9)
14	New Hampshire	(1.0)
49	New Jersey	(28.8)
16	New Mexico	(4.1)
39	New York	(17.3)
27	North Carolina	(12.4)
15	North Dakota	(1.8)
33	Ohio	(15.4)
22	Oklahoma	(8.3)
25	Oregon	(11.8)
8	Pennsylvania	8.3
1	Rhode Island	46.3
29	South Carolina	(13.7)
5	South Dakota	11.7
19	Tennessee	(6.6)
37	Texas	(16.8)
24	Utah	(11.5)
42	Vermont	(18.8)
21	Virginia	(8.1)
44	Washington	(20.4)
26	West Virginia	(12.3)
29	Wisconsin	(13.7)
38	Wyoming	(17.2)

RANK ORDER

RANK	STATE	PERCENT CHANGE
1	Rhode Island	46.3
2	Nebraska	27.8
3	Iowa	24.8
4	Idaho	17.3
5	South Dakota	11.7
6	Kansas	9.6
7	Alabama	9.1
8	Pennsylvania	8.3
9	Mississippi	6.6
10	Montana	6.4
11	Hawaii	5.7
12	Colorado	4.8
13	Alaska	4.0
14	New Hampshire	(1.0)
15	North Dakota	(1.8)
16	New Mexico	(4.1)
17	Florida	(4.7)
18	Illinois	(6.3)
19	Tennessee	(6.6)
20	Massachusetts	(7.2)
21	Virginia	(8.1)
22	Oklahoma	(8.3)
23	Maine	(10.7)
24	Utah	(11.5)
25	Oregon	(11.8)
26	West Virginia	(12.3)
27	North Carolina	(12.4)
28	Delaware	(12.5)
29	South Carolina	(13.7)
29	Wisconsin	(13.7)
31	Arizona	(14.0)
32	Nevada	(14.9)
33	Ohio	(15.4)
34	California	(15.6)
34	Georgia	(15.6)
36	Connecticut	(16.0)
37	Texas	(16.8)
38	Wyoming	(17.2)
39	New York	(17.3)
40	Kentucky	(17.6)
41	Missouri	(18.1)
42	Vermont	(18.8)
43	Indiana	(18.9)
44	Washington	(20.4)
45	Michigan	(20.6)
46	Louisiana	(22.5)
47	Minnesota	(24.0)
48	Arkansas	(25.3)
49	New Jersey	(28.8)
50	Maryland	(28.9)
	District of Columbia	(9.3)

Source: Morgan Quitno Press using data from Federal Bureau of Investigation
"Crime in the United States" (Uniform Crime Reports, 1996 and 1999 editions)
*Forcible rape is the carnal knowledge of a female forcibly and against her will. Assaults or attempts to commit rape by force or threat of force are included. However, statutory rape without force and other sex offenses are excluded.

Robberies in 1995

National Total = 580,509 Robberies*

RANK	**STATE**	**ROBBERIES**	**% of USA**		**RANK**	**STATE**	**ROBBERIES**	**% of USA**

RANK	STATE	ROBBERIES	% of USA	RANK	STATE	ROBBERIES	% of USA
18	Alabama	7,900	1.4%	1	California	104,611	18.0%
40	Alaska	937	0.2%	2	New York	72,492	12.5%
20	Arizona	7,329	1.3%	3	Florida	42,485	7.3%
32	Arkansas	3,122	0.5%	4	Illinois	39,139	6.7%
1	California	104,611	18.0%	5	Texas	33,667	5.8%
30	Colorado	3,604	0.6%	6	Pennsylvania	22,858	3.9%
25	Connecticut	5,345	0.9%	7	New Jersey	22,486	3.9%
37	Delaware	1,425	0.2%	8	Maryland	21,334	3.7%
3	Florida	42,485	7.3%	9	Ohio	19,931	3.4%
11	Georgia	14,777	2.5%	10	Michigan	17,885	3.1%
35	Hawaii	1,553	0.3%	11	Georgia	14,777	2.5%
45	Idaho	279	0.0%	12	North Carolina	12,896	2.2%
4	Illinois	39,139	6.7%	13	Tennessee	11,732	2.0%
19	Indiana	7,844	1.4%	14	Louisiana	11,662	2.0%
36	Iowa	1,507	0.3%	15	Missouri	10,863	1.9%
33	Kansas	2,775	0.5%	16	Massachusetts	9,137	1.6%
28	Kentucky	4,001	0.7%	17	Virginia	8,718	1.5%
14	Louisiana	11,662	2.0%	18	Alabama	7,900	1.4%
43	Maine	334	0.1%	19	Indiana	7,844	1.4%
8	Maryland	21,334	3.7%	20	Arizona	7,329	1.3%
16	Massachusetts	9,137	1.6%	21	Washington	7,209	1.2%
10	Michigan	17,885	3.1%	22	South Carolina	6,461	1.1%
23	Minnesota	5,702	1.0%	23	Minnesota	5,702	1.0%
31	Mississippi	3,530	0.6%	24	Wisconsin	5,384	0.9%
15	Missouri	10,863	1.9%	25	Connecticut	5,345	0.9%
46	Montana	253	0.0%	26	Nevada	4,966	0.9%
39	Nebraska	1,067	0.2%	27	Oregon	4,332	0.7%
26	Nevada	4,966	0.9%	28	Kentucky	4,001	0.7%
44	New Hampshire	314	0.1%	29	Oklahoma	3,788	0.7%
7	New Jersey	22,486	3.9%	30	Colorado	3,604	0.6%
34	New Mexico	2,604	0.4%	31	Mississippi	3,530	0.6%
2	New York	72,492	12.5%	32	Arkansas	3,122	0.5%
12	North Carolina	12,896	2.2%	33	Kansas	2,775	0.5%
49	North Dakota	64	0.0%	34	New Mexico	2,604	0.4%
9	Ohio	19,931	3.4%	35	Hawaii	1,553	0.3%
29	Oklahoma	3,788	0.7%	36	Iowa	1,507	0.3%
27	Oregon	4,332	0.7%	37	Delaware	1,425	0.2%
6	Pennsylvania	22,858	3.9%	38	Utah	1,309	0.2%
41	Rhode Island	914	0.2%	39	Nebraska	1,067	0.2%
22	South Carolina	6,461	1.1%	40	Alaska	937	0.2%
47	South Dakota	189	0.0%	41	Rhode Island	914	0.2%
13	Tennessee	11,732	2.0%	42	West Virginia	781	0.1%
5	Texas	33,667	5.8%	43	Maine	334	0.1%
38	Utah	1,309	0.2%	44	New Hampshire	314	0.1%
49	Vermont	64	0.0%	45	Idaho	279	0.0%
17	Virginia	8,718	1.5%	46	Montana	253	0.0%
21	Washington	7,209	1.2%	47	South Dakota	189	0.0%
42	West Virginia	781	0.1%	48	Wyoming	86	0.0%
24	Wisconsin	5,384	0.9%	49	North Dakota	64	0.0%
48	Wyoming	86	0.0%	49	Vermont	64	0.0%
					District of Columbia	6,864	1.2%

Source: Federal Bureau of Investigation
"Crime in the United States 1996" (Uniform Crime Reports, October 4, 1997)
*Revised figures. Robbery is the taking or attempting to take anything of value by force or threat of force.

Percent Change in Number of Robberies: 1995 to 1999

National Percent Change = 29.4% Decrease*

RANK	STATE	PERCENT CHANGE
39	Alabama	(32.9)
47	Alaska	(39.6)
4	Arizona	(0.6)
44	Arkansas	(35.2)
49	California	(42.6)
16	Colorado	(15.2)
28	Connecticut	(24.2)
2	Delaware	4.7
29	Florida	(24.8)
10	Georgia	(12.3)
38	Hawaii	(32.8)
24	Idaho	(20.1)
37	Illinois	(32.0)
19	Indiana	(17.2)
35	Iowa	(30.3)
30	Kansas	(26.2)
26	Kentucky	(20.8)
42	Louisiana	(34.9)
33	Maine	(27.2)
45	Maryland	(36.1)
43	Massachusetts	(35.1)
27	Michigan	(21.1)
36	Minnesota	(31.3)
11	Mississippi	(12.4)
41	Missouri	(34.2)
7	Montana	(9.9)
1	Nebraska	18.5
16	Nevada	(15.2)
21	New Hampshire	(18.2)
46	New Jersey	(36.7)
5	New Mexico	(1.0)
47	New York	(39.6)
6	North Carolina	(6.3)
12	North Dakota	(12.5)
34	Ohio	(27.7)
31	Oklahoma	(26.5)
40	Oregon	(34.0)
22	Pennsylvania	(18.3)
14	Rhode Island	(13.8)
8	South Carolina	(10.8)
50	South Dakota	(45.5)
32	Tennessee	(26.7)
13	Texas	(12.7)
9	Utah	(11.5)
3	Vermont	1.6
25	Virginia	(20.3)
23	Washington	(19.4)
18	West Virginia	(15.4)
20	Wisconsin	(17.4)
15	Wyoming	(14.0)

RANK	STATE	PERCENT CHANGE
1	Nebraska	18.5
2	Delaware	4.7
3	Vermont	1.6
4	Arizona	(0.6)
5	New Mexico	(1.0)
6	North Carolina	(6.3)
7	Montana	(9.9)
8	South Carolina	(10.8)
9	Utah	(11.5)
10	Georgia	(12.3)
11	Mississippi	(12.4)
12	North Dakota	(12.5)
13	Texas	(12.7)
14	Rhode Island	(13.8)
15	Wyoming	(14.0)
16	Colorado	(15.2)
16	Nevada	(15.2)
18	West Virginia	(15.4)
19	Indiana	(17.2)
20	Wisconsin	(17.4)
21	New Hampshire	(18.2)
22	Pennsylvania	(18.3)
23	Washington	(19.4)
24	Idaho	(20.1)
25	Virginia	(20.3)
26	Kentucky	(20.8)
27	Michigan	(21.1)
28	Connecticut	(24.2)
29	Florida	(24.8)
30	Kansas	(26.2)
31	Oklahoma	(26.5)
32	Tennessee	(26.7)
33	Maine	(27.2)
34	Ohio	(27.7)
35	Iowa	(30.3)
36	Minnesota	(31.3)
37	Illinois	(32.0)
38	Hawaii	(32.8)
39	Alabama	(32.9)
40	Oregon	(34.0)
41	Missouri	(34.2)
42	Louisiana	(34.9)
43	Massachusetts	(35.1)
44	Arkansas	(35.2)
45	Maryland	(36.1)
46	New Jersey	(36.7)
47	Alaska	(39.6)
47	New York	(39.6)
49	California	(42.6)
50	South Dakota	(45.5)
	District of Columbia	(51.3)

Source: Morgan Quitno Press using data from Federal Bureau of Investigation
  "Crime in the United States" (Uniform Crime Reports, 1996 and 1999 editions)
*Robbery is the taking or attempting to take anything of value by force or threat of force.

Robbery Rate in 1995

National Rate = 220.9 Robberies per 100,000 Population*

ALPHA ORDER				RANK ORDER		
RANK	STATE	RATE		RANK	STATE	RATE
15	Alabama	185.8		1	Maryland	423.1
22	Alaska	155.1		2	New York	399.7
20	Arizona	173.8		3	California	331.2
31	Arkansas	125.7		4	Illinois	330.8
3	California	331.2		5	Nevada	324.6
37	Colorado	96.2		6	Florida	299.9
21	Connecticut	163.2		7	New Jersey	283.0
12	Delaware	198.7		8	Louisiana	268.6
6	Florida	299.9		9	Tennessee	223.2
10	Georgia	205.2		10	Georgia	205.2
30	Hawaii	130.8		11	Missouri	204.0
47	Idaho	24.0		12	Delaware	198.7
4	Illinois	330.8		13	Pennsylvania	189.3
26	Indiana	135.2		14	Michigan	187.3
41	Iowa	53.0		15	Alabama	185.8
34	Kansas	108.2		16	Texas	179.8
36	Kentucky	103.7		17	North Carolina	179.2
8	Louisiana	268.6		18	Ohio	178.7
45	Maine	26.9		19	South Carolina	175.9
1	Maryland	423.1		20	Arizona	173.8
24	Massachusetts	150.4		21	Connecticut	163.2
14	Michigan	187.3		22	Alaska	155.1
32	Minnesota	123.7		23	New Mexico	154.5
29	Mississippi	130.9		24	Massachusetts	150.4
11	Missouri	204.0		25	Oregon	137.9
43	Montana	29.1		26	Indiana	135.2
40	Nebraska	65.2		27	Washington	132.7
5	Nevada	324.6		28	Virginia	131.7
44	New Hampshire	27.4		29	Mississippi	130.9
7	New Jersey	283.0		30	Hawaii	130.8
23	New Mexico	154.5		31	Arkansas	125.7
2	New York	399.7		32	Minnesota	123.7
17	North Carolina	179.2		33	Oklahoma	115.6
50	North Dakota	10.0		34	Kansas	108.2
18	Ohio	178.7		35	Wisconsin	105.1
33	Oklahoma	115.6		36	Kentucky	103.7
25	Oregon	137.9		37	Colorado	96.2
13	Pennsylvania	189.3		38	Rhode Island	92.3
38	Rhode Island	92.3		39	Utah	67.1
19	South Carolina	175.9		40	Nebraska	65.2
46	South Dakota	25.9		41	Iowa	53.0
9	Tennessee	223.2		42	West Virginia	42.7
16	Texas	179.8		43	Montana	29.1
39	Utah	67.1		44	New Hampshire	27.4
49	Vermont	10.9		45	Maine	26.9
28	Virginia	131.7		46	South Dakota	25.9
27	Washington	132.7		47	Idaho	24.0
42	West Virginia	42.7		48	Wyoming	17.9
35	Wisconsin	105.1		49	Vermont	10.9
48	Wyoming	17.9		50	North Dakota	10.0
					District of Columbia	1,239.0

Source: Federal Bureau of Investigation
"Crime in the United States 1996" (Uniform Crime Reports, October 4, 1997)
*Revised figures. Robbery is the taking or attempting to take anything of value by force or threat of force.

Percent Change in Robbery Rate: 1995 to 1999

National Percent Change = 32.0% Decrease*

ALPHA ORDER

RANK	STATE	PERCENT CHANGE
39	Alabama	(34.8)
48	Alaska	(41.1)
8	Arizona	(12.3)
43	Arkansas	(36.9)
49	California	(45.3)
20	Colorado	(21.7)
26	Connecticut	(24.3)
3	Delaware	(0.4)
33	Florida	(29.4)
16	Georgia	(18.9)
36	Hawaii	(32.6)
27	Idaho	(25.8)
37	Illinois	(33.7)
18	Indiana	(19.2)
35	Iowa	(30.9)
32	Kansas	(28.7)
22	Kentucky	(22.9)
40	Louisiana	(35.4)
28	Maine	(27.9)
45	Maryland	(37.7)
42	Massachusetts	(36.2)
24	Michigan	(23.7)
37	Minnesota	(33.7)
12	Mississippi	(14.7)
41	Missouri	(35.9)
5	Montana	(11.3)
1	Nebraska	16.4
29	Nevada	(28.3)
21	New Hampshire	(21.9)
46	New Jersey	(38.2)
4	New Mexico	(4.1)
47	New York	(39.8)
6	North Carolina	(11.8)
7	North Dakota	(12.0)
31	Ohio	(28.4)
29	Oklahoma	(28.3)
44	Oregon	(37.5)
14	Pennsylvania	(17.7)
9	Rhode Island	(13.9)
13	South Carolina	(15.7)
50	South Dakota	(45.6)
34	Tennessee	(29.7)
15	Texas	(18.4)
16	Utah	(18.9)
2	Vermont	0.0
23	Virginia	(23.2)
25	Washington	(24.0)
11	West Virginia	(14.3)
19	Wisconsin	(19.4)
10	Wyoming	(14.0)

RANK ORDER

RANK	STATE	PERCENT CHANGE
1	Nebraska	16.4
2	Vermont	0.0
3	Delaware	(0.4)
4	New Mexico	(4.1)
5	Montana	(11.3)
6	North Carolina	(11.8)
7	North Dakota	(12.0)
8	Arizona	(12.3)
9	Rhode Island	(13.9)
10	Wyoming	(14.0)
11	West Virginia	(14.3)
12	Mississippi	(14.7)
13	South Carolina	(15.7)
14	Pennsylvania	(17.7)
15	Texas	(18.4)
16	Georgia	(18.9)
16	Utah	(18.9)
18	Indiana	(19.2)
19	Wisconsin	(19.4)
20	Colorado	(21.7)
21	New Hampshire	(21.9)
22	Kentucky	(22.9)
23	Virginia	(23.2)
24	Michigan	(23.7)
25	Washington	(24.0)
26	Connecticut	(24.3)
27	Idaho	(25.8)
28	Maine	(27.9)
29	Nevada	(28.3)
29	Oklahoma	(28.3)
31	Ohio	(28.4)
32	Kansas	(28.7)
33	Florida	(29.4)
34	Tennessee	(29.7)
35	Iowa	(30.9)
36	Hawaii	(32.6)
37	Illinois	(33.7)
37	Minnesota	(33.7)
39	Alabama	(34.8)
40	Louisiana	(35.4)
41	Missouri	(35.9)
42	Massachusetts	(36.2)
43	Arkansas	(36.9)
44	Oregon	(37.5)
45	Maryland	(37.7)
46	New Jersey	(38.2)
47	New York	(39.8)
48	Alaska	(41.1)
49	California	(45.3)
50	South Dakota	(45.6)

District of Columbia (48.0)

Source: Morgan Quitno Press using data from Federal Bureau of Investigation
   "Crime in the United States" (Uniform Crime Reports, 1996 and 1999 editions)
*Robbery is the taking or attempting to take anything of value by force or threat of force.

Aggravated Assaults in 1995

National Total = 1,099,207 Aggravated Assaults*

RANK	STATE	ASSAULTS	% of USA
20	Alabama	17,169	1.6%
38	Alaska	3,179	0.3%
18	Arizona	20,909	1.9%
27	Arkansas	9,435	0.9%
1	California	186,458	17.0%
24	Colorado	11,194	1.0%
34	Connecticut	7,022	0.6%
39	Delaware	3,173	0.3%
2	Florida	101,302	9.2%
10	Georgia	29,318	2.7%
43	Hawaii	1,564	0.1%
40	Idaho	3,088	0.3%
5	Illinois	73,163	6.7%
19	Indiana	20,211	1.8%
32	Iowa	7,894	0.7%
35	Kansas	6,920	0.6%
29	Kentucky	8,571	0.8%
9	Louisiana	29,484	2.7%
45	Maine	1,007	0.1%
14	Maryland	25,697	2.3%
7	Massachusetts	30,626	2.8%
6	Michigan	41,070	3.7%
31	Minnesota	7,939	0.7%
28	Mississippi	8,628	0.8%
17	Missouri	22,296	2.0%
46	Montana	972	0.1%
36	Nebraska	4,821	0.4%
30	Nevada	8,395	0.8%
48	New Hampshire	646	0.1%
16	New Jersey	22,830	2.1%
26	New Mexico	10,098	0.9%
4	New York	74,351	6.8%
8	North Carolina	30,615	2.8%
50	North Dakota	340	0.0%
11	Ohio	28,433	2.6%
21	Oklahoma	16,121	1.5%
25	Oregon	10,638	1.0%
15	Pennsylvania	24,927	2.3%
42	Rhode Island	2,429	0.2%
12	South Carolina	27,577	2.5%
44	South Dakota	1,012	0.1%
13	Tennessee	25,783	2.3%
3	Texas	80,380	7.3%
37	Utah	4,196	0.4%
49	Vermont	450	0.0%
23	Virginia	12,901	1.2%
22	Washington	15,602	1.4%
41	West Virginia	2,584	0.2%
33	Wisconsin	7,602	0.7%
47	Wyoming	959	0.1%

RANK	STATE	ASSAULTS	% of USA
1	California	186,458	17.0%
2	Florida	101,302	9.2%
3	Texas	80,380	7.3%
4	New York	74,351	6.8%
5	Illinois	73,163	6.7%
6	Michigan	41,070	3.7%
7	Massachusetts	30,626	2.8%
8	North Carolina	30,615	2.8%
9	Louisiana	29,484	2.7%
10	Georgia	29,318	2.7%
11	Ohio	28,433	2.6%
12	South Carolina	27,577	2.5%
13	Tennessee	25,783	2.3%
14	Maryland	25,697	2.3%
15	Pennsylvania	24,927	2.3%
16	New Jersey	22,830	2.1%
17	Missouri	22,296	2.0%
18	Arizona	20,909	1.9%
19	Indiana	20,211	1.8%
20	Alabama	17,169	1.6%
21	Oklahoma	16,121	1.5%
22	Washington	15,602	1.4%
23	Virginia	12,901	1.2%
24	Colorado	11,194	1.0%
25	Oregon	10,638	1.0%
26	New Mexico	10,098	0.9%
27	Arkansas	9,435	0.9%
28	Mississippi	8,628	0.8%
29	Kentucky	8,571	0.8%
30	Nevada	8,395	0.8%
31	Minnesota	7,939	0.7%
32	Iowa	7,894	0.7%
33	Wisconsin	7,602	0.7%
34	Connecticut	7,022	0.6%
35	Kansas	6,920	0.6%
36	Nebraska	4,821	0.4%
37	Utah	4,196	0.4%
38	Alaska	3,179	0.3%
39	Delaware	3,173	0.3%
40	Idaho	3,088	0.3%
41	West Virginia	2,584	0.2%
42	Rhode Island	2,429	0.2%
43	Hawaii	1,564	0.1%
44	South Dakota	1,012	0.1%
45	Maine	1,007	0.1%
46	Montana	972	0.1%
47	Wyoming	959	0.1%
48	New Hampshire	646	0.1%
49	Vermont	450	0.0%
50	North Dakota	340	0.0%
	District of Columbia	7,228	0.7%

Source: Federal Bureau of Investigation
   "Crime in the United States 1996" (Uniform Crime Reports, October 4, 1997)
*Revised figures. Aggravated assault is an attack for the purpose of inflicting severe bodily injury.

Percent Change in Number of Aggravated Assaults: 1995 to 1999

National Percent Change = 16.6% Decrease*

ALPHA ORDER

RANK	STATE	PERCENT CHANGE
30	Alabama	(16.9)
23	Alaska	(12.8)
31	Arizona	(17.4)
27	Arkansas	(15.5)
43	California	(26.8)
33	Colorado	(20.6)
12	Connecticut	(7.0)
4	Delaware	10.0
19	Florida	(11.9)
21	Georgia	(12.3)
25	Hawaii	(14.1)
38	Idaho	(22.2)
36	Illinois	(21.9)
44	Indiana	(31.9)
37	Iowa	(22.0)
8	Kansas	(0.5)
22	Kentucky	(12.6)
41	Louisiana	(23.6)
17	Maine	(10.9)
18	Maryland	(11.3)
25	Massachusetts	(14.1)
16	Michigan	(9.8)
19	Minnesota	(11.9)
47	Mississippi	(39.6)
31	Missouri	(17.4)
1	Montana	36.0
2	Nebraska	12.6
48	Nevada	(40.5)
29	New Hampshire	(16.6)
40	New Jersey	(22.9)
5	New Mexico	7.2
34	New York	(20.8)
24	North Carolina	(12.9)
46	North Dakota	(36.5)
49	Ohio	(41.3)
35	Oklahoma	(21.4)
39	Oregon	(22.3)
3	Pennsylvania	11.9
45	Rhode Island	(33.1)
15	South Carolina	(8.2)
42	South Dakota	(23.9)
6	Tennessee	3.6
13	Texas	(7.9)
14	Utah	(8.0)
7	Vermont	1.8
9	Virginia	(2.6)
28	Washington	(16.5)
NA	West Virginia**	NA
10	Wisconsin	(5.0)
11	Wyoming	(6.9)

RANK ORDER

RANK	STATE	PERCENT CHANGE
1	Montana	36.0
2	Nebraska	12.6
3	Pennsylvania	11.9
4	Delaware	10.0
5	New Mexico	7.2
6	Tennessee	3.6
7	Vermont	1.8
8	Kansas	(0.5)
9	Virginia	(2.6)
10	Wisconsin	(5.0)
11	Wyoming	(6.9)
12	Connecticut	(7.0)
13	Texas	(7.9)
14	Utah	(8.0)
15	South Carolina	(8.2)
16	Michigan	(9.8)
17	Maine	(10.9)
18	Maryland	(11.3)
19	Florida	(11.9)
19	Minnesota	(11.9)
21	Georgia	(12.3)
22	Kentucky	(12.6)
23	Alaska	(12.8)
24	North Carolina	(12.9)
25	Hawaii	(14.1)
25	Massachusetts	(14.1)
27	Arkansas	(15.5)
28	Washington	(16.5)
29	New Hampshire	(16.6)
30	Alabama	(16.9)
31	Arizona	(17.4)
31	Missouri	(17.4)
33	Colorado	(20.6)
34	New York	(20.8)
35	Oklahoma	(21.4)
36	Illinois	(21.9)
37	Iowa	(22.0)
38	Idaho	(22.2)
39	Oregon	(22.3)
40	New Jersey	(22.9)
41	Louisiana	(23.6)
42	South Dakota	(23.9)
43	California	(26.8)
44	Indiana	(31.9)
45	Rhode Island	(33.1)
46	North Dakota	(36.5)
47	Mississippi	(39.6)
48	Nevada	(40.5)
49	Ohio	(41.3)
NA	West Virginia**	NA

District of Columbia (36.2)

Source: Morgan Quitno Press using data from Federal Bureau of Investigation
 "Crime in the United States" (Uniform Crime Reports, 1996 and 1999 editions)
*Aggravated assault is an attack for the purpose of inflicting severe bodily injury.
**Not comparable.

Aggravated Assault Rate in 1995

National Rate = 418.3 Aggravated Assaults per 100,000 Population*

ALPHA ORDER

RANK	STATE	RATE
21	Alabama	403.7
8	Alaska	526.3
11	Arizona	495.7
22	Arkansas	379.8
6	California	590.3
26	Colorado	298.7
37	Connecticut	214.4
14	Delaware	442.5
2	Florida	715.1
20	Georgia	407.1
45	Hawaii	131.8
32	Idaho	265.5
4	Illinois	618.5
23	Indiana	348.3
30	Iowa	277.8
31	Kansas	269.8
35	Kentucky	222.0
3	Louisiana	679.0
47	Maine	81.1
9	Maryland	509.7
10	Massachusetts	504.2
15	Michigan	430.1
41	Minnesota	172.2
25	Mississippi	319.9
18	Missouri	418.8
46	Montana	111.7
27	Nebraska	294.5
7	Nevada	548.7
49	New Hampshire	56.3
28	New Jersey	287.4
5	New Mexico	599.3
19	New York	410.0
17	North Carolina	425.5
50	North Dakota	53.0
33	Ohio	255.0
12	Oklahoma	491.8
24	Oregon	338.7
38	Pennsylvania	206.5
34	Rhode Island	245.4
1	South Carolina	750.8
44	South Dakota	138.8
13	Tennessee	490.5
16	Texas	429.3
36	Utah	215.1
48	Vermont	76.9
40	Virginia	194.9
29	Washington	287.3
43	West Virginia	141.4
42	Wisconsin	148.4
39	Wyoming	199.8

RANK ORDER

RANK	STATE	RATE
1	South Carolina	750.8
2	Florida	715.1
3	Louisiana	679.0
4	Illinois	618.5
5	New Mexico	599.3
6	California	590.3
7	Nevada	548.7
8	Alaska	526.3
9	Maryland	509.7
10	Massachusetts	504.2
11	Arizona	495.7
12	Oklahoma	491.8
13	Tennessee	490.5
14	Delaware	442.5
15	Michigan	430.1
16	Texas	429.3
17	North Carolina	425.5
18	Missouri	418.8
19	New York	410.0
20	Georgia	407.1
21	Alabama	403.7
22	Arkansas	379.8
23	Indiana	348.3
24	Oregon	338.7
25	Mississippi	319.9
26	Colorado	298.7
27	Nebraska	294.5
28	New Jersey	287.4
29	Washington	287.3
30	Iowa	277.8
31	Kansas	269.8
32	Idaho	265.5
33	Ohio	255.0
34	Rhode Island	245.4
35	Kentucky	222.0
36	Utah	215.1
37	Connecticut	214.4
38	Pennsylvania	206.5
39	Wyoming	199.8
40	Virginia	194.9
41	Minnesota	172.2
42	Wisconsin	148.4
43	West Virginia	141.4
44	South Dakota	138.8
45	Hawaii	131.8
46	Montana	111.7
47	Maine	81.1
48	Vermont	76.9
49	New Hampshire	56.3
50	North Dakota	53.0
	District of Columbia	1,304.7

Source: Federal Bureau of Investigation
   "Crime in the United States 1996" (Uniform Crime Reports, October 4, 1997)
*Revised figures. Aggravated assault is an attack for the purpose of inflicting severe bodily injury.

Percent Change in Aggravated Assault Rate: 1995 to 1999

National Percent Change = 19.1% Decrease*

ALPHA ORDER

RANK ORDER

RANK	STATE	PERCENT CHANGE
28	Alabama	(19.1)
19	Alaska	(14.9)
41	Arizona	(27.1)
25	Arkansas	(17.7)
43	California	(30.3)
40	Colorado	(26.6)
11	Connecticut	(7.2)
4	Delaware	4.6
24	Florida	(17.4)
27	Georgia	(18.9)
18	Hawaii	(14.0)
42	Idaho	(27.8)
35	Illinois	(23.8)
45	Indiana	(33.5)
33	Iowa	(22.7)
8	Kansas	(3.8)
19	Kentucky	(14.9)
36	Louisiana	(24.1)
13	Maine	(11.7)
16	Maryland	(13.5)
22	Massachusetts	(15.5)
14	Michigan	(12.6)
19	Minnesota	(14.9)
47	Mississippi	(41.2)
29	Missouri	(19.6)
1	Montana	34.0
3	Nebraska	10.7
49	Nevada	(49.7)
30	New Hampshire	(20.2)
38	New Jersey	(24.8)
5	New Mexico	3.8
31	New York	(21.1)
26	North Carolina	(18.0)
46	North Dakota	(35.7)
48	Ohio	(41.9)
34	Oklahoma	(23.2)
39	Oregon	(26.4)
2	Pennsylvania	12.6
44	Rhode Island	(33.2)
15	South Carolina	(13.2)
37	South Dakota	(24.4)
7	Tennessee	(0.7)
17	Texas	(13.9)
23	Utah	(15.7)
6	Vermont	0.3
9	Virginia	(6.2)
32	Washington	(21.2)
NA	West Virginia**	NA
12	Wisconsin	(7.3)
10	Wyoming	(6.9)

RANK	STATE	PERCENT CHANGE
1	Montana	34.0
2	Pennsylvania	12.6
3	Nebraska	10.7
4	Delaware	4.6
5	New Mexico	3.8
6	Vermont	0.3
7	Tennessee	(0.7)
8	Kansas	(3.8)
9	Virginia	(6.2)
10	Wyoming	(6.9)
11	Connecticut	(7.2)
12	Wisconsin	(7.3)
13	Maine	(11.7)
14	Michigan	(12.6)
15	South Carolina	(13.2)
16	Maryland	(13.5)
17	Texas	(13.9)
18	Hawaii	(14.0)
19	Alaska	(14.9)
19	Kentucky	(14.9)
19	Minnesota	(14.9)
22	Massachusetts	(15.5)
23	Utah	(15.7)
24	Florida	(17.4)
25	Arkansas	(17.7)
26	North Carolina	(18.0)
27	Georgia	(18.9)
28	Alabama	(19.1)
29	Missouri	(19.6)
30	New Hampshire	(20.2)
31	New York	(21.1)
32	Washington	(21.2)
33	Iowa	(22.7)
34	Oklahoma	(23.2)
35	Illinois	(23.8)
36	Louisiana	(24.1)
37	South Dakota	(24.4)
38	New Jersey	(24.8)
39	Oregon	(26.4)
40	Colorado	(26.6)
41	Arizona	(27.1)
42	Idaho	(27.8)
43	California	(30.3)
44	Rhode Island	(33.2)
45	Indiana	(33.5)
46	North Dakota	(35.7)
47	Mississippi	(41.2)
48	Ohio	(41.9)
49	Nevada	(49.7)
NA	West Virginia**	NA

District of Columbia (31.8)

Source: Morgan Quitno Press using data from Federal Bureau of Investigation
"Crime in the United States" (Uniform Crime Reports, 1996 and 1999 editions)
*Aggravated assault is an attack for the purpose of inflicting severe bodily injury.
**Not comparable.

Property Crimes in 1995

National Total = 12,063,935 Property Crimes*

ALPHA ORDER

RANK	STATE	CRIMES	% of USA
26	Alabama	179,294	1.5%
45	Alaska	30,097	0.2%
12	Arizona	316,355	2.6%
34	Arkansas	102,780	0.9%
1	California	1,536,830	12.7%
24	Colorado	185,705	1.5%
28	Connecticut	134,188	1.1%
44	Delaware	31,790	0.3%
3	Florida	939,288	7.8%
8	Georgia	385,005	3.2%
37	Hawaii	81,938	0.7%
39	Idaho	47,444	0.4%
5	Illinois	527,572	4.4%
18	Indiana	238,317	2.0%
33	Iowa	106,504	0.9%
30	Kansas	114,558	0.9%
29	Kentucky	115,298	1.0%
15	Louisiana	246,132	2.0%
42	Maine	39,132	0.3%
14	Maryland	267,625	2.2%
20	Massachusetts	221,971	1.8%
7	Michigan	429,223	3.6%
21	Minnesota	190,911	1.6%
32	Mississippi	108,195	0.9%
19	Missouri	237,278	2.0%
41	Montana	40,246	0.3%
38	Nebraska	68,140	0.6%
36	Nevada	86,203	0.7%
46	New Hampshire	29,170	0.2%
11	New Jersey	326,056	2.7%
35	New Mexico	94,508	0.8%
4	New York	674,342	5.6%
9	North Carolina	359,256	3.0%
50	North Dakota	17,817	0.1%
6	Ohio	437,424	3.6%
27	Oklahoma	161,693	1.3%
22	Oregon	189,765	1.6%
10	Pennsylvania	354,623	2.9%
43	Rhode Island	38,378	0.3%
23	South Carolina	186,656	1.5%
47	South Dakota	20,799	0.2%
16	Tennessee	241,315	2.0%
2	Texas	940,033	7.8%
31	Utah	112,417	0.9%
49	Vermont	19,395	0.2%
17	Virginia	240,084	2.0%
13	Washington	314,213	2.6%
40	West Virginia	41,093	0.3%
25	Wisconsin	184,665	1.5%
48	Wyoming	19,517	0.2%

RANK ORDER

RANK	STATE	CRIMES	% of USA
1	California	1,536,830	12.7%
2	Texas	940,033	7.8%
3	Florida	939,288	7.8%
4	New York	674,342	5.6%
5	Illinois	527,572	4.4%
6	Ohio	437,424	3.6%
7	Michigan	429,223	3.6%
8	Georgia	385,005	3.2%
9	North Carolina	359,256	3.0%
10	Pennsylvania	354,623	2.9%
11	New Jersey	326,056	2.7%
12	Arizona	316,355	2.6%
13	Washington	314,213	2.6%
14	Maryland	267,625	2.2%
15	Louisiana	246,132	2.0%
16	Tennessee	241,315	2.0%
17	Virginia	240,084	2.0%
18	Indiana	238,317	2.0%
19	Missouri	237,278	2.0%
20	Massachusetts	221,971	1.8%
21	Minnesota	190,911	1.6%
22	Oregon	189,765	1.6%
23	South Carolina	186,656	1.5%
24	Colorado	185,705	1.5%
25	Wisconsin	184,665	1.5%
26	Alabama	179,294	1.5%
27	Oklahoma	161,693	1.3%
28	Connecticut	134,188	1.1%
29	Kentucky	115,298	1.0%
30	Kansas	114,558	0.9%
31	Utah	112,417	0.9%
32	Mississippi	108,195	0.9%
33	Iowa	106,504	0.9%
34	Arkansas	102,780	0.9%
35	New Mexico	94,508	0.8%
36	Nevada	86,203	0.7%
37	Hawaii	81,938	0.7%
38	Nebraska	68,140	0.6%
39	Idaho	47,444	0.4%
40	West Virginia	41,093	0.3%
41	Montana	40,246	0.3%
42	Maine	39,132	0.3%
43	Rhode Island	38,378	0.3%
44	Delaware	31,790	0.3%
45	Alaska	30,097	0.2%
46	New Hampshire	29,170	0.2%
47	South Dakota	20,799	0.2%
48	Wyoming	19,517	0.2%
49	Vermont	19,395	0.2%
50	North Dakota	17,817	0.1%
	District of Columbia	52,697	0.4%

Source: Federal Bureau of Investigation
 "Crime in the United States 1996" (Uniform Crime Reports, October 4, 1997)
*Revised figures. Property crimes are offenses of burglary, larceny-theft and motor vehicle theft.

Percent Change in Number of Property Crimes: 1995 to 1999

National Percent Change = 15.4% Decrease*

ALPHA ORDER				RANK ORDER		
RANK	STATE	PERCENT CHANGE		RANK	STATE	PERCENT CHANGE
4	Alabama	(4.4)		1	Mississippi	0.3
42	Alaska	(23.3)		2	North Carolina	(1.3)
38	Arizona	(19.3)		3	Delaware	(2.7)
16	Arkansas	(10.2)		4	Alabama	(4.4)
48	California	(31.5)		5	Texas	(4.7)
36	Colorado	(18.7)		6	Ohio	(5.3)
46	Connecticut	(25.6)		7	New Mexico	(5.6)
3	Delaware	(2.7)		8	Kansas	(6.0)
28	Florida	(13.9)		8	Missouri	(6.0)
10	Georgia	(6.7)		10	Georgia	(6.7)
49	Hawaii	(33.4)		11	South Carolina	(6.8)
43	Idaho	(23.4)		12	Pennsylvania	(8.9)
24	Illinois	(13.2)		13	Tennessee	(9.1)
32	Indiana	(15.4)		14	New Hampshire	(10.0)
40	Iowa	(20.7)		15	Nebraska	(10.1)
8	Kansas	(6.0)		16	Arkansas	(10.2)
20	Kentucky	(11.5)		17	Washington	(10.6)
18	Louisiana	(10.9)		18	Louisiana	(10.9)
20	Maine	(11.5)		18	Utah	(10.9)
38	Maryland	(19.3)		20	Kentucky	(11.5)
44	Massachusetts	(24.6)		20	Maine	(11.5)
27	Michigan	(13.8)		22	Virginia	(12.4)
33	Minnesota	(16.9)		23	South Dakota	(12.7)
1	Mississippi	0.3		24	Illinois	(13.2)
8	Missouri	(6.0)		25	Oklahoma	(13.3)
31	Montana	(15.2)		25	Wisconsin	(13.3)
15	Nebraska	(10.1)		27	Michigan	(13.8)
29	Nevada	(14.3)		28	Florida	(13.9)
14	New Hampshire	(10.0)		29	Nevada	(14.3)
45	New Jersey	(25.4)		30	Rhode Island	(14.9)
7	New Mexico	(5.6)		31	Montana	(15.2)
47	New York	(27.4)		32	Indiana	(15.4)
2	North Carolina	(1.3)		33	Minnesota	(16.9)
34	North Dakota	(17.2)		34	North Dakota	(17.2)
6	Ohio	(5.3)		34	Vermont	(17.2)
25	Oklahoma	(13.3)		36	Colorado	(18.7)
37	Oregon	(19.1)		37	Oregon	(19.1)
12	Pennsylvania	(8.9)		38	Arizona	(19.3)
30	Rhode Island	(14.9)		38	Maryland	(19.3)
11	South Carolina	(6.8)		40	Iowa	(20.7)
23	South Dakota	(12.7)		40	Wyoming	(20.7)
13	Tennessee	(9.1)		42	Alaska	(23.3)
5	Texas	(4.7)		43	Idaho	(23.4)
18	Utah	(10.9)		44	Massachusetts	(24.6)
34	Vermont	(17.2)		45	New Jersey	(25.4)
22	Virginia	(12.4)		46	Connecticut	(25.6)
17	Washington	(10.6)		47	New York	(27.4)
NA	West Virginia**	NA		48	California	(31.5)
25	Wisconsin	(13.3)		49	Hawaii	(33.4)
40	Wyoming	(20.7)		NA	West Virginia**	NA
					District of Columbia	(36.6)

Source: Morgan Quitno Press using data from Federal Bureau of Investigation
   "Crime in the United States" (Uniform Crime Reports, 1996 and 1999 editions)
*Property crimes are offenses of burglary, larceny-theft and motor vehicle theft.
**Not comparable.

Property Crime Rate in 1995

National Rate = 4,591.3 Property Crimes per 100,000 Population*

ALPHA ORDER

RANK	STATE	RATE
26	Alabama	4,215.7
15	Alaska	4,982.9
1	Arizona	7,500.1
29	Arkansas	4,137.7
18	California	4,865.1
16	Colorado	4,956.1
32	Connecticut	4,097.3
25	Delaware	4,433.8
3	Florida	6,630.6
10	Georgia	5,346.5
2	Hawaii	6,902.9
33	Idaho	4,079.4
23	Illinois	4,459.6
30	Indiana	4,106.8
38	Iowa	3,747.5
22	Kansas	4,466.2
45	Kentucky	2,987.0
7	Louisiana	5,668.6
44	Maine	3,153.3
11	Maryland	5,307.9
40	Massachusetts	3,654.4
21	Michigan	4,495.0
28	Minnesota	4,141.2
35	Mississippi	4,011.7
24	Missouri	4,456.8
19	Montana	4,626.0
27	Nebraska	4,162.5
8	Nevada	5,634.2
49	New Hampshire	2,540.9
31	New Jersey	4,103.9
9	New Mexico	5,608.8
39	New York	3,718.3
14	North Carolina	4,993.1
48	North Dakota	2,779.6
36	Ohio	3,922.7
17	Oklahoma	4,932.7
4	Oregon	6,041.5
46	Pennsylvania	2,937.6
37	Rhode Island	3,876.6
12	South Carolina	5,081.8
47	South Dakota	2,853.1
20	Tennessee	4,591.2
13	Texas	5,020.5
6	Utah	5,762.0
43	Vermont	3,315.4
41	Virginia	3,627.7
5	Washington	5,785.5
50	West Virginia	2,248.0
42	Wisconsin	3,604.6
34	Wyoming	4,066.0

RANK ORDER

RANK	STATE	RATE
1	Arizona	7,500.1
2	Hawaii	6,902.9
3	Florida	6,630.6
4	Oregon	6,041.5
5	Washington	5,785.5
6	Utah	5,762.0
7	Louisiana	5,668.6
8	Nevada	5,634.2
9	New Mexico	5,608.8
10	Georgia	5,346.5
11	Maryland	5,307.9
12	South Carolina	5,081.8
13	Texas	5,020.5
14	North Carolina	4,993.1
15	Alaska	4,982.9
16	Colorado	4,956.1
17	Oklahoma	4,932.7
18	California	4,865.1
19	Montana	4,626.0
20	Tennessee	4,591.2
21	Michigan	4,495.0
22	Kansas	4,466.2
23	Illinois	4,459.6
24	Missouri	4,456.8
25	Delaware	4,433.8
26	Alabama	4,215.7
27	Nebraska	4,162.5
28	Minnesota	4,141.2
29	Arkansas	4,137.7
30	Indiana	4,106.8
31	New Jersey	4,103.9
32	Connecticut	4,097.3
33	Idaho	4,079.4
34	Wyoming	4,066.0
35	Mississippi	4,011.7
36	Ohio	3,922.7
37	Rhode Island	3,876.6
38	Iowa	3,747.5
39	New York	3,718.3
40	Massachusetts	3,654.4
41	Virginia	3,627.7
42	Wisconsin	3,604.6
43	Vermont	3,315.4
44	Maine	3,153.3
45	Kentucky	2,987.0
46	Pennsylvania	2,937.6
47	South Dakota	2,853.1
48	North Dakota	2,779.6
49	New Hampshire	2,540.9
50	West Virginia	2,248.0
	District of Columbia	9,512.1

Source: Federal Bureau of Investigation
"Crime in the United States 1996" (Uniform Crime Reports, October 4, 1997)
*Revised figures. Property crimes are offenses of burglary, larceny-theft and motor vehicle theft.

Percent Change in Property Crime Rate: 1995 to 1999

National Percent Change = 18.5% Decrease*

ALPHA ORDER

RANK	STATE	PERCENT CHANGE
3	Alabama	(7.0)
40	Alaska	(25.1)
46	Arizona	(28.7)
15	Arkansas	(12.6)
49	California	(34.7)
39	Colorado	(24.9)
41	Connecticut	(25.7)
5	Delaware	(7.5)
33	Florida	(19.3)
18	Georgia	(13.7)
48	Hawaii	(33.3)
47	Idaho	(28.8)
23	Illinois	(15.4)
30	Indiana	(17.4)
37	Iowa	(21.4)
9	Kansas	(9.2)
18	Kentucky	(13.7)
11	Louisiana	(11.5)
14	Maine	(12.4)
36	Maryland	(21.3)
42	Massachusetts	(25.8)
29	Michigan	(16.6)
34	Minnesota	(19.8)
1	Mississippi	(2.3)
7	Missouri	(8.5)
28	Montana	(16.5)
12	Nebraska	(11.6)
44	Nevada	(27.5)
20	New Hampshire	(14.0)
43	New Jersey	(27.2)
8	New Mexico	(8.6)
45	New York	(27.6)
4	North Carolina	(7.2)
27	North Dakota	(16.3)
2	Ohio	(6.2)
22	Oklahoma	(15.3)
38	Oregon	(23.4)
6	Pennsylvania	(8.3)
21	Rhode Island	(15.0)
13	South Carolina	(11.9)
17	South Dakota	(13.2)
16	Tennessee	(12.9)
10	Texas	(10.9)
31	Utah	(18.4)
32	Vermont	(18.5)
25	Virginia	(15.7)
25	Washington	(15.7)
NA	West Virginia**	NA
23	Wisconsin	(15.4)
35	Wyoming	(20.7)

RANK ORDER

RANK	STATE	PERCENT CHANGE
1	Mississippi	(2.3)
2	Ohio	(6.2)
3	Alabama	(7.0)
4	North Carolina	(7.2)
5	Delaware	(7.5)
6	Pennsylvania	(8.3)
7	Missouri	(8.5)
8	New Mexico	(8.6)
9	Kansas	(9.2)
10	Texas	(10.9)
11	Louisiana	(11.5)
12	Nebraska	(11.6)
13	South Carolina	(11.9)
14	Maine	(12.4)
15	Arkansas	(12.6)
16	Tennessee	(12.9)
17	South Dakota	(13.2)
18	Georgia	(13.7)
18	Kentucky	(13.7)
20	New Hampshire	(14.0)
21	Rhode Island	(15.0)
22	Oklahoma	(15.3)
23	Illinois	(15.4)
23	Wisconsin	(15.4)
25	Virginia	(15.7)
25	Washington	(15.7)
27	North Dakota	(16.3)
28	Montana	(16.5)
29	Michigan	(16.6)
30	Indiana	(17.4)
31	Utah	(18.4)
32	Vermont	(18.5)
33	Florida	(19.3)
34	Minnesota	(19.8)
35	Wyoming	(20.7)
36	Maryland	(21.3)
37	Iowa	(21.4)
38	Oregon	(23.4)
39	Colorado	(24.9)
40	Alaska	(25.1)
41	Connecticut	(25.7)
42	Massachusetts	(25.8)
43	New Jersey	(27.2)
44	Nevada	(27.5)
45	New York	(27.6)
46	Arizona	(28.7)
47	Idaho	(28.8)
48	Hawaii	(33.3)
49	California	(34.7)
NA	West Virginia**	NA

District of Columbia (32.3)

Source: Morgan Quitno Press using data from Federal Bureau of Investigation
    "Crime in the United States" (Uniform Crime Reports, 1996 and 1999 editions)
*Property crimes are offenses of burglary, larceny-theft and motor vehicle theft.
**Not comparable.

Burglaries in 1995

National Total = 2,593,784 Burglaries*

ALPHA ORDER

RANK	STATE	BURGLARIES	% of USA
21	Alabama	43,586	1.7%
45	Alaska	5,055	0.2%
13	Arizona	59,762	2.3%
32	Arkansas	24,763	1.0%
1	California	353,895	13.6%
25	Colorado	35,001	1.3%
29	Connecticut	29,095	1.1%
43	Delaware	6,491	0.3%
2	Florida	215,657	8.3%
9	Georgia	76,324	2.9%
37	Hawaii	13,832	0.5%
41	Idaho	9,069	0.3%
5	Illinois	108,555	4.2%
19	Indiana	47,676	1.8%
34	Iowa	21,527	0.8%
31	Kansas	27,404	1.1%
30	Kentucky	28,389	1.1%
15	Louisiana	53,481	2.1%
42	Maine	9,015	0.3%
16	Maryland	53,320	2.1%
17	Massachusetts	49,669	1.9%
8	Michigan	86,872	3.3%
24	Minnesota	36,756	1.4%
28	Mississippi	30,505	1.2%
18	Missouri	49,649	1.9%
44	Montana	5,060	0.2%
38	Nebraska	10,344	0.4%
35	Nevada	20,235	0.8%
46	New Hampshire	4,806	0.2%
10	New Jersey	69,533	2.7%
33	New Mexico	24,383	0.9%
4	New York	146,562	5.7%
6	North Carolina	101,995	3.9%
50	North Dakota	2,248	0.1%
7	Ohio	93,539	3.6%
22	Oklahoma	41,694	1.6%
26	Oregon	34,640	1.3%
11	Pennsylvania	67,815	2.6%
40	Rhode Island	9,234	0.4%
20	South Carolina	46,083	1.8%
48	South Dakota	3,942	0.2%
12	Tennessee	60,086	2.3%
3	Texas	202,642	7.8%
36	Utah	15,623	0.6%
47	Vermont	4,451	0.2%
23	Virginia	39,388	1.5%
14	Washington	59,265	2.3%
39	West Virginia	10,329	0.4%
27	Wisconsin	31,416	1.2%
49	Wyoming	2,938	0.1%

RANK ORDER

RANK	STATE	BURGLARIES	% of USA
1	California	353,895	13.6%
2	Florida	215,657	8.3%
3	Texas	202,642	7.8%
4	New York	146,562	5.7%
5	Illinois	108,555	4.2%
6	North Carolina	101,995	3.9%
7	Ohio	93,539	3.6%
8	Michigan	86,872	3.3%
9	Georgia	76,324	2.9%
10	New Jersey	69,533	2.7%
11	Pennsylvania	67,815	2.6%
12	Tennessee	60,086	2.3%
13	Arizona	59,762	2.3%
14	Washington	59,265	2.3%
15	Louisiana	53,481	2.1%
16	Maryland	53,320	2.1%
17	Massachusetts	49,669	1.9%
18	Missouri	49,649	1.9%
19	Indiana	47,676	1.8%
20	South Carolina	46,083	1.8%
21	Alabama	43,586	1.7%
22	Oklahoma	41,694	1.6%
23	Virginia	39,388	1.5%
24	Minnesota	36,756	1.4%
25	Colorado	35,001	1.3%
26	Oregon	34,640	1.3%
27	Wisconsin	31,416	1.2%
28	Mississippi	30,505	1.2%
29	Connecticut	29,095	1.1%
30	Kentucky	28,389	1.1%
31	Kansas	27,404	1.1%
32	Arkansas	24,763	1.0%
33	New Mexico	24,383	0.9%
34	Iowa	21,527	0.8%
35	Nevada	20,235	0.8%
36	Utah	15,623	0.6%
37	Hawaii	13,832	0.5%
38	Nebraska	10,344	0.4%
39	West Virginia	10,329	0.4%
40	Rhode Island	9,234	0.4%
41	Idaho	9,069	0.3%
42	Maine	9,015	0.3%
43	Delaware	6,491	0.3%
44	Montana	5,060	0.2%
45	Alaska	5,055	0.2%
46	New Hampshire	4,806	0.2%
47	Vermont	4,451	0.2%
48	South Dakota	3,942	0.2%
49	Wyoming	2,938	0.1%
50	North Dakota	2,248	0.1%
	District of Columbia	10,185	0.4%

Source: Federal Bureau of Investigation
"Crime in the United States 1996" (Uniform Crime Reports, October 4, 1997)
*Revised figures. Burglary is the unlawful entry of a structure to commit a felony or theft. Attempts are included.

Percent Change in Number of Burglaries: 1995 to 1999

National Percent Change = 19.0% Decrease*

ALPHA ORDER				RANK ORDER		
RANK	STATE	PERCENT CHANGE		RANK	STATE	PERCENT CHANGE
13	Alabama	(11.3)		1	North Dakota	4.0
42	Alaska	(25.1)		2	West Virginia	(0.3)
25	Arizona	(17.3)		3	Nebraska	(1.8)
16	Arkansas	(12.4)		4	North Carolina	(3.5)
50	California	(36.8)		5	Mississippi	(4.6)
39	Colorado	(22.9)		6	Texas	(6.1)
48	Connecticut	(33.7)		7	Georgia	(6.4)
32	Delaware	(19.2)		8	Utah	(6.6)
23	Florida	(15.9)		9	Ohio	(7.0)
7	Georgia	(6.4)		10	Washington	(7.8)
45	Hawaii	(31.9)		11	Louisiana	(10.7)
22	Idaho	(15.7)		12	Indiana	(10.9)
35	Illinois	(20.4)		13	Alabama	(11.3)
12	Indiana	(10.9)		14	Michigan	(11.7)
37	Iowa	(21.0)		15	New Mexico	(11.9)
34	Kansas	(20.2)		16	Arkansas	(12.4)
21	Kentucky	(14.8)		17	Nevada	(13.0)
11	Louisiana	(10.7)		18	South Carolina	(14.0)
24	Maine	(16.5)		19	Missouri	(14.4)
31	Maryland	(18.9)		20	Tennessee	(14.5)
47	Massachusetts	(33.6)		21	Kentucky	(14.8)
14	Michigan	(11.7)		22	Idaho	(15.7)
41	Minnesota	(24.6)		23	Florida	(15.9)
5	Mississippi	(4.6)		24	Maine	(16.5)
19	Missouri	(14.4)		25	Arizona	(17.3)
43	Montana	(25.2)		25	Oklahoma	(17.3)
3	Nebraska	(1.8)		27	Pennsylvania	(17.4)
17	Nevada	(13.0)		27	South Dakota	(17.4)
40	New Hampshire	(23.1)		29	Virginia	(17.7)
46	New Jersey	(32.4)		30	Wisconsin	(18.4)
15	New Mexico	(11.9)		31	Maryland	(18.9)
49	New York	(36.4)		32	Delaware	(19.2)
4	North Carolina	(3.5)		33	Wyoming	(20.0)
1	North Dakota	4.0		34	Kansas	(20.2)
9	Ohio	(7.0)		35	Illinois	(20.4)
25	Oklahoma	(17.3)		36	Vermont	(20.5)
38	Oregon	(22.8)		37	Iowa	(21.0)
27	Pennsylvania	(17.4)		38	Oregon	(22.8)
44	Rhode Island	(31.3)		39	Colorado	(22.9)
18	South Carolina	(14.0)		40	New Hampshire	(23.1)
27	South Dakota	(17.4)		41	Minnesota	(24.6)
20	Tennessee	(14.5)		42	Alaska	(25.1)
6	Texas	(6.1)		43	Montana	(25.2)
8	Utah	(6.6)		44	Rhode Island	(31.3)
36	Vermont	(20.5)		45	Hawaii	(31.9)
29	Virginia	(17.7)		46	New Jersey	(32.4)
10	Washington	(7.8)		47	Massachusetts	(33.6)
2	West Virginia	(0.3)		48	Connecticut	(33.7)
30	Wisconsin	(18.4)		49	New York	(36.4)
33	Wyoming	(20.0)		50	California	(36.8)
					District of Columbia	(50.3)

Source: Morgan Quitno Press using data from Federal Bureau of Investigation
   "Crime in the United States" (Uniform Crime Reports, 1996 and 1999 editions)
*Burglary is the unlawful entry of a structure to commit a felony or theft. Attempts are included.

Burglary Rate in 1995

National Rate = 987.1 Burglaries per 100,000 Population*

ALPHA ORDER

RANK	STATE	RATE
19	Alabama	1,024.8
30	Alaska	836.9
4	Arizona	1,416.8
20	Arkansas	996.9
12	California	1,120.3
21	Colorado	934.1
27	Connecticut	888.4
26	Delaware	905.3
1	Florida	1,522.4
17	Georgia	1,059.9
9	Hawaii	1,165.3
36	Idaho	779.8
24	Illinois	917.6
31	Indiana	821.6
38	Iowa	757.5
16	Kansas	1,068.4
39	Kentucky	735.5
8	Louisiana	1,231.7
40	Maine	726.4
18	Maryland	1,057.5
32	Massachusetts	817.7
25	Michigan	909.7
35	Minnesota	797.3
11	Mississippi	1,131.1
23	Missouri	932.6
45	Montana	581.6
41	Nebraska	631.9
5	Nevada	1,322.5
49	New Hampshire	418.6
28	New Jersey	875.2
2	New Mexico	1,447.1
33	New York	808.1
3	North Carolina	1,417.6
50	North Dakota	350.7
29	Ohio	838.8
6	Oklahoma	1,271.9
13	Oregon	1,102.8
47	Pennsylvania	561.8
22	Rhode Island	932.7
7	South Carolina	1,254.6
48	South Dakota	540.7
10	Tennessee	1,143.2
15	Texas	1,082.3
34	Utah	800.8
37	Vermont	760.9
44	Virginia	595.2
14	Washington	1,091.2
46	West Virginia	565.0
42	Wisconsin	613.2
43	Wyoming	612.1

RANK ORDER

RANK	STATE	RATE
1	Florida	1,522.4
2	New Mexico	1,447.1
3	North Carolina	1,417.6
4	Arizona	1,416.8
5	Nevada	1,322.5
6	Oklahoma	1,271.9
7	South Carolina	1,254.6
8	Louisiana	1,231.7
9	Hawaii	1,165.3
10	Tennessee	1,143.2
11	Mississippi	1,131.1
12	California	1,120.3
13	Oregon	1,102.8
14	Washington	1,091.2
15	Texas	1,082.3
16	Kansas	1,068.4
17	Georgia	1,059.9
18	Maryland	1,057.5
19	Alabama	1,024.8
20	Arkansas	996.9
21	Colorado	934.1
22	Rhode Island	932.7
23	Missouri	932.6
24	Illinois	917.6
25	Michigan	909.7
26	Delaware	905.3
27	Connecticut	888.4
28	New Jersey	875.2
29	Ohio	838.8
30	Alaska	836.9
31	Indiana	821.6
32	Massachusetts	817.7
33	New York	808.1
34	Utah	800.8
35	Minnesota	797.3
36	Idaho	779.8
37	Vermont	760.9
38	Iowa	757.5
39	Kentucky	735.5
40	Maine	726.4
41	Nebraska	631.9
42	Wisconsin	613.2
43	Wyoming	612.1
44	Virginia	595.2
45	Montana	581.6
46	West Virginia	565.0
47	Pennsylvania	561.8
48	South Dakota	540.7
49	New Hampshire	418.6
50	North Dakota	350.7
	District of Columbia	1,838.4

Source: Federal Bureau of Investigation
   "Crime in the United States 1996" (Uniform Crime Reports, October 4, 1997)
*Revised figures. Burglary is the unlawful entry of a structure to commit a felony or theft. Attempts are included.

Percent Change in Burglary Rate: 1995 to 1999

National Percent Change = 22.0% Decrease*

ALPHA ORDER

RANK	STATE	PERCENT CHANGE
12	Alabama	(13.7)
40	Alaska	(26.9)
41	Arizona	(27.0)
15	Arkansas	(14.7)
50	California	(39.7)
43	Colorado	(28.8)
46	Connecticut	(33.8)
35	Delaware	(23.2)
29	Florida	(21.2)
11	Georgia	(13.5)
45	Hawaii	(31.8)
30	Idaho	(21.7)
33	Illinois	(22.4)
9	Indiana	(13.0)
30	Iowa	(21.7)
34	Kansas	(22.9)
19	Kentucky	(16.9)
7	Louisiana	(11.3)
20	Maine	(17.2)
28	Maryland	(21.0)
48	Massachusetts	(34.7)
14	Michigan	(14.5)
42	Minnesota	(27.2)
4	Mississippi	(7.1)
17	Missouri	(16.7)
36	Montana	(26.3)
3	Nebraska	(3.5)
37	Nevada	(26.4)
37	New Hampshire	(26.4)
47	New Jersey	(34.0)
15	New Mexico	(14.7)
49	New York	(36.6)
6	North Carolina	(9.2)
1	North Dakota	5.1
5	Ohio	(7.8)
24	Oklahoma	(19.3)
39	Oregon	(26.8)
18	Pennsylvania	(16.8)
44	Rhode Island	(31.4)
23	South Carolina	(18.7)
21	South Dakota	(17.9)
22	Tennessee	(18.1)
8	Texas	(12.3)
13	Utah	(14.4)
30	Vermont	(21.7)
27	Virginia	(20.8)
9	Washington	(13.0)
2	West Virginia	0.9
26	Wisconsin	(20.4)
25	Wyoming	(20.0)

RANK ORDER

RANK	STATE	PERCENT CHANGE
1	North Dakota	5.1
2	West Virginia	0.9
3	Nebraska	(3.5)
4	Mississippi	(7.1)
5	Ohio	(7.8)
6	North Carolina	(9.2)
7	Louisiana	(11.3)
8	Texas	(12.3)
9	Indiana	(13.0)
9	Washington	(13.0)
11	Georgia	(13.5)
12	Alabama	(13.7)
13	Utah	(14.4)
14	Michigan	(14.5)
15	Arkansas	(14.7)
15	New Mexico	(14.7)
17	Missouri	(16.7)
18	Pennsylvania	(16.8)
19	Kentucky	(16.9)
20	Maine	(17.2)
21	South Dakota	(17.9)
22	Tennessee	(18.1)
23	South Carolina	(18.7)
24	Oklahoma	(19.3)
25	Wyoming	(20.0)
26	Wisconsin	(20.4)
27	Virginia	(20.8)
28	Maryland	(21.0)
29	Florida	(21.2)
30	Idaho	(21.7)
30	Iowa	(21.7)
30	Vermont	(21.7)
33	Illinois	(22.4)
34	Kansas	(22.9)
35	Delaware	(23.2)
36	Montana	(26.3)
37	Nevada	(26.4)
37	New Hampshire	(26.4)
39	Oregon	(26.8)
40	Alaska	(26.9)
41	Arizona	(27.0)
42	Minnesota	(27.2)
43	Colorado	(28.8)
44	Rhode Island	(31.4)
45	Hawaii	(31.8)
46	Connecticut	(33.8)
47	New Jersey	(34.0)
48	Massachusetts	(34.7)
49	New York	(36.6)
50	California	(39.7)
	District of Columbia	(46.9)

Source: Morgan Quitno Press using data from Federal Bureau of Investigation
   "Crime in the United States" (Uniform Crime Reports, 1996 and 1999 editions)
*Burglary is the unlawful entry of a structure to commit a felony or theft. Attempts are included.

Larcenies and Thefts in 1995

National Total = 7,997,710 Larcenies and Thefts*

ALPHA ORDER

RANK ORDER

RANK	STATE	THEFTS	% of USA
26	Alabama	120,967	1.5%
46	Alaska	21,891	0.3%
12	Arizona	207,763	2.6%
33	Arkansas	69,935	0.9%
1	California	902,456	11.3%
21	Colorado	136,184	1.7%
29	Connecticut	87,401	1.1%
45	Delaware	22,329	0.3%
3	Florida	612,311	7.7%
8	Georgia	264,872	3.3%
36	Hawaii	59,907	0.7%
39	Idaho	35,560	0.4%
5	Illinois	357,143	4.5%
17	Indiana	163,618	2.0%
31	Iowa	78,645	1.0%
30	Kansas	78,855	1.0%
32	Kentucky	76,906	1.0%
16	Louisiana	166,667	2.1%
41	Maine	28,444	0.4%
15	Maryland	178,126	2.2%
22	Massachusetts	135,586	1.7%
7	Michigan	280,712	3.5%
20	Minnesota	138,414	1.7%
34	Mississippi	67,967	0.8%
18	Missouri	162,430	2.0%
40	Montana	32,797	0.4%
38	Nebraska	52,044	0.7%
37	Nevada	54,563	0.7%
44	New Hampshire	22,698	0.3%
13	New Jersey	206,339	2.6%
35	New Mexico	61,478	0.8%
4	New York	425,184	5.3%
10	North Carolina	234,911	2.9%
49	North Dakota	14,421	0.2%
6	Ohio	297,624	3.7%
27	Oklahoma	103,727	1.3%
24	Oregon	133,075	1.7%
9	Pennsylvania	236,991	3.0%
43	Rhode Island	24,780	0.3%
25	South Carolina	126,416	1.6%
47	South Dakota	15,976	0.2%
19	Tennessee	147,143	1.8%
2	Texas	632,468	7.9%
28	Utah	89,202	1.1%
50	Vermont	14,150	0.2%
14	Virginia	181,333	2.3%
11	Washington	224,861	2.8%
42	West Virginia	27,724	0.3%
23	Wisconsin	134,623	1.7%
48	Wyoming	15,774	0.2%

RANK	STATE	THEFTS	% of USA
1	California	902,456	11.3%
2	Texas	632,468	7.9%
3	Florida	612,311	7.7%
4	New York	425,184	5.3%
5	Illinois	357,143	4.5%
6	Ohio	297,624	3.7%
7	Michigan	280,712	3.5%
8	Georgia	264,872	3.3%
9	Pennsylvania	236,991	3.0%
10	North Carolina	234,911	2.9%
11	Washington	224,861	2.8%
12	Arizona	207,763	2.6%
13	New Jersey	206,339	2.6%
14	Virginia	181,333	2.3%
15	Maryland	178,126	2.2%
16	Louisiana	166,667	2.1%
17	Indiana	163,618	2.0%
18	Missouri	162,430	2.0%
19	Tennessee	147,143	1.8%
20	Minnesota	138,414	1.7%
21	Colorado	136,184	1.7%
22	Massachusetts	135,586	1.7%
23	Wisconsin	134,623	1.7%
24	Oregon	133,075	1.7%
25	South Carolina	126,416	1.6%
26	Alabama	120,967	1.5%
27	Oklahoma	103,727	1.3%
28	Utah	89,202	1.1%
29	Connecticut	87,401	1.1%
30	Kansas	78,855	1.0%
31	Iowa	78,645	1.0%
32	Kentucky	76,906	1.0%
33	Arkansas	69,935	0.9%
34	Mississippi	67,967	0.8%
35	New Mexico	61,478	0.8%
36	Hawaii	59,907	0.7%
37	Nevada	54,563	0.7%
38	Nebraska	52,044	0.7%
39	Idaho	35,560	0.4%
40	Montana	32,797	0.4%
41	Maine	28,444	0.4%
42	West Virginia	27,724	0.3%
43	Rhode Island	24,780	0.3%
44	New Hampshire	22,698	0.3%
45	Delaware	22,329	0.3%
46	Alaska	21,891	0.3%
47	South Dakota	15,976	0.2%
48	Wyoming	15,774	0.2%
49	North Dakota	14,421	0.2%
50	Vermont	14,150	0.2%
	District of Columbia	32,319	0.4%

Source: Federal Bureau of Investigation
   "Crime in the United States 1996" (Uniform Crime Reports, October 4, 1997)
*Revised figures. Larceny and theft is the unlawful taking of property without use of force, violence or fraud.
Attempts are included. Motor vehicle thefts are excluded.

Percent Change in Number of Larcenies and Thefts: 1995 to 1999

National Percent Change = 13.0% Decrease*

RANK	STATE	PERCENT CHANGE
3	Alabama	(1.1)
46	Alaska	(23.9)
36	Arizona	(19.3)
15	Arkansas	(8.6)
48	California	(26.8)
38	Colorado	(19.8)
41	Connecticut	(20.7)
1	Delaware	1.4
27	Florida	(12.8)
13	Georgia	(6.4)
49	Hawaii	(32.5)
47	Idaho	(24.6)
21	Illinois	(10.6)
32	Indiana	(15.2)
42	Iowa	(20.8)
2	Kansas	1.1
17	Kentucky	(9.9)
19	Louisiana	(10.2)
22	Maine	(10.7)
34	Maryland	(17.3)
37	Massachusetts	(19.7)
33	Michigan	(15.8)
30	Minnesota	(14.9)
6	Mississippi	(3.0)
6	Missouri	(3.0)
28	Montana	(13.3)
25	Nebraska	(12.2)
43	Nevada	(20.9)
14	New Hampshire	(6.6)
45	New Jersey	(22.0)
6	New Mexico	(3.0)
39	New York	(20.5)
4	North Carolina	(1.9)
44	North Dakota	(21.1)
10	Ohio	(3.2)
16	Oklahoma	(9.7)
31	Oregon	(15.0)
11	Pennsylvania	(3.9)
18	Rhode Island	(10.1)
12	South Carolina	(5.1)
24	South Dakota	(12.1)
6	Tennessee	(3.0)
5	Texas	(2.9)
26	Utah	(12.4)
35	Vermont	(18.0)
23	Virginia	(11.8)
29	Washington	(14.5)
NA	West Virginia**	NA
20	Wisconsin	(10.3)
40	Wyoming	(20.6)

RANK	STATE	PERCENT CHANGE
1	Delaware	1.4
2	Kansas	1.1
3	Alabama	(1.1)
4	North Carolina	(1.9)
5	Texas	(2.9)
6	Mississippi	(3.0)
6	Missouri	(3.0)
6	New Mexico	(3.0)
6	Tennessee	(3.0)
10	Ohio	(3.2)
11	Pennsylvania	(3.9)
12	South Carolina	(5.1)
13	Georgia	(6.4)
14	New Hampshire	(6.6)
15	Arkansas	(8.6)
16	Oklahoma	(9.7)
17	Kentucky	(9.9)
18	Rhode Island	(10.1)
19	Louisiana	(10.2)
20	Wisconsin	(10.3)
21	Illinois	(10.6)
22	Maine	(10.7)
23	Virginia	(11.8)
24	South Dakota	(12.1)
25	Nebraska	(12.2)
26	Utah	(12.4)
27	Florida	(12.8)
28	Montana	(13.3)
29	Washington	(14.5)
30	Minnesota	(14.9)
31	Oregon	(15.0)
32	Indiana	(15.2)
33	Michigan	(15.8)
34	Maryland	(17.3)
35	Vermont	(18.0)
36	Arizona	(19.3)
37	Massachusetts	(19.7)
38	Colorado	(19.8)
39	New York	(20.5)
40	Wyoming	(20.6)
41	Connecticut	(20.7)
42	Iowa	(20.8)
43	Nevada	(20.9)
44	North Dakota	(21.1)
45	New Jersey	(22.0)
46	Alaska	(23.9)
47	Idaho	(24.6)
48	California	(26.8)
49	Hawaii	(32.5)
NA	West Virginia**	NA

District of Columbia (32.9)

Source: Morgan Quitno Press using data from Federal Bureau of Investigation
    "Crime in the United States" (Uniform Crime Reports, 1996 and 1999 editions)
*Larceny and theft is the unlawful taking of property without use of force, violence or fraud. Attempts are included.
Motor vehicle thefts are excluded.
**Not comparable.

Larceny and Theft Rate in 1995

National Rate = 3,043.8 Larcenies and Thefts per 100,000 Population*

ALPHA ORDER

RANK	STATE	RATE
29	Alabama	2,844.3
12	Alaska	3,624.3
2	Arizona	4,925.6
31	Arkansas	2,815.4
28	California	2,856.9
11	Colorado	3,634.5
36	Connecticut	2,668.7
21	Delaware	3,114.2
4	Florida	4,322.4
9	Georgia	3,678.3
1	Hawaii	5,046.9
23	Idaho	3,057.6
25	Illinois	3,019.0
30	Indiana	2,819.5
33	Iowa	2,767.2
22	Kansas	3,074.3
47	Kentucky	1,992.4
7	Louisiana	3,838.5
43	Maine	2,292.0
14	Maryland	3,532.8
45	Massachusetts	2,232.2
27	Michigan	2,939.7
26	Minnesota	3,002.5
39	Mississippi	2,520.1
24	Missouri	3,050.9
8	Montana	3,769.8
19	Nebraska	3,179.2
13	Nevada	3,566.2
48	New Hampshire	1,977.2
38	New Jersey	2,597.1
10	New Mexico	3,648.5
42	New York	2,344.4
18	North Carolina	3,264.9
44	North Dakota	2,249.8
35	Ohio	2,669.0
20	Oklahoma	3,164.3
5	Oregon	4,236.7
49	Pennsylvania	1,963.1
40	Rhode Island	2,503.0
15	South Carolina	3,441.8
46	South Dakota	2,191.5
32	Tennessee	2,799.5
16	Texas	3,377.8
3	Utah	4,572.1
41	Vermont	2,418.8
34	Virginia	2,740.0
6	Washington	4,140.3
50	West Virginia	1,516.6
37	Wisconsin	2,627.8
17	Wyoming	3,286.3

RANK ORDER

RANK	STATE	RATE
1	Hawaii	5,046.9
2	Arizona	4,925.6
3	Utah	4,572.1
4	Florida	4,322.4
5	Oregon	4,236.7
6	Washington	4,140.3
7	Louisiana	3,838.5
8	Montana	3,769.8
9	Georgia	3,678.3
10	New Mexico	3,648.5
11	Colorado	3,634.5
12	Alaska	3,624.3
13	Nevada	3,566.2
14	Maryland	3,532.8
15	South Carolina	3,441.8
16	Texas	3,377.8
17	Wyoming	3,286.3
18	North Carolina	3,264.9
19	Nebraska	3,179.2
20	Oklahoma	3,164.3
21	Delaware	3,114.2
22	Kansas	3,074.3
23	Idaho	3,057.6
24	Missouri	3,050.9
25	Illinois	3,019.0
26	Minnesota	3,002.5
27	Michigan	2,939.7
28	California	2,856.9
29	Alabama	2,844.3
30	Indiana	2,819.5
31	Arkansas	2,815.4
32	Tennessee	2,799.5
33	Iowa	2,767.2
34	Virginia	2,740.0
35	Ohio	2,669.0
36	Connecticut	2,668.7
37	Wisconsin	2,627.8
38	New Jersey	2,597.1
39	Mississippi	2,520.1
40	Rhode Island	2,503.0
41	Vermont	2,418.8
42	New York	2,344.4
43	Maine	2,292.0
44	North Dakota	2,249.8
45	Massachusetts	2,232.2
46	South Dakota	2,191.5
47	Kentucky	1,992.4
48	New Hampshire	1,977.2
49	Pennsylvania	1,963.1
50	West Virginia	1,516.6
	District of Columbia	5,833.8

Source: Federal Bureau of Investigation
"Crime in the United States 1996" (Uniform Crime Reports, October 4, 1997)
*Revised figures. Larceny and theft is the unlawful taking of property without use of force, violence or fraud.
Attempts are included. Motor vehicle thefts are excluded.

Percent Change in Larceny and Theft Rate: 1995 to 1999

National Percent Change = 16.2% Decrease*

<table>
<tr><td colspan="3">ALPHA ORDER</td><td colspan="3">RANK ORDER</td></tr>
<tr><td>RANK</td><td>STATE</td><td>PERCENT CHANGE</td><td>RANK</td><td>STATE</td><td>PERCENT CHANGE</td></tr>
<tr><td>4</td><td>Alabama</td><td>(3.8)</td><td>1</td><td>Kansas</td><td>(2.3)</td></tr>
<tr><td>43</td><td>Alaska</td><td>(25.8)</td><td>2</td><td>Pennsylvania</td><td>(3.3)</td></tr>
<tr><td>45</td><td>Arizona</td><td>(28.7)</td><td>3</td><td>Delaware</td><td>(3.6)</td></tr>
<tr><td>16</td><td>Arkansas</td><td>(11.0)</td><td>4</td><td>Alabama</td><td>(3.8)</td></tr>
<tr><td>47</td><td>California</td><td>(30.2)</td><td>5</td><td>Ohio</td><td>(4.1)</td></tr>
<tr><td>44</td><td>Colorado</td><td>(25.9)</td><td>6</td><td>Mississippi</td><td>(5.5)</td></tr>
<tr><td>39</td><td>Connecticut</td><td>(20.9)</td><td>7</td><td>Missouri</td><td>(5.6)</td></tr>
<tr><td>3</td><td>Delaware</td><td>(3.6)</td><td>8</td><td>New Mexico</td><td>(6.1)</td></tr>
<tr><td>29</td><td>Florida</td><td>(18.2)</td><td>9</td><td>Tennessee</td><td>(7.1)</td></tr>
<tr><td>23</td><td>Georgia</td><td>(13.5)</td><td>10</td><td>North Carolina</td><td>(7.7)</td></tr>
<tr><td>48</td><td>Hawaii</td><td>(32.4)</td><td>11</td><td>Texas</td><td>(9.3)</td></tr>
<tr><td>46</td><td>Idaho</td><td>(29.9)</td><td>12</td><td>Rhode Island</td><td>(10.2)</td></tr>
<tr><td>22</td><td>Illinois</td><td>(12.8)</td><td>13</td><td>South Carolina</td><td>(10.3)</td></tr>
<tr><td>27</td><td>Indiana</td><td>(17.2)</td><td>14</td><td>New Hampshire</td><td>(10.7)</td></tr>
<tr><td>41</td><td>Iowa</td><td>(21.5)</td><td>15</td><td>Louisiana</td><td>(10.8)</td></tr>
<tr><td>1</td><td>Kansas</td><td>(2.3)</td><td>16</td><td>Arkansas</td><td>(11.0)</td></tr>
<tr><td>19</td><td>Kentucky</td><td>(12.2)</td><td>17</td><td>Maine</td><td>(11.6)</td></tr>
<tr><td>15</td><td>Louisiana</td><td>(10.8)</td><td>18</td><td>Oklahoma</td><td>(11.9)</td></tr>
<tr><td>17</td><td>Maine</td><td>(11.6)</td><td>19</td><td>Kentucky</td><td>(12.2)</td></tr>
<tr><td>33</td><td>Maryland</td><td>(19.4)</td><td>20</td><td>Wisconsin</td><td>(12.5)</td></tr>
<tr><td>40</td><td>Massachusetts</td><td>(21.0)</td><td>21</td><td>South Dakota</td><td>(12.6)</td></tr>
<tr><td>30</td><td>Michigan</td><td>(18.5)</td><td>22</td><td>Illinois</td><td>(12.8)</td></tr>
<tr><td>28</td><td>Minnesota</td><td>(17.9)</td><td>23</td><td>Georgia</td><td>(13.5)</td></tr>
<tr><td>6</td><td>Mississippi</td><td>(5.5)</td><td>24</td><td>Nebraska</td><td>(13.8)</td></tr>
<tr><td>7</td><td>Missouri</td><td>(5.6)</td><td>25</td><td>Montana</td><td>(14.6)</td></tr>
<tr><td>25</td><td>Montana</td><td>(14.6)</td><td>26</td><td>Virginia</td><td>(15.1)</td></tr>
<tr><td>24</td><td>Nebraska</td><td>(13.8)</td><td>27</td><td>Indiana</td><td>(17.2)</td></tr>
<tr><td>49</td><td>Nevada</td><td>(33.1)</td><td>28</td><td>Minnesota</td><td>(17.9)</td></tr>
<tr><td>14</td><td>New Hampshire</td><td>(10.7)</td><td>29</td><td>Florida</td><td>(18.2)</td></tr>
<tr><td>42</td><td>New Jersey</td><td>(23.9)</td><td>30</td><td>Michigan</td><td>(18.5)</td></tr>
<tr><td>8</td><td>New Mexico</td><td>(6.1)</td><td>31</td><td>Vermont</td><td>(19.2)</td></tr>
<tr><td>38</td><td>New York</td><td>(20.7)</td><td>32</td><td>Washington</td><td>(19.3)</td></tr>
<tr><td>10</td><td>North Carolina</td><td>(7.7)</td><td>33</td><td>Maryland</td><td>(19.4)</td></tr>
<tr><td>36</td><td>North Dakota</td><td>(20.3)</td><td>34</td><td>Oregon</td><td>(19.5)</td></tr>
<tr><td>5</td><td>Ohio</td><td>(4.1)</td><td>35</td><td>Utah</td><td>(19.7)</td></tr>
<tr><td>18</td><td>Oklahoma</td><td>(11.9)</td><td>36</td><td>North Dakota</td><td>(20.3)</td></tr>
<tr><td>34</td><td>Oregon</td><td>(19.5)</td><td>37</td><td>Wyoming</td><td>(20.6)</td></tr>
<tr><td>2</td><td>Pennsylvania</td><td>(3.3)</td><td>38</td><td>New York</td><td>(20.7)</td></tr>
<tr><td>12</td><td>Rhode Island</td><td>(10.2)</td><td>39</td><td>Connecticut</td><td>(20.9)</td></tr>
<tr><td>13</td><td>South Carolina</td><td>(10.3)</td><td>40</td><td>Massachusetts</td><td>(21.0)</td></tr>
<tr><td>21</td><td>South Dakota</td><td>(12.6)</td><td>41</td><td>Iowa</td><td>(21.5)</td></tr>
<tr><td>9</td><td>Tennessee</td><td>(7.1)</td><td>42</td><td>New Jersey</td><td>(23.9)</td></tr>
<tr><td>11</td><td>Texas</td><td>(9.3)</td><td>43</td><td>Alaska</td><td>(25.8)</td></tr>
<tr><td>35</td><td>Utah</td><td>(19.7)</td><td>44</td><td>Colorado</td><td>(25.9)</td></tr>
<tr><td>31</td><td>Vermont</td><td>(19.2)</td><td>45</td><td>Arizona</td><td>(28.7)</td></tr>
<tr><td>26</td><td>Virginia</td><td>(15.1)</td><td>46</td><td>Idaho</td><td>(29.9)</td></tr>
<tr><td>32</td><td>Washington</td><td>(19.3)</td><td>47</td><td>California</td><td>(30.2)</td></tr>
<tr><td>NA</td><td>West Virginia**</td><td>NA</td><td>48</td><td>Hawaii</td><td>(32.4)</td></tr>
<tr><td>20</td><td>Wisconsin</td><td>(12.5)</td><td>49</td><td>Nevada</td><td>(33.1)</td></tr>
<tr><td>37</td><td>Wyoming</td><td>(20.6)</td><td>NA</td><td>West Virginia**</td><td>NA</td></tr>
<tr><td></td><td></td><td></td><td></td><td>District of Columbia</td><td>(28.3)</td></tr>
</table>

Source: Morgan Quitno Press using data from Federal Bureau of Investigation
   "Crime in the United States" (Uniform Crime Reports, 1996 and 1999 editions)
*Larceny and theft is the unlawful taking of property without use of force, violence or fraud. Attempts are included.
Motor vehicle thefts are excluded.
**Not comparable.

Motor Vehicle Thefts in 1995

National Total = 1,472,441 Motor Vehicle Thefts*

ALPHA ORDER				RANK ORDER			
RANK	STATE	THEFTS	% of USA	RANK	STATE	THEFTS	% of USA
26	Alabama	14,741	1.0%	1	California	280,479	19.0%
40	Alaska	3,151	0.2%	2	Florida	111,320	7.6%
9	Arizona	48,830	3.3%	3	Texas	104,923	7.1%
35	Arkansas	8,082	0.5%	4	New York	102,596	7.0%
1	California	280,479	19.0%	5	Illinois	61,874	4.2%
27	Colorado	14,520	1.0%	6	Michigan	61,639	4.2%
23	Connecticut	17,692	1.2%	7	New Jersey	50,184	3.4%
42	Delaware	2,970	0.2%	8	Pennsylvania	49,817	3.4%
2	Florida	111,320	7.6%	9	Arizona	48,830	3.3%
11	Georgia	43,809	3.0%	10	Ohio	46,261	3.1%
34	Hawaii	8,199	0.6%	11	Georgia	43,809	3.0%
43	Idaho	2,815	0.2%	12	Massachusetts	36,716	2.5%
5	Illinois	61,874	4.2%	13	Maryland	36,179	2.5%
16	Indiana	27,023	1.8%	14	Tennessee	34,086	2.3%
37	Iowa	6,332	0.4%	15	Washington	30,087	2.0%
33	Kansas	8,299	0.6%	16	Indiana	27,023	1.8%
30	Kentucky	10,003	0.7%	17	Louisiana	25,984	1.8%
17	Louisiana	25,984	1.8%	18	Missouri	25,199	1.7%
45	Maine	1,673	0.1%	19	North Carolina	22,350	1.5%
13	Maryland	36,179	2.5%	20	Oregon	22,050	1.5%
12	Massachusetts	36,716	2.5%	21	Virginia	19,363	1.3%
6	Michigan	61,639	4.2%	22	Wisconsin	18,626	1.3%
25	Minnesota	15,741	1.1%	23	Connecticut	17,692	1.2%
31	Mississippi	9,723	0.7%	24	Oklahoma	16,272	1.1%
18	Missouri	25,199	1.7%	25	Minnesota	15,741	1.1%
44	Montana	2,389	0.2%	26	Alabama	14,741	1.0%
38	Nebraska	5,752	0.4%	27	Colorado	14,520	1.0%
29	Nevada	11,405	0.8%	28	South Carolina	14,157	1.0%
46	New Hampshire	1,666	0.1%	29	Nevada	11,405	0.8%
7	New Jersey	50,184	3.4%	30	Kentucky	10,003	0.7%
32	New Mexico	8,647	0.6%	31	Mississippi	9,723	0.7%
4	New York	102,596	7.0%	32	New Mexico	8,647	0.6%
19	North Carolina	22,350	1.5%	33	Kansas	8,299	0.6%
47	North Dakota	1,148	0.1%	34	Hawaii	8,199	0.6%
10	Ohio	46,261	3.1%	35	Arkansas	8,082	0.5%
24	Oklahoma	16,272	1.1%	36	Utah	7,592	0.5%
20	Oregon	22,050	1.5%	37	Iowa	6,332	0.4%
8	Pennsylvania	49,817	3.4%	38	Nebraska	5,752	0.4%
39	Rhode Island	4,364	0.3%	39	Rhode Island	4,364	0.3%
28	South Carolina	14,157	1.0%	40	Alaska	3,151	0.2%
48	South Dakota	881	0.1%	41	West Virginia	3,040	0.2%
14	Tennessee	34,086	2.3%	42	Delaware	2,970	0.2%
3	Texas	104,923	7.1%	43	Idaho	2,815	0.2%
36	Utah	7,592	0.5%	44	Montana	2,389	0.2%
50	Vermont	794	0.1%	45	Maine	1,673	0.1%
21	Virginia	19,363	1.3%	46	New Hampshire	1,666	0.1%
15	Washington	30,087	2.0%	47	North Dakota	1,148	0.1%
41	West Virginia	3,040	0.2%	48	South Dakota	881	0.1%
22	Wisconsin	18,626	1.3%	49	Wyoming	805	0.1%
49	Wyoming	805	0.1%	50	Vermont	794	0.1%
					District of Columbia	10,193	0.7%

Source: Federal Bureau of Investigation
"Crime in the United States 1996" (Uniform Crime Reports, October 4, 1997)
*Revised figures. Includes the theft or attempted theft of a self-propelled vehicle. Excludes motorboats, construction equipment, airplanes and farming equipment.

Percent Change in Number of Motor Vehicle Thefts: 1995 to 1999

National Percent Change = 22.1% Decrease*

ALPHA ORDER

RANK	STATE	PERCENT CHANGE
20	Alabama	(10.9)
24	Alaska	(15.6)
34	Arizona	(21.7)
29	Arkansas	(17.5)
47	California	(39.9)
8	Colorado	1.9
45	Connecticut	(36.1)
6	Delaware	2.5
27	Florida	(16.3)
17	Georgia	(8.4)
48	Hawaii	(43.2)
44	Idaho	(32.6)
26	Illinois	(15.8)
35	Indiana	(24.9)
31	Iowa	(18.9)
40	Kansas	(27.1)
22	Kentucky	(13.7)
28	Louisiana	(16.5)
9	Maine	1.3
42	Maryland	(29.7)
43	Massachusetts	(30.2)
16	Michigan	(7.9)
25	Minnesota	(15.7)
1	Mississippi	39.2
18	Missouri	(8.8)
32	Montana	(20.6)
12	Nebraska	(5.4)
3	Nevada	14.8
30	New Hampshire	(18.7)
41	New Jersey	(29.5)
13	New Mexico	(6.0)
48	New York	(43.2)
4	North Carolina	14.4
19	North Dakota	(9.8)
23	Ohio	(15.3)
36	Oklahoma	(25.4)
46	Oregon	(38.2)
33	Pennsylvania	(21.2)
15	Rhode Island	(7.6)
7	South Carolina	2.0
10	South Dakota	(2.3)
38	Tennessee	(25.9)
21	Texas	(12.3)
11	Utah	(2.8)
2	Vermont	14.9
14	Virginia	(7.3)
5	Washington	12.4
NA	West Virginia**	NA
37	Wisconsin	(25.8)
39	Wyoming	(26.0)

RANK ORDER

RANK	STATE	PERCENT CHANGE
1	Mississippi	39.2
2	Vermont	14.9
3	Nevada	14.8
4	North Carolina	14.4
5	Washington	12.4
6	Delaware	2.5
7	South Carolina	2.0
8	Colorado	1.9
9	Maine	1.3
10	South Dakota	(2.3)
11	Utah	(2.8)
12	Nebraska	(5.4)
13	New Mexico	(6.0)
14	Virginia	(7.3)
15	Rhode Island	(7.6)
16	Michigan	(7.9)
17	Georgia	(8.4)
18	Missouri	(8.8)
19	North Dakota	(9.8)
20	Alabama	(10.9)
21	Texas	(12.3)
22	Kentucky	(13.7)
23	Ohio	(15.3)
24	Alaska	(15.6)
25	Minnesota	(15.7)
26	Illinois	(15.8)
27	Florida	(16.3)
28	Louisiana	(16.5)
29	Arkansas	(17.5)
30	New Hampshire	(18.7)
31	Iowa	(18.9)
32	Montana	(20.6)
33	Pennsylvania	(21.2)
34	Arizona	(21.7)
35	Indiana	(24.9)
36	Oklahoma	(25.4)
37	Wisconsin	(25.8)
38	Tennessee	(25.9)
39	Wyoming	(26.0)
40	Kansas	(27.1)
41	New Jersey	(29.5)
42	Maryland	(29.7)
43	Massachusetts	(30.2)
44	Idaho	(32.6)
45	Connecticut	(36.1)
46	Oregon	(38.2)
47	California	(39.9)
48	Hawaii	(43.2)
48	New York	(43.2)
NA	West Virginia**	NA

District of Columbia (34.7)

Source: Morgan Quitno Press using data from Federal Bureau of Investigation
   "Crime in the United States" (Uniform Crime Reports, 1996 and 1999 editions)
*Includes the theft or attempted theft of a self-propelled vehicle. Excludes motorboats, construction equipment, airplanes and farming equipment.
**Not comparable.

Motor Vehicle Theft Rate in 1995

National Rate = 560.4 Motor Vehicle Thefts per 100,000 Population*

ALPHA ORDER

RANK	STATE	RATE
34	Alabama	346.6
19	Alaska	521.7
1	Arizona	1,157.7
36	Arkansas	325.4
2	California	887.9
29	Colorado	387.5
17	Connecticut	540.2
26	Delaware	414.2
3	Florida	785.8
11	Georgia	608.4
7	Hawaii	690.7
42	Idaho	242.0
18	Illinois	523.0
23	Indiana	465.7
43	Iowa	222.8
37	Kansas	323.5
41	Kentucky	259.1
13	Louisiana	598.4
49	Maine	134.8
5	Maryland	717.6
12	Massachusetts	604.5
9	Michigan	645.5
35	Minnesota	341.5
32	Mississippi	360.5
22	Missouri	473.3
40	Montana	274.6
33	Nebraska	351.4
4	Nevada	745.4
47	New Hampshire	145.1
10	New Jersey	631.6
20	New Mexico	513.2
14	New York	565.7
38	North Carolina	310.6
44	North Dakota	179.1
25	Ohio	414.9
21	Oklahoma	496.4
6	Oregon	702.0
27	Pennsylvania	412.7
24	Rhode Island	440.8
30	South Carolina	385.4
50	South Dakota	120.9
8	Tennessee	648.5
15	Texas	560.4
28	Utah	389.1
48	Vermont	135.7
39	Virginia	292.6
16	Washington	554.0
46	West Virginia	166.3
31	Wisconsin	363.6
45	Wyoming	167.7

RANK ORDER

RANK	STATE	RATE
1	Arizona	1,157.7
2	California	887.9
3	Florida	785.8
4	Nevada	745.4
5	Maryland	717.6
6	Oregon	702.0
7	Hawaii	690.7
8	Tennessee	648.5
9	Michigan	645.5
10	New Jersey	631.6
11	Georgia	608.4
12	Massachusetts	604.5
13	Louisiana	598.4
14	New York	565.7
15	Texas	560.4
16	Washington	554.0
17	Connecticut	540.2
18	Illinois	523.0
19	Alaska	521.7
20	New Mexico	513.2
21	Oklahoma	496.4
22	Missouri	473.3
23	Indiana	465.7
24	Rhode Island	440.8
25	Ohio	414.9
26	Delaware	414.2
27	Pennsylvania	412.7
28	Utah	389.1
29	Colorado	387.5
30	South Carolina	385.4
31	Wisconsin	363.6
32	Mississippi	360.5
33	Nebraska	351.4
34	Alabama	346.6
35	Minnesota	341.5
36	Arkansas	325.4
37	Kansas	323.5
38	North Carolina	310.6
39	Virginia	292.6
40	Montana	274.6
41	Kentucky	259.1
42	Idaho	242.0
43	Iowa	222.8
44	North Dakota	179.1
45	Wyoming	167.7
46	West Virginia	166.3
47	New Hampshire	145.1
48	Vermont	135.7
49	Maine	134.8
50	South Dakota	120.9
	District of Columbia	1,839.9

Source: Federal Bureau of Investigation
    "Crime in the United States 1996" (Uniform Crime Reports, October 4, 1997)
*Revised figures. Includes the theft or attempted theft of a self-propelled vehicle. Excludes motorboats,
construction equipment, airplanes and farming equipment.

Percent Change in Motor Vehicle Theft Rate: 1995 to 1999

National Percent Change = 24.9% Decrease*

<table>
<tr><td colspan="3">ALPHA ORDER</td><td colspan="3">RANK ORDER</td></tr>
<tr><td>RANK</td><td>STATE</td><td>PERCENT CHANGE</td><td>RANK</td><td>STATE</td><td>PERCENT CHANGE</td></tr>
<tr><td>19</td><td>Alabama</td><td>(13.3)</td><td>1</td><td>Mississippi</td><td>35.6</td></tr>
<tr><td>24</td><td>Alaska</td><td>(17.7)</td><td>2</td><td>Vermont</td><td>13.1</td></tr>
<tr><td>40</td><td>Arizona</td><td>(30.9)</td><td>3</td><td>North Carolina</td><td>7.6</td></tr>
<tr><td>28</td><td>Arkansas</td><td>(19.7)</td><td>4</td><td>Washington</td><td>6.0</td></tr>
<tr><td>47</td><td>California</td><td>(42.8)</td><td>5</td><td>Maine</td><td>0.3</td></tr>
<tr><td>10</td><td>Colorado</td><td>(5.9)</td><td>6</td><td>Delaware</td><td>(2.6)</td></tr>
<tr><td>44</td><td>Connecticut</td><td>(36.3)</td><td>7</td><td>South Dakota</td><td>(2.8)</td></tr>
<tr><td>6</td><td>Delaware</td><td>(2.6)</td><td>8</td><td>Nevada</td><td>(2.9)</td></tr>
<tr><td>31</td><td>Florida</td><td>(21.5)</td><td>9</td><td>South Carolina</td><td>(3.6)</td></tr>
<tr><td>20</td><td>Georgia</td><td>(15.3)</td><td>10</td><td>Colorado</td><td>(5.9)</td></tr>
<tr><td>48</td><td>Hawaii</td><td>(43.1)</td><td>11</td><td>Nebraska</td><td>(7.1)</td></tr>
<tr><td>45</td><td>Idaho</td><td>(37.4)</td><td>12</td><td>Rhode Island</td><td>(7.7)</td></tr>
<tr><td>25</td><td>Illinois</td><td>(17.8)</td><td>13</td><td>North Dakota</td><td>(8.8)</td></tr>
<tr><td>35</td><td>Indiana</td><td>(26.7)</td><td>14</td><td>New Mexico</td><td>(9.0)</td></tr>
<tr><td>28</td><td>Iowa</td><td>(19.7)</td><td>15</td><td>Virginia</td><td>(10.7)</td></tr>
<tr><td>39</td><td>Kansas</td><td>(29.6)</td><td>16</td><td>Michigan</td><td>(10.8)</td></tr>
<tr><td>21</td><td>Kentucky</td><td>(15.9)</td><td>17</td><td>Utah</td><td>(10.9)</td></tr>
<tr><td>23</td><td>Louisiana</td><td>(17.1)</td><td>18</td><td>Missouri</td><td>(11.2)</td></tr>
<tr><td>5</td><td>Maine</td><td>0.3</td><td>19</td><td>Alabama</td><td>(13.3)</td></tr>
<tr><td>43</td><td>Maryland</td><td>(31.4)</td><td>20</td><td>Georgia</td><td>(15.3)</td></tr>
<tr><td>41</td><td>Massachusetts</td><td>(31.3)</td><td>21</td><td>Kentucky</td><td>(15.9)</td></tr>
<tr><td>16</td><td>Michigan</td><td>(10.8)</td><td>22</td><td>Ohio</td><td>(16.1)</td></tr>
<tr><td>27</td><td>Minnesota</td><td>(18.6)</td><td>23</td><td>Louisiana</td><td>(17.1)</td></tr>
<tr><td>1</td><td>Mississippi</td><td>35.6</td><td>24</td><td>Alaska</td><td>(17.7)</td></tr>
<tr><td>18</td><td>Missouri</td><td>(11.2)</td><td>25</td><td>Illinois</td><td>(17.8)</td></tr>
<tr><td>32</td><td>Montana</td><td>(21.8)</td><td>26</td><td>Texas</td><td>(18.1)</td></tr>
<tr><td>11</td><td>Nebraska</td><td>(7.1)</td><td>27</td><td>Minnesota</td><td>(18.6)</td></tr>
<tr><td>8</td><td>Nevada</td><td>(2.9)</td><td>28</td><td>Arkansas</td><td>(19.7)</td></tr>
<tr><td>33</td><td>New Hampshire</td><td>(22.3)</td><td>28</td><td>Iowa</td><td>(19.7)</td></tr>
<tr><td>41</td><td>New Jersey</td><td>(31.3)</td><td>30</td><td>Pennsylvania</td><td>(20.7)</td></tr>
<tr><td>14</td><td>New Mexico</td><td>(9.0)</td><td>31</td><td>Florida</td><td>(21.5)</td></tr>
<tr><td>49</td><td>New York</td><td>(43.4)</td><td>32</td><td>Montana</td><td>(21.8)</td></tr>
<tr><td>3</td><td>North Carolina</td><td>7.6</td><td>33</td><td>New Hampshire</td><td>(22.3)</td></tr>
<tr><td>13</td><td>North Dakota</td><td>(8.8)</td><td>34</td><td>Wyoming</td><td>(25.9)</td></tr>
<tr><td>22</td><td>Ohio</td><td>(16.1)</td><td>35</td><td>Indiana</td><td>(26.7)</td></tr>
<tr><td>36</td><td>Oklahoma</td><td>(27.2)</td><td>36</td><td>Oklahoma</td><td>(27.2)</td></tr>
<tr><td>46</td><td>Oregon</td><td>(41.4)</td><td>37</td><td>Wisconsin</td><td>(27.6)</td></tr>
<tr><td>30</td><td>Pennsylvania</td><td>(20.7)</td><td>38</td><td>Tennessee</td><td>(29.0)</td></tr>
<tr><td>12</td><td>Rhode Island</td><td>(7.7)</td><td>39</td><td>Kansas</td><td>(29.6)</td></tr>
<tr><td>9</td><td>South Carolina</td><td>(3.6)</td><td>40</td><td>Arizona</td><td>(30.9)</td></tr>
<tr><td>7</td><td>South Dakota</td><td>(2.8)</td><td>41</td><td>Massachusetts</td><td>(31.3)</td></tr>
<tr><td>38</td><td>Tennessee</td><td>(29.0)</td><td>41</td><td>New Jersey</td><td>(31.3)</td></tr>
<tr><td>26</td><td>Texas</td><td>(18.1)</td><td>43</td><td>Maryland</td><td>(31.4)</td></tr>
<tr><td>17</td><td>Utah</td><td>(10.9)</td><td>44</td><td>Connecticut</td><td>(36.3)</td></tr>
<tr><td>2</td><td>Vermont</td><td>13.1</td><td>45</td><td>Idaho</td><td>(37.4)</td></tr>
<tr><td>15</td><td>Virginia</td><td>(10.7)</td><td>46</td><td>Oregon</td><td>(41.4)</td></tr>
<tr><td>4</td><td>Washington</td><td>6.0</td><td>47</td><td>California</td><td>(42.8)</td></tr>
<tr><td>NA</td><td>West Virginia**</td><td>NA</td><td>48</td><td>Hawaii</td><td>(43.1)</td></tr>
<tr><td>37</td><td>Wisconsin</td><td>(27.6)</td><td>49</td><td>New York</td><td>(43.4)</td></tr>
<tr><td>34</td><td>Wyoming</td><td>(25.9)</td><td>NA</td><td>West Virginia**</td><td>NA</td></tr>
<tr><td></td><td></td><td></td><td></td><td>District of Columbia</td><td>(30.3)</td></tr>
</table>

Source: Morgan Quitno Press using data from Federal Bureau of Investigation
   "Crime in the United States" (Uniform Crime Reports, 1996 and 1999 editions)
*Includes the theft or attempted theft of a self-propelled vehicle. Excludes motorboats, construction equipment, airplanes and farming equipment.
**Not comparable.

Hate Crimes in 1999

National Total = 7,876 Reported Hate Crimes*

ALPHA ORDER

RANK	STATE	HATE CRIMES	% of USA
NA	Alabama**	NA	NA
45	Alaska	5	0.1%
8	Arizona	252	3.2%
43	Arkansas	8	0.1%
1	California	1,949	24.7%
16	Colorado	148	1.9%
17	Connecticut	135	1.7%
30	Delaware	37	0.5%
6	Florida	267	3.4%
31	Georgia	36	0.5%
NA	Hawaii**	NA	NA
33	Idaho	34	0.4%
9	Illinois	247	3.1%
20	Indiana	111	1.4%
35	Iowa	31	0.4%
28	Kansas	41	0.5%
23	Kentucky	71	0.9%
44	Louisiana	6	0.1%
38	Maine	22	0.3%
11	Maryland	230	2.9%
4	Massachusetts	443	5.6%
5	Michigan	407	5.2%
13	Minnesota	225	2.9%
46	Mississippi	2	0.0%
21	Missouri	83	1.1%
37	Montana	27	0.3%
32	Nebraska	35	0.4%
22	Nevada	75	1.0%
39	New Hampshire	20	0.3%
2	New Jersey	617	7.8%
40	New Mexico	16	0.2%
3	New York	590	7.5%
35	North Carolina	31	0.4%
46	North Dakota	2	0.0%
10	Ohio	232	2.9%
27	Oklahoma	42	0.5%
19	Oregon	123	1.6%
15	Pennsylvania	185	2.3%
28	Rhode Island	41	0.5%
25	South Carolina	52	0.7%
42	South Dakota	14	0.2%
18	Tennessee	127	1.6%
7	Texas	262	3.3%
24	Utah	59	0.7%
40	Vermont	16	0.2%
14	Virginia	203	2.6%
11	Washington	230	2.9%
34	West Virginia	32	0.4%
26	Wisconsin	49	0.6%
46	Wyoming	2	0.0%

RANK ORDER

RANK	STATE	HATE CRIMES	% of USA
1	California	1,949	24.7%
2	New Jersey	617	7.8%
3	New York	590	7.5%
4	Massachusetts	443	5.6%
5	Michigan	407	5.2%
6	Florida	267	3.4%
7	Texas	262	3.3%
8	Arizona	252	3.2%
9	Illinois	247	3.1%
10	Ohio	232	2.9%
11	Maryland	230	2.9%
11	Washington	230	2.9%
13	Minnesota	225	2.9%
14	Virginia	203	2.6%
15	Pennsylvania	185	2.3%
16	Colorado	148	1.9%
17	Connecticut	135	1.7%
18	Tennessee	127	1.6%
19	Oregon	123	1.6%
20	Indiana	111	1.4%
21	Missouri	83	1.1%
22	Nevada	75	1.0%
23	Kentucky	71	0.9%
24	Utah	59	0.7%
25	South Carolina	52	0.7%
26	Wisconsin	49	0.6%
27	Oklahoma	42	0.5%
28	Kansas	41	0.5%
28	Rhode Island	41	0.5%
30	Delaware	37	0.5%
31	Georgia	36	0.5%
32	Nebraska	35	0.4%
33	Idaho	34	0.4%
34	West Virginia	32	0.4%
35	Iowa	31	0.4%
35	North Carolina	31	0.4%
37	Montana	27	0.3%
38	Maine	22	0.3%
39	New Hampshire	20	0.3%
40	New Mexico	16	0.2%
40	Vermont	16	0.2%
42	South Dakota	14	0.2%
43	Arkansas	8	0.1%
44	Louisiana	6	0.1%
45	Alaska	5	0.1%
46	Mississippi	2	0.0%
46	North Dakota	2	0.0%
46	Wyoming	2	0.0%
NA	Alabama**	NA	NA
NA	Hawaii**	NA	NA
	District of Columbia	4	0.1%

Source: Federal Bureau of Investigation
"Crime in the United States 1999" (Uniform Crime Reports, October 15, 2000)
Figures are for reporting law enforcement agencies. Participating agencies covered 85 percent of the U.S. population. Fifty-six percent of the incidents were motivated by racial bias; 16.5 percent by religious bias; 16 percent by sexual-orientation bias; and 11 percent by ethnicity/national origin bias.
***Not available.*

Rate of Hate Crimes in 1999

National Rate = 3.4 Hate Crimes per 100,000 Population*

ALPHA ORDER

ALPHA ORDER

RANK	STATE	RATE
NA	Alabama**	NA
31	Alaska	1.9
5	Arizona	5.6
46	Arkansas	0.3
4	California	5.9
17	Colorado	3.6
11	Connecticut	4.2
7	Delaware	4.9
34	Florida	1.8
11	Georgia	4.2
NA	Hawaii**	NA
27	Idaho	2.7
6	Illinois	5.2
17	Indiana	3.6
41	Iowa	1.1
1	Kansas	12.3
28	Kentucky	2.6
47	Louisiana	0.2
34	Maine	1.8
9	Maryland	4.4
2	Massachusetts	8.2
9	Michigan	4.4
8	Minnesota	4.7
47	Mississippi	0.2
31	Missouri	1.9
17	Montana	3.6
29	Nebraska	2.3
13	Nevada	4.1
20	New Hampshire	3.4
3	New Jersey	7.6
37	New Mexico	1.4
22	New York	3.2
43	North Carolina	0.4
43	North Dakota	0.4
24	Ohio	2.9
38	Oklahoma	1.3
16	Oregon	3.7
36	Pennsylvania	1.6
13	Rhode Island	4.1
38	South Carolina	1.3
31	South Dakota	1.9
24	Tennessee	2.9
38	Texas	1.3
26	Utah	2.8
22	Vermont	3.2
20	Virginia	3.4
13	Washington	4.1
30	West Virginia	2.2
42	Wisconsin	0.9
43	Wyoming	0.4

RANK ORDER

RANK	STATE	RATE
1	Kansas	12.3
2	Massachusetts	8.2
3	New Jersey	7.6
4	California	5.9
5	Arizona	5.6
6	Illinois	5.2
7	Delaware	4.9
8	Minnesota	4.7
9	Maryland	4.4
9	Michigan	4.4
11	Connecticut	4.2
11	Georgia	4.2
13	Nevada	4.1
13	Rhode Island	4.1
13	Washington	4.1
16	Oregon	3.7
17	Colorado	3.6
17	Indiana	3.6
17	Montana	3.6
20	New Hampshire	3.4
20	Virginia	3.4
22	New York	3.2
22	Vermont	3.2
24	Ohio	2.9
24	Tennessee	2.9
26	Utah	2.8
27	Idaho	2.7
28	Kentucky	2.6
29	Nebraska	2.3
30	West Virginia	2.2
31	Alaska	1.9
31	Missouri	1.9
31	South Dakota	1.9
34	Florida	1.8
34	Maine	1.8
36	Pennsylvania	1.6
37	New Mexico	1.4
38	Oklahoma	1.3
38	South Carolina	1.3
38	Texas	1.3
41	Iowa	1.1
42	Wisconsin	0.9
43	North Carolina	0.4
43	North Dakota	0.4
43	Wyoming	0.4
46	Arkansas	0.3
47	Louisiana	0.2
47	Mississippi	0.2
NA	Alabama**	NA
NA	Hawaii**	NA
	District of Columbia	0.8

Source: Morgan Quitno Press using data from Federal Bureau of Investigation
   "Crime in the United States 1999" (Uniform Crime Reports, October 15, 2000)
*Figures are for reporting law enforcement agencies. Participating agencies covered 85 percent of the U.S. population. Fifty-six percent of the incidents were motivated by racial bias; 16.5 percent by religious bias; 16 percent by sexual-orientation bias; and 11 percent by ethnicity/national origin bias.
**Not available.

Criminal Victimization in 1999

Each year the Bureau of Justice Statistics conducts the National Criminal Victimization Survey (NCVS). Unlike the FBI's Uniform Crime Reports, which collects crime data from law enforcement agencies, the NCVS information is obtained through interviews with victims of crime.

Type of Crime	Number of Victimizations	Victimization Rates*
All crimes	28,779,800	NA
Personal crimes	7,564,680	33.7
Crimes of violence	7,357,060	32.8
Completed violence**	2,278,260	10.1
Attempted/threatened violence	5,078,790	22.6
Rape/Sexual Assault	383,170	1.7
Rape/attempted rape	200,880	0.9
Rape	141,070	0.6
Attempted rape	59,810	0.3
Sexual assault	182,290	0.8
Robbery	810,220	3.6
Completed/property taken	530,250	2.4
With injury	189,080	0.8
Without injury	341,170	1.5
Attempted to take property	279,970	1.2
With injury	78,080	0.3
Without injury	201,890	0.9
Assault	6,163,670	27.4
Aggravated	1,503,280	6.7
With injury	449,160	2.0
Threatened with weapon	1,054,110	4.7
Simple	4,660,400	20.8
With minor injury	998,310	4.4
Without injury	3,662,090	16.3
Personal theft**	207,630	0.9
Property crimes	21,215,110	198.0
Household burglary	3,651,580	34.1
Completed	3,064,390	28.6
Forcible entry	1,174,780	11.0
Unlawful entry without force	1,889,610	17.6
Attempted forcible entry	587,190	5.5
Motor vehicle theft	1,068,130	10.0
Completed	807,730	7.5
Attempted	260,400	2.4
Theft	16,495,400	153.9
Completed**	15,963,770	149.0
Less than $50	5,700,280	53.2
$50-$249	5,789,210	54.0
$250 or more	3,394,140	31.7
Attempted	531,640	5.0

Source: U.S. Department of Justice, Bureau of Justice Statistics
"Criminal Victimization 1999: Changes 1998-99 with Trends 1993-99" (Bulletin, August 2000, NCJ-182734)
*Rates are per 1,000 persons age 12 or older or per 1,000 households. In 1999, there were 224,568,370 persons age 12 or older and 107,159,550 households. **Completed violent crimes include rape, sexual assault, robbery with or without injury, aggravated assault with injury, and simple assault with minor injury. The NCVS is based on interviews with victims and thus cannot measure murder. Personal theft includes pick pocketing, purse snatching and attempted purse snatching not shown separately. Completed theft includes thefts with unknown losses.

VII. APPENDIX

A-1   Population in 2000

A-2   Population in 1999

A-3   Population in 1995

A-4   Urban Population in 1999

A-5   Rural Population in 1999

A-6   Population 10 to 17 Years Old in 1999

A-7   Total Area of States in Square Miles in 1999

Population in 2000

National Total = 281,421,906*

ALPHA ORDER

RANK	STATE	POPULATION	% of USA
23	Alabama	4,447,100	1.6%
48	Alaska	626,932	0.2%
20	Arizona	5,130,632	1.8%
33	Arkansas	2,673,400	0.9%
1	California	33,871,648	12.0%
24	Colorado	4,301,261	1.5%
29	Connecticut	3,405,565	1.2%
45	Delaware	783,600	0.3%
4	Florida	15,982,378	5.7%
10	Georgia	8,186,453	2.9%
42	Hawaii	1,211,537	0.4%
39	Idaho	1,293,953	0.5%
5	Illinois	12,419,293	4.4%
14	Indiana	6,080,485	2.2%
30	Iowa	2,926,324	1.0%
32	Kansas	2,688,418	1.0%
25	Kentucky	4,041,769	1.4%
22	Louisiana	4,468,976	1.6%
40	Maine	1,274,923	0.5%
19	Maryland	5,296,486	1.9%
13	Massachusetts	6,349,097	2.3%
8	Michigan	9,938,444	3.5%
21	Minnesota	4,919,479	1.7%
31	Mississippi	2,844,658	1.0%
17	Missouri	5,595,211	2.0%
44	Montana	902,195	0.3%
38	Nebraska	1,711,263	0.6%
35	Nevada	1,998,257	0.7%
41	New Hampshire	1,235,786	0.4%
9	New Jersey	8,414,350	3.0%
36	New Mexico	1,819,046	0.6%
3	New York	18,976,457	6.7%
11	North Carolina	8,049,313	2.9%
47	North Dakota	642,200	0.2%
7	Ohio	11,353,140	4.0%
27	Oklahoma	3,450,654	1.2%
28	Oregon	3,421,399	1.2%
6	Pennsylvania	12,281,054	4.4%
43	Rhode Island	1,048,319	0.4%
26	South Carolina	4,012,012	1.4%
46	South Dakota	754,844	0.3%
16	Tennessee	5,689,283	2.0%
2	Texas	20,851,820	7.4%
34	Utah	2,233,169	0.8%
49	Vermont	608,827	0.2%
12	Virginia	7,078,515	2.5%
15	Washington	5,894,121	2.1%
37	West Virginia	1,808,344	0.6%
18	Wisconsin	5,363,675	1.9%
50	Wyoming	493,782	0.2%

RANK ORDER

RANK	STATE	POPULATION	% of USA
1	California	33,871,648	12.0%
2	Texas	20,851,820	7.4%
3	New York	18,976,457	6.7%
4	Florida	15,982,378	5.7%
5	Illinois	12,419,293	4.4%
6	Pennsylvania	12,281,054	4.4%
7	Ohio	11,353,140	4.0%
8	Michigan	9,938,444	3.5%
9	New Jersey	8,414,350	3.0%
10	Georgia	8,186,453	2.9%
11	North Carolina	8,049,313	2.9%
12	Virginia	7,078,515	2.5%
13	Massachusetts	6,349,097	2.3%
14	Indiana	6,080,485	2.2%
15	Washington	5,894,121	2.1%
16	Tennessee	5,689,283	2.0%
17	Missouri	5,595,211	2.0%
18	Wisconsin	5,363,675	1.9%
19	Maryland	5,296,486	1.9%
20	Arizona	5,130,632	1.8%
21	Minnesota	4,919,479	1.7%
22	Louisiana	4,468,976	1.6%
23	Alabama	4,447,100	1.6%
24	Colorado	4,301,261	1.5%
25	Kentucky	4,041,769	1.4%
26	South Carolina	4,012,012	1.4%
27	Oklahoma	3,450,654	1.2%
28	Oregon	3,421,399	1.2%
29	Connecticut	3,405,565	1.2%
30	Iowa	2,926,324	1.0%
31	Mississippi	2,844,658	1.0%
32	Kansas	2,688,418	1.0%
33	Arkansas	2,673,400	0.9%
34	Utah	2,233,169	0.8%
35	Nevada	1,998,257	0.7%
36	New Mexico	1,819,046	0.6%
37	West Virginia	1,808,344	0.6%
38	Nebraska	1,711,263	0.6%
39	Idaho	1,293,953	0.5%
40	Maine	1,274,923	0.5%
41	New Hampshire	1,235,786	0.4%
42	Hawaii	1,211,537	0.4%
43	Rhode Island	1,048,319	0.4%
44	Montana	902,195	0.3%
45	Delaware	783,600	0.3%
46	South Dakota	754,844	0.3%
47	North Dakota	642,200	0.2%
48	Alaska	626,932	0.2%
49	Vermont	608,827	0.2%
50	Wyoming	493,782	0.2%
	District of Columbia	572,059	0.2%

Source: U.S. Bureau of the Census
"First Census 2000 Results" (December 28, 2000, http://www.census.gov/main/www/cen2000.html)
*Resident population.

Population in 1999

National Total = 272,690,813*

ALPHA ORDER

ALPHA ORDER

RANK	STATE	POPULATION	% of USA
23	Alabama	4,369,862	1.6%
48	Alaska	619,500	0.2%
20	Arizona	4,778,332	1.8%
33	Arkansas	2,551,373	0.9%
1	California	33,145,121	12.2%
24	Colorado	4,056,133	1.5%
29	Connecticut	3,282,031	1.2%
45	Delaware	753,538	0.3%
4	Florida	15,111,244	5.5%
10	Georgia	7,788,240	2.9%
42	Hawaii	1,185,497	0.4%
40	Idaho	1,251,700	0.5%
5	Illinois	12,128,370	4.4%
14	Indiana	5,942,901	2.2%
30	Iowa	2,869,413	1.1%
32	Kansas	2,654,052	1.0%
25	Kentucky	3,960,825	1.5%
22	Louisiana	4,372,035	1.6%
39	Maine	1,253,040	0.5%
19	Maryland	5,171,634	1.9%
13	Massachusetts	6,175,169	2.3%
8	Michigan	9,863,775	3.6%
21	Minnesota	4,775,508	1.8%
31	Mississippi	2,768,619	1.0%
17	Missouri	5,468,338	2.0%
44	Montana	882,779	0.3%
38	Nebraska	1,666,028	0.6%
35	Nevada	1,809,253	0.7%
41	New Hampshire	1,201,134	0.4%
9	New Jersey	8,143,412	3.0%
37	New Mexico	1,739,844	0.6%
3	New York	18,196,601	6.7%
11	North Carolina	7,650,789	2.8%
47	North Dakota	633,666	0.2%
7	Ohio	11,256,654	4.1%
27	Oklahoma	3,358,044	1.2%
28	Oregon	3,316,154	1.2%
6	Pennsylvania	11,994,016	4.4%
43	Rhode Island	990,819	0.4%
26	South Carolina	3,885,736	1.4%
46	South Dakota	733,133	0.3%
16	Tennessee	5,483,535	2.0%
2	Texas	20,044,141	7.4%
34	Utah	2,129,836	0.8%
49	Vermont	593,740	0.2%
12	Virginia	6,872,912	2.5%
15	Washington	5,756,361	2.1%
36	West Virginia	1,806,928	0.7%
18	Wisconsin	5,250,446	1.9%
50	Wyoming	479,602	0.2%

RANK ORDER

RANK	STATE	POPULATION	% of USA
1	California	33,145,121	12.2%
2	Texas	20,044,141	7.4%
3	New York	18,196,601	6.7%
4	Florida	15,111,244	5.5%
5	Illinois	12,128,370	4.4%
6	Pennsylvania	11,994,016	4.4%
7	Ohio	11,256,654	4.1%
8	Michigan	9,863,775	3.6%
9	New Jersey	8,143,412	3.0%
10	Georgia	7,788,240	2.9%
11	North Carolina	7,650,789	2.8%
12	Virginia	6,872,912	2.5%
13	Massachusetts	6,175,169	2.3%
14	Indiana	5,942,901	2.2%
15	Washington	5,756,361	2.1%
16	Tennessee	5,483,535	2.0%
17	Missouri	5,468,338	2.0%
18	Wisconsin	5,250,446	1.9%
19	Maryland	5,171,634	1.9%
20	Arizona	4,778,332	1.8%
21	Minnesota	4,775,508	1.8%
22	Louisiana	4,372,035	1.6%
23	Alabama	4,369,862	1.6%
24	Colorado	4,056,133	1.5%
25	Kentucky	3,960,825	1.5%
26	South Carolina	3,885,736	1.4%
27	Oklahoma	3,358,044	1.2%
28	Oregon	3,316,154	1.2%
29	Connecticut	3,282,031	1.2%
30	Iowa	2,869,413	1.1%
31	Mississippi	2,768,619	1.0%
32	Kansas	2,654,052	1.0%
33	Arkansas	2,551,373	0.9%
34	Utah	2,129,836	0.8%
35	Nevada	1,809,253	0.7%
36	West Virginia	1,806,928	0.7%
37	New Mexico	1,739,844	0.6%
38	Nebraska	1,666,028	0.6%
39	Maine	1,253,040	0.5%
40	Idaho	1,251,700	0.5%
41	New Hampshire	1,201,134	0.4%
42	Hawaii	1,185,497	0.4%
43	Rhode Island	990,819	0.4%
44	Montana	882,779	0.3%
45	Delaware	753,538	0.3%
46	South Dakota	733,133	0.3%
47	North Dakota	633,666	0.2%
48	Alaska	619,500	0.2%
49	Vermont	593,740	0.2%
50	Wyoming	479,602	0.2%
	District of Columbia	519,000	0.2%

Source: U.S. Bureau of the Census
"State Population Estimates" (December 29, 1999, http://www.census.gov/population/estimates/state/st-99-3.txt)
Includes armed forces residing in each state.

Population in 1995

National Total = 262,803,276*

ALPHA ORDER

RANK	STATE	POPULATION	% of USA
23	Alabama	4,262,731	1.6%
48	Alaska	601,345	0.2%
22	Arizona	4,306,908	1.6%
33	Arkansas	2,480,121	0.9%
1	California	31,493,525	12.0%
25	Colorado	3,738,061	1.4%
28	Connecticut	3,265,293	1.2%
46	Delaware	718,265	0.3%
4	Florida	14,185,403	5.4%
10	Georgia	7,188,538	2.7%
40	Hawaii	1,180,490	0.4%
41	Idaho	1,165,000	0.4%
6	Illinois	11,884,935	4.5%
14	Indiana	5,791,819	2.2%
30	Iowa	2,840,860	1.1%
32	Kansas	2,586,942	1.0%
24	Kentucky	3,855,248	1.5%
21	Louisiana	4,327,978	1.6%
39	Maine	1,237,438	0.5%
19	Maryland	5,023,650	1.9%
13	Massachusetts	6,062,335	2.3%
8	Michigan	9,659,871	3.7%
20	Minnesota	4,605,445	1.8%
31	Mississippi	2,690,788	1.0%
16	Missouri	5,324,610	2.0%
44	Montana	868,522	0.3%
37	Nebraska	1,635,142	0.6%
38	Nevada	1,525,777	0.6%
42	New Hampshire	1,145,604	0.4%
9	New Jersey	7,965,523	3.0%
36	New Mexico	1,682,417	0.6%
3	New York	18,150,928	6.9%
11	North Carolina	7,185,403	2.7%
47	North Dakota	641,548	0.2%
7	Ohio	11,155,493	4.2%
27	Oklahoma	3,265,547	1.2%
29	Oregon	3,141,421	1.2%
5	Pennsylvania	12,044,780	4.6%
43	Rhode Island	989,203	0.4%
26	South Carolina	3,699,943	1.4%
45	South Dakota	728,251	0.3%
17	Tennessee	5,241,168	2.0%
2	Texas	18,679,706	7.1%
34	Utah	1,976,774	0.8%
49	Vermont	582,827	0.2%
12	Virginia	6,601,392	2.5%
15	Washington	5,431,024	2.1%
35	West Virginia	1,820,560	0.7%
18	Wisconsin	5,137,004	2.0%
50	Wyoming	478,447	0.2%

RANK ORDER

RANK	STATE	POPULATION	% of USA
1	California	31,493,525	12.0%
2	Texas	18,679,706	7.1%
3	New York	18,150,928	6.9%
4	Florida	14,185,403	5.4%
5	Pennsylvania	12,044,780	4.6%
6	Illinois	11,884,935	4.5%
7	Ohio	11,155,493	4.2%
8	Michigan	9,659,871	3.7%
9	New Jersey	7,965,523	3.0%
10	Georgia	7,188,538	2.7%
11	North Carolina	7,185,403	2.7%
12	Virginia	6,601,392	2.5%
13	Massachusetts	6,062,335	2.3%
14	Indiana	5,791,819	2.2%
15	Washington	5,431,024	2.1%
16	Missouri	5,324,610	2.0%
17	Tennessee	5,241,168	2.0%
18	Wisconsin	5,137,004	2.0%
19	Maryland	5,023,650	1.9%
20	Minnesota	4,605,445	1.8%
21	Louisiana	4,327,978	1.6%
22	Arizona	4,306,908	1.6%
23	Alabama	4,262,731	1.6%
24	Kentucky	3,855,248	1.5%
25	Colorado	3,738,061	1.4%
26	South Carolina	3,699,943	1.4%
27	Oklahoma	3,265,547	1.2%
28	Connecticut	3,265,293	1.2%
29	Oregon	3,141,421	1.2%
30	Iowa	2,840,860	1.1%
31	Mississippi	2,690,788	1.0%
32	Kansas	2,586,942	1.0%
33	Arkansas	2,480,121	0.9%
34	Utah	1,976,774	0.8%
35	West Virginia	1,820,560	0.7%
36	New Mexico	1,682,417	0.6%
37	Nebraska	1,635,142	0.6%
38	Nevada	1,525,777	0.6%
39	Maine	1,237,438	0.5%
40	Hawaii	1,180,490	0.4%
41	Idaho	1,165,000	0.4%
42	New Hampshire	1,145,604	0.4%
43	Rhode Island	989,203	0.4%
44	Montana	868,522	0.3%
45	South Dakota	728,251	0.3%
46	Delaware	718,265	0.3%
47	North Dakota	641,548	0.2%
48	Alaska	601,345	0.2%
49	Vermont	582,827	0.2%
50	Wyoming	478,447	0.2%
	District of Columbia	551,273	0.2%

Source: U.S. Bureau of the Census
"State Population Estimates" (December 29, 1999, http://www.census.gov/population/estimates/state/st-99-3.txt)
Includes armed forces residing in each state. This updates earlier 1995 population estimates.

Urban Population in 1999

National Total = 239,366,953 Urban Population*

ALPHA ORDER

RANK	STATE	POPULATION	% of USA
23	Alabama	3,558,024	1.5%
42	Alaska	425,501	0.2%
16	Arizona	4,480,386	1.9%
30	Arkansas	1,732,012	0.7%
1	California	32,505,049	13.6%
21	Colorado	3,686,552	1.5%
25	Connecticut	2,802,999	1.2%
40	Delaware	650,719	0.3%
4	Florida	14,275,312	6.0%
9	Georgia	6,224,694	2.6%
38	Hawaii	866,566	0.4%
39	Idaho	833,469	0.3%
NA	Illinois**	NA	NA
15	Indiana	4,822,870	2.0%
28	Iowa	1,974,400	0.8%
NA	Kansas**	NA	NA
NA	Kentucky**	NA	NA
22	Louisiana	3,657,831	1.5%
37	Maine	893,730	0.4%
14	Maryland	4,884,284	2.0%
10	Massachusetts	6,164,782	2.6%
7	Michigan	8,753,895	3.7%
20	Minnesota	3,883,178	1.6%
31	Mississippi	1,630,761	0.7%
19	Missouri	4,226,664	1.8%
NA	Montana**	NA	NA
34	Nebraska	1,256,307	0.5%
32	Nevada	1,609,211	0.7%
NA	New Hampshire**	NA	NA
8	New Jersey	8,143,000	3.4%
33	New Mexico	1,427,286	0.6%
3	New York	17,319,841	7.2%
11	North Carolina	5,872,472	2.5%
43	North Dakota	418,630	0.2%
6	Ohio	9,881,625	4.1%
27	Oklahoma	2,708,139	1.1%
26	Oregon	2,789,813	1.2%
5	Pennsylvania	10,955,043	4.6%
36	Rhode Island	991,000	0.4%
24	South Carolina	3,026,244	1.3%
41	South Dakota	452,063	0.2%
17	Tennessee	4,355,218	1.8%
2	Texas	18,355,842	7.7%
29	Utah	1,889,713	0.8%
44	Vermont	353,046	0.1%
12	Virginia	5,789,375	2.4%
13	Washington	5,210,571	2.2%
35	West Virginia	1,042,524	0.4%
18	Wisconsin	4,246,989	1.8%
45	Wyoming	349,192	0.1%

RANK ORDER

RANK	STATE	POPULATION	% of USA
1	California	32,505,049	13.6%
2	Texas	18,355,842	7.7%
3	New York	17,319,841	7.2%
4	Florida	14,275,312	6.0%
5	Pennsylvania	10,955,043	4.6%
6	Ohio	9,881,625	4.1%
7	Michigan	8,753,895	3.7%
8	New Jersey	8,143,000	3.4%
9	Georgia	6,224,694	2.6%
10	Massachusetts	6,164,782	2.6%
11	North Carolina	5,872,472	2.5%
12	Virginia	5,789,375	2.4%
13	Washington	5,210,571	2.2%
14	Maryland	4,884,284	2.0%
15	Indiana	4,822,870	2.0%
16	Arizona	4,480,386	1.9%
17	Tennessee	4,355,218	1.8%
18	Wisconsin	4,246,989	1.8%
19	Missouri	4,226,664	1.8%
20	Minnesota	3,883,178	1.6%
21	Colorado	3,686,552	1.5%
22	Louisiana	3,657,831	1.5%
23	Alabama	3,558,024	1.5%
24	South Carolina	3,026,244	1.3%
25	Connecticut	2,802,999	1.2%
26	Oregon	2,789,813	1.2%
27	Oklahoma	2,708,139	1.1%
28	Iowa	1,974,400	0.8%
29	Utah	1,889,713	0.8%
30	Arkansas	1,732,012	0.7%
31	Mississippi	1,630,761	0.7%
32	Nevada	1,609,211	0.7%
33	New Mexico	1,427,286	0.6%
34	Nebraska	1,256,307	0.5%
35	West Virginia	1,042,524	0.4%
36	Rhode Island	991,000	0.4%
37	Maine	893,730	0.4%
38	Hawaii	866,566	0.4%
39	Idaho	833,469	0.3%
40	Delaware	650,719	0.3%
41	South Dakota	452,063	0.2%
42	Alaska	425,501	0.2%
43	North Dakota	418,630	0.2%
44	Vermont	353,046	0.1%
45	Wyoming	349,192	0.1%
NA	Illinois**	NA	NA
NA	Kansas**	NA	NA
NA	Kentucky**	NA	NA
NA	Montana**	NA	NA
NA	New Hampshire**	NA	NA
	District of Columbia	519,000	0.2%

Source: Morgan Quitno Press using data from Federal Bureau of Investigation
    "Crime in the United States 1999" (Uniform Crime Reports, October 15, 2000)
*Estimated totals for urban areas, defined by the F.B.I. as Metropolitan Statistical Areas and other cities outside
such areas. National total includes states not shown separately.
**Not available.

Rural Population in 1999

National Total = 33,324,047 Rural Population*

ALPHA ORDER

RANK	STATE	POPULATION	% of USA
19	Alabama	811,976	2.4%
40	Alaska	193,499	0.6%
33	Arizona	297,614	0.9%
18	Arkansas	818,988	2.5%
23	California	639,951	1.9%
29	Colorado	369,448	1.1%
26	Connecticut	479,001	1.4%
42	Delaware	103,281	0.3%
17	Florida	835,688	2.5%
3	Georgia	1,563,306	4.7%
31	Hawaii	318,434	1.0%
27	Idaho	418,531	1.3%
NA	Illinois**	NA	NA
8	Indiana	1,120,130	3.4%
13	Iowa	894,600	2.7%
NA	Kansas**	NA	NA
NA	Kentucky**	NA	NA
21	Louisiana	714,169	2.1%
30	Maine	359,270	1.1%
34	Maryland	287,716	0.9%
43	Massachusetts	10,218	0.0%
9	Michigan	1,110,105	3.3%
14	Minnesota	892,822	2.7%
6	Mississippi	1,138,239	3.4%
5	Missouri	1,241,336	3.7%
NA	Montana**	NA	NA
28	Nebraska	409,693	1.2%
39	Nevada	199,789	0.6%
NA	New Hampshire**	NA	NA
44	New Jersey	0	0.0%
32	New Mexico	312,714	0.9%
15	New York	877,159	2.6%
1	North Carolina	1,778,528	5.3%
38	North Dakota	215,370	0.6%
4	Ohio	1,375,375	4.1%
22	Oklahoma	649,861	2.0%
25	Oregon	526,187	1.6%
11	Pennsylvania	1,038,957	3.1%
44	Rhode Island	0	0.0%
16	South Carolina	859,756	2.6%
35	South Dakota	280,937	0.8%
7	Tennessee	1,128,782	3.4%
2	Texas	1,688,158	5.1%
37	Utah	240,287	0.7%
36	Vermont	240,954	0.7%
10	Virginia	1,083,625	3.3%
24	Washington	545,429	1.6%
20	West Virginia	764,476	2.3%
12	Wisconsin	1,003,011	3.0%
41	Wyoming	130,808	0.4%

RANK ORDER

RANK	STATE	POPULATION	% of USA
1	North Carolina	1,778,528	5.3%
2	Texas	1,688,158	5.1%
3	Georgia	1,563,306	4.7%
4	Ohio	1,375,375	4.1%
5	Missouri	1,241,336	3.7%
6	Mississippi	1,138,239	3.4%
7	Tennessee	1,128,782	3.4%
8	Indiana	1,120,130	3.4%
9	Michigan	1,110,105	3.3%
10	Virginia	1,083,625	3.3%
11	Pennsylvania	1,038,957	3.1%
12	Wisconsin	1,003,011	3.0%
13	Iowa	894,600	2.7%
14	Minnesota	892,822	2.7%
15	New York	877,159	2.6%
16	South Carolina	859,756	2.6%
17	Florida	835,688	2.5%
18	Arkansas	818,988	2.5%
19	Alabama	811,976	2.4%
20	West Virginia	764,476	2.3%
21	Louisiana	714,169	2.1%
22	Oklahoma	649,861	2.0%
23	California	639,951	1.9%
24	Washington	545,429	1.6%
25	Oregon	526,187	1.6%
26	Connecticut	479,001	1.4%
27	Idaho	418,531	1.3%
28	Nebraska	409,693	1.2%
29	Colorado	369,448	1.1%
30	Maine	359,270	1.1%
31	Hawaii	318,434	1.0%
32	New Mexico	312,714	0.9%
33	Arizona	297,614	0.9%
34	Maryland	287,716	0.9%
35	South Dakota	280,937	0.8%
36	Vermont	240,954	0.7%
37	Utah	240,287	0.7%
38	North Dakota	215,370	0.6%
39	Nevada	199,789	0.6%
40	Alaska	193,499	0.6%
41	Wyoming	130,808	0.4%
42	Delaware	103,281	0.3%
43	Massachusetts	10,218	0.0%
44	New Jersey	0	0.0%
44	Rhode Island	0	0.0%
NA	Illinois**	NA	NA
NA	Kansas**	NA	NA
NA	Kentucky**	NA	NA
NA	Montana**	NA	NA
NA	New Hampshire**	NA	NA
	District of Columbia	0	0.0%

Source: Morgan Quitno Press using data from Federal Bureau of Investigation
    "Crime in the United States 1999" (Uniform Crime Reports, October 15, 2000)
*Estimated totals for rural areas, defined by the F.B.I. as other than Metropolitan Statistical Areas and other cities
outside such areas. National total includes states not shown separately.
**Not available.

Population 10 to 17 Years Old in 1999

National Total = 31,310,547

RANK	STATE	POPULATION	% of USA
24	Alabama	477,563	1.5%
46	Alaska	91,185	0.3%
21	Arizona	568,426	1.8%
34	Arkansas	301,922	1.0%
1	California	3,708,731	11.8%
23	Colorado	485,779	1.6%
29	Connecticut	372,155	1.2%
47	Delaware	80,513	0.3%
4	Florida	1,594,645	5.1%
9	Georgia	899,684	2.9%
42	Hawaii	122,724	0.4%
39	Idaho	163,646	0.5%
5	Illinois	1,385,402	4.4%
13	Indiana	690,683	2.2%
30	Iowa	343,173	1.1%
32	Kansas	327,097	1.0%
25	Kentucky	440,729	1.4%
22	Louisiana	550,080	1.8%
41	Maine	145,275	0.5%
20	Maryland	585,989	1.9%
15	Massachusetts	654,546	2.1%
8	Michigan	1,185,798	3.8%
18	Minnesota	606,973	1.9%
31	Mississippi	342,000	1.1%
17	Missouri	650,331	2.1%
43	Montana	111,907	0.4%
36	Nebraska	210,285	0.7%
37	Nevada	208,830	0.7%
40	New Hampshire	146,156	0.5%
10	New Jersey	874,739	2.8%
35	New Mexico	225,979	0.7%
3	New York	1,918,576	6.1%
11	North Carolina	854,263	2.7%
48	North Dakota	79,131	0.3%
7	Ohio	1,314,259	4.2%
27	Oklahoma	411,253	1.3%
28	Oregon	383,249	1.2%
6	Pennsylvania	1,339,308	4.3%
44	Rhode Island	109,029	0.3%
26	South Carolina	432,482	1.4%
45	South Dakota	95,375	0.3%
19	Tennessee	598,221	1.9%
2	Texas	2,474,558	7.9%
33	Utah	307,963	1.0%
49	Vermont	69,490	0.2%
12	Virginia	742,949	2.4%
14	Washington	683,118	2.2%
38	West Virginia	192,107	0.6%
16	Wisconsin	651,927	2.1%
50	Wyoming	63,577	0.2%

RANK	STATE	POPULATION	% of USA
1	California	3,708,731	11.8%
2	Texas	2,474,558	7.9%
3	New York	1,918,576	6.1%
4	Florida	1,594,645	5.1%
5	Illinois	1,385,402	4.4%
6	Pennsylvania	1,339,308	4.3%
7	Ohio	1,314,259	4.2%
8	Michigan	1,185,798	3.8%
9	Georgia	899,684	2.9%
10	New Jersey	874,739	2.8%
11	North Carolina	854,263	2.7%
12	Virginia	742,949	2.4%
13	Indiana	690,683	2.2%
14	Washington	683,118	2.2%
15	Massachusetts	654,546	2.1%
16	Wisconsin	651,927	2.1%
17	Missouri	650,331	2.1%
18	Minnesota	606,973	1.9%
19	Tennessee	598,221	1.9%
20	Maryland	585,989	1.9%
21	Arizona	568,426	1.8%
22	Louisiana	550,080	1.8%
23	Colorado	485,779	1.6%
24	Alabama	477,563	1.5%
25	Kentucky	440,729	1.4%
26	South Carolina	432,482	1.4%
27	Oklahoma	411,253	1.3%
28	Oregon	383,249	1.2%
29	Connecticut	372,155	1.2%
30	Iowa	343,173	1.1%
31	Mississippi	342,000	1.1%
32	Kansas	327,097	1.0%
33	Utah	307,963	1.0%
34	Arkansas	301,922	1.0%
35	New Mexico	225,979	0.7%
36	Nebraska	210,285	0.7%
37	Nevada	208,830	0.7%
38	West Virginia	192,107	0.6%
39	Idaho	163,646	0.5%
40	New Hampshire	146,156	0.5%
41	Maine	145,275	0.5%
42	Hawaii	122,724	0.4%
43	Montana	111,907	0.4%
44	Rhode Island	109,029	0.3%
45	South Dakota	95,375	0.3%
46	Alaska	91,185	0.3%
47	Delaware	80,513	0.3%
48	North Dakota	79,131	0.3%
49	Vermont	69,490	0.2%
50	Wyoming	63,577	0.2%
	District of Columbia	36,767	0.1%

Source: U.S. Bureau of the Census
"State Population Estimates by Age" (http://www.census.gov/population/estimates/state/stats/st-99-10.txt)

Total Area of States in Square Miles in 1999

National Total = 3,717,796 Square Miles*

ALPHA ORDER

RANK	STATE	MILES	% of USA
30	Alabama	52,237	1.4%
1	Alaska	615,230	16.6%
6	Arizona	114,006	3.1%
28	Arkansas	53,182	1.4%
3	California	158,869	4.3%
8	Colorado	104,100	2.8%
48	Connecticut	5,544	0.2%
49	Delaware	2,396	0.1%
23	Florida	59,928	1.6%
24	Georgia	58,977	1.6%
47	Hawaii	6,459	0.2%
14	Idaho	83,574	2.3%
25	Illinois	57,918	1.6%
38	Indiana	36,420	1.0%
26	Iowa	56,276	1.5%
15	Kansas	82,282	2.2%
37	Kentucky	40,411	1.1%
31	Louisiana	49,651	1.3%
39	Maine	33,741	0.9%
42	Maryland	12,297	0.3%
45	Massachusetts	9,241	0.3%
11	Michigan	96,705	2.6%
12	Minnesota	86,943	2.3%
32	Mississippi	48,286	1.3%
21	Missouri	69,709	1.9%
4	Montana	147,046	4.0%
16	Nebraska	77,358	2.1%
7	Nevada	110,567	3.0%
44	New Hampshire	9,283	0.3%
46	New Jersey	8,215	0.2%
5	New Mexico	121,598	3.3%
27	New York	53,989	1.5%
29	North Carolina	52,672	1.4%
18	North Dakota	70,704	1.9%
34	Ohio	44,828	1.2%
20	Oklahoma	69,903	1.9%
10	Oregon	97,132	2.6%
33	Pennsylvania	46,058	1.2%
50	Rhode Island	1,231	0.0%
40	South Carolina	31,189	0.8%
17	South Dakota	77,121	2.1%
36	Tennessee	42,146	1.1%
2	Texas	267,277	7.2%
13	Utah	84,904	2.3%
43	Vermont	9,615	0.3%
35	Virginia	42,326	1.1%
19	Washington	70,637	1.9%
41	West Virginia	24,231	0.7%
22	Wisconsin	65,499	1.8%
9	Wyoming	97,818	2.6%

RANK ORDER

RANK	STATE	MILES	% of USA
1	Alaska	615,230	16.6%
2	Texas	267,277	7.2%
3	California	158,869	4.3%
4	Montana	147,046	4.0%
5	New Mexico	121,598	3.3%
6	Arizona	114,006	3.1%
7	Nevada	110,567	3.0%
8	Colorado	104,100	2.8%
9	Wyoming	97,818	2.6%
10	Oregon	97,132	2.6%
11	Michigan	96,705	2.6%
12	Minnesota	86,943	2.3%
13	Utah	84,904	2.3%
14	Idaho	83,574	2.3%
15	Kansas	82,282	2.2%
16	Nebraska	77,358	2.1%
17	South Dakota	77,121	2.1%
18	North Dakota	70,704	1.9%
19	Washington	70,637	1.9%
20	Oklahoma	69,903	1.9%
21	Missouri	69,709	1.9%
22	Wisconsin	65,499	1.8%
23	Florida	59,928	1.6%
24	Georgia	58,977	1.6%
25	Illinois	57,918	1.6%
26	Iowa	56,276	1.5%
27	New York	53,989	1.5%
28	Arkansas	53,182	1.4%
29	North Carolina	52,672	1.4%
30	Alabama	52,237	1.4%
31	Louisiana	49,651	1.3%
32	Mississippi	48,286	1.3%
33	Pennsylvania	46,058	1.2%
34	Ohio	44,828	1.2%
35	Virginia	42,326	1.1%
36	Tennessee	42,146	1.1%
37	Kentucky	40,411	1.1%
38	Indiana	36,420	1.0%
39	Maine	33,741	0.9%
40	South Carolina	31,189	0.8%
41	West Virginia	24,231	0.7%
42	Maryland	12,297	0.3%
43	Vermont	9,615	0.3%
44	New Hampshire	9,283	0.3%
45	Massachusetts	9,241	0.3%
46	New Jersey	8,215	0.2%
47	Hawaii	6,459	0.2%
48	Connecticut	5,544	0.2%
49	Delaware	2,396	0.1%
50	Rhode Island	1,231	0.0%
	District of Columbia	68	0.0%

Source: U.S. Bureau of the Census
    "1990 Census of Population and Housing" (Series CPH-1)
*Total of land and water area. These totals are revised. Excludes territorial water which was included in previous reports.

IX. SOURCES

Administrative Office of the U.S. Courts
Statistics Division
One Columbus Circle, NE
Washington, DC 20544
202-502-2600
www.uscourts.gov

American Correctional Association
4380 Forbes Blvd.
Lanham, MD 20706-4322
800-222-5646
www.corrections.com/aca

Bureau of the Census
3 Silver Hill & Suitland Roads
Suitland, MD 20746
301-457-2800
www.census.gov

Bureau of Justice Assistance
810 Seventh Street, NW
4th Floor
Washington DC 20531
202-616-6500
www.ojp.usdoj.gov/BJA/

Bureau of Justice Statistics Clearinghouse
810 Seventh Street, NW
Washington, DC 20531
202-307-0765
www.ojp.usdoj.gov/bjs/

Children's Bureau
Administration for Children & Familes; HHS
370 L'Enfant Promenade, SW
Washington, DC 20447
202-401-9215
www.acf.dhhs.gov

Drugs and Crime Clearinghouse of the Office of National Drug Control Policy
Box 6000
Rockville, MD 20849-6000
800-666-3332
www.whitehousedrugpolicy.gov

Federal Bureau of Investigation
J. Edgar Hoover FBI Building
935 Pennsylvania Avenue, NW
Washington, DC 20535-0001
202-324-3000
Internet: http://www.fbi.gov

Juvenile Justice Clearinghouse
Box 6000
Rockville, MD 20849-6000
800-638-8736
www.ojjdp.ncjrs.org

National Archive of Crime and Justice Programs
Inter-University Consortium for Political
  and Social Research
P.O. Box 1248
Ann Arbor, MI 48106
800-999-0960
www.icpsr.umich.edu/NACJD/home.html

National Association of State Alcohol and Drug Abuse Directors, Inc.
808 17th Street, NW
Suite 410
Washington, DC 20006
202-293-0090
www.nasadad.org

National Center for State Courts
300 Newport Avenue
Williamsburg, VA 23185
757-253-2000
www.ncsc.dni.us/

National Institute of Justice
810 Seventh Street, NW.
Washington, DC 20531
(202) 307-2942
www.ojp.usdoj.gov/nij

National Clearinghouse on Child Abuse and Neglect
330 C Street, SW
Washington, DC 20447
800-394-3366
www.calib.com/nccanch/

National Criminal Justice Reference Service (NCJRS)
Box 6000
Rockville, MD 20849-6000
800-851-3420
www.ncjrs.org

Substance Abuse and Mental Health Services Administration
U.S. Department of Health and Human Services
5600 Fishers Lane
Rockville, MD 20857
301-443-8956
www.samhsa.gov

Victims of Crime Resource Center
810 Seventh Street, NW.
Washington, DC 20531
800-627-6872
www.ojp.usdoj.gov/ovc/

X. INDEX

Admissions to prisons 77, 78
Agencies, law enforcement 270
Aggravated assault, 1995: 486-489
Aggravated assault, arrests for 13, 14, 202-204
Aggravated assault, by weapon used 370-378
Aggravated assault, clearances 42
Aggravated assault, in rural areas 433-435
Aggravated assault, in urban areas 430-432
Aggravated assault, juvenile arrests for 202-204
Aggravated assault, number of 365, 367, 370,
   373, 375, 377, 430, 433, 486, 487
Aggravated assault, rate 368, 371, 431,
   434, 488, 489
Aggravated assault, time between 366
AIDS, deaths in prison 95-97
AIDS, prisoners with 98, 99
Alcohol, usage by teens 246
Alcohol & drug treatment, expenditures for
   133-135
Alcohol & drug treatment, admissions 120-130
Alcohol & drug treatment, admissions by race
   125-130
Alcohol & drug treatment, admissions by sex
   121-124
Alcohol & drug treatment, juveniles in 248, 249
Appeal or bond, prisoners released on 89
Arrest rate, violent crime 6
Arrest rates 2, 4, 6, 8, 10, 12, 14, 16, 18, 20, 22, 24,
   26, 28, 30, 32, 34, 36, 185, 188, 191, 194, 197,
   200, 203, 206, 209, 212, 215, 218, 221, 224, 227,
   230, 233, 236,
   Arrests 1-36, 184-237
Arrests, aggravated assault 13, 14, 202-204
Arrests, arson 23, 24, 217- 219
Arrests, burglary 17, 18, 208-210
Arrests, crime clearances 37-46
Arrests, crime index offenses 3, 4, 187-189
Arrests, driving under influence 27, 28, 223-225
Arrests, drug abuse violations 29, 30, 226-228
Arrests, larceny and theft 19, 20, 211-213
Arrests, motor vehicle theft 21, 22, 214-216
Arrests, murder 7, 8, 193-195
Arrests, offenses against families and children
   35, 36, 235-237
Arrests, property crime 15, 16, 205-207
Arrests, prostitution & commercialized vice 33,
   34, 232-234
Arrests, rape 9, 10, 196-198
Arrests, robbery 11, 12, 199-201
Arrests, sex offenses 31, 32, 229-231
Arrests, violent crime 5, 6, 190-192
Arrests, weapons violations 25, 26, 220-222
Arrests of juveniles 184-237
Arson, arrests for 23, 24, 217-219

Arson, juvenile arrests for 217-219
Bank robberies 364
Black juvenile custody rate 242
Black state prisoners 60-62, 69, 70
Black prisoners under death sentence 69, 70
Bond or appeal, prisoners released on 89
Burglary, 1995: 494-497
Burglary, arrests for 17, 18, 208-210
Burglary, time between 386
Burglary, clearances 44
Burglary, in rural areas 445-447
Burglary, in urban areas 442-444
Burglary, juvenile arrests for 208-210
Burglary, number of 385, 387, 442, 445, 494, 495
Burglary, rate 388, 389, 443, 446, 496, 497
Capacities, prisons 52
Capital punishment 63-76
Car theft, 1995: 502-505
Car theft, arrests 21, 22, 214-216
Car theft, clearances 46
Car theft, number of 395, 397, 454, 456, 457,
   459, 502, 503
Car theft, in rural areas 457-459
Car theft, in urban areas 454-456
Car theft, rate 398, 399, 455, 458, 504, 505
Car theft, time between 396
Cases, federal criminal 305, 306
Child abuse, victims of 250-261
Child abuse fatalities 260, 261
Children and families, arrests for offenses against
   35, 36, 235-237
Children and families, juvenile arrests for
   offenses against 235-237
Clearances, crime 37-46
College and university crime 460-465
Commercialized vice and prostitution, arrests
   for 33, 34, 232-234
Commercialized vice and prostitution, juvenile
   arrests for 232-234
Commuted death sentences 75, 76
Conditional prison releases 82-87
Correctional institutions, prisoners in 47-51
Correctional officer, inmates per 115
Correctional officers, by sex 113, 114
Correctional officers, turnover rates 116
Correctional officers 112-116
Corrections, expenditures for 156-168
Corrections, payroll 180
Court commitments, admissions to prison
   through 78
Crime, clearances 37-46
Crime, in 1995: 466-505
Crime, property, number of 379-382, 490-493

X. INDEX (continued)

Crime, time between 310, 316, 326, 345, 351, 366, 380, 386, 391, 396

Crime, universities and colleges 460-465

Crime, violent, 315-323, 470-473

Crime index offenses, arrests for 3, 4, 187-189

Crime rates 313, 314, 319, 320, 322, 328, 329, 331, 334, 347, 348, 349, 353, 354, 356, 368, 369, 371, 383, 384, 388, 389, 393, 394, 398, 399, 401, 404, 407, 410, 413, 416, 419, 422, 425, 428, 431, 434, 437, 440, 443, 446, 449, 452, 455, 458, 468, 469, 472, 473, 476, 477, 480, 481, 483, 484, 485, 488, 489, 492, 493, 496, 497, 500, 501, 504, 505, 507

Crime rates, rural 404, 410, 416, 422, 428, 434, 440, 446, 452, 458

Crime rates, urban 401, 407, 413, 419, 425, 431, 437, 443, 449, 455

Criminal cases, federal 305-307

Custody juveniles in 239-242

Death penalty 63-76

Death sentences, by race 67-70

Death sentences, by sex 64-66

Death sentences overturned 75, 76

Deaths, prisoner 91-97, 100, 101

Driving under influence, arrests for 27, 28, 223-225

Driving under influence, juvenile arrests 223-225

Dropout rate, high school 243

Drug abuse violations, arrests for 29, 30, 226-228

Drug abuse violations, juvenile arrests 226-228

Drug & alcohol abuse services, expenditures for 131-137

Drug & alcohol prevention services 136, 137

Drug & alcohol treatment, admissions 120-130

Drug & alcohol treatment, admissions by race 125-130

Drug & alcohol treatment, admissions by sex 121-124

Drug & alcohol treatment, juveniles in 248, 249

Drug & alcohol treatment, units 119

DUI, arrests 27, 28, 223-225

DUI, juvenile arrests 223-225

Emotionally abused children 256, 257

Employees, correctional institutions 108-114

Employment, justice system 264-267

Employment, law enforcement agencies 273-278

Employment, local police dept 287-290

Employment, sheriffs' dept 292-295

Employment, special police agencies 297-300

Employment, state law enforcement 279-285

Escaped prisoners 80, 90

Escapees returned 80

Executions 71- 73

Expenditures, per inmate 165

Families and children, arrests for offenses against 35, 36, 235-237

Families and children, juvenile arrests for offenses against 235-237

Federal law enforcement officers 262, 263

Female correctional officers 114

Female law enforcement officers 284, 285

Female prisoners 53-56, 65, 66

Females, in drug and alcohol treatment 123, 124

Females, under sentence of death 65, 66

Guns, crimes involving 321-323, 330-335, 355-357, 370-372

Handguns, murders involving 333-335

Hate crimes 506, 507

High school dropout rate 243

HIV/AIDS, prisoners testing positive for 98, 99

Incarceration rate 50, 51, 54, 58, 61

Incarceration rate, by race 58, 61

Inmate expenditures 165

Inmates, jail 118

Inmates, prison 47-51

Jail inmates 118

Judges, salaries of 181-183

Judgeships, U.S. district court 303, 304

Judicial and legal services, expenditures for 169-177

Justice activities, expenditures for 138-146

Justice system, payroll 178-180

Juvenile arrests 185-237

Juvenile arrests, aggravated assault 202-204

Juvenile arrests, arson 217- 219

Juvenile arrests, burglary 208-210

Juvenile arrests, driving under influence 223-225

Juvenile arrests, drug abuse violations 226-228

Juvenile arrests, larceny and theft 211-213

Juvenile arrests, motor vehicle theft 214-216

Juvenile arrests, murder 192-195

Juvenile arrests, offenses against families and children 235-237

Juvenile arrests, property crime 205-207

Juvenile arrests, prostitution and commercialized vice 232-234

Juvenile arrests, rape 196-198

Juvenile arrests, robbery 199-201

Juvenile arrests, sex offenses 229-231

Juvenile arrests, violent crime 190-192

Juvenile arrests, weapons violations 220-222

Juvenile custody rate 240-242

Juveniles, in alcohol and drug treatment 248, 249

Juveniles, in custody 239-242

Knives, crimes involving 340, 341, 358, 359, 373, 374

Larcenies and thefts, time between 391

Larceny and theft, 1995: 498-501

Larceny and theft, arrests for 19, 20, 211-213

Larceny and theft, clearances 45

X. INDEX (continued)

Larceny and theft, in rural areas 451-453
Larceny and theft, in urban areas 448-450
Larceny and theft, juvenile arrests for 211-213
Larceny and theft, number of 390, 392, 448, 451, 498, 499
Larceny and theft, rate 393, 394, 449, 452, 500, 501
Law enforcement agencies 270
Law enforcement officers, by sex 283-285
Law enforcement officers 262, 263, 268, 269, 274-276, 279-285, 287-289, 293, 294, 297-299
Legal and judicial services, expenditures for 170-178
Local and state government expenditures, corrections 156-168
Local and state government expenditures, judicial and legal services 169-177
Local and state government expenditures, justice activities 138-146
Local and state government expenditures, police protection 147-155
Local police department employment 287-290
Male correctional officers 113
Male law enforcement officers 283
Males, in drug and alcohol treatment 121, 122
Males under sentence of death 64
Marijuana, usage by teens 247
Motor vehicle theft, 1995: 502-505
Motor vehicle theft, arrests for 21, 22, 214-215
Motor vehicle theft, clearances 46
Motor vehicle theft, in rural areas 457-459
Motor vehicle theft, in urban areas 454-456
Motor vehicle theft, juvenile arrests for 214-215
Motor vehicle thefts, number of 395, 397, 454, 457, 502, 503
Motor vehicle theft, rate 398, 399, 455, 458, 504, 505
Motor vehicle theft, time between 396
Murder, 1995: 474-477
Murder, arrests for 7, 8, 192-195
Murder, clearances 39
Murder, in rural areas 415-417
Murder, in urban areas 412-414
Murder, juvenile arrests for 192-195
Murder, number of 325, 327, 330, 332, 333, 336, 338, 340, 342, 412, 415, 474, 475
Murder, rate 328, 329, 331, 334, 413, 416, 476, 477
Murder, time between 326
Murder, weapon used 330-343
Neglect, child victims of 250, 251, 258-261
Neglect and abuse, fatalities from 260, 261
Offenses, crime index 3, 4, 187-189
Officers, by sex 283-285
Officers, correctional 112-116
Officers, federal 262, 263
Officers killed 301, 302
Officers, law enforcement 262, 263, 268, 269, 274-276, 279-285, 287-289, 293, 294, 297-299
Officers, local police 287-290
Officers, sheriffs' depts. 291-294
Officers, special police 297-299
Officers, state law enforcement 279-285
Overturned death sentences 75, 76
Parole, prisoners released on 84
Parole, violators returned to prison 79
Payroll, corrections 180
Payroll, police 179
Police, government expenditures for 147-155
Police, payroll 179
Police, special 296-300
Prison capacities 52
Prison employees 108-114
Prisoner deaths, by AIDS 95-97
Prisoner deaths, by illness 93, 94
Prisoner deaths, by suicide 100, 101
Prisoner deaths 91-97, 100, 101
Prisoner releases, conditional 82-86
Prisoner releases, on appeal or bond 89
Prisoner releases, parole 84
Prisoner releases, probation 85
Prisoner releases, supervised mandatory release 86
Prisoner releases, unconditional 87, 88
Prisoner releases 82-89
Prisoners, by race 57-62, 67-70
Prisoners, by sex 53-56, 64-66
Prisoners, change in number 48
Prisoners, change in rate 51
Prisoners, escaped 80, 90
Prisoners, executed 71-73
Prisoners, female 54-56, 65, 66
Prisoners, under death sentence 63-70
Probation, adults on 104, 105
Probation, prisoners released on 85
Property crime, 1995: 490-505
Property crime, arrests for 15, 16, 205-207
Property crime, average time between 380
Property crime, clearances 43
Property crime, juvenile arrests for 205-207
Property crime, number of 379, 382, 436, 439, 490, 491
Property crime, per square mile 381
Property crime, rate 383, 384, 437, 440, 492, 493
Property crime, rural 439-441
Property crime, universities and colleges 464, 465
Property crime, urban 436-438
Prostitution, arrests for 33, 34, 232-234
Prostitution, juvenile arrests for 232-234
Rape, 1995: 478-481

X. INDEX (continued)

Rape, arrests for 9, 10, 196-198
Rape, clearances 40
Rape, in rural areas 421-423
Rape, in urban areas 418-420
Rape, juvenile arrests for 196-198
Rape, number of 344, 346, 418, 421, 478, 479
Rape, rate 347, 348, 419, 422, 480, 481
Rape, time between 345
Releases, from prisons 81-89
Rifles, murders involving 336, 337
Robbery, 1995: 482-485
Robbery, arrests for 11, 12, 199-201
Robbery, bank 364
Robbery, by weapon used 355-363
Robbery, clearances 41
Robbery, in rural areas 427-429
Robbery, in urban areas 424-246
Robbery, juvenile arrests for 199-201
Robbery, number of 350, 352, 355, 358, 360, 362, 364, 424, 427, 482, 483
Robbery, rate 353, 354, 356, 425, 428, 484, 485
Robbery, time between 351
Rural crime 403-405, 409-411, 415-417, 421-423, 427-429, 433-435, 439-441, 445-447, 452-453, 457-459
Salaries, judges 181-183
Sex offenses, arrests for 31, 32, 229-231
Sex offenses, juvenile arrests for 229-231
Sexual abuse, children 254, 255
School, weapons at 240, 241
Sheriffs' department employees 292-295
Sheriffs' departments 291
Shotguns, murders involving 338, 339
Special police 296-299
State & local government expenditures, corrections 156-168
State & local government expenditures, judicial and legal services 169-177
State & local government expenditures, justice activities 138-146
State and local government expenditures, police protection 147-155
State law enforcement officers 279-285
Suicides, prisoner 100, 101
Supervised mandatory releases 86
Theft and larceny, 1995 498-501
Theft and larceny, clearances 45
Theft and larceny, in rural areas 451-453
Theft and larceny, in urban areas 448-450
Theft and larceny, number of 390, 392, 448, 451, 498, 499
Theft and larceny, rate 393, 394, 449, 452, 500, 501
Thefts and larceny, time between 391
Unconditional prison releases 87, 88

University and college crime 460-465
Urban crime 400-402, 407, 408, 412-414, 418-420, 424-426, 430-432, 436-438, 442-444, 448-450, 454-456
Vice and prostitution, arrests 33, 34, 232-234
Vice and prostitution, juvenile arrests 232-234
Violent crime, 1995: 470-474
Violent crime, arrests for 5, 6, 190-192
Violent crime, clearances 38
Violent crime, juvenile arrests 190-192
Violent crime, number of 315, 317, 318, 321, 406, 409, 470, 471
Violent crime, per square mile 318
Violent crime, rates 319, 320, 322, 407, 410, 472, 473
Violent crime, rural 409-411
Violent crime, universities and colleges 462, 463
Violent crime, urban 406-408
Weapons, and violent crime 321-323
Weapons at school 244, 245
Weapons violations, arrests for 25, 26, 220-222
Weapons violations, juvenile arrests for 220-222
White juvenile custody rate 241
White state prisoners 57-59, 67, 68
White prisoners under death sentence 67, 68
Wiretaps 308

CHAPTER INDEX

Arrests

Corrections

Drugs and Alcohol

Finance

Juveniles

Law Enforcement

Offenses

HOW TO USE THIS INDEX

Place left thumb on the outer edge of this page. To locate the desired entry, fold back the remaining page edges and align the index edge mark with the appropriate page edge mark.